PRESENT VALUE OF AN ANNUITY OF $1 PER PERIOD (P/A, i, n)

N	0.50%	0.67%	0.75%	1%	2%	3%	4%	5%	6%	7%	8%	9%
2	1.9851	1.9802	1.9777	1.9704	1.9416	1.9135	1.8861	1.8594	1.8334	1.8080	1.7833	1.7591
3	2.9702	2.9604	2.9556	2.9410	2.8839	2.8286	2.7751	2.7232	2.6730	2.6243	2.5771	2.5313
4	3.9505	3.9342	3.9261	3.9020	3.8077	3.7171	3.6299	3.5460	3.4651	3.3872	3.3121	3.2397
5	4.9259	4.9015	4.8894	4.8534	4.7135	4.5797	4.4518	4.3295	4.2124	4.1002	3.9927	3.8897
6	5.8964	5.8625	5.8456	5.7955	5.6014	5.4172	5.2421	5.0757	4.9173	4.7665	4.6229	4.4859
7	6.8621	6.8170	6.7946	6.7282	6.4720	6.2303	6.0021	5.7864	5.5824	5.3893	5.2064	5.0330
8	7.8230	7.7652	7.7366	7.6517	7.3255	7.0197	6.7327	6.4632	6.2098	5.9713	5.7466	5.5348
9	8.7791	8.7072	8.6716	8.5660	8.1622	7.7861	7.4353	7.1078	6.8017	6.5152	6.2469	5.9952
10	9.7304	9.6429	9.5996	9.4713	8.9826	8.5302	8.1109	7.7217	7.3601	7.0236	6.7101	6.4177
12	11.6189	11.4958	11.4349	11.2551	10.5753	9.9540	9.3851	8.8633	8.3838	7.9427	7.5361	7.1607
14	13.4887	13.3242	13.2430	13.0037	12.1062	11.2961	10.5631	9.8986	9.2950	8.7455	8.2442	7.7862
16	15.3399	15.1285	15.0243	14.7179	13.5777	12.5611	11.6523	10.8378	10.1059	9.4466	8.8514	8.3126
18	17.1728	16.9089	16.7792	16.3983	14.9920	13.7535	12.6593	11.6896	10.8276	10.0591	9.3719	8.7556
20	18.9874	18.6659	18.5080	18.0456	16.3514	14.8775	13.5903	12.4622	11.4699	10.5940	9.8181	9.1285
22	20.7841	20.3997	20.2112	19.6604	17.6580	15.9369	14.4511	13.1630	12.0416	11.0612	10.2007	9.4424
24	22.5629	22.1105	21.8891	21.2434	18.9139	16.9355	15.2470	13.7986	12.5504	11.4693	10.5288	9.7066
26	24.3240	23.7988	23.5422	22.7952	20.1210	17.8768	15.9828	14.3752	13.0032	11.8258	10.8100	9.9290
28	26.0677	25.4648	25.1707	24.3164	21.2813	18.7641	16.6631	14.8981	13.4062	12.1371	11.0511	10.1161
30	27.7941	27.1088	26.7751	25.8077	22.3965	19.6004	17.2920	15.3725	13.7648	12.4090	11.2578	10.2737
32	29.5033	28.7311	28.3557	27.2696	23.4683	20.3888	17.8736	15.8027	14.0840	12.6466	11.4350	10.4062
36	32.8710	31.9118	31.4468	30.1075	25.4888	21.8323	18.9083	16.5469	14.6210	13.0352	11.7172	10.6118
40	36.1722	35.0090	34.4469	32.8347	27.3555	23.1148	19.7928	17.1591	15.0463	13.3317	11.9246	10.7574
50	44.1428	42.4013	41.5664	39.1961	31.4236	25.7298	21.4822	18.2559	15.7619	13.8007	12.2335	10.9617
60	51.7256	49.3184	48.1734	44.9550	34.7609	27.6756	22.6235	18.9293	16.1614	14.0392	12.3766	11.0480
80	65.8023	61.8471	59.9944	54.8882	39.7445	30.2008	23.9154	19.5965	16.5091	14.2220	12.4735	11.0998
120	90.0735	82.4213	78.9417	69.7005	45.3554	32.3730	24.7741	19.9427	16.6514	14.2815	12.4988	11.1108
180	118.5035	104.6403	98.5934	83.3217	48.5844	33.1703	24.9785	19.9969	16.6662	14.2856	12.5000	11.1111
240	139.5808	119.5539	111.1450	90.8194	49.5686	33.3057	24.9980	19.9998	16.6667	14.2857	12.5000	11.1111
300	155.2069	129.5641	119.1616	94.9466	49.8685	33.3286	24.9998	20.0000	16.6667	14.2857	12.5000	11.1111
360	166.7916	136.2830	124.2819	97.2183	49.9599	33.3325	25.0000	20.0000	16.6667	14.2857	12.5000	11.1111

N	10%	11%	12%	13%	14%	15%	16%	18%	20%	25%	30%	40%
2	1.7355	1.7125	1.6901	1.6681	1.6467	1.6257	1.6052	1.5656	1.5278	1.4400	1.3609	1.2245
3	2.4869	2.4437	2.4018	2.3612	2.3216	2.2832	2.2459	2.1743	2.1065	1.9520	1.8161	1.5889
4	3.1699	3.1024	3.0373	2.9745	2.9137	2.8550	2.7982	2.6901	2.5887	2.3616	2.1662	1.8492
5	3.7908	3.6959	3.6048	3.5172	3.4331	3.3522	3.2743	3.1272	2.9906	2.6893	2.4356	2.0352
6	4.3553	4.2305	4.1114	3.9975	3.8887	3.7845	3.6847	3.4976	3.3255	2.9514	2.6427	2.1680
7	4.8684	4.7122	4.5638	4.4226	4.2883	4.1604	4.0386	3.8115	3.6046	3.1611	2.8021	2.2628
8	5.3349	5.1461	4.9676	4.7988	4.6389	4.4873	4.3436	4.0776	3.8372	3.3289	2.9247	2.3306
9	5.7590	5.5370	5.3282	5.1317	4.9464	4.7716	4.6065	4.3030	4.0310	3.4631	3.0190	2.3790
10	6.1446	5.8892	5.6502	5.4262	5.2161	5.0188	4.8332	4.4941	4.1925	3.5705	3.0915	2.4136
11	6.4951	6.2065	5.9377	5.6869	5.4527	5.2337	5.0286	4.6560	4.3271	3.6564	3.1473	2.4383
12	6.8137	6.4924	6.1944	5.9176	5.6603	5.4206	5.1971	4.7932	4.4392	3.7251	3.1903	2.4559
13	7.1034	6.7499	6.4235	6.1218	5.8424	5.5831	5.3423	4.9095	4.5327	3.7801	3.2233	2.4685
14	7.3667	6.9819	6.6282	6.3025	6.0021	5.7245	5.4675	5.0081	4.6106	3.8241	3.2487	2.4775
15	7.6061	7.1909	6.8109	6.4624	6.1422	5.8474	5.5755	5.0916	4.6755	3.8593	3.2682	2.4839
16	7.8237	7.3792	6.9740	6.6039	6.2651	5.9542	5.6685	5.1624	4.7296	3.8874	3.2832	2.4885
17	8.0216	7.5488	7.1196	6.7291	6.3729	6.0472	5.7487	5.2223	4.7746	3.9099	3.2948	2.4918
18	8.2014	7.7016	7.2497	6.8399	6.4674	6.1280	5.8178	5.2732	4.8122	3.9279	3.3037	2.4941
19	8.3649	7.8393	7.3658	6.9380	6.5504	6.1982	5.8775	5.3162	4.8435	3.9424	3.3105	2.4958
20	8.5136	7.9633	7.4694	7.0248	6.6231	6.2593	5.9288	5.3527	4.8696	3.9539	3.3158	2.4970
21	8.6487	8.0751	7.5620	7.1016	6.6870	6.3125	5.9731	5.3837	4.8913	3.9631	3.3198	2.4979
22	8.7715	8.1757	7.6446	7.1695	6.7429	6.3587	6.0113	5.4099	4.9094	3.9705	3.3230	2.4985
23	8.8832	8.2664	7.7184	7.2297	6.7921	6.3988	6.0442	5.4321	4.9245	3.9764	3.3254	2.4989
24	8.9847	8.3481	7.7843	7.2829	6.8351	6.4338	6.0726	5.4509	4.9371	3.9811	3.3272	2.4992
25	9.0770	8.4217	7.8431	7.3300	6.8729	6.4641	6.0971	5.4669	4.9476	3.9849	3.3286	2.4994
30	9.4269	8.6938	8.0552	7.4957	7.0027	6.5660	6.1772	5.5168	4.9789	3.9950	3.3321	2.4999
40	9.7791	8.9511	8.2438	7.6344	7.1050	6.6418	6.2335	5.5482	4.9966	3.9995	3.3332	2.5000

INTRODUCTION TO FINANCIAL MANAGEMENT

SIXTH EDITION

INTRODUCTION TO FINANCIAL MANAGEMENT

Lawrence D. Schall

Professor of Finance and Business Economics
University of Washington

Charles W. Haley

Professor of Banking and Finance
University of Washington

McGRAW-HILL, INC.

New York   St. Louis   San Francisco   Auckland   Bogotá   Caracas   Hamburg
Lisbon   London   Madrid   Mexico   Milan   Montreal   New Delhi   Paris
San Juan   São Paulo   Singapore   Sydney   Tokyo   Toronto

INTRODUCTION TO FINANCIAL MANAGEMENT

1 2 3 4 5 6 7 8 9 0 DOC DOC 9 5 4 3 2 1 0

ISBN 0-07-055117-0

This book was set in Times Roman by Better Graphics, Inc.
The editors were Kenneth A. MacLeod and Bob Greiner;
the production supervisor was Louise Karam.
The cover was designed by Joan Greenfield.
New drawings were done by Fine Line Illustrations, Inc.
R. R. Donnelley & Sons Company was printer and binder.

Library of Congress Cataloging-in-Publication Data

Schall, Lawrence D.
  Introduction to financial management / Lawrence D. Schall, Charles
  W. Haley.
    p.   cm.
  Includes bibliographical references and index.
  ISBN 0-07-055117-0
  1. Corporations—Finance.   I. Haley, Charles W.   II. Title.
  H34011.S33   1991
  858.15—dc20   90-20838

ABOUT THE AUTHORS

LAWRENCE D. SCHALL is Professor of Finance and Business Economics at the University of Washington's Graduate School of Business. He received his M.A. and Ph.D. in economics from the University of Chicago. Professor Schall has published numerous articles on various finance and economics topics and has coauthored four books in finance and accounting. He has conducted numerous seminars for business managers and owners and has been a consultant to business firms and to the U.S. Government. In recognition of his accomplishments in both research and teaching, Professor Schall has been the recipient of the Bank of America Excellence Award and the Burlington Northern Foundation Award.

CHARLES W. HALEY is Professor of Finance at the University of Washington. He received a BSE from the University of Michigan and his M.B.A. and Ph.D. in finance from Stanford University. Professor Haley is a coauthor of *The Theory of Financial Decisions* and has designed three bank management simulations. He has been the Managing Editor of the *Journal of Financial and Quantitative Analysis* and Associate Editor for three other journals. His teaching and research has focused on financial management of business firms and financial institutions. He has been on the faculties of the Stonier Graduate School of Banking and the Pacific Coast Banking School since 1971.

CONTENTS

ix

PREFACE

In this edition our primary goal is to provide students with a thorough foundation in finance. For many students the introductory course is the only exposure to finance, and we cover all the material that we believe is essential to a comprehensive understanding of financial management. In today's world such an understanding must include international aspects of finance, and we have integrated international issues throughout. Although the text covers a wide range of topics and issues, we have treated the material at an introductory level in all cases. Our method has been to explain the main issues very carefully in order to provide the student with an intuitive understanding of finance concepts and an appreciation of the way those concepts are applied in practice.

The text does not neglect students who will be taking additional courses in finance. Basic principles, techniques, and institutional aspects needed for effective analysis of business finance cases are well covered. A foundation for more advanced theoretical courses is provided in the chapter appendixes and in Chapters 6 and 9. Throughout we have tried to ensure that our approach here is consistent with current theory. Students completing a course of study using this book should be well prepared for courses in investments because of our stress on risk and return in the financial markets and our coverage of the basic characteristics of securities and markets.

The book is designed for undergraduate one-quarter or one-semester courses, although it is unlikely that all chapters can be assigned in a single course. If supplemented by cases and readings, it will be suitable as the primary text for courses extending two quarters or more. Instructors using this text for an introductory course for MBA students will find that Chapters 6 and 9 and the appendixes to Chapters 4, 5, 8, 9, 12, and 17 enable them to approach basic finance on a more advanced level.

We have made a special effort to provide an integrated discussion of the topics covered. Nevertheless, the book has been designed to offer great flexibility in choosing the order of presentation of most chapters. Furthermore, many chapters have one or more sections that can be deleted without any loss of continuity. Appendixes in several chapters explore major concepts in greater depth. These are intended as supplements to the basic coverage in the text and are designed for use by well-prepared undergraduate and beginning graduate students.

The first six chapters provide an introduction to the book and an introduction to finance in general. In Part 1 we examine the general nature of financial management, the financial system, taxes and other legal issues, organization, compound-interest calculations, risk, and the principles of market valuation.

Parts 2 through 4 cover the basic concepts and techniques of financial management. Part 2 is concerned with long-term decisions involving investments and financing, including dividend policy. Part 3 explores techniques of financial analysis, including ratio analysis, funds flow, break-even analysis, and forecasting. Part 4 deals with the problems of managing the firm's current assets and current liabilities. The discussion in Part 4 is unusual in that the firm's working capital decisions are explicitly linked to the discussion of long-term investment and financing decisions in Part 2.

Parts 5 deals with several special topics that are often not covered in an introductory course. This section covers leasing as a method of financing, the characteristics of securities involving options including convertible debt and warrants, holding companies, mergers, and acquisition.

CHANGES IN THE SIXTH EDITION

In this edition we decided to reorganize the text. The two objectives in this reorganization were to integrate international aspects of financial management throughout and to make all topics more accessible to students. The specific changes include:

1 Integration of international material into all chapters where it is relevant. This includes the majority of chapters.
2 A new Chapter 3 on the legal environment including organizational form, taxes, and bankruptcy. The tax treatment is up to date as of the beginning of 1990.
3 A new Chapter 9 on special topics in capital budgeting. Chapter 8 now provides the fundamentals of capital budgeting.
4 A new Chapter 11 that describes the major types of securities issued by firms and the issuing process. Chapter 12 focuses on the decision as to which securities to issue.
5 Current asset management is now covered in two chapters—Chapter 17 dealing with inventory and accounts receivable management and Chapter 18 dealing with cash and securities management.
6 The majority of problems are new or revised from the fifth edition and many of them have an international focus.

TEXT ORGANIZATION AND SUPPLEMENTARY MATERIALS

Although this book has been written to offer substantial latitude in selecting which chapters to cover and their order of presentation, we suggest that certain chapters be taught in a given order. Chapters 4, 5, 7, 8, 11, 14, 16, and 17 are prerequisites for certain other chapters. Specifically, Chapter 4 should precede Chapter 5, and Chapters 4 and 5 should precede all of Part 2 (Chapters 7 through 13). We recommend that the chapters in Part 2 be taught in sequence. However, not all of this material need be covered. A complete discussion of the possibilities for alternative sequences is included in the *Instructor's Manual* for the text. Many instructors may choose to assign Chapters 14, 15, and 16—which cover financial statement analysis, break-even analysis, and forecasting, respectively—early in the course. This can be done with no difficulty, although the discussion of financial leverage in Chapter 15 is most effectively taught if it is presented after Chapter 12. A sequence that we find quite workable in one quarter consists of Chapters 1 through 5, 7 through 14 and 16 through 20.

Students come to the basic finance course with a wide range of prior preparation in accounting, mathematics, and economics. We have assumed minimal background in these areas, but we do expect that students have had at least one quarter of financial accounting shortly before taking the class. Able students should be capable of mastering the material almost without regard to their previous formal course work. We have tried to make the book as self-contained as possible and, through extensive use of examples, to make it suitable for self-study. Many of the problems are suitable for solution using a microcomputer, and a software disk designed for this text is available.

As an aid to students, many instructors recommend a study guide when such is available. The *Study Guide* written by Thomas E. Stitzel serves as an excellent review and supplement to this book. It contains additional solved problems as well as questions in a programmed learning format. We believe that many students will find this supplement helpful.

The *Instructor's Manual* includes a substantial amount of supplementary teaching material, as well as recommended course outlines, a test bank, and answers to text questions and problems. Overhead transparencies are available upon adoption.

The test items are available from McGraw-Hill, Inc., on the Rhtest microcomputer system for computerized test generation. These systems can be obtained by contacting your local McGraw-Hill representative.

The *Computer Models* software package contains a series of spreadsheets to solve many of the problems contained within the text. The spreadsheets are arranged by chapters and cover the major topics of the text.

ACKNOWLEDGMENTS

Many people have aided us in this project. Our students provided us with numerous comments that have resulted in substantial improvements over earlier versions of the text. Colleagues at the University of Washington and elsewhere have reviewed drafts of the manuscripts, and we are very grateful for their help. Our thanks go to Durwood Alkire, Henry H. Barker, William J. Bertin, Zvi Bodie, Don Boyd, Gregory Breen, Stephen G. Buell, Brian T. Carroll, Jess Chua, John Crockett, Fred Delva, Mark Dorfman, Eugene F. Drzycimski, Russell Ezzell, James F. Feller, John K. Ford, Michael Giliberto, John H. Hand, David Heskel, George W. Hettenhouse, Pat Hill, Gailen L. Hite, Lee Hoover, Michael

H. Hopwell, Donald Houthaker, James Hugon, F. Lee Hull, Richard Johnson, Ann Kremer, Gene Laber, John B. Major, Rita M. Maldonado-Bear, Robert McDonald, Robert McGee, Judy Elmore Maese, Allen Michel, Michael Miller, Donald A. Nast, Gerald Newbould, Terrence W. O'Keefe, Robert T. Patton, Gerald W. Perritt, Herb Phillips, Jerry Platt, Arthur Rasher, Bill Resler, Michael Rice, Ralph Ringgenberg, Rick Rivard, William Sartoris, William L. Scott, John Settle, Bernard A. Shinkel, Joel Shulman, Donald G. Simonson, Ronald Sprecher, Thomas E. Stitzel, Timothy Sullivan, Howard E. Van Auken, Nikhil Varaiya, Marc Vellrath, James A. Verbrugge, Jerry A. Viscione, Ernest W. Walker, Michael C. Walker, Ralph Walking, Larry White, Roger Wong, Gene Wunder, Francis Yeager, and J. Kenton Zumwalt. We would also like to thank J. S. Butler, Vanderbilt University; Albert R. Eddy, Loyola College; Ali M. Fatemi, Kansas State University; James F. Feller, Middle Tennessee State University; Norman Gardner, Boise State University; Irene Hammerbacher, Iona College; Eric Haye, St. John's University; F. Lee Hull, California State University; Ronald Hutchins, Eastern Michigan University; George K. Keyt, Southwest Texas State University; David J. Kim, Indiana State University; Robert T. LeClair, Villanova University; Wayne E. Mackie, Saginaw Valley State University; Surendra K. Mansinghka, San Francisco State University; Thomas E. McCue, George Washington University; Robert B. McElreath, Jr., Clemson University; Susan Moeller, Northeastern University; Jerry B. Poe, Arizona State University; Dennis P. Sheehan, Purdue University; Patrick M. Shen, Michigan Technological University, School of Business and Engineering; A. Charlene Sullivan, Purdue University; Robert A. Wallace, Gannon University; and John R. Weigel, Elmhurst College. We owe a great deal to Steven Thorley, who did research on the international aspects of finance in assisting us on this book, and wrote the first drafts of a major portion of the international finance sections. Mazhar Siddiqi did a wonderful job in reviewing many parts of the book and in supervising important stages of our production process. Special thanks go to Grant McQueen, who wrote "Computer Spreadsheets for Financial Analysis" (following Chapter 16), and to Marilyn Johnson, who prepared the initial draft of "Venture Capital" (following Chapter 11). We are indebted to Charles D'Ambrosio, who provided us with encouragement and advice throughout the development of the book and helped us at numerous junctures. The cash management discussion in Chapter 18 benefited greatly from a tutorial given by Bernell Stone at the 1986 Financial Management Association Meetings. Betty Schall provided us with important advice and assistance in writing Chapter 3. Paul Allen, Terence Barron, Jean-Claude Bosch, Gregg Brauer, Susan Doolittle, Keith Hauschulz, Doug Hensler, Paul Makens, Ellen Morgan, Thomas Munro, John Settle, Michael Sherry, and Kaj Svarrer developed many of the end-of-chapter questions and problems and provided us with helpful suggestions for the text material. We are very grateful to Ellen Morgan for her meticulous preparation of the index, and to Teresa Ho for her excellent efforts on the *Instructor's Manual* and the index.

The editorial staff at McGraw-Hill has been a critical resource for us. Kaye Pace, Editor in Chief of Business and Economics, gave us early encouragement and support on this project. Finance Editors Suzanne BeDell and Kenneth MacLeod guided this edition through its various stages and were encouraging supporters at every turn. And we remain deeply indebted to Marjorie Singer, whose numerous recommendations and suggestions were invaluable in our writing the first and second editions; her legacy lives on in the sixth edition. Finally, the book could not have been written without the continued support of Anne Haley.

Lawrence D. Schall
Charles W. Haley

PART ONE

THE ENVIRONMENT OF FINANCIAL DECISIONS

Part 1 consists of six chapters in which we present the general background for individual and company financial decisions. Chapter 1 is an introduction to business finance and to this text. Here we discuss the nature and objectives of financial management. In Chapter 2 we examine the American financial system: the network of financial institutions and markets that is an important part of the financial manager's environment. Chapter 3 covers other aspects of this environment, the legal form of business organizations, the tax laws that affect financial decisions, and financial distress. Whereas the material in the first three chapters is largely descriptive, in Chapter 4 we develop a fundamental financial concept, the time value of money. We show here how to solve a variety of basic financial problems involving time and money. Chapter 5 explains how securities (bonds and stocks)
are valued in the market, and examines the theory of efficient markets. In an appendix, we discuss the term structure of interest rates. Chapter 6 explores the concept of risk and shows how risk affects the value of securities. We introduce a model of financial market equilibrium—the Capital Asset Pricing Model—and discuss its implications for financial management.

The material in Part 1 is important not just to the managers of business firms. Most of the topics covered are of equal importance to an individual concerned with such financial problems as borrowing money and choosing alternative ways of investing personal savings. The remainder of the text is almost exclusively concerned with problems faced by financial managers; but these first six chapters cover financial concepts that are useful to everyone.

CHAPTER ONE

FINANCIAL MANAGEMENT AND GOALS

This is a book about financial decisions—the financial decisions of a company. We will examine concepts which apply to giant corporations such as Exxon and General Motors and to small obscure companies which produce products you may never see. The underlying financial principles are essentially the same for all companies big or small: There are goals to be defined and facts to be considered using methods of analysis that are consistent with the goals. This book discusses those goals and presents those analytical methods within the context of important contemporary issues and the practices of modern financial management.

The financial decisions of a company can affect many groups in society. This chapter examines the two most controversial relationships: between the stockholders (owners) and management (which makes most of the decisions), and between the company and the rest of society. Each of these relationships can involve mutual benefit or serious conflict. The first part of this chapter discusses the problems that can create conflicts, and explains how these differences are, at least in part, resolved. We then inquire into the nature of finance as a discipline, and into the functions and objectives of the financial manager as a practitioner of this discipline.

THE CORPORATE OBJECTIVE

To perform effectively, the financial manager must have a clear understanding of the company's goals. We will begin by distinguishing between policies and goals. We then ask who determines the policies and goals of a company—its stockholders, management, or society—and, equally important, what goals are ordinarily pursued by firms in practice.

One of the most important goals of business firms is maximization of the owners' interest in the firm (maximization of value of the corporation's shares),[1] though nowadays social considerations can also be an

---

[1] As explained in Chap. 3, a corporation is a company whose owners are called "shareholders" or "stockholders." Each shareholder owns pieces of paper called "stock certificates" or "shares," which represent the owner's interest in the company. If a company has a total of 100,000 shares outstanding, the owner of 1000 shares owns 1 percent of the firm.

important company objective—for example, helping to save energy or minimizing pollution. The policies of a company are *the strategies it employs to achieve its goals*. Company policy may involve such questions as whether to try to speed up growth by buying existing businesses, how much to invest in research and development, and what degree of risk to accept in launching new products.

A company's goals and policies are determined—theoretically—by the owners (the shareholders or stockholders) as represented by an elected board of directors. The board's responsibility is to make major policy decisions affecting the firm and to hire the day-to-day management team. In practice, however, the board of directors usually consists of a slate which is proposed by the company's management and which includes the top echelon of the management team. Thus, in reality, the shareholders delegate to management enormous powers to "run the company"—that is to say, to set its goals and shape its policies. There are two good reasons for this. The first is that it would be impractical and inefficient to transmit to management the views of every stockholder on every issue. Second, the owners recognize that professional managers, because of their training and expertise, are better qualified than they are to operate the business. This delegation of authority is acceptable to most stockholders, so long as the company's performance is satisfactory in terms of dividend payments and earnings.

Owner and Management Objectives

Small businesses are usually managed by their owners. For such firms there cannot be any conflicts between owners and managers, since they are the same people. But most large firms are run by professional managers who, by law, represent the stockholders. The duty of management is to pursue the goals of the stockholders in a manner consistent with the law.

During the past decade, a whole body of financial theory—called *agency theory*—has emerged which, in part, deals with the relationship between stockholders and management and the costs imposed on stockholders when conflicts between the two exist. Conflicts between management and shareholders may arise because the managers place their own interests ahead of those of the shareholders. They may, for example, grant themselves excessive salaries and perquisites. Or management may pursue expansionary policies simply to increase the company's size even though the growth does not enhance earnings per share prospects (for some, it's more fun to manage a billion dollar company than a $500 million company; also, salaries and perquisites are generally larger the bigger the company). Or the shareholders may feel that management, in order to maintain its position, has painted an unrealistically rosy picture of the company's performance. There are many well-known cases in which management concealed major mistakes and even illegal acts. A notorious example was the Equity Funding scandal of 1973, in which audacious frauds and other hocus-pocus committed by management remained hidden from the stockholders—and from government regulatory authorities—for as long as nine years. It was ultimately revealed that the company's reported profits were nonexistent and that more than

$100 million of its assets had been faked. The stockholders lost several hundred million dollars. Equity Funding's president and eighteen officers and employees of the company pleaded guilty to charges brought against them and were sentenced to varying jail terms.

But quite apart from the issue of wrongdoing, it is extremely difficult for the average shareholder to know what marks to award to management. On the one hand, it is impossible for a stockholder without exceptional expertise to know how much better the firm's performance might have been if different policies had been adopted. On the other hand, difficulties occur that are due to circumstances beyond management's control. For example, one cannot really blame cigar makers for the decline in the popularity of cigars, or blame the manufacturers of plastic toys for the sharp increase in materials costs after the oil embargo of 1973.

The question that naturally follows is "What assurances are there that management will serve, rather than exploit, the stockholders?" There are several mechanisms that protect the shareholder's position. **Stock option** plans, under which operating officers become part owners of the company, help align management's interests with the stockholders' interests. A similar function is served when part of executive compensation is a cash or stock bonus which depends on the company's earnings or on some other performance measure. Executives of many large corporations—such as International Harvester, Pillsbury, and Honeywell—have received huge bonuses under such plans. It is not uncommon for over 50 percent of a top executive's compensation to be in the form of nonsalary rewards (e.g., bonuses and stock options) pegged to company performance. There is also the threat of bad publicity by a disgruntled stockholder who can embarrass management and create discontent among other stockholders if the grievances are well founded. Stockholder complaints can result in a change of management, especially if the stockholder leading a movement is a major investor in the company. Corporate boards and managers also face legal liability for their actions. For example, since 1980 all corporate directors have had to sign the corporation's 10K report to the SEC; the effect of this has been to increase the board's accountability for the report's contents. Broadened director liability has made it increasingly difficult for corporations to recruit directors, even for hefty director fees. Although this has primarily been a problem for smaller companies, it has also affected some of the larger, well-known firms (for example, Control Data Corporation and Allegheny International, Inc.).

As an added protection to shareholders, corporate boards now include an increasing number of outside directors who have no direct ties with management. Among those serving in this capacity on several boards are former President Gerald R. Ford, former Secretary of Commerce Juanita M. Kreps, and former Federal Reserve Board governor Andrew Brimmer.

The possibility of an outside takeover of the company can also be a powerful deterrent to mismanagement. Although the small shareholders may not have the requisite knowledge to judge management's performance, there are well-financed outsiders who do have such knowledge. Such parties are constantly on the lookout for opportunities to purchase a company with unrealized potential. It should be pointed out that in practice, although takeovers do often occur, many takeover attempts either never go beyond the planning stage or fail. Many takeover efforts are abandoned early because of the cost. This is so whether the parties involved are outsiders or an insurgent group of stockholders. If the takeover is attempted through large purchases of stock, the price offered will have to be substantially above the current market price in order to induce existing stockholders to sell out. Furthermore, management will often successfully resist a takeover attempt by using any of a variety of tactics, including lawsuits or a merger with another firm which is friendly to management. If the takeover is targeted at electing a new slate of directors without massive purchases of stock, all the company's stockholders have to be contacted and persuaded individually to cast their votes at the annual meeting for the newly proposed slate of directors. The promotional, legal, and other expenses involved in such an undertaking run to large numbers. What's more, the chances of success—judging from the historical record—are not encouraging. To begin with, the existing board of directors has a significant advantage; it is entitled to use the company's funds to defend its position through mailings to stockholders. More important, the inertia of stockholders—coupled with their normal distrust of insurgents or outsiders—usually ensures victory for the incumbent board, unless it is guilty of dishonesty or company performance has been conspicuously bad.

Having emphasized the large costs of stockholder revolts and takeover bids, it should be noted that takeovers are frequent occurrences. Indeed, many companies, such as Textron and International Telephone and Telegraph (IT&T), have grown into giant conglomerates by acquiring other companies and making them more profitable. A mismanaged company with depressed stock prices can be a particularly attractive acquisition if the buyer has the know-how to turn the company around.

The Corporation and Society

To economist John Kenneth Galbraith and muckraker-consumer advocate Ralph Nader, large corporations are all too often unscrupulous and antisocial, and are in dire need of house-training and socialization, preferably through strict government controls (or nationalization). They argue that, without government involvement, wealth inequalities will become unacceptably great, the environment will be ruined, and social injustice will reign unchallenged. Not so, assert economist Milton Friedman, social commentator Irving Kristol (editor of *Public Interest* and columnist in *The Wall Street Journal*), and other ardent defenders of capitalism. They hold that the primary function of a business firm is to make a profit by producing products demanded in the marketplace. Not only is an unfettered capitalism conducive to economic efficiency but, they say, perhaps more importantly, to liberty and democracy.

Unfortunately, we cannot resolve the debate here. But we *can* say that the debate is a reflection of a generally divided opinion about how much nonbusiness (government, labor, consumer groups, etc.) involvement in business decisions is best, and of the fact that substantial involvement is almost certain. Government financial intervention (for example, the 1980 $1.5 billion United States loan guarantee for Chrysler) and regulatory intervention may change form, or even diminish, but a return to the pre-1960 philosophy of "what's good for General Motors is good for the country" (quoted from Charles Wilson, former Secretary of Defense and former head of General Motors) is highly unlikely. What policies should a firm adopt and what goals should it pursue in such an environment? From a moral standpoint there is no generally acceptable answer, for people differ on what is or is not moral. From a legal standpoint, the answer is much clearer: Management should adopt policies that are lawful and which satisfy stockholder wishes. Stockholders want the value of their ownership interest to be as great as possible, which means a company policy that emphasizes earnings. Corporate stockholders generally do not like to mix their investment portfolios with their social concerns; perhaps not too surprisingly, the General Motors shareholders voted 97.27 percent against expanding the board of directors to include "public" representatives and voted 97.56 percent against the creation of a Committee for Corporate Responsibility. It should be pointed out, though, that maximization of share values usually means obeying the laws, such as antipollution statutes, that compel firms to protect society's interests. Violation of such laws can be very expensive in terms of government fines and hostile consumer reactions. Since share value maximization is the most important target for management, let us take a closer look at this objective.

The Firm's Objective

We will assume in this book that shareholders and management (which represents shareholders) prefer policies that maximize the market value of the company's shares. Share values depend on the firm's earnings, since earnings are used to pay dividends and to reinvest in productive assets that will generate earnings in later years. But the risk as well as the level of earnings is important to shareholders. It is true that stockholders always prefer that the company achieve greater earnings per share than less. However, when a particular policy is adopted, the *future* effect on earnings is ordinarily uncertain. Shareholders may, for example, prefer policy A that provides completely safe (certain) future company earnings of $50,000 per year over "risky" policy B that will result in earnings as high as $100,000 or as low as zero, with an equal chance for all amounts between zero and $100,000. Both policies imply an average of $50,000 per year in the firm's earnings, but B is clearly less certain than A.[2] It is likely that in a market of investors who do not like risk the value of the firm's shares will be greater under policy A than under policy B. Later

---

[2] The average earnings under policy B are computed by simply taking the midpoint between the highest ($100,000) and lowest (zero) possible earnings outcomes, since all outcomes from zero to $100,000 are equally likely. The $50,000 is therefore a middle estimate of the earnings outcome of policy B.

chapters in the book will examine in detail the impact of risk on company policy.

Using share value maximization as the objective does not mean that management is concerned with day-to-day fluctuations in the stock market. It is true that as long as existing stockholders and other investors in the market have accurate and timely information on the firm's activities, better performance will mean a higher market price for the stock. However, information may not be immediately available to investors, and there may be different views as to what the available information implies about the firm's future performance. Hence, the real concern of management is to maximize share value over the long term.

Figure 1-1 illustrates the interactions between a firm's owners, its management, and society. The details of these interactions differ from company to company. And for virtually all firms the relationships vary over time as a result of changes in our social and economic institutions.

*Is Share Value
Maximization
Ethical?*

In the wake of insider trading scandals, defense contract overcharges, and alleged cover-ups of environmental damages, managers are being pressured to give more consideration to ethical principles in their business decisions. Does this mean that an objective of share value maximization leads to unethical decisions or that this objective itself is unethical? The answers to these questions are subject to differences of opinion because there is no general agreement in all cases on what is ethical. However, there is a basic principle that ethical behavior by managers requires them to consider the impact of any action or decision they make on other people. In business firms "other people" include

FIGURE 1-1

*Formulation of
company objectives
and policies. The
firm's objectives are
primarily based on
owner preferences and
on the economic and
legal environment;
however, the objectives
that are sought by the
firm may be affected
by management
attitudes. The policies
to achieve the
objectives are
developed by
management and
influenced by legal and
economic factors.*

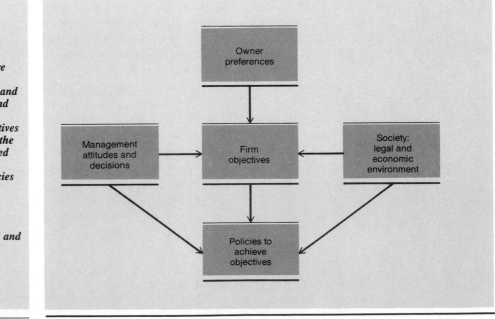

shareholders, employees, customers, and people in the communities where the company conducts its business. These are the people who are most likely to be affected by a business decision.

Share value maximization as an objective tells the manager to consider the impact of decisions on the firm's shareholders. This can be viewed by itself as a guiding principle or rule for ethical behavior by managers. It is based, in part, on the concept that, as employees of a company, managers have a responsibility to act in the best interest of those who hire them, the firm's owners. It is also based on theories that economic efficiency will be highest if managers follow this rule. Furthermore, many believe that share value maximization leads to an enlightened self-interest that produces socially responsible behavior. According to a recent survey, the managers of major U.S. corporations believe that share value maximization requires them to maintain high standards of ethical behavior in all their business dealings.[3]

Most corporations today have published guidelines for ethical conduct by their employees. These guidelines are presumably consistent with the corporate objective. Does this mean that following the rules is sufficient? Not really, since the rules cannot cover all the possible situations that can arise and may, from time to time, be in conflict. Philosophers have attempted for centuries to develop general guiding principles for ethical behavior. The major principles or theories are utilitarianism, egalitarianism, respect for others' rights, and libertarianism.

- Utilitarianism is concerned with the results of actions and holds that ethical decisions are those that provide "the greatest good for the greatest number" of people. Utilitarianism focuses on costs and benefits and essentially says that ethical decisions are those that produce the highest net benefits. This approach tends to be very attractive to managers, as it fits generally with other business and economic concepts. A variation of this theory is concerned with rules for decisions that, if generally applied, will produce maximum long run net benefits. As we noted above, share value maximization is an example of such a rule.
- Egalitarianism is also concerned with results and holds that actions (or rules) that produce equal benefits for everyone are ideal and those that produce unequal benefits are acceptable only if they produce some benefits for everyone, especially those least well off. This doctrine places the greatest weight on the distribution of benefits and costs in contrast to utilitarianism, which emphasizes maximizing aggregate net benefits.
- Rights theories are concerned with the reasons for making decisions (not so much the results), with an emphasis on individual rights. A

---

[3] The Business Roundtable, *Corporate Ethics: A Prime Business Asset,* New York, 1988. For example, a company that lies to its customers will lose their trust, the sales and profits of the company will decrease, and, therefore, share value will decrease.

basic rule for ethical behavior is "never treat people only as means, but always also as ends." The rights doctrine was the basis for the Bill of Rights of the U.S. Constitution.

● Libertarianism is also concerned with processes. The fundamental idea is one of individuals freely (without coercion) entering into agreements with each other. Ethical behavior involves keeping one's promises and agreements. This theory is also consistent with standard business practices.

The main point here is that there are many dimensions of ethical behavior, and the principles described above may provide conflicting guides as to what is ethical in a particular situation. Different cultures often have different standards as to what is ethical. There is another rule: "When in Rome, do as the Romans do." American business managers posted abroad must often consider this adage.

An important question is "How serious must be the conflict between share value maximization and other guiding principles before a manager must decide that an action that benefits the shareholders is not ethical or that an action that will harm the shareholders is ethical?" There is no clear-cut answer. But ethical behavior probably means asking the question often.

THE KEY ROLE OF FINANCE

The Financial Manager

The financial manager plays a central role in the company. As summarized in Table 1-1, the manager's duties include budgeting, raising funds in the capital markets, evaluating investment projects, and planning the company's marketing and pricing strategies. An individual manager is often a specialist, with a knowledge of many areas of finance but particular expertise in one or two specialities. The breadth of the finance function is so great that in many companies it includes personnel from several departments and involves may echelons of management.

TABLE 1-1
Major finance-related functions in a firm

1. Financing and investments: supervising the firm's cash and other liquid holdings, raising additional funds when needed, and investing funds in projects
2. Accounting and control: maintaining financial records; controlling financial activities; identifying deviations from planned and efficient performance; and managing payroll, tax matters, inventories, fixed assets, and computer operations
3. Forecasting and long-run planning: forecasting costs, technological changes, capital market conditions, funds needed for investment, returns on proposed investment projects, and demand for the firm's product; and using forecasts and historical data to plan future operations, e.g., planning services and uses of cash
4. Pricing: determining the impact of pricing policies on profitability
5. Other functions: credit and collections, insurance, and incentive planning (pensions, option plans, etc.)

The talents required of financial managers are rapidly expanding and, because of this, corporations are increasingly looking outside their existing ranks for individuals to fill the post of chief financial officer. The greater demands placed on financial executives results from two factors. First, financial analytic techniques and financial securities have become significantly more complex. Second, more companies now have operations or raise capital overseas. This means that the financial executive must be familiar not only with the customs and institutions of this country, but also with those of foreign countries, especially countries with important money market centers (major European nations and Japan).

The crucial role played by the finance staff has not gone unrecognized in executive promotions. Finance people have headed many corporate giants, including General Motors, General Electric, CBS, Anaconda, and Twentieth Century-Fox. This ascendency of finance people to top corporate positions is not surprising. Finance is concerned with the lifeblood of a company, money: how it is obtained to finance the business and how it should be used to assure the business's success. Clearly, skill in this area is an extremely valuable asset in managing a company.

Corporate Organization

The assignment of finance functions to individuals and departments will depend upon the size of the company. The larger the company, generally the greater the degree of specialization of tasks, and the greater the proliferation of positions and departments. A smaller firm would consolidate many duties into fewer departments.

Generally, corporations are required by state law to have a president, a secretary, and a treasurer. Historically, the chief finance officer has been the treasurer. In recent years, two other positions have evolved—the controller and the financial vice president. The controller supervises most of the accounting and control functions listed in Table 1-1, and the treasurer supervises or participates in most of the remaining finance functions. The treasurer oversees the company's liquid assets, liabilities, payroll and cashier activities, credits and collections, forecasting, capital budgeting and investments, and financing. The treasurer is an active participant in long-range financial planning. In the corporate hierarchy, the financial vice president is above the usually coequal controller and treasurer. The financial vice president supervises all financial operations and planning and advises the board of directors on financial matters.

Although the finance functions shown in Table 1-1 are generally performed by staff specifically assigned to those tasks, nonfinance personnel in other areas also participate in the financial decision-making process. For example, although cost recording and control are accounting and finance functions, the determination of standard costs and the responsibility for correcting for variations from realizable standards rests with the production department. Similarly, it is the task of the sales department to estimate the level of sales for various pricing policies; this information is utilized in financial planning to estimate profit levels for each price structure. Planning funds for operations and capital budgeting is a joint decision-making process conducted by the production, sales, and finance personnel. Thus, the need for a new machine might be determined by the production department, which submits its request to the division head (who is in part a financial manager). If the expenditure is not greater than a prescribed dollar amount, say, $20,000, the decision as to whether to acquire the machine would be made at this point. If the outlay is above that amount, the requisition would be submitted for approval to the home office with the division head's recommendation (and supporting data). The home office financial staff, and perhaps the board of directors, would then approve or disapprove the proposed investment, based upon data relating to projected production and sales, and the availability of funds to finance the investment.

FINANCE AS A DISCIPLINE

The focus of this text is on the financial management of business firms; however, the field of finance is much broader. Put simply, finance is a body of facts, principles, and theories dealing with the raising (for example, by borrowing) and using of money by individuals, businesses, and governments. Although our primary concern here will be with managerial finance, essential aspects of individual financial planning and of financial institutions will be covered.

The individual's financial problem is to maximize his or her well-being by appropriately using the resources available. Finance deals with how individuals divide their income between consumption (food, clothes, etc.) and investment (stocks, bonds, real estate, etc.), how they choose from among available investment opportunities, and how they raise money to provide for increased consumption or investment.

Firms also have the problem of allocating resources and raising money. Management must determine which investments to make and how to finance those investments. Just as the individual seeks to maximize his or her happiness, the firm seeks to maximize the wealth of its owners (stockholders).

Finance also encompasses the study of financial markets and institutions, and the activities of governments, with stress on those aspects relating to the financial decisions of individuals and companies. A familiarity with the limitations and opportunities provided by the institutional environment is crucial to the decision-making process of individuals and firms. In addition, financial institutions and governments have financial problems comparable to those of individuals and firms. The study of these problems is an important part of the field of finance.

The central topic of this text is business financial management. In addition to a knowledge of strictly company financial affairs, an appreciation of the individual's investment behavior and preferences is critical to a full understanding of managerial finance. Managers are representatives of existing shareholders; they must contract with new stockholders and creditors in raising funds. They are also concerned with financial institutions because these institutions conduct the firm's activities in financial markets. A sensitivity to the financial attitudes and concerns of these various parties is crucial to management's effectiveness.

THE ORGANIZATION OF THIS BOOK

This text provides the background and tools required for effective financial management. Of course, topics can be dealt with here only on an introductory level. Additional readings are recommended for those interested in going further. Part 1 describes the general environment for individual and company financial decisions. Financial institutions, markets, and securities, as well as basic finance concepts such as the time value of money, risk, and valuation of securities, are introduced here. Part 2 examines the long-term investment and financial structure decisions of the company. The chapters cover risk and its relationship to capital budgeting and firm financing. Capital budgeting techniques and investment risk evaluation are explained in detail. The characteristics of alternative financing methods and the problem of choosing the appropriate methods are covered. Also included is a discussion of dividend policy and its relationship to a firm's financing policy. Part 3 describes tools of analysis that are useful for evaluating company performance and planning company operations. Part 4 discusses management of short-term assets and liabilities, and the relevance of short-run planning to long-term financial and marketing strategies. Part 5 deals with certain special problems confronting many firms: leasing, the use of convertibles and warrants, and business combinations.

SUMMARY

The primary objective of shareholders and management is generally maximization of the value of the owners' interest in the company (maximization of the value of the firm's shares). Conflicts arise between stockholders, management, and society at large. Differences between stockholders and management can be minimized by various factors, such as stock option plans that make managers part owners, or the possibility of the company's takeover by dissatisfied parties who would replace the existing management. Socially oriented company policies are sometimes encouraged by prodding from stockholders but more often by laws (e.g., antipollution statutes). Any such laws are ordinarily viewed by management as constraints within which the company seeks to maximize profits.

The financial manager is a key person in the business organization, frequently rising to the top post in the firm. The finance function includes a wide variety of responsibilities, including budgeting and investing funds, accounting, product pricing, and forecasting.

The field of finance embraces many subareas, including personal finance, financial institutions, and managerial finance. This is a text on managerial finance, that is, on the financial management of business firms. However, we will touch upon other finance areas that are important in fully understanding business financial management.

CHAPTER TWO

THE FINANCIAL SYSTEM: DOMESTIC AND INTERNATIONAL

The financial system provides the background for all business enterprises. This system consists of the institutions and markets that serve companies and individuals in financing the acquisition of goods and services, in investing capital, and in transferring the ownership of securities. A knowledge of our financial system is important not only for financial managers, but for informed citizens as well.

An efficient financial system is essential to a healthy economy. Its primary role is the distribution of capital in the economy. For example, the personal savings of an individual, placed in a bank, can be loaned to another individual to buy a house or to a business firm to build a plant. Thus the activity of the financial system affects every citizen.

We begin by outlining the nature of the services provided by the financial system and the institutions providing them. We then look at the various types of securities that are issued and traded in the domestic financial markets and the factors that determine the general level of interest rates in the economy. The final section deals with international financial markets and exchange rates.

SERVICES PROVIDED BY THE FINANCIAL SYSTEM

The primary role of the financial system in the economy is to aid in transforming the **savings** (income minus expenditures on goods and services in a given time period) of some individuals and companies into **investment** (purchases of physical assets that are used to produce goods and services) by others. *The financial system provides the principal means by which a person who has saved money out of current income can transfer these savings to someone else who has productive investment opportunities and needs money to finance them.*[1] This transfer of money almost always results in the creation of a **financial asset**, which is

---

[1] The "persons" described in this section can be individuals, business firms, farmers, governmental units, etc.

a claim against the future income and assets of the person who issued the asset. From the viewpoint of the issuer, this claim is a **financial liability**. Therefore, for every financial asset owned by someone there is a corresponding financial liability for the issuer. Financial assets are the basic "products" of the financial system.

Types of Financial Assets

Financial assets fall into three general classes: money, debt, and stock. At the present time, money is issued by the federal government as paper currency and coins, and by some financial institutions as demand deposits and NOW accounts.[2] Debt is issued by practically everyone including governments, whereas stock is issued only by business firms. Our emphasis in this chapter will be on the creation of debt and stock because they are issued by business firms, whereas money is issued only by the federal government and financial institutions and is the medium of exchange for transactions in goods, services, and the other financial assets. Debt and stock are very important to financial managers. The issuer of debt promises to pay the creditor a specified amount of money at a future date, whereas the issuer of stock is selling ownership of the corporation. A stockholder is entitled to a share of the profits once the claims of the debtholders are satisfied. The precise amount of money to be paid to the owner of stock is not spelled out in advance as it is in the case of debt. Thus the stockholders (owners of stock) of a firm receive income from the firm only after its creditors (owners of debt) are paid what is owed them.

There are many different types of debt in the financial system. We will examine the major types issued by individuals, governments, and businesses in this chapter. Chapters 11 and 12 will discuss in detail the kinds of debt used by business firms. An important part of financial management is the intelligent use of debt in raising money for the company.

The two basic types of stock are **common stock** and **preferred stock**. Common stock represents the ownership of corporations. The owners of the common stock of a firm are the owners of the firm. The extent of ownership by any person depends on the number of shares of common stock held by the person relative to the total number of shares outstanding. For example, if the firm has 1000 shares of common stock outstanding, someone owning 100 shares would own 10 percent of the firm. Preferred stock is much less significant than common stock in terms of the amount outstanding. The owners of preferred stock are paid divi-

---

[2] Commercial banks provide demand deposit accounts (checking accounts) to everyone. Commercial banks, mutual savings banks, and savings and loan associations also issue NOW accounts to individuals and certain other types of customers such as nonprofit organizations. NOW stands for "negotiable order of withdrawal" and these accounts are essentially interest-bearing demand deposits. Most credit unions offer "share draft" accounts that are similar to NOW accounts. Demand deposits could be classified as debt, since they represent money that must be paid by the issuing financial institution on the demand of the owner. However, since checks drawn on demand deposits are widely used as a means of payment, they are usually classified as money.

*The Creation
and Transfer
of Financial
Assets*

dends before any dividends can be paid to the common stockowners. Many financial managers think of preferred stock as being similar to debt. When we say "stockholders" we always mean the owners of common stock, not the owners of preferred stock.

We have said that the primary role of the financial system is to serve the saving-investment process of the economy. The basic instruments in this process are the financial assets created when money is transferred from one person to another.

A direct transfer of money occurs when a person who wants to acquire money issues a financial asset (debt or stock) and sells it to someone who has money available. For example, a person starting a small business might issue shares of stock to friends and relatives in exchange for money. He or she might also borrow money from them (issue a debt claim in exchange for money). The financial asset issued in this process is simply a piece of paper which indicates the nature of the asset and which meets legal requirements for establishing the claim (debt or stock) in case disagreements arise between the two parties involved. Financial institutions such as security **brokers** and **dealers** are often used to facilitate direct transfers. A broker is in contact with people who have money and wish to own financial assets.[3] Thus a borrower can approach a broker who will arrange for the actual transfer of money from the investor to the borrower in exchange for financial assets. A dealer actually purchases the financial assets of borrowers and then sells them to investors. Brokers simply act as "go-betweens"; they don't actually own the financial assets and they charge a commission for their services. Dealers buy and sell financial assets; their income depends on the difference between the price they pay for an asset and the price they sell it for.

Sales of financial assets by the issuer, regardless of whether brokers or dealers are involved, are called **primary market transactions**. In contrast, most of the activity of brokers and dealers involves financial assets that have been issued *in the past* and are being sold by someone other than the person who originally issued them. There are **secondary markets** for existing financial assets just as there is a market for used cars. In these secondary markets, people who own the assets are able to sell them to others. The existence of secondary markets provides advantages to everyone. For an investor there is a greater choice of financial assets to purchase, since the investor isn't limited to purchasing newly issued ones. Also, someone who purchased the asset in the past can raise money now by selling it rather than having to wait until the original issuer pays it off. The secondary markets are of particular importance to the owners of common stock, since these securities need never be paid

---

[3] These people are often called "investors" since they wish to invest in financial assets. In order to distinguish between people who *have* money to invest and people who *need* money, we shall refer to people who have money as "investors" and people who need money as "borrowers."

off, so long as the corporation that issued the stock continues in existence.

As noted above, primary markets are those in which financial assets are originally issued. Since the amount of existing financial assets is much greater than the amount of new ones being issued, there is a great deal more activity in the secondary markets.

Indirect methods for transferring money involve the use of a group of financial institutions called **financial intermediaries**, for example, banks. Financial intermediaries purchase the financial liabilities of firms and individuals; they also borrow by issuing their own financial liabilities. As a simple example, consider a bank that has loaned money obtained from savers to a person who is buying a house. The new financial assets that have been created here are a home mortgage owned by the bank and savings accounts owned by savers. In a direct transaction there would be only one financial asset—the mortgage owned by savers.[4] There are several advantages to money transfers performed by financial intermediaries.

1   *Flexibility and liquidity.* The intermediary is able to provide large sums of money to a borrower by pooling the savings of several investors. Moreover, the intermediary can provide investors with financial assets which may be money or readily convertible into money at the same time that it is making loans which will not be repaid for a long time.

2   *Diversification.* By purchasing the debt issues of many different borrowers, the intermediary is able to increase the chances that most of the money lent will be repaid. Therefore, it is able to provide relatively low-risk assets to investors. The federal government further decreases the risk by insuring accounts in several types of financial institutions from losses.

3   *Convenience.* Intermediaries offer a variety of financial services to their customers besides loaning money and creating financial assets. It is convenient for a single person (individual or business) to deal with a single firm that can supply whatever services are needed.

4   *Expertise.* The intermediary, because it is continuously purchasing financial assets issued by many borrowers, becomes expert in the process. A single person, whether borrower or investor, is apt to be much less knowledgeable as to exactly what the proper form of the assets should be.

The services provided by the financial system and its component institutions also include various forms of insurance (life, health, fire, etc.), the facilitation of consumer and business transactions through the monetary system, and loans to consumers for purchase of goods and

---

[4] Technically, a mortgage is a pledge of property as collateral for a loan, and the debt instrument (e.g., a note) represents the financial asset. Following common usage, we use the term ''mortgage'' here to refer to the financial asset backed by the collateral.

services (as compared with financing investment in productive assets). Figure 2-1 summarizes the overall structure of the financial system and the general methods of creating and transferring financial assets. Borrowers such as business firms, governmental units, and individuals raise money by issuing financial assets either directly to investors or to financial intermediaries. Investors acquire financial assets directly from the borrowers, from financial intermediaries (indirectly financing borrowers), or through purchases of previously issued securities. Brokers and dealers (including investment bankers discussed later in the chapter) facilitate the creation and transfer of new financial assets from borrowers to investors and the transfer of previously issued financial assets from their owners to investors.

FINANCIAL INSTITUTIONS

The financial system consists of the financial markets and the financial institutions that, in many respects, create the markets. It is difficult to separate these two aspects of the system; however, we will look first at the financial institutions themselves and then describe the markets and the financial assets that are bought and sold in them.

Deposit-Type Financial Institutions

There are four types of financial institutions in the United States that accept demand or savings deposits—commercial banks, savings banks, savings and loan associations, and credit unions. They accept the money deposited by individuals, businesses, and governmental units and lend this money to other individuals, businesses, and governmental units.

FIGURE 2-1
The creation and transfer of financial assets.

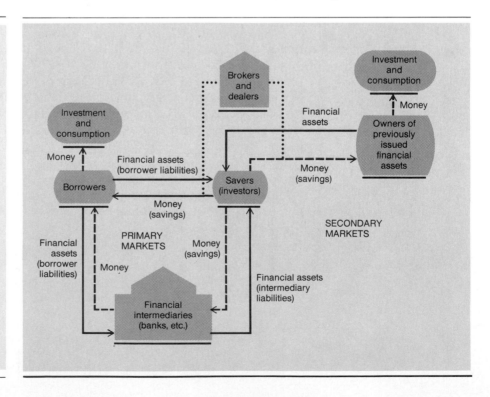

Commercial banks are by far the largest type of financial institution measured in terms of the amount of financial assets they hold. There are over 12,000 commercial banks in the United States. They hold substantial numbers of securities issued by governmental units, lend heavily to individuals both for purchases of homes and for other needs, and are a major source of credit to business firms (included as "other loans"). Commercial banks sometimes refer to themselves as "department stores of finance." They are very important to financial managers and their services are discussed in detail in Chapters 18 and 19.

Savings and loan associations and **savings banks** acquire the majority of their funds in the form of savings deposits by individuals. They then lend those funds to finance home purchases. Both make other types of loans to individuals and business; but primarily they (1) lend to individuals who wish to buy homes and (2) accept the deposits of individuals. Savings and loan associations are found in every state. They are second only to commercial banks in assets among all financial institutions and their assets have been growing faster than the commercial banks' assets. Savings banks are not as widespread as savings and loan associations. In the Northeast, where they are very active, savings banks have aggressively expanded the financial services provided to individuals. Many savings and loan associations have become savings banks to obtain the title of "bank," which better reflects the breadth of services they now offer.

Credit unions are institutions established to provide credit to individuals who share some common bond, such as working for the same firm. While they are relatively small financial institutions, there are many of them throughout the country (approximately 18,000 at the end of 1989) and they are growing rapidly. The members of the credit union provide the funds primarily in the form of savings accounts to lend out to other members who need money. Credit unions usually provide the least expensive kind of consumer credit available.

*Insurance
Companies*

Insurance companies can be divided into two types—life, and property and casualty. The two types play distinctly different roles in the financial system. To see why this is so, you must understand the nature of insurance contracts.

A basic insurance contract or **policy** involves the payment of a periodic fee or **premium** to the company in exchange for a promise to pay the insured if the peril that is being insured against occurs. For example, if you insure your house against loss through fire for $60,000 and the house burns down, you will collect $60,000 from the insurance company. The insurance company collects premiums from a large number of people to provide funds to pay the small number who actually have losses.

All basic insurance policies sold provide the insurance companies with investable funds, since the premiums are paid in advance. However, these funds are relatively temporary. To illustrate, suppose an insurance company collected $1 million in premiums at the beginning of the year on basic insurance policies covering perils for one year and sold no more insurance thereafter. By the end of the year, if the losses were as predicted, the only money left in the insurance company would be the profit on the insurance—perhaps $30,000 or so. The rest of the money would have been paid out in claims to policyholders and in operating expenses.

In contrast to basic insurance, life insurance policies often *incorporate a savings element*. A portion of the premium paid is set aside just as if it were a savings deposit in a bank. This portion earns interest, and the total accumulates over time as more premiums are paid and interest is added. The total amount saved is called the **cash value** of the policy. Policyholders who wish to cancel their insurance get the cash value paid to them. Because of this savings element, life insurance companies accumulate large amounts of money available for investment. In this activity they perform financial intermediation just like the deposit-type financial institutions. The importance of life insurance companies in the financial system is based more on their ability to accumulate funds for investment than on their stated business of providing insurance.

As a result of the savings component in life insurance policies, life insurance companies as a group are much larger in total assets than are property and casualty insurers, which only issue basic insurance. Life insurance companies hold large amounts of corporate securities and are a major source of business financing. They invest heavily in mortgages— both home mortgages, which they acquire through mortgage companies (discussed later in this chapter), and mortgages on commercial real estate.

Other Financial Institutions

There is a wide variety of other private financial institutions operating in the financial system.

Pension funds are established to provide income to retired or disabled persons in the economy. Pension funds for the employees of state and local governments invest heavily in corporate bonds and stocks and some mortgages. Private pension funds established by business firms are most often managed by the trust departments of commercial banks and by life insurance companies. The principal type of financial asset held by private pension funds is corporate stock.

Mutual funds are financial institutions established to invest the money of numerous individuals in securities of various types for the benefit of the individuals. The fund pays a fee to a management company consisting of professionals in the field of investments. These professionals manage the fund's assets, which are derived from selling "shares" to individuals. Mutual fund shares are a financial asset whose value equals the value of the securities and cash owned by the fund. The distinctive feature of mutual funds is that persons owning shares in the fund have a right to sell them back to the fund at their current asset value whenever they wish to do so. The fund is obligated to redeem the shares it issues, and mutual fund shares are not traded in secondary markets. The importance of these institutions in the financial system is that they provide an easy way for individuals to invest in a diversified portfolio of stocks and bonds. They are primarily active in the secondary markets.[5]

Mutual funds tend to specialize in their securities investments. Many funds invest almost exclusively in corporate stocks, and some of these stock funds concentrate on particular areas such as energy companies or insurance companies. One fund, Japan Fund, invests in stocks issued by Japanese corporations. Some funds hold mixed portfolios of stocks and bonds and others invest only in bonds. The dominant type of mutual fund is one that came into being in 1974—the money market mutual fund. Money market funds constituted more than half of all mutual fund assets at the end of 1989. They invest in short-term, low-risk securities (money market securities) issued by banks, other corporations, and the United States government that are described later in this chapter.

Finance companies raise their money by issuing securities and borrowing from commercial banks. They use their funds to make short- and intermediate-term loans to individuals and business firms. Finance companies can be broken into three types. **Sales finance companies** invest in consumer installment loans, especially automobile loans; the largest sales finance company is General Motors Acceptance Corporation, a subsidiary of General Motors. They also, as a group, lend money to business firms. **Personal finance companies** make small cash loans to individuals. Most people are aware of their activities from their substantial advertising programs. Household Finance Company and Beneficial Finance Company are personal finance companies. **Commercial finance companies** make large cash loans to business firms. Their activities are largely confined to high-risk customers who find it difficult to obtain financing from banks.

DOMESTIC FINANCIAL MARKETS AND SECURITIES

Financial markets exist wherever financial transactions occur. By financial transaction we mean the creation or transfer of a financial asset. This contrasts with the exchange of money for real goods or services, which would not be categorized as a financial transaction. People who transfer funds from checking accounts to savings accounts are operating in the financial markets just like those who buy government bonds, common stocks, or any other financial assets. From this example we can see that the financial markets are pervasive throughout the economy. Indeed, if we include purchases of goods on credit, virtually everyone in the country is active in them.

Financial markets are usually described by the financial assets being traded. Just as we can speak of the automobile market, we can speak of

---

[5] Mutual funds are a type of investment company. They are sometimes referred to as "open-end" investment companies because they are continuously selling and redeeming their shares. Mutual funds are much larger than other types of investment companies (such as "closed-end" investment companies, which do not redeem their shares) and therefore are the only type covered here.

the savings market or the corporate bond market. We will divide the domestic financial markets into two general classes—money markets and capital markets. *Money markets deal in short-term debts whereas capital markets deal in long-term debts and stock.* The only markets we will examine are those that are national in scope. The stock market is a national market. It is very easy for a miner in Butte, Montana to purchase General Motors stock that was previously owned by a seventy-two-year-old retiree residing in Fort Myers, Florida. The basic transaction might take place within five minutes after the miner placed an order to buy and the retiree placed an order to sell the stock, although the paperwork would take several days to complete.

In contrast to the stock market, the market for consumer credit is primarily a local one. For individuals and small firms, local financial markets can be quite important; however, medium-sized and large firms are more concerned with the money and capital markets presented here.

The Money Market

Knowledge of the operations of the money market is a measure of sophistication in the financial world. The securities traded are among the most esoteric of financial assets: federal funds, commercial paper, Treasury bills, banker's acceptances, certificates of deposit, and other short-term debt instruments. To be considered a money market security, a financial asset must have little or no risk of loss to the purchaser. The money market is centered in New York but operates through a national network of commercial banks and securities dealers. It serves as the basic glue that holds the financial system together because it is the part of the financial system which acts most directly in preventing appreciable differences in local and regional interest rates. The existence of a national money market, more than any other single aspect of the financial system, makes it possible to speak of a general level of interest rates that applies to the economy as a whole. In order to understand this, let us examine the financial assets that are issued and traded in the market.

Federal Funds Depository financial institutions offering checking accounts are required to have reserves as a percentage of the amount of these accounts. The bulk of these reserves are deposits in Federal Reserve banks. Federal funds are simply these deposits that can be "bought" and "sold" in the money market. A "sale" of federal funds is a *loan* by one institution to another. The loan is usually for one day only or over a weekend. The total volume of such loans can exceed $20 billion per day, and the basic trading unit is $1 million.

The interest rate on federal funds is one of the most volatile interest rates in the economy. It reflects daily, even hourly, changes in the financial markets. Most transactions in the economy for goods and services as well as for financial assets involve the use of checks drawn on deposits in commercial banks. As funds are withdrawn and deposited throughout the economy, some banks accumulate more deposits with the Federal Reserve than they need to cover their reserve requirements. Other banks have shortages. Federal funds provide a mechanism for banks with excess reserves to provide them to banks with shortages. Therefore, the demand and supply of federal funds depends on transactions throughout the economy and is sensitive to all kinds of changes in the financial system. Also, the Federal Reserve itself operates in the money markets as a means of implementing monetary policy by buying and selling United States government securities. The actions of the Federal Reserve have appreciable impact on the federal funds market, because a purchase of securities by the Federal Reserve is paid for by increasing the reserve accounts of member banks, and a sale results in a decrease in those deposits. The Federal Reserve uses the interest rate on federal funds as an index of the impact of its activities in the money markets.

Treasury Bills   Every Monday at 1:30 P.M. (New York time), the U.S. Treasury closes the bidding on its weekly 91-day and 182-day debt issues. Later in the afternoon the successful bidders, primarily financial institutions, will be told how much of some several billions of dollars in bills being sold they have just bought. Payment is due and the actual bills will be delivered on Thursday. Once a month a similar process will occur for nine- and twelve-month bills. The United States government is continuously borrowing money to pay for expenditures in excess of tax receipts and to pay off maturing debt issues. Treasury bills are short-term (one year or less) debts of the federal government of the United States. The **par value** or **face value** of a bill is the amount of money that will be paid to the purchaser when the bill is due. The interest return to an investor is provided by the difference between the par value of the bills and the price the investor pays for them. This difference is called the **discount** on the bill. For example, a bill might initially be sold by the Treasury for $950 to be redeemed for its par value of $1000 a year later. The original purchaser would earn $50 on an investment of $950 if it is held for a year. There is an active secondary market in bills, and the investor can also sell the bill before it matures. The seller will receive the current market price of the bill, which will be less than the par value of $1000.

U.S. Treasury bills are the most popular of the money market securities in terms of total volume outstanding and also in terms of their use by many different types of investors, because they are backed by the United States government and have short maturities. The minimum unit of purchase is $10,000, which puts bills within the reach of many individual investors and most business firms.

Banker's Acceptances   Banker's acceptances are the oldest form of money market paper. Their equivalent was first used in the Roman Empire, and during the Renaissance the banking houses in Italy brought them to a high state of development. A banker's acceptance (or just acceptance) is a short-term debt issued by a business firm on which a large commercial bank has guaranteed payment to the investor so that it becomes a liability of the bank. In other words, a bank has backed the debt with its own credit standing. The purchaser of an acceptance does not have to worry about the risk of the borrower but only whether the bank is strong.

These securities vary in face value depending on the size of the underlying commercial transaction. They are sold at a discount from face value similar to Treasury bills. Acceptances are usually created as the result of a sale of goods from one business firm to another when the goods will be in transit for a few months as is typical in international trade, and they arise primarily from import and export activity.

Commercial Paper   Commercial paper is a short-term debt (usually three to six months maturity) of a business firm or financial institution which has been sold in the market. It is also issued at a discount from face value. The use of this method of financing is discussed in Chapter 19. There is almost as much commercial paper outstanding as Treasury bills; however, commercial paper is a debt issued by a private firm, and private firms (even very large ones) have been known to fail. Interest rates on commercial paper usually are well above the rates on Treasury bills.

CDs and Other Money Market Securities   Negotiable certificates of deposit (CDs) are large interest-bearing deposits in a bank. They have fixed maturities, normally under one year, and they pay interest at maturity. They cannot be withdrawn from the bank prior to their maturity date. The owners of the certificates can sell them in the money market prior to maturity, and there is an active secondary market for them.

The maturing bonds of governmental units and corporations are also included in the money market. A bond issued in 1970 that matures on December 31, 2000, was at the time of issue a long-term debt with a thirty-year maturity. However, on January 1, 1999, it is due in one year and thus is in the money market. The distinction between the bond market and the money market is somewhat arbitrary. The two markets merge for low-risk debt issues with maturities somewhere between one and three years. Also there are debt securities issued by state and local governments that have original maturities of less than one year. The United States government issues notes with maturities ranging from one to ten years, and corporations sometimes issue notes with maturities of three to ten years. Consequently, there is no way to draw a firm line that distinguishes the bond market from the money market; they blend together and strongly influence each other.

The Capital Markets   The capital markets consist of the markets in which the intermediate- and long-term securities of individuals, business firms, and governmental units are issued and traded. They are frequently subdivided into three parts—the bond market, the mortgage market, and the stock market. There are some fairly important differences among them. We will describe briefly each of the three components, focusing on obligations of individuals and governmental units, since corporate securities are described in depth later in the book.

Issuing Capital Market Securities   There are four ways to issue debt and stock. One way is direct in the sense discussed earlier: The firm, individual, or governmental unit goes to someone else, usually a financial institution, and obtains money by borrowing or selling stock. More money is raised directly than by all other methods combined, and this is the only way individuals borrow. A second way is the **auction approach** used by the U.S. Treasury, as in the issue of Treasury bills. The Treasury invites bids by investors, who submit both the prices and amounts they wish to acquire. The Treasury then accepts as many bids as it needs to raise the amount of money required, taking the highest bids first. The Treasury is the only user of this method in the United States.[6] A third method, used by state and local governments, and to some extent by business firms (primarily gas, electric, and telephone companies) to issue debt securities, is **underwriting through competitive bids**. The borrower announces that it wishes to issue, say, $20 million in bonds to mature in twenty-five years. A single financial institution or a group of financial institutions (called a **syndicate**) can submit a bid for the entire issue. The bidder with the lowest interest cost to the issuer wins the entire issue and will then try to sell it in smaller portions to investors. The aspect that makes this procedure "underwriting" is that the winner is buying the issue to sell to someone else rather than lending the money directly. Financial institutions whose primary business is underwriting are called **investment bankers**. The fourth method, **negotiated underwriting**, is used by business firms to issue both bonds and stock. In negotiated underwritings the interest rate (or price) is set by negotiations between an investment banker and the issuing firm. This method is discussed in Chapter 11.

The Bond Market   Bonds are debts of federal, state, and local governmental units and large corporations. They normally are issued in units of $1000 maturity or par value and have a fixed-interest payment made semiannually. The total annual interest is expressed as a percentage of the maturity value and is called the **coupon rate**. For example, a 7 percent coupon bond would pay $70 (0.07 × $1000) per year in two semiannual installments of $35 each until maturity, when the bond is to be redeemed for $1000.

While the money market is fundamentally centered in New York City, the bond market is dispersed. State and local government bonds in particular are traded throughout the country as are, to a lesser extent,

---

[6] Bids are on the basis of price rather than interest rate since there is no interest payment on bills, and notes and bonds are issued with fixed coupon rates (refer to the next section for a definition).

the corporate bonds. However, the focus of activity in these securities is still New York, as it is for the issues of the federal government.

Governments and Agencies   In the language of the bond market, there are two groups of federal securities—"governments" and "agencies." "Governments" are notes and bonds issued by the U.S. Treasury and guaranteed by the federal government. They are considered to be the safest long-term debt securities available. The distinction between a note and a bond is maturity. Notes have original maturities of up to ten years, and bonds have original maturities of over ten years. Also, notes are usually issued in units of $5000, whereas bonds usually have $1000 as the minimum unit.

"Agencies" are securities issued by various federal agencies that have been established by the federal government to issue their own debt securities and use the money for a variety of purposes. The bonds issued by federal agencies have become an important part of the bond market in recent years. The major organizations and their bonds are listed in the *Federal Reserve Bulletin*. The interest rates on agencies are slightly higher than comparable rates for government bonds.

Municipal Bonds   People who deal in the bond market refer to the debt issues of state and local governmental units as **municipal bonds** or "munis." The major distinguishing feature of these securities compared with all other securities in the financial markets is that the interest paid to investors is not taxed by the federal government. Since the interest is exempt from federal income taxes, these bonds are also referred to as **tax-exempt bonds**. This tax-exempt feature means that most state and local governments are able to issue bonds at lower interest costs than the federal government.

There are several types of municipal bonds. The most common are the **general obligation bonds** issued by a town, city, county, or state. These bonds are backed by the taxing power of the governmental unit involved and therefore can be considered a debt of everyone who lives in that area. Another type is **revenue bonds**. These bonds are to be paid off from the revenues derived from a specific public project. For example, roads and bridges may be financed with revenue bonds to be repaid with tolls. Dormitories and student centers at state colleges and universities are also frequently financed with revenue bonds, and student fees are used to repay them. A third type, **industrial development bonds**, is of interest to business firms. These bonds are issued to build plants to attract new industry to an area. A business firm rents the plant, and the rental payments are used to repay the bonds. In effect, the local government is using the tax-exempt feature of the bonds as a way to provide cheap financing to a business firm.

Corporate Bonds   Business firms issue many types of debt; however, only large firms issue bonds. Smaller firms deal directly with lenders such as banks and insurance companies. Bonds generally have longer-term maturities than direct loans and are usually issued to pay for capital expenditures such as new plant and equipment. The many different types of corporate bonds are described in Chapters 11 and 12.

The Mortgage Market Although local primary mortgage markets have existed for a long time, an appreciable national secondary market for the mortgages on individual residences has developed only within the last two decades. The federal government established three major organizations to purchase mortgages from the financial institutions that originally made the loans. The three organizations are the Federal National Mortgage Association ("Fannie Mae"), which is now a semiprivate corporation; the Government National Mortgage Association ("Ginnie Mae"); and the Federal Home Loan Mortgage Corporation ("Freddy Mac"). A national market for mortgages provides several benefits; among these are the reduction of regional differences in mortgage rates and the increased availability of mortgage financing even in periods of tight money.

Most mortgages today are paid off in equal monthly (residential mortgages) or quarterly (commercial mortgages) installments over the life of the debt, which may extend to thirty or forty years. The interest rate on residential mortgages is usually somewhat higher than the rate on low-risk corporate bonds. A specialized type of financial institution, the **mortgage company**, operates in this market, as do commercial banks, savings and loan associations, and savings banks. Mortgage companies are different from the other financial institutions in that they do not keep the mortgages they originate but rather sell them in blocks to large investors such as life insurance companies and pension funds. The mortgage company collects the monthly payments and forwards them to the ultimate owner of the mortgage. Mortgage companies are the investment bankers of the mortgage market.

The Stock Market When the stock market is mentioned, most people think of the New York and the American Stock Exchanges. These two stock exchanges plus ten regional stock exchanges and the over-the-counter market constitute the domestic secondary markets for the stock issues of private corporations.

The organized stock exchanges are themselves only a way to bring buyers and sellers together via their representatives, the brokerage firms. Stock brokers are the financial institutions that buy and sell securities at the orders of their customers. Most large brokers are members of the stock exchanges and have representatives of their firm on the "floors" of the exchanges to make purchases and sales. However, the stock issues of several thousand smaller firms do not meet the criteria required for a listing on the New York Stock Exchange or the somewhat less demanding requirements of the other exchanges. A network of brokers and dealers has evolved to undertake transactions in unlisted stocks. This is the **over-the-counter** market. (It should be noted that some large companies which do qualify for listing on the stock exchanges have chosen to remain in the over-the-counter market.)

Now that we have looked at the structure of the U.S. financial system, let us examine the basic prices in the system—interest rates.

INTEREST RATES

Interest rates are the *prices* of credit in the financial markets. They are usually measured as an annual percentage rate of the amount borrowed; for example, 6 percent per year is $6 interest per year per $100 borrowed. Interest rates also are the earning rates on financial assets. One person's liability is another person's asset. Therefore, interest rates as prices of credit are equivalent to interest rates as earning rates—it just depends on whether you are borrowing or lending.

Different types of financial assets will have different interest rates. However, all market interest rates usually vary together over time. This means that we can speak of "high" or "low" interest rates without having to be specific about the interest rate of a particular financial asset. For example, if interest rates are "high" on corporate bonds, they will usually also be "high" on home mortgages, state and local bonds, etc. The general level and variation of interest rates over the past fifty years is illustrated in Figure 2-2. Even though corporate bonds differ greatly from Treasury bills, the interest rates on these two financial assets do show similar general trends.

What causes interest rates to change over time? There are several theories that seek to explain this phenomenon. The one most often used

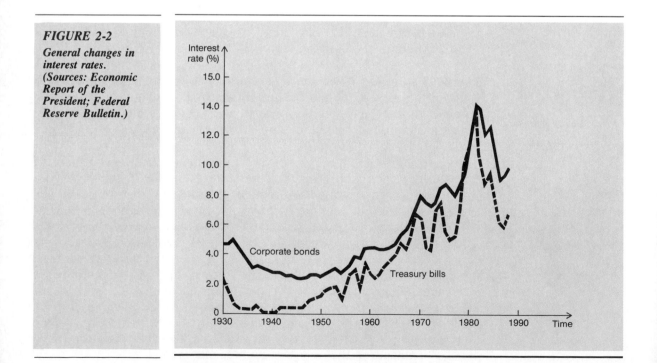

FIGURE 2-2

General changes in interest rates. (Sources: Economic Report of the President; Federal Reserve Bulletin.)

Loanable Funds

by financial managers is based on fluctuations in the supply of and demand for loanable funds. In addition, the prospects for changes in the general level of prices for goods and services, inflation or deflation, will affect the level of interest rates.

Loanable funds are the dollars available for purchases of new financial assets at a given point in time. Loanable funds, like any other commodity, are subject to the laws of supply and demand. Thus, if large amounts of dollars are available for investment, the interest rate will be low, just as the price of oranges decreases when there is a bumper crop.

The *supply* of loanable funds consists of the savings of individuals and business firms and changes in the amount of money in the economy. Savings is the difference between current income and current expenses including taxes and is usually the major source of loanable funds. The federal government can increase the money supply by printing more currency, but the major changes in money supply are due to the expansion of checking accounts in the banking system. Changes in the money supply are controlled by the Federal Reserve Board by adjusting the amount of reserves on deposit in the Federal Reserve banks.

The *demand* for loanable funds comes primarily from those persons who wish to borrow money to finance investment. They may include business firms that want to expand their operations or increase their productivity through modernization; federal, state, and local governments that usually spend more than they take in from taxes and must borrow funds to make up the deficit; and individuals who require funds for the purchase of houses or other durable goods. In addition, firms and individuals may wish to increase their holdings of money relative to other financial assets. This also is part of the demand for loanable funds.

As you might expect, an increase in the demand for loanable funds without a corresponding increase in the supply causes interest rates to rise until supply and demand are in balance. The general level of interest rates at any time is primarily determined by individuals' desires for current expenditures relative to their incomes (which determines savings) and the amount of investment opportunities available.

Inflation

The expectation of future inflation may alter the level of interest rates by changing the supply of and demand for loanable funds. If people expect prices to rise in the future, there is an incentive to purchase goods and services now rather than later (at higher prices). This has the effect of reducing savings and increasing investment in productive assets.

People owning existing financial assets sell them to get money to purchase physical assets, thereby pushing down the prices of financial assets and pushing up the rates of return (interest rates) paid on financial assets. Lenders require higher interest rates because the dollars they will receive in the future in repayment of the debt will have less purchasing power due to the inflation. The result is that interest rates are higher when people expect high rates of inflation than when people expect low rates of inflation.

There is a theoretical relationship between the expected rate of inflation and observed interest rates called the **Fisher equation** after its originator, economist Irving Fisher. The observed (nominal) interest rate is considered to be the sum of two factors—the real rate of interest and the expected rate of inflation.[7]

Observed interest rate = real interest rate + expected rate of inflation

The real interest rate is determined by the productivity of investment in the economy and the preferences of individuals regarding present consumption versus future consumption. The real rate is thought to be relatively stable over time and, in the United States, to be approximately 2 percent. If the real rate of interest is 2 percent and the expected rate of inflation is 10 percent, the Fisher equation indicates that we should observe actual interest rates to be 12 percent. Figure 2-3 shows how interest rates on Treasury bills have moved with the rate of inflation as measured by changes in the Consumer Price Index. As you can see, the rate of inflation does appear to have a strong impact on interest rates.

INTERNATIONAL FINANCIAL MARKETS

The description of the American financial system just completed could, with a few changes, apply to the financial systems of most developed countries. For example, the British equivalents of American savings and loan associations are called building societies; housing finance companies in Japan serve much the same function. One of the most striking

---

[7] The equation is an approximation since factors such as taxes and uncertainty in the rate of inflation are not included. However, it has proved to be useful empirically.

FIGURE 2-3

Inflation and interest rates. Annual rates of change in the Consumer Price Index and average annual interest rates on U.S. Treasury bills of three months' maturity. (Source: Economic Report of the President)

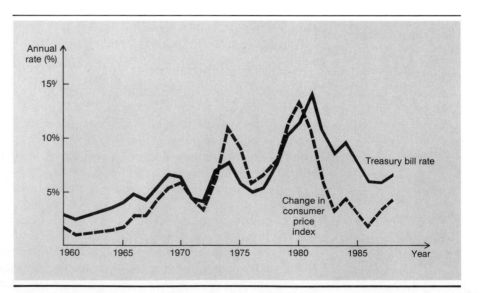

trends of the past decade is the globalization of financial markets. **Globalization** refers to the increasing integration of domestic financial markets into international ones. Large commercial banks, investment banks, and securities brokerage firms operate in many different countries. Banks that are headquartered in Asia and Europe are operating in the United States, and banks headquartered in the United States are operating in Europe and Asia. It is possible for Americans to buy securities listed on the Tokyo Stock Exchange and for Japanese to buy securities listed on the New York Stock Exchange. American business firms may raise money by issuing securities in Europe, and European business firms may raise money by issuing securities in America. *The Wall Street Journal* routinely provides information on securities prices in financial markets around the world.

There are also international financial markets that operate across country borders and are distinct from the domestic financial systems of each country. There are international money and capital markets and markets for foreign exchange.

*International Money
and Capital Markets*

The international money markets arise from the deposit of major currencies in financial institutions outside of the country of issue; for example, a bank in London accepting a U.S. dollar deposit. The primary currencies involved are the U.S. dollar, British pound (sterling), deutsche mark, Japanese yen, and Swiss franc. The markets originated in Europe based on U.S. dollar deposits and, hence, were (and often still are) referred to as the Eurodollar markets. Now there are markets of this sort in Japan, Singapore, Hong Kong, and Bahrain (Asiadollar markets), and there are more currencies in use. The terms ''Eurocurrency markets'' and ''offshore markets'' are now sometimes used. Japanese yen in Japan are just yen; Japanese yen in London are Euroyen. However, the dominant currency is still the U.S. dollar and the majority of the volume is in the European financial centers. The basic reasons for the existence of these markets are the avoidance of government regulations and taxes in the countries whose currencies are used.

The offshore money markets are used by large corporations and governmental agencies that wish to borrow short-term funds or make short-term deposits. Interest rates on the deposits tend to be slightly higher than those available in the country of origin for the currency because the deposits are free from many domestic regulations and expenses, such as the depository insurance fees paid by banks to the Federal Deposit Insurance Corporation. Interest rates on the loans can be slightly lower than those available in the domestic money markets for the same reasons. Eurocurrency interest rates on both loans and deposits are frequently tied to the London interbank offer rate (LIBOR), which is similar to the federal funds rate in the United States. The transactions are large, equivalent to $1 million or more.

There are also offshore markets for medium and long-term debt. Loans extending beyond one year are called Eurocredits. Three- to ten-year maturities are common, and the interest rates are usually pegged to

*Foreign Exchange
Markets*

LIBOR and may change semiannually. Eurobonds are long-term public debt issues similar to those issued domestically except that they are issued outside of the country whose currency is used. Both fixed rate and floating rate Eurobonds are issued.

The currencies of different countries are traded in the foreign exchange markets. The markets are located in all major financial centers of the world (New York, London, Tokyo, Hong King, Singapore, and others). These markets are interconnected via telecommunications so that one might consider there to be only a single, global market for currencies with several trading centers, one or more of which are open at some time throughout the 24-hour global trading day.

Suppose you are planning a trip to Germany. You will need to have German currency, or deutsche marks (DM), so that you can make purchases while you are there. How many marks can you obtain with, say, $500? The relationship between the values of two currencies is called the exchange rate. The exchange rate between dollars and marks can be stated as dollars per mark or marks per dollar; for example, $0.50 per mark of DM2.0 per dollar. At this exchange rate $500 would exchange into (purchase) $2.0 \times \$500 = DM1000$. Note that one exchange rate is the reciprocal of the other: $0.5 = (1/2.0)$. Exchange rates of major world currencies, expressed both as dollars per foreign currency unit and as currency units per dollar, are listed in *The Wall Street Journal* each day. The names of several countries' currencies and exchange rates relative to United States dollars are shown in Table 2-1. Notice the wide range of relative currency values that exist at a point in time. In addition, Table 2-1 indicates that precise wording is needed when dealing with

TABLE 2-1
Selected currencies and exchange rates

| Country | Currency | Exchange rate, U.S. $ | |
		January 1988	January 1989
Australia	Dollar	.711	.871
Austria	Schilling	.086	.077
Canada	Dollar	.778	.839
France	Franc	.179	.160
Germany	Deutsche mark (mark)	.605	.545
India	Rupee	.077	.066
Italy	Lira	.00082	.00074
Japan	Yen	.0078	.0079
Netherlands	Guilder	.538	.483
Spain	Peseta	.0089	.0087
Sweden	Krona	.167	.159
Switzerland	Franc	.743	.640
United Kingdom	Pound	1.801	1.774

Source: Federal Reserve Bulletin.

*Factors Determining
Exchange Rates*

currencies. It is not sufficient to say a bushel of wheat sells for $2.50. You must say whether it is $2.50 United States, $2.50 Australian, or $2.50 Canadian. Similarly, more than one country denominates its currency in pounds, in pesos, in francs, and so forth.

Exchange rates are determined in the foreign exchange market and reflect the supply and demand for each currency. The demand for a given country's currency is based on people's needs to make payments in that currency, plus speculative demand, plus government demand. Payments requiring foreign exchange are made for several reasons: purchases of goods being exported from the country, purchases of goods and services by foreign tourists in the country, financial assets being acquired by foreign investors, and direct investments in plant and equipment by foreign corporations establishing productive facilities in the country. Speculative demand for a currency is based on expectations that the currency will appreciate (increase in value) relative to other currencies. Government demand reflects attempts by the government of a country to maintain its currency's value relative to the values of other currencies.

The supply of a currency in the foreign exchange market comes from people who presently own the currency and wish to exchange it for foreign currencies. Importers who wish to pay for goods purchased abroad buy foreign currencies, thus supplying their own currency to the foreign exchange market. Tourists exchange their home country's currency for the currencies of the countries they are visiting. Anyone holding currency X who would prefer to hold some other country's currency is a source of supply of currency X. For example, if you are a citizen of country X and are worried about high rates of inflation, political instability, or possible confiscation of your assets in country X, you might prefer to transfer funds out of country X into more secure assets in country Y.

Inflation   Although changes in exchange rates result from changes in the supply and demand for currencies, this explanation does not provide a very helpful answer to the question of why exchange rates change. We must look for the more fundamental factors that affect the supply and demand for currencies. One factor is the relative rate of inflation in different countries. If the rate of inflation is 10 percent per year in country X and 1 percent per year in country Y, the purchasing power of country X's currency is declining faster than the purchasing power of country Y's currency. As a result, the exchange rate of country X's currency will tend to decline relative to country Y's currency. If people could freely transfer money from one country to another and could freely purchase goods and services throughout the world, the goods and services that can be purchased for $100 in the United States, for example, would be the same as those available in France if $100 is exchanged into French francs. Exchange rates therefore tend to vary so as to provide similar purchasing power in each country. Differences in inflation rates among countries result in changes in exchange rates.

Interest Rates   A second factor influencing exchange rates is relative interest rates. If investors can earn 4 percent interest per year in country *Y* and 8 percent per year in country *X*, they will prefer to invest in securities of country *X* provided that the rate of inflation is the same in both countries. As people buy currency *X* with currency *Y*, the exchange rate of country *X*'s currency will appreciate relative to country *Y*'s. The increased demand for securities in country *X* relative to country *Y* also tends to reduce the interest rate differential between the two countries. This occurs because the prices of country *X*'s securities rise (reducing their yield to new investors) and the prices of country *Y*'s securities fall (increasing their yield to new investors).[8]

Government Policies and Other Factors   Governments have an enormous influence on exchange rates through tariffs, quotas, foreign exchange restrictions, and fiscal and monetary policies (which affect inflation and interest rates). In addition, the political stability of a country affects the risks of investing in that country. Governments often actively intervene in the foreign exchange markets, buying and selling currencies to support the value of their currency relative to others. In some cases governments do not allow their currencies' values to be established in the foreign exchange market. For example, the communist countries have traditionally not been tied into the international financial system, and their exchange rates have been set by government decree.

*Spot and Forward
Rates*

The **spot** rate of exchange between two currencies is today's rate of exchange for currencies being bought and sold for immediate delivery. The **forward** rate of exchange is a rate agreed on today with the actual delivery of the currency to take place at a *future* time, usually 30, 90, or 180 days from now. Forward exchange rates are therefore prices set today for currency exchanges that will occur in the future.

Forward rates may be greater than the current spot rate (premium) or less than the current spot rate (discount). For example, the following exchange rates were quoted in *The Wall Street Journal* for transactions on November 17, 1989.

	British pounds, £	Japanese yen, ¥
	1.5695	0.006932
30-day forward	1.5612	0.006945
90-day forward	1.5446	0.006964
180-day forward	1.5217	0.006985

The first figure shown in each case was the spot rate for that day, $1.5695 per pound for example. The other rates are the forward rates for con-

---

[8] The interest rate (yield) provided by a financial asset is inversely related to its price (see Chap. 5).

tracts of the time specified. Forward rates on the pound are at a discount from the spot rate, whereas forward rates for the yen are at a premium. Purchase of a forward contract for exchange of £100 into dollars 180 days later (May 16, 1990) would assure the purchaser that £100 could be exchanged into $152.17 (£100 × $1.5217) regardless of the spot rate in effect on May 16, 1990.

SUMMARY

The primary role of the financial system is to facilitate savings and investment in the economy. Financial assets (and corresponding liabilities) are the basic products of the system. There are three general classes of financial assets—money, debt, and stock. Each of these classes may be subdivided into several types. Money consists of currency and demand deposits, and stock consists of preferred stock and common stock. There are many different types of debt categorized by the issuer (individuals, businesses, governmental units, or financial institutions) and by the nature of the debt contract (loans, mortgages, bonds, etc.).

New financial assets are created in the primary markets. Money or goods are exchanged for a financial asset. Savers may deal directly with those persons needing money for the purchase of goods and services or indirectly through financial intermediaries.

Financial intermediaries create financial assets desired by savers, and they lend money to those who need it. The major financial intermediaries are the commercial banks, savings and loan associations, mutual savings banks, life insurance companies, and credit unions.

Many of the financial transactions in the economy do not involve the creation of financial assets. Instead, existing financial assets are purchased and sold in the secondary markets. In practice, little distinction is made between primary and secondary markets, and financial markets are most often described by the types of assets issued or traded in them. The money markets and capital markets are national in scope in contrast to the markets for savings, consumer installment loans, etc., which are local.

Short-term debt securities of business firms, governmental units, and financial institutions are issued and traded in the money markets. Money market financial assets include federal funds, Treasury bills, banker's acceptances, CDs, and commercial paper. The money market serves an important role in eliminating regional differences in interest rates.

The capital market is often divided into the bond market, the mortgage market, and the stock market. The long-term debt issues of governmental units and business firms are traded in the bond market. Mortgages on residential property owned by individuals are the principal security traded in the mortgage market. The stock market is almost completely a secondary market where previously issued shares of stock in business firms are traded.

Interest rates are the prices of credit. They differ according to the type of financial asset, and they vary over time. The general level of interest rates changes because of changes in the supply of and demand for loanable funds. Changes in expectations regarding the rate of inflation are an important factor in causing interest rates to change.

The domestic financial markets in the United States are linked to the financial markets in other countries around the world. There is a global financial system with large financial institutions operating in many different countries. There are also international, offshore markets that operate independently of national boundaries.

Monetary units or currencies vary from country to country. Exchange rates express the relationship between the values of different currencies. Spot rates are the rates on current exchanges of currencies, and forward rates are the current rates for future exchanges. Exchange rates change over time because of differences in inflation, interest rates, and government policies of countries.

QUESTIONS

1 What is a financial asset? How are financial assets created and transferred?
2 Explain the differences between money, debt, and stock. How does preferred stock differ from common stock?
3 If you obtain a student loan, is this a primary or a secondary market transaction? Explain.
4 The United States government issued a bond with a $6\frac{3}{4}$ percent coupon rate that matures in 1993. How much interest would you receive every six months if you bought five of these bonds which have a maturity value of $1000 each?
5 Distinguish between brokers and dealers. In which type of secondary market would you expect to find each?
6 Distinguish between money markets and capital markets. What types of assets are traded in each?
7 Why is there a difference between the interest rates on corporate bonds and U.S. Treasury bills shown in Figure 2-2?
8 "During periods of inflation it is better to be a borrower than a lender." Discuss.
9 What is the difference between a Swiss investor buying Swiss franc bonds in Switzerland and the same person buying Swiss franc bonds in London?
10 What factors can cause the exchange rate between two countries' currencies to change?
11 Suppose that you plan to spend a semester at a British university six months from now. Your room, board, and tuition will be £3000. What could you do to be sure in advance of the U.S. dollar cost of your expenses?

PROJECT

Using Tuesday's *Wall Street Journal* as a source, collect the most recent twelve weekly values for interest rates on federal funds, ninety-day Treasury bills, a Treasury note due in 1995, and the 10 percent Treasury bonds due in 2005–2010. Plot the values on a graph (rate versus date). What conclusions can you draw? Find the articles discussing the Monday Treasury bill auctions. Why are the rates changing? (For the interest rate on the notes and bonds use the values reported as "yield.")

PROBLEMS

1 The current interest rate on a one-year U.S. Treasury bill is 8 percent.

  a If the real rate of interest in the United States is 2 percent per year, what rate of inflation is expected next year according to the Fisher equation? [Ans.: 6%]

  b Suppose that a news report comes out tomorrow morning saying that inflation is being reduced significantly and a new forecast for inflation over the next 12 months is 3.5 percent. If people in general believe this forecast, what will be the rate of interest on one-year U.S. Treasury bills tomorrow afternoon?

2 Use the foreign exchange rates for January 1989 in Table 2-1 to calculate the amount of U. S. dollars the following currencies will exchange for.

1. 100 deutsche marks	[Ans.: $54.50]
2. 100 rupees	
3. 100 krona	
4. 10,000 lira	[Ans.: $7.40]
5. 10,000 yen	

3 Obtain a recent copy of *The Wall Street Journal* and calculate the currency exchanges of problem 2. How do these figures compare to those obtained in problem 2?

4 Use the exchange rates in Table 2-1 for January 1989 to answer the following:

  a How many Italian lira can be acquired for $7.40 U.S.? [Ans.: see no. 4 in table in problem 2]

  b How many Swedish krona can be acquired for $15.90 U.S.?

  c How many Japanese yen can be acquired for $120 U.S.? [Ans.: 15,190 yen]

5 Use the exchange rates in Table 2-1 for January 1989 to calculate the following:

  a How many Austrian schillings can be acquired with $100 U.S.?

  b How many French francs can be acquired with $100 U.S.?

  c How many French francs can be acquired with 1298.70 Austrian schillings?

  d How many British pounds can be acquired with $100 Canadian?

6 Suppose *The Wall Street Journal* reports the following exchange rates for country Flint whose currency is the stone:

Flint (stone)	0.2400
30-day forward	0.2380
90-day forward	0.2365
180-day forward	0.2305

a Is the forward rate on the stone at a discount or premium relative to the U.S. dollar?

b Suppose you executed a thirty-day futures contract to exchange 100,000 stones into U.S. dollars. How many dollars would you get thirty days from now? [Ans.: $23,800]

c Suppose you executed a 180-day futures contract to exchange $100,000 U.S. into stones. How many stones would you get 180 days from now?

THE LEGAL ENVIRONMENT: BUSINESS ORGANIZATION, TAXES, AND BANKRUPTCY

Benjamin Franklin once wrote, "In this world nothing is certain but death and taxes." By choosing a suitable form of organization, a business firm can outlive its original owners. However, neither the firm nor its owners can escape taxes. Business organization and taxes are closely related because the taxes paid by a company and its owners depend on how the company is organized. This chapter first describes the various alternative forms of business organization and then examines the federal income tax on individuals and businesses. We then address another legalistic topic—one sometimes even more depressing than taxes—corporate bankruptcy and liquidation. The final section briefly describes the multinational corporation and the tax treatment of income earned from foreign operations. The common thread throughout this chapter is the importance of legal issues in the decision process. Invariably, the financial manager will have to turn to lawyers and accountants in dealing with business organization, taxes, and financial distress. However, some familiarity with these issues on the part of the financial executive is helpful in understanding what the attorneys and accountants have to offer.

BUSINESS ORGANIZATION

The three principal types of business organization are the proprietorship, the partnership, and the corporation. A **proprietorship** is a business owned by one person, a **partnership** is owned by two or more people or entities but usually not more than ten, and a **corporation** may be owned by any number of people from one to several million. Corporations differ from partnerships and proprietorships in that the firm itself is a legal "person" apart from its owners. In a proprietorship or partnership the owners are a part of the business. As shown in Table 3-1, although proprietorships and partnerships far outnumber corporations, corporations generate 90 percent of business revenues and are a much larger economic force than the noncorporate sector.

Proprietorship

Most businesses are owned by one person and are proprietorships. A proprietorship can be established simply by beginning to sell a product or perform some service. Except for the licensing required of many businesses, proprietorships are very easy to establish and are subject to very little government regulation. The owner is responsible personally for any debts of the business. For tax purposes, the income (or losses) of the business is part of the personal income of the owner.

Partnership

A partnership is owned by two or more persons. The owners must agree on how much time and money each will contribute to the business and how the profits will be divided. Partnerships are not regulated to any great extent by the government and are very easy to establish. Partnership income is taxed as the personal income of the partners. In a **general partnership** each partner is responsible for debts incurred by the business; however, profits of the business and the ownership of its assets may be divided in any way agreed on by the partners. Often there is a formally written partnership agreement specifying the arrangement.

Another type of partnership, called a **limited partnership**, is permitted in many states. In a limited partnership there must be at least one general partner. A general partner is personally liable for any of the partnership's debts. The limited partners usually invest money in the partnership and share in the profits; however, unlike the general partner, they are not personally liable for the company's debts, and the most that they can lose is the amount they have invested in the business.

If a partner leaves the partnership or dies, or a new partner is brought into the partnership, the old partnership dissolves. Most partnership agreements have special provisions for the purchase of the ownership interest of a partner who cannot continue in the business.

Corporation

The corporation is the most important form of business organization in the United States. Although only 20 percent of all businesses are corporations, they account for 90 percent of the total revenues of firms. Corporations are established by obtaining a charter from a state, usually the state in which the primary operations of the business are located. Large firms often choose to be chartered in Delaware because its charter provisions are more flexible than those of most other states. The corporation can own assets, borrow money, and perform business functions without directly involving its owners, who are also called **shareholders** or **stockholders**. The stockholder's ownership interest in the corporation is determined by the number of shares of common stock he or she owns. Corporations are taxed differently from other types of businesses, and

---

TABLE 3-1
Business organizations

	Number (thousands)	Percent	Revenues (billions)	Percent
Proprietorships	11,929	71	540	6
Partnerships	1,714	10	368	4
Corporations	3,277	19	8,398	90
Total	16,920	100	9,306	100

41

CHAPTER 3
**The legal environment:
business organization,
taxes, and bankruptcy**

the owners are not responsible for the debts incurred by the corporation. The corporation is a legal method of permitting the affairs of a business to be separated from personal affairs of its owners.

To form a corporation, the corporate founders prepare **articles of incorporation** which usually indicate the name of the proposed corporation, corporate purpose, number of directors and the names and addresses of the directors, amount of stock authorized, and the duration of the corporation (if it is to be limited). The articles are sent to the secretary of state of the state in which incorporation is sought. If the articles are approved, the corporation receives its **certificate of incorporation** and becomes a legal entity. The corporation is governed by the state's corporation laws, by the corporation's articles of incorporation, and by the corporate bylaws, which are rules drawn up by the corporation's founders and approved by the board of directors (the bylaws may be changed later by the board of directors with the shareholders' approval). The bylaws concern such matters as the rights of the shareholders (for example, whether they have the first rights to any new shares issued by the corporation), special aspects of the corporation's organization (for example, the existence of permanent committees), and how the board of directors is to be elected (for example, whether majority rule or cumulative voting is to be used).

Corporations have three important advantages over sole proprietorships and partnerships: limited liability, unlimited life, and ease in transferring ownership. The stockholders are not liable for the debts of the corporation; that is, there is limited liability for stockholders. The most that the shareholders can lose is what they have already invested in the corporation. The corporation usually has unlimited life and continues to exist even if the shareholders die or sell their shares. Relative to sole proprietorships and partnerships, transferability of ownership is especially easy for a corporation because of the convenient division of the ownership interest into shares and because of the corporation's limited liability and unlimited life features.

THE FEDERAL INCOME TAX

The federal tax on the incomes of individuals and corporations constitutes the largest single source of revenue received by any governmental unit. The income tax is determined as a percentage of *taxable income*, which is defined as total or gross income less exemptions and deductions. Tax laws influence business investment and financing decisions in several ways, which will be discussed in later chapters. In this section we will examine some of the basic characteristics of the federal income tax. State and local income taxes vary considerably but generally follow similar patterns.

Taxation of the incomes of individuals and businesses by the federal government was authorized by the Sixteenth Amendment, which was passed in 1913.[1] Congress enacts the income tax laws (the tax code), and

---

[1] Although the Sixteenth Amendment ushered in the general income tax on a permanent basis, there was an income tax for approximately three years during the Civil War and a minor corporate excise tax (based on corporate income) beginning in 1909.

the U.S. Treasury Department issues detailed regulations defining or interpreting the specifics of the laws. Taxpayers are responsible for reporting their incomes to the Internal Revenue Service (IRS), which is a federal agency that collects taxes and issues rulings interpreting the tax code and the Treasury Department regulations. Federal courts resolve conflicts between taxpayers and the IRS. There is also a special court, the Tax Court, in which taxpayers may contest the rules and decisions of the IRS. This system has one primary purpose—to make sure that those taxes owed to the federal government are assessed fairly and are collected.

Individual Income Taxes

Personal taxable income equals gross income (wages, salaries, rents, dividends, interest, capital gains, etc.) *minus* business, investment, and personal deductions from gross income. Various items are excluded from gross income and are not taxable. Examples of nontaxable items are municipal bond interest, life insurance proceeds, and gifts received (large gifts are subject to a separate gift tax levied on the giver). Business deductions from gross income include expenses and losses incurred in business. Investment deductions include expenses incurred to hold and maintain investments, such as interest cost and fees for investment advice. Personal deductions include interest payments (e.g., on a home mortgage), property taxes, and charitable contributions. A taxpayer without significant personal deductions can take a standard deduction (in 1989, $3100 for single taxpayers and $5200 for married taxpayers filing jointly). A larger standard deduction applies to blind or aged persons. A taxpayer is also permitted one exemption (two exemptions for a joint return) plus an added exemption for each person in the family whom the taxpayer supports. The exemption was $2000 in 1989. Like itemized and standard deductions, the exemptions are deducted in computing taxable income. The standard deduction and exemptions are indexed to inflation.

Gross income includes capital gain income. A capital gain results when an asset is sold for more than it cost; a capital loss results when it is sold for less than it cost.[2] If the asset was owned by the seller for one year or less at the date of sale, the capital gain or loss is **short-term**; if the asset was owned for more than one year, the gain or loss is **long-term**. All short-term and long-term gains are included in taxable income and are taxed at the same rate as other income.[3] The tax treatment of a capital

---

[2] Gains on investments (e.g., stock, bonds, and real estate) and personal use assets (e.g., a home) are subject to capital gains taxation. Losses on nondepreciable investments are deducted as capital losses for tax purposes; losses on personal use assets are not tax deductible. If an asset is depreciable (only business and investment assets, and not personal use assets, may be depreciated), the gain is the sales price received minus the depreciated cost (where depreciated cost is original cost less accumulated depreciation); if this difference is negative, there is a loss equal to the depreciated cost minus the sales price received.

[3] Currently there is no difference in the tax rates applicable to long-term and short-term capital gains. However, the law still requires that long-term gains and short-term gains be reported separately. Furthermore, there are provisions in the law that imply that, in the future, long-term gains may be treated more favorably than short-term gains.

43

CHAPTER 3
The legal environment:
business organization,
taxes, and bankruptcy

loss (which arises if an asset is sold for less than its original cost minus any depreciation) is more complicated and will not be described here, but generally the loss deduction is extremely limited. Capital gains (or losses) can be incurred on stocks, bonds, real estate, collectibles (stamps, antiques, etc.), and on most other types of assets held by individuals for investment purposes. Capital gains on assets held for personal use are taxed, but capital losses on personal assets are not tax deductible.

To illustrate the capital gain computation, assume that Clara Boyd bought 100 shares of Harbor Corporation stock last year for $10 per share, a total investment of $1000. If she sold the 100 shares in the current year for $1500, she would have a capital gain of $500 and would include the entire $500 in her current taxable income.

Table 3–2 shows the individual tax rate structure for 1989. Notice that there is a "hump" in the marginal tax rate structure; the marginal rate rises to 33 percent and then falls back to 28 percent for high taxable incomes. The result of this is to make the taxpayer's average tax rate 28

TABLE 3-2
1989 *tax rates taking into account the additional 5 percent tax*

	Taxable income[a]	Rate
Married individuals filing joint returns	$ 0–$ 30,950	15%
	$30,951–$ 74,850	28%
	$74,851–$155,320	33%
	over $155,320	28%
Heads of households	$ 0–$ 24,850	15%
	$24,851–$ 64,200	28%
	$64,201–$128,810	33%
	over $128,810	28%
Single taxpayers	$ 0–$ 18,550	15%
	$18,551–$ 44,900	28%
	$44,901–$ 93,130	33%
	over $ 93,130	28%
Married individuals filing separate returns	$ 0–$ 15,475	15%
	$15,476–$ 37,425	28%
	$37,426–$117,895	33%
	over $117,895	28%

[a] Amounts shown as the maximum taxable income subject to the 33% rate (e.g., $93,130 for a single taxpayer) are increased by $11,200 for each personal exemption claimed in 1989 (and will be indexed for inflation after 1990). The taxpayer is allowed one personal exemption (two exemptions on a joint return) plus an additional exemption for each dependent supported by the taxpayer. Thus, a single taxpayer with one dependent has two exemptions, and that taxpayer rate schedule is as follows: 15% for taxable income from $0 to $18,550; 28% for taxable income from $18,551 to $44,900; 33% for taxable income from $44,901 to $115,530; and 28% for taxable income over $115,530. The $115,530 is computed as $115,530 = $93,130 plus (2 × $11,200) for the two exemptions.

percent if taxable income is high ($155,320 or above for married individuals filing joint returns, $128,810 or above for a head of household, $93,130 or above for a single taxpayer, and $117,895 or above for a married individual filing a separate return).[4]

Virtually all income from investments is subject to federal income taxes (interest on municipal bonds is an important exception). Investment income includes dividends from stock; interest from promissory notes, bonds, and accounts at financial institutions; income from renting or leasing real estate, equipment, or other assets; and capital gains from selling virtually any kind of investment, including stocks, bonds, real estate, equipment, and collectibles (such as rare stamps, coins, and art).

In order to ensure that taxpayers do not reduce their taxes below a certain point through the use of "tax preferences," the tax code provides for an alternative minimum tax (AMT). Tax preferences are such items as tax-exempt interest on certain bonds, rapid depreciation on investments (e.g., on real estate), some types of investment losses, and a part or all of some charitable contributions. A taxpayer must pay the *greater* of the tax computed in the usual way or the taxpayer's AMT. For example, if a taxpayer has a usual tax of $20,000 and an AMT of $25,000, the tax that must be paid is $25,000.

Taxes on Owners of Small Businesses   Business income (revenues less expenses) earned by a proprietorship or partnership is treated for tax purposes as the personal income of its owners. If a small business is incorporated, the owners may have the option to be taxed either as a corporation or somewhat like a partnership.[5] In either case, though, any salaries and dividends paid to the owners will be taxed as their personal income. If the business is taxed as a corporation, salaries would be deductible in determining the corporation's taxable income but the dividends would not be deductible.

*Corporate Income
Taxes*

Taxable income for corporations is determined in essentially the same way as for all businesses. Business expenses including wages, salaries, materials costs, depreciation allowances, and interest expenses are subtracted from the firm's revenues for the year. Other deductions include losses from previous years and depletion allowances (such as deprecia-

---

[4] Table 3-2 shows the **marginal tax rate** (the tax rate on the last dollar of taxable income) for income in each taxable income range. For example, for a single taxpayer with a taxable income of $50,000, the marginal tax rate is 33 percent. The **average tax rate** is the tax paid divided by taxable income. For example, a single taxpayer with a taxable income of $50,000 would pay a tax of $11,843 [computed as 0.15($18,550) + 0.28($44,900 − $18,550) + 0.33($50,000 − $44,900)]. The average tax rate would be just under 24 percent (=$11,843/$50,000) and the marginal tax rate would be 33 percent.

[5] A small corporation with no more than thirty-five shareholders can usually elect to be taxed somewhat like a partnership, provided that it meets certain other requirements. Corporations taxed as partnerships are termed "small business corporations" by the IRS. They are also known as "S" corporations in reference to the subchapter of the tax code providing this option.

45

CHAPTER 3
The legal environment:
business organization,
taxes, and bankruptcy

tion) for oil, mining, and other extractive industries. Some types of revenues are excluded from taxable income in whole or in part; for example, interest earned on the debt securities issued by state and local governments is not subject to federal income tax.

The average corporate tax rate (percentage of corporate taxable income paid in taxes) increases with the level of corporate taxable income up to a limit of 34 percent. That is, the corporate tax is progressive. Table 3-3 shows the corporate tax rate schedule. To illustrate, a corporation with a taxable income of $80,000 would pay taxes of

$$(\$50,000 \times 15\%) + (\$25,000 \times 25\%) + (\$5000 \times 34\%) = \$15,450$$

In this example, the average tax rate is approximately 19.3 percent ($15,450/$80,000) and the marginal tax rate is 34 percent (since a tax rate of 34 percent applies to the last dollar of taxable income, i.e., to the 80,000th dollar). In making financial decisions, corporations must determine the taxes on the additional income resulting from the decision. Thus, the marginal tax rate is used.

The $15,450 tax calculated above would be the annual income tax of a corporation earning $80,000. Corporations are required (as are all taxpayers) to pay taxes essentially as the taxable income is earned. Payments of estimated taxes are made quarterly on April 15, June 15, September 15, and December 15. Thus, a corporation estimating its taxes at $15,450 for the year would pay $3862.50 in each quarter. If its income actually turned out to be less or more than $80,000, the corporation would either get a refund or pay more taxes at the end of the year.

Like individual taxpayers, corporations are subject to an alternative minimum tax (AMT). The corporation must pay the larger of its tax

---

TABLE 3-3
1989 corporate income tax rates

Taxable income	Marginal tax rate, %
Up to $50,000	15
$50,001 to $75,000	25
Over $75,000[a]	34

[a] An extra tax of 5 percent is imposed on income in excess of $100,000 and up to $335,000. This implies a *marginal* corporate tax rate of 39 percent on taxable income above $100,000 and up to $335,000, and a marginal corporate tax rate of 34 percent for all taxable income above $335,000. A corporation with a taxable income of $335,000 or above pays 34 percent of taxable income in taxes (e.g., a corporation with $1 million in taxable income would pay a tax of $340,000). Therefore, for a corporation with a taxable income above $335,000, both the marginal and the average tax rates are 34 percent. To illustrate, a corporation with a taxable income of $200,000 pays a tax of $61,250 [equal to 0.15($50,000) + 0.25($25,000) + 0.34 ($25,000) + 0.39($100,000)]. A corporation with a taxable income of $500,000 pays a corporate tax of $170,000 [0.34($500,000) = 0.15($50,000) + 0.25($25,000) + 0.34($25,000) + 0.39($235,000) + 0.34($165,000)].

computed in the usual way and its alternative minimum tax. The purpose of the AMT is to prevent corporations from reducing their taxes below a certain point through the use of favored income (for example, municipal bond interest, which is tax exempt) or tax preference deductions (for example, rapid depreciation deductions or depletion deductions that exceed an asset's cost).

Corporations, like proprietorships and partnerships, can earn capital gains. But, whereas the capital gains of proprietorships and partnerships are included in the personal taxable income of the owners, corporate capital gains are taxed at the corporate level. All corporate capital gains are included in corporate taxable income and taxed like other corporate income.[6]

One difference between corporations and other businesses is that only part of the dividends received from a corporation's ownership of stock in the U.S. corporations is taxable. The taxable fraction of the dividends received by corporation X from corporation Y depends on the percentage of Y owned by X. If X owns no more than 20 percent of Y, then 30 percent of the dividends received by X from Y is taxable to X. If X owns more than 20 percent but less than 80 percent of Y, only 20 percent of the dividends is taxable. If X owns 80 percent or more of Y, none of the dividend paid by Y to X is taxable to X.

Business Losses If a firm's taxable income is negative (i.e., expenses are greater than revenues), the firm has a loss for the year and pays no income taxes. In addition, the loss becomes a potential deduction from income in other years. The loss for the current year may be either *carried back* or *carried forward*. If the loss is carried back, the firm will receive a cash refund of taxes paid in past years. If the loss is carried forward, less taxes will be paid on income in future years than would otherwise be paid. Losses may be carried back no further than three years and be carried forward no further than fifteen years. The law requires that losses that are carried back be deducted first from the earliest year (three years ago); if taxable income in that year was insufficient to offset the loss, the remaining loss would be deducted from the second year back and so on out to fifteen years in the future.[7] To see how this works, we will consider an example. For simplicity we will assume that there is a single tax rate of 50 percent on business income.

Suppose a firm has a loss of $50,000 in 1991, and had taxable income and paid taxes in the three preceding years as follows:

---

[6] For corporations with taxable income between $100,000 and $335,000, the *marginal* tax rate is 39 percent because of the 5 percent added tax on corporate income (see Table 3-3). For corporations, capital losses may not be deducted against ordinary corporate income and can only be used to offset capital gains. If there is a net capital loss, the loss may be carried back three years and then forward five years.

[7] The taxpayer may elect not to carry back a loss at all and simply to carry the loss forward, a choice preferred by the taxpayer if, for example, the taxpayer's marginal tax rate is expected to be much higher in the future than it was during the past three years. *If the loss is carried back, however, it must first be carried back three years, then two years, etc.*

47

CHAPTER 3
**The legal environment:
business organization,
taxes, and bankruptcy**

	1988	1989	1990
Taxable income	$10,000	$20,000	$30,000
Taxes paid	$ 5,000	$10,000	$15,000

The firm would submit a special form to the IRS covering these three years. As much of the $50,000 loss as possible would be shown as a deduction from the last three years' taxable income in order to determine the tax refund. The computations would be as follows:

	1988	1989	1990
Original taxable income	$10,000	$20,000	$30,000
Less part of the 1991 loss	$10,000	20,000	20,000
Amended taxable income	0	0	10,000
Taxes on amended income	0	0	5,000
Taxes previously paid	5,000	10,000	15,000
Tax refund	$ 5,000	$10,000	$10,000

The firm would get an immediate tax refund of $25,000. The entire loss of $50,000 has been deducted from income in the three prior years.

If taxable income in the three preceding years was less than the loss in 1991, any unused portion of the loss could be carried forward. If taxable income in 1990 had been only $10,000, we would have the following:

	1988	1989	1990	Total
Original taxable income	$10,000	$20,000	$10,000	$40,000
Less part of 1991 loss	10,000	20,000	10,000	40,000
Amended taxable income	0	0	0	0
Taxes on amended income	0	0	0	0
Taxes paid	5,000	10,000	5,000	20,000
Tax refund	$ 5,000	$10,000	$ 5,000	$20,000

The firm has only been able to deduct $40,000 from prior years' income, so it would receive an immediate tax refund of $20,000. The unused portion of the loss, $10,000, would have to be carried forward and applied as a deduction from income in 1992. If income in 1992 were insufficient to use up the loss, the balance would be carried forward to 1993; if 1993 income were insufficient to use up all the remaining loss, the unused loss balance would be carried to 1994, and so on out to 2006. If the firm did not earn at least $10,000 in those next fifteen years (i.e., 1992–2006), the unused portion of the $10,000 loss carryforward would be lost as a possible deduction.

These same general rules also apply to proprietorships. However, the rules for partnerships are much more complex.

Two topics will be covered in this section: the concept of depreciation and its tax effects, and the treatment of gains and losses from the sale of business assets. The appendix to this chapter provides additional information on the various methods of depreciation.

Depreciation   Most physical assets do not last indefinitely. Machine tools, buildings, and apple trees, for example, may have productive uses for many years, but eventually they will wear out or become obsolete and have little value to anyone. **Economic depreciation** is the decrease in the market value of an asset over a period of time, such as one year. We are concerned, however, with the depreciation provided for in the tax laws. You will recall that business expenses in general are tax deductible. If a firm pays its employees $20,000 in a year, that amount can be deducted from the firm's total income. However, if a firm spends $20,000 on a new machine, it will be able to treat only a portion of the initial cost as a deductible expense each year. The expenditure of $20,000 must be deducted in installments as depreciation over several years.

In the Economic Recovery Tax Act of 1981, the term **cost recovery** was introduced as a substitute for the term ''depreciation,'' and the depreciation allowed under that act is defined by the **Accelerated Cost Recovery System (ACRS)**. The ACRS is described below. In most cases in this text, we will use the familiar term ''depreciation'' rather than ''cost recovery.''

The Tax Reform Act of 1986 revised the previous Accelerated Cost Recovery System. Under the current system, as shown in Exhibit 3-1 personal property (property that is not real estate) is assigned to one of six ACRS classes (three-, five-, seven-, ten-, fifteen-, and twenty-year classes). Costs in the three-, five-, seven-, and ten-year classes are recovered (depreciated) over three, five, seven, and ten years, respectively, using 200 percent declining balance or straight-line depreciation (see Appendix 3A on depreciation methods).[8] The taxpayer determines

---

[8] For real estate, all acquisitions are assumed for cost recovery purposes to have been acquired in the middle of the month in which the property was actually acquired, and disposed of in the middle of the month in which the actual disposition of the property took place. Therefore, a building purchased on January 3, 1990, and sold on March 25, 1991, would be assumed, in computing depreciation for tax purposes, to have been acquired on January 15, 1990, and disposed of on March 15, 1991. For personal property (property other than real estate), the assumed date of acquisition is July 1 of the year of acquisition and July 1 of the year of disposition (regardless of when during the year the asset acquisition and disposition actually took place). Therefore, one-half of a year's depreciation is allowed in the year of acquisition and one-half of a year's depreciation is allowed in the year of disposition. An exception to this rule for personal property applies if more than 40 percent (in dollar value) of acquisitions for the year occur in the last quarter of the year. In this case, all personal property is assumed to have been acquired in the middle of the quarter of acquisition and disposed of in the middle of the quarter of disposition.

49

CHAPTER 3
**The legal environment:
business organization,
taxes, and bankruptcy**

whether the double declining balance or straight-line method is used. The tax code indicates that the taxpayer will switch to straight-line depreciation when it optimizes the depreciation deductions. Costs of assets in the 15- and 20-year ACRS classes are amortized using the 150 percent declining balance or straight-line method (the taxpayer makes the choice), with switching to straight-line to optimize deductions.

Real estate falls into either the 27.5-year ACRS class (residential property, such as apartments) or the 31.5-year ACRS class (nonresidential property, such as office buildings or warehouses). All real estate must be depreciated on a straight-line basis.

EXHIBIT 3-1
Cost recovery (depreciation) methods for assets

ACRS class and method	ADR midpoint[a]	Type of property
3-year, 200% declining balance or straight-line	4 years or less	Includes some race horses; excludes cars and light trucks
5-year, 200% declining balance or straight-line	More than 4 years to less than 10	Includes cars and light trucks, semiconductor manufacturing equipment, qualified technological equipment, computer-based central-office switching equipment, some renewable and bio-mass power facilities, and research and development property
7-year, 200% declining balance or straight-line	10 years to less than 16	Includes some equipment and machinery, office furniture, single-purpose agricultural and horticultural structures and railroad track; includes property with no ADR midpoint
10-year, 200% declining balance or straight-line	16 years to less than 20	Rare
15-year, 150% declining balance or straight-line	20 years to less than 25	Includes sewage treatment plants, telephone distribution plant and comparable equipment for two-way voice and data communication
20-year, 150% declining balance or straight-line	25 years or more	Excludes real property with ADR midpoint of 27.5 years or more; includes municipal sewers
27.5-year, straight-line	N/A	Residential rental property
31.5-year, straight-line	N/A	Nonresidential real property

[a] Asset depreciation range, which is an IRS guideline.

In computing depreciation under the ACRS, we completely ignore the asset's salvage value and actual expected useful life. For example, assume that an asset with a three-year ACRS class life is to be depreciated using the 200 percent declining balance method. The asset was purchased for $900,000 on March 12, 1990, but for cost recovery purposes is assumed to have been purchased on July 1, 1990.[9] Depreciation using the 200 percent declining balance method involves deductions of $600,000, $200,000, and $100,000 in years one, two, and three (see Appendix 3A). One-half of a year's depreciation is allowed in the first year and in the fourth year. Therefore, depreciation is as shown below.[10]

Year	Cost recovery deduction
1990	$300,000
1991	$400,000
1992	$150,000
1993	$ 50,000

Gains and Losses on Depreciable Assets   This section deals with gains and losses realized on disposing of depreciable assets used in a trade or business. Although part or all of the gains are in many cases treated as long-term capital gains, the losses are generally treated as ordinary losses. That is, gains may be taxed at low rates but losses can be used to offset ordinary income which is taxed at high rates (the best of both worlds!).[11] Since there are differences between personal property (property other than real estate) and real property (real estate), we will discuss them separately.

Let's first consider personal property. Suppose a firm purchased a machine for $40,000 in 1986 and sold the asset in 1989. Assume that the accumulated depreciation on the machine for tax purposes up to the 1989 sale date is $15,000; therefore, the book value of the asset (initial cost less accumulated depreciation) is $25,000. If the machine is sold for more

[9] See footnote 8.

[10] In 1990, one-half of the first year's $600,000 cost recovery deduction (i.e., $300,000) is deducted. In 1991, the cost recovery is the remaining half of the first year's $600,000 ($300,000) plus one-half of the second year's $200,000 ($100,000) for a total cost recovery deduction of $400,000. In 1992, the deduction is the remaining half of the second year's $200,000 ($100,000) plus one-half of the third year's $100,000 ($50,000) for a total 1992 cost recovery deduction of $150,000. The remaining half of the third year's cost recovery amount of $100,000 ($50,000) is deducted in 1993.

[11] Currently, the corporate tax rate on corporate capital gains (short-term or long-term) is the same as the corporate tax rate on other income. However, there is a provision in the tax law that stipulates that in the future the corporate tax rate on capital gains may be fixed at a maximum rate of 34 percent. A similar situation applies in the case of individual taxes (see footnote 3). In computing taxes on gains, long-term gains and losses are netted against one another to compute a net long-term gain or loss for the year; similarly for short-term gains and losses. These nets are then netted together to determine the tax consequences of capital transactions.

51

CHAPTER 3
**The legal environment:
business organization,
taxes, and bankruptcy**

than its $25,000 book value but for less than its $40,000 initial cost, the entire gain (sales price *minus* book value) is treated as ordinary income. For example, if the machine were sold for $30,000, the gain, treated as ordinary income, would be $5000. If the machine is sold for more than its original cost of $40,000, the difference between the selling price and the $40,000 original cost is treated as a long-term capital gain and the $15,000 difference between the $40,000 original cost and the $25,000 book value is ordinary income. For example, if the machine were sold for $50,000, $10,000 of the gain would be treated as a long-term capital gain and $15,000 of the gain would be treated as ordinary income.[12] If the machine is sold for less than its $25,000 book value, the difference between the $25,000 book value and the selling price is an ordinary loss and is deductible from taxable income (like an ordinary business expense).

Real property is treated differently from personal property. Consider first real property acquired before 1987 under the tax law that applied before 1987. For *nonresidential* real estate, if straight-line depreciation has been used, any gain (sales price minus depreciated book value) is treated as a capital gain and any loss is treated as an ordinary loss. If accelerated depreciation has been used, the tax treatment is the same as with personal property (see above). For *residential* real estate, if straight-line depreciation has been used, any gain is treated as a capital gain; if accelerated depreciation has been used, part of the gain will be treated as ordinary income (will be recaptured) and the remainder will be treated as a capital gain.[13] Assuming that the real estate (residential or nonresidential) has been used in a trade or business, any loss upon disposition of the real estate will be treated as an ordinary loss and will be deductible from ordinary taxable income. For real property acquired after 1986, straight-line depreciation must be used. Any gain upon disposition is treated as a capital gain. If the real property was used in a trade or business, any loss upon disposition will be treated as an ordinary loss and be deductible from ordinary income.[14]

Beginning in 1984, if a company has ordinary losses from selling assets, some of the capital gains produced by sales of other assets in later years will be treated as ordinary gains (to the extent of the earlier years' ordinary losses). For example, if Hoyt Corporation had ordinary losses of $2 million on assets sold in 1988 and, in 1989, had capital gains of $5

---

[12] The machine example used here is a simplification, since gains and losses on all business asset sales during the year are combined in computing taxes, and therefore the tax effect of a particular asset often depends on other asset gains and losses. (See footnote 11.)

[13] The part of the gain taxed as ordinary income equals *the lesser of* (1) the gain and (2) the accumulated depreciation that was actually taken on the building *minus* the accumulated depreciation that would have been taken *if* straight-line depreciation had been used.

[14] The discussion here ignores Section 291 which, for corporations, causes some depreciation recapture for residential and nonresidential property depreciated using the straight-line method and causes additional depreciation recapture for residential property that was acquired before 1987 and that was depreciated using an accelerated method.

million on 1989 asset sales, $2 million of the $5 million of the 1989 gains would be treated as ordinary income in computing Hoyt's 1989 federal income tax.

FIRM FAILURE, REORGANIZATION, AND LIQUIDATION

Most of this book deals with ongoing business firms, not those experiencing bankruptcy or liquidation. This section examines some of the problems confronting a company in financial or economic failure, the outcome of which may be bankruptcy or liquidation.

Definition of Failure

The failure of a firm can be economic or contractual. A firm is an **economic failure** if it cannot be operated profitably even if it were properly managed and debt-free. The best solution to economic failure is liquidation of the firm. **Financial failure** (or **contractual failure**) occurs when the firm is unable to meet its contractual obligations to its creditors. Financial failure can occur whether or not a firm is an economic failure.

Liquidation means the termination of the firm as a going enterprise and the sale of the assets for the price that they will bring in the market. Whenever a firm's value as an ongoing enterprise is less than its value in liquidation, the firm is an economic failure and should be liquidated. Firms in this condition are often referred to as "being worth more dead than alive." For example, a firm may have no debt and be earning $10,000 a year. However, if the liquidation value of its assets were $500,000, the firm would be earning only 2 percent on its assets ($10,000/$500,000 = 2 percent). Even though this firm is not a financial failure (since it has no creditors), the firm should liquidate because it is an economic failure.

In the remainder of this chapter we will look at firms suffering from financial failure and perhaps from economic failure. If the financial failure is accompanied by economic failure, the firm should and probably will be dissolved and liquidated. If the financial failure is not accompanied by economic failure, the firm may continue in existence under either a voluntary adjustment or a reorganization.

Bankruptcy is a condition in which the firm is unable to pay its debts (is a financial failure) and its assets are surrendered to the court for administration. Bankruptcy proceedings may result in liquidation or may provide for an arrangement or a reorganization under which the firm continues to operate.

Frequency and Causes of Failure

Figure 3-1 shows the failure rate of business firms since 1929. Research by Dun and Bradstreet and by others indicates that failure is particularly common among new firms—those that have been in existence less than five years.[15] Furthermore, as might be expected, the failure rate is lower

---

[15] Under the Dun and Bradstreet's definition of failure, business failures include firms that ceased operations following assignment of bankruptcy; ceased with a loss to creditors after such actions as execution, foreclosure, or attachment; voluntarily withdrew leaving unpaid obligations; were involved in court actions such as receivership, reorganization, or arrangement; or voluntarily compromised with creditors.

53

CHAPTER 3
**The legal environment:
business organization,
taxes, and bankruptcy**

for large firms and is lower in times of prosperity than during periods of recession and depression. Large firms are not, of course, immune to failure, as evidenced by the recent and highly publicized failures of Wilson Foods, Braniff Airlines, Manville Corporation, and the biggest bankruptcy filing in U. S. history, Texaco Inc. (which was temporarily bankrupt; for details, see the topical essay "The Merger Game," which follows Chapter 23). The most important single cause of business failure has historically been the inability of the company to effectively promote the product and generate sufficient sales. Difficulties in collecting on receivables and in controlling operating expenses have also been frequent causes of failure.

The sharp increase in the business failure rate since 1978 (see Figure 3-1) has been largely due to three factors: recessions, high interest rates, and a liberalized bankruptcy law which has made bankruptcy filing and failure easier for U.S. businesses. Even with a strong economy and moderate interest rates, the new legal environment is likely to mean a continuation of a higher rate of bankruptcy than in past decades.

Voluntary Remedies for Financial Distress

If a firm is unable to meet its commitments to creditors, an agreement to avert bankruptcy may be reached between the firm's creditors and owners. The agreement may take one of several forms, but it usually results in a continuation of the firm under existing ownership. In some

FIGURE 3-1

*Historical business
failure rate per 10,000
concerns.*

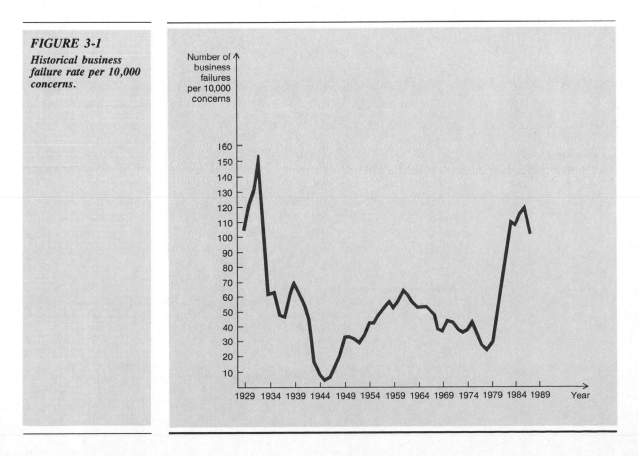

cases the firm may be terminated. Below we consider adjustments that allow the firm to survive.

It is important to stress that voluntary agreements are *voluntary*—no court or trustee supervises the settlement. Any creditor who refuses to take part in the agreement may press a claim, blocking the agreement for all creditors. However, this may result in more financial loss to the creditor than would cooperating with the other creditors to arrange a settlement with the debtor. Often small claims—those under $50 or $100—are fully paid, with the creditors having the larger claims remaining as parties to the voluntary agreement. Those creditors participating in the accord with the firm will usually appoint a committee among themselves to deal with the debtor firm. Voluntary remedies include extension, composition, and temporary assumption of firm control by creditors.

In an **extension** the creditors agree to *postpone* payments on the debt for a given period in order to mitigate the debtor firm's current difficulties. To get the creditors to agree to the extension, the firm's owners may have to provide security, such as mortgages on the firm's assets or the personal property of the company's owners.

Under a **composition**, creditors agree to *receive less* than the amount originally owed to them, for example, $0.80 for every dollar of debt. Creditors may agree to a composition because they feel that the only other alternative is to force the firm into bankruptcy and liquidation, with the possible result that they would receive even less than under the composition.

An agreement may be reached under which a creditor's committee representing the creditor group assumes temporary control of the firm. The hope is that the committee will be able to ameliorate the situation sufficiently for the debts to be retired, after which old management can resume control.

General Bankruptcy Provisions

The financial distress of business firms and individuals is regulated by the federal Bankruptcy Code.[16] Chapter 11 of the Code deals with debtor reorganizations. Chapters 7 and 11 contain all the remedies available to corporations. Most liquidations are covered by Chapter 7. Chapter 13 provides for a remedy for individuals and businesses which are neither corporations nor partnerships and which have unsecured debts less than $100,000 and secured debts of $350,000 or less. An unsuccessful Chapter

[16] The Bankruptcy Code contains four titles. Only Title I concerns us here because Titles II to IV are very technical in nature. The seven chapters of Title I (all odd-numbered) contain all substantive statutory laws concerning bankruptcy: Chapter 1 contains general provisions; Chapter 3 covers the court administration of a case; Chapter 5 deals with creditors' claims; Chapter 7 explains the liquidation process; Chapter 9 has special rules and procedures for municipalities; Chapter 11 (of particular relevance here) consolidates the debtor relief provisions of the repealed Chapters X, XI, and some of the Chapter XIII of the old Bankruptcy Act.

55

CHAPTER 3
**The legal environment:
business organization,
taxes, and bankruptcy**

13 plan may be converted to a Chapter 11 plan or to a Chapter 7 liquidation.

Either the debtor or the creditors or stockholders may initiate a petition if the firm is insolvent, as defined by the Bankruptcy Code. Under the Code, *insolvency* means that the firm is not paying its debts as they come due, or that, within 120 days before the involuntary petition is filed, a custodian (other than a trustee) was authorized to take charge of all or substantially all the debtor's property. A hearing is held after the filing of an involuntary petition if the debtor challenges the petition. At the hearing, the bankruptcy court determines whether the firm is insolvent under the above definition.

*Chapter 11
Reorganizations*

Under Chapter 11 reorganizations, a debtor may petition the bankruptcy court for a reorganization under which the debtor will eliminate its debts by making only partial or delayed payments to creditors. A creditor, a creditor's committee, or the stockholders may file a plan if the debtor fails to do so within 120 days after filing the petition.

The firm's creditor and ownership claims are divided into classes containing claims similar in type. Common stock and preferred stock are separate classes. Within each class of creditor, two-thirds of the amount of debt and a numerical majority of the claims must approve of the plan for the class itself to be deemed to have approved the plan. Holders of two-thirds of the amount of stock in each class of stockholder must approve the plan for the class to approve it.

In order for the classes of claims against the firm to make an informed decision on the proposed plan, the proponent of the plan must make a disclosure statement to each class before its vote on the proposal. After the necessary disclosures are made, their adequacy has been determined by the court, and the classes of claims have voted, the bankruptcy court will confirm or reject the proposed plan.

After the plan is confirmed, the payments in cash, property, or securities are made to the creditors and stockholders, and the debtor is discharged from all affected debts (however, if the debtor is a corporation or a partnership and if the plan involves the complete liquidation of the debtor, special rules apply).

The reorganization plan may provide for the issuance of new securities to the firm's creditors in order to reduce the debt payment burden. Often, the firm's assets are only sufficient to cover some of the debt claims, in which case the equity claims of stockholders and the claims of some or all unsecured creditors may be completely eliminated, that is, entirely unpaid and dissolved.

Reorganization and Priority   Under reorganization, new securities are issued to some or all of the firm's creditors and perhaps to its preferred and common stockholders, depending upon the value of the firm upon reorganization. Usually, senior claims are honored in full before junior claims receive anything. To illustrate, assume that the firm's balance sheet as of the end of the period preceding reorganization was as shown in Exhibit 3-2. Remember that balance sheet asset figures are at book value ($18 million) and not liquidation value. Assume that the liquidation value of the firm's assets is $4 million, but its going concern value is estimated to be $6 million. The estimated value of the securities to be issued under the new capital structure created under reorganization is $6 million. The total liabilities of $8 million exceed the new value of the firm, and so the old stockholders receive nothing under the reorganization. The stockholders' equity interest in the firm has been eliminated because the firm is insolvent (assets of $6 million are less than liabilities of $8 million). Assume that the $6 million in new securities to be issued will be in the form of $2 million in 6 percent bonds, $1 million in $6\frac{1}{2}$ percent subordinated debentures, $1 million in 7 percent preferred stock, and $2 million in common stock. Values of the claims of each creditor and the distribution of the new securities to those creditors are shown in Exhibit 3-3. The holders of the notes receive $3 million in new bonds and new subordinated debentures in satisfaction of their original $3 million claim. The subordinated debenture holders receive new preferred stock and new common stock worth a total of $2,250,000, and the general unsecured creditors receive $750,000 in common stock. Thus, only the note holders receive new securities with a value equal to the original claim against the firm. This is because the notes are repaid before the subordinated debenture holders receive anything.[17]

The Code may allow priorities which differ from those shown above. For example, senior creditors with large claims may wish to allow the old stockholders to retain some interest in the firm. This may be done over the protests of the junior creditors if the dissenting classes of junior creditors are to receive a "fair and equitable" portion of the proceeds from implementation of the plan.

---

[17] The distribution of securities parallels the distribution of cash under liquidation, as described in the section below on liquidation.

EXHIBIT 3-2
Balance sheet

Assets	$18,000,000
Liabilities	
Notes payable	3,000,000
Subordinated debentures*a*	4,000,000
General unsecured creditors	1,000,000
Stockholders' equity	10,000,000

a Subordinated to the notes payable. The general unsecured creditors are not affected by the subordination.

57

CHAPTER 3
**The legal environment:
business organization,
taxes, and bankruptcy**

Decision to Reorganize or Liquidate In evaluating the reorganization plan, the court, the security holders, and the SEC, if involved, must decide whether the firm's going concern value after reorganization will exceed its liquidation value. Reorganization is justified only if the firm is not an irreversible economic failure. If, even after a reorganization, it is likely to be an economic failure, the firm should be liquidated and not reorganized.

To estimate the going concern value, future revenues, costs, and earnings must be forecast, using available information regarding expected sales, labor and material input costs, and any other factors relating to the firm's operations. The choice between reorganization and liquidation will vary from situation to situation. For example, if the firm were a chain of retail clothing stores that had overexpanded into unprofitable geographic regions, liquidation value of the land and buildings might be very high but the business itself would be an economic failure. Even better management could not generate the sales needed to make

---

EXHIBIT 3-3
Old claims and new claims under reorganization

Old security	Old claim	New claim with reorganization[a]
Notes	$3,000,000	$3,000,000
Subordinated debentures	4,000,000	2,250,000
General unsecured debt claims	1,000,000	750,000

**Distribution of new securities
under new claim with reorganization**

Old security	Received under reorganization
Notes	$2,000,000 in 6% bonds
	$1,000,000 in 6½% subordinated debentures
Subordinated debentures	$1,000,000 in 7% preferred stock
	$1,250,000 in common stock
General unsecured debt claims	$750,000 in common stock

[a] Because in this illustration the debentures are subordinated only to the notes, the general unsecured creditors are unaffected by the subordination and therefore receive what they would if no subordination agreement existed (per dollar owed this equals the amount contractually owed divided by the dollars available for the debt repayment). Since the securities distributed have a value of $6 million but creditor claims equal $8 million, general unsecured creditors receive 75 percent ($6,000,000/$8,000,000) of their claim, i.e., $750,000 in securities (0.75 × $1,000,000). The remaining $5,250,000 in securities is divided between the notes and subordinated debenture holders; however, since the notes are senior to the debentures under the subordination, they are paid in full (securities worth $3 million) and the remaining $2,250,000 in securities goes to the debenture holders.

the firm profitable. Liquidation would be preferable to an attempt to reorganize in this case. On the other hand, the firm might be a poorly managed manufacturing firm with good markets for its products and owning specialized equipment with little liquidation value. Reorganization rather than liquidation might be justified.

Liquidation

If the creditors estimate that the going concern value of the firm is less than its liquidation value, they may seek to liquidate the firm's assets and distribute the proceeds among the creditors. There are two ways to effect liquidation: nonjudicial liquidation and bankruptcy. Under either, the proceeds from the liquidation are distributed among the firm's creditors. The remainder of the chapter explores these topics in detail.

Nonjudicial Liquidation   Under a nonjudicial liquidation, the firm and its creditors privately settle the firm's debt. The courts are not involved. A trustee is generally appointed by the creditors to supervise the orderly liquidation of the firm's assets and the distribution of the proceeds. Not infrequently the trustee is the adjustment bureau of a local or national creditors association.

All creditors must consent to the settlement, since any one of them is free to block it and place the firm in bankruptcy through court action. As noted below, under a bankruptcy the priority rule applies under a bankruptcy liquidation; that is, senior claims are ordinarily fully paid before junior claims are met at all. Therefore, for senior claimants to agree to a nonjudicial liquidation, they will demand priority treatment. If they are denied priority, they may move to throw the firm into bankruptcy. Consequently, the settlement under assignment will generally conform to the priority rule.

Liquidation under Bankruptcy   If a reorganization fails or a nonjudicial liquidation cannot be worked out, a firm may enter into a liquidation under Chapter 7 of the Code. (The procedure is the same whether the firm itself voluntarily files for bankruptcy or an involuntary bankruptcy petition is filed by the creditors.) The federal bankruptcy court appoints a referee who then arranges a meeting of the creditors. At the meeting, claims are proved and a trustee is elected by the creditors. The trustee's responsibility is to liquidate the firm's assets in an orderly manner and to distribute the proceeds to the claimants. Upon completion of the payment to the creditors, the trustee prepares an accounting that is presented to the creditors and to the referee.

Under the priority guidelines provided by Chapter 7 the distribution of the proceeds from liquidation must conform to the following priority of claims (highest priority first):

1   Expenses associated with preserving, supervising, and liquidating the bankrupt's estate. These are called administration expenses.
2   Unsecured claims arising after the filing of an involuntary petition but before the appointment of a trustee.

59

CHAPTER 3
**The legal environment:
business organization,
taxes, and bankruptcy**

3 Wages, salaries, and commissions, not to exceed $2000 per claimant, earned within ninety days prior to the filing of the bankruptcy petition.
4 Claims for contributions to employee benefit plans arising within 180 days before commencement of the proceeding or the debtor's cessation of business, whichever occurs first. This item is limited by a statutory formula.
5 Certain consumer claims, not exceeding $900, arising from purchase, lease, or rental of goods or services.
6 Some government tax claims.
7 Secured and unsecured creditors' claims in order of priority.
8 Payment of dividends to preferred stockholders.
9 Payment of dividends to common stockholders.

Item 7 needs some clarification. Secured creditors have first right to that property which was used to secure their claims. To the extent that such property is insufficient to cover the amount owed to them, the secured creditors join the unsecured creditors in dividing the remaining liquidation proceeds. If the proceeds from the sale of the security property more than meet the secured claims, the remaining funds are used to pay unsecured creditors. If proceeds from the sale satisfy creditor claims, then the remaining amount is payable to stockholders.

THE INTERNATIONAL LEGAL ENVIRONMENT

The Multinational Corporation

The international trade of goods and services has throughout history been an important part of world economics. Export and import companies have traditionally provided commodities for and acquired commodities from foreign markets, but, since the 1950s, a new type of business organization has emerged: the multinational corporation (MNC). The MNC is not limited to export and import activity; it makes direct investments—in manufacturing facilities, for example—in foreign countries. In most cases, the MNC, the parent company, establishes a subsidiary in a foreign country and invests through the subsidiary.

Each of the fifty largest (in terms of sales) U.S. manufacturing firms is a multinational corporation. American giants, such as Exxon, IBM, Dow Chemical, and Merck, acquire at least half of their revenues from their foreign operations. Firms in the United States were the first to develop multinational status, but in the last twenty years, companies in Western Europe and, more recently, Japan have established or acquired foreign subsidiaries. Collectively, Britain, The Netherlands, Switzerland, West Germany, Canada, and Japan have invested more outside their borders than has the United States. The foreign-based MNCs with sizable operations in the United States include England's Barclays Bank, Ltd.; Switzerland's Nestle Alimentana; France's Michelin; and West Germany's Volkswagen.

Why have corporations decided to expand internationally instead of simply exporting or importing goods and services? One important reason has been to avoid government-imposed tariffs and trade sanctions. To sell American-made products in France, for example, a cosmetics manufacturer would have to pay a French tariff; tariffs are not imposed if the products are manufactured by the cosmetics firm's Franch subsidiary. Although trade barriers have become less restrictive in many countries, there are additional advantages to manufacturing a product closer to its final market. These include a faster response to market changes, lower transportation costs, and better after-sales service. Even without the imposition of a French tariff, American-made cosmetics—because of fast-paced changes in style—might be out of fashion by the time they arrive in France. Part of Volkswagen's decision to begin production in the United States was the three-month shipping time and the costs required to transport its cars from West Germany to North America.

A second factor that has promoted the rise of the MNC has been differences in technical knowledge, managerial skills, and production costs among countries. MNCs based in large industrialized nations can often supply technical and managerial expertise to their subsidiaries in countries that offer plentiful natural resources and lower labor costs. Over time, this technical and managerial knowledge is usually acquired by the residents of the less developed country, and new, locally owned firms may eliminate the MNC's competitive edge. A final reason that many corporations invest abroad is the difference in tax laws and tax benefits accorded to companies with foreign operations.

*Taxation of
Multinationals*

Although corporate tax law for domestic U.S. firms is complicated, the taxation of MNCs with operations in several foreign countries—each with its own laws, rates, and deductions—can be overwhelming. Nonetheless, there are some basic tax considerations for MNCs based in the United States.

One tenet of the U.S. tax system is that corporations are taxed only on income earned in or returned to the United States. A somewhat arbitrary distinction is made, however, between the foreign branches of the U.S. company and foreign subsidiaries (subsidiaries are separate corporations whereas branches are not). The income earned by a foreign branch is treated as income earned in the United States and is taxed accordingly. The income of a foreign subsidiary is not taxed by the U.S. government unless and until it is transferred to the parent company in the form of dividends, interest, or royalties. In addition, the **foreign tax credit** (FTC) in U.S. tax law, as well as various bilateral tax treaties with other countries, is designed to prevent the possibility of taxing foreign earnings twice. In general, if income earned abroad has already been taxed by the host country, the MNC receives a foreign tax credit and must pay only the amount necessary to bring the total tax bill in line with U.S. tax rates. If the tax rate in the foreign country is higher than that of the United States, the foreign tax credit received is limited to the taxes due under U.S. tax law.

To illustrate, let's examine subsidiaries in two foreign countries, Lowtax Land and the Republic of Hightax. The corporate tax rate in Lowtax is 30 percent; the rate in Hightax is 60 percent. The Republic of Hightax also imposes a 10 percent withholding tax on dividends paid to

61

CHAPTER 3
The legal environment:
business organization,
taxes, and bankruptcy

its U.S. parent corporation. The U.S. tax rate is 40 percent. The subsidiaries in Lowtax and Hightax both have $100 in profits they wish to repatriate to the United States immediately. Exhibit 3-4 illustrates the tax computation for both subsidiaries.[18]

The details of U.S. tax law for multinational corporations are very complex. Tax evasion schemes and the laws instituted to prevent them can be quite involved. One aspect of international operations that is particularly important in this regard is transfer prices. When a company provides a foreign affiliate with an intermediate product or managerial service, the price charged for that commodity is somewhat arbitrary, for both companies are owned by the same investors. The price stated for accounting purposes is called the **transfer price**, which can have a major impact on the accounting profits—and the taxes—of the two companies. For example, if goods are being shipped to a subsidiary in a country with a high tax rate, it is in the MNC's best interest to charge a high price for those goods so that the book profits are shifted to the relatively lower tax rate country. In the United States, the IRS tries to expose instances in which profits and taxes have been intentionally shifted to other countries.

SUMMARY

A proprietorship is owned by one individual. The owner is responsible for all the firm's debts. For tax purposes, the income from the proprietorship is included in the owner's personal income. Partnerships are businesses

---

[18] This example assumes that the two subsidiaries are owned by separate United States parent companies. If they were both owned by the same company, then the FTC received for taxes paid to the Republic of Hightax would be $50, bringing the total United States taxes due on foreign-source income to zero.

EXHIBIT 3-4
Foreign and United States taxes on foreign subsidiary income

	Lowtax		Hightax
1. Profit before tax		$100	$100
2. Foreign corporate tax		30	60
3. Aftertax profit		$ 70	$ 40
4. Dividend withholding tax		0	4
5. Dividend to U.S.		$ 70	$ 36
6. U.S. tax on $100 profit	$40		$40
7. Credit for foreign tax rates paid (up to the 40% due under U.S. law)	30		40
8. U.S. taxes due [(6) − (7)]		10	0
9. Aftertax dividend [(5) − (8)]		$ 60	$ 36

owned by two or more people who share in the profits or losses. The income from the partnership is treated as personal income to the partners, and each partner is taxed according to the proportion of the business that he or she owns. The partnership dissolves if one of the partners leaves the partnership or dies.

Corporations are legal entities established by obtaining a certificate of incorporation from the state in which the business operates. A corporation may have one or more owners who are called stockholders or shareholders; each stockholder's ownership interest in the business is determined by the number of shares of stock owned. Corporations are taxed separately from the owners. The stockholders of a corporation enjoy limited liability in that creditors of the corporation cannot require stockholders to pay any of the corporation's debts from their personal assets or incomes. Because the corporation exists apart from its owners, a stockholder can sell his or her shares to other people without involving the rest of the owners. The corporation can continue to exist even if the owners die.

An individual's taxable income is the individual's total income less a variety of exemptions, deductions, and exclusions. Personal income tax rates depend on marital status. A corporation is taxed on its net income after expenses. Both the personal and corporate income taxes are progressive in that the rates increase as income rises. A corporation can elect to be taxed as a partnership if it has no more than thirty-five shareholders and meets certain other conditions.

If a business (incorporated or unincorporated) incurs a loss for the current year, the loss may be carried back as a deduction from taxable income of the three prior years so as to produce a refund to the firm of taxes previously paid. If taxable income in the past is less than the loss, losses may be carried forward as deductions from taxable income for the next fifteen years.

Depreciation is a tax deductible expense allowed firms with certain types of business assets, including fruit orchards, machinery, and buildings. The ACRS (Accelerated Cost Recovery System) assigns property, on the basis of its type, to a class life category; the class life category determines how a property may be depreciated for tax purposes. Either accelerated or straight-line depreciation may be used.

Part or all of a gain on disposing of a depreciable asset used in a trade or business may, in some cases, be treated for tax purposes as a capital gain. The part that is not treated as a capital gain is "recaptured depreciation" and that part is taxed as ordinary income. Generally, any losses on disposing of depreciable business assets are ordinary losses for tax purposes (i.e., are deductible from ordinary taxable income).

Failure of a corporation is economic if the company cannot earn a reasonable return on its investments. Failure is contractual or financial if the firm cannot meet its commitments to creditors. A company that is an incurable economic failure (whether or not it is a financial failure) should go out of business and liquidate its assets, since it cannot earn a reasonable return on investment. With financial failure but no economic failure, the firm will have to make some adjustment in order to satisfy

63

CHAPTER 3
The legal environment:
business organization,
taxes, and bankruptcy

unpaid creditors. This adjustment may involve only postponement of payment on the debt or may require the extreme remedy of a corporate reorganization.

Private agreements between the firm and its creditors to avert bankruptcy include extensions, compositions, or temporary assumption of managerial control of the firm by creditors. Under an extension, creditors accept a postponement of their payments, whereas under a composition the creditors accept only partial payment in satisfaction of the debt.

Adjustments that permit the company to continue in existence may also be effected through court action under Chapter 11 of the Bankruptcy Code. Under Chapter 11, a firm may petition the court to approve a plan that provides for settlement of the company's debts and specifies the steps required for a reorganization. The reorganization can also be initiated by the firm's creditors. After the court approves the petition, a trustee may be appointed to draw up the reorganization plan and to supervise the company's assets until the plan goes into effect. The old management will often be left in control. Under reorganization, the old securities of the corporation are retired and new securities are issued to those people with claims against the company. Creditors with senior claims usually receive securities with a value covering the amount owed to them before junior claimants receive anything.

If a company is an economic failure, it will be liquidated. Liquidation may proceed under a private settlement between the company and its creditors or with court supervision under Chapter 7 of the Bankruptcy Code. In either case, senior claimants are ordinarily fully paid before junior claimants receive anything.

Multinational corporations (MNCs), which are corporations with overseas operations, face an especially complex legal environment. Most large U.S. firms are MNCs, many deriving more revenues from foreign than from domestic sources. Expanding abroad has been a way of avoiding tariffs and other trade restrictions and of obtaining access to natural resources and low-cost labor. U.S. corporations are generally given some tax relief to compensate for taxes paid to foreign governments.

QUESTIONS

1 Compare and contrast the three types of business organizations. Why are large businesses almost always corporations?
2 How does being a limited partner differ from owning stock in a corporation, assuming that the percentage of ownership is the same in both cases?
3 What are the tax advantages to a stockholder of having the stock appreciate in value instead of receiving cash dividends?
4 List the advantages and disadvantages to a business of being taxed as a corporation rather than as a partnership.
5 If the total depreciation over the life of a machine is the same under all depreciation methods, what is the advantage of accelerated depreciation over the straight-line method?
6 Distinguish between economic failure and financial failure.

7 Under what conditions should a firm be liquidated?
8 Distinguish among the three basic types of voluntary remedies of financial distress: extension, composition, and temporary assumption of control of the firm by creditors.
9 What rationale can you give for creditors accepting less than the face value of their claim when a firm is in financial distress?
10 What is the priority of claims rule as it is used in reorganizations and liquidations? When may it be modified?

PROJECTS

1 Research and prepare a table showing percentages in terms of numbers and gross revenues (sales) accounted for by proprietorships, partnerships, and corporations for the following lines of business: grocery stores, airplane manufacturers, construction contractors, men's clothing manufacturers, and security brokers and dealers. Evaluate the variations in percentages. (Use the IRS publication *Business Income Tax Returns* for the most recent year available.)
2 Talk with a lawyer who specializes in bankruptcy cases and inquire about the significance of legal costs, accounting fees, and so on, that are involved in bankruptcy. Ask about the importance of business disruptions caused by creditor (or trustee) takeover if the bankrupt firm is not liquidated but is continued by the creditors as a going enterprise.

DEMONSTRATION
PROBLEMS

DP1 The Blake Company forecast of taxable income for 1990 is $80,000.
   a Using the tax schedule in Table 3-3, compute Blake's estimated tax for 1990 and its expected quarterly payments.
   b Through the third quarter Blake made payments according to the estimates made in *a* above. However, at the end of the year, Blake discovered that the firm had earned only $90,000 total for the year. What was the firm's fourth-quarter tax payment?

SOLUTION TO DP1:
a Estimated annual tax = 0.15($50,000) + 0.25($25,000)
                       + 0.34($5000) = $15,450
   Quarterly payment = $15,450/4 = $3862.50

b Taxes owed = 0.15($50,000) + 0.25($25,000)
                + 0.34($15,000) = $18,850
   Taxes already paid = $3,862.50(3) = $11,587.50
   Fourth-quarter payment = $18,850 − $11,587.50
                      = $7262.50

DP2 The book value of Marginal Foods, Inc., assets is shown below. The liquidation value of the assets is $25 million. Assume a

65

CHAPTER 3
**The legal environment:
business organization,
taxes, and bankruptcy**

going concern value of $35 million. Also assume the bonds are subordinated to all other liabilities. Marginal has defaulted on its debt and is in bankruptcy. Determine how much the stockholders and each class of creditor will receive.

Marginal Foods, Inc. balance sheet

Assets		$40,000,000
Liabilities:		
General creditors...................	$15,000,000	
Notes payable......................	5,000,000	
Subordinated bonds................	16,000,000	
Total liabilities		36,000,000
Stockholders' equity		$ 4,000,000

SOLUTION TO DP2:
The firm will be reorganized and new securities will be issued since the going concern value exceeds liquidation value. The marshalling of securities will take place according to the priority of the claims on the assets of the firm. Inasmuch as the going concern value of the firm is less than the book value of its debt by $1 million, the stockholders will not participate at all in the reorganization.

Since the claims of creditors exceed the going concern value by $1 million there will be some give there as well. The subordinated bonds, by the nature of the subordination agreement, will absorb the entire $1 million deficiency. Therefore, the value of the securities received will be as follows:

Proceeds upon reorganization

	Value of securities received
General creditors	$15,000,000
Notes payable	5,000,000
Subordinated bonds	15,000,000
Stockholders	0
Total	$35,000,000

PROBLEMS

1 In April 1990, Carl Stanley bought 4000 shares of Grand Foods at $40 per share. The tax rate on any dividends from the stock is 30 percent.

    a What personal taxes on this investment would Carl have paid if he sold the stock in June 1990 for $50 per share, having received dividends of $2 per share? [Ans.: $14,400]

    b What would Carl's taxes on the stock have been if he sold the stock in February 1991 for $90 per share and received (during the ten-month holding period) dividends of $6 per share? [Ans.: $67,200]

2 Flexicorp has a seven-year history of income and expenses as shown below. What would Flexicorp's actual taxes paid (or received) in each year have been, making use of tax carrybacks and carryforwards? Assume a tax rate of 50 percent.

Year	1	2	3	4	5	6	7
Revenues	$15,000	$25,000	$100,000	$60,000	$ 80,000	$160,000	$40,000
Expenses	25,000	30,000	55,000	60,000	100,000	80,000	80,000

3 In 1989, Berger Corporation purchased a $100,000 machine. Berger's asset purchases are spread out evenly over the year. The depreciable life of the machine is five years. Straight-line depreciation is used for tax purposes. Berger's tax rate is 34 percent.

    a What is the depreciation per year on the machine?

    b What is the book value of the machine on July 1, 1991?

    c How much tax must be paid on the sale if the firm sells the machine on September 30, 1991, for $40,000? Assume that this is the only asset sold by the firm during the year.

    d How much tax must be paid if the firm sells the asset for $150,000 on September 30, 1991?

4 Todler Corporation is facing reorganization under Chapter 11 of the Bankruptcy Act with the following existing capital structure:

	Book value
Bonds	$ 30,000,000
General unsecured creditors	40,000,000
Preferred stockholders	50,000,000
Common stockholders	100,000,000
	$220,000,000

The trustee for the reorganization has estimated the liquidation value of Todler's assets at $100 million and the value of Todler as a going concern at $140 million and in this light has proposed the following new capital structure for the reorganized firm.

67

CHAPTER 3
**The legal environment:
business organization,
taxes, and bankruptcy**

Unsecured debt	$ 20,000,000
Income debentures	20,000,000
Preferred stock	20,000,000
Common stock	80,000,000
	$140,000,000

If the court accepts this plan, what will be the distribution of the new securities to the old security holders?

5 The book value of the assets of Drop Corporation is shown below. The notes are subordinated to the bank loans. The going concern value of Drop is $3 million. ($3 million is the value of the company's debt and equity if the firm continues to operate.)

Drop Corporation balance sheet		
Assets		$20,000,000
Liabilities		
Bank loans	$5,000,000	
Subordinated notes	3,000,000	
General creditors	8,000,000	
Total liabilities		$16,000,000
Stockholders' equity		$ 4,000,000

What will each type of creditor and stockholder receive under each of the following assumptions:
a The firm's assets are liquidated for $20 million.
b The firm's assets are liquidated for $15 million.
c The firm's assets are liquidated for $10 million.
d The firm's assets are liquidated for $5 million.

DEPRECIATION METHODS

Three methods of depreciation will be described below: straight-line, declining balance, and sum-of-the-years' digits. We will illustrate the depreciation methods using an asset that cost $20,000, has a depreciable life of five years, and has a $5000 salvage value. Under the Accelerated Cost Recovery System (ACRS), salvage value is assumed to be zero in computing depreciation; however, we will assume a $5000 salvage value below in order to illustrate the general application of the depreciation methods. Under ACRS, assets may be depreciated using the straight-line method or using an accelerated method that approximates the declining balance method assuming the half-year convention (see footnotes 8 and 10).

Under straight-line depreciation, the annual depreciation charge is:

$$\text{Annual depreciation} = \frac{\text{initial cost} - \text{salvage value}}{\text{depreciable life}} \qquad (3\text{-}1)$$

In the example, the depreciation is $3000 per year [($20,000 − $5000)/5 years].

The declining balance method (either 150 percent, 175 percent, or 200 percent declining balance) provides higher depreciation in the early years of the asset's life than it does in the later years. To calculate the depreciation allowance using the double-declining method (i.e., the 200 percent declining method), use the following formula:

$$\text{Current depreciation} = \left[\frac{2}{\text{depreciable life}}\right] \times \text{current book value} \qquad (3\text{-}2)$$

where the current book value of the asset equals its original cost *minus* total depreciation to date. In our example, the depreciation allowance would be $(\frac{2}{5})$20,000 = 8000 in the first year. Notice that we do not have to consider salvage value initially and that the initial book value is simply the cost of the machine. For the second year, we calculate the new book value as the cost minus the depreciation previously taken, which equals $20,000 − $8000 = $12,000. Depreciation for the second year is $(\frac{2}{5})$12,000 = 4800. Later years are treated in a similar fashion. If the book value of the asset in the last year of its depreciable life is greater than the salvage value, the entire difference

69

CHAPTER 3
**The legal environment:
business organization,
taxes, and bankruptcy**

is taken as depreciation. In the above example, the machine would have a book value of $2592 at the beginning of the fifth year ($20,000 initial cost minus $17,408 accumulated depreciation). For the 150 percent and 175 percent declining balance methods, simply replace the 2 in Eq. (3-2) with a 1.5 and 1.75, respectively.

The sum-of-the-years'-digits method determines the depreciation in each year as a portion of the original cost less salvage value. This method also provides higher depreciation in the early years relative to the later years. To determine depreciation, we first compute a factor equal to the sum-of-the-years' digits. For example, the factor for an asset being depreciated over five years is $5 + 4 + 3 + 2 + 1 = 15$. The factor may also be computed using the following formula:

$$\text{Factor} = \text{depreciable life} \times \left(\frac{\text{depreciable life} + 1}{2}\right) \tag{3-3}$$

In the example above:

$$\text{Factor} = 5 \left(\frac{5 + 1}{2}\right) = 15$$

Depreciation in year t is now determined as:

$$\text{Depreciation}_t = (\text{cost} - \text{salvage value}) \times \left(\frac{\text{depreciable life} + 1 - t}{\text{factor}}\right) \tag{3-4}$$

where the first year is considered year 1 ($t = 1$). The depreciation in the first year would be:

$$\text{Depreciation}_1 = (\$20,000 - \$5000) \left(\frac{5 + 1 - 1}{15}\right) = \$5000$$

For the second year

$$\text{Depreciation}_2 = (\$20,000 - \$5000) \left(\frac{5 + 1 - 2}{15}\right) = \$4000$$

The depreciation for the fifth and last year would be $1000.

ANCIENT TIMES

When a Neolithic farmer some 7000 years ago borrowed additional seed grain to expand his land under cultivation, he had no idea what he was starting. By 3000 B.C. loans of grain and silver with repayment in kind were commonplace in ancient Sumer. Going interest rates were $33\frac{1}{3}$ percent per year on barley loans and 20 percent per year on silver loans. Not long afterward groups of merchants established trading associations that were the predecessors of the modern corporation.

The Code of Hammurabi (about 1800 B.C.) regulated financial transactions in Babylon. Such banking operations as deposits, transfers to another party (checks), and loans were widespread. Business partnerships of various types were codified, and requirements for security arrangements in loans (assets pledged to the lender) were set out. During the sixth century B.C., merchant bankers were active in Babylon. These firms engaged in activities similar to those of the great European merchant bankers of the nineteenth century, the Rothschilds: making loans to individuals, businesses, and governments; entering into partnerships with other firms to engage in some joint commercial venture; accepting, transferring, and paying interest on deposits; and purchasing existing loans secured by land (equivalent to buying a mortgage

¹ The major sources for this essay are Sidney Homer, *A History of Interest Rates* (New Brunswick: Rutgers University Press, 1963); Samuel Eliot Morrison, *The Oxford History of the American People* (New York: Oxford University Press, 1965); and Arthur Stone Dewing, *The Financial Policy of Corporations* (New York: Ronald Press, 1953).

in twentieth-century secondary markets). Interest rates on loans in this period were 10 percent to 20 percent per year depending on the type of loan. Thus the Babylonians developed relatively sophisticated financial capabilities quite early in history, and, as we shall see, there were few significant advances beyond this point for the next 2000 years.

The Greeks' contribution to finance was minimal compared with their contributions in other areas. They did develop and extend the types of loans made. By the fourth century B.C., unsecured loans became common. Interest rates were generally lower than in Babylon. A well-secured loan in second-century B.C. Athens could be obtained at an annual rate of 6 percent. On the other hand, many of the city-states of Greece had very poor credit ratings, and loans made by individuals to some cities carried interest rates as high as 48 percent per year.

A common financial arrangement throughout the Mediterranean area in ancient times was the "sea loan." Typically this was a loan secured by a ship or by its cargo made at the beginning of a voyage. If the voyage was successful, the lender was repaid; otherwise he was not. During stable periods the interest rate charged was about 30 percent. When there was active warfare or piracy, interest rates were 60 percent to 100 percent. This financial arrangement was essentially a partnership with one partner (the lender) being limited in the amount received but having first claim on any proceeds from the voyage.

The Romans, whose economy was based on agriculture and tribute from other nations, were not particularly interested in business and finance. It is known that joint stock

71

CHAPTER 3
**The legal environment:
business organization,
taxes, and bankruptcy**

companies with limited liability for the owners existed in Rome, but it is not clear where they originally were developed. The Romans were the original "cheap money" people. Low interest rates were considered desirable as a goal of public policy. They established a legal maximum on interest rates of $8\frac{1}{3}$ percent per year. After 443 B.C., a creditor charging more than this rate was liable for quadruple damages under Roman law. Later the maximum rate was raised to 12 percent, where it remained for several hundred years. During prosperous times the actual rates charged were usually well below the maximum, down to 4 percent on occasion.

One shouldn't conclude from this discussion that finance in those early times was not very different from the present day. Organized financial markets did not exist. Borrowing was usually undertaken to finance trade or for personal needs, and loans were short-term—one year or less. Large private corporations did not exist, and governmental units were infrequent borrowers, in part due to their generally poor credit standing. Temples in Babylon and Greece were heavily engaged in lending. Relatively few private banking firms existed. The penalities for default on a loan were severe— personal slavery in Babylon and Rome.

EARLY CHRISTIANITY AND USURY

The early Christian doctrine of usury—the tenet that charging interest on a loan is immoral—had a profound influence on the development of finance for 1000 years. Loans were viewed as an aid to a neighbor in distress. To profit from a neighbor's distress by charging him interest was viewed as evil. This concept, which has philosophical appeal,

was applied to loans for commercial purposes as well. The secular authorites vacillated between the absolute prohibition against interest demanded by the Church and the Roman tradition of regulation and legal maxima. Therefore, although individuals could band together in business partnerships and share in the profits from commercial activities, borrowing money to engage in such activities was inhibited.

In time some of the obvious differences in the purpose of loans became apparent. Commercial activity began to increase during the twelfth century, and this forced the development of financial arrangements which avoided the doctrine of usury while serving the basic purpose of providing compensation to a lender. Some leaders of the Protestant Reformation— Luther, Zwingli, and Calvin—defended interest on loans as proper, provided the rate was not injurious or extortionary. Calvin fixed the maximum legal rate in Geneva in 1547 at 5 percent per year.

THE DEVELOPMENT OF SECONDARY MARKETS FOR SECURITIES

During the twelfth and thirteenth centuries, two types of long-term "securities" developed that could be resold. The first was the "census," which originated early in the Middle Ages. A census was the right to obtain a portion of the returns from agricultural property. Originally the returns were a share in the harvest; later annual money payments were substituted. A landowner could sell a census (borrow money) on his property without the buyer (lender) being considered a usurer. A variety of different types developed. A census might have fixed payments and a fixed maturity and resemble a mortgage loan of today. Some censuses were perpetuities, paying a fixed amount forever. Others ceased with the death of one of the parties. A secondary market of sorts existed for these contracts. The owner of the census could sell it to another person, but trading in these securities was not active.

A more extensive secondary market developed in Venice. The Republic of Venice forced its wealthier citizens to "loan" money to the government in order to finance its defense budget. In return the Republic paid 5 percent per year interest. Principal repayments were made occasionally, depending on the condition of the Venetian finances, but interest payments on these loans were made regularly for 100 years. Essentially the loans were government bonds. No paper certificates were issued, but a record of the owner of the "bonds" was kept and the ownership was freely transferable. The prices of these securities were quoted daily as an active market for them developed. Over the period in which they were outstanding, market prices varied from 20 percent of face value during wartime to over 100 percent during prosperous periods when they were being repaid.

FINANCE FROM 1100 TO 1750

The financial development of Western Europe, beginning in the twelfth century, is characterized by increasing trade and the resulting demand for short-term commercial loans and for methods of dealing in foreign exchange. Long-term debt contracts of various sorts arose in this period, including the equivalent of mortgages on real estate and of government bonds that were often perpetuities without promise of principal repayment. These government securities were issued by the independent cities of Italy and Germany and by Holland, and secondary markets developed from them. This period also saw the development of government-sponsored banks. The Bank of England was established in 1654.

What distinguishes this period from modern times is the limited nature of the financial institutions and the lack of large private corporations. Most of the banking activities were carried out through partnerships, often within a single family. Banking per se was often incidental to the basic purpose of the business—to engage in trade and commercial activities. The Medicis of Florence, who were leading bankers in the fifteenth century, are a well-known example of this. The family contained merchants, bankers, princes, and popes. They maintained offices throughout Europe, North Africa, and the Near East and engaged in a wide range of international trading and banking activities, while acquiring large land holdings and political power in Italy.

By 1750 financial affairs in Europe could be characterized as well developed in the areas of government finance and the financing of international trade. Business finance was dominated by speculators. Many companies were promoted, and their stock was actively traded. Amsterdam was the financial capital of Europe. The stock of the Dutch East India Company was traded on the Amsterdam Exchange, along with commodities and the bonds of local and foreign governments. Trading methods such as margin purchases, short sales, and futures contracts had been developed. Insurance, invented in the seventeenth century, had become a means by which private investors speculated on shipping ventures.

73

CHAPTER 3
**The legal environment:
business organization,
taxes, and bankruptcy**

THE NINETEENTH CENTURY

In many respects the nineteenth century was the "golden age" of finance. The industrial revolution brought heavy demands for capital investment. New companies were formed in great numbers to exploit new technologies. Preferred stock was developed in the first half of the century, and limited liability for corporate stockholders was common by the middle of the century. The railroad boom in the United States attracted large amounts of British capital. Even the Bank of England held some American railroad bonds. Long-term interest rates were fairly low (2 to 4 percent), despite the demand for money. The invention of paper currency in the eighteenth century combined with large gold discoveries kept the money supply expanding, while rapid increases in productivity kept inflation rates down. London replaced Amsterdam as the world's major financial center.

During this period the major consumer financial institutions were established: savings banks, "building societies" (savings and loan associations), and cooperative credit associations (credit unions). Commercial banks were almost exclusively concerned with the affairs of their business customers.

Prior to the American Revolution there were no chartered (incorporated) banks in the thirteen American colonies. Money was in generally short supply, and many business transactions were based on the barter of commodities. After the revolution several banks received charters from state governments. In 1791 the First Bank of the United States was chartered by Congress at the urging of Secretary of the Treasury Alexander Hamilton. The bank was founded to expand the credit available in the economy, but its charter was not renewed in 1811 because it had been badly managed and because agricultural interests in the country were opposed to renewal.

In 1816 the Second Bank of the United States was chartered. As a financial institution serving the interests of the growing country, it

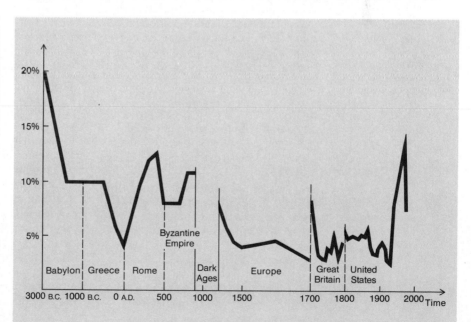

Historical interest rates. (Rates shown after A.D. 1200 are for long-term, low-risk securities. Earlier interest rates are for short-term debts.) (Sources: Homer, "A History of Interest Rates" and Federal Reserve Bulletin.)

was well conceived. Unfortunately, the bank fell prey to Andrew Jackson's mistrust of "monied interests" and its policies of keeping the paper money issued by local banks within bounds aroused intense antagonism. The Second Bank's charter expired in 1836. The bankers of New York City picked up the leftover pieces of the bank (which had been headquarterd in Philadelphia) and proceeded to construct a vastly greater stronghold of financial power than had been dreamed of by its original management. The ultimate result was that the farmers and frontiersmen who had opposed the bank gained nothing, but the financial center of the United States moved from Philadelphia to New York. There was not to be another central government bank in this country until the Federal Reserve Bank was established in 1913.

The period 1836 to 1863 was the era of "wildcat banking." Anyone could start a bank and issue currency. The currency of most of these banks was not considered to be worth its face value. The most beneficial thing that wildcat banking did was to encourage the development of the American engraving industry. With every bank issuing its own paper currency, there was a lot of engraving work to do.

In 1863 the National Banking Act provided for the federal chartering of commercial banks (national banks) and imposed a tax on private bank currency issues that effectively eliminated them.

Nineteenth-century interest rates in the United States varied widely from one part of the country to the other. A tradition of 5 percent to 6 percent interest on long-term debt became established in the East, and rates stayed mostly in this range for secure debt instruments. In the West things were different. In specific cases mortgages on ranchland were obtained at 36 percent annual interest. Savings banks in Los Angeles at midcentury were paying 15 percent on deposits. The problem was the lack of a well-developed financial system to ease the movement of money from East to West. The discrepancies in rates spawned several political movements as well as a distrust in the West of "Eastern bankers" that persists to some extent today.

UNITED STATES FINANCE IN THE TWENTIETH CENTURY

The nineteenth century was the heyday of private financiers. In the twentieth century the federal government assumed a dominant role in the American financial system. The stock market collapse of 1929 to 1932 wiped out the fortunes of many people and dispelled the notion that Wall Street financiers had financial matters well under control. Legislation passed during the 1930s made the stock market less of a private club of speculators and stripped financial power from the major banking houses of the time by forcing a division between commercial banking and investment banking. The House of Morgan—the great banking firm established by J. P. Morgan that dominated the financial scene in the early part of the century—was split into two firms still active today as major financial institutions: Morgan, Stanley, and Company, investment bankers; and Morgan Guaranty Trust, a commercial bank.

Financially the twentieth century is also characterized by the dispersion of financial power, the proliferation of financial instruments, and an emphasis on personal finance. The stock market is dominated by financial institutions that rely on individual investors for their funds.

75

CHAPTER 3
**The legal environment:
business organization,
taxes, and bankruptcy**

Financial institutions woo consumer accounts with all the marketing skills they can bring to bear. The average person can borrow money to finance cars, boats, and appliances. Such financing was not widely available until after World War II.

Interest rates, after staying fairly low during the early part of the century, dropped to minimal levels during the 1930s and stayed relatively low until 1965. Since then we have been living in a complex and rapidly shifting financial environment. Interest rates have moved up and down rapidly and at times have reached levels unprecedented in the history of the United States. In 1981, the United States government had to pay more than 16 percent to borrow money for two years. A reduction in the rate of inflation brought relief in the mid-1980s as interest rates dropped in response and remained at lower levels into the 1990s.

The financial markets are now international in scope. The major financial centers of the world—New York, London, Hong Kong, Singapore, Zurich, and Tokyo—are closely linked together by electronic communications and financial institutions.

CHAPTER FOUR

THE TIME VALUE OF MONEY

A well-known fact of economic life is that money is not free and can be downright expensive. In this chapter, we look at some methods of comparing cash flows that occur over time. The ability to make such comparisons is very useful for both business managers and individuals in making financial decisions. The techniques described in this chapter are universal. They apply in France or Singapore as they do in the United States. The examples are all expressed in dollars, but they could just as well be expressed in yen.

Financial calculators and computers that can quickly solve time-value problems are readily available. But these mechanical tools provide solutions only after you have structured the problem. Correctly setting up the problem requires a clear understanding of the time-value concept and of the implied interest rate relationships. This chapter provides that understanding.

WHY MONEY HAS TIME VALUE

In Chapter 2 we defined interest rates as prices of credit in the economy. From the viewpoint of an individual or a business firm, the practical consequences of interest rates are apparent. If you have some spare cash now, you can invest it in liquid and low-risk assets such as a savings deposit in a bank and receive more money later. If you borrow money now, you must repay a larger amount in the future (the amount borrowed *plus* interest). The result is that $100 in hand today is worth more than $100 to be received a year from now because $100 today can be invested to provide $100 plus interest next year. The existence of interest rates in the economy therefore provides money with its time value quite apart from the attitudes of any one person or the investment opportunities available to a particular firm.

In the first part of this chapter we will assume that we know the interest rate which gives money its time value. The last section is devoted to the problem of determining an unknown interest rate on a loan or investment when all the cash flows are known.

If you borrow $200 for one year and agree to repay the lender $220 at the end of the year, the interest cost of borrowing is $20. The rate of interest is $20/$200 = 0.10 or 10 percent per year. All the mechanics of compound interest are illustrated in this simple example. Let's examine the basic cash flows of the example. There are really only two cash flows of importance here, your initial inflow of cash of $200 and the payment of $220 one year later. If we take the date of borrowing as time 0 and the date of repayment as time 1 (one year from time 0), these flows can be represented in the cash flow diagram shown in Figure 4-1. This diagram is drawn from the viewpoint of the borrower. If you were the lender instead of the borrower, your cash flows would be as shown in Figure 4-2.

The general relationship among the variables in the example can be expressed as

Repayment = amount borrowed plus interest payment

and, since the interest charged is usually expressed as a rate or percent of the amount borrowed

Repayment = amount borrowed + (rate × amount borrowed)

FIGURE 4-1

The cash flows associated with borrowing $200 for one year at an interest rate of 10 percent.

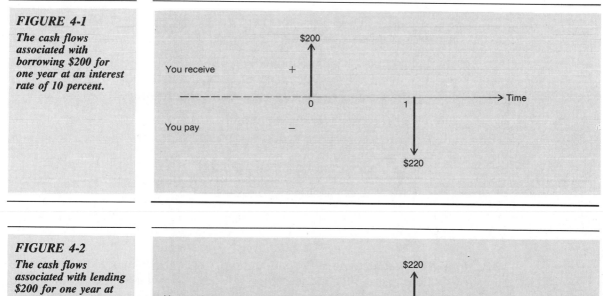

FIGURE 4-2

The cash flows associated with lending $200 for one year at an interest rate of 10 percent.

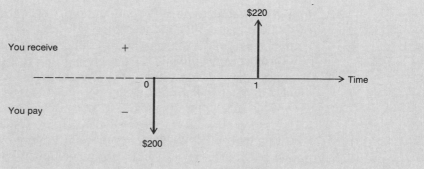

or, by rearranging the terms,

$$\text{Repayment} = (\text{amount borrowed})(1 + i) \tag{4-1}$$

where i is the interest rate. In our example,

$$\$220 = \$200(1 + 0.10)$$

$$= \$200(1.10)$$

$$= \$220$$

Suppose that you just purchasd a used Honda from Friendly Dan, the Cycle Man, for $200. He is kind enough to give you up to one year to pay off the purchase price with only 1 percent *per month* interest charge on the outstanding balance. At the end of the first month, you would owe $200(1.01) = $202. What if you didn't pay this amount at the end of the first month? Since you owe $202 at the end of the first month, you would owe $202(1.01) = $204.02 at the end of two months. At the end of three months you would owe $204.02(1.01) = $206.06. Another way of showing the amount owed at the end of three months is

First month: (1.01)($200)
Second month: (1.01)(1.01)($200)
Third month: (1.01)(1.01)(1.01)($200)

or

$(1.01)^3 \$200 = (1.0303) \$200 = \$206.06$

The interest is being compounded monthly. At the end of twelve months you would have to pay $(1.01)^{12} \$200 = (1.1268) \$200 = \$225.36$. This example illustrates the following general relationship.

If P is a present or initial amount

F is a future amount

i is the interest rate *per time period*

n is the number of time periods

then,

$$F = P(1 + i)^n \tag{4-2}$$

In the example, P is the amount borrowed now and F is the future payment (amount borrowed plus interest). However, the formula also applies when P is the amount invested now and F is the amount received in the future (initial investment plus interest). Equation (4-2) is the basic relationship in time-value-of-money methods. All the other relationships we will discuss later are developed from this one.

The only difficult part of Eq. (4-2) is raising $(1 + i)$ to the nth power. Unless you have a calculator handy, finding $(1.01)^{12}$, for example, takes quite a while. For this reason, there are many published tables available giving values of $(1 + i)^n$ for various values of i and n. Appendix A in the back of this book contains a fairly complete set of tables of interest rate factors. Table 4-1 shows some typical values for $(1 + i)^n$. The time periods in the table can be days, months, quarters, years, or whatever time period is appropriate for your problem.

Returning to the example, if you wished to know how much you would owe on the motorcycle at the end of four months at an interest rate of 1 percent per month, you would go to the table and look across the row for four periods and under the 1 percent column, finding this value of $(1.01)^4 = 1.0406$. The amount owed at the end of four months is therefore $(1.0406) \$200 = \$208.12$.

Example Problem In 1626 Peter Minuit purchased Manhattan Island from the Indians for about $24 worth of trinkets. If the Indians had taken cash instead and invested it to earn 6 percent compounded annually, how much would the Indians have had in 1986, 360 years later?

Table 4-1 doesn't go out to 360. So, in the absence of a calculator that would give us $(1.06)^{360}$, we will have to solve this problem in steps.

First, how much would the Indians have in 1726 at the end of the first 100 years, which is the highest value for n in the table? We see that the value of $1 at 6 percent per year for 100 years is $339.30; therefore, the value of $24 compounded at 6 percent per year for 100 years is

$$F_{100} = \$24(1 + .06)^{100}$$

$$= \$24(339.3)$$

$$= \$8143$$

We can now consider the $8143 as invested at $t = 0$ and see what its value would be at the end of the next 100 years compounded at 6 percent per year. At the end of the second century (1826) the $8143 invested in 1726 would again have grown by a factor of 339.3.

TABLE 4-1
Future compound value of $1: $(1 + i)^n$

Number of periods (n)	Interest rate per period (i)						
	1%	2%	4%	6%	8%	10%	12%
1	1.0100	1.0200	1.0400	1.0600	1.0800	1.1000	1.1200
2	1.0201	1.0404	1.0876	1.1236	1.1664	1.2100	1.2544
3	1.0303	1.0612	1.1249	1.1910	1.2597	1.3310	1.4049
4	1.0406	1.0824	1.1699	1.2625	1.3605	1.4641	1.5735
5	1.0510	1.1041	1.2167	1.3382	1.4693	1.6105	1.7623
10	1.1046	1.2190	1.4802	1.7908	2.1589	2.5937	3.1058
12	1.1268	1.2682	1.6010	2.0122	2.5182	3.1384	3.8960
15	1.1610	1.3459	1.8009	2.3966	3.1722	4.1772	5.4736
20	1.2202	1.4859	2.1911	3.2071	4.6610	6.7275	9.6463
25	1.2824	1.6406	2.6658	4.2919	6.8485	10.835	17.000
60	1.8167	3.2810	10.52	32.99	101.3	304.5	897.6
100	2.7048	7.2446	50.505	339.3	2,200.0	13,780.0	83,522.0

$$F_{200} = F_{100}(1.06)^{100}$$

$$= \$8143 \ (339.3)$$

$$= \$2,762,919.90$$

or approximately \$2.763 million. By 1926, at the end of the third 100 years, the value would have increased another 339.3 times.

$$F_{300} = F_{200} \ (1.06)^{100}$$

$$= \$2.763 \text{ million } (339.3)$$

$$= \$937.5 \text{ million}$$

For the sixty years from 1926 to 1986 the \$937.5 million would grow to

$$F_{360} = F_{300} \ (1.06)^{60}$$

$$= \$937.5 \text{ million } (32.99)$$

$$= \$30.93 \text{ billion}$$

This value is approximately \$50 per square foot of Manhattan Island! Maybe Peter didn't make that good a buy.

Note that this problem could have been solved more simply by observing initially that $(1.06)^{360} = (1.06)^{100}(1.06)^{100}(1.06)^{100}(1.06)^{60}$. We could have simply multiplied $(339.3)(339.3)(339.3)(32.99)$ to arrive at[1]

$$(1.06)^{360} = 1288.6 \times 10^6$$

This factor multiplied by \$24 provides us with \$30.93 billion, the same answer as above.

Double Your Money   If you look at Table 4-1 in the 6 percent column, you see that the factor for twelve periods is 2.0122. This means that \$1 invested at 6 percent per year will grow to \$2.01, or very nearly double, in twelve years. This is an example of a rule of thumb called the **rule of 72**. This rule works as follows: If you wish to know how long it will take to double your money at a given interest rate, divide the rate into 72 and the result is the number of years it will take. In this case $\frac{72}{6} = 12$. The rule works pretty well for most interest rates.[2] For example, the rule of 72 would say that it will take seventy-two years to double your money at

---

[1] This is an application of the rule for combining exponents which says that

$$N^{A+B} = (N^A)(N^B)$$

For example,

$$2^5 = (2^3)(2^2) = (8)(4) = 32$$

[2] A more accurate method is the **rule of 69**:

$$\text{Number of periods to double} = 0.35 + \frac{69}{\text{interest rate}}$$

For a development of the rule of 69 and a comparison with the rule of 72, see J. P. Gould and R. L. Weil, "The Rule of 69," *Journal of Business*, 49(3) (July 1974), pp. 397–398.

1 percent per year. In fact, it will take about seventy years. The rule says that it would take 3.6 years to double your money at 20 percent ($\frac{72}{20}$); in fact, it will take 3.8 years. The rule works the other way too. You can estimate the interest rate required to double your money in a given number of years by dividing the number of years into 72. For example, you must earn about 7.2 percent per year to double your money in ten years. The rule of 72 is a handy thing to remember.

Present Value

In the problems discussed above we were calculating the future value (or payment) of an amount invested (or borrowed) at a given rate of interest. In many problems, you would like to know the present amount that will grow to a given future value. Suppose you are faced with the following problem. You wish to save a portion of the earnings from your summer job this year to make your first tuition payment next fall, a year from now. Tuition will be $600 and the bank will pay you 5 percent compounded annually. How much must you put in the bank now in order to have $600 next year? The future amount you need is $600 and the interest rate is 5 percent. Let P be the amount put into savings now. From Eq. (4-2) we know that

$$F = P(1 + i) \tag{4-3}$$

Solving Eq. (4-3) for P, we get

$$P = \frac{F}{1 + i} \tag{4-4}$$

and

$$P = \frac{\$600}{1.05}$$

$$= \$571.43$$

The amount $571.43 is called the **present value** of $600 to be received one year from now at the interest rate of 5 percent per year. The general relationship for the present value of a future amount to be received n periods from now at an interest rate of i per period is derived from Eq. (4-2) just as the one-period relation was. Equation (4-2) was

$$F = P(1 + i)^n$$

Solving for P,

$$P = \frac{F}{(1 + i)^n} \tag{4-5}$$

In solving problems where P is the unknown amount, if we know the value of $(1 + i)^n$, you can remember to divide the future amount by that factor in order to find the present value. Alternatively, note that Eq. (4-5) can be expressed as

$$P = F\left[\frac{1}{(1 + i)^n}\right] \tag{4-6}$$

Tables generally provide values for the term in the brackets so that when you wish to find the present value of a future amount you can *multiply* by the present value factor $1/(1 + i)^n$ rather than *divide* by the compound amount factor $(1 + i)^n$. This was done originally because it is easier for people doing hand calculations to multiply than divide. To take a trivial example, if $(1 + i)^n = 1.05$, then $1/1.05 = 0.9524$. Which is easier to calculate, $0.9524 \times \$100$ or $\$100/1.05$? With widespread use of calculators, this doesn't matter so much. We retain the approach as a convenience in setting up and solving problems.

We can use the value of $1/1.05 = 0.9524$ to solve the previous example. From Eq. (4-6) the present value of $F = \$600$ is

$$P = \$600(0.9524)$$

$$= \$571.43$$

We now have two interest factors to keep track of, the **compound amount factor** $(1 + i)^n$ and the **present value factor** $[1/(1 + i)^n]$. As a way of remembering what these factors do, we use a special notation to express them. The compound amount factor is

$$(F/P, i, n) = (1 + i)^n \tag{4-7}$$

This factor is used to find the future value of a present amount at i percent for n periods. The compound amount factor is always greater than 1.0 for i greater than zero, indicating that a present amount will always grow to a larger future value.

The present value factor is

$$(P/F, i, n) = \frac{1}{(1 + i)^n} \tag{4-8}$$

This factor is used to find the present value of a future amount. The present value factor is always less than 1.0 for i greater than zero, indicating that a future amount has a smaller present value. A dollar in the future is worth less than a dollar today, as we said at the beginning of the chapter. Moreover, the further out in the future a dollar is, the less it is worth today. For example, at an interest rate of 6 percent the value today of a dollar received one year from now is

$$P = \$1(P/F, 6\%, 1)$$

$$= \$1\left[\frac{1}{1.06}\right]$$

$$= \$1(0.9434)$$

$$= \$0.9434$$

Using Table 4-1 to obtain the value of $(1.06)^2 = 1.1236$ we see that the value today of a dollar received two years from now is

$$P = \$1(P/F, 6\%, 2)$$

$$= \$1\left[\frac{1}{(1.06)^2}\right]$$

$$= \$1\left(\frac{1}{1.1236}\right)$$

$$= \$1(0.8900)$$

$$= \$0.89$$

Therefore, at an interest rate of 6 percent, a dollar to be received one year from now is worth 94.34 cents today, whereas a dollar to be received two years from now is worth only 89 cents today.

Note that the higher the interest rate is, the less a dollar in the future is worth today. At an interest rate of 5 percent, a dollar to be received in one year is worth 95.24 cents today, but at an interest rate of 6 percent, that dollar is only worth 94.34 cents today.

Values for all the interest rate factors for various interest rates are shown in Appendix A at the back of the book. The headings in the tables of Appendix A are based on the symbols defined above. If you look at the table for 6 percent under the column headed P/F, you will find 0.8900 in the row for $n = 2$. We will be discussing the use of these tables after we look at some more difficult problems.

Annuities

An **annuity** is a series of periodic payments or receipts of equal amounts; for example, $100 per year for ten years. A typical house mortgage repayment schedule is an annuity. Figure 4-3 shows the cash flow diagram for any annuity of A for n periods contrasted with present (P) and future (F) amounts. As an example of one type of problem involving annuities, suppose you plan to save $1000 each summer for the next

FIGURE 4-3
Cash flow diagrams.

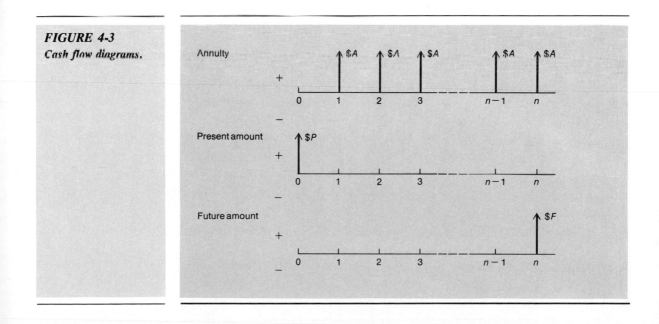

three years. You can earn 5 percent per year on this money. How much could you withdraw from the bank three years from now? A cash flow diagram of the problem we are describing is shown in Figure 4-4, where F is the unknown amount to be determined. From the cash flow diagram you can see that the first savings deposit planned is one year from the present. At the end of the summer two years from now you will have that $1000 plus the interest earned on it as well as a newly deposited $1000, or $1000(1.05) + $1000. Therefore, the total in the account at the end of two years will be $2050. At the end of the third summer you will have accumulated savings and interest of $2050(1.05) = $2152.50 plus an additional $1000 in new savings. You would therefore have a total future amount of $3152.50, that is

$$F = \$3152.50$$

Future Values and Annuities   There is an easier way to solve such problems. To see how, let's look at the savings program a different way. At the end of the third summer the $1000 saved in the first year would have been earning interest for two years. Therefore, the first summer's savings contributed $1000 (1.05)^2 = $1000 (1.1025) = $1102.50. The savings from the second summer earned interest for one year, $1000 (1.05) = $1050. The savings from the third year were just deposited and earned nothing. Adding them together,

$$F = \$1000(1.05)^2 + \$1000(1.05) + \$1000$$

$$= \$1102.50 + \$1050 + \$1000$$

$$= \$3152.50$$

We can express the computations above in terms of an annual amount A (which was $1000 in the example) and the interest rate i.

$$F = A(1 + i)^2 + A(1 + i) + A$$

Alternatively, we can write the relationship as

$$F = A[(1 + i)^2 + (1 + i) + 1] \tag{4-9}$$

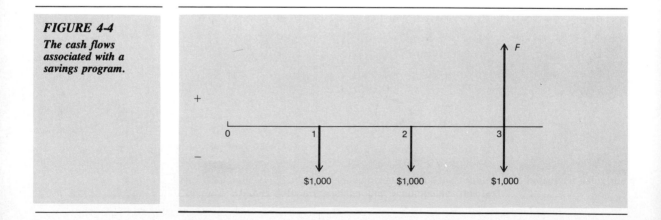

FIGURE 4-4

*The cash flows
associated with a
savings program.*

The term in the brackets is another interest factor that is sometimes called the **annuity compound amount factor**.[3] It expresses the value at the end of three periods of a three-period annuity of $1 per period invested at an interest rate of i percent. We can represent this factor for n periods and i percent per period in our notation as $(F/A, i, n)$. It is used to find the future value of an annuity and always has a value greater than 1.0. Notice from Figure 4-3 that the future value F occurs at the same point in time as does the last annuity amount A; the last annuity amount therefore earns no interest. Values for the annuity compound amount factor are also found in tables such as the ones in Appendix A.

In the example above, the factor is

$$1.1025 + 1.05 + 1.0 = 3.1525$$

To solve our problem, we would need only to look in the 5 percent table in Appendix A under the column headed F/A and along the row for $n = 3$ to find the value of 3.1525 and multiply it by $1000 to get our answer of $3152.50.

Now suppose you wanted to have $3152.50 available to you at the end of the summer three years from now. How much would you have to deposit each summer at an interest rate of 5 percent starting one year from now assuming that you save equal amounts each year? We know the answer is $1000 per year, but how can we calculate it? It's simply the reverse of the problem above. Now we are given the future amount and wish to know the annual amount.

There is a factor used to find the annuity that must be invested to provide a future value. It is called the **sinking fund factor** and is expressed as $(A/F, i, n)$. This factor is a number between zero and 1.0. In order to solve our problem, we need to know $(A/F, 5\%, 3)$. If you now look in the 5 percent table of Appendix A down the column headed A/F and along the row for $n = 3$, you will find

$$(A/F, 5\%, 3) = 0.3172$$

To determine the annual savings required to accumulate to a future value of $3152.50, you need to perform the following calculations:

$$A = \$3152.50(A/F, 5\%, 3)$$

$$= \$3152.50(0.3172)$$

$$= \$1000$$

In general, to find the annuity A given the future amount F, use the sinking fund factor

$$A = F(A/F, i, n) \tag{4-10}$$

---

[3] The general form of the annuity compound amount factor $(F/A, i, n)$ is the sum of a series of individual compound amount factors:

$$(F/A, i, n) = (1 + i)^{n-1} + (1 + i)^{n-2} + \cdots + (1 + i) + 1.0 = \frac{(1 + i)^n - 1}{i}$$

Note that the sinking fund factor is equal to the reciprocal of the annuity compound amount factor:

$$(A/F, 5\%, 3) = \frac{1}{(F/A, 5\%, 3)}$$

$$= \frac{1}{3.1525}$$

$$= 0.3172$$

The sinking fund factor is very useful in developing savings plans designed to reach a particular goal. Many corporate bond issues require the firm to make regular payments into a sinking fund set up to retire the bonds at the end of a specified number of years. This is where the factor gets its name, since it is used to find out how large the payments (annuity) must be to make the sinking fund equal the amount of the bond issue when the bonds must be paid off.

Present Values and Annuities   In many problems you will want to know the present amount that must be invested today in order to provide an annuity for several periods. For example, suppose your grandmother wished to deposit enough money now to meet your tuition payments for the next three years of $2000 per year. The interest rate is 5 percent per year. The cash flows are shown in Figure 4-5.

One way to solve this problem is to treat it as three smaller problems of finding the present values given the future amounts.

1   How much must be invested today to provide $2000 one year from now?

$$P = \$2000(P/F, 5\%, 1)$$

$$= \$2000\left[\frac{1}{1.05}\right]$$

FIGURE 4-5

*The present value of
three annual amounts.*

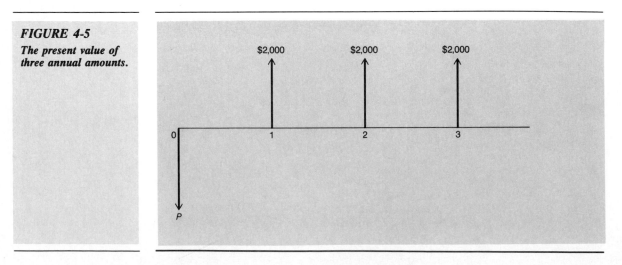

= $2000(0.9524)

= $1904.80

2 How much must be invested today to provide $2000 two years from now?

$P = \$2000(P/F, 5\%, 2)$

$= \$2000\left[\dfrac{1}{(1.05)^2}\right]$

$= \$2000(0.9070)$

$= \$1814$

3 How much must be invested today to provide $2000 three years from now?

$P = \$2000(P/F, 5\%, 3)$

$= \$2000\left[\dfrac{1}{(1.05)^3}\right]$

$= \$2000(0.8638)$

$= \$1727.60$

The total amount that must be deposited is the sum of the three values calculated above; so

$P = \$1904.80 + \$1814 + \$1727.60$

$= \$5446.40$

This computational scheme can be written in a more general form as

$$P = \dfrac{A}{1 + i} + \dfrac{A}{(1 + i)^2} + \dfrac{A}{(1 + i)^3}$$

$$= A\left[\dfrac{1}{1 + i} + \dfrac{1}{(1 + i)^2} + \dfrac{1}{(1 + i)^3}\right] \qquad (4\text{-}11)$$

The terms in the brackets are a simple sum of single payment present value factors. Values for such sums are tabulated as an interest factor called the **annuity present value factor**.[4] We can denote the factor as $(P/A, i, n)$, the present value of an annuity. The annuity begins (the first A occurs) one period *after* the present amount P occurs (this was illustrated earlier in Figure 4-3). The value for $(P/A, 5\%, 3)$ is

$(P/A, 5\%, 3) = 0.9524 + 0.9070 + 0.8638$

$= 2.7232$

---

[4] The general relationship for the annuity present value factor is

$(P/A, i, n) = \dfrac{1}{1 + i} + \dfrac{1}{(1 + i)^2} + \cdots + \dfrac{1}{(1 + i)^n} = \dfrac{1 - (1 + i)^{-n}}{i}$

This value can be found in the 5 percent table in Appendix A. For our problem above we could have determined P as

$$P = A(P/A, i, n)$$

$$= \$2000(P/A, 5\%, 3)$$

$$= \$2000(2.7232)$$

$$= \$5446.40$$

This brings up another issue: How accurate do you really need to be in calculating such values? The answer is: Not nearly so accurate as we have been in our calculations. For many practical purposes, three-place accuracy is sufficient in solving interest rate problems. An answer of $5450 is often just as good as $5446.40. There are some situations in which greater accuracy is desirable, but you should be able to identify them when they are encountered. The values in the tables of Appendix A are accurate to four or five figures to permit more precise results if you want them. For very precise results, a calculator or computer can be used with the formulas in Appendix 4A at the end of this chapter. Also, many calculators have built-in financial functions. Their use is also discussed in Appendix 4A. Most of the time it is safe to round off the factors to three places.

In some problems you might want to know the annuity that can be provided from a given present amount of money. For example, suppose your grandmother (a lovely person) gave you $5446.40. You plan to deposit it in a savings account paying 5 percent and spend the entire amount plus interest over the next three years. How much could you withdraw each year with equal annual withdrawals? You know the answer already to be $2000 per year. After the third withdrawal, the deposit balance would be zero since $2000 per year is equivalent to (has the same present value as) $5446.40 today. In this case we wanted to know the annuity that results from a given present amount. The general representation of this interest factor is $(A/P, i, n)$. It is the reciprocal of the annuity present value factor

$$(A/P, i, n) = \frac{1}{(P/A, i, n)} \tag{4-12}$$

In our previous example $(P/A, 5\%, 3) = 2.7232$. The corresponding value for $(A/P, 5\%, 3)$ is $1/2.7232 = 0.3672$. You can check this by looking in the 5 percent table of Appendix A under the column headed A/P at $n = 3$.

$(A/P, i, n)$ is sometimes called the **capital recovery factor** since it can be used to determine what income is necessary to recover a capital investment given the rate of interest on the investment. It can also be called the **loan repayment factor**, since it is used to find the payments needed to pay off a loan. For example, suppose you worked for "Friendly Dan, the Cycle Man," and wished to set up monthly payment plans for motorcycle purchases. In order to find the monthly payments that would pay off a given purchase in twelve months at an interest rate of 1 percent per month, you would need to know $(A/P, 1\%, 12)$. The value of this factor is 0.0888, which you can get from the 1 percent table in Appendix A. The required payments (A) given the purchase price (P) would be

$$A = 0.0888 \, P$$

For a motorcycle costing \$600, the purchaser must pay $(0.0888)\$600 = \$53.28$ per month.

Perpetual Annuities A perpetual annuity (or "level perpetuity") is an annuity that is expected to continue forever. This type of cash flow pattern is often used for illustrative purposes both by us and by other authors because the present value of such annuities can be calculated very easily. The annuity present value factor when the number of periods becomes large (n approaches infinity) is simply $1/i$. Therefore the present value P of a perpetual annuity A beginning one period from the present is

$$P = \frac{A}{i} \tag{4-13}$$

The present value, using an 8 percent interest rate, of \$100 per year beginning in one year and to be received forever is

$$P = \frac{A}{i}$$

$$= \frac{\$100}{0.08}$$

$$= \$1250$$

Summary of Interest Factors

Three pairs of interest factors are useful in solving problems involving money paid or received at different points in time. If you are using a calculator to solve problems, it is as easy to divide as it is to multiply and you would need to have available only one factor from each of the three pairs. But you must keep track of which one is needed, and having all six is helpful. Values for the six factors are included in tables in Appendix A under the appropriate headings. The examples given below all use the 5 percent table at $n = 5$. Appendix 4A provides an algebraic formula for each factor, instructions for using calculators to compute the factors directly, and some hints on using financial calculators.

Single Payments or Receipts To find the future value of a present amount, use the compound amount factor:

$$F = P(F/P, i, n)$$

where

$$(F/P, i, n) = (1 + i)^n$$

This is the amount $1 will grow to in n periods invested at i percent per period. The future value of $100 invested for five years at 5 percent is $F = \$100(1.2763) = \$127.63$.

To find the present value of a future amount, use the present value factor:

$$P = F(P/F, i, n)$$

where

$$(P/F, i, n) = \frac{1}{(F/P, i, n)}$$

This is the amount that must be invested today to have $1 n periods from now at i percent per period. The present value of $127.63 to be received five years from now given a rate of 5 percent is $P = \$127.63(0.7835) = \$100$.

Annuities (Equal Payments or Receipts in Each Period) To find the future value of an annuity, use the annuity compound amount factor:

$$F = A(F/A, i, n)$$

where

$$(F/A, i, n) = (1 + i)^{n-1} + (1 + i)^{n-2} + \cdots + (1 + i) + 1$$

This is the amount (F) accumulated by investing $1 each period for n periods at an interest rate of i per period. F is the amount accumulated at the time the last investment is made; therefore the last investment earns no interest. The future value of $100 per year for five years at 5 percent is $F = \$100(5.5256) = \$552.56$.

To find the annuity required to accumulate to a future value, use the sinking fund factor:

$$A = F(A/F, i, n)$$

where

$$(A/F, i, n) = \frac{1}{(F/A, i, n)}$$

This is the amount (A) which must be invested each period for n periods at an interest rate of i per period to obtain $1 in period n at the time the last investment is made. The last investment of amount A earns no interest. The annual savings required to accumulate to $552.56 in five years at 5 percent is $A = \$552.56(0.1810) = \$100$.

To find the present value of an annuity, use the annuity present value factor:

$$P = A(P/A, i, n)$$

where

$$(P/A, i, n) = \frac{1}{(1 + i)} + \frac{1}{(1 + i)^2} + \cdots + \frac{1}{(1 + i)^n}$$

This is the amount which must be invested to provide an annuity of $1 per period for n periods at a rate of i percent per period. The annuity begins one period after the investment is made. The present value of $100 per year for five years at 5 percent is

$$P = \$100(4.3295)$$

$$= \$432.95$$

To find the annuity provided by a present amount, use the capital recovery or loan repayment factor:

$$A = P(A/P, i, n)$$

where

$$(A/P, i, n) = \frac{1}{(P/A, i, n)}$$

This is the annuity provided for n periods by investing $1 at a rate of i percent per period. The annual income for five years provided by a present investment of $432.95 at 5 percent is $A = \$432.95(0.2310) = \$100$.

SOLVING PROBLEMS WHEN THE INTEREST RATE IS KNOWN

Using the Tables

We have been using the tables in our examples above, but now let's examine them more carefully. Table 4-2 contains part of the table of factors in Appendix A for an interest rate of 6 percent per period. There is one such table for each interest rate included in the appendix. The range of rates provided is from $\frac{1}{3}$ to 50 percent. Each of the six factors is included in the table. In order to use the tables, you merely look up the value of the factor for the rate and number of periods desired. Note that

TABLE 4-2
*Interest rate of 6 percent**

n	F/P	P/F	F/A	A/F	P/A	A/P
1	1.0600	.9434	1.0000	1.0000	.9434	1.0600
2	1.1236	.8900	2.0600	.4854	1.8334	.5454
3	1.1910	.8396	3.1836	.3141	2.6730	.3741
4	1.2625	.7921	4.3746	.2286	3.4651	.2886
5	1.3382	.7473	5.6371	.1774	4.2124	.2374
6	1.4185	.7050	6.9753	.1434	4.9173	.2034
7	1.5036	.6651	8.3938	.1191	5.5824	.1791
8	1.5938	.6274	9.8975	.1010	6.2098	.1610
9	1.6895	.5919	11.4913	.0870	6.8017	.1470
10	1.7908	.5584	13.1808	.0759	7.3601	.1359

* The complete table for a 6 percent rate can be found in Appendix A.

each column in Table 4-2 is headed by the descriptive notation for the factor. The second column is headed F/P. This column contains the values of $(F/P, 6\%, n) = (1.06)^n$ for the values of n shown in the first column. For example, what is the value of $(F/P, 6\%, 5)$? Find the number in Table 4-2 that corresponds to $(F/P, 6\%, 5)$. The correct value is 1.3382.

Let's look at a problem using Table 4-2. Suppose you are trying to decide whether you should buy four tires expected to last for 20,000 miles or a set expected to last for 40,000 miles. You drive an average of 10,000 miles per year and expect to keep the car at least another four years. The 20,000-mile tires will cost $90 now and the 40,000-mile tires will cost $180. The cash flow diagrams for this problem are shown in Figure 4-6. Figure 4-6a shows the cash costs of buying 20,000-mile tires now at $90 and assumes that the same set is expected to cost you $100 two years from now. Figure 4-6b shows a single purchase of 40,000-mile tires. We will transform the two cash flows for the 20,000-mile tires to their present value. This gives us the cost of 20,000-mile tires in terms of dollars today which can be compared with the cost today of 40,000-mile tires. The present value of $90 today and $100 two years from now assuming an interest rate of 6 percent is

$$P = \$90 + \$100(P/F, 6\%, 2)$$

Look up $(P/F, 6\%, 2)$ in Table 4-2. Its value is 0.89. The present value of the cost of buying 20,000-mile tires is therefore

$$P = \$90 + \$100(0.89)$$

$$= \$90 + \$89.00$$

$$= \$179$$

Since the present value of the cost of the 40,000-mile tires is $180, you would save money with the 20,000-mile tires.

Beginning students usually encounter several difficulties involving interest rate problems. One such difficulty is recognizing the factors and tables to use in solving a particular problem. This difficulty is easily overcome with the familiarity gained from solving practice problems and reviewing the example problems on a step-by-step basis. Another difficulty arises when the cash flows in the problem are complicated and

FIGURE 4-6

Cash flows from
alternative
tire purchases.

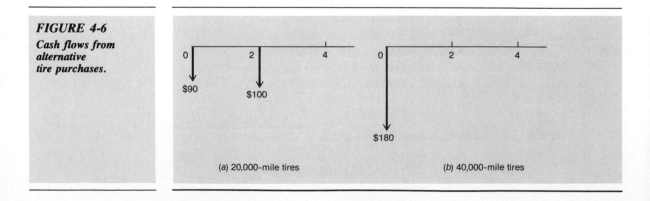

(a) 20,000-mile tires   (b) 40,000-mile tires

don't fit the simple examples we have been using. Here, too, practice helps, but that is not enough. There is a section later on about what to do when the cash flows vary from period to period.

A further difficulty arises when the available tables don't have the exact factor you need to solve your problem. For example, we don't have a table here for an interest rate of $7\frac{1}{2}$ percent. If your problems involve this rate, you have two choices. First, you can compute the factors you need using a calculator or a computer as discussed in Appendix 4A at the end of the chapter. Second, if your problem doesn't require a high degree of accuracy, you can interpolate in the tables you do have. Interpolation is sort of like averaging two numbers to get an "in-between" value. For example, if you wish to know the compound amount factor for five years at an annual rate of $7\frac{1}{2}$ percent, you are looking for $(F/P, 7\frac{1}{2}\%, 5)$. The tables provide the following values (look them up to check):

$$(F/P, 7\%, 5) = 1.4026$$

and

$$(F/P, 8\%, 5) = 1.4693$$

The value for $(F/P, 7\frac{1}{2}\%, 5)$ will be in between these two values. Figure 4-7 illustrates the problem. Since $7\frac{1}{2}$ percent is halfway between 7 percent and 8 percent, the value for the $7\frac{1}{2}$ percent factor will be approximately halfway between the 7 percent factor and the 8 percent factor. The distance between the two factors (difference in their values) is

$$1.4693 - 1.4026 = 0.0667$$

One-half of the difference is $0.0667/2 = 0.0333$. The value for $(F/P, 7\frac{1}{2}\%, 5)$ is therefore (approximately) $1.4026 + 0.0333 = 1.4359$. Interpolation can also be used when the number of periods in your problem is not in the tables. For example, if you want $(P/A, 6\%, 41)$ and all you have is $(P/A, 6\%, 40)$ and $(P/A, 6\%, 44)$, you can interpolate between the two known values to find the unknown one. Try this problem using the 6 percent table in Appendix A. Note that 41 is one-fourth of the distance from 40 to 44. The correct answer is $15.0463 + 0.0842 = 15.1305$. Interpolation is also useful in finding unknown interest rates, as we show later in the chapter.

FIGURE 4-7
Interpolation.

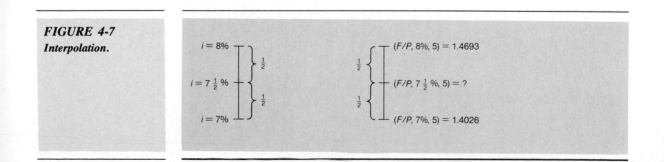

Variable Cash Flows

When you are faced with a problem that doesn't fit the simple situations we have been looking at, the first thing to do is to draw a cash flow diagram. Since any interest problem can be solved by applying the proper set of factors, once you identify the cash flows you can decide what factors you need. Take the example as shown in Figure 4-8a. If you wish to find the present value of the annual cash flows shown given an interest rate of 6 percent per year, either of the following two methods will work.

The first method is to consider the cash flows as being a $20 per year annuity beginning in year 2 plus a single amount of $80 in year 1, as shown in Figure 4-8b. We can first calculate the present value (P_1) of the $20 per year annuity in years 2, 3, and 4 as of the end of the first year. At 6 percent,

$$P_1 = \$20(P/A, 6\%, 3)$$

$$= \$20(2.673)$$

$$= \$53.50$$

The annuity has now been converted to a value equivalent to a cash receipt of $53.50 at the end of year 1. We can add to this figure the $80 receipt in year 1 to get the total equivalent cash receipt at this time, $80 + $53.50 = $133.50.

$$P_0 = \$133.50(P/F, 6\%, 1)$$

$$= \$133.50(0.9434)$$

$$= \$126$$

FIGURE 4-8

Analyzing variable cash flows.

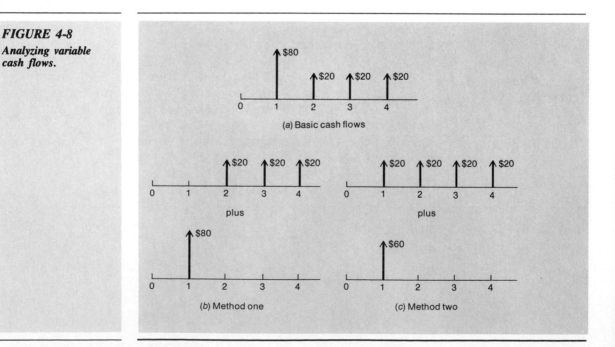

The alternative method is to evaluate the cash flow as being an annuity of $20 beginning at the end of the first year plus a receipt of $60 in that time as illustrated in Figure 4-8c. The present value is then the sum of the present values of the two cash flows.

$$P = \$20(P/A, 6\%, 4) + \$60(P/F, 6\%, 1)$$
$$= \$20(3.465) + \$60(0.9434)$$
$$= \$126$$

As another example, suppose you wished to know what the cash flows of Figure 4-8a would accumulate to at the end of four years from today (time 0 in the figure) if deposited to earn 6 percent. Using the second method, the future value would be

$$F = \$20(F/A, 6\%, 4) + \$60(F/P, 6\%, 3)$$
$$= \$20(4.375) + \$60(1.191)$$
$$= \$159$$

Note that the $60 is compounded for only three periods since the deposit will only be in the account for that length of time from year 1 to year 4. The annuity factor, $(F/A, 6\%, 4)$, is for four periods since there are four $20 payments, one in each period.

If the cash flows vary from period to period, then you must handle each period's cash flow individually. For example, suppose you wish to find the present value of the cash flows shown in Figure 4-9. At an interest rate of 6 percent per year the present value of all the cash flows is simply the sum of the present values of each one.

$$P = \$20(P/F, 6\%, 1) + \$25(P/F, 6\%, 2) + \$30(P/F, 6\%, 3)$$
$$\quad + \$28(P/F, 6\%, 4)$$
$$= \$20(0.9434) + \$25(0.8900) + \$30(0.8396) + \$28(0.7921)$$
$$= \$18.87 + \$22.25 + \$25.19 + \$22.18$$
$$= \$88.49$$

FIGURE 4-9
Variable cash flow.

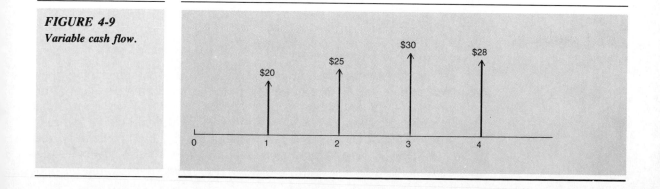

Finding future values would be done in a similar fashion but using $(F/P, i, n)$ instead of $(P/F, i, n)$. If you wish to transform a set of variable cash flows into an annuity, the easiest thing to do is to first find the present value of the cash flows, as done in the example. Then use the capital recovery factor $(A/P, i, n)$ to convert that present value into its equivalent annuity. If, for example, you wished to know the annuity equivalent to the cash flows of Figure 4-9, it can be determined by using the present value of $88.49 that we have already found.

$$A = \$88.49(A/P, 6\%, 4)$$
$$= \$88.49(0.2886)$$
$$= \$25.54$$

That is, the cash flows of Figure 4-9 are equivalent to an annuity of $25.54 per year for four years at 6 percent.

Example Problem Assume that you are twenty-five years old and wish to retire at age sixty. You expect to be able to average a 6 percent annual rate on savings over your lifetime. You would like to save enough money to provide $8000 per year beginning at age sixty-one in retirement income to supplement other sources (social security, pension plans, etc.). One problem you face is estimating how long you wish the $8000 per year to continue on retirement. Suppose you decide that the extra income need be provided for only twenty years (up to age eighty). The problem is how to organize your savings program prior to retirement so that you will have enough money to support a supplementary retirement income of $8000 per year for twenty years. Try to draw a cash flow diagram of this problem assuming that some savings will be made each year up to age sixty.

The initial part of this problem is fairly simple. You should find the amount of money you must have at age sixty in order to provide $8000 per year for twenty years. In other words, you need to know the present value (as of age sixty) of a twenty-year annuity of $8000 per year. The factor needed is therefore $(P/A, i, n)$, the annuity present value factor.

$$P_{60} = \$8000(P/A, 6\%, 20)$$
$$= \$8000(11.4699)$$
$$= \$91,760$$

At age sixty a savings account of $91,760 earning 6 percent interest per year will permit you to take out $8000 per year beginning one year after retirement and continuing for twenty years. Notice that we are making the simplifying assumption that you draw out $8000 annually. In practice, you would probably withdraw smaller amounts more frequently, for example $650 or so per month beginning at age sixty. However, the assumption of annual withdrawal is a fairly good approximation and makes the problem easier to solve. Also, for simplicity, we can round off the $91,760 to an even $92,000 as our target savings goal.

A simple savings program would be to deposit the same amount each year. To find out the annual amount invested at 6 percent needed to accumulate to $92,000 at age sixty, thirty-five years from now, what factor should be used? We wish to find the annuity that will accumulate to a future value, $(A/F, i, n)$, the sinking fund factor.

$$A = \$92,000(A/F, 6\%, 35)$$

$$= \$92,000(0.0090)$$

$$= \$828$$

Therefore, you would have to save $828 per year for thirty-five years to have $92,000 at the end.

Suppose you felt that the most you could afford to save presently and until age forty-five would be $500 per year. See if you can figure out how much you would have to save each year from age forty-five to sixty in order to end up with $92,000. [Hint: The $500 saved per year for the first twenty years would be worth $500(F/A, 6\%, 20) = \$18,400$ at age forty-five. By age sixty this amount would grow to $18,400(F/P, 5\%, 15) = \$44,000$.] The answer is $2064 per year needed to be saved from age forty-five to age sixty.

Time and Timing

In this book, in problems where the cash flows cover several years, we simplify our calculations by putting all the cash received or paid during a given year at the end of the year. This is an approximation to simplify the problem. The savings-retirement problem shown earlier is an example. You would probably be making monthly deposits into your savings account during the savings period and variable withdrawals during retirement. Unless there is some reason to want a high degree of accuracy, treating the cash flows as single annual amounts is a reasonable way to keep down the complexity of a given problem. Of course, some problems demand that months or quarters or some other period be used—for example, finding the monthly payments on a mortgage. In this text, however, when we say that some amount of money is to be received in year 5, what we usually mean is that the money is assumed to be received five years from now as a single receipt.

FINDING AN UNKNOWN INTEREST RATE

In many problems you will know the amounts of all the cash flows and would like to determine what the interest rate is. Business investments are often evaluated using their **rate of return**, which is the interest rate expected to be earned by the investment.

Essentially we can identify two general situations in which you might wish to find the interest rate based on the cash flows—a loan agreement and an investment opportunity. When you are borrowing money, you receive an amount of money today in return for an agreement to pay more money back in the future. When you invest, you pay money out today in the expectation that you will receive more money in return sometime in the future. When you deposit money in a bank savings account, you are lending money to the bank with the expectation that the bank will pay you back with interest. Similarly, when the bank loans money to you, the bank is making an investment and expects you to pay the money back with interest.

The result is that, except for the direction of the cash flows, a loan is like an investment. The rate of return the bank earns on its investment in a loan to you is the same as the interest rate you will pay to the bank. The point is that finding interest rates on loans is the same as finding rates of return on investments. In each case the interest rate implicit in a series of cash flows is that rate which sets the present value of future cash flows equal to the initial outlay or receipt. We begin by showing how to perform the analysis of different sorts of loans and we then give examples of finding the rate of return on an investment. The stress here is on calculations by hand or using simple calculators. There are calculators and computer programs available which will calculate the interest rate for you. Some will do so only for the simple cash flow patterns described in the next sections; others will find the interest rate for variable cash flows discussed later. Even if you own one of the more powerful calculators, you should understand what the calculator is doing, and the training in this chapter will help you set up problems properly.

Simple Cash Flows

There are four payment schedules or cash flow patterns for which we can find the interest rate without using tables although tables can be used in these cases as well.

The first simple case: *You borrow money and promise to pay an equal annual amount of interest every year forever*. This is a perpetual annuity and is not a very common type of loan. (The British government has issued perpetual bonds, however.) We can use Eq. (4-13) presented earlier to find the interest rate

$$P = \frac{A}{i} \qquad (4\text{-}13)$$

$$i = \frac{A}{P} \qquad (4\text{-}14)$$

where A is the annual amount.[5] Therefore, if you borrowed $50 on the promise to pay $5 per year forever, the interest rate would be $5/$50 = 0.10 or 10 percent per year.

The second case: *You borrow money and repay the loan within one*

---

[5] This can be proved mathematically using the formula in Appendix 4A for the annuity present value factor and letting the value for n approach infinity.

year or less with a single payment. In this case, let P be the amount borrowed now (principal) and F be the amount repaid later. We wish to find the interest rate i given P, the principal, and future payment F.

$$F = (1 + i)P$$

$$F = P + iP$$

$$F - P = iP$$

$$i = \frac{F - P}{P} \tag{4-15}$$

$$i = \frac{F}{P} - 1 \tag{4-15a}$$

In other words, if you borrow \$50 and repay \$55 in one year, you are paying (\$55 − \$50)/\$50 = 0.10 or 10 percent per year. If the loan were for less than a year, you would compute the interest rate as in Eq. (4-15), and then scale up to an annual basis. For example, if you borrow \$100 for six months and repay \$105, the rate would be \$5/\$100 or 5 percent for six months or 10 percent per year.[6] Many securities—for example, Treasury bills—have single payments.

The third simple case: *You borrow P dollars today, pay A dollars every year for n years, and at the end pay back P dollars*. The interest rate for this type of loan is computed according to Eq. (4-14). Corporate bonds have payments like this. For example, if you borrow \$50 now, pay \$5 a year for six years (beginning one year from now), and then pay back the \$50 at the end of the sixth year, your interest cost is 10 percent per year (\$5/\$50). It's like a series of one-year loans. Think of it in this way: At the end of every year you pay the interest of \$5 and pay back the original \$50 borrowed, then turn around and immediately reborrow the \$50. You end up on balance just paying \$5 per year until the last year when you no longer borrow.

The fourth case is not as simple; it arises when the cash flows from an investment grow at a constant rate. This case is presented in Appendix 4A.

There are two more simple cash flow patterns for which the interest rate can be determined fairly quickly. However, a simple formula does

---

[6] This 10 percent figure is the annual **nominal interest rate**, assuming a 5 percent six-month rate and two six-month compounding periods. The annual **effective interest rate**, using a 5 percent six-month rate, would be 10.25 percent, which is computed as $(1.05)^2 - 1 = 10.25\%$. The 10.25 percent rate is the annual rate assuming that interest is compounded. In general, if the rate for q months, in decimals, is signified by x (for example, $x = .05$ if the rate is 5 percent), then the annual effective rate equals

Annual effective rate $= (1 + x)^{12/q} - 1$

In the example, $x = .05$, $q = 6$ (6 months), and the annual effective rate is 10.25 percent.

not apply.[7] The first of these is where there is *a single payment but the loan is outstanding longer than one year*. Suppose you borrow $1000 and agree to pay off the borrowing three years from now with a payment of $1260. What annual rate of interest are you being charged? We know that the compound amount factor can be used to find the future payment equivalent to the principal of a loan made today.

$$F = P(F/P, i, n)$$

and in this case,

$$\$1260 = \$1000(F/P, i, 3)$$

Solving for the value of the factor, we get

$$(F/P, i, 3) = \frac{\$1260}{\$1000}$$

$$= 1.260$$

We now need to find that interest rate which provides a value for the compound amount factor of 1.260 at $n = 3$. To do this, you must go to the tables and look through them until you find the right value or one close to it. A good starting point can be found by noting that the average annual interest cost is $260/3 = \$87$ or roughly 8.7 percent of $1000. The exact annual interest rate will be less than the average rate since you are not really paying anything until the end of three years. If you try 8 percent first, you will find that $(F/P, 8\%, 3) = 1.260$. Therefore, the rate you are paying is 8 percent per year.

However, what if the payment were $1275? The factor you would be looking for is 1.275, which is greater than the value for 8 percent yet less than the value for 9 percent, $(F/P, 9\%, 3) = 1.295$. The rate must be between 8 percent and 9 percent. If you wish to be more accurate than that, you can interpolate to provide a fairly good approximation. This is

---

[7] In the case of a single-payment loan (or investment) when the future payment will be made n years from now, the interest rate can be determined easily using a calculator with a power function (y^x). The procedure is as follows:

$$F = P(F/P, i, n)$$
$$F = P(1 + i)^n$$
$$(1 + i)^n = \frac{F}{P}$$
$$1 + i = \left(\frac{F}{P}\right)^{1/n}$$
$$i = \left(\frac{F}{P}\right)^{1/n} - 1$$

Find the ratio F/P and then calculate $(F/P)^{1/n}$ using the y^x function where $y = F/P$ and $x = 1/n$. In the text example, $F/P = 1.26$ and $n = 3$.

$$i = (1.26)^{1/3} - 1$$
$$= 1.080 - 1$$
$$= 8.0\%$$

similar to the procedure followed earlier in the chapter, except that now we are trying to find the interest rate rather than the factor. The answer by interpolation is 8.43 percent.

The second payment pattern which can be analyzed easily using the tables is *an annuity*. For example, if a loan of $1000 requires annual payments of $250 per year for five years, what is the interest rate being charged? We know that the loan payment can be found by using the loan repayment factor $(A/P, i, n)$. Therefore,

$$\$250 = \$1000(A/P, i, 5)$$

and

$$(A/P, i, 5) = \frac{\$250}{\$1000}$$

$$= 0.250$$

Now go to the tables and try to find a value for $(A/P, i, 5)$ equal to 0.250. You know the rate will be less than 25 percent ($250/$1000) since that would apply to a perpetuity and these payments stop after five years. Try a much lower rate, say, 12 percent. $(A/P, 12\%, 5) = 0.277$. That's too large a value, so you know the interest rate must be lower than 12 percent. The lower the interest rate, the lower the payments must be. You will find that $(A/P, 8\%, 5) = 0.250$. The answer is, therefore, 8 percent. If the value of the factor for the unknown rate does not equal the value for a factor in the tables, interpolate between the factor values for the two interest rates that most closely bracket the unknown rate.

Now let's find the interest rate on an installment loan when the lender doesn't provide one. Friendly Dan advertises that you can buy a $600 motorcycle for $27 down and $28.50 per month for twenty-four months. He tells you that the finance charge is only $111, which he calculated as the difference between the total amount of your payments and the amount you owed (borrowed) initially, or $(24 \times \$28.50) - (\$600 - \$27) = \$111$. What interest rate are you paying? The solution to this problem is similar to the one just above. You are dealing with an annuity and therefore use the formula

$$A = P(A/P, i, n)$$

Substituting in the appropriate values, we have

$$\$28.50 = \$573(A/P, i, 24)$$

$$(A/P, i, 24) = \frac{\$28.50}{\$573}$$

$$= 0.0497$$

Looking through the tables for a value of $(A/P, i, 24) = 0.0497$, we find that $(A/P, 1\frac{1}{2}\%, 24) = 0.0499$. The value for the next lowest rate in the table is $(A/P, 1\frac{1}{4}\%, 24) = 0.0485$. The interest rate therefore is between $1\frac{1}{4}$ percent and $1\frac{1}{2}$ percent per month. Interpolating to get a more exact rate,

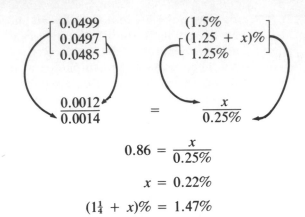

$$0.86 = \frac{x}{0.25\%}$$

$$x = 0.22\%$$

$$(1\tfrac{1}{4} + x)\% = 1.47\%$$

Therefore, Friendly Dan is charging 1.47 percent per month, or 12(1.47%) = 17.6 percent per year.

Variable Cash Flows

Finding an unknown interest rate when the cash flows do not match one of the patterns shown above is more difficult. You must first set up an equation expressing the time-value equivalence of the cash flows. This equation will usually contain two or more interest factors in it involving the unknown rate.[8] Then you must try out different interest rates until you find one for which the equation will balance. This procedure is illustrated by the following example of an investment-type problem.

Suppose you would like to determine the interest rate you would earn from buying a bond and holding it to maturity. This interest rate is called the **yield to maturity** of the bond. The cash flows from buying and owning the bond are shown in Figure 4-10. The bond's current price is $850, it pays an annuity of $60 per year for ten years, and it will mature in ten years paying its face value of $1000 at that time. If the price of the

---

[8] If it contains only one factor, you must have a version of one of the simple cases.

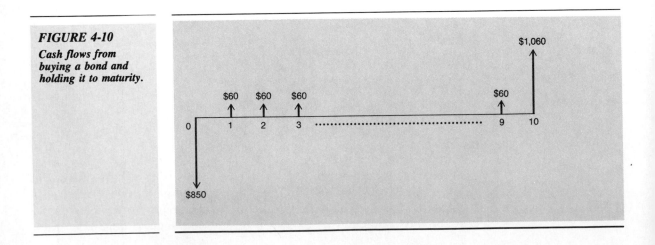

FIGURE 4-10

Cash flows from buying a bond and holding it to maturity.

bond were $1000 today, we know that the yield to maturity (interest rate) on the bond would be $60/$1000 = 6 percent per year from our earlier discussion. However, since the price is only $850, we know that the yield to maturity must be greater than 6 percent. The time-value equation for the cash flows is

$$\text{Present price of the bond} = \begin{array}{c}\text{present value of}\\\text{interest payments}\end{array} + \begin{array}{c}\text{present value of}\\\text{principal payment}\end{array}$$

$$\$850 = \$60(P/A, i, 10) + \$1000(P/F, i, 10)$$

The problem is to find that interest rate which will make the right side of the equation equal $850. The right side of the equation is the present value (P) of the future cash receipts from owning the bond given the interest rate. We can think of the problem as finding that interest rate which will make $P = \$850$. Since we know the rate is greater than 6 percent, let's try 7 percent.

$$P_{7\%} = \$60(P/A, 7\%, 10) + \$1000(P/F, 7\%, 10)$$
$$= \$60(7.024) + \$1000(0.5083)$$
$$= \$930$$

This value of P is too large. In order to get a lower present value, we need to use a higher interest rate. Suppose we try 10 percent.

$$P_{10\%} = \$60(P/A, 10\%, 10) + \$1000(P/F, 10\%, 10)$$
$$= \$60(6.145) + \$1000(0.3855)$$
$$= \$754$$

Since the present value at 10 percent is too low, the correct rate must lie between 10 percent and 7 percent. Now that we have bracketed the true rate, we can either try some more values (8 percent or 9 percent) or we can interpolate. Let's interpolate.

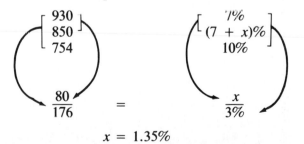

$$x = 1.35\%$$

The estimated rate is therefore 7 percent + 1.35 percent = 8.35 percent. If we wanted to get a more accurate estimate of the true rate, we could compute P at 8 percent and 9 percent and interpolate between those values instead of between 7 percent and 10 percent. The narrower the spread is, the more accurate is the interpolation. If we did this, our new estimate would be 8.26 percent. This answer is accurate to the second decimal place.

The Rate of Return on Common Stock   As a final example of finding an unknown interest rate, let's look at the problem of finding the rate of return earned on an investment in common stock. Suppose you purchased ten shares of stock in a company four years ago at a price of $50 per share. Your total investment was $500 (10 × $50). The company paid you the following dividends:

	First year	Second year	Third year	Fourth year
Dividend per share	$ 2.00	$ 2.00	$ 2.50	$ 3.00
Total dividends received	20.00	20.00	25.00	30.00

The current price of the stock is $60. What rate of return have you earned on your investment if you sell the stock now? The proceeds from sale of your shares will be $600 (10 × $60). The cash flow diagram for the investment is shown in Figure 4-11. We are assuming that you have just received $30 in dividends for the current year, four years after the stock was purchased. Time is measured from the date of the original investment. To find the rate of return earned on the investment, we must find that interest rate which makes the present value of the cash receipts in years 1 to 4 equal to the amount invested. A direct expression is to treat each cash receipt as a single future amount:

$$\$500 = \frac{\$20}{1 + i} + \frac{\$20}{(1 + i)^2} + \frac{\$25}{(1 + i)^3} + \frac{\$630}{(1 + i)^4}$$

$$\$500 = \$20(P/F, i, 1) + \$20(P/F, i, 2) + \$25(P/F, i, 3) + \$630(P/F, i, 4)$$

FIGURE 4-11
*Cash flows from a
common stock
investment.*

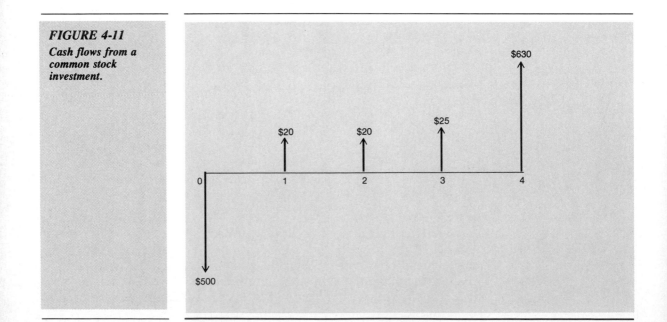

This is the most general approach and will work for any set of future cash flows. However, using this approach, you must work with as many different interest rate factors as you have future cash flows, four in this example. Often the problem can be reduced somewhat by separating out any annuities in the flows. In this case we have a two-period annuity of $20; so the following expression is also correct:

$$\$500 = \$20(P/A, i, 2) + \$25(P/F, i, 3) + \$630(P/F, i, 4)$$

Now we need to work with only three factors instead of four.[9]

As we did in the previous example, we must try out different interest rates until we find two that bracket the true rate. Then we must interpolate between the two to estimate the value of the true rate. How can we know where to begin? There is no simple answer to the question. As you gain experience in solving these problems, your initial guesses will improve. Generally one examines the cash flow pattern and compares it with one of the simple cases discussed earlier. In this example we received $95 in dividends plus $100 capital gains for an average annual return of $49 per year. This is an average return of approximately 10 percent ($49/$500) on our investment. Since the true interest rate must be lower than 10 percent as most of the returns were not obtained until the fourth year, let's try 9 percent as a starting rate and go from there.

$$P_{9\%} = \$20(P/A, 9\%, 2) + \$25(P/F, 9\%, 3) + \$630(P/F, 9\%, 4)$$

$$= \$20(1.759) + \$25(0.772) + \$630(0.708)$$

$$= \$500.52$$

That is very close to $500, the initial investment. The true rate must be slightly over 9 percent, and in many practical problems, you could stop here. To get a better estimate, we must use the next higher rate in the tables, 10 percent.

$$P_{10\%} = \$20(P/A, 10\%, 2) + \$25(P/F, 10\%, 3) + \$630(P/F, 10\%, 4)$$

$$= \$20(1.736) + \$25(0.751) + \$630(0.683)$$

$$= \$483.79$$

This rate is obviously much too high. We can try interpolation at this point

---

[9] Although there is no advantage in this example, the following expressions are also equivalent and in many situations can be used to simplify problems:

$$\$500 = \$20(P/A, i, 3) + \$5(P/F, i, 3) + \$630(P/F, i, 4)$$

and

$$\$500 = \$20(P/A, i, 4) + \$5(P/F, i, 3) + \$610(P/F, i, 4)$$

In general, if you have a stream of future cash flows, $F_1, F_2, F_3, \ldots, F_n$, their present value can always be expressed as

$$P = A(P/A, i, n) + (F_1 - A)(P/F, i, 1) + (F_2 - A)(P/F, i, 2)$$
$$+ (F_3 - A)(P/F, i, 3) + \cdots + (F_n - A)(P/F, i, n)$$

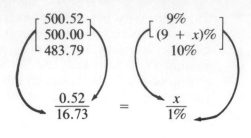

$$x = 0.03\%$$

This gives us an estimated rate of return of 9 percent + 0.03 percent or 9.03 percent per year. A still more exact figure would require use of a sophisticated calculator or a computer program. The actual rate is 9.046 percent.

SUMMARY

Interest rates give money its time value. Compound interest methods are used to solve problems when money is to be paid or received at different points in time. The basic principles of compound interest were described and illustrated through examples which serve two purposes: (1) to show how to solve problems involving compound interest and (2) to illustrate the range of problems requiring the use of compound interest techniques in real life. There are two general types of decisions that require some consideration of time value. One type of decision involves investing (or saving) money now in order to receive future cash benefits. The other type involves borrowing (or dissaving) now to make current expenditures at a cost of having less money in the future.

The present value of future income is one of the key concepts of finance. Present value provides a way to compare alternative income or cost streams that differ in time and/or amounts.

Interest rate factors are used to provide numerical solutions to financial problems. The six major interest factors are:

The **compound amount factor** *(F/P, i, n): This is the value n periods from now of $1 invested today at a rate of interest of i percent per period. To find the value F of P dollars invested today, multiply P by (F/P, i, n):*

F = P(F/P, i, n)

The **present value factor** *(P/F, i, n): This is the value today of $1 to be received n periods from now given an interest rate of i percent per period. To find the present value P of F dollars to be received n periods from now, multiply F by (P/F, i, n):*

P = F(P/F, i, n)

The **annuity compound amount factor** *(F/A, i, n): This factor is the value at the end of n periods resulting from an investment of $1 per period for n periods at a rate of i percent per period. To find the future value F of an annuity of A dollars per year, multiply A by (F/A, i, n):*

F = A(F/A, i, n)

The **sinking fund factor** *(A/F, i, n): This factor is the amount that must be invested each period for n periods at i percent per period to produce $1 at the end of n periods. To find the annuity A needed to accumulate to F dollars in n periods, multiply F by (A/F, i, n):*

$$A = F(A/F, i, n)$$

The **annuity present value factor** *(P/A, i, n): This factor is the value today of an annuity of $1 provided at the end of each period beginning one period from now and ending n periods from now given an interest rate of i percent. To find the present value P of A dollars per period, multiply A by (P/A, i, n):*

$$P = A(P/A, i, n)$$

The **capital recovery or loan repayment factor** *(A/P, i, n): This factor is the amount of money which must be paid each period for n periods in order to pay off a loan of $1 given an interest rate of i percent. It is also the amount of money that must be received in each period for n periods to provide an interest rate of i percent on $1 invested today. To find the annuity A equivalent to P dollars, borrowed or invested today, multiply P by (A/P, i, n):*

$$A = P(A/P, i, n)$$

The *interest factors are also used to find unknown interest rates. If the cash flow pattern does not fit one of the simple cases shown in the chapter, then a trial-and-error procedure must be used to determine the rate.*

1 People often assume that an increase in interest rates will encourage more savings by individuals. Suppose that you are saving to pay for future tuition. Will an increase in interest rates cause you to save more or less money today?

2 Two banks offer savings accounts with a stated interest rate of 6 percent per year. For bank *A* the actual rate is $1\frac{1}{2}$ percent per quarter compounded quarterly. For bank *B* the actual rate is $\frac{1}{2}$ percent per month compounded monthly. Will one of the two banks provide more interest than the other assuming that no withdrawals are made from the account for one year? Why?

3 What happens to the present value of an annuity if the interest rate rises? What happens to the future value?

4 Why is $(A/F, i, n)$ called the sinking fund factor?

5 Given an investment that will provide a stream of future cash flows, what is the relationship between the present value of the future cash flows and the rate of return on the amount invested?

6 In Chapter 2 we said that an increase in the expected rate of inflation should increase interest rates. Suppose that you own a bond paying a fixed amount of money each year and read in the newspaper that inflation is expected to increase. Should you be happy, sad, or not concerned?

PROJECT

Obtain information about savings and savings certificate accounts offered by at least two financial institutions in your town (the number to be fixed by your instructor). Which one would appear to be the most desirable if (1) you may wish to withdraw money at any time; (2) you will not withdraw any money for at least one year; (3) you would like to withdraw interest every three months, but the principal can remain in the account for at least four years; (4) you do not intend withdrawing any money for six years? (See problem *31*.)

DEMONSTRATION PROBLEMS

DP1 How much money should you put in a savings account at the end of each month in order to have $2000 in the account at the end of five years? Assume that the same amount will be saved each month and that the account pays $\frac{1}{2}$ percent interest per month.

SOLUTION TO DP1:
Five years = 60 months. The amount to be saved each month A is

A = $2000(A/F, \frac{1}{2}\%, 60)$

$\quad$ = $2000(0.0143)$

$\quad$ = <u>$28.60</u> per month

DP2 You are considering making an offer to buy some land for $25,000. Your offer will be to pay $5000 down and for the seller to carry a contract for the remaining $20,000. You would like to pay off the contract over six years at an interest rate of 12 percent per year. For the first year you wish to pay interest only each month. For the remaining five years, you are willing to pay off the contract in equal monthly installments. What will be your monthly payment for years 2 through 6 if the seller agrees to your terms?

SOLUTION TO DP2:
Since no payments will be made on the principal amount of $20,000 until the second year, the contract will be paid off over five years (60 months) with interest. The interest rate of 12 percent per year is 1 percent per month. Therefore,

Monthly payment = $20,000(A/P, 1\%, 60)$

$\quad\quad\quad\quad\quad\quad\quad$ = $20,000(.0222)$

$\quad\quad\quad\quad\quad\quad\quad$ = <u>$444.00</u>

DP3 In December 1988 Dana Walker purchased fifty shares of common stock in Ranac Corporation at a price of $22 per share. Dana sold the stock in December 1992 for $30 per share. The following dividends per share were received by Dana:

Year	1989	1990	1991	1992
Dividends	$1.00	$1.00	$1.25	$1.50

a Does the rate of return (interest rate) earned from owning this stock depend on the number of shares purchased? Why or why not?

b What was the rate of return before taxes from owning the stock?

SOLUTION TO DP3:

a No, the number of shares owned is a "scale" factor which affects all dollar figures per share in the same way. The rate of return is the same whether ten shares or a million shares were purchased.

b The cash flow diagram for the investment is

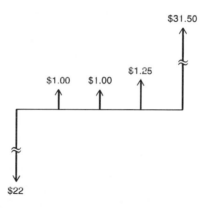

To find the rate of return, express the initial investment as the present value of the cash flows received.

$22 = $1(P/F, i\%, 1) + $1(P/F, i\%, 2) + $1.25(P/F, i\%, 3) + $31.50(P/F, i\%, 4)$

Try $i = 13\%$:

$22 = $1(.8850) + $1(.7831) + $1.25(.6931) + $31.50(.6133)$

$= $.89 + $.78 + $.87 + 19.32

$= 21.86

Try $i = 12\%$:

$22 = $1(.8929) + $1(.7972) + $1.25(.7118) + $31.50(.6355)$

$= $.89 + $.80 + $.89 + 20.02

$= 22.60

Interpolating

$21.86	13%
$22.00	$(12 + X)\%$
$22.60	12%

$$\frac{.60}{.74} = \frac{X}{1\%}, \ X = .81\%, \ i = \underline{12.81\%} \text{ per year}$$

PROBLEMS

1   What is the present value (today) of the following cash flows at an interest rate of 12 percent per year?
  a $100 received today.
  b $100 received five years from now. [Ans.: $56.74]
  c $100 received 10,000 years from now.
  d $100 received each year beginning one year from now and ending ten years from now. [Ans.: $565.02]
  e $100 received each year beginning one year from now and continuing forever.

2   What is the value of the following investments five years from now at an interest rate of 8 percent per year, 2 percent per quarter, or $\frac{2}{3}$ percent per month depending on the compounding period?
  a $100 invested today with interest compounded annually. [Ans.: $146.93]
  b $100 invested today with interest compounded quarterly. [Ans.: $148.59]
  c $100 invested today with interest compounded monthly. [Ans.: $148.98]

3   Find the future value of the following investments; the interest rate is 8 percent per year, compounded annually:
  a $100 is invested each year beginning one year from now and continuing through year 10, when the proceeds are withdrawn. [Ans.: $1448.66]
  b $100 is invested each year starting today and continuing through year 10, when the proceeds are withdrawn. [Ans.: $1664.55]
  c $100 is invested each year beginning one year from now and continuing through year 9. The proceeds are to be withdrawn in year 10. [Ans.: $1348.66]

4   a   If you put $1000 into a savings certificate today paying interest of 10 percent per year, how much money will you have in the account after six years if no withdrawals are made from it until then? How much of this is interest?
  b   Suppose you withdraw the interest every year. What will be your total earnings? Why does this differ from the interest earned in a?

5   If you wish to have $10,000 ten years from now, how much money must you invest today in a savings certificate that pays 8 percent per year?

6 How much money should you put in a savings account at the end of each month in order to have $10,000 in the account at the end of ten years? Assume that the same amount will be saved each month and that the account pays $\frac{1}{2}$ percent interest per month.

7 Suppose that you invest $1000 in a savings account today paying interest of 6 percent per year. You expect to save $600 per year, which will be placed into the account at the end of each year beginning one year from now (the last $600 deposit occurring in six years). How much money will you have in the account after six years?

8 Suppose that you invest $1000 in a savings account today paying interest of 6 percent per year ($\frac{1}{2}$ percent per month). You expect to save $600 per year, which will be invested at a rate of $50 at the end of each month for 72 months (the first $50 investment occurring one month from now). How much money will you have in the account after six years? Compare the answer here with the answer for problem **7** above. Explain the difference in results from the two savings programs.

9 George Clever, who lives in Chicago, Illinois, received an offer in the mail to invest $5000 in a Mexican bank savings account which pays 25 percent annual interest in pesos. The account permits no withdrawals for four years and is guaranteed by the Mexican government. At current exchange rates, $5000 will exchange into 15 million Mexican pesos. If George invests the money today, how many pesos would he receive four years from now? Do you see any exchange rate problems with this opportunity?

10 The day you were born your parents bought a "baby bond" for $500. This bond repays its purchase price plus $6\frac{1}{2}$ percent per year interest, compounded annually, on your twenty-first birthday. You have just turned twenty-one. Happy birthday. How much money will you be getting from your "baby bond"?

11 You would like to have $5000 in savings at the end of five years. How much money, in equal annual amounts, must be invested at the end of each of the next five years in order to achieve your goal? Your current savings balance is $500 and the interest rate you expect to earn over the next five years is 6.5 percent per year.

12 Calculate the following:

a The monthly payments required on a $2000 loan bearing a 15 percent per year interest rate ($1\frac{1}{4}$ percent per month). The loan is to be paid back in eighteen equal monthly installments.

b The total amount of interest paid over eighteen months for the loan in **a**.

c The monthly payments on a thirty-year mortgage for $25,000. The interest rate is 9 percent per year ($\frac{3}{4}$ percent per month).

d The total amount of interest paid over thirty years for the loan in **c**.

13 You own an apartment house that provides a net income to you of $2000 per month. What is the maximum twenty-year mortgage loan you could obtain such that the payments on the loan could be made entirely from the apartment income? Assume a 9 percent annual interest rate ¾ percent per month) and monthly payments on the mortgage.

14 Your grandfather left you $40,000 when he died. You can invest the money to earn 9 percent per year.

 a If you spend $7227 per year out of this inheritance, how long will the money last?

 b If you spend $3600 per year, how long will the money last?

 c What is the most you can spend in equal annual amounts from the inheritance for the next 20 years?

15 You work for a company that provides a pension plan for which the company contributes 50 percent of the amount you contribute. For example, if you specify that $100 of your monthly salary is to go into the plan, the company will add $50 to make the total contribution $150 per month. The plan guarantees an annual interest rate of 8 percent (compounded monthly). If you believe you can safely earn 12 percent per year (compounded monthly) by investing the money yourself, is it worthwhile belonging to the company plan? Assume that you plan to retire in thirty years and that you will set aside $80 per month regardless of the approach used.

16 You are the parent of a four-year-old girl and plan to begin saving next year on her fifth birthday (on September 2, 1992) for her college education. You wish to provide $15,000 per year for four years beginning when she is eighteen. How much money in thirteen equal annual installments must be invested each year until she is seventeen (on September 2, 2004) to meet this goal if you earn 9 percent on your investment?

17 Sandy Triton is an avid scuba diver who lives in Boston. Since New England waters are very cold, Sandy has decided to purchase a dry suit for diving. After some investigation, Sandy must decide which one of two suits to buy—a "Norway" suit for $750 or an "Oregon" suit for $300. The major difference between the two is that the Norway should last for 300 dives whereas the Oregon suit will need to be replaced after 100 dives. Sandy has $750 in a savings account paying 8 percent interest, which can be used to pay for either suit. Which suit would be most economical for Sandy to buy? Analyze Sandy's problem for each of the following assumptions.

 a Sandy expects to make 25 cold water dives per year for the next twelve years.

 b Sandy expects to make 50 cold water dives per year for the next six years.

18 Ole Hanson wants to save money to meet two objectives. First he would like to be able to retire twenty years from now and have a retirement income of $30,000 per year for at least thirty years. Second he would like to purchase a fishing boat five years from now at an estimated cost of $20,000. He can afford to save only

$6000 per year for the first ten years. Ole expects to earn 8 percent per year on average from investments over the next fifty years. What must his minimum annual savings be from years 11 through 20 to meet his objectives?

19 One year ago you borrowed $10,000 at an annual interest rate of 12 percent (1 percent per month) to be repaid in thirty-six monthly installments of $332.14 each. You have made twelve payments on the loan.

    a What is the current balance remaining on the loan? (Hint: What is the relationship between the present value of the remaining payments to be made on the loan and its current balance?)

    b What will be the balance owed on the loan one year from now if all payments are made as scheduled?

    c What is the dollar amount of interest to be paid on the loan in the coming year? (Hint: The answers to *a* and *b* are very useful in answering *c*.)

20 Compute the annual interest rate or rate of return that you will earn on the following investments:

    a A U.S. Treasury bill that has a current price of $930 and will pay $1000 at maturity one year from now. [Ans.: 7.53 percent]

    b A U.S. Treasury bill that has a current price of $950 and will pay $1000 at maturity six months from now. [Ans.: 10.53 percent]

    c A U.S. Treasury note selling at its maturity value ($1000), paying 9 percent coupon interest per year, and maturing in five years.

    d An acre of vacation property with a current price of $5000 that you expect to be able to sell for $6475 in three years. There are no other expenses or income from this property.

    e A preferred stock with a current price of $90 paying $10.80 dividends per share per year forever.

21 Compute the annual interest rate for the following investments:

    a A U.S. Treasury bill which matures in ninety-one days with a quoted price of $97.50 per $100 maturity value.

    b A share of common stock purchased one year ago at a price of $42 per share and just sold for $48. No dividends were received.

    c A share of common stock purchased one year ago for $21 and sold yesterday for $18 after receipt of a dividend check for $1.

    d A share of common stock purchased for $30 three years ago and just sold for $30. Dividends of $2.10 were received at the end of each of the three years of ownership.

22 Benito Rubio borrowed 5000 bolivars (B) from his older brother in Caracas, Venezuela. Benito promised to repay the loan in two annual installments of B3000 each. What rate of interest is Benito paying his brother? (Approximate the answer to the nearest whole percentage by inspection of the tables.)

23 Determine the annual interest rate on the following debt contracts:

   a A $25,000 mortgage with monthly payments of $209.80 to be paid off in twenty-five years.

   b Solve the problem in **a** considering that the lender is charging a 2 percent fee at the time the loan is taken out so that the actual amount being lent to you is less than $25,000. [Ans.: 9.29 percent]

   c An installment loan for $2000 that has monthly payments of $66 for the thirty-six months and an additional "balloon" payment of $150 in the last month.

24 You are in the market for a new, high-performance windsurfing board. A dealer offers you financing on the $1500 you need to buy the board at a "low 10 percent annual interest rate" for twenty-four months. Your payments are determined as follows:

$$\text{Annual interest} = 10\% \text{ of } \$1500 = \$150 \text{ per year}$$

$$\text{Total due} = \text{principal plus 2 years interest}$$

$$= \$1500 + 2(\$150)$$

$$= \$1800$$

$$\text{Monthly payment} = \frac{\$1800}{24 \text{ months}}$$

$$= \$75 \text{ per month}$$

This procedure is called "add on" interest. What is the actual annual rate of interest being charged on this loan?

25 You need to borrow $3000 to buy a powerboat. The boat dealer offers (low, low) monthly payments of $99 for thirty-six months with an additional "balloon" payment of $300 in the last month. What annual interest rate is the dealer charging you on the $3000 loan?

26 Four years ago your mother invested $10,000 in the Alpha Mutual Fund to provide money for your college education. All dividends were reinvested in the fund. Now the money is needed. The value of the shares in the fund is $14,116. What annual rate of return was earned on the original $10,000 investment?

27 On January 16, 1990, Clara Hatfield invested $2000 in the common stock of Ace Novelties. Ace pays dividends quarterly on April 15, July 15, October 15, and January 15 of each year. Clara sold her stock on July 16, 1991, after receiving $30 in dividends each quarter.

   a Suppose that Clara sold her Ace stock for $1820. What annual rate of return did she earn?

   b Suppose that Clara sold her Ace stock for $2000. What annual rate of return did she earn?

   c Suppose that Clara sold her Ace stock for $2194. What annual rate of return did she earn?

28 In December 1988, exactly four years ago, you purchased shares in a mutual fund for $500. Although all the dividends were reinvested in the fund, you had to pay personal taxes at a rate of 20 percent on the dividends paid into your account each year. The current value of the shares you own, including those obtained from dividend reinvestment, is $705.80. If the shares are sold, you will be subject to a capital gains tax of 20 percent (capital gains = proceeds from sale − original cost of all shares). The dividends paid and reinvested are shown below.

Year	1989	1990	1991	1992
Dividends	$30	$32	$36	$40

a What is your pretax rate of return to date?

b If you sell all the shares now, what will be your aftertax rate of return? (Assume that taxes are paid in the same year that dividends are paid and that all payments and receipts are at the end of the year.)

29 In problem *17* above, Sandy Triton is concerned that 8 percent might not be the correct interest rate to use. Sandy would like to know what the rate of interest would have to be to make the two suits of equivalent present value. Sandy plans to make 50 cold water dives per year for the next six years.

30 Your father has asked your advice on the following problem. He has a mortgage loan on the family home that was made several years ago when interest rates were lower. The loan has a current balance of $40,000 and will be paid off in twenty years by paying $330 per month. He has discussed paying off the loan ahead of schedule with an officer of the bank holding the mortgage. The bank is willing to accept $36,000 right now to pay it off completely. What interest rate, expressed as an annual rate, would your father earn by paying off the loan now rather than making monthly payments for twenty years? Your father is currently earning 9 percent on his investments. Would it be worthwhile paying off the loan if he has the money available?

31 Two years ago Kareem Casey invested $5000 in a savings certificate account with a seven-year maturity and an annual interest rate of 9 percent compounded monthly. Interest rates are higher now and Kareem is considering withdrawing the current balance in the account (no withdrawals of principal or interest have occurred) and investing the money in a higher-yielding asset. However, the bank will deduct a "penalty for early withdrawal" equal to the first six months' interest paid on the account.

a What is the current balance in the account?

b What will be the balance at maturity, five years from now, if no withdrawals are made?

c How much money will Kareem receive if he closes out the account now?

d   What interest rate must Kareem earn on an alternative investment to obtain as much money in five years' time as he would
have by keeping the certificate? Assume annual compounding
on the alternative investment.

e   If Kareem keeps the certificate for one more year, will the interest rate he must earn then to make withdrawal worthwhile
be higher, lower, or the same as the rate calculated in *d*?
Why?

The ■ indicates that all or a significant part of the problem can be solved using the
Computer Models Software package that accompanies this text.

FORMULAS AND COMPUTATIONAL METHODS

This appendix serves as a reference and an aid to solving problems when tables that fit a particular problem are not available. Here we provide mathematical formulas for calculating the basic interest rate factors presented in Chapter 4. These formulas can be used to calculate the values for a factor for any given interest rate and time period. We also provide formulas for the present value of growing or declining streams, which were not discussed in the chapter. We describe some methods to compute the factors using the formulas and discuss the use of financial calculators.

FORMULAS FOR THE BASIC INTEREST RATE FACTORS

1 a Compound amount factor:

$$(F/P, i, n) = (1 + i)^n \tag{4-16}$$

b Present value factor:

$$(P/F, i, n) = \frac{1}{(1 + i)^n} = (1 + i)^{-n} \tag{4-17}$$

2 a Annuity compound amount factor:

$$(F/A, i, n) = \frac{(1 + i)^n - 1}{i} \tag{4-18}$$

b Sinking fund factor:

$$(A/F, i, n) = \frac{i}{(1 + i)^n - 1} \tag{4-19}$$

3 a Annuity present value factor:

$$(P/A, i, n) = \frac{(1 + i)^n - 1}{i(1 + i)^n} = \frac{1 - (1 + i)^{-n}}{i} \tag{4-20}$$

b Capital recovery (loan repayment) factor:

$$(A/P, i, n) = \frac{i(1 + i)^n}{(1 + i)^n - 1} = \frac{i}{1 - (1 + i)^{-n}} \tag{4-21}$$

The formulas are grouped into the three pairs of factors for which one member of the pair is the reciprocal of the other.

There are two major advantages to knowing the factors rather than relying on tables. First, you may not have tables available for the interest rate i and time period n that you require. The formulas apply to any interest rate, for example, 8.375 percent, or time period, for example, eighteen years. The second advantage is the ease with which the formulas can be programmed into programmable calculators or computers. If one of these devices is available, there is no need for tables at all when you know the formulas.

FORMULAS FOR GROWING OR DECLINING STREAMS

In many situations the future stream of cash payments or receipts grows or declines at constant rates. We will examine two types of growth and decline—arithmetic and compound.

Arithmetic Growth or Decline

Arithmetic or *linear growth* occurs when a stream of cash increases by a constant *dollar* amount each period. For example, Figure 4-12a shows a stream of cash receipts growing at a rate of $10 per period. Similarly, Figure 4-12b shows a stream of cash receipts declining arithmetically at a rate of $10 per period. This is also called linear growth or decline because if the figures are plotted on a graph, the points lie on a straight line, dollars versus time.

The most straightforward method of evaluating such streams is to split them into two pieces—an annuity plus (or minus) the growth (decline) element. For example, the stream of Figure 4-12a can be considered an annuity of $20 per period for five periods plus a growth element of $10 per period. Similarly the stream of Figure 4-12b is an annuity of $50 per period for five periods less a decline element of $10 per period. The present value of the total stream is therefore the present value of the annuity portion plus the present value of the growth element or minus the present value of the decline element. This is illustrated in

FIGURE 4-12
*Arithmetic growth and
decline.*

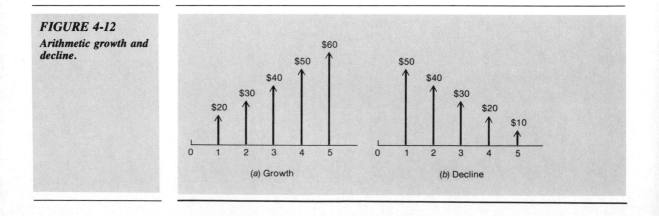

Figure 4-13 for the growing stream of Figure 4-12a. Once we calculate the present value of the stream, we can compute the equivalent annuity or future value if they are desired. Let G be the amount of growth or decline per period, $10 in the examples. We can represent the present value per dollar of growth or decline as an interest rate factor $(P/G, i, n)$ so that the present value of the growth element is

$$P = G(P/G, i, n) \tag{4-22}$$

The formula for this factor is

$$(P/G, i, n) = \frac{1}{i}\left[\frac{1 - (1 + i)^{-n}}{i} - n(1 + i)^{-n}\right]$$

$$= \frac{1}{i}[(P/A, i, n) - n(P/F, i, n)] \tag{4-23}$$

Therefore, values for this factor can be easily calculated using tables for the two basic present value factors when they are available. Otherwise, the formulas can be used.

For example, suppose $i = 10$ percent. Then, using the tables,

$$(P/A, 10\%, 5) = 3.791$$

$$(P/F, 10\%, 5) = 0.621$$

$$(P/G, 10\%, 5) = \frac{1}{0.10}[3.791 - 5(0.621)]$$

$$= \frac{1}{0.10}(0.686)$$

$$= 6.86$$

The present value of the growing stream in Figure 4-12a is

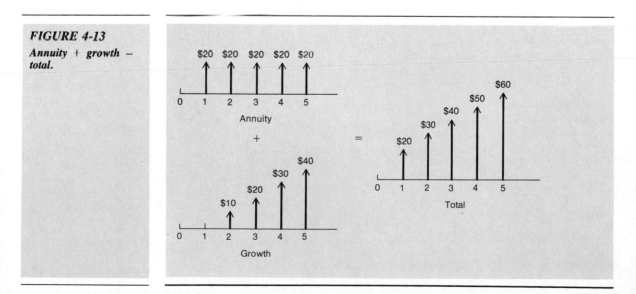

FIGURE 4-13
Annuity + growth = total.

$$P = A(P/A, 10\%, 5) + G(P/G, 10\%, 5)$$

$$= \$20(3.791) + \$10(6.86)$$

$$= \$144.42$$

The present value of the declining stream in Figure 4-12b is

$$P = A(P/A, 10\%, 5) - G(P/G, 10\%, 5)$$

$$= \$50(3.791) - \$10(6.86)$$

$$= \$120.95$$

*Compound Growth
or Decline*

Compound growth occurs when a stream of cash payments or receipts grows at a constant *percentage* rate per period. For example, the rate of growth might be 10 percent per period. If the initial (period 1) value is $100, and the stream grows for five periods, the values would be as shown in Figure 4-14a. Note that the dollar increase in each period is not constant as in the case of arithmetic growth but increases instead. Similarly, a compound rate of decline of 10 percent per period is illustrated in Figure 4-14b.

Let F_1 be the amount of the cash flow in period 1. This is the base value which grows or declines. That is, the cash flow n periods from now is $F_1(1 + g)^{n-1}$ where g is the rate of growth or decline. The present value of such cash flow streams can be calculated from one of the two formulas presented below.[10] The choice of formula depends on the relationship between the growth rate g and the interest rate i.

---

[10] We can derive these formulas as follows: The present value of a stream of cash flows that grows or declines at a constant compound rate of g for n periods is

$$P = \frac{F_1}{1 + i} + \frac{F_1(1 + g)}{(1 + i)^2} + \frac{F_1(1 + g)^2}{(1 + i)^3} + \cdots + \frac{F_1(1 + g)^{n-1}}{(1 + i)^n} \qquad (a)$$

Case 1: $g = i$, then (a) becomes

$$P = \frac{F_1}{1 + i} + \frac{F_1(1 + i)}{(1 + i)^2} + \frac{F_1(1 + i)^2}{(1 + i)^3} + \cdots + \frac{F_1(1 + i)^{n-1}}{(1 + i)^n}$$

$$= \frac{F_1}{1 + i} + \frac{F_1}{1 + i} + \frac{F_1}{1 + i} + \cdots + \frac{F_1}{1 + i}$$

$$= \frac{nF_1}{1 + i} \qquad (b)$$

Case 2: $g \neq i$, multiply both sides of (a) by $(1 + g)/(1 + i)$, to obtain (c)

$$P\left(\frac{1 + g}{1 + i}\right) = \frac{F_1(1 + g)}{(1 + i)^2} + \frac{F_1(1 + g)^2}{(1 + i)^3} + \frac{F_1(1 + g)^3}{(1 + i)^4} + \cdots + \frac{F_1(1 + g)^n}{(1 + i)^{n+1}} \qquad (c)$$

Subtract (c) from (a), to obtain

$$P - P\left(\frac{1 + g}{1 + i}\right) = \frac{F_1}{1 + i} - \frac{F_1(1 + g)^n}{(1 + i)^{n+1}}$$

$$P\left[1 - \frac{1 + g}{1 + i}\right] = \frac{F_1}{1 + i}\left[1 - \frac{(1 + g)^n}{(1 + i)^n}\right]$$

$$P\left[\frac{i - g}{1 + i}\right] = \frac{F_1}{1 + i}\left[1 - \left(\frac{1 + g}{1 + i}\right)^n\right]$$

$$P = \frac{F_1}{i - g}\left[1 - \left(\frac{1 + g}{1 + i}\right)^n\right] \qquad (d)$$

1 If g equals i, then

$$P = \frac{nF_1}{1 + i} \tag{4-24}$$

2 If g is not equal to i, then

$$P = \frac{F_1}{i - g}\left[1 - \left(\frac{1 + g}{1 + i}\right)^n\right] \tag{4-25}$$

A useful special case is when n is very large (approaching infinity) and g is less than i. In this case $[(1 + g)/(1 + i)]^n$ approaches zero as n becomes large. The present value of a stream of this type is

$$P = \frac{F_1}{i - g} \tag{4-26}$$

This is the constant perpetual growth case mentioned in Chapter 4 and used in several later chapters.

In applying Formula (4-25) we need values for $[(1 + g)/(1 + i)]^n$. For computational purposes the following approaches may be used. First, suppose that g is less than i, but n is not large so that (4-26) is inaccurate. Define a new interest rate i^*

$$i^* = \left(\frac{1 + i}{1 + g}\right) - 1 \tag{4-27}$$

Then

$$\left(\frac{1 + g}{1 + i}\right)^n = \left(\frac{1 + i}{1 + g}\right)^{-n} = (1 + i^*)^{-n} \tag{4-28}$$

The quantity $(1 + i^*)^{-n}$ is the present value factor $(P/F, i^*, n)$ which may be found in tables for some values of i^* and/or calculated as explained below.

If g is greater than i, we can define a new interest rate i'

$$i' = \left(\frac{1 + g}{1 + i}\right) - 1 \tag{4-29}$$

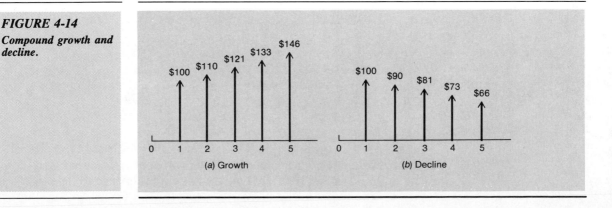

FIGURE 4-14

Compound growth and decline.

(a) Growth

(b) Decline

Then

$$\left(\frac{1 + g}{1 + i}\right)^n = (1 + i')^n = (F/P, i', n) \tag{4-30}$$

We may be able to use interest rate tables to find $(F/P, i', n)$ or calculate the value as explained below.

To illustrate the use of "interest rates" $i*$ and i', let's calculate the present values of the streams shown in Figure 4-14 using an interest rate i of 8 percent. Figure 4-14b is a stream with

$$F_1 = \$100$$

$$g = -0.10$$

$$n = 5$$

Since g is less than i, compute $i*$ as

$$i* = \left(\frac{1 + i}{1 + g}\right) - 1$$

$$= \frac{1.08}{0.90} - 1$$

$$= 20\%$$

We need $(P/F, 20\%, 5)$, which is available in the 20 percent table and is found to be 0.4019. Then, applying the general formula (4-25)

$$P = \frac{F_1}{i - g}\left[1 - \left(\frac{1 + g}{1 + i}\right)^n\right]$$

$$= \frac{\$100}{0.08 + 0.10}[1 - 0.4019]$$

$$= \$332.28$$

The stream of Figure 4-14a has

$$F_1 = \$100$$

$$g = 0.10$$

$$h = 5$$

Since g at 10 percent is greater than i at 8 percent, compute i' as

$$i' = \left(\frac{1 + g}{1 + i}\right) - 1$$

$$= \frac{1.10}{1.08} - 1$$

$$= 1.85\%$$

Now we need to find $(F/P, 1.85\%, 5)$, which is not readily available in interest rate tables. Our choices are to use an approximation by rounding off the interest rate to fit a table we do have (in this case to 2 percent), to use interpolation in the tables, or to compute $(1.0185)^5$. Since $(F/P,$ $1.85\%, 5) = 1.096$, the value of the growing stream in Figure 4-14a is

$$P = \frac{F_1}{i - g}\left[1 - \left(\frac{1 + g}{1 + i}\right)^n\right]$$

$$= \frac{\$100}{0.08 - 0.10}[1 - 1.096]$$

$$= (-\$5000)(-0.096)$$

$$= \$480$$

Calculating Interest Rate Factors

If you examine the formulas presented above, you will see that the only difficult part to calculate is $(1 + i)^n$ or $(1 + i)^{-n}$. These are the compound amount factor and the present value factor, respectively. Therefore all the other factors can be calculated easily once one of these has been found.

Three types of calculators available at low cost are useful in obtaining factor values.

1 Even the most basic "financial" or "business" calculators contain $(P/F, i, n)$ as a built-in function. As we noted above, once you have a number for the present value factor [$(P/F, i, n) = (1 + i)^{-n}$], finding any other factor is easy using the appropriate formula. We will discuss the use of financial calculators below.

2 "Scientific" calculators usually have a function described as a^x, y^x, or similar notation. Let $a = 1 + i$ and $x = n$; now $(1 + i)^n$ can be calculated with this function.

3 Calculators lacking the needed functions can also be used to compute $(1 + i)^n$ by successive multiplication. That is,

$$(1 + i)^n = (1 + i)(1 + i)(1 + i) \cdots (1 + i)$$

n times. This process is greatly facilitated if the calculator has memory. The quantity $(1 + i)$ can be stored and then recalled for use in multiplying the result of the prior multiplication.

Using Financial Calculators

There are several inexpensive (under $40) calculators available that have financial functions. Their instructions show how to use them in solving many of the simple problems illustrated in this chapter. Here are some additional tips and guidelines for their use.

Most of the calculators are set up to solve problems which involve any combination of a present amount P, an annuity for n periods A, and a future amount F occurring n periods from now. We can express the present value of an annuity and a future amount as

$$P = A(P/A, i, n) + F(P/F, i, n) \tag{4-31}$$

Financial calculators will usually find the value of any one of the five variables in this equation (P, A, F, i, n) given values of the other four. Some will not solve for n and a few will not solve for interest rate i. You should check for such limitations before purchase. The ability to solve for an unknown interest rate is especially desirable.

A financial calculator which can solve problems of the form of Eq. (4-31) can be used to generate any interest factor desired.[11] Therefore, it can be used to solve any problem involving the time value of money. Having such a calculator available is equivalent to having a complete set of tables for all values of i and n.

To obtain an interest rate factor from a calculator, key in values for i and n. Then key in 1 for one of P, F, or A, zero for another, and follow the calculator's procedure to solve for the remaining variable. For example, suppose you wish to find $(P/A, 6.8\%, 12)$. You would key in 6.8% for i, 12 for n, 0 for F, and 1 for A. Now have the calculator solve for the remaining variable, P. The number displayed on the calculator will be $(P/A, 6.8\%, 12)$. Note that all factors contain a ratio of the form X/Y as in $(X/Y, i, n)$. To find the "X/Y factor," you give "Y" the value of 1 and solve for "X."

If your problem only involves a simple combination of P, A, and F where one of the three may be zero, a financial calculator will calculate the answer directly from the numbers in your problem. If your problem is more complicated, you will have to solve it in steps. You can use the calculator just as you would use tables with the advantages that you do not have to find table values and that the arithmetic is done for you. Since it is rare that you will want to know the value of the interest factor itself, you will normally key in the dollar value for "Y" that fits your problem. You will obtain $Y(X/Y, i, n)$ as the result, where "X" and "Y" can be any pair of P, A, or F.

As an example of solving a more complicated problem, suppose that you wish to know what your payments will be on loans to finance your college education. Interest on the loans is being accumulated and compounded annually until graduation. After graduation the loans must be paid off in monthly installments over five years. You just began your junior year and you currently owe $2800. One year from now, you expect to borrow an additional $3000. Two years from now you must begin making monthly payments. How large will those payments be? The interest rate charged is 8.4 percent.

No financial calculator is going to solve this problem directly for you because it is not in the simple form required. However, you can use a financial calculator to solve the problem fairly quickly, as follows:

1 Find out how much you will owe at the beginning of your senior year. This will be the future value of $2800 in one year, plus $3000 borrowed at that time. The future value of $2800 in one year at i = 8.4 percent can be obtained from a calculator as $3035.20. Adding

---

[11] This is so because the factors are all mathematically related. For example,

$$(A/P, i, n) = 1/(P/A, i, n),$$

and $(F/A, i, n) = (P/A, i, n)/(P/F, i, n)$

$3000 to this amount yields $6035.20 owed at the beginning of your senior year.

2 Find out how much you will owe two years from now when you begin repayment. This will be the future value of $6035.20 in one year at 8.4 percent and can be obtained from a calculator as $6542.16.

3 Finally, calculate the annuity for 60 months (5 years × 12 months) required to repay $6542.16 at a monthly interest rate of 0.7 percent (8.4 percent/12). The answer is $133.91 per month.

A financial calculator is a great convenience in solving financial problems.

CHAPTER FIVE

SECURITY PRICES

In Chapter 1 we said that the objective of financial management was to maximize the price of the firm's common stock, given legal and ethical considerations. This chapter examines how the market prices of common stock, bonds, and other securities are determined and how risk affects those prices. Appendix 5A explains how to use and interpret stock and bond price data available in financial publications. Appendix 5B explains why the interest rates on securities of different maturities may not be the same. In Chapter 6 we discuss risk measurement and the impact of risk on security prices in more depth. In later chapters, we show how specific decisions by management affect stock prices.

Chapters 5 and 6 explain the four basic principles stated below. The first three principles are introduced in Chapter 5 and the fourth is explained in Chapter 6.

1   The current market price of a security is the present value of the future payments to the owner of the security.
2   The discount rate that is used to determine the present value depends on:
    a   The current level of interest rates.
    b   The riskiness of the income provided by the security.
    c   The attitudes of investors toward risk.
3   Market prices of securities tend to reflect existing information. In investing in marketable securities you cannot profit from having information that is widely disseminated, since market prices already fully reflect that information.
4   The risk in owning a security depends on how well you can predict the future cash receipts from owning it and how well it fits with the other assets that you own.

With these points in mind, let's look first at the relationship between prices and present values.

PRICES AND PRESENT VALUES

The benefits from owning a security are the future cash flows—such as interest payments, principal payments, and dividends—that are paid to the owner. The current market price of the security is the amount of money one has to pay to obtain the future cash flows. Securities are traded in financial markets with many buyers and sellers. The price of a security at a point in time is what the highest bidders are willing to pay for the future cash flows that will be produced by the security. The question is: What is the relationship between the market price of a security and its future cash flows? A fundamental principle of finance is that *the market price of a security is the present value of its future cash flows*.

The discount rate (interest rate) used to determine the present value depends on several characteristics of the cash flows as we discuss later. For now, suppose that the cash flows are known for certain and that there is only one interest rate that applies in the market today, regardless of when the cash flows are received in the future.[1] To illustrate the equivalence of prices and present values, let's look at an example.

Suppose that the market interest rate i is 6 percent per year and you are considering the purchase of a U.S. Treasury bill maturing in one year. It will pay $1000 to the owner one year from now. The present value of $1000 one year from now at a rate of 6 percent per year is

$$\text{Present value} = \frac{\$1000}{1 + i}$$

$$= \frac{\$1000}{1 + 0.06} = \frac{\$1000}{1.06}$$

$$= \$943.40$$

If you purchase the bill at a price of $943.40, what rate of return will you earn for the year? The $1000 will pay you back the current price plus interest.

$$i = \frac{\$1000 - \text{price}}{\text{price}}$$

$$= \frac{\$1000 - \$943.40}{\$943.40} = \frac{\$56.60}{\$943.40}$$

$$= 0.06 \text{ or } 6\%$$

Purchasing the bill at a price equal to the present value of 6 percent provides a rate of return to the investor of 6 percent. If the price were not equal to the present value of $943.40, then the rate of return on the bill would not be 6 percent.

If the market interest rate is the same for all riskless securities, then dollar prices will differ among these securities only to the extent that the cash payments differ in timing or amount. Exhibit 5-1 shows the market prices for several securities assuming that the market interest rate for all of them is 6 percent per year. The only things the securities shown in Exhibit 5-1 have in common are the rate of return of 6 percent provided

---

[1] Appendix 5B explains why the interest rates today may be different for cash to be received at different times into the future.

to the purchasers of the securities and that all future payments are known for sure.

Now let's see how prices adjust to a given interest rate. For a given stream of future payments, the lower the price that is paid, the higher is the interest rate or rate of return received. This basic characteristic is illustrated using a security that pays $10 per year to the owner forever. If the price of this security is $200, investors will earn 5 percent per year.

$$\text{Rate} = \frac{\$10}{\$200} = 5\%$$

If the price is $100, investors will earn 10 percent per year.

$$\text{Rate} = \frac{\$10}{\$100} = 10\%$$

Similarly, if the price is $50, investors will earn 20 percent per year.

EXHIBIT 5-1
Example of security prices at an interest rate of 6 percent per year

1. *One-year bill ($100 maturity value[a])*

   $$\text{Price} = \frac{\$100}{1.06}$$
   $$= \$100 \ (P/F, \ 6\%, \ 1)$$
   $$= \$100 \ (0.9434)$$
   $$= \$94.34$$

2. *Five-year note (7 percent coupon rate,[b] $100 maturity value)*

   $$\text{Price} = \frac{\$7}{1.06} + \frac{\$7}{(1.06)^2} + \cdots + \frac{\$107}{(1.06)^5}$$
   $$= \$7 \ (P/A, \ 6\%, \ 5) + \$100 \ (P/F, \ 6\%, \ 5)$$
   $$= \$7 \ (4.2124) + \$100 \ (0.7473)$$
   $$= \$104.22$$

3. *Twenty-year bond (5 percent coupon rate, $100 maturity value)*

   $$\text{Price} = \frac{\$5}{1.06} + \frac{\$5}{(1.06)^2} + \cdots + \frac{\$105}{(1.06)^{20}}$$
   $$= \$5 \ (P/A, \ 6\%, \ 20) + \$100 \ (P/F, \ 6\%, \ 20)$$
   $$= \$5 \ (11.4699) + \$100 \ (0.3118)$$
   $$= \$88.53$$

[a] For debt securities such as bonds that pay the entire principal at maturity, the terms maturity value, principal amount, face value, and par value all refer to the same quantity.
[b] The coupon rate is the interest payment expressed as a percentage of the face value; the face value equals maturity value for these securities.

Suppose that the rate of interest in the market is 10 percent. If the price of a security paying $10 per year forever is $200, no one would wish to own it and the price would fall. If the price of the security were $50, everyone would find it to be an attractive investment and the price would rise. At a price of $100, this security would not be especially attractive or unattractive and there would be no tendency for the price to change. The rate of return earned on the security at a price of $100 is the market interest rate of 10 percent.

New securities issued in the market are subject to the same conditions as securities already being traded. The decisions by investors as to whether or not they wish to buy the new security, and the self-interest of the issuer, cause new securities to have the same interest rate as old securities. For example, suppose that the market interest rate is 6 percent, but a company issues bonds with a coupon rate of 5 percent. The bonds have $100 maturity value per bond and will mature in twenty years. In other words, the firm will pay $5 interest each year and $100 in year 20 to the purchaser of the bonds. From example 3 in Exhibit 5-1, we know that investors will earn 6 percent on these bonds if they pay $88.53 per bond. Since investors can earn 6 percent on other securities in the market, no one would pay the firm more than $88.53, as the rate of return would be less than 6 percent if a higher price were paid. On the other hand, if the firm offered the bonds at a price below $88.53, everyone would like to buy them since the bonds would provide a higher rate of return than available in the market. However, it would be foolish for the firm's financial managers to do this, since the firm would then be paying a higher interest rate than is necessary to raise money.

Given this equality between prices and present values, let's examine how the prices and market interest rates of fixed-income securities such as bonds are determined.

FIXED-INCOME SECURITIES: BONDS

A fixed-income security provides a stream of cash payments to its owner that have been promised by the issuer (borrower) at the time the security was originally issued (when the money was borrowed). Debt contracts such as bonds and mortgages are the most common fixed-income securities, although preferred stocks are also of this type. The promised stream of cash payments are fixed at the time of issue, and the payments are the *maximum* amounts that the issuer will pay. However, if the payments are at all uncertain (risky), there is a chance that the promised payments won't be made; the issuer may default on the debt.

Let's get a better idea of what fixed-income securities are all about by looking at two bonds that are traded on the New York Exchange. One bond was issued by Navistar (formerly named International Harvester). It has a 9 percent coupon rate and matures in 2004. The other bond was issued by Amoco, with a coupon rate of 9.2 percent and maturity in 2004. Both bonds promise to pay the owner coupon interest each year until maturity, and both promise to pay their maturity values (principal) on maturity. Prices for the two bonds in February 1987 were $89 for the Navistar bond and $105 for the Amoco bond.[2]

The yield to maturity on each bond is the interest rate on the bond given the current price and the promised payments (coupon interest and principal) for that bond. The general equation used to find the yield to maturity, i, on a bond maturing in n periods is

$$\text{Price} = \frac{\text{interest}}{1 + i} + \frac{\text{interest}}{(1 + i)^2} + \cdots + \frac{\text{interest} + \text{principal}}{(1 + i)^n} \qquad (5\text{-}1)$$

or, equivalently,

$$\text{Price} = \text{interest}(P/A, i, n) + \text{principal}(P/F, i, n) \qquad (5\text{-}2)$$

In 1987, both bonds had approximately seventeen years until maturity ($n = 17$). To determine i for the Navistar bond, we used Eq. (5-2) as follows:

$$\$89 = \$9(P/A, i, 17) + \$100(P/F, i, 17)$$

The 9 percent coupon rate means that bondholders will receive $9 each year per $100 maturity value. The yield to maturity, i percent, is the interest rate that makes the equation balance. Applying the procedure of Chapter 4, we find that the yield to maturity for the Navistar bond was 10.406 percent, or approximately 10.4 percent. Similarly, for the Amoco bond the relationship was

$$\$105 = \$9.20(P/A, i, 17) + \$100(P/F, i, 17)$$

and the yield to maturity of the Amoco bond was found to be 8.6 percent.[3] Why would anyone have paid $105 for the Amoco bond when

---

[2] These prices were reported in *The Wall Street Journal*. Bonds usually have maturity values of $1000 per bond. Therefore, a price of $50 per $100 maturity value implies an actual price of $500 per bond. Treasury bills have maturity values of $10,000 per bill, and most notes (one-year maturity securities) have maturity values of $5000 per note. Prices of these and other fixed-income securities are normally quoted per $100 maturity value (see Appendix 5A for examples). For this reason, the calculations of yield to maturity and other examples are shown on the basis of $100 maturity value.

[3] The issuers of most bonds pay interest twice each year at one-half of the coupon rate. Therefore the owner of a $1000 Navistar bond with a coupon rate of 9 percent would actually receive $45 (9 percent/2 of $1000 = $45) every six months. In the text, we found the yield to maturity on the Navistar bond by discounting the annual interest payments. A more accurate way to compute the yield to maturity of the bond is to determine the semiannual yield, then multiply by 2. For example, the price of the Navistar bond was $89 per $100 maturity value and that bond matured in seventeen years. Someone who purchased one bond at the beginning of 1987 would receive 34 payments of $45 each (a $45 payment every 6 months) plus $1000 at maturity if all payments are made. The semiannual yield to maturity is obtained from the relationship

$$\$890 = \$45(P/A, i, 34) + \$1,000(P/F, i, 34)$$
$$i = 5.196 \text{ percent}$$

The annual yield to maturity is then 2×5.196 percent $= 10.392$ percent. The difference between the yield estimated on the basis of annual payments and the yield based on semiannual payments is not large. The yield to maturity assuming annual payments for seventeen years for this bond is 10.406 percent rather than 10.392 percent, a difference of only 0.014 percent. Notice that you obtain the same yield by expressing all values per $100 maturity value rather than using the actual dollar amounts on the bond. For example, you also obtain $i = 5.196$ percent as the solution to $\$89 = \$4.50(P/A, i, 17) + \$100(P/F, i, 17)$.

the Navistar bond was only $89? If you bought the Navistar bond and held it to maturity and if Navistar made all the promised payments, you would have earned 10.4 percent per year on your investment, much more than from the Amoco bond. Why buy Amoco? Because investors must have believed that there was significant risk that Navistar would not make all the promised payments.

The yield to maturity on a bond is the *most* you can earn by holding it to maturity. If any of the payments are not made when due to the owners of a bond, the owners will earn less than the yield to maturity on their purchase price. For many bonds there is significant risk that you will earn less than the yield to maturity. In the case of Navistar, investors assessed the chance of earning less as being fairly large.

Premiums, Discounts, and Par The Amoco bond was trading at a **premium**—its market price of $105 is greater than its maturity value of $100. (Remember that prices are quoted per $100 of maturity value.) Bonds sell at a premium when their coupon interest rates (9.2 percent) are greater than their yields to maturity (8.6 percent). The Navistar bond was trading at a **discount**—its market price of $89 is less than $100. Bonds sell at a discount when their coupon interest rates (9.0 percent) are less than their yields to maturity (10.4 percent). Suppose that the market price of a bond is equal to its maturity value of $100—the bond is trading at **par**. If investors require exactly the same yield as the coupon rate of a bond, the market price of the bond will be $100. In Chapter 4 the "third simple case" of finding an unknown interest rate was when P dollars are borrowed (invested) today, A dollars are paid (received) each period, and P dollars are paid (received) at the end of some number of periods. In this case the interest rate (yield to maturity) for this set of cash flows is simply A divided by P. For bonds, A/P is also the coupon rate of interest. Thus, when the market price of a bond is equal to its maturity value, the yield to maturity equals the coupon rate on the bond.

*Bond Ratings
and Yields*

There are several ways to analyze or compare how risk affects the prices of bonds. One widely used method is based on the yield to maturity. Two bonds of the same "quality" or risk should have the same yield to maturity. Under this approach, risk is not measured precisely. Instead, bonds are classified or organized into risk groups; all the bonds within the same group should have approximately the same yield. Two financial service firms provide widely used classification systems in the United States and abroad—Standard & Poor's Corporation and Moody's Investor Services. Their classifications differ somewhat, but the two services provide comparable ratings in the lower-risk classes, as shown in Table 5-1.

Amoco bonds were rated Aaa by Moody's; Navistar bonds were rated B. As Moody's says about its B-rated bonds, they "generally lack characteristics of a desirable investment." By this Moody's means that a conservative investor should avoid B bonds since they are fairly risky. In most cases, the lower the rating for a bond, the higher will be its yield to maturity. This is so because the ratings reflect the risk of bonds as

TABLE 5-1
Bond classifications

Standard & Poor's		Moody's	
AAA	Highest grade	Aaa	Best quality
AA	High grade	Aa	High quality
A	Upper medium grade	A	Upper medium grade
BBB	Medium grade	Baa	Medium grade
BB	Lower medium grade	Ba	Possess speculative elements
B	Speculative	B	Generally lack characteristics of a desirable investment
CCC	Vulnerable to default	Caa	Poor; may be in default
CC	Subordinated to other debt with CCC rating	Ca	Speculative to a high degree; often in default
C	Subordinated to other debt with CCC$^-$ rating	C	Lowest grade
CI	Income bonds not paying interest		

evaluated by the rating firms who are experts in this area. However, all bonds of a given rating (A, for example) don't necessarily have the same yield to maturity. Some A bonds will yield about the same as Aa bonds, and some will have yields close to those on Baa bonds. The reason is that the classification scheme is only approximate, and many investors do their own "rating." Thus, if the A-rated bonds of a particular company appear more risky than the average A-rated bond, they will have a higher yield than the average A-rated bond and vice versa. Even the highest rated corporate bonds are not riskless. There is always the possibility that a private corporation cannot pay its debts. Investors seeking the least risk can purchase U.S. government bonds. Since the U.S. government has the power to tax and to print money, it would never need to default on its obligations. The debt issues backed by the "full faith and credit" of the United States are considered to be the safest available with respect to guaranteed payment of principal and interest. Bond yields therefore scale up from the rates available on U.S. government securities (except for bonds with special features such as tax exempt interest or convertibility into common stock).

The yields required on bonds of a given rating are not constant over time but vary due to changes in the general level of interest rates. Also the "spread" or difference between the yields on bonds of different ratings varies over time, depending on the general outlook for the economy. Figure 5-1 shows the average yields to maturity for samples of U.S. government bonds, Aaa bonds, and Baa bonds since 1929. Note that during times of general economic uncertainty such as the 1930s the difference between the yield on the three classes of bonds widens, especially the difference between Baa and Aaa bonds, as investors require a much higher yield on the more risky Baa bonds than on the safer Aaa bonds. Compare the situation in 1932 with that of 1970. In both years the yield on Baa bonds was over 9 percent. In 1932, the higher rate on Baa bonds was due to concern over the risk of the bonds, as the Aaa rate was only 5 percent. In 1970 it was primarily due to the high general level of interest rates as reflected by the correspondingly high rates on U.S. government and Aaa bonds.

Earlier in the chapter we stated the principle that the market price of a security is the present value of the future cash flows from the security. We are now able to state a second fundamental principle:

The discount rate that determines the present value of a security's cash flows depends on the riskless rate of interest plus a premium that depends on the risk of the cash flows from the security.

The more risk there is, the higher the premium will be.

This principle is illustrated by the data shown in Table 5-2 which shows the actual average rates of return from 1926 to 1988 on four types of securities. These data show that common stocks on average provided a much higher rate of return than corporate bonds. The corporate bonds used in the calculation all had high ratings. Even so, the corporate bonds provided higher rates of return than the government bonds and Treasury bills. In other words, investors on average have been paid premiums for

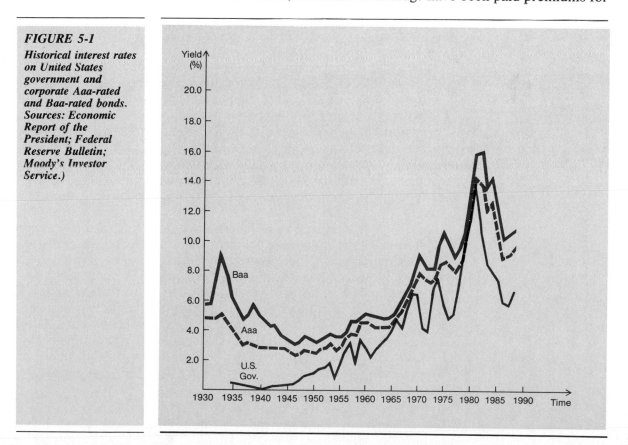

FIGURE 5-1

Historical interest rates on United States government and corporate Aaa-rated and Baa-rated bonds. Sources: Economic Report of the President; Federal Reserve Bulletin; Moody's Investor Service.)

TABLE 5-2
Average rates of return on selected securities 1926–1988

Security	Average annual rate of return	Risk premium (relative to Treasury bills)
Common stocks	12.1%	8.5%
Corporate bonds	5.3	1.7
Government bonds	4.7	1.1
Treasury bills	3.6	0

Source: Stocks, Bonds, Bills, and Inflation, 1989 Yearbook, Ibbotson Associates.

risk in owning corporate bonds and common stock, and the premium was much higher for stock than it was for highly rated corporate bonds. The existence of these premiums is consistent with the idea that investors dislike risk (are risk-averse) and must be compensated for bearing it.

VARIABLE-INCOME SECURITIES: COMMON STOCK

Fixed-income securities promise to provide specified cash payments to their owners. Variable-income securities, such as common stock, do not. The yield to maturity of a bond can be calculated precisely and provides a reference point in determining its price. There is no such reference point for common stock, but there is also no ceiling on how much you can earn from owning stock.

The financial returns from owning any asset come from two basic sources: periodic income (dividends on stock or interest on debt) and the amount you realize at the end of your ownership (selling price or maturity payments). In order to determine the value of the asset, you must estimate both the periodic income and the ultimate receipts from sale or maturity, and usually neither is known for sure. The returns from common stock ownership are especially uncertain since there are no promised interest or maturity payments. Future dividends are uncertain; and, since common stock has no maturity, any future sales price is uncertain as well.

Let's look at the problem of determining the value of the common stock of a corporation. Suppose you were to purchase one share of stock in Andes Company at $20 per share. One year from now you receive a dividend of $1 and sell the stock for $22. You earned $1 in dividends plus $2 in capital gains on the sale for a total of $3. Your rate of return is $3/$20 = 15 percent. Now suppose you kept the stock for two years and received dividends of $1 the first year and $1.50 the second year. At the end of the second year you sell the stock for $23.80. What rate of return did you earn? To find out you must find the rate of return i that makes the following equation balance:

$$\$20 = \frac{\$1}{1 + i} + \frac{\$1.50}{(1 + i)^2} + \frac{\$23.80}{(1 + i)^2}$$

$$= \$1\,(P/F, i, 1) + \$1.50\,(P/F, i, 2) + \$23.80\,(P/F, i, 2)$$

The rate is again 15 percent.[4] We can express the valuation relationship in a more general form. Let P_0 be the price of the stock now, D_1 be dividends in one year, D_2 be dividends in two years, and P_2 be the price at the end of the second year, two years from now. Then

$$P_0 = \frac{D_1}{1 + i} + \frac{D_2 + P_2}{(1 + i)^2}$$

$$= D_1(P/F, i, 1) + (D_2 + P_2)(P/F, i, 2) \qquad (5\text{-}3)$$

Equation (5-3) applies to any stock held for two years. The use of our notation $(P/F, i, n)$ is cumbersome here, so we will stop using it. Suppose a stock was held for three years. The relationship would be

$$P_0 = \frac{D_1}{1 + i} + \frac{D_2}{(1 + i)^2} + \frac{D_3 + P_3}{(1 + i)^3} \qquad (5\text{-}4)$$

In general, if you owned the stock for n years,

$$P_0 = \frac{D_1}{1 + i} + \frac{D_2}{(1 + i)^2} + \cdots + \frac{D_n + P_n}{(1 + i)^n} \qquad (5\text{-}5)$$

What we have developed here is a general expression to obtain a rate of return i given the purchase price of the stock, dividends paid on it, and the selling price at the end of n periods. This expression will help us determine the value of a stock.

We can consider the stream of dividends and the final price to be *forecasted* magnitudes as of today. Associated with these forecasts is uncertainty; no one can be sure what the future dividend payments and the price of common stock for a company will be. Nevertheless, investors must expect to earn a reasonable rate of return from owning the stock or else they wouldn't own it. The rate of return required by investors in the market depends on the uncertainty of the dividends and future price and on the riskless rate of interest. We will designate the rate of return *required* by investors to be k.

For example, suppose that investors in the market expect that the price one year from now of a share of stock in the Star Company will be $55 and the company is forecast to pay a dividend of $2.50 next year.[5] Also suppose that the required rate of return k is 15 percent based on investors' assessment of the uncertainty as to what the dividend and price will actually be. The price today would be

$$P_0 = \frac{\$2.50 + \$55}{1.15}$$

$$= \$50$$

---

[4] At $i = 15\%$

$\$20 = \$1(P/F, 15\%, 1) + \$1.50(P/F, 15\%, 2) + \$23.80(P/F, 15\%, 2)$

$\quad = \$1(.8696) + \$1.50(.7561) + \$23.80(.7561)$

$\quad = \$20$

[5] We are assuming for the example that dividends are paid once per year. In practice, dividends are usually paid once per quarter.

P_0 is the present value of the expected $2.50 dividend and expected $55 share price using a discount rate k of 15 percent. If it actually turns out that the dividend is $2.50 and the share price is $55, the investor will have earned a 15 percent rate of return [that is, $i = 15$ percent using Eq. (5-5)]. This example reveals what we mean by the required rate of return (discount rate) k. Investors discount (value) the future dividends and share price using rate k. Valuing shares in this way means that, if future dividends and future share price turn out as expected ($2.50 and $55 in the above example), the investors will actually earn rate k (15 percent) on their investment ($50).

We can show that the value of a share can be expressed entirely in terms of the future dividends on the share. One year from now the price of the stock depends on what income (dividends) the stock is expected to provide people buying the stock then. Therefore, *the price of the stock today can be viewed as the present value of all expected future dividends, using the interest rate* k *required to compensate the owners of the stock for the time value of money and the risk of those expected dividends.* If the last payment to any owner is at time m, then [6]

$$P_0 = \frac{D_1}{1 + k} + \frac{D_2}{(1 + k)^2} + \cdots + \frac{D_m}{(1 + k)^m} \qquad (5\text{-}6)$$

After time m, the price of the stock (or asset) would be zero since there would be no further income to the owners. At time m, either the assets of the firm are being liquidated or the firm is being sold in entirety to someone and all cash received from the sale is paid out. In any case, D_m is the last payment to the stockholders of the company. For many companies the last dividend may be many years into the future, and therefore m is very, very large. Huge, well-established firms such as

---

[6] As proof of Eq. (5-6), suppose you were planning to own the stock for only one year, then

$$P_0 = \frac{D_1}{1 + k} + \frac{P_1}{1 + k} \qquad (1)$$

The price of the stock one year from now, P_1, must be based on what investors expect to receive in future years; for example,

$$P_1 = \frac{D_2}{1 + k} + \frac{P_2}{1 + k} \qquad (2)$$

Substituting Eq. (2) into Eq. (1), we get

$$P_0 = \frac{D_1}{1 + k} + \frac{D_2}{(1 + k)^2} + \frac{P_2}{(1 + k)^2} \qquad (3)$$

Now we can look at P_2 as being

$$P_2 = \frac{D_3}{1 + k} + \frac{P_3}{1 + k} \qquad (4)$$

Substituting Eq. (4) into Eq. (3), we get

$$P_0 = \frac{D_1}{1 + k} + \frac{D_2}{(1 + k)^2} + \frac{D_3}{(1 + k)^3} + \frac{P_3}{(1 + k)^3} \qquad (5)$$

We can continue this argument until we reach D_m, which is the last payment (including the proceeds from liquidating the company) made to owners, and we arrive at Eq. (5-6). One problem with this approach is that we have no assurance that k is the same value for each future period.

IBM and General Motors are expected to continue existence for a long time. But even for large firms, there may be considerable uncertainty as to when time m is. For example, dividends may cease due to the firm's bankruptcy, and the firm might go bankrupt any time in the future.

Equation (5-6) expresses in mathematical form the proposition that the market price (or value) of common stock is the present value of all expected future receipts (the D's) from owning the stock. This is so, regardless of whether the people now owning the stock plan to continue owning it until time m, since the value at any future time (period 3, for example) will depend on the expectations regarding receipts in period 4 and thereafter. Let's look at a special case of Eq. (5-6) which is used widely in finance, constant perpetual growth.

The Constant Growth Model

If investors expect dividends to be a constant amount, D dollars per year beginning one year from now and continuing forever, common stock is like a perpetuity. In this case Eq. (5-6) reduces to a much simpler relationship, which is the present value of a perpetual annuity:

$$P_0 = \frac{D}{k} \tag{5-7}$$

This formula applies when there is no growth expected in the firm's dividend payments, as in the case of preferred stock. There is a more general relationship that applies when the rate of growth is constant.

Suppose that dividends per share for a firm are expected to be $1 next year. Two years from now the expected dividend is $1.06 per share. In three years the dividend is expected to be $1(1.06)^2 = \$1.1236$, in four years $1(1.06)^3 = \$1.1910$, etc. These dividends are expected to grow at a compound rate of 6 percent per year. If this growth is expected to continue for the foreseeable future (forever, to be precise), then we have an example of the constant growth case.

Let D_1 be the dividend expected in the coming year and g be the expected growth rate. The dividend in any year t is expected to be

$$D_t = D_1(1 + g)^{t-1} \tag{5-8}$$

Equation (5-8) summarizes the general situation. In our example we had:

t	1	2	3	4	$\cdots$
D_t	$1.00	$1.06	$1.1236	$1.1910	$\cdots$

The series of dividends D_t in this example can be expressed compactly using Eq. (5-8) as

$$D_t = \$1(1.06)^{t-1}$$

If the expected stream of dividend payments fits the pattern of Eq. (5-8), then we have constant growth. At time $t = 0$, the present value of this stream of dividends is

$$P_0 = \frac{D_1}{k - g} \tag{5-9}$$

Note that, when $g = 0$, Eq. (5-9) reduces to Eq. (5-7), the no-growth case.

The derivation of Eq. (5-9) was provided in Appendix 4A. The important things to know about the derivation are (1) that it is purely a mathematical result given the assumptions of constant perpetual growth (g) and constant required rate of return (k), and (2) that the growth rate g must be less than the rate of return k in order for the model to make sense.[7]

If we substitute a 6 percent growth rate and a dividend next year of $1 into the formula, we get

$$P_0 = \frac{\$1}{k - 0.06}$$

In order to do anything more, we need a value for k (or P). Suppose $k = 10$ percent. Then the price of the stock would be

$$P_0 = \frac{\$1}{0.10 - 0.06} = \$25$$

The formula can be used to illustrate the relationship between future prices and dividend streams that we discussed earlier. Suppose that expectations do not change from this year to next year and that $1 in dividends is actually paid. What will be the price of the stock next year? The price next year will be the present value of expected future dividends. Next year, the expected growth rate in dividends remains 6 percent by assumption. Also, the expected dividend one year from then will be $1.06. If k is 10 percent, the price next year will be[8]

---

[7] Equation (5-9) is undefined if g equals k and is negative if g exceeds k. If g is equal to or greater than k, we can use Eq. (5-6) to show that P_0 is infinite. But, no share can have an infinite price in the world we know; and therefore no share can yield a dividend that is expected to grow, *forever*, at a rate g that equals or exceeds the discount rate k.

[8] The constant growth model implies that an equation like Eq. (5-9) applies at any point in time. For example, at time 1 (one year from now), using $D_2 = D_1(1 + g)$ from Eq. (5-8),

$$P_1 = \frac{D_2}{k - g} = \frac{D_1(1 + g)}{k - g} \tag{a}$$

where P_1 is the price at time 1, D_2 is the dividend expected to occur at time 2, g is the expected constant dividend growth rate and k is the discount rate. In general, for the constant growth model [where $D_{t+1} = D_1(1 + g)^t$ using Eq. (5-8)]:

$$P_t = \frac{D_{t+1}}{k - g} = \frac{D_1(1 + g)^t}{k - g} \tag{b}$$

Also, the rate of growth per period in the price of a share under the constant growth model is rate g. To see this, use (b):

Rate of growth
in stock price $= \dfrac{P_{t+1} - P_t}{P_t}$
during period t

$$= \frac{\dfrac{D_1(1 + g)^t}{k - g} - \dfrac{D_1(1 + g)^{t-1}}{k - g}}{\dfrac{D_1(1 + g)^{t-1}}{k - g}}$$

$$= g$$

$$P_1 = \frac{\$1.06}{0.10 - 0.06} = \$26.50$$

As of now (time 0), we are expecting a dividend of $1 and a price for the stock of $26.50, both to occur one year from now. If the required rate of return is 10 percent, what should the current price be? The present value at 10 percent of $1 plus $26.50 received in one year is

$$P_0 = \frac{\$26.50 + \$1}{1 + k}$$

$$= \frac{\$27.50}{1.10} = \$25$$

We get the same price as before, which demonstrates the consistency of the "stream of dividends" approach with the "dividends plus future price" approach to stock valuation.

A final point is that Eq. (5-9) can be rewritten to express k in terms of prices, dividends, and growth rate. Solving (5-9) for k gives

$$k = \frac{D_1}{P_0} + g \qquad\qquad (5\text{-}10)$$

The first term on the right-hand side of the equation is called the *dividend yield* of the stock, dividend over price. Here the dividend yield is based on the expected future dividend, D_1. The dividend yield in our example was $1/$25 = 4 percent. Given estimates of the dividend yield and of the growth rate in dividends, g, we can use Eq. (5-10) to estimate the required rate of return on the stock. We do this in Chapter 7.

In the constant growth model, the growth rate in dividends is also the expected rate of growth of the stock price. In our example the price of the stock was expected to grow from now to next year by 6 percent, which is the same as the dividend growth rate.[9]

$$\frac{\$26.50 - \$25}{\$25} = \frac{\$1.50}{\$25} = 6\%$$

Equation (5-10) therefore reveals that the required rate of return on stock is composed of two parts: (1) expected dividend yield, D_1/P_0, and (2) the expected rate of price appreciation or capital gains rate, g.

Variable Growth

Few firms grow at the same annual rate throughout their lives. Many firms grow very rapidly in their early stages, especially those in new industries created by technological innovation. Growth rates of 30 to 50 percent per year for several years in a row are not uncommon. However, eventually the rapid pace slows and these firms begin to grow at rates much closer to the average in the economy. Most firms have periods of interrupted growth from time to time due to downturns in the economy or special problems in the firm or its industry. Yet these firms too might be expected to resume more normal growth after a while. The constant

---

[9] See footnote 8.

growth model can be used in the valuation of a firm that is expected to have unusually high or low growth followed thereafter by constant growth.

The valuation procedure is to value the dividends expected during the unusual period and then to use the constant growth model to value the dividend stream expected thereafter. To illustrate, suppose that Zilogic Corporation's dividends are expected to grow at a rate of 40 percent per year for the next three years. At the end of three years, Zilogic growth is expected to drop to a long-run average of 8 percent per year. Zilogic just paid a dividend of $1.00 per share. Assume that the rate of return required by investors for this stock is 12 percent. What should Zilogic's stock price be?

Zilogic's expected dividend stream is illustrated in Figure 5-2 and stated below.

Date	Growth rate during previous period	Dividend per share
0 (now)		$1.00
1	40%	$1.00(1.4) = $1.40
2	40%	$1.40(1.4) = $1.96
3	40%	$1.96(1.4) = $2.74
4	8%	$2.74(1.08) = $2.96
5	8%	$2.74(1.08)^2 = $3.20
6 and on	8%	

FIGURE 5-2

Variable dividend growth example.

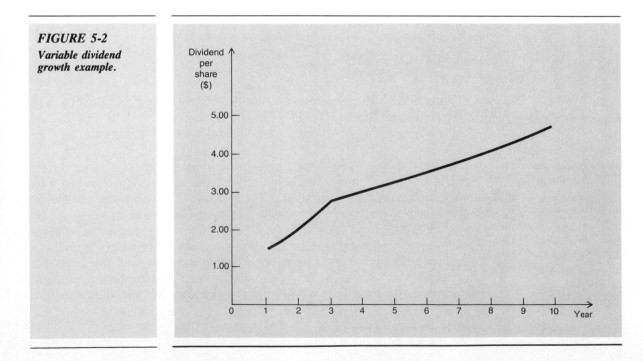

Notice that the dividends to be valued consist of three payments of $1.40, $1.96, and $2.74 in one, two, and three years, and then a stream of perpetually growing dividends (at 8 percent per year) that begins in four years. First, let's use the constant growth model to compute the expected price of Zilogic stock at date 2, right after the $1.96 dividend for year 2 has been paid. Label this price as P_2 and the expected dividend at date 3 as D_3. The dividend expected at date 3 is the base for future growth at 8 percent per year. Thus, we get the following for P_2.

$$P_2 = \frac{D_3}{k - g}$$

$$= \frac{\$2.74}{.12 - .08}$$

$$= \$68.50$$

Next we can value all the dividends to compute the value of a share now (P_0). This is done as follows:

$$P_0 = \frac{D_1}{(1 + k)} + \frac{D_2}{(1 + k)^2} + \frac{P_2}{(1 + k)^2}$$

$$= \frac{\$1.40}{(1.12)} + \frac{\$1.96}{(1.12)^2} + \frac{\$68.50}{(1.12)^2}$$

$$= \$1.25 + \$1.56 + \$54.61$$

$$= \$57.42$$

We could get the same answer by going one more year out in the future to estimate the stock price; however, this requires another calculation. That is, we could determine the price of the stock under constant growth at date 3 (P_3) as:

$$P_3 = \frac{D_4}{k - g}$$

$$= \frac{\$2.96}{.12 - .08}$$

$$= \$74.00$$

And calculate P_0 as:

$$P_0 = \frac{D_1}{(1 + k)} + \frac{D_2}{(1 + k)^2} + \frac{D_3}{(1 + k)^3} + \frac{P_3}{(1 + k)^3}$$

$$= \frac{\$1.40}{(1.12)} + \frac{\$1.96}{(1.12)^2} + \frac{\$2.74}{(1.12)^3} + \frac{\$74.00}{(1.12)^3}$$

$$= \$1.25 + \$1.56 + \$1.95 + \$52.67$$

$$= \$57.43$$

THE EFFICIENT MARKETS HYPOTHESIS

As we discussed, a company's current stock price is based on investor expectations about future dividends and stock price. These expectations depend on the information investors have about the company and its future prospects. It would seem to follow that investors who have superior information, or who can evaluate information more effectively than others, might be able to find stocks that are likely to provide a rate of return higher than the rate required by the market; that is, they might be able to find "bargains." Some might even argue that diligently reading *The Wall Street Journal* (an excellent source of business information) is a path to riches.

However, simply reading *The Wall Street Journal* does not make someone—even someone who has taken four finance courses—an investment hotshot who can consistently pick stocks with extraordinarily high returns. The reason: Most large investors (individual and institutional) and most investment advisors (upon whom investors depend for picking stocks) either read *The Wall Street Journal* or have information sources providing the same information as does *The Wall Street Journal*. Consequently, the market prices of publicly traded stocks very quickly reflect that information. If the president of Exxon announces a major new oil discovery at 10:00 A.M. on a Monday morning, the price of Exxon stock will rise within minutes. To gain an edge, the investor must have accurate information before everyone else does. The **efficient markets hypothesis** is that information spreads quickly in the market and is reflected immediately in security prices. A type of information (for example, accounting data in a company's annual report) is "fully reflected" in prices if there is no investment strategy using that type of information that will allow an investor to do consistently better than other investors. We say that the market is *efficient* with respect to a particular set of information if market prices reflect that information. Efficient markets prevent an investor from exploiting information because prices have already adjusted to take that information into account.

Markets can be efficient with respect to some kinds of information but not others. For example, prices may fully reflect *publicly available* information but not reflect information possessed *only* by those very close to the corporation (e.g., the firm's directors and top executives). Thus, Henry Investor could not "beat the market" (earn an extraordinarily high rate of return for the risk involved) using the publicly available statistics published in *The Wall Street Journal*. But Henry might be able to make a killing by using information given to him by his Uncle Ted, a mining company geologist, on a new silver discovery in Nevada that has not been publicly announced. Of course, Henry and Ted might also have to collaborate in choosing an attorney to defend themselves against charges of illegally trading on insider information.

The concept of efficiency can be applied to any market; for example, the market for bonds, for potatoes, or for medical care. Most empirical research on efficiency has used stock market data. Also, recognize that when we say that a market is efficient, we *only* mean that prices fully reflect information and not that there are no brokerage fees in buying and selling stocks or that your broker can make twenty sales calls in an hour.

Using types of information as the basis for categorization, Eugene Fama of the University of Chicago has conveniently categorized market efficiency as either weak form, semistrong form, or strong form. Let's look at each of these.

Weak Form Efficiency   This form of efficient markets implies that knowledge of the past price trends of stocks cannot be used to pick those stocks that will turn out, in the future, to generate extraordinarily high returns. The argument used to explain weak form efficiency is that, if everyone knows about past price trends (the information is publicly available), the current price reflects that information since it is used by investors in deciding what stocks are worth. Any investor with past price information will not have an advantage over other investors in picking stocks, since they have the same information. An enormous amount of empirical research supports the weak form efficiency notion.[10]

Semistrong Efficiency   Semistrong efficiency implies that a knowledge of *all publicly available* information will provide no advantage. The reason is that existing prices reflect all public information, good or bad. If a firm is doing well, buyers and sellers of the stock will immediately bid the current price to a high level. If the firm is doing poorly, the stock's price will immediately fall. Unless new information is provided to the market in the future, the future price of the stock will not experience extraordinary changes. If the market is semistrong efficient, all the information available to the market is currently impounded in market prices.

A substantial amount of empirical work has been done to test the semistrong efficiency argument. The findings offer qualified support for the theory. The market has been shown to adjust quickly to certain types of new information, such as dividend increase announcements and earnings announcements.[11] However, other studies have found that market prices may not reflect all information that could be used to earn an extraordinary rate of return.[12] Thus, asset prices probably reflect most publicly available information, but the degree of this efficiency depends on the type of information and the type of asset being traded. For

---

[10] See, for example, Arnold B. Moore, "Some Characteristics of Changes in Common Stock Prices," in Paul H. Cootner, *The Random Character of Stock Market Prices* (Cambridge, Mass.: M.I.T., 1964), pp. 139–161; Eugene F. Fama, "The Behavior of Stock Market Prices," *Journal of Business*, vol. 38, no. 1 (January 1965), pp. 34–105; Clive W. J. Granger and Oskar Morgenstern, "Spectral Analysis of New York Stock Market Prices," *Kyklos*, 16 (1963), pp. 1–27.

[11] See E. F. Fama, L. Fisher, M. Jensen, and R. Roll, "The Adjustment of Stock Prices to New Information," *International Economic Review*, vol. 10, no. 1 (February 1969), pp. 1–21; Myron S. Scholes, "The Market for Securities: Substitution versus Price Pressure and the Effects of Information on Share Prices," *Journal of Business*, vol. 45, no. 2 (April 1972), pp. 179–211; Ray Ball and Philip Brown, "An Empirical Evaluation of Accounting Income Numbers," *Journal of Accounting Research*, 6 (Autumn 1968), pp. 159–178.

[12] For example, Jaffe found that publicly available information on inside trading could have been used to select stocks which produced an above average rate of return. See Jeffrey F. Jaffe, "Special Information and Insider Trading," *Journal of Business*, vol. 47, no. 1 (July 1974), pp. 410–429.

example, the real estate market may not be as efficient as the stock market because information about individual properties is more costly to obtain than is information about publicly traded stocks (which are analyzed continuously by security analysts).

Strong Form Efficiency   Markets are strong form efficient if prices reflect *all* information. With strong form efficiency, an investor could not profit even from information possessed by those closest to the situation ("inside information"). The theory behind this is that those who have inside information (or the select group they talk to) will buy or sell the stock of the company (or whatever asset is relevant) and thereby cause its price to adjust to a realistic level in light of that information. Again the empirical results are mixed. Studies of mutual fund performance (fund managers are more likely to have inside information than are average investors) indicate that they do not consistently outperform a randomly selected portfolio of stocks of a risk similar to that of the fund.[13] This suggests that any inside information obtained by fund managers was already reflected in market prices and therefore did not, on average, produce superior results. (It could also imply that fund managers simply didn't get much inside information.)

There is also evidence that suggests that inside information can be used profitably. Niederhoffer and Osborne concluded that specialists on the major United States exchanges (traders on the floor of the exchanges who specialize in certain stocks) are able to use trading information to earn exceptional returns.[14] Scholes and also Lorie and Niederhoffer found that corporate officers may be able to benefit from use of privileged information.[15] It appears, therefore, that true insiders (company officers) or traders can gain by using privileged information but outsiders, such as fund managers, who get "hot tips" are less successful.

*Efficient Markets
and Insider Trading
Violations*

If markets were completely efficient in the strong form sense, no one could profit from inside (or "insider") information about a company because the company's stock price would already fully reflect that information. Recent newsworthy events show that it is sometimes possible to profit greatly from the use of insider information. In 1986 and 1987, the Securities and Exchange Commission filed insider trading charges

---

[13] For example, see M. C. Jensen, "The Performance of Mutual Funds in the Period 1954–1964," *Journal of Finance*, 33 (May 1968), pp. 389–416; N. E. Mains, "Risk, the Pricing of Capital Assets, and the Evaluation of Investment Portfolios: Comment," *Journal of Business*, 50 (July 1977), pp. 371–384.

[14] See Victor Niederhoffer and M. F. M. Osborne, "Market Making and Reversal on the Stock Exchange," *Journal of the American Statistical Association*, 61 (December 1966), pp. 897–916.

[15] See M. S. Scholes, "The Market for Securities: Substitution versus Price Pressure and the Effects of Information on Share Prices," *Journal of Business*, vol. 45, no. 2 (April 1972), pp. 179–211; James H. Lorie and Victor Niederhoffer, "Predictive and Statistical Properties of Insider Trading," *Journal of Law and Economics*, 11 (1968), pp. 35–53.

against arbitrageur Ivan Boesky and against a number of investment bankers from several major Wall Street firms. The accused had earned many millions of dollars through stock trades based on nonpublic information (or by providing nonpublic information to traders). Boesky's punishment set records. He agreed to pay the equivalent of $100 million in settlement, was barred from the securities business for life, and was sentenced to a three-year prison term. The Boesky affair followed another well-publicized insider trading case which demonstrated that prosecutions can extend to very high places. In January 1984, then Deputy Secretary of Defense W. Paul Thayer was charged with passing on insider information about LTV Corporation to eight of his friends. Thayer was later sentenced to four years in prison and was ordered to disgorge $550,000 for his illegal trading activities.

There is no definition in the statutes of "insider trading," but case law is quite clear on who can be charged with an insider trading violation under Section 10b-5, the antifraud provision of the Securities and Exchange Act of 1934. For the purpose of Section 10b-5, an "insider trader" is anyone who, *directly or indirectly*, knowingly receives nonpublic material information from a corporate source and trades on that information. An insider trader can therefore be someone with no association with the company as well as someone with direct ties (corporate director, officer, employee, outside lawyer or accountant, etc.). The nonpublic information must have been intended to be used for a corporate purpose and not by an insider for his or her personal gain, and the information must be material in the sense that there is a substantial likelihood that a reasonable investor would consider it important in making the investment decision.

The Enforcement Division of the Securities and Exchange Commission (SEC) enforces the insider trading regulations. The SEC's methods include various electronic systems for monitoring and checking stock market transactions to detect and investigate abnormal trading activity. However, by far the most common method of catching an insider trader is through a tip to the SEC staff from an informant. The penalties imposed on someone convicted of insider trading include an injunction against trading, temporary or permanent barring from the brokerage industry, civil penalties up to three times the profits made (or losses avoided) as a result of the insider trading, and criminal referral to the United States Attorney's Office (often resulting in criminal prosecution and a jail sentence). The risks involved in insider trading reach well beyond the potential loss on the trades themselves.

Implications of Market Efficiency

We have pointed out that the evidence suggests that the United States stock market is quite efficient with respect to publicly available information and somewhat efficient in reflecting insider information. What are the implications of these findings for the investor and the financial manager?

First, we can infer that the market is not fooled by accounting manipulations which do not affect the real assets and cash flows of the firm. For example, accounting income changes which are due only to changes in how operations are reported but which do not affect cash flows (such as a switch from straight-line to accelerated depreciation for financial reporting but not for tax purposes) will not affect share prices.[16] The important point here is that the financial manager will not be able to raise share prices by sleight-of-hand tactics; all that matters is real performance (assets, liabilities, cash flows, etc.).

Second, investors and financial managers should not try to outguess the market unless they have information which is not publicly available and, even in that case, caution is warranted. With efficient markets, security prices reflect available information and therefore one cannot outsmart the market using that information. This dictum applies to an individual investor building a personal portfolio or to a firm buying marketable securities (Treasury bills, another corporation's stock or bonds, etc.) for its own account or for an employee pension fund. One can expect to earn the normal rate of return on the type of security purchased, and no more. This also applies to a financial manager who is trying to decide when to issue securities. In an efficient market, the prices of securities are unbiased estimates of security values, and unless the manager has information that the market does not have, trying to time the issue of securities to take advantage of supposed "mispricing" will not, on average, provide superior results.

Third—and this is directly related to the second point above—a company should not seek a merger with another company simply because, on the basis of information that is also available to investors in the market, its management feels the stocks of the two companies form a nice stock portfolio for the stockholders. The stockholders have similar information and can create their own stock portfolios. A merger is justified only if the acquiring firm's management feels either that it has information not already reflected in stock market prices that it can use to find exceptional bargains in the market, or that a merger will produce cash flow benefits (e.g., due to lower production costs resulting from economies of scale) because the merging companies mesh so well. The issue of firm diversification is discussed again in Chapters 10 and 23.

Fourth, if markets are efficient with respect to a particular type of information (e.g., publicly available information) and therefore prices fully reflect that information, then we cannot use that information to predict tomorrow's prices. That is, we cannot use the information to find temporarily undervalued or overvalued assets. For example, assume that the market is semistrong efficient (prices reflect all publicly available information). Then, the July 1 price of a share of stock fully reflects all information that is publicly available on July 1. Might you, on the basis of the July 1 information, conclude that the July 2 price will be much

---

[16] For empirical evidence that book depreciation methods do not affect share prices, see R. S. Kaplan and R. Roll, "Investor Evaluation of Accounting Income Information: Some Empirical Evidence," *Journal of Business*, 45 (April 1972), pp. 225–257.

higher or much lower than the July 1 price? Well, if you could, then that would mean that the July 1 price did not *already* reflect the July 1 information. There would be a contradiction in assuming that prices already reflect publicly available information and also in assuming that we can use the information to predict the future price. The July 2 price is unpredictable using the July 1 information. Another word for "unpredictable" is "random." Financial theorists often say that share prices follow a "random walk," which is another way of saying that tomorrow's price is unpredictable using today's information.[17]

Fifth, with market efficiency, market prices reveal a great deal of useful information. For example, if a firm's share price has been steadily declining while stock prices in general have been stable or rising, it is clear that the market has become progressively more pessimistic about the firm's prospects. We could use this information to predict whether the firm will go bankrupt.[18] Similarly, changes in the general level of stock prices can be used to forecast ups and downs in the general economy. Stock prices depend on investors' expectations about profitability in the coming periods, and when investors anticipate a general economic downturn, share prices fall. As it turns out, investors are pretty good at foretelling fluctuations in the economy. As a result, the general level of stock prices is a good leading indicator of actual business trends.

SUMMARY

The basic message of this chapter is that the market price of a financial asset is the present value of the future cash payments to the owner of the asset. When the payments are known for sure, the riskless rate of interest determines the present value. Risky streams of payments are more difficult to analyze.

Fixed-income assets, such as bonds, have a stated promised stream of cash payments to the owners; variable-income assets, such as common stock, do not provide a promised stream, but instead may in the future pay more or less than the income that they are currently providing. One method of valuing fixed-income securities is based on the yield to maturity. Two fixed-income securities with the same degree of uncertainty in their payments should have the same yield for the degree of risk involved. Then the value of a fixed-income security would be the present value of the promised payments using that yield as the interest rate.

---

[17] We are using the term "random walk" loosely here. Technically, prices follow a random walk if successive price changes are independent of one another and are identically distributed (i.e., have the same probability distributions). Market efficiency does not actually imply that prices conform to a random walk. Prices in an efficient market can follow a "submartingale," under which the probability distributions of price changes shift over time.

[18] On the use of share prices for this purpose, see W. H. Beaver, "Market Prices, Financial Ratios and the Prediction of Failure," *Journal of Accounting Research*, 6 (Autumn 1968), pp. 179–192.

The second method of valuation is applicable to all types of income-producing assets. The value of an asset can be thought of as the present value of the expected stream of payments using (for discounting purposes) the rate of return that is appropriate for the degree of risk of the payments. For example, the value of common stock can be thought of as the present value of the expected dividends that will be paid to present and future owners of the stock.

The risk-adjusted discount rate or required rate of return that should be used in valuing the expected income from an asset depends on the general level of interest rates in the economy and the degree of risk. The greater the risk, the higher is the rate of return required by investors.

The efficient markets hypothesis states that a security's current price reflects all the information currently available to the market. The weak form of the hypothesis considers only the past price history of the security. The semistrong form considers all publicly available information including the price history. The strong form of the hypothesis considers all information that is currently known by anyone in the market. Tests of the hypothesis suggest that the United States market is probably fairly efficient in the semistrong sense.

QUESTIONS

1   In a world of no risk, explain why financial assets might have different prices. What is the common element to all financial assets in such a world?

2   In the world of idealized certainty (i.e., no risks, no taxes, and perfect markets for financial assets), would the following situations be possible? (In each case, support your answer.)
   a   Two financial assets providing the same cash flows selling at different prices
   b   Two financial assets selling at the same price but providing different cash flows to the owner
   c   Two financial assets selling at the same price but providing different rates of return (interest rates)

3   Suppose that currently the yield to maturity on Aaa bonds is 9 percent. The Fritz Company is planning to issue bonds with a coupon rate of 9 percent. The bonds will be rated Aa. Will Fritz bonds sell at their face (maturity) value? Why or why not?

4   If the price of a share of common stock depends on the dividends paid to the stockholders, why do we find stocks of companies that have never paid a dividend selling at prices greater than zero and in many cases at a high multiple of the company's earnings per share?

5   Is the yield to maturity of a bond an adequate measure of its desirability as an investment? Why or why not?

6   Does the fact that a bond is rated AAA mean that it is a good investment for you? Why or why not?

7   Assuming that the stock market is efficient with respect to past prices (weak form efficiency) but no more efficient than that,

which of the following investment situations is likely to result in unusually high returns? Why or why not?

a The price of a stock has declined for five consecutive days. It "looks cheap and is due for a recovery."

b An analysis of General Motors' automobile sales for the past two months as reported in *The Wall Street Journal* shows that the company is experiencing increased sales of its most profitable cars. Your broker, who performed the analysis, recommends that you buy GM stock.

c In your statistics course you learned a technique for forecasting time series data. You have programmed the technique on your personal computer and are using it to forecast future stock prices based on past stock prices. You have found a stock with a current price of $40 per share that your computer forecasts will rise to $80 within one year.

8 If the stock market is strong form efficient, will anyone be able to earn unusually high returns from investing in stocks? Explain your answer.

(Question *9* draws on Appendix 5A.)

9 Explain what the figures mean in the following quotations taken from *The Wall Street Journal*.

a

Treasury bonds and notes

Rate	Maturity	Bid	Asked	Bid chg.	Yld.
13.75	Aug 04	148.19	148.25	−.07	8.03

b

Bonds	Cur. yld.	Vol.	Close	Net chg.
Sears 8s06	8.3	60	$95\frac{7}{8}$	$+\frac{3}{8}$

c

52 Weeks High	52 Weeks Low	Stock	Sym.	Div.	Yld. %	P–E ratio	Sales 100s	High	Low	Close	Net chg.
$74\frac{1}{2}$	$48\frac{5}{8}$	Xerox	XRX	3.00	4.1	19	5192	$73\frac{3}{8}$	$72\frac{1}{4}$	$73\frac{1}{8}$	...

PROJECTS

1 Suppose that you have $10,000 to invest. Explore several alternatives open to you, using *The Wall Street Journal* and other sources of information to find the going rates of return. Try to rank these investments in increasing order of risk according to your own

judgment. Estimate the risk premiums in these investments using the rate on Treasury bills for the riskless rate. Which investments would you make?

2 Using *The Wall Street Journal*, look up the prices of the 9 percent Navistar and Amoco bonds discussed in this chapter for each quarter during the past four years. Compute the yields to maturity for each bond and plot them on a graph over time. Relative to the Amoco bonds, what appears to have happened to the risk of the Navistar bonds?

**DEMONSTRATION
PROBLEMS**

DP1 You are considering investing in a U.S. Treasury note that pays $80 in interest per year and $1000 at maturity two years from now.

  If the yield to maturity on the note is 8 percent, what is its current price?

  At what price would the note sell for today if the interest rate is 6 percent per year?

SOLUTION TO DP1:

a The price can be calculated, but note that the coupon rate on the note is the annual interest payment divided by the maturity value.

$$i = \frac{\$80}{\$1000} = 8\%$$

Since the coupon rate is equal to the yield to maturity, the note must have a price equal to its maturity value of $1000.

b The price of the note is the present value of the coupon interest and principal payments. Therefore,

Price = $80(*P/A*, 6%, 2) + $1000(*P/F*, 6%, 2)

  = $80(1.8334) + $1000(0.8900)

  = $1036.67

DP2 As financial manager of the Beta Corporation, you have planned to issue $50 million worth of bonds. The bonds will mature in twenty years. Current interest rates on bonds of different ratings are

Rating	Aaa	Aa	A	Baa	Ba	B
Rate	7.5%	7.7%	8.0%	9.0%	10.0%	11.0%

a Suppose you set an 8 percent coupon rate on the bonds. How must they be rated in order to sell at face value?

b If the bonds will be rated as Baa, what is likely to be their price per $100 face value? (Assume annual coupon payments will be made.) What will be the proceeds to the company at that price?

SOLUTION TO DP2:

a Since the yield on the bonds if sold at par would be 8 percent, they must be rated "A".

b Baa bonds currently yield 9 percent, so the Beta bonds must also yield 9 percent. Since the price of the bonds is the present value of the coupon and principal payments per $100 face value.

$$\text{Price} = \$8(P/A, 9\%, 20) + \$100(P/F, 9\%, 20)$$

$$= \$8(9.1285) + \$100(0.1784)$$

$$= \$90.87$$

This is the price per $100 face value. The price per dollar of face value issued would be

$$\text{Price} = \$90.87/\$100$$

$$= \$0.9087 \text{ per dollar}$$

The proceeds from issuing $50 million in face-value bonds would be

$$\text{Proceeds} = \$0.9087(\$50 \text{ million})$$

$$= \underline{\$45,435 \text{ million}}$$

DP3 Dividends on Velocity Corporation stock are expected to grow at a rate of 12 percent per year indefinitely. Next year's dividend is projected to be $1.20 per share. The rate of return required by investors on Velocity stock is 16 percent. What is the price per share of Velocity stock?

SOLUTION TO DP3:

$$P_0 = \frac{D_1}{k - g}$$

$$= \frac{\$1.20}{0.16 - 0.12}$$

$$= \frac{\$1.20}{0.04}$$

$$= \underline{\$30}$$

PROBLEMS

1 *a* Suppose that the market interest rate is 10 percent per year. You purchase a U.S. Treasury bill that pays $1000 to its owner one year from now. How much would you pay at the most for the bill? [Ans.: $909.09] *b* If you purchase the bill at a price of $909.09, what interest rate will you earn on the bill for the year?

 2 A U.S. Treasury note is available in the market; it pays $100 in interest per year and $1000 at maturity two years from now.

a If the yield to maturity on the note is 10 percent, what is its current price? [Ans.: $1000]

b Given that the current price is $1000, at what price must you be able to sell the note one year from now (after the first year's interest is received) to earn 10 percent on your investment if you buy the note today? [Ans.: $1000]

c At what price would the note sell today if the interest rate is 8 percent per year? [Ans.: $1035.67]

d Given that the current price is $1035.67, at what price must you be able to sell the note one year from now to earn 8 percent on your investment if you buy the note today? [Ans.: $1018.52]

e Suppose that you purchase the note at a price of $1000 to yield 10 percent per year. One year later the market interest rate has changed to a new rate of 8 percent. What will be the price of the note at that time? [Ans.: $1018.52]

f Given your answer from *e*, what interest rate would you obtain if you sold the note after one year (after receiving interest)? What rate will you earn if you hold it to maturity instead of selling it?

g Suppose that you purchase the note at a price of $1035.67 to yield 8 percent per year. One year later the market interest rate has changed to a new rate of 10 percent. What will be the price of the note at that time? What interest rate will you earn if you sell it then? What rate will you earn if you hold it to maturity?

3 The rate of interest is 8 percent per year.

a How much should an investor pay today for a security that will pay $1000 for sure a year from now?

b How much should the investor pay for a security that pays $1000 for sure two years from now and nothing at the end of the first year?

c How much must a security pay at the end of two years to entice the investor to pay the same price as in *a*? (Nothing is paid at the end of the first year.)

4 You have been offered the opportunity to purchase a mortgage contract on a house for $4000. The contract provides its owner with five payments of $1000 per year with the next payment due one year from now. The market interest rate is 10 percent per year.

a What rate of return would you earn if you paid $4000 for the contract? Is $4000 a fair price for it?

b What is the maximum price you should be willing to pay for the contract?

5 As financial manager of Argus, Inc., you have planned to issue $40 million in bonds. The coupon rate is to be 9 percent with coupon interest to be paid annually. The entire $40 million face (maturity) value will be due in ten years. Current interest rates are:

Rating	Aaa	Aa	A	Baa	Ba	B	Caa
Rate	8.8%	9%	9.3%	9.6%	10%	10.5%	11.2%

a What rating must the bonds have in order to sell at face value?

b If the bonds are rated Ba, what is likely to be their price per $100 face value?

c Given your answer from *b*, what must be the face value of the issue if sufficient bonds are sold so as to provide $40 million in cash to Argus?

6 Investors currently expect that the dividends per share of Fantastic Corporation will grow at a rate of 14 percent per year for the foreseeable future. Dividends next year are expected to be $2.40 per share. The risk of Fantastic's dividend stream is such that investors require a 16 percent rate of return on the stock.

a What is the price per share of Fantastic's common stock?

b Suppose that new information on Fantastic comes into the market such that the expected growth rate is reduced to 8 percent per year (but the expected dividend next year is still $2.40). What will be the new price of Fantastic's stock?

c What do the results from *a* and *b* tell you about the sensitivity of stock prices to changes in expectations?

7 The Denver Saddle Burr Company (DSBC) is expected to pay a $2.00 dividend per share of common stock next year. DSBC's current stock price is $40. Investors expect the firm's dividends to grow at a rate of 6 percent per year forever.

a What rate of return do investors appear to require on DSBC's stock?

b Your analysis of DSBC's published financial statements suggests that the long-run growth rate will be around 8 percent per year. The stock market is semistrong efficient. What rate of return should you expect to earn on DSBC's stock?

8 Dividends on STB stock next year are expected to be $2.40 per share. The current price of STB stock is $60 per share. You believe that the required rate of return on STB stock is 12 percent. What long-run growth rate of dividends for STB is consistent with the above information?

9 To cope with continued inflation, the Government of Mexico issued a changing coupon bond in the New York bond market. The bond has a maturity value of $1000 and a term to maturity of 5 years. Coupon payments are made annually. In the first year, a 10 percent coupon is promised. Thereafter, the coupon *rate* increases by 15 percent per year, compounded annually. If the rate of return required on this bond is 20 percent, what is the current price of this bond?

10 Caper Hall is a security analyst with the brokerage firm of Allen, Hamlin, and Osborne. As an investor you wish to purchase the shares of BMI Inc. common stock presently selling for $20 per share. Caper estimates that the current dividend per share of $2.00 would decline at a 10 percent annual rate for the coming two years and then grow at a constant 5 percent annual rate into the foreseeable future.

   a Show the expected dividend stream on a time line.
   b If investors require a 15 percent rate of return on BMI's common stock, what price per share should it sell for?
   c Should you buy any shares of BMI's common stock? Explain.

SOURCES OF
FINANCIAL INFORMATION

Information on financial markets, economic trends, and individual companies is available from a wide range of sources. Here we provide a guide to most of the major sources and show how to interpret quotations on stocks and bonds.

**DAILY
SECURITIES
DATA**

Most newspapers carry some information on the daily activity in the securities market, but *The Wall Street Journal* (*WSJ*) covers more securities and provides more complete information than almost any other easily available source. The *WSJ* publishes a wide variety of articles on business and financial activities as well as data on commodity prices, foreign exchange rates, option prices, bond quotations (including both corporates and governments), and stock quotations. The data are always to be found in the last eight or nine pages of each issue.

Stock Quotations

The location of data on the trading activity of the stock issued by a particular company depends on whether the stock is listed on one of the stock exchanges or not. The *WSJ* provides information on all the listed securities that were actually traded in a given day plus information on the stock of many other companies.

Companies are shown alphabetically (names abbreviated) in three groups: NYSE Composite, Amex Composite, and Over-the-Counter. Therefore, if you are looking for information on a stock and you don't know whether it is listed or not, you must examine all three groups. The NYSE Composite provides information on stocks listed on the New York Stock Exchange and several other exchanges, excluding those stocks listed on the American Stock Exchange that are shown under Amex Composite. Other, nonlisted, stocks are shown as Over-the-Counter. An example of the information provided for listed stocks is shown in Exhibit 5-2.

Both common and preferred stocks are traded on stock exchanges. The quotation for Abbott Laboratories is a common stock quotation; the Alabama Power stock is a preferred stock, as indicated by "pf" following the abbreviated name for the company. The first two columns show the highest and lowest prices at which the stock had traded during the past 52 weeks. The annual dividend is shown following the trading symbol for the company's common stock. Common stock dividends are calculated as four times the most recent quarter's "regular" dividend unless indicated otherwise by a footnote. Footnotes are found at the end of the list of quotations. "Yld." is the current dividend yield of the stock (dividends/price). The price-earnings ratio is the ratio of the closing price to the most recent year's earnings per share reported by the company and is provided only for common stocks, as preferred stockholders generally do not share in earnings after preferred dividends have been paid. Sales, given in hundreds, are the number of shares of the stock that were traded (bought and sold) during the day. There were 357,200 shares of Abbott Lab's common stock traded that day. The "z70" for Alabama Power preferred stock sales indicates that the total number of shares traded was 70. The next three columns give the highest, lowest, and last price at which trading occurred during the day. The price of Abbott Labs at the close decreased $\frac{3}{8}$ of $1 ($0.375) from the closing price on the previous day of trading.

Bond Quotations

The *WSJ* provides very little information on the bonds issued by state and local governments. Your best source of price and related information on these issues is a local brokerage firm. Information on new state and local issues is provided, however.

Corporate and federal government issues are covered in much greater detail. Corporate bonds may be listed on either the American Exchange or the New York Exchange, and data on listed, traded issues are provided daily. Many listed bonds do not trade every day; therefore you must often look at several days' listings before you will find data on a particular bond. Moody's manuals (see below) indicate the listing of bonds issued by corporations. Exhibit 5-3 shows example quotations for corporate bonds. Data on all bonds, notes, and bills issued by the U.S. Treasury, most bonds issued by federal agencies, and some other governmental units are provided in a separate section of the *WSJ*. Exhibit 5-4 shows example data for U.S. Treasury issues.

Corporate Bonds   Each bond issue that is listed on the New York Exchange that was traded on the previous trading day is shown in *The Wall*

EXHIBIT 5-2
Quotations for listed stocks: NYSE composite transactions reported in The Wall Street Journal

52 weeks		Stock	Sym.	Div.	Yld. %	PE	Vol. 100s	High	Low	Close	Net chg.
High	Low										
$62\frac{5}{8}$	33	AbbotLab	ABT	.84	1.4	26	3572	$61\frac{7}{8}$	$60\frac{7}{8}$	$61\frac{1}{4}$	$-\frac{3}{8}$
$106\frac{1}{2}$	94	AlaPwr pf		9.00	8.6	. . .	z70	105	105	105	. . .

Street Journal. As shown in Exhibit 5-3, companies such as American Telephone and Telegraph (AT&T) have more than one bond issue, and so each one must be identified separately. The identification is by company name (AT&T), coupon rate of interest (7s, pronounced "sevens," refers to a 7 percent coupon rate), and year of maturity (01, meaning 2001). The current yield is the coupon rate divided by the closing price, not the yield to maturity, which is more relevant to the investor and is explained in Chapter 5. The "cv" for the Control Data bonds means that these securities are convertible into common stock and no current yield is provided. The "high," "low," and "close" indicate prices (per $100) maturity (or par value) during the trading day. "Net change" is the difference between the closing price on this day and the prior day's close.

Treasury Bonds and Notes U.S. Treasury notes and bonds pay coupon interest and therefore can be identified by their coupon rate and maturity. In Exhibit 5-4 "Rate" refers to coupon rate. The 9.50 percent note maturing in October 1994 is identified as a note by the "p" following the maturity date. (The "p" also means that the note is exempt from nonresident withholding taxes. The "k" on the 9.00 percent security identifies it as a bond with the same lack of withholding taxes.) The distinction between notes and bonds is based on initial maturity and is not important for most investors. The hyphenated maturity for the 12 percent bond means that the bond may be called (principal paid) in 2008, but otherwise will mature in 2013. "Bid" and "Asked" refer to dollar prices per $100 maturity value and are expressed in $\frac{1}{32}$ of $1. "Yield" is the yield to maturity based on the bid price. See Appendix 5B for a discussion of why the yield may vary with maturity. Note that if investors believe that the 12 percent bond may be called in 2008, they will compute "yield to call" and use this in making their decisions as well as yield to maturity. Yield to call is calculated in the same fashion as yield to maturity using the number of periods until the call date (August 2008) in place of the number of periods until the maturity date (August 2013).

Stripped Treasuries and Treasury Bills Stripped Treasuries and Treasury bills have no coupon payments; therefore, their coupon rate is shown as

---

EXHIBIT 5-3
*Listed corporate bond quotations: New York Exchange Bonds,
as reported in* The Wall Street Journal

Bonds	Cur yld.	Vol.	Close	Net chg.
ATT 6s00	7.3	22	82¾	−⅜
ATT 7s01	7.9	120	88⅝	−⅛
CtlDat 8½11	cv	37	86	+1

.00. A stripped Treasury is a Treasury note or bond that has had the coupon interest payments separated from the principal payment. The rights to the interest payments are sold separately from the rights to the principal payment. The security maturing November 2018 has a claim to principal payments of the 9.00 percent bond shown below. (The "b" indicates that it is the principal payment of a bond.) The price of the stripped security is very low relative to its maturity value of $100 because investors receive no cash payments until maturity. The yield to maturity is slightly lower than the yield on the underlying bond. This is due to compensation to the firms that perform the stripping service. Treasury bills are quoted differently from the other securities. The maturity date is more specific (March 8, 1990) and the bid or asked amounts shown are the annualized discounts from the maturity value. The bid of 7.67 indicates a discount of approximately 1.92 percent or a price per $100 maturity value of $98.08 since the bill matures about one quarter from the date of the price quote (7.67/4 equals 1.92). The annualized yield to maturity at this price is shown as "Yield."

SOURCE GUIDE

The table on the following page is a general guide to financial information. It is organized in two sections. The first section is a quick reference list organized by the type of information. The second section is organized by source and provides a capsule summary of the nature of the information provided in a given source.

Generally, when you are in doubt as to where to find some specific type of financial information, consult the person at the reference desk of your library.

EXHIBIT 5-4
United States government securities quotations reported in The Wall Street Journal, *December 6, 1989*

		Treasury bonds, notes and bills			
Rate	**Maturity**	**Bid**	**Asked**	**Bid Chg.**	**Yield**
		Government bonds and notes			
9.50	Oct 94p	106.14	106.18	−.08	7.84
12.00	Aug 08–13	137.14	137.20	−.10	8.07
9.00	Nov 18k	111.27	111.31	−.12	7.94
		Stripped Treasuries			
.00	Nov 18b	11.03	11.10	−.02	7.67
		Treasury bills			
.00	Mar 08 '90	7.67	7.63	+.09	7.88

Type of information	Sources
Current prices and yields on securities	*The Wall Street Journal, Commercial and Financial Chronicle, Bank and Quotation Record, Moody's Bond Record*, stock brokers
Average interest rates on various financial assets	*The Wall Street Journal, Federal Reserve Bulletin, Economic Report of the President*
Stock and bond market activity	*The Wall Street Journal, Statistical Bulletin of the Securities and Exchange Commission, Commercial and Financial Chronicle*
Aggregate financial data	*Federal Reserve Bulletin, Economic Report of the President*
Individual company data	Annual reports of the company, various manuals of Moody's, *Standard & Poor's Corporation Records, Fitch's Corporation Manuals, Value Line Investment Survey*
General business data	*Survey of Current Business, Statistical Abstract of the United States, Business Statistics*

Selected publications	Type of information
Business Week	General coverage of business affairs
Barron's	Security markets, individual securities, analysis of individual companies
Forbes	Analysis of individual companies, general articles on financial topics
Fortune	General coverage of business affairs, size rankings of major United States and foreign corporations, with summary data
Dun's Reviews	Bankruptcy data, average financial ratios for various industries, general financial articles
The Economist	General coverage of international business
Federal Reserve Bulletin	Wide variety of monetary, banking, and financial statistics; reviews of financial trends
Survey of Current Business	A wide variety of business statistics; see *Business Statistics* for historical data taken from this source
Monthly Bulletin of the Securities and Exchange Commission	Data on stock market activity and corporate securities issues
Monthly reviews of various Federal Reserve banks	Each Federal Reserve bank (New York, St. Louis, etc.) publishes a monthly review containing articles on financial and economic activity plus various types of data on national and regional trends

THE TERM STRUCTURE
OF INTEREST RATES

On August 24, 1981, U.S. Treasury securities maturing in one year had a yield to maturity of 17.2 percent per year whereas ten-year maturity securities had a yield of 15.3 percent. Five years later, on August 25, 1986, one-year maturity Treasury securities had a yield of 5.7 percent per year whereas ten-year maturity Treasury securities had a yield of 7.2 percent.[19] These data illustrate first that interest rates change over time for reasons explained in Chapter 2 and, second, that the rates which apply at a point in time to one maturity need not be the same as the rate for other maturities. Thus, the market interest rate on a given date depends not only on the risk of the cash flows but also on when the cash flows occur. The relationship between interest rates and the timing of a cash flow is called the term structure of interest rates or, more simply, the yield curve. The yield curves for U.S. Treasury securities on August 24, 1981, and August 25, 1986, are shown in Figure 5-3. The price quotations and yield used in developing the yield curve for August 25, 1986, are shown in Exhibit 5–5. For an explanation of these quotes, see Appendix 5A.

The yield curve is rarely "flat"; that is, interest rates usually vary with the timing of the cash flows. This poses two questions: (1) How are cash flows valued when the yield curve is not flat, and (2) what factors determine the shape of the yield curve? Let's answer the first question first.

THE TIME VALUE OF MONEY REVISITED

In Chapter 5 we established the principle that the market value of a certain (known for sure) stream of future cash flows is the present value of those cash flows. We assumed that there was only one interest rate currently applicable for all riskless streams. Now we are saying that, in fact, the market interest rate applicable to a cash flow occurring one year from now could be 11 percent whereas the interest rate applicable to a cash flow occurring two years from now could be 12 percent. What then will be the market value of an asset that pays $111 to be received for

---

[19] Reported in *The Wall Street Journal,* August 25, 1981 and August 26, 1986.

certain in one year and $125 to be received for certain in two years and nothing thereafter? The answer is quite simple: it is the sum of the present values of the two cash flows using the applicable interest rates. That is

$$V = \frac{\$111}{1.11} + \frac{\$125}{(1.12)^2}$$

$$= \$100 + \$99.65$$

$$= \$199.65$$

In general, then, we can express the value of any stream of certain future cash flows as the sum of the present values of the individual cash flows using rates i_1 for cash flows one period from now (F_1), i_2 for cash flows two periods from now (F_2), etc.

$$V = \frac{F_1}{1 + i_1} + \frac{F_2}{(1 + i_2)^2} + \frac{F_3}{(1 + i_3)^3} + \cdots + \frac{F_n}{(1 + i_n)^n} \qquad (5\text{-}11)$$

Rates i_1, i_2, i_3, etc., are the rates of interest for cash to be delivered at times 1, 2, 3, etc., respectively. These interest rates are the yields to maturity for zero-coupon securities (securities that provide only a single cash payment at maturity). These interest rates are usually referred to as zero-coupon yields. Zero-coupon yields are reported for Treasury bills and stripped Treasury notes and bonds in *The Wall Street Journal* (see Appendix 5A).

FIGURE 5-3

The term structure of interest rates: August 24, 1981 and August 25, 1986.

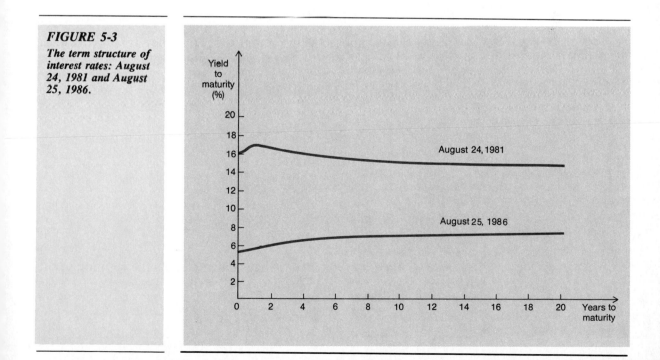

EXHIBIT 5-5
Data used in plot of yield curve for August 25, 1986 as displayed in
The Wall Street Journal

U.S. Treasury bills			
Mat. date	Bid	Asked	Yield
	Discount		
11–28	5.35	5.32	5.40
2–19	5.39	5.35	5.57
8–6	5.41	5.39	5.69

Treasury bonds and notes					
Rate	Mat. date	Bid	Asked	Bid chg.	Yld.
$10\frac{1}{2}$s	1988 Aug *n*	107.28	108	+.1	6.12
$13\frac{7}{8}$s	1989 Aug *n*	119.18	119.22	+.2	6.48
$10\frac{3}{4}$s	1990 Aug *n*	113.24	114	+.4	6.68
$14\frac{7}{8}$s	1991 Aug *n*	132.29	133.5	+.8	6.88
$8\frac{5}{8}$s	1993 Aug	108.13	108.21	+.3	7.03
8s	1996–01 Aug	103.23	104.7	+.4	7.37
$8\frac{3}{8}$	2003–08 Aug	107.6	107.14	+.7	7.59

Source: The Wall Street Journal, *Aug. 26, 1986.*

The yield to maturity of a coupon-bearing bond is a complex weighted average of the zero-coupon yields with weights that depend on the magnitude of the cash flows in each period. For example, suppose that the zero-coupon yields for the next three years are as follows:

$i_1 = 7\%$, $i_2 = 7.5\%$, and $i_3 = 8\%$

A bond with a 7% coupon rate and three years to maturity will have a market price equal to:

$$V = \frac{\$7}{(1.07)} + \frac{\$7}{(1.075)^2} + \frac{\$107}{(1.08)^3}$$

$$= \$6.54 + \$6.06 + \$84.94$$

$$= \$97.54$$

The yield to maturity (y) on the bond is calculated as the solution to the equation:

$$\$97.54 = \frac{\$7}{(1 + y)} + \frac{\$7}{(1 + y)^2} + \frac{\$107}{(1 + y)^3}$$

$$y = 7.95\%$$

The bond's yield to maturity of 7.95 percent is less than the zero-coupon yield for year 3 (i_3 = 8 percent) because it reflects the lower rates for years 1 and 2 (i_1 = 7 percent, i_2 = 7.5 percent). However, the bond's yield is close to 8 percent because most of the cash flow from the bond occurs in year 3.

THE SHAPE OF THE YIELD CURVE

Sometimes the yield curve slopes upward with long-term rates higher than short-term rates. This has been the most common shape in the twentieth century. At other times the curve is roughly flat; occasionally it is "humped" with the intermediate-term rates higher than both short-term and long-term rates. In the past ten years, the curve has frequently been downward sloping with short-term rates higher than long-term rates, often with a hump at one year or so, as was shown in Figure 5–3 for August 24, 1981. Figure 5-4 illustrates these four basic shapes. Several factors have been proposed to explain the shape of the curve. The three major factors are expectations of future interest rates, risk, and differences in the preferences of borrowers and lenders (investors) for different maturities.[20]

Interest Rate Expectations

Expectations of future interest rates strongly influence the yield curve. Everything else equal, when market participants (borrowers and lenders) expect interest rates to rise in the future, current long-term rates should

[20] For a thorough discussion of term structure theories, see James Van Horne, *Financial Market Rates and Flow* (Englewood Cliffs, N. J.: Prentice-Hall, 1978), pp. 78-135.

FIGURE 5-4

Four shapes of the yield curve.

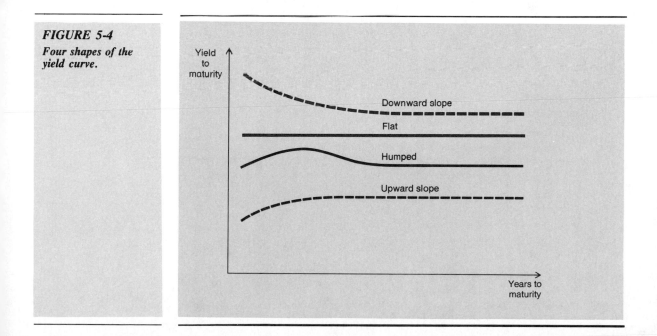

be higher than current short-term rates. For example, suppose that the yield curve is currently flat and investors expect that interest rates will not change. The current discount rates for cash flows for all future times are equal to 10 percent. This yield curve is shown as "I" in Figure 5-5. Suppose that expectations change and market participants now expect future interest rates to rise above current levels. Current borrowers will now tend to borrow long-term (issue long-term bonds rather than short-term notes) to avoid paying higher interest rates in the future. Lenders will tend to invest in short-term assets so that they can reinvest later at higher rates. (They will buy short-term notes and avoid long-term bonds.) Prices of long-term bonds should therefore fall (since supply exeeds demand) relative to short-term notes (where demand exceeds supply). As prices fall, interest rates rise and the result will be a new equilibrium set of interest rates. The yield curve will be upward sloping with long-term rates higher than short-term rates. Short-term rates may end up at 10 percent or fall to a lower level. This is illustrated by yield curve "II" in Figure 5-5. Therefore, an upward-sloping yield curve is consistent with expectations of higher interest rates in the future. Similarly, if the shape of the yield curve depends only on expectations about future rates, a downward-sloping yield curve indicates that the market believes interest rates will fall in the future and a flat yield curve indicates that no change in rates is expected.

Interest Rate Risk

Even if we are examining securities that have certain cash flows such as U.S. Treasury securities, there is risk due to changing interest rates. Investors in long-term securities are exposed to the risk that interest rates will rise, thereby making the value of the securities fall. If these investors believe that they may sell their securities prior to maturity,

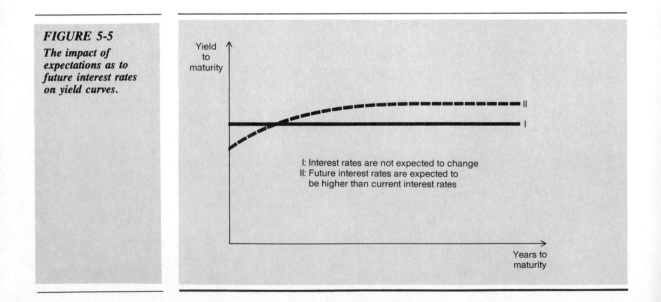

FIGURE 5-5

The impact of expectations as to future interest rates on yield curves.

they will be concerned about this risk. We can say these investors are exposed to price risk. On the other hand, investors in short-term securities who plan to reinvest the cash flows in the market are exposed to the risk that interest rates will fall. Indeed all investors who plan to reinvest coupon interest payments or the proceeds from maturing securities are exposed to uncertainty in their future incomes due to changing interest rates. This is so because, if interest rates fall, the earnings on the reinvested money will also fall. We can say that these investors are subject to one sort of interest rate risk or the other. There are investment strategies that may be pursued to minimize interest rate risk for a given investor, but we will not explore them here.[21]

The effects of interest rate risks on the shape of the yield curve are not totally clear, but many people believe that there is liquidity preference on the part of most investors; that is, a premium must be paid in long-term rates relative to short-term rates to induce investors to give up the liquidity of short-term investment. This view is based in part on the notion that the investors are concerned about the price risk of long-term bonds because they may sell the bonds prior to maturity. To get these investors to purchase long-term bonds, a premium must be paid over the short-term rate. In addition, the major issuers of securities have long-term needs for funds (for example, corporations financing plant and equipment). They prefer to issue long-term debt because they want to be assured of the interest rate they will have to pay; if they borrow short-term, they risk that refinancing the short-term debt will involve an interest rate above current levels. A preference of investors for short-term securities and a preference of borrowers for long-term debt issues implies that the yield curve on average should be upward sloping. That is, long-term interest rates should be higher than short-term interest rates on average. For the past fifty years this, in fact, has been true. Figure 5-6 illustrates the combined effects of risk premiums on long-term bonds and expectations. Yield curve "I" is based purely on expectations and assumes that investors do not expect interest rates to change. Yield curve "II" shows how the actual yield curve looks when risk premiums are added to these expectations.

Supply-Demand Conditions

A third factor thought to influence the shape of the yield curve is the relative supply and demand for securities of different maturities apart from expectations and risk considerations. The concept here is that many of the borrowers and lenders in the market have preferences for particular maturities. Pension funds and insurance companies prefer to buy long-term securities because they have long-term predictable obligations. These investors would rather not be bothered with the need to reinvest the proceeds from maturing short-term securities. Some corpo-

---

[21] See L. Fisher and R. L. Weil, "Coping with the Risk of Interest-Rate Fluctuations: Returns to Bondholders from Naive and Optimal Strategies," *Journal of Business*, 44 (October 1971), pp. 408–431.

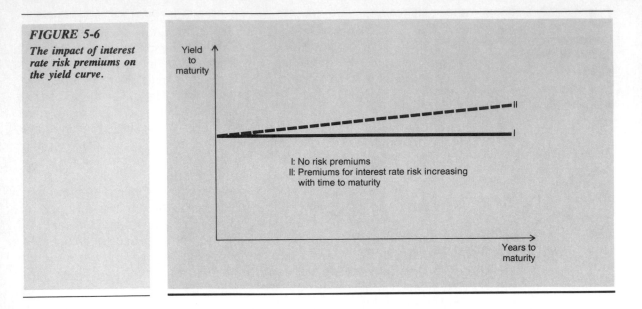

rate borrowers such as public utilities issue large amounts of long-term securities to finance new plants. Since these borrowers need the money for many years, they would rather not be bothered with the need to refinance short-term debts. If, say, the utilities want to borrow a lot of long-term money at a time when long-term investors are short of funds, long-term interest rates will tend to rise since the supply of long-term securities exceeds the demand. Conversely if long-term investors have a lot of money to invest when long-term borrowers need very little, long-term rates will tend to fall. Therefore, in order to understand the shape of the yield curve, one must examine the financial circumstances of all the major sectors of the economy. This supply-demand influence on the yield curve operates in conjunction with expectations and risk to determine the actual shape of the curve.

YIELD CURVES FOR RISKY FIXED-INCOME SECURITIES

We have been looking at government securities' yield curves for which the cash payments to the owner are assumed to be known with certainty. What about fixed-income securities paying uncertain future cash flows (that is, where there is default risk)? Although the data are less easily obtained, we can develop yield curves for fixed-income securities of different risk classes based on their yields to maturity. For example, we can estimate a yield curve for Aaa securities and a yield curve for Aa securities. The result, at a point in time, should look something like the curves shown in Figure 5-7. As a frame of reference we have included the yield curve on government securities which have no default risk. Note that in Figure 5-7, as the maturity increases, the difference between the yield curves increases. For example, the difference between the yields on ten-year Baa bonds and ten-year A bonds is greater than the difference between the yields on one-year Baa bonds and one-year A bonds. This is due to the greater uncertainy in the amount that will actually be paid (greater default risk) as the distance into the future increases.[22] In principle, every borrower faces a particular yield curve at a point in time, and financial managers use this information in deciding on the maturity of debt to be issued. An understanding of yield curves is, therefore, an important part of financial management.

[22] We normally find an increasing difference in yields between yield curves of different risk classes as the maturity increases, but the differences have been exaggerated in Figure 5-7.

FIGURE 5-7

The impact of default risk premiums on the yield curves.

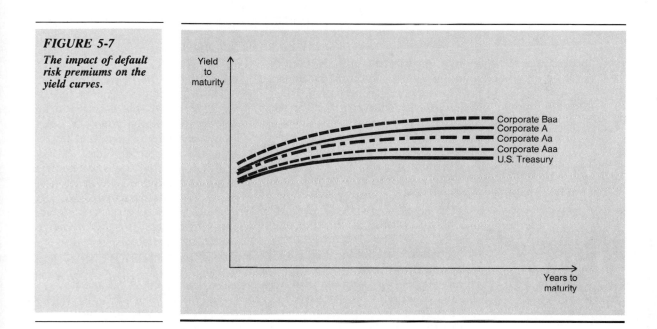

As any racing handicapper knows, betting at the track offers no free rides: A chance at tremendous gains by betting on a longshot is just that, a longshot. This is nothing new. Bigger potential gains usually mean bigger risks. Investors have a wide array of choices in putting their money to work earning more money for the future. The essential problem the investor faces is to choose the set of investments that has the best risk-return characteristics from the investor's standpoint. Keep in mind that an investor is concerned with the overall risk of his or her portfolio and, in assessing a particular investment, the investor should consider how much that asset will add to both the expected return and the risk of the total portfolio.

The investment choices made by investors determine the types of securities (stocks, bonds, convertibles, etc.) companies will issue and determine which firms will find it easy to obtain capital. Thus, for example, if there is optimism about the real estate market, firms with real estate oriented activities (construction, land developers, real estate investment trusts, and so forth) will find it easier to finance investment and consequently these firms will tend to expand. Disenchantment with real estate would dampen investment in that sector of the economy. Investor attitudes therefore represent a basic determinant of where capital expenditures will take place in the economy.

What are the investment possibilities open to investors? How do they compare in terms of returns? In terms of risk? These are the subjects of this essay.

A PIECE OF AMERICAN INDUSTRY

What could be safer than owning a piece of American industry, a share of the backbone of our economy? Indeed, there is a well-known San Francisco attorney who advocates a people's capitalism with workers and management alike owning stock in their companies so that everyone can share in the rewards of being a capitalist. The seductive idea of being a part owner of the great companies of America is not without qualifications, however; even a good thing can be acquired at a price so high that the bargain is no longer attractive. In the late 1920s common stocks were touted as a guaranteed source of income and wealth. The allure was irresistible and stock prices escalated to dizzying heights. But then came disillusionment and despair as the stock market experienced the worst collapse in its history. From September 1929 to July 1932, the bears were in control. United States Steel plummeted from $262 per share to $22 per share. Montgomery Ward from $136 per share to $4 per share, and General Motors from $73 per share to $8 per share. Many lesser securities fell to less than 1 percent of their 1929 highs (or disappeared entirely).

It was not until the early 1950s that the stock market recovered from the monumental collapse of 1929–1932. Although there were several intermittent drops between 1942 and 1968, that period saw a general steep rise in equity prices. From April 1942 to December 1968, the Standard and Poor's average rose nearly fourteenfold, from 7.84 to 106.5. That is an increase of approximately 10.3 percent per year (7.1 percent per year real return, that is, when adjusted for inflation) and it doesn't include dividends paid on the stocks. The average price of stocks of smaller companies increased by considerably more. A very impressive performance and one that lulled many investors in the late 1960s into believing that it could go on forever. It didn't go on forever. From December 1968 to December 1989, the Standard & Poor's Composite rose by 249 percent and consumer prices rose by 263 percent, implying a real *decline* in the Standard & Poor's Composite average of approximately 4 percent over the twenty-one-year period.

The above observations are supported by a number of rigorous analyses of stock performance. Fisher and Lorie studied common stock returns for the period of 1926 to 1965; the pretax return, including dividends, from 1926 to 1965 was 9.3 percent compounded annually.[1] The real pretax rate of return (the rate adjusted for inflation) was about 7.7 percent per year for the 1926 to 1965 period. For someone in a relatively high tax bracket, aftertax returns fell to 7.1 percent compounded annually before adjusting for inflation and to about 5.6 percent per year after an adjustment for inflation. A more recent study by Ibbotsen and Sinquefield found that the pretax return (dividends plus capital gains) from 1926 to 1988 was 10 percent for stocks (a real rate of return of about

6.9 percent per year).[2] However, Ritter and Urich found that common stocks yielded a real rate of return from 1968 to 1983 of only 1 percent per year.[3] Over very long periods of time (twenty-five years or more), stocks have usually provided what most would regard as a reasonable rate of return. But, over short or even intermediate time spans, stocks have been less predictable and have often performed poorly.

Interestingly, stocks do not in the short run appear to provide a good protection against inflation. Sharp rises in the general price level often produce declines in stock prices. Real estate, for example, seems to be a better inflation shelter in the short run. However, over the very long run, it appears that stocks do protect against inflation since revenues, expenses, and net profits all tend to increase with inflation. Of course, the long run can be a long time, and for an investor with a short planning horizon (say, under ten years), stocks may not be the ideal medium.

PLAYING IT SAFE: FIXED-INCOME ASSETS

For those whose nerves cannot tolerate the possibility of the wide daily fluctuations in wealth that can accompany stock investments, fixed-income assets may be the answer. Fixed-income securities are those

---

[1] Lawrence Fisher and James H. Lorie, "Rates of Return on Investments in Common Stock: The Year by Year Record, 1926–65," *The Journal of Business*, vol. 41, no. 3 (July 1968), pp. 291–316.

[2] *Stocks, Bonds, Bills and Inflation, 1989 Yearbook*, Ibbotson Associates.

[3] Lawrence S. Ritter and Thomas J. Urich, "The Role of Gold in Consumer Investment Portfolios," *Monograph Series in Finance and Economics*, Salomon Brothers Center for the Study of Financial Institutions, Graduate School of Business, New York University, 1984.

that have a fixed promised dollar return (interest and principal payments), such as bonds. From 1926 to 1988 the annual pretax yield was 5 percent per year on long-term corporate bonds and was 4.4 percent per year on long-term United States government bonds.[4] These average rates of return on bonds are about 5 percent less per year than those from stocks, a very substantial price to pay for the added safety of bonds. Furthermore, stocks have tax advantages that are not available on bonds.[5]

There are fixed-income investments other than corporate bonds. Perhaps the most important of these are savings accounts at financial institutions. Savings accounts yield even less than the highest-grade corporate bonds, usually at least $\frac{3}{4}$ percent less per year and therefore savings accounts compare even less favorably on a return basis with stocks than do corporate bonds. United States government bonds, notes, and bills also yield less than do corporate bonds.

In spite of the yield disadvantage of all these fixed-income securities relative to stocks, it cannot be said that fixed-income securities are worse than stocks. It depends on the investor's taste for risk and return. For those who are very risk averse, it may be best to sacrifice the 5 percent or 6 percent in real return per year to avoid the high anxiety that

they may suffer from investing in stocks.

Since interest rates move up and down with changes in inflation, short-term fixed-income securities have been a good inflation hedge. As a security matures and the investor is paid off, the funds can be reinvested at the going interest rate in the market. In periods of significant inflation, short-term fixed-income securities have outperformed stocks. Of course, long-term fixed-income assets (those that mature far into the future) suffer price declines as interest rates rise (for example, due to inflation) and these securities do not represent a good hedge against unanticipated inflation.

KEEPING YOUR FEET ON THE GROUND

To paraphrase Will Rogers, land must be a very good investment, since the need for land is always growing but they aren't making much of the stuff anymore. How has real estate performed as an investment? It depends on the kind of real estate. The annual compound rate of increase in the price of a single-family house was 3.7 percent from 1890 to 1981 but, from 1944 to 1981 it was approximately 9 percent (stock prices rose at an average annual rate of about 6.3 percent from 1944 to 1981). From 1968 to 1988, the average annual housing price increase was 8.9 percent. However, keep in mind that the above rates of appreciation exclude the rental income that could be provided by a house. The basic point made here is that since World War II a single-family house has been a very good investment.

Farmland is an alternative form of real estate investment, one that has experienced significant price appreciation over the years. Reilly, Marquardt, and Price found that farm

---

[4] Ibbotsen, op. cit.

[5] A significant portion of the income on stocks is capital gains. The tax on capital gains can be postponed by not selling the stock. Most income on bonds is in the form of interest which is taxed in the year received (i.e., the tax cannot be postponed). Also, a corporation is taxed on only 20 percent of the dividends it receives from U.S. corporations, whereas the corporation pays taxes on all interest it receives on corporate debt securities it owns.

real estate in the United States increased at an average rate of 3.64 percent per year from 1919 to 1974.[6] However, since World War II farmland price increases have been significantly greater. From 1970 to 1990 the average annual increase was 6 percent.

Like homes and farmland, commercial, multifamily residential (apartments), and industrial real estate have been good hedges against inflation. Over long periods of time they have on average provided returns that have been competitive with stocks. A critical component of the returns on these types of properties is the tax benefit from depreciation, and, when significant changes in tax laws occur, property owners can be affected markedly. As with most investments, there are wide variations in returns depending on location and on the quality of property management.[7]

COLLECTING AND HOARDING FOR PROFIT

There are many kinds of assets which have historically been regarded as collectors' items or expensive consumption goods which have turned out to be extremely good investments. Examples include jewelry, precious metals, rare coins, photographs, clocks, stamps, paintings, antiques, books, and nostalgia. From the early 1970s to the end of the decade, some types of precious gems increased in value at rates between

[6] See Frank K. Reilly, Raymond Marquardt, and Donald Price, "Real Estate as an Inflation Hedge," *Review of Business and Economic Research*, vol. 12, no. 3 (Spring 1977), pp. 1–19.

[7] For an excellent review of real estate return studies see Stephen E. Roulac, "Can Real Estate Returns Outperform Common Stocks?" *The Journal of Portfolio Management* (Winter 1976), pp. 26–43.

10 percent and 20 percent per year. During the 1960s and 1970s, collectibles increased in value over 10 percent per year on average, far better than the return on stocks during the same time period. The following table shows the price increases for the 1970 to 1990 period for several of the more popular investments:

Investment	Compound annual increase in value from 1970 to 1990
Chinese ceramics	13.3%
Gold	11.5
Silver	5.5
Old master paintings	10.9
Coins	16.6
Diamonds	10.4
Consumer Price Index	6.3

Along with the potential for large gains, there are important disadvantages to the collecting-for-profit game. First, collectibles are very risky. For example, the early 1980s saw substantial declines in the prices of gold, silver, photography collections, and many other collectibles. Even during the 1960s and 1970s, some items experienced significant price declines and other items sat for years without any appreciation. Second, most collectibles generate no income during the holding period (no interest, dividends, etc.). Third, collectibles are very illiquid and selling commissions are ordinarily high—10 percent to 25 percent or even more. This means that an item must markedly increase in price just to cover the commission on resale. Fourth, obtaining sufficient knowledge—or expert advice—is more difficult with collectibles than with many other types of investments. The collectibles market is less perfect than, say, the market for investment-grade bonds or even stocks and it is very easy to overpay out of ignorance. The implication of all that is that, for most people, it is probably wise to put most of one's material wealth in other types of assets such as stocks, real estate, and bonds.

CHAPTER SIX

RISK AND RETURN

Risk is present whenever future events are not completely predictable and some events are preferable to others. In Chapter 5, we showed that the price of a security is the present value of the cash flows to the owner of the security, where the discount rate used in computing the present value reflects the risk of the cash flows. This chapter explores risk in more depth. We explain how risk can be measured and how it affects the discount rates in the security market. The following fundamental principle is presented:

The risk from investing in a financial asset depends on the relationship between the cash flows of that asset and the cash flows from other assets owned by an individual.

Associated with this principle is the concept of diversification, which is also developed in this chapter. We begin by looking at the problem of measuring risk.

MEASURING RISK: FUNDAMENTALS

In financial decisions it is often helpful to have an objective measure of risk. Such a measure should be independent of how much a given person dislikes risk. In other words, we would like to be able to separate the degree of risk in a situation from the feelings of different people toward bearing risk. We can then look at the question of how much risk is involved in a particular decision as a separate issue from the question of whether enough incentive is provided to warrant bearing the risk. The amount of incentive required for a given amount of risk will vary from person to person depending on how risk-averse each person is.

The main reason for having measures of risk is to enable us to make better decisions. To be useful, a risk measure should enable us to rank alternative risky ventures (such as investments). If there are two possibilities being analyzed, *A* and *B*, it is often important to know whether *A* is riskier than *B* or vice versa. A good measure of risk should also tell us *how much more risky A is than B*. Is *A* twice as risky or ten times as risky as *B*? Is *B* risky at all? It would be best if the risk measure had a value of zero for a riskless venture (a venture with future consequences that are now known with certainty). The risk measure should also increase numerically as the degree of risk increases.

Although we will begin our discussion by examining the case of investing in only one asset, investors are generally concerned with the risk of their total investment in many assets. The risk of investing in an asset depends on how that investment affects the overall risk of all the assets owned by the investor. For now let's assume that only one asset is owned; in a later section we will consider the implications of investing in more than one asset.

Risk and Probability Distributions

Risk measurement procedures are usually based on a particular method of organizing financial problems—through **probability distributions**. A probability distribution is a way to describe the possible future values for a quantity. In the following example we will describe a **discrete probability distribution**, which is a distribution of a variable that can have a limited (finite) number of values (for example, the number of phone calls your stockbroker will receive before noon tomorrow). Later, we will consider a **continuous probability distribution**, which is a probability distribution of a variable that can achieve any value over some range (for example, your broker's blood pressure at noon tomorrow).

Suppose you are thinking about purchasing stock A, which has a current price of $50 per share and pays no dividends. If you buy it, you plan to sell the stock one year from now. The return you will get when you sell depends only on the price of the stock at the time you sell. You therefore want to consider what price the stock might sell for in one year. To illustrate the concept of a discrete probability distribution, we will assume that there is a limited number of prices your stock might achieve one year from now. You decide there is no chance that the stock will sell for less than $40 per share or more than $80 per share. You estimate that there is one chance in ten or a 10 percent chance that the price will be $40, a 20 percent chance that the price will be $50, a 40 percent chance that it will be $60, a 20 percent chance that it will be $70, and a 10 percent chance that it will be $80. The result of this analysis is shown in Exhibit 6-1 and in Figure 6-1 with the "chances" shown as decimals (20 percent

EXHIBIT 6-1
Price of stock A *in one year*

Price of stock A	Probability
$40	.10
$50	.20
$60	.40
$70	.20
$80	.10

is 0.2). We have labeled the vertical axis as "probability," since the "chances" are probabilities, and what you have done is to develop a probability distribution for the price of the stock.

There are two characteristics of this probability distribution that are useful in deciding whether this stock is worth owning—the expected value and the standard deviation. The **expected value** or **mean** of a probability distribution measures the average value that the variable (stock price in this case) will have. We calculate the expected value by multiplying the probability of getting each price times that price and adding up the results for all possible prices. The general equation for the expected value is

$$\text{Expected value} = p_1X_1 + p_2X_2 + \cdots + p_nX_n \qquad (6\text{-}1)$$

where p_1 is the probability of obtaining amount X_1, p_2 is the probability of obtaining amount X_2, etc. In this example

$$\text{Expected value} = .1(\$40) + .2(\$50) + .4(\$60) + .2(\$70) + .1(\$80)$$

$$= \$60$$

Therefore the expected price is $60. However, we know that we may not be able to sell the stock for $60. There is uncertainty as to what the price really will be.

The **standard deviation** of a probability distribution measures the dispersion or variability around the expected value. The standard deviation is a measure of the reliability of the expected value and therefore a measure of the risk or uncertainty of the stock price. In other words, given an estimate of the future price as $60, the standard deviation measures how "fuzzy" that estimate is. The higher the standard deviation, the more fuzzy or spread out is the probability distribution. For example, the price of stock B in Figure 6-2b has a greater standard deviation than the price of stock A in Figure 6-2a. We are less certain about the price that will be achieved by stock B.

FIGURE 6-1

Probability distribution of the price of stock A.

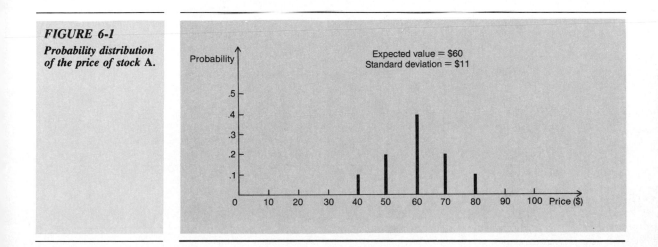

The standard deviation is computed by first taking the difference of each possible value from the expected value, squaring the differences, weighting the squared values by the probability of getting that price, and then summing the weighted squares. The sum is called the **variance** of the distribution and it can also be used to measure risk. The formula for the variance is

$$\text{Variance} = p_1(X_1 - \overline{X})^2 + p_2(X_2 - \overline{X})^2 + \cdots + p_n(X_n - \overline{X})^2 \quad (6\text{-}2)$$

where p_1 = the probability of X_1

p_2 = the probability of X_2, etc.

$\overline{X}$ = the expected value of the distribution

The standard deviation is the square root of the variance

$$\text{Standard deviation} = \sqrt{\text{variance}} \quad (6\text{-}3)$$

The standard deviation of the price of stock A (see Exhibit 6-1) is calculated as follows:

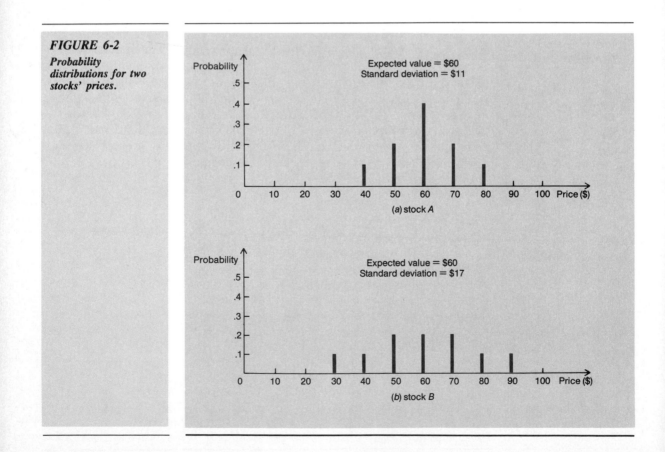

FIGURE 6-2

Probability distributions for two stocks' prices.

$$\text{Variance} = .1(\$40 - \$60)^2 + .2(\$50 - \$60)^2 + .4(\$60 - \$60)^2 \\ + .2(\$70 - \$60)^2 + .1(\$80 - \$60)^2$$

$$= .1(400)(\$^2) + .2(100)(\$^2) + .4(0)(\$^2) + .2(100)(\$^2) \\ + .1(400)(\$^2)$$

$$= 120(\$^2)$$

and

$$\text{Standard deviation} = \sqrt{120(\$^2)}$$

$$= \$10.95$$

Notice that, because we are squaring dollar quantities in computing the variance, we end up with "dollars squared" in the variance. The standard deviation—the square root of the variance—is expressed in dollars, not dollars squared. So the standard deviation of the price is approximately $11.

The Standard Deviation as a Risk Measure

There are four important features of the standard deviation as a measure of risk:

1 Only differences between the expected value and the values that can occur affect the size of the standard deviation. If only one value is possible, say, $60, it would have a probability of 1.0. The expected value would be $1.0(\$60) = \$60$ and the variance and standard deviation would be zero since $1.0(\$60 - \$60)^2 = 0$. Since there is no fuzziness to your estimate of $60, you are certain that the price will be $60 and there is no risk in this case. When there is no risk, the standard deviation is zero. If there is any risk at all, the standard deviation is greater than zero.

2 The differences are squared in the calculation. This means that prices far away from the expected value increase the standard deviation much more than those close to the expected value. (The square of a large number is very much greater than the square of a relatively small number.) Using the standard deviation as a measure of risk implies that big differences from the expected value involve much more risk than small differences.

3 The squared differences are multiplied by the probability that the actual value will deviate from the expected value. Therefore, the smaller the chance a particular value will occur, the less effect it has on the standard deviation.

4 The standard deviation is the square root of the sum of the squared differences (weighted by their probabilities). The standard deviation has the same measurement units as the expected value and can be compared directly with it.[1]

---

[1] The standard deviation is a more convenient measure of risk than the variance for this reason. The variance is in terms of dollars squared.

Now that we have developed the standard deviation as a measure of risk, what can we use it for? First, it tells us something about how uncertain the price is. For most probability distributions there is very little chance that the actual value will be more than twice the standard deviation away from the expected value. In the stock A example, two times the standard deviation of $11 is $22. In this example, the price is certain to be between $38 ($60 − $22) and $82 ($60 + $22). We can also look at the standard deviation relative to the expected value.[2] In the example the standard deviation is 18 percent of the expected value ($11/$60 = 0.18). This tells us that the actual price is likely to be fairly close to the expected price of $60. There is only moderate uncertainty. If the standard deviation were 1 percent of the expected price instead of 18 percent, there is little uncertainty as to what the price will be. If the standard deviation were 50 percent of the expected price, then there would be a great deal of uncertainty.

The standard deviation can also be used to compare two alternatives. Suppose you evaluated stock B and came up with the probability distribution shown in Figure 6-2b. A comparison with the probability distribution for stock A in Figure 6-2a (same as stock A in Figure 6-1) should lead you to the conclusion that the future price of stock B is more uncertain than the future price of stock A.

Stock B has an expected value of $60 and a standard deviation of $17, as compared with stock A, which has the same expected value and a standard deviation of $11. The standard deviation for B is larger, which reflects the greater "spreading out" of the probability distribution of B's future price. Therefore, much more uncertainty exists about the actual future price of stock B than about that of stock A.

Rates of Return

The above examples illustrate the uncertainty in future prices. However, this uncertainty is also directly translated into uncertainty about the rates of return which will be earned by an investor. For example, given that the current price of stock A is $50, let's convert the *future* prices in Exhibit 6-1 and Figure 6-1 into rates of return. An actual price of $40 at the end of the year would provide a rate of return of ($40 − $50)/$50 = −0.2 or −20 percent. That is, we had $50 invested in the stock at the beginning of the year and ended up with only $40 at the end of the year, a loss of 20 percent. We can convert all the prices into their equivalent rates of return as shown in Exhibit 6-2. We now have a "new" probability distribution as shown in Figure 6-3. Again the standard deviation is in the same units (percent) as the expected rate of return, and its value of 22 percent measures the uncertainty as to the expected rate of return of 20 percent.

Rates of return are frequently used in analyzing securities such as stocks and bonds. The basic point here is that we can translate uncertain

---

[2] The ratio of the standard deviation to the expected value is called the **coefficient of variation** and is sometimes used as a separate measure of risk. The coefficient of variation is discussed further in Chap. 10.

EXHIBIT 6-2

Probability distribution of rate of return on stock A

Future price	$40	$50	$60	$70	$80
Rate of return, %	−20	0	20	40	60
Probability	.1	.2	.4	.2	.1

future dollar values into their corresponding percentage rates of return given the price of the asset. We can also obtain the mean and standard deviation of the rate of return by dividing the dollar amounts by the current price. For example, the 22 percent standard deviation of the rate of return can be calculated as $11/$50.

Continuous Probability Distributions

Whenever you are dealing with a variable, such as the rate of return on a stock that can take a large number of possible values, you may wish to use a *continuous* probability distribution instead of the discrete distributions shown in Figures 6-1, 6-2, and 6-3. Since stock prices are quoted in eighths of a dollar, there are 320 (8 × 40) possible stock prices in the range of $40 to $80 for a stock and hence 320 possible rates of return in this range. If the stock might pay a dividend that is also uncertain, the number of possible rates of return would increase enormously. In Figure 6-4, a continuous distribution for the rate of return on stock *A* is shown along with the discrete distribution of Figure 6-3.

In a continuous distribution the probability of obtaining a single value such as a rate of return of precisely 10.0 percent is nil. Instead, we measure the probability of obtaining any value within a specified range as the area under the curve. For example, in Figure 6-4 the probability of obtaining a rate of return between 10 percent and 30 percent is .4 (the shaded area under the curve between the 10 percent and 30 percent rates of return in Figure 6-4). This is the same as the .4 probability of obtaining a 20 percent rate of return in the discrete distribution of Figure 6-3.

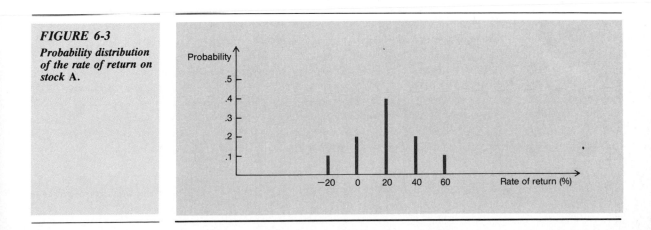

FIGURE 6-3

Probability distribution of the rate of return on stock A.

Continuous distributions are usually described by summary measures such as the expected value and standard deviation. The calculation of these measures for continuous distributions is a topic for statistics courses.

PORTFOLIO RISK AND DIVERSIFICATION

The Diversification Concept

"Don't put all your eggs in one basket" is a simple way to express the desirability of **diversification**. Diversification means investing in at least two assets that differ. If all your money is invested in one risky asset, the rate of return you earn depends solely on what happens to the income and market value of that one asset. If you invest in two nonidentical assets, in order for you to get a low or negative return on your money, both investments must turn out badly. Taken individually, each asset might be equally risky. However, if you put half of your money in one and half in another, you may come out with less risk on your total investment than you would have by investing all your money in a single asset. This is so because high returns from one asset may offset low returns from the other. Investors, both individuals and firms, are concerned with the risk of their total investment, and diversification can reduce this risk.

To see how diversification can reduce or even eliminate risk, imagine that you are considering investing $200 in the stock of two different companies—a taxicab company and a bus company. During boom times, people ride in taxis and the taxi company does well, but the bus company does poorly. In recessions, people take the bus and the bus company does well, but the taxi company does poorly. Assume that the probability of boom is .5 and the probability of recession is also .5. The rates of return from the two stocks are shown in Exhibit 6-3. The expected rate of return from investing in each stock is 10 percent (.5 × 40% + .5 × −20%) and investing $200 in either stock by itself is risky. However, suppose that you put $100 in taxi stock and $100 in bus stock. During boom times, your investment in taxi stock will earn $40 but your investment in bus stock will lose $20, for a net return of $20 on

---

FIGURE 6-4

Continuous and discrete probability distributions of the rate of return on stock A.

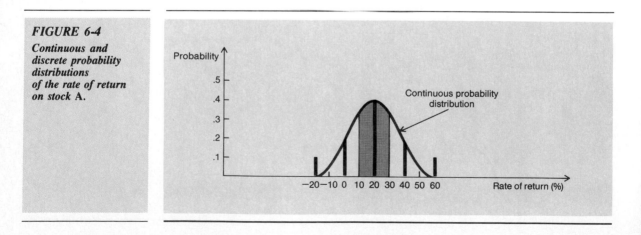

your investment of $200 or 10 percent ($20/$200). In recessions, your investment in bus stock will earn $40 but your investment in taxi stock will lose $20, again for a net return of $20 or 10 percent. Therefore, regardless of what happens to the economy, you earn 10 percent on your investment and have eliminated risk.

Risk was eliminated through diversification in this example because a high return from the taxi stock was associated with a low return from the bus stock and vice versa. The statistical term for this behavior is perfect negative correlation. **Correlation** is a measure of the degree to which two variables, such as the rates of return on two stocks, move together.[3] It takes on numerical values that range between -1.0 and 1.0. In the taxicab-bus example above, the correlation was -1.0. Whenever a high return for one stock tends to occur at the same time a low return occurs for another stock, the correlation between the two stocks is negative (less than zero). If a high return for one stock tends to occur when a high return occurs for another stock, the correlation between the two is positive (greater than zero). For example, suppose a yacht company stock will return 60 percent in a boom economy and -40 percent in a recession. The yacht stock's returns are positively correlated (correlation of 1.0) with the returns from the taxi stock. A zero correlation would describe a situation when there is no particular relationship between the returns.

---

[3] The correlation between two variables X and Y is calculated in two steps. First, the **covariance** is calculated. The covariance is a direct measure of the relationship between the two variables. It is expressed in the product of the units of X and Y, for example, $\$^2$.

$$\text{Covariance} = p_1(X_1 - \overline{X})(Y_1 - \overline{Y}) + p_2(X_2 - \overline{X}Y_2 - \overline{Y}) + \cdots + p_n(X_n - \overline{X})(Y_n - \overline{Y})$$

where X_1 and Y_1 are a pair of values for X and Y occurring with probability p_1; X_2 and Y_2 are another pair of values occurring with probability p_2, etc. $\overline{X}$ and $\overline{Y}$ are the expected values of X and Y, respectively. Second, the standard deviations of X and Y are calculated according to the procedure explained earlier in the chapter. Let SD_X be the standard deviation of X and SD_Y be the standard deviation of Y. The correlation of X and Y is:

$$\text{Correlation} = \frac{\text{covariance}}{\text{SD}_X\ \text{SD}_Y}$$

EXHIBIT 6-3
Rates of return on investing in taxicab stock, bus stock, and both taxicab and bus stocks

		Rate of return earned		
	Probability	Invest all in taxicab stock	Invest all in bus stock	Invest half in each of taxicab and bus stocks
Boom	.5	40%	-20%	10%
Recession	.5	-20%	40%	10%

Two points were illustrated by the example. First, diversification is a way of reducing risk. By owning more than one security, you were able to eliminate all risk in the example. Unfortunately, negative correlations among security returns are quite rare since the returns of most securities available to investors tend to be dependent on the behavior of the overall economy. Therefore, security returns tend to be positively correlated, but with a correlation less than 1.0. Statistical studies of stock returns indicate that most stocks in the United States have a correlation with the United States stock market which lies somewhere between 0.5 and 0.6. Diversification can reduce risk but not eliminate it. The second point is that an investor should not be concerned about the risk of individual securities, but rather with the risk of the investor's total portfolio of securities, and with how investing in a particular security affects the risk of the entire portfolio.

International Diversification

If diversification among the securities of domestic firms reduces risk, it would seem that diversifying internationally would be even better. To the extent that foreign economies do not move in concert with the domestic economy, diversification into the securities of firms doing business in those economies is desirable. It is not even necessary to purchase securities in overseas markets, although many investors choose this method. Within the major securities markets around the world, it is possible to purchase stock in large multinational corporations that do business in many different countries. The United States securities markets offer several choices for achieving international diversification. In addition to stocks of U.S.–based multinational firms, stocks of over 100 foreign corporations are traded in the United States. In addition there are many mutual funds that have portfolios of foreign securities including several that specialize in particular countries. These are popular with foreign investors that lack the ability to achieve such diversification within their own domestic markets.

However, international diversification is not perfect. First, there is some added risk in foreign securities due to exchange rate changes that is not present for domestic securities. Second, the increase in economic dependencies among countries has reduced the advantages of international diversification. For example, the October 1987 stock market crash in the United States was echoed in stock markets around the world. Although there are still some risk-reduction opportunities through international diversification, investors cannot escape the risk of the global economy.

With these points in mind, let's examine how the risk and return on a portfolio is affected by the securities in it.

Portfolio Risk and Return

The rate of return from a portfolio of securities is the weighted average of the returns from the individual securities included in it. The weights are the proportions of each security in the portfolio. For example, if you invest 40 percent of your money in a stock that returns 20 percent and 60 percent of your money in a stock that returns 5 percent, the actual return on your total investment in this portfolio will be

Actual return $= 0.4(20\%) + 0.6(5\%)$

$= 11\%$

The actual return on a portfolio tells you how well your investment has performed in the past. However, if you are trying to decide what to invest in, you are concerned with the *future* performance of your portfolio and should calculate the expected rate of return. The computation procedure for the expected returns is similar to the one used to find the actual return. Suppose that you had expected to earn 15 percent on the security that constitutes 40 percent of the portfolio and had expected to earn 10 percent on the security that constitutes 60 percent of the portfolio. Your expected return on the portfolio was

Expected rate of return $= 0.4(15\%) + 0.6(10\%)$

$= 12\%$

The general formula for the expected rate of return on a portfolio of n securities ($\bar{r}_P$) is simply

$$\bar{r}_P = w_1\bar{r}_1 + w_2\bar{r}_2 + \cdots + w_n\bar{r}_n \tag{6-4}$$

where $w_1 =$ the proportion invested in security 1, etc.

$\bar{r}_1 =$ the expected rate of return on security 1, etc.

The formula for the standard deviation of the rate of return on a portfolio of n securities is rather complicated, since it contains the standard deviations of each security and the correlations between every pair of securities.[4] Instead of presenting it, we shall show numerically how diversification affects portfolio risk as measured by the standard deviation.

Suppose that you currently own stock A, which has a probability distribution of its rate of return as was shown in Figure 6-3. All your money is invested in this stock; thus the expected rate of return on your

---

[4] The standard deviation for a two-security portfolio (SD_P) is calculated as the square root of the variance of the portfolio's rate of return. The variance is calculated as

$(SD_P)^2 = w_1^2 SD_1^2 + w_2^2 SD_2^2 + 2w_1w_2 \, Corr_{12} \, SD_1 \, SD_2$

where

$w_1 =$ the proportion invested in security 1

$w_2 =$ the proportion invested in security 2 ($w_2 = 1 - w_1$ in this case)

SD_1 and $SD_2 =$ the standard deviations of the rates of return on securities 1 and 2, respectively

$Corr_{12} =$ the correlation between the returns on securities 1 and 2

Then

$SD_P = \sqrt{(SD_P)^2}$

total investment is the expected rate of return on stock A, 20 percent. The standard deviation of the rate of return on stock A, and therefore on your total investment, is 22 percent. You are considering diversifying your investment by selling half of the shares you own in A and purchasing stock C. Half your investment will be in stock A and half in stock C. Stock C also has an expected rate of return of 20 percent and a standard deviation of 22 percent, the same as for stock A. Will you gain any advantage from this restructuring of your portfolio of stock?

First you should note from Eq. (6-4) that the expected rate of return on the new portfolio of A and C (r_{AC}) will be 20 percent, because both securities have an expected rate of return of 20 percent. The weighted average rate of return is 20 percent since, using Eq. (6-4):

$$\bar{r}_{AC} = .5(\bar{r}_A) + .5(\bar{r}_C)$$

$$= .5(20\%) + .5(20\%)$$

$$= 20\%$$

Any benefit from diversification in this case must result from a reduction in risk as measured by standard deviation. If there is to be a benefit, the standard deviation of the rate of return on the portfolio of A and C must be lower than 22 percent, which is the standard deviation of each of A and C owned individually. Will any reduction occur? The answer depends on the correlation between the rate of return on A and the rate of return on C.

The standard deviation of the portfolio of A and C for all possible values of the correlation is shown in Figure 6-5.[5] We assume in the figure that the investment is half in A and half in C, and that stocks A and C each have an expected return of 20 percent and a standard deviation of return of 22 percent. If the returns from stock A and stock C have a correlation of 1.0, then the rate of return on a portfolio of A and C together has the same standard deviation as the rate of return of stock A by itself. In this case purchasing stock C is no different from keeping all your investment in stock A because stock C achieves the same rate of return that stock A does. For example, if A has a rate of return of -20 percent, C also has a rate of return of -20 percent. In practice, the returns from two different stocks will never be perfectly correlated; most likely the correlation of returns will be greater than zero but less than

---

[5] All results reported here and in Figure 6-5 are based on the formula in footnote 4. For example, we calculate the standard deviation of the portfolio consisting of 50 percent stock A and 50 percent stock C, when the correlation between A and C is 0.5, as follows:

$$(SD_P)^2 = w_A^2 \, SD_A^2 + w_C^2 \, SD_C^2 + 2w_A \, w_C \, Corr_{AC} \, SD_A \, SD_C$$

$$= (0.5)^2 \, (22\%)^2 + (0.5)^2 \, (22\%)^2 + 2(0.5)(0.5)(0.4)(22\%)(22\%)$$

$$= 338.8 \, (\%)^2$$

$$= \sqrt{338.8 \, (\%)^2}$$

Therefore,

$$SD_P = 18.4\%$$

1.0. *The positive correlation of stock returns is due to the dependence of returns of most stocks on general economic conditions.* Suppose the correlation between the returns on stock A and stock C is 0.4. In this case, the standard deviation of the returns on the portfolio of A and C is 18.4 percent, less than the standard deviation of the individual stocks. Thus there is an advantage to diversifying by owning two stocks rather than one. Indeed, such an advantage will obtain for all correlations less than 1.0. An implication of this simple example is that the correlation of the returns from a single asset with the returns from the other assets held by the investor strongly influences the risk of the total portfolio. The lower the correlation, the more effective is diversification.

Finding securities with low correlations is difficult; however, there is another way to reduce risk—increasing the number of securities in the portfolio. Increasing the diversification of a portfolio by adding additional securities whose returns are not perfectly correlated with the returns of the other securities can reduce portfolio risk up to a point. This diversification effect is illustrated in Figure 6-6. We assume in this figure that each stock has (individually) an expected return of 20 percent and a standard deviation of 22 percent, the same as for stocks A and C above, and that the correlation between each pair of stock returns is 0.5. Each stock in a given portfolio is owned in equal dollar amounts. Thus, in a five-stock portfolio, 20 percent is invested in each of the five stocks.

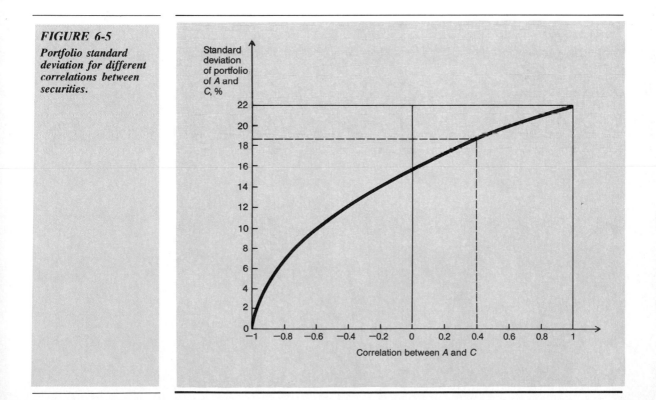

FIGURE 6-5

Portfolio standard deviation for different correlations between securities.

Figure 6-6 shows that increased diversification reduces portfolio risk. Note, however, that investing in more than ten stocks reduces risk only slightly below the level for the ten-stock portfolios. It does not take a great deal of diversification to obtain most of the benefits.

Our analysis to this point can be summarized as follows:

1 Investors who dislike risk should be concerned about the standard deviation of the rate of return on their total investment portfolios. *An implication is that, in evaluating the risk of a particular asset, what matters is how that asset affects the risk of the entire portfolio.*
2 Diversification reduces portfolio risk.
3 The contribution of an individual asset to portfolio risk depends on the standard deviation of the asset's returns, the correlation of the asset's returns with returns of the other assets in the portfolio, and the proportion of the portfolio represented by that asset.

The technique of determining how to put together a desirable investment portfolio is beyond the scope of this text. However, we have covered the basic principles here. Now we shall see what they imply for the pricing of securities in the marketplace assuming that the market is dominated by investors who understand these principles.

FIGURE 6-6

*Impact on portfolio
standard deviation of
diversification among
positively correlated
securities.*

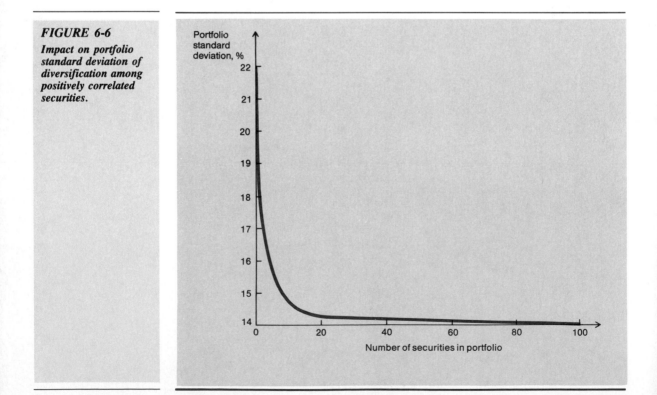

We showed in Figure 6-6 that there was a limit to the amount of risk reduction that can be achieved by diversification among positively correlated securities. This is a mathematical result and one might ask how well it applies to actual stocks. Imagine performing the following experiment. Choose *at random* portfolios of common stocks from the newspaper, each portfolio containing a *different* number of stocks. Track the performance of each portfolio by computing both its actual annual rate of return each year for several years and the standard deviation of its annual returns.[6] Now plot the standard deviation for each portfolio against the number of stocks in the portfolio. The results will look like those shown in Figure 6-7, which is very similar to Figure 6-6. Figure 6-7 shows that diversification, at least of this random variety, will eliminate some but not all risk from a portfolio. The only risk remaining in a well-diversified portfolio is the risk of the market as a whole (since a well-diversified portfolio is a cross section of the total market). This means that the returns from all well-diversified portfolios are highly correlated

---

[6] The standard deviation of the returns from a particular portfolio indicates how much the returns from the portfolio fluctuated from year to year over the time period studied. If the time period studied was from 1973 to 1988, to compute the portfolio's standard deviation we would first compute the average annual rate of return on the portfolio over the sixteen-year period (equal to the sum of the annual rates of return divided by sixteen). We would then use Eq. (6-2) to compute the variance, where in Eq. (6-2): $\overline{X}$ = the average annual rate of return on the portfolio over the sixteen-year period; $p_1 = p_2 = \cdots = p_{16} = \frac{1}{16}$; and X_1 = portfolio rate of return in 1973, X_2 = portfolio rate of return in 1974, . . . , X_{16} = portfolio rate of return in 1988. The standard deviation equals the square root of the variance.

FIGURE 6-7

Impact on portfolio standard deviation of random diversification.

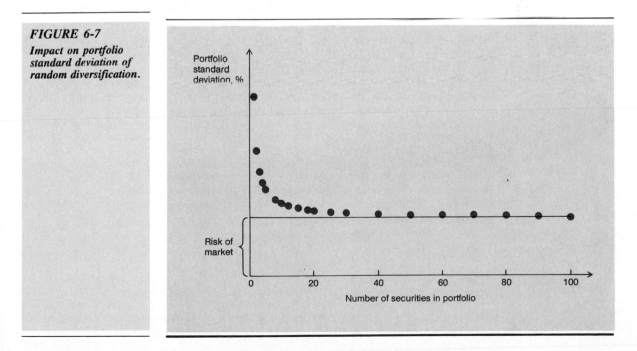

(close to 1.0) and therefore move up and down together with the entire market.

Beta as a Measure of Risk

Let's assume that investors are diversified.[7] We know from the previous section that an investor is concerned with the risk of his or her entire portfolio, and that the relevant risk of a particular security is the effect the security has on the risk of the entire portfolio. This leads us to the following important proposition:

The contribution of a security to the risk of a diversified portfolio is measured by the security's beta. The higher a security's beta, the more the security raises the risk of the diversified portfolio.

A security's beta indicates how closely the security's returns move with the returns from a diversified portfolio. Since the returns from a diversified portfolio move with the market as a whole, beta also measures how closely the security's returns move with the market.[8] Securities differ in their risk and therefore in their betas. A beta of 1.0 for a given stock means that, if the total value of stocks in the market moves up by 10 percent, the stock's price will also move up, on average, by 10 percent, and if the market declines by 10 percent, the stock's price will decline, on average, by 10 percent. If a stock has a beta of 2.0, its price will, on average, rise by 20 percent when the market rises by 10 percent and fall by 20 percent when the market falls by 10 percent. And a stock with a beta of 0.5 will on average rise or fall by 5 percent as the market rises or falls by 10 percent, respectively. A stock with a -0.5 beta will, on average, rise by 10 percent when the market *falls* by 20 percent, and on average fall by 10 percent when the market rises by 20 percent (negative beta securities are extremely rare). The beta of the market as a whole is 1.0. The beta of a fully diversified portfolio of risky assets is also 1.0 since it is simply a sample of the market as a whole.

---

[7] By "diversified" we mean that each investor's portfolio is representative of the market as a whole and that the portfolio's beta is 1.0. The same basic arguments hold as long as investors' portfolios are perfectly correlated with the market. Under certain conditions (for example, those assumed in deriving the Capital Asset Pricing Model, which is described in detail in Appendix 6A), investors who own any risky assets are best off with portfolios that are representative of the market or perfectly correlated with the market. As illustrated in Figure 6-7, ownership of even a small number of securities can provide close to complete diversification. Even if investors are not fully diversified in the sense just described (with portfolios that are identical to or perfectly correlated with the market) but are only fairly well diversified, the general concepts presented in this chapter still hold as good approximations.

[8] Beta for stock J is usually defined as

$$\text{Beta}_J = \frac{\text{Corr}_{JM}\,\text{SD}_J}{\text{SD}_M}$$

where Corr_{JM} is the correlation of stock J's return with the market return; SD_J is the standard deviation of stock J's return; and SD_M is the standard deviation of the market's return. Alternatively, beta for a security is the covariance of the security's rate of return with the rate of return on the market divided by the variance of the market's rate of return. Thus beta is simply the scaled covariance of the security's rate of return.

The beta of any portfolio of securities is the weighted average of the betas of the securities, where the weights are the proportions invested in each security. For example, if $400 is invested in stock A and $600 is invested in stock B (40 percent in A and 60 percent in B), and if A has a beta of 1.0 and B has a beta of 1.5, then the portfolio made up of A and B has a beta of:

Beta of the combined investment in A and B = .4(1.0) + .6(1.5) = 1.3

Thus, the beta of a diversified portfolio (beta = 1.0) is simply the weighted average of the betas of a large number of securities that are representative of the market (these securities comprising the diversified portfolio).

The above description of beta helps us see why beta makes sense as a measure of a security's risk. Assume that you already own a diversified portfolio of securities (portfolio's beta = 1.0) and are considering adding one more security, say stock Z. Since your portfolio is diversified, we know (from the discussion a couple of paragraphs ago) that the returns from your portfolio move with the market's overall returns (i.e., up and down together). What will adding stock Z do to the risk of your portfolio? If stock Z has a high beta (beta greater than 1.0), that is, on average its price moves closely and sharply with the market, it also on average moves closely and sharply with the value of your diversified portfolio. But that means that it will increase your portfolio's risk by making your portfolio's value bounce up and down more violently than it would if stock Z were not in the portfolio. It follows that, *for a diversified investor, a high-beta security is a high-risk security because adding it to the portfolio increases the risk of the portfolio.*

On the other hand, if stock Z has a low beta (beta less than 1.0) or a negative beta (beta less than 0.0), its returns on average do not move closely with the market or with your diversified portfolio. Indeed, the value of a negative beta stock on average moves contrary to the value of your portfolio, and therefore the stock reduces the risk of the total portfolio. The lesson here is that, *for a diversified investor, a low- or negative-beta security is a low-risk security because adding it to the portfolio reduces the risk of the portfolio.*[9]

How do you determine the beta of a particular stock? A stock's beta can be estimated statistically from the history of its returns. Betas for most companies with publicly traded stock are available in publications such as the *Value Line Investment Survey* and *Standard & Poor's Stock Reports*. These betas are calculated for the United States stock market; that is, they do not consider the potential for international diversification by United States investors. Some estimates of betas for different stocks

---

[9] As a technical note, if the investor's portfolio is representative of the market (i.e., is diversified, as assumed here), it must already contain a small amount of security Z (or a security like Z). It can be shown mathematically that the contribution of security Z to the investor's diversified portfolio's risk, given that security Z is a small fraction of that portfolio, can be measured by security Z's beta.

are shown in Table 6-1. Note, however, that here betas are estimated from historical data. The beta for a firm's stock can shift over time, due to changes in the investment and financing policies of the firm and other changes in the economic condition of the firm and its industry (for example, deregulation).

Let's summarize. We have made the following points about beta as a measure of risk:

1 The value of a diversified portfolio moves with the market as a whole (up and down together).
2 Beta measures how sharply and closely a security's price moves on average with the market, and therefore (given point 1) beta measures how closely a security's price moves with the returns from a diversified portfolio.

TABLE 6-1
Beta values for selected common stocks

Company	Beta	Company	Beta
American Express	1.35	IBM	.95
Anheuser-Busch	.95	Kellogg	1.00
Apple Computer	1.35	Lockheed	1.20
AVON Products	1.00	Merrill Lynch & Co.	1.20
BankAmerica Corp.	1.00	Navistar International	1.25
Bethlehem Steel	1.50	National Semiconductor	1.45
Caesars World	1.45	Polaroid	1.25
Caterpillar Tractor	1.20	Proctor & Gamble	.90
Coca-Cola	.95	Savannah Foods	.60
Con. Edison	.70	Sears, Roebuck	1.15
Control Data	1.25	Texas Instruments	1.40
Deere & Co.	1.10	Tootsie Roll Ind.	1.05
Exxon Corporation	.80	U.S. Steel (USX)	1.00
Federal Express	1.10	Wang Labs-B	1.30
Ford Motor	1.15	Woolworth	1.20
General Motors	.95	Xerox	1.20
Goodyear Tire	1.15	Zenith Electronics	1.45
Homestake Mining	.65		
Hughes Supply	.95		

Source: Value Line Investment Survey, August 18, 1989

3   Adding a high-beta (beta greater than 1.0) security to a diversified portfolio increases the portfolio's risk, and adding a low-beta (beta less than 1.0) or negative-beta (beta less than 0.0) security to a diversified portfolio reduces the portfolio's risk.

We can conclude that, in a world of well-diversified investors, a security's beta is an important indicator of risk, and therefore a determinant of what people are willing to pay for the security. In the next section, we discuss security markets and beta.

The Security Market Line

We now have a measure of risk for individual stocks (beta) that is appropriate for diversified investors who care only about the risk of their total portfolio as measured by the standard deviation of the rate of return on the portfolio. We observe that investors are generally risk-averse (that is, they prefer less risk to more risk) and not willing to bear risk without getting something for it. For securities, that something is a higher expected rate of return. However, in a market dominated by diversified investors, the relevant risk for an individual stock is how the stock's value moves with the market, which we measured by beta. Given some additional conditions that are discussed in Appendix 6A, we can arrive at a theory of market risk and return called the Capital Asset Pricing Model (CAPM). The CAPM says that properly priced securities should provide an expected rate of return to investors equal to the rate of interest on riskless securities (U.S. Treasury bills) plus a premium for bearing risk. The risk is measured by the security's beta. Any security with a beta of 1.0, the same as the beta for the entire market, will have an expected rate of return equal to the rate of return expected on average for the market. In the CAPM there is a linear relationship between a stock's beta and the expected rate of return on that stock. This relationship is called the security market line and is shown in Figure 6-8.

The security market line shows the current risk-return tradeoff in the market. It should be thought of as showing what expected rates of return must be provided to investors to compensate them for bearing risk. In other words, the security market line indicates the "going" rate of return in the market for a given amount of risk. Every security having that amount of risk should provide the same expected rate of return to investors; this expected rate of return is equal to the rate of return required for that degree of risk.

We can see this more clearly by expressing the security market line as an equation.

$$k_J = i + (k_M - i)\text{beta}_J \tag{6-5}$$

where k_J = the required rate of return for security J

i = the riskfree rate of interest

k_M = the expected rate of return for the market as a whole

beta_J = security J's beta value

The symbol k will be used throughout the book to represent a rate of return required by investors in the security markets. In the CAPM, a properly priced security will provide an expected rate of return equal to the rate of return required for all securities having the same beta. If this is not true, the price will change. For example, suppose that the stock of Felix Industries has a beta of 1.5 and that the current rate of interest on U.S. Treasury securities (which is usually taken to be the riskfree rate) is 7.8 percent. The difference between the market rate of return and the riskless rate ($k_M - i$) is called the market risk premium. Assume that the market risk premium is estimated to be 6.1 percent based on historical rates of return. This security market line with a riskfree rate of 7.8 percent and a market risk premium of 6.1 percent is shown in Figure 6-9. The rate of return required in the market for stocks with a beta of 1.5 is:

$$k_J = i + (k_M - i)\, \text{beta}_J$$
$$= 7.8\% + (6.1\%)1.5$$
$$= 17\%$$

Suppose that the average investor in the market expects that Felix will pay a $2.00 dividend in one year's time and that the expected price of Felix stock in the market in one year is $28. The current price of Felix stock is $25. Thus the rate of return expected by the average investor for Felix is 20 percent, where this rate is calculated as follows:

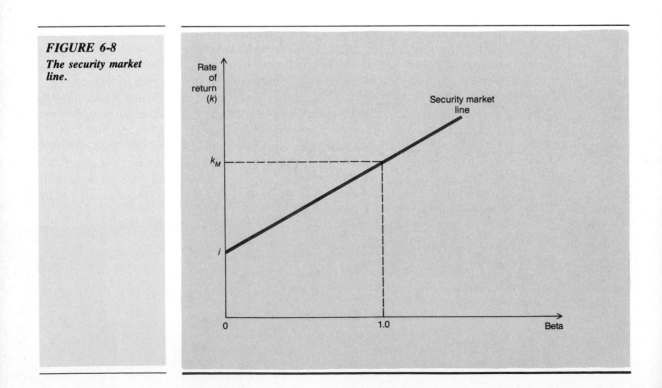

FIGURE 6-8
The security market line.

$$\text{Expected rate of return} = \frac{\$28 + \$2 - \$25}{\$25}$$

$$= 20\%$$

Felix stock is underpriced as it provides too high an expected rate of return relative to the required rate of return. Felix stock has an expected rate of return that plots above the security market line in Figure 6-9. Investors can only expect to obtain 17 percent on other stocks in the market with a beta of 1.5, so they will be eager to buy Felix stock with its expected rate of return of 20 percent. In an efficient market, this underpricing will not persist as investors will bid the price up quickly. The price will adjust until the expected rate of return equals 17 percent. The price for which this is true can be calculated as the present value of the future dollar returns discounted at 17 percent, i.e.,

$$\text{Price} = \frac{\$28 + \$2}{1.17}$$

$$= \$25.64$$

A price of \$25.64 for Felix stock provides an expected rate of return of 17 percent. Notice that we are using the same basic concept of the market price of a security's being the present value of its cash returns that was introduced in Chapter 5. We discount the expected return (price plus dividend) at the market discount rate of 17 percent to find the current price that provides an expected rate of return of 17 percent to the investor.

The rates of return shown by the security market line are interest rates that have been adjusted for risk. Their magnitudes are determined by the activities of all investors in the market. The market risk premium

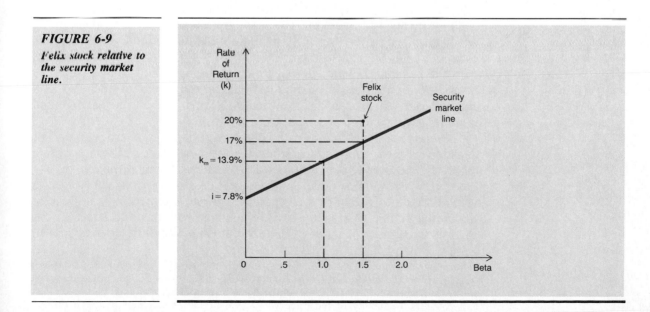

FIGURE 6-9

Felix stock relative to the security market line.

depends on the attitudes of investors toward bearing risk. The riskfree rate depends on the overall supply and demand for money in the economy. The security market line rates apply at a given point in time and are subject to change with changes in the economy. In particular we know that riskfree interest rates can change dramatically over relatively short periods of time. We know little about how the market risk premium changes and usually assume that it is constant.

Implications and Applications of the CAPM

The CAPM expresses the following important ideas in a relatively simple way:

1 The required rate of return on all financial assets depends in part on the riskless rate of interest.
2 Investors should be concerned primarily with risks that cannot be diversified away by holding portfolios of securities rather than single securities.
3 Investors require a premium for bearing risk, and the risk premium for a security is equal to the market risk premium times the security's beta, which measures its relative market risk.
4 If all investors are risk-averse and have similar expectations, the only way to increase the expected return from an investment in securities is to take on increased risk. Conversely, the higher the risk, the greater is the expected return.

The CAPM wraps up these ideas in a tidy package summarized by the security market line in Eq. (6-5). The CAPM is used in several ways. In Chapter 7, we show how the CAPM and beta may be used to estimate the required rate of return on a company's common stock. In Chapter 10, we discuss its application in the evaluation of risky investment projects involving real assets (as compared to financial assets). In Chapter 12, the CAPM is used to explain why the use of debt (borrowed funds) by business firms increases the risk and, therefore, increases the rate of return required by the firm's stockholders. In addition, the CAPM can be used as a basis for measuring how successful the manager of a securities portfolio has been. Financial researchers have used the model to analyze a variety of important problems in financial management and also as a way of controlling for risk in empirical research. These topics are treated in more advanced finance courses.

Although the CAPM has proved to be quite useful, there remains the question of how well it describes the pricing of securities in actual markets. The answer is that no one is quite sure. A big problem in testing the CAPM is that the model is based on investor expectations and it is very difficult to measure and evaluate people's expectations. Despite this problem and others, the CAPM has been supported to some extent by tests using historical data.[10] The market risk premium does appear to

---

[10] Several tests of the CAPM are presented and discussed in M. C. Jensen (ed.), *Studies in the Theory of Capital Markets* (New York: Praeger, 1972). For a critique of the empirical work, see Richard Roll, ''A Critique of the Asset Pricing Theory's Tests: Part 1: On Past and Potential Testability of the Theory,'' *Journal of Financial Economics*, 4 (March 1977), pp. 129–176.

be positive and beta seems to be the best single measure of risk; however, we cannot explain very well the risk premiums that are observed. The empirical validity of the CAPM remains controversial. Financial experts recognize that the CAPM is too simple, and more complicated asset-pricing models have been developed. However, simplicity is itself an advantage in dealing with difficult problems. The model does contain some of the most important elements of financial analysis under risk, and for many practical and research problems it is still the best model available.

ADVANCED PRICING MODELS

Although the CAPM is useful in many applications, it does not work well for every financial asset. In particular, it does not apply to complex securities, such as convertible bonds, that involve an option to acquire another asset, such as common stock. A different approach is required for complex securities; see Chapter 22 and the essay on options that follows it. In addition, many people believe that the CAPM is too simple to describe fully the pricing of even basic securities like common stock. The CAPM assumes that all risk in owning a security can be summarized in a single measure, beta, that relates the security's returns to the market's return. These people argue that more than one factor is involved in asset pricing and that a more elaborate model is required. The current contender for the title "best asset pricing model" is called Arbitrage Pricing Theory (APT).

APT specifies that one or more basic economic factors influence the returns on securities, rather than necessarily only one factor, as in the CAPM. These factors can include, for example, changes in U.S. industrial production, inflation, and the term structure of interest rates. Securities may vary in the degree to which they are influenced by the factors, and therefore they may differ in risk. Investors try to achieve as high an expected return as possible at any given level of exposure. The result is that, in equilibrium, the expected return on each security is a function of the sensitivity of the security's return to each factor.

For example, suppose that there are three (and only three) factors affecting security returns. Under APT, the expected rate of return on security j (k_j) is:

$$k_j = a + p_1 b_{1j} + p_2 b_{2j} + p_3 b_{3j}$$

where the p's are the market risk premiums that apply to each factor and the b's measure the sensitivity of the security's return to the factor. For example, if $p_1 = .03$ and $b_{1j} = 2$, then security j's expected return is increased by 6 percent (2 × .03) because of its sensitivity to factor 1. The b's are conceptually similar to the CAPM beta of a security, which measures the sensitivity of a security's return to the return on the market portfolio. Therefore APT can be described as having one or more betas with appropriate risk premiums—one for each economic factor that is priced in the market—in contrast to the CAPM, which has only a single beta and market risk premium.

APT does not tell us what the factors are, however. It is an abstract theory that leaves the definition of the factors to empirical analysis. Indeed it is possible that APT describes the behavior of markets accurately but that the market rate of return used in the CAPM summarizes the impact of all the factors quite well. There is a great deal of research currently going on that compares the APT to the CAPM and that is developing the theory in a form that may make it useful to business financial managers and investment portfolio managers.

SUMMARY

In dealing with future monetary payments or receipts, a probability distribution is often useful in assessing the degree of risk. Two of the more important quantitative measures of risk are the standard deviation and correlation. The standard deviation measures the uncertainty as to the returns of an asset or portfolio of assets. The correlation measures the degree to which the returns of one asset vary with the returns of another asset or portfolio. The total risk of a portfolio of assets depends on the standard deviations and correlations of the individual assets.

Through diversification, investors can reduce the risk of owning risky securities. Diversification—which means investing in more than one security—reduces risk if the returns from the securities in the portfolio are not perfectly correlated with each other. The only risk remaining in a fully diversified portfolio is the risk of the market as a whole. A measure of the contribution by an individual security to the risk of a fully diversified portfolio is the security's beta.

Beta measures how closely a security's returns vary with the returns of all securities in the market. If investors are generally well diversified, a security's beta will be an important determinant of the price of the security.

The security market line expresses the relationship between the expected rate of return required by investors and the risk of the security. In the capital asset pricing model (CAPM), the security market line is

$$k_J = i + (k_M - i)\, beta_J \tag{6-5}$$

where k_J = *the required rate of return on security J*

i = *the riskfree rate of interest*

k_M = *the expected rate of return for the entire market*

$beta_J$ = *the value of beta for security J*

The CAPM has many uses in finance and is the dominant model of risk and return in the financial markets.

QUESTIONS

1   In 1929 a department store (Frederick and Nelson) obtained a lease on a 700,000-square-foot store in downtown Seattle for a fixed payment of $91,000 per year for 99 years. Do you think that a department store in your town could obtain a fixed payment lease for 99 years today? Why or why not?

2 Rank the following portfolios in order of their degree of diversification from least diversified to most diversified:

 a Half common stock and half bonds of ITT, a company which has a wide range of business activities in many different countries.

 b Equal amounts of stock in five firms in five different industries.

 c Equal amounts of stock in three computer companies.

 d The stocks of ten companies selected by throwing darts at a newspaper listing of stock prices.

 e Shares of a $10 billion internationally diversified mutual fund.

3 Suppose that you currently own 100 shares of General Motors Company stock. This is your only risky investment. Is it likely that you could achieve greater returns on your investment with less risk? Why or why not?

4 Can you think of any alternatives to the standard deviation as a measure of risk for investment returns? How would your measures compare with standard deviation? (There is no single correct answer to this question.)

5 Investors are thought to be concerned about the uncertainty in the returns on their investments as measured by the standard deviation of the returns. Why, then, should such investors be interested in the beta of a security?

6 Explain what the security market line is, using words only.

(*Note:* The following questions are based on Appendix 6A.)

7 Suppose there were a law prohibiting borrowing to invest in securities. All other assumptions of the CAPM hold. Sketch the resulting capital market line (curve). How do you think that the passage of such a law would affect the prices of securities that have large betas (for example, betas greater than 1.5)?

8 What is the difference between the capital market line and the security market line?

PROJECT

Using a source such as the *Value Line Investment Survey*, identify four or more stocks with betas greater than 1.2 and four or more stocks with betas less than 0.8. Examine the history of these stocks. Do the high-beta stocks appear to be more risky than the low-beta stocks? Do the high-beta stocks appear to provide higher average returns than the low-beta stocks? Can you identify any characteristics of the companies which determine whether one will have a high-beta or a low-beta stock?

DEMONSTRATION PROBLEM

DP1 Automotive Computer Systems (ACS) sells electronic components to automobile manufacturers. Its sales, profits, and stock price are highly correlated with the economy as a whole. The current price of ACS stock is $20 per share. Your assessment of the possible dollar returns (stock price plus dividends) from owning one share of the stock for one year and their associated probabilities are as follows:

Dollar return	$14	$18	$20	$22	$24	$26
Probability	.1	.1	.3	.2	.2	.1

a What are the expected rate of return and standard deviation of the rate of return for an investment of $20 in ACS stock?
b What are the expected rate of return and standard deviation of the rate of return for an investment of $2000 in ACS stock?

SOLUTION TO DP1:
a At a price of $20, the rates of return are

Rate of return	−30%	−10%	0%	10%	20%	30%
Probability	.1	.1	.3	.2	.2	.1

Expected rate of return = $.1(-30\%) + .1(-10\%) + .3(0\%)$
$+ .2(10\%) + .2(20\%) + .1(30\%)$

$= \underline{5\%}$

Variance = $.1(-30\% - 5\%)^2 + .1(-10\% - 5\%)^2$
$+ .3(0\% - 5\%)^2 + .2(10\% - 5\%)^2$
$+ .2(20\% - 5\%)^2$
$+ .1(30\% - 5\%)^2$

$= .1(1225\%^2) + .1(225\%^2) + .3(25\%^2)$
$+ .2(25\%^2) + .2(225\%^2) + .1(625\%^2)$

$= 265\%^2$

Standard deviation = $\sqrt{265\%^2}$

$= \underline{16.28\%}$

b Same answer as in *a*. The amount of the investment does not affect the expected rate of return and its standard deviation.

PROBLEMS

1 You are considering purchasing stock in Massive Manufacturing Company. The current price per share is $40. You have the following expectations regarding the price of the stock one year from now (no dividends are expected):

Future price	$20	$30	$40	$50	$60	$80
Probability	.1	.2	.2	.2	.2	.1

a What is the price expected to be one year from now? [Ans.: $46]

b If the price turns out to be $46, what rate of return will you have earned? [Ans.: 15 percent]

c Determine the probability distribution of the rates of return on this stock. What is the expected rate of return as calculated from this probability distribution? Compare this answer to the rate of return calculated in *b*. Should the two be equal? Why or why not?

d Using the probability distribution of *c*, calculate the standard deviation of the rate of return on the stock. [Ans.: 42.13 percent]

2 Sasquatch Automotive Company is about to introduce its first product, a car that operates with sawdust as fuel. If the car sells well, the firm could make enormous profits; however, its failure could very well bankrupt the company. The current price of the stock is $20 per share. The interest rate on riskless assets is 10 percent per year. The returns from owning the stock are positively correlated with the overall economy. Your assessment of the dividends and price of the stock next year for the various possibilities and their associated probabilities is:

	Total failure	Partial failure	Partial success	Total success
Probability	.2	.3	.4	.1
Dividend	$0	$ 0	$ 1	$ 5
Stock price	$0	$10	$24	$75

a Calculate the expected total dollar return (dividend plus price) and the expected rate of return from owning one share of Sasquatch stock for one year.

b Given the above information, would you purchase the stock?

c Suppose that investors in the market on average require an expected rate of return of 25 percent on stock of this degree of risk. What price should the stock sell for if investors in general share your assessment of the prospects for Sasquatch?

d Calculate the rate of return for each possibility, given the price of $20 per share and again using the price determined in *c*. Compare the results of the two sets of calculations. How do changes in current prices affect rates of return given a set of future possibilities?

3 Four Square Industries (FSI) assembles microcomputers from off-
the-shelf parts. Movements in its stock price are highly correlated
with the stock market as a whole. The current price of FSI stock
is $40 per share. FSI pays no dividends. Your assessment of the
possible prices of FSI stock one year from now and their
associated probabilities are as follows:

Stock price	$20	$30	$40	$50	$60
Probability	.1	.2	.3	.2	.2

a What are the expected rate of return and standard deviation of
the rate of return for an investment of $4000 in FSI stock?
b The riskless rate of interest is currently 6 percent. Does FSI
stock appear to be a good investment at its current price of
$40 per share?
c If other investors in the market agree with your assessment of
the distributions of dollar returns from FSI stock, what will
happen to the stock price?

4 The stock of Hamburger Heaven (HH) tends to perform well
relative to other stocks during depressions. On the other hand,
the stock of Sizzlin Steaks (SS) tends to do especially well during
boom periods. The following table represents your assessment of
the probabilities of boom and depression next year and of the
dollar returns (dividend plus price) the two stocks will have. Both
stocks are currently selling for $100 per share. Compare the
expected returns obtained from investments of (1) $1000 in HH
stock, (2) $1000 in SS stock, and (3) $500 in HH stock plus $500
in SS stock. Evaluate the risks of the alternative investment
strategies. Which would you prefer? Why?

Economic conditions next year	Boom	Depression
Probability	.6	.4
Return of HH stock	$120	$100
Return of SS stock	$150	$ 80

5 Suppose that the riskless rate of interest is 10 percent and that we
can measure risk for a security by its beta, which is 0.0 for a
riskless security. The expected rate of return required by the
market for a security with a beta of 1.0 is known to be 15 percent.
a Graph the security market line.
b What would be the expected rate of return on stock X, which
has a beta of 0.5?
c You are considering the purchase of a stock with a current
price of $50 per share. You expect to receive $3 per share in
dividends next year and to be able to sell the stock for $55 in

one year. What is the expected rate of return from owning the stock for one year?

d The stock in **c** is estimated to have a beta of 1.2. What should its expected rate of return be, according to your expectations and the security market line of **a** above? If many other people agree with you, what should be the price of the stock?

6 The riskless interest rate is 8 percent and the expected rate of return on the market portfolio is 14 percent. Using the PM and Eq. (6-1):

a Draw the security market line.

b What should be the expected rate of return for a security with a beta of 2.0?

7 A friend of yours holds stock in the four companies shown below with their current market values and betas. The riskless rate of interest is 8 percent and you believe that the long-run risk premium in the market is 6 percent. Assume that the CAPM applies.

Stock	Value	Beta
A	$2,500	1.2
B	$2,000	0.9
C	$4,500	1.0
D	$1,000	1.5
Total	$10,000	

a What is the current beta of the portfolio?

b What is the expected rate of return for the portfolio? [Hint: There are two ways to compute this.]

c Is it likely that your friend could obtain a safer investment portfolio with the same expected rate of return as the current portfolio?

(*Note:* Problems 8 through 11 are based on Appendix 6A.)

8 Mercedes Balboa lives in Brazil where the rate of inflation is very high. She estimated the expected rate of return and standard deviation for five portfolios as shown below. Mercedes can borrow at a 30 percent rate of interest and can invest in riskless securities at 30 percent. Which of the five portfolios would be best for Mercedes to invest in, if Mercedes is willing to assume some risk? Why?

	Portfolio				
	A	B	C	D	E
Expected rate of return	30%	35%	40%	45%	50%
Standard deviation	5%	15%	20%	25%	30%

9 You have found that the average rate of return on a large sample of stocks which is representative of the entire market is 12 percent. The standard deviation of the rate of return on this sample is 4.5 percent. The riskless rate of interest is 6 percent.

a What is your best estimate of the market price of risk in the capital market? Draw the capital market line.

b Draw the security market line. Why does it differ from the capital market line?

c The stock of Webb International has a beta of 1.5. What is your best estimate of the required rate of return on this stock?

10 Gamma Computer's stock is currently selling at a price of $20 per share. You have analyzed the company and have developed the following estimates:

Expected total dollar return in one year	$30
Standard deviation of dollar returns	$12
Correlation of Gamma's return with the market return	0.6

a Gamma stock's beta calculated from the past history of the stock's price is 2.5. Assuming that the security market line of problem **6** applies, is Gamma stock correctly priced according to your estimates?

b The standard deviation of the market's rate of return is 24 percent. Given the data above, what should the price of Gamma's stock be? [Hint: Try Eq. (6-8).]

c Based on the price calculated in *b*, what should be the expected rate of return and beta for Gamma's stock? Are these values consistent with the security market line?

(*Note:* Part *c* is fairly difficult.)

11 The stock price of Resource Industries (RI) is highly sensitive to economic conditions whereas the price of Midwest Utilities (MU) is less so. You are considering purchasing a portfolio of the two securities and have made the following probability estimates.

	Economic condition		
	Recession	Normal	Inflation
Probability	.2	.5	.3
Rate of Return—RI	−20%	10%	30%
Rate of Return—MU	−10%	20%	0%

a What are the expected rates of return and standard deviations of the rates of return from 100 percent investment in each stock?

b What are the expected rates of return and standard deviations of the following portfolios?

      A   30 percent in RI and 70 percent in MU
      B   50 percent in RI and 50 percent in MU
      C   70 percent in RI and 30 percent in MU

c Examine the results of *a* and *b* above. Do they suggest that some portfolios might be more desirable than others? (*Note:* For your information, the correlation between the rates of return of RI and MU is 0.28.)

The ⬛ symbol indicates that all or a significant part of the problem can be solved using the *Computer Models* software that accompanies this text.

PORTFOLIO THEORY AND THE CAPITAL ASSET PRICING MODEL

Portfolio theory shows how investors can combine securities into portfolios that provide maximum returns for a given degree of risk. The essentials of portfolio theory were presented in Chapter 6. The Capital Asset Pricing Model (CAPM) is a theory about how the prices and interest rates on risky financial assets (securities) are determined in the capital market. The CAPM combines the principles of portfolio theory with certain assumptions regarding investor expectations and market characteristics. The model provides a precise relationship between the risk of a security, as measured by its beta value, and its required rate of return. In brief, the key insights of the CAPM are:

1 A security's risk is measured by its beta value.
2 The required rate of return on a security depends on the riskless rate of interest, the market risk premium, and the security's beta.
3 Investors should own risky securities only as part of a highly diversified portfolio of such securities.
4 The only way to increase the expected rate of return from investment is to take on additional risk.

Although the assumptions made in the model present an abstract and idealized description of the capital markets, statistical analysis of actual rates of return on securities provides some support to the CAPM. Portfolio theory and the CAPM are important parts of modern finance theory and their concepts are used by security analysts, portfolio managers, and business financial managers to help them increase returns and minimize risk.

In the following pages, we develop the model in a step-by-step fashion, first examining the underlying assumptions and ideas, and then building on them. We begin with a review of portfolio theory, which is useful both in its own right and as the foundation of the CAPM.

PORTFOLIO THEORY

Portfolio theory provides investors with a method of selecting securities that will provide the highest expected rate of return for any given degree of risk or that will provide the minimum amount of risk for any given expected rate of return. Here, we present the concepts and assumptions of portfolio theory that are essential for understanding the CAPM.

Suppose that the only risk that an investor cares about is the standard deviation of the returns from the money he or she has available to invest. The investor dislikes risk and wishes to obtain as large an expected return as is possible for any given level of risk (i.e., any given standard deviation). This investor has a single period time horizon; that is, the only returns of immediate concern are those that occur one period from now. For convenience we assume that the period is one year, the funds are invested now, and that dividends or interest on the investment are received one year from now. The returns in one year include dividends, interest payments, and the change in market value (based on selling prices) of the securities owned by the investor.

Portfolio theory assumes that the amount of money an investor has available to invest is some given amount. The investor's problem can then be analyzed entirely in terms of possible rates of return that can be earned on that given amount.

Let's now look at the options available to our investor. Suppose, for the moment, that only two securities are being considered—stock of company A and stock of company B. The investor could purchase A's stock or B's stock or any combination (portfolio) of the two; the expected rate of return and standard deviation resulting from all the possible portfolios of A and B will look something like the curve in Figure 6-10. The precise shape of the curve depends on the correlation between

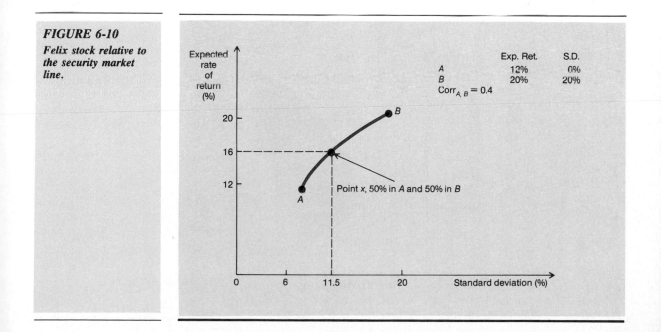

FIGURE 6-10

Felix stock relative to the security market line.

the returns from A and the returns from B.[11] The correlation between A and B in Figure 6-10 is 0.4. Point x on the curve shows the expected return and standard deviation for a portfolio with 50 percent of the investor's money invested in A and 50 percent invested in B.

Figure 6-10 is simply a picture of the risk and expected return from the possible portfolios containing stocks A and B, including the alternatives of 100 percent in A and 100 percent in B (points A and B). Given this information the investor can choose the most desirable alternative based on his or her tastes regarding risk and return. A relatively risk-averse person might choose A alone, whereas most people would probably choose some combination of A and B.

*The Efficient
Frontier*

Many more choices are open to investors. There are over 1400 different stocks traded on the New York Stock Exchange alone. Imagine that the expected rate of return and standard deviation of a large number of risky securities and of all portfolios of those assets are shown in a figure like Figure 6-11 (the shaded region in the figure). Ideally, you would like to

---

[11] Equations that define the curve were provided in Chap. 6. For two risky securities, A and B, the expected return on a portfolio ($\bar{r}_P$) with fraction w invested in security A and $(1 - w)$ in security B is

$$\bar{r}_P = w\bar{r}_A + (1 - w)\bar{r}_B \tag{a}$$

The standard deviation of the rate of return on the portfolio (SD_P) can be determined by taking the square root of:

$$(SD_P)^2 = w^2 (SD_A)^2 + (1 - w)^2 (SD_B)^2 + 2w(1 - w)SD_A \, SD_B \, Corr_{A,B} \tag{b}$$

where $Corr_{A,B}$ is the coefficient of correlation between r_A and r_B.

FIGURE 6-11

*Risk and return for all
possible portfolios of
risky securities.*

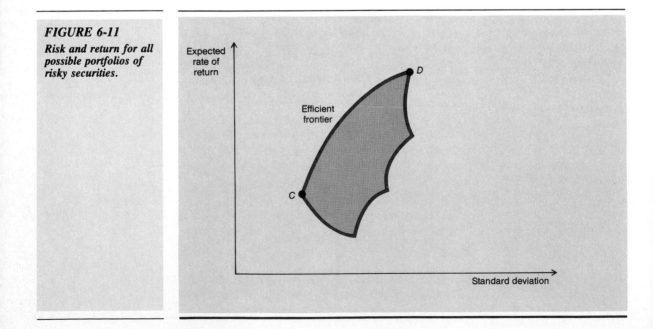

include all the risky financial assets available for investment in the economy in this figure, so that you could consider all possible choices. If this information were available (including the ability to identify which assets are represented by every point on the figure), what could you do with it?

If you are like our investor, you will only be interested in acquiring assets or portfolios of assets that plot along the upper left edge of the shaded region. These assets and portfolios provide higher expected returns and less risk than any other risky investment shown. This curve, indicated by the heavy line from point C to point D, is called the **efficient frontier**. Given the expectations used to generate the figure, investment opportunities along the efficient frontier are better than (dominate) all other opportunities. You can achieve either a higher expected return with the same risk, or the same expected return and a lower risk, from an investment on the efficient frontier than from any other possible risky investment shown in the shaded region.

The concept of an efficient frontier can be applied to any number of securities under consideration for investment. The efficient frontier for two securities A and B is the curve connecting points A and B in Figure 6-10. Of course, the more securities that you include for consideration, the more likely you are to find superior opportunities.

*Borrowing
and Lending
Opportunities*

There are, however, two other alternatives available: investing in a riskless asset (lending), and borrowing to invest additional funds in risky assets. Borrowing increases the total amount available for investment. The amount invested will be your initial capital plus the amount borrowed. Suppose for simplicity, that the rate of interest i that you can earn from investing in a riskless asset is equal to the rate of interest that you pay to borrow in order to finance additional investment in risky assets. Then the risk-return combinations that you can obtain lie along a straight line passing through i, the riskless rate, and the point on the graph representing all funds invested in the risky asset (or portfolio) with no borrowing. As you increase the proportion of your initial capital that is invested in risky assets, both the expected rate of return and the risk increase. In Figure 6-12, point P represents the expected rate of return and standard deviation from investment in a portfolio of risky assets. The section of the line drawn through i and P that lies between i and P represents the possible risk-return combinations available from investment in the riskless asset and in P. At i, all your capital is invested in the riskless asset; at P, all your capital is invested in P. The portion of the line extending beyond P to the upper right represents the risk-return combinations available from borrowing and investing the total amount (borrowed funds plus capital) in P. The more money that is borrowed, the greater is both the risk and expected return on your own capital.

To see how this works, suppose that you put 40 percent of your money in a riskless asset (one-year Treasury bill) offering an interest rate of 10 percent and the rest of your money (60 percent) in a portfolio of risky assets that has an expected rate of return of 15 percent and a standard deviation of 8 percent. The expected rate of return on your capital $\bar{r}_C$ will be the weighted average of the two returns.

$$\bar{r}_C = (0.4 \times 10\%) + (0.6 \times 15\%)$$

$$= 13\%$$

The standard deviation of the rate of return on your capital SD_C will be the proportion invested in the risky portfolio times its standard deviation.[12]

$$SD_C = 0.6 \times 8\%$$

$$= 4.8\%$$

On the other hand, if you were to *borrow* an amount equal to 50 percent of your capital at 10 percent interest and invest the total (150 percent of capital) in the same risky portfolio, the expected rate of return on your capital would be

$$\bar{r}_C = (-0.5 \times 10\%) + (1.5 \times 15\%)$$

$$= 17.5\%$$

---

[12] To see this mathematically, assume that you invest a proportion w in risky asset A and a proportion $(1 - w)$ in riskless asset B. Since B is riskless, $SD_B = 0$. Using Eq. (b) of footnote 11, the standard deviation of combination C made up of A and B is the square root of:

$$(SD_C)^2 = w^2(SD_A)^2 + (1 - w)^2 (SD_B)^2 + 2w(1 - w)SD_A \, SD_B \, Corr_{A,B}$$

$$= w^2(SD_A)^2$$

FIGURE 6-12

Determining the best portfolio, when borrowing and investing in a riskless security are available.

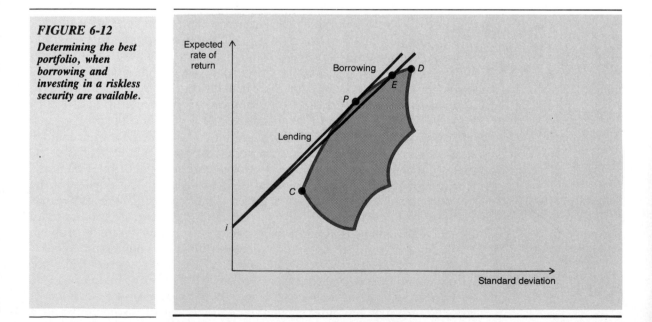

We weight the 10 percent interest rate by -0.5 because you have to *pay* interest on borrowed funds equal to 50 percent of your capital. We weight the 15 percent expected rate of return on the risky asset by the proportion of your capital, 150 percent, invested in it. The standard deviation of the rate of return on your capital is still equal to the proportion of your money invested in the portfolio (150 percent) times the portfolio standard deviation.

$$SD_C = 1.5 \times 8\%$$

$$= 12\%$$

Given the mechanics of these investment alternatives, an interesting result occurs. Examine Figure 6-12 and notice that the opportunities using borrowing or lending with investment in portfolio P dominate all other investment possibilities shown; that is, you will be able to obtain higher return with less risk.

The opportunities along the borrowing-lending line through P are also superior to borrowing or lending with any other portfolios or securities. For example, compare the line through P with the line through E, another portfolio on the efficient frontier. The opportunities provided by borrowing or lending in combination with investment in E, as represented by the line through E, are not as desirable as opportunities you have by investing in P instead. For any point on the line through E (except at i) you can find a point on the line through P that will provide a higher expected return with less risk. *Therefore, the only portfolio of risky assets of interest to the investor is P.*

The problem for the individual investor can thus be described as follows:

1 Determine the efficient frontier.
2 Find the portfolio or portfolios that, in combination with borrowing or lending, provide the best set of investment alternatives (e.g., determine the best borrowing-lending line).
3 Choose the investment package on the best borrowing-lending line that best suits the investor's tastes for risk and return.

An important point here is that, out of all the possible risky asset portfolios, there is only one (portfolio P) that the investor would consider purchasing. As we will see, unless the investor has expectations about particular securities that are greatly different from those held by most other investors in the market, the portfolio will be a highly diversified portfolio of assets similar to the portfolio of a well-diversified mutual fund.

THE CAPITAL ASSET PRICING MODEL

So far we have been discussing the situation faced by a single investor. We assumed that, in selecting a portfolio, this investor:

1 Is concerned only with the return over a single period.
2 Has a specific amount of money to invest.

3 Likes high expected portfolio return and low standard deviation of portfolio return.

4 Has estimates of the expected rates of return and the standard deviations from all portfolios of risky assets.

5 Is able to borrow and to lend at the same (riskless) rate of interest.

In addition, suppose that we assume the following:

6 Securities are bought and sold in a highly competitive market with no transaction costs (such as brokerage fees).

7 All investors have the same expectations regarding the future returns from owning securities (same expected rates of return and standard deviations for all portfolios).

8 Taxes do not bias investors in favor of one investment over another.[13]

These assumptions describe a world in which investors may differ in their wealth and their attitudes toward risk, but in which *they all have the same opportunities and expectations*. They all dislike risk and view the standard deviation of the return on their capital as the appropriate measure of risk. They can freely invest in any combination of riskless and risky securities and can borrow, if they so desire, to finance securities' purchases. *Therefore the relationships shown in Figure 6-12 must be the same for every investor*. All investors will agree that P represents the best portfolio of risky assets to own if any risky assets are to be owned. Since all risky assets must be owned by someone, portfolio P must contain every risky security in the market. If a security is not included in P, it means that no one would want to own it, at least at its current price. The price will therefore fall. As the price falls, the security's expected rate of return will increase and eventually everyone will agree that it should be included in P. Thus, P is the *market portfolio* that contains all risky securities.[14] Given this conclusion and our assumptions, all other implications and results of the Capital Asset Pricing Model follow from the mathematics of portfolio theory.

The Capital Market Line

We designate the market portfolio as portfolio M and the rate of return on the riskless asset as i. Figure 6-13 illustrates capital market equilibrium at a point in time when all security prices have adjusted to reflect current expectations, investor attitudes toward risk, etc. All investors hold portfolios that lie along the line passing through i and M. This line is called the **capital market line**. The line can be written as an equation

$$k_C = i + s\,\text{SD}_C \tag{6-6}$$

where k_C is the equilibrium expected rate of return and SD_C is the equilibrium standard deviation of the rate of return on an investor's

[13] This assumption implies either no taxes on security returns or, if there are taxes, they do not affect the choice of which securities to own.

[14] We describe a portfolio by the proportions of the various securities contained in it. The proportion of a security in the market portfolio is the total market value of that security divided by the total market value of all securities in the market.

capital. Coefficient s is the slope of the capital market line, often called the "market price of risk," and equals

$$s = \frac{k_M - i}{SD_M} \qquad (6\text{-}7)$$

where k_M is the expected rate of return and SD_M is the standard deviation of the rate of return for the market portfolio.

The capital market line shows the expected rate of return and risk for the investment alternatives available to investors from investing in **M** *and borrowing or lending at the riskfree rate* i. The investment opportunities represented by the capital market line are the best ones that are available in the market. The value of s indicates the risk-return tradeoff by investors in the market. For example, suppose that the expected rate of return on the market portfolio is 15 percent, the standard deviation for the market portfolio is 20 percent, and the riskless rate is 9 percent. From Eq. (6-6):

$$s = \frac{15\% - 9\%}{20\%}$$

$$= 0.3$$

A value of 0.3 for s means that for an increase of one percentage point in standard deviation, investors require an increase of 0.3 percentage point in expected rate of return.

The Security Market Line

Although the capital market line provides us with information about the general risk-return tradeoff in the market, it does not indicate the relationship between risk and return for individual securities. However, given the capital market line and the mathematical relationships that

FIGURE 6-13

Equilibrium in the capital market and the capital market line.

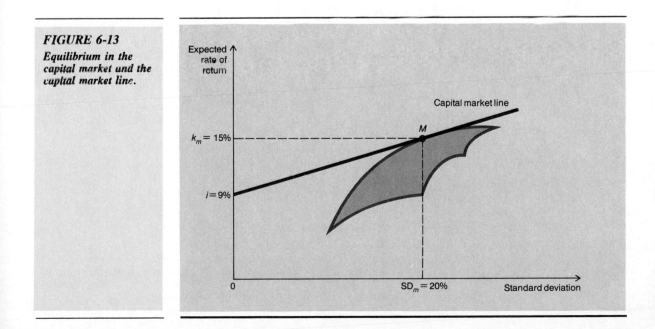

apply to the market portfolio and the securities that are included in the portfolio, we can develop the relationship between risk and return for individual securities.

The mathematics are complex, but the logic is as follows. Each risky security in the market is included in the market portfolio. Investors who invest in risky securities do not own a security by itself, but, as explained above, own a part of the market portfolio M which contains all risky securities. *In assessing an individual security, investors are concerned with how the total risk and return of the market portfolio is affected by including that particular security in it*. The expected rate of return on the market is simply the average rate of return on all securities in it. However, the market standard deviation depends not only on the standard deviations of the securities in the market portfolio, but also on the correlations between the securities. Consequently, the risk of an individual security for investors holding the market portfolio depends both on the standard deviation of the security's rate of return *and* the correlation of the security's rate of return with the rates of return on the other securities in the market.[15]

In equilibrium, given the capital market line, the expected rate of return on a security J is given by the security market line

$$k_J = i + s \; \text{Corr}_{JM} \; \text{SD}_J \tag{6-8}$$

That is, the equilibrium expected rate of return (k_J) equals the riskless interest rate (i) plus a premium for risk. This premium consists of the slope coefficient of the *capital* market line (s), which measures the risk-return tradeoff of investors, times the correlation of the rate of return on the security with the market's rate of return (Corr_{JM}) times the standard deviation of the security's rate of return (SD_J). The measure of risk here, $\text{Corr}_{JM} \; \text{SD}_J$, represents the contribution security J makes to the risk of the market portfolio. *All other risk associated with security J is diversified away*. For example, a security with returns that are highly correlated with the market (say, $\text{Corr}_{JM} = 0.9$) and a standard deviation (SD_J) of 20 percent would have a risk of 0.9×20 percent, or 18 percent. Even when included in the market portfolio with all the other securities in the economy, most of the risk of this security cannot be diversified away. However, another security with returns that do not vary much with the market (say, $\text{Corr}_{JM} = 0.2$) and a standard deviation of 25 percent would have a risk of only 10 percent (0.2×25 percent). Much of the risk of

---

[15] The standard deviation of any portfolio P can be determined from the following expression:

$$(\text{SD}_P)^2 = \sum_{H=1}^{n} \sum_{J=1}^{n} w_H \; w_J \; \text{Corr}_{HJ} \; \text{SD}_H \; \text{SD}_J$$

where w_H is the proportion of security H in the portfolio, and SD_H is the standard deviation of the rate of return on security H; similarly for w_J and SD_J. Corr_{HJ} is the correlation between the returns of securities H and J. In applying this formula, it is important to recognize that the correlation of a security's returns with its own returns, Corr_{HH}, is 1.0.

owning this security is eliminated when owned as part of the market portfolio.

One way to understand why the correlation with the market is so important in determining a security's risk is to imagine what would result if the returns from securities did not vary with any common factor. That is, if all securities' returns were uncorrelated with each other. How would the return on the market portfolio consisting of a large number of these securities behave? When some securities are experiencing high returns, others will be experiencing low returns, since all returns vary independently. If there is a sufficiently large number of securities in the market, the market portfolio's return will equal the average return for all securities with no appreciable uncertainty.[16] On the other hand, suppose that all securities' returns vary together in lock step. Then, no matter how many securities you own, the return on your portfolio will have the same uncertainty (standard deviation) as the average standard deviation of the securities in it. There are no benefits to diversification in this case.

An alternative form of the security market line uses beta as a measure of risk. Recall from Chapter 6 that beta measures the responsiveness of a security's rate of return to the rate of return of the market. A security's beta can be expressed as

$$\text{Beta}_J = \frac{\text{Corr}_{JM}\ \text{SD}_J}{\text{SD}_M} \tag{6-9}$$

Using this definition of beta and the equation for the slope coefficient s, Eq. (6-7), we can write the security market line of Eq. (6-8) as

$$k_J = i + (k_M - i)\ \text{beta}_J \tag{6-10}$$

Equation (6-10) captures the basic insight of the CAPM. The expected rate of return of an individual security, in equilibrium, depends on the riskless interest rate, investor attitudes toward risk as measured by the market risk premium ($k_M - i$), and the risk of the security measured by its beta. The security market line using beta as the risk measure for a security was shown in Figure 6-8. All portfolios and securities fall along the security market line in equilibrium. Beta for the market itself is 1.0 as implied by the definition of beta, Eq. (6-9), since correlation of the return on the market with itself is 1.0. Therefore the expected rate of return for securities with betas equal to 1.0 is the expected rate of return on the market.

Asset Prices

Equations (6-8) and (6-10) tell us what the expected rate of return will be for an asset that is priced "correctly" according to the security market

---

[16] This is based on the law of large numbers which says, in this context, that the standard deviation of the average return on the market will equal the average standard deviation of the securities in the market divided by the square root of the number of securities. Thus, with 10,000 securities, the standard deviation of the market return will be only 1 percent ($1/\sqrt{10,000} = \frac{1}{100}$ of the average of the standard deviations of the securities' returns themselves.

EXHIBIT 6-4
Example price calculation applying Eq. (6-11) to stock A of Figure 6-1

Stock A

Expected dollar return $(\overline{R}_A) = \$60.00$

Standard deviation of dollar return $(SD_{RA}) = \$11.00$

Correlation of stock A's returns with the market $(Corr_{AM}) = 0.6$

Market data

Slope of the capital market line $(s) = 0.3$

Riskless interest rate $(i) = 10\%$

Estimated market price (V_A)

$$V_A = \frac{\overline{R}_A - s\ Corr_{AM}\ SD_{RA}}{1 + i} \qquad \text{(Eq. 6-11)}$$

$$= \frac{\$60.00 - (0.3)(0.6)(\$11.00)}{1.10}$$

$$= \frac{\$60.00 - \$1.98}{1.10}$$

$$= \$52.75$$

line. However, it is also useful to be able to determine what the "correct" price should be directly. The ability to estimate the market price of an asset, given knowledge of the probability distribution of the asset's returns and the market parameters common to all assets (i and s), is especially convenient if the asset or security has not previously been traded in the market. For example, suppose you wish to estimate the stock price of a company that is issuing stock to the public for the first time. To do this, we restate Eq. (6-8) in terms of dollar return and prices. The resulting equation for the value of security J (V_J) is[17]

---

[17] Equation (6-11) is derived as follows:

1 The expected return (k_J) for an asset J that is "correctly priced" according to the CAPM will be [from Eq. (6-8)]

$$k_J = i + s\ Corr_{JM}\ SD_J \qquad \text{(a)}$$

2 The expected rate of return is also

$$k_J = \frac{\overline{R}_J}{V_J} - 1 \qquad \text{(b)}$$

where $\overline{R}_J$ is the expected dollar return one period from now from security J, and V_J is the current market value of security J.

3 The standard deviation of the rate of return of the security (SD_J) equals the standard deviation of the dollar return of the security (SD_{RJ}) divided by its price.

$$SD_J = \frac{SD_{RJ}}{V_J} \qquad \text{(c)}$$

4 Using relationships (b) and (c) to substitute for k_J and SD_J in (a) we can solve for V_J and the result is Eq. (6-11).

$$V_J = \frac{\overline{R}_J}{1 + k_J}$$

$$= \frac{\overline{R}_J - s\,\mathrm{Corr}_{JM}\,\mathrm{SD}_{RJ}}{1 + i} \tag{6-11}$$

where $\overline{R}_J$ is the expected dollar return one year from now to the owners of security J and SD_{RJ} is the standard deviation of the dollar returns. The other variables in Eq. (6-11) (s, Corr_{JM}, and i) are the same as those in Eq. (6-8). Equation (6-11) can be used to estimate the market value of any asset for which the required data arc available. Exhibit 6-4 provides an example application.

THE FIRM'S INVESTMENT, FINANCING, AND DIVIDEND DECISIONS

Part 2 comprises seven chapters that deal with the firm's fundamental considerations in making its investment, financing, and dividend decisions. The sequencing of these chapters roughly follows the sequence of decisions made by the financial manager. In the light of past investment, financing, and dividend decisions, the finanacial manager estimates the firm's cost of capital for use as a standard to evaluate proposed investments. The cost of capital is the rate of return investors require on their investment in the firm. Procedures for estimating its numerical value are presented in Chapter 7. Management then uses the cost of capital to evaluate investments of the same risk and financed in the same way as those historically undertaken by the firm. The techniques used in this process are covered in Chapters 8 and 9. Procedures for dealing with investments that differ in risk are covered in Chapter 10.

Application of the methods of business investment planning covered in Chapters 8 through 10 results in a planned capital expenditure program for the firm. The financial manager must now consider how these expenditures are to be financed. Chapter 11 examines the major sources of financing used by business firms. Chapter 12 explains how management decides which sources to use. If this financing method differs significantly from that used in the past, the cost of capital estimate may be revised, and a change may be made in the capital budget that was initially chosen. The final financing and investment program followed by the firm depends on the cost and availability of financing.

A major source of financing is earnings retained by the firm instead of being paid out as dividends. Chapter 13 discusses the factors that influence policies for dividend payments to shareholders and how the firm formulates the policy best suited to its particular situation.

CHAPTER SEVEN

THE COST OF CAPITAL

A company's **cost of capital** is the average rate of return required by investors in the company's securities. This average rate is often used as a minimum acceptable rate of return for new investments being considered by the firm. Under appropriate conditions, the cost of capital is the interest rate or discount rate to use in computing the market value of the cash flows generated by an investment. The cost of capital is also used in setting the rates that regulated companies (e.g., electric utilities) can charge their customers. In this chapter we explain the conditions under which a company's cost of capital can be used to evaluate business investments. We present methods for estimating the rates that are required on the various types of securities (debt and stock) used by the firm. Then we show how to combine these rates into an estimate of the company's cost of capital.

BASIC CONCEPTS

A company's cost of capital is calculated as a weighted average of the costs of the securities used to finance the firm's investments. The cost of each type of security is multiplied by its proportion (which sums to 1.0) of the total amount of all securities issued by the firm. For example, suppose that the firm uses debt costing 5 percent and stock costing 15 percent. If the proportion of debt used is 40 percent and the proportion of stock used is 60 percent, then the cost of capital k_a is

$$\text{Cost of capital} = \text{debt proportion} \times \text{debt rate}$$
$$+ \text{stock proportion} \times \text{stock rate} \tag{7-1}$$
$$k_a = 0.40 \times 5\% + 0.60 \times 15\%$$
$$= 2\% + 9\%$$
$$= 11\%$$

This calculation raises two questions: (1) Why is the company's cost of capital useful in evaluating investment proposals and (2) how can the components (costs and proportions) be determined? We first discuss the use of the cost of capital because this provides the basis for specifying how the components should be determined.

There are two basic conditions for using the company's cost of capital to evaluate new investments.

1 The new investments being considered have the same risk as the typical or average investment undertaken historically by the firm.
2 The financing policy of the firm is not affected by the investments that are made.

The first condition means that the company's cost of capital should be used to evaluate only investments of the same risk as the average investment made in the past; that is, the new investments must not change the business risk of the firm if they are undertaken. The second condition means that the relative amounts of the different types of securities used by the firm should not change as a result of undertaking any of the new investments being evaluated; that is, the financing of the new investments must not change the financial risks of the firm.

Evaluating new investments when these conditions are not met is a much more difficult problem. We show how to deal with investments of differing risks in Chapter 10 and discuss financing issues in Chapters 11 and 12. However, the concepts developed here are useful in dealing with the more complex situations. Now let's see why the cost of capital is a proper measure of the minimum acceptable rate of return on investment when the two conditions apply.

Suppose a firm is considering an investment such as purchasing a new machine costing $1000 that will be financed with a debt issue of $400 and a stock issue of $600. Assume that the interest cost of the debt is 5 percent and that the stockholders require an expected rate of return of 15 percent on their investment of $600. If the cash returns from the investment are expected to continue at the same level forever and all of it is paid out in interest and dividends, how large must the annual cash flow be to justify the expenditure of $1000?

The cash flow from the investment must cover at a minimum the interest cost of the debt and provide a satisfactory dividend return to shareholders.

$$
\begin{aligned}
\text{Minimum acceptable cash flow} &= \text{interest cost} + \text{minimum dividends} \\
&= \text{debt rate} \times \text{debt issue} \\
&\quad + \text{stock rate} \times \text{stock issue} \qquad (7\text{-}2) \\
&= 5\% \times \$400 + 15\% \times \$600 \\
&= \$20 + \$90 \\
&= \$110
\end{aligned}
$$

The minimum acceptable rate of return on this investment is the minimum acceptable cash flow divided by the amount of the investment or $110/$1000 = 11 percent. Since Eq. (7-2) expresses the minimum acceptable cash flow in terms of the financing used, let's divide both sides of that equation by the amount of the investment.

$$\frac{\text{Minimum acceptable cash flow}}{\text{Investment}} = \frac{\text{debt rate} \times \text{debt issue} + \text{stock rate} \times \text{stock issue}}{\text{investment}}$$

$$= \text{debt rate} \times \frac{\text{debt issue}}{\text{investment}}$$

$$+ \text{stock rate} \times \frac{\text{stock issue}}{\text{investment}}$$

$$= \text{debt rate} \times \text{proportion of debt}$$
$$+ \text{stock rate} \times \text{proportion of stock} \qquad (7\text{-}3)$$

$$= 5\% \frac{\$400}{\$1000} + 15\% \frac{\$600}{\$1000}$$

$$= 5\%(0.4) + 15\%(0.6)$$

$$= 11\%$$

Therefore we can compute a minimum acceptable rate of return using Eq. (7-3). Now compare Eq. (7-3) with our initial statement of the cost of capital, Eq. (7-1). The minimum acceptable rate of return and the cost of capital (k_a) are equal. If the project has an expected rate of return higher than 11 percent, it should be accepted since the cash returns from the investment will provide shareholders with dividends in excess of their minimum requirements.

We have shown by means of a simple example that the *minimum acceptable rate of return on an investment is equal to an average of the rates of return that investors require on the securities they own.*[1] This is a company's cost of capital. The concept is illustrated in Figure 7-1. This figure shows the security market line of Chapter 6 with the risks and market rates of return of the debt and stock as indicated. The cost of capital reflects the average risk (business and financial risks) of the total company and is therefore based on the risk-return relationship in the security markets as represented by the security market line.

General Formula for the Average Cost of Capital

Now we have the basic concept of the cost of capital and why it is a valid measure. Let's express it as a general formula. If the firm uses n different types of financing, each type j with its own costs k_j and in proportion p_j, then the firm's cost of capital k_a is

$$k_a = p_1 k_1 + p_2 k_2 + \cdots + p_n k_n \qquad (7\text{-}4)$$

---

[1] In the numerical illustration above, the debt rate used was the effective rate on debt adjusted for corporate income taxes. Figure 7-1 ignores corporate tax effects.

FIGURE 7-1

The cost of capital and the security market line.

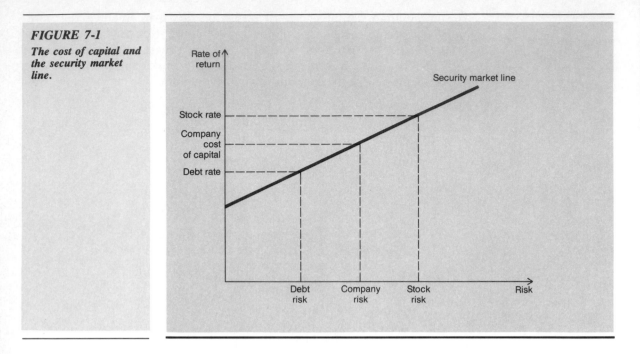

If the firm uses three types of financing (for example, bonds, preferred stock, and common stock) with costs of 5, 8, and 12 percent each and in proportions 30, 20, and 50 percent, respectively, then

$$k_a = p_1k_1 + p_2k_2 + p_3k_3$$

$$= 0.30(5\%) + 0.20(8\%) + 0.50(12\%)$$

$$= 1.5\% + 1.6\% + 6\%$$

$$= 9.1\%$$

Despite the apparent precision of the formula, the cost of capital is often difficult to estimate exactly. There are several variations of the definitions of the proportions and the costs used in the same general formula. There are also some practical problems in estimating the costs regardless of what definition is used.

Our stress here is on the underlying logic of the procedure and the basic estimates needed to determine the general magnitude of a firm's cost of capital. At this point we know that the proportions used are to be based on the financing plans of the firm and that the costs depend on the market interest rates required by investors in the firm's securities. We need now to identify the proportions and the costs more precisely so that they can be estimated from real data. Let's look at the costs first.

DETERMINING THE COST RATES

We need to know how to estimate the percentage cost rates [the k's in Eq. (7-4)] of each type of financing source used by the firm in order to calculate the average cost of capital. We will look at three types of financing used by firms: debt, preferred stock, and equity where equity includes common stock, and retained earnings.[2] Although the details of each type differ somewhat, our basic procedure is similar for all of them.

The rates we wish to estimate are those which the firm must provide to investors in order to finance the firm's investments in new plant, equipment, etc. However, we don't know what those investments will be yet, since the cost of capital is used as a criterion for determining what investments to undertake. This would seem to pose a dilemma. We need to know the financing rates in order to get a cost of capital to evaluate investments. However, we don't know how much money will be needed and therefore can't plan the financing until we evaluate the investments. The solution to the problem is based on our two basic conditions that investment risk and financing policies remain unchanged.

We estimate the rates of return that investors in the firm's securities currently require. These security market rates reflect the current business and financial risks of the firm. The current business risk of the firm is the same as the risk of the typical or average investment made by the firm historically. Recall that the cost of capital is appropriate for evaluating only investments of this degree of risk. Similarly, the current financial risk of the firm is determined by past financing decisions. We assumed that the financing policy of the firm will not change so that we could use current market rates which reflect current financial risk.

Our procedure is, therefore, to estimate rates of return currently required by investors in the firm's securities. Under some circumstances this will be very difficult to do, and alternative approaches will be suggested to deal with these cases. However, it is important to know what the desired result is, namely, the market rates of returns which are required by the investors who supply money to the firm.

The Rate on Debt

In measuring the interest cost of debt financing, two questions arise.[3]

1   How should the use of several different types of debt be handled?
2   How should income taxes be taken into account?

---

[2] Any operational method of estimating the cost of capital for a firm involves some degree of approximation, and the procedure presented here is no exception. We are ignoring the out-of-pocket costs of raising money (underwriting fees and other flotation costs, loan set-up fees, etc.). These costs do not affect the market rates required by investors, but do affect the net dollar proceeds from borrowing and issuing stock. The presence of such costs makes the choice of investments and their financing interdependent. Simply incorporating these costs in a single cost of capital rate for the firm can lead to serious errors except in very unusual circumstances. In Chapter 12, we show how to deal with interdependent investment and financing decisions.

[3] A third issue that will not be explored here is whether the promised rate (yield to maturity) or expected rate on the debt should be used. In theory, the rate of return that investors expect to earn on the debt (the **expected rate**) is more appropriate. The expected rate is less than the promised rate if there is any chance of default. However, we will use the promised rate for three reasons. First, the expected rate is difficult to estimate, whereas the promised rate can always be calculated. Second, unless the debt is very risky (rated below Ba), the promised rate produces sufficiently accurate results. Third, the promised rate is used in actual business practice.

224

PART 2
**The firm's investment,
financing, and dividend
decisions**

The first question raises the possibility that the firm may use more than one type of debt. For example, there are several different kinds of bonds that the firm could issue. The interest and principal payments on a bond issue may be subordinated to those in other debt issues so that the investors in the subordinated bonds get paid only after the others have been paid. Since these bonds are more risky than ordinary bonds, a higher interest rate must be paid on them.

When there is more than one debt issue outstanding, we can estimate the current rate on debt by calculating the average rate.[4] For example, suppose the firm has two long-term debt issues outstanding—a "senior" bond and a "subordinated" bond, where the holders of the subordinated bond get paid only if the holders of the senior bond have been paid first. Let's examine a specific case. The following data are assumed:

	Senior bonds	Subordinated bonds
Maturity value	$20 million	$10 million
Market value	$18 million	$10 million
Coupon rate	9%	11%
Yield to maturity	10%	11%

The average interest rate required by the bondholders of the firm is calculated using the *market values* of both kinds of bonds and their *yields to maturity* as follows:

Total market value of bonds = $18 + $10 = $28

$$\text{Average rate on bonds} = 10\% \left(\frac{\$18}{\$28}\right) + 11\% \left(\frac{\$10}{\$28}\right)$$

$$= 10.36\%$$

We use current market value and yield to maturity in this calculation because these reflect current interest rates in the market. The firm is assumed to be able to issue new senior and subordinated bonds with an average interest rate of 10.36 percent. Maturity values and coupon rates reflect interest rates at the time the debt was originally issued, and these historical values are not relevant to current decisions.

Income Tax Effects   Our second question concerned the impact of taxes on debt rate. The answer is that the effective cost of debt is lower than the interest rate paid to creditors because the firm can deduct interest payments in the determination of taxable income, thereby reducing taxes. The amount of the reduction in taxes and the effective cost of debt

---

[4] An alternative to computing the average rate on debt is to consider each type of debt a separate financing source and include it as a part of the cost of capital calculation. However, there are advantages to estimating an average rate on the debt, as will be shown when the method is applied later in the chapter.

depend on the tax rate. The higher the tax rate, the lower the effective interest rate on debt. For example, look at the data in Exhibit 7-1. There are two firms, A and B, that have identical earnings before interest and taxes. Firm A has no debt, whereas firm B has $2000 in outstanding debt and pays an interest rate of 10 percent. The firms' incomes are calculated using three tax rates, 0, 25, and 50 percent, and the resulting values of the net incomes are compared. If no taxes were paid, the only difference between the net incomes of the two firms would be due to the interest expense incurred by firm B of $200. In this case we would say that the effective rate on the debt was equal to the interest rate of 10 percent ($200/$2000 = 10 percent). If the tax rate is 25 percent, the impact of the debt interest on net income is only $150 due to the tax deductibility of interest. The effective rate on debt is therefore only $150/$2000 = 7.5 percent. Similarly, at a 50 percent tax rate the effective rate is only $100/$2000 − 5 percent. The general formula for the effective rate is

$$\text{Effective rate} = \text{interest rate} \times (1.0 - \text{tax rate}) \qquad (7\text{-}5)$$

where the interest rate used is the average market interest rate on the firm's debt. We use the effective rate as the cost of debt in calculating the firm's cost of capital.

The Rate on
Preferred Stock

Preferred stock is similar to common stock in that it has no maturity. Once issued, it may remain outstanding as long as the firm continues in existence. Cash payments (called **preferred dividends**) to the owners of this security are a fixed amount, for example $5 per share per year, and usually no dividends can be paid to the common stockholders unless the preferred stockholders have been paid. In this respect preferred stock is much like a bond with its fixed interest payments. However, the dividends paid to preferred stockholders are not tax deductible.

EXHIBIT 7-1

Tax rates and the effective rate on debt

	0% tax rate		25% tax rate		50% tax rate	
	Firm A	**Firm B**	**Firm A**	**Firm B**	**Firm A**	**Firm B**
Earnings before interest and taxes	$1,000	$1,000	$1,000	$1,000	$1,000	$1,000
Interest	0	200	0	200	0	200
Taxable income	$1,000	$ 800	$1,000	$ 800	$1,000	$ 800
Taxes	0	0	250	200	500	400
Net income	$1,000	$ 800	$ 750	$ 600	$ 500	$ 400
Difference[a]		$200		$150		$100
Effective rate[b]		10%		7.5%		5%

[a] Net income of firm A − net income of firm B.
[b] (Difference in net income)/$2000 of outstanding debt for firm B.

The fixed cash payments to the owner plus the absence of tax deductibility means that we can estimate the rate on preferred stock by simply dividing the preferred dividend per share by the current price per share since the dividend can be considered a level perpetual payment.

$$\text{Preferred rate} = \frac{\text{dividend}}{\text{price}} \qquad (7\text{-}6)$$

For example, Consolidated Edison's preferred stock, which pays $5 per share, was selling recently at a price of $64. The rate was therefore $5/$64 or 7.8 percent.

Sometimes firms have more than one issue of preferred stock outstanding. In this situation the average current rate on all preferred issues can be used as was done for debt issues.

The Rate on Common Stock

The rate on common stock (and retained earnings) is the rate most difficult to estimate.[5] The stock rate is the rate of return required by the stockholders of the firm. However, as we discussed in Chapter 5, there are no fixed contractual payments for common stock as there are for other securities issued by the firm. Stockholders have expectations as to what future dividends are, but it's difficult for the financial manager to determine the expected values. Many firms pay no dividends for long periods of time, either because they prefer to finance through use of retained earnings to the greatest extent possible or because they have not been profitable. Several methods of estimating the rate on stock are in use. We will examine four of them here. As we will see, no method is free of problems, and often more than one is used to provide the financial manager with a reasonable estimate of the rate.

Historical Rate of Return The first method is to determine the historical rate of return actually earned by the shareholders. Take the most recent five or ten years and calculate the rate of return earned by an investor who purchased stock at the beginning of the study period, held it to the present, and sold it at current prices. The historical rate of return includes both dividends and any change in the price of the stock from the beginning of the period to the end. This procedure is based on the assumption that investors, on average, earn what they expect to earn. Furthermore, the method requires that (1) there were no significant changes in investor expectations as to the future performance of the firm during the study period, (2) no significant changes in the level of interest rates have occurred, and (3) investor attitudes toward risk haven't

---

[5] We will use the market value of the firm's stock later in determining the equity financing proportion. Since this market value reflects the entire value of the stockholders' ownership interest in the firm, there is no distinction between stock and retained earnings. See the end of Chapter 12 for more discussion of this issue.

changed. Unfortunately, such conditions are very unusual, and this method must be used only with great caution. Historical rates of return differ considerably, depending on the time periods chosen.

As a simple example, suppose that five years ago the price of the firm's stock was $50. Dividends of $6 per share were paid each year, and today the stock is still selling for $50. The average rate of return for an investor who bought the stock for $50 has been $6/$50 = 12 percent per year. Using the historical method, 12 percent would be an estimate of the current required rate of return on the stock.

Estimates of Future Dividends The second method is for the financial manager to estimate what investors expect the future dividend stream of the firm will be and to use the current price of the stock to determine stockholders' expected rate of return. The basic relationship for the price of the firm's stock was provided in Chapter 5. There we said that the price would be equal to the present value of the expected dividends given the risk-adjusted rate (k_s) required by investors. If we know the price and the expected dividends, we can determine the required rate of return from the equation.

$$P = \frac{D_1}{1 + k_s} + \frac{D_2}{(1 + k_s)^2} + \frac{D_3}{(1 + k_s)^3} + \cdots + \frac{D_m}{(1 + k_s)^m} \tag{7-7}$$

That is, given the current price P and the values for future dividends D_t, we can calculate k_s.

Determining the dividends expected by investors is not easy. However, if the firm has maintained some regular pattern of dividend payments in the past, it is not unreasonable for investors to expect this pattern to continue in the future. Suppose, for example, that for the past ten years the firm has paid an average dividend of $6 per share per year with no trend toward higher or lower payments and the earnings of the firm have also shown no trend up or down. Under these circumstances, it would be reasonable to assume that investors view the firm as paying a level perpetual dividend of $6 per share and therefore

$$P = \frac{\$6}{k_s}$$

If the current price of the stock is $50,

$$k_s = \frac{\$6}{P}$$

$$= \frac{\$6}{\$50}$$

$$= 12\%$$

A more typical firm would increase dividends over time. We know of a simple model of growing dividends that can be used to estimate k_s, the constant growth model of Chapter 5. In this model dividends are ex-

228

PART 2
**The firm's investment,
financing, and dividend
decisions**

pected to grow at a compound rate of g per year. If D_1 is the dividend expected next year, then

$$P = \frac{D_1}{k_s - g} \tag{7-8}$$

or

$$k_s = \frac{D_1}{P} + g \tag{7-9}$$

To use this model, we must assume that investors expect the dividends of the firm to grow indefinitely at a rate of g. This would be reasonable if the firm had consistent growth in the past and no significant changes appear likely in the future. It may not be easy to estimate what investors expect as next year's dividend and the long-run average growth rate, but it is less difficult to do this than to try to estimate what investors expect in every future year.

As an example, suppose that, historically, dividends have grown at a rate of 6 percent per year and management expects to pay $2 per share next year. Assuming that nothing has changed about the firm that would warrant a change in expectations regarding future growth, those two figures can be used with the current price of the stock to estimate k_s. If the current price is $40, then k_s would be estimated as

$$k_s = \frac{\$2}{\$40} + 0.06$$

$$= 11\%$$

If the actual circumstances of the business do not fit the constant growth model, then the problem of estimating the required rate of return becomes much more difficult because it may be very hard to estimate the future dividends expected by investors. For example, what should be done for firms that are not paying dividends? Through 1989, Pan American Airlines had not paid any dividends since 1967. Some new businesses have never paid a dividend. For such firms some other method must be used. The historical rate of return is one possibility although, as we indicated, there are potential problems in using this method. The rate of return earned by Pan American stockholders was negative in most of the years from 1967 through 1989 and approximately zero for the five-year period 1984–1989.

Using the Stock's Beta   A third method for estimating the stock rate k_s is based on the stock's beta value. The CAPM discussed in Chapter 6 specifies that the required rate of return on stock depends on its beta. The relationship is

$$k_s = \text{riskless rate} + \text{risk premium} \times \text{beta} \tag{7-10}$$

We can use this equation to estimate the stock rate if we have values for the riskless rate of interest, the market risk premium, and the stock's beta. We obtain the riskless rate for this purpose from the current rate on long-term government bonds as reported in publications such as *The Wall Street Journal*.[6] The market risk premium is more difficult to estimate. To obtain a rough idea of its magnitude, we can use the difference between the long-run average rate of returns on stocks and government bonds. Using the data in Table 5-2, this difference for the period 1926 to 1988 was 7.4 percentage points. Thus we estimate the market risk premium to be about 7 percentage points.

The beta for a company's stock can be obtained from published sources or estimated by the financial manager. Value Line and Merrill Lynch provide estimates of beta for the 1000 or so largest companies. For such companies, the published beta can be used. Estimating beta for a smaller company requires some statistical analysis. This is a topic for more advanced courses. In either case the value of beta is based on the historical relationship between the rate of return on the stock and the rate of return in the market. Therefore the procedure is accurate only if the business and financial risks of the firm have not changed over the period studied and are not expected to change.

As an example, beta for Pan Am's stock was estimated by Value Line to be 1.00 in 1989. Long-term government bond rates were about 7.5 percent in December 1989. We can therefore estimate the required rate of return on Pan Am's stock in December 1989 to be

Stock rate $= 7.5\% + 7\% \times 1.0$

$\qquad = 14.5\%$

Using Debt Rates   All three methods described above use historical data to estimate the stock rate. However, any use of historical data to reflect current views of investors assumes that investor views haven't changed recently. What if you are not willing to make that assumption? For example in 1981 Du Pont (a major chemical company) acquired Conoco (a major oil company) by borrowing about $4 billion. Clearly the business risk and the financial risk of the combined company might be different from that of either Du Pont or Conoco prior to the acquisition. How then in late 1981 could one estimate Du Pont's stock rate? The fourth approach takes the current rate on debt issued by the firm and assumes that the stockholders require an appreciably higher rate than that. Actual rates of return on common stocks average four to six percentage points higher than rates of return on corporate bonds. In Du Pont's case, this would imply that the company's stockholders required

---

[6] Some people suggest that the short-term Treasury bill rate be used as the riskless rate. This is appropriate if you wish to estimate a short-term rate on stock. We use long-term government bond rates because we wish to estimate the long-term required rate of return on stock for use in evaluating long-term investments. Our procedure is theoretically valid only under highly restrictive assumptions. However those assumptions are necessary to justify use of the CAPM to estimate long-term required rates of return.

230

PART 2
**The firm's investment,
financing, and dividend
decisions**

a rate of 18 to 20 percent since the firm's bonds were yielding around 14 percent at that time. This approach provides a very crude estimate of the stock rate, but it is based on current market rates and can be used when other approaches are suspect. It also is useful as a rough check on the magnitude of an estimate derived by another method.[7]

DETERMINING THE PROPORTIONS

In calculating the cost of capital we multiply the rate for each type of financing by the proportion of that type used by the firm. Now that we know how to determine the rates, we need to specify the proportions [the p's in Eq. (7-4)].

Several alternative ways to specify the proportions are used in practice. These include using the existing proportions on the firm's balance sheet, the proportions of financing planned for the current capital budget, the expected future financing proportions, and the current proportions of the market values of the firm's outstanding securities. Each may provide a cost of capital suitable for investment decisions in some cases; however, we recommend the use of market value proportions for two reasons.

First, it is difficult to determine the proportions of the types of financing that will be used to provide money for current and future investments before the profitability and amount of investment expenditures are known. Yet the financial manager must estimate the cost of capital before deciding which investments would be in the stockholders' interests. The current market value proportions of the firm's outstanding securities *are* known at the time investment decisions are made; therefore there is no need to forecast the financing methods that will be used.

Second, the best estimates of the rates associated with the various financing sources are those currently required on the firm's existing securities in the market. These rates reflect investors' assessments of the current business and financial risk of the firm and, coupled with investor expectations of future income, determine the current market value of the firm's securities. The cost of capital computed with current market rates and market value proportions is the average rate of return (adjusted for the tax deductibility of debt interest) required by investors in the firm's securities. Given the assumption that the firm's business and financial risk will not be changed, the cost of capital computed with market rates and market value proportions is a valid measure of the minimum rate of return required on new investments for them to be in the stockholders' interests. Indeed, under the assumptions used here, the present value of the expected cash flow from an investment using this cost of capital is a direct estimate of the increase in the market value of the firm's common

---

[7] There is yet another method that is sometimes used, E/P = (earnings per share)/(price per share). This method can be applied to firms not paying dividends, but it requires (a) that the firm be profitable, (b) that current earnings are neither abnormally high nor low, and (c) that the firm is not expected to have investments earning more than its cost of capital on average now and in the future.

stock from undertaking the investment. This is not true of other approaches even though they may indicate correctly, under some conditions, which investments should be undertaken.

For example, we calculate the proportions in the following way, using the market values of the securities currently outstanding:

Outstanding securities	Market value	Proportion
Debt	$ 4.0 million	0.40
Preferred stock	1.0 million	0.10
Common stock	5.0 million	0.50
Total	$10.0 million	1.00

CALCULATION OF A FIRM'S COST OF CAPITAL

Now that we know how to obtain the components, let's put them together in the calculation of the cost of capital for a firm. We will use modified data from an actual firm to illustrate the procedure.

Basic Brands, Inc. (not true name) is a consumer products company with well-established brand names. We are estimating the cost of capital for the firm at the beginning of 1990 for use in evaluating investment proposals in 1990. Data for Basic Brands are shown in Exhibit 7-2.

As discussed above, the required return on common stock is the most difficult value to estimate. The difficulties arise from trying to determine what shareholders are expecting with regard to the future performance of the firm. Since the firm's earnings and dividends have been growing fairly steadily since 1984 (in fact, dividends per share have risen every year for twenty-three years), the constant growth model appears appropriate. The problem, then, is one of estimating the future growth rate of dividends expected by investors. The historical growth rate of dividends provides a starting point. However, dividends have grown faster than earnings because an increasing percentage of earnings have been paid out. Suppose we assume that stockholders expect dividends to grow in the future at the same rate that earnings have grown at over the past six years, which is 10.8 percent per year. For 1990 let's assume $2.60 per share was expected since the firm declared a $0.65 dividend for the last quarter of 1989, which would imply an annual dividend of $2.60 if the quarterly rate were maintained. Applying Eq. (7-9), given a current stock price of $62,

$$k_s = \frac{D}{P} + g$$

$$= \frac{\$2.60}{\$62} + 0.108$$

$$= 15\%$$

What if investor expectations as to future dividends for Basic Brands were based on past dividend growth rather than past earnings growth?

This would be reasonable if investors expected earnings to grow somewhat faster in the future than in the past, thereby allowing the firm to continue its high rate of dividend increase. Using the historical dividend growth rate of 11.3 percent as an estimate of future dividend growth, we get

$$k_s = \frac{D}{P} + g$$

$$= \frac{\$2.60}{\$62} + 0.113$$

$$= 15.5\%$$

Therefore, the dividend growth method gives us values for k_s of 15 to 15.5 percent. Applying the beta method, we obtain a much lower number. Beta for Basic Brands was estimated to be 0.85. Interest rates on long-term government bonds in January 1990 were 7.4 percent. Using

---

EXHIBIT 7-2

Financial data for Basic Brands, Inc.: outstanding debt, preferred stock, and common stock as of December 31, 1989 (dollar figures in millions)

	Book value	Market value	Interest rate, %[a]
Bonds (7¾% due 2003)	$ 45	$ 41	8.9
Bonds (9½% due 2004)	50	52	8.9
Bonds (14% due 1992)	75	89	8.9
Other debt[b]	210	215	8.9
Total debt	$380	$397	8.9
Preferred stock[c] ($3.50)	$ 40	$ 20	7.0
Common stock	$620	$824	

	1984	1985	1986	1987	1988	1989	Average growth rate, %
			Common stock data				
Dividends per share	$1.45	$1.60	$1.77	$2.05	$2.28	$2.48	11.3
Earnings per share	2.97	3.73	4.21	4.83	4.86	4.95	10.8
Price per share	$29					$62	
Rate of return earned by stockholders 1984–1989: 18.7%							

[a] Interest rates on the three bond issues and other debt were set at the rate (8.9 percent) on the recently issued debt of the firm, which is selling closest to par (9½s of 2004). This was considered the best estimate of the current market rate on debt. None of the debt issues is subordinate to any other.
[b] Other debt consists of eight different types of debt, none of which is publicly traded. Market value is based on interest rates provided in the firm's annual report, using 8.9 percent as the estimated market rate that would apply.
[c] $100 par value; current market price is $50 per share.

the estimated market risk premium of 7 percent, we apply Eq. (7-10) to obtain

k_s = riskless rate + risk premium × beta

= 7.4% + 7% × 0.85

= 13.35%

The debt rate method (adding 4 to 6 percent to the debt rate to compute the equity rate) would yield values for k_s of 13 to 15 percent. Given this information and the other estimates of k_s computed above, let's use 14 percent as our estimate of equity rate k_s.

It should be apparent that estimating the stock rate is not a cookbook procedure. The best one can hope for is to be able to devise a reasonably good approximation to the "real" value, which cannot be directly observed. Note also that the actual historical rate of return to the stockholders has been 18.7 percent, which is much higher than our other estimates. This reflects in part a stock market rally in 1989.

Given a 1990 corporate income tax rate of 34 percent, we have all the information needed to calculate the cost of capital for Basic Brands. The calculations are shown in Exhibit 7-3 and result in an estimated cost of capital of 11.3 percent. This rate would be appropriate to evaluate investment opportunities available at the beginning of 1990.

THE COST OF CAPITAL FOR FOREIGN INVESTMENTS

The use of a firm's cost of capital to evaluate new investments assumes two conditions: (1) that the project has the same level of risk as the firm's existing projects and (2) that the project does not affect corporate financing policy. Both of these conditions are likely to be violated when the corporation initiates projects outside the country.

Foreign projects, particularly those in which the firm enters a country for the first time, are often riskier than existing domestic investments. The additional risks of international investments include

---

EXHIBIT 7-3
Cost of capital calculation for Basic Brands, Inc.

	Amount[a]	Proportion[b]	Rate, %	Prop. × Rate, %
Debt	$ 397	0.32	5.9[c]	1.9
Preferred stock	20	0.02	7.0	.1
Common stock	824	0.66	14.0	9.3
Total	$1,241	1.00		11.3

Cost of capital k_a = 11.3%

[a] These amounts are market values from Exhibit 7-2.
[b] Proportion is market value of financing type divided by total market value.
[c] Interest rate on debt is adjusted for tax rate of 34 percent. 8.9%(1 − 0.34) = 5.9.

234

PART 2
**The firm's investment,
financing, and dividend
decisions**

exchange rate risk and political uncertainties, such as expropriation. These risks can often be managed, but the fact that the risk may be different for foreign projects requires the firm to modify its calculation and use of the cost of capital. The risks peculiar to foreign investments are discussed in Chapter 9; adjustments for investments with differing risk are covered in Chapter 10.

The financing of foreign projects often includes foreign capital. A multinational corporation establishing operations in a new country will typically set up a foreign subsidiary. For various reasons, such as restrictions on the repatriation of earnings (under which interest and dividend payments are returned to the parent company), the firm often obtains part of its financing locally, within the foreign country. The subsidiary's funding sources may include local ownership (equity) and local debt, as well as funds from the parent company. The foreign subsidiary's retained earnings can also be used for new projects in the country. Because of differences in tax laws and accounting regulations, the retained earnings of the subsidiary may have a different cost than the retained earnings of the parent. For foreign investments with project-specific financing requirements, we must employ the general formula for the cost of capital, Eq. (7-4), using the proportions and costs of financing of the subsidiary. For example, an Italian-based multinational corporation that is considering the establishment of a manufacturing plant in Brazil might finance the Brazilian subsidiary with 60 percent of its own debt and equity, 10 percent equity from local Brazilian investors, 20 percent equity from the Brazilian government, and 10 percent in local cruzado-denominated bank loans. The cost of these sources of capital will be the rates of return required by the parent, by local and government investors, and by local Brazilian banks, respectively. Although the same principles apply, the calculation of the cost of capital for foreign projects is often more complicated than the calculations for domestic projects.

SUMMARY

The cost of capital for a firm is often used to evaluate investment projects. It is the minimum acceptable rate of return on new investments from the viewpoint of investors in the firm's securities. The cost of capital is suitable for investments with the same risks as past investments made by the firm, provided that the firm's financing policy does not change from what it has been in the past.

In order to assign a value to the cost of capital, we must estimate the rates of return required by investors in the firm's securities (including all borrowings) and average those rates according to the market values of the various securities currently outstanding. The rates are determined as follows:

1   The debt rate is the average market interest rate on the firm's debt issues adjusted for the tax deductibility of interest. For bonds the current yield to maturity is ordinarily used as the market rate.
2   The rate on preferred stock is the promised dividend payment on the preferred stock divided by the price of the stock.

3   The stock rate is the most difficult rate to estimate. The average historical rate of return earned by stockholders is sometimes used as an estimate of what stockholders currently require. If the firm seems to provide a constant growth in dividends, then the expected dividend yield on the stock plus the estimated growth rate of dividends is used to estimate the rate. A third method is to use the beta of the stock, current government bond rates, and the market risk premium to estimate the stock rate. Another method is to base the estimated stock rate on the current interest rate of the firm's debt plus a premium for the added risk of the stock.

QUESTIONS

1   Why is the cost of capital the minimum acceptable rate of return on an investment?

2   Under what conditions is the firm's cost of capital a valid criterion for new investment opportunities?

3   Why is it difficult to determine the rate of return required by investors in the firm's common stock?

4   Which method of calculating the rate on common stock would be most appropriate for the following firms:

  a   A profitable firm that has never paid a dividend but has had steady growth in earnings.

  b   An electric utility that has paid a dividend every year since 1895.

  c   A firm that had grown very rapidly until two years ago, when over-capacity problems in the industry produced severe price cutting in the firm's major product line. At the same time management decided to invest heavily in facilities to manufacture a new product. So far the manufacturing process has not worked properly. The firm lost $50 million last year, and the price of its common stock has dropped 80 percent in the past two years.

5   Is the cost of debt to the firm the debtholders' required rate of return as measured by the yield to maturity? Why or why not?

6   If the firm has several different types of long-term debt outstanding, does it make any difference in principle if an average debt rate is calculated for use in computing the cost of capital rather than treating each debt type separately with its own proportion and rate in the cost of capital formula? Does it make any difference in practice?

7   Would you expect all the firms in a given industry to have approximately the same cost of capital? Why or why not?

8   Do you think that the cost of capital for a firm is fairly constant over time? Explain. What are the implications of your answer for business use of the cost of capital?

9   How could one find the cost of capital for a proprietorship or partnership? Can you think of any ways to do this? What problems are present for these firms that are not present for corporations?

10 A U.S.–based forest products firm is planning capital expenditures for its Indonesian subsidiary. The firm's current cost of capital has been estimated to be 11 percent. The subsidiary is financed with a mix of equity from the parent and local debt issues. Should the firm use 11 percent as the cost of capital for its Indonesian subsidiary? Why or why not?

PROJECT

Choose a business firm and estimate its cost of capital as of some particular date. The following guides may be helpful in this project:

1 A large company will be easier to obtain data for than a small company; however, large companies are often more complicated to analyze.
2 Choose a date immediately following an available annual report for the company. The annual report will serve as a very important source of data on the firm's financial affairs.
3 Appendix 5A provides additional sources of data.
4 Avoid firms with bonds or preferred stock that are convertible into common stock. Convertible securities are difficult to analyze.
5 Many firms use large amounts of short-term debt, have long-term debt with interest rates that are tied to short-term interest rates, or have debt denominated in foreign currencies. Treat these items as was done for "other debt" in the Basic Brands example in the chapter.
6 Read the footnotes to the financial statements in the annual report. Leases are a form of debt. Their estimated value will be found in the balance sheet or in footnotes.

DEMONSTRATION PROBLEM

DP1 The Crunchy Cookie Company has had its problems in the past, but management currently expects the firm to be able to maintain a fairly steady growth rate of 8 percent per year in earnings and dividends. Crunchy's common stock had been selling at a rather depressed price of $15 per share until the annual stockholders meeting, where management outlined its future investment and operating plans. The current price is now $25 per share. The $2.00 per share dividend that had been paid each year since 1969 is not expected to change next year, even though earnings will be higher, because of the need to finance a complete modernization of the firm's bakery. However, in future years dividends will be increased as earnings rise. The annual meeting was rather lively as several major stockholders were very concerned about the company's prior performance. One stockholder noted that her 1988 investment in the company had provided a rate of return (given the price of $15 per share obtained prior to the meeting) of only 5.8 percent. This, she caustically remarked, was much less than she would have earned in U.S. government bonds purchased at the same time.

Further, she noted that she would have been better off being a
bondholder of the company than a stockholder. The company's
bonds are currently yielding 9 percent. What is your best
estimate of the required rate on Crunchy's common stock?
(*Note:* There is no single exact answer to this problem.)

SOLUTION TO DP1:

Approach the problem using several methods.

1　Historical rate of return is 5.8 percent. This is very low and
should be ignored—below U.S. government bond rate.

2　Management's forecast of 8 percent growth and current price
of $25.

$$k_s = \frac{\$2.00}{\$25} + 0.08$$

$$= 16\%$$

3　Historical dividends and previous price—no growth.

$$k_s = \frac{\$2.00}{\$15}$$

$$= 13.3\%$$

4　Interest rate on firm's bonds of 9 percent plus a premium of
4 percent to 6 percent provides a range of 13 percent to 15
percent.

Conclusion k_s is probably less than 16 percent since investors
have reason to believe management could be overly optimistic.
On the other hand, the stock price did rise sharply, so investors
didn't discount management's opinion entirely. Suppose
investors are forecasting a growth rate in the range of 5 percent
to 7 percent. This would suggest a value for the stock rate of
between 13 percent and 15 percent which is consistent with the
range developed from the debt rate and close to the 13.3 percent
estimated using the previous price. Best guess 14 percent.

PROBLEMS

1　Drysdale Store has the following issues outstanding:

	Senior bonds	Subordinated bonds
Market value	$20 million	$20 million
Maturity value	$24 million	$20 million
Yield to maturity	14%	16%
Coupon rate	10%	16%

a　What is the before-tax interest cost to the firm of each of the
two types of debt issues?

b　What is the average rate on the bonds?

238

PART 2
**The firm's investment,
financing, and dividend
decisions**

c Assuming a 46 percent tax rate, what is the effective rate on the bonds?

2 Calculate the required rate of return (k_s) for common stock under the following situations:

a Firm A has paid a $5 dividend for the past fifteen years and investors expect it to continue to do so in the future. The current price of A's stock is $40 per share.

b Firm B's dividends per share have grown at a constant rate of 8 percent a year. Investors expect a dividend of $1.50 next year. The current price of a share of the firm's stock is $20.

c Firm C pays no dividends and the beta for its common stock is estimated to be 1.0. The current interest rate on government bonds is 12 percent and the market risk premium is 6 percent.

3 Determine the rates to be used in cost of capital calculations for the following securities. Assume that they are issued by different firms and that the corporate income tax rate is 40 percent.

a A seven-year (original maturity) note with a coupon interest rate of 10 percent. The note matures in five years and has a current market price of $90 per $100 maturity value.

b A bond issue is scheduled to mature in twenty years, bearing a coupon rate of 16 percent; however, the firm's management has announced plans to pay off the bonds one year from now after paying the interest due for the year. The bondholders would receive the maturity value at that time. The current price for the bonds as reported in the newspaper is $104.

c A preferred stock pays $5 dividends per $100 par value. The current market price is $40.

d The historical average rate of return earned by owners of the firm's common stock has been about 17 percent per year until very recently. The dividends of the firm have grown at an average rate of 13 percent per year over the same period. A major investment advisory service has issued a report that is somewhat critical of the firm's management and forecasts dividends and earnings to grow no faster than the overall growth rate in the general economy. The price of the firm's stock reacted sharply to the report, dropping from $100 per share to $50 per share. The long-run economic growth rate for the U.S. economy is generally thought to be 6 percent per year. The stock's dividends for next year are expected to be $5 per share.

4 Calculate the proportions to be used in calculating the cost of capital for each of the following sets of data on different firms:

a

	Balance sheet data	Market value
Bonds	$8 million maturity value	$ 8 million
Preferred stock	$4 million par value	$ 2 million
Common stock	$6 million book value	$10 million

Bond price = $100 per $100 maturity value

Preferred stock price = $50 per $100 par value

Common stock price = $10 per share

(There are 1 million shares of common stock outstanding.)

b There are two types of securities outstanding for the firm—bonds with a maturity value of $5 million and 100,000 shares of common stock. The current market price for the bonds is $90 per $100 maturity value, and the price of the stock is $45 per share.

c

Balance sheet data	
Bonds (8% due 2002)	$10.0 million
Common stock (200,000 shares at $5 par value)	1.0 million
Surplus	1.5 million
Retained earnings	5.5 million
Total equity	$ 7.0 million

Market price for bonds = $80

Market price for stock = $60

d

Balance sheet data	
Long-term debt	$5 million
Preferred stock ($100 par)	$1 million
Book value of common stock	$6 million

Other data	
Common stock	2 million shares outstanding; current price = $4 per share
Preferred stock	These securities are not traded and no market prices are available. However, the stock is recently issued, and the dividend rate being paid by the firm is approximately equal to current market rates.
Long-term debt	Current price = $80 per $100 maturity value

5 As a financial analyst for Hawk Manufacturing Corporation (HMC), you have been asked to develop an estimate of the required rate of return that HMC should use in evaluating typical investment proposals. HMC's management plans to maintain its current capital structure of 30 percent debt and 70 percent equity (based on estimates of current market values). HMC's outstanding debt securities carry an average interest cost of 7.3 percent of their book value. Management estimates that the average rate in

240

PART 2
The firm's investment,
financing, and dividend
decisions

the market for new debt issues comparable to those currently outstanding would be 9 percent if the firm's financing policies are maintained. The average rate of return (dividends plus price appreciation) on HMC's common stock for the past ten years has been 16 percent. Management believes, however, that stockholders require a rate of return of 15 percent under present market conditions. HMC's tax rate is 34 percent. Is there sufficient information provided here to make the estimate called for above? If not, what is needed? If so, what is your estimate?

6 Kerry Malatesta is considering opening a bookstore in a small town which does not currently have one. She estimates that initial capital requirements would be $50,000, of which $30,000 would be borrowed at an interest rate of 15 percent and $20,000 would come from her personal funds. Given alternative investment opportunities in the capital market of comparable risk, Kerry believes that a minimum expected rate of return of 20 percent on her investment would be required to make a bookstore worthwhile. The bookstore would be incorporated and the corporate tax rate would be 25 percent (ignore personal taxes).

a What is the minimum acceptable cash flow from the bookstore? (Assume level cash flows and ignore principal payments on the debt.)

b What is the minimum acceptable return on the total investment in the project, given your answer from a?

c Calculate the cost of capital for the bookstore and compare it to your answer for b.

7 Undersea Sports, Inc. is a rapidly growing manufacturer of scuba gear established in 1981. The chief financial officer has asked you to prepare an estimate of the rate of return required by investors in Undersea's stock at the beginning of 1991. You have compiled the data shown below. Prepare a brief report which provides the estimate asked for and explains the basis of your estimate.

	Earnings per share	Dividends per share	Year-end share price
1990	$3.00	$0.60	$34.80
1989	2.40	0.40	32.00
1988	1.85	0.30	27.50
1987	1.10	0.20	22.80
1986	0.50	—	12.75
1985	0.08	—	3.20

Management is projecting $0.80 dividends per share for 1991. A recent report on the scuba industry forecast a long-run growth in sales of 9 percent per year. Security analysts have estimated a beta of 1.4 for Undersea's stock. The firm can issue debt at an interest rate of 9 percent, a premium of 2 percentage points over the current U.S. Treasury bond rate of 7 percent. The interest rate on Treasury bills is 4.8 percent. Recent studies have provided the following historial data:

Average rate of return on common stocks	10.5%
Average rate of return on AAA bonds	6.5%
Average rate of return on U.S. Treasury bonds	6.0%
Average rate of return on U.S. Treasury bills	5.5%

Given this information, what is your best estimate for the rate of return required by investors on Undersea's common stock?

8 Undersea Sports, Inc. has a variety of investment possibilities that management must evaluate. As part of this process you have been asked to estimate Undersea's current cost of capital. In addition to the data provided in problem 7 above, you have collected the following information:

Balance sheet (000s) (12/31/90)			
Current assets	$15,000	Current liabilities	$ 8,500
Plant & equipment	35,000	Bonds	20,000
Total assets	$50,000	Preferred stock	4,000
		Common stock (1 million shares)	500
		Retained earnings	17,000
		Total	$50,000

Market data (January 20, 1991)			
	Bonds	**Preferred stock**	**Common stock**
Price	$105	$80	$34.80
Yield*	9.0%	9.5%	1.7%

* Yield for bonds is "yield to maturity." Yield for preferred stock and common stock is 1990 dividend divided by price.

The bonds pay a 10 percent coupon rate of interest and the preferred stock pays a dividend of $7.60 per share ($100 par). Undersea's 1991 marginal income tax rate will be 32 percent. What is your estimate of the firm's cost of capital?

CHAPTER EIGHT

FUNDAMENTALS OF CAPITAL BUDGETING

Each year United States nonfarm businesses spend roughly $300 billion on new plant and equipment—factories, machines, tools, pollution control equipment, and transportation facilities, among other things. Unlike current assets, which are discussed in Chapters 17 and 18, these assets, called **capital assets**, are used by the company in the physical process of producing goods and services and are ordinarily used for a number of years. Because the dollar amounts involved are so large, businesses carefully plan and evaluate expenditures for capital assets. The plan for expenditures is called a **capital budget**. The process of determining both how much to spend on capital assets and which assets to acquire is called **capital budgeting**.

This chapter presents the basic concepts of capital budgeting. The budgeting procedure is first examined and then the techniques used to evaluate proposals are described. Several important issues, including inflation and capital rationing, are discussed. The chapter ends with a look at the attitudes of business toward the various capital budgeting techniques.

THE CAPITAL BUDGETING PROCESS

Most firms prepare at least a short-run budget that indicates planned capital outlays for the current and immediately forthcoming periods. Many firms also prepare intermediate and long-term capital budgets that project capital requirements for three to five, and sometimes even ten, years into the future. Capital budgets are based on sales forecasts and on the anticipated plant and equipment needed to meet those expected sales.

Many items in the capital budget originate as proposals from plant and division management. These proposals, with supporting data, are submitted to senior management for consideration. Project recommendations may also come from top management, especially if a corporate stategic move is involved (for example, a major expansion or entry into a new market). Review of a proposed project may involve lengthy discussions between senior management and those members of lower management at the division and plant level who will be involved with the project if it is adopted. Generally, the list of proposals is studied by senior management and its staff and a subset of the list is accepted and a capital budget prepared. The budget is then submitted to the board of directors for approval.

In many cases, the process just described is modified for small dollar-value capital expenditures. For example, division managers may be permitted to spend up to some given amount, say, $50,000, for capital replacements and other outlays in a given year. All capital expenditures above that amount would require approval by central management.

A capital budgeting system under which proposals originate with top management is referred to as a **top-down system**, and one in which proposals originate at the plant and division level is referred to as a **bottom-up system**. Sometimes ''top-down'' signifies that approval authority rests with senior management and ''bottom-up'' signifies that the authority resides at lower levels. Actually, most large corporations are a mixture of both these approaches. Investment ideas emerge from below and above and authority is usually divided between senior management, which approves large projects, and division management, which has discretion up to some limit. The issue is therefore one of emphasis. Since World War II there has been a gradual shift in the direction of decentralization and a greater use of the bottom-up approach.

Economic conditions are constantly changing and even the best projections of future operations usually require revision over time. Capital budgeting is no exception. Investment plans are continually reformulated as new information regarding demand for the firm's products, changes in technology, and costs of production become available. Intermediate and long-term capital budgets are then revised accordingly. The new information not only provides a clue as to the appropriate level of future capital outlays, but it also reflects upon past investment decisions. The wisdom or error of previous decisions is revealed by the success or failure of particular projects. Information on the progress and profitability of the firm's past investments is useful in several respects. It pinpoints sectors of the firm's activities that may warrant further financial commitments; or it may call for retreat if a particular project becomes permanently unprofitable. The outcome of an investment also reflects on the performance of those members of management associated with the project. Finally, past errors and successes may provide clues regarding the weaknesses and strengths of the capital budgeting process itself.

The remainder of this chapter examines alternative procedures for evaluating investment opportunities. These techniques relate to the capital budget in two ways. First, they set forth profitability criteria that investments must satisfy in order to be accepted. The criteria are used by firms to estimate the amount of funds that they can invest profitably.

244

PART 2
**The firm's investment,
financing, and dividend
decisions**

These estimated amounts are incorporated into the firm's intermediate or long-term capital budget. Since these figures are only predictions of future capital outlays, they will usually have to be revised as the actual investment date approaches. At this stage the second role of capital budgeting analysis comes into play. When the time arrives to determine the exact amount to invest and where, capital budgeting techniques such as present value and internal rate of return are used. As is explained next, the analysis of an investment first requires an estimation of its cash flows.

CASH FLOW FROM AN INVESTMENT

Under each method of analysis described in this chapter, it is necessary to consider the costs and benefits of each investment opportunity. These methods for evaluating projects are based on the marginal or incremental **cash flow** from each project. The marginal cash flow from an investment is the change in total firm cash flow from adopting that investment.

Computing Cash Flow

What is cash flow, and why is cash flow the proper measure of a project's costs and benefits? Cash flow is money paid or received by the firm as a result of undertaking the project. We can express cash flow for any period in terms of the relevant costs and benefits associated with an asset (or "project") for that period:

$$
\begin{aligned}
\text{Net cash flow from the project} = {}& \text{project cash inflows} \\
& - \text{project cash outflows} \\[6pt]
= {}& \text{project revenues} \\
& - \text{project expenses other} \\
& \quad\text{than depreciation} \\
& - \text{project capital expenditures} \\
& - \text{project income taxes} \qquad (8\text{-}1)
\end{aligned}
$$

where

$$
\begin{aligned}
\text{Project income taxes} = {}& \text{tax rate} \times (\text{project revenues} \\
& - \text{project expenses other} \\
& \quad\text{than depreciation} \\
& - \text{depreciation}) \qquad (8\text{-}1a)
\end{aligned}
$$

The term in parentheses in Eq. (8-1a) is the computed taxable income from the project.[1] Project revenues in Eq. (8-1) include all cash received from customers for the firm's product (cash sales and collections of accounts receivable). Expenses other than depreciation include cash

---

[1] Equation (8-1) is only an approximation. Cash revenues and expenses are usually not equal to taxable revenues and tax deductible expenses because revenues and expenses for tax purposes are ordinarily computed on an accrual rather than a cash basis. However, in most cases the differences can be safely ignored, as is done here.

outlays for labor, materials, and other items required by the use of the asset but do *not* include interest on firm debt.[2]

Depreciation affects the cash flow of Eq. (8-1) only through its impact on income taxes. Depreciation is not a cash expense (does not involve any expenditure of cash); it is simply a way to spread the cost of an asset (a capital expenditure) over the asset's life. From a cash flow standpoint, the capital expenditure is recorded as a cash outflow *when the asset is acquired* and not over its useful life. This will be illustrated below in an example.

It is very important to note that taxes are computed as though the project were financed entirely with equity funds. Interest on debt is not included as an expense in determining project income taxes in Eq. (8-1a). In other words, in computing aftertax cash flow, you are ignoring the method of financing the investment. Financing method is reflected in the cost of capital that takes account of the benefit derived from the tax deductibility of interest (see Chapter 7). As we will see later in the chapter, this cost of capital is used in evaluating the cash flow.

Since a project's cash flow is the change in total firm cash flow resulting from adopting the investment, a method for determining the cash flow from an investment is to compare the firm's cash flow with and without that investment. The difference between the two is the additional cash flow due to the investment. To illustrate, assume that an investment costs $1200, has a life of twelve years, has an expected aftertax liquidation value at the end of the twelve years of $200, and is depreciated for tax purposes on a straight-line basis at $100 per year ($1200/12 years). (*Recall from Chapter 3 that salvage value is assumed to be zero in computing depreciation for tax purposes*.) The corporate tax rate is 30 percent. At the time the asset is acquired, the net cash flow is simply the capital expenditure, which is an outlay (a negative cash flow) of $1200. The computation in Exhibit 8-1 shows that the net cash flow for years 1 to 11 is $205. The net cash flow for year 12 is the $205 from using the asset during year 12 (computed as in Exhibit 8-1) *plus* the aftertax liquidation value of $200 that is received from selling the asset at the end of year 12; this adds up to a year 12 net cash flow of $405 ($205 + $200). The asset cash flows are shown in Exhibit 8-2.

---

[2] Equation (8-1) includes all cash inflows and outflows associated with the project, and it is cash flows (and their timing) that matter. Project revenues in Eq. (8-1) are cash sales plus collections of accounts receivable (*cash* received) from customers, and this is not typically equal to sales on the income statement (which are on an accrual basis and include increases in accounts receivable). Similarly, project expenses other than depreciation in Eq. (8-1) are *cash* payments to labor, suppliers, etc., and this usually differs from expenses on the income statement (which are on an accrual basis). In some cases, it may be convenient to estimate cash revenues and expenses using accrued sales and expenses and then making adjustments for changes in working capital (current assets minus current liabilities) during the period. See the discussion in Chap. 20 for an illustration of the use of changes in current assets and current liabilities in making cash flow estimates.

EXHIBIT 8-1
Determining the annual cash flow on an investment

	Firm's cash flow without the investment (1)	Firm's cash flow with the investment (2)	Added cash flow due to the investment (col. 2 − col. 1) (3)
Annual revenues (R)	$2,000	$2,400	$400
Annual expenses other than depreciation (E)	1,500	1,650	150
Taxes:			
Revenues less expenses ($R - E$) $500		$750	$250
Less depreciation 200		300	100
Taxable income (TI) $300		$450	$150
Tax (30% of TI)	90	135	45
Net cash flow ($R - E -$ tax)	$ 410	$ 615	$205

Summary of above results:		
Revenues from the investment		$400
Less:		
Expenses other than depreciation	$150	
Taxes	45	
Total		195
Annual aftertax cash flow		$205

Assumptions:

Life of asset = 12 years
Price of asset = $1,200
Tax rate = 30%
Salvage value at end of year 12 = $200

The approach for determining and analyzing the cash flow from an investment can be summarized in the following three steps:

1 Determine the change in the firm's cash flow from acquiring the new asset. This can be done by using the Exhibit 8-1 method of comparing the firm's cash flow with and without the asset. *All* changes in cash flow due to the investment must be taken into ac-

EXHIBIT 8-2
Net cash flow from the investment

Time	Net cash flow
Time 0 (when asset acquired)	− $1,200
Each year for years 1 to 11	$ 205
Year 12	$ 405

count, including any salvage value cash proceeds when the asset is sold.

2 Put the results of the step *1* computation in tabular form, showing the timing and amount of the cash flow (for example, as in Exhibit 8-2).

3 Analyze the cash flow using net present value or internal rate of return (these methods are described below) to determine whether the investment should be made.

Why is cash flow the proper measure of the costs and benefits of an investment? The answer is that cash flow represents the true inflow and outflow of purchasing power for the firm. When an asset is purchased, such purchasing power is sacrificed; when a net cash flow is earned on the asset in later periods, purchasing power is received. The future cash flow from an asset is the money generated by the asset that is available for payment to the firm's stockholders and bondholders as dividends and interest or to finance further investment. It is the stream of purchasing power provided by the asset and is therefore the measure of that asset's productivity.

A firm's cash budget (discussed in Chapter 16) and a firm's cash flow should be distinguished. The cash budget shows the forecasted cash transactions of the firm (or some subentity such as a division) for some stated time period. It is an estimate of cash receipts and cash disbursements based on an analysis of past performance and on the firm's plans for the future. A cash budget is used for planning operations and financing. Exhibit 16-4 illustrates a cash budget. The firm's forecasted cash flow [cash flow as defined in Eq. (8-1)] is readily computed using the data in the cash budget. Notice that, in contrast with the cash budget, cash flow does not include the cash effects of capital transactions (for example, interest payments, dividends, and stock and bond sales), but it represents the net cash flow generated by the firm's assets (or a single asset) that is available to those financing the company (stockholders and bondholders). Also, cash flow is often calculated for an individual investment and not just for an operating entity such as a department, division, or firm. Cash flow is used primarily to assess an investment's desirability, whereas a cash budget is ordinarily used for overall planning.

Cash Flow and Uncertainty

Generally, future cash flows are uncertain, and only estimates of these flows are available for evaluating an investment proposal. The estimate that is often used is **expected cash flow**, which will be discussed in Chapter 10. In the present chapter, we assume that all investments have the same level of risk. Further, we assume that a numerical estimate can be made of the cash flow in each future year from any investment. The cash flow estimate is an "educated guess" based upon available information. It is ordinarily somewhere between the highest and lowest possible figures that can be expected, in other words, a middle estimate. In Chapter 10 we will be more precise. Since in this chapter all investments are assumed to be of identical risk, all will be evaluated using the same cost of capital, k. Rate k can be viewed as the minimum acceptable rate of return on the investment. In the examples of this chapter, k will be 10 percent.

EVALUATION
TECHNIQUES

After the cash flows have been estimated, they are evaluated to determine whether the investment should be undertaken. Several techniques are available to evaluate investment proposals. The chief ones are:

1 Present value
2 Internal rate of return (or simply rate of return)
3 Payback period
4 Accounting rate of return

A fifth approach that uses a profitability index will be discussed in the section on capital rationing.

Present Value

The time-value-of-money concept discussed in Chapter 4 can be used to evaluate the cash flows from an investment. The **present value** of a cash flow is what it is worth in today's dollars. Present value incorportaes the time-value principle by **discounting** future dollars (computing their present value) using the appropriate discount rate (interest rate). In investment analysis, this discount rate is the cost of capital.

The present value rule states that an investment should be adopted only if the present value of the cash flow it generates in the future exceeds its cost, that is, if it has a positive **net present value (NPV)**. The net present value of an asset equals

$$NPV = \frac{\text{present value of}}{\text{future cash flows}} - \text{initial cost}$$

$$= \frac{CF_1}{1 + k} + \frac{CF_2}{(1 + k)^2} + \cdots + \frac{CF_n}{(1 + k)^n} - I$$

$$= CF_1(P/F, k, 1) + CF_2(P/F, k, 2)$$
$$+ \cdots + CF_n\,(P/F, k, n) - I \tag{8-2}$$

where CF_1 = cash flow in period 1

CF_2 = cash flow in period 2, etc.

I = initial outlay or cost

k = cost of capital

The $(P/F, k, 1)$, $(P/F, k, 2)$, etc., terms are the present value factors discussed in Chapter 4.

If the future cash flow is a level annuity of CF per period for n periods (all cash flows are equal), then Eq. (8-2) becomes

$$NPV(\text{annuity}) = \frac{CF}{1 + k} + \frac{CF}{(1 + k)^2} + \cdots + \frac{CF}{(1 + k)^n} - I$$

$$= CF(P/A, k, n) - I \tag{8-3}$$

NPV is the net benefit that accrues to the firm from adopting the investment. A positive NPV means that the project yields a rate of return exceeding the cost of capital k. In this case, NPV is the total value in current dollars of the extraordinary return (the return above the cost of capital) earned by the investment. If a project's NPV $= 0$, it is just earning the cost of capital and is therefore just barely, or marginally, acceptable. If NPV is negative, less than the cost of capital is earned by the project; that is, the project is not even earning the required rate of return, and it should therefore be rejected.[3]

In Appendix 8A, it is shown that the net present value of an investment is equal to the benefit of the investment to shareholders and that therefore net present value is a valid guide to project selection.

The Accept-Reject Decision   Sometimes an investment decision involves the acceptance or rejection of a given opportunity and not the comparison of several alternatives. The present value method specifies that such an investment should be adopted if its NPV is greater than zero; if NPV $= 0$, it is a matter of indifference whether the project is accepted; and if NPV is less than zero, the project should be rejected.[3]

To illustrate the present value method, assume that a restaurant can buy a new sign that will increase net cash flow by attracting new customers. The choice is either to buy the particular sign or to obtain no new sign at all. The sign costs $3500, will last five years, and will increase net cash flow by an estimated $1000 in each of the next five years. Using Eq. (8-3) and assuming a cost of capital k of 10 percent, the NPV equals

$$\text{NPV} = \frac{\$1000}{1 + 0.10} + \frac{\$1000}{(1 + 0.10)^2} + \cdots + \frac{\$1000}{(1 + 0.10)^5} - \$3500$$

$$= \$1000(P/A, 10\%, 5) - \$3500$$

$$= \$1000(3.791) - \$3500$$

$$= \$3791 - \$3500 = \$291$$

Since the NPV of $291 is positive, the sign should be purchased. The $3791 is the value in today's dollars (the present value) of the future benefits from the asset, and the $3500 is the cost in today's dollars: The difference is the net gain, $291.

Choices between Alternatives   Many, perhaps most, investment decisions involve a choice from among several mutually exclusive alternatives rather than the simple accept-reject decision of a single alternative. Two alternatives are mutually exclusive if adopting one means that the other

---

[3] As is explained later in this section, we are assuming that the firm can obtain additional funds for investment at the cost of capital. At the end of the chapter, capital rationing (limited funds available) is considered in detail.

will not be adopted (for example, to buy machine A or machine B or neither, but not both). The present value rule dictates that the alternative having the highest NPV is best and it is accepted if, and only if, its NPV is positive (indifference if NPV = 0).

Cash flows from sign	
Initial outlay (I)	$3,500
Increase in annual cash flow for next 5 years	$1,000

As an example, assume that a manufacturer is comparing two machines for its production line: the deluxe model, which costs $3000 and will raise net estimated cash flow by $900 per year for the next five years, and the economy model, with a smaller capacity, which costs $2000 and will raise net estimated cash flow by $610 per year for the next five years.

Cash flows of machine alternatives		
	Deluxe machine	**Economy machine**
Initial outlay (I)	$3,000	$2,000
Increase in annual cash flow for next 5 years(CF)	$ 900	$ 610

Using Eq. (8-3), we can compute the NPV of each, assuming a cost of capital of 10 percent:

$$\text{NPV(deluxe model)} = \$900(P/A, 10\%, 5) - \$3000$$
$$= \$900(3.791) - \$3000$$
$$= \$412$$

$$\text{NPV(economy model)} = \$610(P/A, 10\%, 5) - \$2000$$
$$= \$610(3.791) - \$2000$$
$$= \$313$$

The deluxe model is superior, since its NPV of $412 exceeds the economy model's NPV of $313. Further, since the deluxe model has an NPV exceeding zero, it should be purchased.

The Net Present Value Method Summarized The net present value rule can be summarized as follows:

1 In an accept-reject decision, the investment is adopted if its NPV is positive. We are indifferent if its NPV = 0, and the investment is rejected if its NPV is negative.

2 In comparing mutually exclusive investment alternatives (at most, one alternative is to be accepted), we first determine which alternative has the highest NPV and reject all the other alternatives. We then accept the alternative with the highest NPV if its NPV exceeds zero. We are indifferent if its NPV = 0 and reject the alternative if its NPV is negative.

The above rules assume that the firm can obtain funds at the cost of capital (through borrowing, selling shares, etc.) as long as those funds can be profitably employed. Indeed, if this were not so, then "cost of capital" would have little meaning since "cost" means the price that must be paid to obtain something, in this case, capital or funds to finance investment. Later in this chapter, we will examine the case in which capital is limited or "rationed." In Chapters 10 and 12 we consider cases in which the cost of capital depends on the risk of the investment and the size of the capital budget.

The Internal Rate of Return

We can look at the above capital budgeting problems in a somewhat different way. Instead of discounting the cash flows at the cost of capital to determine net present value, we can ask the following question: What rate of return does the project earn? If the rate of return exceeds the cost of capital k, it is a profitable project since the cost of capital is the minimum required rate of return. If the project's rate of return just equals k, it is only marginal (we are indifferent as to whether it is accepted). If the project's rate of return is less than the cost of capital, it should be rejected.

Determining the IRR In Chapter 4 we discussed methods for determining an unknown interest rate, for example, the rate earned on a share of stock. An internal rate of return is the rate we expect to earn on an investment project. The IRR is that rate which discounts a project's cash flow to an NPV of zero. Letting r signify the IRR, an investment's IRR is that rate r which satisfies the following relationship:

$$0 = \frac{CF_1}{1 + r} + \frac{CF_2}{(1 + r)^2} + \cdots + \frac{CF_n}{(1 + r)^n} - I$$

$$= CF_1(P/F, r, 1) + CF_2(P/F, r, 2) + \cdots + CF_n(P/F, r, n) - I \tag{8-4}$$

If the cash flow returns are a level annuity, that is, if $CF_1 = CF_2 = \cdots = CF_n = CF$, then Eq. (8-4) becomes

$$0 = \frac{CF}{1 + r} + \frac{CF}{(1 + r)^2} + \cdots + \frac{CF}{(1 + r)^n} - I$$

$$= CF(P/A, r, n) - I \tag{8-5}$$

To illustrate the above method, assume that project H costs $3000 and generates cash flows of $2400 in the first year and $1440 in the second year. The cash flows are stated on the following page.

252

PART 2
The firm's investment,
financing, and dividend
decisions

Cash flows of project H
$I = \$3,000$
$CF_1 = \$2,400$
$CF_2 = \$1,440$

Using Eq. (8-4), we find that the rate of return on project H is 20 percent ($r = 20\%$) since:

$$0 = \frac{\$2400}{1.2} + \frac{\$1440}{(1.2)^2} - \$3000$$

$$= \$2000 + \$1000 - \$3000$$

Now that we have examined how an IRR is computed, let us take a closer look at what the IRR number really measures.

The Rate of Return Concept   To examine more closely what we mean by an investment's IRR assume a project requiring an initial outlay I and producing a stream of future net cash flows $CF_1, CF_2, \ldots, CF_n$, over the coming n periods. When we say that the project's IRR is some amount r, we mean that if at time 0 (now) we were to put amount I into a fund actually earning rate of return r each period, we could withdraw from the fund amount CF_1 one period from now, amount CF_2 two periods from now, and so on including CF_n n periods from now, and exactly exhaust the fund at the end of the n periods. It is similar to the idea developed in Chapter 4 of purchasing an annuity currently that pays a future income and provides a rate of return equal to the interest rate. Here, for an investment project, the price of the annuity is I, the income it provides is the $CF_1, CF_2, \ldots, CF_n$ stream, and the rate of return is r. We can illustrate this concept using project H above.

The rate of return on project H is 20 percent. As illustrated in Figure 8-1, if we deposit $3000 at time 0 in a fund, we will have $3600 in the fund at time 1 assuming a 20 percent rate of return earned during the first period. Since we want to produce a cash flow $CF_1 = \$2400$, we withdraw $2400 from the fund at time 1 and leave $1200 in the fund. One period later, at time 2, the $1200 has earned 20 percent and has therefore grown to $1440 ($1200 + 0.20 × $1200), which we can now withdraw to produce our time 2 cash flow of $1440.

A project with the cash flows $I = \$3000$, $CF_1 = \$2400$, and $CF_2 = \$1440$ therefore implies that 20 percent per period is being earned on the $3000 investment.

Another insight into the IRR approach emerges by examining Eqs. (8-4) and (8-5). To compute the IRR on an investment, we plug in I and the cash flows CF_1 to CF_n into (8-4) or (8-5) and then solve for r. Since (8-4) and (8-5) are simply present value equations with the present value equal to zero, in determining r we are determining that interest rate which would imply that the investment has a net present value of zero. Keep in mind that the interest rate we used in Eqs. (8-2) and (8-3) is k, the cost of capital, and this will equal r, the IRR, only if $r = k$, that is, only if the project has an actual NPV equal to zero. (Remember in our discussion of present value that we said that if NPV $= 0$, the project is just earning the cost of capital k.) If NPV *exceeds* zero using cost of capital k, then ordinarily r exceeds k, and the project is earning a rate of return that exceeds the cost of capital.[4]

In Figure 8-2 the relationships between NPV, k, and r are shown. At the cost of capital k of 10 percent, the NPV of project H equals

$$\text{NPV(project H)} = \frac{\$2400}{1.1} + \frac{\$1440}{(1.1)^2} - \$3000$$

$$= \$2182 + \$1190 - \$3000$$

$$= \$372$$

The NPV(project H) schedule shows an NPV $= \$372$ at a discount rate of 10 percent. Each point on the schedule shows the NPV of project H along the vertical axis for each discount rate shown along the horizontal axis. Notice that if the discount rate k were 20 percent, NPV(project H) $= 0$; therefore, internal rate of return r for project H is 20 percent, since r is that rate which sets the NPV equal to zero [see Eq. (8-4)]. In short, we can view the internal rate of return, r, as the cost of capital which would just make the project marginally acceptable (NPV $= 0$). Project H

---

[4] Actually, a positive NPV necessarily implies that the investment's rate of return exceeds the cost of capital only if the investment involves an initial outlay (cost) and produces a nonnegative cash flow return in future periods. This is the type of investment considered in the examples in this chapter.

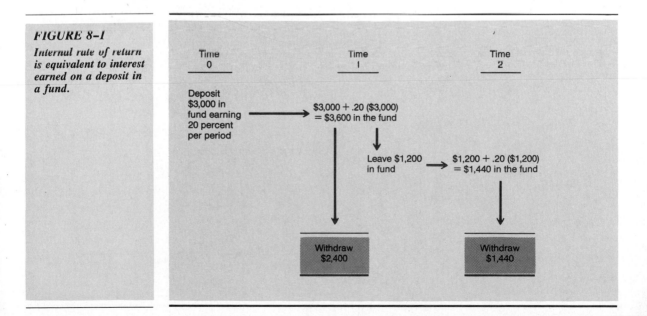

FIGURE 8-1

*Internal rate of return
is equivalent to interest
earned on a deposit in
a fund.*

would be just marginally acceptable (NPV = 0) if the cost of capital k equaled 20 percent, and therefore its IRR is 20 percent; but since k equals 10 percent, project H earns more than the cost of capital (r exceeds k) and is quite profitable (it has a positive NPV).

The Accept-Reject Decision The IRR method requires that if a particular investment is either to be accepted or rejected (and not to be compared with some alternative investment), it should be accepted if its IRR exceeds the cost of capital. The rationale is that if an investment earns more than the cost of the funds used to finance it, it should be adopted. We can apply the rule to the restaurant sign example used earlier. The sign costs $3500 and produces a net cash flow of $1000 in each of the next five years. Using Eq. (8-5) to determine r, the IRR, we solve the following:

$1000(P/A, r, 5) = $3500

or

$$(P/A, r, 5) = 3.5$$

Using the tables, we find that $r = 13.2$ percent, that is, $(P/A, 13.2\%, 5) = 3.5$.[5] The project returns 13.2 percent per year, and this exceeds the cost of capital k of 10 percent. Therefore, the sign should be purchased, a conclusion that is consistent with that reached earlier using net present value.

---

[5] Using interpolation (see Chap. 4), we find that $(P/A, 13.2\%, 5) = 3.5$.

FIGURE 8-2

Determining the IRR by examining the NPV of cash flows for various discount rates.

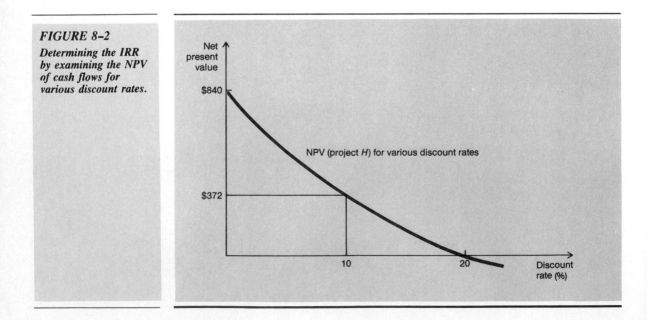

Choices between Alternatives—the Incremental Approach The IRR method can be used to compare two or more alternative investments when at most one alternative is to be accepted (mutually exclusive options). However, it is somewhat more difficult to use than is the present value method in the same situation and must be applied rather carefully. The IRR procedure consists of first determining which alternative investment is the most profitable by applying the incremental approach (described below) and then determining whether that most profitable alternative is sufficiently profitable to adopt. The alternative is adopted only if its IRR exceeds the cost of capital. (It is shown in the next section that it is incorrect to simply select the investment with the highest IRR.)

To demonstrate the method, we can refer back to the example involving a comparison between the deluxe machine (alternative D) and the economy machine (alternative E). We assume as before that the cost of capital is 10 percent. The cash flows were as shown below:

| | Time | | | | | | |
Alternative	0	1	2	3	4	5	IRR
Deluxe machine (D)	−$3,000	$900	$900	$900	$900	$900	15.2%
Economy machine (E)	−$2,000	$610	$610	$610	$610	$610	16.0%

To compare alternatives D and E using the IRR method, we must first ask whether the additional (or incremental) investment of $1000 in D as compared with E is justified. In other words, we look at the *difference* between D and E. The difference between the cash flows of the two alternatives is:

	0	1	2	3	4	5	IRR
D − E	−$1,000	$290	$290	$290	$290	$290	13.8%

If we pick D instead of E, an additional investment of $1000 must be made and we would expect to receive an additional $290 per year for five years. The IRR on the additional investment is found to be 13.8 percent by using the IRR equation. If the firm's cost of capital k is less than 13.8 percent, then D is preferred to E; if k is greater than 13.8 percent, E is better than D. Since the cost of capital equals 10 percent (by assumption), D is preferred to E. If the cost of capital were 15 percent, then E would be chosen over D because the additional investment required by D does not provide a high enough rate of return.

The next step is to decide whether the better alternative, D, is sufficiently profitable to be acceptable. D is acceptable since its rate of return of 15.2 percent exceeds the cost of capital of 10 percent.

If we have more than two alternatives available, then we must pick the best one by making a series of comparisons. Suppose there are four alternatives: A, B, C, and D. We can start off with any two and find out which one is the better of the two by the procedure just illustrated. Suppose we look at A and B first and decide that A is better. Then we could compare A with C in the same way. Suppose that A is again more profitable. Finally we must compare A with D. Suppose D is better than A. By this process we could determine that D is the best of the four alternatives. Now we need only to decide whether D is worth undertaking at all by comparing its rate of return with the cost of capital as we did above; D should be adopted if, and only if, its rate of return exceeds the cost of capital.

A common error in using the IRR method to compare two alternatives is to choose the one with the higher IRR (rather than using the incremental approach). Although this is a very natural mistake, it can mean adopting less profitable investments. This is clear from the above example since we found that, if the cost of capital were less than 13.8 percent (10 percent in the example), D was preferred to E even though D had the lower IRR (15.2 percent vs. 16.0 percent). It may appear strange that the firm should pass up a 16.0 percent investment (E) for a 15.2 percent investment (D). But, the 16 percent is *not* "passed up" since we can view D as being a package of two investments with the following characteristics:

	0	1	2	3	4	5	NPV	IRR
E	− $2,000	$610	$610	$610	$610	$610	$313	16.0%
D − E	− $1,000	$290	$290	$290	$290	$290	$ 99	13.8%
D	− $3,000	$900	$900	$900	$900	$900	$412	15.2%

Accepting D instead of E means taking on the investment package E *and* (D − E). E is an investment of $2000 with a rate of return of 16 percent and (D − E) is an investment of $1000 with a rate of return of 13.8 percent. The average rate of return on the total package [D = E + (D − E)] is 15.2 percent. Therefore, taking D over E means effectively investing in E plus another investment (D − E) that has a rate of return of 13.8 percent. If (D − E) is a good investment, which it is since 13.8 percent exceeds the cost of capital of 10 percent, you will want to take D in preference to E, since with D you in effect get investment E plus another good investment (D − E).

To further emphasize the error in simply choosing the investment with the highest IRR, assume two mutually exclusive investments, investment A involving an initial outlay of $1 and returning $10 one year hence (an IRR of 900 percent) and investment B involving an initial cost of $100,000 and returning $200,000 one year later (an IRR of 100 percent). If the cost of capital is 10 percent, the NPV(A) = $8.09 and the NPV(B) = $81,820. It should be clear that B is preferred to A even though A has the higher IRR. This is an extreme example used to highlight the need to use the incremental approach described above.

Although actual situations are not so blatantly obvious, the same principle will still apply.

In the examples we just examined, the alternatives differed in the amount of initial investment; however, this is not the only situation in which simply picking the option with the highest rate of return can lead to problems. Alternatives with the same initial investment but having unequal lives or just markedly different cash flow patterns over identical lives can also present this problem (see Appendix 8B, Section 1). In general, therefore, picking the alternative with the highest rate of return can be incorrect. Instead, the incremental approach outlined here should be used.

IRR, Present Value, and Reinvestment Rate Assumptions   Although, as we just noted, simply picking the mutually exclusive investment with the highest IRR can lead to mistakes, there is a special case in which the investment with the highest IRR is best. In this case, the alternative with the highest IRR is the one that would also be chosen using the incremental IRR method or the present value method. The special case arises if the mutually exclusive investments require the same initial outlay and if the future cash flows from each investment can be reinvested by the firm in other projects which earn that investment's IRR until some particular future date, where that future date is the same for all the mutually exclusive projects. For example, mutually exclusive investments A and B might each involve an initial outlay of $1000 in 1991; A has a three-year life and an internal rate of return of 20 percent, and all future cash flows generated by A will be reinvested by the firm in other projects to earn 20 percent per year (A's IRR) until 1997; and B has a four-year life and an internal rate of return of 30 percent, and all future cash flows will be reinvested to earn 30 percent per year (B's IRR) until 1997. In this special case, B is better than A because B has the higher IRR. B would also be chosen using the incremental rate of return and the present value methods. This special case is discussed in greater detail in Section 2 of Appendix 8B. It should be pointed out that this case does *not* often occur in practice, and it is ordinarily *not* correct to choose the mutually exclusive option with the highest IRR. In general, either the incremental IRR method or the present value method should be used in choosing from among mutually exclusive investments.

There is a broader issue than the specialized case just discussed above. This issue relates to how the rate of return that can be earned on *future* investments of the firm depends on which *current* investments are adopted. As explained in Section 1 of Appendix 8B, if the profitability of future investments (regardless of how profitable) does *not* depend on which current investments are adopted, then we can ignore the future investments in evaluating current projects. This was the assumption made above in explaining the present value and IRR methods, and both these methods are completely consistent and valid in this case. There are situations, however, in which investments lead to future profitable op-

258

PART 2
**The firm's investment,
financing, and dividend
decisions**

portunities that would not be available to the firm if the investments had not been undertaken. For example, firms that established footholds in foreign countries in the 1950s often found that they had an advantageous position in those foreign markets even in the 1980s. If the choice of current investments affects the rate of return that can be earned on future investments, then in evaluating current projects it becomes necessary to analyze the cash flows from the current investments *and* also the cash flows from the future investment opportunities that depend on the current investments. Either the present value method or the IRR method can be used to analyze these present and future project cash flows. Both present value and IRR are appropriate for such an analysis whether it is assumed that the future investments earn a rate of return equal to the cost of capital, equal to each investment's IRR, or equal to any other rate, and whether the future investments are financed by reinvesting the future cash flows from current investments or are financed by any other source. The method of analyzing this type of problem is presented in detail in Section 3 of Appendix 8B.

IRR and Present Value Compared   In most situations the internal rate of return method properly applied and present value provide the same choices. The IRR approach has the advantage of providing a rate of return that is easy to interpret and for that reason is particularly popular in industry. On the other hand, computing a rate of return is usually more difficult than computing a present value, although, with electronic calculators and computers readily available, this is not a serious drawback. In addition, the incremental IRR method, as we have seen, is conceptually more complex when choosing among alternatives. Most important, in some cases the cash flows imply more than one internal rate of return or no meaningful rate of return at all.[6] In these cases, the IRR method cannot be used whereas present value can be. Finally, as is explained in the previous section and in Appendix 8B, even if special reinvestment rate assumptions are made regarding the current projects being evaluated, the present value method appropriately applied is the easiest method to use.

   Overall, it is our judgment that present value is superior to internal rate of return as a capital budgeting approach. Any problem that can be treated with IRR can also be analyzed using present value, whereas the

---

[6] Some cash flows imply more than one internal rate of return or only rates of return involving $\sqrt{-1}$ (imaginary numbers). In these cases the IRR method cannot be used. Such problems will not arise if the cash flow involves an initial outflow (I_0) and positive cash flows thereafter. They can arise if some future cash flows are negative (cash outflows). For example, if an investment involves initial outlay $I_0 = \$10$, time 1 cash flow $CF_1 = \$150$ and time 2 cash flow $CF_2 = -\$140$, then the internal rates of return are 0 percent and 440 percent. For a complete discussion of the problems with the internal rate of return method, see Haley and Schall, *The Theory of Financial Decisions*, 2d ed. (New York: McGraw-Hill, 1979), Appendix 3a.

reverse is not the case. In Appendix 8A, it is shown that the gain to shareholders from an investment equals its net present value and the NPV is therefore a proper guide to selecting investments.[7]

The Payback Period
Method

The **payback period** is the length of time it takes to recover the initial investment on a project. For example, if a $1000 investment returns an aftertax cash flow per year of $400, the payback period is $2\frac{1}{2}$ years ($1000/$400). The payback period method dictates acceptance of a project only if the project has a payback period less than some level specified by management. In comparing two alternative options using this method, the one with the smaller payback period is preferred and is accepted if its payback period is less than the specified requirement.

The payback period approach has a number of problems. First, there is no consideration of returns after the required payback period. Assume that the firm has projects Q and R from which to choose and has set the required payback period at three years. Thus, only if the project recovers the entire investment within three years is the project acceptable. From Exhibit 8-3, we can see that the payback period of Q is 2 years and the payback period of R is 2.1 years. Both projects meet the three-year requirement, but Q is preferred since its payback period is less. However, notice that R returns a cash flow at time 3 of $1000, whereas Q returns only $25 after its two-year payback period. These post-payback period returns are ignored in using the method since the standard is based entirely on the time required to recover capital. Beyond the

---

[7] If we were to take into account flotation (sales) costs of issuing securities, investor costs in buying and selling securities, and personal tax effects, net present value has to be amended (so do IRR and other capital budgeting techniques). This topic is not appropriate for discussion here but has been explored in the financial literature. One proposed approach is the use of "adjusted present value"; see S. Myers, "Interaction of Investment and Financing Decisions," *Journal of Finance* (March 1974), pp. 1–25.

EXHIBIT 8-3
Payback period comparison

		Cash flows	
	Time	Q	R
Initial investment	0	−$1,000	−$1,000
Returns	1	200	600
	2	800	300
	3	25	1,000
Payback period		2 years	2.1 years
Net present value at cost of capital of 10 percent		−$ 138	$ 545

260

PART 2
The firm's investment,
financing, and dividend
decisions

payback period, returns are disregarded. Even though payback dictates the choice of Q, at a 10 percent cost of capital the present value of Q is −$138 and of R is $545. Present value, therefore, dictates the selection of R, the opposite result from that using payback.[8] A primary reason for the different results for the two methods is that, in contrast to payback, present value does not ignore returns beyond the payback period.

Notice secondly that payback also ignores the pattern of returns within the payback period; i.e., the time value of money is not taken into account. Compare assets S and T described in Exhibit 8-4. S and T each have a payback period of two years and are therefore equivalent on this basis. However, since we know that a dollar received sooner is better due to the time value of money, project T is the better investment as indicated by the greater net present value of T. Payback completely fails to account for the differences in the pattern of returns.

In spite of the flaws in the payback period method, it is still widely used. Three rationales have been offered in payback's defense. First, after the required payback period the uncertainty may be so great for some projects that requiring recovery of capital within that period is a good way to avoid undue risk. However, this argument does not confront the time-value-of-money problem within the payback period illustrated above for investments S and T (Exhibit 8-4). Furthermore, risk is rarely so great that returns beyond that period should be completely ignored. As explained in Chapter 10, if risk is increasing over time, the discount rate used under the present value method can be adjusted to take this increasing risk into account. A second argument sometimes advanced in support of payback is that in practice it is generally used with other criteria which do account for the time value of money and for

---

[8] It is easily shown that the IRR method using incremental analysis also dictates the choice of R.

EXHIBIT 8-4
Payback period comparison

	Time	Cash flows S	Cash flows T
Initial investment	0	− $500	− $500
Returns	1	100	400
	2	400	100
	3	500	500
Payback period		2 years	2 years
Net present value at a cost of capital of 10%[a]		$297	$322

[a] NPV(S) = 0.9091 ($100) + 0.8264 ($400) + 0.7513 ($500) − $500 = $297;
NPV(T) = 0.9091 ($400) + 0.8264 ($100) + 0.7513 ($500) − $500 = $322.

the post-payback period returns. But this is a roundabout way of saying that these two latter considerations must be taken into account. If this is so, why not employ the present value criterion in the first place?

The third, and probably weakest, argument used to defend payback is its simplicity. The expense of a more careful analysis is generally more than compensated for by better investment decisions. Further, with the availability of present value tables and computers, any computational advantages of payback have become negligible.

In conclusion, payback has very little to recommend it and can be highly misleading. A comparison of available approaches clearly favors the present value and IRR methods.

*Accounting Rate
of Return*

The accounting rate of return (ARR) equals the average annual aftertax accounting profit generated by the investment divided by the average investment. That is,

$$\text{ARR} = \frac{\text{average annual profit from investment}}{(I + S)/2} \tag{8-6}$$

where S is the salvage or liquidation value of the asset at the end of its useful life, and therefore $(I + S)/2$ is the average investment in the asset during its useful life. ARR is a misleading measure of the benefits from an asset for two reasons: Profit does not generally equal the asset's cash flow and may have a pattern very much different from that of cash flow and, second, the time value of money is ignored by the ARR method.

To illustate the ARR method, assume two assets, F and G, each of which requires an initial outlay I of $20,000. Each asset lasts for four years and is depreciated on a straight-line basis with zero salvage value (S) at the end of the four years; depreciation is therefore $5000 per year on F or G. These data and the accounting profit for each asset are shown in Exhibit 8-5. If the cost of capital were 10 percent, asset F with a net

EXHIBIT 8-5

Comparison of accounting rate of return (ARR) and present value

	Asset F		Asset G	
	Annual profit	**Cash flow**	**Annual profit**	**Cash flow**
1	$11,000	$16,000	$ 1,000	$ 6,000
2	11,000	16,000	1,000	6,000
3	2,000	7,000	1,000	6,000
4	2,000	7,000	25,000	30,000
Total	$26,000	$46,000	$28,000	$48,000
ARR[a]	65%		70%	
NPV		$17,808		$15,410

[a] ARR = (Total profit/4 years) ÷ $10,000.

present value of $17,808 would be preferred to asset G with a net present value of $15,410. But, using ARR, G is preferred to F since G's ARR of 70 percent exceeds F's ARR of 65 percent. Present value produces the correct results, and therefore ARR can lead to the wrong choices.[9]

INDUSTRY USE OF CAPITAL BUDGETING TECHNIQUES

Until the 1960s, only the largest firms in capital-intensive industries employed advanced capital budgeting tools (e.g., present value and internal rate of return). Other firms used simpler and less satisfactory techniques such as payback and accounting rate of return. Although the less accurate techniques are still widely employed, a majority of the largest 250 United States firms in terms of capital outlays use either present value or internal rate of return for capital expenditure analysis. Surveys of large United States firms by Klammer and by Schall, Sundem, and Geijsbeek revealed that the use of the present value and IRR approaches has greatly increased since the 1950s.[10] By 1970, a significant majority of firms had at least one member of the company staff assigned to full-time capital budgeting. Not surprisingly, the companies using the more sophisticated capital budgeting methods were those with larger investment budgets, e.g., oil and chemical firms.

The increase in the use of present value and internal rate of return demonstrates that companies will adopt improved methods of analysis if they produce earnings benefits. The benefits accrue because better choices are made in selecting projects and in determining the amount to be invested. There is a cost to employing superior techniques, however. Since more information is required, computers may be needed to perform the analysis, and personnel with an understanding of these techniques must be found (and paid a salary commensurate with their talents). For these reasons, small firms and less-capital-intensive firms have been slower to adopt the newer approaches. However, as the costs of obtaining information and employing computers decline, and as understanding of the approaches becomes more widespread, more firms will find it profitable to modernize their capital budgeting procedures.

[9] It is assumed in Exhibit 8-5 that aftertax profit equals cash flow less depreciation. This will be so if cash revenues R and cash expenses E are revenues and expenses for tax purposes. Then cash flow = $R - E -$ taxes, and profit = $R - E -$ depreciation $-$ taxes = cash flow $-$ depreciation. Also, the definition of the ARR stated in Eq. (8-6) is one of many alternative definitions that have been proposed; one of these alternatives uses I in the denominator instead of $[(I + S)/2]$ as in (8-6). All the commonly proposed ARR measures are inferior to present value as capital budgeting criteria because they do not evaluate cash flow or do not *properly* take into account the time value of money.

[10] See Thomas Klammer, "Empirical Evidence of the Adoption of Sophisticated Capital Budgeting Techniques," *Journal of Business* (July 1972); and Lawrence D. Schall, Gary L. Sundem, and William R. Geijsbeek, Jr., "Survey and Analysis of Capital Budgeting Methods," *Journal of Finance* (March 1978).

We have introduced several techniques for assessing the desirability of capital investment projects. Of the techniques discussed, present value and internal rate of return are most likely to lead to choices that benefit shareholders. The example problems below illustrate several situations that are commonly encountered in practice. We use the present value method in the solutions; problem **13** at the end of the chapter requires that the example problems below be solved using the IRR approach. The first problem involves an asset addition that reduces costs but does not affect revenues; the second problem deals with an asset addition that increases sales *and* costs; and the third problem involves the replacement of an existing asset with a new asset. In the problems below we assume for simplicity that, for tax purposes, depreciation is spread over the asset's useful life and is computed assuming a zero salvage value for the asset.

Asset Addition:
Asset Reduces Costs

Assume that Streak Wholesalers is considering the acquisition of a delivery truck that will allow Streak to do its own shipping rather than purchase shipping services from another firm. The new asset, a truck, is not a substitute for an old one already in operation and is therefore defined here as an asset addition (rather than replacement). Suppose that the benefits from the truck would be a reduction in shipping costs. By reducing costs, the net cash flow of the firm as a whole is increased. The estimates of the costs and benefits associated with this investment decision are shown in Exhibit 8-6. Notice that although the truck reduces annual shipping costs by $15,000, additional expenses for a driver and for upkeep of the truck are also taken into account. These expenses are $13,000 per year, and therefore the return from acquiring the truck before taxes is $2000 per year. Taxes are then deducted in order to determine the aftertax benefit from making the new investment. Since the truck is a depreciable asset for tax purposes, depreciation must be deducted from the increased returns due to the truck in order to determine the part of the returns that is taxable; in the example, this taxable return is $1200. Applying a tax rate of 30 percent and subtracting the resulting taxes of $360 produces a net cash return from the asset of $1640 per year. As shown in Exhibit 8-6, the net present value of the project is $2722 and therefore the project should be accepted. The truck would be a good investment.

Asset Addition:
Asset Increases Sales
and Costs

In the above example, it was assumed that the firm's sales were unaffected by the acquisition of the delivery truck. The benefits from the truck were a reduction in operating expenses. It is also possible that a new investment has an impact on the firm's sales as well as upon operating costs. For example, assume that a new machine, if purchased, will enable the firm to increase annual sales by $6000, increase cost of goods sold by $2500, and increase operating expenses by $500, producing a new rise in firm's pretax cash flow of $3000 annually ($6000 −

EXHIBIT 8-6
Asset addition: Asset reduces costs

Truck purchase price:
  $6,400 (Truck will last 8 years with an $800 liquidation value)[a]

Returns per period for 8 years:
  Reduction in shipping expenses $15,000
  Deduct: Salary for driver $9,000
        Upkeep, gas, etc. 4,000
  Return before taxes ($15,000 − $9,000 − $4,000) $2,000

Taxes:
  Pretax return .... $ 2,000
  Deduct: Depreciation on truck[b] 800
  Net taxable income .... $ 1,200
  Tax at 30% (0.30 × $1,200) 360
  Increase in annual net cash flow ($2,000 − $360) $1,640

Time	Cash flow
0 (cost)	− $6,400
1–7 (returns per year)	$1,640
8 (return)	$2,440[c]

Net present value at 10% (cost of capital):
  NPV = $1,640 (P/A, 10%, 7) + $2,440 (P/F, 10%, 8) − $6,400
    = $1,640 (4.868) + $2,440 (0.4665) − $6,400
    = $2,722

[a] A zero salvage value is assumed in computing tax deductible depreciation.
[b] Depreciation on a straight-line basis = $6,400 cost /8 years = $800 per year.
[c] Aftertax cash flow from use + aftertax salvage value = $1,640 + $800 = $2,440.

$2500 − $500). Let the new machine cost $6000 and have a five-year life with no salvage value. Using the same method as before, it is shown in Exhibit 8-7 that the change in aftertax cash flow is $2460 per year. The net present value of the machine is $3326, and it should therefore be purchased.

Replacement of an Existing Asset

Firms frequently consider the possibility of replacing assets currently in operation. Even if the old asset is economically productive, the new asset may be sufficiently more productive to warrant the replacement. In determining whether to replace, the crucial question is whether the added initial expenditure for the new asset (less the market value received from liquidating the old asset) is justified by the increase in the firm's cash flow (aftertax cash flow from new asset minus aftertax cash from the asset being replaced). That is, are the incremental cash flow benefits from the changeover sufficient to warrant the initial investment rquired by the replacement? An example will clarify the approach.

A new machine costing $24,000 can be acquired to replace a machine presently in use ("old" machine); the old machine was purchased four years ago for $5000 and has a current liquidation value of $3000. Assume initially that the current liquidation value of the old machine equals its book value for tax purposes and that, therefore, there is no gain or loss on sale of the old machine. (Later we explain how to deal with tax gains and losses on asset sales.) Therefore, the net outlay required to acquire the new machine is $21,000, the amount to be paid for the new machine

---

EXHIBIT 8-7
Asset addition: Asset increases sales

Machine purchase price:
  $6,000 (Machine will last 5 years with no salvage value)[a]

Returns per period for 5 years:
  Increase in sales $6,000
  Deduct: Increases in cost of goods sold
    ($2,500) and operating expenses ($500) 3,000
  Return before taxes ($6,000 − $3,000) $3,000

Taxes:
  Pretax return $3,000
  Deduct: Depreciation on machine[a] 1,200
  Net taxable income $1,800
  Tax at 30% (0.30 × $1,800) 540
  Increase in annual net cash flow ($3,000 − $540) $2,460

Time	Cash flow
0 (cost)	−$6,000
1–5(returns per year)	$2,460

Net present value at 10% (cost of capital):
  NPV = $2,460 (P/A, 10%, 5) − $6,000
      = $2,460 (3.791) − $6,000
      = $3,326

---

[a] The machine has no salvage value for tax purposes and a zero estimated liquidation value in five years; therefore annual depreciation equals (machine's cost)/(machine's useful life) = $6,000/5 years = $1,200 per year.

less the amount received for the old machine. The old machine could be maintained in service for six years and the new machine has a life of six years.[11] The year 6 aftertax liquidation value of the old machine will be zero and the year 6 aftertax liquidation value of the new machine will be $5000. As shown in Exhibit 8-8, the new machine will increase output and thereby raise sales by $1500, will reduce nondepreciation production expenses by $7000, and will consequently raise pretax net returns (sales − nondepreciation expenses) by $8500. The $7000 expense reduction equals the cost savings due to more efficient production with the new machine less any increased expenses involved in producing the additional units sold. The firm's aftertax cash flow increases by $7000 per year for the six years due to use of the new machine. In year 6, there is an added cash flow of $5000 due to liquidation of the new machine; the total cash flow increase in the sixth year due to the new machine is therefore $12,000 ($7000 + $5000).

As shown in Exhibit 8-8, the additional cash flows due to the replacement are an added outlay of $21,000 initially, an increase of $7000 per year for the next five years, and an increase of $12,000 in the sixth year. The cash flow has a net present value of $12,311, and therefore the replacement should be made.

The Treatment of Gains and Losses on Asset Sales[12]   In the above problem we assumed that the current liquidation value of the old machine equaled its current book value (both $3000) and therefore there was no gain or loss on selling the old machine. If the liquidation value differs from the book value for tax purposes ("tax basis" of the asset), there will be a gain or loss on the sale of the old asset that must be included in the analysis. It is important to note that the tax effect of a gain or loss on a single asset depends on the gains and losses incurred during the period on *other* asset dispositions, since gains and losses are combined in computing taxable income. Furthermore, the tax treatment of real estate is different from the tax treatment of other business assets. The implication of all this is that no simple rule can be applied in computing the taxability of a gain or loss on an individual asset. The overall situation of

---

[11] The example presented below makes the simplifying assumption that the remaining life of the old asset currently being used by the firm equals the life of a new asset being considered as a replacement. This assumption, although unrealistic, allows us to present the basic approach to replacement problems. This approach is appropriate even when the lives of the old and new assets differ. However, if the remaining life of the old asset does not equal the life of the new asset, then we have to consider future replacements and we encounter the problem of comparing investments with unequal lives. This complicates the analysis but does not alter the basic method for computing or analyzing the cash flows. The problem of comparing investments with unequal lives is discussed later in this chapter.

[12] See Chap. 3 on gains and losses on depreciable assets.

EXHIBIT 8-8
Replacement problem

1. Initial outlay:

Price of new machine $24,000
Current aftertax liquidation value of old machine 3,000
Net outlay for new machine $21,000

2. Firm's annual cash flow for the next six years (years 1 to 6) with old and new machine excluding year 6 salvage value of new machine

Cash flow variable	With old machine (a)	With new machine (b)	Change due to new machine (col. b − col. a)
1. Sales	$100,000	$101,500	$1,500
2. Nondepreciation expenses	57,000	50,000	− 7,000
3. Sales − nondepreciation expenses [(1) − (2)]	43,000	51,500	8,500
4. Depreciation[a]	10,500	14,000	3,500
5. Taxable income [(3) − (4)]	32,500	37,500	5,000
6. Taxes [0.30 × (5)]	9,750	11,250	1,500
7. Net cash flow [(3) − (6)]	33,250	40,250	7,000

3. Year 6 salvage value:

Year 6 aftertax liquidation value of new machine $5,000
Year 6 aftertax liquidation value of old machine   0
Added year 6 asset liquidation cash flow with new machine $5,000

Time	Additional cash flow due to new machine
0 (cost)	− $21,000
1–5 (annual return)	7,000
6 (return)	12,000[b]

4. Net present value of replacement (at 10% cost of capital):

NPV (replacement) = $7,000 (P/A, 10%, 5)
                  + $12,000 (P/F, 10%, 6) − $21,000
                  = $7,000 (3.791) + $12,000 (0.5645) − $21,000
                  = $12,311

[a] Depreciation on the old machine is assumed to be $500 per year; depreciation on new machine = ($24,000/6 years) = $4,000 per year; firm's depreciation on all *other* assets = $10,000 per year.
[b] $12,000 in year 6 = $7,000 from asset's use + $5,000 aftertax salvage value.

268

PART 2
**The firm's investment,
financing, and dividend
decisions**

the firm regarding asset gains and losses on *all* assets sold during the period must be known.[13]

To see how to treat a gain in analyzing an asset replacement, assume that the old machine in the example in Exhibit 8-8 has a liquidation value of $5000 (instead of $3000). This implies a taxable gain of $2000 (liquidation value − book value). Assume that the tax rate on the gain is 30 percent (in light of other asset dispositions made during the period); the tax is therefore $600 (0.30 × $2000). The current aftertax liquidation value of the old machine is $4400, the $5000 current liquidation value less the $600 tax on the gain. This $4400 amount would replace the "current liquidation value of the old machine" of $3000 at the top of Exhibit 8-8. The net outlay for the new machine therefore becomes $19,600 ($24,000 − $4400), and the net present value of the replacement becomes $13,711, instead of the $12,311 shown at the bottom of Exhibit 8-8.

If an asset is sold at a loss (at less than book value), the loss is a tax deductible expense that reduces taxes payable by the firm. To illustrate, assume that the liquidation value of the old machine in the Exhibit 8-8 example is $2000 (instead of $3000), which is less than the $3000 book value. This implies a loss upon liquidation of $1000 (book value − liquidation value). The $1000 loss is tax deductible and this tax deduction reduces the firm's taxes. Assume that the tax deduction of $1000 reduces firm taxes by $300 in the example. The $300 tax benefit is added to the $2000 liquidation value to compute the net liquidation value of the old machine, which is therefore $2300. This $2300 amount replaces the $3000 at the top of Exhibit 8-8; the net outlay for the new machine therefore becomes $21,700 ($24,000 − $2300), and the net present value of the replacement becomes $11,611 instead of $12,311.

SUMMARY

The enormous cost of new capital equipment purchased each year by United States industry has motivated firms to carefully budget capital expenditures. Most firms prepare short-run budgets, and many companies plan capital outlays for the next three to five years. These budgets are estimates and are often revised as new information becomes available.

The additional aftertax cash flow generated by an investment is the relevant measure of the investment's productivity to the firm. The cash flow can be evaluated using present value, internal rate of return, payback, or benefit cost. Using present value, a project should be accepted only if its net present value is positive. In comparing mutually exclusive

[13] Ordinarily, if an asset used in a business has been held no longer than six months when it is sold (retired), a gain on the sale is treated as ordinary income and a loss is treated as an ordinary loss in the year of sale. If the asset is not real estate and was held more than six months, a gain on the asset may in part be treated as a long-term capital gain (under Sections 1231 and 1245 of the Internal Revenue Code) if the sale price exceeds the original cost of the asset. If the sale price is equal to or less than original cost (which is more typical), all the gain is ordinary income because of depreciation recapture under Section 1245. The treatment of real estate (Section 1250) is more generous than the treatment of non-real estate in that a larger proportion of gains on real estate may be subject to long-term capital gains taxation.

investment alternatives (alternatives only one of which can be accepted), that with the highest net present value is the most profitable and should be adopted provided that its net present value is positive.

The internal rate of return (IRR) method specifies that only investments with an IRR greater than the cost of capital should be accepted. In comparing mutually exclusive options, the incremental method should be used. This method determines whether the additional cash flows of one alternative relative to another justify the former's acceptance. The IRR approach is often more cumbersome to use than is present value and in some cases is not applicable because of analytical problems. Present value is therefore recommended as the preferred evaluation technique.

The payback period method dictates acceptance of projects only if they return the cost of the investment within a specified period of time (the payback period). This method ignores the time value of money and does not take into account cash flows after the payback period. The accounting rate of return method requires that the investment with the highest accounting rate of return be adopted if the rate exceeds a specified level. As with payback, this method ignores the time value of money. Payback period and accounting rate of return are distinctly inferior to net present value and internal rate of return as capital budgeting criteria.

The use of sophisticated capital budgeting techniques has been primarily limited to large, capital-intensive firms. However, present value and IRR are rapidly gaining in acceptance and may eventually replace payback, accounting rate of return, and other less accurate methods.

QUESTIONS

1 What information is required to determine the cash flow from an investment opportunity?
2 Why do we use cash flow in evaluating an investment?
3 Depreciation is a noncash expense. Why, then, is it necesary to compute depreciation in order to perform a proper cash flow analysis?
4 Intuitively, what does an internal rate of return show?
5 What are the advantages and disadvantages of the net present value method relative to the internal rate of return method?
6 The TOPCOA Industrial Corporation has been using the payback evaluation technique for a number of years. Recently, you have been hired by the firm as a financial analyst. Prepare a convincing memo to the vice president for finance explaining your rationale for using another technique of investment evaluation. In your memo you want to be objective. Are there any situations in which the payback period method can be useful in capital budgeting analysis?
7 A recent graduate of the Wellduke Business School commented: "Capital budgeting is simple; just divide the investment's net income after taxes by the amount of the investment and compare this to the cost of financing the investment. If the return on investment is greater than the cost of financing, accept the investment." Comment critically.

270

PART 2
**The firm's investment,
financing, and dividend
decisions**

8 Define the terms "cost of capital," "discount rate," and "minimum acceptable rate of return," and explain why they are equal to one another in project evaluation.

9 Early in the chapter it was noted that intermediate- and long-term capital budgets are revised periodically. As a part of such a revision process, suppose a firm is reviewing the progress of a specific venture that has been in operation for five years. Outline the considerations that are relevant in performing the review process.

10 Assume that the federal government is considering the following four new policies to stimulate investment by private firms:

   a Allow each firm to reduce its taxes by 5 percent of the dollar amount the firm invests (e.g., if a firm invests $100, the firm can reduce its taxes by $5).

   b Allow firms to deduct 5 percent of the cost of new assets from their taxable income in the year the asset is acquired.

   c Pay firms a cash subsidy of 5 percent of the cost of new assets in the year the asset is acquired.

   d Allow firms to increase depreciation above what is currently allowed in the year an asset is acquired by 5 percent of the cost of the asset and to reduce future years' depreciation on the asset by 5 percent of the asset's cost; that is, to allow firms to accelerate depreciation by raising the current depreciation deduction by 5 percent of the asset's cost with an equal reduction in future depreciation.

   Carefully compare these four policies in terms of the probable relative impact of each on a firm's level of investment.

PROJECT

Refer to library sources (e.g., the *Federal Reserve Bulletin*, the *Economic Report of the President*, the *Survey of Current Business*) and examine the past annual levels of investment, national income, federal income taxes, profits, and dividends in the United States. Try to find breakdowns of investment by industry or by sector of the economy. Also investigate forecasts of investment by industry, by sector, and for the entire United States economy.

*DEMONSTRATION
PROBLEMS*

DP1 Diaz Microfilm, Inc., is comparing two new processes for its plant. Each process would have an expected useful life of ten years. The initial investment and annual cash return from each process are shown below.

	Process A	Process B
Initial investment	$200,000	$300,000
Annual cash flow for years 1 through 10	$ 35,000	$ 60,000

a Analyze the above problem using the net present value method. Perform the analysis for each of the following costs of capital:

1 12 percent

2 15 percent

Compare your results for the two costs of capital.

b Analyze the problem using the internal rate of return method assuming a cost of capital of 15 percent.

SOLUTION TO DP1:

a *Process A*

$$\text{NPV (@ 12\%)} = -\$200,000 + \$35,000(P/A, 12\%, 10)$$
$$= -\$200,000 + \$35,000(5.6502)$$
$$= -\$2242$$

$$\text{NPV (@ 15\%)} = -\$200,000 + \$35,000(P/A, 15\%, 10)$$
$$= -\$200,000 + \$35,000(5.0188)$$
$$= -\$24,342$$

Process B

$$\text{NPV (@ 12\%)} = -\$300,000 + \$60,000(P/A, 12\%, 10)$$
$$= -\$300,000 + \$60,000(5.6502)$$
$$= -\$39,012$$

$$\text{NPV (@ 15\%)} = -\$300,000 + \$60,000(P/A, 15\%, 10)$$
$$= -\$300,000 + \$60,000(5.0188)$$
$$= -\$1128$$

Conclusion: Process A is not acceptable, and process B is acceptable, with a cost of capital of 12% or 15%.

b To compare investments on the basis of internal rate of return, we use the incremental internal rate of return method. We first compute the incremental cash flows.

	A	B	(B − A)
Initial cost	$200,000	$300,000	$100,000
Annual cash flow for years 1 through 10	$ 35,000	$ 60,000	$25,000

Using the incremental cash flows above (incremental cost = $100,000 and incremental annual cash flow = $25,000), we compute the incremental IRR. That is, we want the IRR for:

Outlay: $100,000

Annual cash flow: $25,000

The incremental IRR (r) is the solution to:

$$0 = -\$100,000 + \$25,000(P/A, r, 10)$$

$$r = 21.55\%$$

272

PART 2
The firm's investment,
financing, and dividend
decisions

Conclusion: B is superior to A since the incremental IRR exceeds the cost of capital (21.55% > 15%). B is acceptable since its IRR exceeds 15% (it is left to you to compute B's IRR).

DP2 Jeanette Fraser has spent fifteen years as a management consultant assisting others in starting new companies and in running ongoing businesses. Jeanette's ambition has long been to own her own firm. She now has the opportunity to purchase Vantage Technologies, which manufactures parts for medical testing equipment. Jeanette and her partners can buy Vantage for $4 million. Vantage is expected to have costs and revenues for the next ten years and for the subsequent years as shown below.

	First ten years	After the first ten years
Annual cash revenues	$5,000,000	$7,000,000
Annual nondepreciation expenses	3,000,000	4,500,000
Capital outlays	700,000	600,000
Depreciation	500,000	600,000

Vantage has a corporate tax rate of 30 percent. The company has no debt and is expected to remain permanently debt-free. All net cash flow (net of corporate taxes) will be paid out to the owners as a dividend. Jeanette wants to earn at least 18 percent per year (before personal taxes) on the $4 million investment in Vantage. Use the net present value method to determine whether Jeanette should buy Vantage Technologies.

SOLUTION TO DP2:
Using Eqs. (8-1) and (8-1a), we can compute the net cash flow for Vantage.

$$\text{Net cash flow} = \text{revenues} - \text{expenses other than depreciation} - \text{capital expenditures} - \text{income taxes} \quad (8\text{-}1)$$

$$\text{Income taxes} = \text{tax rate} \times (\text{revenues} - \text{expenses other than depreciation} - \text{depreciation}) \quad (8\text{-}1a)$$

First ten years' annual cash flow:

$$\text{Income taxes} = .30(\$5,000,000 - \$3,000,000 - \$500,000)$$

$$= \$450,000$$

$$\text{Net cash flow} = \$5,000,000 - \$3,000,000 - \$700,000 - \$450,000$$

$$= \$850,000$$

Subsequent years' annual cash flow:

Income taxes = .30($7,000,000 − $4,500,000 − $600,000)

= $570,000

Net cash flow = $7,000,000 − $4,500,000 − $600,000
− $570,000

= $1,330,000

Summary of cash flows:

First ten years: $850,000 per year
Subsequent years: $1,330,000
Initial outlay: $4,000,000

Net present value = −$4,000,000 + $850,000($P/A$, 18%, 10)
+ $1,330,000($P/A$, 18%, ∞)($P/F$, 18%, 10)

= −$4,000,000 + $850,000(4.4941)
+ $1,330,000(5.5556) (.1911)

= $1,232,013

Since the net present value is positive, Jeanette should purchase Vantage Technologies.

DP3 Sola Insulation Materials is considering a $270,000 outlay for a new cutter that will reduce costs. The cutter will last twenty years and will have a zero liquidation value at the end of the twenty years. Nondepreciation cost reductions resulting from the new cutter are forecast at 3 percent of the current $2 million per year. Sola's annual revenues of $4 million will remain unaffected. The cutter will be depreciated over twelve years on a straight-line basis; this depreciation will be added to a current depreciation allowance for the firm of $500,000 per year on existing plant and equipment. The firm's tax rate is 30 percent. Sola's cost of capital is 15 percent.

a Set up a cash flow analysis like Exhibit 8-1 in the text for this problem.

b Compute the net present value, internal rate of return, payback period, and accounting rate of return for this project. Should the project be adopted?

SOLUTION TO DP3:

a Incremental investment is $270,000. Annual depreciation in years 1 to 12 = $270,000/12 years = $22,500.

274

PART 2
The firm's investment,
financing, and dividend
decisions

Years 1 to 12

	Firm cash flow w/o investment	Firm cash flow with investment	Change in cash flow
Annual revenues (R)	$4,000,000	$4,000,000	$ 0
Annual expenses other than depreciation (E)	$2,000,000	$1,940,000	−$60,000
Taxes			
R − E	$2,000,000	$2,060,000	$60,000
Less depreciation	500,000	522,500	22,500
Taxable income (TI)	$1,500,000	$1,537,500	$37,500
Tax @ 30% of TI	450,000	461,250	11,250
Net cash flow (R − E − tax)	$1,550,000	$1,598,750	$48,750

Years 13 to 20

	Firm cash flow w/o investment	Firm cash flow with investment	Added cash flow
Annual revenues (R)	$4,000,000	$4,000,000	$ 0
Annual expenses other than depreciation (E)	$2,000,000	$1,940,000	−$60,000
Taxes			
R − E	$2,000,000	$2,060,000	$60,000
Less depreciation	500,000	500,000	0
Taxable income (TI)	$1,500,000	$1,560,000	$60,000
Tax @ 30% of TI	450,000	468,000	18,000
Net cash flow (R − E − tax)	$1,550,000	$1,592,000	$42,000

Life of asset:	20 years
Price of asset:	$270,000
Effective tax rate:	30%
Discount rate:	15%

Summary

Date	Added cash flow
Now	− $270,000
Years 1–12	48,750
Years 13–20	42,000

b *Net present value:*

$$\text{NPV at } 15\% = \$48,750(P/A, 15\%, 12) + \$42,000$$
$$(P/A, 15\%, 8)(P/F, 15\%, 12) - \$270,000$$
$$= \$48,750(5.4206) + \$42,000(4.4873)(.1869)$$
$$- \$270,000$$
$$= \$29,479 > 0; \text{ therefore accept.}$$

Internal rate of return (r): The IRR (r) is the solution to:

$$0 = \$48,750(P/A, r, 12) + \$42,000(P/A, r, 8)(P/F, r, 12)$$
$$- \$270,000$$

Using interpolation (see Chapter 4);

$$\text{NPV at } 16\% = \$48,750(5.1971) + \$42,000(4.3436)(.1685)$$
$$- \$270,000$$
$$= \$14,098$$
$$\text{NPV at } 18\% = \$48,750(4.7932) + \$42,000(4.0776)(.1372)$$
$$- \$270,000$$
$$= -\$12,835$$

Using interpolation;

$$r = \left(\frac{\$14,098}{\$14,098 + \$12,835}\right) 2\% + 16\% = 17.05\%$$

Since the internal rate of return (r) of 17.05% exceeds the discount rate of 15%, the project should be accepted.

Payback period:

$$\text{Payback period} = \frac{\$270,000}{\$48,750} = 5.54 \text{ years}$$

Accounting rate of return (ARR):

$$\text{ARR} = \frac{\text{average accounting income}}{\text{average investment}}$$

Accounting income $= R - E -$ depreciation $-$ tax. From part *a*, accounting income is $26,250 in years 1 to 12 and is $42,000 in years 13 to 20. The average accounting income is therefore $32,550 ($=$ $651,000 total profit over the 20

276

PART 2
**The firm's investment,
financing, and dividend
decisions**

years/20 years). The average investment is $270,000/2 = $135,000. Therefore,

$$ARR = \frac{\$32,550}{\$135,000} = 24.11\%$$

PROBLEMS

[*Note*: In the following problems, depreciation for tax purposes should be computed using the following assumptions: (1) the asset has a zero salvage value; (2) a full year's depreciation should be assigned to the year in which the asset is acquired; and (3) unless otherwise indicated, depreciation is spread over the asset's useful life.]

1 Lambda Corporation has annual cash revenues of $750,000, annual cash expenses of $250,000, and annual depreciation of $200,000. These figures are expected to remain the same permanently if Lambda continues to subcontract out to other companies certain phases of its production process. If Lambda invests $350,000 in new machinery and discontinues the subcontracting, it will be able to increase its sales and reduce its per unit costs. With the new machinery, the firm's annual cash revenues will increase to $900,000 and annual cash expenses will increase to $320,000. The new machinery has a ten-year life, with no salvage value for tax purposes and no expected end-of-life liquidation value. The machinery will be depreciated for tax purposes on a seven-year straight-line basis ($50,000 per year). At the end of the ten-year life of the machinery, the company's cash flow will return to what it would have been without the new machinery unless a replacement for the machinery is purchased at that time. The firm's tax rate is 30 percent, both with and without the new equipment.

a Set up a cash flow analysis table for this problem like Exhibit 8-1 in the text to determine the cash flow from the machinery.

b Assuming that the appropriate discount rate on the investment is 15 percent, use the net present value method to determine whether the investment should be made.

2 Platonic Sportswear just bought a new loom for $90,000. The salvage value for computing depreciation and the estimated liquidation value of the asset at the end of three years are both zero. The future cash flow and profit generated by the loom are:

Year	Cash flow	Profit
1	$50,000	$20,000
2	50,000	20,000
3	35,000	5,000

Compute the following for the loom:

a Internal rate of return [Ans.: IRR = 24.9 percent]

b Net present value using a cost of capital of 15 percent [Ans.: NPV = $14,298]

c Payback period [Ans.: 1.8 years]

d Accounting rate of return [Ans.: 33.3 percent]

3 If the cash inflows from the loom in problem **2** could be kept fully invested until the end of year 3, earning a rate of return of 30 percent per year, how much would the cash flow accumulate to at the end of year 3? [Ans: $184,500]

4 P. Carter ("Bubbles") Dodd IV speculates in political memorabilia. He purchased a truckload of Hubert Humphrey 1968 Presidential campaign posters and buttons for $8,000. Bubbles expects to be able to sell the truckload in one year for $10,000 (net of taxes). The memorabilia generate no other cash flows. Bubbles' cost of capital is 20 percent. Using both the net present value method and the IRR method, determine whether Bubbles should purchase the truckload of memorabilia. [Ans.: NPV = $333 and IRR = 25%; therefore Bubbles should purchase the memorabilia]

5 Assume that the investment described in problem **4** will give Bubbles Dodd a return of $10,000 in two years. Using the information in problem **4**, apply the net present value method and the IRR method to determine whether Bubbles should make the investment.

6 Little Pumpkin Cookie Shoppe is considering the purchase of a new cookie cutting machine. The cookie cutter will cost $30,000 and, because of increased cookie output, will increase net cash flow by $6000 per year for the next ten years. The cookie cutter has a zero liquidation value at the end of its useful life of ten years. Little Pumpkin's cost of capital is 20 percent. Compute the cookie cutters:

a NPV

b IRR

c Payback period

7 Dimples Baby Products is deciding whether it should buy a new vegetable masher for manufacturing its product "Vegey Goo," a smooth, creamy, vegetable pablum for infants. The masher will cost $40,000 and will increase the firm's cash flow by $8000 per year for the next fifteen years (assume that the first $8000 occurs one year hence.) At the end of the fifteen years it is expected that the masher can be sold for $4000 (this is net of taxes). What is the masher's:

a NPV using a cost of capital of 15 percent?

b IRR?

c Payback period?

8 Flag Carwash is considering the purchase of new car wash equipment in order to expand its operations. Two types of options are

278

PART 2
**The firm's investment,
financing, and dividend
decisions**

available: a low-speed system with an $18,000 initial cost and a high-speed system with a $26,000 initial cost. Each system has a twenty-five-year life and a zero end-of-life liquidation value. The net cash flows associated with each investment are:

	Low-speed system	High-speed system
Initial cost	$18,000	$26,000
Annual cash flow for years 1 through 20	$2,800	$3,900

a   Analyze the above problem using the NPV method. Perform the analysis for each of the following costs of capital:

    (1)   12 percent [Ans.: NPV(low-speed system) = $7416
                                    NPV(high-speed system) = $9400]

    (2)   14 percent
    (3)   16 percent
    Compare your results for the three cases.

b   Analyze the problem using the IRR method, using each of the above costs of capital (12 percent, 14 percent, and 16 percent).

9   Hank Sykes and his wife, Hyacinth, have long dreamed of owning their own business. A recent inheritance has made realizing this dream possible. Cranberry farming has a particular attraction for the Sykes because Hank's family has for generations been in farming and both Hank and Hyacinth have very strong hands and arms (which will help in working the cranberry bog). The Sykes can acquire 40 acres of cranberry bog land for $8000 per acre. In addition to the bog land cost, a capital investment of $48,000 will be necessary to set up operations. The $48,000 in capital assets will be depreciated on a straight-line basis over twelve years. Assume also a zero market value of the capital assets at the end of the fifteen years. Each acre of land is expected to yield 150 barrels of cranberries per year, and berry prices are anticipated to remain at $20 per barrel indefinitely. Cash expenses will be 30 percent of the gross receipts from selling the cranberries. In addition, the Sykes will pay themselves total annual salaries of $30,000 ($15,000 each), which is what they would have to pay two other people to perform the work of operating the cranberry farm and exactly what the Sykes can earn in alternative employment. This $30,000 in salaries to the Sykes is to be deducted in computing company cash flow. The Sykes plan to sell the bog land in fifteen years, and they expect the land to increase in value at the rate of 5 percent per year over that time period. The tax rate applicable to all company income except the gain from selling the bog land is 30 percent; the tax rate on the gain from selling the bog is 15 percent. The appropriate discount rate on the firm's cash flows is 12 percent. Answer the following:

a Why must the salaries of Hank and Hyacinth be included among company expenses in computing the firm's cash flow? Would the $30,000 in salaries have to be deducted as an expense if the Sykes decided not to pay themselves a salary?

b Compute each year's net cash flow from the investment in the cranberry business.

c Should Hank and Hyacinth invest in the cranberry bog?

10 Elixir Press is considering a $300,000 capital outlay for a new printing press which will reduce printing costs. The press will last twenty years and will have a zero liquidation value at the end of the twenty years. Nondepreciation cost reductions resulting from the new press are forecast at a 3 percent of the current $2 million per year. Elixir's annual revenues of $4 million will remain unaffected. The press will be depreciated over twelve years on a straight-line basis; this depreciation will be added to a current depreciation allowance for the firm of $500,000 per year on existing plant and equipment. The firm's tax rate is 50 percent. The new press will be eligible for a 10 percent investment tax credit. Elixir's cost of capital is 15 percent.

a Set up a cash flow analysis like Exhibit 8-1 in the text for this problem.

b Compute the net present value, internal rate of return, payback period, and accounting rate of return for this project. Should the project be adopted?

11 Assume that Elixir Press buys the printing press described in problem *10*. In addition, assume that Elixir, as a result of purchasing the new printing press, could reduce the sales price of its unabridged dictionary from $50 to $48. Because of the price reduction, the number of books sold will rise from 80,000 to 85,000, and production costs will rise from $2 million to $2.04 million. Except for these additional effects of the new press, all the facts stated in problem *10* still apply. Which one of the three following options should Elixir adopt?

a Purchase the new press but keep its old price ($50) and old output (80,000 units).

b Acquire the new press and cut its price (to $48) and increase its output to 85,000 units.

c Not purchase the press and simply keep its old price ($50) and output (80,000 units).

Use the present value method to solve this problem. Assume that Elixir's cost of capital is 15 percent.

12 Consider the following three projects, each of which has an investment cost of $130 and a life of three years.

280

PART 2
The firm's investment,
financing, and dividend
decisions

Year	Net cash flow		
	A	B	C
1	$90	$ 20	$ 40
2	60	70	30
3	30	110	100

a Which project is called for by the payback method?
b Compute NPV for each project at discount rates of 0 percent, 5 percent, 10 percent, 15 percent, 20 percent, and 30 percent. Plot the results (with NPV on the vertical axis). Which investment is superior for each of these discount rates?
c Find the IRR of each project.
d Note that IRR corresponds to the rate where the curve crosses the horizontal axis. From your plot, make some inference as to why two projects cannot be compared by comparing IRR.

13 Solve the problems of Exhibit 8-6 (page 264), Exhibit 8-7 (page 265), and Exhibit 8-8 (page 267) using the internal rate of return method.

14 Sandra Hayden owns a large microcomputer retail outlet. She is considering a new location for her store, and has the opportunity to purchase a store in the main business district for $500,000 (land $200,000, building $300,000). The store will require an additional $60,000 outlay for remodeling. Its depreciation base for tax purposes will be $360,000 ($300,000 for the building plus $60,000 for the remodeling improvements), and the depreciation will be on a straight-line basis over eighteen years (i.e., depreciation will be $20,000 per year). Sandra plans to use only half of the available space in the new store for her own business and will lease out, under a twenty-five-year lease, the other half of the store for $30,000 per year. At the end of the twenty-five years, the entire structure will be demolished (assume that the removal costs will be negligible and can be ignored). The value of the land at the end of the twenty-five years is expected to be $400,000.

Sandra is now at the end of the tenth year of a twelve-year lease at her present location, but she can get out of the lease by paying a $5000 tax deductible penalty. Her tax deductible lease payments at the current location are $10,000 per year. At the end of the twelve-year lease, Sandra can get a renewal for an additional twenty-five years at $14,000 per year.

Sandra's annual cash revenues are $840,000, and her cash expenses other than lease rentals and taxes are $500,000. These items will remain unchanged if Sandra stays at her present location, but will increase by 40 percent if she moves to a new location. Sandra's tax rate is 30 percent and she uses a 15 percent cost of capital for discounting cash flows. Should Sandra move to the new location?

15 Solve problem *14* but assume that the value of the land at the new location will increase at 5 percent per year over the twenty-five-year period and assume that the new property will be sold by Sandra at the end of the twenty-five years. Also, assume that a 30 percent tax rate will apply to the gain from selling the property at the end of the twenty-five years (the gain will equal the value of the land at the end of the twenty-five years minus the $200,000 original cost of the land). Assume no real estate brokerage costs or sales taxes in selling the property.

16 Pepé's Ski Shop is contemplating replacing its equipment for injecting foam into the lingings of downhill ski boots to provide a custom fit. The foaming machine currently in use was purchased eight years ago for $24,000, has been completely depreciated, and has a current market value of $4200. Pepé is considering the following two *mutually exclusive* alternative replacements:

Alternative 1: A similar but larger-capacity machine costing $45,000. Pepé estimates that this machine will increase annual revenues by $18,000 and increase annual nondepreciation expenses by $6500, implying a net pretax cash flow increase of $11,500 per year over its estimated fifteen-year life. It is expected that the new machine will have an actual aftertax liquidation value of $2000 at the end of fifteen years. The machine will be depreciated for tax purposes on a straight-line basis over fifteen years (assume a zero salvage value for computing depreciation).

Alternative 2: The latest in boot-foaming technology—a high-pressure machine capable of injecting a new ultralight foam with exceptional insulating characteristics and high resistance to breakdown. Since ultralight foam represents the frontier in ski boot technology, Pepé anticipates that cachet-conscious skiers will pay a premium to have boots foamed by this process. As a result he estimates that this process will provide an increase in annual revenues of $36,000 and an increase in annual nondepreciation expenses of $15,500, implying an increase in annual pretax cash flow of $20,500 over the fifteen-year life of the process. This alternative requires an initial outlay of $75,000 for equipment. The equipment is expected to have a zero actual liquidation value at the end of fifteen years. the machine will be depreciated for tax purposes on a straight-line basis over fifteen years (assume a zero salvage value for computing depreciation).

Pepé estimates his cost of capital at 12 percent, uses straight-line depreciation on all his equipment, and faces a marginal tax rate of 40 percent of the foreseeable future. The 40 percent tax rate applies to all taxable income, including any gain from selling the old foaming machine.

a Pepé has offered you a new pair of ski boots if you can help him make the correct choice. Should Pepé select alternative 1 or alternative 2? Assume no investment tax credit.

282

PART 2
**The firm's investment,
financing, and dividend
decisions**

b If the equipment of alternatives 1 and 2 qualified for a 10 percent investment tax credit, would your recommendation change?

17 Marination Products, Inc., manufactures face creams and other cosmetics. It is evaluating two proposals for replacing antiquated laboratory equipment. The existing equipment was purchased seven years ago at a cost of $40,000 and is completely depreciated for tax purposes. The old equipment can be sold now for $15,000 and the tax on the sale would be $3000. It is expected that the equipment could be sold one year from now for $9000, the tax on the sale being $2000. The equipment's aftertax sale value twelve years from now is forecast to be $1000. Technology in Marination's industry is rapidly changing and the firm is comparing two replacement alternatives:

Alternative 1: Replace now with equipment that will cost $80,000 and will be depreciated for tax purposes on a straight-line basis over ten years ($8000 per year). Marination expects to keep the equipment for twelve years and then sell it for $10,000 (net of taxes on the sale). It is forecast that the new equipment will raise annual revenues by $25,000 and annual nondepreciation expenses by $7000. These revenue and expense changes begin one year hence and will continue for eleven additional years.

Alternative 2: Replace the existing facilities in one year for an investment of $100,000 one year from now. This replacement will incorporate a new technology that is not currently available. The equipment will be depreciated for tax purposes on a straight-line basis over ten years ($10,000 per year) and is expected to be kept for eleven years (i.e., until twelve years from now). The disposal value (net of taxes on the sale) of the equipment twelve years from now is expected to be $20,000. It is forecast that the new facilities will increase annual company revenues by $25,000 and annual nondepreciation expenses by $4000. The annual revenue and expense increases will begin two years from now and continue until twelve years from now.

Marination has a 30 percent corporate tax rate and has cost of capital of 14 percent. Compare alternative 1, alternative 2, and retention of the existing equipment for twelve more years.

The ▪ symbol indicates that all or a significant part of the problem can be solved using the *Computer Models* software package that accompanies this text.

WHY AN INVESTMENT'S NET PRESENT VALUE EQUALS ITS BENEFIT TO CURRENT STOCKHOLDERS

In calculating the net present value for project selection in the text of this chapter, we assumed that a project's NPV is the net gain to stockholders from the project. Criteria for investments under the NPV technique are:

1 If the firm can obtain funds (borrow funds or sell new shares) to finance profitable investments, for mutually exclusive investments, the one with the highest positive NPV should be adopted; and, in making accept-reject decisions, an investment should be adopted if and only if its NPV is positive.
2 If the firm faces a budget constraint, the set of projects with the highest positive total NPV should be adopted.

In this appendix, we explain why the NPV of a project equals the gain to current ("old") shareholders from that project. Current or old shareholders are those who own the firm when the investment decision is being made and do *not* include any new shareholders who buy additional shares of the company's stock that are sold to finance the investment. We will consider two kinds of financing of the investment: first, the use of idle cash (described below) and, second, the use of borrowing or selling new shares.

FINANCING WITH THE FIRM'S CASH

Idle cash is cash that has a value equal to its face value because it does not produce an above-average rate of return by serving the firm in a productive capacity. The cash has a value equal to its face amount *and is the property of stockholders*. If the cash is spent, it is therefore a sacrifice of that cash by the company's shareholders.

An investment paid for with idle cash is an exchange of cash in the amount I (amount of investment) for the newly acquired assets. The value of the cash given up is I; for example, an investment I of $100,000 of idle cash is a sacrifice by stockholders of the $100,000. The new asset obtained by investing I provides the firm with an added future cash flow. The net gain equals the present value of the returns from the investment less the cost of investment. That is, the net gain to stockholders equals

284

PART 2
The firm's investment,
financing, and dividend
decisions

$$\begin{pmatrix} \text{Gain to} \\ \text{stockholders} \end{pmatrix} = \begin{pmatrix} \text{the present value of the} \\ \text{future cash flow from the} \\ \text{new assets acquired} \end{pmatrix} - \begin{pmatrix} \text{cash surrendered} \\ \text{in making the} \\ \text{investment} \end{pmatrix}$$

$$= \frac{CF_1}{1 + k} + \frac{CF_2}{(1 + k)^2} + \cdots + \frac{CF_n}{(1 + k)^n} - I$$

$$= \text{NPV}$$

Terms CF_1, CF_2, . . . , CF_n are the cash flows from the project in periods 1, 2, . . . , n; k is the discount rate; and I is the initial investment in the project (the cash expended on the project). The above relationship indicates that the net gain to shareholders is simply the NPV of the project. The net present value method is therefore appropriate if the investment is financed with idle cash.

FINANCING WITH FUNDS FROM BORROWING OR NEW STOCK

We wish to show that if the funds to finance new investment are acquired by selling *new* shares (in amount S^N) or through borrowing (selling new bonds in amount B^N), then the effect on the wealth of current shareholders (those owning the "old" stock) from the investment and its financing will equal the investment's NPV. This net wealth gain will be reflected in a rise in the market value of the firm's old shares by an amount equal to the project's NPV. Old shares refer to the stock outstanding *not* including the new shares issued (S^N).

To show that the effect on the value of the firm's *old shares* from a project is the project's NPV whether it is financed with new stock S^N, new bonds B^N, or a combination of the two, assume the following:

S = the market value of the old shares assuming the investment in a new project is made and is financed with some combination of new stock and new bonds

S' = the market value of the old shares assuming the investment is *not* made

B = the market value of the firm's old bonds (not including new bonds to finance the investment) if the investment is made

B' = the market value of the old bonds if the investment is *not* made

S^N = the market value of new shares sold to finance the investment

B^N = the market value of new bonds sold to finance the investment

V = the market value of the firm (value of all outstanding stocks and bonds) if the new investment is made

V' = the market value of the firm if the new investment is *not* made

New shares S^N and new bonds B^N are issued to finance investment and are not issued if there is no investment. Therefore, with investment of amount I financed with S^N and B^N we know that

$$S^N + B^N = I \tag{8-7}$$

For example, new investment of amount $100,000 might be financed with $40,000 of new stock and $60,000 of new borrowing (bonds); thus, $I = \$100,000$, $S^N = \$40,000$, and $B^N = \$60,000$.

Since, by definition, the value of the firm equals the value of all outstanding stocks and bonds, with the investment the firm's value is

$$V = \begin{pmatrix} \text{value of the} \\ \text{firm with the} \\ \text{investment} \end{pmatrix} = \begin{pmatrix} \text{value of all shares} \\ \text{outstanding with} \\ \text{the investment} \end{pmatrix} + \begin{pmatrix} \text{value of all bonds} \\ \text{outstanding with} \\ \text{the investment} \end{pmatrix}$$

$$= S + S^N + B + B^N \tag{8-8}$$

Furthermore, the value of the firm if the investment is *not* undertaken (signified by V') equals

$$V' = \begin{pmatrix} \text{value of the firm} \\ \text{without the} \\ \text{investment} \end{pmatrix} = \begin{pmatrix} \text{value of all shares} \\ \text{outstanding without} \\ \text{the investment} \end{pmatrix} + \begin{pmatrix} \text{value of all bonds} \\ \text{outstanding without} \\ \text{the investment} \end{pmatrix}$$

$$= S' + B' \tag{8-9}$$

We know that the change in the value of the old shares due to the investment equals $S - S'$, the value of the shares with the investment less the value without the investment. By rearranging (8-8) it is clear that $S = V - B - B^N - S^N$ and by rearranging (8-9) we know that $S' = V' - B'$. Subtracting S' from S, the change in old share values is

$$S - S' = (V - B - B^N - S^N) - (V' - B')$$

$$= V - B - B^N - S^N - V' + B'$$

$$= V - V' - (S^N + B^N) - (B - B') \tag{8-10}$$

From Eq. (8-7) recall that $(S^N + B^N) = I$ and let $(B - B') = 0.$[14] Equation (8-10) becomes

$$\begin{pmatrix} \text{Change in old share value} \\ \text{due to the investment} \end{pmatrix} = S - S' = (V - V') - I \tag{8-11}$$

The change in the firm's total value in Eq. (8-11), $V - V'$, is the additional value of the firm due to the investment. $V - V'$ is the present value of the future cash flow from the new assets. Since I is the current cost of the new assets, it follows that the right-hand side of Eq. (8-11) is the NPV of the new investment. Therefore, if investment is financed

---

[14] The assumption that $B - B' = 0$ means that the new investment and its financing by selling additional shares or bonds does not affect the value of the *old* bonds. If the value of the old bonds were affected by a new investment—for example, by reducing the likelihood of bankruptcy (thereby making the old bonds less risky and consequently more valuable)—then the value of the new investment to stockholders would equal the investment's net present value less the change in the value of the old bonds. This assumption that the old bonds do not change in value is made throughout this book and is generally made in actual business practice. This is because it not only simplifies the analysis but is ordinarily a realistic assumption. For a discussion of this point, see Haley and Schall, *The Theory of Financial Decisions*, chap. 12.

286

PART 2
**The firm's investment,
financing, and dividend
decisions**

with funds from the sale of some combination of new stocks and bonds, the increase in the value of the old shares equals the net present value of the investment.

An example will help clarify the above concept. Assume that the firm is considering an investment outlay of $10,000 that would be financed with $6000 from borrowing ($B^N$ = $6000) and $4000 from the sale of new stock (S^N = $4000). If the new investment *is not* adopted, the value of the currently outstanding stock would be $500,000 ($S'$ = $500,000) and the value of the currently outstanding bonds would be $400,000 ($B'$ = $400,000). The value of the firm (V') therefore would be $900,000. Assume that if the new investment *is* adopted, the value of the firm would be $915,000 ($V$ = $915,000), the present value of the additional aftertax cash flow to stockholders and bondholders from the new assets therefore being $15,000 (the rise in the value of the firm's total aftertax cash flow being $915,000 − $900,000). The *net present value of the investment* is therefore $5000, $15,000 less the cost of the assets of $10,000. *The increase in the value of the old shares* is consequently $5000. The data associated with the problem are shown in Exhibit 8-9.

EXHIBIT 8-9
Equality of NPV and the change in old share values

	Without the investment	With the investment
1. Value of old shares	$500,000	$505,000
2. Value of old bonds	400,000	400,000
3. New stock sold for the investment	0	4,000
4. New bonds sold for the investment	0	6,000
5. Value of all stock outstanding [= (1) + (3)]	500,000	509,000
6. Value of all bonds outstanding [= (2) + (4)]	400,000	406,000
7. Value of firm (V) [= (5) + (6)]	900,000	915,000

Gain to old shareholders = rise in value of old shares = $505,000 − $500,00 = $5,000. Net present value of the investment = (present value of future cash flows from the investment) − (cost of investment) = (V − V') − I = ($915,000 − $900,000) − $10,000 = $5,000.

CHOICES BETWEEN MUTUALLY EXCLUSIVE INVESTMENTS: INTERNAL RATE OF RETURN VERSUS PRESENT VALUE

The three sections of this appendix cover the following:

1 The use of the present value and internal rate of return methods in comparing mutually exclusive investments assuming either that future investment opportunities are not dependent on current investments or that all future investments will yield exactly the cost of capital. We show that the present value or the *incremental* IRR method must be used and that simply selecting the investment with the highest IRR is usually not the proper approach; that is, it can lead to adoption of the less profitable investment.

2 The special case mentioned on page 257 in which the best investment from among a set of mutually exclusive investments is the one with the highest IRR. In the discussion below, it is shown that the investment with the highest IRR is the best one as long as certain conditions hold. It is also the investment that would be chosen using the incremental IRR method or the present value method.

3 The general approach for analyzing investments when the firm's future investment opportunities *depend on which investments are currently adopted*. This approach is valid whether the future reinvestment rates (the rates of return on future investments) are equal to the firm's cost of capital, the current investments' IRRs, or some other rate.

We assume throughout this appendix that the firm can obtain funds at the cost of capital. Capital rationing was considered in a separate section in the body of Chapter 8.

1. FUTURE INVESTMENTS INDEPENDENT OF CURRENT INVESTMENTS

It should be noted at the outset that if the profitability of future investment opportunities is not dependent on current investments, then it is correct to evaluate current investments using the present value and IRR techniques described in the text, with the incremental IRR approach applied if one is selecting from among mutually exclusive alternatives. This is true regardless of the rate of return that the firm expects to earn

288

PART 2
**The firm's investment,
financing, and dividend
decisions**

on future investments as long as those future investments do not depend on currently adopted projects. In this case, the *current* projects are accepted or rejected on the basis of the cash flows that they generate, and the *future* projects are accepted or rejected on the basis of the cash flows that they generate. Both present and future projects are evaluated using the firm's cost of capital, either as a discount rate or as a minimum acceptable rate of return.

A second important point is that, in evaluating current investments, we can ignore any future project that depends on current investments as long as that future project is expected to earn a rate of return not exceeding the firm's cost of capital. The reason that such future investments can be ignored is that all future projects earning less than the cost of capital will not be adopted, since they have a negative NPV (and so are irrelevant), and all future projects earning exactly the cost of capital have a zero net present value and therefore do not affect shareholder wealth (they are just marginally acceptable). In this situation, we can apply the present value and internal rate of return methods to the cash flows of current investments as explained in the text. In this section of Appendix 8B the use of the present value and incremental rate of return methods will be illustrated for the present case that allows us to ignore *future* investments. In this case it is ordinarily incorrect simply to select the mutually exclusive investment with the highest IRR. This was shown to be so in the text (pages 255–257) if the investments being compared require different initial outlays. We show below that choosing the investment with the higher IRR can lead to errors even if the mutually exclusive investments have the same lives and require the same initial outlay. Either the incremental rate of return method or the present value method should be used.

EXHIBIT 8-10
Cash flows from mutually exclusive investments A and B

	A	B	A − B
Time:			
Now	− $1,000	− $1,000	$ 0
Year 1	50	1,200	− 1,150
Year 2	100	100	0
Year 3	1,536	40	1,496
IRR (r)	20%	30%	14%[a]
NPV (at 10% rate)	$283	$204	$79

Conclusion: Choose A since $283 exceeds $204.

[a] The 14% rate is the IRR of the (A − B) cash flows; the added outlay of $1,150 in year 1 produces an added return of $1,496 in year 3, the rate of return being 14% per year. Since 14% exceeds the cost of capital rate of 10%, A is superior to B using the incremental IRR method [the (A − B) increment has an IRR that exceeds the cost of capital].

To illustrate the principles involved, assume that the firm has two mutually exclusive investment opportunities, A and B, which each require an initial outlay now of $1000. The cash flows from A and B are shown in Exhibit 8-10. Assume that the cost of capital is 10 percent. Observe that although the 30 percent internal rate of return of B, $r(B)$, exceeds $r(A) = 20$ percent, the net present value of A, NPV(A), of $283 exceeds NPV(B) = $204. A is the superior investment. Also, notice that the incremental rate of return is 14 percent, which exceeds the cost of capital of 10 percent; therefore the incremental IRR method also correctly leads to a choice of A over B. Figure 8-3 shows the net present values of A and B for various discount rates. If the discount rate (cost of capital) is less than 14 percent, the NPV(A) exceeds NPV(B) (the case in the example where the cost of capital was assumed to be 10 percent); if the cost of capital were exactly 14 percent, NPV(A) = NPV(B) and we would be indifferent between A and B; and if the cost of capital were greater than 14 percent, NPV(B) would exceed NPV(A) and B would be preferred to A.

2. REINVESTMENT AT THE IRR FOR MUTUALLY EXCLUSIVE INVESTMENTS WITH THE SAME I

Assume that the firm is comparing two or more mutually exclusive investments and that conditions **a**, **b**, and **c** below apply to those investments:

a All the investments involve the same initial (current) dollar outlay.
b Each investment provides the firm with the special opportunity to reinvest the investment's future cash flows at a rate of return equal to the investment's IRR.
c The reinvestment opportunity described under *b* above lasts until T periods from the current investment (i.e., the funds can remain

FIGURE 8-3
The NPV of investments A and B at different discount rates.

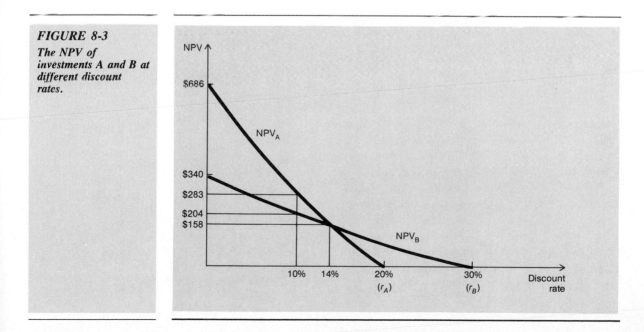

reinvested earning the internal rate of return until T periods hence), where T is the same for all the mutually exclusive opportunities being compared *and* T is no less than the life of the longest lived of the mutually exclusive investments (e.g., if the longest-lived investment has a five-year life, T is no less than five years).

Conditions **a**, **b**, and **c** were noted in the text on page 257. It was observed that **a**, **b**, and **c** hold infrequently in practice. In those cases in which **a**, **b**, and **c** do hold, the mutually exclusive investment with the highest IRR is also that which provides the highest NPV and is the investment that would be chosen using the incremental rate of return method. We will use an example to show this.

Assume that investments C and D are being evaluated by the firm at time 0. The firm's cost of capital is 10 percent. C and D each require an initial outlay of $1000 (condition **a**). The cash flows of C and D are shown in Exhibit 8-11. The IRR of C [signified $r(C)$] is 20 percent, and the future cash flows from C can be reinvested until time 5 at a rate of return of 20 percent per period; that is, by investing in C now, the firm obtains the opportunity to reinvest C's future cash flows in new projects that also earn 20 percent per period (until time 5). C is identical to A in Exhibit 8-10 except that we are now assuming that the future cash flows from A are reinvested at A's IRR. The IRR of D, $r(D)$, is 35 percent, and the future cash flows from D can be reinvested to earn 35 percent until time 5. Thus, condition **b** is satisfied. Note that T in condition **c** is equal to 5 in this example; therefore, condition **c** is satisfied since 5 is greater than the three-year life of project C, the longer-lived project. Since the firm's cost of capital is only 10 percent, we know that the firm will, if C is adopted, reinvest C's cash flow at the reinvestment opportunity rate of 20 percent

---

EXHIBIT 8-11
Comparing mutually exclusive investments with cash flows that are reinvested at the internal rate of return

	C	D
Time:		
Now	− $1,000	− $1,000
Year 1	50	1,350
Year 2	50	0
Year 3	1,596	0
IRR (r)	20%	35%
NPV of above cash flows at 10% (ignoring reinvestment)	$286	$227
Year 5 terminal amount (V_5)	$2,488	$4,484
NPV of V_5 at 10%	$545	$1,784

Conclusion: Choose D since $1,784 exceeds $545.

and will, if D is adopted, reinvest D's cash flow at the reinvestment opportunity rate of 35 percent. Assuming such reinvestment, the firm will accumulate at time 5 the terminal amount $V_5(C) = \$2488$ if C is adopted and amount $V_5(D) = \$4484$ if D is adopted. $V_5(C) = \$2488$ results by investing, at a rate of 20 percent per period, C's time 1 cash flow of $50 for four periods (to time 5), reinvesting C's time 2 cash flow of $50 for three periods, etc. $V_5(D) = \$4484$ results by reinvesting at 35 percent per period D's time 1 cash flow of $1350 for four periods to time 5. Notice that for any T in condition **c** (where $T = 5$ in the present example)

$$V_T = (1 + r)^T I = (F/P, r, T)I \tag{8-12}$$

Equation (8-12) follows, since reinvesting all cash flows at the internal rate of return r is equivalent to simply investing I for T periods with all funds kept invested for the T periods earning rate r per period. This is like putting I in a bank account earning r each period and leaving all interest in the account along with the principal until the end of the T periods.

The objective is to maximize the present value of the returns from the investment (using the cost of capital) and, using (8-12),

$$NPV(C) = \frac{V_5(C)}{(1 + k)^5} - I \tag{8-13}$$

$$= \frac{[1 + r(C)]^5 I}{(1 + k)^5} - I = \frac{(1.2)^5 \, \$1000}{(1.1)^5} - \$1000$$

$$= \frac{\$2488}{(1.1)^5} - \$1000 = \$545$$

$$NPV(D) = \frac{V_5(D)}{(1 + k)^5} - I \tag{8-14}$$

$$= \frac{[1 + r(D)]^5 I}{(1 + k)^5} - I = \frac{(1.35)^5 \, \$1000}{(1.1)^5} - \$1000$$

$$= \frac{\$4484}{(1.1)^5} - \$1000 = \$1784$$

Notice from Eqs. (8-13) and (8-14) that as long as C and D involve the same I, T, and cost of capital k—which is the case here since $I = \$1000$, T = five years, and $k = 10$ percent for both investments—the investment with the higher V_T is preferred. We can see from Eq. (8-12) that this is equivalent to choosing the investment with the higher internal rate of return.

Although simply selecting the alternative with the highest IRR is the easiest selection method under the present assumptions (**a**, **b**, and **c** above), it should be clear that the net present value method also leads to the correct choice. The procedure is simply to compute the terminal value, V_T, of each mutually exclusive investment and choose the investment with the highest terminal value since, with the same initial outlay and *T* for all the investments, highest terminal value also means highest NPV.

3. REINVEST-MENT RATES IN GENERAL

In general, if future investment opportunities are affected by current investments, then those future opportunities must be taken into account in evaluating projects. All effects of current investments on the future cash flows must be taken into account, including future capital projects and returns from those projects. The net present value or incremental IRR methods can be applied in this case. It is not in general correct to choose the investment with the highest internal rate of return.

To illustrate the correct approach, assume that the firm is comparing mutually exclusive investments E and F that require current outlays of $2000 and $5000 in the current period. E has a life of two years (returns annual cash flows of $1500 at the end of years 1 and 2), and the funds from E can be reinvested at a 20 percent rate of return until the end of year 4. E also provides the opportunity to invest an additional $1000 at the end of the third year (three years hence) at 20 percent per year for one year. After year 4, investment E provides no special reinvestment opportunities, and all funds are withdrawn from E and its reinvestment projects at the end of year 4. Exhibit 8-12 describes these cash flows.

Investment F is a three-year project (returns annual cash flows of $2500 from years 1 through 3) but provides no special reinvestment opportunities.

Do we choose E or F? *The preferred investment is that with the greater net present value of future cash flows, taking into account any reinvestment opportunities earning more than the cost of capital. The objective is to choose that investment plan which maximizes the net present value of cash flows.*

The net present value of E is computed by assuming that the $1500 cash flows of years 1 and 2 are reinvested to earn 20 percent per year

---

EXHIBIT 8-12
Cash flows from investment E and reinvestment

Time	Inflows (1)	Investment (2)	Net cash flow (col. 1 − col. 2) (3)	
Now		$2,000	− $2,000	
Year 1	$1,500	1,500	0	Net funds invested
Year 2	1,500	1,500	0	in project
Year 3		1,000	− 1,000	
Year 4			5,952	Funds withdrawn from project at end of year 4 [$V_4(E)$]

until the end of year 4; $1000 is also invested at the end of year 3 until the end of year 4 at a rate of return of 20 percent. The total amount accumulated at the end of year 4 [$V_4(E)$] is $5952. The net present value of E is computed as follows:

$$\text{Amount accumulated at end of year 4 with E} = V_4(E)$$

$$= \$1500(1.2)^3 + \$1500(1.2)^2 + \$1000(1.2)$$

$$= \$5952$$

$$\text{Present value of new funds invested in E} = I(E) = \$2000 + \frac{\$1000}{(1.10)^3} = \$2751$$

$$\text{Net present value of E } [NPV(E)] = \frac{V_4(E)}{(1.10)^4} - I(E)$$

$$= \frac{\$5952}{(1.10)^4} - \$2751 = \$1314$$

For investment F, the net present value equals

$$NPV(F) = \frac{\$2500}{1 + 0.10} + \frac{\$2500}{(1.10)^2} + \frac{\$2500}{(1.10)^3} - \$5000$$

$$= \$2500(P/A, 10\%, 3) - \$5000$$

$$= \$2500(2.487) - \$5000 = \$1218$$

Since $NPV(E) = \$1314$ exceeds $NPV(F) = \$1218$, E is preferred; and since $NPV(E)$ is positive, E should be adopted.

CHAPTER NINE

CAPITAL BUDGETING: SPECIAL TOPICS

Chapter 8 provided the primary tools for performing capital budgeting analysis. A variety of special problems that frequently arise in practice were ignored. These include comparison of alternatives with different lives, inflation, interrelated investments, capital rationing, and capital budgeting in an international environment. Methods of addressing these problems are presented in this chapter.

COMPARING INVESTMENTS WITH DIFFERENT LIVES

Until now, in comparing mutually exclusive investments we have assumed that the lives of the investments were the same. Often two or more options being compared do not have equal lives. Strictly speaking, to analyze such investments using present value or IRR, it is generally necessary to evaluate them for equal periods of time. To do this, we merely ask: "What would we do after the shorter-lived asset expires, if we were to obtain it instead of acquiring the longer-lived asset?" The examples below will illustrate the problem and its solution. We will then observe that in many cases an approximation technique is adequate and that often we need not evaluate the investments for exactly equal periods of time.

Assume that a firm is comparing machines M_1 and M_2. M_1, which will last six years, costs $1000 at time 0 and will yield a net cash flow of $400 per year. M_1, if purchased, will be replaced at time 6 by M_1', which will cost $1200 and will yield $400 per year (from time 7 to time 12). M_2 will last for twelve years, will cost $1800 at time 0, and will yield $400 per year for twelve years. The point here is that the comparison should be between the NPV of M_1 and M_1' [signified NPV($M_1 + M_1'$)] and the NPV of M_2 [signified NPV(M_2)]. We can see from Exhibit 9-1 that this comparison leads us to choose M_1 now and to replace it with M_1' at time 6 rather than to obtain M_2 now, since NPV($M_1 + M_1'$) = $1048 and NPV($M_2$) = $926. It is improper to simply compare the NPV of M_1 (ignoring the replacement with M_1' at time 6) with the NPV of M_2. If we had done this, we would have chosen M_2 since NPV(M_2) = $926 and NPV($M_1$) = $742.

EXHIBIT 9-1

Comparison of investments with different lives

Time	Cash flows		
	M_1	M_1'	M_2
Time 0 (cost)	$-\$1,000$		$-\$1,800$
Time 1–6 (returns per year)	400		400
Time 6 (cost)		$-\$1,200$	
Time 7–12 (returns per year)		400	400

$$NPV(M_1) = -\$1,000 + \$400 \; (P/A, \; 10\%, \; 6)$$
$$= -\$1,000 + \$400 \; (4.355) = \underline{\$742}$$

$$NPV(M_1 + M_1') = \$400 \; (P/A, \; 10\%, \; 12)$$
$$- \$1,000 - \$1,200 \; (P/F, \; 10\%, \; 6)$$
$$= \$400 \; (6.814) - \$1,000$$
$$- \$1,200 \; (0.5645) = \underline{\$1,048}$$

$$NPV(M_2) = \$400 \; (P/A, \; 10\%, \; 12) - \$1,800$$
$$= \$400 \; (6.814) - \$1,800$$
$$= \underline{\$926}$$

Conclusion: Buy M_1 now and replace with M_1' at time 6 since $NPV(M_1 + M_1')$ exceeds $NPV(M_2)$.

In the above example, the two options [option $(M_1 + M_1')$ and option M_2] had identical time durations of twelve years. Often, to establish identical durations for options being compared, it is necessary to forecast replacements many years into the future.[1] In such cases, it is ordinarily adequate to make the options only approximately, and not exactly, of the same duration.

For example, it would ordinarily be acceptable to compare the alternative of machines M_1 and M_1' (twelve-year total life) with the alternative involving M_2, even if M_2 had only an eleven- or even ten-year life; the discrepancy would be one or two years occurring a decade into the future. The importance of a time discrepancy between two investment alternatives is dependent upon three things:

---

[1] For example, if asset X and its future replacement each last ten years (replacement at time 10, time 20, etc.) and asset Y and each of its future replacements last thirteen years (replacement at time 13, time 26, etc.), we would have to analyze cash flows for the next 130 years (the shortest period ending when replacements of both X and Y also end). However, as noted below, adequate accuracy usually requires consideration of only a limited time period. Note also that this section assumes that investment (e.g., a replacement) in any particular time period does not depend on previous investment. Thus, in the above example, the NPV of any year 12 replacement does not depend on whether M_1 and M_1' or M_2 was used in the first twelve years. See Appendix 8B, Section 3, on analyzing investments that affect or depend on investment in other periods.

296

PART 2
**The firm's investment,
financing, and dividend
decisions**

1 *The shorter the discrepancy is, the less important it is.* Thus, we had to consider the replacement of M_1 and M_1' in the above example because a six-year discrepancy between M_1 and M_2 was too large to ignore.

2 *The further into the future the life discrepancy is, the less important it is.* For example, if we were considering alternative buildings for a vacant piece of land, we could ordinarily compare the NPV of a building with a forty-year life with the NPV of a building with a fifty-year life and ignore what each would be replaced with at the end of its life. The ten-year discrepancy occurs forty to fifty years into the future and can be ignored in most cases. The reason is that the NPV of cash flows occurring far in the future is usually very small.[2]

3 *The closer the rate of return on future investments is to the cost of capital, the less important are any time discrepancies.* This is because the NPV = 0 for any future investment that just earns the cost of capital. *If the NPV on future investment is zero, then the time discrepancy can be ignored.* For example, assume that M_1' in the above example has the cash flows shown below instead of those shown in Exhibit 9-1.[3]

Time	Cash flow of M_1'
t_6 (cost)	− \$1,200.00
$t_7 - t_{12}$ (returns per year)	\$ 275.55

$$\text{NPV}(M_1') \text{ at time } 6 = \$275.55(P/A, 10\%, 6) - \$1200$$
$$= \$275.55(4.355) - \$1200$$
$$= \$1200 - \$1200 = 0$$

NPV$(M_1') = 0$; that is, *it adds nothing* to the NPV of M_1 and M_1' combined. We can just ignore M_1' and directly compare the six-year asset M_1 with the twelve-year asset M_2. Assuming that M_1 and M_2 have the cash flows and NPVs as shown in Exhibit 9-1 and M_1' has the cash flows and NPV shown above, the NPV$(M_1 + M_1')$ = NPV(M_1) = \$742, since NPV(M_1') = 0. We choose M_2 since NPV(M_2) = \$926, which exceeds NPV(M_1) of \$742.

---

[2] Even a very large net present value far into the future has a small value when discounted to the present using an economically realistic discount rate. For example, \$1,000,000 at time 50 discounted to time 0 (now) has a value of \$8500 if the discount rate is 10 percent [$(P/F, 10\%, 50) = 0.0085$]. Of course, the larger is the future amount, the further into the future it must be for it to become insignificant when discounted to the present.

[3] If M_1' cost \$1200 at time 6 and yields \$275.55 per year for years 7 through 12, it has an IRR of exactly 10 percent [$(A/P, 10\%, 6) = 0.2296$]. At a cost of capital of 10 percent, the NPV of M_1' is zero at time 6, as is shown in the text computation below.

To summarize, in order to provide an exactly correct comparison between mutually exclusive options, the two alternatives must have equal lives. An alternative here refers to a particular course of action that ordinarily involves an investment now and may involve further investments (replacements) in the future. Often it is not practical or possible to establish equal lives for two alternatives. In this case, it is generally correct to ignore time discrepancies if they are small, or if they occur far into the future, or if the rates of return on investments subsequent to the ones being considered are close to the cost of capital (that is, if such future investments have small NPVs).

The above conclusions also apply if we are using the IRR approach in comparing alternatives. We must ordinarily use equal lives for the alternatives for an exactly correct answer. However, as with the present value method, this rule is subject to the above qualifications.

INFLATION AND CAPITAL BUDGETING

Inflation in the early 1990s is not what it was even a few years ago. But it is still with us, as is the possibility of a resurgence to significantly higher levels. Economists are still divided as to what causes inflation. Fortunately, the financial manager's task is enormously simpler than that of the macroeconomist.

In an inflationary environment, the financial manager should know how to incorporate inflation into capital budgeting analysis. The job is surprisingly simple. The capital budgeting analyst should merely predict the actual dollar cash flows that will occur, taking into account the inflationary trend. For example, if the firm sells product X and the aftertax cash flow generated by sale of a single unit is expected to rise (due to inflation and any other factors) at the rate of 5 percent per year from the current level of $1, then the aftertax cash flow to be discounted is $1 per unit of product X sold this year, $1.05 per unit next year, $1.1025 (= 1.05 × $1.05) the year after next, and so forth to year 5, when the cash flow will be $1.276 per unit. Thus, the firm should use its expectations regarding inflation to estimate the actual dollar cash flows to be earned, and then use those expected actual flows in the analysis. The inflationary trend must be estimated, and usually this is done by selecting an estimate made by economists or by forecasting firms such as Chase Econometrics and Data Resources. These forecasts are sometimes published in financial periodicals or are available for a fee from the forecasters.

The appropriate discount rate to employ is still the market rate currently used by investors to discount cash flows of a similar risk. *Market rates take into account inflationary expectations*, and a greater expected rate of inflation will mean that investors will require a higher rate of return. This is the reason that interest rates on bonds and the borrowing rate at banks (including the prime rate charged the banks' biggest and least risky customers) increase as inflation accelerates. Figure 9-1 illustrates the similar historical patterns of the general price level and market discount rates (an average of long-term Baa bond rates in the figure).

The essence of this approach is that the proper rate to apply in discounting a cash flow is the rate investors apply to cash flows of similar risk. This rate will necessarily take into account inflationary trends. To illustrate the method, assume that a store is considering the purchase of a display case for $1500 that has an anticipated useful life of three years. If there were no inflation, the added sales due to the display case would be $2500 per year, increased cost of goods sold would be $1300, added nondepreciation expenses (i.e., expenses other than depreciation) would be $200, and the rise in the firm's taxes would equal $300. Thus, aftertax cash flow from the case would equal $700 per year ($700 = $2500 − $1300 − $200 − $300) for three years. However, with the expectation of continued inflation, the selling price of the product and the magnitude of the costs will rise. Assume that the expected cash flows (taking into account inflationary expectations) are as shown in Exhibit 9-2.

Notice from the table that the impact of inflation on sales may differ from the impact on costs. Let the discount rate appropriate to the cash flow be 12 percent; that is, the rate of return required by investors for cash flows of similar risk is 12 percent. The net present value of the display case is the discounted value of the cash flows in Exhibit 9-2 less the $1500 initial cost of the case; that is,

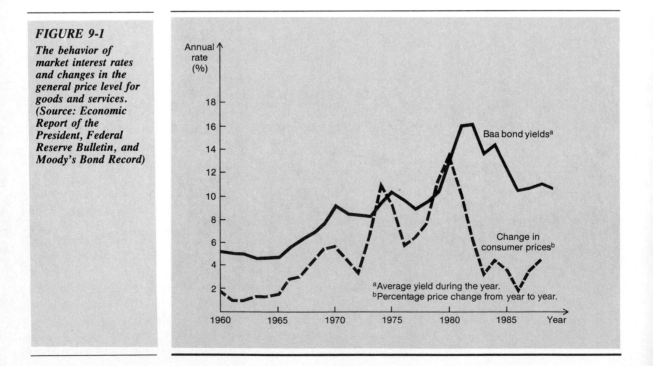

FIGURE 9-1
The behavior of market interest rates and changes in the general price level for goods and services. (Source: Economic Report of the President, Federal Reserve Bulletin, and Moody's Bond Record)

$$NPV = \frac{\$750}{1.12} + \frac{\$800}{(1.12)^2} + \frac{\$900}{(1.12)^3} - \$1500$$

$$= 0.8929(\$750) + 0.7972(\$800) + 0.7118(\$900) - \$1500$$

$$= \$448$$

The expected future dollar cash flows are discounted, and the current market discount rate used by investors is used for discounting. The cash flows are estimated so that they reflect anticipated inflation, and the current discount rate reflects the inflationary expectations of investors.

INTERRELATED INVESTMENT OPPORTUNITIES

Up to this point we have considered investment choices that either involved accepting or rejecting a particular project or involved a choice between two mutually exclusive options, e.g., whether the truck purchased would be a Ford or a Chevrolet. Frequently, however, two or more investments are being evaluated, any or all of which can be accepted. Furthermore, the investments may affect one another's profitability. In this case, the decision involves selecting the set of investments having the highest net present value and accepting the set if its net present value is positive. To illustrate, assume that Blue Grass Realty owns two adjacent plots of land, plot 1 and plot 2. Intuitively we know that what is constructed on plot 1 may influence the profitability of what is constructed on plot 2. The two land uses are economically interdependent. Blue Grass has decided that its only options for plot 1 are to construct a rest home on it or leave it vacant; its only options for plot 2 are to construct an amusement park on it or leave it vacant. Its options are therefore to construct the rest home and not the amusement park, to construct the amusement park and not the rest home, to con-

---

EXHIBIT 9-2

Cash flows from the display case with inflation

	Year 1	Year 2	Year 3
Increase in sales		$2,700	$2,900	$3,200
Deduct:			
Increase in cost of goods sold	$1,400	$1,500	$1,600
Increase in other nondepreciation expenses	250	275	300
Increase in taxes	300	325	400
Total deductions		1,950	2,100	2,300
Change in firm's aftertax cash flow		$ 750	$ 800	$ 900

struct both, or to construct neither. Assume that to leave both plots vacant produces a zero cash flow and requires a zero investment. Also assume for simplicity that all options involve the same risk and the same cost of capital of 10 percent.[4] The costs and payoffs of each decision involving the construction of one or both of the amusement park and rest home are shown in Exhibit 9-3. It is not surprising that the total cash flow from both the amusement park and rest home together ($24,000) falls far short of even the rest home alone ($50,000 per year). The home would not be too restful (and patrons therefore few) with merry-go-round music and children's screams wafting through the air. The net present value of the rest home on plot 1, with plot 2 left vacant (no amusement park), is the highest of the three choices, and would be the option selected, since its present value of $200,000 is positive.

The above example suggests a general guideline for analyzing a set of interdependent options. If we have any set of investments which have *interdependent* cash flows, e.g., investments A, B, and C, the following procedure is appropriate in determining the best course of action:

1   Determine the combinations of the interdependent options that are possible. For three interdependent options, A, B, and C, if none is mutually exclusive of any of the others (that is, all can be simultaneously adopted), then the possible combinations (which involve adopting at least one option) are:

A but not B or C   B and C but not A
B but not A or C   A and C but not B
C but not A or B   A, B, and C together
A and B but not C

2   Determine the initial outlay, the future aftertax cash flows, and the net present value of each of the combinations of options identified in step *1* above (seven combinations in the above example of A, B, and C).

3   Choose the combination of options analyzed in step *2* above with the highest net present value. If that highest net present value is positive, adopt that combination; if negative, reject that combination along with all the other combinations; if zero, you are indifferent concerning investment in that combination, and reject all the other combinations.

This procedure was followed in the amusement park–rest home example. In step *1*, we defined the combinations of options as the amusement park and not the rest home, rest home and not amusement park, or both. In step *2*, we determined the initial outlay, future cash

---

[4] If different options involve different risk, then they will warrant different discount rates (costs of capital). For example, if the rest home were riskier than the amusement park, the former might warrant a 14 percent discount rate and the latter a 10 percent discount rate; and the two together might justify an 11 percent discount rate. The issue of differing risk is discussed in Chap. 10.

flows, and net present value of each option (shown in Exhibit 9-3). In step *3*, we chose the rest home alternative since it had the highest net present value and that net present value was positive.

Are all options of the firm interdependent in some way, and must every combination of investment opportunities be analyzed in choosing a capital budget? Fortunately, the problem is not as bad as that. Although strictly speaking all a firm's activities are somewhat dependent (i.e., affect one another's profitability), many options are approximately independent and can therefore be evaluated as separate projects. For example, if plots 1 and 2 of Blue Grass Realty were in different parts of the city, the land uses on each could be individually evaluated. In that case, the rest home on plot 1 could be accepted or rejected, and the amusement park on lot 2 could be independently accepted or rejected. We would then not have to consider as a separate possibility the construction of both the amusement park and the rest home. Notice that if we had done this in the case of the adjacent (and therefore interdependent) plots described in Exhibit 9-3, we would have erroneously accepted the amusement park and the rest home, since each if done without the other has a positive net present value ($20,000 and $200,000, respectively). *With interdependencies that are significant we cannot consider each investment option individually.* This is so since the cash flow figures relating to the options as individual investments do not apply if more than one of the investments are undertaken. This is clearly illustrated in Exhibit 9-3, since the cash flow of the amusement park and rest home together ($24,000) is not equal to the cash flow of the amusement park alone ($12,000) plus the cash flow of the rest home alone ($50,000).

As a closing point, note that investments can be geographically near one another and still be economically independent. For example, if a new roof on a firm's manufacturing plant does not affect the profitability of a new truck, then the roof and truck are independent. If the roof and truck were independent of all other investment options being considered, then the project evaluation procedure would involve evaluating the roof

---

EXHIBIT 9-3
Interrelated investment opportunities

	Only amusement park	Only rest home	Amusement park and rest home
I_0	$100,000	$300,000	$400,000
Annual expected perpetual aftertax cash flow	$ 12,000	$ 50,000	$ 24,000
Net present value at 10%[a]	$ 20,000	$200,000	−$160,000

[a] NPV(only amusement park) = $12,000(10) − $100,000 = $20,000 where 10 is the 10% annuity present value factor for a perpetual annuity (see Appendix A); NPV(only rest home) = $50,000(10) − $300,000 = $200,000; NPV(amusement park and rest home) = $24,000(10) − $400,000 = −$160,000.

302

PART 2
**The firm's investment,
financing, and dividend
decisions**

CAPITAL
RATIONING

and truck separately. The roof would be built if, and only if, its net present value were positive, and the truck would be purchased if, and only if, its net present value were positive.

Sometimes, only limited funds are available for investment and, at least in the short run, no additional capital is obtainable from external sources. This might occur if the decision unit is not an entire firm but a division with a given capital allocation for investment determined by the parent company. The problem is how the division manager should use the funds that are available. Capital constraints are also common for government agencies with fixed appropriations.[5]

The present value approach to treating the capital constraint problem is to invest the funds that are available in that set of projects with the highest total net present value. That is, the goal is to maximize the net present value of the entire current investment.[6] For example, assume a fixed sum of $100,000 is available for an investment. Also, assume that the firm can invest in some combination of projects A through D. The data associated with each project are shown in Exhibit 9-4. Assume that A and B are mutually exclusive (cannot both be done), as would be so, for example, if A were a restaurant and B were a gas station on a given plot of land that has room for only one or the other. Also note that since we have only $100,000 to invest, we cannot do both C and D, nor can we do both A and D, because each combination involves an initial outlay of $110,000. Therefore, given the mutual exclusivity of A and B and the budget constraint of $100,000, the possible project combinations are A and C, B and C, and B and D. If B and C are done, there is $10,000 left over, since together they require only $90,000 of the $100,000 available. In Exhibit 9-5 the net present value of each feasible combination of

---

[5] If the reason that the firm cannot obtain capital at an acceptable rate (acceptable cost of capital) is that outsiders realistically view the firm's investment opportunities as unattractive, no capital rationing exists. This would simply be a case of a firm with investment opportunities that do not offer sufficient risk-return qualities to attract investors. Similarly, capital rationing does not exist just because credit is tight and funds in the economy are extremely expensive; the firm's resulting high cost of capital should nevertheless be used to evaluate current investments. If the company's investments do not provide a rate of return at least equal to this cost of capital (i.e., imply a positive NPV), they should be rejected since the firm can earn the cost of capital by simply investing (lending) its funds in the market. No investment that is inferior to such market opportunities should be accepted.

[6] We are assuming in this discussion of capital rationing that the constraint on funds exists only in the current period and not in future periods. The same general concepts apply with multiperiod constraints, but the analysis is far more complex; an additional consideration that becomes important with multiperiod constraints is the rate at which funds can be reinvested by the firm in each period. For a proof of the validity of the method presented here, see Edwin Elton, "Capital Rationing and External Discount Rates," *Journal of Finance* (June 1970).

projects is shown. The $60,000 net present value of the combination of A and C equals the net present value of A ($40,000) plus the net present value of C ($20,000), which were stated in Exhibit 9-4. The net present value of a combination of B and C equals the sum of the net present values of B and C, and the net present value of the combination of projects B and D equals the sum of the net present values of B and D. Note that the $10,000 that is unspent if B and C are adopted has a *net present value* of zero since, if it is invested at the market rate, the benefits received will be worth $10,000, producing a net present value of zero.[7] Since the net present value of the combination of projects A and C

[7] In order for an investment to have a positive NPV, the present value of the investment's future returns must exceed the investment's initial cost. The $10,000 invested at the going market rate of return will produce future benefits with a present value of $10,000, and therefore the investment has a zero *net* present value (i.e., a zero extraordinary return).

EXHIBIT 9-4

Net present values of the firm's investment opportunities with capital rationing

Opportunity	Present value of future returns (1)	Initial outlay (2)	Net present value (col. 1 − col. 2) (3)
A	$90,000	$50,000	$40,000
B	50,000	40,000	10,000
C	70,000	50,000	20,000
D	65,000	60,000	5,000

EXHIBIT 9-5

Net present values of alternative firm capital outlays with capital rationing

Possible combinations of opportunities	Net present value of entire capital budget[a]
A and C	$60,000[b]
B and C	30,000[c]
B and D	15,000

[a] Computed by adding the net present values from Exhibit 9-4; for example, the net present value of A and C is $40,000 + $20,000, the sum of the net present values of A and C.

[b] A and C is the best combination.

[c] See text discussion and footnote 7 on why the unspent $10,000 is not added to the $30,000 in computing the net present value.

is the greatest, as can be seen from Exhibit 9-5, this is the combination that should be selected.[8]

The above method for dealing with a capital constraint problem is valid because investors want the cash flow generated by the investment to have the highest value possible. This value is determined by discounting the cash flow at the market interest rate appropriate to the riskiness of the cash flow.[9] The method is quite general and can be applied to investments even if they are interdependent (if they affect one another's cash flows or are mutually exclusive). However, if all the firm's investments are independent of one another (they do *not* affect one another's cash flows and are *not* mutually exclusive), then a simplification of the above procedure is possible. (It is extremely important to note that this profitability index procedure should *not* be used in comparing mutually exclusive options or in analyzing investments that, if adopted together, will affect one another's cash flows.) *The procedure is to rank the firm's investments by the ratio of the net present value per dollar of initial investment that they provide (NPV/I), and then select those investments with the highest NPV/I until the budget is exhausted.* NPV/I is referred to as the **profitability index**.[10] This procedure selects for adoption the combination of investments within the budget constraint that has the highest total net present value.

To illustrate, assume that the firm has up to $100,000 to invest and no more. Exhibit 9-6 indicates the firm's investment opportunities, their costs (I), NPVs, and profitability indices. The firm should invest its funds in projects A through F, a total outlay of $98,000. This leaves $2000 ($100,000 budget limit minus $98,000 invested). The $2000 is insufficient to accept either of the remaining opportunities with positive NPVs (G and H), and so the $2000 can be held for future investment, be paid out in dividends, or be used to reduce company debt.

---

[8] Dynamic programming can greatly facilitate the analysis of the combinations of investment opportunities. This problem is often referred to as the "knapsack problem": see Harvey M. Wagner, *Principles of Operations Research*, 2d ed. (Englewood Cliffs, N.J.: Prentice-Hall, Inc., 1975).

[9] For a complete discussion, see Elton, op. cit. Notice that the investments that make up the capital budget can differ in risk (for example, A, B, and C may be of different risk). As will be explained in Chap. 10, the cash flow from any combination of investments should be discounted at that rate appropriate to the riskiness of the total cash flow generated by that combination of investments. Thus, in the example, the cash flow from A and C might be discounted at 10 percent whereas the discount rate for the cash flow from B and C might be 12 percent. In this chapter we are assuming that all investments have the same risk and are therefore evaluated using the same cost of capital (discount rate).

[10] The profitability index is also often defined as $(NPV + I)/I$ = (present value of future net cash flows)/(initial outlay); this ratio is sometimes referred to as the benefit-cost ratio and using this ratio to rank investments leads to the same decisions as using the profitability index as defined here. Also, I is in some contexts defined as the present value of present and future capital outlays associated with the investment; for capital rationing in the *current* period, it is proper to define I as *current* capital outlays, as is done here. Multiperiod capital rationing is not examined here (see footnote 6).

EXHIBIT 9-6
Simplified present value procedure for capital rationing

Project	Initial outlay (I)		NPV	Profitability index (NPV/I)
A		$50,000	$80,000	1.6
B		10,000	15,000	1.5
C	$98,000	20,000	10,000	0.5
D		15,000	6,000	0.4
E		2,000	800	0.4
F		1,000	300	0.3
G		5,000	1,000	0.2
H		3,000	300	0.1
I		4,000	0	0

A problem may arise in using the above procedure that involves those investments that are just marginally acceptable (on the border between being accepted and rejected, for example, E, F, and G in Exhibit 9-6). The problem can arise if the projects that are accepted on the basis of highest profitability index do not fully exhaust the capital available. Thus, let the NPV of project G in Exhibit 9-6 equal $1200 instead of $1000; G's profitability index would become 0.24, still below the profitability index of project F. Using the above profitability index procedure, A through F would still be selected and G would be rejected. However, notice that it would be more profitable (a higher total NPV for all projects combined) to select G and reject E and F since the NPV of G is now $1200, whereas the total NPV of E and F is only $1100.[11] Therefore, the profitability index procedure is misleading in this case in selecting from among the marginal investments. The way to avoid an error of this type is simply to examine the investments close to the budget limit (the marginal investments) and make sure that an error is not being made.

It should be pointed out that completely inflexible budget constraints are not common for large businesses. This is particularly true in the long run, that is, if sufficient time is available to inform sources of capital of the firm's profitable investment opportunities. A budget constraint means that a limited quantity of capital is available *regardless of the profitability of the company's investments*. Such a limited capital situation can arise for small businesses because of the inability of manage-

---

[11] With E and F we have $2000 left over. However, the *net* present value of any investment of that $2000 will be zero; that is, the value of what is received on the investment of $2000 will equal $2000. Any investment outside the firm that earns just the normal rate of return has a zero *net* present value. All the investments with positive net present values should be included in the analysis of Exhibit 9-6 in determining the allocation of the $100,000.

306

PART 2
**The firm's investment,
financing, and dividend
decisions**

ment to convince outside sources of capital of the attractiveness of the company's opportunities.[12] A large firm with profitable investments can usually either borrow additional funds or sell additional shares of stock to finance the investments. Of course, it will have to pay the going rates on the acquired funds, but this will be reflected in the cost of capital used to evaluate the investments. Similarly, if a division of a company has attractive projects, the division head can generally present his or her proposals to central management, which will ordinarily allocate funds to the division if the investment proposals merit support.

INTERNATIONAL CAPITAL BUDGETING

A multinational corporation's capital budgeting decisions are complicated by issues that single-country firms do not face. Cash flow estimation procedures must consider the effects of blocked funds, transfer prices, fees and royalties, and currency exchange rates, all of which are discussed below. The assessment of risk is more involved for foreign investment projects because of exchange rate fluctuations and political uncertainties. But the rewards for multinational corporations that successfully identify profitable foreign projects can more than compensate for these complications and increased risk.

Foreign Project Cash Flow Estimation

Most MNCs are organized as a parent company with subsidiaries in foreign countries. The profits of the subsidiaries are transferred to the parent and, ultimately, to the investors. To motivate MNCs to reinvest their profits locally, many governments establish laws and regulations that partially block the repatriation of earnings. In addition, differences in tax rates make the timing and nature of cash flow repatriation an important variable for the corporation. As a result of fund transfer and tax laws, the cash flow earned by the foreign subsidiary may differ from the cash flow going from the subsidiary to the parent. The financial manager of an MNC should use the parent corporation's perspective in valuing cash flows.

As an extreme example, suppose a large MNC like Exxon is considering an investment in a small Latin American nation, whose government requires that all subsidiary earnings be reinvested in the country. If a subsidiary is established, it might operate quite profitably, but if the earnings can never be returned to Exxon, the parent company will clearly be unwilling to make the initial investment.

Normally, the subsidiary's profits are not blocked entirely, but the timing and nature of earnings repatriation is regulated and has tax implications for the parent firm. Consequently, MNCs use several methods of profit transfer, in addition to a straightforward payment of interest or dividends, from the subsidiary to the parent. For example, transfer prices for goods being shipped between the subsidiaries and the parent

---

[12] See footnote 5.

can be adjusted so that profits are realized where they're needed. By raising the price that Ford charges its English manufacturing subsidiary for automobile engines, the corporation can increase the profits of its American plant (the English subsidiary will show a matching decrease in profits). A parent company can also receive cash payments from a subsidiary in the form of fees and royalties for management services, research and development, and patent or trademark use. Because the subsidiary is controlled by the parent, the price charged for such services is somewhat arbitrary. Royalty and fee charges can be adjusted to circumvent profit repatriation regulations and unfavorable tax laws.

While these practices complicate cash flow estimation procedures, the underlying capital budgeting principles are comparable to those for domestic projects. *A project's net present value is based on the incremental cash flows to the parent.* For example, a project's fees and royalties are costs from the subsidiary's perspective, but, for the parent corporation, they should be considered additional positive cash flow that would not have been received without the project. Likewise, market prices, not transfer prices, should be used to determine a project's profitability and cash flow. For example, if Ford sells engines to its foreign subsidiary for $2000 each and the engines cost Ford $1200 each (including shipping costs), Ford is earning a profit of $800 per engine even if the transfer price of $2000 is treated as a "cost" for booking or regulatory purposes.

Currency exchange rates complicate international cash flow analysis. Earnings from foreign operations must be exchanged for the home currency before being paid out as interest or dividends to the parent company's investors. If the earnings are retained by the MNC, but are reinvested in a different foreign subsidiary in a different foreign country, the earnings still need to be exchanged from one currency to another. Market-determined exchange rates fluctuate over time and, from the perspective of the parent, can have a profound effect on a project's cash flow. The analysis of foreign investment projects must include a forecast of expected future exchange rates.

International investments are subject to the same kinds of uncertainty characterizing domestic investments. They also involve certain additional risks that domestic companies do not face. These risks fall into two categories: (1) exchange rate risks that result from fluctuations in currency exchange rates, and (2) political risk due to changes in the political environment of a foreign country. Exchange rates affect the value of future cash flows in terms of the domestic currency, the book value of foreign assets and liabilities, and the competitiveness of foreign subsidiaries. Political risk includes tax and regulatory changes, the possibility that a firm's funds will be blocked, and the expropriation or nationalization of assets without compensation.

Exchange Rate Risk

The potential for exchange rate changes imparts three kinds of risk on the company: economic exposure, competitive risk, and accounting exposure.

Economic Exposure   The risk that exchange rate fluctuations will alter the home currency value of future cash flows, changing the present value of a firm's project, is termed **economic exposure.** To illustrate, assume that Blass Products, Inc., a U.S. company, is considering the establishment of a subsidiary in England to manufacture and sell a line of technical instruments. Blass has estimated the initial cash requirements and expected future cash flows. The cash flow forecasts were estimated in English pounds because this currency will be used to cover initial expenses and to receive future revenues. The initial cash requirements, however, will be supplied by the U.S. parent company. The current dollar/pound exchange rate can be used to translate the initial cash requirements from English pounds into dollars, but what will the exchange rate be in three or four years, when the project starts to generate positive cash flows and when the parent company's shareholders in the United States expect to reap the rewards of their investment? The level of future exchange rates is uncertain, and so the project takes on a greater risk than it would have if future currency exchanges were not required.

Exhibit 9-7 gives a simple example of how different future exchange rates can have an effect on the net present dollar value of a foreign project. In the exhibit, notice that the exchange rate is declining over the life of the project, and so the pounds translate into fewer and fewer dollars as each year passes. In part A of the exhibit, the exchange rate is declining at 2 percent per year, and in part B of the exhibit the exchange rate is declining at 4 percent per year. To compute the net present value or internal rate of return for the project, use the cash flow figures in dollars (the last column in the exhibit) and apply the net present value and internal rate of return methods described in Chapter 8.

Competitive Risk   Another type of exchange rate risk, **competitive risk,** relates to the impact of exchange rate fluctuations on the competitive position and long-term profitability of a subsidiary. To illustrate, assume that the technical instruments manufactured by Blass Ltd. are made using English labor and materials but are sold primarily outside England. If the British pound were to fall in value, the foreign price of Blass's product would drop. This make Blass's product more competitive, thereby increasing sales. Since the production costs (in pounds) will not be directly affected because the inputs of production are British, the increased foreign demand for Blass's products will mean greater profits for the subsidiary. If the pound were to appreciate on the international market, however, Blass's competitive position would deteriorate, and sales and profits would decrease.

Protecting a firm against competitive exchange rate risk is possible in some cases. The corporation's basic strategy would be to internationally diversify its output or sources of input supply so that changes in one currency's exchange rate can be offset by shifting production or input purchases to places where the exchange rate is more advantageous. For example, a rise in the value of the pound might depress Blass's export sales, but if Blass Products, Inc., the parent corporation, also has a subsidiary making the same product in a country where the currency has depreciated, the decline in Blass's sales might be counterbalanced by the sales of the other subsidiary. Similarly, with the rise in the value of the pound, it might be advantageous for Blass Ltd. to switch its purchases of inputs from a domestic supplier to a foreign supplier (since the rise in the pound has made imports into England less costly). Clearly, international diversification for production and input purchases is not always easy or practical, especially if there are important advantages, such as the availability of technical skills, in locating production in particular places or in consolidating production in one place because of economies of scale. If a particular input is only obtainable from a single source, supplier diversification may not be possible.

Accounting Exposure   The risk that changes in the value of the home currency will change the book value of the firm's equity is called **accounting exposure.** To illustrate, assume that Blass Products, Inc., now

---

EXHIBIT 9-7
*Impact of future exchange rate changes on the net present value
of a British project for a United States company*

Assumption A: Dollar/pound exchange rate declines by 2% per year

Time	Cash flows, £	Exchange rate $/£	Cash flow, $
0	− 100,000	2.00	− 200,000
1	25,000	1.96	49,020
2	25,000	1.92	48,058
3	25,000	1.88	47,116
4	25,000	1.85	46,192
5	50,000	1.81	90,573
Net present value at 10% cost of capital			$7,469
Internal rate of return			11.3%

Assumption B: Dollar/pound exchange rate declines by 4% per year

Time	Cash flows, £	Exchange rate, $/£	Cash flow, $
0	− 100,000	2.00	− 200,000
1	25,000	1.92	48,077
2	25,000	1.85	46,228
3	25,000	1.78	44,450
4	25,000	1.71	42,740
5	50,000	1.64	82,193
Net present value at 10 % cost of capital			− $4,466
Internal rate of return			9.2%

310

PART 2
**The firm's investment,
financing, and dividend
decisions**

has an ongoing subsidiary, Blass Ltd., in England. Blass Ltd. has assets worth £100,000 and liabilities of £60,000. Suppose that the exchange rate is $2/£1, which means that, in U.S. dollars, the subsidiary's assets are worth $200,000 and the liabilities total $120,000. If the pound increases in value to $3/£1, there would be an increase in the dollar level of the Blass's assets to $300,000 and liabilities to $180,000. A rise in the value of the foreign currency (the pound) causes a dollar gain on the foreign assets (the asssets can be coverted into more dollars) and a dollar loss on the foreign liabilities (more dollars would be required to pay off the liabilities). In contrast, if the pound fell in value to $1/£1, there would be a decrease in the dollar level of Blass's assets to $100,000 and a decrease in its liabilities to $60,000. A decline in the value of the foreign currency causes a dollar loss on the foreign assets (the assets can be converted into fewer dollars) and a dollar gain on the foreign liabilities (fewer dollars would be required to pay off the liabilities). The figures in the example are shown in Exhibit 9-8.

If Blass's assets exceed its liabilities, there is a net gain in terms of dollars if the pound rises in value and a net loss if the value of the pound falls. This highlights an interesting point: The risk exposure depends on foreign assets minus foreign liabilities (that is, the foreign subsidiary's equity). Thus, when £1 = $2, the equity is $80,000. If the pound appreciates to $3, the equity increases to $120,000; the gain of $40,000 equals a gain of $100,000 on the assets (which increase in dollar value from $200,000 to $300,000) minus a loss of $60,000 on the liabilities (which increase from $120,000 to $180,000).

If the worth of an investment is measured by the net present value of future cash flows, wouldn't the company only worry about its economic exposure and not be concerned about accounting exposure? Why is accounting exposure important? The answer is that taxes are calculated based on financial statement gains and losses, including currency translation gains and losses. Taxes are a cash outflow and greater uncertainty about taxes can be a source of risk.

A company can eliminate its accounting exposure by reducing the net equity position of the company, in terms of a foreign currency, to

---

EXHIBIT 9-8
Impact of an exchange rate change on the dollar balance sheet of a British subsidiary.

	If exchange rate is £1 = $2		If exchange rate is £1 = $3		If exchange rate is £1 = $1	
	In pounds	In dollars	In pounds	In dollars	In pounds	In dollars
Assets	£100,000	$200,000	£100,000	$300,000	£100,000	$100,000
Liabilities	60,000	120,000	60,000	180,000	60,000	60,000
Equity	40,000	80,000	40,000	120,000	40,000	40,000

zero. That is, any claims to the foreign currency (expected foreign project cash flows, assets in the foreign country, etc.) must be exactly offset by liabilities denominated in the same foreign currency. Thus, a parent corporation can eliminate accounting exposure by making sure that its net equity position in the subsidiary is zero. For example, Blass Products could have Blass Ltd. borrow £40,000 (see Exhibit 9-8), convert those pounds to dollars, and repatriate the dollars to the United States. After this transaction. Blass Ltd. would have assets worth £100,000 and liabilities of £100,000, and Blass Products would have a zero equity position in Blass Ltd.

Political Risk

All firms, domestic and multinational, are subject to changes in tax rates or business regulations. But multinational firms, particularly those that operate in less economically developed countries, are exposed to the possibility of blocked funds and the expropriation of their assets. **Blocked funds** are earnings of a foreign subsidiary that cannot be fully repatriated to the parent company. For example, a developing country might allow only 50 percent of locally earned profits to leave the country in any given year. The regulation will typically set limits on the amount and timing of allowable earnings repatriation. The corporation should incorporate information about such government controls into its capital budgeting cash flow estimation before making a commitment to the foreign country. The risk is that unknown changes in the political situation—a change in government, for example—could result in unanticipated restrictions on earnings repatriation.

The greatest political risk is asset **expropriation.** Sovereign countries have ultimate control of the assets within their borders, and a government may seize the assets of the local subsidiary of an MNC without compensation if it so chooses (even though this will make it difficult for that country to attract foreign investment in the future). The danger of expropriation is particularly great for investments that involve the natural resources of underdeveloped countries, since such resources often represent a large portion of the national wealth and are regarded by nationals as part of the country. One of the more famous expropriations was in Chile in 1971, when the new Marxist government of President Salvador Allende seized, among other things, Anaconda's copper mines and equipment without compensation. Although few foreign ventures are as ill-fated as Anaconda's in Latin America or some of the international oil firms' holdings in the Middle East, the risk of foreign expropriation or blocked funds is an ever-present threat to multinational corporations.

To deal with the foreign government intervention risk that confronts U.S. companies abroad, the United States government established the Overseas Private Investment Corporation (OPIC). This agency insures the firm against losses due to the inconvertibility into dollars of investments in a foreign country or the income from those investments. Other OPIC programs insure against expropriation and nationalization, and losses that result from war or revolution. Only certain properties can be

312

PART 2
**The firm's investment,
financing, and dividend
decisions**

insured by the agency, and each individual project must be approved for eligibility. The fees charged by OPIC total a specified percentage of the value of the insured property. The percentages are the same for all firms and all investments, regardless of risk, but they do vary according to the type of coverage (inconvertibility, expropriation, or war).

SUMMARY

If investments being compared have different lives, then a completely correct analysis usually requires that future investments be taken into account. In many situations this is not necessary, however, and the net present values of the investments can be directly compared in the usual manner.

In the presence of inflation, the firm should still use the actual cash flows that are anticipated in computing NPV. The discount rate that is appropriate is, as in the case of no inflation, that rate used by investors to discount cash flows with a similar risk to be the one being analyzed. This approach is valid, since the cash flow and the discount rate will both take the inflation into account and the investment's NPV will be its net benefit to the stockholders in terms of current dollars.

Investment opportunities may affect one another's cash flows if both are adopted, for example, a gas station and a restaurant next door to one another. In this case, the cash flows and net present values from undertaking each project alone and from undertaking them together must be computed. That combination of opportunities (an opportunity taken alone or with one or more of the interrelated opportunities) that produces the highest NPV is best and should be adopted if its NPV is positive.

A capital rationing problem exists if the firm does not have and cannot obtain (through borrowing or selling new shares) sufficient funds to adopt all projects with a positive NPV. In this case, the firm should adopt that set of investments not exceeding its budget constraint which has the highest total NPV. Under certain conditions, a shortcut analytic approach is applicable. This approach specifies that the firm should adopt those investments with the highest profitability indices. A budget constraint generally does not exist for large firms. Such a constraint is ordinarily a short-run problem that may occur for small firms or for corporate divisions.

A multinational firm faces special problems in its capital budgeting since all cash flows have to be translated from the foreign currency into dollars. Multinational firms also face risks that are not relevant to domestic projects. One risk is that of exchange rate fluctuations. These cause a change in the dollar value of cash flows from foreign projects, can cause a change in the company's competitive position, and can produce changes in book equity value that result in tax effects. Another source of risk is political. Funds from foreign operations can be blocked from repatriation to the home country, and foreign operations are subject to the risk of expropriation by foreign governments. Firms can insure against some kinds of risk through the Overseas Private Investment Corporation.

1 In forecasting a project's flow, how would you incorporate your expectations about future inflation?
2 How does the discount rate used in computing a present value depend on inflation?
3 Strictly speaking, all activities of a firm are interdependent; that is, they affect one another's cash flows. Therefore, any new investment in some way—directly or indirectly—affects the cash flows of every other investment the firm adopts. Since this is so, how can we justify ever evaluating a new investment by itself, i.e., without considering how it effects the cash flows of every other investment we are considering? What are the advantages and disadvantages of ignoring interdependencies?
4 What types of entities are most likely to face a capital budget constraint?
5 You are operating a business unit that faces a capital budget constraint. Does the capital budgeting method that you will use depend on whether or not the opportunities you are evaluating affect one another's cash flow (i.e., are they economically dependent on one another)? If so, how?
6 What are the critical differences between domestic and foreign investments from the standpoint of capital budgeting analysis?

Interview the capital budgeting analysts at several small firms, and several large firms, to determine whether they assume a capital budget constraint (capital rationing) in their analysis of projects and, if so, how they take the constraint into account in the analysis.

DP1 The management consulting firm of Toady, Chill & Minion (TCM) is evaluating two computer systems to meet its needs over the next ten years (all depreciation is on a straight-line basis with no salvage value assumed). TCM is considering the two following choices:

Choice A: Buy ten used Apple II's and four Apricots for $20,000. These computers are depreciable for tax purposes over three years, with no salvage value assumed. It is expected that the computers will be sold after two years for total proceeds of $4,000 (net of taxes). The Apples and Apricots will be replaced by an advanced IBM system which is expected to last eight years and which is expected to cost $60,000. The IBM system will be depreciated over three years, with no salvage value for tax depreciation purposes. It is expected that the IBM system will be sold at the end of the eight-year holding period (ten years from now) for $5,000 (net of taxes).
Choice B: Buy a new IBM system for $70,000. The system will last for ten years and will have a zero salvage value for com-

314

PART 2
The firm's investment,
financing, and dividend
decisions

puting depreciation for tax purposes. The system will be depreciated over three years. It is expected that the IBM system will be sold in ten years for $1,000 (net of taxes).

The services provided over the next ten years under choice A and choice B are the same. Also, we know that both choice A and choice B have a positive NPV; the problem is to choose the better of the two alternatives. TCM is in the 40 percent tax bracket and has a 15 percent cost of capital. Is choice A or choice B preferable?

SOLUTION TO DP1:
The objective is to minimize the net present value of the costs net of the depreciation tax shelter benefits and net of the salvage values of the computers. The depreciation benefit equals the firm's tax rate (40%) times the depreciation taken.

Choice A
Computer costs: $20,000 now (at time 0) for the Apples and Apricots; $60,000 at time 2 (two years from now) for the IBM system.
Depreciation tax benefits: On the Apples and Apricots, the depreciation per year in years 1 and 2 will be $6667, and the tax savings will be .4($6667) = $2667. On the IBM's, the depreciation per year in years 3, 4, and 5 will be $20,000 and the tax savings will be .4 ($20,000) = $8000.
Liquidation proceeds: The firm expects to receive $4000 (net of taxes) at time 2 and $5000 at time 10.

$$
\begin{aligned}
\text{NPV of costs} = {} & \$20,000 + \$60,000(P/F, 15\%, 2) \\
& - \$2667(P/A, 15\%, 2) \\
& - \$8000(P/F, 15\%, 2)(P/A, 15\%, 3) \\
& - \$4000(P/F, 15\%, 2) \\
& - \$5000(P/F, 15\%, 10)
\end{aligned}
$$

$$
\begin{aligned}
= {} & \$20,000 + \$60,000(.7561) - \$2667(1.6257) \\
& - \$8000(.7561)(2.2832) - \$4000(.7561) \\
& - \$5000(.2472)
\end{aligned}
$$

$$= \$42,959$$

Choice B
Initial cost = $70,000
Annual depreciation tax savings = .4($70,000/3) = $9333

Liquidation proceeds in ten years = $1000

$$
\begin{aligned}
\text{NPV of costs} = {} & \$70,000 - \$9333(P/A, 15\%, 3) \\
& - \$1000(P/F, 15\%, 10)
\end{aligned}
$$

$$= \$70,000 - \$9333(2.2832) - \$1000(.2472)$$

$$= \$48,444$$

Conclusion: Since choice A costs less, choice A is better.

DP2   A parcel of land was worth $200,000 on January 1, 1991. The increase in the general level of prices (inflation) was 6 percent during the year from January 1, 1991 to December 31, 1991.

   a If the real value of the land (value in terms of purchasing power) was the same on December 31, 1991 as on January 1, 1991, what was the dollar value of the land on December 31, 1991?

   b If the real value of the land was 10 percent greater on December 31, 1991 than it was on January 1, 1991, what was the dollar value of the land on December 31, 1991?

SOLUTION TO DP2:

a In order that the land have the *same* purchasing power on December 31 as on January 1, its value must be 6 percent greater because of inflation; that is, the December value must be

Value (December 31 if same real value as on January 1)

$$= (1 + \text{inflation rate}) \times \text{value (January 1)}$$

$$= (1 + .06) \$200,000 = \underline{\$212,000}$$

It takes $212,000 on December 31 to buy what $200,000 could buy on January 1.

b Since we want the real value (purchasing power) to be 10 percent greater than on January 1, we must make the $212,000 ten percent larger. So,

Value (December 31 if 10% greater real value than on January 1)

$$= (1 + \% \text{ change in real value}) \times \$212,000$$

$$= (1 + .10) \$212,000 = \underline{\$233,200}$$

DP3   Coleen Garner is president of Garner Search, an executive recruiting company. She is evaluating ways to serve more effectively Garner Search's rapidly growing client base and to ensure that the growth will continue. Three options are under consideration:

A.   Purchase a computer and computer software to maintain company records and to assist in matching potential employers and executive employees.

B.   Advertise the firm's services.

C.   Develop seminars to promote Garner Search at major corporations.

   The present value of the costs for A, B, and C are $50,000 for A, $100,000 for B, and $40,000 for C. The cost of each of A, B, and C does not depend on whether the other options are adopted (e.g., A costs $50,000 whether or not B or C is adopted).

316

PART 2
**The firm's investment,
financing, and dividend
decisions**

The present value of the benefits from A without B or C is $40,000, from B without A or C is $120,000, and from C without A or B is $35,000. Because both the advertising (B) and the seminars (C) increase Garner Search's clientele, and because the computer enhances the company's ability to serve its clients, the present value of the benefits of A and B (without C) is $200,000 and of A and C (without B) is $175,000. The present value of the benefits of B and C (without A) is $140,000. The present value of the benefits from A, B, and C together is $225,000.

Which of the three options—A, B, and C—should Garner Search adopt?

SOLUTION TO DP3:
To solve this problem compare the net present values of all the possible combinations of the three options and adopt the combination with the highest net present value.

Combination	Investment (1)	Present value of benefits (2)	Net present value [(2) − (1)] (3)
A only	$ 50,000	$ 40,000	− $10,000
B only	100,000	120,000	20,000
C only	40,000	35,000	− 5,000
A and B	150,000	200,000	50,000
A and C	90,000	175,000	85,000[a]
B and C	140,000	140,000	0
A, B, and C	190,000	225,000	35,000

[a] The combination of A and C has the highest net present value ($85,000) and, since that net present value is positive, the combination should be adopted.

DP4 Wong Instruments has the following projects that it can adopt:

Project	Initial outlay	Net present value
A	$ 50,000	$ 70,000
B	90,000	120,000
C	60,000	120,000
D	100,000	10,000
E	250,000	150,000
F	80,000	20,000
G	40,000	40,000

Assuming: (1) the initial outlay is the only cash outflow for each project, (2) the projects are *not* mutually exclusive, and (3) the cash flows of the projects are *not* interdependent:

a Rank the projects in order of desirability on the basis of profitability index.

b If the firm has a limited capital budget of $550,000, which projects should it choose?

SOLUTION TO DP4:

PI = profitability index = NPV/*I*

a

Project	Initial outlay	NPV	PI
C	$ 60,000	$120,000	2.0
A	50,000	70,000	1.4
B	90,000	120,000	1.33
G	40,000	40,000	1.0
E	250,000	150,000	.6
F	80,000	20,000	.25
D	100,000	10,000	.10

b It should adopt C, A, B, G, and E. This requires an initial outlay of $490,000, which is less than the $550,000 that is available.

PROBLEMS

1 Rosebud Florists needs a truck and is evaluating the following two choices for meeting its needs over the next ten years:

Choice A: Buy a used Ford truck for $3000. The truck will be depreciated for tax purposes assuming a five-year life with no salvage value. It is expected that the truck will be sold after four years for $500 (net of taxes): the first Ford truck will then be replaced with another used Ford truck that is expected to cost $7200 and last six years with no salvage value for tax depreciation purposes and no liquidation value at the end of the six years. It is planned that the second Ford truck will be held for the entire six-year period.

Choice B: Buy a new Chevrolet truck for $8000. The Chevrolet will last for ten years and will have a zero salvage value for computing depreciation for tax purposes. The expected aftertax liquidation value of the truck at the end of the ten years is $1000. It is planned that the Chevrolet truck will be kept for the entire ten years.

318

PART 2
**The firm's investment,
financing, and dividend
decisions**

The services provided by the Ford trucks and the Chevrolet truck are the same. Furthermore, it is clear that choice A and choice B have a positive NPV: the problem is to choose the better of the two alternatives. If Rosebud Florists is in the 40 percent tax bracket, uses straight-line depreciation for tax purposes on all its trucks, and has a 12 percent cost of capital, is choice A or choice B preferable?

2 Alvarez Corporation manufactures chemical products and is evaluating two new processes for producing a particular compound. Demand for the compound will be small during the next five years and will then increase. Process A requires equipment that is appropriate for small output levels; A will be replaced in five years with process B, which will utilize equipment with an eighteen-year life. B is capable of meeting large output requirements. The alternative to using processes A and B is to install currently (time 0) process C, which employs equipment with an estimated life of twenty years. The costs of A, B, and C are:

Time of outlay	Expected capital outlay for process		
	A	B	C
Now (time 0)	$1.5 million		$3 million
Five years hence		$5 million	

The future annual net cash flows from each process are:

Time of cash flow (years)	Annual cash flow		
	A	B	C
1–5	$500,000		$400,000
6–20		$800,000	$700,000
21–23		$800,000	

The discount rate is 12 percent. Answer the following:

a Should the firm adopt A and B or adopt C? Justify your approach. (What about the three-year time discrepancy between the A-B combination and C?)

b If the life of process C were only fifteen years instead of twenty years, would your approach to the problem be different? Explain.

3 A particular home was worth $90,000 on January 1. The increase in the general level of prices (inflation) was 10 percent during the year from January 1 to December 31.

a If the real value of the house (value in terms of purchasing power) was the same on December 31 as on January 1, what was the dollar value of the house on December 31? [Ans.: $99,000] *b* If the real value of the house was 4 percent greater on December 31 than it was on January 1, what was the dollar value of the house on December 31? [Ans.: $102,960]

4 Hi Daniels just purchased a plot of vacant land for $150,000. The net cash flow from the property during the next four years will be zero. The best use of the land is simply to let it remain vacant for at least the next four years.

  a If the property increased in value by 8 percent per year during the next four years, what is its value in four years? What pretax annual rate of return has Hi Daniels earned on the property during the four years?

  b If after four years the property has increased in value by 8 percent per year during the past four years, is Daniels concerned about the inflation rate that occurred during the four-year period? Why?

  c If Hi Daniels expects a pretax annual real rate of return on the land of 8 percent and he expects an annual inflation rate of 5 percent, what does he expect the land to be worth in four years?

5 The Rainbow Paint and Dye Company wants to know whether to go ahead and market a promising new product, Formula Z paper dye. The firm is calculating depreciation on a five-year basis. Formula Z will be phased out and replaced by a still more advanced dye process after five years. The table below indicates relevant projected cost and revenue data for each of the ensuing five years stated in *beginning of 1991 prices*.

	1991	1992	1993	1994	1995
Revenues	$200,000	$260,000	$360,000	$330,000	$298,000
Depreciation expenses	24,000	24,000	24,000	24,000	24,000
Selling expenses	40,000	30,000	15,000	10,000	5,000
Production costs	107,000	138,000	202,000	174,000	161,000

Assume that the above flows occur at the *end* of the year (end of 1991, end of 1992, etc.). All the above projections are at *beginning* of 1991 prices; i.e., they assume there will be no inflation after 1990. But in fact substantial inflation is expected. The projected inflation rate is 9 percent per year over the five-year period, and this rate is expected to apply uniformly to all prices (except depreciation). The 9 percent rate is the best estimate of top economists and is the forecast generally accepted by the public. Depreciation is expected to equal the amounts shown in the table above. However, all the cash flow items in the table (all the items other than depreciation) will be greater in nominal terms by an amount just sufficient to adjust for inflation; thus, the dollar amounts *in purchasing power terms* will be those stated in the table. Therefore, to compute the expected *dollar* cash flows, the data in the table (except depreciation) must be inflated by an inflation factor; for example, by (1.09) for the end of 1991 cash flows, by (1.09)^2 for the end of 1992 cash flows, etc.

The investment needed to initiate the Formula Z project is $120,000 at the *beginning* of 1991. At the end of 1995 all assets associated with the Formula Z project will be sold for $100,000 (in *beginning* 1991 prices). The firm's tax rate is 50 percent, and this tax rate is applicable to all net income and to any dollar gain on selling the assets at the end of 1995 (there is a gain if the asset is sold for a price that exceeds its end-of-1995 book value). If the firm's current cost of capital is 16 percent, is this project worthwhile? In solving the problem keep in mind that actual dollar amounts should be used, *not* amounts stated in beginning of 1991 dollars.

6 Unicorn Grocery Stores is considering three methods of stimulating business: a blitz advertising campaign (A), replacement of existing signs with new signs for all its stores (B), and the introduction of a delivery service that will require the purchase of a fleet of delivery trucks (C). The initial outlays for each alternative are:

Investment	Initial outlay
A Advertising campaign	$300,000
B Signs	400,000
C Delivery system	400,000

If A is done but B is not, A has an NPV (present value of added future cash flows less the $300,000 initial outlay) of $250,000. If B is done but A is not, B has an NPV of $110,000. The advertising draws customer attention to the signs. The NPV of doing both A and B is $460,000. The NPV of the delivery system, C, is $180,000. Its NPV is not dependent on whether A or B is adopted, and the NPV of A or B does not depend on whether C is adopted. Assuming that the firm has no budget constraint (can obtain funds at the cost of capital to finance any investment with a positive NPV), which of investments A, B, and C should Unicorn adopt? [Ans.: Adopt A, B, and C]

7 Solve problem 6 assuming that the firm can invest only up to $700,000; that is, the firm has a $700,000 capital constraint. [Ans.: Adopt A and B]

8 The Piker Paper Products Company currently manufacturers paper napkins, towels, tissues and bags. The company has been

considering expanding its successful business. It is evaluating three options:

A. Expand its paper bag line.
B. Produce custom ordered and printed bags.
C. Expand into a line of paper party accessories.

The returns from A, B, and C are as follows:

A. The expansion of the paper bag line will required an initial investment in machinery of $150,000 and an additional initial outlay of $40,000 for plant improvements. The present value of the future cash flows generated by A is $250,000.
B. Custom ordered and printed bags would call for a relatively small current investment of $50,000 for the purchase and installation of a printing press. The present value of the future cash flows from B is $95,000.
C. To expand into a party accessories line will require a printing press somewhat more sophisticated than that needed for B. Also, new cutting and fabricating machinery will be needed. The required initial outlay is $275,000. The present value of the future cash flows from C is $380,000 assuming A and B are not done.

If A and B (but not C) are both done, a more efficient higher-capacity bag line will be justified. The total outlay for A and B together will be $260,000, but because of increased efficiency and lower operating costs the present value of the future cash flows generated by A and B together is $410,000.

If B and C (but not A) are done, the printing press used in the party accessories line will also be available for the custom printing of bags. This option would therefore eliminate all but $10,000 of the initial investment required for B. The initial outlay for B and C together is therefore $285,000. There are no other interdependencies between B and C.

If A and C (but not B) are done, there will be no interdependencies. The party accessory line will not compete with the bags for sales, and the production operations will be separate. The initial outlay for A and C together is therefore $465,000, and the present value of the future cash flows from A and C is $630,000.

If A, B, and C are all done, the advantages noted above from doing both A and B and from doing both B and C will still be available. However, the adoption of all three projects will require added plant space requiring an additional plant expansion cost of $200,000. If A, B, and C are done, the initial outlay will be $615,000, and the present value of future cash flows from A, B, and C will be $790,000.

Which options should Piker Paper Products adopt?

9 Magnum Calculators is considering an number of plant improvement investments and has allocated $315,000 to do the job. Under consideration are the following projects. Assume that the net annual cash inflows are all perpetuities.

322

PART 2
The firm's investment,
financing, and dividend
decisions

Project	Outlay	Net annual inflows
A. Computerize stamping and assembly	$300,000	$57,000
B. Revamp asembly line	100,000	20,000
C. Increase warehouse space	100,000	12,000
D. Install new climate control system	20,000	22,000
E. Expand shipping dock	30,000	7,500

Not all these projects can be considered independently of one another. The following information may help clarify some of the relationships:

A and B are alternative (mutually exclusive) proposals for the same assembly line.
If A is done, then the option of expanding the shipping dock (E) would cost only $10,000 because it could be done conveniently by the contractors on A.
If B is done, then $5,000 can be saved on the installation of the shipping dock (E). Also, under these circumstances, there would be an increase in shipping efficiency so that the shipping dock expansion would generate $9000 per year instead of $7500.
All other combinations are independent (do not affect one another's cash flows). The cost of capital is 15 percent. Which projects should be adopted?

10 Gretto's Tool & Die has $1 million available for current investment. It has evaluated its options and has found that only four investments—A, B, C, and D—have positive net present values. A, B, C, and D are entirely independent of one another (the adoption of one investment does not affect the initial cost or future cash flows from any of the others). The data for these investments are as shown below:

Investment	Initial outlay	Present value of future cash flows from the investment
A	$500,000	$650,000
B	200,000	390,000
C	400,000	570,000
D	300,000	600,000

Which investments should the firm adopt?
11 Solve problem 10 but assume that A has a present value of future cash flows equal to $670,000 instead of $650,000.

12 The Plush Mountain Shopping Center Association is an incorporated entity comprising the merchants in the center. As a corporation, the center has accumulated $450,000 in cash. The $450,000 is the maximum amount Plush Mountain has available for investment. The center would like to begin a development on an adjacent vacant plot of land which it can buy for $220,000. On this land it can do one or more of the following:

A. Build a three-tier parking structure.
B. Build an ice-skating rink to be operated by the corporation.
C. build and operate a movie theater.
D. Erect a fabulous sign advertising the shopping center.

The parking structure will cost $120,000 to build (in addition to the acquisition of the land for $220,000), and by providing added customer convenience, is expected to yield an NPV of $75,000. The skating rink will cost $150,000 over and above the land acquisition, and will yield an NPV of $90,000. The theater will cost $180,000 in addition to the land cost and will yield an NPV of $100,000. All NPVs are computed with the $220,000 cost of the land included in the initial outlay.

The land can accommodate both the skating rink and the same amount of parking space if the three-tier parking building and the rink are built as a single structure. The parking structure would cost only $90,000 to build over and above the cost of the rink, and the combination skating rink–parking building would yield an NPV of $290,000. The parking structure would provide needed parking for the rink. Similarly, the theater and parking structure could be done for a *total* of $225,000, excluding the land, yielding an NPV of $275,000. The rink plus the theater would be infeasible because of insufficient parking. D may be done for $40,000, and no matter which of A, B, or C are done, D yields an NPV of $90,000 *if* the land has been acquired (i.e., not net of the $220,000 land cost); D would therefore not be done alone. Rank all the possible investment combinations and select the best combination that can be done for no more than $450,000.

13 Gourmet Fast Foods has the following projects available during the coming year:

Project	Initial outlay	Net present value
A	$ 40,000	$11,000
B	100,000	28,000
C	120,000	25,000
D	200,000	45,000
E	240,000	65,000
F	300,000	95,000
G	300,000	80,000

324

PART 2
**The firm's investment,
financing, and dividend
decisions**

Assuming: (1) the initial outlay is the only cash outflow for each project, (2) the projects are *not* mutually exclusive, and (3) the cash flows of the projects are *not* interdependent;

a Rank of the projects in order of desirability on the basis of profitability index.

b If the firm has a limited capital budget of $680,000, which projects should it choose?

c The cash flows for project F are revised as follows:

Project	Initial outlay	Net present value
F	$280,000	$90,000

Now answer *a* and *b* again.

14 Gear Corporation has the following projects available during the coming year:

	Initial outlay	Net present value	Internal rate of return
A	$ 200,000	$ 300,000	25%
B	500,000	500,000	15
C	300,000	540,000	30
D	1,000,000	1,200,000	22
E	700,000	600,000	18
F	500,000	200,000	20
G	3,000,000	1,500,000	10
	$6,200,000		

The projects are not mutually exclusive; that is, acceptance of one project will not exclude acceptance of any of the others. Furthermore, adoption of any one of the projects does not affect the cash flows from adoption of any of the other projects. A cost of capital of 15 percent was used to calculate net present values.

a Rank the projects according to their internal rates of return and according to their profitability indices.

b The firm is able to raise only $2,000,000 to finance the entire capital budget. Which projects should the firm choose?

c What is the total net present value of the projects chosen in *b*?

15 Corbetron Corporation, a United States–based manufacturer of toasters and other small appliances, is considering placing a final assembly and sales facility in the (hypothetical) South American country of Toltica. Financial analysts, familiar with the region, estimate that the initial cost of the facility in terms of the local currency will be T3,000,000 (three million tolticanos). This translates into $750,000 in U.S. currency at the current exchange rate of 4 tolticanos per dollar. The net cash flow that can be repatri-

ated back to Corbetron is expected to be T1,000,000 per year before inflation, for six years, at which time the entire unit will be turned over to the local government. Inflation in Toltica has always been high at about 30 percent a year, so the actual cash flow in nominal terms will be T1,300,000 for the first year, T1,690,000 for the second year, and so on, up to T4,826,809 in the sixth year. Because of the high level of inflation in Toltica compared to the United States rate of about 5 percent, the currency exchange rate is expected to increase by 25 percent a year starting at the current rate of 4.00 T/$. For example, the exchange rate at the end of the first year will be 5.00, and at the end of the second year it will be 6.25, and on up to 15.26 at the end of the sixth year. What is the net present value of the project to Corbetron in terms of U.S. dollars if the discount rate is 15 percent? Make a table of the tolticano cash flow after inflation for each year and the expected currency exchange rate for that year. Use these rates convert the tolticanos into dollars and then discount the dollar cash flows at a discount rate of 15 percent. [Ans.: $320,558]

16 In problem 15, the government of Toltica has promised to allow Corbetron to operate in the country for six years. However, there will be a Tolitican election in just four years that could bring in a political party which is opposed to the foreign control of local assets. Assuming that Corbetron's plant and equipment is expropriated without compensation after four years of operation, is the project advisable? What if the unfriendly party takes over the country in a military coup after just three years? (Ans.: Yes, because NPV is positive at $32,654; no, because NPV is negative at −$134,489)

The ▪ symbol indicates that all or a significant part of the problem can be solved using the *Computer Models* software package that accompanies this text.

CHAPTER TEN

RISK ANALYSIS AND CAPITAL BUDGETING

In Chapter 8 we assumed that all investments being considered for inclusion in a company's capital budget had the same risk as those undertaken in the past, on average, by the firm. Thus the firm's cost of capital could be used as a discount rate or minimum acceptable rate of return in evaluating the desirability of each investment project. Projects normally vary in their risks, and the firm's cost of capital will not be the proper discount rate to use in evaluating all of them. The analysis of risky investment projects is one of the most difficult and debated issues in finance. Many different approaches are used and no single approach is generally recognized as best in all situations.

In this chapter we present several procedures for evaluating investments that differ in degree of risk. We begin with an explanation of the problem and follow this with a description of some relatively simple procedures that do not require the explicit measurement of risk. Then we show how to analyze the estimated cash flows of an investment to determine which of the economic factors affecting the cash flows may be the major contributors to the project's risk. Next we explain how risk can be measured using probability distributions of a project's cash flows. We then describe how risky projects are evaluated and how the risk assessment procedures discussed earlier in the chapter are used in the evaluation. In the final section we apply the Capital Asset Pricing Model to evaluate risky investments.[1]

PROBLEMS IN EVALUATING RISKY INVESTMENTS

Suppose that you are the financial manager of a company and that three different investment projects have been proposed. The first project involves the burning of industrial waste to produce steam to generate electricity for the firm's use. The second project is to increase the production capacity of the firm. The third is to begin manufacturing a new product. Each of these investments is risky in the sense that no one

---

[1] Problems in the financing of investments and of interactions between investment and financing decisions are covered in Chap. 12.

currently knows for certain what the future cash flows resulting from these investments will be. The degree of uncertainty is different for each project and may also vary over time for a particular project. For example, the cash flows from generating electricity are probably more certain than those from manufacturing the new product. The cash flows from generating electricity next year are probably more certain than those from generating electricity ten years from now.

The initial step in any project analysis is to choose a method of project evaluation. The choice will depend on the costs and benefits of each possible method. Some methods in this chapter require significant time and expense. These methods are usually reserved for large-scale risky projects for which accurate risk estimates may prevent management from making costly errors. The authors know of a firm that built a $50 million semiconductor plant based on very limited analysis. The plant turned out to be a $50 million disaster and has been shut down. Management admits (privately) that if they had more carefully analyzed the risks at the beginning, they would not have made this mistake. When the project cash flows are relatively certain or when the potential cost of an error is small, extensive risk analysis is not economically advisable.

All methods of analyzing a risky project have three things in common:

1   A framework for analysis
2   An assessment of the project's risk
3   An adjustment for the degree of risk

Procedures for assessing risk and adjusting for it vary among different methods of analysis. The financial manager may assess risk by judgment or by an elaborate computer analysis of the project's cash flows. The manager may adjust the cash flow estimates to reflect their risk or may adjust the discount rate used to compute the present value of the cash flows. Most of the methods found in theory and in practice use the discounted cash flow approach described in Chapter 8 as their basic framework. The methods discussed here are based on this framework with some variations.[2]

INFORMAL METHODS OF RISK ANALYSIS

There are three methods of risk analysis found in practice that use discounted cash flow techniques and that do not require numerical measures of risk. All are based on managerial judgment as to the risk of a project. They are:

1   Use of conservative estimates of project cash flows
2   Use of judgment as to whether the project is sufficiently profitable to compensate for its risk

[2] A theoretical procedure for adjusting the cash flow estimates to their "certainty equivalents" is presented in Appendix 10A. In this procedure, riskless interest rates are used to determine the present values of future, adjusted cash flows.

3 Use of a classification system for projects with prespecified minimum acceptable rates of return (discount rates) for each classification

All three methods share a common problem; they do not directly consider how investors will value the cash flows from a project that is undertaken. Therefore, they are not very accurate in determining whether undertaking a project will benefit the owners of the firm. To compensate for this inherent lack of accuracy, the methods are relatively easy to apply. Under the proper conditions, all of them can provide reasonable results.

Conservative Estimates

Perhaps the oldest and still most widely used method of dealing with risk is to make conservative estimates of the cash flows. The firm's cost of capital is used to evaluate the cash flows from all projects regardless of their risk. For example, as a financial manager evaluating the proposal to manufacture a new product, you might take the sales projections and reduce them by 20 percent. Then you might increase the cost per unit manufactured by 10 percent. If the project's revised cash flows have a positive net present value based on the firm's cost of capital, you might then decide the project is worthwhile undertaking. There are three major problems with this procedure. First, it does not handle low-risk projects very well. If the project offers significantly less risk than the typical firm project, it may be erroneously rejected unless it is extremely profitable.[3] Second, the procedure requires a great deal of judgment by the financial manager. To properly account for risk, high-risk cash flows should be adjusted differently from low-risk cash flows. Without additional analysis, it isn't clear how large the adjustment should be (10 percent, 20 percent, or what?). Third, if the people who originate the projects find out that you are adjusting their estimates, they may compensate by providing overly optimistic estimates. This can result in a game played between the financial manager and operating personnel that does not contribute to sound decisions or to good personal relationships.

Judgmental Risk Evaluation

Under the most common procedure using judgmental risk evaluation, the financial manager computes, or asks the project originator to compute, the project's internal rate of return. The financial manager decides whether the internal rate of return is "high enough" given the perceived risk of the project. This judgment of the financial manager is based on past experience and current conditions in the capital markets. The firm's cost of capital may be used as a comparison rate. For example, suppose

---

[3] If a project's cash flows have less risk than is typical for the firm's past investments, a discount rate that is less than the firm's cost of capital is needed to correctly compute the net present value of the expected cash flows. Therefore, using the firm's cost of capital as the discount rate will cause some desirable investments to be rejected even when the expected cash flows are properly discounted. Applying conservative estimates to the cash flows compounds the problem.

the internal rate of return on a project is calculated to be 16 percent based on the best available estimates of the future cash flows. The firm's cost of capital is estimated to be 12 percent. If the project is thought to be only slightly more risky than the typical project or less risky, it will be undertaken. If the project is thought to be extremely risky, it will be turned down. A capable financial manager can use this approach with some success, avoiding large errors. It is often used in small- and medium-sized firms.

Project Classification

In many large firms with decentralized decisions, a more formal procedure, project classification, is used. The project classification method is based on the assumption that broad groups of projects will have similar risks. Classification schemes in use are typically based on the purpose of the project and on the product line of the division. The corporate finance staff will estimate a separate cost of capital for each division as if the division were an independent firm. Frequently estimates of the cost of capital for other firms in industries similar to the division's industry are made using the techniques described in Chapter 7. For example, a diversified petroleum firm might estimate separate costs of capital for its divisions: exploration and development, tanker operations, pipelines, petrochemicals, refining, and marketing. Within each division several different discount rates for projects might be established. A relatively low discount rate might be used for cost reduction investments involving known technology. An average discount rate might be used for investments involving expansion of existing facilities or cost reduction investments using new technology. A high discount rate might be used for investments involving new products. These discount rates are provided to division financial managers for use in their evaluations of projects.

Project classification has two major advantages. First, when interest rates are relatively stable, the discount rates do not have to be changed often. Therefore, they can be estimated with some care initially.[4] Second, once in place, they are objective criteria that can be communicated throughout the organization. This inhibits the game playing that may occur when more judgmental methods are used.

The major disadvantage of project classification in its application is that the classification schemes used by most companies are very limited and do not recognize risk differences among projects within the same classification. For example, not all new products in the petrochemical division are likely to be of equal risk. Likewise, there may be several alternative methods of producing a product all involving similar levels of technology. However, some methods may be more readily adaptable to different products than others, making investment in these production

---

[4] The frequent, large changes in interest rates during the past decade have reduced this advantage. For example, the average rate on Aaa corporate bonds increased by over 3 percentage points during 1981. From January 1986 to January 1987 the Aaa rate dropped by 1.5 percentage points. Corporations should now review their discount rates at least once a year. Some firms revise their discount rates quarterly.

330

PART 2
**The firm's investment,
financing, and dividend
decisions**

methods less risky. Ford Motor Company closed down one of the most efficient (low-cost) V8 engine plants in the world because the plant could not be used economically to produce the small engines then in demand. However, other Ford plants that were less efficient at engine production in general were also more flexible and Ford transferred production to them. The investment in these, more flexible plants was less risky than investment in the V8 engine plant.

SENSITIVITY ANALYSIS

The approaches described in the preceding section used estimates (expected values) of the cash flows for a project and various forms of judgmental risk evaluation. Most of the procedures used to measure the risk of a project require the development of probability distributions. However, the first technique we examine, sensitivity analysis, may be used alone or in conjunction with analysis of probability distributions.

The net cash flow from a project depends on many variables, each of which must be estimated. For example, suppose we wish to calculate the net cash flow from a project to generate electricity from industrial waste to replace power currently being purchased from the electric utility. We must estimate the investment outlay, the amount of waste available for burning, the costs of operating and maintaining the generating equipment, the amount of electricity generated, and the probable price of the electricity if we continue to purchase it from the electric utility rather than generate it. Sensitivity analysis is a systematic way to determine which of the factors affecting project cash flow are most important. The method is used to assess the degree of risk in the project and indicates areas where additional effort to produce better (less uncertain) estimates might be justified. The basic procedure is to recalculate the net present value using assumptions that differ from those used to produce the original net cash flow estimates. The purpose of the analysis is to assess how "sensitive" the net present value is to changes in assumptions about the underlining economic factors.[5] There are many variations in this basic procedure; we illustrate one approach below.

Suppose that the electricity generating project has estimated cash flows as shown in Exhibit 10-1. The firm uses the project classification method, and 9 percent is the discount rate normally applied to cost reduction projects by the firm. Given these estimates, the NPV of the project is positive, indicating that the project is acceptable. As financial manager, you decide to perform a sensitivity analysis by first examining

---

[5] Sensitivity analysis can be summarized as follows:

a Develop numerical estimates of the partial derivatives of the dependent variables (NPV or IRR) with respect to the economic variables (e.g., electricity price) that determine net cash flow.

b Evaluate the degree of uncertainty of those variables having large impacts (large partial derivatives).

c Use the information to assess the project's risk or as a guide to where additional efforts in refining estimates (reducing uncertainty) might be made.

how sensitive the esimated NPV is to an error of 10 percent in the estimates of the economic factors affecting the cash flows. To do this, you recalculate the NPV using revised values for each factor taken one at a time, as shown in Exhibit 10-2. Here the initial cost and annual depreciation are assumed to be known so that these components need not be investigated further.

From the data in Exhibit 10-2 you find that the NPV is most sensitive to errors in the forecasts of the price of electricity and the volume of power generated. If the forecasts are off 10 percent in the wrong direction, the NPV of the project falls from a positive $27,000 to a negative $69,000. The NPV is also fairly sensitive to errors in the life of the project. On questioning the plant manager, who originated the project, you find that the volume of power is unlikely to vary much more than 2 percent from forecast as the supply of industrial waste (fuel) is ample and the technology is well known. The major sources of risk in this project are uncertainties in the future price of electricity and the life of the project. At this point, sensitivity analysis has made its contribution. You have zeroed in on the crucial risk factors in the decision: the electricity

---

EXHIBIT 10-1
Electricity generating project with equal annual cash flows assumed

---

Initial cost $1,000,000
Estimated life .... 10 years
Depreciation $100,000/year
Operating costs $50,000/year
Power generated .... 1 million kWh/year
Price of purchased electricity .... $0.25/kWh (expected average price over 10 years)
Tax rate .... 40 percent
Discount rate .... 9 percent

Electricity savings = (price) × (power generated)
    = $0.25 × 1 million kWh
    = $250,000

Taxes = (tax rate) × (electricity savings − operating costs − depreciation)
    = 0.4 ($250,000 − $50,000 − $100,000)
    = $40,000

Net cash flow = electricity savings − operating costs − taxes
    = $250,000 − $50,000 − $40,000
    = $160,000

Present value of net cash flow = (6.4177)$160,000 = $1,027,000 (rounded)

NPV = $27,000

332

PART 2
**The firm's investment,
financing, and dividend
decisions**

EXHIBIT 10-2
Sensitivity analysis of electricity generating project

Factor	Estimate	Revision	Revised net cash flow	Revised NPV
Life	10 years	9 years	No change	− $41,000
Operating costs	$50,000	$55,000	$157,000	$8,000
Power generated	1 mil kWh	900,000 kWh	$145,000	− $69,000
Electricity price	$0.25	$0.225	$145,000	− $69,000
Tax rate	40%	44%	$156,000	$1,000

price and the project's life. The next step could be an attempt to estimate the probability distribution of net cash flow. In applying probability analysis, which is described below, the major effort would be placed on estimating the probability distribution of the electricity price and the project life since these are now known to be critical variables. Other possibilities include examining alternative "scenarios" for combinations of electricity price, project life, operating costs, etc. Sensitivity analysis is a flexible method that provides useful information; but it does not tell you what decision should be made.

**RISK AND
PROBABILITY
DISTRIBUTIONS**

The most advanced techniques of project risk analysis use the probability distributions of the cash flows from the project.[6] There are two problems here—first, how to obtain the distributions and, second, what to do with them once you have them. Our emphasis is on the second problem since the project originator is usually the one who provides the probability distributions for the financial manager to evaluate.

Recall from Chapter 6 that a probability distribution may be either discrete or continuous. Figure 10-1 illustrates the two types. The choice of which type to use in project analysis depends on convenience and the degree of accuracy needed in describing the possible values that may occur. In this chapter we use discrete distributions throughout for convenience. Summary measures are commonly used to describe a probability distribution. The **expected value** (mean) of the distribution is a measure of where the center is. The **standard deviation** (or variance) measures the spread of values around the expected value. The **correlation coefficient** is a measure of the relationship between two variables. There are several other statistical measures, but these three are the ones most frequently used.

Financial managers often use estimated probability distributions to assess the degree of risk in a project. Once the risk is assessed, an adjustment to the discount rate or the project's expected cash flows will

---

[6] Readers who do not feel comfortable with the concept of probability distribution, standard deviation, etc., should review Chap. 6 before proceeding with this section.

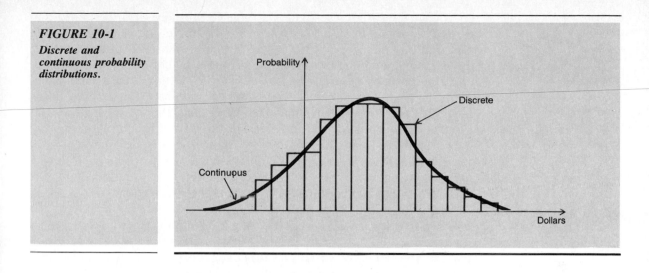

FIGURE 10-1
Discrete and continuous probability distributions.

be made. The adjustment for the degree of risk can be done by judgment or by objective calculations. Objective methods for risk adjustment are still in the process of development; however, we illustrate one such method based on the Capital Asset Pricing Model later.

Measuring Risk

In Chapter 6 we discussed the use of the standard deviation as a measure of uncertainty. In dealing with the cash flows from a project, however, an alternative measure is useful. To illustrate the issues, let's look at a project that uses industrial waste to generate electricity. The initial equipment investment is known to be $1 million, and the investment has an economic life of five years.[7] Probability distributions of the net cash flow from the project for years 1 and 5 are shown in Figure 10-2. The degree of uncertainty in the cash flows increases with time. This is shown both by the standard deviation of cash flows ($80,000 in year 1 versus $240,000 in year 5) and by another measure, the coefficient of variation (.4 in year 1 versus .8 in year 5).

Coefficient of Variation The coefficient of variation (CV) of a probability distribution is defined as

$$CV = \frac{\text{standard deviation}}{\text{expected value}} \tag{10-1}$$

In computing the CV, the standard deviation is divided by the expected value in order to adjust for the scale or magnitude of the cash flow. The standard deviation measures the uncertainty of the cash flow and is measured in the same units (dollars here) as the expected value. The

---

[7] In many cases the initial cost and life of an investment are also uncertain. Uncertainty in the amount of initial investment poses some special problems for analysis that are dealt with in more advanced texts.

334

PART 2
The firm's investment,
financing, and dividend
decisions

coefficient of variation provides a relative measure of uncertainty that can be expressed in percentage form. For example, the year 1 coefficient of variation can be expressed as 40 percent. When dealing with cash flows, the coefficient of variation provides a better measure of the uncertainty than does the standard deviation. To take an extreme example, suppose that the standard deviation of cash flow A and of cash flow B is $20,000. Also assume that the expected value of cash flow A is $20,000 whereas the expected value of cash flow B is $2 million. CV for A is 1.0, or 100 percent, whereas CV for B is .01, or 1 percent. For practical purposes, cash flow B is virtually certain whereas cash flow A is highly uncertain. This difference in uncertainty is reflected by the coefficient of variation but not by the standard deviation.

Correlation in Project Risk Analysis   We have identified two related measures of the uncertainty of a project's cash flow—the standard deviation and the coefficient of variation. However, only part of the uncertainty affects the risk of the project, the part that cannot be diversified away by investors in the firm. This part depends on the correlation of the project's cash flow with the returns from the other assets owned by the investors.

Two points are relevant here. First, any project of the company is owned by the company's shareholders and is therefore a part of the portfolios of assets owned by the shareholders. Second, the risk of a project (from the shareholders' perspective) depends on how it affects the risk of the shareholders' portfolios, and this depends on how the project blends with the rest of those portfolios. For any given standard deviation of cash flow from the project, the higher is the correlation of the project's cash flows with the cash flows of the other assets in the

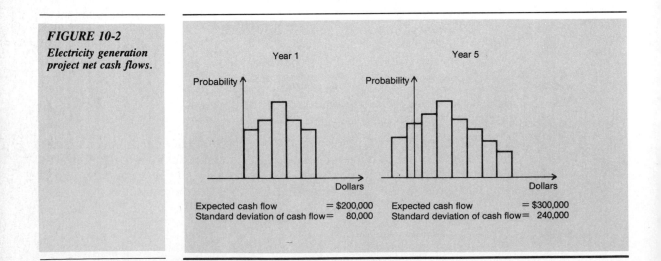

FIGURE 10-2

Electricity generation project net cash flows.

shareholders' portfolios, the more the project increases the risk of the portfolios and therefore the greater is the project's risk.[8]

If you are a manager of a company trying to maximize the market value of the company's shares, what should you suppose about the asset compositions of the portfolios owned by your existing shareholders and by potential shareholders (who establish the market price for your company's stock)? For large United States companies, the best assumption is that existing and potential investors in your company's shares have diversified portfolios with returns that move closely with the United States economy. On average, the economy is simply the sum total of all investors' portfolios and is therefore a reasonable measure of what investors own.

If we assume that the cash flows from investors' portfolios move closely with the economy, then, for any given standard deviation of cash flow from a project, the higher the correlation of the project's cash flows with the economy, the more the project increases the risk of investors' portfolios and the higher is the risk of the project. Estimating the correlation of a project's cash flows with the economy may be done by an analysis of historical relationships such as the relationship between the price of electricity and GNP. Often the cash flows of the project will be very highly correlated with the cash flows of an existing operating unit or division within the firm. In such cases the historical correlations between the cash flows of the division and the economy may be used as an estimate of the correlations of the project's cash flows with the economy. Alternatively, there may be another firm which has observable cash flows similar to those of the project. The historical correlation for this firm could be used. Determining an appropriate correlation can be a difficult task, but some estimate must be made to properly assess the risk of the project.

ESTIMATING PROBABILITY DISTRIBUTIONS

Two techniques used in estimating probability distributions should be known by the financial manager. They are simulation and decision tree analysis. We look at each one separately.

Simulation

If complete probability distributions for the cash flows are desired, computer simulation is normally used. This approach is typically applied to large-scale projects where the benefits of the complete analysis are sufficient to justify the time and effort involved. The basic procedure is to estimate, for each time period, separate probability distributions for

---

[8] For details on the relationship between a single asset's standard deviation and correlation with the portfolio's returns and the effect of the asset on the portfolio's risks, see Chap. 6 (the sections on Portfolio Risk and Diversification, Risk and Return in the Securities Markets, and Appendix 6A).

336

PART 2
The firm's investment,
financing, and dividend
decisions

each uncertain factor affecting net cash flow (sales price, labor cost, etc.). The probability distributions may be discrete or continuous. A computer program that contains the equation for net cash flow [Eq. (8-1), for example] generates values for each factor from its probability distribution for the first time period of the project's life and computes the net cash flow. This process is repeated for each period of the analysis to produce a set of net cash flows for the project. Then a new set of net cash flows is generated by the same procedure. After many such cash flows have been developed, the result is a series of probability distributions for the net cash flow, one for each time period. The mean (expected) value for each period, the standard deviation, and any other desired measures are calculated by the computer program. The reason computers are used is that a large number of computations is involved. The simulation process for analyzing investment in a manufacturing facility to produce a new product is illustrated in Figure 10-3.

Decision Trees

In some situations, the development of probability distributions of net cash flows requires an evaluation of future decisions. Decision tree analysis is used in these cases. Decision tree analysis is usually done with a diagram that has "branches," thus the name. The branches reflect alternative future decisions and possible states of the world. For example, suppose that you are trying to decide whether to invest $1 million in a pilot plant for a new process to produce synthetic rubber. Based on the results of the pilot plant operations, you will then decide whether or not to proceed with synthetic rubber manufacturing. The probability of favorable results from the pilot plant is .5 and the probability of un-

---

FIGURE 10-3

An example of the input and output for the simulation analysis of an investment.

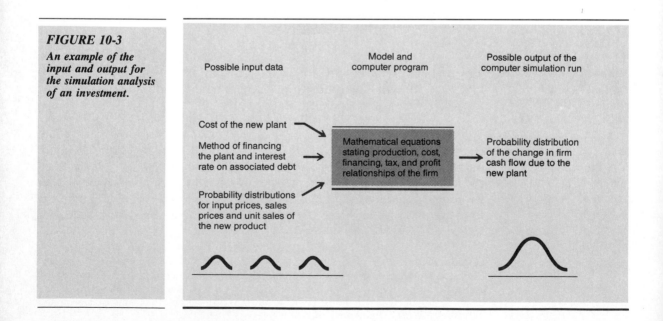

favorable results is also .5. The net cash flow from the project will depend on whether demand for the product is high or low as well as on the cost of the manufacturing process as obtained from the pilot plant operations. Figure 10-4a illustrates the original problem.

The idea behind decision tree analysis is that, of all the possible future decisions, you should include only the ones you might actually make in deciding whether to invest in the pilot plant today. If the outcome of the pilot study is unfavorable, the best future decision is not to invest in a synthetic rubber plant since the present value of the future cash flows, even when there is high demand for the product, is less than the cost of building a full-scale plant. There is no need to consider the possibility of investing in the plant when it will not be profitable to do so. On the other hand, if the outcome of the pilot study is favorable, building the full-scale plant appears to be the best decision. At worst, under conditions of low demand, the plant is a break-even investment. Therefore, the alternative of not building the plant when the pilot study is favorable can be eliminated from consideration. Decision tree analysis shows how to prune out future possibilities and, therefore, to develop more accurate probability distributions. Figure 10-4b illustrates the results of the pruning.

COMPANY DIVERSIFICATION AND PROJECT ANALYSIS

We noted earlier that, for large United States companies, the correlation of a project's cash flows with the United States economy was an important measure of risk from the perspective of the firm's stockholders. We did not consider the impact of the project on the risk of the firm itself. Should the firm be considered a portfolio of projects and should management try to minimize the risk of the firm's portfolio? The answer is *no*. The reason is that investors are able to diversify on their own, and they are not willing to pay extra for a firm's shares just because the firm is diversified; that is, they are not willing to pay a premium for someone else (firm management) to do what they can do themselves.

To illustrate the above point, assume that firm *A* could buy firm *B* (which is in a line of business different from *A*'s) and thereby diversify. The new firm would be called firm *AB*. Also assume that the total income of firm *AB* is exactly equal to the sum of the incomes of firms *A* and *B* separately (i.e., there are no economies of scale or other savings from combining). Will investors pay more for the shares of firm *AB* than for the shares of firms *A* and *B* separately? That is, will the value of firm *AB* be greater than the sum of the values of firms *A* and *B* if unmerged? The answer is *no*. Even if firms *A* and *B* were separate, the investors could do their own diversifying by simply buying shares in firm *A* and shares in firm *B*; they don't need a merger to produce the diversification benefits. The values of firms *A* and *B* if they are not merged (V_A and V_B) will reflect the diversification benefits investors can gain from combining shares of *A* and *B* into portfolios and will equal the value of the merged

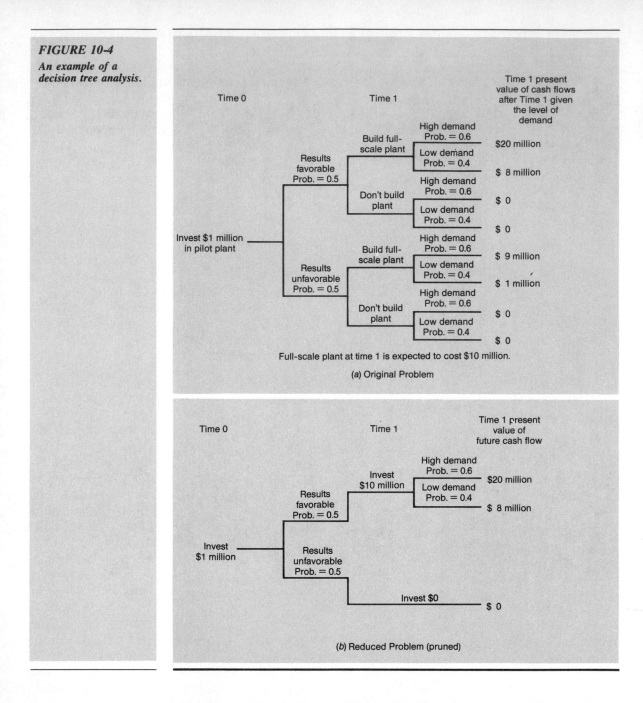

FIGURE 10-4

An example of a decision tree analysis.

Time 0   Time 1   Time 1 present value of cash flows after Time 1 given the level of demand

Invest $1 million in pilot plant

Results favorable Prob. = 0.5

Build full-scale plant — High demand Prob. = 0.6 → $20 million
Low demand Prob. = 0.4 → $ 8 million

Don't build plant — High demand Prob. = 0.6 → $ 0
Low demand Prob. = 0.4 → $ 0

Results unfavorable Prob. = 0.5

Build full-scale plant — High demand Prob. = 0.6 → $ 9 million
Low demand Prob. = 0.4 → $ 1 million

Don't build plant — High demand Prob. = 0.6 → $ 0
Low demand Prob. = 0.4 → $ 0

Full-scale plant at time 1 is expected to cost $10 million.

(a) Original Problem

Time 0   Time 1   Time 1 present value of future cash flow

Invest $1 million

Results favorable Prob. = 0.5

Invest $10 million — High demand Prob. = 0.6 → $20 million
Low demand Prob. = 0.4 → $ 8 million

Results unfavorable Prob. = 0.5

Invest $0 → $ 0

(b) Reduced Problem (pruned)

firm (V_{AB}), that is, $V_{AB} = V_A + V_B$. The same principle applies if B is not a separate firm but is simply a new project of firm A. The value of project B to the firm is simply V_B, the value of the income stream from B to investors. That is, we simply use the appropriate risk-adjusted market discount rate to discount the cash flow from B. We do not have to worry about how the income stream from project B correlates (diversifies with) the income stream from firm A.[9]

The important message is that, since investors can do their own diversifying, firms do not have to be concerned with diversification and can ignore correlation between project returns.[10] Management's job is to find projects with positive net present values; in other words, projects generating cash flows with values to investors that are greater than the projects' costs.

RISK AND PROJECT EVALUATION

So far we have been examining methods of analyzing and measuring the risk of a project. Sensitivity analysis is used to determine the economic factors and cash flow components that are the major sources of uncertainty for the project. Simulation and decision trees are used to generate probability distributions. We looked at three summary measures of a cash flow distribution (standard deviation, coefficient of variation, and correlation) and discussed their importance in measuring risk. Now let's see how we can use the information from cash flow probability distributions to evaluate an investment project.

Suppose that you are provided the following data for a project: the expected net cash flows (including the initial outlay), the standard deviations of the cash flows, and the correlation of each period's cash flows with the economy. An example of such data is shown in Exhibit 10-3. What do you do next? One possibility is to compute the internal rate of return for the project, which is 16.6 percent, and use judgment to determine whether the internal rate of return is high enough to justify undertaking the project. The difference between this approach and the "judgmental risk evaluation" method described earlier is that now you have numerical risk measures of the project's cash flows to aid in making a judgment. Of course, to apply judgment in this case you will need experience in dealing with the risk measures as well as knowledge of current capital market conditions. An alternative procedure is to compute the net present value of the project.

---

[9] If CF_A is the cash flow stream of firm A without project B, CF_B is the added flow provided by project B, and CF_{AB} is firm A's cash flow if it adopts project B (where $CF_{AB} = CF_A + CF_B$), then it follows that: $V_{AB} = V_A + V_B$, where V_{AB} is the value of firm A if project B is adopted, V_A is the value of firm A if project B is not adopted, and V_B is the value that CF_B would have as an individual stream in the market. The principle that the total value of a set of combined income streams (V_{AB}) equals the sum of the values of the streams separately ($V_A + V_B$) is commonly referred to as the "value additivity principle."

[10] The firm may be able to benefit from a reduction in costs associated with financial planning and financial distress if the uncertainty in the firm's cash flows is reduced. This benefit of diversification is very difficult to quantify and informal, judgmental procedures are used to account for it.

EXHIBIT 10-3
Summary data for project (initial cost $1 million)

	Year				
	1	2	3	4	5
Expected net cash flow (CF)	$200,000	$300,000	$400,000	$400,000	$300,000
Standard deviation (SD)	$ 80,000	$120,000	$240,000	$320,000	$240,000
Correlation with economy (Corr)	0.50	0.50	0.50	0.50	0.50
Coefficient of variation	0.4	0.4	0.6	0.8	0.8

Project Net Present Value

To apply the net present value technique, the present value of the cash flow in each period must be computed. Since the risk of the cash flows in Exhibit 10-3 varies from period to period, the discount rates applicable to the cash flows may also vary. A general expression for the present value of future cash flows with varying discount rates is

$$PV = \frac{CF_1}{1 + k_1} + \frac{CF_2}{(1 + k_2)^2} + \frac{CF_3}{(1 + k_3)^3} + \cdots + \frac{CF_n}{(1 + k_n)^n} \qquad (10\text{-}2)$$

where CF_1 = expected cash flow in year 1

$\quad k_1$ = discount rate appropriate for the risk of the year 1 cash flow

$\quad CF_2$ = expected cash flow in year 2

$\quad k_2$ = discount rate appropriate for the risk of the year 2 cash flow

$\quad \cdots$ and so on for n years

The net present value (NPV) of the investment is then

$$NPV = PV - \text{initial cost} \qquad (10\text{-}3)$$

To solve Eq. (10-2), we need estimates of expected cash flows CF_1, $CF_2, \ldots, CF_n$ and of discount rates $k_1, k_2, \ldots, k_n$. The expected cash flows are implied by the cash flow probability distributions discussed earlier in the chapter. Once the expected cash flows have been computed, the problem becomes one of determining the discount rates.

Estimating Discount Rates

There are several ways to estimate the discount rates to be used in project evaluation. We describe two approaches here and present another, based on the Capital Asset Pricing Model, in the next section.

The financial manager can use judgment and knowledge of current conditions in the capital markets to arrive at values for the discount rates. The manager performs no statistical analyses but simply makes an educated guess as to what discount rate investors use to value assets with a risk similar to that of the project being analyzed. Only a single discount rate that reflects the average risk of the stream might be used (rather than a different discount rate for each future time period's expected cash flow). The discount rate estimate might involve setting the discount rate equal to the current interest rate on U.S. government securities plus a premium for risk. The manager could use judgment to determine the premium appropriate to the risk of the cash flow in each period.

A more time-consuming, but less subjective, approach is to search for a particular asset traded in the capital market with cash flows of similar risk to the project's cash flows. The market rate of return on the traded asset can be estimated and then used as a discount rate for the project's cash flows. For example, assume that your company is planning to buy Rome Footwear, a shoe manufacturer. If there are other shoe manufacturers with cash flows of similar risk and growth patterns, and if those shoe manufacturers have publicly traded securities, you can estimate the discount rate which discounts each firm's cash flow to its current market value. An average of those discount rates could be used to value Rome Footwear's cash flows. Suppose that Ranger Shoes is very similar to Rome Footwear. If Ranger Shoes has expected cash flow $CF_1, CF_2, \ldots, CF_n$ and has current firm value (stock plus bonds) of amount V_0, the implied market risk-adjusted discount rate for Ranger is k, where k is the solution to:[11]

$$V_0 = \frac{CF_1}{1 + k} + \frac{CF_2}{(1 + k)^2} + \cdots + \frac{CF_n}{(1 + k)^n} \tag{10-4}$$

Rate k in Eq. (10-4) is the discount rate used by investors to discount Ranger's expected cash flow to its current market value. We could apply this method to several similar companies to estimate their k's, and the average of these k's could be used to value the cash flows from Rome Footwear.[12]

A problem with the above approach is that it may be quite difficult and expensive to find assets with cash flows that have a risk similar to that of the project. For some types of projects, such as a commercial

---

[11] The n in Eq. (10-4) is the anticipated life of Ranger Shoes, and therefore n might be very large.

[12] We could simply use Ranger's discount rate k in Eq. (10-4) to value Rome Footwear, rather than use an average of several companies' k's. However, there may be errors in estimating future cash flows or current market values. Assuming that such errors tend to cancel out by using a sample of several firms, a better estimate of k is likely if an average of several firm's k's, rather than just one firm's k, is used.

342

PART 2
The firm's investment,
financing, and dividend
decisions

office building, the approach may be feasible. For other projects, such as a plant to manufacture a new type of computer memory chip, the approach is likely to fail because similar risk assets are not traded in the market.

APPLYING THE CAPM TO PROJECT ANALYSIS

In Chapter 6 we showed that the rates of return required by investors in the capital market could be expressed as a simple function of the betas of securities in the market. The equation for the rate of return on a security if the Capital Asset Pricing Model (CAPM) applies is:

$$k_J = i + (k_M - i)\text{beta}_J \tag{10-5}$$

In this equation, k_J is the required rate of return on security J which has a risk of beta_J; i is the riskless rate of interest, and k_M is the expected rate of return on the market portfolio. Therefore, if we can estimate the beta for a cash flow, we can determine the rate of return or discount rate that would apply to the cash flow if it were available in the capital market. A set of such discount rates could then be used in Eq. (10-2) to estimate the market value of the cash flows from an investment. Once we have discount rates for all the cash flows from an investment, the rates can be used to discount the expected cash flows to obtain the net present value from undertaking the investment. If the net present value is positive, the investment is desirable; if the net present value is negative, the investment should not be undertaken.

For example, suppose that $k_M = 14$ percent, $i = 8$ percent, and therefore the market risk premium $(k_M - i)$ is 6 percent. Also assume that we have a project with an expected cash flow one year from now of $100, an expected cash flow two years from now of $150, and no further cash flows after that. Let the initial outlay on the project be $175. If the cash flow one year from now has a beta value of 1.0, using Eq. (10-5) we compute the discount rate for that cash flow as

$$k_1 = 8\% + (6\%)1.0$$

$$= 14\%$$

Similarly if the cash flow two years from now has a beta of 1.2, the value of k_2 is:

$$k_2 = 8\% + (6\%)1.2$$

$$= 15.2\%$$

The net present value of the project is therefore:

$$\text{NPV} = -\$175 + \frac{\$100}{1.14} + \frac{\$150}{(1.152)^2}$$

$$= \$25.75$$

Since the NPV is positive, the project should be accepted.

The major difficulty with the above approach is estimating the betas. A cash flow's beta depends on the correlation of the cash flow with the economy and the cash flow's coefficient of variation. The larger are these two measures of risk, the larger is the beta of the cash flow. However, the precise relationships are complex and their specification is a topic for advanced courses.[13]

An alternative to estimating the beta for each period's cash flow is to estimate a single average beta for the entire stream of cash flows from the project. This beta can then be used to determine a single discount rate for all the cash flows. Of course, if the cash flows differ in their risk, this approach is only an approximation. A way to determine a single beta is to identify an asset already existing in the market which has cash flows that are similar in risk to the cash flows from our project. We can estimate the beta for the existing asset and use it for our project. For example, if our investment project is a steel mill, we could look at the betas of steel companies to estimate the project's beta.

In conclusion, there is no easy solution to the problem of evaluating risky investment projects. All known methods involve some degree of judgment by the financial manager and many require extensive analysis without providing a definite answer. We have presented an overview of the tools available at this time.

EVALUATING FOREIGN INVESTMENTS

Foreign investment projects may be analyzed in much the same fashion as domestic projects—the same methods discussed above may be used. There are additional sources of risk as discussed in Chapter 9 (foreign exhange risk, political risk, etc.) in such projects, and these risks should be reflected in the cash flows and in the discount rates used to evaluate them. For example, suppose a Japanese firm is considering establishing a new plant in Singapore. The relevant cash flows are the yen that the Japanese firm will be able to generate from the plant. The amount of yen cash flows generated will depend on the currencies obtained from sale of the plant's output, the exchange rates of these currencies to yen and the ability to convert these currencies to yen. Since the operating costs of

---

[13] Beta for an asset A which has a single cash flow occurring one period from now can be expressed as:

$$\text{Beta}_A = \left(\frac{1 + i}{k_M - i}\right)\left(\frac{1}{1 - s \, \text{Corr CV}} - 1\right)$$

where i = the riskless interest rate
k_M = the expected rate of return on the market portfolio
s = the slope of the capital market line [see Eq. (6-7)]
Corr = the correlation of asset A's cash flow with the market
CV = the coefficient of variation of asset A's cash flow

The relationship for multiperiod cash flows is more complex. For an analysis of some of the difficulties in using asset betas, see S. C. Myers and S. M. Turnbull, "Capital Budgeting and the Capital Asset Pricing Model: Good News and Bad News," *Journal of Finance*, 32 (May 1977), pp. 321–332.

the plant will be in Singapore dollars, the exchange rate of the Singapore dollar relative to the yen will also affect the net cash flow. Thus the probability distributions of the cash flows will depend in part on the probability distributions of the relevant exchange rates. This is an added complication to the estimation of cash flows but does not change the fundamental problem.

There is an additional complication involving the degree of international diversification of the stockholders of the firm undertaking the project. Suppose that the stockholders are not internationally diversified. In this case the relevant correlation of project cash flows is the correlation with the domestic economy. This implies that the firm may be able to provide risk-reduction benefits to its stockholders through its international diversification. In this case, even though foreign project cash flows appear highly risky, the applicable discount rate may be quite low because the cash flows are not correlated with changes in the domestic economy.

On the other hand, suppose the stockholders are well diversified internationally. Foreign projects are less likely to provide any additional diversification benefits. The discount rates in this case should depend on the degree of correlation with some measure of global economic conditions.

Foreign projects tend to be larger than the average project undertaken by a given firm and, therefore, are often evaluated with formal methods of risk assessment such as simulation. However, they are inherently more complicated to analyze than are domestic projects. Therefore, judgmental evaluation plays an important role in the decision process as well.

SUMMARY

Not all investment opportunities available to business firms have the same risk. Good decisions about which investments to make require that differences in risk be reflected in the analysis of those investments. Most of the methods used in practice are based on managerial judgment about project risk. Firms using discounted cash flow analysis typically adjust the discount rate or minimum acceptable rate of return to reflect the degree of risk. High-risk projects are evaluated using a higher discount rate than low-risk projects. In some cases, the estimates of project cash flows are lowered to reflect their risk.

Numerical risk analysis techniques include sensitivity analysis and the estimation of the probability distributions of the cash flows. Sensitivity analysis is done by revising the estimates of the components of the expected cash flows from the project to see how much the net present value changes as a result of the revision. Computer simulation is used to estimate the probability distribution of the cash flows for large-scale projects. The probability distributions of the cash flows are developed by repetitive sampling from probability distributions of the components of the cash flows. Decision tree analysis is used to eliminate from consideration those future outcomes that would result only if management made poor future decisions.

The primary measures of risk that are obtained from probability distributions are the standard deviations of the cash flows and their correlations with the economy. The coefficient of variation equals the standard deviation of a cash flow divided by the expected value. It is superior to the standard deviation as a risk measure because it compensates for the size of the cash flow. If the owners of the firm are well diversified, the firm's managers need not be concerned about diversification of the firm's investments. Each investment opportunity can be evaluated on its own merits.

Numerical risk measures can be combined with judgment to produce discount rates that reflect the risks of the cash flows. The Capital Asset Pricing Model provides an objective method of determining discount rates based on the betas of the project's cash flows.

Foreign investment projects are more complex than domestic projects since they are subject to additional sources of risk. The evaluation of such projects usually involves use of both judgmental and formal methods. An important consideration is the degree of international diversification by the firm's stockholders.

QUESTIONS

1 Why might the use of conservative cash flow estimates for projects cause rejection of more low-risk projects than high-risk projects?

2 Is judgmental risk evaluation better suited to small firms or to large firms? Why?

3 What is the major advantage of the project classification approach relative to judgmental risk evaluation?

4 Why is the standard deviation of an investment's cash flow an inadequate measure of the investment's risk?

5 What are we assuming about investors in the firm when the correlation of a project's cash flow with the economy is used as one of the measures of the project's risk?

6 Assume that a firm has raised $10 million by selling new shares and bonds to finance its entire current capital budget, which involves investing in many individual projects. What is the reasoning for using different risk-adjusted discount rates for investments of different risk if they are financed from the same $10 million source of funds?

7 If you are considering an investment in an apartment building and have estimated the expected future cash flows from the building, how might you go about estimating a proper discount rate for the investment to determine the apartment's net present value?

8 Midwest Resources engages in several distinct lines of business organized into separate divisions including natural gas pipelines, natural gas exploration and development, coal mining, and electric

power generation. The financial manager has carefully estimated discount rates for each line of business for use in capital budgeting decisions at the divisional level. Each division is provided with the discount rate to be used for projects in that division. New discount rates are calculated quarterly. Evaluate the approach used by Midwest.

9 As a financial analyst in the gas pipeline division of Midwest Resources, you have been given the task of estimating a discount rate to be used in evaluating typical (normal risk) projects in the division. The chief financial officer of Midwest has specified that divisional discount rates must reflect current capital market rates and the degree of risk in the division.

   a Will the CAPM help you in this task? What are the advantages and disadvantages of using it?

   b How will you estimate the beta for a typical project?

10 Discuss the practical limitations of:

   a Performing computer simulations over more than a two- or three-year horizon period.

   b Doing a decision tree analysis for more than a two- or three-year period.

11 As chief financial officer of a medium-sized United States corporation, you have been asked to determine an appropriate discount rate to be used to evaluate capital expenditures for a new subsidiary located in Hungary. This is the first overseas venture for the company whose stockholders are not diversified internationally. The current cost of capital is estimated to be 11 percent. How would you proceed with this task? Do you think that the discount rate for the typical project undertaken by the Hungarian subsidiary is likely to be higher than, lower than, or equal to 11 percent? Why?

PROJECT

Visit one or more large firms in your area and inquire how the firms perform their capital budgeting analyses. Among the questions you might want to ask are:

1 How much does the firm spend each year on capital outlays?

2 What capital budgeting techniques are employed (present value, IRR, payback, accounting rate of return, etc.)?

3 If a cost of capital is used, how is the cost of capital determined and what is its numerical magnitude?

4 If cash flow is used in evaluating projects, how is it computed?

5 How is risk assessed for a particular investment, e.g., using probability distributions, subjective assessment without quantification, no assessment at all, etc.?

6 How is risk accounted for in analyzing investments, e.g., by using risk-adjusted discount rates?

DP1 The production manager of Alliance Industries has proposed that an automated paint machine be purchased to replace the one currently being used. The new machine will require an initial expenditure of $400,000 and is estimated to provide aftertax cost savings of $1.00 per item painted. Special tax provisions have permitted the original cost of the equipment to be deducted upon installation so no depreciation is taken for tax purposes. The $400,000 initial expenditure is net of all tax savings. The production manager has indicated that 80,000 units per year will be painted with this equipment and that it will last for 10 years. The machine will require maintenance expenses of $10,000 per year (after taxes), which are largely unaffected by the volume painted. Alliance requires a minimum rate of return of 8 percent on cost-reducing investments. Perform a sensitivity analysis on this investment proposal. The factors of concern are the cost savings per unit, the number of units painted, the life of the machine, and the maintenance costs.

SOLUTION TO DP1:

The NPV of the paint machine project is calculated as follows:

Initial investment = $400,000

Annual aftertax cash flow = $1 per unit × 80,000 units
$$- \$10,000$$

$$\begin{aligned}
\text{NPV} &= \$70,000(P/A, 8\%, 10) - \$400,000 \\
&= \$70,000(6.7101) - \$400,000 \\
&= \$469,707 - \$400,000 \\
&= \$69,707
\end{aligned}$$

To perform a sensitivity analysis of the basic factors, we recompute the NPV after changing each one by a specified percentage. Here we use 10 percent.

Factor	Revised estimate	Revised net cash flow	Revised NPV
Cost savings per unit	$0.90	$62,000	$16,026
Number of units	72,000	$62,000	$16,026
Machine life	9 years	No change	$37,283
Maintenance cost	$11,000	$69,000	$62,997

Clearly the critical factors are the cost savings per unit and number of units painted. Errors in these have the greatest impact on NPV.

348

PART 2
**The firm's investment,
financing, and dividend
decisions**

DP2 Rework the synthetic rubber plant example shown in Figure
10-4, showing both the original problem and the reduced problem when all the following revised forecasts apply:

a If the full-scale plant is not built, the pilot plant has a salvage value of $0.4 million. Otherwise the salvage value is
zero.

b If results from the pilot plant are unfavorable and a full-scale
plant is built, the present value of the cash flows at time 1
under high-demand conditions is $8 million and under low-
demand conditions is $3 million.

SOLUTION TO DP2:

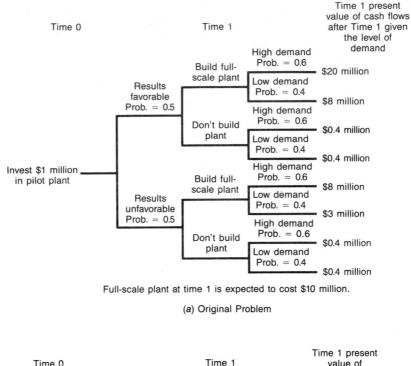

Full-scale plant at time 1 is expected to cost $10 million.

(*a*) Original Problem

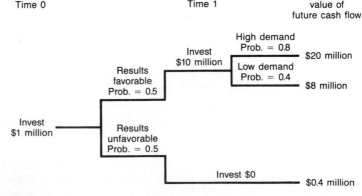

(*b*) Reduced Problem (pruned)

1 Organic Compost Company uses the project classification method of evaluating investment proposals. The minimum acceptable rates of return for different types of projects are:

Cost reduction: 9%
Expansion of existing products: 10%
New products: 12%

As chief financial officer you have received the following proposals:

I Installation of new spreader to reduce labor costs. Initial outlay is $100,000. Annual savings after tax is $15,000 per year for ten years.

II A plant to produce granular fertilizer from industrial waste. There is no comparable product on the market. Initial outlay is $1 million. Annual net cash flow after taxes is forecast to be $250,000 for six years.

Which investment (I, II, both, or neither) do you recommend that Organic undertake?

2 Boston Utilities has traditionally followed a conservative investment policy, avoiding high-risk ventures. Its cost of capital is estimated to be 10 percent. A district manager has proposed that the company build a plant that converts garbage into electricity. The technology involved has never been used on this scale before and the state utilities commission insists that the firm bear the full risk of the project. Any losses incurred cannot be passed on through higher rates to the utility's customers. The initial investment in the plant would be $20 million, and it is forecast to provide an aftertax cash flow of $2.5 million per year for 30 years. How should this investment be evaluated? What would your recommendation be, given only the information provided here?

3 Clearcut Lumber Company is considering investment in a new plywood manufacturing facility. The initial cost of the plant will be $400,000. Annual cost and revenue items are shown below. The discount rate is 15 percent. Perform a sensitivity analysis on this project. Clearcut's effective tax rate is zero.

Economic life of the plant: 20 years
Volume of plywood produced: 2 million square feet per year
Price per square foot of plywood sold: $0.25
Labor cost per square foot of plywood produced: $0.05
Lumber cost per square foot of plywood produced: $0.10
Operating costs of plant: $100,000 per year

4 Tastee Bananas, Inc., is considering investment in a plant to produce dried banana chips. The Vice President for Finance of Tastee is concerned that there may be significant deviations from the forecasted values of the economic variables which determine the profitability of the investment. You are asked to evaluate the impact of errors in these forecasts. Tastee pays corporate income taxes at a rate of 33 percent, which is not expected to change over the life of the plant. The plant will be depreciated (straight-line) for tax purposes over 20 years. If subsequent economic conditions make the plant unprofitable to operate, its salvage value is expected to equal its depreciated book value at the time it is closed. Initial investment in facilities will be $2 million and the discount rate for investments of this type is 12 percent. The following forecasts have been developed.

Economic life of the plant: 20 years
Volume of banana chips produced: 1 million pounds per year
Price received for banana chips: $2.00 per pound
Labor cost: $0.25 per pound produced
Raw materials cost: $0.95 per pound produced
Other variable costs: $0.10 per pound produced
Nonvariable operating expenses: $240,000 per year

5 *a* Rank the following projects according to their coefficients of variation:

Project	Expected cash flow	Standard deviation of cash flow
A	$ 40,000	$ 10,000
B	400,000	16,000
C	500,000	150,000
D	800,000	160,000

b If each project has a correlation with the ecomomy of 0.4, which project is the most risky from the perspective of a highly diversified stockholder?

6 Norton Sports owns bowling alleys and tennis courts throughout the United States. Norton is evaluating a new project that will house a variety of sports facilities, including tennis, bowling, and swimming, in one location. The initial (time 0) cost of the project will be $4.5 million. The project is regarded by Norton as quite risky. The estimated expected annual cash flows and their associated discount rates for computing present values are shown below:

Time	Expected annual cash flow	Risk-adjusted discount rate
1	$400,000	12%
2	600,000	16%
3 and thereafter	800,000	18%

Norton management feels the higher discount rate is appropriate for more distant future cash flows because of markedly increasing uncertainty about them.

What is the net present value of the project?

7 Rework the synthetic rubber plant example shown in Figure 10-4, showing both the original problem and the reduced problem given the following: There is another option—a small-scale plant can be built at a cost of $5 million. If results from the pilot plant are favorable and a small-scale plant is built, the present value of the cash flows at time 1 under high-demand conditions is $12 million and under low-demand conditions is $8 million. If results from the pilot plant are unfavorable and a small-scale plant is built, the present value of the cash flows at time 1 under high-demand conditions is $6 million and under low demand conditions is $5 million.

8 Advanced Controls Corporation (ACC) is evaluating a proposal to develop an energy-saving water heater control valve. The Engineering Department believes that an expenditure of $200,000 will result in a new valve design that offers significant benefits over products currently on the market. The development effort will take one year. Three outcomes are possible. There is a 20 percent probability the project will be completely unsuccessful, with no workable design being developed. There is a 30 percent probability that a new product will be produced and that the design can be patented to prevent its novel features from being copied by other valve manufacturers. Finally, there is a 50 percent chance that a successful but unpatentable design will result; but, if market demand for the valve is high, other firms could copy it and compete with ACC. The risk associated with design development is considered high enough to require a 20 percent discount rate.

If the new valve design is developed, a decision must be made as to how it should be manufactured. The most efficient manufacturing facility requires an initial investment of $3 million and offers significant cost savings if operated near capacity. A less efficient facility can be built with an initial investment of only $1.6 million, but with higher costs of manufacturing the valves.

Market acceptance for the valve is highly uncertain. ACC will not know what the final demand for the valve will be until it has been placed on the market. Although there are the usual risks present throughout the life of the facility, much of the initial uncertainty will be resolved one year after the decision is made to invest in a manufacturing facility. Management believes that the appropriate discount rate to reflect the risk of the initial market uncertainty is 15 percent. ACC management has estimated the present values of the net cash flows from all alternatives under two market demand conditions—high and low. These conditions are considered to be equally likely at the moment. The present

352

PART 2
The firm's investment,
financing, and dividend
decisions

values are calculated given conditions two years from now; that is, they are the estimated values two years hence of the cash flow streams expected from a given set of circumstances. They are summarized in the table below (in millions).

| | Facility decision | |
	$1.6 mil	$3.0 mil
Patented design, high demand	$5.0	$8.0
Patented design, low demand	2.4	3.2
No design patent, high demand	3.0	5.5
No design patent, low demand	0.8	1.3

a   Develop a decision tree diagram of ACC's problem.
b   Should the design project be undertaken? In determining your answer, you should first try to determine which facility is appropriate, given the outcome of the design effort. It is desirable to show an intermediate diagram after you have determined the appropriate facility.

9   A financial analyst working for ACC (see problem 8) has just recognized that an option was not considered. In the worst case, if the valve cannot be manufactured and sold profitably, ACC could abandon the project and sell the facility. For purposes of analysis, management considers this option as creating a choice between continued operations or abandonment to be made after market acceptance is known. The present values shown above were based on an assumption of continued operations. If the project is abandoned after the facility is built, the year 2 present value of the resulting cash flows for the $3 million facility is estimated to be $1.8 million and the abandonment value of the $1.6 million facility is estimated at $1 million.
a   Develop a decision-tree diagram for the ACC valve development project incorporating this new information.
b   Solve the problem showing intermediate steps.
c   (This assumes that problem 8 has been solved separately.) How has the evaluation of the overall project been affected by the abandonment option? Did the option affect any intermediate decisions?

10 The Organic Compost Company has decided to estimate a separate discount rate for the fertilizer plant project of problem 1-11. The beta for the project is thought to be the same as the beta of firms currently reclaiming industrial waste. The estimated beta is 1.5. The riskfree rate is 6 percent, and the market risk premium is

6 percent. Should Organic undertake the project?

(*Note:* Problem *11* is based on Appendix 10A.)

11 A project has an expected cash flow two years hence of $200. The certainty equivalent factor $a_2 = 0.90$ for this cash flow and the riskless interest rate is 8 percent. What risk-adjusted discount rate applies to this cash flow?

CERTAINTY EQUIVALENTS AND RISK-ADJUSTED DISCOUNT RATES

Throughout this text the discount rates used to evaluate cash flows are "risk-adjusted." The discount rate that applied to a zero-risk cash flow is identified as the "riskless" rate of interest. The firm's cost of capital reflects the average risk of the firm's securities as shown in Figure 7-1. The security market line of Chapter 6 shows the relationship in the market between risk and the required (risk-adjusted) rate of return on a security. The dominant theme of Chapter 10 is how to determine what (risk-adjusted) discount rate to use to evaluate the cash flows from a project. However, there is an alternative to the use of risk-adjusted discount rates, the **certainty equivalent approach**. Here we present this approach and show how it is applied to business investment decisions.

RISK ANALYSIS USING CERTAINTY EQUIVALENTS

The certainty equivalent approach to analyzing risky investments is to determine the riskless cash flow stream that is just as good as the risky cash flow anticipated from a project and then to discount that riskless stream at the riskless rate of interest to obtain its present value.

To illustrate, assume that investment S is being evaluated and that it will require an initial $300 outlay (for simplicity, assume that this initial cost is known with certainty) and will generate an expected cash flow of $100 per year during the next two years and an expected cash flow of $200 in the third year. Assume that the correct risk-adjusted discount rate for the cash flows is 10 percent and that the riskless rate of interest is 6 percent (rate of return earned in the economy on riskless assets). We could use the procedure described in Chapter 8 and simply compute the NPV of the asset using the 10 percent discount rate. An alternative is to use the certainty equivalent approach, which involves determining the riskless future stream of returns that has the same value to investors as does the risky cash flow stream from the asset. Exhibit 10-4 is an example of such riskless amounts.[14] Thus, in this illustration, investors

---

[14] The numbers in col. 2 of Exhibit 10-4 are those, as shown below, that are consistent with a riskless interest rate of 6 percent and a risk-adjusted discount rate of 10 percent. In

EXHIBIT 10-4
Certainty equivalents for asset S

Time (t)	Expected cash flow (1)	Riskless amount equivalent to risky flow (2)	Certainty equivalent factor a_t (col. 2 ÷ col. 1) (3)
Now	−$300	−$300	1.00
Year 1	100	96	.96
Year 2	100	93	.93
Year 3	200	178	.89

currently (when initial outlay of $300 is made) would be indifferent between receiving $96 one year hence for certain and owning the risky asset year 1 cash flow with expected dollar return of $100. That is, investors are currently indifferent between a sure thing of $96 received in year 1 and the cash flow probability distribution with an expected level of $100. Similarly, investors currently would be just as happy to know that they will receive $93 for certain in year 2 as they would be to own the risky asset year 2 stream that has an expected payoff of $100 in year 2. And investors are currently indifferent between receiving $178 in year 3 and receiving the risky asset's year 3 cash flow with an expected value of $200. The reason investors are indifferent between the riskless stream and the risky stream with a *higher* expected level is that investors do not like risk. The asset provides an *expected* return of $100 in year 1, but the amount that actually will occur might be much less, for example, perhaps only $80 or even less; so, investors would be just as happy with $96 for sure.

Column 3 in Exhibit 10-4 shows the certainty equivalent factors, a_t, where the t subscript stands for the time period. Factor a_t states the amount of money received for certain in future period t that is just equivalent (just as good in the eyes of investors) to a period t cash flow probability distribution with $1 of expected return. Thus, investors are currently indifferent between $0.96 received for certain in year 1 and a year 1 cash flow probability distribution from project S with an expected level of $1. The lower is a_t, the less the year t risky cash flow is worth, i.e., the riskier it is perceived as being.[15] A lower a_t means that fewer

general, for investors who do not like uncertainty, we know that the numbers in col. 2 must be less than those in col. 1 for any cash inflows that are uncertain.

[15] Actually, a_t depends on both the perceived riskiness of the period t cash flow and how investors feel about incurring risk in period t. Therefore, a decline in a_t, as t rises could occur because of increased risk or because of an increased dislike of risk, or both, as t increases. For simplicity we are assuming in the text discussion that the dislike of risk, or risk aversion, is the same for all t; given this assumption, a fall in a_t with greater t necessarily implies more risk as t rises, i.e., as we look further into the future.

356

PART 2
The firm's investment,
financing, and dividend
decisions

dollars received for certain in year t are equivalent for the year t risky stream. In the example of Exhibit 10-4, we are assuming that investors view the stream as more risky as they look further into the future; for this reason, a_t is decreasing as t increases, falling from $a_0 = 1$ down to $a_3 = 0.89$.

The above discussion implies that

$$\begin{pmatrix} \text{Risky period } t \text{ cash flow} \\ \text{with expected level CF}_t \end{pmatrix} \quad \text{has the same value as} \quad \begin{pmatrix} a_t \text{CF}_t \text{ received for} \\ \text{certain in period } t \end{pmatrix}$$

This implies that the present value to investors of the risky cash flow equals the present value of the equivalent riskless amount $a_t\text{CF}_t$. That is,

$$
\begin{array}{l}
\text{Present value of} \\
\text{the risky cash flow} \\
\text{discounted at} \\
\text{risk-adjusted rate } k_t
\end{array}
= \frac{\text{CF}_t}{(1 + k_t)^t}
$$

$$
= \frac{a_t\text{CF}_t}{(1 + i)^t} =
\begin{array}{l}
\text{present value of} \\
\text{the riskless amount} \\
\text{discounted at the} \\
\text{riskless rate } i
\end{array}
\tag{10-6}
$$

In Eq. (10-6), k_t is the risk-adjusted discount rate used to discount the period t expected cash flow, CF_t; i is the rate of return in the economy earned on riskless assets (the riskless rate of interest) and is therefore the rate used by investors to discount riskless amounts.[16] We use the riskless rate i in Eq. (10-6) to discount $a_t\text{CF}_t$ since $a_t\text{CF}_t$ is a riskless amount, i.e., is a riskless dollar amount that would be equally desirable as the risky cash flow from the asset.

In the Exhibit 10-4 example, $k_t = k = 10$ percent for all t. That is, the certainty equivalent factors a_t imply that investors view the cash flow risk as justifying a 10 percent risk-adjusted rate of return to discount the cash flow. To see this, let's use (10-6) and compute the net present value of the cash flows using the risk-adjusted discount rate method and the certainty equivalent method. Using a risk-adjusted discount rate of 10 percent, the NPV equals (where I is the initial outlay)

$$\text{NPV} = \frac{\text{CF}_1}{1 + k} + \frac{\text{CF}_2}{(1 + k)^2} + \cdots + \frac{\text{CF}_n}{(1 + k)^n} - I \tag{10-7}$$

$$= \frac{\$100}{1.10} + \frac{\$100}{(1.10)^2} + \frac{\$200}{(1.10)^3} - \$300$$

$$= \$91 + \$83 + \$150 - \$300 = \$24$$

---

[16] The riskless rate is assumed here to be constant over time to simplify the discussion. All relationships can be generalized to nonconstant rates by setting $i = i_t$.

Using the certainty equivalent approach, with $i = 6$ percent, the net present value equals

$$\text{NPV} = \frac{a_1 \text{CF}_1}{1 + i} + \frac{a_2 \text{CF}_2}{(1 + i)^2} + \cdots + \frac{a_n \text{CF}_n}{(1 + i)^n} - I \tag{10-8}$$

$$= \frac{(.96)\$100}{1.06} + \frac{(.93)\$100}{(1.06)^2} + \frac{(.89)\$200}{(1.06)^3} - \$300$$

$$= \$91 + \$83 + \$150 - \$300 = \$24$$

NPV in Eqs. (10-7) and (10-8) must be equal since they are simply two different ways of computing the same value. We can use a risk-adjusted rate k which is greater than i, as in (10-7), or, instead, we can adjust the cash flows in the numerator to take care of risk and then discount the risk adjusted cash flows at the riskless rate, as in (10-8). Both the risk-adjusted discount rate k and the certainty equivalent factors a_t are selected so as to correctly reflect the riskiness of the investment.

An important characteristic of using a constant discount rate to value risky cash flows is illustrated by the certainty equivalent factors in Exhibit 10-4. The certainty equivalent factors decline from 1.0 to 0.89 which means that the cash flow is riskier the further we look out into the future. Using a constant discount rate $k = 10$ percent is apparently consistent with this increasing risk since it produces the correct present value in Eq. (10-7) of $24. Let's examine this in a more general format.

RISK ADJUSTMENT IN DISCOUNT RATES

Using Eqs. (10-2) and (10-3), we can express net present value as

$$\text{NPV} = \frac{\text{CF}_1}{1 + k_1} + \frac{\text{CF}_2}{(1 + k_2)^2} + \cdots + \frac{\text{CF}_n}{(1 + k_n)^n} - I \tag{10-9}$$

where k_t is the risk-adjusted discount rate for discounting the period t expected cash flow CF_t. We also know that, using certainty equivalents, NPV also equals (where i is the riskless rate)

$$\text{NPV} = \frac{a_1 \text{CF}_1}{1 + i} + \frac{a_2 \text{CF}_2}{(1 + i)^2} + \cdots + \frac{a_n \text{CF}_n}{(1 + i)^n} - I \tag{10-10}$$

The NPVs in (10-9) and (10-10) are equal, and so is each term in (10-9) equal to the corresponding certainty equivalent term in (10-10); that is,

$$\frac{\text{CF}_t}{(1 + k_t)^t} = \frac{a_t \text{CF}_t}{(1 + i)^t} \tag{10-11}$$

Equation (10-11) implies

$$a_t = \frac{(1 + i)^t}{(1 + k_t)^t} = \left[\frac{1 + i}{1 + k_t}\right]^t \tag{10-12}$$

and, that

$$k_t = \frac{1 + i}{(a_t)^{1/t}} - 1 \tag{10-13}$$

358

PART 2
The firm's investment,
financing, and dividend
decisions

Notice from Eq. (10-12) that if k_t is the same for all t, that is, if we use the same discount rates for all future period cash flows regardless of how far into the future the flows will occur, then a_t falls as t rises. For example, if $k = 10$ percent and $i = 6$ percent, then $a_1 = .96$, $a_2 = .93$, $a_3 = .89$ (these were the figures in Exhibit 10-4). But with a_t falling as t gets bigger, we are saying that risk is becoming greater the further into the future cash flow occurs, since, as explained in the text, a smaller a_t means that the cash flow is riskier (investors are willing to take a smaller certain amount for each dollar of expected cash flow). For any constant k ($k_t = k$ for all t) in (10-12), a_t must decline as t rises, implying that a constant k means rising risk. (See Figure 10-5.)

If the risk is constant, then the a_t in (10-12) are the same for all t, and k_t must decrease as t increases. For example, with $i = 6$ percent and $a_t = .96$ for all t, substituting these values into Eq. (10-13) we find that $k_1 = 10$ percent, $k_2 = 8.2$ percent, $k_3 = 7.4$ percent, etc. Having risk constant as we look into the future means that we use a smaller and smaller k for cash flows further into the future in computing a present value in Eq. (10-9). This is illustrated in Figure 10-5.

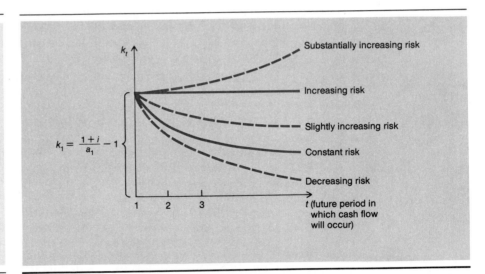

FIGURE 10-5

Behavior of k_t for different risk assumptions. If k_t falls less sharply (or is constant or rising) than the constant risk schedule indicates, then risk is assumed to be rising; if k_t falls more sharply than the constant risk schedule indicates, then risk is assumed to be falling.

Risk is not simply a take it or leave it matter—risk can be changed and controlled by any of a variety of techniques. Below we discuss ways of making costs and revenues more predictable. These risk reduction strategies are often not free, and whether they are profitable in a particular situation will depend on circumstances.

INSURANCE

Perhaps the purest antidote for risk is **insurance**. There are many kinds of insurance, including insurance to cover physical damage, theft and loss of life or health (for example, of a key business executive), loss of revenues (e.g., to provide a lessor with insurance against a lessee's not paying the lease rentals), and even default on a mortgage. Leasing rather than buying an asset is a way of purchasing insurance against a large decline in the salvage value of the asset; part of the lease rental is really a fee to the lessor (the asset's owner) for bearing the salvage value risk.

LONG-TERM ARRANGEMENTS

Peabody International, a major energy and environment control firm, found that costs often ran far ahead of expectations, largely because of inflation. The solution: Peabody often obtains fixed commitments from subcontractors before placing its own bids on new projects. The risk reduction strategy used by Peabody involves a long-term contract which guarantees the supply of a critical input at a prearranged price. The same strategy is being used when a company negotiates a long-term credit line with a bank: The company is guaranteeing a supply of funds even if there's a general credit crunch. A firm can also reduce uncertainty about its ability to sell its product by negotiating a long-term sales contract with a customer.

INDEXING

Risks due to uncertainty about the future purchasing power of the dollar (inflation uncertainty) and about future interest rates can be shifted from one party to another by agreeing beforehand to make adjustments as prices or interest rates change in the future. For example, labor contracts and supply contracts often have **escalator clauses** under which the price of the good or service being supplied is adjusted for inflation. The **real price** (i.e., the price in terms of dollars of a fixed purchasing power) is thereby held constant. Variable rate mortgages carry interest rates which move up and down with the general level of interest rates (for example with the United States Treasury bill rate). This means that the mortgage lender will always receive an interest rate which is roughly in line with current interest rates. Long-term supply contracts for goods or services that involve price indexing actually protect both the buyer and the seller against inflation risks since the indexing keeps the real price (that is, the price in terms of purchasing power) constant. With a fixed price and no indexing both parties are exposed to risk. If inflation is greater than expected, the supplier will be worse off and the buyer will be better off than expected; but, if inflation turns out to be lower than expected, the supplier will be better off and the buyer worse off than expected.

360

PART 2
The firm's investment,
financing, and dividend
decisions

IMPROVING INFORMATION

"Don't test the depth of the river with both feet" is an African proverb. This concept applies to investments. Risk can be reduced by obtaining more information before accepting a project and by maintaining a current flow of information about those projects which have been adopted. Obtaining information, and properly evaluating that information, is perhaps the key technique for reducing risk. An example of this is the use by Turner Construction Company of a computerized system which uses up-to-date information on work progress, costs, weather, and other relevant factors in scheduling and controlling projects. Information and information analysis is not free and should be expanded only as long as the incremental benefits exceed the incremental costs. Usually, though, at least a small investment in information collection and analysis is justified.

CHANGES IN MODUS OPERANDI

Different methods of producing or marketing a product can have different risks. Rotary well drilling is faster than cable drilling, but it involves the risk of drilling right past a water table, the result being an unusable well. Acting as an intermediary (broker) between a computer lessor and a user involves less inventory risk than buying computers from a manufacturer and leasing them to users, since computers can become obsolescent almost overnight. This realization at one time motivated Itel Corporation to become a broker. Whether adopting the lower-risk approach is desirable will depend on the relative costs and returns, as well as risks, of the available choices.

OPTIONS

An **option** is an arrangement which gives the optionholder the right to compel someone else to do something. Options take many forms. The right to buy (or sell) a building for $1 million at any time over the next year, the right to obtain up to $500,000 from a bank at any time over the next year under a revolving credit line, or the right to purchase up to 5000 tons of coal at any time over the next three years are all options. Options reduce risk for the optionholder by providing flexibility through additional choices. This involves less risk than having to adopt a fixed course of action with fewer choices (for example, of buying, or of not buying, the building or the coal now, or of borrowing or not borrowing the money now). An option is not a "heads I win, tails you lose" transaction; the optionholder must pay a price for the option. This price may take the form of a fixed dollar amount; for example, I pay you $25,000 now for the option to buy your building for $1 million at any time over the next year (if I don't buy, you keep the $25,000). The option price may also take the form of a fee per unit time; for example, $\frac{1}{2}$ percent per year on any part of the $500,000 credit line *not* drawn down (borrowed). Since the option has a price, a decision must be made as to whether the added flexibility afforded by the option is worth the price. That depends on the situation.

HEDGING IN THE FUTURES MARKETS

You manufacture a chocolate-coated candy called Chocolate Surprise. You are about to sign a one-year fixed-price contract to supply Chocolate Surprise to a national chain of food stores. There is a great deal of uncertainty concerning the price of cocoa over the coming year and you would like to eliminate this risk without having to store huge quantities of cocoa. There is a very simple way to solve this problem: Purchase cocoa for future delivery by buying cocoa futures contracts in the commodities futures market. The buyer of a futures contract is entitled to delivery of the commodity at a specified future date and at a price that is agreed upon today. Futures markets exist for most agricultural products, minerals, metals, and for certain types of financial instruments (for example, U.S. Treasury bills). Financial futures provide a way to hedge against future changes in interest rates (see the essay Inflation and Innovation in the Financial Markets after Chapter 12).

RAISING INTERMEDIATE AND LONG-TERM FUNDS

The preceding discussion of capital budgeting showed how investment opportunities are evaluated and combined into a planned capital budget. In this chapter and in Chapter 12 we examine the problems faced by a financial manager in deciding how to obtain money to finance a capital budget. Our focus will be on equity financing and on debt with a maturity of over one year. We first briefly describe the four major financing sources used by firms—debt, preferred stock, common stock, and retained earnings. Then each type of financing is discussed in detail. Next we explain how a company accesses the capital markets in raising capital. Finally, we describe international sources of business financing.

GENERAL CHARACTER-ISTICS OF FINANCING METHODS

Debt, preferred stock, and common stock are fund sources that are *external* to the firm, whereas retained earnings represent an *internal* source of funds. Provided that management can convince outsiders of the desirability of investing in or loaning money to the firm, there is virtually no limit to the amount of money that can be raised from external sources.[1] In contrast, retained earnings are limited by the profits of the firm net of any dividends to its owners.

Common stock and retained earnings both represent money contributed by the firm's owners rather than by its creditors or preferred stockholders. The owners of the firm receive income only after all obligations due its creditors and preferred stockholders have been paid.

Tables 11-1 and 11-2 provide a breakdown of the financing used by nonfinancial corporations. Notice that the major source of corporate financing is internal funds (retained earnings and depreciation). Debt financing is second to internal funds and is sometimes used almost as

---

[1] There is no practical limit to the amount of money the firm can raise as long as those with funds to invest in the firm (new stockholders or lenders) feel that the money will be invested in assets that provide an acceptable rate of return. However, the cost of financing may be quite high, particularly for small firms and firms with very risky investments. For very small unincorporated businesses, convincing outsiders that investing in the firm will provide an acceptable rate of return may be very difficult.

363

CHAPTER 11
**Raising intermediate and
long-term funds**

TABLE 11-1

*Financing sources used by nonfinancial corporations,
as a percentage of total financing*

	Internal funds	Debt	Common and preferred stock
1959–1963	60%	35%	5%
1964–1968	63	36	1
1969–1973	50	44	6
1974–1978	59	39	2
1979–1983	70	29	1
1984–1987	74	40	−14[a]

[a] The negative number indicates that stock repurchases exceeded new stock sales.
Source: Statistical Abstract of the U.S., 1989.

TABLE 11-2

*New issues of securities by United States corporations
(in millions of dollars)[a]*

	Common stock[b]	Preferred stock[b]	Bonds	Total
1970	$ 7,240	$ 1,390	$ 30,315	$ 38,945
1971	9,291	3,670	32,123	45,090
1972	9,694	3,367	28,896	41,957
1973	7,750	3,372	22,268	33,391
1974	3,994	2,253	32,066	38,313
1975	7,405	3,458	42,756	53,619
1976	8,305	2,789	42,262	53,356
1977	7,861	3,916	42,015	53,792
1978	7,526	2,832	36,872	47,230
1979	7,751	3,574	40,139	51,464
1980	16,858	3,631	53,206	73,694
1981	23,552	1,797	45,092	70,441
1982	25,449	2,690	53,636	84,198
1983	44,366	7,213	68,370	119,949
1984	18,510	4,118	109,903	132,531
1985	29,010	6,505	165,754	201,269
1986	50,316	11,514	355,293	417,123
1987	43,225	10,123	325,648	378,996
1988	35,911	6,544	350,988	393,443

[a] Gross proceeds (offering price times number of units sold).
[b] Underwritten issues only.
Source: Federal Reserve Bulletin.

364

PART 2
**The firm's investment,
financing, and dividend
decisions**

heavily as internal funds. Although common stock and preferred stock are relatively minor sources of financing in aggregate, they can be quite significant for an individual firm in a given year.

Table 11-3 outlines the important characteristics of the alternative financing sources. The remaining sections of this chapter provide details.

DEBT FINANCING

When a company borrows money, it promises in the debt agreement to repay the money borrowed (the principal) plus interest on specified future dates. If the payments are not made on time and in the proper amount, the debtholders can take a variety of actions to force payment,

TABLE 11-3
Characteristics of financing sources

Debt	Preferred stock	Common stock	Retained earnings
1. Firm must pay back money with interest.	1. Similar to debt in that preferred dividends are limited in amount to rate specified in agreement (like interest rate).	1. Money is raised by selling ownership rights.	1. Lowers amount of money available for current dividends but can increase future dividends.
2. Interest rate is based on risk of principal and interest payments as perceived by lenders.	2. Dividends are not legally required, but no common dividends can be paid unless preferred dividends are paid; also usually cumulative, and passing dividend for a stated number of years may give preferred stockholders voting rights.	2. Value of stock is determined by investors.	2. Stockholders forego dividend income, but they do not lose ownership rights as occurs if new common stock is issued.
3. Amount of money to be repaid is specified by debt contract.	3. No maturity but usually callable.	3. Dividends are not legally required.	3. Funds are internal— no need for external involvement.
4. Lenders can take action to get their money back.	4. Usually no voting rights except as per (2) above.	4. Creates change in ownership.	4. Cost of issuing securities is avoided.
5. Lenders get preferred treatment in liquidation.	5. Preferred dividends are not tax deductible.	5. Shareholders have voting rights.	
6. Interest payments are tax deductible.		6. Common dividends are not tax deductible.	

365

CHAPTER 11
**Raising intermediate and
long-term funds**

depending on the terms of the debt agreement. They may take some of the firm's assets, cause management to be fired, or even force the firm to sell all its assets and thereby force it out of business. They can prevent any payments being made to shareholders (owners) or preferred stockholders before the debtholders have been paid. The debtholders have priority over the other security holders in receiving money from the firm, but the amount of money to be paid to the debtholders is limited to what has been specified in the debt agreement. For example, if the firm owes a bank $2 million, which is to be paid in one year with interest of $200,000, the bank must be paid $2.2 million, but only this amount. Debt financing also differs from other sources of financing in that interest payments are tax deductible to the corporation (dividends are not tax deductible).[2]

Although there are many forms of debt, all debtholders are guaranteed a prior claim over stockholders to the firm's income. That is, *creditors receive what is contractually promised to them before stockholders receive anything.*

For the purposes of financial decisions, three characteristics that all financing methods share are especially important: priority over other security holders, tax deductibility of interest, and a limit on the amount that will be paid to the creditor.

Bonds

A **bond** is a long-term (virtually always with a term of at least ten years) promissory note issued by a corporation. The contract between the corporation and lender is referred to as the **bond indenture**. The indenture ordinarily specifies that the creditor will receive regular interest payments, usually semiannually, during the term of the debt and then receive the **face value** or **maturity value** of the bond at maturity date. For example, a twenty-year $1000 bond promising a **coupon rate** of 10 percent per year sold on January 1, 1989, will pay $100 per year (.10 × $1000) until January 1, 2009; the $100 annual interest will commonly be paid in two $50 semiannual installments. On the maturity date, January 1, 2009, the corporation will also pay the lender the bond's maturity value of $1000.

The *market value* of a bond (what investors would be willing to pay for the bond) is the discounted value (present value) of the dollar payments promised to the bondholder using the market interest rate to discount those payments. Bond valuation was described in Chapter 5.

Provisions of the Bond Contract Bonds may be secured or unsecured. Unsecured bonds, called **debentures**, are issued against the general credit of the corporation, whereas secured bonds are backed by a pledge of specific assets. This section discusses general provisions that apply to both kinds of bonds. The special characteristics of unsecured and secured bonds are examined later.

---

[2] Chapter 12 provides details on the tax differences between equity and debt.

366

PART 2
**The firm's investment,
financing, and dividend
decisions**

Keep in mind that a provision in the bond agreement that protects the bondholders generally means greater constraints on the firm. The provision makes the bonds more attractive to lenders and means the firm can borrow at a lower interest rate than without such a provision. Whether a particular provision is included in a bond contract will depend on the company's situation (which determines how burdensome the provision is) and on the attitudes of lenders (how much they value the provision).

Terms and Enforcement of the Bond Agreement   The bond contract or indenture specifies the terms agreed upon by the corporation and bondholders. The indenture stipulates the payments to be made by the corporation to the bondholders, the identity of any property that is pledged, the call provisions, and any restrictions on the firm to protect the interests of the bondholders. These restrictions are called **protective covenants**. They relate to the right of the firm to pay dividends, to the need to maintain a given level of working capital, and to any other requirements needed to ensure the capacity of the firm to meet its debt obligations. Such restrictions are an important protection to bondholders.

A trustee, frequently a commercial bank, is assigned to represent the bondholders by ensuring that the bond contract meets legal requirements and that the corporation fulfills the terms of the debt contract once the bonds are issued. If the corporation violates a provision of the bond indenture, it is in **default**. It is the duty of the trustee to protect the bondholders if the firm is in default. Bond issues in excess of $1 million and registered with the Securities and Exchange Commission are subject to the Trust Indenture Act of 1939. This federal act provides that the indenture terms must be clear and not deceptive and that the trustee act strictly in behalf of the bondholders.

Call Provision   The call provision in the bond agreement provides that the firm can repurchase ("call") the bonds after they are issued at some stipulated **call price**, which is generally above the face value of the bonds. The difference between the call price and the bond's face value is referred to as the **call premium**. For example, if a $1000 (face value), thirty-year, $7\frac{1}{2}$ percent bond can be called by the firm for $1075, the call premium is $75 ($1075 − $1000). The premium is frequently equal to one year's coupon payment ($75 on a $7\frac{1}{2}$ percent, $1000 bond). Sometimes the call premium declines over time; it might be $75 the first year the bonds are outstanding, $72.50 the second year, and so on, the premium declining by $2.50 per year for thirty years to zero at the maturity date.

Investors would prefer that there be no call provision, since it means that the firm can force them to sell back their bonds at a particular price. For example, assume that a $1000, 8 percent, twenty-year bond is issued on January 1, 1989, at par (that is, for $1000) and has a call provision that allows the firm to repurchase the bond at any time for $1050. The investor pays $1000 for the bond and, if the firm does not call the bond,

367

CHAPTER 11
**Raising intermediate and
long-term funds**

will receive an interest payment of $80 per year for twenty years, plus $1000 at the end of that period. Assume that interest rates in the market fall to 6 percent because of a change in economic conditions after the bond is issued and the firm decides to call the bond on January 19, 1991. The corporation will probably wish to call the bond in this case, since it can now borrow at 6 percent instead of 8 percent. Is the investor worse off than if the firm could not call the bond? The answer is clearly yes. If there were no call option, the value of the bond (using a 6 percent discount rate) would be $1217—the present value of $80 per year for eighteen years (January 1991 to January 2009) plus the present value of the $1000 face value received in eighteen years.[3] However, the firm pays the bondholder only $1050 (the call price) for the bond. To compensate the bondholder for the call provision disadvantage, bonds with such a provision generally pay a somewhat higher coupon rate. Thus, if the $1000 bond were issued at par, without a call provision it might have a coupon rate (and yield to maturity) of 7 percent; with the call provision, issuing the bond at par might require a coupon rate (and yield to maturity) of 8 percent.

Sinking Fund Provision   The bond agreement may include a sinking fund provision that requires the corporation to retire a given number of bonds in certain specified years. The funds for retirement are transferred to a trustee who retires the bonds. The stipulated means of retirement may be calling the bonds or purchasing them in the open market. For example, if the firm issued $10 million of twenty-year bonds on January 1, 1989, it might agree to retire 5 percent of the bonds ($500,000 of par value) in each year beginning in 1990. Sinking fund provisions vary significantly and may require that only some or all of the bonds be retired before maturity. The sinking fund retirements may begin immediately or several years after issuance of the bonds. For example, for the twenty-year bonds issued on January 1, 1989, the indenture might require the retirement of 5 percent of the bonds in the years 1999 to 2008, with the remaining bonds retired at maturity on January 1, 2009.

Other Provisions   A bond indenture restriction might limit the dividends the firm may pay, require the firm to maintain a minimum current ratio or level of working capital, or limit the amount of further company borrowing. For small firms, there are often restrictions on corporate officers' salaries or on company investments. Such restrictions on firm operations are rarely found in public bond offerings, but they are common in privately placed debt.

Secured Debt   Secured debt is backed by particular corporate assets that are specified in the bond indenture as security on the debt. In the event of bankruptcy, the secured bondholder has first claim to the assets

---

[3] Using the factors of Chap. 4, the value of the bond = $80 (*P/A*, 6%, 18) + $1000(*P/F*, 6%, 18) = $80(10.828) + $1000(0.3503) = $1217.

securing those bonds. A **mortgage** is used to pledge real property (land or buildings), and a **chattel mortgage** is used to pledge personal property (property that is not real property).

A given secured bond issue may have a senior claim to specific assets, in which case the bonds would be referred to as **first mortgage bonds**. The claim to the assets may be subordinate to that of other creditors, in which case the bonds carry a junior mortgage on the property and would be referred to as second mortgage bonds or third mortgage bonds, etc. This situation is analogous to the familiar first, second, and third mortgages on residential real estate.

A mortgage may relate to specific land and buildings or may be a **blanket mortgage** covering all the real property owned by the corporation. Instead of a mortgage (which is a security interest in real estate), the firm may use personal property (property that is not real estate) as collateral on the bonds. If equipment is used, the bonds are referred to as **equipment trust certificates**. This type of security has been used frequently by railroads. Sometimes securities (stock or bonds owned by the corporation) or inventory or other intangible assets (e.g., patents) are used as collateral, in which case the debt securities issued by the corporation would be referred to as **collateral trust bonds**. Collateral trust bonds are most frequently issued by railroads and by holding companies (companies whose primary assets are the stock issued by its subsidiaries).

An illustration of a mortgage bond is provided by Inland Steel's first mortgage $8\frac{7}{8}$ bonds, maturing on April 15, 1999. The properties securing the bonds are the following:

1 The Indiana Harbor Works and certain parcels of land in East Chicago, Indiana
2 Certain iron ore properties in Michigan and Minnesota
3 The coal properties of the company in Jefferson County, Illinois
4 Approximately 400 acres of vacant land in Porter County, Indiana

The mortgage is open-ended, with the indenture permitting the issuance of additional debt under the mortgage so long as interest is adequately covered by the firm's income.

Unsecured Debt Unsecured bonds, or debentures, are backed by the general credit of the corporation, that is, by all the firm's assets that are not pledged as security on secured debt. These bonds are not secured by any specific property. Large corporations with excellent credit standings—for example, AT&T; General Motors; and Sears, Roebuck—are those most likely to issue debentures instead of secured bonds. The type of assets owned by the firm also affects the choice between issuing secured or unsecured debt. Whereas a railroad with large fixed assets may find it advantageous to issue secured bonds, a firm with liquid or intangible assets, as for example, a publishing company (whose assets may largely be in the form of copyrights and goodwill), will generally have to resort to unsecured debt.

369

CHAPTER 11
**Raising intermediate and
long-term funds**

Bond indentures frequently include a **negative pledge clause**, stipulating that the firm will not issue any new debt that takes priority over the debentures in their claim to the firm's assets. This may apply to assets acquired in the future as well as to those already owned by the firm.

The company may issue **subordinated debentures.** An issue of debt is subordinated to another if it has a lower-priority claim to the firm's assets in the event of bankruptcy. If debt issue A is subordinated to debt issue B, then in the event of firm liquidation the issue B creditors must be fully paid (all principal and interest due) before the issue A creditors are paid anything. Debentures are often subordinated to bank loans and other short-term debt. Subordinated debt allows the firm to increase its borrowing without jeopardizing the security position of senior debt. Thus the firm can obtain senior loans at a relatively low interest cost by specifying that any further debt will assume a subordinate position.

Are Bonds Risky for Investors?

It used to be that investing in corporate bonds was for widows, orphans, and the highly risk-averse. This is no longer true for two reasons. First, uncertainty about future inflation means that, even if a bond has no default risk, there is risk in what the future interest and principal payments will buy. If inflation turns out to be very high, the payments received by the bondholder will not buy as much as they would if inflation turns out to be low. The interest rate (coupon rate) on the bond will be high enough to compensate the bondholder for this inflation risk.

A second source of risk is default. In recent years, corporations (as well as individuals and the U.S. government) have increased their borrowing relative to their incomes. We have become a highly leveraged society. Greater corporate borrowing means higher corporate default risk. Some of the recent borrowing has been associated with leveraged buyouts (which are discussed in the chapter on mergers) which involve increased company debt, and assets sales, which increase the risk exposure of existing bondholders. As a result, bond values can plummet simply because of the increased likelihood of default. The investment grade bonds of RJR Nabisco, Inc., fell 20 percent in 1988 after management proposed the largest leveraged buyout in history.

In a sense, debt has assumed part of the role of equity as a form of risk capital. Bondholders now assume some of the risks formerly associated with equity. For example, when Storage Technology Corporation came out of its Chapter 11 bankruptcy in 1987, bondholders were paid not only cash and new bonds but also sufficient equity to make them one-third owners. If default becomes a more prevalent phenomenon, the possibility of becoming a stockholder will become more a part of being a bondholder.

Some Other Forms of Debt

In addition to the standard forms of debt described above, a variety of less conventional debt instruments have evolved.

Income Bonds **Income bonds** are unsecured debt requiring payment of interest only to the extent earned by the firm. For example, if the annual

370

PART 2
**The firm's investment,
financing, and dividend
decisions**

interest on the bonds is $100,000 and the firm earns only $50,000 (before interest and taxes), the company has to pay only $50,000 interest on the income bonds. If the firm has earned $150,000, $100,000 in interest would be paid on the income bonds.

Income bonds have been used by companies whose capacity to meet interest and principal payments is questionable, for example, after corporate reorganizations (especially railroad reorganizations). Income bonds have also been used by some small companies as a replacement for outstanding preferred stock. An advantage of income bonds is that interest on those bonds, as on other bonds, is tax deductible, but the interest need not be paid unless the company has sufficient earnings to pay the interest.

Income bond indenture provisions vary. Interest payments are sometimes cumulative; that is, if they are not paid in a given period, they must be paid in future periods if earned by the firm. Sinking fund provisions are common, and some income bonds are convertible into common stock.

Variable-Rate (Floating Rate) Bonds A **floating rate bond** pays interest which fluctuates with prevailing interest rates, rather than being fixed over the life of the bond. For example, the interest rate on Citicorp's 1992 floating rate bond is 1 percent above the rate on ninety-day Treasury bills. In 1980, General Motors Acceptance Corporation issued ten-year notes which yielded 13.45 percent during the first two years and a floating yield thereafter (adjusted annually and tied to the ten-year Treasury bond rate). Petro-Lewis sold bonds in 1980 with an interest rate which varies with the price of "sweet" crude oil from West Texas.

The rationale behind variable interest rate debt is that, in a period of volatile interest rates, many borrowers and lenders do not want to engage in a long-term fixed interest rate contract. One option, of course, is to borrow or lend on a short-term basis at the going market interest rate and to continue to do so from period to period. An alternative is a long-term floating rate security. A floating rate security provides the borrower and lender with what is equivalent to a series of short-term loans, but without the trouble (and cost) of reborrowing or relending every few months on a short-term basis. Also, the borrower is assured of long-term financing with a long-term loan, whereas this is not necessarily so with short-term debt (the firm may simply be unable to renew or renegotiate a short-term loan).

Low- and Zero-Coupon Bonds Northwest Industry's thirty-year bonds were originally issued with a coupon rate of only 7 percent even though other bonds with similar ratings were yielding roughly 14 percent at the time. The Northwest Industry bonds were sold at a 47 percent discount from par (at a price of $527.50 for a bond with a $1000 face value payable at maturity and paying $70 per year in interest); the yield to maturity on the bonds was 13.5 percent. The coupon on General Motors Acceptance Corporation's ten-year debentures is even lower, zero!

371

CHAPTER 11
**Raising intermediate and
long-term funds**

What are the advantages of low-coupon debt? **Low- zero-coupon bonds** are issued at a discount (that is, at below face value) and are referred to as original discount bonds. These bonds provide most or all of the cash payment (interest and principal) when the bond matures. This may be attractive to a lender (bondholder) who does not want the inconvenience of reinvesting periodic interest payments or who wants to lock in his or her investment at current interest rates. An ordinary bond which pays high coupon payments involves uncertainty about the rate of return the bondholder will be able to earn in the future by reinvesting those coupons. Also, low-coupon bonds are generally callable at a price far above the issuance price (for example, at face value), which means that even if market interest rates fall and the bond's price rises substantially, the bonds will not be called (this inability to call a bond at a resonable price is, of course, a disadvantage to the issuing firm). Low-coupon bonds do have the disadvantage that, even though the coupon is small or zero, the bondholder must pay income taxes on a pro rata share of the discount as well as taxes on the coupon.[4] Apparently, investors have found these bonds to be especially attractive because they have sold with yields to maturity roughly $\frac{1}{4}$ to $\frac{3}{4}$ percent below comparably rated regular bonds.

Low-coupon bonds allow the borrower to postpone to maturity most or all of the interest and principal payments on the loan. This means that, in effect, the firm is able to borrow more money for a longer period of time. Furthermore, each year the firm may deduct for tax purposes a part of the bond discount even though the discount isn't paid until maturity.[5]

Put Bonds   **Put bonds** allow the bondholder to return the bonds to the issuer in return for a cash payment equal to the bond's face (par) value. For example, in 1976 Beneficial Corporation issued bonds which mature in 2001 and which allow the bondholder, after June 15, 1983, to turn in the bond to Beneficial in return for the par value of $1000. In return for the put option, put bonds yield a little less than ordinary bonds.

Project Financing   **Project financing** involves debt that is a claim against a particular project and not against the parent company. These are privately placed loans, usually with major banks. The projects for which such financing has been made available have generally been very large (commonly mineral extraction and mineral processing projects). Project

---

[4] For example, assume a twenty-year, 4 percent, $1000 bond that is issued for $400 (implying a yield to maturity of approximately 12 percent). In computing taxable income each year, a bondholder would have to include in other ordinary income (not capital gains) both the $40 coupon *and* a portion of the discount. The entire discount will be amortized into ordinary income over the life of the bond (certain exceptions to this apply if the bond is sold by the investor who originally purchased the bond from the corporation).

[5] Thus, in the illustration of footnote 4, each year the corporation could deduct for tax purposes the $40 coupon plus a portion of the discount.

financing allows the parent corporation to limit or even eliminate its liability exposure (the degree to which the parent is liable is subject to negotiation). Of course, liability limitation is not free since the banks will charge an interest rate which reflects the loan's risk.

Junk Bonds Low-grade debt or **junk bonds**—referred to more kindly as "high-yield securities"—are bonds below investment grade in quality (rated below Baa by Moody's and below BBB by Standard and Poor's). Since the late 1970s, the public's appetite for this kind of security has blossomed. About 20 percent of public debt offerings from 1983 through mid-1986 was of the low-grade variety. Roughly half of this debt has been issued by companies involved in mergers (or in defending against mergers), leveraged buyouts (see Chapter 23), and other restructurings. The low-grade debt arising in restructurings is most often downgraded debt that was previously of investment grade, where the downgrading has occurred because the issuing company involved in the restructuring has taken on much more debt. The initial takeover of companies is generally financed with short-term debt (bank loans or commercial paper), not with junk bonds. Some low-grade issues are convertible into stock or have warrants attached (which give the warrantholder the option to buy the company's stock at a specified price). Other issues include a variable interest rate (sometimes with the right to exchange the variable rate debt for fixed rate debt) or an interest rate which is pegged to certain commodity prices.

Historically, the yields on low-grade debt have more than compensated for the risks, on average yielding roughly 4 percent more than high-grade corporate debt. However, the higher average return has clearly been a compensation for greater risk. A 1989 study by Moody's Investors Service found that 3.3 percent of junk-bond issuers defaulted *each year* between 1970 and 1988. During the same period, the annual default rate for issuers of investment-grade bonds was only .06 percent. During the ten-year period ending in 1988, 18.9 percent of issuers of Ba bonds defaulted and 32.9 percent of issuers of the B bonds defaulted, whereas only .8 percent of issuers of Triple-A bonds defaulted. At the end of the 1980s, much of the bloom was off the junk-bond rose as many well-known borrowers ran into trouble (including Eastern Airlines, Resorts International, and Campeau Corporation). Investors began to avoid particularly risky issues and many merger deals dependent on junk-bond financing were canceled as lenders backed off. At the beginning of the 1990s it appeared that lenders would show more selectivity than they did in the dizzy heights of junk-bond financing in the mid-1980s.

Interest Rate Swaps An interest rate swap is exactly what it sounds like—an exchange of interest payments between two parties. Typically, one party pays a fixed interest rate and the other party pays a floating interest rate (like the prime rate plus 1 percent). For example, Americorp, a United States manufacturer, might agree to pay Britbank, a London bank, 12 percent per year interest for five years on a principal

373

CHAPTER 11
**Raising intermediate and
long-term funds**

amount of $10 million; and Britbank may simultaneously agree to pay Americorp an interest rate of LIBOR minus 0.5 percent per year for five years on a principal amount of $10 million. (LIBOR, or London Interbank Offer Rate, is the rate at which banks in London lend to other banks; LIBOR fluctuates like the prime rate in the United States.) Only interest payments change hands under this arrangement since there is no principal owed by either party to the other. The principal amount in the transaction—$10 million in the above example—serves only as a basis for computing the interest payments and is referred to as the "notional principal." The timing of the interest payments is a matter of negotiation. If the payments in our example are quarterly, then each quarter Americorp pays Britbank $300,000 in interest, and Britbank pays Americorp interest of $10 million times the going LIBOR minus 0.5 percent (e.g., if LIBOR were 10.5 percent for that quarter, Britbank would pay Americorp $250,000 interest for the quarter).

To see how benefits can accrue under the above arrangement, assume that Americorp can borrow $10 million in the United States on a fixed or floating rate basis under the terms shown below.

Americorp's borrowing opportunities	
Type of loan	**Annual interest cost**
Fixed interest rate	15 percent
Floating interest rate	LIBOR plus 2 percent

Assume that Britbank has a stronger financial position than Americorp and can borrow $10 million in Europe under the following terms.

Britbank's borrowing opportunities	
Type of Loan	**Annual interest cost**
Fixed interest rate	12.25 percent
Floating interest rate	LIBOR

Suppose that Americorp wants to borrow on a fixed rate basis and Britbank wants to borrow on a floating rate basis. The above situation provides an opportunity for Americorp and Britbank to work together through an interest rate swap and end up ahead. Imagine an interest rate swap that requires Americorp to pay Britbank a fixed interest rate of 14.5 percent for the $10 million it needs and requires Britbank to pay Americorp LIBOR minus 0.5 percent on the $10 million it needs. Americorp pays less than the 15 percent fixed rate it would have to pay if it borrowed from a United States bank, and Britbank pays less than LIBOR, which is what it would have to pay if it borrowed on a floating rate basis in Europe. Exhibit 11-1 shows the transactions Americorp and Britbank would make in performing the swap we have just described.

374

PART 2
**The firm's investment,
financing, and dividend
decisions**

It can be shown that an interest rate swap can produce gains (ignoring transaction costs) for both parties if the fixed interest rate the corporation must pay in the United States minus the fixed rate the bank must pay in Europe is greater than the floating rate the corporation must pay in the United States minus the floating rate the bank must pay in Europe. Applying this rule to the above example, there were gains because (15 percent minus 12.25 percent) is greater than (LIBOR + 2 percent minus LIBOR).

Interest rate swaps generally involve an intermediary financial institution (for example, a commercial bank) which deals with the two parties. The United States corporation and the European bank in the above example would not transact directly and would probably not even know each other's identity. Swaps generally involve borrowings of at least $5 million. The floating rates may be tied to LIBOR, prime, or the rate on Treasury bills, certificates of deposit, or even commercial paper. The parties may both be United States corporations, with one seeking fixed interest rate financing (like Americorp) and the other floating rate financing (like Britbank).

EXHIBIT 11-1
Interest rate swap

Americorp conducts the following transactions:
    Americorp borrows $10 million in the United States on a floating annual interest rate of LIBOR plus 2 percent.

(1) Interest cost to Americorp	LIBOR + 2 percent

Americorp pays Britbank interest on $10 million at a fixed annual rate of 12 percent.

(2) Interest cost to Americorp	12 percent

Americorp receives from Britbank interest on $10 million at the annual rate of LIBOR minus 0.5 percent.

(3) Interest income to Americorp	LIBOR − 0.5 percent
Net interest paid by Americorp [(1) + (2) − (3)]	14.5 percent

Britbank conducts the following transactions:
    Britbank borrows $10 million in Europe at a fixed annual interest rate of 12.25 percent.

(4) Interest cost to Britbank	12.25 percent

Britbank pays Americorp interest on $10 million at a floating annual interest rate of LIBOR minus 0.5 percent.

(5) Interest cost to Britbank:	LIBOR − 0.5 percent

Britbank receives from Americorp interest on $10 million at the fixed annual interest rate of 12 percent.

(6) Interest income to Britbank:	12 percent
Net interest paid by Britbank [(4) + (5) − (6)]	LIBOR − 0.25 percent

375

CHAPTER 11
**Raising intermediate and
long-term funds**

Interest rate swaps were introduced in late 1981. Initially used by giant international firms, swaps have become a popular financing tool for United States corporations. By 1990, the worldwide level of outstanding debts (including notional principal) involving swaps was well over $200 billion (up from around $3 billion in early 1982).

PREFERRED STOCK

Preferred stock is a hybrid of debt and common stock financing. Preferred stockholders have a prior claim relative to common stockholders to the firm's income after interest and taxes and to the firm's assets in the event of bankruptcy. Preferred stock is subordinate to all debt with regard to earnings and assets. If the firm liquidates, creditors are paid before preferred and common stockholders receive anything. After payment to creditors, the preferred stockholders are paid the par value of their shares, plus any preferred dividends in arrears or for the current period. Anything remaining goes to the common stockholders.

Dividend Payments

The firm need not pay dividends on preferred stock as long as it also fails to pay dividends on the common stock. Therefore, the existence of preferred stock does not increase the probability of firm bankruptcy. Indeed, any added capital provided by the issuance of preferred stock reduces the likelihood of bankruptcy by increasing the firm's capital. Preferred share dividends are generally stated as a percentage of the preferred's par value, e.g., a dividend of 8 percent of par with a par of $100 would be $8 per year.[6] If the preferred stock does not have a par value, the dividend payment is merely stated by itself, e.g., as an annual dividend of $8 per preferred share. Preferred dividends must be paid before any dividends can be paid to common stockholders.

Preferred stock is usually **cumulative**, which means that all past unpaid dividends on the preferred stock must be met before any dividends can be declared on the common stock. For example, if the firm has a $10 million (par) 8 percent preferred stock issue outstanding, the annual preferred dividend would be $800,000. Assume that the firm did not pay dividends in 1990 and 1991 but is considering paying a dividend on the common stock in 1992. Under a cumulative preferred dividend provision, before the common dividend can be paid, the preferred dividends owed for 1990 and 1991, plus the preferred dividend for 1992, must

---

[6] The par value of preferred stock is similar to the par value of a bond and is used to express the dividend payment (as a percentage of par). The *market value* of a preferred share is rarely equal to its par value. Market value equals the present value of future dividends on the preferred stock using the market discount rate (*not* the dividend rate as a percentage of par). For example, assume a $100 par preferred stock paying an annual 8 percent dividend ($8 dividend = 0.08 × $100), and assume that the preferred stock is not expected to be called in the future (perpetual dividend). If investors want to earn 10 percent on their investment in the stock, its market value is the $8 dividend discounted at 10 percent, which equals $8 (*P/A*, 10%, ∞) = $8(10.0) = $80. An investor paying $80 for the preferred stock will earn 10 percent annually on the $80 investment as long as the stock is held, assuming that the dividend is actually paid each year.

first be paid—a total preferred dividend of $2,400,000 ($800,000 for each of the years 1990, 1991, 1992).

The cumulative dividend provision is important protection for the preferred stockholders. Without the cumulative provision the firm could greatly reduce preferred dividends by paying large infrequent dividends, rather than smaller annual dividends, on the common stock. Thus, in the example above but with noncumulative preferred stock, payment of large dividends to common stockholders once every three years would only require a payment of $800,000 to preferred stockholders once every three years; however, paying even a small dividend to common stockholders each year would require an $800,000 dividend on the preferred stock every year.

In a **participating preferred** issue, investors may participate equally (or up to a stipulated level) with common stockholders in receiving dividends. With fully participating preferred stock, the dividend distribution involves payment first to preferred stock up to the stipulated amount (e.g., $8 per share on 8 percent $100 preferred stock), then a dividend payment on each common share equal to that paid on a preferred share, and finally, equal payment of the remaining dividends to the common and preferred stock.

Adjustable rate preferred (ARP), which became popular in the mid-1980s, pays dividends that are pegged at a fixed relationship to government security interest rates (e.g., to the highest of the rates on three-month Treasury bills, ten-year Treasury bonds, and twenty-year Treasury bonds). There is generally a stipulated maximum and minimum dividend rate; for example, the ARP agreement might specify that the annual rate never fall below 10 percent or rise above 14 percent. A variant of the ARP is the convertible adjustable preferred (CAP), which has an adjustable dividend but is also convertible to common stock at the option of the preferred shareholder. Many companies have issued ARPs or CAPs, including Sears, Roebuck & Company, Northern Trust Corporation, GATX, and Tidewater, Inc.

Voting Rights

Preferred stockholders usually have only limited voting privileges. Consent of the preferred stockholders may be required for the issuance of additional securities with an equal or higher-priority claim on the firm's assets or earnings, e.g., the issuance of additional debt. Sometimes, the preferred stockholders may elect a minority number of directors, e.g., two out of seven. This privilege of electing directors may be contingent upon the failure of the firm to pay preferred dividends for some specified number of periods.

Other Provisions

The corporation may retain the right to call the preferred shares, generally at a price above par. For example, the firm may be able to call its $100 par preferred shares by paying the shareholders $108 per share, the call premium in this case being $8.

377

CHAPTER 11
**Raising intermediate and
long-term funds**

Periodic retirement of the preferred stock under a sinking fund arrangement may be required, although this provision is far less common than it is with bonds.

The preferred stock may be convertible into common stock at the option of the holder. The preferred stock may also be issued as a unit with warrants to purchase common stock (the unit is the combination of the share of preferred stock and a specified number of warrants).

The preferred stock agreement may require the corporation to maintain a specified current ratio or level of working capital before dividends may be paid on the common stock. A limit may be placed on the issuance of additional debt or preferred stock. The objective of these conditions is to ensure the ability of the firm to pay preferred dividends and to protect the preferred shareholder's investment in the company.

*An Actual Preferred
Stock Issue*

On February 26, 1974, the Appalacian Power Company offered for sale 200,000 shares of 8.52 percent cumulative preferred. The par value of the stock was $100, implying an annual dividend of $8.52 per share (8.52 percent × $100). However, the offering, or selling, price per share to investors was $101 per share, thereby providing them with an actual annual dividend yield of 8.44 percent ($8.52/$101). These terms are shown below.

Shares (in thousands)	Par value	Annual dividend yield (dividend/par)	Offering price	Actual yield (dividend/offering price
200	$100	8.52%	$101	8.44%

The stock is callable as a whole or in part at varying prices over time: at $110.28 from the date of issuance through February 28, 1979; at $108.94 through February 28, 1984; at $105.82 through February 28, 1989; and at $103.59 thereafter. Some of the conditions designed to protect the preferred stockholders' interest were as follows:

1   Consent of the holders of a majority of the total number of preferred shares then outstanding is needed to issue additional preferred stock unless the firm's net income and gross (pretax) income relative to preferred dividends (on old and any new preferred stock) and interest on the firm's debt are at certain specified levels.
2   Consent of the holders of a majority of the total number of preferred shares is required for the firm to issue or assume additional unsecured debt, if the result is to cause the firm's debt burden to exceed a certain specified level.
3   Dividends on the firm's *common stock* will be restricted if the firm's debt-equity ratio exceeds a specified level.

This preferred stock issue contains most of the provisions that we described earlier.

COMMON STOCK

We have already discussed many features of common stock. In Chapters 1 and 2 we defined the stockholders as the firm's owners and described the financial institutions through which shares are traded. Chapter 3 described some of the characteristics of a corporation and the taxation of stockholder income. Chapters 5 and 6 explained how common stock is valued in the market. This section takes a further look at what is meant by common stock financing, and then discusses the rights and privileges associated with share ownership, the process of issuing new shares, and the listing of stock.

Financing with Common Stock

A firm can raise money by issuing common stock and selling the shares to investors, who become new owners if they were not already stockholders of the firm. Let us assume here that a firm raising money by issuing common stock is selling the stock to new investors as opposed to its existing owners ("old" owners). Although this assumption does not always hold in practice, it greatly simplifies the discussion without making any significant difference to the results.

The sale of common stock divides the ownership of the firm into two parts—that part owned by the old owners and that part owned by the purchasers of the new stock. Suppose that 20,000 shares are held by the old owners and an additional 5000 shares are sold. There would now be 25,000 shares outstanding. The original owners who had 100 percent of the firm now have only 80 percent (20,000/25,000), and the new shareholders who bought 5000 shares have 20 percent (5000/25,000). If the firm now pays $100,000 in dividends, the money must be distributed equally among the shares. In this example, the old shareholders would be entitled to 80 percent of $100,000, while the new shareholders would be entitled to 20 percent of $100,000.

The amount of money raised by issuing a given number of new shares depends on what the new shareholders believe their proportionate interest in the firm is worth. Suppose that the total value of the firm's stock after financing (therefore, including the new shares) and investment has taken place is expected to be $1 million. The new shareholders would then be willing to pay 20 percent of $1 million, or $200,000, to the firm for 5000 shares. This amounts to $40 per share ($200,000/5000). In practice, management decides how much money is needed ($200,000), estimates the price that new investors will be willing to pay for the shares ($40), and from this information determines the number of shares that must be issued (5000).

The shareholders as owners have voting rights through which they elect the firm's directors, who determine corporate policy. The new shareholders therefore acquire 20 percent of the voting power. In many cases firms are reluctant to sell common stock because the new shareholders may not agree with the policies followed by the management elected by the old shareholders. This is especially true of small businesses where the old shareholders usually are the firm's management. For example, the president of a small company who is also its largest

379

CHAPTER 11
**Raising intermediate and
long-term funds**

shareholder might lose control of the business if the company sold a large enough number of shares to other people. The new shareholders could then determine policy or even fire the president.

A major advantage of common stock financing over debt financing is the absence of any requirement to make payments to the shareholders. If the firm borrows money and then runs short of cash when a debt payment comes due, it may have to sell some of its assets to make the payment or be forced out of business by the creditors. On the other hand, the firm does not have to pay dividends to its shareholders, and it never has to repay the money the new shareholders invested. The owners of common stock who want to get back their original investment must either find someone to buy their stock or try to have the company liquidated. Common stock financing has only slight advantages over preferred stock financing in these respects since failure to pay a preferred dividend is not nearly so serious as failure to pay interest, and the money obtained from sale of preferred stock never need be repaid.

*Rights and Privileges
of Share Ownership*

Income and Claim to Firm Assets   Shareholders are residual claimants of the firm, which means that shareholders receive what is left after all other claims against the company have been met. If the firm becomes bankrupt, shareholders get only what is left after all other claimants (creditors, employees, etc.) have been paid. For example, if income before taxes and interest on debt is $100,000, and if interest on debt is $60,000, stockholders receive before-tax earnings in the current period of $40,000 ($100,000 − $60,000 = $40,000). However, if interest on debt is $120,000, stockholders incur a loss of $20,000 ($100,000 − $120,000 = −$20,000). But being in a residual position also has advantages. If the firm earns $500,000 during the current period, bondholders receive only their fixed interest, say, $60,000, and stockholders receive $440,000. Along with the greater risk of a residual interest goes the chance of a greater reward. This is the concept of financial leverage.

The income to stockholders may be retained by the firm or be paid out as dividends. Dividends are paid after they are declared by the board of directors. In most cases, the firm's income exceeds the dividends and some income is retained by the firm. The retention causes an increase in the value of the firm's shares. If the firm earns $200,000 during the year and pays dividends of $120,000, the value of the firm's shares will rise by $80,000 ($200,000 − $120,000 = $80,000).[7] The shareholders have therefore received benefits in two forms: first, dividends of $120,000, and

---

[7] In reality, share prices will probably not rise by exactly $80,000. This is so because of differential taxes on capital gains and dividends (capital gains are not taxed unless the stock is sold). Furthermore, note that when it is stated here that share value will rise by $80,000, it is meant that the retained earnings will have an upward effect on share value of $80,000. Factors other than current retained earnings (e.g., general stock market trends and expectations about the firm's future earnings) may also affect share value, causing it to rise by more or less than $80,000.

second, an increase in the value of their shares (a capital gain).[8] Companies that reinvest a large fraction of their earnings will have low dividend payments relative to earnings (low "dividend payout ratios") but will have higher than average share value increase each year; that is, more income to shareholders will be in the form of capital gains.

Control   In theory, stockholders control the firm through their right to elect the corporation's board of directors, which appoints management. In practice, stockholder control is somewhat limited. Most often, management selects the board of directors. At the time of the election, management sends stockholders proxy statements requesting that the shareholders assign to management the right to vote their stock. Of course, shareholders may give their proxies to some outside dissident group; but, this is the exception rather than the rule. Stockholders who neither appear at the stockholders meeting nor give their proxies to someone else to vote do not exercise their right to vote, and those who do vote consequently elect the new board of directors. Shareholders usually sign and return the proxies they have received from existing management or simply fail to exercise their vote. Only a small fraction of stockholders attend most annual meetings. As a result, management usually retains control of the corporation and chooses the board of directors.[9] Effective control of a corporation generally does not require even 50 percent ownership of the outstanding common stock. The inertia or apathy of shareholders often ensures that a minority position retains control.

Some firms have both voting and nonvoting common stock. For example, the class B common stock may have the right to vote, whereas the class A common stock may not. The nonvoting stock may or may not have an identical claim to dividends, income, and assets as the voting shares.

Preemptive Rights   The **preemptive right** is the right of existing stockholders to maintain their share of the ownership of the corporation by purchasing any new shares issued by the corporation. For example, if the corporation has 100,000 shares of common stock outstanding and plans to issue 50,000 new shares, a stockholder owning 100 of the 100,000 outstanding shares (0.1 percent) will have the right to purchase

---

[8] An increase in the price of a stockholder's shares is referred to as a capital gain whether or not the shares are sold by the stockholder. The capital gain is referred to as **realized** if the shares are sold for cash (the gain is realized in the form of cash).

[9] Rebelling against the annual stockholders meeting as a waste of time and money, J. B Fuqua, chairman of Fuqua Industries, polled his stockholders some years ago on their reactions to the idea of discontinuing such meetings. He received 99 percent support. Although Delaware law would have allowed discontinuing the annual meetings, they are required by the New York Stock Exchange for all listed firms. So the meetings continue even though no more than a dozen of the Fuqua shareholders generally attend.

381

CHAPTER 11
**Raising intermediate and
long-term funds**

50 of the 50,000 new shares (0.1 percent) before those new shares are offered to anyone else.

Common law provides for the preemptive right. However, some states deny the preemptive right by statute unless it is specifically included in the corporate charter; in other states, the preemptive right exists unless denied under the corporate charter. If the firm issues securities that are convertible into common stock, existing shareholders are generally pemitted under the preemptive right to purchase these convertible securities before they are offered to outsiders. Even when the preemptive right exists, it does not apply to new common stock which is used as payment for property or as payment in a merger acquisition and does not apply to the resale of treasury stock (that is, the sale of stock which was previously brought back by the firm from shareholders) or to the issuance of stock to employees (for example, under a stock option plan). Stockholders may waive the preemptive right upon management's request, for example, if the preemptive right is a hindrance to issuing new shares.

The preemptive right is an important protection to shareholders. Without this right, management could issue stock to individuals favorably inclined to management and thereby retain control of the company. The preemptive right also protects shareholders against dilution of their financial interest in the firm. *If additional shares are sold to new stockholders at a price below the stock's current market price, owners of the old shares will suffer a fall in the market value of their holdings.* For example, assume a firm has 100,000 shares of common stock but no bonds outstanding and a market value of $10 per share; the market value of the firm is therefore $1 million (100,000 × $10). The firm is to issue 50,000 new shares at $4 per share, thereby raising $200,000 of new capital. After issuance of the new stock, the value of the firm is approximately $1,200,000 ($1,000,000 + $200,000 raised by issuing new stock) and there are 150,000 shares outstanding. The market value per share of the stock is $8 ($1,200,000 divided by 150,000 shares = $8) instead of the preissuance price of $10. The original stockholders lose $2 per share of stock owned. The preemptive right ensures that current stockholders get the first chance to buy any new shares at $4 per share.

Right to Inspect the Firm's Books   A stockholder has the right to obtain information from management regarding the firm's operations. However, this right is not unlimited and applies only if the release of such information will not injure the competitive position of the firm. This limitation is imposed in order to protect other stockholders. A stockholder who feels that management is withholding information about its malfeasance or gross negligence in managing the company may take the case to the courts.

Right to Transfer Shares   A shareholder can sell his or her shares without permission from management or other shareholders. The corporation continues to exist regardless of any changes in ownership because of transfers of stock by shareholders. A shareholder may directly sell his or her stock to another party merely by signing that stock (on the back of the certificate) over to the buyer. If the stock is publicly traded, the shareholder may also transfer the stock through a broker. The purchaser of the stock (or the broker) sends the stock certificate, which has been transferred to the purchaser, to a transfer agent representing the corporation. The transfer agent then issues a new certificate under the name of the purchaser so that the new owner may be listed on the firm's books as the owner of record. The new shareholder is now entitled to receive dividends on the shares and has all the rights and privileges associated with stock ownership.

Limited Liability   Because the corporation is a distinct entity under the law, a stockholder is not liable for the debts of the corporation (although, if the corporation is used by stockholders for illegal or morally reprehensible purposes, the stockholders may become liable for the corporation's acts). In contrast, the owner of a sole proprietorship or a general partner of a partnership would be personally liable for the debts of the business.

Stockholder Voting   We noted earlier that one of the rights of stockholders is to elect the board of directors of the corporation. Two types of voting systems are in general use—majority rule and cumulative voting.

Unless otherwise provided by state statute or by the corporate charter, the will of the majority of those voting is effective in electing the board of directors. Each share entitles its owner to one vote; an owner of 100 shares has 100 votes. Each position on the board of directors is voted on individually. Therefore, if six positions were to be filled, an owner of 100 shares would cast 100 votes for a candidate for position 1,100 votes for a candidate for position 2, etc. Thus, someone who owns 51 percent of the firm's shares could elect the candidate it prefers for each position and prevent election of any directors by the minority. For this reason an alternative voting system has evolved, one which gives the minority a greater opportunity for representation on the board. This system is cumulative voting.

Under cumulative voting each shareholder receives a number of votes equal to the number of his or her shares times the number of directors to be elected. For example, if six directors were to be elected, a shareholder with 100 shares would have 600 votes. A shareholder's votes may be applied in support of one candidate, or they may be spread over a number of candidates. With six directors to be elected, a shareholder with 600 votes could cast all 600 votes for a given candidate, or say, 400 votes for one candidate and 200 for a second candidate, and so forth. Under both the majority rule and cumulative voting systems, those candidates receiving the most votes are the ones elected to the board of directors. If six positions on the board were to be filled, and there were twelve candidates, the six candidates with the most votes would win. However, whereas under the majority rule system a majority is able to elect all members of the board, under cumulative voting a significant minority is assured of at least some representation on the board, if it properly distributes its votes among the candidates.[10]

Issuing New Shares

When a company issues new shares, it ordinarily receives, in payment, cash from the investors buying those shares. To show how this is recorded by the firm, assume that Infotex, Inc., has issued 1 million new shares at $11 per share (the price paid by those buying the stock) and that the flotation costs (fees to investment bankers) are $1 million. The net proceeds of Infotex from the sale are $10 million. On its books, Infotex records the sale by increasing both cash and stockholders' equity by $10 million. If the stock has a par value (explained below) of, say, $5 per share, the $10 million increase in stockholders' equity is made up of a $5 million rise in each of the par value and paid-in surplus on the balance sheet. Paid-in surplus is the amount above par value received by a corporation for shares it sells. Exhibit 11-2 shows the balance sheet changes for Infotex from the stock sales assuming that the stock has a par value of $5 per share.

Par value is a per share amount assigned to the corporation's stock by the board of directors. The use of a par value is meant to protect creditors, since in many states the law requires that corporations not make payments to stockholders which reduce shareholders' equity below the total par value of outstanding shares. For example, Infotex cannot reduce stockholders' equity below $20 million after the new shares are issued since this is the total par value of Infotex stock (see Exhibit 11-2).

In some states, corporations are required to set a "stated value" per share rather than a par value per share. As with par value, the firm is not permitted to pay dividends which reduce owners' equity below its stated value.

Generally, the firm will issue new shares at a market price significantly above par or stated value. Except for the restriction placed upon payments to shareholders described above, it is the market price of the shares upon issue that is of significance to shareholders and management. This market price is what new investors are willing to pay for the

---

[10] Let n = the total number of firm shares outstanding, D = total number of directors to be elected, d = number of directors the minority stockholders desire to elect, and X = the number of shares needed to ensure the election of d directors. Then:

$$X = \frac{n \times d}{D + 1} + 1 \qquad \text{(a)}$$

If the minority shareholders own q shares, then they can elect Z directors, where:

$$Z = \frac{(q - 1) \times (D + 1)}{n} \qquad \text{(b)}$$

For example, if n = 1,000,000, D = 10, and d = 2, then, from (a), X = 181,819.18 = 181,819 (fractions are dropped off); i.e., it will take 181,819 shares to guarantee the ability to elect two directors. If the minority shareholders own 300,000 shares, then, using (b), the minority shareholders can necessarily elect (where q = 300,000) Z = 3.3 = 3 (fractions are dropped off) directors.

384

PART 2
**The firm's investment,
financing, and dividend
decisions**

The Listing of Stock

firm's shares and is what management feels is at least a fair payment for the ownership interest being sold to those investors. Generally, it will be market price, and not par or stated value, that is important in financial decisions.

A corporation is referred to as **closely held** if it has relatively few shareholders. An existing group of shareholders may wish to keep the company closely held in order to maintain privacy or maintain full control over operations (and not be answerable to a dissident group of stockholders). However, if a firm has 500 or more shareholders and total assets in excess of $1 million (both conditions must apply), it must publicly disclose its financial position by filing an annual statement with the Securities and Exchange Commission (SEC).[11]

The shares of a **publicly held** corporation are traded publicly in the over-the-counter market or on one of the thirteen organized exchanges in the United States. From the standpoint of the firm, it is debatable whether a listing provides significant gains. As was explained in Chapter 2, both over-the-counter and listed stock transactions usually involve brokers who act as intermediaries between buyers and sellers of the

---

[11] If the company has securities that are convertible to stock, owners of the convertible securities are added to the number of shareholders to determine whether the minimum of 500 shareholders is met (e.g., 400 stockholders and 100 owners of bonds convertible into stock would satisfy the requirement).

EXHIBIT 11-2
Recording the issuance of new shares by Infotex, Inc.

	Balance sheet		Change in balance sheet figures
	Before new shares are issued	After new shares are issued	
Assets			
Cash	$ 5,000,000	$15,000,000	$10,000,000
Other assets	60,000,000	60,000,000	0
Total assets	$65,000,000	$75,000,000	$10,000,000
Liabilities and owners' equity			
Liabilities	$30,000,000	$30,000,000	0
Owners' equity			
Par value	15,000,000	20,000,000	$ 5,000,000
Paid-in surplus	10,000,000	15,000,000	5,000,000
Retained earnings........	10,000,000	10,000,000	0
Total liabilities and owners' equity	$65,000,000	$75,000,000	$10,000,000

stock. SEC regulations are essentially the same for listed and unlisted companies. One might expect a benefit from listing since some financial institutions are permitted (under state laws) to own only listed stocks, and since listed securities enjoy somewhat greater publicity (e.g., trading volume in the stock and price quotations are published in more newspapers if the stock is listed). However, it is not clear from the empirical evidence that the market price of a company's stock is enhanced merely because it is listed on an exchange.

If a firm lists its stock, it must file papers with the exchange and with the SEC. The various exchanges have minimum listing requirements pertaining to assets, earnings, number of shares outstanding, and number of shareholders. The SEC requires that the firm publish both quarterly earnings reports and annual overall financial statements.

RETAINED EARNINGS

Retained earnings are the profits remaining in the firm after dividends are paid. This means that the availability of retained earnings depends on the earnings of the firm and on the policy of the firm regarding dividend payments. Earnings are limited and generally unpredictable, and therefore the financial manager may not be able to rely on the availability of retained earnings to finance investment.

Firms often accumulate funds over a period of years in order to finance investment. For example, investment in 1991 might be financed from retentions of earnings from 1988 through 1991.

Retained earnings substitute most directly as an alternative to common stock, since both represent investment by owners (old or new) of the firm. However, the use of common stock may present problems in maintaining control of the firm by the original shareholders. For this reason many small firms avoid common stock issues. Also the firm must pay various fees and costs to issue stock that are avoided when retained earnings are used.

RAISING INTERMEDIATE- AND LONG-TERM FUNDS

This section looks at some of the more technical aspects of obtaining funds from the capital markets. The discussion focuses on debt issues with a maturity of more than one year and on stock issues.

General Decisions in Raising Funds

Once the company has determined the amount of financing needed and the type of financing to be used (debt, common stock, or some other type), two decisions have to be made. The financial manager must choose between public and private financing, and the maturity of any debt to be issued must be fixed. A **public security issue** is sold to individual and institutional investors. The actual selling is usually handled by an investment banker, who buys the securities from the firm and sells them to investors. If a **private security issue** (or **private placement**) is chosen, the firm approaches one investor or a small number of investors directly and sells the securities to them. The investors in a private issue are usually financial institutions such as pension funds and insurance companies.[12] While a number of factors influence the choice between public and private financing, the major considerations are the size and type of financing needed. Common and preferred stocks are usually sold as public issues, whereas debt is issued publicly and privately. Large issues of long-term debt (over $10 million and over ten years) are more often public issues, whereas smaller and shorter-term debt issues are more often private.

In determining the maturity of new debt, the financial manager might be tempted to rely on the "matching principle," which states that the maturity of the debt should match the period of time for which the money will be needed. This is appropriate if the borrowing is temporary in that once the "need" has passed the debt will be retired. However, it is not appropriate for firms that plan to maintain the debt as a normal part of their outstanding securities. In this case, maturing old debt will be repaid with funds raised by issuing new debt. Determining debt maturity for these firms is largely a decision as to how often the firm wishes to refinance its debt.

Public Securities Issues and Investment Banking

Most companies making a public issue of debt or stock use the services of an investment banker, who does the actual selling of the securities. In some situations, firms do try to sell the securities to the investors themselves. This is called a **direct securities issue** and, for nonfinancial corporations, is largely confined to common stock.

Firms use investment bankers to sell securities to investors when it is cheaper and easier than doing it themselves. Investment bankers specialize in selling new securities issues. They know investor preferences as to the type and features of securities and are organized to contact potential buyers. They normally earn their money on the difference between the price at which they acquire the securities from the firm and the price at which the securities are sold to investors.

Most public issues are sold through **negotiated underwriting**. In this process a firm chooses an investment banker, negotiates the price and conditions of the issue, and sells it to the banker. Underwriting is the process whereby the investment banker purchases the issue from the firm at a given price and then sells the issue to investors. In an underwritten issue, the investment banker bears the risk that it will not sell well. The issuing firm is guaranteed a fixed price. Alternative procedures are also possible.

Some firms, primarily railroads and public utilities, use **competitive bidding**, rather than negotiation, both to pick the investment banker and

---

[12] The terms "issuing securities" or "securities issues" as used in practice generally connote public issues of debt and stock. In the interest of simplicity in our discussion, we use these terms in their broader sense of agreements between a firm and those supplying money to it. Similarly, whereas "investor" typically refers to someone purchasing a public issue of debt or stock, we use the term to refer to anyone providing funds to the company.

387

CHAPTER 11
Raising intermediate and
long-term funds

to determine the price of the issue. In a competitive bidding situation, the firm announces that it wishes to issue securities and invites bids from investment bankers. On large issues several investment bankers join together in a **syndicate** and submit a single bid for the group. The firm specifies the type of security and any conditions or features that it has. The investment bankers then submit bids on the price (or interest rate) for the issue, and the banker making the best bid is awarded the issue.

Whether an investment banker is chosen by negotiation or bidding, the banker acts as an underwriter. An alternative approach is for the firm to ask an investment banker to sell its securities on a **best efforts** or **agency** basis. In this case the investment banker is not acting as an underwriter but merely sells the securities for a commission. This procedure is used either by very large firms that are confident that their securities will sell easily, or (much more frequently) by very small firms, when the investment banker feels the risks of an unsuccessful issue are too high. Table 11-4 provides information on the relative amounts of securities issued through investment bankers. Notice that 79 percent of the dollar volume of all issues is underwritten. Also note that, whereas almost all bonds, notes, and preferred stock are underwritten, a large portion of common stock is sold on an agency basis (33 percent) or direct (8 percent).

Preliminary Discussions A typical security issue begins with discussions by the firm's financial manager with one or more investment bankers, who provide advice on investors' reactions to the company's debt policy, the possible features or conditions of a debt issue, and an estimate of the price or interest rate that investors will require. The financial manager will usually ask for a written proposal on what the security issue might be. When discussions are carried out with more than one banker, the proposals provide a basis for choosing among them. The investment banker chosen in this process is called the **originating house**. Large firms

---

TABLE 11–4
Corporate securities issues by method of issue during 1988ᵃ (dollar figures in millions)

	Underwritten		Agency basis		Direct		Total	
	Amount	Percentᵇ	Amount	Percentᵇ	Amount	Percentᵇ	Amount	Percentᵇ
Bonds and notes	$42,244	94	$ 1,795	4	$1,125	2	$45,164	100
Preferred stock	$ 4,477	97	$ 33	.7	$ 107	2.3	$ 4,617	100
Common stock	$22,166	59	$12,253	33	$3,113	8	$37,532	100
Total issues	$68,887	79	$14,081	16	$4,345	5	$87,313	100

ᵃ Preliminary figures for December 1988.
ᵇ Percentages are based on row totals.
Sources: SEC Monthly Statistical Review and U.S. Securities and Exchange Commission.

388

PART 2
The firm's investment,
financing, and dividend
decisions

often have continuing relationships with an investment banker that last for many years. For large issues, other investment bankers may be brought in to form the **underwriting syndicate**. The originating house will normally serve as the manager of the syndicate and underwrite the largest portion of the issue.

The fees paid to the investment banker for undertaking the issue have two parts—underwriting commissions and sales commissions. The underwriting commission is the payment for risk bearing and the sales commission is the payment for doing the actual selling of the securities. The manager of a syndicate is compensated out of the underwriting commission, and the remaining part (after expenses are deducted) of the underwriting commission is paid to the members of the syndicate in proportion to their original shares of the underwriting. Sales commissions are based on the actual sales of the syndicate members.

Table 11-5 provides some data on the costs of issuing securities through a negotiated underwriting. Notice that issue costs as a percentage of the proceeds decline rapidly until the issue size reaches about $10 million. Also note that the underwriting commission for common stock is higher than the commission for debt. The difference is due to the greater price fluctuation of common stock and hence the greater risk borne by the underwriter.

Setting Up the Issue   Once agreement has been reached between the investment banker and the issuing firm, an evaluation of the firm is made. If new plant and equipment will be purchased with the proceeds of the issue, engineering firms may be hired to analyze the technical aspects

---

TABLE 11-5
Costs of issuing corporate securities (cost expressed as a percentage of issue amount)

Size of issue ($ millions)	Debt, %	Preferred stock, %	Common stock, %
$0–$0.49	12.3	14.5	23.7
$0.5–$0.99	11.0	12.2	20.9
$1–$1.9	10.5	9.8	16.9
$2–$4.9	6.2	5.2	12.4
$5–$9.9	3.1	2.5	8.1
$10–$19.9	1.9	1.8	5.9
$20–$49.9	1.4	1.7	4.6
$50–$99.9	1.2	1.6	3.7
$100 and over	1.0	2.4	3.0

Sources: U.S. Securities and Exchange Commission and Investment Bankers Association.

389

CHAPTER 11
**Raising intermediate and
long-term funds**

of the assets. An accounting firm may be called in to audit the firm's accounts.

A major portion of the preissue activity of the investment banker consists of meeting the requirements imposed by the state and federal agencies regulating new issues. Most of these requirements involve the disclosure of information on the company's operations and financial condition, the ownership of outstanding securities by officers and directors of the firm, and any legal problems the firm may be having. The regulatory authorities are especially concerned that important relevant facts about the company are fully and accurately disclosed to potential investors.

The final price or interest rate to the firm is not usually set until after the registration has been completed. If the firm is issuing bonds and already has outstanding bonds that are being traded in the bond market, the interest rate will be set slightly higher than the market yield on the company's existing bonds. Similarly, if the firm is issuing stock and its stock is currently traded in the stock market, the offering price of the stock will be somewhat lower than the market price at the end of registration. In both cases, how much different the terms of the issue will be from the market rate or price will depend on how stable the market has been recently and is a matter of negotiation between management and the investment banker.

The problem facing a firm that has never had a public issue of the security in question is more difficult. If the firm is issuing bonds and there are no publicly traded bonds outstanding, management and the investment banker must decide what the proper interest rate should be. They will rely primarily on comparisons with other firms that do have outstanding bonds. In addition they may ask for the bonds to be rated by one of the firms that provide such services (as was discussed in Chapter 5). If management and the investment banker know that bonds will be rated A, for example, then they will use the current interest rate on A-rated bonds as a basis for determining the rate on the issue. Rating increases the marketability of a bond issue, since the existence of a rating reduces the amount of work needed by investors to decide whether they wish to buy the issue. For this reason most public debt issues are rated, regardless of whether the firm has currently outstanding bonds or not.

Pricing a New Issue of Common Stock   A firm making its first public issue of common stock [initial public offering (IPO)] is said to be **going public**. Prior to going public the firm would have only a few shareholders, who purchased their stock directly from the firm or who were the founders of the firm and their families. Now, either the firm needs more equity capital than can be provided by retained earnings or the original owners wish to sell a part of their interest in the firm to others. Going public almost always substantially increases the number of shareholders in the firm. There is no established market price for such firms, and an estimate must be made by the firm's management and the investment banker as to

390

PART 2
The firm's investment,
financing, and dividend
decisions

the market value of all the firm's shares once the stock is issued. Once the total market value has been estimated, the estimated price per share is simply the market value divided by the total number of outstanding shares. For example, suppose that the market value of the firm is estimated to be $1 million and there will be 200,000 shares outstanding after issue. Then the estimated price per share is

$$\text{Price} = \frac{\$1,000,000}{200,000 \text{ shares}} = \$5 \text{ per share}$$

Here we are not concerned about the number of *new* shares to be issued, only the total number that will be outstanding after issue.

The total number of shares can be adjusted by the issuer to achieve a price per share that the investment banking firm believes is appropriate. Most underwritten initial public offerings over $1 million are priced between $2 and $15 per share. Suppose that the firm that is going public wishes to issue $5 million in new shares and that the estimated market value of the firm after issue is $20 million. If the investment banker wishes to issue the stock at a price of $20 per share, 1 million shares ($20 million/$20) must be outstanding after issue; 250,000 shares will be sold to new investors ($5 million/$20), and 750,000 shares (1,000,000 − 250,000) will be held by the current owners. What if there were only 50,000 shares currently (preissue) outstanding? Prior to issue there will be a 15 to 1 stock split (750,000/50,000) to provide current stockholders with the appropriate number of shares. On the other hand, suppose that there were 1.5 million shares outstanding prior to issue. In this case, there would have to be a reverse split of 1 for 2 (750,000/1.5 million) to achieve the desired number of shares. The main problem is to estimate the total market value of the common stock.[13]

The basic principles required to estimate the value of common stock were presented in Chapter 5, and they will not be repeated here. There we developed the idea that the value of an asset was the present value of the income produced from it. From the viewpoint of the owners of a firm's common stock, the relevant income is the dividend stream paid by the firm, and the value of the firm's stock is the present value of expected future dividends.

Advantages of Underwriting   The investment banker provides a variety of services including counseling on the type and terms of the securities to be issued, bringing the securities to market, and maintaining a market for common stock after issue. Stock issued through an investment banker will be sold to many investors, creating a broader ownership of the company. To the extent investors in a company are more likely to patronize the company, this may have real benefits in terms of volume of

---

[13] Empirical studies suggest that initial public offerings are more apt to be underpriced than overpriced. See Clifford W. Smith, Jr., "Raising Capital: Theory and Evidence," *Midland Corporate Finance Journal*, 4 (Spring 1986), pp. 6–22.

391

CHAPTER 11
**Raising intermediate and
long-term funds**

business conducted by the company. A broader ownership also makes it less likely that the new shareholders will collaborate in replacing current management. This is an important consideration for firms that are controlled by a few people and that need substantial new equity to finance investments. Finally, there is the advantage of knowing exactly how much money will be raised and at what cost. The firm receives the money when the underwriter pays for the entire issue. The alternative is to have the sale of the securities occur over a period of time with varying prices (or interest rates) depending on the reaction of investors and changing economic conditions. In an underwritten issue the investment banker bears these risks.

Regulation of Public Issues Public securities issues must comply with a variety of state and federal regulations. In 1911, the Kansas State Legislature passed one of the first laws regulating securities issues. A member of the legislature remarked at that time that the new law would prevent sellers of securities from promising the "blue sky" to unsophisticated investors. As a result, such state regulations are called **blue sky laws**. Generally state requirements impose some minimum standards for disclosure of the business and financial affairs of the issuing firm and regulate the activities of investment bankers and securities broker-dealers. The laws in some states set limits on the percentage of the issue that can be paid in compensation to the investment banker.

The principal federal laws in this area are the Securities and Exchange Acts of 1933 and 1934. The 1934 act established the SEC as the primary federal regulatory agency responsible for securities issues and trading. The 1933 act was specifically directed toward regulation of new securities issues. The major result of this law was to force firms issuing securities to the public to disclose fully any information relevant to an investor in the new security being offered. Before a security can be issued, the firm must file a registration statement containing this information that must be approved by the SEC. The registration process may take two to four months to complete. In addition, copies of a condensed version of the registration statement must be made available to prospective investors before they purchase the securities. This package of information is called a **prospectus**.

For purposes of SEC regulation a public issue is one that will be sold to more than approximately twenty-five investors; however, not all public issues need be registered with the SEC. The major exceptions are: (1) small issues, less than $1.5 million in amount during a single year; (2) issues limited to purchase by citizens of a single state; (3) debt issues with maturities of less than 270 days (commercial paper is in this category); and (4) firms in industries already regulated by another federal agency (for example, railroads, which are regulated by the Interstate Commerce Commission).

From an investor's viewpoint it is important to remember that the SEC *does not* prevent firms from issuing trashy securities. Stock may be greatly overpriced, or debt may have too low an interest rate for the risk involved. The firm may even be doing illegal things such as paying bribes to foreign governmental officials. The firm may be unprofitable and close to bankruptcy. All the SEC requires is that complete and accurate information be disclosed. It is up to the individual investor to sort out the trash.

Shelf Registration: Rule 415   In November 1983, the SEC gave permanent approval to Rule 415, which authorizes a process for issuing securities called **shelf registration**. Under shelf registration, a company need only register a security offering once in a period of two years. After the registration has been approved by the SEC, the firm can issue securities at any time and in any amount during the two-year period, so long as the total amount issued does not exceed an amount specified in the registration. For example, a company might register $100 million in bonds. Six months later, the company could issue $50 million, and a year later issue another $40 million without going through another registration. A final issue of $10 million could be made, or not, at the company's discretion. Indeed, none of the $100 million need be issued. Shelf registration eliminates the need for multiple registrations, and therefore saves on issue costs. In addition, the time required to issue is greatly reduced. With a shelf registration in place, a company can raise capital in a few days. A phone call from the financial manager to the firm's investment bankers is sufficient to initiate the process, and the issue might be sold to investors before the day is over. The company will not receive the cash for several days, but it is assured of the financing within a few hours. Shelf registration is only available for the securities of large corporations, but it has become the normal way to issue debt for companies that meet the minimum size limits set by the SEC.

Private Placement

The distinguishing differences between public and private issues include the number of buyers of the securities and the extent of contact between the firm issuing the securities and the buyers. In a public issue many investors will purchase the securities, whereas a private issue will involve only a few investors. A firm making a public issue will not normally have any contact with the investors prior to their becoming stockholders or bondholders of the firm. In a private issue, the firm will be discussing the terms of the issue directly with prospective purchasers. Common stock is much less likely to be privately placed than are debt and preferred stock. In recent years, less than 5 percent of common stock financing has been through private placements, whereas about 20 percent of bond and preferred stock financing has been privately placed.

Public versus Private Issues   Private issues have some definite advantages over public issues. For one thing the firm is spared the time, trouble, and expense of having to register the issue with the SEC and to comply with its requirements. Moreover, since the main requirements of public issues involve disclosure of information about the company, many firms dislike the idea of having to "tell it all" to their employees, their

393

CHAPTER 11
**Raising intermediate and
long-term funds**

competitors, and the general public. Privately placed debt issues provide advantages if the firm gets into difficulties later on. The firm can discuss the problem directly with the lender and make modifications in the debt agreement. For example, a scheduled loan payment might be delayed or financing arranged with the same lender (usually at a higher interest rate). This is much more difficult to do when there are many holders of a public debt issue.

However, private issues have some disadvantages. First, the investor-lender may monitor the operations of the firm much more carefully than the purchaser of a public issue. In the case of common stock financing, the investor or investor group is more likely to try to gain control of the firm. Second, the interest rate paid on debt issues is likely to be higher and the price of common stock issues lower if they are private placements. Therefore, the advantage of lower issue costs for private issues may be partially or completely offset by the higher rate of return required by a private investor. This is especially true for large issues because issue costs tend to be relatively smaller for them (see Table 11-5). Shelf registration has also reduced the cost of public issues for large corporations. Third, it is more difficult to finance large amounts privately than it is to make a public issue. The result is that larger securities issues tend to be public issues, whereas smaller issues tend to be private.

The feature that distinguishes different private placements is not *what types* of securities are issues, but *who* provides the money. Therefore we will look at some of the major private sources of intermediate- and long-term financing.

Commercial Banks Business firms acquire money from commercial banks through two long-term debt arrangements—mortgages and term loans. A mortgage is a loan secured by real estate—land and buildings—that is usually repaid in periodic installments.[14] Mortgage loans to business firms are similar to mortgage loans to individuals except that the maturity of the loan is usually less for business mortgages. Mortgage loans to people buying a house to live in (**residential mortgages**) generally are repaid over a period of fifteen to thirty years. Business mortgages (usually called **commercial mortgages**) infrequently extend past twenty years and may be repaid over only five years. Residential mortgages almost always require equal monthly payments, whereas commercial mortgages are often repaid quarterly. Banks make commercial mortgages to finance manufacturing facilities, stores, and office buildings.

Term loans may or may not be secured by assets of the firm. Payment schedules are highly variable but do not extend beyond ten years. A typical term loan would be paid off in quarterly installments over a period of three to five years. The principal payments are usually

---

[14] The term ''mortgage'' has a particular legal definition. Our use includes other types of loans secured by real estate (e.g., deeds of trust) as well.

394

PART 2
**The firm's investment,
financing, and dividend
decisions**

the same amount each quarter (or month), whereas the interest payments are based on the outstanding balance of the loan. For example, suppose that a firm borrows $100,000 for ten years using a term loan with quarterly payments required. The interest rate is 8 percent per year, or 2 percent per quarter. The loan would require a principal payment of $100,000/40 = $2500 per quarter plus interest on the outstanding balance. In the first quarter, the interest would be $100,000 × 0.02 = $2000, and so the total payment would be $2000 + $2500 = $4,500 in the first quarter. However, in the last quarter the loan is outstanding, the interest payment would be $2500 × 0.02 = $50 for total payment of $2550.

Term loans often carry **restrictive provisions** or constraints on the firm. For example, the loan agreement may require that the firm not pay any dividends in excess of earnings for the year or that the firm maintain working capital equal to a fixed percentage of long-term debt. Most term loans made by banks are **variable-rate** loans. That is, the interest rate may vary over the life of the loan. The rate is usually expressed as a fixed percentage over the bank's current prime rate.[15] For example, the agreement might read that the rate will be "1 percent over prime." If the current prime rate were 9 percent, the current interest rate on the loan would be 10 percent. It is standard practice to vary the interest rate on the loan whenever the prime rate changes. Thus, if the prime rate on February 15 changes from 9 percent to 8 percent, the interest rates on all loans made under this type of arrangement would be adjusted downward. If the prime rate changed again on February 22, the new rate would immediately apply. Under this system, the bank charges the firm periodically (monthly or quarterly) the amount of interest owed for the prior period.

The uncertainty in the interest payments on variable-rate loans has concerned financial managers of business firms. They now often attempt to negotiate a ceiling on the average interest rate over the period of the loan. Such a ceiling is called a **cap**. A loan agreement might specify a cap of, say, 15 percent. This means that if interest rates rise and stay over 15 percent for a long time, future interest payments made by the firm will be reduced so that the 15 percent cap is not exceeded on average. This does not mean that the rate in any given period cannot exceed 15 percent, only that the average interest rate paid on the loan must not be greater than 15 percent per year.

Revolving credits are a type of term loan. With a revolving credit, the bank has made a formal commitment to the borrower to continue lending up to the maximum amount stated in the revolving credit agreement until the end of the agreement. Such agreements are usually established for a one-to-five-year period. Revolving credits have a variable interest rate (changing when the prime rate changes) that is computed on the daily balance of the amount loaned. So long as the borrower abides

---

[15] Base rates other than the prime rate are becoming common in loans to large corporations. The rates used include the rate on short-term certificates of deposit and LIBOR.

395

CHAPTER 11
**Raising intermediate and
long-term funds**

by the terms of the loan (restrictive provisions, etc.), the bank is legally obligated to continue lending. Often, at the end of the revolving credit agreement, there is a provision that the loan may be converted into an ordinary term loan with a regular repayment schedule. Revolving credits are heavily used by large corporations because of the flexibility they provide to the borrower.

Insurance Companies   Life insurance companies are another important source of long-term debt financing for business firms. Term loans, mortgages, and bonds with maturities of over ten years are the types of financing available, and these loans are often at a fixed interest rate. Besides the longer maturity, insurance company term loans differ from bank term loans in that a penalty is often assessed for payments made ahead of schedule. In addition, these loans usually carry a provision prohibiting the firm from prepaying by refinancing the loan in order to gain a lower interest rate. The insurance company does not want the firm to be able to repay the loan early by issuing new debt at a lower rate, because the insurance company would then only be able to invest the money at the lower rates. Since banks generally prefer shorter maturities than insurance companies, it is common for a bank and an insurance company to participate in the same loan. In a fifteen-year term loan, the principal payments made in the first seven years might go the bank, whereas the payments made in the last eight years would go to the insurance company. Of course, the interest would be paid on the balance owed to each party and the interest rate may differ on the two portions, with the rate paid to the bank often being lower than the rate paid to the insurance company.

High interest rates and inflation in the period 1979 to 1982 encouraged the insurance companies to shorten the maturities, to require variable-interest rates, and to add **equity kickers**. Equity kickers are such features as convertibility to common stock, warrants, or the right to share in the income in real estate being financed.

A particularly interesting example of a term loan is the $250 million term loan by Prudential Insurance Company to Chrysler Corporation in 1954. The maturity of the loan was 100 years, with the entire balance due in 2054. Chrysler "took down" the loan in four annual installments of $62.5 million each so that the full amount was not borrowed until 1958. There was a provision in the loan agreement that after 1964 either party could convert the loan into a twenty-year term loan to be repaid annually. The interest rate on the original loan was $3\frac{3}{4}$ percent; however, the rate would drop to $3\frac{1}{2}$ percent if the twenty-year option were taken. Needless to say, with much higher interest rates prevailing in 1964, the insurance company took the option as soon as it could and Chrysler had to begin paying off the loan. The loan was completely paid in 1984, thirty years after the initial borrowing.

Government Financing   The federal government provides financing assistance to business firms in several ways. One form of assistance is

396

PART 2
**The firm's investment,
financing, and dividend
decisions**

direct loans to businesses, for example, advance payments on defense contracts. For items with long lead times in development and production, these payments amount to intermediate-term financing.

The Small Business Administration (SBA) has the authority to make loans to small businesses in general and has special provisions for low-income and other economically disadvantaged persons. The SBA also may guarantee up to 90 percent of a loan made by a private lender (for example, a bank) to a qualified borrower. Loans made or guaranteed by the SBA are ordinarily repaid in monthly installments. Generally, the SBA prefers to guarantee a loan rather than to lend the money directly. Also, neither direct loans nor guarantees will be made unless the firm is unable to get loans on reasonable terms from private sources. Interest rates on SBA or SBA-guaranteed loans are usually below the rates on normal loans made by financial institutions.

A somewhat controversial source of government financial assistance, **industrial development bonds**, is provided by local governments. Industrial development bonds (IDBs), also called industrial revenue bonds, are issued through state or municipal agencies to raise funds which are used by private corporations to finance ventures (for example, $1 million for a McDonald's restaurant in Wetumpka, Alabama). The bonds are issued through investment bankers who acquire the issue through competitive bidding. The unique feature of these bonds is that the interest paid on the bonds is not taxable income to the bondholder and, therefore, the interest rate on the bonds is relatively low. Although the IDBs are issued under the auspices of a state or municipal agency, the bonds are the debt of the corporation for whom the IDBs have been issued. The governmental agency is not liable if the corporation defaults on the bonds. Often, the bond proceeds are used by the corporation to buy plant and equipment (frequently pollution control equipment). In other cases, the government agency will take the proceeds and buy an asset (for example, a factory) and then lease the factory to the corporation; the lease rentals are set so that they are just sufficient to pay off the IDBs. IDB financing has blossomed (exploded!) in recent years. The number of firms using IDBs is enormous and includes such companies as Boise Casade, K-Mart, McDonald's Corporation, Georgia Pacific, ITT, Monsanto, and Weyerhaeuser. This type of financing is of course controversial because it involves a tax subsidy to business (because of the tax exempt interest on the bond).

The use of IDBs grew from virtual nonexistence in 1970 to more than $125 billion outstanding by early 1986. The Tax Reform Act of 1986 sharply reduced the amount of such debt that may be issued, and it is likely that IDBs will be a significantly less important financing device in the future.

Small Business Investment Companies Small business investment companies (SBICs) are private firms licensed under the Small Business Investment Act of 1958 and organized to provide long-term debt and equity financing to small business. The SBA will provide long-term debt

397

CHAPTER 11
**Raising intermediate and
long-term funds**

at low interest rates to an SBIC in amounts that depend on the equity capital of the SBIC.

The SBIC may use its capital only to finance small businesses. The SBA has criteria (which it changes from time to time) for defining "small business." An SBIC may either lend the funds or purchase common stock of the small business. Stock accounts for slightly over half of the financing provided by SBICs. Frequently, the SBIC will purchase convertible debentures (unsecured bonds that can be converted into common stock). The SBIC may not extend financing to a single business in a total amount that exceeds 20 percent of the SBIC's equity capital.

SBICs receive very generous federal tax treatment. Any dividends received from its investments are exempt from the corporate income tax. A loss on its investments is treated by the firm as an ordinary loss (deductible from operating income) rather than as a capital loss. Furthermore, in determining their personal income taxes, the owners of the SBIC may deduct a loss on their investment in the SBIC as a deduction from ordinary income rather than as a capital loss.

In spite of the considerable government incentives to SBICs, they have had only varying success. The history of the SBICs suggest that finding good small business opportunities has generally been quite difficult and costly. Many of the investments made have been to firms which are close to the upper limit of the size requirements for a "small business." The result is that SBICs provide only a minor portion of the financing needs of small businesses.

Other Sources of Financing   In addition to those above, there are many corporations, partnerships, and individuals who provide financing for business firms. One type of financial institution, leasing companies, is discussed later in this book. Business finance companies provide one- to ten-year loans on purchases of equipment. The manufacturers of large, expensive equipment often offer long-term financing to purchasers. There are many venture capital firms and individuals who are willing to provide equity money to promising companies. The more organized groups (including many SBICs) often provide management consulting to a business in which they have invested money.

INTERNATIONAL SOURCES OF CAPITAL

A relatively recent economic development is the integration of the world's capital markets. Single-country firms, as well as multinational corporations, often look to neighboring or overseas countries to obtain their debt and equity financing.

Foreign Debt

Suppose that an Irish contact lens manufacturer floats a bond issue in the United States. The issue would be syndicated by American investment bankers and denominated (the interest and principle paid) in U.S. dollars. The manufacturer's offering would have to comply with all U.S. regulations for corporate bonds, and the bonds would be purchased primarily by U.S. investors. The proceeds would be exchanged for Irish

398

PART 2
**The firm's investment,
financing, and dividend
decisions**

pounds, and then distributed to the Irish lens maker. A bond issued in a foreign country and denominated in the foreign country's currency, as in this example, is called a **foreign bond**.

The motives for using foreign capital markets are cost, in the form of lower interest rates, and the size or depth of the overseas markets. Firms in small countries may be forced to issue their bonds in larger markets to obtain substantial amounts of capital. Switzerland has by far the world's largest foreign bond market (the United States ranks second), and the foreign bonds sold there are normally bought by nonresident investors. That is, both the issuer and purchaser of Swiss bonds are likely to be non-Swiss.

Another type of international debt issue is the **Eurobond**. The distinguishing feature of these bonds, compared with foreign bonds, is that Eurobonds are denominated in the issuer's currency instead of the currency of the country in which they are sold. More importantly, governments do not regulate Eurobonds as strictly as they do local currency bonds. For example, a U.S. firm that issues a dollar-denominated bond in France can bypass many French disclosure and regulatory requirements. In addition, the bond issue does not have to comply with the relatively strict SEC regulations because the security is not sold in the United States. The result is that both issuers and investors often prefer Eurobonds, which are cheaper, because of lower issuance costs, than either foreign or domestic bonds issues.

Foreign Equity

Like a foreign bond, **foreign equity** is obtained by the sale of shares in another country's stock market. Most of the world's major stock exchanges will list foreign company stocks if they meet the local regulatory and listing requirements. More than a hundred foreign companies, for example, are listed on the two major U.S. exchanges in New York. The British, German, and Japanese stock exchanges are also popular listings for foreign corporations. It is not uncommon for large corporations to sell their shares on several major world exchanges at the same time.

A firm, particularly a large firm in a small country, may need the market size and depth that a foreign exchange can offer. For example, in 1986 KLM, the Dutch airline, simultaneously issued new equity in Europe, the United States, and Japan to fund substantial financial requirements that the Dutch market alone could not have provided. Multinational corporations based in large countries also establish foreign listings as a marketing device to increase their international exposure and name recognition. In addition, financial managers often list their shares on several exchanges to decrease the firm's dependence on a single country's market or investor base.

SUMMARY

Debt, preferred stock, and new equity are external methods of financing the company, whereas retained earnings represent an internal source of funds. In terms of importance as a source of financing, retained earnings ranks first, debt second, and, far behind, common stock and preferred

399

CHAPTER 11
**Raising intermediate and
long-term funds**

*stock. Debt has priority over preferred stock, and preferred stock has
priority over common stock, in terms of a claim to income and a claim to
the firm's assets in the event of bankruptcy or liquidation.*

*Long-term debt and preferred stock are fixed-income securities since
they provide the investor with a promised series of future payments. The
interest and face value are specified for bonds, and the dividend rate and
par value are stated for preferred stock. Creditors have a prior claim to the
company's income and to the company's assets if the company liquidates.
The firm must pay the interest and the maturity value on its debt as agreed
upon in the bond contract, or the firm defaults and is subject to legal
action. In contrast, the firm is not obligated to pay dividends on the
preferred stock unless dividends are also paid to common stockholders.
Thus, rather than increasing the probability of bankruptcy, the issuance of
preferred stock lessens bankruptcy risk by raising the total assets of the
firm, thereby strengthening the capacity of the company to meet its debt
obligations.*

*The value of a bond is the discounted worth of the coupon (interest)
payments and maturity value. This discounted value may differ from the
bond's face or maturity value, depending upon the interest rate investors
use to discount the bond payments. The debt agreement, or indenture, may
include provisions to protect bondholders, such as the requirement that the
firm maintain a given working capital position, restrict dividends, refrain
from issuing further debt of the same class, or periodically retire part of
the debt issue. The tax deductibility of interest is a strong inducement to
use debt. This inducement does not exist for preferred stock, since
preferred dividends are not tax deductible to the paying corporation.*

*In addition to the conventional types of debt that are most commonly
used, there is a variety of rather novel debt forms. These forms include
income bonds, industrial development bonds, variable-rate (floating rate)
bonds, low-coupon bonds, put bonds, project financing, low-grade debt,
and swaps.*

*Preferred stock dividends must be paid before any dividends can be
paid on the common stock. Dividends are usually cumulative; that is,
before any dividends can be issued on the common stock, there must be
payment of all past unpaid preferred dividends. Preferred stock may be
participating, in which case preferred shareholders receive dividends on an
equal basis with common stockholders.*

*Financing with debt and preferred stock, rather than with additional
common stock, allows existing common stockholders to retain company
control and to retain claim to any extraordinary company profits. Debt has
the added advantage of interest tax deductibility, whereas preferred stock
does not involve the default risk associated with debt. The choice between
debt and preferred stock as a method of financing will depend upon the
volatility of the firm's income and upon its existing capital structure. Even
a relatively stable company may issue preferred stock rather than additional
debt if its existing debt burden is great.*

*Ownership of common stock entitles the stockholders to the following:
to receive the residual portion (after other investors, e.g., creditors, are*

400

PART 2
The firm's investment,
financing, and dividend
decisions

paid) of the firm's income; to elect the board of directors; in many cases, to purchase any new firm shares before they are sold to outsiders (preemptive right); to inspect the company's books; to transfer their shares; to be immune from liability to the corporation's creditors; and to own a residual claim to the firms' assets in the event of liquidation.

The election of the board of directors may be conducted under the majority rule or cumulative voting procedures. Under the majority rule, ownership of a majority of the shares ensures the power to elect the entire board, whereas under the cumulative voting method votes are distributed so that a significant minority is assured of representation on the board.

A publicly held corporation—that is, one that is owned by many stockholders—may have its stock traded on the over-the-counter market or on an organized exchange. Securities traded on an exchange are referred to as listed. Listing of a stock requires fulfillment of both exchange and SEC requirements.

A firm can raise money by public offerings of its securities and by private placement. A public securities issue is sold to many investors at terms announced in advance, and large issues must be registered with the SEC. Private placement involves direct negotiations between the issuing firm and a few investors and need not be registered with the SEC.

Investment bankers sell the new securities issues of companies to the public. Investment bankers provide several services including advice on the terms of an issue, underwriting, and selling the securities to investors. The underwriting service transfers the risk that the securities will not be purchased at their offering price from the firm to the investment banker. The banker buys the securities from the firm at one price and sells them to the public at a higher price. The difference between the two prices is the compensation to the investment bankers.

In the negotiations between the firm and the investment banker, setting an appropriate price for the securities is a critical problem. For debt issues, a rating is usually obtained from the rating agencies and the interest rate is based on the rates available in the market for debt with the same rating. Pricing a new issue of common stock is especially difficult. Several approaches are used, but the most popular involves estimating an appropriate price-earnings ratio for the stock.

An alternative to a public issue of securities is private placement. In this procedure, the firm may directly negotiate with a few investors or lenders, or it may employ the services of an investment banker to act as the firm's representative in the negotiations. The major advantages of private issues of securities are the lower issue costs and the elimination of delays due to registration requirements on public issues. The terms of private debt issues are also more easily modified later on. In recent years there has been an increase in the private placement of common stock, although debt issues still are the more likely candidates for this approach.

Commercial banks and life insurance companies are the major financial institutions offering long-term funds directly to businesses. Commercial banks offer term loans and mortgages, and life insurance

401

CHAPTER 11
**Raising intermediate and
long-term funds**

*companies offer term loans and bonds. Other sources include federal
agencies, local governments, finance companies, SBICs, and wealthy
individuals.*

*U.S. companies can raise both debt and capital abroad. A foreign bond
is a bond issued by a company in a foreign country and denominated in
the currency of the foreign country. For example, a bond issued by
General Electric in France and denominated in francs would be a foreign
bond. An alternative is a Eurobond, which is a bond denominated in the
issuing company's home currency but issued in another country; for
example, a bond issued by General Electric in France but denominated in
U.S. dollars. An advantage of Eurobonds is that they are not as closely
regulated as are bonds issued in the currency of the country in which they
are sold.*

*Companies frequently issue equity in other countries. Many U.S.
firms' stocks are listed on foreign stock exchanges, and numerous non-
U.S. companies have their stocks listed on U.S. exchanges. This
internationalization of equity markets significantly broadens the potential
capital sources for U.S. and foreign business firms.*

QUESTIONS

1 Compare and contrast debt with preferred stock as alternative
methods of financing.
2 What are the major differences between retained earnings and
other sources of financing?
3 Contrast the promise made to debtholders with the promise made
to stockholders.
4 Define bond, indenture, face value, and coupon rate.
5 Distinguish between debentures and mortgage bonds.
6 Of what value is the cumulative feature found in preferred stock
issues?
7 Itemize the rights of common stockholders. For each right that
you itemize, indicate whether it invariably attaches to common
stock or its inclusion depends on the terms of the stock offering,
which vary from one stock to another.
8 "As an investor in a firm's common stock, I am really interested
in only one thing, namely, that I get a rate of return consistent
with the level of risk that I assume. The management of a company cannot do anything more for me than that, so all this
business about the rights and privileges of stockholders mentioned
in this chapter is just so much baloney." Evaluate this statement.
9 "If an unprofitable company wishes to issue additional shares, no
matter what provisions are contained in the stock contract, the
shares are not likely to have much value." Comment on the validity of this statement.
10 Discuss the advantages and disadvantages of having a residual
claim on the income of the firm.
11 If a firm earns $200,000 and retains half of it, how much would

you expect the value of its shares to increase assuming there are no other influences except earnings retention on the value of the shares?

12 How does a public securities issue differ from a private securities issue?

13 What factors will be considered by the financial manager in choosing between a public issue of common stock and a private issue of common stock?

14 Would the following firms be more likely to use private placement or a public issue? Why? All the firms wish to issue long-term debt.

   a A local appliance dealer.

   b A medium-sized ($60 million annual sales) electronics manufacturer.

   c An electric utility company serving customers in three states.

   d A large electronics manufacturer whose research staff has made a major technological breakthrough. Financing is needed to exploit this new technology as rapidly as possible.

15 What are the distinctive characteristic of an underwritten securities issue as compared with other methods of raising money?

16 Why would a corporation use a negotiated underwriting rather than obtain competitive bids?

17 How is an investment banker compensated for services provided to the corporation?

18 In what ways do governments aid businesses in obtaining financing?

PROJECTS

1 Obtain from a stockbrocker a prospectus for a new bond issue. Examine the provisions concerning priority of payment, collateral (if applicable), restrictions on the firm (on dividends, working capital position, etc.), and any other matters discussed in this chapter.

2 Obtain from your state's secretary of state (or other appropriate official) information on the requirements for forming a corporation in your state and the rights and privileges of stockholders. Compare the provisions of your state law with those outlined in this chapter.

3 Obtain the prospectus for a recent security issue (may be provided by the instructor). Review the prospectus. What types of information does it contain. Determine the following:

   a The issuing firm and the investment banking firm

   b The type of security and the terms (price or interest rate of the issue)

   c What type of issue it is (negotiated, etc.)

   d How much the issue is costing the firm (underwriting fees, etc.), and the part of the cost represented by the investment banking fee

DP1 Find the value of a bond that matures in eighteen years, has a face value of $1000 and a coupon rate of 11 percent, and pays interest annually. Bonds of similar quality and maturity have a yield to maturity of 12 percent.

SOLUTION TO DP1:

$$V = \frac{\$110}{(1 + .12)} + \frac{\$110}{(1 + .12)^2} + \cdots + \frac{\$110}{(1 + .12)^{18}} + \frac{\$1000}{(1 + .12)^{18}}$$

$$= \$110(P/A, 12\%, 18) + \$1000(P/F, 12\%, 18)$$

$$= \$110(7.2497) + \$1000(.1300)$$

$$= \$927.47$$

DP2 Caracas Snacks is planning a capital expansion next year in response to the rapidly increasing demand for its products. It estimates that it will need $15 million and plans to issue preferred stock to finance the expansion. The preferred stock will have a par value of $100 and a 10 percent dividend. Caracas does not plan to retire the preferred stock in the foreseeable future. It has found that similar issues of preferred stock (same risk and maturity characteristics) are yielding 13 percent. Assume that flotation costs are zero.

a What price can Caracas expect to receive for a share of the preferred stock?

b How many shares must it issue to finance the planned expansion?

c What are the advantages of a preferred issue over a bond issue?

d Answer *a* and *b* if flotation costs were 5 percent of the total proceeds received from the preferred stock investors.

SOLUTION TO DP2:

a Dividend $= .10(\$100) = \$10$

$$\text{Price} = \frac{\text{dividend}}{\text{market yield}} = \frac{\$10}{.13} = \$76.92$$

b To raise $15 million by selling preferred stock at $76.92 per share, Caracas must issue:

$$\frac{\$15,000,000}{\$76.92} = 195,008 \text{ (rounded) shares}$$

c Nonpayment of dividends to preferred stock does not place the firm in default. By issuing preferred stock, Caracas is not increasing the debt in its capital structure; if it believes it already has the right amount of debt, the use of preferred stock may be a good choice.

d The price per share received for the preferred stock is unaffected by the flotation costs assuming the $10 per share dividend and the 13 percent required yield. However, the answer to *b* is changed. Caracas receives only 95 percent of the proceeds, and therefore more than $15 million of perferred stock must be sold. That is,

Proceeds to Caracas = .95 (gross proceeds) = $15,000,000

Gross proceeds   = $15,789,474

The number of shares that must be sold equals:

$$\text{Number of shares} = \frac{\$15,789,474}{\$76.92} = 205,271 \text{ (rounded)}$$

DP3   If Ginger Seasonings issues 700,000 new shares of common stock to existing shareholders at a price of $30 a share, what would you expect the price of the common shares to be if it was $45 a share before the issue? There were 2,300,000 shares outstanding before the new shares were issued.

SOLUTION TO DP3:
Value of shares
  outstanding: 2,300,000 shares × 45 per share   = $103,500,000

Value of new
  shares issued: 700,000 shares × $30 per share = $21,000,000

Total value of all shares: $124,500,000
Total number of shares: 3,000,000
Value per share: ($124,500,000/3,000,000 shares) = $41.50

PROBLEMS

1   Morales, Inc., is planning to issue twenty-year bonds with a face value of $1000 per bond to finance expansion of its plant. The bonds pay interest once per year. The market rate of interest (yield to maturity) on bonds of the same risk and maturity as the proposed Morales issue is 14 percent.
  a   If Morales issues the bonds with a 16 percent coupon, what price will one bond sell for? With a 14 percent coupon? With an 8 percent coupon? [Partial ans.: Price with a 16 percent coupon = $1132.50]
  b   Provide an explanation for your answers in *a* above.
2   Primabella Fabrics is planning a capital expansion next year to meet the increasing demand for its products. It estimates that it will need $10 million and plans to issue preferred stock to finance the expansion. The preferred stock will have a par value of $100 and an 11 percent dividend. Primabella does not plan to retire the preferred stock in the foreseeable future. It has found that similar issues of preferred stock (same risk and maturity characteristics) are yielding 12 percent. Assume that flotation costs are zero.

405

CHAPTER 11
**Raising intermediate and
long-term funds**

a What price can Primabella expect to receive for a share of the preferred stock?

b How many shares must it issue to finance the planned expansion?

c What are the advantages of a preferred issue over a bond issue?

3 Below is the balance sheet of Rose Foods, Inc., before it issued 200,000 shares of new common stock at a price of $30 each. The underwriting fees aggregated 5 percent of the total sale. Show the net effect on the company's balance sheet of the sale of the new stock. Assume that the new stock has a par value of $5 per share.

Assets	
Cash	$ 7,000,000
Other assets	56,000,000
Total assets	$63,000,000
Liabilities and owners' equity	
Liabilities	$25,000,000
Owners' equity	
Common stock ($5)	1,000,000
Paid-in surplus	5,000,000
Retained earnings	32,000,000
Total liabilities and owners' equity	$63,000,000

4 If Milton Buttons, Inc., issues 200,000 new shares of common stock to existing shareholders at a price of $25 a share, what would you expect the price of the common shares to be if it was $35 a share before the issue? There are currently 600,000 shares outstanding. Show all calculations.

5 The Enterprise Company plans to raise $2 million through its first public stock issue. The total market value of stock after issue is estimated to be $8 million. There are presently 100,000 shares outstanding held by the Kirk family.

a How many new shares must be issued to raise $2 million? [Ans.: 33,333 shares]

b What is the estimated price per share of the stock after the issue is sold?

c The firm's investment bankers believe that a desirable initial price per share for a firm such as Enterprise is $20. They recommend that, prior to issuing the new stock, the old stock should be "split" with the current shareholders to receive additional shares of stock in proportion to their current holdings. If Jim Kirk owns 50 shares, how many new shares would Jim receive if the investment banker's recommendation were followed?

406

PART 2
**The firm's investment,
financing, and dividend
decisions**

6 Using the data in Table 11-5, estimate the dollar costs that would be incurred by a firm for issuing the following securities:

a $2 million in debt
b $12 million in debt
c $2 million in preferred stock
d $2 million in common stock
e $12 million in common stock

The ⬛ symbol indicates that all or a significant part of the problem can be solved using the *Computer Models* software that accompanies this text.

In 1977, Philip Wilber, ignoring the conventional wisdom that drug stores could only make money selling products at high gross margins, opened a discount drug store in Worthington, Ohio. Eight years later, Drug Emporium had expanded to a chain of 90 stores with annual sales of over $140 million.

Former IBM engineers David G. Morton, Rod Linton, and David Bailey came up with a unique disk drive offering increased storage capabilities. When IBM told them it wasn't interested, the three went out on their own and in 1980 founded Iomega Corp. In 1985, despite a disk-drive industry slump, Iomega had earnings of $15 million on sales of $115.52 million.

Crucial to these entrepreneurs' success was venture capital financing provided by people typically uninterested in actively managing a company but willing to provide financial, marketing, accounting, or technical advice. In return for their money and counsel, these venture capitalists receive a significant percentage of the firm's common stock. If the new business succeeds, the stock will be worth much more than the initial investment. Most ventures do no better than to survive marginally. Indeed, a large percentage of firms completely fail after a few years, with the stockholders receiving little or nothing. The potential for a high return on successful ventures compensates the venture capitalists for the not-so-small chance of making nothing or even losing all their investment.

SELLING AN IDEA TO THE VENTURE CAPITALIST

Venture capitalists prefer opportunities with high growth potential. This has traditionally meant high- and new-technology businesses. In fact, the two largest recipients of venture capital during the early 1980s were the computer and health care industries. There is also an increasing emphasis on nontechnology service firms with innovative approaches to new or existing markets. A neighborhood dry cleaner or bakery would not receive funding. But a *new* type of dry-cleaning establishment or bakery that with capital and management might in several years establish itself in neighborhoods all over the country could very well qualify.

Critical in attracting venture capital are a thorough business plan clearly showing the entrepreneur's understanding of the proposed venture and a credible management team knowledgeable in finance, marketing, sales, R & D (research and development), and operations. Venture capitalists also prefer that the company's founders have a personal financial stake (investment) in the new venture. The investment is a tangible signal of the founders' faith in the venture's potential. It also provides an incentive to make the business succeed.

New firms at any of several stages of growth often approach venture capitalists for financing. The "blueprint" stage involves developing a new product or service. Next comes the "startup" stage, at which point the company is organized and the initial sale of its product or service begun. Firms with a short operating history, but in need of additional capital to continue their growth, often approach venture capitalists for "second round" financing. At this stage, the firm may not yet be profitable. Firms with longer operating histories, but which are still small, may also seek venture capital

408

PART 2
**The firm's investment,
financing, and dividend
decisions**

for "expansion" financing, or if the firm is in financial difficulty, "turnaround" financing. Finally, a small company wishing to grow through acquisition may seek "buy-out" financing.

Venture capital is typically invested in amounts of at least $1 million. As a result, most new businesses do not qualify. Roughly 70 percent of new companies still get at least part of their financing from friends and relatives. Another alternative for an entrepreneur starting small is an "angel." Angels are private investors, often members of investment clubs, who put up the first $20,000 to $200,000 to get a business off the ground. An entrepreneur starting out on a larger scale should carefully study the venture capital community to avoid wasting time, and credibility, by knocking on the doors of firms that have no interest in what the entrepreneur has to offer.

CHOOSING A VENTURE CAPITALIST

There are several criteria an entrepreneur should apply in choosing a venture capitalist (if more than one choice is available). Geographical location is one. There are definite advantages to being located in an area with a large number of venture capital firms. Geographic proximity of the venture capitalist and entrepreneur is important because it gives the financing source a closer watch over the investment and gives the entrepreneur easier access to the venture capitalist's management advice. A disproportionate number of venture capitalists and startup firms specializing in high- and new-technology fields are located in the Boston and San Francisco metropolitan areas. New York, Massachusetts, California, Illinois (Chicago

area), and Texas are the top states in number of venture capital firms.

Stage of development is also an important consideration in determining which venture capitalist to approach. Some venture capitalists, for example, are interested only in blueprints, while others prefer companies with proven track records.

A third very important factor is the venture capitalist's ability and willingness to provide expertise to the project. This usually requires that the venture capitalist have broad experience in the same kind of business, preferably with some successes as well as failures.

WHO ARE THE VENTURE CAPITALISTS?

Originally, most venture capital came from venture capital firms organized by wealthy individuals. Relative newcomers to the venture capital game are investment bankers, commercial banks, and large corporations. These sources usually provide financing to new firms for two reasons: to make a profit on the venture itself and to earn profits by later providing services to the new firm if it succeeds.

Investment bankers are involved in several aspects of the venture capital market. Although they primarily act as intermediaries in bringing together capital providers and entrepreneurs, investment bankers also invest venture capital on their own account, on behalf of wealthy individuals, or as the managers of funds. In addition, they are interested in helping firms meet subsequent financing needs. If the firm ever reaches the stage of issuing securities to the public, the investment banker who helped out initially expects to earn additional returns by handling the firm's new issues.

Many commercial banks, such as Bank of America, First National of

409

CHAPTER 11
**Raising intermediate and
long-term funds**

Boston, and First National of Chicago, have established small business investment companies (SBICs) to provide venture capital. SBICs, which can also be founded by entities other than commercial banks, are licensed by the United States government and must provide management advice in addition to financing. SBICs are usually not interested in blueprint or startup situations. The SBICs bank founder seeks a profit from providing both venture capital and banking services to the company.

Large industrial corporations—including General Electric, Exxon, Texaco, Kodak, 3M, and Xerox—are also active in venture financing. In addition to a high return on their investment, these firms hope to gain access at an early stage to new ideas and technologies useful in their regular operations. In exchange for financing, these firms frequently require a majority ownership position in the new company.

Insurance companies and investment management companies are frequent providers of venture capital. Generally, these investors are passive. They do not take an active role in the company and are interested only in firms with an operating history.

"Finders" are consultants, accountants, lawyers, investment bankers, and others who use their professional contacts to bring entrepreneurs together with the providers of venture capital. For a price, generally ranging from 2 percent to over 10 percent of the principal amount of the financing, finders will expedite an entrepreneur's search for a venture capitalist.

There are also a few foreign venture capital firms—mostly from Europe and Japan—investing in the United States. Some cities and states, such as Buffalo, Alaska, California, and Massachusetts, have established taxpayer-financed venture firms and research/industrial parks to aid small businesses. Even the average investor can be a venture capitalist. Many SBICs and formerly private venture capital firms have mutual funds. These funds diversify risk by spreading the investment dollars among a variety of cash hungry businesses. Shares in these funds are primarily traded in the over-the-counter market.

TRENDS

The venture capital industry is undergoing basic change. In contrast to the rapid growth in the early 1980s, outlays by venture capital firms to entrepreneurial operations during 1984–1987 remained constant at around $3 billion per year. And, instead of backing blueprints or startups, many venture capitalists are now emphasizing expansion financing or investments in companies that plan to grow through mergers and acquisitions or leveraged buyouts. A recent study found a trend away from first-round financing (blueprints or startups) and an increase in expansion and buy-out financings. It also revealed a shift from high- and new-technology investments to service industries.

Several reasons have been suggested to explain these changes, including the maturation of the industry, revised federal tax laws, and the prolonged computer industry slump. Initially, the venture capital business was a collection of small private firms often run by brilliant, idiosyncratic individuals with years of hands-on business management experience. Today, with the entry of pension funds, investment banks, and insurance companies, the business has developed into a large-scale, highly institutionalized industry.

New capitalizations have grown from around $30 million in 1977 to

410

PART 2
**The firm's investment,
financing, and dividend
decisions**

roughly $3 billion per year in the early 1990s—a hundred-fold increase. As the money flowed in, the game changed. New entrants with large funds to manage often lacked the time and experience to provide the managerial advice entrepreneurs needed. Consequently, instead of backing the development of new companies, many are emphasizing late-round financing or investments in companies that plan to grow through acquisition.

Before the Tax Reform Act of 1986, the capital gains from venture capital investments held over six months were subject to a maximum tax rate of 20 percent. Under the new law, profits are taxed as regular personal income at a rate as high as 33 percent. This change has affected some venture capital sources but not others. The higher personal tax rates reduce the incentive to invest for high bracket investors. Some sources of venture capital, such as pension funds, are tax exempt and are therefore not directly impacted by tax rate changes.

CHAPTER TWELVE

FINANCING DECISIONS AND CAPITAL STRUCTURE

In this chapter we examine the problems faced by a financial manager in deciding how to obtain the money needed to finance a given capital budget. We look at the four major financing sources used by firms—debt, preferred stock, common stock, and retained earnings—and examine the methods used to plan a complete financing program.

First we present the factors that should be considered by the financial manager in choosing among financing sources. Then we show the impact of alternative financing plans on the returns and risks to the firm's owners. The problem of long-run policy as to financing sources is examined, and we discuss how the policy chosen affects the cost of capital used to evaluate investment opportunities. This chapter covers the basic financing decisions that must be made by the financial manager and the implications of those decisions for capital budgeting.

ANALYZING EXTERNAL FINANCING METHODS

Financial managers base their financing decisions on the firm's forecasted capital budget. The period of time covered and the amount of care taken in developing this forecast will depend greatly on the size of the firm and its particular situation. A small firm whose present plans are only to acquire a new delivery truck may not do more than estimate when and at what price the truck is to be acquired. A large firm embarking on a major expansion program may forecast its financing needs for several years. For the purposes of this chapter, we assume that the financial manager has undertaken this forecasting-planning process and has developed a clear picture of how much money is needed, during the next year, plus some idea of the likely financing requirements of the firm in the more distant future.[1] The manager knows what sources of financing are currently available and the prices, interest rates, and other characteristics of each source. A critical part of the financial manager's job is deciding on and arranging for external financing. We will discuss

---

[1] Forecasting financial requirements is obviously an important problem for the manager, and methods for doing this are provided in Chap. 16.

the problem of choosing among debt, preferred stock, and common stock first, assuming that external financing is needed. Later we will examine the use of retained earnings.

FRICTO Evaluation

A convenient framework for analyzing alternative financing choices is provided by FRICTO, which is an acronym for:

F = Flexibility
R = Risk
I = Income
C = Control
T = Timing
O = Other

The relative importance of each factor depends on the company's particular situation. The manager should be sure that all the relevant factors have been considered.

The first factor, *flexibility*, refers to the impact of current financing decisions on the future financing options available to the firm. The use of a particular financing method today may narrow the choices that will be available in the future. For example, a debt issue today may impose restrictions on the firm that will make it difficult to issue additional debt next year, forcing the company to resort to equity next year if external financing is required at that time. For a firm that is expected to need additional external financing next year, the relevant decision may not be "stock versus debt" but "debt now and stock next year versus stock now and a choice next year." In addition to needing money to finance expected new investments, companies also want to have a financing reserve (borrowing capacity) to be able to take advantage of unexpected opportunities and to withstand unexpected losses due to strikes, lawsuits, business downturns, etc. The requirement that a firm must meet scheduled interest and principal payments on its debt issues means that debt must be limited in order to maintain a reserve. Financing through stock now may be necessary to allow the firm to be able to borrow later to meet unexpected needs.[2]

Risk and *income* are closely related and so important that we devote much of the remainder of this chapter to their evaluation. *Control* of a firm is a concern of stockholders. If the majority of a firm's stock is presently owned by relatively few stockholders who therefore have control, the controlling owners may be concerned about the impact of financing choices on their ability to maintain this control. They may be unwilling to issue common stock if the amount of money needed would require bringing in so many new stockholders that control would be lost. For large firms with many stockholders, control is rarely a significant factor in the financing decision.

---

[2] The importance and assessment of flexibility is developed in depth by Gordon Donaldson, *Strategy for Financial Mobility* (R. D. Irwin: Homewood, Illinois, 1971).

Timing has become an increasingly important factor in the past decade as the stock and bond markets have undergone extreme fluctuations. There have been periods when only financially strong firms were able to issue bonds easily and other periods when relatively weak firms were able to issue debt at moderate cost. Financial managers speak of "windows" of opportunity in the market for certain types of securities. Similarly, market trends can affect the desirability of issuing stock. The main point is that the state of the capital markets is an important factor in making financing choices.

Other factors besides flexibility, risk, income, control, and timing must also be considered. Each situation is different but some of these other considerations might be:

1 *Collateral values:* What assets are available for use in securing debt?
2 *Flotation costs:* How much will it cost to issue securities?
3 *Speed:* How quickly can money be raised?
4 *Exposure:* Will issuing securities now facilitate issuing them in the future because investors may become more familiar with the firm? Will a stock issue create a broader market for current owners of the firm's stock and raise its value?

Many of these other considerations are discussed in more depth in this and later chapters.

The FRICTO approach to the evaluation of financing decisions does not provide answers. It does provide a systematic approach to making informed decisions. Let's now look at the two big factors of income and risk.

Impact on Shareholder Income

To see how the choice of financing affects the returns to current owners, let's look at an example. Auric Mining Company is planning the development of a mine and processing plant on land owned by the firm. At the present time this land is the firm's only asset. The development costs are $1 million to be paid in the first year. The expected cash flow before taxes from the operation is $480,000 per year. We will assume that all cash flow from the mine will be paid out in taxes, dividends, and interest and that the cash flow is expected to continue forever. Suppose that the owners of Auric don't have any money of their own to finance this venture and that the firm does not have any cash. The $1 million in development costs must be raised by borrowing the money, by issuing preferred or common stock, or by some combination of these methods. We will look at common stock financing first so that we have a basis for the contrast with debt and preferred stock financing.

Before proceeding with the Auric Mining example, we should point out that an important difference between debt and stock (common or preferred stock) is that interest on debt is tax deductible to the corporation whereas dividends on stock are not. This corporate tax effect appears in many of the numerical illustrations below. Since the underlying concepts are the same regardless of the corporate tax rate, to keep

414

PART 2
**The firm's investment,
financing, and dividend
decisions**

the illustrations simple and easy to follow we will usually assume a corporate tax rate of 50 percent, and we ignore depreciation and depletion allowances in computing taxable income. Since World War II, the maximum marginal corporate tax rate has varied from 39 percent (current maximum) to as high as 85.5 percent.

Common Stock   If common stock is issued, the new stockholders will share in the future cash flows. Their share will depend on the percentage ownership they obtain in the firm in return for the $1 million they will be investing in it. The percentage ownership will be a bargain struck between the present owners, as represented by the firm's management, and the investors. In general, the investors will demand at least that the expected rate of return to them will equal the rate of return available in the financial markets on investments of comparable risk. As we know from Chapter 6, the relationship between risk and return in the financial markets is shown by the security market line. If the financial manager acts in the best interests of the *present* owners of Auric, no greater rate of return should be provided to the *new* stockholders than that minimum required. Suppose the required rate of return is 12 percent per year. Then to raise $1 million, stock investors must expect to receive 12 percent per year on $1 million, which is $120,000 per year on the average. The $120,000 represents 50 percent of the aftertax cash flow expected from the mine. Under these conditions, new shareholders must obtain 50 percent of the stock of the company in return for their investment of $1 million. The present owners will be left with the remaining 50 percent of the stock and an expected cash return of $120,000 per year. These values are shown in Exhibit 12-1.

Preferred Stock   Preferred stock may be issued to finance the mine. The dividend rate that must be provided to preferred stockholders will reflect the risks borne by them. Since the preferred stock of a company is usually a less risky security than the common stock, let's assume that the required dividend rate is 10 percent. Preferred dividends on a $1 million preferred stock issue would therefore be $100,000, and the original owners would receive $140,000, as shown in Exhibit 12-1. Under this financing plan, the original owners expect to receive $20,000 more in dividends than if common stock is issued because the rate of return required by the preferred stockholders is less than that required by new investors in common stock.

Debt   Suppose that the $1 million could be raised by borrowing the money at an interest rate of 8 percent per year. Lenders generally do not require as high an interest rate as stockholders because the risk is less. Interest would amount to 8 percent of the $1 million borrowed, or $80,000 per year. The expected aftertax cash flow available to the original owners would therefore be $200,000, as shown in Exhibit 12-1. The original owners would therefore expect to receive $80,000 per year more in income if debt financing were used instead of common stock ($200,000 − $120,000) and $60,000 more if preferred were used ($200,000 − $140,000). These income differences are due to two factors. First, the interest rate on the debt (8 percent) is lower than the rate of return required by new shareholders (12 percent) or by preferred stockholders (10 percent). Of the $80,000 difference between debt and common stock, $40,000 is due to the difference in rates (4 percent of $1 million). Of the $60,000 difference between debt and preferred, $20,000 is due to the difference in rates (2 percent of $1 million). Second, the interest on the debt is tax deductible, and this accounts for the remaining $40,000 difference for both common and preferred stock. When debt financing is used, we see from Exhibit 12-1 that the firm pays only $200,000 in taxes instead of the $240,000 in taxes paid with preferred and common stock financing. Therefore, the original owners benefit both from the lower interest rate on the debt and the tax deductibility of interest.

EBIT-EPS Analysis

An obvious question at this point in the analysis is what happens if the mine doesn't earn $480,000 before interest and taxes each year? We need to examine other levels of earnings. A common method used to evaluate the impact of financing decisions on shareholder income is to analyze the relationship between earnings before interest and taxes (EBIT) and earnings per share (EPS). Since the original stockholders will own the same number of shares regardless of the method of financing, EPS (earnings to common divided by the number of outstanding shares) is

---

EXHIBIT 12-1

The impact of debt and stock financing on expected income

	Common stock	Preferred stock	Debt
Before-tax cash flow	$ 480,000	$ 480,000	$ 480,000
Interest	0	0	(80,000)
Taxable income	$ 480,000	$ 480,000	$ 400,000
Taxes (at 50%)	(240,000)	(240,000)	(200,000)
Earnings after taxes	$ 240,000	$ 240,000	$ 200,000
Preferred dividends	0	100,000	0
Earnings to common	$ 240,000	$ 140,000	$ 200,000
Income to new stockholders ...	$ 120,000	0	0
Income to original owners	$ 120,000	$ 140,000	$ 200,000

Common stock financing:	$1 million raised from new stockholders, in return for 50% of the company's shares
Preferred stock financing:	$1 million raised from investors with a dividend rate of 10% per year
Debt financing:	$1 million raised from lenders with an interest rate of 8% per year

416

PART 2
**The firm's investment,
financing, and dividend
decisions**

directly related to the income belonging to the original owners (EPS ×
number of original shares = original owners' income). The level of EBIT
varies from year to year depending on how successful the firm's operations are. The analysis involves taking each financing method proposed
and plotting on a graph the EPS that would result from a given value of
EBIT. The relationship between EPS and EBIT for each financing
method is a straight line. When the lines representing each method are
plotted on the same graph, we can compare them. To see how this
works. let's use the Auric Mining data in a general procedure. (In the
Auric example, EBIT = before-tax cash flow.)

1 We need information on the existing financing (all common stock
   in this example) used by the firm and related data:
   a The tax rate (50 percent)
   b Interest per year on outstanding debt (none)
   c Preferred dividends (none)
   d Number of shares outstanding (50,000)
2 We need the terms of the alternative financing methods:
   a Debt: interest on debt (8 percent on $1 million = $80,000)
   b Preferred stock: preferred dividends (10 percent of $1 million =
      $100,000)
   c Common stock: number of shares to be issued (50,000)[3]
3 Since the graphical relationship between EPS and EBIT for any
   given financing method is a straight line, only two points on the
   graph are needed to completely determine the line.[4] Therefore,
   given the above information in 2, we need to compute earnings per
   share at two different levels of earnings before interest and taxes
   for each financing method. Choice of the two EBIT values is not
   critical; however, they are usually chosen to be representative of
   levels of EBIT that the firm might have. Calculations of EPS at
   EBIT = $200,000 and EBIT = $600,000 are shown in Exhibit 12-2.
   The results of the calculations are plotted on a graph (Figure 12-1).

   Figure 12-1 shows that at EBIT levels of over $160,000, the debt
issue provides higher values for EPS than does common stock, whereas
when EBIT is below $160,000, the common stock issue is better. This
number can be verified by calculation (recommended as an exercise).
Debt provides higher EPS than preferred stock at all levels of EBIT.

---

[3] Since new shareholders must own 50 percent of the firm according to the earlier
analysis, they must acquire the same number of shares as held by the original owners. The
50,000 figure for the number of shares held by the original owners is simply assumed; from
that assumption the number that must be issued follows.

[4] The relationship between EPS and EBIT can be expressed as

$$\text{EPS} = \frac{(\text{EBIT} - \text{interest})(1 - \text{tax rate}) - \text{preferred dividends}}{\text{total number of shares outstanding}}$$

The financing method chosen fixes the values for interest, the number of shares, and
preferred dividends. So long as the tax rate is a constant, this relationship is a straight line.

Preferred stock provides higher EPS than common at levels of EBIT greater than $400,000.

Financial Leverage   Figure 12-1 illustrates the concept of **financial leverage**.[5] Financial leverage refers to the response of shareholders income to changes in EBIT and is created by debt or preferred stock financing with fixed interest and dividend payments. If the firm is financed entirely with common stock, a given percentage change in EBIT results in the same percentage change in EPS. A 10 percent increase in EBIT results in a 10 percent increase in EPS. However, the use of debt or preferred stock financing increases the responsiveness of EPS to changes in EBIT. For example, when EBIT is $400,000, both common stock and preferred stock financing provide earnings of $2 per share (EPS = $2). A 50 percent increase in EBIT to $600,000 increases EPS with common stock financing to $3, also a 50 percent increase. If preferred stock is used, a 50 percent increase in EBIT leads to an EPS of $4, a 100 percent increase. Financial leverage works both ways, down as well as up. The percentage reduction in EPS is greater than a given percentage of reduction in EBIT when debt or preferred stock financing is used. We will look more explicitly at the negative effects of leverage when we consider risk.

---

[5] It is also referred to as "trading on equity." The British use the term "gearing."

EXHIBIT 12-2
Calculation of the impact of financing methods on earnings per share

	Common stock		Preferred stock		Debt	
EBIT	$ 200,000	$ 600,000	$ 200,000	$ 600,000	$200,000	$ 600,000
Interest (old debt)	0	0	0	0	0	0
Interest (new debt)	0	0	0	0	(80,000)	(80,000)
Taxable income	$ 200,000	$ 600,000	$ 200,000	$ 600,000	$120,000	$ 520,000
Taxes	(100,000)	(300,000)	(100,000)	(300,000)	(60,000)	(260,000)
Earnings after taxes	$ 100,000	$ 300,000	$ 100,000	$ 300,000	$ 60,000	$ 260,000
Preferred dividends (old)	0	0	0	0	0	0
Preferred dividends (new)	0	0	100,000	100,000	0	0
Earnings to common (1)	$ 100,000	$ 300,000	$ 0	$ 200,000	$ 60,000	$ 260,000
Number of old shares	50,000	50,000	50,000	50,000	50,000	50,000
Number of new shares	50,000	50,000	0	0	0	0
Total common shares (2)	100,000	100,000	50,000	50,000	50,000	50,000
EPS [(1)/(2)]	$1.00	$3.00	$0	$4.00	$1.20	$5.20

418

PART 2
**The firm's investment,
financing, and dividend
decisions**

Businesses that have a lot of debt outstanding relative to their assets are often said to be "highly levered," since shareholder income tends to be more variable for such firms than for firms using less debt. A more precise measure of the degree of financial leverage than the proportion of debt used is the ratio of interest payments to EBIT (assuming no preferred stock is used).[6] Lenders and financial managers use this ratio (or

---

[6] The degree of financial leverage can be expressed more generally as a multiplier of the percentage change in EBIT; that is,

Percentage change in EPS = leverage multiplier × percentage change in EBIT

The leverage multiplier can be calculated from the leverage ratio as follows:

$$\text{Leverage ratio} = \frac{\text{interest} + [\text{preferred dividends}/(1 - \text{tax rate})]}{\text{EBIT}}$$

Notice that this ratio equals interest/EBIT when there are no preferred dividends.

$$\text{Leverage multiplier} = \frac{1}{1 - \text{leverage ratio}}$$

For example, with debt financing, interest is $80,000; at an EBIT of $480,000, the leverage ratio equals .167, and the multiplier is 1.2. A 10 percent increase in EBIT from $480,000 will therefore increase EPS by 12 percent.

FIGURE 12-1

*Impact of alternative
financing methods on
EPS.*

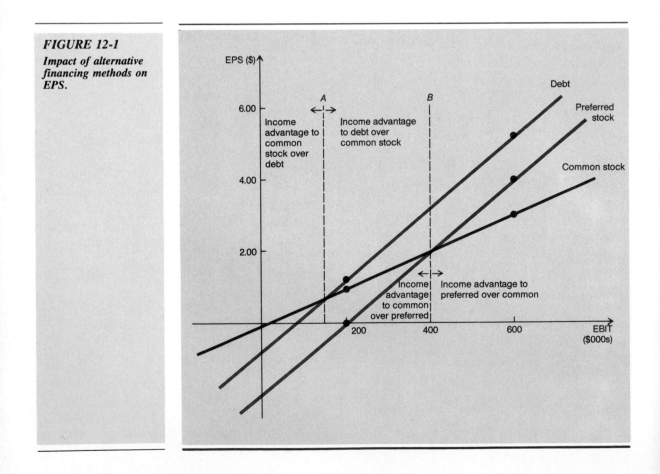

its reciprocal) in evaluating the use of debt by the firm. Additional measures are discussed in Chapter 14.

Impact on
Shareholder Risk

Although debt and preferred stock financing provide income advantages over common stock if the firm does well, they increase the risk if it does not. The most risky financing from the viewpoint of the stockholders is debt because interest and principal payments are contractual obligations of the firm. Preferred dividends need not be paid when earnings are poor, and the money raised from preferred stock financing need never be repaid. Since debt offers the greatest income advantage and the greatest risk, we will focus our discussion here on the choice of debt relative to common stock. We consider preferred stock again later.

There are two types of risk to the owners of a firm, business risk and financial risk. Financial risk depends on the method of financing whereas business risk depends on the nature of the firm's operations. Business risk is directly related to the uncertainty as to the firm's ability to earn a satisfactory rate of return on its investments over the long run. It involves uncertainty as to the demand for the firm's products and the prices of the products. It is related to the degree of control the firm has over its costs, and how readily its assets can be converted into cash if the need arises. Business risk depends on the quality of the firm's management and the ability of management to react to unforeseen events. Fundamentally then, business risk involves uncertainty as to the long-run profitability of the firm (EBIT) and its investments and to the potential value of the firm in liquidation, if it cannot be operated at a profit.

If there were no business risks, the firm could finance as it pleased without affecting the risk to its owners and without paying a high interest rate. If the Auric Mining Company, its owners, and its creditors knew for sure that the mine would produce $480,000 per year forever, there would be absolutely no risk to the owners from borrowing $1 million at an interest rate of 8 percent per year since the $80,000 interest payments could always be paid from the earnings of the mine. If desired, the firm could be completely out of debt in a few years by paying the aftertax cash flow to the lenders until the $1 million debt was paid off. However, the returns from business investments are never certain. Let's look at Auric's financing problem when there is business risk in the mining investment.

To keep the problem simple and to isolate the source of risk, suppose that the costs of mining and the amount of product (gold) to be mined are known for sure. However, the price is uncertain. There are three possible prices.[7] At the low price the mine will provide only $60,000 per year

---

[7] A more realistic assumption that provides the same results is that the "prices" are average price levels for the product. It is not necessary to assume that the price of gold will be constant at, for example, $400 per ounce. The actual price could vary over time, say, between $350 to $450 while averaging $400.

420

PART 2
**The firm's investment,
financing, and dividend
decisions**

in before-tax cash flow net of the costs of mining the gold. At the middle price, the mine will provide $480,000 per year, and at the high price the mine will provide $600,000 per year. The probability of the high price is .35, the probability of the middle price is .55, and the probability of the low price is .10. The expected cash flow *before taxes* is therefore

$$\text{Expected cash flow} = .35(\$600,000) + .55(\$480,000) + .10(\$60,000)$$

$$= \$480,000$$

which equals the before-tax cash flow used in Exhibit 12-1.

If high or middle prices are obtained, there is no problem with debt financing. We can see from Figure 12-1 that the income benefits of debt financing are substantial for EBIT of $480,000 and $600,000. However, there is a 10 percent chance that only $60,000 per year will be generated from the mine due to the low price of gold. If the firm must pay $80,000 in interest on the debt, sufficient money is not available from the mine's operations to meet this obligation. So what will happen? The answer in practice will depend on several things. Auric's owners might continue to operate the mine for a while, paying the $20,000 per year deficit ($80,000 − $60,000) out of their own pockets if they have hopes that prices will increase in the future. Failure to pay the interest would force the firm into bankruptcy and the mine would be sold for whatever it would bring. The lenders would have first claim on the proceeds from such a sale up to $1 million principal amount of the debt. Under the circumstances of the example it is unlikely that the entire property could be sold for as much as $1 million, and so the lenders would take a loss and the owners would receive nothing.[8] In any case, the firm, its owners, and its creditors would be in trouble.

Also, the interest rate charged by lenders will be affected by the possibility that the mine will incur losses. If the entire $1 million is raised from debt and lenders require 8 percent on a safe loan, they will charge a higher rate on this loan; they may even not be willing to lend this amount of money.

In this simple example, the risk to the lender can be eliminated by the firm not borrowing so much money. Suppose only $750,000 is borrowed at 8 percent. The firm is then obligated to pay only 0.08($750,000) = $60,000 per year, which would be covered even in the worst case. Prudent financial managers would limit the amount borrowed to a level where they are confident that the interest can be paid from the firm's income. Exceeding this point subjects the firm and its owners to excessive risk and may also be costly due to higher interest rates being charged.

Using even limited amounts of debt is likely to increase the risk of losses for a firm. A more general situation is depicted in Figure 12-2. The

---

[8] This assumes that Auric is a corporation and that the owners are not personally liable for the debt. Otherwise, the lenders would try to make up any losses by instituting legal action to claim personal assets of the owners.

curves in this figure were drawn assuming the firm's earnings before interest and taxes are represented by the probability distribution shown by curve *A*. Curve *A* is also the income to all shareholders before taxes if no debt is issued. Curve *B* illustrates the effects of financing with some given amount of debt on shareholders' income before taxes. The fixed interest charges change curve *A* to curve *B*. Notice that the likelihood of the firm's incurring a loss has increased appreciably due to the use of debt. Generally the more debt that is used, the greater the risk of loss.

A third aspect of the risk of debt is its impact on the variability of shareholder income. From our discussion of financial leverage, we know that debt financing increases the responsiveness of earnings per share to changes in earnings before interest and taxes. Therefore, the use of debt (or preferred stock) amplifies the inherent variability of EBIT and increases the variability of shareholder income.

For example, suppose that earnings before interest and taxes for the first year of Auric's operations are $200,000 and in the second year are $180,000, a decline of 10 percent. The effects of this decrease in EBIT on Auric's owners are shown in Exhibit 12-3 assuming that the entire investment of $1 million is being financed completely either with common stock or with debt at an 8 percent interest rate. The decrease in income to the original owners is 17 percent with debt financing as compared with the 10 percent decrease with stock financing. With common stock financing all changes, positive or negative, in income are shared among all the shareholders, whereas with debt financing, the lenders receive a fixed interest payment and all changes are borne by the original owners.

Leverage and Beta   EBIT-EPS analysis is widely used by financial managers because it provides a simple picture of the consequences of alter-

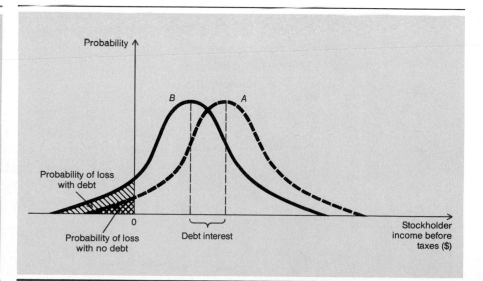

FIGURE 12-2
*Effects of debt
financing on
stockholder income.
Curve **A** shows EBIT
for the firm, which
equals stockholder
income before taxes
when debt is used. The
fixed interest payment
increases the
probability of loss from
that shown as the
crosshatched area
under **A** to that shown
as the hatched area
under **B**.*

native financing methods; however, more sophisticated techniques are available. One approach is to consider the impact of alternative methods on the stockholder's risk as measured by beta. In Chapter 6 we used beta as a summary measure of the risk of a financial asset based on the Capital Asset Pricing Model (CAPM). A precise analysis of the impact of financing on beta is a topic for more advanced courses. Here we provide the basic idea. The beta of a firm's common stock depends on the amount of leverage used by the firm. Measuring leverage as the ratio of debt (and preferred stock) to the total value of all securities issued, beta of the common stock increases with leverage. This is illustrated in Figure 12-3a.[9] Since the risk to the stockholders increases with increased leverage, the stockholders' required rate of return also increases as shown in Figure 12-3b. The problem for the financial manager is to determine how the *value* of the firm's stock will be affected. The higher expected income from leverage will be discounted at a higher rate. Thus the trade-off between risk and return is analyzed in terms of the impact of financing decisions on the value of the firm's stock.

Financial Leverage and Value

We assume that management will want to choose the financing method that provides the greatest financial benefit to current stockholders of the firm. The financial benefits to stockholders are obtained from current dividends and the value of their stock. However, the choice among external financing methods does not affect current dividends, so we first examine the problem of how the choice of external financing affects

[9] The relationship shown in Figure 12-3a was developed from numerical examples by applying the CAPM to several different probability distributions. It applies when the firm issues risky as well as riskless debt.

EXHIBIT 12-3
The impact of debt and common stock financing on the variability of income

	Common stock		Debt	
	First year	Second year	First year	Second year
EBIT	$ 200,000	$180,000	$200,000	$180,000
Interest	0)	0	(80,000)	(80,000)
Taxable income.......	$ 200,000	$180,000	$120,000	$100,000
Taxes (at 50%)	(100,000)	(90,000)	(60,000)	(50,000)
Net income	$ 100,000	$ 90,000	$ 60,000	$ 50,000
Income to original owners	$ 50,000	$ 45,000	$ 60,000	$ 50,000
Dollar change	−$5,000		−$10,000	
Percentage change	−10%		−17%	

stock value. To highlight the issues, we focus on the choice between debt and common stock. The impact of financing leverage on value is one of the most difficult and heavily debated topics in finance. Divergences of opinion exist among financial managers and among financial theorists. Ultimately the financing decision is a matter of judgment for the financial manager. Here we present what is currently known about the problem.

The No-Tax Case Let's examine the simplest possible situation to provide a base for understanding the problem as found in practice. Suppose that a firm's securities (debt, preferred stock, and common stock) are issued and traded in a perfect capital market.[10] All investors in the market have the same probability distributions for the future returns from any securities or from any investments undertaken by the firm. Assume also that there are no costs or penalties (such as legal fees and disruption of operations resulting from default) incurred by the firm if it defaults on debt payments, although the debtholders may take over the firm.[11] All debt issues are perpetual bonds; only interest payments are required. For now we assume that there are no corporate or personal income taxes. Under these conditions, how do financing decisions affect the value of a firm's common stock? Let's use the Auric Mining example to explore the problem.

---

[10] In perfect capital markets, transactions (buying, selling, and issuing securities) involve no transaction costs (such as brokerage fees); investors have equal, costless access to information; and there is a large number of buyers and sellers of securities, none of whom is individually able to affect market prices.

[11] This assumption means that the act of default and the subsequent actions by lenders do not reduce the level of EBIT below what it would have been in the absence of the contractual obligations that have been unfulfilled due to the default (that is, what the EBIT would have been if the firm had been all equity financed).

FIGURE 12-3

*The effects of leverage
on securities' betas
and rates of return in
the CAPM.*

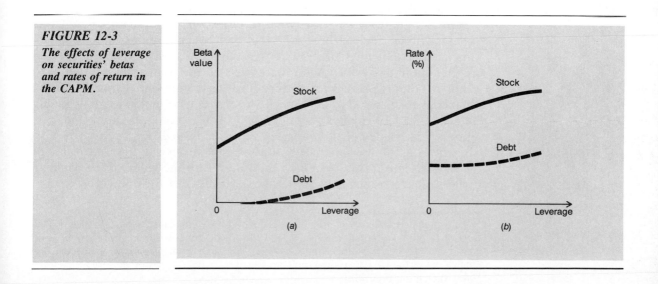

In Exhibit 12-1, the expected income from the mine is $480,000 per year. As before, $1 million must be raised to undertake the investment. Our choice is between debt financing at an interest rate of 8 percent or common stock financing. Investors in common stock are assumed to require an expected rate of return of 12 percent if no debt is used. All income will be paid out as dividends and interest.

If only common stock financing is used, the total market value of the outstanding stock will be the present value of the expected dividends to the stockholders. The expected dividends are a perpetual stream of $480,000 per year since there are no corporate income taxes. The value of the dividends is

$$\text{Market value} = \frac{\text{expected dividends}}{\text{required rate of return}}$$

$$= \frac{\$480,000}{0.12}$$

$$= \$4 \text{ million}$$

If the total market value of common stock is $4 million and if $1 million in stock has been sold to new investors, the value of the original owners' stock must be $3 million. What, then, will the original owners' stock be worth if debt rather than common stock is used to raise $1 million? Financial theory tells us that in this situation the original owners' stock will also be worth $3 million with debt financing.[12] Therefore the value of the original owners' stock is not affected by the financing decision. This is because of two conditions implied by our assumptions. First, the total income being received by investors (stockholders and bondholders) does not depend on how the firm is financed. Second, the total value of the income is the same regardless of how it is split up among different types of securities.[13] (The value of a pie stays the same regardless of how you slice it.) To see how this works, let's look at Auric Mining when debt is used.

In Exhibit 12-4 we show what interest and expected dividend payments will be for various combinations of debt and common stock financing. We have assumed here that the interest rate on debt increases as the amount of debt issued increases. Notice that total payments to security holders is the same under present assumptions regardless of the financing package chosen. Since Auric needs $1 million, raising only $250,000 in debt implies that $750,000 in new common stock must be issued. The values of the various securities issued by the firm are also shown. These values are based on the proposition that the total value of the firm's securities is $4 million, and therefore the value of the original owners' shares remains at $3 million regardless of the choice of financ-

---

[12] The original analysis of the problem was done by F. Modigliani and M. H. Miller, "The Cost of Capital, Corporation Finance, and the Theory of Investment," *American Economic Review*, 48 (June 1958), pp. 261–297. The same conclusion can be reached by application of the CAPM to the problem.

[13] We sketch out the formal argument in Appendix 12A.

ing. In addition this analysis implies that the required rate of return on stock increases with the leverage of the firm. We show a measure of leverage (interest/EBIT) and the expected rate of return on total stock given the expected dividend payments and stock values. Figure 12-4 shows the general behavior of security values and rates of return for the no-tax case. In Figure 12-4c the firm's cost of capital is also plotted. Notice that it is unaffected by the degree of leverage used even though the rates on stock and debt increase with leverage. This implies that the firm's investment decisions are unaffected by the choice of financing in this simplified situation.

The Effects of Corporate Income Taxes Suppose that Auric pays corporate income taxes, but all other assumptions remain the same.[14] If the corporate tax rate is 50 percent, only $240,000 in shareholder income is provided from the mine with common stock used to raise $1 million, as was shown in Exhibit 12-1. The market value of an expected dividend stream of $240,000 is $2 million given a required rate of return of 12 percent. Since $1 million in stock is sold to new investors, the original owner's stock is worth $1 million with stock financing.

The effect of debt financing is significantly different with corporate income taxes than it is in the no-tax case. Since interest payments are tax deductible, issuing $1 million in debt with required interest payments of

---

[14] In general, interest rates in the capital market would probably be different with corporate taxes than with no corporate taxes. We have kept the same rate structure to highlight the important differences between the tax and no-tax cases for an individual firm.

EXHIBIT 12-4
Impact of financial leverage on required rates of return with no taxes

Debt issued....................	$ 0	$ 250,000	$ 500,000	$ 750,000	$1,000,000
Interest rate	—	6%	6.5%	7.0%	8.0%
Expected EBIT	$ 480,000	$ 480,000	$ 480,000	$ 480,000	$ 480,000
Interest	0	15,000	32,500	52,500	80,000
Dividends = net income.......	$ 480,000	$ 465,000	$ 447,500	$ 427,500	$ 400,000
Total returns					
(dividends + interest)	$ 480,000	$ 480,000	$ 480,000	$ 480,000	$ 480,000
Interest/EBIT	0.0	0.03	0.07	0.11	0.17
New stock issued	$1,000,000	$ 750,000	$ 500,000	$ 250,000	$ 0
Value of old stock...........	3,000,000	3,000,000	3,000,000	3,000,000	3,000,000
Total stock value............	$4,000,000	$3,750,000	$3,500,000	$3,250,000	$3,000,000
Debt and stock value	$4,000,000	$4,000,000	$4,000,000	$4,000,000	$4,000,000
Required rate on stock[a].....	12%	12.4%	12.8%	13.2%	13.3%

[a] Calculated as dividends/total stock value.

$80,000 causes shareholder income to drop from $240,000 to $200,000 with the debt issue as shown in Exhibit 12-1. In the no-tax case we found that the required rate of return on stock was 13.3 percent for $1 million in debt financing (see Exhibit 12-4). We note that the financing leverage is the same in both cases. Our measure of financial leverage, interest/EBIT, is not affected by taxes.

$$\frac{\text{Interest}}{\text{EBIT}} = \frac{\$80,000}{\$480,000}$$

$$= 0.167$$

If the degree of leverage is the same, the risk-return relationship in the capital market is the same, and the business risk is the same, then the required rate of return on stock should be the same.

Indeed financial theory tells us that this is so.[15] With a required rate

---

[15] See Haley and Schall, op. cit., p. 301. This result is an implication of both the Modigliani-Miller analysis of the problem [F. Modigliani and M. H. Miller, "Taxes and the Cost of Capital: A Correction," *American Economic Review*, 53 (June 1963), pp. 433–443]. and of the CAPM when the Security Market Line is the same under the tax and no-tax cases.

FIGURE 12-4

The effects of leverage on securities' values and rates of return with perfect markets and no taxes.

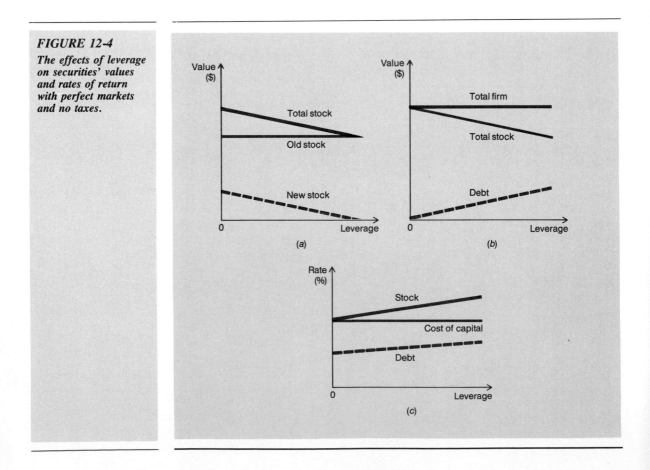

of return of 13.3 percent and expected dividends of $200,000 per year, the stock value with $1 million in debt financing will be

$$\text{Stock value} = \frac{\$200,000}{0.133}$$

$$= \$1,500,000$$

Since the value of the original owners' shares with stock financing was only $1 million, the stockholders will prefer debt financing.

To understand why debt increases value, consider the total cash payments made to security holders (i.e., to stockholders and bondholders). In the no-tax case the amount of money paid in dividends and interest is expected to be $480,000 per year regardless of the financing method used. With taxes, debt financing increases the total expected payments from the firm because the firm pays lower taxes. When common stock is used, the total expected payments to security holders are $240,000 (all dividends) and the firm pays taxes of $240,000. When $1 million in debt is issued, expected total payments to security holders rise to $280,000 ($200,000 dividends plus $80,000 interest) and taxes drop from $240,000 to $200,000. By financing with debt instead of common stock, $40,000 more is expected to be paid to security holders and $40,000 less is expected to be paid to the government. The value of the additional $40,000 is reflected in a higher value for the old stock with debt financing.

The implications of this analysis when the amount of debt issued varies are shown in Exhibit 12-5.

EXHIBIT 12-5
Impact of financial leverage on stock value with corporate income taxes

Debt issued....................	$ 0	$ 250,000	$ 500,000	$ 750,000	$1,000,000
Interest rate	—	6%	6.5%	7.0%	8.0%
Expected EBIT	$ 480,000	$ 480,000	$ 480,000	$ 480,000	$ 480,000
Interest	0	15,000	32,500	52,500	80,000
Taxable income...............	$ 480,000	$ 465,000	$ 447,500	$ 427,500	$ 400,000
Taxes (@ 50%)	240,000	232,500	223,750	213,750	200,000
Net income....................	$ 240,000	$ 232,500	$ 223,750	$ 213,750	$ 200,000
Interest/EBIT.................	0	0.03	0.07	0.11	0.17
Required rate on stock[a]........	12%	12.4%	12.8%	13.2%	13.3%
Value of total stock[b]...........	$2,000,000	$1,875,000	$1,750,000	$1,625,000	$1,500,000
New stock issued	$1,000,000	$ 750,000	$ 500,000	$ 250,000	0
Value of old stock[c]............	$1,000,000	$1,125,000	$1,250,000	$1,375,000	$1,500,000

[a] From Exhibit 12-4.
[b] Value of total stock = net income (dividends)/required rate on stock.
[c] Value of old stock = value of total stock − new stock issued.

428

PART 2
**The firm's investment,
financing, and dividend
decisions**

Compared to the no-tax case of Exhibit 12-4, we see that taxes reduce the net income (dividends) to stockholders. However, the degree of financial leverage (interest/EBIT) is the same at each level of debt and, therefore, the required rate of return on the stock is the same as in the no-tax case. We calculate the total value of the stock as the present value of the income to the stockholders. Notice that the total value of stock declines as the amount of debt issued increases. However, by issuing more debt, we are issuing less new stock. The value of the original shareholders' stock increases with the increased use of debt.

Figure 12-5 displays the data of Exhibit 12-5 in graphical form. Leverage is measured as interest/EBIT. In Figure 12-5a, the values of the old stock and new stock issued sum to the total stock value. Notice as the degree of leverage increases, total stock value declines but the value of the old stock increases. In Figure 12-5b, the value of the stock plus the value of the debt equals the total value of the firm. Note that total firm value increases with leverage. In Figure 12-5c, the behavior of the required rates on debt and stock and of the firm's cost of capital are shown. Notice that, despite the increased rates on debt and stock, the cost of capital decreases as leverage increases under the assumptions here.

We have found that the existence of corporate taxes coupled with the tax deductibility of interest implies that debt financing is superior to

FIGURE 12-5

*The effects of leverage
on securities' values
and rates of return
with perfect markets
and corporate taxes.*

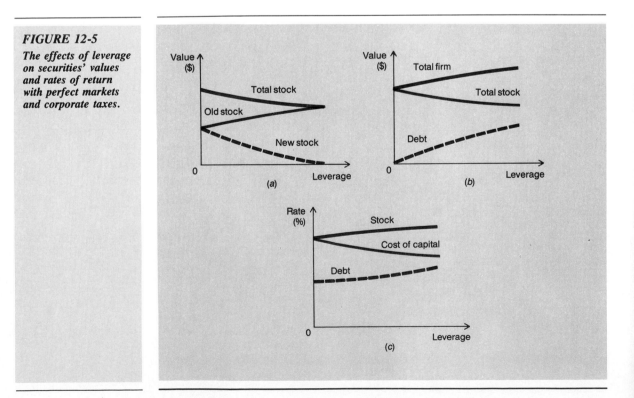

common stock. What about financing with preferred stock? Preferred dividends are not tax deductible; therefore, preferred stock financing results in the same value for the original owners' stock as common stock financing. The implications for small business finance are interesting. Although we won't analyze the problem in detail, we can indicate the general results. The advantage of debt financing results from a reduction in *corporate* income taxes. If a business is not paying corporate taxes,[16] then the no-tax case applies and there is no advantage to debt relative to any other method of obtaining money from external sources, such as bringing in a new partner.

The Effect of Personal Taxes   Taxes on the income received by investors in the firm's securities (personal taxes) greatly complicates the analysis. Personal taxes affect the choices among all types of financing including retained earnings. We discuss the impact of these taxes on dividend–retained earnings policies in Chapter 13. Here we present the implications for the use of external financing methods, especially debt. The basic idea is quite simple. Investors (stockholders and bondholders) generally pay lower taxes on a dollar of equity income (dividends and capital gains) than on a dollar of income from corporate debt securities (interest).[17] The tax on investors thus favors equities relative to debt. On the other hand, the corporate tax favors debt relative to equity. This is so because the return provided to the corporation's lenders (interest) is tax deductible to the corporation, whereas the return provided to shareholders (dividends and retained earnings) is subject to the corporate tax. There are therefore two offsetting tax forces that have an effect on the aftertax (personal and corporate) returns provided by debt and equity securities, and therefore on the attractiveness of debt and equity securities to investors.

To illustrate the above point, suppose that the personal tax rate on interest income is 30 percent and that the effective personal tax rate on income to stockholders is zero.[18] This is obviously an extreme case but does help to clarify the effects of personal taxes. Exhibit 12-6 illustrates a company with an EBIT of $500,000 and compares the total aftertax income to investors (shareholders and bondholders) if the company is all equity with the total aftertax income to investors if the company has debt

---

[16] The business may be a proprietorship, a partnership, or a small corporation that has elected to be taxed as a partnership. See Chap. 3.

[17] Taxes on interest must be paid in the year in which the interest or dividend is received. The tax on capital gains (which are primarily generated by common stock and other equities) is not due until the asset is sold. A shareholder can avoid capital gains taxes simply by not selling the shares. Also, most dividends (common or preferred) received by a corporation on stock owned in U.S. corporations is not taxable to the recipient corporation. In contrast, all interest on corporate bonds owned by the corporation is taxable.

[18] This might be approximately true if all earnings are retained and invested to increase the value of the stock and the stockholders defer capital gains taxes by holding their stock indefinitely.

430

PART 2
**The firm's investment,
financing, and dividend
decisions**

(with annual interest of $100,000). The corporate tax rate is assumed to be 30 percent (the same as the assumed personal tax rate on interest income). In this example, the higher personal tax on interest income offsets the lower corporate tax (zero) on interest paid. The total income for security holders produced by the company net of all taxes is the same regardless of the choice of financing.

The above example was meant only to illustrate how personal taxes (which favor equities) can compensate for corporate taxes (which favor debt). Of course, the extent to which personal tax effects offset corporate tax effects depends on the corporate tax rate and on the personal tax rates on debt and equity income. Personal tax rates vary widely among investors. Because of this, the overall tax system (i.e., personal and corporate taxes) does not completely favor either debt or equity financing, but rather encourages a mixture of both debt and equity in the economy.[19]

---

[19] The basic idea is that investors with very high personal tax rates will end up with more aftertax income (net of corporate and personal taxes) if the firm issues them stock (since for them the personal tax on debt interest more than wipes out the corporate tax savings from using debt); and investors with low personal tax rates will end up with more aftertax income if the firm issues them debt securities (since for them the personal tax on debt is not enough to wipe out the corporate tax savings from using debt). The result will be that firms in the economy will issue both debt and equity securities, with high-tax-bracket investors owning equities and low-tax-bracket investors owning debt securities. These points are developed in detail in M. H. Miller, "Debt and Taxes," *Journal of Finance*, 32 (May 1977), pp. 261–275; and H. De Angelo and R. W. Masulis, "Optimal Capital Structure Under Corporate and Personal Taxation," *Journal of Financial Economics* (March 1980), pp. 3–29.

EXHIBIT 12-6
The combined effects of corporate and personal taxes on investors' income

	Firm is all equity	Firm has debt
1. EBIT	$500,000	$500,000
2. Interest paid to bondholders	0	100,000
3. Corporate taxable income	$500,000	$400,000
4. Corporate tax [0.30 × (3)]	150,000	120,000
5. Income to stockholders	$350,000	$280,000
6. Personal tax on stock income [0% × (5)]	0	0
7. Personal tax on bondholder interest income [0.30 × (2)]	0	$ 30,000
8. Income to shareholders after corporate and personal taxes [(5) − (6)]	$350,000	$280,000
9. Income to bondholders after corporate and personal taxes [(2) − (7)]	0	$ 70,000
10. Aftertax income to investors [(8) + (9)]	$350,000	$350,000

Under the Tax Reform Act of 1986, marginal personal tax rates vary from 0 to 33 percent, and marginal corporate tax rates vary from 15 to 39 percent. The Tax Reform Act significantly diminished the personal tax advantage of equities relative to debt by eliminating the low tax rate on long-term capital gains (which applied most often to equities) and, of less importance, by dropping the tax exemption for the first $100 of dividends received by an individual from U.S. corporations. Offsetting this reduction in the personal tax advantage accorded equities, the Tax Reform Act reduced the corporate tax advantage of debt by lowering the marginal corporate tax rates (this reduced the corporate tax benefit from deducting interest expense). On balance, the tax law change probably favored debt relative to equity. That is, if taxes were the only factor influencing capital structure decisions, we would expect to see an increase in debt relative to equity as a result of the new tax code. However, there are factors in addition to taxes which affect capital structure, some of which we consider next.

Complications in Practice If the world were as simple as was assumed above, life would be much easier for financial managers and they would be paid lower salaries. Some of the complications found in practice provide advantages to debt financing whereas other factors favor common stock.

First, the capital markets are not perfect. Information is not costlessly available to everyone; there are costs to investors in buying and selling securities, etc. The lack of perfection in the market implies, primarily, that there may be situations where debt financing (or preferred stock financing) may be unusually costly relative to common stock or vice versa. The financial manager must be alert to market conditions and consider them in making financing decisions. Investment bankers can often provide helpful advice as to the current market situation.

Second, there are legal fees, investment banking commissions, and other expenses involved in issuing securities, as discussed in Chapter 11. It is usually more expensive for a firm to issue preferred stock than to issue debt and more expensive to issue common stock than to issue either debt or preferred stock.

Third, the use of debt financing increases the possibility that the firm may be forced to default on its debt obligations. There are severe costs associated with default. There is often serious disruption of the firm's business activity as top management spends time in negotiations with lenders while lower management starts thinking about alternative jobs. Customers for the firm's products and services begin to look for other sources of supply. The firm may have profitable investment opportunities at the same time its existing business is doing poorly. The firm may be forced to delay or forego making these investments because it cannot finance them. There are also legal and other expenses associated with the legal proceedings in bankruptcy situations. As the firm uses increased amounts of debt financing, the probability that it may default at some future time also increases. At some point the expected costs of

432

PART 2
**The firm's investment,
financing, and dividend
decisions**

default will become large enough to offset any other advantages to debt. At this point other sources of financing will be preferred.

Firms with large amounts of outstanding debt may have other problems. Lenders are reluctant to lend additional money to firms that are highly levered, and they may either not lend the money or charge a very high interest rate to compensate for their exposure to risk. Potential lenders and investors in the firm's securities may not agree with management. They may be unwilling to commit large amounts of new money to a corporation that is already highly levered. This problem may be especially significant for firms with relatively high business risks. The general opinion of financial experts is that, beyond some point, additional leverage is undesirable. This opinion is reflected in the concept of an optimal capital structure.

Optimal Capital Structure The term *capital structure* means the proportions of different types of securities issued by the firm. The optimal (best) capital structure is the set of proportions that maximize the total value of the firm. Although the concept of capital structure applies to all types of securities, for simplicity we will continue to examine only debt and common stock. Figure 12-6 illustrates the general concept as applied to the Auric Mining example. In Figure 12-6a, the two components of total stock value (value of original owners' stock and value of new stock issued) are shown. In Figure 12-6b, the total value of all the firm's

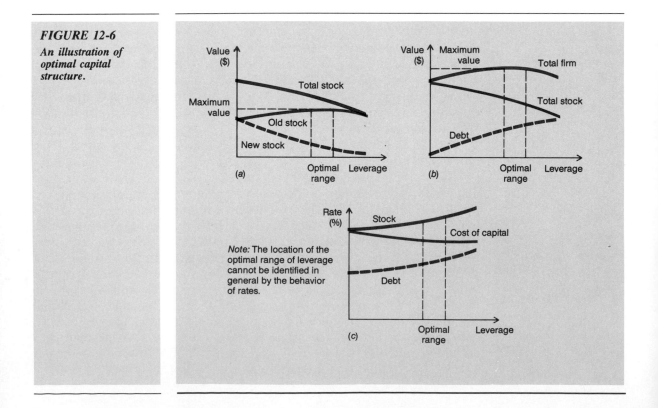

FIGURE 12-6

An illustration of optimal capital structure.

securities, debt plus stock, is shown. Notice that maximum value for the original owners is reached in the same range as maximum value for the entire firm. Management should use the proportion of debt to total value (or, equivalently, that degree of financial leverage) that maximizes the value of the firm since this provides the highest financial return to the original owners.[20]

Contrast the situation depicted in Figure 12-6 with that shown in Figure 12-5. In Figure 12-5 the value of the old shares and the total value of all securities increases with the amount of debt issued. In Figure 12-6, increasing debt is only desirable up to a point; beyond the optimal range, value declines and no more debt should be issued.

How is the financial manager to determine where the range of maximum value is? This is a tough problem. Financial managers must formulate their own policies. One source of information is the behavior of the prices of the firm's securities. If the price of the firm's stock drops on announcement of a new financing program, this is an obvious sign that the planned financing will move the firm outside of the optimal range. Institutional lenders such as banks and insurance companies provide the financial manager with their views on the desirability of financing programs. If the firm must pay unusually high interest rates for its debt issues, this may be a sign that too much debt is being issued. A lowering of ratings on the firm's bonds by the bond-rating agencies is another sign. The firm's investment bankers, who are experts in the issuance of securities, are a major source of information and advice.

Capital Structure and Bond Ratings   Managers of large firms often set a target bond rating for their companies' bonds. Bonds can be divided into two groups: "investment grade" and "junk bonds." Bonds that have ratings of Baa (Moody's) or BBB (Standard & Poor's) or higher qualify as investment grade. Bonds with lower ratings are often called "junk bonds." (Investment bankers who deal in these bonds often refer to them as "high-yield securities." See Table 5-1 for a description of the various ratings.) Firms that are able to issue investment grade bonds pay significantly lower interest rates than firms that issue junk bonds. The difference in interest rates between bonds rated A and bonds rated BBB (or Baa) is also normally larger than the difference between A and AA. Therefore, there is an appreciable interest cost advantage to being A-rated. In addition, high-grade bonds, especially those with ratings of A or better, can be readily issued under most capital market conditions. During periods of economic recession, low-grade bonds are typically given a cool reception by investors, and firms find it difficult and expensive to issue them.

Although there are no precise criteria for determining the rating of a firm's debt, a general idea can be obtained by looking at the financial

---

[20] This is true provided that there are no differences in current dividends. When particular financing choices affect current dividends (as when retained earnings are used), current dividends plus the value of the original owners' shares is a better measure of owner benefits.

characteristics of firms with different ratings. Table 12-1 shows some data for industrial corporations, classified by bond-rating. A firm that wants to maintain a high rating can do so only by keeping its debt within moderate bounds.

Capital Structure and the Cost of Capital Given that management is able to determine the optimal capital structure for the firm, how does this affect the cost of capital? The required rates of return on the firm's securities, debt and stock, will depend on the capital structure chosen. Figure 12-6c shows the behavior of debt rates and stock rates as leverage is increased. Since these rates depend on the capital structure decision, it is important that management measures the cost of capital when the firm has a capital structure in the optimal range; that is, when the firm's value is maximum. Otherwise the computed cost of capital may be seriously in error.

Once management has established the optimal financing policy and allowed time for the securities markets to adjust to the policy, the cost of capital can be measured as described in Chapter 7. The general procedure was and is to determine the current proportions of the outstanding securities and to estimate current capital market rates as inputs to the cost of capital computation.

There are some adjustments to the cost of capital approach that may be necessary under some conditions. These adjustments will be discussed in a later section of the chapter, after we consider financing through internal funds.

RETAINED EARNINGS AND INTERNAL FUNDS

Debt, preferred stock financing, and common stock financing force the financial manager to bargain with "outsiders." Lenders and investors must be convinced of the stability and profitability of the firm's present operations and of the desirability of new investment if they are to provide money at a reasonable cost to the firm and its present owners. The precise terms of these external financing sources will be determined by negotiations between management and the people providing the money. In any case the use of external financing reduces the future

---

TABLE 12-1
Median averages of key ratios of industrial corporations by rating category

	AAA	AA	A	BBB	BB	B
EBIT/interest	10.5	8.2	5.5	3.0	2.5	1.8
Total debt/total capital*a*	18%	25%	29%	34%	46%	64%

a Total debt and total capital exclude current liabilities other than short-term debt and current maturities of long-term debt.
Source: Standard & Poor's Corporation.

income available to the present owners. Financing investment by reducing cash and securities accumulated from the earnings of prior periods and by retaining cash generated from current operations does not present these difficulties. Instead the problem is to convince current shareholders (and perhaps current lenders) that the funds are best used for investment rather than for paying dividends or repaying debt before it is due. Usually this is an easier task because current shareholders and debtholders have already made a commitment to the future of the firm. Indeed, the firm has no legal obligation to pay debtholders prior to the scheduled principal and interest payments. The shareholders present a different problem, however.

The following type of problem has arisen for many companies. Suppose the shareholders have become accustomed to receiving on average about 50 percent of the profits as dividends. Profits and dividends have been growing at an average rate of 5 percent per year for several years. Management is about to embark on a major capital expenditure program that will probably continue for several years. New products will be manufactured and production facilities will be expanded. Management anticipates that these will be profitable investments to make, although only the current opportunities have been evaluated in detail. In any case, some current decisions will commit the firm to investing large amounts of money for two or three years. Based on forecasts of current and future cash flows, a continuation of the 50 percent payout of dividends would imply substantial external financing, at least part of which would have to be in the form of common stock. The use of debt to cover all additional requirements would, in management's judgment, be unwise, as the required amounts would subject the firm to excessive risk. The resulting capital structure would be outside the optimal range. Informal discussions with potential lenders have confirmed this judgment.

Given these circumstances, should management change the dividend policy of the firm to provide additional internal funds, plan to issue common stock as needed in the face of the uncertainties of future market conditions, try to borrow more money, or reduce investments? Notice that each of the above alternatives implies a cost to the current shareholders.

Foregoing profitable investments is not in the best interest of the stockholders unless there is no way to finance them at a reasonable cost. We have shown how the use of too much debt places the firm in a vulnerable position and will produce a lower value of the firm's stock. Therefore the source of the money must be either retained earnings (which implies lower dividend payments) or the sale of common stock. We feel, as do many financial theorists and managers, that usually the shareholders would be better off receiving lower dividends than having the firm issue common stock. This is so for several reasons that vary in relative importance according to the firm's particular situation:

1   If the firm retains earnings instead of paying higher dividends and issuing stock, the price per share of stock should be higher since

436

PART 2
**The firm's investment,
financing, and dividend
decisions**

earnings per share and future dividends per share will be higher if new stock is not issued. The shareholders could therefore get cash benefits from the investment by selling some of their stock. They would receive capital gains on the stock rather than dividends.[21] Those shareholders who will be reinvesting dividends will have to pay personal taxes on those dividends, leaving less money for investment. If the firm invests the money, the resulting capital gain is not taxed until the stock is sold.

2 There is a variety of costs (legal fees, commissions, etc.) associated with issuing common stock. These costs can amount to over 25 percent of the total dollars of stock issued.

3 Temporarily investing retained earnings in marketable securities for purposes of future investment increases both the safety of the firm and its financial flexibility. Selling securities generally provides cash more quickly than would turning to external sources (borrowing or issuing stock) for funds. When the investment is to be made, the securities are liquidated and the proceeds used to finance the capital expenditure. On the other hand, if conditions change for the worse, sales of these securities bring cash quickly to meet debt payments, pay dividends, or pay expenses. Moreover, the existence of these funds does not preclude other financing if desirable. Their absence forces management to seek external sources to finance investment.

4 Sale of common stock may create control problems for the current owners of the firm.

Accordingly, we can see that there are sound reasons for preferring to finance investment through funds generated from operations and accumulated as marketable securities.

Despite the usual advantages to financing with retained earnings, this method of financing is not always possible or desirable. Shareholders may react very negatively to receiving lower dividend payments. It is one thing not to increase dividends as earnings rise and another to reduce them from prior levels. Shareholders may depend upon a given level of dividends, and reducing the dividends may force them to sell shares (and incur brokerage fees) to finance personal expenditures. The higher prices for the firm's stock due to the investment program may not be achieved immediately, and shareholders could be hurt under these conditions. Also, a reduction in dividends may actually cause temporary declines in the firm's stock. Investors may interpret the reduction of the dividend as evidence of weakness in the firm.

It may also be true that the amount of money available from not paying dividends would not be sufficient to avoid issuing some stock if

---

[21] There is a personal tax advantage to selling stock to raise cash rather than receiving dividends. Taxes on the sale of stock are paid only on the gain in value (sale price − purchase price) whereas the entire dividend is taxed. Therefore, less taxes would result from the sale of $1000 in stock than from the receipt of $1000 in dividends.

the investment program is to be maintained. Under these conditions management is likely to be reluctant to risk even temporary declines in the stock price and may continue to pay dividends to support the price. Management will attempt to achieve a balance between the dividends paid and the increased number of shares needed to be sold. It should be clear that, whenever a firm issues stock and also pays a dividend, in effect it is using some of the stock sale proceeds to pay the dividends. This is not an uncommon occurrence.

INTERNATIONAL FINANCING POLICIES

It should come as no surprise that differences in banking regulations, tax laws, and business traditions among countries result in variations in corporate financing practice. West German and Japanese firms, for example, tend to use more debt in their capital structures than do U.S. firms, and that debt is almost entirely in the form of bank loans, rather than bond issues. Most Japanese and German companies borrow from a single bank, which owns a sizable portion of the firm's outstanding shares and positions its officers on the client's board of directors. American managers would deem this degree of bank participation unacceptable, and such activities in the United States are, in fact, illegal.

Another example of the different practices in international financing is the manner in which firms in the United States and many other major economic powers commonly borrow from pension plans and insurance companies. In contrast, the use of pension and insurance funds is virtually nonexistent in France and Italy, where those industries are now socialized. Much of the discussion in this chapter is pertinent to financial policy decisions in any country, but many other points are specific to the regulatory and financial environment in the United States. The managers of foreign firms need an exact understanding of the financial environment of the country in which they operate if they are to be effective decision-makers.

Financing Multinational Corporations

Multinational corporations are typically organized as a parent company with affiliates in several countries. The typically complicated financial policy questions of how much debt and equity to use in new investments are compounded by the complexityy of the MNC's organizational structure. How should each subsidiary—and the corporation as a whole—structure its finance policy? Should the parent company invest in subsidiaries through debt or equity positions? How much funding should be obtained locally? Should internally generated earnings be retained by the subsidiary or paid out as interest or dividends? In answering these questions, the financial manager of the MNC must consider the same FRICTO factors that are relevant for single-country firms. There are, however, several additional considerations that are unique to firms that operate in more than one country.

First, the MNC can take advantage of politically imposed distortions in capital markets. For example, differences in tax laws and rates may allow the corporation to reduce its total tax bill by chananging the debt to equity mix of its subsidiaries, as well as the way in which the parent company realizes ownership of the subsidiaries' earnings. Given that governmental policies and regulations create disparities in the real rate of interest and, consequently, the cost of capital among countries, the MNC has access to a world of financing options and can choose the cheapest international source of funds.

Second, the exchange rate risks and political insecurities faced by MNCs can affect financing policy. One method of reducing exchange rate risk is for the parent company to offset its investments in a foreign country with foreign currency denominated debt. If the net equity position is reduced to zero, the economic impact of exchange rate fluctuations is essentially eliminated (see Chapter 9). The likelihood of political expropriation can be reduced if local residents or the government of an unstable country is given an equity position in the foreign subsidiary. As is the case in most areas of business, financial structure decisions are complicated by the political considerations faced by multinational corporations.

THE IMPACT OF FINANCING ON INVESTMENT

The firm's cost of capital is the standard by which investment projects having the same business risk as the firm are evaluated. We have seen that the magnitude of the cost of capital depends on the firm's capital structure. Therefore the impact of financing decisions on investment decisions is conveyed through the use of the cost of capital. However, there are situations where the procedures of Chapter 7 used to estimate the cost of capital will not provide an appropriate measure for use in evaluating investment projects, even though the projects have the same business risk as the firm. We will consider three common problems here: (1) changes in financing policies, (2) financing large capital budgets, and (3) costs of issuing new securities.

Changes in Financing Policy

Suppose that the financial manager has determined that the present capital structure of the firm is inappropriate. Economic conditions may have changed, or new management may have decided that past policies are not optimal. In any case, calculation of a cost of capital using current proportions of outstanding securities will not reflect the proportions to be maintained in the future. In addition, the required rates of return on the securities are likely to change as capital structure changes. In theory, the solution is simple. A new capital structure for the firm is obtained by issuing new securities and retiring outstanding ones. For example, debt can be rapidly reduced by selling stock and using the proceeds to retire the debt. Once the new capital structure has been achieved, the market rates on the securities can be measured and a new cost of capital can be calculated using the new proportions.

In practice, major changes in capital structure are not often made rapidly. There are several types of costs and fees that would be incurred, such as costs of issuing new securities and penalties imposed on early retirement of debt. Instead, firms usually move gradually toward a new capital structure by disproportionate use of one financing source over another for several years. This procedure has the advantage of not only keeping costs down, but also permitting financial managers to assess the effects of the new policy, to "feel their way" toward the optimal range.

An operational solution to the problem of estimating the new cost of capital when changes are being made gradually is to use, not the current proportions of financing sources, but *the planned future proportions*. The rates used are those currently in effect. We assume here that the new policy has been announced to the market so that current rates on the firm's securities reflect the market's assessment of this new policy. The rates must be continually reevaluated as the actual capital structure changes, but this must be done in any case as capital market conditions change.[22] In 1982, Martin Marietta Corporation took on huge debts (almost $1 billion) in order to avoid a takeover by Bendix Corporation. The debt amounted to 80 percent of its total capital and the firm was too highly levered. It took four years for Martin Marietta to reduce its debt to a more desirable 20 percent of total capital.

For example, if the financial manager believes that an appropriate capital structure for the firm is 30 percent debt, 10 percent preferred stock, and 60 percent common stock, then these are the proportions to be used in calculating the average cost of capital. The new financing policy is announced to the market, and new rates for the firm's securities are estimated based on the prices of outstanding securities after the announcement has been made. These rates are then used with the planned future proportions to calculate a new cost of capital.

Financing Large Capital Budgets

The problem associated with the size of the capital budget can be most simply posed in terms of an example. Suppose that a firm with $10 million in assets is planning its capital expenditure program for the coming year. The financial manager has calculated the firm's cost of capital (using the procedure of Chapter 7) and has found it to be 12 percent. Would it make any difference if the capital expenditures for the year were $10 million or $1 million, given that all investments have positive net present values (all internal rates of return greater than 12 percent)? In most cases the answer would be yes.

If the firm were investing only $1 million, the money probably could come from internal funds and readily available debt (e.g., a bank loan). If the firm is operating profitably and has not exceeded its debt capacity, neither lenders nor shareholders would be disturbed by a $1 million capital budget. However, suppose that the firm must raise $10 million, thereby doubling its assets in one year. In this case, new shares of common stock must be issued or substantial new debt acquired, or, more likely, both sources will be used. In any case, to raise this much new money compared with the past financing requirements of the firm is

---

[22] The theoretical solution to this problem is complex, but the solution recommended here serves as a reasonable approximation.

likely to cause lenders and stockholders to require a higher rate of return than in the past, thereby causing the true cost of capital to be more than 12 percent.

There are several explanations why the cost of capital increases as the capital budget gets larger:

1   If the size of the capital budget is large relative to the size of the firm, external financing from new sources is probably needed. New investors, both stockholders and lenders, will be asked to provide the firm with the money needed to undertake the investment. New investors generally have a more pessimistic view of the firm's future than do "old" investors and often require a higher rate of return because of a greater perceived risk.

2   Investors may also doubt the ability of management to control so much growth. That is, they may believe that the investments taken individually could be profitable, but will not be profitable if undertaken simultaneously. Many new people would have to be hired, trained, and organized; existing production processes may be disrupted; and so on. Therefore the investments may be viewed as being more risky.

3   The firm will incur issue costs if the volume of investment forces it to issue new securities (rather than use internal funds and direct loans from financial institutions). Issue costs pose special problems and are discussed later in this chapter.

Figure 12-7 shows how the size of the capital budget affects the firm's cost of capital. For small budgets the cost of capital for new financing (marginal cost of capital) is the same as the current cost of capital for the firm. As the amount invested and financed increases, the cost of capital for the new financing increases, causing the current cost of capital for the firm to rise. This means that the current cost of capital

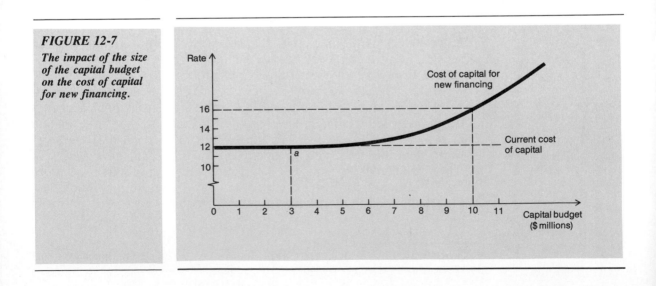

FIGURE 12-7

The impact of the size of the capital budget on the cost of capital for new financing.

is not a reliable standard for evaluating new investments when the volume of investment proposals is large relative to the present size of the firm. Basing investment decisions on the current cost of capital may cause so many investments to be included in the capital budget that the firm's current cost of capital rises, thereby making some of those investments unprofitable to undertake.

For example, suppose that the capital budget would be $10 million if 12 percent were used as the discount rate. That is, there are $10 million in new investments with a positive net present value using a discount rate of 12 percent. However, the $10 million could only be raised at a marginal cost of 16 percent. The correct cost of capital for $10 million in new investment is 16 percent, not the current cost of capital for the firm, which is less than 16 percent. However, if the cost of capital is 16 percent, many of the investments included in the capital budget when 12 percent was used will now be rejected. The internal rate of return on these rejected opportunities is greater than 12 percent but less than 16 percent. The total amount of planned expenditures might be significantly decreased, say, to $3 million, if the minimum acceptable rate of return is set at 16 percent. But if the firm invests only $3 million, the cost of capital for new financing is likely to be less than 16 percent. In Figure 12-7, the cost of capital for $3 million is approximately 12 percent (point *a*). Now the firm may be undertaking too little investment, rejecting investments that offer rates of return less than 16 percent but greater than 12 percent.

The proper capital budget must be determined by finding that amount of expenditures having a cost of capital less than any projects included in the budget but with no profitable projects excluded. The problem is illustrated in Figure 12-8. The expected rate of return on the

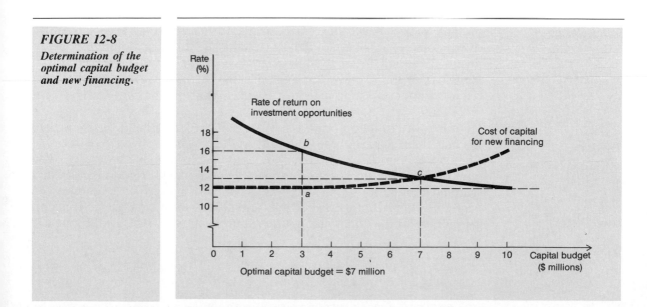

FIGURE 12-8

Determination of the optimal capital budget and new financing.

442

PART 2
**The firm's investment,
financing, and dividend
decisions**

least profitable or marginal investment included in a given capital budget is plotted for different sizes of capital budget. This is the curve that falls as the amount invested increases. In other words, the firm has relatively few projects that have high expected rates of return but quite a few that have low expected rates of return. All investments here are of the same risk, the average business risk of the firm. The cost of capital for new financing is the same curve depicted in Figure 12-7. Using a cost of capital of 16 percent will result in a capital budget of $3 million (point *b*), but a $3 million capital budget can be financed at a cost of capital of 12 percent (point *a*). In this hypothetical case the optimal capital budget has expenditures and requires new financing of $7 million (point *c*). The minimum rate of return on any investment accepted and the cost of capital for new financing are both 13 percent.

In practice, financial managers do not have precise numbers that enable them to draw curves like those in Figure 12-8 and compute an exact answer. The cost of capital curve is especially hard to estimate, and more than two curves are required for investments that differ in risk. Instead, the financial manager evaluates the costs and difficulties involved in raising enough money to support the planned capital budget. If financing is a problem, those investments that were only marginally profitable when evaluated using the original estimate of the cost of capital are eliminated from the capital budget. A revised capital budget is developed and financing requirements are examined. This process is continued until management decides that the returns expected from the remaining projects in the capital budget are sufficient to justify the cost of financing them, and the budget is approved. In other words, the actual process produces results that come close to the ideal case shown in Figure 12-8.

Issue Costs

Whenever the firm raises money from external sources, it incurs some initial costs. This was described in Chapter 11. All costs associated with the process of raising money are called issue costs or flotation costs to distinguish them from the ongoing costs of the payments made to the suppliers of the money—for example, the interest paid to bondholders. Here we are concerned with how issue costs affect the firm's investment decisions.

One way to incorporate issue costs in the investment decision is to include them as part of the cost of capital. Issue costs are one reason that the cost of capital increases as the amount of financing increases. The approach presented here is quite simple and provides good results in a variety of situations. The method assumes that the firm maintains the same capital structure over time and that issue costs are a constant proportion of the dollar amount raised for each type of security issued.[23]

---

[23] The method presented here provides only approximate results, as do all existing methods that include flotation costs through a cost of capital adjustment. More exact methods are significantly more complicated. For a discussion of this issue, see John Ezzell and R. Barr Porter, "Flotation Costs and the Weighted Average Cost of Capital," *Journal of Financial and Quantitative Analysis*, XI, 3 (1976) pp. 403–414.

We need to deal with two concerns. First, we must adjust the cost of each external financing source to include issue costs. Second, we must recognize that the cost of retained earnings differs from the cost of issuing common stock. As we will see, the cost of retained earnings is less than the cost of common stock. Therefore, the financial manager will use retained earnings first. However, the amount of financing from retained earnings is limited by the profits of the firm. If more equity is required to finance investments than is available from retained earnings, common stock must be issued. The use of this more expensive source of equity causes the cost of capital to increase.

A general procedure for estimating the cost of each financing source is as follows:

1. Determine the net amount of money that the firm will receive from the financing source after deducting issue costs.
2. Solve for the effective cost (k) of the financing source.

In the case of debt financing, the effective cost is the discount rate that makes the present value of the aftertax payments equal to the net amount received. That is,

Net amount = present value of future principal and interest payments

$$= \frac{X_1}{1 + k} + \frac{X_2}{(1 + k)^2} + \cdots + \frac{X_n}{(1 + k)^n} \qquad (12\text{-}1)$$

where $X_1, X_2, \ldots, X_n$ are the payments made to the lender net of any taxes associated with the financing. For example, suppose that the cost of issuing $1 million of ten-year bonds is $50,000. The bondholders are paying $1 million in cash, but the firm is receiving $950,000 after all expenses and discounts. The net amount of money the firm will have to use for investment is therefore the gross proceeds of $1 million less the issue costs of $50,000—$950,000. The issue costs on a debt issue are deductible for tax purposes, but they must be amortized over the life of the debt on a straight-line basis. In this example there would be a tax deduction of $5000 per year for ten years resulting from the issue costs of $50,000. Assume that the tax rate for the firm is 40 percent. The tax saving from the issue costs is therefore $2000 per year (0.40 × $5000). Suppose that the interest rate on the $1 million loan is 10 percent; therefore, the interest payments on the bonds are $100,000 per year, all of which is tax deductible. At a 40 percent tax rate, the aftertax interest cost is $60,000 per year [(1 − tax rate) × $100,000]. The annual net aftertax cash payment resulting from the bond issue is the annual after-tax interest expense less the annual tax savings from the issue cost deduction:

Annual aftertax interest = $60,000

Less: Annual tax savings from
      issue cost deduction = <u>2,000</u>

Annual aftertax payment = <u>$58,000</u>

444

PART 2
**The firm's investment,
financing, and dividend
decisions**

To find the aftertax cost of the debt, we must now solve for the interest rate on the net amount received, $950,000. The annual aftertax payments are $58,000. At the end of ten years the firm must pay back $1 million. Therefore, we can solve for the effective aftertax cost of the debt as the rate that makes the present value of the future aftertax principal and interest payments equal to the net amount received:

$$\$950,000 = \$58,000(P/A, k, 10) + \$1,000,000(P/F, k, 10)$$

$$k = 6.5\%$$

In the absence of issue costs, the effective cost of the debt financing would be 6 percent $[(1 - \text{tax rate}) \times 10\%]$. In this example, issue costs of only 5 percent of the amount issued ($50,000/$1 million) significantly raises the effective cost of the debt, from 6 percent to 6.5 percent.

Common stock and preferred stock have indefinite maturities. For these sources we can calculate the effective financing cost by multiplying the estimated market rate by the gross amount of the issue divided by the net amount received:

$$\text{Effective rate} = \text{market rate} \times \frac{\text{gross amount}}{\text{net amount}}$$

For example, suppose that you have estimated the market rate on your company's stock as 15 percent. A stock issue of $2 million will have issue costs of $180,000 (issue costs on stock are not tax deductible). The net amount received from this stock issue will be $1,820,000 ($2,000,000 − $180,000). We compute the effective cost of the stock issue as

$$\text{Effective rate} = 15\% \times \frac{\$2,000,000}{\$1,820,000}$$

$$= 16.5\%$$

For retained earnings we use the market rate on the firm's stock. In the above example, 15 percent was the market rate. Since use of retained earnings avoids the issue costs associated with common stock, no stock will be issued until all available retained earnings have been exhausted. Under the conditions of this analysis, there will be an increase in the cost of capital once we start issuing stock to finance the capital budget. The marginal cost of capital with stock financing is greater than the marginal cost of capital with retained earnings financing because of stock issue costs.

The marginal average cost of capital is the minimum rate of return required on investments of the same risk as the firm. To combine the costs of the individual financing sources and obtain the marginal average cost of capital, we need to know the capital structure proportions for the firm (using the market values of the firm's outstanding stock and debt to compute the proportions). Suppose that these proportions are 60 percent equity and 40 percent from debt. We have two marginal costs of capital—one with retained earnings as the source of equity, and one with new common stock as the source of equity. Using the 6.5 percent cost of debt, the 15 percent cost of retained earnings, and the 16.5 percent cost of new common stock:

With retained earnings:

$$MCC = 0.6 \times 15\% + 0.4 \times 6.5\%$$

$$= 11.6\%$$

With common stock:

$$MCC = 0.6 \times 16.5\% + 0.4 \times 6.5\%$$

$$= 12.5\%$$

Suppose that any capital budget in excess of $6 million would require the use of common stock. Then the minimum acceptable rate of return on investment for capital budgets over $6 million would be 12.5 percent. If the capital budget is $6 million or less, the minimum acceptable rate of return is 11.6 percent. We show this graphically in Figure 12-9.

Issue costs are only one factor causing the marginal cost of capital to rise as the size of the capital budget increases. Under more realistic conditions, the marginal cost of capital increases without the distinct jump shown in Figure 12-9.[24]

---

[24] Figure 12-9 assumes that the only factor affecting the cost of capital is issue costs on new equity that are a fixed proportion of the dollar amount raised. In practice, issues costs per dollar raised vary with the amount raised. Also, as we discussed earlier, the perceived risk of the capital budget (and therefore the cost of capital) can depend on the size of the capital budget. These complications, and others, generally cause the cost of capital to increase gradually as the amount of funds obtained increases.

FIGURE 12-9

*The impact of issue
costs for common stock
on the marginal cost of
capital*

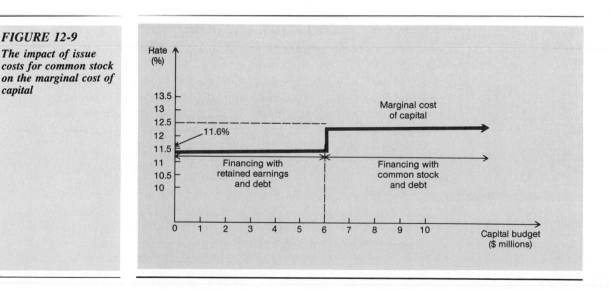

SUMMARY

In developing a plan for financing the firm's capital budget, the financial manager must consider the risks and returns provided by alternative plans. Debt financing increases the financial leverage of the firm and, therefore, both the risk and the return. Debt financing amplifies the basic business risk of the firm. Financial risk is the increase in total risk caused by the use of debt. This is the risk borne by stockholders and the firm because of the requirements to pay the debt interest and principal when due.

The FRICTO framework provides a checklist of factors to consider in the evaluation of financing alternatives. The acronym FRICTO stands for flexibility, risk, income, control, timing, and other factors.

An analysis of the financing problem of business firms leads to the following conclusions:

1   Under idealized conditions with no income taxes, there are no advantages or disadvantages to any given financing plan from the viewpoint of the firm's stockholders.
2   Under idealized conditions with corporate income taxes (but no personal taxes), debt financing provides an advantage over other financing sources because of the tax deductibility of interest.
3   In practice there exists an optimal range for the capital structure of the firm. If the firm finances outside of this range, the value of the firm will decline.

Flexibility in future financing is provided by retaining earnings. Internal financing with retained earnings means that less current dividends will be paid than would be the case with external financing (new stock or debt). Stockholders may be better off receiving lower current dividends for several reasons. First, the price of the firm's stock should increase, reflecting the additional money invested in the firm, and there are personal tax advantages to capital gains instead of dividends. Second, issue costs of common stock are avoided. Third, with internal financing present owners are better able to retain their control of the firm.

When a firm changes its financing policy, its cost of capital is likely to change. The cost of capital should be calculated using the planned future proportions of the various financing sources and the current rates on its securities.

The cost of capital may be affected by the amount of financing required to support the planned capital budget. The capital budget may require revision to ensure that the returns expected from the least profitable investments being undertaken are sufficient to justify the costs of financing them.

QUESTIONS

1   Financial institutions, such as banks, finance their assets with a very high percentage of debt (considering demand and savings deposits as forms of debt). How are they able to do this without exposing their stockholders to a great deal of risk?
2   Describe what happens if a firm finances investment by issuing common stock at an ''unreasonably'' low price because of un-

usual conditions in the security markets. How is this "bad" for the current owners of the firm?

3 Regulated monopolies such as electric utilities and telephone companies use much more debt and preferred stock than do industrial corporations. Why do you think this is so?

4 If the corporate income tax were substantially reduced (say, to a flat rate of 10 percent), how would the types of financing used by corporations be affected?

5 If dividends on common stock and preferred stock were tax deductible expenses for the corporation, what would be the impact on the choice of financing?

6 Company A is in a high-risk business whereas company B is in a low-risk business. Sketch on one graph the behavior of the total value of the firm's securities for each of the two firms as a function of the degree of leverage used under realistic assumptions concerning the impact of leverage. Assume that the stock values of the two firms would be equal if neither firm used any leverage.

7 What is FRICTO? What purpose does it serve?

8 Why might a corporation headquartered in Tokyo choose a different capital structure for its Mexican subsidiary than it has chosen for the total corporation?

PROJECT

Estimate the relative proportions of debt, preferred stock, common stock, and retained earnings used as financing sources for each of the past ten years by nonfinancial corporations. Examine the level of long-term interest rates, corporate profits, and the behavior of the stock market over the same period. Try to explain the variations in financing methods used over this period. See Appendix 5A for sources of this information.

**DEMONSTRATION
PROBLEMS**

DP1 A movie theater is under construction. It will have a 500-seat capacity, and management plans to have 800 showings per year. The ticket price will average $2.50 per person, and total annual operating expenses are almost certain to be $300,000. Management feels fairly confident that the theater will operate at 50 percent capacity on average. An optimistic estimate would be 70 percent, whereas a pessimistic estimate would be 30 percent. The cost of the new theater will be $900,000, of which $100,000 is available from internal funds. Three financing alternatives for the remaining $800,000 are being considered: using all common stock, raising $400,000 from a sale of common stock and $400,000 by borrowing money at an 8 percent annual rate, or borrowing $800,000 at a 10 percent annual rate. Assume common stock can be sold at a price of $100 per share, there is no existing debt or preferred stock outstanding, current

448

PART 2
**The firm's investment,
financing, and dividend
decisions**

shareholders own 10,000 shares of stock, and the income tax rate is 40 percent.

a Develop an EBIT-EPS graph for the three financing alternatives.

b At approximately what percentages of capacity do the alternatives provide the same EPS (comparing financing alternatives two at a time)?

c Evaluate the three alternatives. Which one would you recommend? Is there any additional information that would be helpful in reaching a decision?

SOLUTION TO DP1:

a

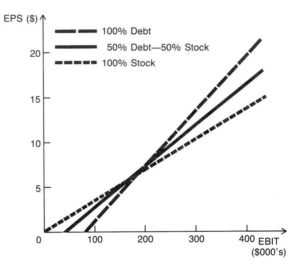

EPS must be calculated at two different levels; choose 50 percent capacity and 70 percent capacity. At 100 percent capacity, total revenues will equal $1 million.

$$
\begin{aligned}
\text{Total revenues} &= \$2.50 \times 800 \times 500 \\
&= \$1 \text{ million}
\end{aligned}
$$

	50% capacity	70% capacity
Total revenues	$500,000	$700,000
Operating expenses	300,000	300,000
EBIT	$200,000	$400,000

Calculation of EPS for each financing alternative and EBIT level are shown below.

	All stock		50–50		All debt	
EBIT	$200	$400	$200	$400	$200	$400
Interest	0	0	32	32	80	80
Taxable income	200	400	168	368	120	320
Taxes (40%)	80	160	67.2	147.2	48	128
Net income	$120	$240	$100.8	$220.8	$72	$192
No. of shares	18,000		14,000		10,000	
Earnings per share	$6.67	$13.33	$7.20	$15.77	$7.20	$19.20

b At 50 percent capacity, the 100 percent debt and the 50 percent stock–50 percent debt alternatives provide the same EPS as per the calculation above.

From the graph, 100 percent debt and 100 percent stock provide the same EPS at EBIT of approximately $180,000. This implies total revenues of $480,000 and, therefore, 48 percent capacity.

Also from the graph, the 100 percent stock and 50 percent stock–50 percent debt alternatives provide the same EPS at an EBIT level of approximately $145,000. This implies total revenues of $445,000 or 44.5 percent capacity.

c At the expected level of sales, the three financing methods do not differ very much. Both debt plans will result in losses if only 30 percent of available seats are sold as per the pessimistic estimate since EBIT is zero in this case. Based on this information, both debt plans seem pretty risky and stock might well be used. To make a final decision it would be helpful to have better estimates or at least some idea of what the probability of operating under 50 percent capacity is.

DP2 Central Pipelines is being formed to build and operate a gas pipeline in the Midwest. The pipeline is estimated to cost $1.4 billion and is expected to earn (EBIT) $196 million per year forever. (Assume no taxes will be paid and all earnings will be distributed as dividends and interest.)

a Assume that, if the plant is financed entirely with common stock, stockholders will require a 14 percent rate of return. What will be the total market value of Central if only common stock is issued in financing the pipeline?

b Assuming perfect capital markets and no costs to bankruptcy, what will be the total value of Central if $600 million in bonds are issued at an interest rate of 10 percent as part of the financing package?

c Given that bonds are issued as in *b*, calculate the rate of return required by stockholders on Central's common stock.

d Assuming that the pipeline will be built, how should it be financed?

SOLUTION TO DP2:

a Total value $= \dfrac{\text{total earnings}}{\text{required rate of return}}$

$= \dfrac{\$196 \text{ million}}{0.14}$

$= \$1.4 \text{ billion}$

b $1.4 billion as per *a* because total value of the firm's securities is not affected by the financing decision under these assumptions.

c Total value = stock value + bond value

If total value is $1.4 billion and $600 million in bonds are issued, then the stock value must be

Stock value = $1.4 billion − $600 million
= $800 million

Dividends to
stockholders = earnings − interest
= $196 million − 10% of $600 million
= $196 million − $60 million
= $136 million

k_s = $136 million/$800 million
= 17%

d The stockholders should be indifferent to the financing methods under the assumptions stated.

PROBLEMS

1 The Sands Corporation currently has 1.8 million shares of common stock outstanding. Management has developed a capital budget calling for total expenditures of $2.4 million in the next six months.

a If new stock can be issued at a price of $12 per share, how many shares must be issued to finance the entire capital budget from common stock?

b What will be the percentage of the firm's stock held by the new shareholders if shares are issued in *a*? [Ans.: 10 percent]

c Last year Sands paid a dividend of $0.50 per share. Management plans to maintain this dividend rate. What were the total dividends paid by the firm last year? What will be the total dividends paid in the coming year if new shares are issued and the dividend rate is maintained? What percentage of the dividends paid in the coming year will be received by the new shareholders?

2 The financial manager of Cheetah Freightlines is considering issuing either debt or preferred stock to finance trucks costing $3 million. The interest rate on debt will be 10 percent whereas the required dividend rate on preferred stock will be 12 percent. The firm's tax rate is 40 percent.

a What annual interest payments will be required on the debt issue?

b How much in additional earnings before interest and taxes must be generated from the new trucks to cover interest on the debt?

c What annual dividends will be required on the preferred stock issue?

d How much in additional earnings before interest and taxes must be generated from the new trucks to cover preferred dividends?

3 The Peachy Computer Company started in business five years ago manufacturing home computers. The firm has grown rapidly and there are now 100,000 shares of common stock outstanding, largely owned by management. Last year's income statement is shown below:

Peachy Computer Company

	Last year actual	Next year projections			
		Stock issue		Debt issue	
Sales	$1,000,000	$1,000,000	$3,000,000	$1,000,000	$3,000,000
Expenses	680,000	800,000	1,600,000		
Operating profit	$ 320,000				
Interest	0				
Taxable income	$ 320,000				
Taxes (25%)	80,000				
Earnings	$ 240,000	$ 150,000			$ 875,000
Earnings per share	$2.40	$0.94			$8.75

Peachy's chief designer, P. I. Tracy, has developed a new combination computer, TV, and telephone in a single package. In order to manufacture this product, new facilities will be required involving a total investment of $2 million. Two financing alternatives are being considered: issuing 60,000 shares of stock or borrowing the $2 million at an interest rate of 15 percent per year. Management has considered two possible future sales projections:

452

PART 2
**The firm's investment,
financing, and dividend
decisions**

a pessimistic projection of $1 million and an optimistic projection of $3 million.

a Calculate the values needed to complete the table.

b Develop an EBIT-EPS graph for the two alternatives.

c Draft a statement to the chief executive officer, A. P. Ricot, explaining the advantages and disadvantages of the alternative financing methods as illustrated by the data in the table and your graph.

4 Office Systems Supplies (OSS) has set out on a major expansion of its manufacturing facilities. The expansion will require $4 million in external financing and is expected to increase earnings before interest and taxes (EBIT) by $800,000 on average. Three financing alternatives are being evaluated: long-term debt, preferred stock, and common stock. Debt can be issued to finance the entire $4 million needed at an interest rate of 8 percent. A $4 million preferred stock issue would require a dividend of 9 percent whereas a $4 million common stock issue would require the firm to issue 200,000 new shares. OSS currently has 600,000 shares of common stock outstanding, no preferred stock, and debt carrying an annual interest cost of $280,000. The income tax rate for OSS is 30 percent. Management considers that EBIT with the new facilities in place is highly unlikely to be less than $400,000 in any year. The expected level of EBIT is $3.0 million per year.

a Develop an EBIT-EPS graph showing the three financing alternatives under assumptions that tax credits will be available in the event of losses and that preferred dividends will be paid even if not earned.

b Compare the three alternatives and indicate which one, in your judgment, seems most appropriate.

c Are there any other alternatives that you believe should be considered based on your evaluation in *b*?

d Suppose that preferred dividends are paid only to the extent they are earned. How would this affect your analysis/evaluation?

5 The Quasar Corporation has no outstanding debt or preferred stock. Management estimates that the required rate of return on Quasar common stock is currently 14 percent. The total market value of the stock is $40 million. An expansion program is planned that will involve $20 million in capital expenditures over the next two years. The estimated net present value of these investments is $5 million based on the current cost of capital of the firm. Therefore, assuming that only equity (common stock and retained earnings) is used to finance the expansion and that capital market rates do not change, the value of the firm's stock would be $65 million in two years.

Quasar's financial manager has suggested that debt be used to finance at least part of the $20 million. The following estimates have been developed:

Debt issued	Debt interest rate, %	Total common stock value	Rate on stock, %	Total value of Quasar securities
$ 0	—	$65 million	14.0	$65 million
5 million	10	62 million	14.2	
10 million	10.2	58 million	14.7	
15 million	10.6	53 million	15.2	
20 million	11	47 million	16.5	

a Determine the total value of Quasar's securities and its cost of capital for each financing alternative given that Quasar's tax rate is 40 percent.

b What financing plan would you recommend and why? (Hint: See Figure 12-6 and discussion.)

6 The QX Corporation has the following investment proposals which passed preliminary screening:

Proposal	Initial outlay	Expected rate of return
A	$ 100,000	30%
B	400,000	25
C	1,200,000	20
D	1,000,000	18
E	800,000	15
F	1,000,000	14
G	2,000,000	13
H	1,500,000	12
Total	$8,000,000	

The firm's current cost of capital is estimated at 11.5 percent. However the financial manager has determined that financing the entire budget of $8 million would result in a higher cost of capital for the firm. Only $3 million could be raised without increasing the cost of capital. The costs of new financing in incremental amounts are estimated to be as follows:

Incremental new financing	Cost of incremental new financing, %
$3.0 million	11.5
2.0 million	12
1.5 million	13
1.0 million	14
0.5 million	15

What should the firm do?

7 Quayle Industries is planning to issue $4 million in twenty-year maturity bonds. The bonds will bear a 10 percent coupon rate of interest and be issued at par. The cost of issuing the bonds will be $300,000. Quayle's tax rate is 40 percent. What is the effective, aftertax cost of the bonds?

8 In order to finance its capital budget, Quayle Industries may have to issue $2 million in common stock. The cost of issuing these securities will be $200,000. Quayle's financial manager has estimated that the market rate on stock is 14 percent. What is the cost of the common stock for use in calculating as marginal cost of capital for Quayle?

(*Note:* Problems *7* and *8* must be solved before problem *9* can be solved.)

9 Quayle Industries maintains a capital structure of 40 percent debt and 60 percent equity. Suppose that Shula issues the securities described in problems *8* and *9* in order to finance its capital budget. What is the marginal cost of capital for Quayle?

10 Gregor Enzac, a recognized genius in the field of entomology, has established a new company called Enz, Inc. The company will produce insects for agricultural pest control and engage in research in this area. Gregor plans to raise $10 million to be used, primarily, to establish facilities for the production of a "super" ladybug species developed by him. Field trials of the ladybug have already resulted in government contracts estimated to provide $500,000 per year in pretax earnings (EBIT) once production is under way. Gregor and his associates have received 100,000 shares of Enz common stock in exchange for the rights to their research and for long-term contracts to work for the company. The problem Gregor faces is how to raise the $10 million in cash. Current interest rates are 6 percent on AAA corporate bonds and 9 percent on B-rated bonds. The tax rate is 40 percent.

As financial advisor to Gregor and his associates, answer the following questions that they have asked:

a "Since AAA bonds have a much lower interest rate than B bonds and interest on debt is tax deductible, why shouldn't we issue $10 million of AAA bonds and not issue any more common stock?"

b "Should we issue $5 million of debt and then raise the remaining $5 million through a preferred stock issue?"

c "If we have to issue some common stock, what factors will determine how many shares must be issued and what price we will obtain?"

The ▓ symbol indicates that all or a significant part of the problem can be solved using the *Computer Models* software package that accompanies this text.

THE MODIGLIANI-MILLER ANALYSIS OF CAPITAL STRUCTURE AND VALUE

As discussed in Chapter 12, under idealized conditions in the capital markets and in the absence of taxes and bankruptcy costs, the value of a firm is unaffected by its financing. Both the total value of a firm's securities and its cost of capital are independent of its capital structure. In this appendix we will provide an illustration of the original analysis of Modigliani and Miller (MM) that provides these results and present the major arguments against the applicability of their results.

THE MM ANALYSIS

Consider two firms that have identical business risks and (for ease of illustration) the same expected level of earnings before interest and taxes. We assume that all business risk is based on the probability distribution of EBIT and that these two firms have identical distributions. Leverage Inc., has $1 million of 8 percent bonds outstanding, and Equity Inc., has no debt. Data on the two firms are shown in Exhibit 12-7. The question at issue here is what the market value of Leverage's common stock and therefore its total value will be. If there is an advantage to debt financing, the total value of Leverage will be greater than that of Equity. If debt financing is undesirable, Leverage's value will be

---

EXHIBIT 12-7
Basic data

	Leverage, Inc.	Equity, Inc.
EBIT	$480,000	$480,000
Interest	80,000	0
Dividends	$400,000	$480,000
Market value—bonds	$1 million	0
Market value—stock	?	$4 million
Total market value	?	$4 million

456

PART 2
The firm's investment,
financing, and dividend
decisions

less than Equity's. We can solve the problem by examining the consequences of first assuming that debt reduces value and then assuming that it increases value. If we find that neither assumption is reasonable, then, logically, total value must be the same for the two firms. In addition, arguing the point in this way will be helpful in illustrating the underlying characteristics of the analysis.

Suppose that the total value for Leverage's securities is only $3.5 million compared with Equity's $4 million. Debt financing has reduced the value of Leverage. Its bonds are worth $1 million, and its stock is worth $2.5 million. Consider an investor who wishes to purchase the rights to an income stream with the risk of Equity. For an investment of $400,000, the investor could purchase 10 percent of Equity's stock and for this amount would have an expected income of 10 percent of Equity's income, or $48,000. The investor now considers investing in Leverage. The investor could purchase 10 percent of Leverage's bonds at a cost of $100,000, which would provide $8000 interest and 10 percent of Leverage's stock at a cost of $250,000 with expected dividends of $40,000. The investor's total expected income from Leverage's securities would be $48,000, and *this income would have a probability distribution identical to that of the income from 10 percent of Equity's common stock.* This is so because the investor would own a 10 percent share in Leverage's earnings before interest and taxes just as he or she would have from purchasing Equity's common stock. The data describing these alternative transactions are shown in Exhibit 12-8. But note that purchasing a 10 percent claim against Leverage's income would cost the investor a

---

EXHIBIT 12-8
Assume debt lowers value

Market value of Leverage's bonds .... $1.0 million
Market value of Leverage's stock .... 2.5 million
Total market value of Leverage .... $3.5 million

Equity's stock value = total value = $4 million

1. Purchase 10% of Equity's stock

Purchase cost = $400,000
Dividend income = $48,000/year

2. Purchase 10% of Leverage's stock and bonds

	Purchase cost	Income
Bonds	$100,000	$ 8,000/year
Stock	250,000	40,000/year
Total	$350,000	$48,000/year

Investors would prefer 2, investing in Leverage's stock and bonds.

total of only $350,000. Obtaining the same expected income ($48,000) from Equity stock would cost the investor $400,000. If you were the investor, which choice would you make? Obviously you would prefer to buy Leverage's securities. In a perfect market, identical substitutes cannot sell at different prices. If all investors agree on the probability distributions of the two firms, their securities must sell at prices that provide the same returns. Either Equity's stock must sell for less than $4 million or Leverage's stock and bonds must sell for more than $3.5 million. *In any case the total value of Leverage's securities cannot be lower than the value of Equity's*; otherwise investors would all prefer to purchase a combination of stocks and bonds issued by Leverage rather than to purchase Equity's stock.

The result established by this example is that a firm using debt financing cannot lower its value below what it would be with all stock financing because investors can always undo the leverage by purchasing a combination of stocks and bonds issued by the firm. However, remember that we are assuming that the probability distribution of EBIT is not affected by financing.

What about the possibility that Leverage's value will be greater than Equity's? Suppose that Leverage's stock has a market value of $3.2 million and a total value of stock plus bonds of $4.2 million. A similar analysis can be performed in this case and the results are shown in Exhibit 12-9. Now investors desiring securities with the same risk as Equity's would purchase Equity's stock because they can get a better return than by purchasing 10 percent of Leverage's stock and bonds. However, what about an investor who is willing to trade off some risk in

---

EXHIBIT 12-9
Assumes debt increases value

Market value of Leverage's bonds............................ $1.0 million
Total market value of Leverage's stock .... 3.2 million
Total market value of Leverage .... $4.2 million

1. Purchase 10% of Equity's stock

Purchase cost = $400,000
Dividend income = $48,000/year

2. Purchase 10% of Leverage's stock and bonds

	Purchase cost	Income
Bonds	$100,000	$ 8,000/year
Stock	320,000	40,000/year
Total	$420,000	$48,000/year

Investors would prefer 1, investing in Equity's stock.

order to achieve a higher rate of return on the investment? An investment of $400,000 in Leverage's stock will provide the investor with an expected return of $50,000 per year, or 12.5 percent ($50,000/$400,000), as compared with only $48,000 per year, or 12 percent, if $400,000 is invested in Equity's stock. Such an investor has another alternative, however. Under the assumptions of this analysis, the investor can borrow at the same interest rate that the company can by using stock as security for the loan. Suppose the investor takes $375,000, borrows an additional $125,000 at 8 percent, and purchases Equity stock with the total amount ($500,000). The results are shown in Exhibit 12-10. The investor's net income is $50,000, the same as if the investor purchased Leverage's stock, and the out-of-pocket outlay is only $375,000 instead of $400,000. Since investors would rather hold Equity's stock alone than a combination of Leverage's stock and bonds, or they would prefer to borrow to invest in Equity's stock rather than hold Leverage's stock by itself, Leverage's stock value must be less than $3.2 million (or Equity's stock must be worth more than $4 million).

One final point is worth making. Suppose the market value of Leverage's stock and bonds is $4 million, made up of $3 million of stock value and $1 million of bond value. Equity's stock value and total value are both $4 million. An investor seeking higher risk and return could invest in Leverage's stock or borrow to invest in Equity's stock. Is risk and return from these two alternative strategies the same given the same dollar outlay by the investor? Exhibit 12-11 evaluates the returns achieved by the two strategies for three different levels of EBIT. Remember, Leverage and Equity are assumed to have identical probability distributions of EBIT (EBIT for the two firms have a correlation of 1.0). We see from Exhibit 12-11 that identical returns are achieved by the two investment alternatives: They have identical risks.

EXHIBIT 12-10
Using personal borrowing when debt is assumed to increase value

---

1. Purchase 12.5% of Leverage's stock

Purchase price = $400,000

Dividend income = $50,000/year

2. Borrowing to invest in 12.5% of Equity's stock

	Purchase cost	**Income**
Stock	$ 500,000	$ 60,000
Borrowing	(125,000)	(10,000)
Net	$ 375,000	$ 50,000

Investors would prefer 2, borrowing to invest in Equity's stock.

We have just shown that Leverage's total value cannot be greater than Equity's total value. We have also shown that Leverage's total value cannot be less than Equity's value. Thus, in the absence of taxes, the values of Leverage and Equity are equal and, therefore, a firm's total value (equity plus debt) does not depend on its financial structure.

*Leverage with
Corporate Taxes*

MM used arguments similar to those above to examine the impact of corporate taxes. They found that debt provides a benefit to the firm because of the tax deductibility of interest payments. The implication of their analysis in this case is that the value of the firm is maximized when its capital structure contains only debt. Although this extreme result is impractical because the Internal Revenue Service would never permit interest payments of this magnitude to be tax deductible, the inference is that firms should use as much debt as they possibly can, subject only to the restrictions of the IRS and the willingness of creditors to lend to the firm.

EXHIBIT 12-11
Assessing the risk from two investment strategies

	EBIT for leverage and equity		
	$80,000	**$480,000**	**$600,000**
Leverage interest	$80,000	$ 80,000	$ 80,000
Leverage dividends	0	400,000	520,000
Strategy A:			
Investor income	$ 0	$ 40,000	$ 52,000
Equity dividends	$80,000	$480,000	$600,000
Strategy B:			
Investor dividends	$ 8,000	$ 48,000	$ 60,000
Investor interest	(8,000)	(8,000)	(8,000)
Investor income	$ 0	$ 40,000	$ 52,000

Strategy A
 Investor purchases $300,000 of Leverage's stock, which has an aggregate market value of $3 million. Investor owns 10% of Leverage's stock.

Out-of-pocket investment = $300,000

Strategy B
 Investor borrows $100,000 at 8% interest rate and buys $400,000 of Equity's stock, which has an aggregate market value of $4 million. Investor owns 10% of Equity's stock.

Out-of-pocket investment = $300,000

Conclusion: **Both strategies provide the same income regardless of the level of EBIT for the firms; therefore the risk is the same for the two strategies.**

460

PART 2
**The firm's investment,
financing, and dividend
decisions**

The results of the MM analysis can be summarized as follows:

A The only benefit of debt financing (relative to equity financing) is the reduction in corporate income taxes due to the tax deductibility of debt interest.

B There is no disadvantage of debt financing relative to equity financing.

Implications for Financing If a firm is not paying corporate income taxes, the financing decision is irrelevant. It doesn't matter one way or the other whether or not debt is used. A firm paying corporate taxes should maximize its use of debt. Debt is superior to any other financing source.

CRITICISMS OF THE MM ANALYSIS

There are four conditions that must be met in order to validate the MM analysis and produce the above results:

1 No costs are imposed on the firm when it defaults on debt payments or goes bankrupt.

2 Investors must be able to do their own borrowing, using "homemade leverage," if they desire higher returns (with higher risk) than the returns provided by debtfree or low-debt firms.

3 Investors must be able to undo the leverage achieved by a corporation by purchasing a proportionate share of all the outstanding claims against corporate income.

4 Personal taxes must be neutral with respect to the choice between debt and equity.

Critics of the MM position have focused their attack on the realism of assuming these four conditions. We can separate these criticisms into two groups. The first group of criticisms is directed toward result **A**, that the only benefit from debt financing is due to the tax deductibility of interest. The second group of criticisms is directed toward point **B**, that there is no disadvantage to debt even if used very heavily. We summarize the various arguments below.

*Arguments
Supporting
Additional Benefits
from Debt*

1 The risk of leverage as perceived by an individual investor borrowing money is different from the investor's perception of the risk of leverage when the corporation borrows the money. Corporate leverage and homemade leverage are not perfect substitutes from the standpoint of the person doing the borrowing. Therefore, individuals will prefer that the corporation rather than they do the borrowing. One reason for this difference is risk in the limited liability of a corporate stockholder. If the corporation borrows and goes bankrupt, individuals lose at most their investment. If the individual borrows to finance stock purchases and the stock becomes worthless, the creditors can take over assets owned by the individual to pay off the debt.

2 The interest rate charged by lenders may be greater for an individual than for a corporation. Therefore, it will be cheaper from the viewpoint of the stockholders to have the corporation do the borrowing.

3 There are legal limitations inhibiting homemade leverage. Mutual funds and trust funds that invest heavily in common stock cannot borrow, and so these investors may prefer corporations with debt.

*Arguments Implying
a Disadvantage to
Debt*

1 The firm is likely to incur costs and suffer penalties if it does not meet its promised principal and interest payments. Legal expenses, disruption of operations, and loss of potentially profitable investment opportunities may result. As the amount of debt in the capital structure increases, so does the probability of incurring these costs. Consequently there are disadvantages to debt, and excessive use of debt may reduce the value of the firm. This is one of the most telling arguments against result *B* above.

2 Investors seeking to undo excessive leverage will incur transaction costs (brokerage fees from buying and selling securities) that would otherwise not need to be paid. Therefore the securities of highly levered firms will sell at somewhat lower prices than MM would predict.

3 Much corporate debt is not marketable. It consists of loans made by banks and other financial institutions. Therefore, investors cannot undo excessive leverage because they cannot purchase a proportionate share of the outstanding claims (stock and debt) against the firm's income.

4 Many institutional investors such as banks and life insurance companies cannot legally purchase low-rated bonds such as those issued by a highly levered corporation. Therefore the interest rates on highly rated, "investment grade" bonds are significantly lower than those on more risky bonds.

5 As firms in general increase their use of debt financing, they provide increasing amounts of interest which is taxed as ordinary income at the expense of capital gains on the stock which is taxed at lower effective rates.

6 The existence of risky borrowing by the firm (risky in the sense that the firm might not be able to repay the debt) can cause the firm to adopt a less profitable investment strategy than it would if it had no risky debt outstanding.

SUMMARY

The Modigliani-Miller (MM) analysis implies that firms are indifferent concerning the method of financing (all combinations of debt and equity are equally good) if there are no taxes, but, with corporate taxes, firms should be financed with virtually all debt. However, the MM model assumes away many factors that can imply that a particular blend of debt and equity financing is best for a given firm.

462

PART 2
The firm's investment,
financing, and dividend
decisions

We should add that existing theoretical models provide only a partial explanation of empirically observed corporate financing behavior, and there are serious difficulties in empirically measuring the impact of leverage on firm value. We do observe that capital structures differ across industries and that, for industries comprising firms with roughly comparable business risks (such as utilities and banks), it is often the case that the firms within an industry have similar capital structures. It is not clear whether this similarity in financing policies is due to "herd instinct" or to a correct determination of optimal capital structure by the companies' managers. The question of optimal capital structure remains a contentious issue in finance.

"May you live in interesting times," is an ancient Chinese curse. One of the aspects of our times that contributes to its "interest" is inflation. **Inflation** is an increase in the general level of prices for goods and services. The reverse of inflation is **deflation**, a reduction in the general level of prices. For the past forty years we have been experiencing some inflation almost continuously, and from the mid-1960s to the early 1980s it was a major problem. The degree of inflation we have faced recently is illustrated by the behavior of an index of consumer prices developed by government statisticians. The table on this page indicates the severity of the inflation since 1965. This essay is an overview of the consequences of inflation, the problems it creates, and the reactions of individuals and firms to it.

Year	Consumer price index (1967 = 100)
1850	25
1875	33
1900	25
1920	60
1930	50
1940	42
1950	72
1960	89
1965	95
1970	116
1975	161
1980	247
1982	289
1984	311
1986	328

THE FINANCIAL IMPACT OF INFLATION

Inflation has two major financial effects. It reduces the value of money and it may increase risk. Here let's look at the impact of inflation on the value of money, and what individuals and businesses are doing to protect themselves against the reduction in the value of the dollar.

The basic impact of inflation is straightforward: A given amount of money will purchase less in the future than it does today. This means, for example, that people living on a fixed income of $500 per month will find it impossible to maintain their standard of living as time passes. Their money income stays the same, but they become poorer as the amounts of goods and services they can buy with their $500 monthly income declines. If prices are increasing at a rate of 10 percent per year, then peoples' incomes must increase at least 10 percent per year for them to stay even. A similar logic applies to investments. If the rate of inflation is 10 percent per year and the rate of return on the investment is 6 percent per year, you are actually earning a negative 4 percent per year on the investment in terms of your ability to purchase goods and services. To gain from the investment, you must earn more than the 10 percent per year inflation rate.

Individuals and businesses have been doing several things to protect themselves against inflation. Employees demand cost of living pay increases. Labor unions seek contracts with employers that provide inflation escalators. These escalators increase wages automatically if the Consumer Price Index or some other measure of the price level increases. For example, a contract might pro-

464

PART 2
**The firm's investment,
financing, and dividend
decisions**

vide that an increase of 10 percent in the Consumer Price Index would result in a 10 percent increase in wage rates. The number of workers covered by major labor contracts with cost of living escalators increased at an unprecedented rate during the 1970s. Congress has responded to pressures from retired people by including cost of living adjustments in social security payments and federal pensions.

INNOVATIONS IN THE FINANCIAL MARKETS

When inflation increases unexpectedly and interest rates increase as well, borrowers are benefited but lenders hurt. In the early 1980s, the hurt to savings and loan associations from interest rate increases was so severe that large numbers of them ceased to operate as separate firms. In order to protect themselves against unanticipated increases in inflation, lenders have developed many new financial arrangements. Moreover some borrowers, in order to appeal to lenders (investors), have developed some ideas of their own.

Most of the innovations in financing can be characterized as belonging to one of two types. These two types are:

1. Variable (instead of fixed) interest rates
2. Equity participations where the lender shares in any increases in the value of the assets being financed

In addition there have been innovations such as "zero-coupon" bonds, which protect investors from decreases in interest rates and several home mortgage plans with payments that increase (contractually) over time to match anticipated increases in a borrower's ability to pay.

Mortgage lenders have been par-

ticularly innovative in designing variable or adjustment rate mortgage loans. Traditionally home mortgages have been long-term, fixed-interest-rate contracts between the borrower and the lender. The critical question for someone buying a house was "can we afford the monthly payment?" However, once the monthly payment on a loan was determined (based on the interest rate on the loan, the amount loaned, and the loan's maturity) that payment was fixed over the entire term to maturity. Now the question is more difficult to answer. Some mortgages (rollovers) have an interest rate and monthly payment that is fixed only for the first five years. At the end of five years, the interest rate may change to the current interest rate and a new monthly payment is determined to run for another five years. Rollover mortgages have been the dominant type of mortgage loan in Canada for many years. There are also many variable rate mortgages with interest rates that change semi-annually. The new rate is based on an index such as the cost of funds of savings and loan associations, the national average rate on new mortgages, the six-month Treasury bill rate, or whatever index agreed to by the borrower and lender. Loans also differ in whether the change in interest rate on the mortgage is reflected in a change in the monthly payment or the loan's maturity date. Often the maturity changes, keeping the same monthly payment. When interest rates increase substantially, however, the monthly payment may not even be enough to pay the monthly interest on the loan. When this happens, the monthly payment is usually increased to make sure the loan will eventually be repaid by the monthly payments. In some cases, the monthly payments are not changed but the loan balance is increased and a balloon payment is required at maturity. We show most types of home mortgages in the table on pages 465–467.

Adjustable interest rates are found in many types of debt contracts other than home mortgages. Some banks are offering variable rate consumer installment loans. The majority of bank loans to corporations have interest rates that change daily. Corporations have been issuing five- to ten-year bonds with variable interest rates usually linked to Treasury securities' rates. In 1982 banks and thrift institutions began offering variable rate time deposits for Individual Retirement Accounts (IRAs).

Equity participations have also become widely used. **Equity partici-** **pation** means that the supplier of money, the lender, shares in any increases (or decreases) in value of the asset being financed. Most of this activity has been in real estate financing. A **shared-appreciation mortgage (SAM)** has a low, fixed rate of interest, but gives the lender a share of any appreciation of the property. In a typical SAM the interest rate is 33 percent lower than the prevailing standard mortgage rate (for example, 8 percent rather than 12 percent). However, when the property is sold, the lender gets 33 percent of any increase in the value of the real estate being financed. Under some agreements, the lender can

---

Varieties of home mortgages

Mortgage type	Interest rate	Maturity	Payments
Conventional	Fixed.	Fixed, often 30 years.	Fixed over term of the loan.
	May be scarce when interest rates are climbing, because lenders do not want to risk being locked into lower income.		
Adjustable rate or variable rate (ARM or VRM)	Indexed to a market rate (for example, 6-month Treasury bill rate). Starting rate may be lower than on conventional because borrower shares risk of rising rates with lender.	Fixed, but sometimes can be extended in lieu of increase in monthly rate rises.	May change when interest rate changes or only at specified intervals, such as annually or every 3 to 5 years. If payments do not increase with interest rates, result may be negative amortization (see GPM below).
Graduated payment (GPM)	Fixed.	Fixed.	Low at start. Increase gradually as predetermined during first 5 or 10 years, then level out.
	Because of lower starting payments, may appeal to young borrowers who anticipate increased income in future years. *Caution:* Early payments may not cover interest due. Unpaid interest is added to outstanding principal, increasing the debt. This is called *negative amortization,* and borrowers may get a shock if they decide to sell in a few years and discover reduced equity in the property. However, some GPMs may include arrangements to prevent negative amortization.		

Mortgage type	Interest rate	Maturity	Payments
Graduated payments adjustable	Adjustable as in ARM or VRM.	Fixed, up to 40 years.	Similar to GPM. During first 10 years may be less than required to fully amortize loan. Adjusted within that period and every 5 years thereafter to insure full payment.
	Federal savings and loans and mutual savings banks were authorized in July 1981 to offer this mortgage, which combines graduated payments with adjustable interest rates. Payment adjustments may be quite large because of these two areas of change.		
Renegotiable rate (RRM)	Fixed for 3 to 5 years, then renegotiated.	Short-term loan (3 to 5 years) but amortized over longer term, usually up to 30 years.	Payments will change as interest rate changes.
	Short-term loan is automatically renewable; but if new interest rate is not acceptable, the borrower must either refinance or sell the property. The interest rate increases permitted each year and over the life of the loan may be limited.		
Shared appreciation (SAM)	Fixed.	Fixed.	Fixed.
	In return for lower interest rate the borrower agrees to share with the lender a percentage of any increase in the value of the home—at specified future dates or when it is sold, whichever occurs first. This plan may appeal to first-home buyer as a way to make the purchase affordable. But remember, increase in value must be shared with the lender; sharing a *decrease* in value may or may not be part of the agreement.		
Wraparound (WRAP)	Fixed.	Fixed.	Fixed.
	The lender combines an existing mortgage on the property (bearing a lower rate) with a new mortgage for the balance needed (at a higher rate) to provide a lower overall cost to the borrower. This is possible only if the existing mortgage is assumable by the buyer. (All FHA and VA mortgages are assumable.)		
Balloon payment	Fixed or adjustable.	Fixed. Traditionally 5 years but may be shorter or longer.	Fixed, usually based on 20- to 30-year amortization, but at end of term debt will not be fully paid. Borrower must pay off remaining "balloon" balance or refinance at prevailing rates.
	Because of short-term and balloon payment, the down payment may be as little as 5 percent.		

Varieties of home mortgages (concluded)

Mortgage type	Interest rate	Maturity	Payments
Reverse annuity (RAM)	May be adjustable.	May be fixed with refinancing option.	Loan due when home is sold or upon death of borrower.
	This plan calls for periodic payments to homeowners based on a loan against their equity in a home. It is designed to appeal to older persons who may be having difficulty living on reduced incomes.		
"Take-back"	Usually fixed.	Usually short term.	Usually a high down payment. May call for balloon payment at maturity.
	This is a loan by the seller of the property, who agrees to take the mortgage in order to facilitate the sale.		
Federal Housing Administration (FHA) insured	Set by FHA. Usually more favorable because of protection afforded lender. Seller may have to pay "points," an amount to raise lender's return to market levels.	Fixed.	Fixed or graduated, depending on FHA options.
	Available from lenders approved by FHA. Properties to be mortgaged must meet FHA requirements.		
Veterans Administration (VA) guaranteed	Fixed. Lower than others but seller may have to pay points.	Fixed. Usually 25–30 years.	Fixed or graduated, depending on VA options.
	Terms are eased because of VA guarantee. No or low down payment. Veterans should check with VA for eligibility requirements and for other assistance related to housing.		
Buy-down	Below market rate, for a specified period or for the life of the loan.	Fixed.	Fixed for term of the buy-down, usually increases thereafter.
	A seller or home builder pays an amount to a lender "up front," who then gives to buyers below-market rate loans. The borrower should realize this arrangement may increase the purchase price of the home.		

Source: Charting Home Mortgages, Federal Reserve Bank of Philadelphia, January 1982.

collect its share of the appreciation after a given number of years (normally ten years) even if the borrower hasn't sold the property (the value being determined by a professional appraiser). Another type of equity participation involves the lender's sharing in the revenues from an income-producing property, such as an office building or shopping center. Some life insurance companies have gone so far as to be co-owners of the property, becoming limited partners of the real estate developer.

468

PART 2
**The firm's investment,
financing, and dividend
decisions**

ARE FINANCIAL FUTURES IN YOUR FUTURE?

Not all the innovation has been confined to the financing area. The variability of interest rates and the desires of businesses and financial institutions to protect themselves against unexpected changes in interest rates has encouraged the development of a new type of financial security—**financial futures**. A **futures contract** is simply an agreement between two parties (individuals or firms) to exchange at some future date an asset for cash at a price that is fixed today. If you agree on January 31 to buy 100 ounces of gold on July 31 at a price of $400 per ounce from your local gold dealer, you have just created a six-months futures contract with the dealer. On July 31 you will have to put up $40,000 and the gold dealer will have to put up the 100 ounces of gold. In this contract $400 is the futures price of gold for delivery on July 31. The current (January 31) price of gold for immediate delivery is called the cash price.

One problem with this arrangement is that both you and the dealer have to have a great deal of trust in each other. The dealer trusts you to have $40,000 on July 31 and you trust the dealer to have the 100 ounces of gold to sell to you on July 31. To avoid this problem (and others), organized markets have been established for buying and selling futures contracts.

There are established futures markets for gold, orange juice, wheat, coffee, and many other commodities. Standardized futures contracts are bought and sold in these markets. All contracts in a given commodity are for a fixed quantity; for example, 100 ounces of gold, 50,000 pounds of cotton, and 10 metric tons of cocoa. Delivery dates are limited to one day in each month so that only the month of delivery need be specified; for example, July 1987, gold futures. The delivery months available for trading at any point in time are limited and vary with the commodity. For example on June 20, 1987, prices were quoted for twelve gold futures contracts listed in *The Wall Street Journal* ranging from July 1987 to February 1989. There were only four barley futures listed, ranging from July 1987 to March 1988.

Futures prices at a given point in time reflect expectations of market traders as to the future cash prices of the commodity. For example, if the cash price of gold six months from now is expected to be higher than the current cash price, the futures price of gold for delivery in six months will be greater than the current cash price. As expectations change, so do futures prices. **Futures prices** are not the cost of buying or selling a contract; they are the price per unit of the commodity in the contract for future delivery (i.e., the price the buyer of the contract agrees to pay for the commodity on the delivery date). In order to buy or sell a contract, you must "post margin" and pay a commission. For example, if you buy a July futures contract for 100 ounces of gold at $400 per ounce in the futures market, the broker with whom you place the order (e.g., Merrill Lynch) will require you to place money in a margin account, about 5 percent of the value of the contract for most commodities. Thus, for a $40,000 gold contract, the required margin would be about $2000. The broker will also charge you a commission, say, $50, for purchasing the contract for you. Once you have purchased this contract, you may either hold it and take delivery of the gold (which is handled through your broker) or, anytime before the July delivery date, sell a July futures contract for 100 ounces of gold, thus "closing out your position." This latter alternative is the most likely. Less than 3 percent of traded contracts are settled by delivery of the actual item. Your gain or loss on the two transactions (purchase and sale of the contract) will depend on what has happened to the July futures price of gold. If the price of July futures has risen since you bought the contract, upon closing out your position you will receive the difference between the prevailing futures price and the $400 futures price when you purchased the contract (less commissions). Thus, for example, if the futures price has risen to $440 per ounce when you close out your position, you will net $4000 less commissions on the deal [($440 − $400) × 100 ounces]. $4000 is a rather nice return on your investment of $2000 in the margin account!

What happens if the price of July gold futures falls instead? Each day your margin account will be reduced by the loss on the contract for that day. When your account drops below a minimum level (maintenance margin), which depends on the contract, you will be asked by your broker to either post more margin (put more money in your account) or to close out your position.

Suppose that you think the price of gold will fall. You can speculate on falling gold prices by selling a gold futures contract. Notice that, when selling contracts in the futures markets, you do not need to own the commodity. If you sell a July gold futures contract in January, you are obligating yourself to hand over 100 ounces of gold in July. You can either be prepared to have 100 ounces of gold to settle the contract, or buy a July futures contract prior to the July delivery date. Buying a July contract gives you the right to obtain 100 ounces of gold on the same delivery date as the contract you sold.

Therefore, buying a July futures contract at anytime before the delivery date will enable you to close out your position without actually having to deliver the gold. So that you don't forget to cover your position, your broker will remind you to close out any open positions prior to the expiration dates of the contracts you own.

Although commodity futures have been used for years, financial futures are a recent development. A financial futures contract is simply a futures contract involving financial assets rather than commodities. The financial assets for which there are active futures markets include foreign currencies (e.g., British pounds), thirteen-week Treasury bills, four- to six-year Treasury notes, fifteen-year Treasury bonds, ninety-day commercial paper, and others. Financial futures can be used to speculate on changes in interest rates (security prices) just as commodity futures can be used to speculate on changes in commodity prices. If you think short-term interest rates are going to rise, sell a one-year Treasury bill futures contract, say, at a price of $90.50. (Prices are stated per $100 of face value.) If interest rates do rise, the price will fall, say, to a price of $89.50. You can close out your position by buying a contract at $89.50. Since each contract in one-year Treasury bills is for $250,000 face value, you will earn $2500 from the transaction. Financial futures have much lower margin requirements than commodity futures, ranging between 0.15 percent to 2 percent of the face value of the contract. You would need only $900 in margin for a single one-year Treasury bill contract.

Financial futures are used by businesses and financial institutions to protect (hedge) against changing interest rates. For example, an airline might be planning to issue $10 million in long-term fixed-rate bonds in six months' time, when a new airplane is to be purchased. The financial manager could protect the airline from an increase in interest rates by selling 100 long-term Treasury bond futures contracts now. The contracts have a face value of $100,000 each so 100 contracts have a face value of $10 million. The financial manager would be planning to buy 100 contracts six months later when the bonds are issued. If interest rates do rise, the gains on the futures transaction will help to offset the higher interest rate on the bond issue. Of course, if interest rates fall, there will be losses on the futures transaction. But in this case the airline will benefit from the lower interest rates on the bonds. In 1981 Pillsbury wished to protect itself from higher interest rates on its short-term borrowing. It sold $60 million in Treasury bill contracts. Interest rates did rise and Pillsbury purchased $60 million in contracts, closing out its position with a profit of $225,000 to help offset its higher borrowing costs. Futures have a bright future as financial managers become adept in using them.

SWAPS

Many smaller companies wishing to borrow money can do so only on a variable interest rate basis, e.g., at the prevailing prime rate plus 2 percent. Other firms, especially large ones with very good credit ratings (often European companies borrowing in Europe), are able to obtain funds on a fixed interest rate basis. But the smaller company may want to pay a fixed rate, and the larger company may prefer to pay a variable rate. To achieve this, the two companies can make an arrangement (a "swap") under which, in effect, the small company pays the fixed interest on the large company's debt. The market for this type of transaction has exploded in the last seven years (growing from $3 billion to over $200 billion in underlying debt). Swaps are discussed in greater detail in Chapter 11.

CHAPTER THIRTEEN

DIVIDEND POLICY AND RETAINED EARNINGS

A corporation can use its earnings to pay dividends to its stockholders, or it can use the funds for other purposes, such as retirement of debt or financing new investments. An increase in dividends involves the payout of firm cash to its shareholders. If management does not want the dividend increase to affect the firm's asset base or level of debt (i.e., if investment policy and financial structure policy are not to change), then the firm will have to issue additional shares to finance the added dividends. A "pure" dividend policy change (i.e., one requiring no alteration of the firm's investment and financial structure policies) involves a change in dividends and an equal dollar change in new share sales (an increase in both or a decrease in both). In general, however, there may be simultaneous changes in more than one policy. For example, a company may decrease its dividend and use the funds to expand its investment (a mixture of dividend policy and investment policy changes), to pay off some of its debt (a mixture of dividend policy and financial structure policy changes), or to increase investment and retire debt (a simultaneous change in all policies). The implications of all this is that dividends, investment, and financing are very closely related.

In the first section of this chapter, we describe the dividend payment procedure. We then discuss the various factors that influence the firm's dividend policy and examine the alternative dividend policies that are followed in practice. Later sections of the chapter cover dividend reinvestment plans, stock dividends and splits, and share repurchases.

THE DIVIDEND PAYMENT PROCEDURE

Generally, firms pay dividends once per quarter, that is, four times per year. Normally, dividends are set at a level that the firm feels is sustainable even during the years of poor earnings. The firm projects its anticipated earnings and desired long-term payout ratio given the investment opportunities it anticipates, and sets a dividend payout ratio that it feels it can maintain. This dividend, which is planned with the firm's long-run situation in mind, is referred to as the **regular dividend**. In addition, some firms pay an **extra dividend** at the end of the year once the firm's earnings are known and investment needs have been determined.

472

PART 2
**The firm's investment,
financing, and dividend
decisions**

The first step in the dividend payment procedure is the announcement by the board of directors that a specified dividend will be paid to shareholders of record at some particular future date. For example, the board of directors of Serrento Corporation announces on February 15, 1991, that dividends of $0.50 per share will be payable to all shareholders of record on March 18, 1991 payment being made on April 8, 1991. A shareholder of record on a given date is someone who is recorded on the company's books at the close of business on that date as the owner of specific shares of stock. In the example, if Serrento Corporation were informed on March 18, or before, of a transfer of shares, the new owner (buyer) receives the dividend; if the corporation were notified of the sale on March 19 or thereafter, the old owner (seller) receives the dividend.

Since there is a lag of several days from the time a sale transaction takes place to the time the firm is informed of the transaction, a sale on, say, March 16 would not generally be recorded on the company's books until after the record date of March 18; that is, the seller would still be entitled to the dividend. Because of this lag, the practice is that the right to the dividend goes with the stock up to, but not including, four business days before the record date; a buyer of the stock four business days before the record date or thereafter does not acquire the right to the dividend. The stock is referred to as **ex-dividend** four days before the record date or thereafter, since the stock no longer provides the right to the dividend. For example, assume that Bill Seller owns 100 shares of Serrento Corporation stock. There are five business days between Friday, March 11, 1991, and March 18, 1991. Therefore, if Bill Seller sells the stock on or before March 11, 1991, the purchaser, Alex Buyer, also acquires the right to the dividend; but if Alex Buyer purchases the stock on March 12 or thereafter, the claim to the dividend remains with Mr. Seller, that is, the stock is ex-dividend. The ex-dividend date is March 12.

The price of the firm's stock will reflect that it has gone ex-dividend. Going ex-dividend will cause the price of the stock to fall by approximately the amount of the dividend. In our example, assuming no other cause for the stock price to change, a share of Serrento stock would sell for $0.50 per share (the amount of the dividend per share) less on March 12 than it did on March 11. If Serrento stock sold for $30 per share on March 11, it would sell for approximately $29.50 per share on March 12. This is so since the buyer of the stock on March 11 is also entitled to the $0.50 dividend; a buyer on or after March 12 is not entitled to the dividend. The dividend checks would be mailed by Serrento Corporation on April 8, 1991, to shareholders of record on March 18, 1991.

FACTORS AFFECTING THE DIVIDEND DECISION

The factors that are important in setting a dividend policy are the profitability of the firm's investment opportunities, taxes, legal considerations, liquidity and debt needs, and various costs that result from the firm's pursuing a particular dividend policy. Let's look at each of these factors.

If the company cannot invest profitably, earnings can be paid out in dividends. On the other hand, if profitable opportunities exist, earnings can be used for their financing. A zero dividend payout is not uncommon for young, rapidly growing firms with good investment opportunities. Financing investments from profits (internal financing) may be preferable to paying larger dividends and financing investments by selling new stock and bonds, because the firm's shareholders prefer capital gains income to dividend income (see the discussion of taxes below). Furthermore, raising external capital involves transaction costs (for example, flotation costs), which are completely avoided by using internally generated funds from operations. Even if current projects are unattractive, when a profitable future investment is foreseen, it may be advisable to invest present earnings in liquid assets (for example, marketable securities) so that the funds will be available later to finance the investment.

Shareholder Taxes As explained in Chapter 3, shareholders pay the same tax rate on capital gains as on dividends.[1] Dividend taxes apply to the entire dividend, and the tax is due in the year in which the dividend is paid. Thus, a taxpayer in the 30 percent tax bracket pays a $15 tax in 1991 on a $50 dividend received in 1991. Taxes on capital gains are payable when the stock is sold (not whenever the stock's price increases), and the tax is on the gain, not on the entire sale proceeds. For example, a share purchased in 1988 for $40 and sold in 1991 for $50 results in a $10 taxable gain in 1991. A shareholder in the 30 percent tax bracket would owe a capital gains tax of $3 in 1991.

An implication of this tax system is that, even if a shareholder's capital gains tax rate and dividend tax rate are equal (e.g., 30 percent), *from a tax standpoint* the shareholder will usually prefer an added dollar of capital gain to an added dollar of dividends. The reason is that the tax on the capital gain can be postponed by not selling all the shares owned, whereas the tax on the dividend cannot be postponed and must be paid in the year in which the dividend is received. To illustrate, assume that Arlo Corporation can adopt either policy A or policy B. Under A, Arlo's share price will be $100 and the dividend per share will be $10, whereas, under B, the share price will be $110 and the dividend zero. There is a $10 per share added capital gain with policy B relative to policy A ($110 − $100), but an added dividend per share of $10 under policy A.

	Policy A	Policy B
Share price	$100	$110
Dividend per share	$10	0

---

[1] An important exception to this applies if the shareholder is a corporation. In general, Corporation X will pay taxes on 30 percent of the dividends it receives from Corporation Y if X owns less than 20 percent of Y; X will pay taxes on 20 percent of the dividends it receives from Y if X owns at least 20 percent, but less than 80 percent, of Y; and X will pay no taxes on the dividends it receives from Y if X owns 80 percent or more of Y.

Suppose that investor X has ten shares of Arlo stock for which X originally paid $50 per share. Exhibit 13-1 compares X's position under policy A with two strategies X can select under policy B. Under strategy I, X retains the ten shares and, under strategy II, X sells one share to raise cash. Suppose first that X wants to keep his or her funds invested in the shares of Arlo. Strategy I with policy B is better than policy A because X can completely avoid current taxes under strategy I and keep an investment worth $1100. The added $100 of share value (10 shares × $10 per share) under policy B relative to policy A will not be taxed until X sells shares. Under policy A, shareholder X is forced to pay dividend taxes of $30 on the $100 of dividends and has only $1070 of wealth remaining ($1000 in stock and $70 in cash). Now suppose X wants some cash. With strategy II and policy B, X can sell one share and end up with Arlo shares worth $990 and cash (aftertax sale proceeds) of $92. This is better than X's $1000 in stock and $70 in cash (aftertax dividend) under policy A. Again, investor X prefers that Arlo adopt policy B. Note that, with strategy II and policy B, capital gains taxes are paid only on the one share sold; no tax is currently paid on the gain on the nine shares not sold.

EXHIBIT 13-1
Shareholder X's financial position under policy A and policy B

Policy A	
1. Market value of X's shares	$1,000
2. Dividends on X's shares	$ 100
3. Tax on dividends (@ 30%)	$ 30
4. Aftertax dividends [(2) − (3)]	$ 70

Policy B	
Strategy I: X retains all ten shares	
1. Market value of X's shares	$1,100
2. Aftertax dividends	0

Strategy II: X sells one share, retains nine shares	
1. Market value of X's nine shares	$ 990
2. Aftertax dividends	0
3. Proceeds from share sale	$ 110
4. Tax on share sale:	
Sale price $110	
Original cost 50	
Gain $ 60	
Tax on gain (@ 30%)	$ 18
5. Aftertax cash proceeds [(3) − (4)]	$ 92

The ability to postpone personal taxes on capital gain income encourages firms to finance investment from retained earnings and to keep dividends lower than would be the case if capital gains were not allowed this tax advantage (e.g., if capital gains were taxed whenever the share price rose whether or not the stock were sold). Why is this so? Each dollar that is earned and retained by the firm as cash or invested by the firm in a productive asset raises the firm's value and the value of currently outstanding shares. The retained earnings thus raise share price and generate capital gains. This price rise is taxed only when the shares are sold. If, on the other hand, the firm were not to retain the earnings but to pay them out in dividends, a tax on the dividend would be payable immediately. The ability to postpone personal taxes by retaining funds in the corporation encourages companies to pay lower dividends than they would if such tax postponement were not permitted.[2]

The Tax Reform Act of 1986 made two changes affecting capital gains and dividends. By far the more important was the elimination of a special lower tax rate on **long-term capital gains** (gains on assets held more than six months). The other change was removal of a tax exemption on the first $100 of annual dividend income received by a taxpayer from U.S. corporations. The net effect of these two changes was to reduce significantly the advantage of capital gains relative to dividends. Capital gains were left with one important advantage, the opportunity to postpone taxes.

It should be kept in mind that at this point we have considered only personal tax effects on dividend policy. As we will see, some of the other factors (tax and nontax) influencing dividends may bias in favor of dividend income rather than capital gains.[3]

Tax on Excessive Firm Retentions Is a corporation able to pay out no dividends and permit its shareholders to earn all income in the form of capital gains? It can, *if* the funds that would have been paid in dividends are used to purchase productive assets by the firm and not merely retained in the form of cash and cash substitutes (stocks and bonds, Treasury bills, etc.). If the firm accumulates cash and cash substitutes beyond a limit deemed reasonable by the Internal Revenue Service in meeting the firm's liquidity needs, a special surtax will be imposed on the firm's improper accumulations. Although this penalty is unlikely to be

---

[2] It is easily shown that if investors incur negligible brokerage fees in buying and selling securities and if information about a firm can be obtained by investors at a nominal cost, then a tax bias in favor of capital gains relative to dividends implies that firms will never finance an investment by selling new shares if the investment can be financed from retained earnings. That is, management will reduce dividends to provide funds for an investment before it will sell new shares to obtain the funds. On this see R. C. Stapleton, "Taxes, the Cost of Capital and the Theory of Investment," *The Economic Journal* (December 1972), pp. 1273–1292.

[3] The dividend policy implications of taxes and various other relevant factors are discussed later in this chapter in the section "The Dividend Policy Debate."

476

PART 2
**The firm's investment,
financing, and dividend
decisions**

imposed, it does discourage flagrant attempts by corporations to avoid paying dividends.

Corporate Taxes From Chapter 12, you will recall that the tax deductibility of interest encourages firms to use more debt financing (and therefore less equity financing) than they would if interest were not tax deductible. This means that more of the corporation's cash flow will be paid out as interest on debt and less will be paid out as dividends.

Legal Commitments and Requirements

Contractual Restrictions The contract between the firm and its creditors or between the firm and its preferred stockholders may include constraints on the firm's activities for protection of the lenders' or preferred stockholders' investments. A common constraint is that dividends may be paid only out of profits earned in periods after the debt contract becomes effective. Preferred stock contracts, which provide for cumulative dividends to preferred stockholders, stipulate that there will be no dividend payment to common stockholders until current and all unpaid past preferred dividends have been paid.

Statutory Constraints on Capital Impairment Most state laws provide that dividends in the form of cash or property may not exceed retained earnings (accumulated profits) plus paid-in surplus. That is, the firm may not pay dividends if the owners' equity (assets minus liabilities) is no greater than the outstanding stock's total par value or, if the stock has no par value, the outstanding stock's "legal" or "stated" capital (a value designated by the firm's board of directors). This requirement is imposed to ensure that the assets of the firm exceed liabilities by a minimum cushion in order to protect the creditors. This cushion (the par value of the firm's stock) may be small in relation to the assets and liabilities of the firm, but it nevertheless provides at least some safety margin to creditors. A second statutory limitation on dividends often applies if the firm is insolvent. Most states prohibit an insolvent firm from paying dividends.[4]

The Firm's Liquidity and Debt Needs

A firm will generally hold some liquid assets, such as cash and marketable securities, to meet planned or unexpected cash requirements. The rate of return on such liquid assets, net of the costs of supervising them (for example, the costs of managing the portfolio of marketable securities), is generally low, and excessive accumulation of such assets is therefore unprofitable. To eliminate excess liquid assets, unneeded cash and proceeds from selling excess marketable securities can be paid out as a dividend or be used to retire debt. A deficiency of liquid assets may encourage the company to curtail dividends.

---

[4] The definition of insolvency varies from state to state. In some cases it means that the firm is simply unable to pay its debts, whereas, in other states, it means that assets are less than liabilities.

Costs of External Financing and of Dividend Payments   A firm may maintain a low dividend payout so that it can avoid external financing of its investments. The greater is the cost of obtaining external financing, the greater will be the incentive to finance internally from the firm's profits. The costs of external capital include underwriting costs, brokerage commissions and fees, bank loan set-up costs, legal and accounting fees, and the expense of management's time in arranging outside financing. These costs are avoided by financing internally. Furthermore, the transaction costs involved in paying dividends (e.g., bookkeeping and postage costs) are avoided if no dividends are paid. The firm's out-of-pocket expenses are always less with internal financing than with external financing.

Stockholder Transaction Costs   Investors incur costs when they buy or sell an asset such as stock. In the case of stock, this cost appears as a brokerage commission and as time spent by the shareholder in conducting the transaction. If shareholders want cash for living expenses or for investments in different assets (for example, in the shares of other firms), the transaction costs to them will be less if they have dividend income than if they have to sell their shares in order to obtain the cash. From a purely transaction cost standpoint (for example, ignoring tax considerations), investors who want cash will prefer dividends to capital gains of the same dollar amount.

On the other hand, some shareholders may prefer to keep their capital invested. If the firm pays them a dividend, they have to reinvest it themselves and pay a brokerage commission. But, if the firm retains the dividend and invests it, shareholders will receive a capital gain that involves no transaction costs to them. In contrast to those who want cash and prefer dividends, investors who wish to keep their funds in the firm prefer income in the form of capital gains rather than in the form of dividends.

Because of differing preferences among investors for capital gains and dividends, firms with high dividend payouts will tend to attract investors who want cash income (dividends), and firms with low dividend payouts will tend to attract investors who want to keep their funds invested. This attraction of investors to companies with dividend policies that meet the investors' preferences is referred to as the **clientele effect**. The clientele effect encourages corporations to maintain stable, predictable dividends because most investors do not like uncertainty about the timing and magnitude of their dividends and capital gains. Unexpectedly low dividends may force a shareholder to sell shares to raise cash (which means brokerage fees and perhaps the payment of capital gains taxes). Unexpectedly large dividends for investors who had planned to keep their funds invested will mean the cost of reinvesting the cash (brokerage fees) and the immediate payment of taxes on the dividends received. It follows that firms with unstable, unpredictable dividend policies will be relatively unattractive to investors. The shares of such companies will sell for a lower price than they would if the company had a stable, predictable dividend.

Two important dimensions of a firm's dividend policy are:

1 *Dividend stability:* whether dividends remain fixed or fluctuate from period to period
2 *Long-run dividend payout ratio:* the long-run average percentage of earnings paid out in dividends

Policy variables **1** and **2** are distinct from one another. Dividends can be stable or unstable whether the percentage of earnings paid out as dividends is high or low.

In examining the two policy variables, we will consider the factors the firm must evaluate in determining its optimal policy and the empirical evidence concerning United States corporate behavior. The actual experience of corporations indicates which factors are most important.

Dividend Stability

Alternative Policies and the Evidence Regardless of the policy determining the long-run dividend payout ratio, year-to-year fluctuations in dividends may follow any one of several guidelines:

1 *Stable dividend payout ratio.* This policy requires that the percentage of earnings paid out (dividend payout ratio = dividends ÷ earnings) each year is held stable. The result is dividends that fluctuate proportionately with earnings.
2 *Stable dollar dividend.* The dollar level of dividends is relatively stable from period to period or follows a steady upward or downward trend over time.
3 *Stable dollar dividend plus an "extra" dividend.* The company pays out a stable (in dollar level) regular dividend plus an added dividend at the end of particularly prosperous years.

Historical evidence suggests that whereas the first policy is rare, a stabilized dollar dividend is maintained by most major United States corporations. The third policy is practiced by a small minority, perhaps 10 percent, of large firms, with General Motors the most prominent example.

Figure 13-1 shows that earnings (net aftertax income) have historically been far more volatile than dividends, although both have trended upward since the 1930s depression. A classic study by John Lintner indicated that firms adjust their dollar dividends only gradually as earnings vary from year to year.[5] He also found resistance by corporations to reducing dividends below the amount paid in the previous period. Later studies by Brittain and by Fama and Babiak provided results generally consistent with those of Lintner.[6]

---

[5] See John Lintner, "Distribution of Income of Corporations among Dividends, Retained Earnings, and Taxes," *American Economic Review*, 46 (May 1956), pp. 97–113.

[6] See John A. Brittain, "The Tax Structure and Corporate Dividend Policy," *American Economic Review* (May 1964), pp. 272–287; Eugene F. Fama and Harvey Babiak, "Dividend Policy: An Empirical Analysis," *Journal of the American Statistical Association* (December 1968), pp. 1132–1161.

An Explanation of Dividend Stability The primary goal of company policy is to benefit shareholders. To justify a stable dollar dividend policy, we must show that stockholders are made better off by this policy. Several explanations for investors' preferring stable dollar dividends have been suggested.

First, investors may use dividends to cover living expenses, which are usually rather stable from period to period. A radical decline in dividend income may force investors to sell shares to obtain funds for living expenses, and a radical rise in dividends may produce excess cash that investors will want to reinvest. Selling shares or investing dividends involves brokerage fees and other expenses, including the investor's time. These costs are avoided if dividends are stable and predictable and the investor consequently does not have to sell shares or reinvest dividend income.

FIGURE 13-1

Aftertax profits, dividends, and retained earnings of U.S. corporations. (Source: Federal Reserve Bulletin).

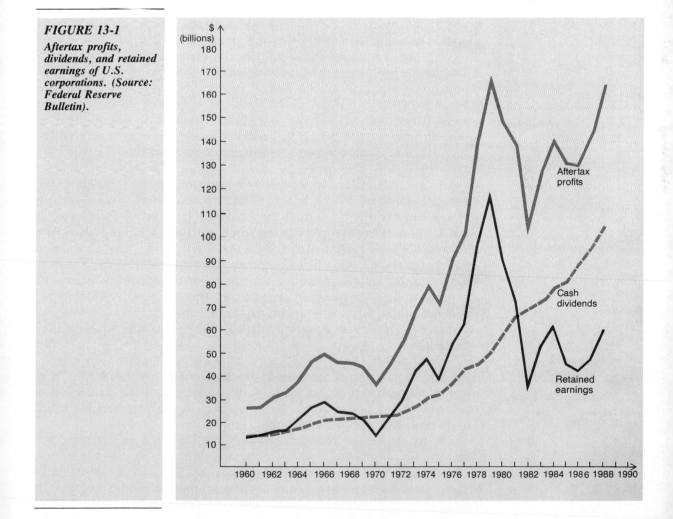

Second, the level of current dividends conveys information to investors on the *future* dividend-paying capacity (earning capacity) of the firm. If investors know that the firm will raise or lower dividends only if management foresees a permanent earnings increase or decrease, respectively, then the level of dividends informs investors about management's expectations about earnings. A cut in dividends implies poor earnings expectations, no change implies earnings stability, and a dividend increase implies management's optimism about earnings. On the other hand, a company with an erratic dividend poicy is, in effect, not providing such information, thereby increasing the risk of the shares. Stable dividends that are based on long-run earning power of the company therefore reduce share riskiness and consequently increase the value of the shares to investors.

A third factor encouraging stable dividends is the requirement by many states that financial institutions, for example, mutual savings banks, insurance companies, and mutual funds, may invest in only those stocks with good dividend records. These institutions are a significant force in the market, and their demand for the company's stock can enhance its price (which benefits the shareholders). Also, federal laws covering pension plans encourage the purchase of stocks with high, stable dividends.

Long-Run Dividend Payout Ratio

The above discussion concerned the first aspect of dividend policy, stability from year to year. We noted that firms tend to keep dividend payments stable from period to period. The second aspect of dividend policy is the long-run average percentage of earnings that the firm pays out in dividends. The firm may plan a high or low long-run dividend payout ratio regardless of its policy concerning period-to-period stability. In actuality, we find that, although most firms have relatively stable dollar dividends, firms differ markedly in terms of their long-run payout ratios. Large, mature companies such as General Motors, Du Pont, and Exxon tend to have high dividend payout ratios, whereas smaller, rapidly growing firms, such as Bally Manufacturing, Hewlett-Packard, and Tandy, often have low dividend payout ratios or pay no dividends at all. The question arises as to whether there is a "correct" dividend policy for a given firm or indeed for all firms. Below, we address this issue and provide guidelines for setting a company's dividend policy.

The Dividend Policy Debate

There is controversy as to whether dividend policy matters at all! There are two schools of thought: the **imperfect markets school**, which argues that dividend policy matters, and the **perfect markets school**, which argues that dividend policy is irrelevant.

The imperfect markets school holds that various types of imperfections (transaction costs, costs of obtaining information, and tax biases) make dividend policy important. One branch of this school asserts that a firm is better off paying *small dividends* and financing investments internally than it would be paying larger dividends and financing investments externally by selling new shares. Internal financing is viewed as superior (cheaper) to external equity financing because, with the former, the firm's current owners earn income as capital gains rather than as dividends (an advantage due to personal tax effects; see the discussion of shareholder taxes earlier in this chapter).[7] Also, flotation costs are avoided with internal financing, and dividend payment accounting and postage costs are avoided if these dollars are reinvested rather than paid out as a dividend. Using internal rather than external equity financing therefore means a lower cost of equity capital and a lower average cost of capital for evaluating investments. An implication is that the cost of capital and the level of investment will depend on the type of equity financing that is available. Thus, it is argued, a firm will invest more if it has internal funds available than if it has to resort to the more costly external equity financing.

A second branch of the imperfect markets school contends that firms should pay *large dividends* even if it means selling new shares to do so. The argument goes something like this: "Firms should pay large dividends even if new shares have to be sold to finance the dividends because investors need the dividends for living expenses. Large dividends provide the needed income without the shareholders' having to sell their shares (which would involve brokerage fees). Although firms incur costs in selling new shares to pay dividends, firm managements are more astute in choosing the proper time to sell (that is, they can sell shares when the stock is overpriced and then store up the cash proceeds to pay big dividends for several periods); investors, on the other hand, are less astute and may, if dividends are small, be forced to sell their shares when they are underpriced. Second, by paying large dividends the firm is showing that it can *really* generate cash returns for the shareholders. That is, dividends are viewed by investors as less risky than capital gains and therefore the firm's shares will be worth more if income is in the form of dividends rather than capital gains." The argument that management is more astute in timing the sale of shares assumes that management has better information about share price trends and values than do shareholders. This is a debatable point which has not been resolved. However, the second argument concerning the advantage of paying dividends to reduce share risk is clearly specious. When a firm sells shares to pay dividends, it is doing nothing more than what share-

---

[7] For theoretical arguments and empirical evidence consistent with this view see, for example, M. J. Brennan, "Taxes, Market Valuation and Financial Policy," *National Tax Journal*, 22 (December 1970), pp. 417–427; R. H. Litzenberger and K. Ramaswamy, "The Effect of Personal Taxes and Dividends on Capital Asset Prices: Theory and Empirical Evidence," *Journal of Financial Economics*, 7 (June 1979), pp. 163–195; and R. C. Stapleton, op. cit. (footnote 2). It should be pointed out that these studies examine time periods in which capital gains tax rates were significantly lower than dividend tax rates. This is no longer the case, although there does remain the tax advantage to capital gains in that the tax on a capital gain can be postponed by not selling the shares (see the discussion of taxes at the beginning of this chapter).

482

PART 2
**The firm's investment,
financing, and dividend
decisions**

holders could do for themselves (since shareholders could sell their own shares and receive the proceeds directly). A firm policy of selling shares each period to pay dividends therefore provides shareholders with no reduction in share risk and no benefits.[8]

Imperfect markets theory advocates of both the small and the large dividend payment persuasions hold that, because of brokerage fees and other imperfections, firms should maintain a *stable* dividend (see the previous section on dividend stability). As is discussed in the next section, the *smoothed residual dividend policy* conforms to the imperfect markets view. It dictates that the firm should maintain a stable dollar dividend and set the dividend level so that equity investment (investment not financed by borrowing) is financed internally (with retained earnings) to the greatest possible degree rather than by selling new shares since internal financing is cheaper.

Confronting the imperfect markets school are those who believe that dividend policy does not matter. We will call this the perfect markets school. The members of the perfect markets school hold that the costs of internal and external equity financing are the same and therefore that the type and level of investment made by the firm do not depend on whether funds are raised internally or externally. The firm can, in any period, choose whatever dividend it deems appropriate, and any excess of equity investment over internally available funds will be financed by selling new shares.

The perfect markets theory begins with a famous proof by Miller and Modigliani that dividend policy is irrelevant in a world of no imperfections (that is, no transaction costs, no tax biases, etc.).[9] Modigliani and Miller do assume risk and uncertainty, however. Perfect markets theory proponents then go on to argue that transaction costs are not all that great and other imperfections do not really matter. For example, the tax bias favoring capital gains relative to dividends is not important because, through various types of tax shelters, dividend tax rates can be reduced to capital gains tax rates.[10] Furthermore, there is no need to stabilize dividends just to convey a positive image to investors; informed investors (informed by financial analysts who specialize in gathering, analyzing, and disseminating information about companies) will value the firm

---

[8] Some arguments in favor of higher dividends to reduce share risk actually involve changes in firm investment policy; that is, these arguments involve a confusion between dividend policy and investment policy effects. For the debate on this point and on other related points, see M. J. Gordon, "Dividends, Earnings and Stock Prices," *Review of Economics and Statistics*, 41 (May 1959), pp. 99–105; M. J. Brennan, "A Note on Dividend Irrelevance and the Gordon Valuation Model," *Journal of Finance*, 26 (December 1971), pp. 1115–1122.

[9] M. H. Miller and F. Modigliani, "Dividend Policy, Growth and the Valuation of Shares," *Journal of Business*, 34 (October 1961), pp. 411–433.

[10] See M. H. Miller and M. S. Scholes, "Dividends and Taxes," *Journal of Financial Economics*, 6 (December 1978), pp. 333–364.

on the basis of its underlying financial health, not on the basis of its dividend policy. Finally, since some investors prefer high dividends and low capital gains (for example, financial institutions which may invest in only those firms with good, stable dividend records), and other investors prefer low dividends and high capital gains, there is a clientele for the shares of a firm regardless of its dividend payment policy.[11] In short, the market price of a firm's shares does not depend in any significant way on dividend policy.

Who is right? Well, let's look at the evidence.[12] A study by Fama, which supports the perfect markets view, concludes that the evidence is consistent with the notion that a firm's investment and dividend policies are independent.[13] A study by Black and Scholes largely supports Fama's findings.[14] These results confront a significant body of contrary findings supporting the imperfect markets theory. Pye examined 330 United States firms and found that an abnormally low proportion of firms that issued new stock also paid dividends.[15] This suggests that firms tend to utilize retained earnings to finance investment before employing external stock financing. Similar conclusions were reached by Higgins, who found that, consistent with the residual payout policy, dividends vary positively with earnings and negatively with investment.[16] Dhrymes and Kurz found that a desire to maintain stable dividends may hamper investment by reducing internal funds available for capital expenditures. Furthermore, their results suggest that investment reduces the dividend payout, as predicted by a residual payout policy.[17] Baumol, Heim, Malkiel, and Quandt observed that the rate of return earned on internally financed investment was significantly lower than that earned on invest-

---

[11] See F. Black and M. S. Scholes, "The Effects of Dividend Yield and Dividend Policy on Common Stock Prices and Returns," *Journal of Financial Economics*, 1 (May 1974), pp. 1–22. Black and Scholes argue that all dividend policies we observe at equilibrium for a particular type of firm (one with similar investment and financial structure policies) must be equally desirable (must produce the same share values) or some firms would switch to a different dividend policy which produces higher share values. That is, all dividend policies we have observed must be equally good (must produce like share values) because inferior policies will be abandoned by firms.

[12] For a pointed discussion of the state of uncertainty concerning dividend policy, see Fischer Black, "The Dividend Puzzle," *Journal of Portfolio Management*, 2 (Winter 1976).

[13] See E. F. Fama, "The Empirical Relationships between the Dividend and Investment Decisions of Firms," *American Economic Review*, 64 (June 1974), pp. 304–318.

[14] See Black and Scholes, op. cit. (footnote 11).

[15] See Gordon Pye, "Preferential Tax Treatment of Capital Gains, Optimal Dividend Policy, and Capital Budgeting," *Quarterly Journal of Economics* (July 1972), pp. 226–242.

[16] See Robert C. Higgins, "The Corporate Dividend-Saving Decision," *Journal of Financial and Quantitative Analysis* (March 1972), pp. 1527–1541.

[17] See P. Dhrymes and M. Kurz, "Investment, Dividends, and External Finance Behavior of Firms," in R. Ferber (ed.), *Determinants of Investment Behavior* (New York: National Bureau of Economic Research, 1967).

484

PART 2
**The firm's investment,
financing, and dividend
decisions**

ments financed externally.[18] This is consistent with the view that more must be earned on externally funded capital outlays because external financing is most costly. Litzenberger and Ramaswamy found that investors may prefer a dollar of capital gains to a dollar of dividends, suggesting that stockholders do not want increased dividends which are financed by new share sales (which reduce the owners' capital gains by diluting their ownership in the firm).[19]

What are the implications if you are setting your company's dividend policy? First, shareholders will likely want the company to maintain a stable dividend from period to period. As explained earlier, radical declines in dividends may force some shareholders to sell shares, and sharp rises in dividends may force some shareholders to reinvest the excess dividend. These transactions and the associated brokerage fees and other costs are avoided if dividends are stable.

Second, the firm's shareholders are probably best off if the company has a long-term policy of minimizing reliance on new shares to finance operations. If necessary, sell shares if internally generated cash and borrowed funds are insufficient to finance investment. But, because taxes on shareholders are so important, do not regularly sell additional shares to pay bigger dividends. An added dollar of dividends financed by new share sales raises the existing shareholders' dividends by one dollar and reduces their capital gains by roughly one dollar. This increases the present value of shareholder taxes because dividend taxes must be paid immediately whereas capital gains taxes can be delayed by not selling all the shares held (see Exhibit 13-1 and the related discussion). The tax advantage of capital gains over dividend income means that shareholders are generally made worse off if the company sells stock to pay bigger dividends. The name for a policy of stable dividends with minimum reliance on new share financing is the **smoothed residual dividend policy**, which is discussed below.

Third, if the company has excess cash that it wants to pay out to shareholders, it is better from a tax standpoint to buy back shares from the shareholders than to pay them dividends. As explained at the end of this chapter, dividends are taxed at the ordinary income tax rate, which is much higher than the long-term capital gains tax rate that usually applies to any gains on shares that a stockholder sells back to the company.[20]

---

[18] See W. J. Baumol, P. Heim, B. G. Malkiel, and R. E. Quandt, "Earnings Retention, New Capital and the Growth of the Firm," *The Review of Economics and Statistics*, 52 (November 1970), pp. 345–355.

[19] See R. H. Litzenberger and K. Ramaswamy, op. cit. (footnote 7).

[20] For example, Arrow Corporation could pay $100 to a shareholder either by paying the shareholder a $100 dividend or by buying $100 worth of the shareholder's Arrow Corporation stock. The shareholder pays a much larger tax on the $100 dividend than on the $100 received for the Arrow stock. For details, see the section on repurchasing stock at the end of this chapter.

The most prominent dividend policy based on the theory that internal financing is cheaper than external financing is referred to as the **residual dividend policy**. Many companies follow this strategy.

Let's begin by examining the residual concept. Funds for corporate investment come from borrowing, retained earnings, and the sale of stock. We refer to investment funded by equity capital sources (retained earnings and stock sales) as **equity investment**. In each period, management determines the proportions of new investments to be financed by borrowing and by equity capital. The desired proportions depend on financial market conditions and on target debt levels set by management. The dividend *under a residual dividend policy equals* the amount left over from earnings after *equity* investment. If equity investment equals earnings, no dividends are paid. If equity investment is greater than earnings, no dividends are paid and new shares are sold to cover any equity investment not covered by earnings. And, if equity investment is less than earnings, *all* such investment is covered from earnings (no new shares sold) and what is left over from earnings is paid out as a dividend. *Dividends are therefore merely a residual remaining after all equity investment needs are fulfilled.* Notice that a residual policy minimizes the use of external equity financing (sale of new shares) since, by this policy, equity investment has a higher-priority claim to earnings than do dividends.

Corporations have employed three general approaches in putting the residual dividend policy into practice. Before describing these approaches, we will define the following variables:

D_t = dividend paid in year t

I_t^e = investment in year t that is financed from equity sources (retained earnings and stock sales)

E_t = earnings in year t

q_t = dividend payout ratio in year t where $q_t = \dfrac{D_t}{E_t}$

1 *Pure residual dividend policy.* Following this approach, the corporation will set the dividends paid each year so that, if equity investment I_t^e equals or exceeds earnings E_t, then dividends will be zero; and if I_t^e is less than E_t, then dividends will be

$$D_t = E_t - I_t^e$$

2 *Fixed dividend payout ratio.* Dividends under this approach equal a constant proportion (q_t) of yearly earnings. This can be expressed as

$$D_t = q_t \cdot E_t$$

If the percentage paid in dividends is 40 percent, for example, this would equal

$$D_t = q_t \cdot E_t = 0.4E_t$$

486

PART 2
The firm's investment,
financing, and dividend
decisions

The percentage q_t is set so that, over the long run, dividends are equal to earnings minus equity investment.

3   *Smoothed residual dividend policy.* Under this approach, dollar dividends have a stable pattern. Dividends over the long-run equal earnings minus equity investment (dividends are zero if, on average, equity investment exceeds earnings).

Exhibit 13-2 shows dividends for 5 years under each of the above three approaches. Under the fixed dividend payout ratio policy the ratio (percent) used is 40 percent. The pure residual dividend policy can produce highly volatile dividends, particularly if investment and earnings move in opposite directions from period to period (from years 2 to 3 and from years 3 to 4 in the Exhibit 13-2 example). The fixed dividend payout ratio residual dividend policy lets dividends fluctuate directly with earnings and will be as volatile as those earnings.

The smoothed residual dividend strategy generally produces the most stable dollar dividend. In a period in which earnings exceed dividends plus equity investment (years 1, 2, and 4 in Exhibit 13-2), the firm increases its holdings of liquid assets (cash and marketable securities). These holdings are used later for dividends and investment in periods in which dividends plus investment exceed earnings (years 3 and 5). The smoothed residual policy minimizes dependence on external financing of equity investment and provides a stable dollar dividend.

The residual dividend policy refers to the second policy variable on page 478, the long-run dividend payout ratio. All three residual dividend policies—pure residual policy, fixed payout ratio residual policy, and smoothed residual policy—follow the same basic long-run dividend payout ratio strategy: They set the ratio so that, on average over the long run, dividends will equal what is left over from earnings after the earnings are used to finance equity investment. But these three residual dividend policies differ with regard to the first policy variable noted earlier, dividend stability. A pure residual policy does not seek

---

EXHIBIT 13-2
Earnings, equity investment, and dividends of a company using a residual payout policy

	Year					Total
	1	2	3	4	5	
Earnings E_t	$140	$180	$130	$200	$150	$800
Equity investment I_t^e	80	60	130	110	100	480
Pure residual dividend D_t	60	120	0	90	50	320
Fixed dividend payout ratio dividend D_t (ratio = .4)	56	72	52	80	60	320
Smoothed residual dividend D_t	50	60	60	70	80	320

whereas the fixed dividend payout ratio residual policy achieves stability in terms of the payout ratio, and the smoothed residual dividend policy achieves stability in terms of the dollar level of dividends.

DIVIDEND REINVESTMENT AND OTHER BENEFIT PLANS

Many firms allow stockholders to request that the firm not pay them a dividend but, instead, that it automatically reinvest the dividend in the company's shares. AT&T, Exxon, General Motors, and Uniroyal are among the numerous firms providing this option. Automatic reinvestment is easier and less costly in terms of brokerage fees than would be reinvestment of a dividend by the stockholders themselves (by using the dividend to buy the firm's stock on the open market). Stockholders who do not want to reinvest in the company can simply choose to receive the dividend. It should be pointed out that the automatic reinvestment of a shareholder's dividends still necessitates the shareholder to pay ordinary income taxes on the dividend, so there is no tax advantage from automatic reinvestment. The advantage of the plan lies in the opportunity to avoid brokerage fees in purchasing additional shares of the company's stock.[21]

Automatic dividend reinvestment plans have been available since the late 1960s. Lately companies have heightened the attraction of reinvestment by offering shareholders the chance to purchase new shares at a discount below the stock's market price. These discount-reinvestment plans—known as DRPs—have been offered by some of the best-known corporations, incuding AT&T, Allied Chemical, Kemper, and Crocker National. A discount of approximately 5 percent from the existing market price is common. The DRP plans have become so popular that some companies have provided dividend reinvestment to preferred stockholders and interest reinvestment to bondholders (allowing the preferred stockholders and bondholders to purchase shares of the firm's common stock at a discount).

Another bonus offered by many companies to stockholders is the opportunity of discount purchases of the company's merchandise. A stockholder of Borden Company should not be surprised to find accompanying the quarterly dividend check an offer to buy a five-pound pippin (wheel) of cheddar cheese for 20 percent below retail value. A stockholder of Cope Allman International Ltd. could add an adventurous wardrobe touch by purchasing a sheepskin jacket at a 10 percent discount. Other companies making available similar merchandise benefits to shareholders include J. J. Heinz, Quaker Oats, Castle and Cooke, and GAF Corporation.

All the above benefits are meant to raise the firm's share price by making the shares more attractive. Many stockholders of a company may personally avail themselves of a dividend reinvestment plan or a

---

[21] In some cases, a shareholder of a utility may elect to exclude from taxable income part of the dividends received from the utility.

bargain sale of merchandise. Those shareholders who do not care to take advantage of these programs also benefit if the programs appeal to investors in the market and consequently raise the company's share price.

STOCK DIVIDENDS AND STOCK SPLITS

A **stock dividend** is a payment in the form of additional shares of stock instead of cash. A **stock split** is essentially the same. When a stock splits, shareholders are given a larger number of shares for the old shares they already own. In either case, each shareholder retains the same percentage of all outstanding stock that he or she had before the stock dividend or split.[22] Thus, for example, a 10 percent stock dividend would mean that each shareholder was given one share of stock for every ten shares already owned. Under a two-for-one stock split, each shareholder would be given one additional share of stock for every share already owned, thus doubling the number of shares owned by each stockholder.[23]

The effects of a stock dividend or a stock split can be summarized as follows:

1 There is no change in the firm's assets or liabilities or in shareholders' equity (assets less liabilities).
2 There is a fall in *per share* earnings, book value, and market price, and an offsetting rise in the number of shares held by each stockholder. Each stockholder, therefore, has no change in the total book value, total earnings, or total market value of all shares held since he or she owns the same percentage of the firm after the stock dividend or stock split as before.

A stock dividend or split does not change the assets of the firm, since nothing is received by the firm for new shares issued. The firm's debt is also unchanged by the stock dividend or split, since the debt is in no way involved. It follows that the total shareholders' equity (the firm's total assets less debt) is also unchanged. Since shareholders each retain their old percentage of the total shareholders' interest, each has the same

---

[22] There is a difference in the accounting procedure for treating stock dividends and stock splits. Under generally accepted accounting principles, a stock split is a stock distribution exceeding 25 percent (that is, more than one new share per four existing shares), and a stock dividend is a distribution of 20 percent or less (one new share or less per five existing shares). A distribution above 20 percent and up to 25 percent can be treated for accounting purposes either as a stock dividend or split. To record a stock dividend, the fair market value of the stock is transferred from the retained earnings account to the paid-in capital account. In contrast, a stock split merely requires restating the par value of the stock; e.g., a two-for-one split of stock with an initial par value of $10 per share would only necessitate a change in the par of the common stock to $5 per share.

[23] If a stockholder is entitled to a fraction of a share under a stock dividend or split, then the company will pay cash in place of the fractional share. For example, with a 2 percent stock dividend, a stockholder with ten shares is entitled to two-tenths of a share (2 percent × 10 shares). The firm would pay the stockholder two-tenths of the fair market value of a share in cash. If the market price per share were $20, the stockholder would receive $4 (0.2 × $20).

claim to real assets after the stock dividend or split as before. The total value of a stockholder's shares will consequently be the same before and after the new shares are issued. The stockholders therefore do not gain or lose as a result of the new shares (see the discussion at the end of this section for qualifications). An example will clarify this point.

Assume that the X. Y. Zoro Company (XYZ Co.) is planning a 25 percent stock dividend (one new share paid for each four already owned). The stock dividend will increase the number of shares outstanding from 800,000 to 1 million. The firm's assets, the firm's debt, the stockholders' equity (assets minus debt), and the firm's income are left unchanged. Since the number of shares outstanding has increased, however, the *per share* book value, earnings, and market price decline. This is shown in Exhibit 13-3. Why has market price fallen in the same proportion as earnings and book value? Because a share of stock is nothing more than a claim on the assets and earnings of the firm; if the assets and earnings per share fall exactly by 20 percent, as is the case here, then it is reasonable for the share price to also fall by 20 percent. Notice that the shareholder is completely unaffected by the stock dividend. This is so because the fall in the figures per share in Exhibit 13-3 are exactly compensated for by the increase in the shareholder's number of shares owned. Consequently, the total book value, total earnings, and total market value of the shares the stockholder owns are the same after the stock dividend as before. To see this, assume a shareholder owned 100 shares of XYZ stock before the stock dividend and owns 125 shares after the stock dividend. The total book value of the shares owned *before* the stock dividend was $1000 (100 shares owned × $10 per share); the total book value *after* the stock dividend of 25 shares is also $1000 (125 shares owned × $8 per share). Total earnings on the shareholder's shares are also unchanged since earnings on the shares before the dividend were $200 (100 shares × $2 earnings per share) and earnings after

---

EXHIBIT 13-3
The effects of a stock dividend

	Total for firm before and after stock dividend	Figures before stock dividend (800,000 shares outstanding)[a]	Figures after stock dividend (1 million shares outstanding)[b]
Equity book value[c]	$ 8,000,000	$10	$ 8
Earnings[d]	1,600,000	2	1.60
Market value of shares	32,000,000	40	32

[a] This column is the total for the firm (col. 1) divided by 800,000.
[b] This column is the total for the firm (col. 1) divided by 1 million.
[c] Equity book value equals firm assets less liabilities as represented on the company balance sheet.
[d] Earnings equals net income to shareholders after taxes and after interest on debt.

the dividend are also $200 (125 shares × $1.60 earnings per share). Nor does the total market value of the shareholder's portfolio change; it was $4000 (100 shares × $40 per share), and after the stock dividend is still $4000 (125 shares × $32 per share).

In short, all that has happened is that the firm has printed extra pieces of paper called additional shares and distributed them proportionally to all stockholders. Each shareholder's fraction of the equity owned is unchanged, and the equity represents the same underlying company assets less liabilities.

Sometimes a firm *reduces* the number of shares outstanding through a **reverse split**. Each shareholder is required to exchange with the corporation the shares owned for a smaller number of shares, e.g., to exchange each four shares owned for one share in return. This action frequently follows a decline in the price of the company's stock over several years. Colt Industries, Studebaker, and United Whelan are among corporations that have engaged in a reverse split after suffering financial difficulties. As with a stock dividend or split, the reverse split does not alter the fraction of the company's equity owned by each shareholder, and the company's equity represents the same underlying assets less liabilities as before.

In spite of the fact that stock dividends and splits do not change the underlying assets, liabilities, or equity of the firm, there is some empirical evidence that the total market value of a company's equity increases when the stock dividend or split occurs (roughly a 2 to 6 percent increase).[24] One explanation for this is that the decline in the price *per share* (resulting from the stock dividend or split) causes the stock to enter a better price range, allowing investors to purchase round lots (multiples of 100 shares) rather than odd lots (fewer than 100 shares). The advantage is reduced brokerage fees, since such fees are greater on odd-lot purchases than on round-lot purchases. Thus, even though the firm's underlying equity is not changed by the stock dividend or split, there is a benefit (reflected in share price) because the shares are cheaper to trade. Another explanation for the equity value increase is that companies engage in stock dividends and splits when management anticipates improved future firm cash flows. That is, investors view the dividend or split as good news about the company's prospects. It is not the stock dividend or split itself that has changed the company's underlying operations or financial position. Rather, the dividend or split is an announcement from management (which presumably has the best information about the company's activities) that operations have already improved. Further empirical research is needed to determine whether either of these explanations, or some other explanation, is correct.

---

[24] See M. S. Grinblatt, R. W. Masulis, and S. Titman, "The Valuation Effects of Stock Splits and Stock Dividends," *Journal of Financial Economics*, 13 (September 1984), pp. 461–490, and see the references cited therein.

In 1987, General Motors announced that it would buy back over $5 billion of General Motors shares from its shareholders by the year 1990, the largest stock buy-back in United States history. Other major buy-backs announced in 1987 were those of Hewlett Packard ($750 million), IBM ($570 million), and Heinz ($340 million). In the early 1970s, the dollars paid out in stock repurchases represented only about 15 percent of dividends paid. By the late 1980s, funds paid out in repurchases well exceeded dividend payments.

Stock purchased by the issuing firm is referred to as **treasury stock**. The corporation can purchase its shares in the open market (like any investor buying shares through a broker), through a direct private transaction with the stockholder or through a tender offer (an announcement to shareholders that the firm will buy back a specified number of shares at a particular price during a stated time period). Open market purchases are more common and generally smaller in magnitude than tender offers. Private purchases are least important. Shares purchased as treasury stock are not retired but are held by the firm for possible resale or for use as payment, for example, in buying another company.

Treasury stock carries no stockholder privileges; thus it receives no dividends and does not have the voting right. If treasury stock is resold, it is again outstanding (is no longer treasury stock) and carries with it the same rights and privileges associated with the other outstanding common stock of the firm. A sale of treasury stock is essentially the same as the sale of any other stock issued by the company.

Treasury stock is *not* an asset of the firm. If the firm owns a share of its own stock, it owns a claim against itself (like owing yourself money). To see this, merely imagine that the firm holds some treasury stock and then destroys that stock (say, burns the certificates). Has the firm lost anything in the process? No, except the paper certificates that have been destroyed. In effect, by burning the certificates, the corporation has eliminated equity ownership claims against itself. Contrast this with securities of *other* companies owned by the firm. If the firm owns securities issued by another company, these securities are assets since they are claims against the real assets of the other company.

Why would a firm purchase its own shares? One good reason is to provide the company's shareholders with tax savings. A company can pay out cash to its stockholders either by paying dividends or by buying back some of the stockholders' shares. Treasury stock purchases can have a tax advantage for the shareholders as compared with dividend payments. Dividends are fully taxed whereas treasury stock payments are taxed only to the extent that they exceed what the shareholder originally paid for the shares sold back to the company. For example, assume that Alice Brown originally bought 200 shares of the company's stock for $6 per share but that the stock is currently selling for $10 per share (an unrealized gain of $4 per share). Assume that Alice Brown's tax bracket is 30 percent. If the firm were to pay her a dividend of $100, all of that dividend would be taxable, resulting in a tax of $30. But, if the company were to pay her $100 for ten of her shares, she would realize a gain of $40 (10 shares × $4 realized gain per share); the capital gains tax on the $40 gain would be $12 rather than the $30 of tax on the dividend. It should be noted, however, that if the treasury stock purchase does not meet certain requirements, the entire distribution ($100 in the above example) will be treated as a dividend (subject to ordinary income taxation) and not as a sale of stock subject to capital gains treatment.[25]

Another motive for treasury stock purchases is the existence of government controls limiting dividends. Such controls existed during a wage- price freeze in the early 1970s. Firms repurchased shares in record amounts during that period.

Companies sometimes purchase treasury shares to block a takeover bid by an outside group. Management may believe that the outside purchaser will mismanage the company; or the members of management may be worried about their jobs (new owners sometimes fire old managers). Thus, if an outsider were offering $40 per share to existing shareholders for their stock, the firm might make a counter-bid of $45 per share. Companies sometimes buy the shares of existing shareholders who threaten to attempt a takeover of the company unless their shares are purchased for an amount above the going market price (see the essay The Merger Game after Chapter 23 for details).

Firms may buy back shares to obtain shares for a particular use, for example, for a stock option plan (under which the shares are sold to employees) or for acquiring another company (the stock being used as payment for the purchased company). Purchases of treasury stock for specific uses is a questionable practice. It is generally easier and cheaper simply to issue additional shares. Issuing shares involves none of the brokerage fees or other transaction costs usually associated with treasury stock purchases.

What happens to a company's stock price when the company buys back its shares? Several empirical studies have found that, on average, the stock's price permanently increases after a share repurchase is announced, and that the share repurchase tends to be followed by extraordinary earnings increases for the company.[26] One interpretation

---

[25] A treasury stock purchase (stock repurchase) is *not* treated as a dividend to the shareholder (and is treated as a sale of stock subject to capital gains tax treatment) if any *one* of the following four conditions holds:

1 The percentage ownership of the shareholder falls by more than one-fifth (e.g., if 10 percent of the firm's shares is owned by the shareholder before the repurchase and less than 8 percent is owned after the repurchase) *and* the shareholder owns less than 50 percent of the firm's shares after the repurchase.

2 All the shareholder's stock in the company is acquired under the stock repurchase.

3 The repurchase is not ''equivalent to'' a dividend. Indications that the repurchase is equivalent to a dividend would be a history of the corporation's not paying significant dividends or a repurchase that is pro rata among the shareholders (same percentage of each shareholder's stock acquired under the repurchase).

4 The repurchase of railroad stock under some conditions of bankruptcy.

If none of the above four conditions holds, then a purchase of a shareholder's stock will normally be treated as a dividend subject to ordinary income taxes.

[26] See, for example, L. Y. Dann, ''Common Stock Repurchases: An Analysis of Returns to Bondholders and Stockholders,'' *Journal of Financial Economics*, 9 (June 1981), pp. 113–138; and T. Vermaelen, ''Common Stock Repurchases and Market Signalling: An Empirical Study,'' *Journal of Financial Economics*, 9 (June 1981), pp. 139–183.

of this is that before a repurchase is decided on by management, management foresees an earnings rise that is not yet foreseen by the market. Management concludes that the shares are undervalued and has the company repurchase its shares. But investors know that when shares are repurchased, it often signals that the company's management believes the shares are undervalued because of likely future earnings increases. This motivates investors to bid up the share's price when the stock repurchase is announced. The price rise is sustained after the share repurchase because the company's earnings actually turn out to be high.

SUMMARY

Earnings can be paid out as dividends or be retained for internal use. The level of dividends a firm chooses to pay is influenced by a variety of factors.

1 *Taxes.* Personal taxes on shareholders favor capital gains relative to dividends and encourage the company to reinvest earnings rather than to pay them out in dividends. Taxes on the firm's excess retentions of cash and cash substitutes encourage companies to pay dividends. Corporate income taxes, because of interest tax deductibility, favor debt financing; in the long run this reduces equity financing and reduces the firm's *total* dividends relative to what they would be if interest were not tax deductible.

2 *Investment opportunities.* Exceptional corporate investment opportunities encourage reinvestment of earnings and low dividends.

3 *Contractual restrictions.* Dividends may be restricted by debt or preferred stock contracts and by state regulations prohibiting payment of dividends if stockholders' equity does not exceed the par or stated value of outstanding stock.

Some earnings may be used to increase the firm's liquidity or to pay off debts rather than be paid out as dividends. The transaction costs in raising external funds and in paying dividends encourage the firm to finance investment with retained earnings and to therefore curtail dividends. Because of the transaction costs paid by stockholders in buying and selling shares, for example, brokerage fees, stockholders prefer that dividends are stable rather than erratic. Investors differ regarding the proportions of their income that they prefer in dividends and in capital gains. A firm will therefore attract a "clientele" or type of investor preferring the company's particular dividend payout policy. This clientele ordinarily wants the company to follow its established dividend policy and to maintain relatively stable (unerratic) dollar dividends.

Two important aspects of dividend policy are stability from period to period and the long-run proportion of earnings paid out in dividends. Dividend payments are relatively stable because investors prefer predictable and level rather than volatile dividend income.

Two theories have been formulated to explain corporate dividend policy. The imperfect markets theory holds that dividend policy is quite

494

PART 2
The firm's investment,
financing, and dividend
decisions

important, whereas the perfect markets school argues that dividend policy is irrelevant. One branch of the imperfect markets school argues that firms should use earnings to finance profitable investments rather than pay out the earnings as dividends; another branch argues that firms should pay out a portion of their earnings as dividends even if it means financing investments by selling new shares. One dividend strategy conforming to the imperfect markets theory is the smoothed residual dividend policy. Under this policy, there is an attempt to keep the dollar level of dividends equal to earnings less equity investment (investment that is not financed by borrowing). Additional shares are sold only if there is an unexpected shortage of cash to maintain a stable dividend and meet investment needs, as would be so, for example, if a very large project is undertaken that completely absorbs earnings and excess liquid reserves.

Stock dividends and stock splits involve the distribution of additional shares of stock to the firm's stockholders. Each stockholder's fraction of the firm's equity owned is unchanged, and the total equity continues to represent the same underlying company assets less liabilities. However, the announcement of a stock dividend or split may raise total equity value. Possible explanations of this are that the stock dividend or split conveys favorable information to the market about management's expectations concerning the company or that it puts the shares into a more attractive price range.

Stock that is repurchased by the issuing firm is called treasury stock. Companies repurchase their own shares to produce tax benefits for shareholders, to avoid government constraints on dividends, to fight a takeover bid by another company, or to obtain stock for a particular purpose (e.g., for use in a stock option plan).

QUESTIONS

1 In what way are dividend policy and retention of earnings related to the financing of the firm's investments?

2 Investors presumably buy a firm's shares in order to receive a return on their investment. Further, it would seem that the more profitable are the firm's investments, the higher that return would be. Since the return to shareholders can take the form of dividends, why do we say that more profitable investment opportunities for the firm *lower* the firm's dividend payments?

3 It has been repeatedly stated that as long as a firm has a *productive use* for them, earnings should be retained. What do you think the term "productive use" means?

4 How can stockholder income tax considerations affect the dividend policy of firms?

5 It has been said that the tax deductibility of interest *lowers* a firm's total dividend payments. What is a rationale for this proposition?

6 Why might a firm borrow $100,000 and simultaneously pay a dividend of $100,000; that is, wouldn't it be wiser not to borrow and pay no dividend since there are transaction costs in

borrowing (e.g., bond flotation costs) and in paying a dividend (accounting costs, postage, etc.)?

7 It is stated in the text that the personal income tax bias in favor of capital gains relative to dividend income leads firms to pay less dividends than they would pay if no such bias existed. In a particular year, in determining whether to change its level of dividends from the previous year, would you expect personal income taxes to be more of a consideration for a large corporation with one million shareholders, or to a small company earning $1 million per year and having only six shareholders?

8 What role do stockholder transaction costs play in determining corporate dividend policies?

9 What are the major factors that ordinarily would discourage a firm from issuing new shares to raise funds to pay higher dividends on existing shares? What might offset these factors and encourage a firm to sell shares and use some or all of the proceeds to pay dividends? Explain.

10 How can a stable dividend policy be said to reduce the riskiness associated with the shares on which the cash dividends are paid?

11 Describe the "perfect markets" theory of dividend policy and contrast it with the imperfect markets view.

12 If Poe Sleep Tablets declared a cash dividend on March 14, 1991, payable to all shareholders of record on April 25, 1991, and you bought the stock on April 23, 1991, were you a shareholder of record? In other words, would you be entitled to receive the cash dividend? If nothing else affected the price of Poe's stock and the company declared a $1 cash dividend, what would you expect the price of the stock to be when it went ex-dividend? Assume the stock was selling at $30 just prior to the ex-dividend date.

13 When a firm buys back some of its shares from stockholders it pays money for those shares (treasury stock). Yet, we say that the treasury stock is not a real asset of the firm (the treasury stock could be destroyed with no loss) since it is simply a claim of the firm against itself. Why would the firm pay money for treasury stock if it is not an asset? Aren't remaining stockholders (those who have not sold their shares back to the company) worse off as a result of the treasury stock purchase since the company has paid out dollars for something that isn't really an asset? Explain.

PROJECTS

1 Find three stocks that have recently split and examine their price behavior before and after the splits.

2 Ascertain the dividend policy of a company in your area by talking with the firm's management. Inquire as to why the particular policy is followed and analyze the policy in light of the discussion of this chapter. Consider whether the policy is in the best interest of stockholders.

DP1 Scamp Industries, Inc., had earnings this year of $5,000,000, retained $2,000,000 of those earnings, and had 400,000 shares outstanding. What were the dividends per share?

SOLUTION TO DP1:

$$\text{Dividends} = \text{earnings} - \text{earnings retained}$$

$$\$3,000,000 = \$5,000,000 - \$2,000,000$$

$$\text{Dividends per share} = 3,000,000/400,000 \text{ shares}$$

$$= \$7.50 \text{ per share}$$

DP2 Magic Clinics, Inc., a national chain of health maintenance organizations, had earnings of $20 million in 1990. Since 1977, earnings grew at a steady rate of 11 percent per year. Dividends in 1990 were $9 million. Earnings in 1991 were exceptionally high, $30 million, and investment was $14 million. It is expected that earnings will not stay at the high level but will settle back down to the long-run 11 percent per year growth rate (expected 1992 earnings of around $24,642,000, etc.). Assuming each of the following, what were dividends in 1991?

a Magic follows a stable long-run dividend payout ratio of 45 percent.

b Magic follows a stable dollar dividend payout policy.

c Magic follows a pure residual dividend policy; assume that 30 percent of the 1991 investment is financed with debt.

d 1991 investment is financed 60 percent with debt and 40 percent with retained earnings. All earnings not invested are paid out as dividends.

e 1991 investment is financed 30 percent with debt, 30 percent with retained earnings, and 40 percent from the sale of new shares. All earnings not invested are paid out as dividends.

SOLUTION TO DP2:

a The earnings for 1991 assuming the 11 percent growth rate would have been $22,200,000. Therefore, in 1991:

$$\text{Dividend} = \text{payout ratio} \times \text{earnings}$$

$$= .45(\$22,200,000)$$

$$= \$9,990,000$$

b A stable dollar dividend policy means the dollar amount paid out in dividends will remain constant, except for a long-run growth adjustment factor. Dividends in 1990 were $9 million. Assuming an 11 percent upward adjustment for 1991, dividends in 1991 equal:

$$\text{Dividend} = \$9,000,000(1.11)$$

$$= \$9,990,000$$

c Under a pure residual dividend policy the equity portion of any investment is financed entirely with retained earnings to the extent earnings are available. Since 30 percent of the $14 million in investment will be financed by debt, 70 percent come from equity sources.

$$\text{Required equity} = \$14,000,000 \times (.70)$$

$$= \$9,800,000$$

Since 1991 earnings exceed the required equity investment, all the $9,800,000 of equity investment will come from earnings.

$$\text{Dividend} = \text{earnings} - \text{retained earnings}$$

$$= \text{earnings} - \text{equity investment}$$

$$= \$30,000,000 - \$9,800,000$$

$$= \$20,200,000$$

d Earnings retained $= \$14,000,000(.40)$

$$= \$\ 5,600,000$$

$$\text{Dividend} = \text{earnings} - \text{retained earnings}$$

$$= \$30,000,000 - \$5,600,000$$

$$= \$24,400,000$$

e Only 30 percent of the investment will come from internal sources.

$$\text{Required internal equity investment} = \$14,000,000(.30)$$

$$= \$4,200,000$$

$$\text{Dividend} = \text{earnings} - \text{retained earnings}$$

$$= \$30,000,000 - \$4,200,000$$

$$= \$25,800,000$$

DP3 Binge Hats has 5 million shares of common stock outstanding, and earnings per share are $6. Binge has a dividend payout ratio of 30 percent. The firm is considering a 4 for 1 stock split to lower the price of the common stock from $160 per share to a more attractive level. What will be the effect of the stock split on

a EPS?
b Dividends per share?
c Price per share?
d Total market value of the firm's shares?
e The value of the holdings of Sparky Malone, who currently owns 2000 shares of Binge stock?

498

PART 2
**The firm's investment,
financing, and dividend
decisions**

SOLUTION TO DP3:

a Total earnings before stock split = total earnings after stock split

$$= \$6 \times 5 \text{ million shares}$$

$$= \$30 \text{ million}$$

Number of shares outstanding after split = 4 × 5 million shares

$$= 20 \text{ million shares}$$

EPS after split = $30 million/20 million shares
$$= \$1.50$$

b Dividends before split = $6 × .30 = $1.80

Total dividends before split = $1.80 × 5 million shares

$$= \$9 \text{ million}$$

Dividends per share after split = $9 million/20 million shares

$$= \$0.45 \text{ per share}$$

c Market value before split = $160 × 5 million shares

$$= \$800 \text{ million}$$

Price per share after split = $800 million/20 million shares

$$= \$40$$

d Market value after split = $800 million

e Before the split, Spanky's holdings were worth:

2000 shares × $160 = $320,000

After the split, Spanky's holdings are worth:

8000 shares × $40 = $320,000

Note that his total dividend payment also remains unchanged:

Before split: $1.80 × 2000 shares = $3600
After split: $.45 × 8000 shares = $3600

PROBLEMS

1 If Isle Manufacturing had earnings of $750,000, retained $350,000, and had 50,000 shares outstanding, what were the dividends per share?

2 Skip Popkins owns 4000 shares of Mode Fibers, which he bought in 1974 for $12 per share. The tax rate on Skip's dividends and capital gains is 30 percent. In 1991, Skip received $1.00 per share in dividends from the Mode Fibers stock. Skip sold 1500 shares of his Mode Fibers stock at the end of 1991 for $20 per share. Answer the following:

a What were Skip's dividends and realized capital gains in 1991

on the Mode Fibers shares (realized capital gains equal gains
on shares that are sold)? [Ans.: Dividends = $4000 and
realized capital gains = $12,000]

b What taxes did Skip pay in 1991 on the Mode Fibers stock?
[Ans.: Tax on dividends = $1200; tax on realized capital
gains = $3600]

(*Note:* The following problem demonstrates how a differential tax
treatment of dividend income and long-term capital gains affects the
aftertax returns on a stock investment.)

3 On January 1, 1991, Lemma Grey bought 200 shares of Goliath
Paints Inc. (GP) for $8 per share and 200 shares of Aorta Candies
(AC) for $10 per share. The dividends and end-of-year share
prices for GP and AC are shown in the table below for the years
1991 and 1992.

Dividends and price per share of GP and AC		
	1991	**1992**
GP:		
Dividends/share during year	$ 1	$ 2
Price per share on December 31 (ex-dividend)	8	12
AC:		
Dividends/share during year	1	1
Price per share on December 31 (ex-dividend)	15	20

Lemma Grey is in the 40 percent tax bracket, and this rate is
applicable to all dividend income from GP and AC; the tax rate
on any long-term capital gain (gain on stock held more than one
year) is 20 percent. Solve the following:

a Compute the dividends Lemma received during 1991 and
compute the increase in the value of her GP and AC shares
during 1991. What is the total return (dividend plus share value
increase) for each stock?

b Compute the taxes paid by Lemma in 1991 on her GP and AC
stock if she sold no shares in 1991.

c Assume that Lemma sells half her GP shares and half her AC
shares on December 31, 1992. Compute the total taxes paid by
Lemma in 1992 on all her GP and AC shares.

4 Flash Tools had earnings of $14 million in 1990. Since 1968,
earnings grew at a steady rate of 9 percent per year. Dividends in
1990 were $6,720,000. Earnings in 1991 were exceptionally high,
$20,000,000, and investment was $10,000,000. It is expected that
earnings will not stay at the high level but will settle back down
to the long-run 9 percent per year growth rate (expected 1992
earnings of around $16,650,000, etc.). Assuming each of the
following, what were dividends in 1991?

500

PART 2
**The firm's investment,
financing, and dividend
decisions**

    a Flash follows a stable long-run dividend payout ratio of 48 percent.

    b Flash follows a stable dollar dividend payout policy.

    c Flash follows a pure residual dividend policy; assume that 25 percent of the 1991 investment is financed with debt.

    d 1991 investment is financed 70 percent with debt and 30 percent with retained earnings. All earnings not invested are paid out as dividends.

    e 1991 investment is financed 35 percent with debt, 35 percent with retained earnings, and 30 percent from the sale of new shares. All earnings not invested are paid out as dividends.

5 Signet, Inc., has shares with a market value of $1,500,000 and debt of $700,000. Signet's management is considering two dividend policy alternatives: (I) to pay no dividends on existing shares, and (II) to sell new shares that provide net (net of any flotation costs) proceeds to Signet of $370,000 and then immediately pay $370,000 to existing (not including new) stockholders.

    a Assume that the flotation costs in selling the new shares are zero.

        (1) Compare the total value of the firm's shares under policies I and II (value of existing shares under I compared with the value of the existing and new shares under II). [Ans.: The value of the shares under policies I and II is $1,500,000]

        (2) Compare the wealth position (dividends and value of shares owned) of existing shareholders under policies I and II.

        (3) What factors favor policy I? When might policy II be justified?

    b Assume that under policy II the new shares are sold for a price of $400,000 (assume this to be a fair price) and that flotation costs are $30,000; the $370,000 difference is received by Signet and paid as a dividend. Answer questions 1, 2, and 3 under *a* above.

    c Compare the results under *a* and *b* above and observe how stock issuance flotation costs discourage the use of stock flotations simply to pay dividends.

6 The board of directors of Dual Manufacturing Company is meeting to determine the dividend to be paid to common shareholders during the next year (1992). Dual has profitable investment opportunities amounting to $9,000,000 and expects income after taxes to be $16,200,000, which can be retained or paid out as dividends. Dual has a target book debt to book equity ratio of 45 percent and pursues a pure residual dividend policy. The firm's current (before the new investment) book debt to book equity ratio exactly equals its target of 45 percent. How much should Dual pay out in dividends for the year?

7 Assume that Dual Manufacturing Company has, as in problem **6**, $16,200,000 in expected 1992 aftertax earnings, $9,000,000 in investments, and a firm target debt-equity ratio (using book values) of 45 percent. However, assume that because of past policies the company has the following balance sheet:

Balance sheet, December 31, 1991			
Assets	$25,500,000	Debt	$17,600,000
		Equity	7,900,000
			$25,500,000

If Dual wishes to attain its target debt to equity ratio of 45 percent, how much should the firm pay out in dividends in 1992?

8 HMS Incorporated is planning an investment in dress manufacturing equipment in order to increase production by 125 percent. The new equipment will cost $3,500,000 and HMS's current-period aftertax earnings are $11,250,000. HMS plans to maintain its present debt-equity ratio (in book terms) of 1/4.

a If HMS follows a pure residual dividend policy and has 1,000,000 shares outstanding, what should the current period dividend per share be?

b If HMS maintains a fixed dividend payout ratio of 85 percent, how much external equity financing will be required in the current period?

9 King Lear Engineering, Inc. (KLE) forecasts that total net income for the next five years will equal $25 million and total capital investment will equal $20 million. KLE wishes to formulate a short-run dividend policy that meets all three following objectives:

1. Maintain an average dividend payout ratio over the five-year planning period of 50 percent (but not necessarily 50 percent in each year).

2. Provide shareholders with a "stable" dividend stream over the planning period—where "stable" connotes either level, increasing at an approximately constant rate, or increasing from period to period by approximately equal dollar increments.

3. Maintain KLE's current debt-equity ratio (in book value terms) of 3/7 in every year.

KLE will continue its current policy of financing strictly with debt or equity (no preferred stock). Answer questions *a* and *b* below for each of the three different anticipated scenarios (in the table which follows) for the behavior of annual net income (E_t) and annual capital investment requirements (I_t) over the five-year planning horizon.

502

PART 2
The firm's investment,
financing, and dividend
decisions

Year (t)	Scenario I		Scenario II		Scenario III	
	E_t	I_t	E_t	I_t	E_t	I_t
1	$ 4.13	$ 3.30	$ 7.00	$ 3.00	$ 4.00	$ 2.90
2	4.56	3.65	1.00	3.90	4.10	3.70
3	4.99	3.99	5.80	4.50	3.70	4.10
4	5.44	4.35	6.00	4.50	6.00	5.40
5	5.88	4.71	5.20	4.10	7.20	3.90
	$25.00	$20.00	$25.00	$20.00	$25.00	$20.00

(in millions of dollars)

a What are the annual equity financing requirements (I_f^e) under
each scenario?

b What would the annual dividends be under each scenario if
KLE followed a "pure residual" dividend policy? Would such
a policy be consistent with KLE's three stated short-run policy objectives? Why or why not?

10 Consider the following projections for Hoff Instruments, Inc.:

Year	EBIT
1991	$1,000,000
1992	1,500,000
1993	1,900,000
1994	2,200,000
1995	2,500,000

Hoff has (December 1990) total assets of $2,300,000, liabilities (all
in the form of bonds paying a 14 percent coupon rate with ten
years to maturity) of $1,000,000, and equity of $1,300,000. As
Hoff's financial manager, you are considering alternative future
dividend policies in light of the fact that Hoff is undergoing a
$1,250,000 capital expansion program over the next five years.
The expansion will take place at equal dollar costs in each of the
next five years ($250,000 each year) and will be half-financed with
equity funds. The debt financing will be in the form of six-year
$125,000 notes, with one note issued in each of the five years
1991 to 1995. Each note requires interest payments of 15 percent
annually ($18,750 per year) with all the principal ($125,000) paid at
the end of six years. Assume that Hoff's tax rate is 40 percent.

a What would be the dividend in each of the next five years under a pure residual dividend policy?

b Determine the dividend payout ratio and each year's total dividend payout assuming that Hoff follows a long-run residual
payout policy with a stable dividend payout ratio. Determine

the dividend payout assuming that total equity investment plus dividends over the five years exactly equals total earnings over the five years. Cite any years in which new external financing might be required.

c Suggest a schedule of dividends for the next five years assuming a smoothed residual dividend schedule. The total dividends plus equity investment over the five years need only approximate total earnings over the five years.

d Having made the recommendations called for in *a, b,* and *c* of this problem you have noticed that the dividend growth under the expansion plan as it is now (given any one of the three policies in *a, b,* and *c*) would be much faster than the 10 percent rate Hoff has had to date. You feel that Hoff might not be able to maintain such a trend through the 1990s. The board of directors has decided that it does not want to convey to investors the impression that the rapid rate of dividend increase can be permanently sustained. Comment on the following courses of action that Hoff might adopt to reduce dividend payments:

(1) Retire some of the outstanding 14 percent bonds.

(2) Finance the expansion plan completely with retained earnings.

(3) Enlarge the expansion program and finance the added expansion with retained earnings.

(4) Acquire liquid assets with funds in excess of those required to maintain a 10 percent to 14 percent dividend growth rate.

(5) Adopt an alternative dividend policy (perhaps a stable dollar dividend plus an "extra" dividend).

11 Mama Fregossi's Foods, Inc., has declared a 30 percent stock dividend. Its shares are selling for $25 each. You own 200 shares.

a How many shares will you have after the stock dividend is paid?

b What would you expect the price of the shares to be after the stock dividend is paid.?

12 On March 24, 1991, the directors of Lyle's Worm Farms, Inc., declared a 2 percent stock dividend payable on May 10 to stockholders of record on April 14.

a On what day would you have had to buy stock in order to be a shareholder of record?

b At the time the company announced the stock dividend, it also announced that it will omit its $0.10 cash dividend, which it had paid in each of the four previous quarters. Furthermore, at the time the stock dividend and the cash dividend omission were announced, it was also pointed out that for the six years prior to March 1991, the company had paid $0.50 quarterly. What does this information suggest about Lyle's Worm Farms, Inc.?

504

PART 2
**The firm's investment,
financing, and dividend
decisions**

c On April 8, the day on which the common stock went ex-dividend, the price per share of stock was $11.25. If all else remained the same between April 7 and April 8, what would you have expected the price of stock to have been on April 7? (Hint: Consider just the impact of the stock dividend. The market price already reflects the fact that the cash dividend has been eliminated.)

13 Simple Simon's Savings & Loan has 1,700,000 shares of common stock outstanding, and earnings per share amount to $3. Simple Simon's S & L has a dividend payout ratio of 50 percent. The firm is considering a 4 for 1 stock split to lower the price of the common stock from $60 per share to a more attractive level. What will be the effect of the stock split on

a EPS?

b Dividends per share?

c Price per share?

d Total market value of the firm's shares?

e The value of the holdings of Harley Penmoor, who currently owns 1000 shares of Simple Simon's?

(*Note:* The following problem shows how a differential tax treatment of dividend income and long-term capital gains affects the relative taxation of a dividend distribution and a treasury stock purchase.)

14 Martha Burney owns 4000 shares of Generic Brands Corporation Martha paid $20 per share for the stock in 1980. In July 1992, Generic paid a dividend of $0.50 per share and in August 1992 made a treasury stock purchase, buying up 15 percent of all outstanding Generic Brands stock. Martha sold 1000 of her 4000 shares back to Generic for $30 per share. In 1993 Martha sold her remaining 3000 shares in the market for $35 per share. Assume that Martha's tax rate on dividend income is 40 percent and that her tax rate on long-term capital gains is 16 percent.

a What tax did Martha pay on her 1992 Generic dividends and on the capital gains she realized on the shares she sells back to Generic in 1992?

b What capital gains tax did Martha pay on the Generic shares she sold in 1993?

PART THREE

FINANCIAL ANALYSIS AND FORECASTING

Part 3 covers several important techniques for evaluating and forecasting financial data. Chapter 14 presents the two major approaches for analyzing financial statements: ratio analysis and funds flow analysis. Chapter 15 deals with profit planning. Profits are shown to depend on fixed and variable production costs, on sales volume, and on financial leverage. Chapter 16 examines techniques for forecasting important financial variables, such as sales, costs, and cash flows. Good forecasts are critical to effective financial planning by management.

All the analytical methods covered in Part 3 use accounting data to evaluate a company's current activities and to plan for the future. They are useful both to financial managers and to those outside the firm, such as financial institutions that lend money to the company and investors who purchase the company's securities.

CHAPTER FOURTEEN

FINANCIAL STATEMENT ANALYSIS

The body of information describing even the smallest firm is enormous. To be useful, this information must be organized into an understandable, coherent, and sufficiently limited set of data. Financial statement analysis can be very helpful in this respect. Data from a firm's financial statements can be used to determine the firm's financial ratios and flow of funds. The company's financial ratios can be compared with target values that are deemed appropriate for the company. The **funds flow statement** shows how a firm obtained and used the resources at its disposal during a time period. It can also pinpoint areas of mismanagement and potential danger. As with all shortcut methods of analysis, ratios and funds flow data must be used only in the light of other relevant facts.

FINANCIAL STATEMENTS

We will be concerned primarily with two types of firm financial statements: the **balance sheet** and the **income statement**. The balance sheet states the company's assets, liabilities, and stockholders' equity (net worth) at a *particular date*, for example, at December 31, 1991. The balance sheet of Macro Toy Company is shown in Exhibit 14-1. Asset values are usually shown at cost (what the company paid for the assets), and the stated liabilities indicate the amount owed. Stockholders' equity is simply the difference between assets and liabilities.

The income statement reveals the performance of the company during a *particular period of time*, for example, for the year ended December 31, 1991. It shows the revenues from sales and various costs, including interest expense and taxes, which the company has incurred during the period. Macro Toy Company's income statement is presented in Exhibit 14-2.

There are two other frequently used financial reports, the statement of retained earnings and the sources and uses of funds statement. The statement of retained earnings indicates the magnitude and causes of changes in the firm's retained earnings due to the year's activities. Retained earnings are the accumulated corporate profits that have been kept by the company over the years, that is, earnings not paid out in dividends, not used to purchase back the firm's shares (treasury stock), etc. The sources and uses of funds statement—which is discussed later in this chapter—shows where the company obtained funds during the year and how the funds were used.

RATIO ANALYSIS

Types of Ratios

The people whose job it is to analyze a firm's financial position will differ in the ratios they find useful. For example, short-term creditors are primarily interested in the firm's short-run performance and level of liquid assets (cash, marketable securities, accounts receivable, etc.). Long-term creditors and stockholders are concerned with the long-term as well as the short-term outlook. Management uses all the financial ratios to gauge performance.

How to determine what ratio levels are satisfactory is discussed later in this chapter. But first, using an example, we will describe the ratios that are especially useful in financial analysis. We will then explore how ratio analysis should be used in actual business applications and where the necessary information for computing ratios can be found.

Any given ratio reflects a particular aspect of a company. But usually that's not sufficient. That particular ratio and what it indicates must be viewed in the context of other ratios and other facts concerning the company. A historical illustration of this point is the case of Penn Central Corporation, which shortly before its collapse in 1970 had a seemingly

---

EXHIBIT 14-1
Macro Toy Company balance sheet as of December 31, 1991

Assets		Liabilities	
Cash	$ 70,000	Accounts payable	$ 150,000
Marketable securities	30,000	Notes payable to bank (8%)	200,000
Accounts receivable, net	450,000	Accruals	20,000
Inventories	350,000	Federal income taxes payable	80,000
Total current assets	$ 900,000	Total current liabilities	$ 450,000
		Mortgage bonds (6%)	150,000
Gross plant and equipment	$2,100,000	Debentures (7%)[a]	400,000
Allowance for depreciation	(500,000)	Total liabilities	$1,000,000
Net plant and equipment	$1,600,000		

Stockholders' equity	
Common stock	$ 500,000
Retained earnings	1,000,000
Stockholders' equity	$1,500,000

Total assets	$2,500,000	Liabilities plus equity	$2,500,000

[a] The annual sinking fund contribution is $24,000.

safe ratio of debt to total assets. Amazingly, the perilous condition of Penn Central was generally undetected even by sophisticated analysts and financial institutions. Their error was a failure to perceive that the company's operations were generating insufficient cash flow and that its assets were highly illiquid (primarily real estate and railroad properties that could not readily be sold at a reasonable price). The credit "crunch" of early 1970 made it impossible for Penn Central to borrow enough to stave off a liquidity crisis, and bankruptcy ensued. In this case, the relationship between debt and assets, isolated from other considerations, was misleading.

Four types of ratios are used in analyzing the financial position of a company.

1 **Liquidity ratios** indicate the company's capacity to meet short-run obligations.
2 **Leverage ratios** indicate the company's capacity to meet its long-term and short-term debt obligations.

EXHIBIT 14-2
Macro Toy Company income statement for year ended December 31, 1991

Net sales		$5,400,000
Cost of goods sold....................................		4,400,000
Gross margin on sales.................................		$1,000,000
Operating expenses:		
Selling	$200,000	
General and administrative[a].....................	330,000	
Lease payments	20,000	
Total operating expenses.........................		550,000
Operating income......................................		$ 450,000
Add: Other revenues (interest on		
marketable securities plus royalties)		3,000
Operating income plus other revenues		$ 453,000
Less other expenses:		
Interest on bank note	$ 16,000	
Interest on mortgage	9,000	
Interest on debentures	28,000	
Total interest expense........................		53,000
Income before taxes		$ 400,000
Federal income taxes (at 40%)		160,000
Net income (net profit)[b]..............................		$ 240,000
Dividends		$ 70,000
Increase in retained earnings............................		170,000

[a] This includes depreciation expense of $100,000.
[b] This equals net income available to common shareholders since there are no preferred dividends.

3 **Activity ratios** indicate how effectively the company is using its assets.

4 **Profitability ratios** indicate the net returns on sales and assets.

Each of these four types of ratios will be defined and examined within the context of an example involving the Macro Toy Company.

Macro Toy Company manufactures games for children and adults. Relative to other firms in its industry, Macro is highly innovative and is willing to take above-average risks in developing and marketing new products. In addition to its regular line, the company produces a number of expensive, special-order toys. Because of its innovativeness and special-order service, the firm is somewhat more risky than the toy industry as a whole. Furthermore, the company recently discontinued production of an unprofitable product, resulting in significant unutilized capacity at its plant.

Exhibits 14-1 and 14-2 show the balance sheet and income statement of Macro for the year ended December 31, 1991. The ratios describing Macro's financial condition were calculated from data in these two statements and are listed in column 5 of Table 14-1 (p. 512). Table 14-1 also shows ratios in column 3 that are considered average for the toy industry; and in column 4 it shows ratios that Macro must meet under current circumstances if it is to maintain its aggressive and innovative policies, and yet remain financially healthy and attractive to investors and creditors.

Later in this chapter, we will demonstrate the methods used to determine the values of the ratios in column 4, which are considered financially appropriate for Macro's particular situation.

Liquidity Ratios Liquidity ratios measure the firm's ability to fullfill *short-term* commitments out of its liquid assets. Assets are "liquid" if they are either cash or relatively easy to convert into cash (for example, through sale). Short-term creditors are generally very interested in the liquidity ratios. The current ratio and the quick ratio are the most commonly used liquidity ratios.

Current Ratio The current ratio equals current assets divided by current liabilities. Current assets are viewed as relatively liquid, which means they can generate cash in a relatively short time period. Current liabilities are debts that will come due within a year. If the current ratio is too low, the firm may have difficulty in meeting short-run commitments as they mature. If the ratio is too high, the firm may have an excessive investment in current assets or be underutilizing short-term credit.

For Macro the current ratio equals

$$\text{Current ratio} = \frac{\text{current assets}}{\text{current liabilities}}$$
$$= \frac{\$900,000}{\$450,000}$$
$$= 2$$

A poor current ratio may imply that only one or that several of the specific current assets and liabilities are at an undesirable level. Thus, a low current ratio could mean that cash, marketable securities, accounts receivable, or inventory should be increased. Similarly, a low current ratio may mean that one or more of the debts—accounts payable or notes payable, or accruals, or provisions for taxes—should be reduced.

Macro's current ratio is 2. However, as indicated in Table 14-1, the acceptable current ratio for Macro is 2.6. It might seem that current assets equal to twice current liabilities should be sufficient. However, recall that Macro is a high-risk business. Macro's special-order toy inventories are not very liquid, and are potentially salable only at a large discount. Furthermore, there may be a delay in collecting accounts receivable. The firm could sell the accounts receivable to a factor (a firm specializing in the purchase of accounts receivable from other companies). But, even if the receivables are sold, less than the $450,000 owed to Macro by its customers (see balance sheet, Exhibit 14-1) would be realized since the factor will demand a profit on the transaction. In short, Macro's current position should be improved and is a justifiable concern to management and to the firm's short-term creditors.

Quick Ratio or Acid Test Ratio   The quick, or acid test, ratio measures the firm's ability to meet short-term obligations from its most liquid assets. In this case, inventory is not included with other current assets because it is generally far less liquid than the other current assets. The quick ratio equals current assets, excluding inventory, divided by current liabilities. That is,

$$\text{Quick ratio} = \frac{\text{current assets} - \text{inventory}}{\text{current liabilities}}$$

$$= \frac{\$900,000 - \$350,000}{\$450,000}$$

$$= 1.22$$

The quick ratio for Macro reflects the same weak position reflected by the current ratio. Macro's quick ratio of 1.22 is significantly less than the acceptable level of 1.7 shown in column 4 of Table 14-1. The same reasons for concern that applied to the current ratio are relevant here.

Leverage Ratios   Leverage ratios measure the extent of the firm's total debt burden. They reflect the company's ability to meet its short- *and* long-term debt obligations. The ratios are computed either by comparing fixed charges and earnings from the income statement or by relating the debt and equity (stockholders' investment) items from the balance sheet. Leverage ratios are important to creditors, since they indicate whether or not the firm's revenues can support interest and other fixed charges, as well as whether or not there are sufficient assets to pay off the debt if the firm liquidates. Shareholders, too, are concerned with leverage, since interest is a company expense that increases with greater debt. If

TABLE 14-1
Ratio definitions and values for Macro Toy Company

Ratio (1)	Ratio formula (2)	Industry average (3)	Appropriate ratio level for Macro Toy Company (4)	Actual Macro Toy Company ratios (5)
Liquidity ratios				
Current	$\dfrac{\text{Current assets}}{\text{Current liabilities}}$	2.4	2.6	2.0
Quick	$\dfrac{\text{Current assets} - \text{inventory}}{\text{Current liabilities}}$	1.2	1.7	1.22
Leverage ratios				
Debt	$\dfrac{\text{Total debt}}{\text{Total assets}}$	0.45	0.4	0.4
Debt-equity[a]	$\dfrac{\text{Long-term debt}}{\text{Stockholders' equity}}$	.48	.43	.37
Times interest earned	$\dfrac{\text{Earnings before taxes} + \text{interest}}{\text{Interest charges}}$	6	6.5	8.55
Fixed-charges coverage	$\dfrac{\text{Income available for meeting fixed charges}}{\text{Fixed charges}}$	3.2	3.5	4.19
Activity ratios				
Inventory turnover	$\dfrac{\text{Cost of goods sold}}{\text{Average inventory}}$	5	9	11
Average collection period, days	$\dfrac{\text{Average accounts receivable}}{\text{Average credit sales per day}}$	56	46	30
Fixed-assets turnover	$\dfrac{\text{Sales}}{\text{Fixed assets}}$	11	10	3.375
Total assets turnover	$\dfrac{\text{Sales}}{\text{Total assets}}$	7	6.5	2.16
Profitability ratios				
Gross profit margin, %	$\dfrac{\text{Sales} - \text{cost of goods sold}}{\text{Sales}}$	12	14	18.5
Net operating margin, %	$\dfrac{\text{Operating income}}{\text{Sales}}$	5	6	8.33
Profit margin on sales, %	$\dfrac{\text{Net income}}{\text{Sales}}$	3.5	4	4.44
Return on total assets, %[b]	$\dfrac{\text{Net income} + \text{interest}}{\text{Total assets}}$	9.6	10.5	11.72
Return on equity, %[c]	$\dfrac{\text{Net income}}{\text{Stockholders' equity}}$	13.5	15	16

[a] Sometimes current debt or total debt, rather than long-term debt, is used in computing this ratio.

[b] Return on total assets as defined here [(net income + interest)/total assets] is sometimes referred to as the "operating return on total assets." Also, the term "return on total assets" is often used to refer to net income/total assets; however, as explained later in the section on the Du Pont system, the ratio (net income/total assets) is not very meaningful.

[c] See footnote 8, this chapter, for a company with preferred stock as well as common stock outstanding.

borrowing and interest are excessive, the company may become bankrupt.

The more predictable are the returns of the firm, the more debt will be acceptable, since the firm will be less likely to be surprised by circumstances that prevent fulfilling debt obligations. Utilities have historically had relatively stable incomes; they have also been among the industries with the heaviest debt. In contrast, furniture manufacturers and auto producers are cyclical businesses and normally include a far lower proportion of debt in their capital structures.

Recall that Macro is more risky than most firms in its industry. Consequently, a more conservative level for the leverage ratios is warranted. For this reason, the three leverage ratio levels indicated in Table 14-1 that are appropriate for Macro (col. 4) differ from those for the industry as a whole (col. 3).

Debt to Total Assets Ratio This ratio equals total debt (total liabilities) divided by total assets. That is, using the Exhibit 14-1 balance sheet data,

$$\text{Debt to total assets ratio} = \frac{\text{total debt}}{\text{total assets}}$$

$$= \frac{\$1.0 \text{ million}}{\$2.5 \text{ million}}$$

$$= 0.4$$

The debt to total assets ratio is also called the debt ratio. Generally, creditors prefer a low debt ratio since it implies a greater protection of their position. A higher debt ratio generally means that the firm must pay a higher interest rate on its borrowing; beyond some point, the firm will not be able to borrow at all.

Macro's debt ratio of 0.4 is satisfactory in that it is less than the maximum acceptable level of 0.45 for the firm indicated in Table 14-1. Recall that Macro's current ratio and quick ratio were too low. Since the firm's overall leverage is not excessive, it could reduce its current liabilities and keep total debt (long-term debt plus current liabilities) at a satisfactory level by borrowing long-term and using these funds to retire some of its short-term (current) obligations. Thus, Macro might borrow an additional $100,000 on a long-term basis (long-term debt rises from $550,000 to $650,000 in Exhibit 14-1) and use the money to pay off $100,000 in current liabilities (reducing current liabilities from $450,000 to $350,000). This would not affect the firm's debt ratio (total debt remains at $1,000,000), but by reducing current liabilities, it would produce a more satisfactory relationship between current assets and current liabilities.

Debt to Equity Ratio This ratio equals the firm's debt divided by its equity, where debt can be defined as total debt or as long-term debt. We will use long-term debt since it is so frequently employed, and because it provides added information not provided by the debt ratio discussed above. Using Exhibit 14-1 data, the debt-equity ratio equals

$$\text{Debt-equity ratio} = \frac{\text{long-term debt}}{\text{stockholders' equity}}$$

$$= \frac{\$550,000}{\$1,500,000}$$

$$= 0.37$$

where Macro's long-term debt equals its mortgage bonds plus its debentures. A high debt-equity ratio (using long-term debt in the numerator) implies that a high proportion of long-term financing is from debt sources, that is, the firm is using a great deal of financial leverage. Long-term creditors generally prefer to see a modest debt-equity ratio since it means greater protection (a larger equity cushion) and a greater stake in the company's future for equity holders (implying a greater stockholder motivation to see the company prosper).

Macro's debt-equity is satisfactory since it is less than the maximum desirable level of 0.43 specified in Table 14-1. Therefore, Macro can increase its long-term borrowing (e.g., to pay off some current liabilities, as discussed above) and still maintain an acceptable debt-equity level.

Times Interest Earned Ratio   The times interest earned ratio equals earnings before interest and taxes (EBIT) divided by interest. EBIT can be computed by simply adding interest expense ($53,000) to income before taxes ($400,000). In Exhibit 14-2, the times interest earned ratio equals net income before taxes plus interest expense all divided by interest expense:

$$\text{Times interest earned ratio} = \frac{\text{EBIT}}{\text{interest expense}}$$

$$= \frac{\$400,000 + \$53,000}{\$53,000}$$

$$= 8.55$$

Times interest earned reflects the firm's ability to pay interest out of earnings. Macro's times interest earned ratio of 8.55 means that Macro's earnings available to pay interest is 8.55 times the interest that is due. From Table 14-1, this is more than the appropriate level for Macro of 6.5. Creditors can feel confident that the interest will be paid, since interest is amply covered by EBIT. Notice that the numerator in the ratio, EBIT, is earnings *before* interest expense and taxes since all of EBIT is available for payment of interest. If interest equalled Macro's EBIT of $453,000, times interest earned would be 1; the company could just pay its interest and would pay no corporate income taxes since taxable income would be zero (earnings before interest and taxes − interest expense = taxable income, that is, $453,000 − $453,000 = 0). Keep in mind that EBIT fluctuates from year to year, and it may in the future fall far short of current EBIT. Therefore, a current times interest earned ratio greatly exceeding unity is desirable because it means that interest on currently outstanding debt will very likely be paid in coming years.

Fixed-Charges Coverage Ratio The fixed-charges coverage ratio equals income available to meet fixed charges divided by fixed charges. Fixed charges include all fixed dollar outlays, including debt interest, sinking fund contributions, and lease payments. A fixed charge is a cash outflow that the firm cannot avoid without violating its contractual agreements. The firm periodically deposits money in a sinking fund that is eventually used to pay off the principal of the long-term debt for which the fund was set up. Lease payments are made by Macro to lessors (owners) of equipment that is used by Macro in its operations. The fixed-charges coverage ratio therefore equals[1]

Fixed-charges coverage ratio

$$= \frac{\text{income available for meeting fixed charges}}{\text{fixed charges}}$$

$$= \frac{\text{operating income + lease payments + other income}}{\text{interest + lease payments + before-tax sinking fund contribution}}$$

$$= \frac{\$450{,}000 + \$20{,}000 + \$3000}{\$53{,}000 + \$20{,}000 + \$40{,}000} = \frac{\$473{,}000}{\$113{,}000}$$

$$= 4.19$$

The fixed-charges coverage ratio is significant since it indicates how much income there is to pay for all fixed charges. Macro's position is satisfactory since its actual ratio of 4.19 exceeds the minimum acceptable level of 3.5 for the firm, as shown in Table 14-1.

---

[1] The bond agreement may require the firm to make periodic payments into a sinking fund that will eventually be used to retire the debt. If the sinking fund contribution is not made, the firm defaults. Sinking fund payments are not tax deductible and therefore must be made from the firm's aftertax income. Notice that the fixed-charges coverage ratio is the number of dollars available from current operations to pay fixed charges divided by the amount that *must be* earned before taxes to assure the payment of fixed charges and also pay the firm's taxes. Fixed charges other than sinking fund payments are tax deductible, and therefore to cover them the firm need only earn pretax amounts equal to those fixed charges. However, to cover the non-tax-deductible sinking fund contribution of $24,000, the firm must earn more than $24,000 in pretax returns. Thus, assuming a corporate tax rate of 40 percent,

$$\text{Pretax dollars needed to cover sinking fund} \times (1.0 - \text{tax rate}) = \text{sinking fund payment}$$

and therefore,

$$\text{Pretax dollars needed to cover sinking fund} = \frac{\text{sinking fund payment}}{1.0 - \text{tax rate}}$$

$$= \frac{\$24{,}000}{1.0 - 0.4} = \frac{\$24{,}000}{0.6} = \$40{,}000$$

The firm needs $40,000 in pretax earnings to cover the $24,000 in sinking fund payments.

Activity Ratios   Activity ratios show the intensity with which the firm uses its assets in generating sales. These ratios indicate whether the firm's investments in current and long-term assets are too small or too large. If investment is too large, it could be that the funds tied up in that asset should be used for more productive purposes. For example, the firm may have unused plant capacity that it could sell and then use the proceeds in some profitable way. If investment is too small, the firm may be providing poor service to customers or inefficiently producing its product. For example, the firm might benefit from an increase in inventories because current stocks are inadequate to efficiently service customers.

Under the approach shown here, we assume that the purpose of the analysis is to evaluate average performance over the year. Therefore, average levels of the assets for the year are used. The alternative approach would be to examine whether current (for example, December 31, 1991) levels of the assets are at proper levels. Under this latter approach the end-of-period levels of the assets would be used.

We will assume for simplicity that the asset balances for Macro did not fluctuate much during the year and that end ∩f-year asset balances approximate the average asset levels during the year. However, to illustrate the technique for computing an average asset level when there are variations during the year, we assume in computing the inventory turnover ratio that Macro's inventories did change significantly during the year. End-of-year asset balances are used for all the other ratios. It will also be assumed throughout that sales did not fluctuate significantly during the year.[2]

Inventory Turnover   Inventory turnover equals cost of goods sold divided by average inventory. Therefore, both balance sheet and income statement data must be used. Inventory may have changed significantly during a given year, and it is particularly important here to use a yearly average rather than the year-end inventory amount. For Macro, the beginning-of-the-year inventory is not shown on the balance sheet in Exhibit 14-1. But let's assume that beginning (December 31, 1990) inventory was $450,000; the balance sheet shows that the December 31, 1991, inventory is $350,000; therefore

$$\text{Average inventory for year} = \frac{\$450,000 + \$350,000}{2}$$

$$= \$400,000$$

---

[2] If sales fluctuate during the year, it is not correct to compare annual sales with asset balances (either end-of-year or a simple average for the year) in computing activity ratios. For example, the accounts receivable at December 31 reflect sales during the latter part of the year, and therefore average daily sales in the latter part of the year should be compared with the accounts receivable at year-end to compute the implied collection period. If performance over the entire year is to be assessed, then a separate collection period should be computed for several points during the year, for example, using quarterly accounts receivable balances and each quarter's sales. Also see footnote 4, this chapter.

and

$$\text{Inventory turnover} = \frac{\text{cost of goods sold}}{\text{average inventory}}$$

$$= \frac{\$4,400,000}{\$400,000}$$

$$= 11$$

Since inventories are valued in terms of their cost, cost of goods sold rather than sales was used in computing inventory turnover in our example. Although sales is less accurate than cost of goods sold for calculating this ratio, sales is often used in practice. Also, if inventory fluctuates seasonally, for example, is high at the middle of the year but low at the beginning and end of the year, then it's somewhat complicated to calculate the average. Nevertheless, the average should be used.[3]

Inventory absorbs fluctuations in deliveries so as to avoid stockouts. A low inventory turnover implies a large investment in inventories relative to the amount needed to service sales. Excess inventory ties up resources unproductively. On the other hand, if the inventory turnover is too high, inventories are too small and it may be that the firm is constantly running short of inventory (out of stock), thereby losing customers. The objective is to maintain a level of inventory relative to sales that is not excessive but at the same time is sufficient to meet customer needs.

A substantial portion of Macro's business is special-order merchandise that is not inventoried, and consequently Macro's appropriate inventory turnover ratio is higher (since inventories are lower) than for the industry. However, Macro's inventory turnover of 11 is higher even than the level of 9 deemed appropriate for the firm (see Table 14-1) and may suggest that Macro is understocked with inventory. It may also be that inventories are being used with exceptional efficiency. Further investigation would be needed to provide the answer.

Average Collection Period   The average collection period is a measure of how long it takes from the time the sale is made to the time the cash is collected from the customer. To compute this figure, the average credit sales per day is determined by dividing the year's credit sales by 360. The average credit sales per day is then divided into year-end accounts receivable or into average accounts receivable for the year. Assume for simplicity that the level of accounts receivable has not varied significantly during the year and that year-end and average accounts

---

[3] For example, with quarterly data available, the average could be computed by taking inventories at the beginning of the year plus each end-of-quarter inventory balance and dividing the total by 5. An even more accurate average would be the inventory balance at the beginning of the year plus each end-of-month inventory balance all divided by 13.

receivable are therefore about the same.[4] Also assume that all Macro Toy Company's sales are made on credit. Thus,

$$\text{Average credit sales per day} = \frac{\text{annual credit sales}}{360 \text{ days}}$$

$$= \frac{\$5,400,000}{360 \text{ days}}$$

$$= \$15,000/\text{day}$$

$$\text{Average collection period} = \frac{\text{accounts receivable}}{\text{average credit sales per day}}$$

$$= \frac{\$450,000}{\$15,000/\text{day}}$$

$$= 30 \text{ days}$$

The average collection period indicates the firm's efficiency in collecting on its sales. It may also reflect the firm's credit policy. If customers are given more time to pay, then the collection period will generally be greater. A long collection period is not necessarily bad, since a stringent credit policy requiring customers to pay faster may lead to a reduction in sales. However, the longer time in collecting on sales from a lax credit policy is a cost to the firm, and it can only be justified if it produces greater sales. The sooner the firm receives the cash due on sales, the sooner it can put that money to work earning interest. That is, the cost of a long collection period is a return (interest) lost on these funds.

Given that the firm has a particular credit policy (it requires payment by customers within a given time period), some acceptable average collection period is implied. If the collection period is too long, remedial measures must be implemented. The weakness may be slow billing procedures, ineffective incentives to get customers to pay on time, or poor selection of customers in extending credit. Macro's collection period of thirty days is well within the acceptable level for the firm of forty-six days (shown in Table 14-1).

---

[4] If sales are stable during the year but accounts receivable fluctuate significantly during the year, an average rather than a year-end accounts receivable estimate would be preferable. It should be noted that with seasonal or other fluctuations in credit sales during the year the average collection period computed as shown in the text above will also fluctuate during the year *even though* collections are stable over the year (that is, even though the fraction of credit sales still uncollected one month after the sale, two months after the sale, etc., is the same from month to month). Also, with fluctuating sales, a stable collection period figure may be implied even though collections are slowing (deteriorating). The implication is that the average collection period figure must be used with caution if the business has significant credit sales fluctuations during the year. On this point, see Wilbur G. Lewellen and Robert W. Johnson, "Monitoring Accounts Receivable," *Harvard Business Review* (May–June 1972).

Fixed-Assets Turnover This ratio is computed by dividing net sales by fixed assets (net plant and equipment) and equals

$$\text{Fixed-assets turnover} = \frac{\text{sales}}{\text{fixed assets}}$$

$$= \frac{\$5,400,000}{\$1,600,000}$$

$$= 3.375$$

This ratio indicates how intensively the fixed assets of the firm are being used.[5] An inadequately low ratio implies excessive investment in plant and equipment relative to the value of the output being produced. In such a case, the firm might be better off to liquidate some of those fixed assets and invest the proceeds productively (or to pay off its debt, or to distribute the proceeds as dividends).[6]

Macro has an exceptionally low fixed-assets turnover of 3.375 relative to the proper level of 10 shown in Table 14-1. Recall that Macro's plant has significant unused capacity. The implication is that the firm would do better to move to smaller facilities unless it anticipates a significant increase in production and sales.

Total-Assets Turnover Total-assets turnover equals sales divided by total assets; therefore,

$$\text{Total-assets turnover} = \frac{\text{sales}}{\text{total assets}}$$

$$= \frac{\$5,400,000}{\$2,500,000}$$

$$= 2.16$$

Total-assets turnover reflects how well the company's assets are being used to generate sales. Total-assets turnover for Macro is well below the appropriate level of 6.5 shown in Table 14-1. This is due to the excessive investment in fixed assets noted earlier. Recall also that the firm has an inadequate current ratio (current assets/current liabilities). Therefore, if it were to liquidate some of its fixed assets, such as plant and equipment, some of the funds generated could be used to increase current assets (such as inventories) or to decrease current liabilities (for example, pay off the bank notes) so as to raise the current ratio to an acceptable level.

---

[5] If fixed assets have changed significantly during the year, an average fixed-asset level for the year should be used (see the average inventory calculation for the inventory turnover ratio). Average assets would also be used in computing the total-assets turnover ratio and the return on total assets.

[6] The use of a balance sheet (book) asset value (cost less accumulated depreciation) as a measure of the market liquidation value of the asset may be misleading, particularly if market values have changed since the asset was purchased by the firm. However, book magnitudes usually provide a useful, albeit rough, estimate of the company's situation.

Profitability Ratios Profitability ratios measure the success of the firm in earning a net return on sales or on investment. Since profit is the ultimate objective of the firm, poor performance here indicates a basic failure that, if not corrected, would probably result in the firm's going out of business.

Gross Margin The gross profit margin is gross profit (sales minus cost of goods sold) divided by sales. Thus, for Macro,

$$\text{Gross profit margin} = \frac{\text{sales} - \text{cost of goods sold}}{\text{sales}}$$

$$= \frac{\$5,400,000 - \$4,400,000}{\$5,400,000}$$

$$= 18.5\%$$

Marco's gross profit margin is very impressive since it far exceeds the target of 14 percent shown in Table 14-1.

The gross margin reflects the effectiveness of pricing policy and of production efficiency (that is, how well the purchase or production cost of goods is controlled). Of course, if the gross margin is increased by raising the price of the firm's product, the product may become uncompetitive, producing a falloff in sales. Therefore, a company may find it advantageous to lower the price, and therefore lower the gross profit margin, if it increases sales so much as to increase total profits.

Net Operating Margin The net operating margin equals net sales minus the sum of cost of goods sold and operating expenses, all divided by net sales. That is,

$$\text{Net operating margin} = \frac{\text{operating income}}{\text{sales}}$$

$$= \frac{\text{sales} - \text{cost of goods sold} - \text{total operating expenses}}{\text{sales}}$$

$$= \frac{\$5,400,000 - \$4,400,000 - \$550,000}{\$5,400,000}$$

$$= \frac{\$450,000}{\$5,400,000}$$

$$= 8.33\%$$

The net operating margin indicates the profitability of sales before taxes and interest expense. Nonoperating revenues (for example, interest on marketable securities and royalties) are not included in the returns, and nonoperating expenses (such as interest) are not deducted. Nonoperating income and expense items are those not directly associated with the production or sale of the firm's product (note that interest expense is a financing cost and not a production cost). The purpose of this ratio is to measure the effectiveness of production and *sales* of the company's product in generating pretax income for the firm. For any given level of sales, the higher the net operating margin the better.

Macro's net operating margin of 8.33 percent is superior to both the industry average of 5 percent and the level of 6 percent deemed appropriate for Macro.[7]

Profit Margin on Sales   This ratio equals net income divided by sales.

$$\text{Profit margin on sales} = \frac{\text{net income}}{\text{sales}}$$

$$= \frac{\$240,000}{\$5,400,000}$$

$$= 4.44\%$$

By itself, profit margin on sales provides little useful information since it mixes the effectiveness of sales in producing profits (reflected by the net operating margin) with the effects of the method of financing on profits (since net income is after deduction of interest on debt and of taxes, which are affected by interest). Macro's appropriate profit margin on sales shown in Table 14-1 is the level management seeks given its current debt level; it would be misleading to compare Macro's profit margin on sales with the profit margin of companies with different degrees of debt financing. In contrast, the net operating margin (operating income/sales) is useful since it reflects pricing policy relative to costs, a useful index for decision making. Later in this chapter, we will see that profit margin on sales is used, in combination with another ratio, to compute return on investment.

Return on Total Assets   This ratio equals net income plus interest on debt, divided by total assets.

$$\text{Return on total assets} = \frac{\text{net income} + \text{interest expense}}{\text{total assets}}$$

$$= \frac{\$240,000 + \$53,000}{\$2,500,000}$$

$$= 11.72\%$$

Return on total assets is the total after-corporate-tax return to stockholders and lenders on the total investment that they have in the firm. It

---

[7] The net operating margin can be expressed as

Net operating margin $= 1 -$ operating ratio

where the operating ratio is equal to (cost of goods sold + operating expenses)/sales.

The ratio of operating income to total assets could be used to measure the effectiveness of sales and pricing policies and of operations in generating income. This ratio is useful in gauging efficiency since it abstracts from financing effects (operating earnings are earnings before deductions for interest on debt and taxes). Notice that this ratio can be computed from ratios described in the text since

$$\frac{\text{Operating income}}{\text{Total assets}} = \frac{\text{operating income}}{\text{sales}} \times \frac{\text{sales}}{\text{total assets}}$$

$$= \text{net operating margin} \times \text{total-assets turnover ratio}$$

is the rate of return earned by the firm as a whole for all its investors, including lenders. Macro's rate of return on total assets of 11.72 percent is significantly above the appropriate rate for the firm of 10.5 percent shown in Table 14-1. In an overall sense, Macro can therefore be viewed as a successful company.

Return on Equity This ratio equals the net income available to common stockholders (i.e., net income minus dividends on any preferred stock) divided by the common stockholders' equity.[8]

$$\text{Return on equity} = \frac{\text{net income to common stockholders}}{\text{common stockholders' equity}}$$

$$= \frac{\$240,000}{\$1,500,000}$$

$$= 16\%$$

Management's objective is to generate the maximum return on shareholders' investment in the firm. Return on equity is therefore the best single measure of the company's success in fulfilling its goal. Macro's return of 16 percent is above the minimum desired level of 15 percent. In the next section we will discuss interrelationships between various ratios and will show how return on equity can be expressed in terms of many other ratios.

*Use of Ratios:
Macro Company
Revisited*

So far, we have defined fifteen ratios and noted their significance. Below, we explain how the firm's target ratio levels—deemed appropriate for the firm—relate to industry ratio levels. We then discuss ratio interrelationships and ratio trends. Finally, we discuss certain problems with using financial statement information.

Firm Standards versus Industry Averages Companies that produce the same products generally confront similar problems. This would seem to imply that to evaluate a firm, it would be reasonable to compare that firm's ratios with the average ratio levels for companies in the same industry. This is valid in some cases, but it's only a rough approximation—sometimes very rough! There are at least two reasons that industry averages must be used cautiously.

First, as with individual firms, entire industries may be prosperous or sick. Using an industry standard to evaluate a firm implies that the industry performance is satisfactory on the average. However, this is not so for ailing industries (for example, railroads). To make the judgment that an individual firm within the industry is healthy because it conforms to industry averages would be wrong in such cases. However, it would

---

[8] For a firm with preferred stock as well as common stock outstanding, a separate return on total equity (common stock and preferred stock) and on common equity alone can be computed. The return on total equity equals (net income)/(common and preferred equity); and the return on common stock equals (net income − dividends due preferred stock for the period)/(common stock equity); common stock equity equals total equity minus preferred equity (where preferred equity = preferred par *plus* preferred paid-in surplus).

be fair to say that if a firm's ratios are as good as the industry's, it is likely that the firm's management is doing at least an average job in view of industrywide conditions, for example, conditions relating to demand for the industry's products or to supply of its inputs.

Second, companies within an industry vary in size and the individual firm's products and services are not all exactly the same. This implies possible differences in risk and operating conditions. Therefore, the same ratio levels may not be appropriate for all companies in the industry. For example, some firms in the publishing industry may produce lower-risk technical and reference materials, whereas other firms publish higher-risk fiction and popular magazines. Riskiest of all is the underground press, which has had great successes, such as *The Village Voice* and *L. A. Free Press*, but many disasters, such as the *San Francisco Balloon* and *The Washington Rebel*.

Another thing to consider is that many firms straddle more than a single industry. To evaluate these firms properly, it is necessary to take into account the proportion of their activities in each industry. It may even be advisable to calculate separate sets of ratios for operations in each industry. The larger is the firm being analyzed, the more likely it is that it will have multi-industry activities and that separate ratios for several lines of activity will have to be computed.

What standards should be used to establish the proper ratios for a particular firm? From the shareholders' standpoint, ratios should be at those levels which mean that the company will generate the best stream of net income over time—simply put, income per share with most desirable risk-return properties. Creditors seek assurance that their principal and interest on the debt will be paid, implying a preference on their part for the firm to be prosperous and for the liquidity and leverage ratios to be equal to or greater than some minimal safe level.

The inventory turnover ratio and operating ratio values should imply that the firm is expanding sales and minimizing costs for any given level and quality of output. Excessive debt means an unacceptable likelihood of default on the debt, something that should be avoided since bankruptcy is disastrous to shareholders and to creditors. This risk is reflected in the liquidity and leverage ratios. The profitability ratio should reflect an adequate return on investment given the risk of the company's activities. In any case, a firm's particular objectives and circumstances must be reflected in the ratio levels that are deemed appropriate for the company. Industry averages can, in most cases, offer no more than a general guide. The firm's ratios should coincide with the industry average ratios only if the firm's objectives and circumstances are typical of the industry and the industry is made up of successful and well-managed companies.

In establishing the appropriate ratio levels for Macro Toy Company (col. 4, Table 14-1), it was assumed that the industry ratio levels (col. 3) were satisfactory for an average firm in the toy industry. That is, the industry is efficient and moderately prosperous and therefore provides a good average standard of performance. Macro Toy Company, however, is not representative since it has an exceptionally high volume of special-order sales and is relatively risky (greater uncertainty regarding future sales or costs, earnings, etc.). Because there is more than average risk, this firm should have a lower debt ratio and a higher interest coverage, as well as a higher than normal profitability (to compensate for greater risk). This is reflected in the appropriate ratio values for Macro, which differ from the values of the ratios for the entire industry. Also, since Macro does many special-order projects, it will not require as large an inventory of finished products as competing companies with primarily mass production products. Therefore, Macro needs a higher inventory turnover ratio (a lower level of inventory relative to sales) than do its competitors in the industry.

Interrelationship of Ratios   Ratios must be evaluated together, not individually. For example, Macro Toy Company has a low current ratio (inadequate liquidity) but a better than adequate debt ratio, interest coverage, and profitability. The firm, therefore, is in a good position to seek additional long-term debt or equity financing if needed. As noted earlier, the current ratio could be improved (increased) by increasing long-term debt and using the proceeds to pay off short-term debt. Recall also that the firm has a high fixed-assets ratio, implying that some of the production facilities could be sold and the funds used to reduce current liabilities. Even if the firm does not reduce its current (short-term) liabilities, creditors can take note that the firm will be able to resort to long-term financing or sell its fixed assets to pay off short-term debts when they come due. Short-term creditors must be concerned not only with the current liquidity position of the firm, but also with its overall position. The current or quick ratios alone do not reveal the entire story. Indeed, another firm with an excellent current ratio but rapidly deteriorating overall position might be far riskier for creditors. This is not to suggest, however, that the liquidity ratios are irrelevant. Higher liquidity ratios mean that the firm is better prepared to pay off debts that are coming due, without having to resort to long-term borrowing (which may be expensive or even impossible if the company is in financial distress).

Expressing the return on equity in terms of other ratios is especially revealing:

$$\text{Return on equity} = \underbrace{\frac{\text{net income}}{\text{operating income}} \times \overbrace{\frac{\text{operating income}}{\text{sales}}}^{\substack{\text{net} \\ \text{operating} \\ \text{margin}}}}_{\text{profit margin on sales}} \times \overbrace{\frac{\text{sales}}{\text{total assets}}}^{\substack{\text{total-} \\ \text{assets} \\ \text{turnover}}} \times \overbrace{\frac{\text{total assets}}{\text{equity}}}^{\substack{1\ + \\ \text{debt-} \\ \text{equity ratio}^9}}$$

_____

[9] [Total assets/equity] = [(equity + debt)/equity] = 1 + [debt/equity] = 1 + debt-equity ratio.

Notice from the above equation that, even if one of the above four ratios comprising return on equity is low, return on equity may still be high. For example, if the net operating margin is very low compared with those of other firms in the industry, the return on equity may be high if the firm has a high total-assets turnover ratio or high debt ratio (assets are large relative to equity). An example of this might be a firm which cuts the sales price of its product (and therefore lowers its operating income and its profit margin on sales) but consequently greatly expands its sales (producing a high total-asset turnover) and therefore has a high return on equity. Another example is a firm which has a great deal of debt relative to equity (i.e., a large debt ratio and therefore a large total assets/equity) but has a pretax return on investment which exceeds the interest rate (and therefore has a satisfactory profit margin on sales).[10] The high (total assets/equity) ratio can mean very large return on equity. This situation is common in the real estate industry. These examples illustrate that a particular ratio level may appear only satisfactory or even poor (for example, a low net operating margin or a high debt ratio), but this may be part of a calculated strategy of management to achieve a high overall performance (a high return on equity). One benefit of expressing return on equity in terms of other ratios, as in the above equation, is that it reveals how policy changes in various areas can affect return on equity. It provides some insight into what factors determine firm profitability.

Trends over Time   Historical information can be useful in diagnosing a firm just as it is in medically diagnosing a patient. Whether the fever is rising or falling can be as important as its level. When a firm's weaknesses are revealed, the immediate reaction is to consider remedies. However, if trends indicate that the situation is improving, it may be that no remedy is needed. Indeed, attempted remedies may make things worse.

Time trends are important in another sense. Pricing and credit policies, production methods, and other areas of managerial control can be varied, all affecting the firm's performance. A survey of past policies and their effects on the firm, as reflected in such performance measures as the above ratios, can be a very helpful guide in formulating future policies.

An additional word of caution regarding the forecasting of future trends: Historical data are suggestive but not conclusive. A financial

---

[10] Note that interest is a tax deductible expense. Also, *if* an investment earns (before corporate taxes) more than the interest rate paid on borrowed funds used to finance the investment, the investment will generate additional profit for the firm's owners. Of course, the sword cuts both ways: If the investment return is less than the interest rate, losses will be produced by the investment. An implication is that, simply raising (total assets/equity) (that is, raising the debt-equity ratio for any given level of total assets and any given operating income) will not necessarily raise return on equity. This is so because greater debt means more debt interest expense, which in turn means lower net income and lower (net income/operating income) since more of the operating income must be paid out to creditors.

variable changing in one direction in the past may not continue to move in that direction in the future. Therefore, to determine if a variable is settling at some level or maintaining its trend, additional information regarding the company and the industry must be obtained.

Examining Macro's trends over time in Figure 14-1, notice that the liquidity ratios at the end of 1990 and 1991 are markedly below the levels of previous periods, implying that the current and quick ratios may be only temporarily depressed. Inadequate liquidity may, therefore, not reflect chronic mismanagement, but merely an extraordinary situation that will soon be corrected. However, the fact that the liquidity deficiency in 1991 is even greater than at the end of the previous year suggests that the problem should be investigated.

The debt ratio has not changed much. From Figure 14-1, we see that sales have declined due to the discontinuation of an unprofitable line. This has increased profits per dollar of sales (increase in the operating margin) but has also created unused plant capacity and a resulting fall in assets turnover (sales/fixed assets and sales/total assets). The firm's profitability has increased, suggesting that the rise in the operating

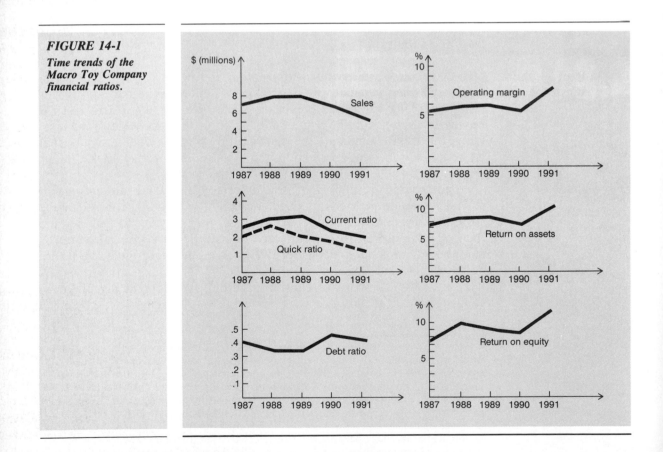

FIGURE 14-1

Time trends of the Macro Toy Company financial ratios.

margin has more than compensated for the fall in sales. Of particular interest to the analyst would be projections of future sales. Additional information would be needed to formulate such a sales forecast.

We should point out that in order to properly forecast a company's future performance (and the implied financial ratios), it is essential that the forecaster have some understanding of the company's production, marketing, and financial plans. The economic feasibility of those plans (in light of data concerning the firm, the industry, and the economy as a whole), and the ability of the company's management to fulfill its plans, should be carefully studied in any evaluation. Financial statement data alone are ordinarily insufficient for the task. A close familiarity with the circumstances behind the financial statements is essential.

The analysis of ratio interrelationships and trends over time is the essence of many modern techniques of financial statement analysis. Several ratios can be simultaneously considered with each ratio weighted by its relative importance (the weights being determined by a statistical study of historical data); the weighted average of the ratio magnitudes gives a number which can be used for predictive purposes, for example, to forecast financial distress. This approach is used in what is referred to as "discriminant analysis." Another ratio technique for forecasting performance involves analysis of rates of change in ratios over time. The traditional method of examining only a few ratios at one point in time is gradually being replaced by these more effective approaches.[11]

Using Financial Statement Information   Financial ratios are generally based on balance sheet and income statement figures. However, there are potential problems with these numbers.

Balance sheet asset figures do not ordinarily equal the actual market values of the assets, and balance sheet liability figures often do not equal what it would actually cost to retire the outstanding liabilities. Assets are listed on the balance sheet at cost (what the company paid for the asset) less depreciation, or, for certain assets (e.g., marketable securities and inventories) at the *lower* of cost or market. Therefore, for Macro Toy Company in Exhibit 14-1, the actual market value of plant and equipment might be $5 million and the actual market value of inventories might be $450,000, even though the figures shown on the balance sheet are $1.6 million and $350,000, respectively. Furthermore, the debentures shown

---

[11] On the use of multiple ratios and ratio changes over time see E. I. Altman, "Financial Ratios, Discriminant Analysis and the Prediction of Corporate Bankruptcy" *Journal of Finance* (September 1968), pp. 589–609; W. H. Beaver, "Market Prices, Financial Ratios, and the Prediction of Failure," *Journal of Accounting Research* (Autumn 1968), pp. 179–192; B. Lev, *Financial Statement Analysis: A New Approach* (Englewood Cliffs, N.J.: Prentice-Hall, 1974); and G. Foster, *Financial Statement Analysis* (Englewood Cliffs, N.J.: Prentice-Hall, 1978).

on the balance sheet at $400,000 may have a market value of, say, only $350,000 (that is the company could retire the bonds by buying them in the market for only $350,000).[12]

Similar observations apply to the income statement. The quantities shown on the income statement are not actually cash flows in the period covered by the income statement (for example, the year 1991 in Exhibit 14-2), but, instead, are amounts computed according to generally accepted accounting principles. For example, in Exhibit 14-2, although depreciation is included as a general and administrative expense, depreciation is not an actual outlay during 1991. Rather, it is some percentage of what was spent on plant and equipment in past periods. Similarly, net income shown on the income statement is an amount computed according to generally accepted accounting principles. This net income is usually not, for example, equal to the dividends paid during the year or to the change in the shareholders' wealth during the year. The change in shareholders' wealth during the year equals the dividends *plus* capital gains (change in the market value of the company stock) for that year.

What does all this mean for ratio analysis? First, we should note that, except for long-term assets like plant and equipment, balance sheet values for assets and liabilities are usually ''in the ball park'' and are therefore good rough measures of actual asset and liability magnitudes. Ratios based only on these values are therefore generally quite useful. Whenever long-term assets are included in a ratio, though, market values for those assets should also be obtained unless there is good reason to believe that the balance sheet figures approximate true market value. Market values for assets are often shown as supplementary information on the balance sheet.

Second, although income statement net income is only one version of income (it is conventional historical cost income computed under generally accepted accounting principles), it is useful as a very rough guide for assessing and comparing companies. It is not the only guide, however. Another basis of evaluation is funds flow, which we discuss later in this chapter.[13]

---

[12] The $400,000 shown on Macro's balance sheet in Exhibit 14-1 is the amount Macro borrowed when it issued the debentures. If, on balance sheet date December 31, 1991, interest rates are much higher than the 7 percent rate on the bonds, the bonds would sell in the market for much less than $400,000.

[13] In addition to conventional historical cost income, the accounting profession has developed two other income measures, current cost income and general price level adjusted income (also referred to as historical cost–constant dollar income). Still other bases for evaluation that are used are current and forecasted firm dividends and current and forecasted firm operating cash flow. As a practical matter, ratio analysis based on the balance sheet and income statement (as described in the chapter) is still the most widely used method of evaluation. It is likely, though, that techniques using actual cash flows rather than income statement net income will become increasingly important in the future.

DU PONT SYSTEM

Around World War I the DuPont Company introduced a method of financial analysis that has won general recognition for its usefulness and has, in one form or another, been adopted by most major United States firms. Its purpose is to provide management with a measure of performance in the form of a return on investment, or ROI. Two common versions of ROI are net income to total assets, Eq. (14-1) below, and return on equity, Eq. (14-2) below (this is the same return on equity discussed earlier).

$$\text{ROI (total assets)} = \frac{\text{sales}}{\text{total assets}} \times \frac{\text{net income}}{\text{sales}} = \frac{\text{net income}}{\text{total assets}} \qquad (14\text{-}1)$$

$$\text{ROI (equity)} = \frac{\text{sales}}{\text{total assets}} \times \frac{\text{total assets}}{\text{stockholders' equity}} \times \frac{\text{net income}}{\text{sales}}$$

$$= \frac{\text{net income}}{\text{stockholders' equity}} \qquad (14\text{-}2)$$

The issues of interest here are: Which of the two above equations is more useful? How can the firm control its ROI if it is too low? And, perhaps most important, how good a measure of performance is ROI?

If a choice is to be made between the two ROI equations, the second should be selected. Net income is the return to those providing *equity* capital, that is, the dollar return on equity. The proper measure of return *on total assets* is *not* net income divided by total assets [Eq. (14-1)] but is net income *plus* interest on debt divided by total assets (this is the return on total assets ratio that was discussed earlier in this chapter). Although Eq. (14-1) is often used in practice, it is very misleading and can produce results at variance with Eq. (14-2) and with the return on total assets ratio described earlier. Indeed, it is easily shown that one company can have a greater return on equity and a greater total return (net income + interest) on total assets than another firm but still have a lower ROI using Eq. (14-1) because the latter firm—the one with the higher ROI using (14-1)—has less debt.[14] Our conclusion is that if we want to measure return on total assets, we should use the (net income + interest)/total assets ratio previously described in this chapter. On the other hand, if we wish to use net income as the numerator in an ROI index of performance, then we are interested in return on net worth and we should use Eq. (14-2), which is also a valid measure of performance.

---

[14] For example, assume that firm *A* has profits of $1.1 million, assets of $10 million, and no debt; so, ROI (total assets), ROI (equity), and return on total assets are 11 percent. Compare this to firm *B* that has profits of $1 million, assets of $10 million, and debt of $4 million and pays $400,000 per year in interest. Firm *B* has an ROI (total assets) of 10 percent (less than firm *A*'s) but has a higher ROI (equity) ($1 million/$6 million = $16\frac{2}{3}$ percent), and a higher return on total assets [($1 million + $400,000)/$10 million = 14 percent] than does firm *A*. Therefore, using ROI (total assets), firm *A* is outperforming firm *B*; but using ROI (equity) and return on total assets, firm *B* is outperforming firm *A*.

Can the firm raise its ROI by increasing its assets turnover (sales/total assets) or by increasing its margin on sales (net income/sales)?[15] Assets turnover is dependent on the company's line of business. Retailers such as grocery stores and automobile dealers generally have high assets turnovers, whereas utilities, real estate–based service companies (such as hotels), and the capital-intensive manufacturers ordinarily have relatively low assets turnovers. Assets turnover tends to decline as the period of time required for the company to produce the product increases and as the proportion of costs going into physical plant increases. Table 14-2 presents ratios for several industries. Assets turnover can be increased by the more efficient use of available assets and the elimination of any excess capacity (unused plant). However, there is ordinarily an upper limit on assets turnover that is determined by the nature of the business.

Profit margin on sales is highly sensitive to pricing policy (which is influenced by competitive conditions), cost control, and the level of sales. Profit margin tends to increase with the level of sales because of the existence of fixed operating costs, such as depreciation on plant (this is referred to as "operating leverage," which is discussed in Chapter 15).

---

[15] As is clear from Eq. (14-2), ROI (equity) is also dependent upon the ratio of total assets to stockholders' equity. As shown in footnote 9, this ratio can be expressed in terms of the firm's debt ratio since we know from a balance sheet that total assets equal firm total liabilities plus stockholders' equity.

TABLE 14-2
Ratios for various industries

Industry	Sales / Total assets	Sales / Equity[b]	Income[a] / Sales	Income[a] / Equity[b]	Debt / Equity[b]
Grocery and meat retailers	6.2	19.9	1.05%	20.9%	2.2
Auto retailers— new and used	4.9	19.7	1.70%	33.4%	2.9
Motels, hotels, and tourist courts	0.8	4.21	4.75%	20.0%	4.3
Electronic components and accessories	1.9	4.71	6.05%	28.5%	1.4
Detective agencies	3.2	13.81	1.81%	25.0%	1.8
Aircraft manufacturers	1.5	3.23	4.93%	15.9%	1.3

[a] Before-tax income.
[b] Total stockholders' equity.
Source: Robert Morris Associates.

Firms that keep per unit costs down and keep sales up are those with high sales profitability and usually high ROIs. Profit on sales generally varies more within a given industry than does assets turnover.

Regardless of the ROI measure that is used [Eq. (14-1), Eq. (14-2), or return on total assets described earlier in the chapter], ROI is only a very rough measure of performance. Only under very unusual circumstances will the actual rate of return being earned on the firm's assets equal the computed ROI. This is due to the definition of ROI, which uses accounting net income rather than cash flow and uses accounting depreciation in computing net income and net assets. Accounting depreciation is generally not equal to actual depreciation, and therefore net income and asset values are distorted. In spite of these deficiencies, it is true that ROI and the real rate of return tend to move together; a high ROI over several accounting periods ordinarily means a high real rate of return, and therefore, ROI is a rough index of performance. It can be used in comparing the relative performance of different firms or of divisions within a firm.

Since the mid-1960s, ROI has been the target of criticism as a basis of performance measurement. The central issue is that ROI is not a very accurate index of true rate of return earned on the company's assets. Although ROI is likely to survive for some time, it is also likely that the ROI concept will eventually be significantly altered or abandoned in favor of more useful measures of performance.

SOURCES OF INFORMATION ON FIRM AND INDUSTRY RATIOS

Data for computing the ratios of particular firms can be obtained from the annual and interim financial reports of the firm and from investment advisory services such as Moody's, Standard & Poor's, and Value Line. Brokerage houses, particularly those with large research departments, distribute financial information on all companies listed on the national exchanges and on some of the larger firms traded in the over-the-counter market. Data can also be obtained from the firm directly. However, company officials may be reluctant to provide a great deal of help for fear of violating Securities and Exchange Commission "inside information" regulations or of disclosing information valuable to competitors.

There are several sources of information on the various sectors of the economy (for example, manufacturing, retailing, wholesaling) and on particular industries. Some of these sources are noted below.

Dun & Bradstreet   Dun & Bradstreet annually publishes key business ratios, including fourteen key ratios for firms in 125 types of retailing, wholesaling, manufacturing, and construction. A large sample of data is used in computing each of the ratios, and values are provided for the upper quartile (top fourth), median, and lowest quartile (bottom fourth).

Robert Morris Associates   In its annual statement studies, this association of bank loan officers provides ratio data on 156 lines of business activity. Eleven ratios are provided for each line with the information derived from the financial statements of firms that the banks deal with. A breakdown is provided showing the relationship of the ratio levels to firm size, although the companies in the samples tend to be large.

Trade Associations   Many trade associations compile data on financial ratios for various industries. Examples are the National Retail Furniture Association and the National Hardware Association.

Government Agencies   The Federal Trade Commission and the Securities and Exchange Commission jointly publish the *Quarterly Financial Report for Manufacturing Corporations*, which provides income statement and balance sheet data based upon a wide sample of manufacturing corporations. The data analysis is presented by industry groups and by firm asset size. The United States Department of Commerce and the Small Business Administration frequently publish studies covering large and small businesses, often including information on the standard financial ratios.

Other Sources   In its semiannual publication, *The Barometer of Small Business*, the Accounting Corporation of America provides income statement and balance sheet data for companies grouped by sales volume and by geographic region. The National Cash Register Company publishes information on expense percentages for firms in fifty-seven lines of business.

THE PURPOSES OF RATIO ANALYSIS

Ratios are a shortcut method of conveying certain crucial facts about a firm's operations and financial situation. When creditors provide funds to a firm, their primary interest is the future capacity of that company to repay the debt. This is true of short-term and long-term lenders. Before extending a loan, banks and other financial institutions generally apply ratio analysis to a prospective borrower's financial statements. The results of the analysis can be a determining factor in whether or not the loan is made. Ratio analysis is also among the tools used by Moody's and Standard & Poor's in rating the bonds of corporations.

Short-term creditors are particularly concerned with the firm's liquidity ratios, since the existing or near-term current assets are generally used to liquidate short-term debts. The overall condition of the firm, however, is also important, because the general financial health of a firm reflects its ability to repay even short-term debt. A strong current asset position can deteriorate rapidly if the company is losing money or is reducing its current assets through capital investment or payments to creditors or stockholders. On the other hand, even if the firm's current liquidity position is weak, if its long-run financial strength seems assured, short-term creditors will be protected as long as the company can borrow funds from long-term sources to pay off short-term liabilities. Therefore, the long-run outlook for the firm is relevant to short-term lenders to the extent that it affects the borrower's capacity to obtain additional outside financing as a means of repaying short-term debts.

Long-term lenders are concerned with any financial ratio that reflects the ability of the firm to meet long-run debt requirements. They are concerned with the liquidity ratios as a measure of both the firm's policy and ability with respect to liquidating short-term debt. The leverage ratios interest lenders because they reflect how much the company is presently in debt. Only in exceptional situations would the lender examine activity ratios, since for most lending purposes the profitability ratios offer a sufficiently good measure of the firm's operating effectiveness.

In evaluating the firm as an investment prospect, security analysts frequently examine the financial ratios. The analyst is interested in the desirability of the firm's stocks and bonds as an investment and in any information reflecting upon the firm's operating efficiency and financial strength. For regulated industries—for example, utilities, airlines, and railroads—financial ratios will be of interest to government agencies, both for the purpose of appraising the financial health of the regulated firm and for rate setting (setting the prices the firms may charge customers).

The management of a firm is concerned with all aspects of its operations and its relations with creditors, investors, and the government. The firm's ability to fulfill commitments to creditors (liquidity and leverage ratios) and to minimize costs (activity and profitability ratios) determines whether it will meet its ultimate objective of providing shareholders with a maximum return (reflected in the profitability ratios). Financial ratio analysis is therefore not just a device for outsiders. It is also useful as a managerial tool.

FUNDS FLOW ANALYSIS

The determination of the sources of cash flowing into the firm and the uses of that cash by the firm is referred to as sources and uses of funds analysis, or simply, as funds flow analysis. We are using "funds" here to refer to cash; later in this section we will examine funds flow using working capital as funds. Funds flow analysis provides a comprehensive view of a firm's receipts and outlays. It is particularly useful for monitoring how well a firm realizes its established plans for obtaining funds (from its sales as well as its lenders and investors) and for using those funds. Lenders are interested in a sources and uses statement because it provides an excellent overview of what transpired during the year.

Funds (cash) sources and uses are associated with specific types of changes:

Sources of funds involve:

1 A decrease in assets, or
2 An increase in liabilities, or
3 An increase in stockholders' equity (from a rise in paid-in capital or in retained earnings)

Uses of funds involve:

1 An increase in assets, or
2 A decrease in liabilities, or

3 A decrease in stockholders' equity (from a decrease in paid-in capital or in retained earnings)

Sources of generating cash are selling assets (decrease in assets), borrowing money (increase in liabilities), issuing and selling new shares (an increase in paid-in capital), or retaining net income earned rather than paying it out in dividends (an increase in retained earnings).

These funds would then be used in the following ways: to purchase assets (an increase in assets), to retire debt (a decrease in liabilities), to retire common or preferred stock by purchasing it or calling it in (decrease in paid-in capital and perhaps retained earnings), or a loss (negative income) incurred by the firm (a decrease in retained earnings).[16] Since every dollar must have a source and a use, the total sources of funds must equal the total uses of funds.

An example will help to clarify the concept of sources and uses of funds. In the illustration we will first use the **comparative balance sheet approach** for determining the sources and uses of funds during the period. This approach is based on changes in each balance sheet account from one statement date to the next. Exhibit 14-3 shows the balance sheet figures for the Macro Toy Company for the periods ending December 31, 1990, and December 31, 1991, and the differences between them are either sources or uses of funds. Notice that a decrease in assets is a source of funds, and an increase in assets is a use of funds. For example, Macro's net accounts receivable decreased by $150,000 during the year, reflecting collections on those accounts (a source of funds). Inventories rose by $70,000, and this rise involved a use of funds.

Increases in liabilities and owners' equity accounts are sources of funds and decreases are uses of funds. Exhibit 14-4 summarizes the transactions generating funds and requiring (using) funds.

For example, the $5,000 rise in Macro's accruals (amounts owed to those providing goods or services to Macro) is a source of funds (funds in effect lent to Macro by the suppliers). The $25,000 decrease in Macro's mortgage bonds is a use of funds to pay off some of that debt.

The data from the sources and uses statement of Exhibit 14-3 suggest healthy performance and growth. Retained earnings increased by $170,000; debt declined by $40,000 (a decrease in accounts payable, mortgage bonds, and debentures of $60,000, and an increase in accruals and federal income taxes payable of $20,000); and assets expanded by $150,000. These data used in conjunction with the other measures of financial position (for example, income statement, various ratios, and an assessment of the firm's business plans) would provide a complete picture of Macro's condition.

Two areas of confusion concerning the sources and uses statement should be mentioned. First, notice that net income and dividends do not appear as a source and a use of funds, respectively. This is because the

---

[16] A company is said to "call" its preferred stock or bonds when it exercises its right to buy back the security from the preferred stockholder or bondholder at a price specified in the initial preferred stock or bond contract.

two have been netted to produce the "increase in retained earnings" entry. The $170,000 of increase in retained earnings (source of funds) is really the difference between the net income of $240,000 (a source) and dividends of $70,000 (a use). The net income and dividends figures for Macro are shown in Exhibit 14-2 . Note that since we are illustrating the comparative balance sheet approach to funds flow analysis, we use balance sheet data (that is, we use retained earnings figures and not net income and dividends figures, which are income statement data). Of course, we could deviate somewhat from the comparative balance sheet approach in Exhibit 14-4 and include the $240,000 of net income as a source of funds, and the $70,000 in dividends as a use of funds, with no entry for the increase in retained earnings.

The second area of confusion relates to depreciation. Notice in Exhibit 14-2 that depreciation expense was $100,000 during 1991, but the change in the allowance for depreciation indicated in Exhibit 14-3 was only $60,000. The reason for this is that there were asset retirements during 1991 and, when the assets were retired, the allowance for de-

---

EXHIBIT 14-3

Macro Toy Company comparative balance sheets and sources and uses of funds (cash) statement (in thousands of dollars) for the year ended December 31, 1991

	Dec. 31, 1990	Dec. 31, 1991	Sources	Uses
Assets				
Cash	$ 100	$ 70	$ 30[a]	
Marketable securities	20	30		$ 10
Net accounts receivable......................	600	450	150	
Inventories	280	350		70
Gross plant and equipment	1,790	2,100		310
Allowance for depreciation	(440)	(500)	60	
Total assets.....................................	$2,350	$2,500		
Liabilities and stockholders' equity				
Accounts payable..............................	$ 160	$ 150		10
Notes payable.................................	200	200		
Accruals......................................	15	20	5	
Federal income taxes payable....................	65	80	15	
Mortgage bonds	175	150		25
Debentures	425	400		25
Common stock paid-in capital...................	480	500	20	
Retained earnings..............................	830	1,000	170	
Total liability and stockholders' equity..............	$2,350	$2,500	$450	$450

[a] The decrease in cash of $30,000 is indicated as a "source" in order to balance sources and uses since, ignoring the cash account, uses of cash minus sources of cash equal $30,000. We can view the $30,000 decline in cash as a source since it involves drawing $30,000 out of the firm's cash balances, and that is a "source" of cash.

EXHIBIT 14-4

Macro Toy Company statement of sources and uses of funds (cash), 1991 (in thousands of dollars)

Sources of funds (cash)		
Assets	Decrease in cash[a]	$ 30
	Decrease in accounts receivable	150
	Increase in allowance for depreciation	60
Liabilities	Increase in accruals	5
	Increase in income taxes payable	15
Owners' equity	Sales of additional common stock	20
	Increase in retained earnings	170
		$450
Uses of funds (cash)		
Assets	Purchase of marketable securities	$ 10
	Increase in inventories	70
	Increase in gross fixed assets	310
Liabilities	Decrease in accounts payable	10
	Decrease in mortgage bonds	25
	Decrease in debentures	25
		$450

[a] See footnote *a*, Exhibit 14-3.

preciation associated with those retired assets (in the amount of $40,000) was written off the books (that is, cancelled).[17] The change in the

---

[17] When an asset is disposed of or retired, the entry to the books is:

	Debit	Credit
Proceeds from asset dispositions	xxx	
Allowance for depreciation on retired asset	xxx	
Loss on disposition sale	xxx	
Gross book value of retired asset		xxx
Gain on disposition sale		xxx

For Macro Toy Company, assume that the total book value of the retired assets in the example was $70,000, the allowance for depreciation $40,000 (therefore a net book value of $30,000), the disposition sale proceeds $45,000, and therefore the gain on the sale $15,000 (proceeds − net book value). The entry would be:

	Debit	Credit
Proceeds from asset dispositions	$45,000	
Allowance for depreciation on retired assets	40,000	
Gross book value of retired assets		$70,000
Gain on disposition sale		15,000

allowance for depreciation during the period was therefore as shown in
the table below.

Allowance for depreciation, 12/31/90	$400,000
Depreciation expense during 1991	100,000
Allowance for depreciation associated with assets retired during 1991	(40,000)
Allowance for depreciation, 12/31/91	$460,000
Change in allowance for depreciation during 1991	$ 60,000

In the above comparative balance sheet analysis of Macro Toy
Company we used cash as funds. We could also have done the analysis
defining funds as working capital (current assets minus current liabilities). Using working capital, we would have examined changes in all
nonworking capital accounts (all accounts other than those that include
current assets or current liabilities) and identified those changes as
sources and uses of working capital.[18] Rather than explore the comparative balance sheet method of computing sources and uses of working
capital, let's look at an approach for determining the sources and uses of
funds which does not use comparative balance sheets and which ordinarily uses working capital to define funds (although the method can
also use cash to define funds). This alternative approach simply identifies the fund sources and uses and categorizes them as associated with
operations (i.e., generated by net income and depreciation), with investment (i.e., with acquiring new assets or retiring old assets), and with
capital transactions (with financing activities, for example, borrowing or
retiring debt, selling new shares, paying dividends). The **statement of
changes in financial position** itemizes the sources and uses of funds and is
included in a company's annual report. Funds here are normally defined
as working capital. Such a statement for Macro Toy Company is shown
in Exhibit 14-5.

---

[18] The reader is invited to perform this exercise. The sources of working capital in the
example total $250,000 and this is computed by adding the $60,000, $20,000, and $170,000
amounts in the Sources column of Exhibit 14-3. The uses of working capital total $360,000
and this is computed by adding the $310,000, $25,000 and $25,000 in the Uses column of
Exhibit 14-3. The net change in working capital for 1991 is therefore a decrease of
$110,000 ($360,000 − $250,000). For a further explanation of the sources and uses of
working capital, see the discussion below in the text on the statement of changes in
financial position. Note that, although the computed change in working capital for 1991
will of course be the same whether the comparative balance sheet method (Exhibit 14-3)
or the statement of changes in financial position method (Exhibit 14-5) is used, the total
funds (working capital) uses will differ between the two methods. The total funds sources
will differ also. With the former method, sources and uses total $250,000 and $360,000,
respectively, whereas with the latter method (see Exhibit 14-5), sources and uses total
$350,000 and $460,000. The differences arise because different accounts are used to obtain
the $110,000 working capital change for the period.

The sources and uses shown in Exhibit 14-5 indicate changes in working capital caused by the change in the item indicated. For example, the $240,000 in net income was a source of working capital during the year.

Notice that since funds are working capital and not cash in Exhibit 14-5, it is necessary to provide a separate statement that breaks down working capital into its components in order to identify the component changes. This statement is shown at the bottom of Exhibit 14-5.

EXHIBIT 14-5
Macro Toy Company statement of changes in financial position for the year ended December 31, 1991 (in thousands of dollars)

Sources of funds

Net income	$ 240
Depreciation	100
Disposal of plant (at net book value)[a]	30
Proceeds from sale of newly issued common stock	20
Total	$ 390

Use of funds

Dividends paid to stockholders	$ 70
Expenditures for plant and equipment	380
Retirement of mortgage bonds	25
Sinking fund payment on debentures	25
Total	$500

Decrease in working capital	$ 110
Working capital at beginning of year	560
Working capital at end of year	450

Increase (decrease) in working capital by element

Cash	$ (30)
Marketable securities	10
Net accounts receivable	(150)
Inventories	70
Accounts payable	10
Accruals	(5)
Federal income taxes payable	(15)
Decrease in working capital	$(110)

[a] See footnote 17, this chapter, for the details on the asset disposition. The proceeds from the disposition are $45,000, made up of $30,000 to cover the disposed assets' net book value, and a $15,000 gain (which is included in net income).

It should be pointed out that depreciation is not really a source of funds in the strict sense of the word but is instead, a *noncash charge* that was deducted in computing net income. Depreciation is only a bookkeeping entry and does not involve an expenditure of funds. Depreciation must therefore be added back to net income to get the funds generated by operations. The table below shows the relevant figures for Macro.

Funds from operations (aftertax)	$ 340,000
Depreciation (noncash charge)	(100,000)
Net Income (net profit)	$ 240,000
Dividends (actual cash payment)	(70,000)
Increase in retained earnings	$ 170,000

In Exhibit 14-5, net income and depreciation are shown as funds sources, and dividends are separately indicated as a use. This contrasts with the comparative balance sheet approach of Exhibits 14-3 and 14-4 where income and dividends were netted against one another to produce a net source of $170,000 because of an increase in retained earnings.

As we will see in Chapter 16, which examines budgeting and forecasting, planning requires a forecast of future sales, capital transactions, and applications of funds in purchasing assets and retiring liabilities. Data based on forecasts can be used to prepare a projected or pro forma sources and uses statement. This statement is, in effect, a plan of action based on expected future cash inflows and outflows associated with production, sales, and existing contractual obligations. This statement summarizes a firm's expected financial activities for a specified time period. It is useful both as a planning tool for management and as an indication to creditors of the firm's future capacity to meet its debt obligations.

SUMMARY

Ratios provide the analyst with a set of summary measures of the firm's debt burden, operating efficiency, and profitability. There are four types of financial ratios:

> *Liquidity ratios* indicate the firm's ability to fulfill short-run commitments.
> *Leverage ratios* indicate the firm's debt burden.
> *Activity ratios* indicate how effectively a firm uses assets.
> *Profitability ratios* indicate the net returns on sales and assets.

The ratios are computed from data in a firm's balance sheet and income statement and then compared with levels considered desirable for the firm. In determining what ratio levels would be desirable for a particular company, the average ratios for that company's industry are a helpful guide, recognizing that adjustments should be made to fit the firm's special circumstances. For example, if the company is riskier than the industry average, it may warrant a higher liquidity and a lower debt ratio. Interrelationships between ratios should be examined since each ratio reflects only one aspect of the company. Weakness in one area may be compensated for by strength in another. Changes in ratios over time should be examined, since this information may reveal whether a problem is being solved or new remedies are needed. Deteriorating ratios may also signal difficulties not yet present but looming over the horizon. In computing financial ratios, balance sheet and income statement figures should be used with caution because they may not be the quantities appropriate for the ratio computations.

Data on individual firms, industries, and sectors of the economy are available from a variety of sources. These sources include the company being analyzed, private data collection services and financial institutions, trade associations, and government agencies.

Ratios can be helpful to the firm's short- and long-term creditors, to investors and investment analysts, to government agencies, and to the firm's management. Regardless of the user's purpose, however, ratios provide only a partial description of a firm and should be used in combination with other available information.

Funds flow analysis identifies all sources and uses of funds (cash or working capital) by the firm during the year. The sources and uses statement can be useful to management and to creditors, since it offers a comprehensive view of company activities.

QUESTIONS

1 It is said that a balance sheet measures stocks and an income statement measures flows. Explain.

2 What is a shortcoming of the current ratio as an indicator of the firm's ability to meet short-term obligations?

3 Why would a stockholder ordinarily prefer to see the firm with a current ratio of 3 than a current ratio of 10?

4 Sartre Meditation, Inc., is a nationwide chain of transcendental meditation training studios. Except for its small home office in Faroot, New York, Sartre rents all its studios under long-term leases; on the average, the leases currently have eight years to expiration. In computing all its financial ratios, neither the leased assets' values nor the lease obligations are included on the balance sheet; however, lease rentals are included as expenses on the income statement. Sartre owns its small home office building, and there is an outstanding mortgage on the building, which is the firm's only interest-bearing debt. The entire building is occupied by Sartre employees and no place is rented to outside tenants. Seventy-five percent of Sartre's noninterest expenses are in wages to transcendental meditation experts, with most of the remaining 25 percent going for rent on the studios and advertising; depreciation on the home office building is negligible relative to total expenses. Sartre is generally viewed as being in a very risky type of business.

Harding Poker Chips and Playing Cards, Incorporated, has been in business since 1920 and has well-established, stable markets for its products and highly predictable costs. The firm's new manufacturing facility in Cleveland, Ohio, is its main fixed asset. Harding leases no assets but does have some long-term bonds outstanding.

Assume that Sartre and Harding are both expertly managed and each firm has financial ratios that are appropriate to this line of business. With no further information, what would you expect regarding the relative magnitudes of the ratios stated below for Sartre and Harding (for example, which firm has the larger debt ratio, etc.)? Explain your choice.

a	Debt ratio	*e*	Fixed-assets turnover
b	Times interest earned	*f*	Total-assets turnover
c	Fixed-charges coverage	*g*	Return on total assets
d	Inventory turnover	*h*	Return on net worth

5   Is it possible for a firm to have a consistently high profit margin on sales and yet be unable to meets its debt obligations?

6   Why is it important to analyze the trends in financial ratios as well as their levels at a particular point in time?

7   Sonny Smiles owns a surfboard manufacturing company, Surf, Inc., and is seeking additional capital from the bank for expansion. Sonny tells William Folde, the bank loan officer and Sonny's golf chum, "My firm is a winner and expansion is clearly justified. Why, over the past three years the profit on sales has averaged 1.3 times the industry average and the profit on total assets has averaged 1.1 times the industry level." Evaluate Sonny Smiles' argument.

8   What types of ratios would the following investors be particularly interested in? Explain.
   a   Banks specializing in short-term loans to commercial enterprises
   b   Pension funds wishing to purchase shares of common stock for their portfolios
   c   Individuals purchasing twenty-year bonds
   d   A firm's management

9   Why is depreciation considered a source of funds?

10   In analyzing a firm's balance sheets for December 31, 1990, and December 31, 1991, state whether each of the following is a source or a use of cash:
   a   Purchase of a new machine for $300,000
   b $500,000 received from sale of land
   c   Sale of 2000 shares of common stock for $25 per share
   d   Issuance of $2,500,000 in twenty-year bonds
   e   Repurchase of 3000 shares of common stock
   f   Decrease of $5000 in the allowance for depreciation
   g   Income after taxes of $20,000

h Dividend payments of $0.50 per share on 100,000 shares out-
standing
i Decrease in accounts receivable resulting from a get tough policy toward customers
j Change in inventory from $250,000 in 1990 to $340,000 in 1991

PROJECT

First refer to *Dun's Review* or to the Robert Morris Associates' *Statement* and examine the financial ratios of different industries. Try to
account for the differences. Then obtain the financial statements of
two firms in different industries and compare their ratios with the industry averages. Try to account for the differences between your firms
and the averages for their industries.

**DEMONSTRATION
PROBLEMS**

DP1 The 1991 balance sheet and income statement for Roland, Inc.,
are shown below. Also shown are the standards (target ratios)
set by management for the company. Compute the financial
ratios for Roland and compare them with the standards. Evaluate Roland's performance using the standards.

Roland, Inc., balance sheet, December 31, 1991

Assets	
Cash	$ 120,000
Marketable securities	80,000
Accounts receivable, net..........................	800,000
Inventories	1,000,000
Gross plant and equipment	2,000,000
Allowance for depreciation........................	(800,000)
Total assets......................................	$3,200,000

Liabilities and equity	
Accounts payable..................................	$ 300,000
Notes payable.....................................	500,000
Accruals..	40,000
Long-term debt....................................	860,000
Common stock	500,000
Retained earnings.................................	1,000,000
Total liabilities and equity	$3,200,000

Roland, Inc., income statement for year ended December 31, 1991

Net sales...		$6,000,000
Cost of goods sold		4,500,000
Gross margin on sales		$1,500,000
Operating expenses:		
Selling	$525,000	
General and administrative.............	375,000	
Total operating expenses		900,000
Operating income		$ 600,000
Other revenues		26,000
Gross income......................................		$ 626,000
Less:		
Interest on long-term debt................	$110,000	
Interest on notes payable	86,000	
Total interest		196,000
Income before taxes...............................		$ 430,000
Federal income taxes..............................		145,000
Income after taxes		$ 285,000

	Roland	Standard for comparison
Current ratio	—	2.1
Quick ratio	—	1.1
Debt ratio	—	.5
Times interest earned	—	4.0
Fixed-charges coverage	—	3.2
Inventory turnover[a]	—	7.0
Average collection period[a]	—	34 days
Fixed-assets turnover	—	4.0
Total-assets turnover	—	2.0
Net operating margin	—	12%
Profit margin on sales	—	5%
Return on total assets	—	16%
Return on equity	—	20%

[a] Based on balance sheet and income statement figures.

SOLUTION TO DP1:

$$\text{Current ratio} = \frac{\$2,000,000}{\$840,000} = 2.38$$

Quick ratio $= \dfrac{\$2,000,000 - \$1,000,000}{\$840,000} = 1.19$

Debt ratio $= \dfrac{\$1,700,000}{\$3,200,000} = .53$

Times interest earned $= \dfrac{\$626,000}{\$196,000} = 3.19$

Fixed charges coverage $= \dfrac{\$626,000}{\$196,000} = 3.19$

Inventory turnover[19] $= \dfrac{\$4,500,000}{\$1,000,000} = 4.5$

Average collection period[20] $= \dfrac{\$800,000}{(\$600,000/360 \text{ days})} = 48 \text{ days}$

Fixed asset turnover $= \dfrac{\$6,000,000}{\$1,200,000} = 5$

Total asset turnover $= \dfrac{\$6,000,000}{\$3,200,000} = 1.875$

Net operating margin $= \dfrac{\$600,000}{\$6,000,000} = 10\%$

Profit margin on sales $= \dfrac{\$285,000}{\$6,000,000} = 4.75\%$

Return on total assets $= \dfrac{\$285,000 + \$196,000}{\$3,200,000} = 15.03\%$

Return on equity $= \dfrac{\$285,000}{\$1,500,000} = 19\%$

Roland compares slightly unfavorably. Inventory turnover is slow, the average collection period is quite long, and its net operating margin, profit margin on sales, return on total assets, and return on equity are somewhat below the standard.

DP2 The 1990 and 1991 balance sheets for Sparta Hats, Inc., are given below.
  a Prepare a sources and uses of funds statement for Sparta, using the comparative balance sheet approach.
  b Assume that Sparta had dividends of $20,000 in 1991. Explain the change in retained earnings from $450,000 to $500,000.
  c What transaction or transactions could account for the change in gross fixed assets and in the allowance for depreciation?

---

[19] Assuming year-end inventory level is not significantly different from the average inventory level for the year.
[20] Assuming all sales are on credit terms.

Sparta Hats, Inc., comparative balance sheets (in thousands of dollars)

	Dec. 31, 1990	Dec. 31, 1991	Source	Use
Assets				
Cash	$ 80	$ 180	_____	_____
Marketable securities	70	60	_____	_____
Net accounts receivable ...	300	380	_____	_____
Inventories	200	360	_____	_____
Gross fixed assets ,,,,,,	700	920	_____	_____
Allowance for depreciation	(250)	(300)	_____	_____
Total assets................	$1,100	$1,600	_____	_____
Liabilities and owners' equity				
Accounts payable	$ 100	$ 130	_____	_____
Notes payable	200	150	_____	_____
Accruals	50	70	_____	_____
Long-term debt	200	250	_____	_____
Common stock...........	100	500	_____	_____
Retain earnings	450	500	_____	_____
Total liabilities and owners' equity	$1,100	$1,600	_____	_____

SOLUTION TO DP2:

a

Sparta Hats, Inc., statement of sources and uses of funds for 1991

Sources of funds	(In thousands of dollars)
Decrease in marketable securities	$ 10
Increase in long-term debt	50
Increase in allowance for depreciation	50
Increase in accounts payable	30
Increase in accruals	20
Increase in common stock	400
Increase in retained earnings	50
	$610
Use of funds	
Increase in cash	$100
Increase in accounts receivable	80
Increase in inventories	160
Increase in gross fixed assets	220
Decrease in notes payable	50
	$610

b Change in retained earnings = net income − dividends

$50,000 = net income − $20,000

Net income = $70,000

c The change in gross fixed assets is equal to asset additions less asset reductions (sales and retirements). Since gross fixed assets increased by $220,000, asset additions must have exceeded asset retirements (if any). The change in the allowance for depreciation equals the depreciation expense for the year less any amount in the allowance for depreciation account that was removed during the year because of sales and retirements of assets (the allowance for depreciation on assets sold or retired is removed from the books). An *example* of transactions that could produce the magnitude in the sources and uses statement is as follows:

	(In thousands of dollars)
New assets acquired (at cost)	$270
Old assets sold (at original cost)	$ 50
Allowance for depreciation on old assets sold	$ 30
Sale price of old assets	$ 15
Loss on sale of old assets ($ book value less $ sale price)	$ 5
Depreciation expense during year	$ 80

Accounting entries (in thousands)	Debit	Credit
1 Depreciation expense	$ 80	
Allowance for depreciation		$ 80
2 New assets	$270	
Cash		$270
3 Cash	$ 15	
Allowance for depreciation	$ 30	
Loss on sale of old assets	$ 5	
Old assets		$ 50

The $220 increase (in thousands) in gross fixed assets from $700 on 12/31/90 to $920 on 12/31/91 is due to the $270 addition (entry 2) less the $50 reduction due to the older asset sale (entry 3). The $50 increase in the allowance for depreciation from $250 to $300 is due to the 1991 depreciation expense of $80 (entry 1) less the $30 allowance for depreciation associated with the assets that were sold (entry 3).

PROBLEMS

1 The 1991 balance sheet and income statement for Venice, Inc., are given below. Compute the financial ratios for Venice and compare them with the standard given. Evaluate Venice's performance using the standards.

Venice, Inc., balance sheet, December 31, 1991	
Assets	
Cash	$ 90,000
Marketable securities	60,000
Accounts receivable, net	750,000
Inventories	900,000
Gross plant and equipment	2,160,000
Allowance for depreciation	(360,000)
	$3,600,000
Liabilities and equity	
Accounts payable	$ 270,000
Notes payable (12%)	600,000
Accruals	30,000
Long-term debt (9%)	900,000
Common stock	550,000
Retained earnings	1,250,000
	$3,600,000

Venice, Inc., income statement for year ended December 31, 1991

Net sales		$4,500,000
Cost of goods sold		3,600,000
Gross margin on sales		$ 900,000
Operating expense		
Selling	$340,000	
General and administrative	270,000	
Total operating expenses		$ 610,000
Operating income		$ 290,000
Other revenues		134,000
Gross income		$ 424,000
Less		
Interest on long-term debt	$ 81,000	
Interest on notes payable	73,000	
Total interest		$ 154,000
Income before taxes		$ 270,000
Federal income taxes (50%)		135,000
Income after taxes		$ 135,000

	Venice	Standard for comparison
Current ratio	—	2.2
Quick ratio	—	1.4
Debt ratio	—	.55
Times interest earned	—	2.5
Fixed-charges coverage	—	2.0
Inventory turnover[a]	—	3.8
Average collection period[a]	—	58 days
Fixed-assets turnover	—	2.8
Total-assets turnover	—	1.3
Net operating margin	—	6.0%
Profit margin on sales	—	3.0%
Return on total assets	—	8.2%
Return on equity	—	7.8%

[a] Based on balance sheet and income statement figures.

2 Blue Barn Sea Foods produces canned and frozen seafood products. In 1989 Blue Barn introduced a new product, a combination
sandwich made of deep fried oysters and pork sausages; the new
sandwich was given the name "Piggy Goes to Sea." Piggy Goes
to Sea was an instant sensation. Unfortunately, the success of
Piggy Goes to Sea was offset by the failure of another Blue Barn
product, Squid & Beans. Total sales over the 1989 to 1991 period
were constant. The table below shows certain ratios for Blue Barn

as of the end of each of the indicated three years. Blue Barn pays 40 percent of its taxable income in taxes (taxable income = EBIT − interest expense).

	1989	1990	1991
Current ratio	2.40	2.70	2.80
Quick ratio	1.50	1.00	.70
Debt ratio	.50	.52	.49
Inventory turnover	16	11	7
Average collection period (days)	43	48	52
Fixed-assets turnover	7	7	7
Total-assets turnover	5	4	3
Net operating margin	.10	.08	.06
Profit margin on sales	.06	.05	.03
Return on total assets	.12	.09	.07
Return on equity	.14	.08	.04

a Using the 1989 ratio levels as the standard of comparison, what ratios appear to have deteriorated by 1991?

b What might explain the ratio deterioration and what action might Blue Barn undertake to bring the ratios back in line?

3 Meteor Cabs pays 40 percent of its taxable income in taxes (taxable income = EBIT − interest expense). The table below shows the balance sheet figures and certain ratios for Meteor as of the end of each of the indicated three years.

Balance sheet	1988	1989	1990
Assets			
Current	$500	?	$1,500
Plant & equipment	$900	?	?
Liabilities			
Current	$200	$250	?
Long-term	?	?	?
Stockholders' equity	$600	$680	$ 700
Other data			
Current ratio	?	2.8	5.0
Debt ratio	?	0.60	0.72
EBIT	$280	?	$510
Interest expense	$130	$182	?
Taxes	?	$ 76	?
Times interest earned	?	?	1.7
Return on equity	?	17%	?

a Fill in the unknown amounts (signified by ?) in the table. Total sales over the 1988 to 1990 period remained constant.

b Assume that during the years 1988, 1989, and 1990 the firm sold new shares (no old shares were retired) in the following amounts:

Year	Funds received (paid-in capital) from selling new shares
1988	$100
1989	80
1990	15

Using your answer to *a*, determine the amount of dividends paid during 1989 and 1990.

c Assume that you are analyzing Meteor's situation as of December 31, 1990. Using your answers to *a* and *b*, what is your diagnosis of Meteor?

4 Verity, Inc., manufactures dental equipment. Verity currently (December 31, 1991) has $500,00 in total assets, $200,000 in debt, and $300,000 in common stock and retained earnings. The 1991 income statement for Verity is shown below.

Verity, Inc., income statement for year ended December 31, 1991		
Net sales		$600,000
Cost of goods sold		$420,000
Gross margin on sales		$180,000
Operating expenses		
Selling	$ 36,000	
General and administrative	24,000	
Lease payments	30,000	
Total operating expenses		$ 90,000
Operating income		$ 90,000
Less interest on debt		30,000
Income before taxes		$ 60,000
Federal income taxes (40%)		24,000
Net income		$ 36,000
Dividends		12,000
Increase in retained earnings		$ 24,000

Verity management believes that sales revenues will increase by $200,000 in 1992 if the firm expands its total assets to $750,000. Management feels that, if it finances the expansion using $200,000 in additional debt and $50,000 from selling new shares, its profitability ratios will rise substantially. Verity makes an annual sinking fund payment of $12,000 per year on its long-term debt. With the additional debt, the sinking fund payment will rise to $24,000 per year. The pro forma (forecasted) income statement below reflects management's expectations for the firm's performance if the expansion is undertaken.

Verity, Inc., pro forma income statement for year ended December 31, 1992

Net sales		$800,000
Cost of goods sold		535,000
Gross margin on sales		265,000
Operating expenses		
Selling	$45,000	
General and administrative	30,000	
Lease payments	30,000	
Total operating expenses		$105,000
Operating income		$160,000
Less interest on debt		64,000
Income before taxes		$ 96,000
Federal income taxes (40%)		38,400
Net income		$ 57,600

---

a If Verity undertakes the expansion, what will its time interest earned and fixed-charges coverage ratios be?

b Will the firm's profitability ratios increase as a result of the expansion?

5 Scan Technologies, Inc., manufactures geological equipment. Although Scan's sales have increased each year from 1988 to 1991, profits have remained very low. Furthermore, future sales for 1992 and beyond are highly uncertain because of the entry of new competition into the field. In comparison with other companies in the same industry, Scan Technologies, Inc., is smaller, less well established, and consequently a riskier enterprise. However, except for Scan's greater sales uncertainty, Scan is very similar to other companies in the industry (in terms of personnel, types of products, and methods of production). The industry is growing steadily and is composed mostly of competitive, well-managed firms.

a Compute the key ratios for Scan for the years 1988 through 1991. (See tables below.)

b Graph the trends in each of the ratios.

c Comment on any strengths or weaknesses you found in *a* and *b*.

d What changes do you recommend to improve Scan's condition?

Scan Technologies, Inc., comparative end-of-year balance sheets (all figures in thousands of dollars)

	1988	1989	1990	1991
Assets				
Current assets				
Cash	$ 20	$ 37	$ 30	$ 32
Securities	10	3	5	0
Accounts receivable, net[a]	32	41	45	54
Inventories[a]	88	112	119	134
Total current assets...............	$150	$183	$199	$220
Fixed assets				
Gross plant and equipment	$530	$620	$710	$830
Reserve for depreciation	(78)	(96)	(116)	(152)
Net plant and equipment	$452	$524	$594	$678
Total assets..........................	$602	$707	$793	$898
Liabilities				
Current liabilities				
Accounts payable....................	$ 18	$ 29	$ 45	$ 51
Accrued wages & salaries	12	15	18	19
Taxes payable......................	14	16	20	18
Bank loans (10.0%)	15	44	57	59
Total current liabilities	$ 59	$104	$140	$147
Long-term liabilities				
Mortgage (7.5%, 20 yr)..............	$ 96	$ 88	$ 78	$ 67
Debentures (12%)....................	60	60	60	60
Subordinated bonds (12%)...........	75	125	175	275
Total long-term liabilities	$231	$273	$313	$402
Total liabilities	$290	$377	$453	$549
Stockholders' equity				
Stockholders' equity				
Common stock ($10 par)	$150	$150	$150	$150
Additional paid-in capital	50	50	50	50
Retained earnings....................	112	130	140	149
Total stockholders' equity	$312	$330	$340	$349
Total liabilities and stockholders' equity	$602	$707	$793	$898

[a] Accounts receivable at end of 1987 were $28,000. Total inventory at end of 1987 was $72,000.

*Scan Technologies, Inc., comparative income statements
(all figures in thousands of dollars)*

	1988	1989	1990	1991
Net sales..............................	$840	$980	$1,020	$1,210
Cost of goods sold	691	803	828	1,002
Gross margin on sales	$149	$177	$ 192	$ 208
Operating expenses:				
Selling	$ 30	$ 33	$ 36	$ 48
General and administrative..........	42	45	58	50
Lease payments	20	20	20	20
Total operating expenses	$ 92	$ 98	$ 114	$ 118
Operating income.....................	$ 57	$ 79	$ 78	$ 90
Operating revenues:				
Income from securities	$ 5	$ 6	$ 4	$ 1
Royalties.......................	2	2	3	3
Total other revenues	$ 7	$ 8	$ 7	$ 4
Gross income.........................	$ 64	$ 87	85	$ 94
Other expenses:				
Interest on bank loan...............	$ 0	$ 4	$ 5	$ 7
Interest on mortgage	8	8	7	7
Interest on debentures..............	7	7	7	7
Interest on subordinated bonds......	7	13	25	31
Research	10	15	21	24
Total other expenses	$ 32	$ 47	$ 65	$ 76
Net income before taxes..............	$ 32	$ 40	$ 20	$ 18
Federal income taxes (at 50%)	$ 16	$ 20	10	9
Net income available to shareholders ..	$ 16	$ 20	$ 10	$ 9
Dividends	$ 1	$ 2	$ 0	$ 0
Increase in retained earnings	15	18	10	9

1991 industry ratios

Ratio	Industry 1991 level
Current ratio	1.50
Quick ratio	0.50
Debt ratio	0.40
Times interest earned	5.12
Fixed-charges coverage	2.00
Inventory turnover	7.00
Average collection period (days)	15.00
Fixed-assets turnover	2.50
Total-assets turnover	1.75
Net operating margin	10%
Profit margin on sales	5%
Return on total assets	9%
Return on equity	10%

6 William "Bill" Williams plans to start a printing business. Since industry standards often provide an indication of what a firm's balance sheet will look like, William Williams has obtained the industry ratios for the printing industry to prepare a balance sheet. Using the ratios given, complete the balance sheet below assuming that income after taxes will be $120,000.

Current ratio: 3
Collection period: forty-five days
Inventory turnover: six times (based on sales)
Current liabilties to net worth: 25 percent
Total debt to net worth: 100 percent
Return on equity: 7.5 percent
Profit margin on sales: $3\frac{1}{3}$ percent

Williams Printing Company pro forma balance sheet for the year ended December 31, 1990

Cash	_____	Accounts payable	_____
Accounts receivable	_____	Long-term debt	_____
Inventory	_____	Total debt	_____
Total current assets	_____	Equity	_____
Fixed assets	_____		
Total assets	_____	Total liabilities and equity	_____

7 The balance sheet, income statement, and certain other relevant information for Reggie Corporation, a manufacturer of quality sports apparel, are shown below. Study the information given and then solve the problems that follow.

Additional Information:

Dividends paid = $12,000
Market price per share for common stock (year-end) = $10.50
Quick ratio = 1.2
Working capital
  (current assets − current liabilities) = $100,000
Inventory turnover ratio = 5.5
Average collection period
  (assuming 360-day year) = 36 days

$$\frac{\text{Total liabilities}}{\text{Stockholders' equity}} = 1.75$$

a Complete the balance sheet and income statement (fill in appropriate data where question marks are shown).
b Calculate the following:

  (1) Current ratio
  (2) Earnings per share
  (3) Return on common stockholders' equity (%)
  (4) Fixed-assets turnover
  (5) Times interest earned
  (6) Net operating margin (%)

Reggie Corporation balance sheet, December 31, 1991

Assets	
Cash	?
Marketable securities	$ 35,000
Accounts receivable (net of bad debt allowance)*a*	?
Inventory*a*	?
Total current assets	?
Plant and equipment (net of depreciation)..................	?
Total assets...	?
Liabilities	
Accounts payable*a*	?
Notes payable—bank (12%)	$ 50,000
Other current liabilities	10,000
Total current liabilities................................	?
Long-term debt (10%)	$180,000
Common stock (40,000 shares, $1 par).....................	40,000
Retained earnings	120,000
Total liabilities and stockholders' equity	?

a Monthly levels of accounts receivable, inventory, and accounts payable have not varied significantly during the year; average levels and end-of-year levels are therefore approximately equal.

*Reggie Corporation income statement for year ended
December 31, 1991*

Sales (all credit sales).....................................	$600,000
Cost of goods sold	?
Gross profit	?
Selling and administrative expense	100,000
Operating income	?
Interest expense	24,000
Income before taxes.....................................	?
Income tax (50% tax rate)...............................	?
Net income...	?

8 The 1990 and 1991 balance sheets for Inland Adhesives, Inc., are shown below. Indicate whether each balance sheet change is a source or a use.

  a Prepare a sources and uses of funds statement for Inland Adhesives, Inc., using the comparative balance sheet approach.

  b Assume that Inland Adhesives, Inc., had income after taxes of $300,000 in 1991. Explain the change in retained earnings shown above from $350,000 to $450,000.

  c What transaction or transactions could account for the change in gross fixed assets and in the allowance for depreciation?

*Inland Adhesives, Inc., comparative balance sheets
(in thousands of dollars)*

	Dec. 31, 1990	Dec. 31, 1991	Source	Use
Assets				
Cash	$ 60	$ 180	____	____
Marketable securities	90	140	____	____
Net accounts receivable	240	180	____	____
Inventories	250	360	____	____
Gross fixed assets	780	720	____	____
Allowance for depreciation	(220)	(180)	____	____
Total assets	$1,200	$1,400	____	____
Liabilities and owners' equity				
Accounts payable...........	$ 150	$ 270	____	____
Notes payable..............	200	100	____	____
Accruals..................	100	180	____	____
Long-term debt.............	300	250	____	____
Common stock	100	150	____	____
Retained earnings...........	350	450	____	____
Total liabilities and owners' equity	$1,200	$1,400	____	____

9 Using the data from problem 8, also assume that the following figures apply to Inland Adhesives., Inc., for the year ended December 31, 1991 (in thousands of dollars):

Net income	$300
Depreciation expense	$200
Disposal (retirement of old assets at net book value)	$ 60
Proceeds from new shares issued	$ 50
New long-term borrowing	$100
Retirement of old debt	$150
Expenditures for new plant and equipment	$240
Dividends paid to stockholders	?

a What were the dividends paid during 1991?
b Prepare a Statement of Changes in Financial Position for the year ended December 31, 1991, for Inland (see Exhibit 14-5 in the text).
c If the expenditure for new plant and equipment of $240,000 were not indicated above, could you determine that figure from the other information that is provided in the question? Explain.

The ▮ symbol indicates that all or a significant part of the problem can be solved using the *Computer Models* software package that accompanies this text.

A company's financial statements are an extremely important source of information about the business. The statements should indicate where the company is now, where it has been, and provide useful clues about where it is going. Without the kind of information provided by financial statements, it is almost impossible to evaluate a company. This reliance on financial statements makes it critically important that the data provided are accurate, that is, truthful, and, equally important, that the variables being measured are relevant to the financial statement user's purposes.

GARBAGE IN, GARBAGE OUT

There is a familiar warning to computer users that computer analysis of bad data will produce poor results: garbage in, garbage out. Highly sophisticated financial analysts using inaccurate financial statement data will generally get misleading results. This can be very costly.

Bad information can be unintentionally or intentionally included in the financial statements. Unintentional errors are most likely in areas where judgment is required, for example, in valuing assets. An example is National Cash Register, the Dayton, Ohio, computer company that wrote off $135 million in obsolete inventory (inventory that some say should have long before been revalued). The result was a "big bath" represented by a $60 million loss in a single year.

The most notable cases of misleading financial statements provided by a company have involved fraud, usually without the knowledge of the company's auditors. A classic case involved the fraudulent overstate-

ment of the inventories and accounts receivable of McKesson & Robbins, Incorporated for the year ended December 31, 1937. The fraud was engineered by the president of the corporation and several of his subordinates. Phony invoices, advices, and other documents with fictitious vendors were prepared to conceal a cash outflow of nearly $25 million, only $3 million of which came back to McKesson in collection of receivables or other cash receipts. Although the auditors, Price Waterhouse & Co., were not involved in the fraud, their audit did fail to spot what had been going on. The accounting firm paid heavily for what happened: it returned over $500,000 in audit fees earned from 1933 to 1937.

History's most spectacular case of financial reporting fraud occurred in the early 1970s and involved the complicity of some of the guilty company's auditors. From 1965 to 1972, the chairman and many members of the top management of Equity Funding Corporation of America and its main subsidiary, Equity Funding Life Insurance Company, created $2 billion of phony life insurance policies on nonexisting persons. The policies were then sold to other life insurance companies for cash and the returns from these sales were included in Equity Funding's growing reported earnings. The bogus assets Equity Funding created in this manner greatly exceeded the $75 million in total profits reported over its entire thirteen-year history. The implication is that the company, which had been the darling of Wall Street for many years, may very well have always been a losing operation—a shocking revelation, particularly to those who invested in the company on the basis of its 25 percent annual compound "earnings" growth record. Some of the auditors of Equity Funding were aware of the scheme and were eventually convicted for fraud, along with the involved Equity Funding executives.

What degree of assurance does the reader of an audited financial statement have that the auditors have made an honest effort to uncover any management attempts to distort the reported figures? It appears that fraud is clearly the exception, but it is impossible to know how many unexposed plots have succeeded. It is possible, however, to describe what auditors say they do and what responsibility they are willing to assume. Until recently, CPA firms held that their function was not to uncover management fraud but rather to ensure that the information provided in the financial statements was presented in accordance with generally accepted accounting principles. Since the late 1960s attitudes have changed and, although the CPA companies are not willing to assume responsibility for management dishonesty, the auditors do now employ auditing procedures specifically designed to detect fraud. They are especially cautious about a company showing certain danger signals, such as inadequate working capital or credit, numerous lawsuits (especially by the firm's shareholders), difficulties in collecting from important customers, and inadequate internal controls and auditing.

Although the alert auditor investigates any observed signs of management fraud, the accounting profession is probably right in stating that even a moderately clever management can fool the auditors if it makes a determined effort to do so. To adopt foolproof fraud detection auditing techniques to be applied to all companies, or even to just those companies showing danger signals, would be prohibitively costly. The conclusion for the financial statement user is that there are no guarantees. The only consolation is that it appears that fraud is the infrequent exception and not a common occurrence.

ACCOUNTING WIZARDRY

A good magician does not need a blindfolded audience to create illusions; a quick hand or a confusing sequence of events will do the trick. And the accounting does not need false data to blindfold the reader, proper arrangements and good combinations of numbers are often sufficient to produce the desired result. We can call this accounting wizardry: the appropriate selection of accounting principles to produce a particular conclusion. Accounting principles often permit more than one approach for treating a given financial event. It is this flexibility that allows the accountant wide discretion in computing a company's earnings or balance sheet figures. The accountant has discretion in allocating revenues or costs in such areas as officers' bonuses, revenue recognition on long-term projects, and the treatment of pension costs. Some other important examples follow.

Depreciation

A company can use one depreciation method on its financial statements and a different depreciation method for tax purposes. On the financial statements, for example, the company could maximize current earnings by minimizing depreciation with the straight-line method; at the same time it could use accelerated depreciation to reduce taxable income in order to minimize current taxes.

Inventory Valuation

Valuation of inventories used up during a period affects reported earnings. LIFO (last in, first out) assumes that the inventories sold during the period were the last inventories purchased, whereas FIFO (first in, first out) assumes that the inventories sold during the period were the oldest inventories in stock. In periods of rising inventory prices (such as during times of inflation), LIFO implies a higher value to inventories sold, a higher cost of goods sold, and therefore lower earnings than FIFO. It should be pointed out that with increasing inventory prices, the use of LIFO for tax purposes produces lower taxable income and therefore lower taxes. A firm should generally use LIFO during periods of increasing inventory prices. By law, if a company uses LIFO for tax purposes it must also use LIFO on its financial statements. Thus, if a company uses FIFO on its financial statements simply to report higher earnings, it must also use it in computing taxable income and must therefore pay higher taxes. Use of FIFO is a costly way to pump up reported earnings.

Research and Development Costs

In some instances accounting principles allow research and development costs to be expensed during the period incurred (that is, completely deducted as an expense) or capitalized (recorded as an asset to be depreciated over several years). Current earnings are greater if the research and development costs are capitalized rather than expensed.

Implications for Financial Statement User

What does all this mean for the user of financial statements? First, it means that in interpreting a given year's earnings, the analyst should know which accounting principles were used. Were the computations done on a conservative or liberal basis and what are the implications for both current and future earnings? The notes to the financial statements generally indicate which accounting principles were used. However, it is often impossible to figure out what the figures would have been had different accounting principles been employed. This is an area in which the accounting profession has done a rather poor job.

Second, most accounting choices that increase one year's earnings will decrease the earnings in one or more future periods by the same amount. That is, accounting wizardry generally involves allocation of revenues and expenses to time periods so that more in one year means less in another year. This means that an overstatement of earnings for one period will usually result in an earnings understatement in one or more other periods. An implication is that examination of reported results for several consecutive time periods will ordinarily give a good picture of what the results on average would have been had different accounting choices been made. Therefore, evaluation of a company using financial statement figures should involve analysis of several years' results and not just the results for a single year.

We should point out that, although there is a great deal of room for mischief in managing earnings by making the appropriate accounting choices, the accounting profession in recent years has made an effort to encourage accurate and meaningful financial reporting. There has been an attempt to require that the accounting method used be the one that best fits the economic situation. Although there remains substantial opportunity for accounting wizardry, the possibilities are significantly less than they once were.

CURRENT VALUES VERSUS HISTORICAL VALUES

Financial statement figures are primarily historical-cost-based rather than current-cost-based. In most cases, balance sheet asset values equal what was paid for the asset (less accumulated depreciation) and not what the assets are currently worth. Liabilities are generally shown at the amount that was borrowed, not what would be required to retire the debt.[1] The result is that balance sheet book values may not indicate the actual financial position of the company.

The income statement has failings similar to those of the balance sheet. Revenues and costs are computed on an accrual basis using historical quantities. Thus, depreciation—which is included among expenses—may not equal what is actually being spent to replace plant and equipment. Cost of goods sold is based on the historical cost of inventories used up during the period and not on the inventories' current replacement cost. In short, accounting income (that is, conventional historical cost accounting income) does not equal cash flow and does not equal economic income (the increase in the shareholders' wealth during the period from holding the firm's shares). Interestingly, though, there is abundant evidence that a

company's share price rises when its accounting income turns out to be greater than expected, and falls when its accounting income turns out to be less than expected.[2] This implies that accounting income contains information which investors find highly useful in valuing shares. There is also evidence that share price does not permanently react to unexpected changes in income or income forecasts that do not have cash flow implications (e.g., a change in depreciation method for firm financial statement reporting but not for computing income taxes); that is, investors apparently "see through" accounting manipulations which do not have real implications for the firm's financial position.[3]

---

[1] For example, assume that in 1960 ABC Company issued $5 million of forty-year bonds at face value (i.e., for $5 million) and that the bonds had a coupon yield of 5 percent per year. Because of much higher interest rates in 1986, the bonds might have a 1986 market value of only $3 million. This means that ABC Company could go into the market and buy back its bonds and retire the debt for approximately $3 million, not the $5 million shown on the balance sheet.

[2] See, for example, R. Ball, "Anomalies in Relationships Between Securities' Yields and Yield Surrogates," *Journal of Financial Economics*, 6 (June 1978), pp. 103–126; H. A. Latane and C. P. Jones, "Standardized Unexpected Earnings—1971–1977," *Journal of Finance*, 34 (June 1979), pp. 717–724; W. H. Beaver, R. Clarke, and W. F. Wright, "The Association Between Unsystematic Security Returns and the Magnitude of Earnings Forecast Errors," *Journal of Accounting Research*, 17 (Autumn 1979), pp. 316–340; D. Givoly and J. Lakonishok, "The Information Contents of Financial Analysts' Forecasts of Earnings," *Journal of Accounting and Economics*, 1 (December 1979), pp. 165–185.

[3] See, for example, T. R. Archibald, "Stock Market Reaction to Depreciation Switchback," *The Accounting Review*, 47 (January 1972), pp. 22–30; R. S. Kaplan and R. Roll, "Investor Evaluation of Accounting Information: Some Empirical Evidence," *Journal of Business*, 45 (April 1972), pp. 225–257; W. H. Beaver and R. E. Dukes, "Interperiod Tax Allocation and δ-Depreciation Methods: Some Empirical Evidence," *The Accounting Review*, 48 (July 1973), pp. 549–559; and S. Sunder, "Stock Price and Risk Related to Accounting Changes in Inventory Valuation," *The Accounting Review*, 50 (April 1975), pp. 305–316.

Many of the problems with accounting figures (both balance sheet and income statement) are due to inflation and this has not gone unnoticed by the accounting profession. Statement of Financial Accounting Standards No. 33 requires large corporations to present certain inflation-adjusted data (including two additional measures of income—historical cost constant dollar income and current cost income) in their financial statements. This new disclosure requirement is not a complete solution to the problem, one of which is to provide cash flow rather than just accrual amounts. But it is a significant step in the right direction.

What is the implication for the financial manager who uses accounting data to do financial analysis (including ratio analysis)? It is that accounting figures ordinarily provide useful but very rough measures of financial position and performance. Comparisons based on these figures are far from meaningless. However, the figures are only approximations of what we are really interested in, namely the actual current dollar amounts (market values, cash flows, etc.) which are relevant in making financial decisions.

BREAK-EVEN ANALYSIS AND THE MEASUREMENT OF LEVERAGE

The level and risk of a company's profits are very important to its stockholders and determine the value of the company's shares. This chapter is concerned with the firm's underlying cost factors that affect profits. Break-even analysis, the first topic to be discussed, examines the relationship between output, profits, and costs. It also considers pricing and cost structure changes that can contribute to greater profitability. The latter half of the chapter discusses leverage, which is the existence of fixed costs (costs that do not vary with output) among the company's costs. **Operating leverage** is due to the existence of fixed production costs, whereas **financial leverage** is due to the presence of fixed financing costs (interest). Both operating leverage and financial leverage are major determinants of the level and variability of company profits.

BREAK-EVEN ANALYSIS

Like ratio and funds flow analysis, break-even analysis is used to analyze financial data. Break-even analysis deals with the relationship of profits to costs, to pricing policy, and to volume of output.[1] A knowledge of this relationship enables a financial manager to maximize income (profits) by specifying production methods, pricing, and output volume.

Break-even analysis is primarily concerned with:

1 How income varies with changes in sales volume (if cost structure and output prices are unchanged)
2 How income varies with changes in costs and prices

Net income (that is, aftertax income) equals revenues from sales less all costs, including depreciation, interest on debt, and taxes, as well as labor, materials, advertising, and other current expenses. By comparing the income from different levels of output, under different cost and price

---

[1] Break-even analysis can be used to examine the relationship of revenues and operating costs (ignoring financial costs such as interest); such an analysis deals with the impact of sales fluctuations on earnings before interest and taxes. The discussion presented here will deal, instead, with the impact of sales fluctuations on the firm's pretax and aftertax income (after deducting interest).

structures, the financial manager can choose the best strategies for investment (which products to produce and how) and for marketing (lower sales price versus increased advertising, for example).

We will first discuss the nature of production costs and then proceed to break-even analysis.

*Fixed and Variable
Costs*

Fixed costs are expenditures that *do not vary as output changes*. The cost of office and factory space and equipment, the cost of an executive staff to oversee operations and a production staff to supervise production, real estate property taxes, etc., are usually fixed costs.

Variable costs are expenditures that *vary with the level of output*. Production materials, direct labor, power for production equipment, shipping services, and office materials used directly for purchasing and billing are ordinarily variable costs.

Most costs may be classified as variable or fixed depending upon any of the following:

1 The magnitude of the change in output
2 The amount of time required to change the cost
3 The length of time the change in output is expected to last

If the expenditure varies with output, the cost is variable; if it does not, the cost is fixed. Let's consider each of these cases.

1 Some costs will be fixed in the long and short run, but only for certain ranges of output. For example, a machine may have a production capacity of 50,000 units annually and be the most economical machine to use for any output between 30,000 and 50,000 units. Over the range of 30,000 to 50,000 units, machine cost is fixed; that is, the same machine is used and neither more nor fewer machines are employed. Outside the 30,000-to-50,000 range, machine cost may be variable. Thus, a rise above 50,000 units annually will necessitate additional machinery; machine cost will therefore vary if output rises above 50,000 units.

2 Some costs may be varied if enough time is available but are fixed (cannot be varied) in the short run. For example, a new manufacturing plant may take three years to construct. Existing plant capacity may be 100,000 units of output annually, with production above 70,000 units requiring much higher labor costs due to round-the-clock operation and overtime pay for workers. The company experiences an increase in annual demand from 55,000 to 95,000 units. In the short run (less than three years), the size of the plant cannot change; production plant cost (depreciation, property taxes, etc.) is fixed over the three-year period, even though output has risen from 55,000 to 95,000 units. In the long run (more than three years), the company will expand its plant capacity so as to produce the 95,000 units more economically; in the long run, plant costs are variable.

3 Some changes in output can result in fixed or variable costs. For example, if a decrease in output is considered temporary (perhaps

565

CHAPTER 15
**Break-even analysis and
the measurement of
leverage**

less than one year), a company may be reluctant to reduce its executive staff or certain segments of its production staff. The cost of their salaries is considered fixed. However, if the downturn is permanent, the firm may decide to reduce its staff or liquidate its plant and equipment. These costs are then variable because they change with output. Similarly, the machine discussed in *1* above may be the most economical means of producing 30,000 to 50,000 units annually; but, if yearly output were to fall permanently below 30,000 units, a smaller machine might be warranted. In the long run, machine cost would be variable for output declines to below 30,000 units annually.

Break-even analysis can be applied for short-run changes in output, in which case some costs are fixed due to the time considerations in *2* and *3*, or for long-run changes, in which case such costs are variable. In the discussion below, we will assume that output variations are short run and some costs are fixed, either because they can't be changed in the short run (as in *2*) or because it isn't profitable to change them simply to respond to temporary changes in output (as in *3*).

The costs considered in our discussion of break-even analysis which will be fixed and variable are:

Fixed costs:
  Depreciation on plant and equipment
  Minimum maintenance costs on plant and equipment
  Salaries and wages of executive and research staff
  Rentals on long-term lease agreements
  Office expenses
  Advertising expenses (if not dependent on output)
  Interest on debt
Variable costs:
  Direct labor wages
  Materials costs
  Sales commissions and salaries

To illustrate the cost relationships, assume that Arcan Corporation has the fixed costs and variable costs listed in Exhibit 15-1.

Arcan's fixed costs are $200,000; whatever output during the year may be, these costs are unaffected. For each unit of output, the firm must incur an additional $10 of cost; that is, variable cost is $10 per unit. Arcan's total variable cost depends on the level of output. Exhibit 15-2 shows the costs and sales revenues for Arcan at various output levels. Figure 15-1 illustrates these data. The diagonal total cost line in Figure 15-1 shows the total costs (fixed plus variable) for each level of output. This line corresponds to the total cost column in Exhibit 15-2.

**Income and
Interest Cost**

Break-even analysis can be used to examine the effect of changes in sales on income (either before-tax or aftertax) or on earnings *before* interest and taxes (EBIT). The impact on pretax income and aftertax income (earnings after deducting interest and taxes) will be examined here.

EXHIBIT 15-1
Costs of Arcan Corporation

Fixed costs:

Depreciation	$100,000
Plant maintenance	15,000
Executive salaries	40,000
Lease rentals	8,000
Office expense	12,000
Advertising	5,000
Interest on debt	20,000
Total	$200,000

Variable costs per unit of output:

Labor	$ 3.00
Materials	5.00
Sales commissions	2.00
Total	$10.00

EXHIBIT 15-2
Arcan Corporation cost and profit schedule

Units sold x	Total fixed cost F	Total variable cost vx	Total cost $F + vx$	Sales px	Pretax income (loss) Profit[a] (loss) (sales − total cost)	Net income (loss)[a]
0	$200,000	$ 0	$200,000	$ 0	$(200,000)	$(100,000)
10,000	200,000	100,000	300,000	150,000	(150,000)	(75,000)
20,000	200,000	200,000	400,000	300,000	(100,000)	(50,000)
30,000	200,000	300,000	500,000	450,000	(50,000)	(25,000)
40,000	200,000	400,000	600,000	600,000	0	0
50,000	200,000	500,000	700,000	750,000	50,000	25,000
60,000	200,000	600,000	800,000	900,000	100,000	50,000
70,000	200,000	700,000	900,000	1,050,000	150,000	75,000

Unit selling price p = $15.00
Fixed costs F = $200,000
Unit variable cost v = $10.00
Total cost $(F + vx)$ = $200,000 + $10x$
Break-even point = 40,000 units

[a] Net income refers to aftertax income. We assume a tax rate of 50%. With a loss, we assume a tax credit equal to the tax rate times the loss (a tax loss carryback)

567

CHAPTER 15
**Break-even analysis and
the measurement of
leverage**

Pretax income equals revenues minus all fixed and variable costs; fixed costs (signified as F) include depreciation *and interest*, since both of these are deducted in computing a company's income. Aftertax income (i.e., net income) equals pretax income minus income taxes paid by the firm.

Interest is a fixed cost that arises from **financial leverage** (borrowing); interest is a financial fixed cost. Lease payments are treated here as operating fixed costs. The other fixed costs listed in the previous section are also operating fixed costs. Operating fixed costs create **operating leverage.** Operating leverage is the presence of operating fixed costs in the firm's cost structure. Thus, financial leverage arises from financial fixed costs and operating leverage arises from operating fixed costs. Fluctuations in income due to sales variations are affected by *both* financial leverage and operating leverage, since *all* fixed costs (both financial and operating) are deducted in determining income. Therefore, in break-even analysis using income, we deduct interest as a fixed cost.

In the later sections of this chapter, we will *not* deduct debt interest as a fixed cost in examining operating leverage, since interest is not an operating cost. However, we will deduct interest as a fixed cost when we consider financial leverage and combined leverage (combination of operating and financial leverage).

Measuring Profitability

To calculate profitability using break-even analysis, revenue from sales must be compared with costs. Assume that Arcan sells its output at a price of $15 per unit. Total sales, costs, and income for each level of output are shown in Figure 15-1 and stated in Exhibit 15-2.

At what level of output should the firm operate for maximum profitability, and at which level must it operate in order to just "break even," that is, earn zero income? In answer to the first part, the firm will generally be somewhat uncertain as to the ultimate demand for its product. From Figure 15-1 and Exhibit 15-2, we can see that income increases as the number of units sold increases, assuming the unit variable cost of $10 and sales price of $15. Therefore, Arcan Corporation will seek to maximize its sales. But sales depend as much upon customer demand for the product as upon the willingness of a firm to sell the product. The firm may not be able to sell as much as it is capable of producing. Future demand is generally uncertain and subject only to an estimate.

What sales are necessary for Arcan to break even? We can see from Exhibit 15-2 that income is zero at sales of 40,000 units. This break-even point of 40,000 units is also illustrated in Figure 15-1 by the intersection of the total-cost and sales curves. Sales below 40,000 units mean losses, and sales above 40,000 units generate income.

---

[2] Technically, lease payments are both financial *and* operating fixed costs; the "interest" portion (net return to the lessor) of the lease payment is a financial fixed cost to the lessee, and the rest of the lease payment, which is a return to the lessor to cover the cost (depreciation) of the asset, is an operating fixed cost to the lessee (is like depreciation).

Before analyzing the above problem algebraically, we should clearly understand what is being assumed about the relationship of costs and revenues to sales. We are assuming that certain costs are fixed (at $200,000) over the range of output being considered, that variable costs per unit ($10) are constant over the range of output, and that sales price per unit ($15) is fixed. Later in the chapter we will consider variations in sales price and the effect on the analysis if variable costs per unit change as output changes.

*Determining the
Break-Even Point*

We can solve for the break-even point by trial and error (just by scanning the numbers in Exhibit 15-2 or by examining Figure 15-1) or algebraically. The following variables are needed for an algebraic solution:

x = number of units sold
F = fixed costs = $200,000
v = variable cost per unit = $10
p = sales price per unit = $15
x_b = level of x at the break-even point (break-even x)

We know that

Pretax income = total sales − total costs

$$= px - (vx + F)$$

$$= px - vx - F$$

$$= x(p - v) - F \qquad (15\text{-}1)$$

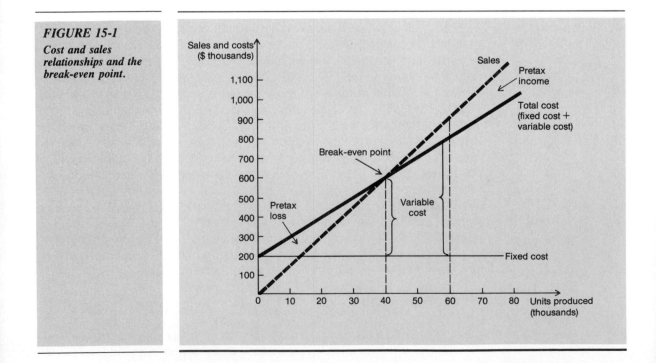

FIGURE 15-1

*Cost and sales
relationships and the
break-even point.*

569

CHAPTER 15
**Break-even analysis and
the measurement of
leverage**

At the break-even point, both pretax and net (aftertax) income are zero. Therefore, to solve for the break-even output x_b, set pretax income in Eq. (15-1) equal to zero and solve. Thus, using (15-1), at the break-even point

$$x_b(p - v) - F = 0$$

$$x_b = \frac{F}{p - v} \tag{15-2}$$

and, therefore

$$\text{Break-even } x = x_b = \frac{F}{p - v} = \frac{\$200,000}{\$15 - \$10} = 40,000 \text{ units}$$

Notice that 40,000 units is the same as the value determined by examining Exhibit 15-2 and Figure 15-1.

What if we want the break-even level of dollar sales? This is just the sales price p times the break-even point in units (x_b). That is,

$$\text{Break-even dollar sales} = px_b = p\left(\frac{F}{p - v}\right)$$

$$= \$15\left(\frac{\$200,000}{\$15 - \$10}\right) = \$600,000$$

From Exhibit 15-2 we see that the dollars of sales at the break-even point of 40,000 units are in fact $600,000. This is also shown in Figure 15-1.

The quantity $(p - v)$ in Eqs. (15-1) and (15-2) is called the **contribution margin**. The contribution margin equals the increase in pretax income from an added unit sold. From Eq. (15-2) we can see that the break-even output x_b is fixed costs divided by the contribution margin.

Sales Price and Cost Changes

Break-even analysis can be useful in analyzing policies which affect sales (for example, changing sales price) or which affect the level of fixed or variable costs. For example, by lowering its sales price, the company may be able to increase total sales. A decline in sales price reduces the contribution margin $(p - v)$ and thereby raises the break-even point x_b, as can be seen from Eq. (15-2). In Figure 15-2, a lower sales price implies a fall in the slope (decrease in steepness) of the total sales schedule. Although income per unit of sales decreases, total sales and income may actually rise. This is illustrated in Figure 15-2. If the decrease in sales price from p_1 to p_2 produces an increase in units sold from q_1 to q_2, then income will increase.

Alternative marketing strategies can be compared using the break-even analysis. The firm might be comparing a new long-term advertising campaign with the alternative of a price reduction in order to increase sales. If the advertising campaign adds amount A to fixed costs, then we could compare the relative benefits of the lower prices with the benefits of the advertising. In Figure 15-3 we see that adoption of the advertising campaign raises sales to q_2 (assuming that unit sales price remains at p_1). Comparing Figures 15-2 and 15-3, we see that advertising increases

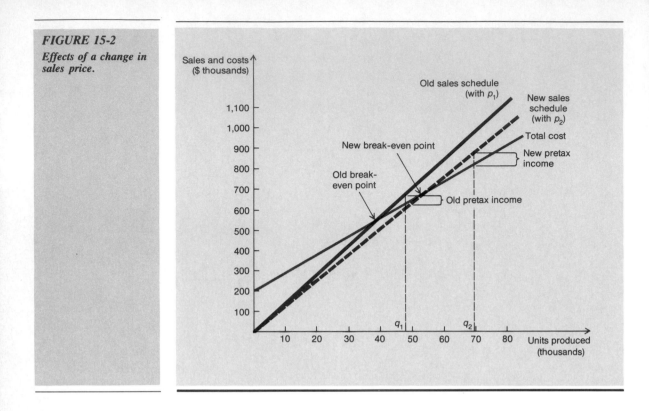

FIGURE 15-2
Effects of a change in sales price.

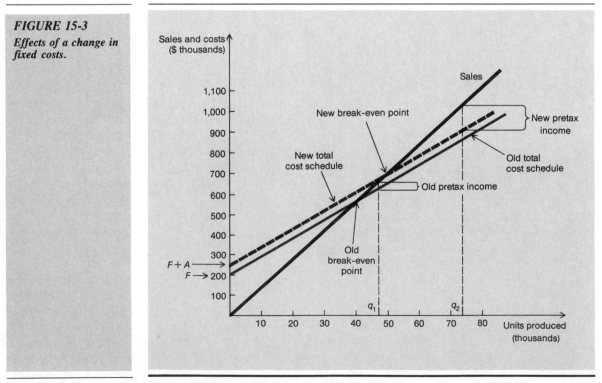

FIGURE 15-3
Effects of a change in fixed costs.

income by more than the increase due to the lower sales price strategy in Figure 15-2. This firm will therefore seek to increase sales and income by advertising rather than by lowering its sales price.

Nonlinear Break-Even Analysis

In the previous discussion it was assumed that costs increased linearly with output; each added unit has the same variable cost. Although this may be valid for some ranges of output, it is not likely to hold over the entire range for an actual firm. Thus, the variable cost of the twenty thousandth unit may be higher or lower than the variable cost of the ten thousandth unit. In Figure 15-4 the cost of an additional unit of output (unit variable cost) is assumed to decrease and then to increase as production increases. Since income equals sales minus total cost, at point q^* the firm's income is maximized (maximum vertical distance between sales and total cost).[3] Notice that there are two break-even points q_b and q'_b. All sales between q_b and q'_b produce positive income. Notice that even if customers demand more than q^* units, the firm will

---

[3] At q^*, the *slope* of the total-cost schedule equals the slope of the sales schedule, implying that the price of output equals the variable cost (marginal cost) of the q^*th unit of output.

FIGURE 15-4
Nonlinear costs.

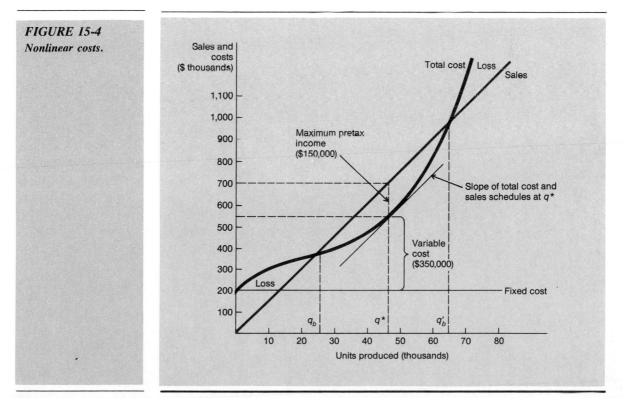

not produce them, since beyond q^* profits are decreasing, that is, profits are greater by selling only q^* units.[4]

Where will the firm operate? As with linear costs, demand for the firm's product is uncertain, and therefore so is the level of sales and production. The firm will not be willing to maintain production and sales above q^* since income is decreasing above that level of output. As long as sales are between q_b and q^*, the firm will earn income. If sales happen to fall below q_b, we can see from Figure 15-4 that the firm will suffer a loss. If this continues, the firm will eventually go out of business. An essential point here is that the exact level of sales is generally unpredictable. The figures tell us only what the firm's income will be for each level of sales. This also was true with linear costs. The analysis using non-linear costs is essentially very similar to that using linear costs.

Limitations of Break-Even Analysis

Even with nonlinear costs, break-even analysis has serious limitations. As we noted earlier, the distinction between fixed and variable costs depends on several assumptions, including the output range that is relevant and the time period involved. A change in assumptions may necessitate an entirely new analysis (new numbers and diagrams). Furthermore, the fixed and variable costs and the price at which the product is to be sold are assumed to be known at each level of output. In real situations, there is often uncertainty as to what costs and price will be for any particular output level. If this uncertainty is incorporated into the break-even framework, the analysis may become unwieldy and another approach may be required. Simplicity is both the virtue and weakness of break-even analysis. Although it can be helpful as a rough guide to decision making, it generally falls far short of being a complete planning tool.

THE CONCEPT OF LEVERAGE

Leverage is the existence of fixed costs among a firm's costs. It is useful to categorize leverage as operating and financial. Operating leverage depends on the company's operating fixed costs (fixed costs other than interest on debt), such as administrative costs, depreciation, advertising expenditures, and property taxes. Financial leverage, which was examined in Chapter 10, depends on financial fixed costs (interest expense, loan fees, etc.). We will see that operating and financial leverage can be joined together to provide a measure of total or "combined" leverage. Before proceeding, assume the following definitions:

---

[4] The firm may in the short run produce more than q^* as a service to customers so that their patronage will not be lost. However, as long as costs and product price do not change (i.e., as long as the sales and cost schedules in Figure 15-4 remain valid), the firm will not produce beyond q^* in the long run since q^* maximizes profit.

573

CHAPTER 15
Break-even analysis and
the measurement of
leverage

F_0 = operating fixed costs (administrative costs, depreciation, etc.)

F_f = financial fixed costs (interest expense, loan fees, etc.)

F = total fixed costs = $F_0 + F_f$

EBIT = earnings before interest and taxes (i.e., pretax income plus interest expense) = $px - vx - F_0 = x(p - v) - F_0$

Operating Leverage

Operating leverage arises when there are fixed *operating* costs in the firm's cost structure. Fixed operating costs do *not* include debt interest (a fixed *financial* cost). With positive (i.e., nonzero) fixed operating costs, a change of 1 percent in sales produces more than a 1 percent change in EBIT. A measure of this effect is referred to as the degree of operating leverage (DOL) and it equals

$$\text{Degree of operating leverage (DOL)} = \frac{\text{percentage change in EBIT}}{\text{percentage change in units sold}}$$

and this can be shown to equal[5]

$$\text{DOL} = \frac{x(p - v)}{x(p - v) - F_0} = \frac{\text{EBIT} + F_0}{\text{EBIT}} \tag{15-3}$$

where x is the output level at which DOL is computed, and p, v, and F_0 are unit sales price, unit variable cost, and operating fixed costs, respectively. Recall that operating fixed costs F_0 for computing DOL *exclude* interest on firm debt since interest is a financial fixed cost.

The greater is a firm's DOL, the more its EBIT will vary with sales fluctuations. We can see from Eq. (15-3) that the firm's cost structure (fixed and variable costs) determines its DOL for any given sales price p. In Exhibit 15-3, two firms with different cost structures are compared. Clear Glassworks has lower fixed costs and higher per unit variable costs than Strand Paper. Both firms charge \$10 (p) for each unit sold. Notice that at an output of 50,000 units, both firms have the same profits (\$60,000). However, as sales fluctuate, the EBIT of Clear Glassworks fluctuates far less than the EBIT of Strand Paper. Strand Paper has a higher DOL. We can see this by computing the DOL for each firm at an x of 50,000 units.

---

[5] Equation (15-3) for DOL is derived as follows:

$$\text{EBIT} = x(p - v) - F_0$$

$$\Delta\text{EBIT} = \Delta x(p - v) \qquad \text{since } p, v, \text{ and } F_0 \text{ do not change } (\Delta \text{ means ``change in'')}$$

$$\frac{\Delta\text{EBIT}}{\text{EBIT}} = \frac{\Delta x(p - v)}{x(p - v) - F_0}$$

$$\frac{\Delta\text{EBIT}/\text{EBIT}}{\Delta x/x} = \frac{\Delta x(p - v)/[x(p - v) - F_0]}{\Delta x/x} = \frac{\Delta x(p - v)}{x(p - v) - F_0} \cdot \frac{x}{\Delta x}$$

$$= \frac{x(p - v)}{x(p - v) - F_0} = \frac{\text{EBIT} + F_0}{\text{EBIT}} = \text{DOL}$$

DOL of Clear Glassworks at an output of 50,000 units

$$= \frac{x(p - v)}{x(p - v) - F_0} = \frac{50{,}000(\$10 - \$7)}{50{,}000(\$10 - \$7) - \$90{,}000} = 2\tfrac{1}{2}$$

DOL of Strand Paper Co. at an output of 50,000 units

$$= \frac{50{,}000(\$10 - \$5)}{50{,}000(\$10 - \$5) - \$190{,}000} = 4\tfrac{1}{6}$$

The above computations indicate that a 1 percent change in sales will produce a $2\tfrac{1}{2}$ percent change in EBIT for Clear Glassworks and a $4\tfrac{1}{6}$ percent change in EBIT for Strand Paper. The EBIT of the firm with the higher DOL (Strand) shows a greater variation with a change in sales. From Exhibit 15-3, you can see that an increase in Strand's sales from 50,000 units to 60,000 units (a 20 percent rise) will raise EBIT from $60,000 to $110,000, an $83\tfrac{1}{3}$ percent rise ($4\tfrac{1}{6}$ times the 20 percent sales rise). The same 20 percent increase in unit sales for Clear Glassworks will increase EBIT from $60,000 to $90,000, only a 50 percent rise ($2\tfrac{1}{2}$ times the 20 percent increase in sales). Notice from the table that a fall in sales below 50,000 units causes a greater percentage decline in Strand's EBIT than in Clear Glassworks' EBIT. A high DOL means large EBIT if sales are great and large losses if sales are depressed. DOL is therefore a measure of firm risk. A high DOL indicates a high risk (a high variability of EBIT if sales vary), as in the case of Strand Paper.

EXHIBIT 15-3
Cost and profit schedules for Clear Glassworks and Strand Paper Company

Clear Glassworks				Strand Paper Company			
Units sold x	Sales px	Total operating cost	EBIT (sales − total cost)	Units sold x	Sales px	Total operating cost	EBIT (sales − total cost)
10,000	$100,000	$160,000	$(60,000)	10,000	$100,000	$240,000	$(140,000)
20,000	200,000	230,000	(30,000)	20,000	200,000	290,000	(90,000)
30,000	300,000	300,000	0	30,000	300,000	340,000	(40,000)
40,000	400,000	370,000	30,000	40,000	400,000	390,000	10,000
50,000	500,000	440,000	60,000	50,000	500,000	440,000	60,000
60,000	600,000	510,000	90,000	60,000	600,000	490,000	110,000
70,000	700,000	580,000	120,000	70,000	700,000	540,000	160,000
80,000	800,000	650,000	150,000	80,000	800,000	590,000	210,000

Unit selling price p = $10	Unit selling price p = $10
Operating fixed costs F_0 = $90,000	Operating fixed costs F_0 = $190,000
Unit variable operating cost v = $7	Unit variable operating cost v = $5
Total operating variable cost vx = $7x	Total variable operating cost vx = $5x
Total operating cost $(F_0 + vx)$ = $90,000 + $7x	Total operating cost $(F_0 + vx)$ = $190,000 + $5x
EBIT break-even point = 30,000 units	EBIT break-even point = 38,000 units

The DOL is also important in production planning. For example, the company may have the opportunity to change its cost structure by introducing labor-saving machinery and thereby increasing fixed capital costs and reducing variable labor costs. This rise in fixed costs and decline in variable costs will increase DOL. In this case, a financial manager would want to evaluate the probability that sales will be high so that the firm can enjoy the increased earnings of increased DOL—and the probability that sales will be low, in which case the higher fixed costs and higher leverage would be disadvantageous. The greater the likelihood of high sales, the more attractive will be the shift to a higher DOL (higher fixed operating cost and lower variable operating cost) method of production.

Operating leverage is often incorrectly used as a synonym for "business risk." Business risk refers to the uncertainty or variability of the firm's EBIT. A company with a highly unpredictable EBIT has high business risk. It is true that the greater is the DOL, the more sensitive is EBIT to a given change in unit sales and that, everything else being equal, a higher DOL means higher business risk. But risk also depends on two other factors: the variability of the firm's sales and the variability of the company's cost and price structures. Let's examine these two other factors.

Assume first that output price and the company's cost structure are known (p, F_0, and v are known, as was the case in our computation of DOL). The DOL indicates how EBIT will change with sales; but, to evaluate the variability of EBIT (the company's risk), we must also know something about the variability of sales. A company with large fixed and low variable costs—for example, a utility or an office building—will have a large DOL, but it may have extremely stable revenues and consequently a stable EBIT and low risk. Conversely, a firm with low fixed operating costs and high variable costs, and therefore a low DOL, may have very unpredictable sales and a highly unpredictable or variable EBIT—for example, a construction firm with most of its costs being wages, material purchases, and equipment rentals.

EBIT can vary not only because sales fluctuate but also because of changes in the company's output price and costs, that is, changes in p, F_0, and v. Indeed, unit sales might remain fixed while EBIT gyrates wildly because of cost or price variations. Also, if price and costs are uncertain, DOL is uncertain, since DOL is defined in terms of p, F_0, and v. In this case, the use of DOL in evaluating business risk is somewhat limited.

The main point here is that DOL is only one measure that can be useful in some situations for determining the behavior of EBIT. The analysis must also examine sales variability and, in many instances, must take into account uncertainty regarding output price and cost structure.

Financial Leverage

Recall from Chapter 12 that financial leverage arises when a company borrows funds. A firm with no debt obligations has no financial leverage. To illustrate the impact of debt on earnings (net income) per share, assume that $500,000 is required to set up the operations of Clear

EXHIBIT 15-4
Three alternative financing plans for Clear Glassworks

Case	Total financing	Debt proportion, %	Dollars of debt (10% interest rate)	Dollars of equity	Number of shares outstanding
A	$500,000	0	$ 0	$500,000	5,000
B	$500,000	20	$100,000	$400,000	4,000
C	$500,000	40	$200,000	$300,000	3,000

Glassworks. Three financing options are described in Exhibit 15-4 and the impact on firm earnings (net income) is shown in Exhibit 15-5: case A, all equity financing (stockholders' investment $500,000); case B, $400,000 of equity and $100,000 of debt financing; and case C, $300,000 of equity and $200,000 of debt financing. The interest rate on all debt is 10 percent.

The degree of financial leverage (DFL) is a measure of the extent of the company's borrowing and is represented by the following formula:

$$\text{Degree of financial leverage (DFL)} = \frac{\text{percentage change in EPS}}{\text{percentage change in EBIT}}$$

which equals[6]

$$\text{DFL} = \frac{x(p - v) - F_0}{x(p - v) - F} = \frac{\text{EBIT}}{\text{EBIT} - F_f} \tag{15-4}$$

---

[6] Equation (15-4) for DFL can be derived as follows:

$$\text{EPS} = \frac{(1 - T)(\text{EBIT} - F_f)}{n} \tag{a}$$

where T = corporate tax rate

F_f = financial fixed costs

n = number of shares

The change in EPS due to a change in EBIT equals

$$\Delta\text{EPS} = \frac{(1 - T)\Delta\text{EBIT}}{n} \tag{b}$$

since T, F_f, and n are constants (do not change as EBIT changes). Therefore, the percentage changes in EPS equals

$$\frac{\Delta\text{EPS}}{\text{EPS}} = \frac{[(1 - T)\Delta\text{EBIT}]/n}{[(1 - T)(\text{EBIT} - F_f)]/n} = \frac{\Delta\text{EBIT}}{\text{EBIT} - F_f} \tag{c}$$

The degree of financial leverage equals the percentage change in EPS divided by the percentage change in EBIT which, using (c), equals

$$\text{DFL} = \frac{\Delta\text{EPS}/\text{EPS}}{\Delta\text{EBIT}/\text{EBIT}} = \frac{\Delta\text{EBIT}/(\text{EBIT} - F_f)}{\Delta\text{EBIT}/\text{EBIT}}$$

$$= \frac{\text{EBIT}}{\text{EBIT} - F_f} = \frac{x(p - v) - F_0}{x(p - v) - F}$$

EXHIBIT 15-5
Illustration of financial leverage—Clear Glassworks

Units sold	EBIT[a]	Interest on debt[b]	Taxes[c]	Net income (loss) (EBIT − interest − taxes)	Earnings per share (net income/ no. of shares)[d]	Rate of return on equity, %[e]
A.	**No debt; equity investment = $500,000 (5,000 shares at $100 per share)**					
10,000	$(60,000)	0	$(30,000)[f]	$(30,000)	$(6.00)	− 6
20,000	(30,000)	0	(15,000)[f]	(15,000)	(3.00)	− 3
30,000	0	0	0	0	0	0
40,000	30,000	0	15,000	15,000	3.00	3
50,000	60,000	0	30,000	30,000	6.00	6
60,000	90,000	0	45,000	45,000	9.00	9
70,000	120,000	0	60,000	60,000	12.00	12
80,000	150,000	0	75,000	75,000	15.00	15
90,000	180,000	0	90,000	90,000	18.00	18
B.	**Debt = $100,000; equity investment = $400,000 (4,000 shares at $100 per share)**					
10,000	$(60,000)	$10,000	$(35,000)[f]	$(35,000)	$(8.75)	− 8¾
20,000	(30,000)	10,000	(20,000)[f]	(20,000)	(5.00)	− 5
30,000	0	10,000	(5,000)[f]	(5,000)	(1.25)	− 1¼
40,000	30,000	10,000	10,000	10,000	2.50	2½
50,000	60,000	10,000	25,000	25,000	6.25	6¼
60,000	90,000	10,000	40,000	40,000	10.00	10
70,000	120,000	10,000	55,000	55,000	13.75	13¾
80,000	150,000	10,000	70,000	70,000	17.50	17½
90,000	180,000	10,000	85,000	85,000	21.25	21¼
C.	**Debt = $200,000; equity investment = $300,000 (3,000 shares at $100 per share)**					
10,000	$(60,000)	$20,000	$(40,000)[f]	$(40,000)	$(13.33)	− 13⅓
20,000	(30,000)	20,000	(25,000)[f]	(25,000)	(8.33)	− 8⅓
30,000	0	20,000	(10,000)[f]	(10,000)	(3.33)	− 3⅓
40,000	30,000	20,000	5,000	5,000	1.67	1⅔
50,000	60,000	20,000	20,000	20,000	6.67	6⅔
60,000	90,000	20,000	35,000	35,000	11.67	11⅔
70,000	120,000	20,000	50,000	50,000	16.67	16⅔
80,000	150,000	20,000	65,000	65,000	21.67	21⅔
90,000	180,000	20,000	80,000	80,000	26.67	26⅔

[a] See Exhibit 15-3 for the computation of EBIT for Clear Glassworks.
[b] Interest rate on debt is 10%, interest on debt = 0.10 × debt.
[c] The tax rate is assumed to equal 50%; taxes = 0.50 × (EBIT − interest on debt).
[d] It is assumed that there are 5,000, 4,000, and 3,000 shares of stock outstanding in cases A, B, and C, respectively. Earnings per share equal net income of the firm divided by the number of shares outstanding.
[e] Rate of return on equity = (net income)/(equity investment) = (net income per share)/$100, where $100 = equity investment per share.
[f] A negative tax means a tax credit due to a negative taxable income [negative (EBIT − interest on debt)].

EPS is aftertax earnings per share. F_0 and F_f are fixed operating and fixed financial costs, respectively, where $F = F_0 + F_f$. Using the Exhibit 15-5 data, DFL at 50,000 units for cases A, B, and C equals:

Case A: $\text{DFL} = \dfrac{\$60,000}{\$60,000 - 0} = 1.0$

Case B: $\text{DFL} = \dfrac{\$60,000}{\$60,000 - \$10,000} = 1.2$

Case C: $\text{DFL} = \dfrac{\$60,000}{\$60,000 - \$20,000} = 1.5$

Therefore, a 1 percent change in EBIT produces a 1 percent change in EPS if Clear Glassworks has no debt, a 1.2 percent change in EPS with $100,000 in debt, and a 1.5 percent change in EPS with $200,000 in debt. Notice from Exhibit 15-5 that *the greater is the leverage, the wider are fluctuations in the return on equity.* This is illustrated in Figure 15-5, where rate of return on equity for each level of EBIT is graphed for

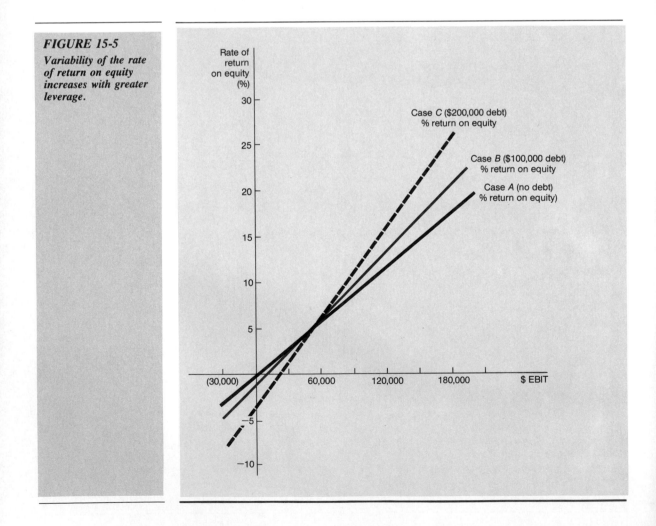

FIGURE 15-5

Variability of the rate of return on equity increases with greater leverage.

funding plans A, B, and C; the steeper the schedule, the greater the change in earnings for a unit change in EBIT.

Combined Leverage

Combined leverage is the measure of the total leverage due to both operating and financial fixed costs. It is easily computed using the DOL and DFL formulas. The degree of combined leverage (DCL) equals

$$\text{Degree of combined leverage (DCL)} = \frac{\text{percentage change in EPS}}{\text{percentage change sales}}$$

which equals

$$\text{DCL} = \frac{x(p - v)}{x(p - v) - F} = \frac{\text{EBIT} + F_0}{\text{EBIT} - F_f} \tag{15-5}$$

where, as before, $F = F_0 + F_f =$ total (operating plus financial) fixed costs.[7] For Clear Glassworks, at an output of 50,000 units ($x = 50,000$) and debt of $100,000,

$$\text{DCL} = \frac{50,000(\$10 - \$7)}{50,000(\$10 - \$7) - (\$90,000 + \$10,000)} = \frac{\$150,000}{\$50,000} = 3.0$$

where, $F = F_0 + F_f = \$90,000 + \$10,000$. At an output of 50,000 units, each 1 percent variation in sales will cause a 3 percent change in EPS. In Exhibit 15-5, a 10 percent rise in sales to 55,000 units will increase earnings per share from $6.25 to $8.125 (a 30 percent increase in EPS) since

$$\begin{aligned}
\text{EPS}_{55,000 \text{ units}} &= \text{EPS}_{50,000} + \text{EPS}_{50,000} \times (\% \text{ change in EPS}) \\
&= \text{EPS}_{50,000} + \text{EPS}_{50,000} \times (\text{DCL} \times \% \text{ change in sales}) \\
&= \text{EPS}_{50,000} + \text{EPS}_{50,000} (3.0 \times 10\%) \\
&= \$6.25 + 6.25(30\%) = \$8.125
\end{aligned}$$

A greater DOL or DFL will raise DCL. DCL is a measure of the overall riskiness or uncertainty associated with stockholders' earnings that arises because of operating and financial leverage.

---

[7] Equation (15-5) for DCL can be derived by observing that DCL = DFL × DOL; that is,

$$\begin{aligned}
\text{DOL} \times \text{DFL} &= \frac{\text{percentage change in EPS}}{\text{percentage change in EBIT}} \times \frac{\text{percentage change in EBIT}}{\text{percentage change in sales}} \\
&= \frac{\text{percentage change in EPS}}{\text{percentage change in sales}} = \text{DCL}
\end{aligned}$$

Therefore, using Eqs. (15-3) and (15-4),

$$\text{DCL} = \text{DOL} \times \text{DFL} = \frac{x(p - v)}{x(p - v) - F_0} \times \frac{\text{EBIT}}{\text{EBIT} - F_f} \tag{a}$$

But, EBIT $= x(p - v) - F_0$, and substituting this into (a) (and noting that $F_0 + F_f = F$),

$$\text{DCL} = \frac{x(p - v)}{x(p - v) - F_0} \times \frac{x(p - v) - F_0}{x(p - v) - F_0 - F_f} = \frac{x(p - v)}{x(p - v) - F} = \frac{\text{EBIT} + F_0}{\text{EBIT} - F_f}$$

which is DCL in Eq. (15-5) in the text.

SUMMARY

Break-even analysis is used to assess the effects of changes in the firm's sales volume, or in cost and price structure, on company profits. An important factor is the relationship between fixed and variable costs. Fixed costs do not vary with output changes, whereas variable costs do vary with output. Most costs can be classified as fixed or variable, depending upon the situation. Break-even analysis can be used to examine the effect of changes in sales price and cost structure on firm profitability. Although linear costs are often assumed in break-even analysis, nonlinear costs as well as variable price can also be assumed. The technique can therefore be adapted to realistic assumptions and often serves as a useful tool in financial planning. However, break-even analysis can become unwieldy if many policy alternatives are being compared. It is therefore generally used in combination with other analytical approaches.

Operating leverage is due to fixed operating costs, such as depreciation on property taxes. The greater are fixed costs relative to variable operating costs, the more variable will be earnings before interest and taxes (EBIT) and the higher will be the firm's degree of operating leverage (DOL). Operating leverage is not the only cause of fluctuations in EBIT, since EBIT can also change with variations in the company's cost structure (level of fixed or per unit variable cost) or sales price.

Financial leverage occurs when the company borrows money. The greater is the firm's debt, the greater will net aftertax earnings per share change due to a given change in EBIT. The degree of financial leverage (DFL) increases directly with increased borrowing. The degree of combined leverage (DCL) indicates the percentage change in net aftertax earnings due to a 1 percent change in sales. DCL rises as operating leverage and financial leverage rise and is therefore a measure of the impact of operating and financial fixed costs on the variability of net income.

QUESTIONS

1 Define and give examples of fixed costs and variable costs.
2 Explain how the following may change the classification of a cost into the fixed or variable class:
 a The magnitude of a change in output
 b The amount of time required to change the cost
 c The length of time the change in output is expected to last
3 Explain what is meant by "contribution margin."
4 In each of the following situations explain what happens to the break-even point in units:
 a The selling price increases and all other variables remain unchanged.
 b The fixed cost increases and all other variables remain unchanged.
 c The variable cost increases and all other variables remain unchanged.
5 In the text it is said that DOL and business risk are often incorrectly used as synonyms. Explain why such usage is

581

CHAPTER 15
**Break-even analysis and
the measurement of
leverage**

incorrect and point out the differences between DOL and business risk.

6 Define the degree of financial leverage (DFL) and explain why it is a measure of risk.

7 Define the degree of combined leverage (DCL) and explain how DCL depends on operating and financial leverage.

PROJECT

Obtain the financial statements of two companies in different industries and compare the firms in terms of the relationship between fixed costs, variable costs, and sales. Assume that the sales price and variable cost per unit of output of one of the companies are the same for all levels of production and compute the company's break-even level of sales, its degree of financial leverage, its degree of operating leverage, and its degree of combined leverage. Hint: To compute break-even dollar sales, note that:

$$\text{Break-even dollar sales} = px_b = p\left(\frac{F}{p-v}\right) = \frac{F}{1 - \dfrac{vx}{px}} = \frac{F}{1 - \dfrac{\text{variable costs}}{\text{sales}}}$$

**DEMONSTRATION
PROBLEMS**

DP1 Lethargo Sports, Inc., manufactures running shoes for the unathletic. Lethargo sells each pair of shoes to retailers for $30. Lethargo's annual fixed costs are $600,000 and Lethargo breaks even with annual sales of 25,000 units (pairs of shoes).

a What is Lethargo's break-even point in dollar sales?

b What is Lethargo's variable cost per unit?

c What is Lethargo's pretax income if 20,000 units are sold?

SOLUTION TO DP1:

a Break-even point in dollar sales = (break-even point in units) × (sales price) = 25,000 × $30 = $750,000.

b Using Eq. (15-2), the break-even point in units, x_b, equals

$$x_b = \frac{F}{p-v}$$

Rearranging the above equaton:

$$v = \frac{x_b p - F}{x_b} = \frac{(25,000)(\$30) - \$600,000}{25,000} = \$6$$

c Using Eq. (15-1), profit at 5000 units of sales equals

Pretax income = total sales − total costs
$$= x(p-v) - F$$
$$= 20,000(\$30 - \$6) - \$600,000$$
$$= -\$120,000$$

DP2 Rand Collections Limited sells miniature gold-plated replicas of famous sports, political, and entertainment personalities. Each

miniature is sold by Rand for $200. Rand's fixed costs are
$200,000. In 1990, Rand sold 6000 miniatures. Total variable
costs for 1990 were $600,000.

a   What was the company's pretax income in 1990?
b   How many miniatures must the company sell just to break
even?
c   For 1991, the company expects a 25 percent increase in fixed
costs.
   (1)   What is the new break-even point in units (miniatures) if
the price remains at $200?
   (2)   By how much should the price per miniature be increased in order for the company to make the same
profit as in 1990, assuming that variable costs and the
number of miniatures sold remain at the 1990 level?
   (3)   The production manager believes that efficiency-increas-
ing measures could be introduced in 1991 which would
reduce per unit variable cost. Assuming that the selling
price remains at $200 per miniature, what reduction in
the variable cost would result in the same break-even
point (in units) as in 1990?

SOLUTION TO DP2:

a   Pretax income = sales − fixed costs − variable costs
$$= \$1,200,000 - \$200,000 - \$600,000$$
$$= \$400,000$$

b   Price per unit = p = $200

Variable cost per unit = v = (total variable cost/units sold)
$$= \$600,000/6000$$
$$= \$100$$

Fixed cost = F = $200,000

Break-even
number of units $= x_b = \dfrac{F}{p - v} = \dfrac{\$200,000}{\$200 - \$100} = 2000$ units

c   (1)   New fixed costs F = $200,000(1.25)
$$= \$250,000$$

New $x_b = \dfrac{\$250,000}{\$200 - \$100} = 2500$ units

   (2)   Pretax income = sales − fixed cost − variable cost
$$= px - F - vx$$

Thus,

$$\$400,000 = p(6000) - \$250,000 - \$600,000$$
$$p = \$208.33$$

The increase in price is therefore $8.33.

583

CHAPTER 15
**Break-even analysis and
the measurement of
leverage**

(3)   Using Eq. (15-2):

$$x_b = \frac{F}{p - v} = \frac{\$250,000}{\$200 - v} = 2000 \text{ units}$$

$$v = \$75$$

Needed reduction in $v = \$25$.

DP3   Brighton Bantamwagon Dealers sells new Bantamwagons, a
modern lightweight English camper automobile. In 1991,
Brighton's earnings before interest and taxes were $400,000. On
January 1, 1991, Brighton increased its debt from $200,000 (on
which annual interest cost was $20,000) to $700,000; the annual
interest on the additional debt is $60,000. The company's tax
rate is 40 percent.

a   What would Brighton's degree of financial leverage be if it
did not increase its debt from $200,000 to $700,000?

b   What is the 1991 degree of financial leverage using the actual
1991 figures?

c   In 1991, what percentage change in aftertax earnings per
share (EPS) would result from a 40 percent increase in
EBIT?

d   In 1991, what percentage increase in EBIT would bring
about a 10 percent increase in EPS?

e   In 1991, Brighton sold 200 campers for $10,000 per camper.
Brighton's fixed operating cost was $300,000 and total vari-
able operating cost was $1.3 million. What was the degree of
combined leverage using the actual 1991 figures?

f   Suppose the 1991 EPS is $3. What would EPS be if unit
sales increased by 20 percent?

g   Compute DOL and check the relation DCL = DOL × DFL
using the data and results of b and e.

SOLUTION TO DP3:

a $DFL = \dfrac{EBIT}{EBIT - F_f} = \dfrac{\$400,000}{\$400,000 - \$20,000} = 1.05$

b $DFL = \dfrac{EBIT}{EBIT - F_f} = \dfrac{\$400,000}{\$400,000 - \$80,000} = 1.25$

c $\dfrac{\Delta EPS}{EPS} = DFL \times \dfrac{\Delta EBIT}{EBIT} = 1.25 \times 40\% = 50\%$ increase

d $.10 = 1.25 \times \dfrac{\Delta EBIT}{EBIT}$

$\dfrac{\Delta EBIT}{EBIT} = \dfrac{.10}{1.25} = 8\%$

e $DCL = \dfrac{x(p - v)}{x(p - v) - F_0 - F_f}$

$v = \dfrac{\$1,300,000}{200} = \$6500$

$p - v = \$10,000 - \$6500 = \$3500$

$DCL = \dfrac{200(\$3500)}{200(\$3500) - \$300,000 - \$80,000} = 2.1875$

f $DCL = \dfrac{\Delta EPS/EPS}{\Delta x/x} = 2.1875$

$\dfrac{\Delta EPS}{EPS} = 2.1875\left(\dfrac{\Delta x}{x}\right)$

$\Delta EPS = 2.1875\left(\dfrac{\Delta x}{x}\right)(EPS)$

$EPS' = EPS + \Delta EPS = EPS + 2.1875\left(\dfrac{\Delta x}{x}\right)EPS$

$= EPS\left(1 + 2.1875\,\dfrac{\Delta x}{x}\right)$

$= \$3.00[1 + 2.1875(.20)]$

$= \$4.3125$

g $DOL = \dfrac{x(p - v)}{x(p - v) - F_0} = \dfrac{200(\$3500)}{200(\$3500) - \$300,000} = 1.75$

$DCL = (DOL)(DFL) = (1.75)(1.25) = 2.1875$

PROBLEMS

1 A manufacturing company is selling its product at a price of $18 per unit. Fixed costs amount to $160,000. Variable cost per unit is $10.
   a Calculate the firm's break-even point in number of units.
   b Calculate the firm's break-even point in dollar sales.
   c What is the company's pretax income if 30,000 units are sold?

2 Cheery Season Products produces candied fruits and meats which are sold both through retail outlets and by mail order. Cheery Season has a new product called "Sweet Tooth," a rum-soaked apricot stuffed with almond chips and brown sugar. Sweet Tooth can be sold to retailers for $34 per case. Cheery Season leases its production facility for $2200 per month under a lease contract that has ten years remaining. The cash expenditure for equipment maintenance, power, telephone, and other fixed operating costs is $3800 per month. Depreciation on the equipment is $18,000 per year. The only other costs of production are labor, materials, and

585

CHAPTER 15
**Break-even analysis and
the measurement of
leverage**

other minor outlays; these costs vary directly with output and
equal $16 per case of Sweet Tooth.

a What are Cheery Season's annual total fixed costs and per unit
(per case) variable cost?

b What is Cheery Season's break-even point in units and in dollar sales?

c What is income (pretax) at 7500 units?

d What is the contribution margin?

e Assume that Cheery Season is selling 7500 units per year and
has the costs and unit sales price indicated in *a* through *d*
above. The company has the opportunity to add a new machine that greatly lowers labor costs: the machine will increase
annual fixed costs to $102,000 but will lower per unit variable
costs to $14. If Cheery Season maintains its sales price at $34
and output at 7500 units, will adding the new machine increase
pretax income?

f Assume that Cheery Season is selling 7500 units and has the
costs and sales price indicated in *a* through *d* above. The com-
pay can lower the sales price to $29 per unit and thereby raise
sales to 10,000 units. What is the effect of the sales price
change on income?

3 Canis Products manufactures a single product, a bubble bath for
dogs. The bubble bath is sold in 1-quart bottles for $20 per bottle.
During, 1990, Canis Products sold $800,000 worth of bubble bath.
During the same year the company's total fixed costs amounted to
$200,000, and the total variable cost on the units sold amounted to
$480,000.

a What was the company's pretax income in 1990?

b How many bottles of bubble bath must the company sell just
to break even?

c For 1991, the company expects a 10 percent increase in fixed
costs because of an increase in property taxes.

(*1*) What is the new break-even point in units (bottles) if the
price cannot be increased above $20?

(*2*) By how much should the price per bottle be increased in
order for the company to make the same profit as in 1990,
assuming that variable costs and the number of bottles
sold remain at 1990 levels?

(*3*) The production manager now believes that productivity
could be improved by using the existing equipment and
personnel more efficiently, thereby reducing variable cost
per unit. Assuming that the selling price remains at $20
per bottle, what reduction in the variable cost would result in the same break-even point (in units) as in 1990?

4 Mickey Mars, president of Pestgo Chemicals, a producer of
pesticides, has provided the following data and forecast for the
company:

Current sales	$15 million
Forecasted sales in 5 years	$20 million
Current variable cost	80% of sales
Current total (operating and financial) fixed cost (including depreciation of $300,000)	$1.5 million

It has recently come to Mars' attention that the firm's high labor and maintenance costs are the result of the obsolete equipment and deteriorating condition of one of the company's plants. Consequently, Mars is considering the replacement of the plant with a new, automated facility. Mars estimates that the new facility will have variable costs equal to 60 percent of sales revenues but annual fixed costs (including depreciation) will increase over their former level (under the obsolete plant) by $3 million.

a Calculate the current earnings before taxes (EBT) of Pestgo.

b What is the sales break-even point for the new plant?

c What is the EBT for the old plant at the forecast level of sales of $20 million? What is the EBT for the new facility at the forecast level of sales of $20 million?

d Compute the degree of operating leverage (DOL) for both the new and the old facilities at the current level of sales and the forecast level of sales. Assume that operating fixed costs are $1 million.

5 Aldo Electronics produces electronic communications equipment. In 1990 the company had $200,000 earnings before interest and taxes. On January 1, 1990, the company borrowed $400,000 at a rate of interest of 10 percent. The company had no previous debt and its tax rate is 50 percent.

a What was the degree of financial leverage prior to 1990?

b What is the 1990 degree of financial leverage using the actual earnings figures?

c In 1990 what percentage change in aftertax earnings per share (EPS) would result from a 50 percent increase in EBIT?

d In 1990 what percentage increase in EBIT would bring about a 20 percent increase in EPS?

e In 1990 the company sold 20,000 items at $60 per item. The fixed operating cost was $600,000, and the total variable operating cost was $400,000. What was the degree of combined leverage using the actual 1990 earnings figures?

f Suppose the 1990 EPS is $2. What would EPS be if unit sales increased by 10 percent?

g Compute DOL and check the relation DCL = DOL × DFL using the data and results of *b* and *e*.

6 Broderick Corporation currently has a degree of combined leverage (DCL) of 3 and a degree of operating leverage (DOL) of 1.5. Broderick plans to purchase new machinery to replace old ma-

587

CHAPTER 15
**Break-even analysis and
the measurement of
leverage**

chinery. The new machinery will increase fixed operating cost but decrease variable cost per unit. Broderick's management believes the DOL will be 1.8 after the investment. Management considers a DCL of 4.5 to be the highest acceptable degree of combined leverage for the firm.

a Calculate the degree of financial leverage before the investment and the maximum acceptable degree of financial leverage after the investment.

b If the new EBIT is expected to be $6,000,000, what is the maximum amount of fixed financial cost the corporation will be able to cover?

c Suppose the fixed financial costs (interest, lease payments, etc.) are $2.4 million before the investment. What is the maximum amount of new borrowing that management will consider to be acceptable if the firm can borrow at an interest rate of 15 percent?

7 Hydro, Incorporated, has just recovered from a severe slump in business and has projected sales of $3,600,000 for next year. Based on the existing production equipment, total fixed operating costs and total variable operating costs are expected to be $1,200,000 and $1,800,000, respectively, so that the EBIT will be $600,000. The selling price per item produced is $50. The firm has a $1,500,000 five-year note outstanding on which it pays interest of 15 percent. Hydro plans to pay off the five-year note with funds borrowed at a lower interest rate. The production manager has suggested the modernization of the old equipment. This would result in a 30 percent increase in fixed operating costs and a 20 percent decrease in per unit variable operating costs.

The general manager agrees with the modernization plan as long as the firm's risk, as measured by the DCL, does not change. This could be made possible by the refunding of the outstanding five-year note. Hydro will borrow $1,500,000 from the bank in order to pay off the note. How much lower must the interest rate on the new $1,500,000 loan be for the modernization plan to become acceptable in the eyes of the manager? Assume that sales price and sales will be unaffected by the cost changes. (Hint: DCL = DFL × DOL.)

CHAPTER SIXTEEN

FINANCIAL FORECASTING AND PLANNING

In Chapters 14 and 15 we discussed financial analyses that are based on past and current financial performance. Although these techniques are helpful in judging what the future performance of the firm may be, they are not forecasts of future performance. To maintain and increase the profitability of the firm, the financial manager must be able to anticipate its future needs for cash. Financial forecasting allows the financial manager to make educated guesses about the future financial condition of the firm. The financial manager also develops budgets that indicate, as time passes, whether the forecasts are proving to be accurate. In this chapter we look at the problem of forecasting future cash requirements and the general financial condition of the firm. We then show how these forecasts are used to develop plans and budgets.

Forecasts are important for several reasons:

1 Cash forecasts show when and how much new financing will be needed, given current operating and investment decisions. This information is used by the financial manager to plan the financing of the firm and to arrange for external sources of funds, such as debt and stock.
2 The data obtained from forecasts provide a basis for the decisions regarding cash management and investment in marketable securities. This is discussed in Chapter 18.
3 Budgets prepared from forecasts provide a way to maintain control over the firm's financial affairs and signal changing conditions that are reflected in the cash flows of the firm. (For example, if cash were expected to increase by $100,000 in June and the increase turned out to be only $50,000, the financial manager would want to know what happened.)
4 Lenders such as commercial banks are favorably impressed by careful financial planning, especially on the part of small businesses where such planning is frequently not done. Evidence of financial planning is very helpful in obtaining loans.
5 Most financial decisions are based on forecasts of the consequences of a particular decision. Forecasting is an essential part of financial management.

In general, forecasting permits the financial manager to be more effective in monitoring the firm's financial affairs, in controlling and investing cash, and in developing financing. These activities increase profits and reduce risk and are therefore vital to the continuing success of the firm.

FORECASTING SINGLE FINANCIAL VARIABLES

Forecasts of the total financial condition of the firm are normally developed from forecasts of individual financial variables. For example, to develop a balance sheet for some future period, it is necessary to forecast accounts receivable and inventory. The forecasts of individual accounts are combined into a forecast of the complete balance sheet. In this section we will look at several approaches to forecasting single financial variables. In the next section we will show how the forecasts of single variables can be combined into an integrated forecast of the financial condition of the firm—balance sheets, income statements, and cash flows.

Most forecasts combine objective analysis of historical data with the subjective insights of the forecaster. In the descriptions of trend, ratio, and statistical forecasting methods that follow, we focus on the objective analytical techniques. When we show how the forecasts of single variables are combined into a forecast of the firm's cash flows, income statement, and balance sheet, examples of objective forecasts modified by management to reflect its judgment will be presented.

Trend Forecasts

Trend forecasts rely solely on historical information about the variable being forecast. The most elementary trend forecast is to predict "no change" from the current value of the variable when information available suggests that there will be no change. For example, if management does not plan to issue or retire any common stock, it would forecast "no change" in common stock outstanding. "No change" forecasts are also used when there is a complete lack of information as to the extent and direction of any change that may occur, in other words, when the current value is the only information available.

More commonly, trend forecasts are based on past trends and seasonability. For example, if sales have grown at an average rate of 8 percent per year, then a forecast for next year's sales might be 8 percent above current levels. Past seasonal patterns are also considered. If sales in December are typically 15 percent of annual sales, then it would seem reasonable that sales for next December might be 15 percent of forecast sales for the year.

All trend forecasts are essentially a projection of recent historical values for the variable into the future. A basic technique used in analyzing the past history of a variable is to plot the values over time. For example, suppose we wish to forecast the level of inventory next month (month 13). The history of inventory levels over the past twelve months is illustrated in Figure 16-1. Based on this history we would forecast inventory in month 13 to be I^*. There are statistical techniques available for performing such projections mechanically; their use is covered in statistics courses.

Trend forecasts are useful, but they do not take into account what else is expected to happen in the firm or the economy. For example, suppose government and private economists are forecasting that a recession will occur next year. If you were forecasting sales of General Motors cars, you might want to forecast lower sales regardless of recent car sales trends, because car sales are affected by general economic conditions. Similarly, if you were forecasting income statement accounts such as cost of goods sold and earnings before interest and taxes, you would want the forecasts for each account to be consistent with forecasted sales. In developing forecasts of single financial variables, the financial manager will want to be sure the forecasts are consistent with each other. Forecasts of one variable are frequently based on a forecast for another variable, which we refer to as the **base variable**.

The levels of assets, liabilities, revenues, and expenses are known to be related to sales volume. The most obvious examples are the revenue and expense accounts; however, assets such as accounts receivable are also related to sales. An increase in sales will usually result in an increase in the level of accounts receivable.[1] Therefore, given a forecast for sales, it is often useful to forecast accounts receivable (or collections) based on past relationships with sales. For example, suppose that the average collection period of the firm is thirty days. This means that there are about one month's sales in accounts receivable. A forecast of accounts receivable for the end of December would equal the sales forecast for December.

Using Ratios in Forecasting   The simplest relationship between two variables is the ratio of the two. Gross margin is a ratio of gross profit to

---

[1] Of course if the increase in sales were confined to customers who pay cash, then an increase in accounts receivable would not occur.

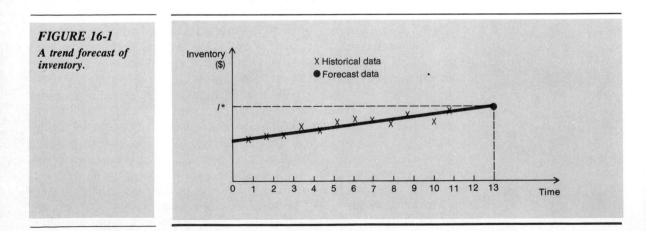

FIGURE 16-1

A trend forecast of inventory.

sales. Ratios, such as those discussed in Chapter 14, can be used in forecasting as described in the following list.

1   The ratio itself is forecast or estimated using historical data. Frequently the average value of the ratio over the past year or two is used, although sometimes a trend forecast with adjustments for seasonality is made. For example, if the firm's gross margin has averaged 30 percent in the past, it might be forecast to remain at 30 percent.

2   The base variable is forecast (sales). The base variable here is the denominator of the ratio. In many cases someone else's forecast of the base variable is used. For example, the marketing manager may provide the financial manager with a sales forecast.

3   The individual financial variable is forecast as

Variable = ratio × base variable

For example, if sales for next year are forecast to be $10 million and the gross margin is forecast to be 30 percent,

Gross profit = gross margin × sales

= 0.30 × $10 million

= $3 million

Sales are the most common base variable in forecasts using ratios since most of the financial variables of the firm are related to sales, at least in the long run. A forecast of sales is often used to provide long-term forecasts for variables that are not directly related to sales in the short run. Plant and equipment would not be likely to vary with sales on a month-to-month basis. However, a forecast of plant and equipment needed by the firm five years from now might be based on the past average ratio of these assets to sales. Accounts payable (and payments to suppliers) are primarily related to purchases. In the short run, purchases may differ appreciably from sales levels. In the short run, therefore, a forecast of accounts payable should be based on expected purchases. In the long run, however, purchases and sales are apt to move together in a fairly stable relationship since goods must be purchased before they can be sold. Therefore, a forecast of sales serves indirectly as a forecast of purchases, and consequently the average ratio of accounts payable to sales can be used as a reasonable basis for a long-range forecast of accounts payable given the sales forecast.

Although sales are the most common base for forecasts using ratios, the general method may be applied using other bases. For example, inventory, wages, or electricity costs might be more related to production levels than to sales. Given a forecast of production, the historical ratio of wages to production might then be used to forecast future wage payments. Similarly, if the ratio of accounts payable to inventory tends to be a constant ratio, a forecast of inventory could serve as a base to forecast accounts payable.

Graphical and Statistical Methods Suppose that it is now 1992 and we
wish to forecast inventory levels over the next five years, 1993 to 1997.
Either trend or ratio methods may be used; however, there are more
accurate alternatives. One of the less complicated of these alternatives is
to examine the past relationship between inventory and sales as illustrated in Figure 16-2. Each point on the graph represents the particular
values of inventory and sales for a given year.

There is a general tendency for higher sales to require higher inventories. Suppose we fit a straight line to these as indicated in Figure
16-2. The line may be drawn by hand or it may be estimated using
statistical methods. The line shows the average past relationship between inventory and sales. If the points lie on a line through the origin
(sales and inventory equal to zero), a fixed ratio between sales and
inventory would be indicated. Since they do not, the ratio method would
not provide accurate forecasts in this case.[2] Given the sales forecast for
1993, inventory for 1993 is forecast as shown. Similarly the 1997 sales
forecast is used to provide an inventory forecast for 1997.

This approach is quite general because it can be based on the relationship between any two items of interest. For example, accounts
payable could be related to inventory just as inventory was related to

---

[2] The equation for the line is

$$I = a + bS$$

where I is inventory, S is sales, and a and b are constants. The ratio of inventory to sales
is

$$\frac{I}{S} = \frac{a + bS}{S} = \frac{a}{S} + b$$

Therefore the ratio is not constant with respect to sales levels unless a is zero.

FIGURE 16-2

*Forecasting inventory
using historical
relationships with
sales.*

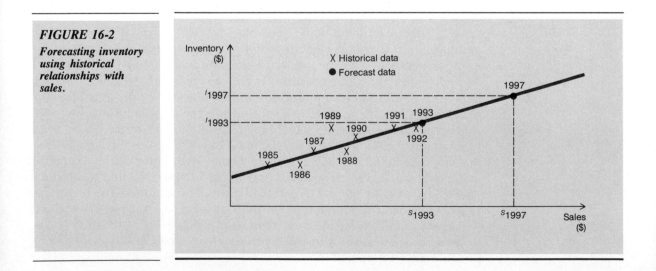

sales in the above case. A forecast of inventory could then be used in conjunction with the line relating accounts payable to inventory to forecast accounts payable.

More elaborate techniques are also available. Statistical techniques can be used to fit a straight line to the data rather than drawing it by hand. It is possible to fit curved lines rather than straight lines if a curved line describes the relationship better. It is also possible to use more than one variable to forecast another. For example, inventory could be related to both the level of sales and the change in sales from the prior period, or it could be related to sales and production. A major advantage of statistical methods is that they provide measures of how well the fitted relationship matches the actual data. Such methods are generally covered in statistics courses.

Problems in Forecasting

The forecasting methods we discussed are "scientific" in the sense that two people applying the same method to generate a forecast should arrive at the same result. Repeatable results, however, do not guarantee accurate forecasts. As we noted earlier, good forecasting relies on good judgment combined with an objective analysis of the data. Therefore a financial manager should approach a forecast by considering the choice of methods available, using the ones that are judged to provide the most reliable results, and deciding whether objective methods alone will be accurate. A financial manager, for example, may want to forecast earnings by multiplying the sales forecast by the expected profit margin. The profit margin can be based on historical patterns, but it might be better to consider the firm's future outlook for prices and costs. If the firm has just undertaken a major cost reduction program, it would not seem reasonable to use historical profit margins as a basis for forecasting future profits. Management can also utilize the judgment of economists as to the future prospects of the industry and the economy. If the economy is headed for increased inflation, then the forecast of sales and prices should take that information into account. Here, the judgment of the financial manager may be much more accurate than scientific methods.

FORECASTING DOMESTIC AND INTERNATIONAL ENVIRONMENTAL VARIABLES

In developing forecasts of firm-specific variables such as sales, interest expense, and inventory, the financial manager must consider forecasts of environmental variables such as inflation rates, interest rates, and exchange rates. For example, if the rate of inflation in the United States is expected to be 5 percent per year for the next five years, forecasted prices and sales of the firm's products in the United States should reflect that forecast in some manner. It should make some difference to the sales forecast whether inflation is expected to be 0, 5, or 10 percent. To the extent that the firm has international activities, forecasts of foreign inflation rates, interest rates, and exchange rates may affect the forecasts for the firm's financial variables. In other words, forecasts of the firm's variables must be conditional on the forecasts of all relevant environmental variables—foreign and domestic.

Should the financial manager or other managers in the firm try to develop their own forecasts of environmental variables? We believe that the answer is "no." The financial markets make such forecasts implicitly in the pricing of financial assets. If the financial markets are efficient in an information sense, as discussed in Chapter 5, current prices of financial assets reflect all currently available information as to future environmental variables. If the financial manager of a firm were to use some other forecast, the manager would be betting against the market. There is no reason to believe that the financial manager of Acme Widgets will be smarter than the collective wisdom of all participants in the financial markets when it comes to forecasts of environmental variables. The manager may know more about the future of Acme Widgets than the market but is not likely to know more about future inflation rates in the United States economy than the market does. Therefore, the problem of the financial manager is to figure out what the market is forecasting for environmental variables and to use those forecasts in making forecasts for the firm's variables.

There are several ways for the financial manager to obtain market forecasts of environmental variables. In Chapter 2 we explained that current interest rates contain in them an implicit forecast of future inflation rates (the Fisher equation). In Appendix 5B we discussed the implicit forecasts of future interest rates that are contained in the term structure of interest rates. The financial manager can use these relationships to estimate market forecasts.

As an alternative to analyzing market data, the financial manager can subscribe to commercial services that provide forecasts of many environmental variables. The services make use of market data and the relationships we describe, as well as other techniques. Their forecasts are widely used by financial market participants and will often be cheaper and provide better estimates than the financial manager could obtain from in-house analysis.

FINANCIAL FORECASTING

So far we have discussed forecasting as if we were solely concerned with the future value of a particular financial variable. However, financial managers usually are more interested in forecasting the total picture. They will use one of the more comprehensive financial forecasting methods—the **cash flow method** or the **balance sheet method**. Both of these approaches forecast the cash position of the firm and make use of single-variable forecasts.

The cash flow method forecasts the cash available to, or needed by, the firm by focusing on the payments and receipts of cash over time. Under this approach, forecasted balance sheets are derived from forecasted cash flows and income statements. The balance sheet method forecasts the balance sheet accounts of the firm and, therefore, the firm's cash position. Both methods start with a sales forecast, and both require a forecast of the firm's income statements.

The balance sheet method is used when a "quick and dirty" forecast is desired for preliminary planning purposes and is also used in long-range planning. The simplest of all approaches to a direct balance sheet forecast is to estimate most of the accounts as a precentage of sales and then to use the sales forecast to generate those accounts. The cash flow method is commonly employed in short-term planning to produce as accurate a forecast as possible. Large firms often make daily cash flow forecasts for the coming month and monthly forecasts for the coming year. They then make quarterly balance sheet forecasts for the next year or two, and annual forecasts for several more years. This permits the financial manager to plan the firm's financing requirements several years into the future while simultaneously focusing on short-run needs that can be forecast with relatively greater accuracy and that require current decisions.

The sales forecast is the backbone of a comprehensive financial forecast because many of the other variables are related to sales. A production schedule, for example, cannot be developed in the absence of a forecast for sales. Any of the methods of forecasting single variables may be used in developing the sales forecast. Careful attention must be paid to competitive conditions within the firm's industry, the outlook for the general economy, and any other factors (such as technological changes in other competing industries) that may have a significant impact on the firm's future sales.

*Income Statement
Forecasts*

Income statement forecasts are widely used in financial planning since an important consideration in any financial decision is the impact of the decision on the firm's profits. The critical variable in any income statement forecast is the sales forecast. The financial manager usually takes the sales forecast provided by the marketing manager and uses it as the base variable in forecasting the variable costs of the goods and services sold. The financial manager will also forecast other income (for example, interest income on securities investment), operating expenses, interest on debt, depreciation, and any other expenses that may be incurred during the forecast period. Given all income and expense items, the financial manager can calculate income taxes owed to the government and arrive at a forecast of net income (profits) for the firm.

Interest costs on outstanding debt and interest income on present securities investment can be forecast accurately since the financial manager knows the interest rates on debt and securities. However, interest costs of new debt and interest income on new securities cannot be forecast accurately until a cash flow or balance sheet forecast has been made. The amount of new borrowing and the cash available for investment are important results from the forecast. Yet neither a cash flow forecast nor a balance sheet forecast can be completed without having an income statement forecast. Fortunately, these interest items are rarely large relative to other financial variables. Therefore standard procedure is to use a "no change" forecast from the previous year. Once a prelimi-

Cash Flow Forecasts

nary estimate of borrowings and securities investment has been made, the forecast can be revised to reflect these items more accurately. This is part of the planning and budgeting process discussed later in the chapter. Exhibit 16-1 illustrates a simple income statement forecast.

To develop accurate cash flow forecasts for a company we need its current balance sheet and its forecasted income statements. We shall develop an example cash flow forecast for January of "year 4" using the forecast income statement in Exhibit 16-1. Exhibit 16-2 shows the firm's balance sheet at the end of December of year 3 and a forecasted income statement for January (which is approximately one twelfth of the forecast for the entire year shown in Exhibit 16-1). Exhibit 16-3 provides an example cash flow forecast for January of year 4 based on the following forecast assumptions.

1 60 percent of the accounts receivable outstanding in December will be collected in January and 10 percent of January sales will be for cash. These two percentages are based on historical relationships as are the ratios below.
2 "Other cash receipts" is primarily interest on securities and is the amount shown on the forecast income statement for January.
3 All accounts payable outstanding in December will be paid in January. January purchases (which will be paid for in February) are expected to be $33,000.

EXHIBIT 16-1
Income statement forecast example (dollar figures in thousands)

	Year 1	Year 2	Year 3	Forecast for year 4	Forecasting method used
Sales revenues..........	$800	$1,000	$1,000	$1,200	Marketing judgment
Cost of goods sold	480	600	600	720	Historical ratio to sales (60%)
Gross profit	$320	$ 400	$ 400	$ 480	
Operating expenses	100	120	145	174	Trend growth rate (20% per year)
Operating profit.........	$220	$ 280	$ 255	$ 306	
Other income...........	10	4	20	20	Same as most recent year
Interest expense	(40)	(64)	(50)	(50)	Same as most recent year
Profit before taxes	$190	$ 220	$ 225	$ 276	
Federal income taxes....	82	91	90	110	Same tax rate as most recent year (40%)
Net profit	$108	$ 129	$ 135	$ 166	

4 Wages paid to employees are based on scheduled production during January. Wages constitute 40 percent of cost of goods sold and the firm expects to operate with level production at a rate of $60,000 worth of goods per month (equal to cost of goods sold).

5 Operating expenses are those shown on the income statement forecast. All operating expenses for this firm are cash outlays.

6 Plant and equipment outlays have been planned in advance. These expenditures are planned to be $30,000 in January.

7 Federal income tax payments are made quarterly. Taxes payable at the end of December will be paid in January.

8 Interest and principal payments on the firm's long-term debt are made quarterly. There are none scheduled for January.

9 Dividends are paid quarterly. Dividends declared in December and shown on the balance sheet as dividends payable will be paid in January.

10 Cash available from securities is the amount of securities on the balance sheet at the end of December. The firm maintains a mini-

---

EXHIBIT 16-2
Balance sheet for December, year 3, and forecast income statement for January, year 4 (dollar figures in thousands)

Balance sheet December 31, year 3		Forecast income statement January, year 4	
Assets		Sales revenues	$100
Cash	$ 20	Cost of goods sold	60[a]
Securities	100	Gross profit	$ 40
Accounts receivable	180	Operating expenses	15
Inventory	230	Operating profit	$ 25
Current assets	$530	Other income	1
Plant and equipment (net)	420	Interest expense	(4)
Total	$950	Profit before taxes	$ 22
Liabilities		Federal income taxes	9
Accounts payable	$ 35	Net profit	$ 13
Taxes payable	28		
Dividends payable	22		
Accrued expenses	18		
Current maturities—LTD	40		
Current liabilities	$143		
Long-term debt	360		
Net worth	447		
Total	$950		

[a] Includes depreciation on plant and equipment of $3,000.

mum cash balance and any extra cash is invested in securities which may be sold as needed to maintain that minimum balance.

11 Funds available (required) equal net cash inflow (outflow) plus cash available from securities. Notice that in developing the cash flow forecast we relied on knowledge of the firm's operations and plans. This knowledge is essential to developing good forecasts.

Balance Sheet
Forecasts

Pro forma (forecasted) balance sheets are commonly used in both short-term (up to one year) and long-term (over one year) financial planning. Short-term planning typically involves use of cash flow forecasts as well as balance sheet and income statement forecasts. The usual procedure in developing these estimates is first to directly forecast the income statements, from which in turn are developed the cash flow forecasts. The pro forma balance sheets are then prepared using the forecasted income statements and cash flows (together with the current balance sheet). Long-term planning commonly employs projected balance sheets and income statements, but not cash flows. The income statements are forecast and data from them are used to develop pro forma balance sheets.

In this section, we will first show how a pro forma balance sheet is developed, based on a cash flow forecast using the example data in Exhibits 16-2 and 16-3. Then we will discuss the forecasting problem when only pro forma balance sheets and income statements are desired.

EXHIBIT 16-3
Cash flow forecast January, year 4 (dollar figures in thousands)

Receipts

Collections	$108	(60% of $180)
Cash sales	10	(10% of $100)
Other receipts	1	(January income forecast)
Total receipts	$119	

Outlays

Payments to suppliers	$ 35	(December accounts payable)
Wages	24	(40% of $60)
Operating expenses	15	(January income forecast)
Plant and equipment	30	(Planned)
Tax payments	28	(December taxes payable are due)
Payments—long-term debt	0	(Not due)
Dividends	22	(December dividends payable)
Total outlays	$154	
Net cash flow	($ 35)	(Total receipts − total outlays)
Cash available—securities	$100	(December balance sheet)
Funds available	$ 65	

Supplemental Balance Sheet Forecasts Given income statement and cash flow forecasts covering a period of time, developing a pro forma balance sheet for the end of the period is primarily a problem of computation rather than forecasting. A supplemental balance sheet must be based on the assumptions and estimates used to forecast the income statement and cash flows of the firm; otherwise the balance sheet would not be consistent with the other forecasts. The general procedure used to forecast balance sheet accounts is as follows:

$$\text{Ending balance} \atop \text{(forecast)} = \text{beginning balance} \atop \text{(known)} + \text{flows in} \atop \text{(forecast)} - \text{flows out} \atop \text{(forecast)}$$

The financial manager takes the current value of the account (beginning balance) and adds the net change in the account derived from the income statement and cash flow forecasts (flows in − flows out) to arrive at the forecast value for the end of the period (ending balance). For example, accounts receivable is forecast as:

$$\text{Ending} \atop \text{accounts} \atop \text{receivable} = \text{beginning} \atop \text{accounts} \atop \text{receivable} + \text{sales on credit} \atop \text{during} \atop \text{period} - \text{collections} \atop \text{during} \atop \text{period}$$

The figure for sales comes from the income statement forecast, and the figure for collections comes from the cash flow forecast.

A pro forma balance sheet for January 31, year 4 and the source of the data used to generate it are shown in Exhibit 16-4. If all calculations are correct and consistent with the forecasts of the income statement and cash flows, the balance sheet will balance as it does here.[3]

Primary Balance Sheet Forecasts Pro forma balance sheets may also be the primary method of forecasting funds required and available. A cash flow forecast will not be made. This is most often used in long-range forecasting and planning. A general procedure is presented below:

1 Income statements are forecast for each period desired. Included is a preliminary estimate of dividend payments.
2 Individual balance sheet accounts are forecast directly using one of the single-variable methods, often as a percentage of sales.
3 The retained earnings account is forecast using the income statement forecast of additions to retained earnings (net income less dividends) and the beginning balance in the account.
4 The balance sheet is balanced by "plugging in" additional cash assets or funds required as needed. That is, all assets and liabilities (including equity accounts) are forecast by whatever method the financial manager considers to be the most accurate. But total assets

---

[3] Most businesses use computer programs to calculate pro forma financial statements. Electronic spreadsheet programs such as Lotus 1–2–3 and Excel are available on personal (micro) computer systems costing less than $1000. However, to use such programs effectively, you need to understand the principles explained in this chapter.

must equal total liabilities plus equity. If the sum of all assets forecast is less than the sum of liabilities plus equity, then the firm must have additional assets (funds available) so that balance is achieved. Similarly, if the sum of liabilities plus equity is less than the asset total, additional liabilities (funds required) must be obtained.

For example, suppose that we wish to forecast the balance sheet of the firm for December 31, year 4 using the income statement forecast from Exhibit 16-1. We will use the "percent of sales" approach by computing most of the balance sheet accounts on December 31, year 3 (from Exhibit 16-2) as a percent of sales in year 3. These percentages are then applied to the sales forecast ($1200) for year 4 to obtain the December 31, year 4 forecast balance sheet. This forecast and the percentages used are shown in Exhibit 16-5. The securities account is being used as a balancing account on the asset side and "Funds Required" is used as a balancing account on the liability side.

EXHIBIT 16-4
Balance sheet forecast January 31, year 4 (dollar figures in thousands)

Assets

Cash	$ 20	(Minimum balance—same as December)
Securities	65	(Cash flow forecast, funds available)
Accounts receivable	162	(December balance of $180 + January credit sales of $90 − collections of $108)
Inventory	230	(December balance of $230 + production of $60 − cost of goods sold of $60)
Current assets	$477	
Plant and equipment	447	(December balance of $420 + outlays of $30 − depreciation of $3)
Total	$924	

Liabilities

Accounts payable	$ 33	(January purchases)
Taxes payable	9	(January taxes)
Dividends payable	0	(Payment made in January)
Accrued expenses	22	(December balance of $18 + interest accrued in January of $4)
Current maturities—LTD	40	(No change indicated)
Current liabilities	$104	
Long-term debt	360	(No change indicated)
Net worth	460	(December balance of $447 + retained earnings of $13)
Total	$924	

Financial managers forecast in order to plan and use forecasts to indicate whether or not their plans are consistent with the goals of the firm. Forecasts therefore are a major part of the planning process. Management uses forecasts to anticipate problems so that action may be taken to alleviate them. Forecasts are used to plan strategies, such as promotional campaigns to increase sales or equipment purchases to reduce production costs or increase productive capacity. Such decisions must be planned well in advance of their implementation. Once management has determined a plan of action for the future, these plans are incorporated into a written **financial budget**. A financial budget is a formal statement of expected values of the financial variables of the firm over a future period. There may be a number of separate budgets for the various activities of the firm showing in detail management's plans for the future. For example, the capital budget would indicate expenditures on the

EXHIBIT 16-5
Direct balance sheet forecast percent of sales approach (dollar figures in thousands)

Sales, year 3 = $1,000	Forecast Sales, year 4 = $1,200		
	December 31 year 3	Percent of sales	Forecast December 31, year 4
Assets			
Cash	$ 20	2%	$ 24
Securities	100	*a*	0
Accounts receivable...........................	180	18	216
Inventory	230	23	276
Current assets	$530		$ 516
Plant and Equipment (net)	420	42	504
Total......................................	$950		$1,020
Liabilities			
Funds required		*a*	2
Accounts payable	$ 35	3.5	42
Taxes payable	28	2.8	33.6
Dividend payable	22	2.2	24.4
Accrued expenses..............................	18	1.8	21.6
Current maturities—LTD	40	*b*	40
Current liabilities.............................	$143		$ 163.6
Long-term debt	360	*b*	320
Net worth.......................................	447	44.7*c*	536.4
Total	$950		$1,020

a Balancing accounts.
b Forecast existing debt using known maturities.
c A better approach would be to add projected retained earnings to net worth since the income statement is normally also forecast as in Exhibit 16-1. Stock issues and dividends are usually planned in advance.

capital projects planned over the budget period. The budget for operating expenses would be broken down by expense categories. The separate, detailed budgets are summarized in a cash budget that shows the various cash flows of the firm similar in form to the cash flow forecast shown in Exhibit 16-5. However, a cash budget would include the sources for financing planned in the future and the use of funds available.

There are two general approaches to developing a financial budget for the total firm—**top-down** and **bottom-up**. Top-down planning begins with a set of overall goals for the firm for the planning period. Then the activities that must take place in order to reach those goals are developed. This approach is most commonly used in long-range planning. Suppose, for example, that management establishes a goal of increasing earnings per share at an average rate of 10 percent per year over the next five years. Management then must determine the revenues that must be obtained in order to reach that goal. These revenue goals are then considered for their implications with respect to the assets required to achieve them, the production requirements, financing requirements, and so forth. The result of this approach is an overall plan or budget for the firm that is consistent with the goal established.

The bottom-up approach begins with estimates of the component activities of the firm. Each product line sold by the firm or each division might be forecast individually. Budgets are established for each area and then added together to provide a total financial plan for the firm. This approach is more like the forecasting procedure discussed earlier in which forecasts of single financial variables are combined into an integrated forecast of cash flows, income statements, and balance sheets.

In large firms both approaches are often used. Management may develop a general plan based on goals it has established. Forecasts of the firm's activities are then made, added together, and compared with the general plan. This dual procedure provides information on aspects of the firm's operations that must be given more attention. Also, it tells management whether the original goals are realistic.

Once the budgets have been established, they may then be used as a means of controlling the firm's operations. Lower-level management personnel can be provided with budgets for their own areas of responsibility and can be asked to operate within the confines of their budget. Budgets used in this way make it more likely that the firm's actual operations will approximate the overall plan.

If actual results deviate appreciably from the budgeted values, management investigates the reasons for the deviations. Depending on the reasons, either the budget will be revised to reflect changing conditions in the firm's environment or action will be taken to bring the firm's operations back into line with the plan.

The planning and budget process in large corporations usually involves a department whose sole activity is planning, and the process is more complicated than we have indicated here. In small firms, planning is usually limited to a forecast of cash flows and financial statements for the coming year and a preliminary plan for financing.

SUMMARY

Forecasting and planning the future financial condition of the firm are important parts of financial management. There are several basic techniques for forecasting single financial variables. These methods are:

1   The use of historical trends for the variable to forecast future values.

2   The use of the ratio of two variables to forecast one given a forecast of the other.

3   The application of statistical methods to historical data to determine the relationship between one or more variables; then one variable can be forecast using forecasts of the others.

4   The application of judgment and subjective evaluation of the future.

The forecasts of individual financial variables can then be combined to develop complete forecasts of the firm's financial position over time. There are two general approaches that may be used. The cash flow method focuses directly on movements of cash into and out of the firm. The balance sheet method relies on forecasts of individual balance sheet accounts. Income statement forecasts are used with both approaches. Each forecast provides somewhat different information about the financial condition of the firm over time, and both may be calculated if the financial manager wishes to have a complete forecast of the financial aspects of the firm's operations.

Forecasts are used as part of the planning and budgeting process of the firm. Budgets are formal plans used as an aid in controlling the firm's operations. Two approaches to planning are in common use. The top-down approach begins with some general goals for the firm for the planning period, and then the activities necessary to achieve these goals are estimated. The bottom-up approach starts with estimates for the separate parts of the firm. These separate plans or budgets are then combined to provide a total plan. Often both approaches are used to ensure consistency of separate budgets with the general goals established by management. The budgets for individual departments or operating units of the firm enable a firm's management to control its operations.

QUESTIONS

1   Why is forecasting an important part of the financial manager's job?

2   How do "trend" forecasts differ from "ratio" forecasts?

3   Under what circumstances would a "no change" forecast be best?

4   What is a "base variable"? What's the most common base variable in financial forecasting, and why is it used so often?

5   A scientific forecasting method provides the same results when used by different people. Does this mean that scientific methods provide the best forecasts?

6   What are pro forma financial statements?

7   What are the principal operating sources of cash receipts for a business firm?

8 There are two general approaches to forecasting a firm's balance sheet at a given future date. What are the two approaches, and under what circumstances is each one used?

9 Describe the two planning procedures discussed in the chapter.

10 Suppose that you are the financial manager of Western Marine Corporation, a company with annual sales of $40 million. Twenty-five percent of your sales are to foreign customers. You have just hired a newly graduated MBA who proposes using advanced statistical techniques and historical time series data to develop forecasts of inflation rates and exchange rates for the countries where your products are sold. Is this likely to prove to be a desirable use of your new employee's talents?

PROJECT

Obtain the annual reports for at least the past two years of a company (may be assigned by your instructor). Using data from the earlier financial statements, forecast the balance sheet and income statement for the year of the most recent annual report that you obtained. Assume that you have accurately forecasted the sales volume for the most recent year; that is, use the year's actual sales as a base variable. Compare your forecasts of all the data other than sales with the actual results. Try to determine why any major errors (greater than 5 percent) occurred.

DEMONSTRATION PROBLEMS

DP1 Income statements for the past two years for Fiber Products are shown below. Sales for 1993 are forecast to be up 20 percent over 1992. Operating expenses are expected to follow their most recent trend. Interest expense is projected to increase to $40,000 because of a planned issue of long-term debt. Management expects that the average income tax rate will be 30 percent in 1993. Other income is not expected to change. All other income statement items are expected to maintain their past relationships to sales. Forecast the 1993 income statement for Fiber Products based on these assumptions.

	1991	1992	1993 (forecast)
Sales	$1,400,000	$1,500,000	
Cost of goods sold	746,000	800,000	
Gross income..........	$ 654,000	$ 700,000	
Operating expense	225,000	250,000	
Operating income	$ 429,000	$ 450,000	
Less interest expense....	(19,000)	(25,000)	
Plus other income.......	10,000	10,000	
Income before taxes.....	$ 420,000	$ 435,000	
Income taxes	160,000	174,000	
Net income.............	$ 260,000	$ 261,000	

SOLUTION TO DP1:

	1993 forecast	Assumptions
Sales	$1,800,000	20% increase over 1992
Cost of goods sold	960,000	53⅓% of sales
Gross income	840,000	
Operating expense	277,500	11.1% trend 1991–1992
Operating income	562,500	
Interest expense	(40,000)	Given
Other income	10,000	No change
Income before taxes	532,500	
Income taxes	159,750	30% of before-tax income
Net income	$ 372,750	

DP2 An analyst working under you has prepared the partially completed balance sheet forecast shown below.

Assets		Liabilities and equity	
Cash.....................		Financing required......,	
Accounts receivable......	$150,000	Accounts payable........	$100,000
Inventory..............	300,000	Other liabilities.........,,,	50,000
Current Assets.......		Current liabilities.....	
Fixed assets............	600,000	Long-term debt..........	$200,000
		Stockholders' equity......	750,000
Total assets.........		Total liabilities and equity.........	

Complete the forecast assuming a minimum cash balance of $30,000.

SOLUTION TO DP2:

Assets		Liabilities and equity	
Cash .... $	50,000	Financing required...... $	0
Accounts receivable	150,000	Accounts payable	100,000
Inventory..............	300,000	Other liabilities.........	50,000
Current assets......	500,000	Current liabilities...	150,000
Fixed assets	600,000	Long-term debt	200,000
Total assets........	$1,100,000	Stockholders' equity....	750,000
		Total liabilities and equity	$1,100,000

Assets forecast = $150,000 + $300,000 + $600,000 + $30,000
(minimum cash balance)

= $1,080,000

Liabilities forecast = $100,000 + $50,000 + $200,000
+ $750,000

= $1,100,000

Assets are less than liabilities by $20,000; therefore, the firm will have additional assets of $20,000. Using cash as a "plug" figure, cash must be $50,000. Financing required is zero. Other missing figures are simply totals.

PROBLEMS

1 Make the following forecasts using the method indicated:
  a Operating expenses have increased at an average rate of 8 percent per year for the past five years. Last year, operating expenses amounted to $50,000. Forecast operating expenses for next year using a trend forecast. [Ans.: $54,000]
  b The cost of goods sold has averaged 75 percent for the past three years. Next year's sales are forecast to be $900,000. Forecast the cost of goods sold for next year using the ratio method. [Ans.: $675,000]
  c General and administrative (G & A) expenses have been as follows:

Year	1988	1989	1990	1991
G & A	$90,000	$99,000	$110,000	$120,000

  Forecast G & A expenses for 1992 using the trend method
  d A construction equipment dealer's bad debt losses as a percentage of average annual accounts receivable have been a fairly steady 2.0 percent per year. As a percentage of sales, bad debt losses have varied between 0.2 and 0.4 percent. In good years many of the firm's customers pay cash; however, the dealer also offers extended credit terms to six months. Sales are forecast to be $3.5 million next year and accounts receivable are expected to average $600,000. Forecast bad debt losses using the ratio method.
2 Wojteki Meats has the following history of sales:

Year	1990	1989	1988	1987	1986	1985	1984
Sales (millions)	$7.1	$6.9	$6.6	$6.4	$6.4	$6.0	$5.5

a Comparing 1990 sales with 1984 sales, calculate the average annual percentage increases over the six-year period. Forecast 1991 sales using this figure.

b Apply a geographical approach to forecasting 1990 sales by fitting a straight line to the data from 1984 to 1990.

c From an examination of the data, which of the forecasts in *a* and *b* appears best?

3 Given the historical data shown, prepare a forecast for purchases in 1993. The value of goods produced (production) in 1993 is forecast to be $2.1 million.

	Year			
	1992	**1991**	**1990**	**1989**
Production (millions)	$2.00	$1.80	$1.75	$1.60
Purchases (millions)	$0.70	$0.55	$0.60	$0.53

4 Given the sales forecast and other information shown below, prepare forecasts of collections and accounts receivable for January, February, and March. Assume that accounts receivable are collected on average, two months after the sales are made.

	Actual		Forecast		
	November	**December**	**January**	**February**	**March**
Sales	$150,000	$175,000	$130,000	$140,000	$200,000
Accounts Receivable	340,000	325,000			
Collections	250,000	190,000			

5 As financial manager of Western Marine products, you are in the process of developing a financial forecast for next year. The marketing manager has supplied a sales forecast of $12 million, an increase of 20 percent from current levels. This forecast assumes that volume will increase by 5 percent and prices will increase by 15 percent. The sales manager has based the price increase on an assumption that the general rate of inflation will be 12 percent per year. Your analysis of financial market date indicates that the financial markets seem to be expecting an inflation rate of only 6 percent. What sales forecast should you use for next year? Why?

6 The financial manager of Saucy Pizza Supplies has found from experience that the collections of accounts receivable in a given month can be estimated as being 20 percent of the current month's sales plus 60 percent of the previous month's sales plus 20 percent of the sales made two months ago. For example, a forecast of August collections would equal 20 percent of August sales + 60 percent of July sales + 20 percent of June sales.

At the beginning of July, a sales forecast for the next six months is as follows:

Month	Sales (thousands)
July	$100
August	$100
September	$120
October	$140
November	$200
December	$200

May sales were $80,000, and June sales were $120,000. Accounts receivable as of June 30 were $112,000.

Using the above data, forecast monthly collections and end-of-month accounts receivable balances for July through December.

7 The financial manager of Central Distributors wishes to forecast the average level of inventory for 1992. Based on a sales forecast, cost of goods sold for 1992 is projected to be $5 million. The following historical data have been collected (dollar figures in the table are in thousands).

Year	Cost of goods sold	Average inventory
1987	$4,000	$ 950
1988	3,800	1,100
1989	4,000	1,020
1990	4,400	1,080
1991	4,600	1,200

a Obtain forecasts of average inventory in 1992 using the following methods:
  (1) "Trend" approach
  (2) "Ratio" approach based on the ratio of inventory to cost of goods sold
b Compare the forecasts obtained in a and indicate which one you prefer.

8 Using the data from problem 7, develop a forecast of 1992 inventory using a graphical approach to obtain the relationship between inventory and cost of goods sold. How confident would you be that the forecast is accurate?

9 Last year's income statement for Detroit Supply is shown below.

	Last year	Next year (forecast)
Sales	$500,000	$550,000
Cost of goods sold	300,000	
Gross income	$200,000	
Operating expenses	90,000	
Interest expense.....................	4,000	
Income before taxes	$106,000	
Income taxes......................	21,500	
Net income	$ 84,500	

Sales for next year are expected to be $550,000. Interest expense is expected to stay the same. The corporate income tax rate will be 15 percent on the first $50,000 of income and 25 percent on income over $50,000. The other income statement items are expected to maintain their past relationship to sales. Forecast next year's income statement using these assumptions.

10 Your brother has a small business and is forecasting the firm's balance sheet for next year. He has arrived at the figures shown below, but doesn't know what to do next. Can you complete the forecast for him? He believes that at least $20,000 should be kept in cash.

Assets		Liabilities and equity	
Cash		Financing required	
Accounts receivable....	$100,000	Accounts payable	$50,000
Inventory	150,000	Other liabilities	20,000
Current assets		Current liabilities	
Fixed assets..........	280,000	Long-term debt........	$120,000
		Stockholders' equity	300,000
Total assets		Total liabilities and equity	

11 Your brother (the same brother as in problem *10*) has just called to say that he forgot to include the impact of a planned sale of one of his stores. The store has a book value of $100,000 (leasehold improvements of $40,000 included in fixed assets plus $60,000 in inventory). Proceeds from the sale would be $120,000 after taxes and would be retained in the business. Revise the forecast balance sheet of problem *10* to reflect the new information.

12 Develop a pro forma balance sheet in the following form for the end of next year given the data provided. Sales for next year are forecast to be $2.0 million.

Assets		Liabilities and equity	
Cash		Financing required ...	
Accounts receivable ..		Accounts payable	
Inventory		Long-term debt	
Fixed assets		Common stock.......	
		Retained earnings	
Total...........		Total...........	

Minimum cash balance = $50,000
Accounts receivable = 15% of annual sales
Inventory = 12% of annual sales
Fixed assets = no change from current level of $850,000
Accounts payable = 4% of annual sales
Long-term debt = $240,000 based on present plans
Common stock = $200,000 (no change)
Retained earnings = $480,000 (current level) plus any additional
                        earnings retained during year
Net income = 5% of annual sales (no dividends planned)

13 The financial manager of Omega Industries wishes to have a forecast for the firm's balance sheet three years from now at the end of year 3. You have been assigned to the task and provided the format and data shown below. Complete the assignment.

Assets		Liabilities and equity	
Cash		Financing required	
Accounts receivable....		Accounts payable......	
Inventory		Long-term debt........	
Fixed assets..........		Common stock	
Retained earnings......			
Total		Total	

Year	1	2	3
Sales forecast	$1,000,000	$1,100,000	$1,200,000

Minimum cash balance = 3% of annual sales
Accounts receivable = 10% of annual sales
Inventory = $50,000 + 12% of annual sales
Fixed assets = $400,000 plus $20,000 per year
Accounts payable = 50% of inventory
Long-term debt = $300,000 less $30,000 per year principal
                        repayment

Common stock = $200,000 (current value; no new issues planned)
Retained earnings = $150,000 (current value) + total additions
Net income per year = 4% of annual sales
Dividends per year = 40% of net income

14 The Deep Six Company manufactures depth sounders for fishing boats. In early January, Deep Six's financial manager, Valerie Steinberg, is in the process of developing a monthly cash flow forecast for the first six months of 1993. Total sales for 1993 are forecast to be $3 million. The following information is available:

Month	Sales forecast (thousands)
January	$ 50
February	70
March	200
April	500
May	900
June	600
Six-month total	$2,320

Sales in November and December 1992 were $40,000 and $20,000, respectively. The depth sounders are sold to retailers who generally buy on credit. It is estimated that 10 percent of sales are for cash, 70 percent are collected in the second month following sales, and 20 percent are collected in the second month following sales. Even though sales are quite seasonal, production is maintained at an even rate throughout the year. No changes in year-end (December) inventories are planned.

Valerie has observed the following historical relationships over the past several years:

Cost of raw material = 50% of sales
Cost of labor = 30% of sales

These relationships are expected to hold during the coming year as well. The raw materials will be purchased evenly over the year in relation to production needs. Payments for raw materials are made during the month following purchase. Labor costs and operating expenses are paid in the month incurred. Total operating expenses are forecast to be $120,000 for the next six months and, like raw materials and labor, will not vary appreciably from month to month. Total depreciation for the next six months is expected to be $60,000 and is included in the cost of goods sold.

Expenditures on plant and equipment are forecast to be $30,000 per month from April through June. Deep Six has an outstanding mortgage, which requires principal payments of $50,000 in June. Interest expenses are estimated to average $9000 per month. The Deep Six Company will continue to pay $10,000 per

quarter in dividends in March and June as they did for the last
two years. A minimum cash balance of $75,000 is required. Quarterly income taxes of $20,000 are due in each of April and June.
Deep Six pays taxes each quarter based on its estimated total
taxes for the year. The tax rate is 25 percent.

Given this information, do the following:

a Develop monthly income statement and cash flow forecasts for
the coming six months, January–June.

b Develop a balance sheet for the month in which the maximum
amount of financing is needed as determined in *a*.

c Develop monthly balance sheets for the coming six months,
January–June. (Note that the balance sheet asked for in *b* will
be included here.)

---

*Deep Six Company financial statements for the fiscal year ending
December 31, 1992.*

Balance sheet at December 31, 1992 (dollar figures in thousands)

Cash	$ 75	Accounts payable........	$ 140
Securities	100	Accrued expenses........	30
Accounts receivable......	150	Mortgage (current portion)	100
Inventory	800	Current liabilities	$ 270
Current assets	$1,125	Mortgage	1,400
Plant and equipment (net)	5,000	Common stock	3,000
Other assets.............	45	Retained earnings........	1,500
Total	$6,170	Total	$6,170

**Income statement for the year ended December 31, 1992
(dollar figures in thousands)**

Net sales	$2,700
Cost of goods sold[a].....................	2,268
Gross profit............................	$ 432
Operating expenses......................	220
Operating profit........................	$ 212
Other income	2
Less interest on debt	(74)
Profit before taxes......................	$ 140
Federal income taxes[b]	35
Net profit	$ 105

[a] Includes materials expenses of $1,350, labor expenses of $810, and depreciation
of $108.
[b] 25 percent tax rate.

A LITTLE HISTORY

Computers changed radically in 1974 when thousands of electronic circuits were put on a small piece of silicon. This first microprocessor developed quickly into Intel Corporation's 8008 (the number is the trade name) and then later the 8080 microprocessor. These early microprocessors opened the door to small desktop computers known as microcomputers. Intel's microprocessor along with MOS Technologies' 6502 were originally packaged with other components in microcomputer kits that were bought by computer hobbyists who assembled the microcomputer themselves. These original machines, although enjoyed by technically advanced pioneers, were hardly practical for the world of corporate finance.

After having some success in 1977 selling a kit called Apple 1, Steve Wozniak and Steve Jobs (engineers for Hewlett-Packard at the time) moved microcomputers a giant step forward by offering the first pre-assembled microcomputer, the Apple II. Shortly thereafter, Tandy/Radio Shack and Commodore introduced their microcomputers, the TRS-80 and PET, respectively. Both machines allowed computer access to nontechnical users. Although freed from assembling the kit and understanding machine language, a user still had to understand the BASIC programming language in order to accomplish even simple tasks. BASIC, with its long list of commands, proved to be a large hurdle to widespread use of microcomputers by business executives.

If a BASIC program was too complicated for wide adoption of microcomputers, wouldn't a familiar interface like an accountant's 13-column ledger sheet overcome this hurdle? This question was answered in 1978 when Don Bricklin and Robert Frankston (two Harvard MBA students) formed Software Arts and developed the first electronic spreadsheet—VisiCalc. VisiCalc was marketed by Personal Software, which later changed its name to Visi-Corp. The combination of Apple II and VisiCalc's spreadsheet resulted in such low costs (measured both in dollars and start-up time) that their adoption by businesses became widespread.

Not all the early microcomputers were Apple computers. Other machines, such as Osborne Computer Corporation's Osborn 1, used a different computer operating system called CP/M that was not compatible with Apple II. In 1980, Sorcim Corporation developed a spreadsheet called Super-Calc, which could run on the CP/M operating system, thus expanding the availability of spreadsheets to all microcomputer users.

Encouraged by the success of VisiCalc, Personal Software developed new products to handle graphing and filing applications and that could share data with VisiCalc through what was called the Data Interchange Format (DIF). This development was significant for two reasons. First, it was perhaps the first attempt to integrate several applications: spreadsheets, graphs, and data management. Second, one of Personal Software's new products, VisiTrend, was developed by Mitch Kapor, who later founded Lotus Development Corporation.

Whereas Apple II and VisiCalc introduced microcomputers to the business world, the development of the IBM PC and Lotus 1–2–3 resulted in the widespread adoption of the microcomputer by businesses. The PC had the advantages of expanded processing power and memory. To take advantage of the PC's power, a new generation of spreadsheets developed. Products like SuperCalc2, VisiCalc Advanced Version, ProCalc, and Multiplan were improvements over their predecessors. However, the most innovative of the new spreadsheets was Lotus 1–2–3. It integrated graphics and data management with its advanced spreadsheet. Developed by Mitch Kapor and Jonathan Sachs, 1–2–3 quickly became the best selling software product for microcomputers.

Since the introduction of IBM's PC and Lotus 1–2–3, there have been continuing improvements in both hardware and software. Computers like IBM's PS/2, advanced new microprocessors and math coprocessors such as Intel's 80386 and 80387, and new laser printers like Hewlett Packard's Laser Jet Series II, have enhanced speed, power, and output quality of spreadsheets. New software developments include spreadsheets that can stack logical pages on top of one another to form a three-dimensional spreadsheet. The 3-D spreadsheet capabilities have proven valuable in situations in which there is a need to consolidate similar spreadsheets from multiple departments into a single summary worksheet. Boeing Computer Services' Boeing Cale 2.0 and Martin Marietta's CalcIT were pioneers in this three-dimensional feature. Lotus recently released version 3.0 of 1–2–3 with 3-D capacity. Additionally, the new version of 1–2–3 can run linear regressions, perform forecasting analysis, access memory beyond the previous 640K limits, and create presentation-quality output.

A recent development in spreadsheets has been the introduction of products like Symphony, Framework, Enable, and Excel that integrate spreadsheets with graphics, data management (organizing and using data), word processing, and communications (the ability to transmit information to another location, usually over telephone lines). Having all these capabilities in one program is convenient but can mean less flexibility, ease of use, and power. An alternative is not to integrate all these capabilities into one program, but to allow the user to let several separate programs (for example, a word processing program and a spreadsheet program) "communicate" with one another. Products like Microsoft's Windows or IBM's Top View allow the stand-alone programs to be integrated. For example, with Windows one could combine graphs and tables from 1–2–3 with text created using a word processor like WordPerfect.

Currently there are many different electronic spreadsheets available. They differ in power, versatility, price, and ease of use, but they are similar in concept and results. In short, the options for spreadsheet users are abundant and constantly improving.

USING SPREADSHEETS

An electronic spreadsheet is nothing more than an electronic adaptation of an accountant's pad of paper. However, instead of being 13 columns by 40 rows, an electronic spreadsheet is 256 columns by 8192 rows (size of Lotus 1–2–3, release 3).

An intersection of a vertical column with a horizontal row is called a cell. A column is usually identified by a letter and a row by a number, and each cell is identified by its row/column coordinates (for example, B9). Each cell can contain a group of letters, numbers, or both. The information in a cell contains one of three types of data: (1) text, like a row description, such as SALES, or a column heading, JANUARY; (2) numerical amounts; and (3) relationships between various cells in the worksheet. Relationships can be arithmetic statements, more complex mathematical formulas (for example, the total of a column of numbers), or special spreadsheet functions (for example, the net present value of a row).

The process of building a spreadsheet is simply customizing the blank "paper" by entering labels and defining all the mathematical relationships. Movement from cell to cell is done with cursor-movement keys or a "mouse" (a handheld device which substitutes for the cursor-movement keys). Cursor movement can also be used to see different parts of the spreadsheet, since only one section of the spreadsheet fits onto the computer screen at a time.

An electronic spreadsheet has several major advantages over paper and an adding machine. The first advantage becomes obvious as you start customizing your spreadsheet. As you enter data and formulas, all the computations are calculated automatically and without error. The electronic spreadsheet lets the computer do all the computing and frees the manager to concentrate on the relationships.

A second benefit of the spreadsheet is in simplifying repetitive administrative tasks. For example, a model built for January's cash budget can be used as a **template**, or prototype, applicable to other months. Since all the relationships have been established, the manager would just have to enter the February, March . . . data into the template and let the computer do the calculations.

A third advantage of an electronic spreadsheet is the ease with which it can be displayed and stored. Once the work is finished, a simple

command prints the results. The spreadsheet can be given a name and filed to be used again later. Furthermore, with most spreadsheets the data can be easily graphed for visual analysis.

A fourth advantage of an electronic spreadsheet is its ability to facilitate decision making. After entering the relevant relationships into the spreadsheet, the decision maker can see the consequences of a decision under various sets of assumptions by changing numbers. For example, a manager, after building a pro forma income statement, could ask "what would happen to the company if a $2 sales price decrease caused sales to go up by 10 percent?" As the manager changes the price and sales volume figures, the computer quickly recomputes the spreadsheet. The manager can then see the effects of the lower price and higher volume in all the modeled parts of the company. Seeing the outcomes under different assumptions is very helpful in deciding what to do. Duplicating this kind of "sensitivity analysis" using hand calculations can be very time consuming.

Before giving an example of a spreadsheet, three cautions are appropriate. First, one wrong entry into an electronic spreadsheet can cause the results to be meaningless. Second, the increased power of electronic spreadsheets facilitates extremely complex financial models and worksheets. Spreadsheet users who do not understand what happens between the spreadsheet's inputs and outputs are likely to make errors either in the spreadsheet or in the decisions based on the spreadsheet. Third, the power of electronic spreadsheets to do sensitivity analysis can lead to what some have called "analysis paralysis." At some point it is necessary to stop the analysis, make a decision, and act.

The following example of a

spreadsheet application uses Lotus 1–2–3; however, most other spreadsheet programs use a very similar technique. The example is of building a pro forma (forecasted) income statement for the first quarter of the year. A step-by-step explanation will not be given but a few exemplary entries will be discussed. Figure 1 shows the actual cell entries in their formula form and Figure 2 shows the resulting display on the screen or printout.

Suppose a manager estimates sales for the first three months of the year to be $10,000, $11,000, and $12,000. The manager also knows from past experience that material and labor expenses are 25 percent and 30 percent of sales, respectively. Furthermore, the manager can forecast the firm's fixed costs, including

---

FIGURE 1
Spreadsheet formulas and data input

	A	B	C	D	E
1					
2					
3					
4		JAN	FEB	MAR	YTD
5		---	---	---	---
6					
7	Sales	10,000	11,000	12,000	@SUM(B7..D7)
8					
9	Variable expenses				
10	Material	+B7*0.25	+C7*0.25	+D7*0.25	@SUM(B10.D10)
11	Labor	+B7*0.30	+C7*0.30	+D7*0.30	@SUM(B11.D11)
12	--------	--------	--------	--------	
13	Contribution	+B7-B10-B11	+C7-C10-C11	+D7-D10-D11	+E7-E10-E11
14					
15	Fixed costs				
16	Depreciation	500	500	500	@SUM(B16.D16)
17	Advertising	750	750	750	@SUM(B17.D17)
18	Administration	1,000	1,000	1,000	@SUM(B18.D18)
19		--------	--------	--------	--------
20	Total fixed costs	@SUM(B16..B18)	@SUM(C16..C18)	@SUM(D16..D18)	@SUM(E16.E18)
21					
22	EBIT	+B13-B20	+C13-C20	+D13-D20	@SUM(B22.D22)
23	Interest Expense	500	500	500	@SUM(B23.D23)
24		--------	--------	--------	--------
25	Profit before tax	+B22-B23	+C22-C23	+D22-D23	+E22-E23
26	Tax @32%	0.32*B25	0.32*C25	0.32*D25	0.32*E25
27		--------	--------	--------	--------
28	Net income	+B25-B26	+C25-C26	+D25-D26	+E25-E26

interest, and expects to pay 32 percent of earnings in taxes. Armed with this knowledge the manager could generate the pro forma income statement in Figure 2.

Notice that in column A and the top 6 rows of the spreadsheet all the titles and accounts names are typed into the appropriate cell. Also, data for sales, fixed costs, and interest expense are entered as amounts for each month. For an example of a formula, look at cell B10. Figure 1 shows the cell entry to be +B7*0.25. The "+" tells Lotus that you are creating a formula, not text. The formula is B7*0.25. This instructs the computer to take the content of cell B7, the sales figure, and multiply it (the * serves as the multiplication symbol) by 0.25 (the material expense ratio). In Figure 2, the product

---

FIGURE 2
Spreadsheet display

	A	B	C	D	E
1			Pro forma income statement		
2			first quarter		
3					
4		JAN	FEB	MAR	YTD
5		---	---	---	---
6					
7	Sales	10,000	11,000	12,000	33,000
8					
9	Variable expenses				
10	Material	2,500	2,750	3,000	8,250
11	Labor	3,000	3,300	3,600	9,900
12		-----	-----	-----	-----
13	Contribution	4,500	4,950	5,400	14,850
14					
15	Fixed costs				
16	Depreciation	500	500	500	1,500
17	Advertising	750	750	750	2,250
18	Administration	1,000	1,000	1,000	3,000
19		-----	-----	-----	-----
20	Total fixed costs	2,250	2,250	2,250	6,750
21					
22	EBIT	2,250	2,700	3,150	8,100
23	Interest expense	500	500	500	1,500
24		-----	-----	-----	-----
25	Profit before tax	1,750	2,200	2,650	6,600
26	Tax @ 32%	560	704	848	2,112
27		-----	-----	-----	-----
28	Net income	1,190	1,496	1,802	4,488

FIGURE 3
Spreadsheet display with changed data

	A	B	C	D	E
			Pro forma income statement		
1					
2			first quarter		
3					
4		JAN	FEB	MAR	YTD
5		---	---	---	---
6					
7	Sales	11,000	12,500	14,000	37,500
8					
9	Variable expenses				
10	Material	2,750	3,125	3,500	9,375
11	Labor	3,300	3,750	4,200	11,250
12		-----	-----	-----	-----
13	Contribution	4,950	5,625	6,300	16,875
14					
15	Fixed costs				
16	Depreciation	500	500	500	1,500
17	Advertising	1,000	1,000	1,000	3,000
18	Administration	1,000	1,000	1,000	3,000
19		-----	-----	-----	-----
20	Total fixed costs	2,500	2,500	2,500	7,500
21					
22	EBIT	2,450	3,125	3,800	9,375
23	Interest expense	500	500	500	1,500
24		-----	-----	-----	-----
25	Profit before tax	1,950	2,625	3,300	7,875
26	Tax @ 32%	624	840	1,056	2,520
27		-----	-----	-----	-----
28	Net income	1,326	1,785	2,244	5,355

is reported in cell B10, which is what is shown on the screen.

Another interesting entry in Figure 1 is in cell B20. The entry @SUM(B16.B18) is a built-in Lotus function that tells the computer to put the sum of cells B16 to B18 into cell B20. Since these three cells contain the monthly fixed costs, the total fixed costs for January are reported in cell B20 as seen in Figure 2.

Suppose the results of a marketing study revealed that if the firm would spend $250 more in advertising each month, then sales in each of the first three months would increase to $11,000, $12,500, and $14,000. Simply by changing three numbers in row 7 and three numbers in row 17, the manager could see how the new ad campaign would affect the company. Figure 3 shows a printout of the income statements under the new assumptions. The first quarter profits have risen from $4488 to $5355, an increase of $867.

Although the example is quite simple, much larger and more complicated spreadsheets can be built. A few common applications include general ledgers, cash budgets, capital budgets, inventory ledgers, tax calculations, check balancing, pro forma balance sheets, accounts payable and receivable ledgers, and payroll worksheets.

PART FOUR

WORKING CAPITAL MANAGEMENT

Working capital management is the management of a company's current assets and current liabilities. Chapters 17 and 18 show how the basic investment concepts of Chapter 8 are modified to deal with the special characteristics of inventory, accounts receivable, cash, and securities—all of which constitute current assets of the firm. Chapter 19 describes the major sources of short-term financing—trade credit (accounts payable), bank loans, and commercial paper—which constitute the most important current liabilities of the firm. Chapter 20 shows how current asset decisions affect the method of financing and link together concepts developed in Part 3 and in the previous chapters of Part 4.

CHAPTER SEVENTEEN

INVENTORY AND ACCOUNTS RECEIVABLE MANAGEMENT

There are four kinds of current assets found in almost all businesses—cash, securities, accounts receivable, and inventories, In this chapter, we examine the financial aspects of inventories and accounts receivable. In the next chapter, we look at cash and securities. We begin with some general rules that apply to investment in any current asset.

CURRENT ASSET MANAGEMENT

The basic principles of asset investment decisions were presented in Chapters 8 through 10. These principles apply to current assets as well as plant and equipment; however, current assets have some unique characteristics that suggest some modifications in the methods of evaluation. First, the amount of investment in each type of current asset may vary from day to day. Therefore, the average amount invested is frequently used in deciding how large the investment should be. Using averages greatly simplifies the analysis. Second, decisions regarding investment in one type of current asset are frequently not independent of decisions regarding other current assets. For example, a change in credit policies that affect accounts receivable may also affect sales and therefore affect the desirable level of inventory. The result is that there is a very large number of alternative levels of investment in each type of current asset. Therefore, in principle, current asset investment is a problem of evaluating a large number of mutually exclusive investment opportunities.

Solution of this problem by the methods presented in Chapter 8 requires that:

1 The financial manager estimates the costs and benefits from each alternative.
2 The net present value must be calculated for each alternative given the discount rate (cost of capital) appropriate to the degree of risk involved.
3 The alternative with the highest net present value be chosen.

However, the net present value approach is rarely used in practice. There are too many alternatives that must be evaluated, and they must be regularly reevaluated since the most profitable level of investment depends on the sales volume of the firm, which is continually changing. Procedures to handle the computational requirements exist, but differ for each asset. Net present values also are somewhat difficult to calculate and interpret for current assets.

So, instead of net present values, an alternative method is used: maximize average net profit with the amount invested treated as its equivalent annual cost. Let us explore this further.

Suppose we are investing $1000 and will continue to receive $100 per year so long as we keep the $1000 invested. At any time, we can choose to withdraw our $1000 and the annual cash flow of $100 stops. This type of investment is described as being **reversible** since the transaction can be "reversed"; we can get the amount of the investment back if we want to. A savings account is a reversible investment. Current assets are usually evaluated as reversible investments.

One characteristic of reversible investments is that net present values are difficult to interpret. How would you calculate the present value of the above investment given a discount rate of 8 percent?

$$\text{NPV} = -\$1000 + \frac{\$100}{1.08} + \frac{\$100}{(1.08)^2} + \cdots + \frac{\$100}{(1.08)^n} + \frac{\$1000}{(1.08)^n}$$

$$= -\$1000 + \$100(P/A, 8\%, n) + \$1000(P/F, 8\%, n)$$

The above NPV is the present value of the net gain, or profit, from the investment. But there is a problem as to what time period n to use. The net present value depends on the time period you choose. However, the nice thing about reversible investments is that *when* the investment period ends is generally not important. To see this, let's calculate the annuity that has a present value equal to the net present value computed above. This annuity is the average net profit per period from the investment.

$$\text{Net profit} = \text{annuity} = \text{NPV}(A/P, 8\%, n)$$

$$= [-\$1000 + \$100(P/A, 8\%, n)$$
$$+ \$1000(P/F, 8\%, n)](A/P, 8\%, n)$$

$$= \$100(P/A, 8\%, n)(A/P, 8\%, n)$$
$$- [\$1000 - \$1000(P/F, 8\%, n)](A/P, 8\%, n)$$

But, $(P/A, 8\%, n) = 1/(A/P, 8\%, n)$, so

$$\text{Net profit} = \$100 - \$1000[1 - (P/F, 8\%, n)](A/P, 8\%, n)$$

The first term on the right-hand side of the above equation is the annual cash flow of $100. The second term is the annual capital cost of the investment of $1000, and this equals 8 percent of $1000 regardless of the number of periods n of the investment.[1]

---

[1] The annual capital cost of an investment of a given amount is the annuity that has the same present value as the amount invested. In other words, we convert an initial amount invested into its equivalent annuity. The annual capital cost for any reversible investment is the discount rate k times the amount of the investment. We can show this mathematically by expressing the interest rate factors in their algebraic form from Appendix 4A.

$$[1 - (P/F, k, n)](A/P, k, n) = [1 - (1 + k)^{-n}]\left[\frac{k}{1 - (1 + k)^{-n}}\right] = k$$

Therefore,

Net profit = $100 − 0.08($1000)

= $100 − $80

= $20

The $80 is the annual capital cost of the $1000 investment at an 8 percent discount rate, and the annual net profit of $20 does not depend on when the investment is reversed. The result is that we can use net profit per period as a criterion for choosing among alternative reversible investments provided that they have the same risks so that the same discount rate applies to each investment. The investment with the highest value of net profit per period is also the investment with the highest net present value, regardless of when the investment is reversed. Investments with positive NPVs have positive net profits; investments with zero NPVs have zero net profits; and investments with negative NPVs have negative net profits.

Another way to look at the problem is to ask how large the annual cash flow must be to have a positive NPV for a reversible investment. If you require 8 percent on an investment of $1000, you must receive at least $80 per year to make it worthwhile. Any amount over $80 provides you with an NPV greater than zero.

Along similar lines you should note that the internal rate of return (IRR) for a reversible investment is simply the annual cash flow divided by the initial investment. In this example the IRR is 10 percent ($100/$1000). The IRR for a reversible investment with equal periodic cash flows corresponds to the yield to maturity on a coupon-bearing bond selling at its maturity value. Therefore we could use IRR in the evaluation of current asset investments if an incremental approach is used. (See Chapter 8 for a description of the incremental approach.)

Many inventory decisions are made on the basis of minimizing cost. The same procedure as above is valid here. Instead of minimizing the net present value of costs, it is easier to minimize total annual cost where the annual capital cost of the investments is the discount rate times the amount invested. We will discuss this further in the next section, which deals specifically with inventory.

Stating our results more generally, if the discount rate is k percent:

$$\text{Net profit} = (1 - \text{tax rate}) \times (\text{annual cash revenues} \\ - \text{annual cash costs}) - k(\text{investment}) \quad (17\text{-}1)$$

$$\text{Total cost} = (1 - \text{tax rate}) \times (\text{annual cash costs}) \\ + k(\text{investment}) \quad (17\text{-}2)$$

where net profit [Eq. (17-1)] and total cost [Eq. (17-2)] are expressed (following standard practice) as dollar amounts per year.

In the analysis below we will treat current asset investments as reversible and therefore select policies that maximize net profit or minimize total cost. The choice between a profit or cost approach depends on the particular problem being analyzed. The use of NPV is examined in

Appendix 17B. Furthermore, in this chapter we will assume that the decisions regarding investment in each asset can be made independently of the decisions regarding other current assets and current liabilities. In Chapter 20, we will show how to deal with more complex problems.

INVENTORY

Managing the level of investment in inventory is like maintaining the level of water in a bathtub with an open drain. The water is flowing out continuously. If water is let in too slowly, the tub is soon empty. If water is let in too fast, the tub overflows. Like the water in the tub, the particular items in inventory keep changing, but the level may stay the same. The basic financial problems are to determine the proper level of investment in inventory and to decide how much inventory must be acquired during each period to maintain that level. Let's examine the various types of inventory to see how each type is used.

Types of Inventory

Business firms keep inventories for many different purposes. Firms that operate equipment often maintain inventories of spare parts so that breakdowns can be quickly repaired. All firms must have some inventories of office supplies such as paper, pencils, and pens. The three most important types of inventory for most business firms are raw materials, work-in-process, and finished goods. **Raw materials** consist of goods purchased from another firm that are used to manufacture a product. **Work-in-process inventory** contains partially completed goods in process of production. **Finished goods** are goods ready for sale. The classification of a particular item depends on the kind of business being discussed. For a coal mining firm, coal is finished goods. For a steel mill, coal is raw materials, as it will be used in the production of steel. Similarly, steel is finished goods for a steel mill, but raw materials for an automobile manufacturer. Once goods have been produced in a form suitable for the consumer (automobiles, refrigerators, furniture, canned food, etc.), they are classified as finished goods. For example, an automobile dealer purchases automobiles from the factory; therefore in a sense they might be considered raw materials for the dealer. However, since the dealer sells a car essentially as it is to the consumer, an inventory of automobiles is considered finished goods.

The inventory of a manufacturing firm contains all three major types of inventory. Wholesalers, retailers, and other firms involved in the distribution of goods from the manufacturer to the ultimate consumer hold finished goods that have been purchased from another firm. The level of investment in inventory differs greatly for firms in different industries. Table 17-1 shows inventory as a percentage of assets for different types of firms. The figures shown are industry averages. You might speculate on why firms in some industries hold much higher inventories than do firms in other industries. Notice also that inventory investment tends to be greater for distribution firms (wholesalers and retailers) than for manufacturers of the same products.

Although the benefits, costs, and risks vary for every kind of inventory, all inventories have two characteristics in common: (1) Costs must be incurred to acquire inventory and (2) there are costs to holding inventory. Let's analyze this basic case before considering other aspects of inventory investment.

Inventory is constantly being used up. This is true regardless of the type of inventory. Raw materials and work-in-process inventories are used in production. Finished goods are being sold. The rate at which the inventory is being used up is called the **usage** or **sales rate**, depending on the type of inventory. We can express this rate as S units of goods per year. For example, a steel mill may be using 10 million tons of coal per year. A grocery store may be selling 50,000 cans of chicken soup per year. To replace the inventory that is being used up, **orders** must be made. An order may be placed with a supplier (coal mine) or within the production facility of the firm. The person managing the finished goods inventory of a steel mill places an order for more steel bars with the production manager of the mill. An order is for some quantity Q.

If the usage rate is constant, orders can be made at even intervals for the same amount each time, and inventory goes to zero just before an order is received. In this case, the number of units in inventory will be as

---

TABLE 17-1
Average inventory investment for selected businesses

	Inventory/assets, %
Manufacturers:	
Apparel	43.5
Aircraft	30.1
Drugs	27.0
Lumber	23.8
Petroleum refining	17.2
Wholesalers:	
Footwear	45.8
Drugs	42.0
Lumber	32.2
Petroleum products	16.7
Retailers:	
Shoes	64.6
Drugs	51.7
Department stores	43.8
Lumber	38.6
Gasoline stations	18.7
Miscellaneous:	
Soft drink bottlers	13.7
Laundry and dry cleaners	5.7
TV stations	2.8

Source: Robert Morris Associates.

shown in Figure 17-1. For example, suppose that the usage rate is 1200 units per year (100 per month) and orders of 100 units are placed every month. When an order is received, there will be $Q = 100$ units in stock. the amount in stock will be reduced, on average, 100 units/30 days $= 3\frac{1}{3}$ units each day, and at the end of the month inventory will be zero.

The average number of units in stock will be $Q/2$. The average level of investment in this item will be the cash outlay required to acquire each unit (C) times the average number of units.

$$\text{Average investment} = \frac{CQ}{2} \tag{17-3}$$

If the cost per unit is $20, average investment in this item will be $20(\frac{100}{2}) = \$1000$.

From the viewpoint of the person managing the inventory, the basic decisions are how much to order, Q, and when to place the order. From the viewpoint of the financial manager, the decision is what level of investment should be made, $CQ/2$. Regardless of who makes the decision, there are four important types of costs that will be incurred: acquisition costs, order costs, holding costs, and the capital costs.

Acquisition Costs and Quantity Discounts Acquisition costs are the cash costs per period of acquiring inventory (either making goods or buying them). These costs can be calculated as the cash outlay per unit C times the usage rate S,

$$\text{Acquisition cost} = CS \tag{17-4}$$

For purchased goods, C is the purchase price; for goods produced by the firm, C is the cash cost per unit produced. Determining C for goods

---

FIGURE 17-1

Inventory levels over time when usage rate is constant.

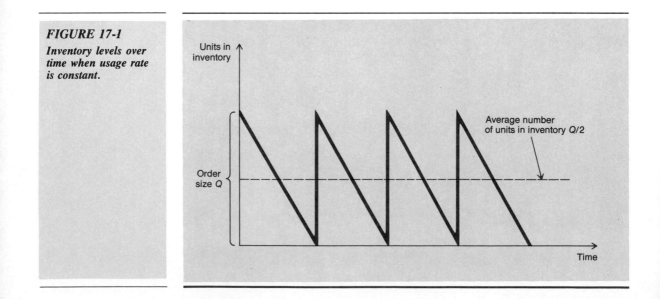

produced by the firm is a difficult problem in cost accounting, so we shall use purchased goods in our examples to keep the variables in the problem clearly defined.

If neither the usage rate S nor the cash outlay per unit C is affected by the order quantity or investment decision, the level of acquisition costs will not affect the decision regarding the level of Q. That is, if acquisition cost is a constant value regardless of the inventory decision, this cost can be ignored in making the decision. However, acquisition costs may vary with the amount ordered, so let's consider this more realistic situation. Note that, although the present example involves purchased goods, the acquisition costs of goods produced by the firm may also vary with the amount ordered; the analysis here also applies to this case.

A **quantity discount** is a reduction in price for ordering more than a minimum quantity of goods at a time. Quantity discounts are usually expressed as a percentage reduction in list price. For example, a discount of 10 percent on orders of 500 units or more for an item with a $20 list price means that the unit price will be $18 ($20 − 0.10 × $20) if the firm orders at least 500 units at a time. Often discounts are available at several levels of order quantity. For example:

Discount, %	Amount ordered (Q)	Price (C)
0	1–99	$20.00
5	100–499	19.00
10	500–999	18.00
15	1,000 and over	17.50

Quantity discounts are normally given to reflect the savings in costs to the supplier from filling large orders. Special, temporary discounts are also occasionally offered when a supplier is overstocked on an item and wishes to reduce inventory quickly.

The effect of a quantity discount is that acquisition cost depends on the quantity ordered Q since the cash outlay per unit C varies with Q. Remember that in analyzing the basic decision we are assuming that the usage rate S is constant. To calculate acquisition cost, we must specify a value for Q. If Q is fifty units, we see from the table above that $C = \$20$ and with a usage rate $S = 1200$ units per year it follows from Eq. (17-4) that

Acquisition cost = $20 × 1200

= $24,000 per year

If $Q = 500$, then $C = \$18$, and

Acquisition cost = $18 × 1200

= $21,600 per year

Order Costs Order costs are the costs that vary with the *number* of orders. In the basic model we assume that every time an order is made, a fixed dollar cost is incurred. For inventories such as work-in-process and finished goods produced by the firm, order costs include any costs of setting up equipment to produce the item. For these inventories the term "set-up costs" is used. Typical types of order and set-up costs are shown in Table 17-2.

The dollar cost of orders in a period depends on how many orders are made in the period and the cost per order. The number of orders per period is

$$\text{Number of orders per period} = \frac{\text{usage rate}}{\text{quantity per order}}$$

$$= \frac{S}{Q} \tag{17-5}$$

With a usage rate of 1200 units per year, if each order is for 10 units, 120 orders must be made per year. However, if 100 units are ordered at a time, only twelve orders per year must be made.

Define the cost per order for a given inventory item as f. The order cost per period for the item is

$$\text{Order cost} = \text{cost per order} \times \text{number of orders}$$

$$= f\frac{S}{Q}$$

$$= \frac{fS}{Q} \tag{17-6}$$

For example, if the cost per order f is \$25 and twelve orders are made per year ($Q = 100$, $S = 1200$), the annual order cost for the item will be

$$\text{Annual order cost} = \$25 \times 12$$

$$= \$300$$

Holding Costs Holding costs are costs due to holding (owning) inventory. Typical kinds of holding costs are shown in Table 17-2. Generally holding cost is calculated as a percentage of the average dollar

---

TABLE 17-2
Typical costs of ordering and holding inventory

Order and setup costs	Holding costs
Transportation costs	Storage costs
Clerical costs of making orders	Fire insurance
Costs of placing goods in storage	Property taxes
Labor costs of equipment setup	Spoilage and deterioration

investment in inventory. The financial manager determines the holding cost rate h by adding up the cost rates for the various kinds of holding costs. For example, suppose the following costs are estimated as percentages of the dollar value of inventory:

$$
\begin{aligned}
\text{Storage costs} &= 2.5\% \text{ per year} \\
\text{Property taxes} &= 1.0\% \text{ per year} \\
\text{Other holding costs} &= 0.5\% \text{ per year} \\
\hline
\text{Holding cost rate } h &= 4.0\% \text{ per year}
\end{aligned}
$$

The holding cost per period is the rate h times average investment in inventory [defined by Eq (17-3)].

Holding cost = holding cost rate × average inventory investment

$$
- h\frac{CQ}{2}
$$

$$
= \frac{hCQ}{2} \tag{17-7}
$$

If 100 units are ordered each time ($Q = 100$) with a price $19 per unit ($C = \$19$), average investment will be $950 ($19 × $\frac{100}{2}$). With a 4 percent annual holding cost rate,

Annual holding cost = $0.04 \times \$950$

$$
= \$38
$$

Capital Cost   Capital cost is the minimum annual dollar return required on the money tied up in inventory. As we discussed earlier in the chapter, a reversible investment can be evaluated on the basis of total costs [Eq. (17-2)] including the capital cost defined here. The discount rate k that applies to investments in inventory may differ for items according to the risk of investing in them.[2] The risks in inventory investment are discussed in the next section. For now we will take the discount rate as given for the item in question.

Capital cost = discount rate × average inventory investment

$$
= k\frac{CQ}{2}
$$

$$
= \frac{kCQ}{2} \tag{17-8}
$$

Given a discount rate k of 10 percent per year and an average investment of $950 ($C = \$19$, $Q = 100$).

Capital cost = $0.10 \times \$950$

$$
= \$95
$$

---

[2] The discount rate (and the average investment) should also reflect the availability and cost of credit from suppliers of a particular item since credit terms affect the dollar cost of inventory.

Total Cost   The total cost of inventory for the basic model can now be expressed by plugging the cost elements we have developed thus far into the general total-cost equation [Eq. (17-2)]:

Total cost = (1 − tax rate) × (acquisition cost + order cost
                                        + holding cost) + capital cost

$$= (1 - \tau) \times \left(CS + \frac{fS}{Q} + \frac{hCQ}{2}\right) + \frac{kCQ}{2} \qquad (17\text{-}9)$$

where τ is the tax rate. The capital cost is not multiplied by $(1 - \tau)$ since k is an aftertax discount rate. (In this book, all discount rates used for investment decisions are rates that apply to after-corporate-tax cash flows; this includes the average cost of capital defined in Chapter 7 and used in Chapter 8.) The decision variable in this equation is Q, the quantity ordered. Alternatively, we would express the total-cost equation as

$$\text{Total cost} = (1 - \tau) \times \left(CS + \frac{fCS}{2I} + hI\right) + kI \qquad (17\text{-}10)$$

where I is the average level of investment ($I = CQ/2$). Regardless of which way the equation is written or whether Q or I is considered to be the decision variable, we wish to minimize total cost.

We will examine two approaches to finding the minimum cost solution. First we will present a special case of the basic model that applies when acquisition costs do not vary with order quantity; then we will show the more general solution.

The EOQ Model   When acquisition costs do not vary with the quantity ordered, the quantity to be ordered that minimizes total cost in Eq. (17-9) can be calculated from a formula. This optimal amount to order is often called the **economic order quantity** or "EOQ" and the formula for its value is

$$\text{EOQ} = \sqrt{\frac{2(1 - \tau)fS}{(1 - \tau)\,hC + kC}} \qquad (17\text{-}11)$$

The EOQ formula is derived by manipulating the total-cost equation [Eq. (17-9)] to find the value of Q that minimizes total cost. This is done in Appendix 17A. A graph of total costs and its two major components, order costs and carrying costs, are shown in Figure 17-2. Carrying costs are holding costs plus capital cost. Both holding costs and capital cost increase with the amount ordered whereas order costs decrease as the quantity ordered increases.

Suppose that the following values are given:

Usage rate	$S = 1200$ units per year
Cost per order	$f = \$25$ per order
Holding cost rate	$h = 4\%$ per year
Discount rate	$k = 10\%$ per year
Tax rate	$\tau = 30\%$
Price per unit	$C = \$20$ per unit for all order quantities

Then, plugging these values into the formula,

$$EOQ = \sqrt{\frac{2(1 - \tau)\,fS}{(1 - \tau)\,hC + kC}}$$

$$= \sqrt{\frac{2(0.7)(25)(1200)}{(0.7)(0.04)(20) + (.10)(20)}}$$

$$= \sqrt{\frac{42,000}{2.56}} = \sqrt{16,406}$$

$$= 128 \text{ units}$$

The optimal amount to order would be 128 units.[3]

Solving the Basic Model The EOQ formula applies only when acquisition costs are not affected by the quantity ordered. To solve the more general case including the possibility of quantity discounts (or any other variations in acquisition costs), the easiest method is to calculate total cost for different amounts to be ordered (Q) given values for the other variables in Eq. (17-9). The value of Q that minimizes total cost can be read from a table of the results of the calculation or determined from a graph of the results.

---

[3] Total cost does not change very much for orders between 120 and 130 units, so a more convenient order quantity than 128 units, such as 130 units or 120 units (10 dozen), might well be used in practice.

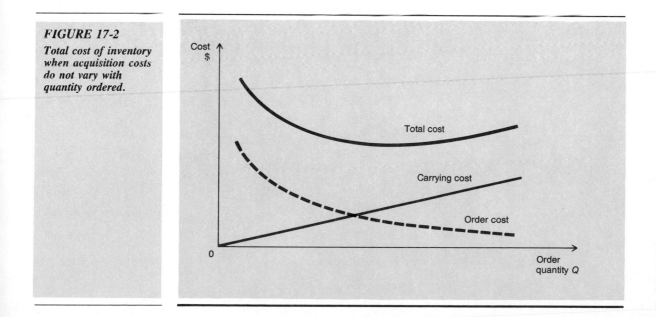

FIGURE 17-2

Total cost of inventory when acquisition costs do not vary with quantity ordered.

Exhibit 17-1 shows several such calculations using the example data, and Figure 17-3 is a graph of total cost as the quantity ordered increases. The "jumps" in the curve reflect the quantity discounts provided at quantities of 100, 500, and 1000 units ordered. As can be seen both from Exhibit 17-1 and Figure 17-3, total cost is minimized at $Q = 500$ units, which means that average inventory investment in this item is

$$I = \frac{CQ}{2}$$

$$= \frac{\$18 \times 500}{2}$$

$$= \$4500$$

The basic inventory decision is to find the order size or average level of investment that produces a minimum total cost. Small, frequent orders allow a low level of investment that has low holding cost and low capital cost, but frequent orders are expensive because of order costs and because quantity discounts may not be available. Large, infrequent orders keep order costs down and may provide quantity discounts that

---

EXHIBIT 17-1
Total cost calculated for various order quantities

Total cost = (1 − tax rate) × (acquisition cost + order cost + holding cost) + capital cost

Quantity Q	Acquisition cost CS	Order cost $\frac{fS}{Q}$	Holding cost $\frac{hCQ}{2}$	Capital cost $\frac{kCQ}{2}$	Total cost
50	$24,000	$600	$ 20	$ 50	$17,284
100	22,800	300	38	95	16,292
120	22,800	250	46	114	16,281
200	22,800	150	76	190	16,308
300	22,800	100	114	285	16,395
400	22,800	75	152	350	16,469
500	21,600	60	180	450	15,738
800	21,600	38	288	720	16,068
1,000	21,000	30	350	875	15,841
1,200	21,000	25	420	1,050	16,062

Assumptions	Quantity discount schedule	
	Quantity (Q)	Price (C)
Usage rate S = 1,200 units per year	1–99	$20.00
Cost per order f = $25 per order	100–499	$19.00
Holding cost rate h = 4% per year	500–999	$18.00
Discount rate k = 10% per year	1,000 and over	$17.50
Tax rate τ = 30%		

cause high holding cost and high capital cost. The best inventory decision is the one that balances all types of costs so that total cost is minimized.

*Benefits from
Inventory Investment*

An alternative way to think of the basic inventory decision is that increasing investment in inventory provides benefits from a reduction in order costs and from the possibility of quantity discounts. This benefit is offset by the increase in holding costs and the requirement that inventory investment provide a satisfactory rate of return, the discount rate k. Now let's look at some other benefits from inventory investment that are not directly related to order quantity.

Avoiding Stockouts   In our development of the basic model we implicitly assumed that the usage rate was known precisely and that we knew exactly when an order would be received once it was placed. These assumptions are not usually valid in practice. Suppose the firm tried to use the solution developed above. The average usage rate is 1200 units per year or 100 units per month. Every five months an order will be placed for 500 units. If it takes a month between the time an order is placed and the time it is received, an order must be placed when the inventory reaches 100 units, which is one month's supply. What happens if the demand for the item is greater than 100 units in the month before the order is received or if the order takes forty-five days to arrive? The firm will not have enough units in stock to satisfy the demand. This is called a **stockout**.

FIGURE 17-3

Total cost of inventory as a function of order quantity.

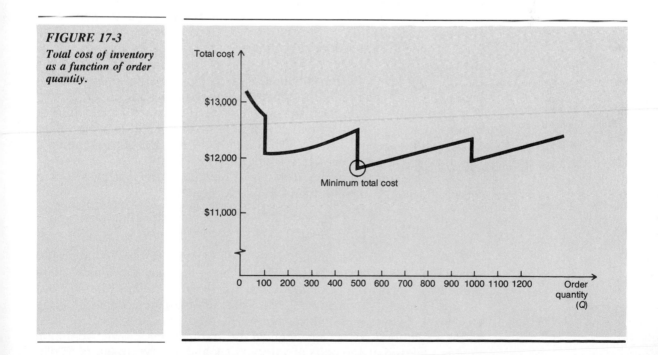

Stockouts are expensive. If the inventory item is finished goods, the customer may buy the goods from someone else; therefore, the profits on the sale will be lost. Even if the customer is willing to wait until the goods arrive, some goodwill is lost. If a firm is often not able to supply goods when customers want them, its reputation suffers and it will lose business—more business than just the orders that were not filled for lack of inventory.

Stockouts of raw materials or work-in-process can cause the production process to stop. This will be expensive because employees will be paid for time not spent in producing goods or, if they are temporarily laid off, the firm will be assessed higher unemployment taxes. Some production processes are so expensive to shut down that management will go to great lengths to avoid running out of raw materials. There exists a company whose business is flying parts to automobile assembly plants so that they won't have to shut down when they run out of a critical item. The cost to the automobile manufacturer of having parts flown in by private jet planes can be several times the cost of the parts themselves. However, paying the high cost of transportation is preferable to shutting down an entire plant.

To avoid stockouts, firms maintain **safety stocks** of inventory. Safety stock is the minimum level of inventory desired for an item given the expected usage rate and the expected time to receive an order. In our example, if an order is placed when the inventory reaches 150 units instead of 100 units, the additional 50 units constitute the safety stock. The manager expects to have 50 units in stock when the new order arrives. The safety stock protects the firm from stockouts due to unanticipated demand for the item or to slow deliveries. Increasing the amount of inventory held as safety stock reduces the chances of a stockout and therefore reduces stockout costs over the long run. The level of inventory investment is, however, increased by the amount of the safety stock.

The best level of safety stock for a given item depends on how much a stockout costs and on the variability of usage rates and delivery times. If the usage rate and the delivery time can be forecast with a high degree of accuracy and if the cost of a stockout is small, then little or no safety stock will be needed. If the circumstances are not so favorable, then a significant investment in safety stock will be desirable.

A simple solution to the problem is to examine the costs associated with a given level of investment in safety stock.

$$\text{Safety stock costs} = (1 - \text{tax rate}) \times (\text{expected stockout cost} + \text{holding costs}) + \text{capital cost} \qquad (17\text{-}12)$$

Holding cost can be calculated as the holding cost rate times the dollar investment in safety stock. Capital cost is the discount rate times safety stock investment. Expected stockout cost must be estimated at various levels of inventory investment. Given the cost estimates, we wish to find that level of investment which minimizes total cost. Exhibit 17-2 illustrates a solution to the problem given the assumptions shown. Minimum cost is achieved at 150 units of safety stock and an investment of $2700.

A complete solution to the problem of determining the proper level of safety stock for an item is complex and beyond the scope of this text. For example, the frequency of orders affects the number of stockouts for any given level of safety stock. Therefore the order quantity decision affects the safety stock decision and, in general, the two decisions must be analyzed together. Since some costs, such as loss of customer goodwill, are very difficult to estimate accurately, safety stocks are typically established by rules of thumb and managerial judgment. Depending on the type of inventory, avoiding stockouts is important to production or marketing management. The financial manager's role in the decision is often that of reminding other members of management that money

---

EXHIBIT 17-2

Total cost of safety stock investment

Total cost = (1 − tax rate) × (expected stockout cost + holding cost) + capital cost

Safety stock u	Investment Cu	Expected stockout cost sN	Holding cost hCu	Capital cost kCu	Total cost
0	$ 0	$2,000	$ 0	$ 0	$1,400
25	450	1,200	18	45	898
50	900	800	36	90	675
100	1,800	400	72	180	510
150	2,700	80	108	270	402
200	3,600	0	144	360	461

Assumptions and definitions

Investment Cu = cash outlay per unit C × number of units of safety stock u
Cash outlay per unit C = $18
Holding cost hCu = holding cost rate h × investment Cu
Holding cost rate h = 4% per year
Capital cost kCu = discount rate k × investment Cu
Discount rate k = 10% per year
Tax rate τ = 30%
Expected stockout cost sN = stockout cost per stockout s × number of stockouts per year N
Stockout cost per stockout s = $40

Stockout estimates

Safety stock u, units	Number of stockouts per year N
0	50
25	30
50	20
100	10
150	2
200	0

invested in inventory should earn at least the cost of capital. Therefore, total avoidance of stockouts by maintaining large safety stocks is usually not the best solution.

Marketing Benefits   So far we have discussed the benefits and costs of investing in individual inventory items. We have not considered the decision as to what items to stock. Generally the wider is the variety of items stocked, the higher total inventory investment will be. What benefits are derived from stocking many types of inventory?

Most items in raw materials and work-in-process inventories of manufacturing firms are necessary in that production cannot proceed without them. The decision as to what items produced by the manufacturer will be kept in finished goods inventories depends on the frequency of customer orders for the item, the time required to produce it, how important rapid delivery times are to customers, and the costs of carrying the item in stock. However, the demand for an item may depend on whether it is normally available. This problem is similar to the problem of determining the proper level of safety stocks. In both cases the sales and profits foregone as a result of not having an item in stock must be evaluated.

A further consideration is the extent to which having a more complete inventory in terms of the number of items stocked increases sales of all items. Most customers purchase more than one item at a time. A manufacturer who stocks a complete line of products is likely to obtain more business on each item than one who stocks only the items in greatest demand.

The decision as to which items to stock is of particular importance to distribution firms such as retailers and wholesalers, since their businesses are based on the availability of goods to meet their customers' demands. Inventory decisions are therefore very much related to the marketing approach used by the firm. For example, Levitz Furniture Corporation virtually revolutionized furniture retailing early in the 1970s by its marketing strategies that included maintaining an unusually large inventory of furniture.

Inventory Speculation   During periods when the prices of purchased items are rising rapidly, firms have an incentive to invest more heavily in inventory than is indicated by the minimum cost calculation. If management believes the price of an item will increase by 10 percent in the next month, substantially more of that item may be ordered than normal. **Inventory speculation** is the term used to describe this extra investment.

The financial manager must keep speculative investment in inventory within prudent limits, since it can be both expensive and risky if carried to extremes. During inflationary periods, interest rates are usually high and so the discount rate is high. An unusually large inventory may require the firm to rent additional storage space as well as to incur all the normal holding costs. There is always the possibility that demand for the item will fall and the firm will be stuck with a large inventory for a long time. This possibility raises the problem of risk in inventory investment. The risks are not inconsequential, so let's look at them.

Risks in Inventory Investment

The main risk in inventory investment is that the market value of inventory may fall below what the firm paid for it, thereby causing inventory losses. The sources of market value risk depend on the type of inventory. Purchased inventory of manufactured goods is subject to losses due to changes in technology. Such changes may sharply reduce final prices of the goods when they are sold or may even make the goods unsalable. This risk is, of course, most acute in products embodying a high degree of technological sophistication, for example, electronic parts. Distributors of personal computers experienced this problem in the early 1980s as prices on some computers dropped 50 percent in less than a year as new designs were introduced. Essentially, firms shouldn't have a lot of buggy whips in stock when buggies are becoming obsolete.

There are also substantial risks in inventories of goods dependent on current styles. The clothing industry is particularly susceptible to the risk of changing consumer tastes. A merchant with a large stock of blue denim pants is in trouble if corduroy becomes the fashion.

Agricultural commodities are a type of inventory subject to risks due to unpredictable changes in production and demand. A bumper crop of a commodity like corn or cocoa can send prices plummeting. Of course, there is also the potential for shortages in these commodities, which cause rapid price rises.

All inventories are exposed to losses due to spoilage, shrinkage, theft, or other risks of this sort. Insurance is available to cover many of these risks and, if purchased, it is one of the costs of holding inventory.

The financial manager must be aware of the degree of risk involved in the firm's investment in inventories. The manager must take those risks into account in evaluating the appropriate level of inventory investment. This can be done by including predictable losses as part of the holding costs and by applying a higher discount rate to those items that are subject to greater risks.

International Inventory Management

In addition to the basic *how much* inventory policy question, an MNC must also decide *where* inventory is to be held. In the absence of political considerations, the answer is wherever the inventory is needed for production (in the case of raw materials) or sales (in the case of finished goods). Like the domestic firm, the international corporation will select the number and the locations of storage facilities that minimize transportation and inventory costs. If the MNC has production facilities and markets in several different countries, this can be a complicated analysis.

There are, however, a number of political and regulatory exceptions that convince firms to deviate from an otherwise optimal inventory policy. If there is any chance of asset expropriation in an unstable country, for example, the MNC should maintain as little inventory there as possible. A mining operation might ship small batches of extracted minerals out of an unstable country as soon as they are processed —even if small shipments are more costly. Instead of outright assets seizure, some governments have simply limited exports. An MNC that is dependent on raw materials from an unstable country may decide to stockpile a large amount of inventory, regardless of holding and capital costs, to combat the possibility of supply disruptions. The multinational firm may also move inventory from one country to another in anticipation of import quotas and tariffs. For example, suppose that an American firm markets a product in France. If the French government announces an increase in import tariffs, the MNC may try to move all its inventory to its French subsidiary before the new tariffs become effective. Difference in property tax rates or regulations can motivate an MNC to transfer more of its inventory to a low tax rate country. Some MNCs hold significant amounts of inventory in offshore ships to avoid property taxes altogether. All these factors complicate international inventory management.

MANAGING ACCOUNTS RECEIVABLE

Accounts receivable is the total of all credit extended by a firm to its customers; therefore this balance sheet account represents unpaid bills owed to the firm. From the viewpoint of the financial manager the dollar amount of accounts receivable can be divided into two parts. One part represents the cash outlays made by the firm in providing the goods that have been sold. The other part is the difference between the cash outlay and the selling prices of the goods. The cash outlay portion is the actual investment by the firm in accounts receivable; the remainder represents accounting profits. The nature of accounts receivable is illustrated by the following example.

Suppose a wholesaler of automobile parts buys mufflers from the manufacturer at a price of $20 each. The wholesaler has invested $20 in each muffler in inventory plus cash expenses associated with inventory investment (holding costs and order costs) of $1 per muffler on average. The cash outlay per muffler is $21. The firm sells ten mufflers to a garage for $26 each on credit. It costs the wholesaler $5 cash expenses to sell and deliver the ten mufflers. The cash outlay by the firm is now $215 for the ten mufflers, $200 initial cost plus $10 inventory expense plus $5 selling and delivery expense. The garage owes the wholesaler $260 for the ten mufflers. This is an account receivable. The cash investment (out-of-pocket costs) in this account is $215 and the remaining $45 represents accounting profits. What has happened is a transformation of real assets, mufflers owned by the wholesaler, into a financial asset, money owed by the garage to the wholesaler.

What if the garage never pays for the mufflers? The wholesaler will lose the $215 it has spent in acquiring, holding, and selling the goods—nothing more.[4] The $215 therefore measures the investment made by the wholesaler in this account.

---

[4] The $45 that was added to the firm's pretax profits when the sale was recorded is a "loss" from the perspective of the firm's accounting, but the net effect of $45 profit less $45 loss is zero.

The basic decision to be made regarding accounts receivable is how much credit to extend to a given customer and on what terms. However, the financial manager sets policies that have a great deal to do with this decision, and it is these policies that we will examine. Let us begin with an analysis of credit extension to a single customer and then see how general credit policies affect this decision and therefore the total investment in accounts receivable.

The Credit Decision

Business firms extend credit to three groups of customers—other business firms, individual consumers, and governmental units. We will confine our analysis to firms selling either to other businesses or to individuals. Governmental units are similar enough to business firms to require no special treatment in an introductory discussion.

Consumer Credit   Businesses selling goods to individual consumers normally provide some sort of credit terms for purchases. The major exceptions are the supermarkets. However, most small merchants do not provide this credit directly themselves; they accept **credit cards**. Sales made with credit cards do not create accounts receivable for the merchant; the issuer of the card (a bank, American Express, etc.) pays the merchant when it is notified of the charge. The issuer of the credit card has the accounts receivable. Large merchants (such as department stores) usually extend credit directly to the consumer. Sales made on credit by these merchants do create accounts receivable for them.

All credit decisions are based primarily on the creditor's assessment of the customer's likelihood of payment. Setting a maximum on the amount of credit offered to a customer limits the exposure of the firm to the risk that the customer won't pay. In deciding to provide credit to a customer, the credit manager must evaluate the chances of nonpayment and estimate the benefits of extending credit. The benefits result from the additional sales obtained and any interest or fees charged for the credit. Consumer credit extending beyond thirty days usually carries with it an interest charge.

Risk assessment is a quantitative analysis of the likelihood that a customer won't pay for goods purchased on credit, and it assists the credit manager in deciding whether credit should be extended to a particular customer. Consumers applying for credit supply information about themselves that the firm evaluates. The firm may also seek information about customers from a credit bureau. Credit bureaus gather information on the credit history of people and sell it to businesses extending credit. People who have failed to pay their bills in the past are viewed as greater credit risks than those who have an unblemished credit record. The information supplied by the individual and the credit bureau is evaluated in terms of the firm's experience with customers having similar characteristics. For example, firms have found that people who own their own home are more likely to pay their bills than those who rent. On the basis of this evidence renters would be looked upon less favorably than home owners when they apply for credit. The types of information asked for may include employment history, income, home ownership, checking and savings accounts, other assets and outstanding debts. The extent of the information asked for depends on the size of the typical credit purchases at the firm. If a large amount of credit is being extended, more information will be requested.

The end result of this risk assessment is the classification of a credit customer into one of a set of **risk classes**. Large firms may use computerized statistical methods. An example classification scheme is shown in Exhibit 17-3.

The general credit policy of the firm will specify which classes of customers will be extended credit. Since the considerations of general credit policy are similar for both business customers and consumers, we will discuss them together after we look at the credit decision for business customers.

Business Credit   The majority of the sales by one business firm to another are made on **open account**. That is, the buyer is not required to pay for the goods immediately on receiving them and does not sign a formal debt contract. The buyer is asked to pay for the goods within a specified period, typically thirty days. The seller may also offer a discount or reduction in the cost of the goods if payment is made sooner. For example, the buyer might get 1 percent off the amount of the invoice if payment is made within ten days. The **credit terms** of the seller involve the specification of the type of account (open account or some other arrangement), the credit period (when payment is due), the size of the discount, and a discount period. A description of various credit terms is provided in Chapter 19 (see Table 19-1). In addition, the seller usually sets a limit on how much credit will be extended to a particular customer. Once the customer has reached the limit, no further sales on credit are made until some of the amount owed is paid off.

Generally, the credit terms of a company selling in a particular market are competitively determined in the market. The firms in a given line of business usually have very similar credit terms, and the credit

---

EXHIBIT 17-3
Risk classification

Class	Average loss ratio, %
1	Negligible
2	0.5
3	1.0
4	4.0
5	10.0
6	25.0
7	50.0

terms of a firm will apply to all customers in that market. Credit terms are not normally varied from customer to customer.[5] This is true of consumer credit as well. The decisions regarding a particular customer are whether or not to extend credit at all and what the maximum amount extended should be.

In making the decision to extend credit to a particular firm, the credit manager will seek information about its financial condition and past history. The primary source of information is credit agencies, such as Dun and Bradstreet, that provide credit ratings and credit reports on firms throughout the country. From this information the credit manager will attempt to determine the degree of risk involved in extending credit to the customer. In other words, the credit manager tries to estimate how likely it is that the firm will pay its bills. If the amount of credit involved is large, and if a cursory investigation suggests that the financial condition of the firm is weak, the credit manager may seek additional information by requesting financial statements from the firm. Techniques such as ratio analysis are often used to evaluate the financial condition of the firm. However, even if there is a significant chance of loss present, the credit manager must also consider the potential profits to be gained from selling to the customer. If the credit manager turns down the request for credit, the customer is likely to buy from someone else. A firm that has no bad debt losses is likely to be turning away many customers to whom it would be profitable to extend credit. Once a customer has been identified as being risky, the limits on credit become important. By restricting the amount of credit extended to a customer with financial problems, the potential loss is limited.

The techniques developed to classify consumers as to credit risk are not easily applied to business firms. Assessing the risk of extending credit to a business firm is much more of an art than a science, and experienced credit managers tend to rely heavily on their assessment of the "moral character" of the firm's owners and managers as it relates to their tendency to pay their creditors. However, if the credit manager has not had past dealings with the people requesting credit, the manager must rely on financial data and on the firm's past record with respect to other creditors.

Customer Attributes Credit managers base their evaluations of the risk in extending credit on their assessments of the attributes of the particular customer. Customer attributes can be summarized by the "five C's" of credit—character, capacity, conditions, capital, and collateral.

> **Character** is a customer's own desire to pay off debts. As indicated above, experienced credit managers consider this to be the most important attribute.

---

[5] Occasionally a customer may negotiate special terms; for example, to be able to delay payment for 90 days instead of 30 days. In such cases, the seller often charges interest for the extended credit.

Capacity is the ability of a customer to pay debts as reflected in the cash flows of the individual or firm.

Conditions are the general economic circumstances of the firm's industry or the individual's employment.

Capital refers to the financial strength of the customer, which depends primarily on the customer's net worth relative to outstanding debt obligations.

Collateral is any asset that the customer has available to pledge against the debt.

These attributes are assessed by examining financial data for the customer and by obtaining credit reports from firms that provide this service such as Dun and Bradstreet (for businesses) or credit bureaus (for individuals).

Credit Policy

Decisions regarding extension of credit to particular customers of the firm are based in part on general credit policy. If the firm has a policy of being fairly restrictive as to its credit terms and the customers to whom it will extend credit, it will have a lower investment in accounts receivable, lower bad debt losses, and very likely lower sales volume. Conversely, as the firm provides easier credit terms and sells on credit to poorer credit risks, its sales will rise but so too will its bad debt losses and level of accounts receivable.

In evaluating a proposed change in credit policy, the financial manager must estimate the impact of the change on the firm's cash flows (collections of accounts receivable, cash sales, cash expenses, and taxes). To highlight the impact of credit policies on accounts receivable, we will look at a firm whose inventories are not affected by changes in sales, as might be true for a firm selling services rather than products. In Chapter 20 we will show how to deal with situations when several current asset and liability accounts are affected by credit policy decisions.

Suppose that the financial manager of an industrial cleaning firm, Cleanall Company, is considering the adoption of a new credit policy. Cleanall, at present, is paid when it completes a job. The typical job takes one week and the company's sales average $2000 per week. Cleanall pays its employees and suppliers weekly. Its variable costs average 75 percent of sales. In a typical week the company would take in $2000 from its customers and pay out $1500 (0.75 × $2000) in cash expenses associated with its sales. The company's cash income therefore averages $500 per week, as shown in Figure 17-4a.

Cleanall is considering offering credit terms to its customers that would allow them to pay four weeks after completion of the work. These terms are expected to increase sales by 20 percent to $2400 per week. Its variable cash expenses would therefore increase to $1800 (0.75 × $2400). Management expects that all customers will pay in four weeks except for some that will not pay at all. Bad debt losses under the new terms are expected to average 1 percent of sales. As a result, cash

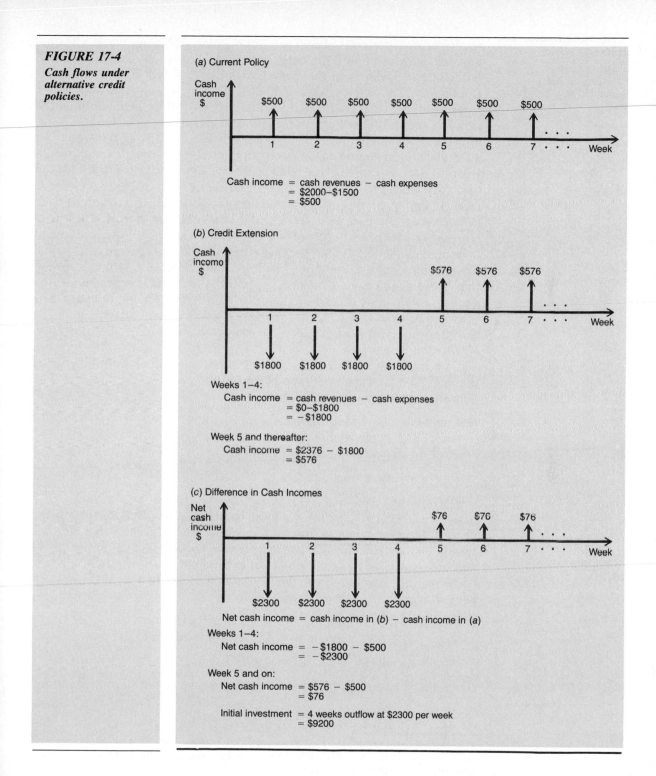

FIGURE 17-4

Cash flows under alternative credit policies.

(a) Current Policy

Cash income $

$500 $500 $500 $500 $500 $500 $500

1 2 3 4 5 6 7 · · · Week

Cash income = cash revenues − cash expenses
= $2000−$1500
= $500

(b) Credit Extension

Cash income $

$576 $576 $576

1 2 3 4 5 6 7 · · · Week

$1800 $1800 $1800 $1800

Weeks 1−4:
Cash income = cash revenues − cash expenses
= $0−$1800
= −$1800

Week 5 and thereafter:
Cash income = $2376 − $1800
= $576

(c) Difference in Cash Incomes

Net cash income $

$76 $76 $76

1 2 3 4 5 6 7 · · · Week

$2300 $2300 $2300 $2300

Net cash income = cash income in (b) − cash income in (a)

Weeks 1−4:
Net cash income = −$1800 − $500
= −$2300

Week 5 and on:
Net cash income = $576 − $500
= $76

Initial investment = 4 weeks outflow at $2300 per week
= $9200

revenues are expected to be 99 percent of sales, $2376 per week. Cleanall will not offer discounts for early payment. Any such discounts would reduce cash revenues in the same fashion as bad debt losses.

Figure 17-4*b* shows what happens if the new policy is adopted at week zero. No cash is received for four weeks, but in the meantime, the firm has cash expenses of $1800 per week at the new sales level. Thereafter cash revenues minus cash expenses average $576 per week. The difference (incremental cash flows) between the two policies is shown in Figure 17-4*c*. We will use the $9200 difference in initial cash flows for the first four weeks as the initial cash investment. The $9200 is an investment in the sense that it is a reduction in the initial (first month) cash flows. After the first four weeks, the firm obtains the benefits of an increase in pretax cash flow of $76 per week. This cash flow is assumed to continue indefinitely, but the investment could be reversed at any time by switching back to requiring cash on completion of all jobs. Suppose that Cleanall has a tax rate of 25 percent. For simplicity, we lump the annual cash income of $3952 (52 weeks and $76 per week) at the end of a year and assume that taxes are paid then.[6] The annual aftertax addition to the firm's cash flow is therefore expected to be $(1 - 0.25)\$3952 = \$2964$.

We can evaluate the desirability of this change in credit policy using the net profit approach outlined earlier in the chapter [Eq. (17-1)].[7] The definition of net profit we will use is

$$
\begin{aligned}
\text{Net profit} = {} & (1 - \tau)(\text{additional cash revenues} \\
& \quad - \text{additional cash expenses}) \\
& - k(\text{additional investment}) \\[6pt]
= {} & \text{additional aftertax cash income} \\
& - \text{additional capital cost.} \qquad\qquad (17\text{-}13)
\end{aligned}
$$

where τ is the firm's tax rate and k is the applicable discount rate. If the change to a new credit policy provides a net profit greater than zero, it should be adopted. We will assume that an appropriate value for k is 11 percent. Later we discuss how k is determined.

With this information in hand we can calculate the net profit expected from the change in credit terms as

$$
\begin{aligned}
\text{Net profit} = {} & \$2964 \text{ increase in aftertax cash income} \\
& - 11 \text{ percent} \times \$9200 \text{ cash investment} \\[6pt]
= {} & \$2964 - \$1012 = \$1952
\end{aligned}
$$

Since the net profit is positive, the new terms are worth implementing.

---

[6] In practice, taxes are usually paid quarterly. Also, taxes are based on sales less expenses associated with sales and do not affect the initial investment. In Appendix 17B, we show what happens to cash flows when taxes are paid quarterly.

[7] We show how the net present value method may be used to evaluate decisions of this sort in Appendix 17B.

Another way to look at the cash investment is to consider what is happening to the firm's accounts receivable. Under the new policy, Cleanall's accounts receivable would increase from zero to $9600 ($2400 sales per week × 4 weeks). However, this increase in accounts receivable overstates the cash investment required to implement the policy. Two things are happening. First, relative to the current policy of cash sales, the firm will not receive $2000 per week for four weeks when the new terms are initially offered. Thus $8000 ($2000 × 4) of the accounts receivable represents the slowdown in cash collections that will occur. That is, if Cleanall institutes the new policy, there will be an initial period of four weeks for which it will not receive the payments that it has been getting. Of the remaining $1600 in accounts receivable, only the additional cash outlays the firm will have to make to achieve higher sales should be counted. The additional cash expenses are $300 per week, and four weeks of those expenses amount to $1200 ($300 × 4). Therefore, the initial cash outlay due to the new policy and reflected in the increase in accounts receivable amounts to:

Additional investment = $8000 due to slower collections
+ $1200 due to increased cash expenses

= $9200

This is the same answer we got by examining the cash flows. The remaining $400 in accounts receivable reflects accounting profit, not cash flows.[8]

This brings us to the next issue, the determination of the discount rate k to apply to this type of investment. As we have discussed in Chapter 10, the appropriate rate depends on the risk. What is the risk in accounts receivable investment?

Risk in Accounts Receivable

Accounts receivable is generally considered a relatively low-risk asset. The basic risk is due to the possibility that the firm will not be able to collect all that is owed to it by its customers. Under normal circumstances the total bad debt losses a firm will experience can be forecast with reasonable accuracy, especially if the firm sells to a large number of customers and does not change its credit policies. These "normal" losses can be considered purely a cost of extending credit. In the Cleanall example above, we subtracted expected losses from expected cash revenues. The real risk arises from the possibility that a significant number of the firm's customers may suddenly get into financial difficulties. For example, suppose an appliance dealer is located near a large industrial plant and 90 percent of its accounts receivable represent credit

---

[8] This is the approach suggested by Edward A. Dyl, "Another Look at the Evaluation of Investment in Accounts Receivable," *Financial Management*, 6 (Winter 1977), pp. 71–74. Note also that if we make an allowance for bad debts of 1 percent, net accounts receivable will be $9504 ($9600 − 0.01 × $9600). However, this reduction in accounts receivable is due to a reduction in the accounting profit, not the cash investment portion.

sales to the plant's employees. If, for some reason, the plant shuts down for an extended period of time, the dealer is likely to be unable to collect an unusually large portion of the accounts receivable. There are companies that provide insurance against unusual losses (credit insurance), and this is one way to reduce the risk. In most cases, accounts receivable is not a particularly risky asset and the discount rate that should be used in evaluating a credit policy is less than the firm's average cost of capital.

The Risks of Foreign Accounts Receivables

There are three reasons why extending credit to foreign customers is riskier than extending it to domestic customers. First, it is more difficult to determine the creditworthiness of firms or individuals in other countries. Differences in business practices, accounting regulations, and culture, as well as the long distances involved, make it expensive to obtain and evaluate foreign credit information. Second, if a foreign customer refuses or is unable to pay, it will be much more difficult and expensive to collect the receivable. Foreign lawyers must be hired, and the firm must rely on a foreign court to enforce the contract. Third, receivables denominated in a foreign currency are subject to currency exchange risk, and the home currency value of foreign accounts carries a greater risk than receivables from a domestic customer, even if they have the same credit rating. Suppose that Marker International, a United States–based manufacturer of ski equipment, sells $10,000 in bindings to a Danish distributor. Given the current exchange rate of 4 Danish krone per dollar, Marker sets the payment terms at 40,000 krone in 90 days. If the exchange rate rises to 5 krone per dollar in the next three months, the value of the payment will drop to $8000.

There are several ways to manage foreign credit and currency exchange risk. If payment is demanded in the home currency, the exchange risk can be transferred to the foreign buyer. For example, Marker could require payment terms of $10,000 (U.S.) in 90 days, giving the Danish distributor the responsibility of bearing the exchange rate. The Danish firm, of course, will want some compensation for taking this risk—a lower price, for example—or it may take its business elsewhere. Marker International could also elect to eliminate the exchange rate risk by an offsetting transaction in the forward exchange market or the money market for Danish krone.

Letters of credit can be used to eliminate foreign credit risk. A letter of credit is essentially a guarantee from the foreign buyer's bank that payment will be made in full. The credit risk is then absorbed by the foreign buyer's local bank, which is in a better position to evaluate the buyer's creditworthiness. The seller can either rely on the creditworthiness of the foreign bank or obtain a confirmation from a domestic bank. Letters of credit are examined in more depth in Chapter 19.

Monitoring Accounts Receivable

After establishing general policies as to credit terms and acceptable credit risks, the financial manager must continuously monitor investment in accounts receivable. The manager will be concerned with the actual payment habits of the firm's customers. The more slowly customers pay, the larger will be the firm's investment in accounts receivable. Some customers may not pay at all, resulting in bad debt losses. The average collection period for accounts receivable provides a simple measurement of the average number of days customers take to pay.

$$\text{Average collection period} = \frac{\text{accounts receivable}}{\text{credit sales per day}} \qquad (17\text{-}14)$$

For example, suppose that accounts receivable on June 30 is $180,000 and that sales made on credit (excluding cash sales) in June were $120,000.[9] Credit sales in June averaged $4000 per day ($120,000/30 days) and

$$\text{Average collection period} = \frac{\$180,000}{\$4000 \text{ per day}}$$

$$- \ 45 \text{ days}$$

If the credit terms provided by the company were 30 days, the financial manager would conclude that customers are paying, on average, 15 days (45 days − 30 days) late. The manager may wish to investigate the problem in more depth at this point. The next stage might be to examine an aging schedule of accounts receivable. An aging schedule categorizes the accounts by the time since the sales were made. For example, the $180,000 balance might have the following aging schedule:[10]

Days outstanding	Accounts receivable	Percent of total
0–30 days	$100,000	56%
31–60 days	40,000	22
61–90 days	25,000	14
Over 90 days	15,000	8
Total	$180,000	100%

The financial manager would be particularly concerned with the accounts that are over 60 days outstanding (over 30 days past due), since these customers might not pay at all. At this point an examination of these customers and their financial condition might be made and efforts made to collect the accounts. Monitoring the ratio of bad debt losses to credit sales is also important if losses are to be controlled. The financial

[9] Generally it is best to use sales for the most recent period corresponding roughly to the expected average collection period. For example, instead of using just June sales, both May and June sales might be used since accounts receivable are clearly greater than June sales.

[10] Another way to express the amount of accounts receivable outstanding is as a percentage of the sales in the period. For example, of the $120,000 sales in June, 83.3 percent ($100,000/$120,000) is uncollected.

manager will be concerned both with the ratio's level (is it larger than anticipated?) and trend (is it increasing or decreasing?).

SUMMARY

This chapter described the problems of determining the level of investment in current assets. Investment in current assets differs from fixed-assets investment because the amount may vary substantially over short periods of time and the investment is reversible. For these reasons, net profit or total cost is used to evaluate alternative average levels of investment.

Decisions regarding manufacturing inventory are complicated by the nature of the manufacturing process, which varies from industry to industry. The general considerations regarding raw materials and finished goods inventories are, however, similar in many respects to those regarding the finished goods inventories of retailers and wholesalers. The factors influencing the decision to invest in inventory include costs of holding inventory, costs of ordering new stock, availability of quantity discounts, and the costs of stockouts. A safety stock of inventory is often carried to reduce the chances of stockouts. There are risks to carrying inventory due to the possibilities of variation in the market value of the goods held and possible deterioration, theft, or spoilage. In addition, the benefits from increased investment are uncertain. The minimum acceptable rate of return or discount rate for inventory investment should reflect the inventory's risk as well as the basic time value of money.

The level of accounts receivable depends primarily on the sales volume of the firm and its credit policy. The basic decisions are whether or not to extend credit to a given customer and what the maximum amount of credit should be. The general credit policy of the firm provides a basis for these decisions and affects the sales volume of the firm. Restrictive credit policies reduce bad debt losses and the amount of investment in accounts receivable relative to sales. However, restrictive policies also limit sales.

PROJECT

Interview the manager of a small local business and find out how current assets are managed. What kinds of decisions are made regarding inventory and accounts receivable?

QUESTIONS

1 What is a "reversible" investment and why is reversibility an important characteristic for analyzing current asset investments?

2 How do the concepts of "net profit" and "total cost" as used in this chapter differ from the normal accounting concepts of profit (net income) and cost?

3 How would the following developments affect the level of investment in inventory by a firm? Specify which types of inventory costs have changed (if any) and whether the costs have increased or decreased.

    a Faster and cheaper transportation of goods.
    b Using an existing computer to generate purchase orders.
    c Expectations of greater future inflation.
    d Changing from English measures (pounds, inches) to metric measures (kilograms, centimeters). Discuss both the short-run and the long-run impact.
    e Increasing the number of models in a product line.
    f An increase in the price per unit of purchased goods.

4 Would you expect the discount rate for investment in an inventory of cocoa to be higher, lower, or the same as the discount rate for investment in an inventory of chocolate bars? Why?

5 In what sense does "safety stock" provide "safety" to a firm? Is there such a thing as being "too safe"?

6 There is potential conflict in inventory decisions between the views of the financial manager and the marketing manager. Why? Why would there be a possible conflict between the financial manager and the production manager regarding inventory?

7 What are the major costs and benefits in establishing a severe credit policy as compared with a more lenient credit policy?

8 In the past four years, the Z Company has not experienced a bad debt loss in its accounts receivable. Sales and profits have increased 10 percent over this period. Evaluate the performance of the Z Company's credit manager.

9 How would you adjust the credit policy of your firm in the following situations? Be as specific as you can.
    a You are trying to attract customers in a wider geographic market.
    b Your customers are paying, on average, thirty days after payment is due.
    c You are asked to manufacture a custom product for a small firm and you are unsure of its financial condition.

10 If accounts receivable are $200,000 as of the end of the year for the Abacus Company, is the firm's investment in accounts receivable $200,000? Why or why not?

11 Does the credit policy of a firm affect its discount rate for investment in accounts receivable? In what ways?

12 Why is inventory management more complex for firms with foreign operations than for firms without them?

13 What is the simplest way to avoid foreign exchange risk in sales on account to foreign customers?

DEMONSTRATION PROBLEMS

DP1 An electronics store sells on average 20 volt-ohm meters (VOMs) per month. VOMs are currently ordered in lots of forty at a time, and the purchase price per VOM is $25. It costs $6 to place an order, and annual holding costs are estimated to be 6 percent of average inventory investment. The discount rate for inventory investment is 12 percent per year. The tax rate is 25 percent.

a   What is the total annual cost of this inventory policy excluding acquisition costs?

b   If any number of VOMs can be ordered at a time, what is the least cost number to order? What would be the store's average investment in VOMs assuming no safety stock is maintained?

c   VOMs are packaged 10 to a case and must be ordered in case lots. How many cases should the store order at a time?

SOLUTION TO DP1:

a   Annual order costs $= \dfrac{fS}{Q}$

$$= \frac{\$6(20 \times 12)}{40}$$

$$= \$36 \text{ per year}$$

Average investment $= \dfrac{CQ}{2}$

$$= \frac{\$25(40)}{2}$$

$$= \$500$$

Annual holding costs $= \dfrac{hCQ}{2} = h(\text{average investment})$

$$= 0.06(\$500)$$

$$= \$30.00$$

Capital cost $= k(\text{average investment})$

$$= 0.12(\$500)$$

$$= \$60$$

Total cost $= (1 - .25)(\$36 + \$30) + \$60$

$$= \$111$$

b   Use the EOQ formula (17-11):

$$Q^* = \sqrt{\frac{2(1 - \tau)fS}{(1 - \tau)hC + kC}}$$

$$= \sqrt{\frac{2(.75)\$6(240)}{(.75(.06)(\$25) + (.12)(\$25)}}$$

$$= \sqrt{\frac{\$2160}{\$4.125}}$$

$$= 22.88 \text{ or } 23 \text{ VOMs per order}$$

c From *b* it would appear that 2 cases (20 VOMs) would be the minimum cost order; however, to be safe calculate total cost at both 20 and 30 VOMs:

Order quantity	(1) Order cost	(2) Holding cost	(3) Aftertax costs	(4) Capital cost	(5) Total cost
20	$72.00	$15.00	$56.25	$30.00	$98.25
30	48.00	22.50	52.88	45.00	97.88

Aftertax costs (3) = $(1 - T)[(1) + (2)]$ where T = tax rate

Total cost = (3) + (4)

Although it doesn't make much difference, 3 cases (30 VOMs) is the minimum cost order in case lots.

DP2 As financial manager of Ace Novelties, you have received some disturbing news. The credit manager has told you that many of the firm's regular customers are having cash flow problems and may start paying their accounts more slowly. Normally, the average collection period of Ace is 25 days. Sales on account are $90,000 per month, and accounts receivable are currently at a level of $75,000. You are concerned about the impact on the cash position of the firm if customers pay more slowly. What would be the impact on cash and accounts receivable if the collection period increased to an average of 35 days from its current level?

SOLUTION TO DP2:
Assuming no change in sales, sales will continue at a rate of $90,000/30 days = $3000 per day. If the average collection period goes to 35 days, accounts receivable will average $3000 × 35 days = $105,000. Since this is entirely due to slower collections, the impact on cash will be the difference between the current accounts receivable level of $75,000 and the new level of $105,000 resulting in a $30,000 reduction in cash. The timing of the reduction in cash depends on when and how fast the slowdown in collections occurs.

DP3 The marketing manager of Ace Novelties has proposed adding a new sales person to solicit customers in Pittsburgh. The additional sales from this expansion are expected to be $146,000 per year. It is estimated that out-of-pocket cash expenses for Ace's products average 80 percent of the selling price and that new customers would pay their accounts, on average, in 25 days. As part of an analysis of the proposal, you are concerned with the initial impact on the cash position of the firm. How would accounts receivable and cash be affected initially from the expanded sales effort?

SOLUTION TO DP3:
The added sales of $146,000 per year amounts to $146,000/365 = $400 per day. If the new customers pay on average in 25 days, added accounts receivable would be $400 × 25 days = $10,000. However, only 80 percent of this represents cash outlays, so the initial impact on the firm's cash position would be 0.80 × $10,000 = $8000. This ignores any impact on cash due to additional inventory required.

PROBLEMS

1 Perform the indicated calculations using a discount rate of 10 percent per year and an income tax rate of 40 percent.

  a Net profit for a reversible investment of $2000 which provides $1200 in additional annual cash revenues and $400 in additional annual cash costs. [Ans.: $280]

  b Total cost for a reversible investment of $1500 with annual cash costs of $600. This is one of several alternative investments that all provide the same level of annual revenues. [Ans.: $510]

  c Calculate the net present value for the investment in *a* assuming that funds are withdrawn (investment is reversed) in five years' time. Check your calculation by using two equivalent procedures.

  d Calculate the present value of costs for the investment in *b* assuming that funds are withdrawn in ten years' time. Check your calculation by using two equivalent procedures.

2 The manager of a farm supply store is evaluating two alternative levels of investment in seed inventory, A or B. Relevant data for the two alternatives are shown below:

	A	B
Average dollar investment	$1,000	$2,000
Monthly cash revenues	$ 600	$ 800
Monthly cash costs	$ 200	$ 390

The discount rate for this investment is 1 percent per month. The income tax rate is 40 percent. In six months' time (at the end of the season) inventories of this item will be reduced to zero. The manager expects to realize the amount invested at that time.

  a Calculate the monthly net profit (as defined in this chapter) for the two alternatives.

  b Calculate the net present value for the two alernatives.

  c Which alternative is best? Does it matter whether net profit or net present value is used to decide on the alternative?

3 A building supply store sells on average twenty-five electrical panels per month. Panels are currently ordered in lots of fifty at a time, and the cost per panel is $30.

a What is the store's average investment in panels assuming no safety stock is maintained?

b If it costs $5 to place an order for panels, what are the annual order costs?

c Suppose holding costs average $0.06 per dollar invested per year. What are the annual holding costs of panels?

d Given a discount rate of 12 percent per year for inventory investment, what is the annual capital cost of inventory investment?

e Given a tax rate of 40 percent, what is the total cost of this inventory policy excluding acquisition cost?

4 Using the data of problem *3*, calculate the total costs (excluding acquisition costs) for the following additional order quantities: 25 panels per order and 75 panels per order. The price per panel is $30 regardless of the amount ordered.

a Which order quantity provides minimum total costs?

b Would inclusion of acquisition costs affect your decision in this case? Why or why not?

5 Suppose the supplier of the panels in problem *3* offers the following quantity discounts from the base price of $30 per panel.

Panels per order	0–49	50–99	100–199	200 or more
Discount from base price	0%	5%	10%	12%

What inventory policy minimizes total cost? (Assume that panel orders are in multiples of twenty-five.)

6 Midwest Electronics manufactures instruments for medical tests. The sales manager of Midwest has been concerned about losing sales because of the low levels of inventory the firm carries. An analysis of losses due to stockouts carried out by a task force set up to investigate the problem suggests the following relationship between average minimum inventory levels and stockout losses:

Average safety stock investment	$100,000	$150,000	$200,000	$250,000
Annual stockout losses (pretax)	$ 50,000	$ 20,000	$ 6,000	$ 0

Holding costs for this type of inventory average 8 percent per year per dollar of inventory. The firm's tax rate is 40 percent, and management estimates the discount rate applicable to this type of investment to be 10 percent.

As financial manager of Midwest Electronics, what level of safety stock would you recommend?

7 Anderson Hardware Supply is a wholesaler located in Denver and sells to small hardware stores in the mountain states. Josh Greene, Anderson's credit manager, has just received a request to extend credit under 30-day payment terms to a store in Missoula, Montana, that would be a new customer for Anderson. An initial order for $5000 of goods has been made. Anderson's cost for these goods is $4000. In addition, Anderson would incur additional expenses of $340 in selling and shipping the goods. What would be the out-of-pocket loss to Anderson if it sells the goods and the customer does not pay?

8 Anderson Hardware Supply has a customer in Boulder, Colorado, that, because of its poor credit standing, has been required to pay cash on delivery of goods. Sales to this customer have averaged $1000 per month. The customer is requesting to be allowed to pay on more normal terms of 30 days credit. Anderson's cost of goods sold is 80 percent of sales and Anderson has been incurring $60 per month in additional expenses in selling to this customer. Anderson's tax rate is 30 percent.

a Assuming that the customer will continue to purchase at the same rate from Anderson if the credit request is denied, what will be the initial cash investment due to the extension of credit?

b Suppose that, if credit is not extended, the customer will stop buying from Anderson. In this situation, what is the initial cash investment due to the extension of credit?

c Suppose that, if credit is extended, the customer will increase purchases to $2000 per month. Out-of-pocket expenses for Anderson will be $1710 at this sales rate. If credit is not extended, the customer will continue to pay cash for $1000 purchases per month. What is the initial cash investment for the extension of credit under these assumptions?

9 Josh Greene, credit manager for Anderson Hardware Supply, has proposed a major overhaul of the firm's credit policies. He has separated the firm's credit customers into two groups—high risk and normal risk. Data for the two groups are shown below.

	Annual sales	Annual cash expenses	Annual bad debt losses	Outstanding accounts receivable
Normal risk	$ 800,000	$720,000	$1500	$ 70,000
High risk	200,000	185,000	5000	35,000
Total	$1,000,000	$905,000	$6500	$105,000

Josh is recommending that the firm stop extending credit to the high-risk group. Anderson would be able to collect 90 percent of the outstanding high-risk accounts if this were done. The remaining 10 percent of the high-risk accounts would be a loss, with a resulting reduction in taxes equalling 30 percent of the loss. Anderson's tax rate is 30 percent. The discount rate applicable in this situation is 8 percent. Evaluate Josh's proposal assuming that all high-risk customers stop buying goods from Anderson.

10 Evaluate Josh Greene's proposal in problem **9** using the assumption that half the high risk customers stop buying goods and the remaining high risk customers will pay cash. Sales revenues and cash expenses for the customers paying cash will be 50 percent of the current sales and cash expenses for those customers. Bad debt losses will be zero under a cash-only policy.

11 Using the information from problem **9**, determine the percentage of high-risk customers willing to pay cash for goods that is required in order for the new policy to break even. Alternatively, what percentage of high-risk customers paying cash would produce the same net profit as the current policy? Assume sales and cash expenses vary proportionately with the percentage of customers continuing to buy from Anderson paying cash. (This problem can be solved without solving problem **9** first.)

The ▪ symbol indicates that all or a significant part of the problem can be solved using the *Computer Models* software package that accompanies this text.

THE ECONOMIC ORDER QUANTITY MODEL

In Chapter 17 we showed how to find the order quantity that minimizes the total cost of inventory investment. The solution method was to calculate total cost [Eq. (17-9)] for different order quantities and to find the minimum either numerically or by examining a graph. The total-cost equation is

Total cost = (1 − tax rate) × (acquisition cost + order cost
+ holding cost) + capital cost

$$= (1 - \tau) \left(CS + \frac{fS}{Q} + \frac{hCQ}{2} \right) + \frac{kCQ}{2} \qquad (17\text{-}9)$$

Suppose that acquisition cost does not vary with order quantity in this equation. Acquisition cost is therefore constant, insofar as the decision regarding Q is concerned, and it will not affect the decision. All variables except Q in Eq. (17-9) are assumed to be constants unaffected by the value of Q. Under these conditions, we can derive a formula for the value of Q that minimizes total cost, Q^*. This value is the economic order quantity in Eq. (17-1). This appendix provides the derivation of Eq. (17-1).

We wish to minimize the total-cost function

$$\text{Total cost} = TC = (1 - \tau) \left(CS + \frac{fS}{Q} + \frac{hCQ}{2} \right) + \frac{kCQ}{2}$$

To do this, calculate the derivative of the total-cost function with respect to Q, the decision variable in this case, and solve for the value of Q that will make the derivative equal to zero (this value of Q is Q^*).

$$\frac{d(TC)}{dQ} = (1 - \tau) \left(\frac{hC}{2} - \frac{fS}{Q^2} \right) + \frac{kC}{2}$$

$$(1 - \tau) \left(\frac{hC}{2} - \frac{fS}{(Q^*)^2} \right) + \frac{kC}{2} = 0$$

$$(Q^*)^2 \left(\frac{hC}{2} + \frac{kC}{2(1 - \tau)} \right) - fS = 0$$

$$(Q^*)^2 = \frac{2(1 - \tau)fS}{(1 - \tau)hC + kC}$$

$$Q^* = \sqrt{\frac{2(1 - \tau)fS}{(1 - \tau)hC + kC}} \qquad (17\text{-}11)$$

The economic order quantity Q^* is the value of Q that minimizes total cost when per unit acquisition costs do not vary with order quantity Q. Besides the convenience of having a simple way to calculate Q^*, Eq. (17-11) is also useful because it indicates how Q^* and therefore the average investment in inventory $CQ^*/2$ is affected by the variables in it. In particular we can see that, as usage rates (sales rates) S increase, the economic order quantity Q^* and the average investment in inventory also increase. However, the increase in investment is not directly proportional to S, but rather proportional to $\sqrt{S}$. Suppose we rewrite Eq. (17-11) in terms of the average level of inventory investment I and rearrange terms

$$I = \frac{CQ^*}{2}$$

$$= \frac{C}{2}\sqrt{\frac{2(1 - \tau)fS}{(1 - \tau)hC + kC}}$$

$$= \left[\sqrt{\frac{(1 - \tau)fC}{2[(1 - \tau)h + k]}}\right]\sqrt{S} \qquad (17\text{-}15)$$

The variables inside the brackets are all cost factors and usually don't change very much. The usage rate S is subject to change. From the formula it is clear that an increase in usage rate with no change in costs will increase average inventory investment in proportion to the square root of S, which is less than S.

THE USE OF NPV IN THE EVALUATION OF CREDIT POLICIES

In Chapter 17, we showed how to evaluate a change in credit policy using the net profit method [Eq. (17-13)]. In this appendix, we discuss the use of net present value (NPV) in credit policy problems. We will use the Cleanall example illustrated in Figure 17-4 as the basis for the discussion. At the end of the section, we briefly compare the NPV and net profit approaches.

In developing the Cleanall example, we made a simplifying assumption that permitted us to calculate net profit easily. We lumped all cash flows at the beginning and end of the year, even though the basic cash flows were weekly in the example. This annualization is obviously an approximation. In this appendix, we show how to use the NPV technique to produce a precise evaluation.

Let's begin by analyzing the proposed change in credit policy assuming that we will revert back to a cash-only policy at the end of 13 weeks. In other words, we are going to use a one-quarter evaluation period to see if the policy is worthwhile. Later, we will look at longer periods.

Cleanall, as is normal practice, pays taxes quarterly, not annually. Therefore, besides the weekly cash flows shown in Figure 17-4, we should add tax payments every 13 weeks. The net cash flows for the cash-only policy and the 13 weeks of a policy of extending credit are shown in Figure 17-5. The net cash flow is $500 per week, with an additional negative cash flow (taxes) of $1625 in week 13. Taxes equal 25 percent of the $6500 profit for the quarter. (Cash sales and expenses equal accrued sales and expenses under the cash sales policy.) The week 13 net cash flow is therefore −$1125 ($500 − $1625). Beginning with week 18, the cash flows under credit extension revert back to those of a cash-only policy, so that an examination only of weeks zero to 17 is needed.

With credit extension, sales increase to $2400 per week, cash expenses increase to $1800 per week, and bad debt losses increase to $24 per week. No cash is received for the first four weeks under the new policy and accounts receivable build up to $9600 (4 weeks sales). Therefore, in weeks 1 through 4, net cash flow is −$1800. Net cash flows after week 4 rise to $576 per week. At the end of 13 weeks, the firm pays taxes

on profits for the quarter. Assuming that Cleanall uses accrual accounting, Cleanall will have recorded 13 weeks of profits at $576 per week or
$7488. Cleanall will pay 25 percent of those profits to the government, a
tax payment of $1872. This means a net cash flow in week 13 of −$1296
($576 − $1872). If Cleanall stops selling on credit after week 13, it will
collect its accounts receivable (less any bad debt losses) when they are
due. Receipts from collections will amount to $2376 per week for weeks
14–17. These collections are the result of reversing the credit sales policy
(i.e., of reverting back to the cash-only sales policy). In addition, the
firm will have $500 from cash sales less expenses. (Note that reverting to
the cash-only sales policy causes sales to return to $2000 per week and
expenses to $1500 per week.) Pretax net cash receipts will therefore be
$2876 per week for weeks 14–17. After week 17, net cash flow per week
is the $500 per week under the cash sales policy.

We can calculate the net present value for the first 17 weeks since
this is the period for which there is a difference in cash flows between the

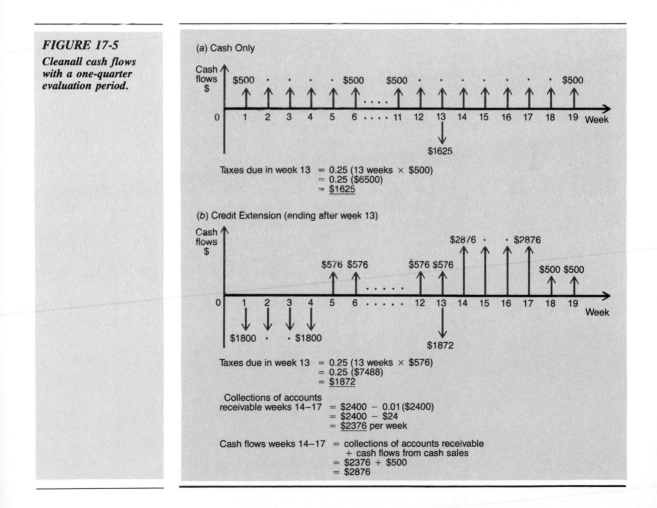

FIGURE 17-5

*Cleanall cash flows
with a one-quarter
evaluation period.*

cash-only policy and the credit extension policy lasting 13 weeks. The easiest approach to computing the present value of the net cash flow is to compute the present value of cash collections less expenses and the present value of taxes, and then deduct the latter from the former. Assume a weekly discount rate of 0.2 percent. We calculate the net present value of the cash-only cash flows for the first 17 weeks as

$$
\begin{aligned}
\text{NPV}_{\text{cash policy}} &= \$500(P/A, 0.2\%, 17) - \$1625(P/F, 0.2\%, 13) \\
&= \$500(16.6978) - \$1625(0.9744) \\
&= \$6766
\end{aligned}
$$

Calculating the NPV of the credit extension cash flows is a bit more complicated. We have

$$
\begin{aligned}
\text{NPV}_{\text{credit policy}} &= -\$1800(P/A, 0.2\%, 4) \\
&\quad + \$576(P/A, 0.2\%, 9)\,(P/F, 0.2\%, 4) \\
&\quad -\$1872(P/F, 0.2\%, 13) \\
&\quad + \$2876(P/A, 0.2\%, 4)(P/F, 0.2\%, 13) \\
&= -\$1800(3.9801) + \$576(8.9107)(0.992) \\
&\quad -\$1872(0.9744) + \$2876(3.9801)(0.9744) \\
&= -\$7164 + \$5091 - \$1824 + \$11{,}153 \\
&= \$7256
\end{aligned}
$$

Since the NPV of the credit policy is higher than the NPV of the cash policy, the credit policy is better even if followed for only 13 weeks. The additional (incremental) NPV from extending credit for 13 weeks is $490 ($7256 − $6766). Now let's extend the evaluation period to one year.

With a one-year evaluation period, the cash-only policy differs from the one-quarter evaluation only in that now Cleanall will have four quarterly tax payments of $1625 at weeks 13, 26, 39, and 52. Under the credit extension policy, the first 13 weeks are the same as in Figure 17-5b. However, now we are not reversing the policy until the end of week 52. Therefore the weekly cash flows of $576 will continue for 52 weeks and there will be quarterly tax payments of $1872. In weeks 53 through 56, the reversing cash receipts of $2876 per week will be obtained. The NPVs of the two policies are now calculated as

$$
\begin{aligned}
\text{NPV}_{\text{cash policy}} &= \$500(P/A, 0.2\%, 56) - \$1625(P/F, 0.2\%, 13) \\
&\quad -\$1625(P/F, 0.2\%, 26) - \$1625(P/F, 0.2\%, 39) \\
&\quad -\$1625(P/F, 0.2\%, 52) \\
&= \$500(52.9279) - \$1625(0.9744) - \$1625(0.9494) \\
&\quad -\$1625(0.9250) - \$1625(0.9013) \\
&= \$26{,}464 - \$1583 - \$1543 - \$1503 - \$1465 \\
&= \$20{,}370
\end{aligned}
$$

$$
\begin{aligned}
\text{NPV}_{\text{credit policy}} = \; & -\$1800(P/A,\, 0.2\%,\, 4) \\
& + \$576(P/A,\, 0.2\%,\, 48)(P/F,\, 0.2\%,\, 4) \\
& -\$1872(P/F,\, 0.2\%,\, 13) - \$1872(P/F,\, 0.2\%,\, 26) \\
& -\$1872(P/F,\, 0.2\%,\, 39) - \$1872(P/F,\, 0.2\%,\, 52) \\
& +\$2876(P/A,\, 0.2\%,\, 4)(P/F,\, 0.2\%,\, 52)
\end{aligned}
$$

$$
\begin{aligned}
= \; & -\$1800(3.9801) + \$576(45.7244)(0.992) \\
& -\$1872(0.9744) - \$1872(0.9494) - \$1872(0.9250) \\
& -\$1872(0.9013) + \$2876(3.9801)(0.9013)
\end{aligned}
$$

$$
\begin{aligned}
= \; & -\$7164 + \$26{,}127 - \$1824 - \$1777 - \$1732 \\
& -\$1687 + \$10{,}317
\end{aligned}
$$

$$
= \$22{,}260
$$

The credit policy is still superior and its margin of superiority has increased. The difference in NPVs is now $1890 as compared to $490, the difference when the two policies were evaluated for one quarter. The credit policy was good for one quarter and is even better if continued for one year.

As a final illustration of the use of NPV, suppose that we extend the evaluation period to forever. That is, suppose that we calculate NPVs assuming a perpetual policy rather than one that is reversed.

The perpetual cash flows are illustrated in Figure 17-6. Note that we retain the assumption of quarterly tax payments. The resulting NPVs are calculated as

$$
\begin{aligned}
\text{NPV}_{\text{cash policy}} &= \$500(P/A,\, 0.2\%,\, \infty) - \$1625(P/A,\, 2.63\%,\, \infty) \\
&= \$500/0.002 - \$1625/0.0263 \\
&= \$188{,}213
\end{aligned}
$$

Since we are dealing with perpetuities it is much simpler to discount tax payments using a quarterly discount rate of 2.63%.[11]

$$
\begin{aligned}
\text{NPV}_{\text{credit policy}} = \; & -\$1800(P/A,\, 0.2\%,\, 4) \\
& + \$576(P/A,\, 0.2\%,\, \infty)(P/F,\, 0.2\%,\, 4) \\
& -\$1872(P/A,\, 2.63\%,\, \infty)
\end{aligned}
$$

$$
= -\$1800(3.9801) + \$576(0.992)/0.002 - \$1872/0.0263
$$

$$
= \$207{,}353
$$

The difference in NPVs is $19,140.

*NPV versus Net
Profit*

In Chapter 17 (page 646) we calculated the additional net profit from adopting the credit policy to be $1952 per year. How does this figure compare with the additional NPVs obtained from adopting the credit policy?

---

[11] Since we are assuming that interest is compounded weekly at a rate of 0.2 percent, the effective quarterly interest rate is 2.63 percent $[(1.002)^{13} - 1]$.

As we have seen, the NPVs for the credit policy are higher than the NPVs of the cash policy regardless of how long the policy is assumed to be in effect. The difference between the NPV of the cash-only policy and the NPV of the credit policy is greater than zero as is the additional net profit, which indicates that the credit policy is preferred. To compare the two procedures, we will calculate the present values of the net profit assuming first the credit policy is in effect for only one year and then that it is in effect forever.

The net present value of $1952 received in one year with a discount rate of 0.2 percent per week is

$$NPV = \$1952(P/F, 0.2\%, 52)$$

$$= \$1952(0.9013)$$

$$= \$1759$$

The net present value of a net profit of $1952 per year forever at a discount rate of 0.2 percent per week (approximately 11 percent per year) is[12]

---

[12] An interest rate of 0.2 percent per week is an effective annual rate of approximately 11 percent $[(1.002)^{52} - 1 \doteq 11\%]$.

FIGURE 17-6

Cleanall cash flows: perpetual.

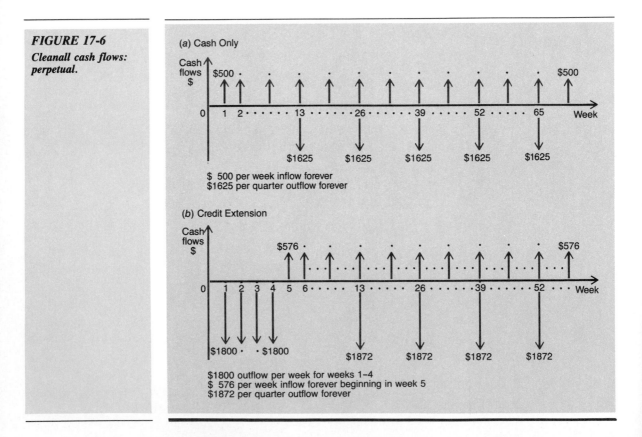

$$\text{NPV} = \$1952(P/A, 11\%, \infty)$$

$$= \$1952/0.11$$

$$= \$17,745$$

We have the following values for NPVs of the difference between the two policies:

Policy Length	NPV using net profit	NPV using cash flow	Error
1 year	$ 1,759	$ 1,890	−6.9%
Forever	$17,745	$19,140	−7.3%

Using the annual net profit approach, which lumps cash flows at the beginning and end of a year, produces a moderate error as compared to the more accurate calculation of NPVs of the cash flows. However, the net profit approach requires much less calculation and does not require specification of a particular evaluation period.

CHAPTER EIGHTEEN

CASH MANAGEMENT

Most payments and receipts of business firms involve checks drawn on demand deposits at commercial banks. Businesses typically pay their employees and suppliers with checks, and their customers pay them in the same way. Relatively few transactions involve the use of currency, and these are primarily retail sales. Both currency and demand deposit balances are "cash," but our focus is on the deposits. In current practice, cash management encompasses management of the firm's cash flows (receipts and payments), maintenance of appropriate cash balances, decisions regarding investment in securities, and decisions regarding short-term borrowing from banks and other sources. In this chapter, we focus on the assets (cash and securities) involved in cash management and on the management of cash flows. In Chapter 19, we examine short-term financing alternatives and, in Chapter 20, we look at cash management as a part of working capital management in general. To show how cash management fits in with other aspects of a firm's operations, we begin with the cash cycle of a firm.

THE CASH CYCLE

In Chapter 16, we discussed cash flow forecasts and cash budgets. There we were concerned with the amount of cash being paid and received by the firm over a period of time, for example, cash inflows and outflows during a month. The firm's **cash cycle** traces the process of a firm's operations that result in cash flows. Since complicated firms have complicated cash cycles, we will describe the cash cycle for a distribution firm which has relatively simple operations. A typical cash cycle is shown in Figure 18-1.

Distribution firms buy goods from suppliers who normally do not require immediate payment. The goods are invoiced when they are shipped (invoice date = shipping date) and recorded as inventory with a corresponding increase in accounts payable when they arrive. This transaction produces an increase in current assets and an increase in current liabilities of the same amount. There are no cash flows at this time. The interval between the time goods are ordered and the time they are received is a concern of inventory management. Cash managers are concerned with the period that begins when goods are received.

As we discuss in Chapter 19, the credit terms of the supplier and a variety of financial considerations determine how long the firm will wait to make payment after receiving goods from a supplier. The firm's **average payment period** is the average length of time the firm waits before paying suppliers. It can be measured as:

$$\text{Average payment period} = \frac{\text{accounts payable}}{\text{purchases per day}} \tag{18-1}$$

For example, if the firm is purchasing goods at a rate of $2500 per day and has outstanding accounts payable of $25,000, its average payment period is ten days ($25,000/$2500 per day). Most firms pay their suppliers by mailing them a check for the amount of the invoice (less any applicable discounts). When the firm mails a check to a supplier, it records a reduction in its deposit account at the bank and a reduction in accounts payable. However, the balance in the account at the bank will not be reduced until the check actually reaches the bank on which the check was drawn. The interval from when the check is mailed to when the check is presented at the bank and the account is reduced (debited) is called the **disbursement time**. As we will see, this is an important concept in managing the firm's cash flows. The firm actually has the use of those funds until the check is presented at the bank. The disbursement time might be four days.

In the meantime, goods are being held in inventory until they are sold. The average length of time goods are in inventory is called the **average inventory period** and is determined by the inventory policies of

FIGURE 18-1

A typical cash cycle for distribution firms.

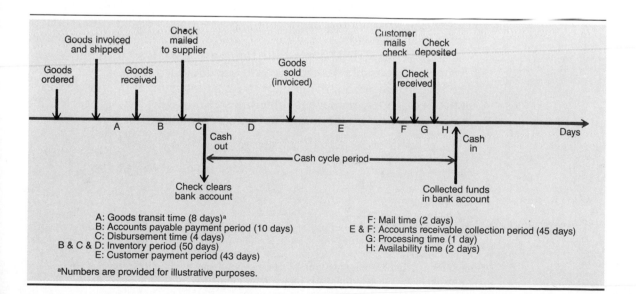

A: Goods transit time (8 days)[a]
B: Accounts payable payment period (10 days)
C: Disbursement time (4 days)
B & C & D: Inventory period (50 days)
E: Customer payment period (43 days)

F: Mail time (2 days)
E & F: Accounts receivable collection period (45 days)
G: Processing time (1 day)
H: Availability time (2 days)

[a]Numbers are provided for illustrative purposes.

the firm. We can measure the average inventory period for a distribution firm as:[1]

$$\text{Average inventory period} = \frac{\text{inventory}}{\text{cost of goods sold per day}} \qquad (18\text{-}2)$$

Therefore, if the firm is selling $2500 worth of goods per day and its inventory is $125,000, the average inventory period for the firm is 50 days ($125,000/$2500 per day).

When goods are sold (invoiced and shipped), inventory decreases by the amount of the cost of the goods sold, and accounts receivable increase by the amount of the invoice (the selling price of the inventory). No cash flows occur yet. The credit terms and payment habits of customers determine the length of the average collection period, which is the average length of time accounts receivable are outstanding [see Eq. (17-14)]. In this example the collection period is 45 days.

The collection period in Figure (18-1) ($E + F$) is comprised of two components—the customer payment period and the mail time. The **customer payment period** (E) is the length of time from when the goods are invoiced and shipped to the time the customer mails a check to pay for the goods, for example, 43 days. The **mail time** (F) is the length of time it takes the firm to receive the check after it was mailed, for example, two days. When the check is received, accounts receivable are reduced by that amount and the firm's cash account is increased. However, a check in the firm's office is not usable cash.

The **processing time** (G) is the time it takes from receipt of a check until the firm to which it was sent updates its records and delivers the check to the bank for deposit—for example, one day. Once the check is deposited, there still may be some delay in having the cash available to pay bills, invest, repay loans, or whatever. The interval between deposit of the check and actually having cash in the account available for use is the **availability time** (H), for example, two days. All these time delays are a concern to cash managers, and later we will discuss methods of reducing their lengths.

The overall period between the time cash is paid out to suppliers and is obtained as usable cash in the firm's account is the **cash cycle period**. The longer this period, the greater the cash investment in current assets of the firm. External analysts sometimes estimate the average cash cycle period for a firm by the following simple formula.

Average cash cycle period = average collection period

+ average inventory period

− average payment period   (18-3)

---

[1] The average inventory period for a manufacturing firm cannot be estimated so easily because inventory includes raw materials and work-in-process as well as finished goods. Equation (18-2) applies only to the inventory period for finished goods inventories. The inventory period for manufacturers, from receipt of raw materials through sale of finished goods, is usually larger than that for distribution firms.

If the average collection period is 45 days, the average inventory period is 50 days, and the average payment period is 10 days, the average cash cycle period is 85 days. However, we can see from Figure 18-1 that Eq. (18-3) is only an approximation. The actual cash cycle period ($D + E + F + G + H$) may not be the same as

$$
\begin{array}{ll}
\text{Collection period} & = E + F \\
+ \text{ inventory period} & = B + C + D \\
- \text{ payment period} & = B \\
\hline
\text{Estimated cash cycle period} & = C + D + E + F
\end{array}
$$

The difference between the estimate and the actual average is $C - G - H$, which reflects any difference between the time the firm has cash due to delays in its suppliers receiving and obtaining funds and the time the firm takes to process checks and have cash available. In our example, this difference is only one day. To some extent, a cash manager's job is to make this difference as large as possible. Let's look at what cash managers do to manage the firm's cash flows.

MANAGING CASH FLOWS

Cash flow management is the management of collection and disbursement procedures so that:

1 Collection from customers is accelerated to make cash available to the firm as soon as possible.
2 Payment to suppliers and other parties is controlled to keep cash available to the firm as long as possible.

Both individuals and firms are concerned with efficient cash flow management.

The individual's strategy for efficient cash flow management is relatively simple. Checks are deposited as soon as possible and bill payments are delayed as long as possible without incurring a finance charge. Credit cards and charge accounts are particularly useful in this respect since the time between purchase and payment can run as long as several months in some instances (with no interest charge). Both business firms and consumers essentially attempt to do the same thing—to minimize the time they are providing someone else with free credit (an interest-free loan) and to maximize their own free credit. This free credit is called "float."

Float is money in the process of being collected. It is measured in dollar-days but normally expressed simply as dollars.[2] Therefore $4 million in float can be $1 million for four days, $2 million for two days, $0.5 million for eight days, or any other combination of amount and time

---

[2] Float is frequently expressed in days as well, for example, a collection float of five days ($F + G + H$ in Figure 18-1). To avoid confusion, we will measure float in dollars and refer to float measured in days as "float time."

with a product of 4 million dollar-days. Float is measured in this way because it translates directly into cash balances. For example, if you can collect money owed to you more quickly, you will have more cash on average over time. A permanent reduction of $1 million in the float arising from collections will provide an increase of $1 million in available cash. Appendix 18A contains a detailed example of the cash flows associated with a reduction in float. There are several different types of float, but the two basic types are collection float and disbursement float.

Speeding Collections

Collection float is money in the process of being received by the firm from its customers. Collection float is created due to the time period from when a customer initiates payment (puts a check in the mail) to the time the cash is available to the firm. Once a customer has initiated the payment—by mailing a check, for example—the firm has collection float. The float ends when the firm has the payment credited to its account as *collected funds available for investment or other uses*.

There are three components of collection float—**mail float, processing float,** and **availability float**. They arise, respectively, from the mail time ($F = 2$ days), the processing time ($G = 1$ day), and the availability time ($H = 2$ days), as shown in Figure 18-1. Suppose that a firm is receiving $1 million per day in checks from its customers. Then the following data apply:

Mail float	= mail time × volume	
	= 2 days × $1 million	= $2 million
Processing float	= processing time × volume	
	= 1 day × $1 million	= $1 million
Availability float	= availability time × volume	
	= 2 days × $1 million	= $2 million
Collection float	= total collection time × volume	
	= 5 days × $1 million	= $5 million

In this example, the float times are averages. The cash manager will wish to consider whether some types of checks are creating more float than others. For example, the $2 million in mail float could be the result of

Check Type	Volume	Mail time	Mail float
A	$ 100,000	4 days	$ 400,000
B	200,000	3 days	600,000
C	300,000	2 days	600,000
D	400,000	1 day	400,000
	$1,000,000	2 days	$2,000,000

In this example, the cash manager would look into reducing mail times for type A and B checks because they have relatively long mail times and contribute 50 percent of the mail float, even though they only constitute 30 percent of the check volume.

Businesses attempt to reduce collection float by methods that reduce the time intervals that create it. Mail time is a problem for a firm whose customers are located in distant areas so that it may take several days to receive checks after they are mailed. Mail time, processing time, and availability time can all be reduced by establishing a **lock box** (a special post office box) in an area where there are many customers. Customers are instructed to send their payments to the lock box address. A local bank picks up the checks and deposits them in the firm's account with that bank. Therefore, lock boxes reduce both mail time and processing time since the checks do not have far to travel and the firm does not have to handle the checks. As we will explain later, availability time may also be reduced because the checks are more likely to be written on accounts in nearby banks. A lock box system can reduce total collection time by one to four days. If checks are being received at a rate of $100,000 per day in the geographic area of the lock box, a reduction of three days would free $300,000 of cash for use by the firm. Large banks offer special zip codes for use by firms. Mail is sent directly to the bank instead of to a post office box; the lock box is at the bank. The mail is sorted by a zip code which identifies the firm receiving the check (the firm has its own zip code). This avoids the need to pick up mail at a post office and speeds the processing of the checks. The use of lock boxes is not free. The bank will charge a fee for the service or require the firm to maintain a minimum level of deposits with the bank. We show how to evaluate the costs and benefits of cash management services later.

Another method of reducing mail and processing time is to persuade customers to permit the use of **preauthorized checks**, which are issued by the company or the company's bank, payable to the company, and drawn on the customer's account. The customer signs an agreement with the company to allow these checks to be issued at specific times and for specific amounts. Preauthorized checks are used primarily in situations where the customer is making a regular monthly payment of a fixed amount, for example, insurance payments and mortgage payments.

Perhaps the most important thing any firm can do to reduce collection float is simply to make sure all checks received are deposited immediately. A reduction in processing time by sorting incoming mail in the morning and depositing checks in the afternoon can benefit even small firms through the reduction in processing float.

Availability float arises from the time interval between the deposit of a check and when that money can be used by the company. The availability time for checks depends on the relationship of the firm with its bank(s), the location of the bank on which the check was written relative to the bank in which it was deposited, and the check clearing procedure used by the bank. Banks have incentives to use efficient clearing procedures and the choice of bank procedures is normally not a concern of the cash manager. However, to understand the problem, one must understand the procedure, which depends on the location of the customer's bank on which the check was written. We will refer to the customer's bank as Bank C and the firm's bank as Bank F. The check clearing process is illustrated in Figure 18-2. If the check was written on an account in Bank F (that is, if C and F are the same bank), the check will clear within the day of deposit and the firm should receive immediate credit for the check. That is, the amount of the deposited check should be immediately available to the firm for its use. If Bank C is in the same city as Bank F, the check should take one day to be collected. That is, the money should be available one day after the deposit was made for local customers of the firm. A small firm that is a good customer of Bank F will usually receive immediate credit (availability) on these checks as well. If Bank C is located far from Bank F, it may take over a week for the check to be collected (presented to Bank C). However, Bank F will normally clear the check through the Federal Reserve System. The Fed

FIGURE 18-2
*The check clearing
process.*

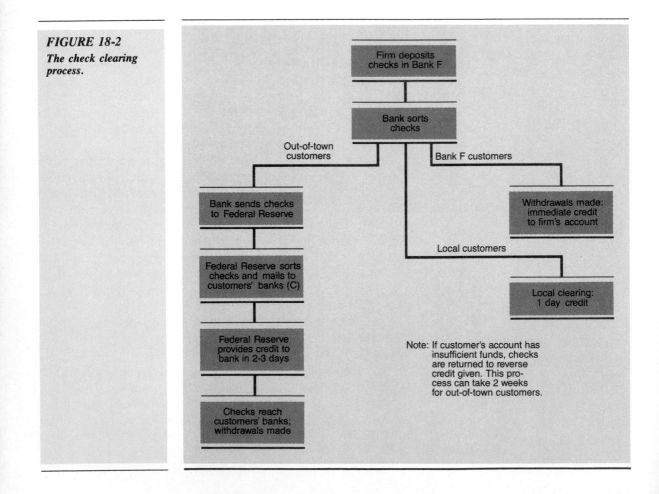

will provide availability of funds to Bank F on a schedule that depends on the distance between Banks C and F, but does not exceed three days. Therefore, the firm could expect Bank F to provide availability within three days so long as Bank C is within the United States. (Checks drawn on foreign banks present more complicated problems, which we will not discuss.) In some cases, if the amounts involved are not large and if the firm is a good customer, the firm might receive immediate credit on these checks, too. However, if Bank F is concerned about whether a check drawn on a distant bank is good (will be honored when it is presented), the bank may not be willing to provide availability for two or three weeks.[3] Other than negotiating better availability with the banks, the primary approach to reducing availability time is to locate depository banks effectively. A large firm with offices around the country will select depository banks that are located in areas where its customers are. By having customers send their checks to the closest office of the firm for deposit in a local bank, the firm can reduce availability time as well as mail time. Having a lock box in the area will serve the same purpose and reduce processing time as well.

At this point it should be clear that there is more than one way to measure cash. From the perspective of the cash manager, the cash that counts is the total of all available balances in the firm's deposit accounts. This cash can be used to pay bills, to repay borrowings, and to invest in interest-bearing securities. It is not the same as the figure that would show on the firm's balance sheet. The balance sheet cash balance (ledger balance) differs from *available* deposit balances as follows:

Balance sheet cash balance = Available deposit balance

+ currency (small for most firms)

+ checks deposited but not yet available

+ checks in hand but not yet deposited

− checks written but not yet presented (cleared)

"Checks deposited but not yet available" is availability float, "checks in hand but not yet deposited" is processing float, and "checks written but not yet presented" is disbursement float.

*Controlling
Disbursements*

Disbursement float is money in the process of being paid by the firm to its employees, suppliers, and other creditors. Disbursement time is the time period from the moment the firm initiates payment (puts a check in the mail) to the moment the cash leaves the firm's account. This float is measured like collection float. Suppose that a firm writes $4000 in checks

---

[3] There are legal restrictions on how long and under what circumstances a bank can delay availability.

each day and that it takes five days on average before those checks are presented for payment at the firm's bank. The firm would have $20,000 ($4000 × five days) in disbursement float. Firms like to have a large disbursement float, in that they want their outstanding checks to take a long time to clear. The longer the delay in clearing, the longer the company has use of the money.

Just as it is important to accelerate collections, it is important to maintain close control over the timing of payments to avoid early payments whenever possible. There are several "controlled disbursement" procedures. Most of these procedures involve the use of one or more banks (disbursement banks) where accounts are maintained exclusively for the purpose of making payments to suppliers and others. **Zero-balance accounts** allow a firm to write checks without having any money on deposit. Each day, the financial manager is notified by the bank of the value of the checks arriving at the bank drawn on the account. The amount needed to cover the checks is wired from a central account in another bank. Large firms may have several zero-balance accounts around the country. In their attempts to increase disbursement float, some firms have adopted the practice of maintaining disbursement accounts in banks that have remote locations relative to the parties they are paying so that the checks take longer to reach the firm's banks. For example, a firm located in Chicago might maintain an account with a bank in Spokane, Washington, on which checks would be written to pay suppliers in Florida. Another procedure is to mail checks from offices that are remote from the suppliers being paid. If a firm headquartered in Chicago has an office in Los Angeles, it might mail checks from that office to pay its Florida suppliers.

Many of the methods of increasing disbursement float impose losses on other parties in devious ways. An increase in disbursement float for a firm either increases the collection float of its suppliers or increases the Federal Reserve's float. An increase in mail time obviously increases the suppliers' mail float, and remote disbursement may increase their availability float. If the suppliers' collection float is being increased, they are likely to be displeased if they are financially astute. This practice is not conducive to good business relationships. Much of the float created by remote disbursement is borne by the Federal Reserve, due to its policies of providing availability on a schedule regardless of how long it actually takes to clear the checks (clearing for out-of-town customers in Figure 18-2). The Fed has actively sought to reduce its float by speeding up its clearing procedures and discouraging banks from selling remote disbursement services to firms. As a consequence of the losses imposed on others, many disbursement procedures might be considered unethical and are not publicized by the firms that practice them.

This discussion of disbursement float is not meant to imply that float maximization is an overriding objective of disbursement control. Many firms have begun to make some payments electronically through the use of **automated clearing houses**. An automated clearing house is simply a computer and software, operated by banks or the Fed, that facilitates direct deposit of money into the accounts of the parties being paid. This is typically used for employee payrolls rather than payments to suppliers. Since funds are immediately transferred from the firm's account to employee accounts, there is no disbursement float in these payments. The savings to the firm in reduced paper work costs and improved employee relations are often greater than the benefits derived from having float. General Motors, which has a very large number of suppliers, has been exploring ways to provide electronic payments to them as well.

Efficient cash management is more difficult for large national firms which have many local facilities paying bills, a number of bank accounts, and customers all over the country. Firms with international operations have even greater problems that are discussed later in this chapter. However, the sums of money involved are generally large enough to justify the use of specialists to keep close watch over cash flows. A one-day speedup in receipts or a one-day slowdown in disbursements may not be terribly important to a firm with cash flows of $1000 per day. For a firm with cash flows of $1 million per day, a one-day speedup means that $1 million in additional funds is available. At 9 percent interest, which has often been available in recent years, $1 million provides interest income of $90,000 per year, which will easily cover the salary of a full-time specialist to manage the firm's cash flows.

MANAGING CASH BALANCES

Cash flow management is concerned with obtaining cash in the form of available balances in the firm's demand deposit accounts. How much cash does a firm need to keep in these accounts? The answer to this question is relevant in determining how much money is available for investment and how much money the firm needs to borrow.

There are two primary reasons for a firm to maintain balances in an account—to have money available to pay checks written on the account and to compensate the bank for services. **Compensating balances** are funds on deposit in the bank that the firm must maintain to pay the bank for loan and deposit services rendered. Traditionally, banks have preferred that they be indirectly compensated for services such as check processing, lock boxes, and funds transfers by having firms keep demand deposits with them. Since (as of 1990) banks do not pay interest on demand deposits, any money kept in these accounts above amounts needed for the firm's own purposes amounts to a zero-interest loan to the bank. The alternative is for the bank to charge an explicit fee for the services. Banks also often require the firm to maintain demand deposit balances as part of a loan agreement. For many large firms, the compensating balance requirements of their banks determine the level of their cash balances—that is, for these firms, no additional balances are maintained. Since compensating balances are frequently part of lending agreements, we will examine them again in Chapter 19. Here we will show how an appropriate level may be determined as compensation for deposit services.

Banks use the following formula to translate a charge for bank services into a compensating balance.

$$\text{Compensating balance} = \text{BSC/ECR} \tag{18-4}$$

BSC is the annualized bank service charge and ECR is the bank's earnings credit rate. The bank will usually calculate the earnings credit rate based on a money market interest rate (for example, the 90 day Treasury bill rate) adjusted for reserve requirements on the deposits. The concept here is that the bank must be able to earn enough on the deposits to equal the service charge. If the reserve requirement is 10 percent, the bank only has use of 90 percent of the funds on deposit. Suppose the Treasury bill rate is six percent. Then the earnings credit rate would be calculated as 90 percent of six percent of 5.4 percent. Suppose that the service charge for the month of January is $90. The annualized January service charge is $1080 (12 × $90) and the compensating balance required is $20,000 ($1080/0.054) from Eq. (18-4). This is the balance that must be maintained for one month to compensate the bank for the January service charge. In practice, the bank would apply the earnings credit rate to the firm's average deposit balance for January to determine whether the service charge was covered. The firm might be asked to keep higher balances in February or to pay a net fee if January balances were below $20,000.

Transaction balances are cash balances held in banks to facilitate daily payments. The firm must have cash in the bank to pay checks written on the account. However, determination of the appropriate amount of transaction balances is not an easy problem.[4] First, since all available balances in the bank can serve as compensating balances, many firms find that compensating balances are more than sufficient to serve for transaction purposes. However, it is useful to have some idea of the transaction balance needed in order to determine the true cost of maintaining a compensating balance.[5] Accordingly, let's consider the factors that must be considered in determining the appropriate transaction balance.

On every business day, checks may be presented against the firm's account for payment. The firm may be depositing checks daily or less frequently and, depending on the situation, funds from those deposits may be available immediately or with some delay. The available balance in the account is:

[4] Two classic papers on the subject are William J. Baumol, "The Transactions Demand for Cash—An Inventory Theoretic Approach," *Quarterly Journal of Economics*, 66 (November 1952), pp. 545–556 and Merton H. Miller and Daniel Orr, "A Model of the Demand for Money by Firms," *Quarterly Journal of Economics*, 80 (August 1966), pp. 413–435. The Baumol paper adapts the EOQ formula [Eq. (17-11)] to determine the average level of cash balances.

[5] The cost of maintaining a compensating balance depends on the additional cash that must be held on deposit relative to the amount that would be held in the absence of the compensating balance; i.e., for transactions purposes.

$$\text{Available balance} = \text{beginning available balance} + \text{receipts}$$
$$- \text{disbursements} \qquad (18\text{-}5)$$

Receipts are funds made available during the day from deposits of currency and from checks being credited to the firm's account from today's deposits or deposits made earlier. Disbursements are currency withdrawals and checks being presented that day. In order to manage the cash position of the firm, the financial manager must know what that available balance is. This requires information from the bank to the manager. Furthermore, the balance can change during the day as the Federal Reserve now presents checks both in the morning and in the afternoon. Having some minimum transaction balance provides a "buffer" for uncertainty in cash receipts and disbursements somewhat akin to a safety stock for inventory. If the beginning balance is too low, the firm may run out of cash when disbursements exceed receipts. In this case, the firm will have to borrow or sell securities (if it has any) to raise money to cover the shortage of funds. These actions involve some transactions costs, much like order costs of inventory. The more frequently such transactions are needed, the higher the costs. On the other hand, holding large balances results in the firm's either foregoing the opportunity to invest in securities or having to borrow more money. Thus, there is a "holding cost" to cash, again similar to the holding cost for inventory.

The financial manager should determine the transaction balance that minimizes total costs. The solution to this problem depends greatly on the size of the firm. For example, suppose that transaction costs are approximately $10 per transaction. That is, it costs $10 every time the manager adds money to the bank account. Also assume that the holding cost is 0.02 percent per day. The holding cost of keeping $50,000 in the account for one day is precisely equal to $10 (0.0002 × $50,000). For a large firm, single transactions in excess of $1 million are normal. The holding cost of keeping $1 million in the account for one day is $200 (0.0002 × $1 million). Therefore, the holding cost for a large firm is much greater than the $10 transaction cost. For large firms, transactions costs are not very significant to the decision as to how much cash to keep. The cash managers of large firms usually make daily transfers. For small firms, the costs of careful cash management (the manager's time devoted to it) may exceed the net benefits of being more efficient. That is, it may not pay small firms to try to maintain cash balances at a level that minimizes transactions and holding costs because it will take too much management time for the benefits derived. Large firms have incentives to keep close track of balances. They may pay the banks to operate zero-balance disbursement accounts. They may also have funds in excess of any compensating balances automatically invested by the bank in overnight repurchase agreements (described in Table 18-2, pp. 684–685). This arrangement is called a "sweep" account because excess cash is "swept" into investments. The financial managers of large firms try to keep cash balances to the barest minimum sufficient to meet transaction requirements and to compensate the bank.

Keeping cash balances at the minimum level requires careful management, especially for companies that have offices and banks in multiple locations. Efficient cash management requires that financial managers know the balances in all corporate bank accounts on a timely basis. For large corporations, timely means daily or even hourly. The information may be obtained via telephone, fax, or other means. Major banks offer balance reporting through computer terminals at the financial manager's office. The manager can access required information on the terminal regarding any account covered by the system. Given this knowledge, the manager can decide where funds should be transferred or invested.

Concentration of cash is the simplest way to gain control of it. Once excess balances in the firm's banks have been identified, the next step is to concentrate the money in an account at one of the firm's major banks. This bank is called a **concentration bank**. The fastest way to move money from one bank to another is wire transfer. Funds transferred by wire become available for use the same day. There are two wire transfer systems in use in the United States. The Fed Wire is operated by the Federal Reserve System, and money transfers are done by bookkeeping entries on the accounts of the banks in the Federal Reserve System. The Bank Wire is a private wire service subscribed to by banks. Transfers over the Bank Wire are made by entries to accounts of the banks that are members. Because wire transfers are relatively more expensive ($3–$10 per transfer) than other methods of moving money, such as checks, they are most often used for transferring amounts in excess of $5000. Systems are now available that allow the financial manager to initiate a wire transfer directly from a computer terminal. These systems can reduce the cost of the transfer.

An alternative to wire transfer is a **depository transfer check**, which costs only a few cents. These are checks drawn on a depository bank (one in which the firm deposits checks and currency) that are payable only to the account in the firm's concentration bank. The concentration bank issues the checks for deposit in the concentration account. Depository transfer checks are not signed. The firm's cash manager simply tells the concentration bank the amounts that should be transferred and the banks that the checks should be drawn on. They are cleared as ordinary checks. Automated depository transfer services are also available from many banks. Under an automated system, the concentration bank creates electronic fund transfers from the depository accounts to the concentration account. Once the cash has been concentrated in a single account, it is under the control of the cash manager.

Figure 18-3 depicts a complete corporate cash management system. Receipts from customers (currency and checks) are deposited in depository banks which are located throughout the country. Sears Roebuck has approximately 4000 depository banks.[6] Depository banks include

---

[6] Sears also has approximately 1000 credit banks, banks at which Sears has established credit lines. This does not mean that Sears deals with 5000 banks. Many of Sears' depository banks also serve as credit banks. Similarly, the concentration bank for most firms is a credit bank and may also be a disbursement bank. Figure 18-3 is an indication of functional relationships only.

any lock box operations. Cash balances may be maintained in depository banks as compensating balances and as transaction accounts for local offices of the firm. Excess funds are transferred daily from these banks to a concentration bank. The critical aspect of this process is information about the balances available at each bank. The corporate cash manager is in direct contact with the concentration bank. The manager must decide what funds are needed in the accounts at the firm's disbursement banks, based on checks already presented that morning and forecasts of presentments in the afternoon. By midmorning the cash manager should know whether additional funds must be obtained by borrowing from the firm's credit banks or by selling securities. Alternatively, the manager may find that excess funds are available for investment in the money market or to repay borrowings. The decision as to what should be done with the excess funds will depend on the alternatives available and on how long a positive cash flow (receipts greater than disbursements) is expected to continue.

EVALUATING CASH MANAGEMENT METHODS

Regardless of the size and complexity of the firm's operations, the same basic approach to analyzing alternative methods of cash management is applicable. This is to compare the costs involved in more efficient management of cash with the benefits derived from the cash released. All cash management methods involve some costs—fees paid to banks, time spent by financial managers, and salaries of personnel. There may also be investment in specialized equipment such as computer terminals or communication devices. The primary benefit arises from the earnings on cash available for investment in securities or the savings in interest cost from reduction of borrowing. If no investment in equipment is involved, we can use net profit [Eq. (17-1)] as the basis for our evaluation of the cash management system. The problem is to estimate the system's cash

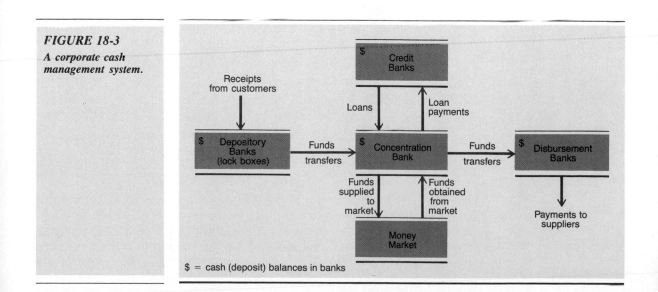

FIGURE 18-3

A corporate cash management system.

$ = cash (deposit) balances in banks

revenues and cash costs. With no equipment investment, we can make an evaluation on a pretax basis and can use net revenue as defined in Eq. (18-6):

$$\frac{\text{Net revenue}}{\text{from system}} = \frac{\text{cash revenue}}{\text{from system}} - \frac{\text{cash costs}}{\text{of system}} \tag{18-6}$$

Cash revenues are normally estimated by first determining the cash provided by the system over a one-year study period. This is measured as gross available balances produced less balances required for compensation or transaction purposes. To be accurate, the daily average of the cash provided should be determined for each month of the year. Then the financial manager must consider how the cash will be used. Normally the cash would be used either for temporary investment in securities or to reduce short-term loans. In either case, the cash can be thought of as providing interest revenues to the firm. Thus, depending on the situation in a given month, either the monthly interest rate on short-term investments or the monthly interest rate on short-term loans would be used to multiply the daily average balance for the month to obtain cash revenues for that month. The cash revenues over a twelve-month period are then added to estimate annual revenues. The reason for this procedure is that the cash provided tends to fluctuate considerably from day to day and from month to month. Therefore, to obtain an accurate evaluation, annual values must be estimated with some attention to monthly variations.

Typically, historical data are used to estimate the monthly average cash provided. These values are then projected into the future based on expected increases in firm activity (sales). Often the firm's bank is willing to provide help in this analysis, if the firm is considering use of the bank's cash management system. A bank competing for the firm's account is also quite likely to provide estimates of the cash released.

To illustrate the procedure, an example calculation of daily average cash provided for a week follows.

Day:	Mon	Tues	Wed	Thurs	Fri	Sat	Sun
Cash available:[a]	$1,400	$1,200	$1,000	$1,400	$2,200	$2,200	$2,200
Minimum required:	$ 200	$ 200	$ 200	$ 200	$ 200	$ 200	$ 200
Cash provided:	$1,200	$1,000	$ 800	$1,200	$2,000	$2,000	$2,000

Total for week: $10,200   Daily average: $1,457

[a] Dollar values in this table are given in thousands.

Thus the daily average cash provided in this example is $1.457 million. If this cash can be invested to earn 0.15 percent per week, cash revenues received by the firm for the week are $2186 (0.0015 × $1.457 million). Suppose that additional fees charged by the bank and other operating expenses incurred by the firm amount to $1500. The firm would have a positive net revenue from the cash management system of $686 ($2186 − $1500). A complete analysis of establishing a new cash management system requires an evaluation period longer than one week; we recommend one year.

If a cash management system involves equipment investment, neither a net revenue nor a net profit approach is appropriate because equipment expenditures are not reversible. (See the discussion of reversibility in the section on net profit and net present value.) The normal capital budgeting procedures described in Chapter 8 must be used to evaluate such systems, but the cash revenues can be estimated using the procedures described here. Now let's look at the securities investment activity of the cash manager.

INVESTING EXCESS CASH

The investment of excess cash is an important activity for most large firms and many smaller ones. Table 18-1 shows the amount of short-term securities investments by several companies.[7] Huge corporations like General Motors and IBM have billions of dollars invested. Large corporations such as Dow Chemical and Hawaian Electric have substantial investments in dollar terms even though the amount may be a small percentage of assets. Investment management for smaller firms, such as Genetech and Sunshine Mining, can be very important because the dollar amount of securities is large and it constitutes a high percentage of their assets. Investment management for Boeing is important no matter how you measure it. There are several reasons why firms have significant securities portfolios. Let's examine them.

---

[7] Most companies do not separate securities with less than three months maturity from cash; therefore, the total of cash and securities is shown in Table 18-1.

TABLE 18-1
Cash and short-term securities investments for selected companies (1988)

Company	(Millions)	Cash + securities/ total assets
Boeing	$ 3,963	31%
Dow Chemical	225	1
General Motors	10,181	6
Genetech	152	23
Hawaiian Electric	73	1
IBM	5,051	7
Sunshine Mining	58	20

Source: Company annual reports.

Firms with seasonal sales patterns usually have periods of one or more months during which they have excess funds. This usually occurs in the months immediately after the peak sales period. At this time, inventory and accounts receivable reach their low point of the year and collections of accounts receivable exceed cash outflows. Firms in industries where sales vary substantially over the business cycle often retain excess cash during recessions in anticipation of an upturn in the economy. As business improves, the funds will be used to finance the additional inventories and accounts receivable needed to support increased sales.

Some firms try to maintain a semipermanent "ready reserve" of securities to ensure that funds will be available to meet unexpected needs for cash. This reason for holding excess funds is sometimes called the **precautionary motive**. The practice of maintaining precautionary balances is characteristic of conservative financial managers.[8] Interestingly, most firms that do this have ready access to bank credit that serves as an alternative source of funds in emergencies and therefore makes precautionary balances somewhat unnecessary. An exception might be small firms operating in risky lines of business. For these firms, a ready reserve could prove highly desirable.

Another reason for holding excess funds is to meet a large planned payment of cash in the near future. Firms often accumulate funds in order to meet taxes, dividends, or payments on long-term debt. A similar situation arises when the firm has raised long-term capital to invest in a new plant. Such financing is often arranged in advance of the actual need for funds, and the proceeds from the sale of the firm's securities are temporarily invested in other securities prior to paying for the plant.

In cases such as these most financial managers will invest in money market securities, often planned so that the securities will mature just before the cash is needed. In the case of precautionary balances, the funds at maturity will be reinvested. The main advantage of money market securities is that they may be sold very quickly with little chance of loss due to changes in interest rates. Table 18-2 lists some methods of short-term investment used by large corporations. Small firms usually confine their investments to Treasury bills, bank (time or savings) deposits, and commercial paper.

There are situations in which firms will accumulate excess funds and invest them over long periods of time. These usually involve the planned long-run expansion of the firm and a desire on the part of the financial manager to finance anticipated needs with internally generated funds rather than with new debt or stock. Also, funds may be accumulated to retire an issue of long-term debt either prior to or at maturity. In such

---

[8] There is a reason for holding liquid assets called the speculative motive, which is not so important for business firms. Cash and short-term securities may be held in order to speculate on a possible increase in interest rates. This would not be typical of a conservative financial manager.

cases, the funds may be invested in long-term debt securities or even common stock.

The decisions as to specific investments in securities depend greatly on conditions in the securities markets and on the circumstances of the firm. The financial managers of large corporations have become very astute in their management of cash and securities.

INTERNATIONAL CASH MANAGEMENT

The objectives of cash management for an MNC are the same as those of any domestic firm: to minimize collection float, avoid excess cash balances, and maximize the earnings on cash accounts. But international cash management is complicated by the banking practices and tax regulation of many different countries. MNCs must be acquainted with the changing government restrictions on capital flow out of each country, as well as deal in multiple currencies and manage the risks associated with exchange rate fluctuations. They need to handle cash collections from around the world—regardless of the distances or mail systems involved. Finally, these corporations are often faced with the lack of international integrated exchange facilities, such as electronic funds transfer systems, that domestic firms in North America and Europe take for granted.

Despite these complications, the MNC is more likely to see the rewards of good cash management than its domestic counterpart. Besides simply being bigger and handling more cash, the firm also transacts business over longer distances, which results in more float time and more potential value from reducing the float. In addition, international firms have access to a world of investment options for short-term funds; domestic firms, in comparison, are limited to local money markets. MNCs are more likely to use electronic funds transfer, lock box systems, and concentration banks than domestic firms, because of the greater distances and greater cash amounts involved. There are alos several cash management practices that are unique to international corporations.

Payments Netting

The MNC is typically organized as a collection of affiliated subsidiary companies in various countries. Manufacturing firms can have a substantial volume of interaffiliate payments if the subsidiaries ship raw materials, subassemblies, and finished products to other units. Besides the long distances, which result in either cable charges or a long float time, international payments incur a currency exchange cost that can total up to 1 percent of the transaction amount. **Payments netting** uses centralized payment information to cancel out cross payments and avoid transaction expenses. As a simple example, if the West German subsidiary of an MNC owes its English counterpart $3 million for subassemblies, and the English subsidiary owes the West German unit $2 million for parts, the amounts can be netted into a single $1 million payment.

Because the transaction needs among the different units can be extremely complex, payments netting can result in a substantial savings.

TABLE 18-2
Methods of short-term investment used by large U.S. corporations

Type	Description	Maturities	Marketability	Minimum denomination[a]
U.S. Treasury bills	Obligation of U.S. government. Treasury issues 3- and 6-month bills weekly, 9-month and 1-year bills monthly. Sold on a discount basis.	Up to 1 year	Excellent	$10,000
Commercial paper: finance company	Unsecured notes of finance companies sold directly to investors who may specify maturity desired. May be coupon bearing but normally sold on a discount basis.	3 to 270 days	None, although issuer may be willing to redeem early	$1,000[b]
Commercial paper: dealer	Unsecured notes of major industrial firms and financial institutions sold through commercial paper dealers. Sold on a discount basis.	15 to 270 days	Generally limited to the issuing dealer	$100,000
Negotiable certificates of deposit	Certificates of time deposits at a commercial bank. Interest paid at maturity. Insured up to $100,000 by Federal Deposit Insurance Corp.	Usually less than 1 year, but may be longer	Good, for major banks	$100,000
Prime banker's acceptance	Time drafts (orders to pay) issued by a business firm (usually an importer) and "accepted" by a bank. Bank effectively guarantees payment to investor. Sold on a discount basis.	Rarely over 6 months	Good, for major banks	$25,000

Short-term tax exempts	Notes of states, municipalities, and other political subdivisions and local agencies. Project notes of public housing agencies may be backed by U.S. government. Interest is exempt from federal income tax.	Up to 1 year	Good	$1,000
Repurchase agreements	Purchase of securities with a guarantee to repurchase by the issuer of the agreement. Essentially a collateralized note. U.S. government obligations are most commonly used. Issuers are usually banks and securities dealers. Known as "repos" or "RPs."	1 day to several weeks	None	$100,000
Eurodollars	Dollar-denominated time deposits in banks or branches outside the United States. Used by multinational corporations.	Usually 30 to 180 days	Variable	$100,000
Foreign securities and deposits	Wide variety available, subject to exchange risks and tax considerations.	Up to 1 year	Variable	Variable

[a] The amounts shown are the minimum values in normal practice. Exceptions do exist.
[b] Minimum order is $25,000.

The crucial requirement of any netting scheme is a centralized payments information system with current payments data from around the world. MNC financial managers must also be aware of the restrictions on payments netting that exist in many countries, including such major economic powers as Japan. Some countries allow netting but only after each transaction is authorized. Other countries place no significant restrictions on nettings.

Cash Pooling

If there are no government restrictions on transferring funds between units, an MNC can centralize cash in one country or subsidiary. A central **cash pool** can meet the precautionary balance needs of several subsidiaries, rather than having each unit maintain its own account. Since unexpected cash needs are not likely to surprise several units at the same time, the central pool can be smaller than the sum of individually maintained cash accounts. The MNC should pool its cash in the country where safety, liquidity, and yield are the highest; this is usually the nation that has a major money market center, where liquid securities are available and a stable currency. Funds may also be held in low tax rate countries, called tax havens, where a subsidiary is set up primarily for cash pooling.

Management Information Systems

Successful payments netting and cash pooling require sophisticated and centralized reporting systems that have daily access to the cash positions and cash needs of the many subsidiaries. With a good information system in place, the financial managers of an MNC can detect and respond to opportunities to optimize corporate funds. If one unit, for example, has idle cash while another is using short-term financing to cover a cash deficit, the corporation can shift the funds that are needed and lower its total financing costs. The value of these systems is particularly high in areas such as Europe, where electronic funds transfer between banks in different countries is available. As in any information system, the costs of data collection, computer hardware and software, and operating personnel must be weighed against the benefits of comprehensive and timely information.

SUMMARY

The management of cash and marketable securities involves four considerations: (1) the minimum cash balance, (2) the amount of excess funds to be invested in marketable securities, (3) the particular securities to be purchased, and (4) efficient management of the firm's cash flow. Financial managers attempt to reduce collection float and to control disbursements in order to increase the funds available for other uses.

In evaluating cash management systems, an analysis of net revenue (annual cash revenues less annual cash costs) is used when no equipment investment is needed. Otherwise standard capital budgeting procedures apply.

International cash management involves a more complex set of considerations than does domestic cash management. Cash receipts and disbursements are usually managed within each country, and only net balances are transferred to the control of the corporate treasurer. Intracompany payments are netted out before any cross-border transfers are made. Funds will be pooled for investment in countries that provide good short-term investment opportunities, low tax rate, and stable currencies. Good information systems are critical to international cash management.

QUESTIONS

1 Define the following terms:
   a Cash cycle period
   b Collection float
   c Availability time
   d Disbursement float
2 What are the three components of collection float, and how can this float be reduced?
3 Explain the difference between compensating balances and transaction balances.
4 The marketing manager of your firm has suggested installing an electronic communications network connecting all the firm's plants and offices around the country. As financial manager, would you find such a network useful in managing the firm's cash position? What kinds of information would you want and how would you use the information?
5 Suppose you are considering various alternative means of investing $2 million that will be needed in ninety days to pay federal income taxes. What alternatives would you consider?
6 A representative of Big City National Bank is trying to obtain your firm's demand deposit account. As part of the bank's sales pitch, a "lock box" system is being heavily promoted. How interested would you be in this system if you were the financial manager of the following businesses:
   a A nationwide chain of self-service laundromats
   b An auto parts wholesaler selling primarily to service stations in the Kansas City metropolitan area
   c A manufacturer of speaker cabinets made on custom order selling to hi-fi dealers on the West Coast
   d A mail-order retail clothing business that allows its customers fifteen days to inspect the merchandise before they have to pay
7 Within the past fifteen years or so retail merchants who provide charge accounts, gasoline companies with credit cards, and similar businesses have shifted from billing all customers at the end of each month to "cycle billing." With cycle billing, customers are billed throughout the month. For example, customers whose last names begin with "A" may be billed on the first day of the month, those with last names beginning with "L" in the middle of the month, those with last names beginning with

"Z" at the end of the month. Any given customer is billed at the same time each month.

a As a customer of a firm who has just switched over, would the change matter to you? In considering the change, would it make any difference whether your personal income is received weekly rather than monthly?

b Discuss the advantages and disadvantages of cycle billing to the business firms. Consider the impact on cash flows, and any costs involved.

8 Large companies in their domestic cash management use concentration banks to centralize cash control. Do multinational firms use the same type of system? Why would an MNC use a different approach?

PROJECT

Suppose you are an assistant to the manager of a small business. The firm has $100,000 cash that will not be needed in its operations for six months. Using *The Wall Street Journal* or other sources, develop a recommendation to the manager concerning how the money should be invested. Include in your recommendation an estimate of the earnings to be achieved and discuss any risks your investment strategy entails.

**DEMONSTRATION
PROBLEMS**

DP1 The financial manager of the CM Company has analyzed both the collection and the disbursement operations of the firm (all times and amounts shown are averages). It takes five days for CM to record a payment as received by the accounts receivable department once its customers initiate payment. Checks are deposited at the bank one day later. The bank provides available balances on the same day as the deposits occur ("immediate availability"). On the other hand, it only takes four days from the time CM mails checks to its suppliers and employees until the checks clear CM's bank account. CM's sales are entirely on open account and amount to $20,000 per day. CM keeps petty cash of $500 on hand and disburses $18,000 per day.

a How large is CM's collection float?

b How large is CM's disbursement float?

c If CM maintains a cash balance of $40,000 on its own books, how large will its available balance be at the bank?

SOLUTION TO DP1:

a Collection time = 5 days + 1 day = 6 days

Collection float = 6 days × $20,000 per day = $120,000

b Disbursement float = 4 days × $18,000 per day = $72,000

c Available balance = book balance + disbursement float
  − currency − processing float
  − availability float

$$= \$40,000 + \$72,000 - \$500 - (1 \text{ day} \times \$20,000) - (0 \text{ days} \times \$20,000)$$
$$= \$91,500$$

DP2 CM Company's bank is changing its policy of immediate availability. (See problem **DP1** for CM Company data.) The bank estimates that the availability time it obtains for checks deposited by CM is 1.5 days and will now make funds available to CM only when funds are available to the bank. However, the bank has a cash collection service that it will offer to CM at a cost of $50 per month. This service should reduce the time it takes for checks to reach the bank by one day. Short-term interest rates are at 7 percent per year, and CM normally has some funds invested in securities. What should CM do?

SOLUTION TO DP2:
One possibility is to try to find another bank that will provide immediate availability. The other alternatives are to go or not go with the bank's collection service. The increase in availability time is irrelevant to the choice between these last two alternatives.

Improved collection of one day would reduce collection float by (1 day × $20,000) = $20,000. The $20,000 can be invested at an annual rate of 7 percent. The net annual revenues from the bank's system would be:

Net revenues = revenues − costs

$$= 7\% \times \$20,000 - \$50 \times 12 \text{ months}$$

$$= \$800 \text{ per year.}$$

Therefore, unless CM can find a bank that will provide immediate availability (and costs and services that are competitive with the current bank), it should go with the improved collection system.

PROBLEMS

1 The cash manager of Roberts Distribution, Inc., Linda Davis, has observed that the average collection period for the firm is 32 days. From an analysis of the postmarks on the envelopes received, Linda estimates that checks are in the mail an average of 4 days before being received at Roberts' office. It takes 6 days on average between the time a check is received and the time funds are made available by Roberts' bank. Annual sales are $29.2 million. How much collection float does Roberts have on average?

2 Linda Davis (see problem *1* for additional information) finds that, when the mail is delivered to Roberts, payments are routed to the accounts receivable department for credit to the appropriate customers' accounts. On average, it takes three days before all checks received are recorded and another two days before the checks are deposited at the bank. Roberts writes an average of $70,000 per day in checks payable to its employees and suppliers. It takes about five days before Roberts' checks are presented at its bank for payment. Roberts' cash on its books, including currency of $1000, averages $175,000 per day.

a What is Roberts' average availability time?
b What is Roberts' average available cash balance in its bank account?

3 Linda Davis (see problems *1* and *2* for additional information) has proposed that a clerk be assigned to open all mail when it is received in the morning. Any checks received should be taken out, the amount recorded, and then deposited in the bank on the same day. The cost of this system would be $8000 per year in additional wages and benefits. Any additional funds generated could be invested at 6 percent per year. Evaluate Linda's proposal.

4 As financial manager of Anderson Hardware Supply, you have been concerned with the impact of increased sales on the firm's available cash. You have gathered the following information (all data are average values).

Payments to suppliers	= $2200 per day
Payment period	= 15 days
Disbursement time	= 3 days
Inventory period	= 60 days
Customer payment period	= 35 days
Collection period	= 38 days
Check collections and deposits	= $2740 per day
Check processing time	= 1.5 days
Availability time	= 2.5 days

a What is the cash cycle period for Anderson? Use two methods to calculate this. Which one is the most accurate? [One of the answers is 83 days.]
b If Anderson increased its purchases by $100 per day with a corresponding increase in sales, what would be the impact on the firm's cash position for the first cash cycle after the increase in purchases?
c What is Anderson's current disbursement float?
d What is Anderson's current processing float?
e What is Anderson's current availability float?
f What is Anderson's current mail float?
g What is Anderson's current collection float?

5 The Steak 'n Tater Company (STC) is franchiser of a national chain of fast-food restaurants. The company sells a variety of supplies to its franchisees, and its cash receipts average $400,000 per day. Based on an analysis of the payments received, STC's management estimates that it takes seven days on average between the time a check is mailed to the firm and the time the money is actually available for use.

    a How much money is being tied up by the seven-day delay?

    b Suppose that the delay could be reduced to five days. How much additional money would be available for other uses?

    c The company's bank has indicated that by introducing special handling of the checks and going to a lock box system the delay could be reduced from seven days to three days. In order to do this, however, the bank says that STC must increase its demand deposits by $600,000; that is, the firm's average balance must increase by that amount. In addition, the firm would incur a variety of additional costs amounting to $70,000 per year. The financial manager of STC plans to invest the money freed by the new cash management system in marketable securities yielding 10 percent per year. Is the new system worth implementing?

6 The Baltimore Oyster Company has average check collections of $5000 per day. By using a messenger service at a cost of $3.00 per working day (assume 250 working days per year), the company could save one day of average check processing time. Any improvements in available cash would enable the company to reduce its loan with the bank which costs 12 percent per year.

    a What net annual revenue could be expected from use of the messenger service?

    b What is the minimum average level of collections that would make use of the messenger service worthwhile?

7 Vesuvius Pizza Company sells supplies to pizza restaurants throughout the eastern United States. Under current procedures, collection float averages $2.8 million (7 days × $400,000 per day). A bank in New York has proposed that Vesuvius establish a lock box there, which is estimated to reduce collection float by $300,000. The manager of the collection department estimates additional costs savings from the reduced volume of checks processed at $3000 per year. The bank's proposal requires Vesuvius to maintain compensating balances with the bank of $100,000. In addition, costs of wire transfer and other items would be $5000 per year. The interest rate applicable to any increase in available cash is 10 percent per year. What are the net revenues from a New York lock box? Is the lock box worthwhile?

8 Trevino Luggage Company (TLC) maintains banking relationships with fourteen banks around the country. Currently a bank in Dallas handles all transactions in the southwest region. Cash re-

ceipts processed through the Dallas bank average $800,000 (600 checks) per day. The bank requires that demand deposit balances of $500,000 be maintained for this service; no fees are involved. TLC's financial manager expects to earn 8 percent per year on short-term securities investments. (Daily check volume is based on 365 days per year.)

a The Dallas bank has offered to renegotiate the terms of its agreement with TLC. The bank wants to institute a per-check charge for processing of $0.05 plus a new (lower) compensating deposit balance. As financial manager for TLC, what is the maximum balance you would be willing to accept, given that you have the alternative of staying with the existing arrangement?

b A bank in Phoenix has approached TLC with the suggestion that it handle all New Mexico and Arizona transactions, currently $200,000 per day. You believe that this arrangement would reduce cash receipt time by 1.2 days on average for transactions in the two states. The Phoenix bank wants a flat fee of $10,000 per year for the service; no balances would be involved. The Dallas bank has indicated that it would require only $400,000 in balances (as compared to the existing requirements of $500,000) if TLC uses the Phoenix bank for New Mexico and Arizona transactions. What do you recommend?

FLOAT REDUCTION AND CASH FLOWS: AN EXAMPLE

In Chapter 18, we discussed the fact that a reduction in float makes cash available for other uses by the firm. We pointed out that, for example, if collections of accounts receivable average $100,000 per day, a reduction of two days of collection time would reduce collection float by $200,000. This $200,000 float reduction results in a onetime increase in the firm's available cash of $200,000. In this appendix, we show exactly how the cash balances increase.

Suppose the firm currently receives and deposits checks from a group of customers at a rate of $100,000 per day. Total collection time (mail time + processing time + availability time) is five days—that is, five days (on average) after a customer mails a check, the firm has cash available in its bank account. The firm is considering establishing a lock box that would reduce collection time to three days, a reduction of two days. Therefore, three days (on average) after a customer mails a check, the firm will have the cash available. Further, assume that the lock box system is scheduled to be implemented on May 1 (5/1). This means that, with the lock box system, checks put in the mail by customers *before* May 1 result in available cash after five days, and checks mailed on May 1 or thereafter result in available cash after three days. Exhibit 18-1 illustrates the timing involved.

We see from Exhibit 18-1 that the immediate effect of the lock box system is to speed by two days the cash made available by checks mailed from May 1 and thereafter. On May 4 and on May 5, with the lock box operating, the firm will obtain $200,000 in available cash (two days of collections) rather than the normal $100,000 per day, an extra $100,000 on each day. Therefore, with the lock box, the firm has an extra $200,000 in total. However, daily cash flows are the same for the two systems after May 3. Therefore, the firm has a onetime (permanent) increase in cash of $200,000.

The $200,000 is a reversible gain. Imagine what happens if the lock box is taken out of operation. There will be two days for which the firm does not receive any cash. Therefore the firm will receive $200,000 less in cash when the policy is reversed.

This example is highly simplified in order to illustrate the point. In practice, cash flows are not even, especially when weekends and holidays are taken into account. That is why we suggested the use of average figures over a year to determine the actual impact of a lock box or other cash management systems.

The added $200,000 cash under the lock box system results from a speedup of collections with no change in recorded sales. If, as is usual, the firm is on an accrual basis for tax purposes, taxes are also unaffected since taxes are based on accrued sales. The $200,000 cash is the benefit from the system. If the firm pays taxes on a cash basis, the speedup of cash collections would result in greater cash inflows for tax purposes and greater taxes in the year the lock box was established. These added taxes would have to be deducted in computing the net benefit of the lock box system.

EXHIBIT 18-1
The effect of a lock box system taking effect on May 1.

Day mailed	Amount mailed	Date cash is available	
		Without lock box	With lock box
4/26	$100,000	5/1	5/1
4/27	100,000	5/2	5/2
4/28	100,000	5/3	5/3
4/29	100,000	5/4	5/4
4/30	100,000	5/5	5/5
5/1[a]	100,000	5/6	5/4
5/2	100,000	5/7	5/5
5/3	100,000	5/8	5/6
5/4	100,000	5/9	5/7

[a] Date of implementation of lock box system.

CHAPTER NINETEEN

SHORT-TERM FINANCING

After planning investment in current assets and forecasting funds required by the firm over the coming year, the financial manager must arrange for financing. The general principles of financing decisions were examined in Chapter 12. After deciding on the combination of debt and equity sources to be used, the financial manager must decide on the particular types of debt financing. Short-term borrowing is typically used to finance temporary investments in current assets. In this chapter we will discuss the principles used by the financial manager in deciding what types of short-term financing to obtain. In Chapter 20 we will examine the problem of how much short-term financing should be used relative to long-term financing.

This chapter will be divided into three main sections covering:

1 The characteristics of major sources of short-term financing, such as bank loans. We will evaluate the advantages and disadvantages of each source of credit and analyze the cost of each credit source to the borrower.
2 The pledging of inventory and accounts receivable to lenders as security for short-term credit. We will describe the types of secured debt agreements used by businesses for short-term financing.
3 The financing of international trade.

MAJOR SOURCES OF SHORT-TERM FINANCING

In choosing a source of short-term financing, the financial manager will be concerned with the following five aspects of each financing arrangement:

1 *Cost.* Generally the financial manager will seek to minimize the cost of financing, which usually can be expressed as an annual interest rate. Therefore, the financing source with the lowest interest rate will be chosen. However, there are other factors that may be important in particular situations.
2 *Impact on credit rating.* Use of some sources may affect the firm's credit rating more than the use of others. A poor credit rating limits the availability, and increases the cost, of additional financing.

3 *Reliability*. Some sources are more reliable than others in that funds are more likely to be available when they are needed.

4 *Restrictions*. Some creditors are more apt to impose restrictions on the firm than are others. Restrictions might include dollar limits on dividends, management salaries, and capital expenditures.

5 *Flexibility*. Some sources are more flexible than others in that the firm can very easily increase or decrease the amount of funds provided.

All these factors must usually be considered before making the decision as to the sources of financing.

The three primary sources of short-term financing for business firms are, in descending order of importance, trade credit, loans from commercial banks, and commercial paper. Both trade credit and commercial paper are unsecured forms of credit, whereas banks make both secured and unsecured loans. A secured loan is one for which the borrower pledges specific assets as security for the loan. Automobile loans are secured consumer loans. Business firms usually pledge accounts receivable or inventory as security for short-term loans. In this section we will consider only unsecured types of credit from the three major sources; secured financing arrangements are covered later in the chapter.

Trade Credit

Trade credit for a business firm is equivalent to a charge account for a consumer. When a firm (the purchaser) buys goods from another firm (the supplier), it normally does not have to pay for those goods immediately. During the period of time before payment becomes due, the purchaser has a debt outstanding to the supplier. This debt is recorded on the purchaser's balance sheet as a liability, **accounts payable**. The corresponding account for the supplier is, of course, accounts receivable, which was discussed in Chapter 17. Normal business transactions therefore provide the firm with a source of short-term financing, trade credit, because of the time between delivery and payment. The amount of financing depends on the volume of purchases and when the purchases are paid for. For example, suppose the firm purchases $1000 of goods every day from its suppliers and always pays thirty days after receiving the goods. The firm would have 30 × $1000 = $30,000 of accounts payable or trade credit outstanding at all times.

An attractive feature of trade credit as a financing source is that it responds readily to an increase in the firm's purchases such as might occur during a seasonal buildup of inventory. If purchases double to $2000 per day, accounts payable will double to 30 × $2000 = $60,000, if the firm continues to pay on a thirty-day schedule.

The cost to the firm for utilizing this financing source depends on several factors, one of which is the credit terms granted by the firm's suppliers. Table 19-1 shows the different terms under which goods are sold. These terms vary considerably according to the industry involved. As we indicated in our discussion of accounts receivable, credit terms

TABLE 19-1
Terms of sale

Terms	Definition	Use
CBD	Cash before delivery: goods must be paid for before shipment is made.	High-risk customers.
COD	Cash on delivery: goods are shipped to customer, who must pay the shipper before taking possession	High-risk customers or those for whom credit information is lacking.
SDDL	Sight draft—bill of lading attached: when goods are shipped, a draft for the purchase price plus a bill of lading (shipping document) is sent to firm's bank for payment. Firm must pay for goods in order to obtain bill of lading needed to get goods from shipper.	Automobile manufacturers, meat packers, and fruit and vegetable canners are typical sellers. Sometimes used by others when large shipments are made.
Net cash (net 7 days; net 10 days; bill to bill)	Goods must be paid for in 7 or 10 days depending on industry. Bill to bill terms require payment on previous delivery when a new one is made.	Retail store purchases of tobacco, produce, fresh meat, and dairy products.
Ordinary terms (2/10, net 30; 2/10, net 60; 1/15, net 30; net 30, etc.)	Terms of 2/10, net 30 provide a discount of 2% if payment is made within 10 days of the invoice date; otherwise payment is due in 30 days.	Many lines of business. Most common trade credit terms.
Monthly billing (2/10, EOM, net 30; 2/10, prox., net 30; 8/10, EOM)	A single payment for all purchases made before the 25th of one month is made in the next month. A cash discount for payment within the first 10 days (2/10) may be quoted. EOM stands for "end of month"; "prox." is an abbreviation of *proximo*, Latin word for "next."	Apparel trades, lumber, books, and other lines of business where several orders may be placed during a given month by the purchasing firm.
Seasonal dating (net 30, January 1; net 30, October 1; 2/10, net 30, January 1)	Payment for all goods shipped prior to the indicated date (Jan. 1) is due per the rest of the terms (net 30; 2/10, net 30).	Businesses with distinct seasons, such as toys, Christmas cards, and school textbooks.
Consignment	Payment for goods is made after they are sold by purchasing firm. Title to the goods remains with original supplier until sale by purchasing firm.	May be used in any business but commonly for rack jobbers in supermarkets, magazines, and photographic supplies.

tend to be fairly similar within a given industry. However, some suppliers may provide more lenient terms than others. If the quality, price, and service provided by the more lenient firms are not inferior to those provided by others, purchasing from those suppliers *may* be to our advantage. Why isn't it *surely* to our advantage?

The answer depends on the nature of the credit terms offered and our alternatives. Suppose two suppliers of comparable products offer the following ordinary credit terms. Supplier *A* sells on terms 2/10, net 30, and supplier *B* sells on terms 2/10, net 60 (see Table 19-1). Since *B* offers better terms than *A*, you might think that it is clearly better to buy from *B*. However, the cash discounts offered by both are the same, 2 percent if the account is paid within ten days.

Suppose you are considering purchasing from *B* and waiting for sixty days before making payment. The cost of foregoing a cash discount (that is, of paying after the ten-day discount period) can be expressed as an annual interest rate as follows:

Annual interest rate = rate per period × number of periods per year

$$= \frac{\text{discount}}{100\% - \text{discount}} \times \frac{365 \text{ days}}{\text{payment period} - \text{discount period}} \quad (19\text{-}1)$$

In the example above the discount is 2 percent, the payment period is sixty days, and the discount period is ten days. Therefore the annual interest rate is

$$\text{Annual interest rate} = \frac{2\%}{100\% - 2\%} \times \frac{365 \text{ days}}{60 \text{ days} - 10 \text{ days}}$$

$$= 0.0204 \times 7.3$$

$$= 0.1489 \text{ or approximately } 15\%$$

The reasoning behind this formula is that, if you do not pay within ten days, you must pay 100 percent of the invoice price of the goods. If you do pay within ten days, you will pay only 98 percent (100% − 2%) of the invoice price. The first ten days (discount period) do not cost you anything. The amount of financing you are really getting after ten days is therefore 98 percent of the invoice price, but you are incurring a dollar cost of 2 percent of the price for the privilege of delaying payment. The ratio 2%/(100% − 2%) expresses the basic interest cost of foregoing the discount for the period involved, .0204 or 2.04 percent. If you pay sixty days (payment period) after the invoice date, you have really gotten only an additional fifty days (payment period − discount period) of credit. You are therefore paying 2.04 percent for fifty days of credit. At an annual rate this amounts to 365 days/50 days × 0.0204 = 15 percent per year.

If you were to buy from supplier *A* and pay thirty days later, it would cost you 37 percent [2%/(100% − 2%) × 365 days/(30 days −

10 days) = 0.37]. By this measure B is still a better deal.[1] However, do you really want to pay 15 percent for short-term financing from supplier B? If you have money invested in securities at 10 percent or can borrow from the bank at 12 percent, you would probably rather take the cash discount no matter which supplier you buy from. Therefore it might not make any difference to you, since both suppliers offer the same discount. If A provided better service, you would prefer A in this case.

Using Eq. (19-1) to compute the annual interest rate enables the financial manager to determine the cost of foregoing cash discounts. This cost is the basic interest cost of trade credit financing. There are other factors that are also important in assessing the desirability and possibilities of using this source of short-term financing.

The dollar volume of a firm's purchases determines the amount of trade credit financing available to it. This type of financing arises only from the firm's not paying immediately for its purchases. As such, it is flexible and very convenient, but rather limited in amount. Trade credit does not provide a direct source of cash to pay other bills. Purchases provide goods, not cash. Moreover, a firm that persistently does not pay its bills when due is apt to develop a poor credit rating. Suppliers may become reluctant to provide credit, requiring the firm to purchase on COD or even CBD terms (see Table 19-1). This can present problems for the firm in several ways.

First, the firm may not be able to find alternative sources of credit (for example, a bank loan). In this case the amount of inventory that the firm can carry may be severely limited, and therefore its sales and profits will fall. Second, the loss of trade credit imposes a cost on the firm and that is not inconsequential. Suppose that the Tight Company is purchasing on terms of net 30 (no cash discount) and is paying after sixty days. If purchases are $1000 per day, the firm would have $60,000 of accounts payable. If Tight paid within thirty days, it would have accounts payable of $30,000. However, delaying payment to sixty days gives Tight a poor credit rating, and suppliers could require the firm to pay cash for goods ordered. Its accounts payable would then shrink to zero. Suppose Tight can borrow from the bank at a rate of 12 percent. If the firm pays its suppliers on time (within thirty days), it will have $30,000 of free credit from suppliers and $30,000 of bank credit at 12 percent. If instead, Tight delays payment to sixty days, it may be required to borrow the entire $60,000 at 12 percent. By paying on time, the firm would be paying 12 percent on $30,000 and 0 percent on $30,000 for an average rate of 6 percent on its short-term financing of $60,000. On the other hand, by delaying payment, Tight would end up paying 12 percent on $60,000. The interest cost of delaying payment is twice the cost of paying on time; in addition, the firm acquires a bad credit reputation.

---

[1] If payment to A were delayed for sixty days, the interest cost would be the same as for B. However, in this case the account is overdue and this may cause problems in the future as discussed below.

Moreover, COD terms impose costs of their own on the firm. Fees are charged by the shipper to collect payment, and cash discounts are not offered to COD customers. Of course, if alternative sources of credit are very expensive and if suppliers are relatively forgiving, it may be desirable to "stretch the payables" (as paying late is called). Occasionally delaying payment or paying only a few days later can be done without disturbing suppliers. However, this practice can be expensive for the firm if carried to extremes.

Bank Loans

The second major source of short-term financing for business firms is loans from commercial banks. Short-term commercial bank loans are generally made in the form of a **note**—a written and signed statement in which the borrower agrees to repay the loan when it is due and to pay interest. Notes may be payable on demand by the bank (demand notes), or payable in thirty days, ninety days, or one year (thirty-day notes, ninety-day notes, etc.). This is in contrast with trade credit, where the only evidence the supplier has of money owed is the purchase request and the invoice. In this section we will discuss some general characteristics of unsecured bank loans. Secured loans are described in more detail in the next section.

Seasonal Loans   Seasonal loans have traditionally been the basic type of credit provided by banks to business firms. Such loans are called **self-liquidating** as they are used to finance temporary increases in inventory and accounts receivable, which are soon converted into cash to repay the loan. For example, textbook publishers have a well-defined pattern of seasonal borrowings. Their borrowings begin in February, as inventory accumulates and books are shipped out to the schools and bookstores, and reach their peak in September/October, at which time payments start pouring in. The majority of seasonal loans are unsecured, although in recent years an increasing number of them have involved collateral. A typical seasonal loan is based on a line of credit previously requested by the firm and approved by the bank.

A **line of credit** is an informal agreement by the bank to lend up to a stated maximum amount to the firm. The bank does not have a legal commitment to supply the funds when the firm requests them, but banks tend to feel a moral obligation to do so. The procedure works as follows for a firm that has been a regular customer of the bank. At the low point of the season, the financial manager estimates funds required for the coming year and then asks the bank for a line of credit equal to the maximum expected need for funds. Usually the firm will provide the bank with its most current financial statement and may include forecasted financial statements to support its request. A financial forecast is especially desirable if the firm is requesting a significant increase in the line of credit. If everything looks reasonable to the bank, one of its officers will write a letter to the firm indicating the amount of the line, the interest rate, and usually a statement that the firm should be "out of the bank" (not borrowing) for at least one or two months during the year.

This latter provision is intended to ensure that the loan is really a short-term seasonal loan and does not involve permanent financing. The firm will then borrow money as it needs it in the form of thirty- or ninety-day notes, where the total outstanding cannot exceed the credit line.[2]

There is another type of credit arrangement, similar to a line of credit, called **revolving credit**. In this case, the bank makes a legal commitment to extend credit up to the maximum. Revolving credit agreements usually involve both seasonal and longer-term financing and extend over several years. The bank may require a fee based on the unused portion of the credit. For example, if the maximum is $500,000 and the firm is currently borrowing $300,000, a fee such as 0.5 percent per year might be charged on the $200,000 not being used in addition to the interest on the $300,000 borrowed.

Bankers consider seasonal lines of credit to be one of the most desirable types of loans to make. The interest rates are often lower on this type of loan than on any other that might be requested by a given firm. However, banks usually require that a firm borrowing under a line of credit maintain a minimum average demand deposit with the bank. This amount is called a **compensating balance** and is expressed as a percentage of the loan. For example, a compensating-balance requirement of 15 percent means that, if the firm is borrowing $100,000, its minimum average checking account at the bank must be $15,000. In addition, there may be a compensating-balance requirement on the unused portion of the credit line. This is invariably a lower percentage than that for the borrowed portion. For example, if the credit line of this borrower were $150,000, then the compensating balance on the unused portion might be 8 percent. When the firm is borrowing $100,000, $50,000 of the credit is unused and an additional $4000 (0.08 × $50,000) balance in the firm's bank account would have to be maintained. Compensating balances would therefore be $15,000 (15 percent of $100,000) on the borrowed portion and $4000 (8 percent of $50,000) on the unused portion for a total of $19,000.

The deposit balances that must be held to meet compensating balance requirements may be a minimum amount at all times or calculated as an average over some period such as a month. There are significant advantages in increased flexibility of cash management and lower costs to the firm of having an average balance count and of having the averaging period be as long as possible. This is a matter of negotiation between the borrower and the bank.

Determining the impact of compensating balance requirements on the cost of a bank loan can be somewhat complicated. Complications

---

[2] In Europe such lines are often executed by the firm's simply writing checks on its account. If there are insufficient funds in the account to cover the checks, the bank will honor the overdraft and create a loan. This arrangement is more flexible since the firm isn't confined to borrowing money over an entire thirty-day period if it needs the funds for only fifteen days. Federal regulations make it difficult for banks to offer this service in the United States.

arise from variations in loan arrangements and when the bank provides services in addition to loans to the firm. A general way to compute the effective annual interest rate of a loan arrangement is to determine the annual cost (interest plus any fees) and divide the annual cost by the amount of money actually made available under the loan arrangement (amount available).

$$\text{Effective interest rate} = \frac{\text{annual cost}}{\text{amount available}} \qquad (19\text{-}2)$$

To show how to apply this general formula, we will look at some common situations.

First, suppose that the firm is borrowing under a simple credit line with a compensating balance on the amount of the loan. No other services are involved. In other words, the bank is only a credit bank for the firm as was illustrated in Figure 18-3. In a straight credit relationship, the firm will maintain deposit balances only to the extent that they are required by the bank. Suppose that the bank requires a 19 percent compensating balance. Then, on a $100,000 loan, the amount actually made available to the firm would only be 81 percent of the loan or $81,000, since $19,000 of the $100,000 borrowed would have to be kept on deposit with the bank. If the interest rate is 10 percent of the loan, the annual cost would be $10,000 (10 percent of $100,000). The effective interest rate is therefore:

$$\text{Effective interest rate} = \frac{\$10,000}{\$81,000} = 12.35\%$$

Alternatively, we can express the effective interest rate in this situation as:

$$\text{Effective interest rate} = \frac{\text{interest rate}}{(1 - \text{CBP})} \qquad (19\text{-}3)$$

$$= \frac{10\%}{(1 - 0.19)}$$

$$= 12.35\%$$

CBP is the compensating balance proportion on the amount borrowed. Equation (19-3) applies to any loan arrangement of this type.

Another formula that can be used in this situation specifies the amount that must be borrowed in order to have a given amount available. Suppose the firm actually needs $100,000. If it borrows $100,000 with a 19 percent compensating balance required, it will only have $81,000 available for use. How much must it borrow to have $100,000 available?

$$\text{Amount borrowed} = \frac{\text{amount needed}}{(1 - \text{CBP})} \qquad (19\text{-}4)$$

$$= \frac{\$100,000}{(1 - 0.19)}$$

$$= \$123,457$$

Determining the amount borrowed when there are compensating balances required on both the amount borrowed and the unused portion of a credit line requires a more complicated formula.

$$\text{Amount borrowed} = \frac{\text{amount needed} + \text{CBPU} \times \text{credit line}}{(1 - \text{CBP} + \text{CBPU})} \qquad (19\text{-}5)$$

where CBP is the compensating balance proportion on the amount borrowed and CBPU is the compensating balance proportion on the unused portion of the credit line. For example, if the firm has a credit line of $150,000, needs $100,000, CBP is 15 percent, and CBPU is 8 percent, then:

$$\text{Amount borrowed} = \frac{\$100,000 + 0.08 \times \$150,000}{(1 - 0.15 + 0.08)}$$

$$= \frac{\$112,000}{0.93}$$

$$= \$120,430$$

Although it is possible to work out formulas for the cost rate in more complex situations, we will show how to apply the general formula, Eq. (19-2), instead. Exhibit 19-1 illustrates the determination of the cost rate for a $150,000 credit line with the following conditions.

1 Compensating balances required are 15 percent of the amount borrowed. In addition, the bank charges a fee of 0.2 percent per year on the unused portion of the credit line.

EXHIBIT 19-1
Determination of the cost rate on a credit line

---

1 Annual cost = interest rate × amount borrowed + annual fees

$$= 0.10 \times \$100,000 + \$100$$

$$= \$10,100$$

2 Amount available = amount borrowed

$$- \text{ compensating balance required}$$

$$+ \text{ balances held for other purposes that can count toward compensating balance requirements}$$

$$= \$100,000 - \$15,000 + \$10,000$$

$$= \$95,000$$

3 Effective interest rate $= \dfrac{\text{annual cost}}{\text{amount available}}$

$$= \frac{\$10,100}{\$95,000}$$

$$= \underline{10.63\%}$$

2 Average usage of the credit line (amount borrowed) over the coming year is expected to be $100,000. Therefore, the average compensating balance required for the line during the year is expected to be $15,000 (15 percent $\times$ $100,000), and the fee on the unused portion of the line is expected to be $100 for the year (0.2 percent $\times$ $50,000).

3 The firm will keep $10,000 on deposit with the bank as transaction balances.

4 The interest rate charged on the amount borrowed is currently 10 percent per year.

The annual cost rate for this credit line is found to be 10.63 percent in Exhibit 19-1.

Interim Financing Short-term bank loans are often used for the initial financing of construction by contractors or of plant and equipment investment by business firms where the ultimate financing will be long term in nature. This use of short-term loans is called **interim financing** (bridge financing), as the loans are intended to cover the funds needed in the interim before the long-term money is made available (bridge the gap between need for funds and availability of long-term financing). Such loans are found most frequently when money is being spent over several months in the construction of apartment houses, shopping centers, or industrial plants. Real estate developers may obtain a commitment from a long-term lender such as an insurance company to provide funds when a project is completed and the bank supplies funds during the period of construction. Manufacturers may use this type of loan prior to issuing long-term securities to finance a new plant. The alternative procedure for these firms would be to issue the securities in advance of their need for funds and invest the proceeds in marketable securities.

Interest Rates on Bank Loans The interest rates on business loans are determined through personal negotiations between the banker and the borrower. The riskier the borrower, the higher is the interest rate on the loan. However, bankers have traditionally refused to make loans to high-risk borrowers, forcing such borrowers to find other sources of credit. Loan rates are usually scaled upward from the bank's prime rate, the rate charged on credit lines to businesses with excellent credit ratings. Major corporations can borrow money in large amounts for 30 days or less at interest rates below the prime rate, although for most business loans the prime rate is the lowest rate available. The prime rate moves in jumps whenever there are significant changes in money market rates. Figure 19-1 shows the prime rate compared with the interest rate on commercial paper for the past few years.

The interest on a loan may be paid in three different ways: the one used is a matter of agreement between the bank and the borrower. The true cost to the borrower depends on which of the three methods is adopted. **Ordinary interest** is paid at the maturity of the note. If you borrow $10,000 at 8 percent per year and repay the loan with interest at the end of one year, you will pay $800 in interest at that time. The true interest rate is 8 percent. The second method of paying interest is used when the bank **discounts** the note. The interest is deducted from the face value of the note when the loan is made. For example, suppose a firm borrows $10,000 on a discount basis for one year at a stated rate of 8 percent per year. The firm would receive only $10,000 − $800 = $9200, the loan amount less the $800 interest. At the end of the year, the firm would pay $10,000. The true interest rate here is determined by dividing the interest by the amount actually received; that is, the rate would be $800/$9200 = 8.7 percent. If the loan is discounted, the true interest rate is therefore higher than the stated rate.

The third method of paying interest is based on a **floating rate**. The interest rate on these loans varies or "floats" with the bank's prime rate using a relationship that is specified in the loan agreement. For example, the rate might be specified as "prime plus 1 percent." Interest would be calculated on the loan each day by adding 1 percent to the prime rate, then expressing the result as a daily equivalent rate [(prime rate + 1.0 percent)/365 days] and multiplying by the loan balance to compute the daily interest. Each month the bank would ask the firm to pay the interest owed from the previous month. In this case, the actual cost of the loan can be determined only after it has been paid off. For the past few years, the majority of business loans have been of this type.[3]

FIGURE 19-1

Bank prime rates and commercial paper rates. (Source: Federal Reserve Bulletin.)

---

[3] See Table 4.23 in the *Federal Reserve Bulletin* for information on terms of lending. This table is usually published about four times per year.

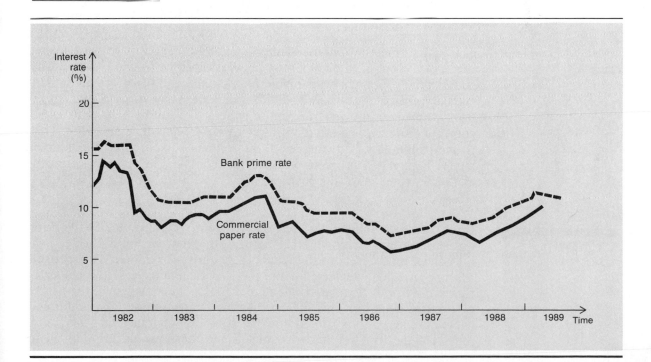

Commercial Paper

Commercial paper is a short-term marketable security sold by business firms to investors—usually other firms, small banks, and financial institutions. It is an unsecured debt of the firm issuing the paper and usually has a maturity of 30 days to 180 days. Maturities are 270 days or less to avoid the registration requirements of the Securities and Exchange Commission (see Chapter 11). Most commercial paper is issued by financial institutions (finance companies and bank holding companies); however, large nonfinancial corporations are also important users of this method of short-term financing. Although commercial paper is sold to investors in amounts as small as $25,000, a firm must issue $5 million or more at a time to access this market.

Many large companies sell their paper directly to investors using their own salespeople to call on potential buyers. Approximately half of the commercial paper outstanding at any given time is sold direct. This large proportion is due to the huge borrowing through direct sales of a few finance companies such as General Motors Acceptance Corporation, Ford Motor Credit, and General Electric Credit. However, most issuers of commercial paper market their paper through dealers who do the actual selling to investors. Dealers charge 0.10 to 0.25 percent of the issue for this service. The main advantage of commercial paper over short-term bank loans is the cost. The interest rate for prime-rated (low risk) issues of commercial paper is normally lower than the prime rate charged by commercial banks. However, most issuers find it desirable (or even necessary) to have lines of credit with commercial banks to backstop their issues of commercial paper. This decision provides protection to the firm if it has financial problems in repaying commercial paper that is coming due. Banks charge 0.2 to 0.5 percent per year fees for such backup lines or require compensating balances. The impact of fees or compensating balances on the cost of commercial paper issues can be determined using the same procedures that apply to bank loans. [Eq. (19-2) applies to commercial paper as well as to bank loans.] The commercial paper market is highly impersonal, and investors are understandably reluctant to purchase the issues of shaky firms. Commercial banks, however, are generally more willing to stand by a customer who gets into difficulty and not to require payment when the loan is due. That is one of the major advantages of bank loans compared to commercial paper. Figure 19-1 provides an historical comparison between commercial paper rates and bank loan rates.

SECURED BORROWING

Firms whose credit ratings are not sufficiently high to qualify them for unsecured loans or commercial paper are often required to pledge a portion of their assets to the lender as security for a loan. The pledged assets are called **collateral** for the loan. The advantage to the lender is that if the firm is liquidated, the lender has first claim against the assets pledged as security. This means that the lender is provided additional protection against loss (in addition to a general claim against the firm's assets) if the firm gets into trouble. Since there are costs involved in establishing and maintaining the security, it is rare that a firm which could borrow on an unsecured basis would elect to pledge assets to secure the loan.

There are several sources for secured short-term loans, with commercial banks, finance companies, and factors being the most important. The most common business assets pledged as security are accounts receivable and inventory. We will look at the use of these two assets separately as financing arrangements differ more by the asset pledged than by the particular lender providing the money.

Accounts Receivable as Collateral

Accounts receivable represent money owed to a business by the individuals or firms to which it has extended credit. Ordinarily, as we discussed in Chapter 17, accounts receivable represent a fairly safe asset for a firm to hold. They usually serve as excellent collateral for loans for the same reasons. In order for a lender whose loan is fully secured by accounts receivable to take a loss, not only must the firm fail but also the money owed to the firm must be uncollectible. From the lender's point of view, however, this does not mean that there is little or no risk in loans secured by accounts receivable. The goods sold by the firm may be returned by the purchaser for various reasons, perhaps because they are defective. This would reduce the amount that could be collected. The firm may be extending credit to high-risk customers in order to increase sales. Thus the accounts receivable could be subject to large bad debt losses. Also, there is the possibility that the borrower may falsify records to show nonexistent accounts. Therefore, lenders rarely loan the full amount of accounts receivable pledged when collateral is deemed necessary.

There are two common approaches to using accounts receivable as collateral. The simpler approach, which is less costly but involves more risk for the lender, is to lend money using all the firm's accounts receivable as collateral. This is called a **general lien** on accounts receivable. The lender may be willing, for example, to loan up to 75 percent of outstanding accounts receivable as part of a secured credit line. The firm is obligated to tell the lender on a regular basis the amount of accounts receivable outstanding. The firm can borrow, as with any credit line, up to the agreed maximum amount.

Another approach is for the borrower to present invoices to the lender as collateral in sufficient amount to cover the amount of the loan; however, the lender may reject some of the accounts as being too risky. In other words, lenders can select the accounts on which they are willing to base loans. In such cases, since lenders have some control over the quality of the collateral, they will be willing to loan a higher percentage of the face value, sometimes 90 percent or more.

As we said, the cost of such arrangements is usually high. The borrower has the costs and problems associated with presenting accounts to the lender, and the lender has the costs involved in keeping track of the accounts pledged. For this reason lenders charge an additional fee to cover costs for secured loans. Finance companies make such loans and will usually charge higher rates than a bank since they are frequently lending to firms that are too risky to qualify for bank credit even on a secured basis.

Factoring Instead of pledging accounts receivable for a loan, some firms sell their accounts receivable to a **factor**. The sale of accounts receivable is called **factoring**. The factor is a financial firm that specializes in this business. Historically, factoring has been most common in the textile industry and most factors were located in the Northeast, although other types of firms also utilize factors and they are found throughout the United States. The typical factoring arrangement is more than just a way to raise money; it usually includes services. The factor may provide credit analysis of the customers and collection of payments due, thereby relieving the firm of most if not all of the expense of maintaining a credit department. The factor may also provide temporary unsecured financing to the firm in addition to the funds furnished by sale of the accounts receivable. While factoring is generally considered an expensive method of financing, these additional advantages may make it the preferred method of short-term financing for some firms.

Credit Cards The widespread use of bank credit cards has virtually revolutionized the financing of accounts receivable at the retail level. Major retailers have for many years provided charge accounts for their customers. With the introduction of bank credit cards, smaller retailers can provide equivalent services to customers holding such cards. From the customer's point of view, acceptance of his or her card by a retailer is as convenient as the extension of credit by the retailer. The retailer is paid immediately by the bank upon submission of the credit invoice; thus the retailer has no investment in accounts receivable and does not actually extend the credit.

For this service the retailer pays the bank a percentage (for example, 3 percent) of the invoiced amount. The arrangement has many of the same characteristics as a complete factoring agreement. The bank does all the credit analysis on the customer and provides immediate funds just as a factor does. The two major differences between a credit card agreement and factoring are, first, credit card customers are consumers whereas the customers of a firm factoring its accounts receivable are other businesses and, second, a credit card customer does not usually perceive the retailer as extending credit whereas the customer of the factoring firm does. This loss of customer identification with the retailer (the customer does not have a charge account at the particular store) is one of the reasons that many large retailers have been reluctant to abandon use of their own charge account systems.[4]

---

[4] A retailer with charge accounts is able to direct specific advertising to its customers and can include promotional material with the bill, etc. However the existence of so many people with credit cards puts continuous pressure on stores to accept the cards. Many stores accept credit cards and also offer their own charge accounts.

Many types of inventory are easily sold and serve as fairly good security for short-term loans, whereas other types of inventory are valueless as collateral from a lender's point of view. The major consideration in the suitability of inventory as a means of securing a loan is the marketability of the inventory. Work-in-process inventories (goods still in the manufacturing process) are almost never considered suitable, since such partially completed products are almost impossible to sell. Many raw materials such as grain, primary metals, and industrial chemicals are good collateral since a ready market exists for them. Manufacturers' finished goods inventories and retail inventories may or may not be good collateral depending on the nature of the goods. New cars, appliances, paper, and lumber are usable as collateral. Clothing, perishable goods, and specialized equipment are not very usable. If an inventory is suitable collateral, the lender will advance some percentage of the total value. The more stable the market value of the inventory, the higher the percentage will be. For example, a commodity such as cocoa, which is subject to wide price variations, would have a lower percentage than a commodity like wheat, which generally does not vary as much in price.

There are several ways in which a lender can gain a secured interest in inventory. Since each of the methods has a somewhat different implication for the cost and flexibility of the financing arrangement, we will consider each separately.

General Lien   Just as was true of accounts receivable, the lender can obtain a lien against all or part of the firm's inventory, whatever the specific items may be. This type of arrangement is very easy to set up, but it doesn't provide much security since there is no telling what the inventory will be like in the event of the firm's liquidation. Since the lender cannot maintain good control over the quality of the collateral, the amount loaned as a percentage of the inventory's value is likely to be small, unless collateral is not a significant element in the credit decision of the lender. The interest rate may also be somewhat higher for this type of inventory loan.

Floor Planning   Floor planning is a type of security arrangement often used in financing automobile dealers, farm and industrial equipment dealers, and sellers of consumer durable goods. Under this type of agreement the goods are specifically identified by the serial numbers of the items in stock. When an item is sold, the proceeds are supposed to be given to the lender in repayment of the loan against that item. As new inventory is purchased, the borrower signs a form describing the items purchased and specifying the terms of the agreement. The lender then pays the supplier for the goods. Periodically a representative of the lender checks out the current inventory of the dealer to make sure that all items covered by the floor plan are still in stock.

Floor plan agreements are fairly inexpensive to administer and provide all the flexibility most borrowers require. The security from the lender's point of view is good provided that the merchandise has not been sold without the lender's being notified. Unfortunately this happens often enough to mean that lenders cannot consider such plans totally secure.

The lender may be a bank, a finance company, or even the manufacturer of the product. Manufacturers engaging in this type of arrangement usually do so in order to encourage their dealers to carry a complete line of goods to boost sales. When such financing is available from the manufacturer, it often carries lower interest rates than the dealer would be able to get from a financial institution.

Warehousing Arrangements   Under warehousing arrangements a third party controls the borrower's access to the goods held as security. Since this party must be paid for its services, this is a relatively expensive procedure. There are two basic types—**field warehouses** and **public warehouses**. In field warehousing arrangements, the warehousing company establishes an area on the borrower's premises as a field warehouse. The company is supposed to maintain strict control over the inventory so that the lender should be able to find out at all times exactly what inventory is there. The borrower has ready access to the goods since they are stored on the borrower's property; however, they must be accounted for continuously. Even with the degree of control afforded by this type of arrangement there have been cases of fraud. The most spectacular case was the Allied Salad Oil scandal of 1963, which caused over $100 million of losses to the lenders involved. Money was lent on salad oil supposedly stored in a field warehouse (large tanks). The tanks turned out to contain water with a little oil floating on top.

Even tighter control over the inventory used as security is provided by public warehouses. In this case the inventory is held in a physical location apart from the borrower's place of business and under control of the warehousing company. The major disadvantage of this type of security arrangement is the cost to the borrower of obtaining the goods for use or for sale. Goods may be moved out of the warehouse only with the consent of the lender. Of course the warehousing company must also be paid for its services. This is the most expensive form of security arrangement.

FINANCING INTERNATIONAL TRADE

In a typical domestic purchase of goods by one business firm from another, the goods are shipped and the purchaser is billed for their value. The seller provides trade credit to the purchaser and bears the risk that the purchaser will not be able to pay for the goods. The credit risks are generally greater in international transactions than in domestic ones. Sellers have less reliable information about purchasers in another country, and it is more difficult to collect debts in a foreign country. Shipping times are much greater in international trade; the goods may be in transit for months. Therefore, the financing burden is much greater because, while the goods are being shipped, neither seller nor purchaser has access to them and yet someone must be financing them. There also may be exchange rate risk associated with the transaction. In this section we describe some of the methods used to deal with foreign exchange risk, credit risk, and financing in international trade.

Foreign Exchange Risk

There is no foreign exchange risk if the buyer (importer) is willing to pay the seller (exporter) when the goods are ordered. The two parties need only agree on the price of the goods—taking into account the current exchange rate between the currencies of the two countries—and complete the transaction. For example, suppose that a United States department store wishes to import 10,000 meters of silk from Thailand. The price of the silk, exported by a Thai silk mill, is to be 200,000 baht (Thai currency). The exchange rate is 20 baht per United States dollar, so the price in United States dollars is $10,000. If the department store immediately buys 200,000 baht and pays the silk mill when it orders the silk, there is no exchange risk and there is no credit risk. However, most international trade involves delayed payments.

Whenever payment is delayed, there is a risk that the exporter's currency will appreciate relative to the importer's currency, but not the reverse. This is so because importation of goods involves money moving from importer to exporter, and because the exporter ultimately wants payment in its own currency. Assuming that no strategy is used to eliminate exchange risk (see next section), the importer's currency will be exchanged for the exporter's currency when the importer pays for the goods. The risk is that the importer's currency will buy fewer units of the exporter's currency than it did when the goods were sold. If the goods are invoiced in the importers currency, the exporter is exposed to the exchange risk. If the goods are invoiced in the exporter's currency, the importer is exposed to the exchange risk.

Suppose that the silk in the example above will be in transit three months and that the Thai exporter is willing to extend credit for this time. If the silk is invoiced at a price of $10,000 (the importer's currency), the silk mill is exposed to the risk that $10,000 will be worth less than 200,000 baht in three month's time; that is, that the baht has appreciated relative to the dollar. If the silk is invoiced at a price of 200,000 baht (the exporter's currency), the department store is exposed to the risk. If the baht appreciates relative to the dollar, it will take more than $10,000 to purchase 200,000 baht when payment is made.

Eliminating Exchange Risk

How can the exchange risk of a delayed payment be eliminated? One way is to cover the transaction in the forward exchange markets as was discussed in Chapter 2. If the goods are invoiced in the importer's currency (dollars, for example), the exporter bears the risk. The exporter can eliminate this risk by selling a forward contract to deliver the importer's currency in exchange for the exporter's currency at the time the sale is made. For example, if the Thai silk mill provides ninety days of credit and invoices the goods at a price of $10,000, it will be receiving $10,000 in ninety days (which it will then convert to baht). Suppose the mill sells a contract for delivery of $10,000 in ninety days' time in exchange for baht. If the forward rate on a ninety-day futures contract is the same as the current spot rate ($0.05), under the forward contract the exporter will be able to deliver the $10,000 and receive 200,000 baht in ninety days' time, regardless of what happens to the exchange rate in the meantime. If the forward rate is at a discount or premium, the amount of baht to be received will be different from 200,000, but in any case the amount will be known at the time the forward contract is made. Indeed, the price of the goods is likely to depend in part on the length of time for which credit will be extended and the cost of covering the transaction in the forward exchange markets.

If the goods are invoiced in the exporter's currency (baht, for example), then the importer bears the exchange risk. In our example, the United States department store could eliminate the risk by selling a forward contract to deliver dollars in exchange for baht at a fixed exchange rate. The contract would be for the amount of dollars needed to obtain 200,000 baht at the ninety-day forward rate.

An alternative method of eliminating exchange risk is through money market transactions. The delayed payment is an asset for the exporter (account receivable) and a liability for the importer (account payable). The party exposed to the exchange risk can eliminate it by creating an offsetting liability or asset in the foreign currency. Suppose that the silk in our example is invoiced at a price of $10,000 to be paid in three months. The Thai exporter has a dollar receivable and is exposed to the exchange risk. The mill could eliminate the risk by obtaining a dollar loan which has a total principal and interest payment of $10,000 at the end of three months. The proceeds from the loan (the present value of $10,000 discounted at the interest rate on the loan) can be exchanged into baht immediately. At the end of the three months, the exporter uses the $10,000 payment on the receivable to pay off the loan.

On the other hand, if the silk is invoiced at a price of 200,000 baht, the United States department store has a baht payable and is exposed to the exchange risk. The store can eliminate the risk by immediately exchanging dollars into baht and investing in a Thai security (asset) which will pay 200,000 baht in three months time. The proceeds from the security can be used to pay the silk mill when the 200,000 baht payment is due in three months.

An analysis of the costs of protection against exchange rate risks is complex and beyond the scope of this book. In many instances firms do not choose to protect against the risk because the costs are too great.

Letters of Credit

As we noted above, immediate payment by the importer (buyer) to the exporter (seller) eliminates the exchange risks of deferred payment and allows the exporter to avoid bearing any credit risk. However, immediate payment means that the importer has money tied up in the goods while they are in transit. Moreover, the importing firm owns goods that will not be in its control and available for inspection for some time. The sellers of any product have an incentive (profits) to ease the problems faced by their customers in acquiring those goods. Only when credit or political risks are very great will the seller demand cash in advance. In some cases, sales will be made on open account, as is customary in domestic transactions. Between these two extremes, a variety of specialized financial arrangements have been developed to facilitate international trade. The most widely used arrangement is based on a **letter of credit**. A letter of credit is a written statement made by a bank that it will pay out money if specified conditions are met. There are several different types of letters of credit; here we will describe the one most often used in United States imports—an irrevocable letter of credit issued by a United States bank.

Import Letters of Credit   Suppose a United States importer wishes to buy goods from a foreign company. The importer orders the goods, asking the seller firm to ship under a letter of credit. The two parties reach agreement on prices, method of shipment, etc. The importer then applies for a letter of credit from a commercial bank. This letter of credit, sent to the exporter, authorizes the exporter to obtain money from the bank by presenting the required documents supporting the sale and shipment of the goods. The exporter is likely to use a bank in its country to handle the paperwork (the negotiating bank). A sample letter of credit is shown in Exhibit 19-2. A glossary of the terms used in the letter and in international trade is shown in Table 19-2.

Notice that there are four parties involved in this transaction—the importer (Osgood and North), the importer's bank (Rainier National Bank), the exporter (Thai Silk Mills), and a bank that will notify the exporter that the letter of credit has been issued (Thai Military Bank). The letter of credit is *irrevocable* by the issuing bank if the *bank* promises to pay the money provided the conditions specified in the letter of credit are met. In such transactions when the importer's bank issues the letter of credit, neither the exporter nor the exporter's bank need have any knowledge of the credit worthiness of the importer. All the credit risk to the exporter is absorbed by the importer's bank, which is in a good position to evaluate the credit of the importing firm. The credit standing of the importer's bank becomes the only concern of the exporting firm and its bank.

Financing under Letters of Credit

Letters of credit are used to reduce the credit risk borne by the exporter. They may or may not involve financing. The letter of credit (L/C) in Exhibit 19-2 specifies that the exporter can draw a draft at sight. This means that the exporter will receive an immediate payment of $10,000, the amount specified in the L/C, when the required documents are presented to the issuing bank (Rainier). Therefore the importer (Osgood & North) is financing the goods in transit. Financing under an L/C is done through the use of time drafts. A time draft is payable at a future date rather than at sight and its tenor (time to payment) will be specified in the L/C, for example, 90 days. The payment may be made either 90 days from the date of the draft or 90 days from sight, as specified in the L/C. A time draft is used when the exporter is providing financing of the

EXHIBIT 19-2
Sample letter of credit

RAINIER NATIONAL BANK
WORLD BANKING DIVISION
P.O. Box 3966 Seattle, Washington 98124 U.S.A.

DATE: January 10, 1985

IRREVOCABLE COMMERCIAL LETTER OF CREDIT	OUR NO.	ADVISING BANK NO.

ADVISING BANK

OUR NO. SEA-92000

Thai Military Bank, Ltd.
34 Phayathai Road
Bangkok 4, Thailand

APPLICANT

Osgood & North
906 Fourth Avenue
Seattle, Washington 98104

BENEFICIARY

Thai Silk Mills Ltd.
P.O. Box 128
Bangkok, Thailand

AMOUNT

US $10,000.00 (TEN THOUSAND AND
NO/100 US DOLLARS)

EXPIRY

March 11, 1985 in Thailand

YOU ARE AUTHORIZED TO DRAW ON US YOUR DRAFTS AT Sight
FOR 100% INVOICE VALUE WHEN ACCOMPANIED BY THE FOLLOWING DOCUMENTS:
Signed Commercial Invoice in quintuplicate;

Packing List in duplicate;
Certificate of Origin;
Beneficiary's Certificate that one set of non-negotiable documents has been airmailed
to Applicant and Seattle Custom Broker, P.O. Box 1092, Seattle, Washington 98123;
Full Set of Clean On Board Marine Bills of Lading issued to the order of shipper
and blank endorsed, evidencing shipment not later than March 5, 1985, Marked
Freight Collect and Notify Applicant and Seattle Custom Broker, P.O. Box 1092,
Seattle, Washington 98123;

SHIPPING TERMS: FOB Vessel, Thailand Port
COVERING: 10,000 Meters Thai Silk

THE AMOUNT OF ANY DRAFT DRAWN UNDER THIS CREDIT MUST BE ENDORSED ON THE REVERSE OF THE ORIGINAL CREDIT. ALL DRAFTS
MUST BE MARKED "DRAWN UNDER RAINIER NATIONAL BANK LETTER OF CREDIT NUMBER SEA-92000 DATED 1-10-85 "

SHIPMENT FROM: Thailand	PARTIAL SHIPMENTS	TRANS-SHIPMENT
TO: Seattle, Washington	Prohibited	Permitted

SPECIAL INSTRUCTIONS:
All bank charges other than those of the issuing bank are for the account of the beneficiary.
Buyer Insures. This letter of credit is available with us by payment and with any bank
for negotiation. The negotiating bank is to forward all documents to us in one airmail.
Drafts and documents to be presented for negotiation not later than 10 days after the Bill of Lading date.

Except so far as otherwise expressly stated, this documentary credit is subject to the "Uniform Customs and Practice for Documentary Credits" (19XX 1983
Revision), International Chamber of Commerce Publication No. XXX 400

WE HEREBY AGREE WITH THE DRAWERS ENDORSERS AND BONA-
FIDE HOLDERS OF DRAFTS DRAWN UNDER AND IN COMPLIANCE
WITH THE TERMS OF THIS CREDIT THAT SUCH DRAFTS WILL BE
DULY HONORED ON DUE PRESENTATION TO THE DRAWEE IF
NEGOTIATED ON OR BEFORE EXPIRY DATE.
jmt

ADVISING BANK NOTIFICATION

Authorized Signature   Authorized Signature

Place, date, name and signature of the advising bank.

04284 R7-79

goods in transit but does not want to assume the credit risk of a sale on account to the importer.

Time drafts also provide the basis for banker's acceptances, a money market security described in Chapter 2. A banker's acceptance is created if the bank issuing the L/C stamps "accepted," with the signature of an authorized bank officer and date on the face of the time draft. The draft then becomes a legal obligation of the bank and a negotiable security. The exporter can sell this security immediately to raise cash at a discount from its face value or can borrow money at a relatively low rate of

---

TABLE 19-2
Definitions of some terms used in international trade[a]

Term	Definition[b]
Accept; acceptance	To agree to pay on a designated date a draft drawn on the party accepting; an acceptance is an accepted draft. (Rainier National Bank would be the party accepting the draft.)
Beneficiary	Party in whose name a letter of credit has been issued or a draft drawn (Thai Silk Mills).
Bill of lading	Document showing that the goods were received by the carrier ("vessel" in which the goods are to be shipped). A "clean" bill of lading shows no indications of defects in the goods or their packing.
Certificate of origin	Document showing the country where the goods originated (Thailand).
Commercial invoice	The bill for the goods issued by the exporter (Thai Silk Mills).
Draft	Instrument by which one party directs another party to make a payment. (Thai Silk Mills would draw a draft against the letter of credit from the Rainier National Bank. The mill might direct the Rainier National Bank to pay $10,000 to Thai Military Bank for the mill's account.)
Free on board (FOB)	A term of sale indicating the point at which the exporter stops paying for transportation costs and the importer begins paying. (Thai Silk Mill would pay all costs involved in getting the silk on the boat. Osgood and North would have to pay for marine insurance and the ocean voyage.)
Open	To establish or issue, as in "to open a letter of credit."

[a] Excluded are those terms defined in the text and included in the glossary at the end of the book.
[b] Remarks in parentheses refer to the text example and Exhibit 19-2.

interest, using the banker's acceptance as collateral for the loan. The cost of this financing may be paid by the importer or by the exporter depending on their agreement, and is usually lower than other financing methods available to the firms. Of course, for this service the bank charges a fee, which can be as high as 2 or 3 percent if the importer is financially weak. Banker's acceptances are widely used in financing international trade.

SUMMARY

The factors that affect the types of short-term financing chosen are interest cost, impact on credit rating, reliability, restrictions, and flexibility. The credit rating of the firm affects the availability of financing and the terms of financing.

Trade credit (accounts payable) is a very important source of credit to small firms and is used to some extent by all firms. Credit terms vary considerably from industry to industry. The amount of trade credit available to the firm depends on its volume of purchases and its credit rating. A major advantage of trade credit as a source of financing is that it increases as the firm's activity increases. The cost of using trade credit is the amount of any discounts foregone so long as the firm pays its bills when they are due. Delaying payment past the due date, while often done, tends to have an adverse impact on the firm's credit rating and may result in suppliers' refusing to provide credit.

Loans from commercial banks are a major source of short-term credit to businesses. Compensating balances are often required by banks. A compensating balance is an amount that the firm must maintain in its checking account with the bank and is stated as a percentage of the credit line. The interest rate charged on a bank loan depends on the credit standing of the firm and the level of short-term interest rates in the economy. The lowest rate charged by banks on credit lines is called the prime rate. Banks sometimes deduct the interest from the principal of the loan in advance. This increases the effective rate of interest.

Commercial paper is a short-term debt security issued by large firms and financial institutions. It can be issued directly to investors or sold through dealers. While the interest cost of commercial paper is usually lower than the rates charged by banks, if the firm becomes unprofitable, it may have trouble refinancing its commercial paper issues.

Lenders such as commercial banks may require a firm whose credit rating is weak to pledge assets as security for a loan. Accounts receivable and inventory are often used as collateral. Accounts receivable are usually the best collateral since the risk to the lender is less with these assets. There are several methods used by lenders to obtain a security interest in accounts receivable. Generally the more control the lender has over the pledged accounts, the less risk there is to the lender but the cost of administering the loan is greater. Lenders frequently require a fee in addition to the interest charge to compensate them for the costs of administration. Factoring is the sale of accounts receivable, but it may also involve other services. Credit cards reduce or eliminate the need of retailers to provide credit to their customers. The credit card company provides the credit, and the merchant is paid immediately on presentation of an invoice.

Inventory may also be pledged as security for a loan. The suitability of inventory as collateral depends on its marketability and on the predictability of its price if it is sold. Floor planning, field warehousing, and public warehousing are methods used by lenders to keep track of inventory used as collateral.

International trade creates special problems for financing. The credit risk is often too high to permit use of sales on open account (trade credit), and foreign exchange risk is also present. Foreign exchange risk may be eliminated through the use of the forward market or money market transactions. Credit risk can be significantly reduced through the use of letters of credit issued by commercial banks. Bankers acceptances are frequently used as a method of financing international trade.

QUESTIONS

1 "The objective of a financial manager is to minimize the cost of financing when seeking short-term funds." Comment on this statement considering other factors that may affect the choice of short-term financing arrangements.

2 Rank the three major sources of short-term financing in terms of availability to the following types of business:
  a A large manufacturer with a high credit rating
  b A medium-sized manufacturer with a good credit rating
  c A small retailer with a fair credit rating

3 What is the basic cost of trade credit and why is it a cost?

4 What determines the amount of trade credit to a firm?

5 "The cost of incurring a bad trade credit reputation is simply the cost of obtaining financing from other sources." Do you agree? Why or why not?

6 Distinguish between a credit line and a revolving credit from the viewpoints of the lender and borrower.

7 Which types of short-term financing would you expect to be used by the following firms:
  a A small open-air market selling fresh seafood and eggs
  b An apparel shop specializing in clothing for taller women
  c A large metropolitan department store
  d A dealer selling new and used cars
  e A contractor constructing the coolers for nuclear reactors
  f A finance company with branch offices nationwide
  g A partnership selling and servicing Whirlpool appliances

8 In 1978 the outstanding short-term borrowings of Pillsbury Co. varied between $30 million and $40 million, mostly in commercial paper. The assistant treasurer, Frances Gamble, reportedly said (*Business Week*, July 8, 1978) that banks were not used "unless we owe them a favor." She also indicated that Pillsbury did borrow from its banks once in the past three years "to let them know

we want a line there if we need it." Why do you think Pillsbury
used commercial paper rather than bank loans as a normal practice? Why did the company use bank loans at all in the preceding
three years?

9 Are accounts receivable generally considered a better source of
collateral than inventories? Why or why not?

10 Given that the following firms use secured financing arrangements, would they be more likely to be pledging inventory,
accounts receivable, or both as collateral? Why?

   a A company manufacturing custom electronic equipment for
major aerospace firms

   b A wholesale lumber dealer

   c A retail appliance (refrigerators, etc.) store

   d A children's clothing manufacturer

11 Distinguish between the following types of secured financial arrangements in terms of advantages and disadvantages to the
borrower:

   a Factoring

   b General lien

   c Floor planning

   d Warehousing arrangements

12 Why would an exporter wish to sell goods under a letter of credit
rather than on open account?

13 In an important letter of credit with payment to be made using a
180-day time draft, what is being financed, who is being financed,
and who is providing financing?

14 Is there any exchange risk when imports are purchased using a
letter of credit? Why or why not?

PROJECTS

1 Obtain a recent annual report of a nonfinancial business. Analyze
the sources of short-term financing currently used by the firm.
Have the amount or composition of short-term financing sources
changed from the previous year? Estimate their costs to the
extent possible. Be sure to read the footnotes to the balance
sheet, where much of the detail on financing will be found.

2 Identify a local firm that has some type of international
transactions (imports or exports) and interview one of its
executives. Find out how the firm handles its financing problems
and deals with exchange risks.

3 Visit a local bank that has an international department. Find out
what kind of services the bank provides for importers and
exporters.

**DEMONSTRATION
PROBLEMS**

DP1 Kaleidoscope Shops purchase $100 per day from a supplier that
asks for payment 30 days after the invoice date (the terms of
sale are net/30). The goods are normally received ten days after
the invoice date.

a If Kaleidoscope pays its bills on time what will its average accounts payable balance be from this supplier?

b Suppose sales (and purchases) increase 10 percent over previous levels, what will the new accounts payable balance be?

c At the new level of purchases in *b*, how much additional financing could Kaleidoscope obtain by paying, on average, twenty days late?

SOLUTION TO DP1

a Purchases of $100 per day $\times$ (30 − 10) days = $2000.

b Purchases of $110 per day $\times$ 20 days = $2200.

c Purchases of $110 per day $\times$ 40 days = $4400 less the answer from *b* of $2200 = $2200.

DP2 Dryland State Bank has granted Camino Yacht Company, Inc., a line of credit of $400,000, under the stipulation that Camino maintain a 15 percent compensating balance in its deposit account with the bank on any loans outstanding and a 10 percent compensating balance for the unborrowed portion of the credit line. Dryland also charges Camino an interest rate of 12 percent for funds borrowed.

a If Camino borrows $300,000 on the line of credit, what is the dollar amount that must be maintained in Dryland as a compensating balance?

b What is the effective interest rate on Camino's borrowings of $300,000 assuming the firm would normally (i.e., even if Camino did not obtain the line of credit) keep $20,000 in the account?

SOLUTION TO DP2

a Line of credit = $400,000
Borrowing = $300,000
Unused portion = $400,000 − $300,000 = $100,000
Compensating balance = 15% of $300,000 + 10% of $100,000
= $45,000 + $10,000
= $55,000

b Interest cost = 12% of $300,000 = $36,000
Available funds = $300,000 − ($55,000 − $20,000)
= $265,000

Effective rate $= \dfrac{\$36,000}{\$265,000} = 13.58\%$

1 Fun furs purchases $300 per day from suppliers whose terms are net/30. The goods are received four days after the invoice dates.

a If Fun Furs pays its bills on time, what will its accounts payable balance be?

b Suppose sales (and purchases) increase 20 percent over previous levels, what will the new accounts payable balance be?

c At the new level of purchases in *b*, how much additional financing could Fun Furs obtain by paying, on average, fifteen days late?

2 Fred's Hobby Shop is a small proprietorship located in an urban shopping center. The terms on purchases of models from a wholesaler are 4/10, net 60. How much would it cost Fred to forego the discount and pay in sixty days rather than ten days? [Ans.: 30.4 percent per year]

3 Suppose that Fred of problem **2** can purchase from either of two wholesalers. The first wholesaler offers terms given in problem **2**, while the second offers a trade discount of 2/15, net 30. Fred can borrow from a bank at 12 percent per year interest cost. What are your recommendations?

4 An approximate formula for the cost of trade credit is often used in place of Eq. (19-1). The approximation is

$$\frac{\text{Annual}}{\text{interest rate}} = \text{discount} \ \times \ \frac{360 \text{ days}}{\text{payment period} - \text{discount period}}$$

a For each of the following trade credit terms calculate the annual interest rate using the exact formula Eq. (19-1) and the approximate formula above assuming that bills are paid when due:

(1) 2/10, net 30   *(3)* 3/10, net 30
(2) 2/10, net 60   *(4)* 5/10, net 90

b Compare your results in *a* for the two formulas. How accurate is the approximation? Would the size of normal monthly purchases under the given terms (for example, $10,000 per month vs. $100,000 per month) affect your findings as to the accuracy of the approximation?

5 Compute the interest cost of foregoing discounts [using Eq. (19-1)] for the following terms assuming bills are paid when due:

a EOM, net 30
b 2/10, EOM, net 30
c 2/15, prox., net 30
d 3/10, net 30, October 1

6 National Corporation has a credit line of $200,000 with Drygulch Bank. Drygulch does not provide any other services to National and requires a 10 percent compensating balance on any borrowing. In addition, Drygulch charges a 0.5 percent annual fee on the unused portion of the line. As part of its overall financing over the next three months, National needs $100,000 in the first month, $130,000 in the second month, and $175,000 in the third month. Drygulch currently charges National an interest rate of 10 percent on its loan.

a What is the average monthly amount that National will need to have available over the next three months?
b What will be National's average monthly borrowing under the line (average usage)?

c What is the annual effective interest rate of this loan? [Ans.: 11.29 percent]

7 Drygulch Bank is offering National (see problem *6*) an alternative loan arrangement. Rather than charging a fee on the unused portion of the line, Drygulch will accept compensating deposit balances equal to 5 percent of the unused portion. Given that National requires the same amounts of money to be available as stated in problem *6*, which loan arrangement is least costly to National?

8 National Corporation is considering using Drygulch Bank as a disbursement bank for payments to suppliers in the Northeast. In this case, National would have an average monthly deposit balance of $9000 that could be used to satisfy compensating balance requirements of their credit line. Determine the effective interest rates for the two loan agreements described in problems *6* and *7*, assuming that National uses Drygulch for disbursements. Which arrangement would be best for National?

9 Bank A offers a one-year loan at an interest rate of 12 percent per year, where the interest is paid at the end of the year when the loan matures. Bank B offers to loan at a stated rate of 11 percent per year but deducts the interest at the beginning of the year. Which bank offers the lower-cost financing?

10 The Bop Corporation uses commercial paper as its primary source of short-term financing. The current interest rate on Bop paper is 6.0 percent. Bop maintains backstop credit lines with banks to support its paper issues. Over the next year, Bop expects to need $20 million in credit lines to support an average of $15 million in outstanding commercial paper. The banks are offering Bop a choice between fees or balances to compensate them for the credit lines. Fees would be 0.4 percent per year of the amount of the credit lines. Alternatively, compensating balances of 8 percent of the lines would be required. Any balances required would be in addition to the deposits normally maintained by Bop. What is the effective annual interest rate for commercial paper financing under each credit line arrangement? Which one should Bop use?

11 Aviary Aircraft Company is considering the use of commercial paper to raise an average of $12 million next year. The interest rate on commercial paper is only 8 percent per year, but Aviary would need a committed bank credit line to issue paper at this rate. Last National Bank is willing to provide the credit line, but requires that Aviary maintain balances equal to 10 percent of the line on deposit with the bank. Aviary's financial manager believes that a $16.0 million credit line would be ample to cover any commercial paper Aviary would issue. Aviary normally maintains a deposit balance of $600,000 with Last National which could count as part of the compensating balances required. What is the effective annual interest rate on the commercial paper issues?

12 The D. Vader Company requires additional short-term financing

of $10.0 million. It has excellent relationships with its bank and its suppliers, and a high credit rating in general. The company maintains normal deposit balances of $400,000. The following sources are available:

a Trade credit. Purchases average $250,000 per day on terms of 2/10, net 60; the $10 million financing need was based on payment within 10 days.

b A 12 percent interest rate loan from the bank that will require 15 percent in compensating balances to be held on deposit with the bank.

c Commercial paper bearing a 11.5 percent interest rate. In order to issue the paper, the firm must maintain backup lines of credit with a bank. The bank will charge an annual fee of 0.4 percent of the credit line and require the firm to maintain 10 percent of the line as deposits at the bank.

Evaluate the cost of each of these three sources. How should Vader obtain the $10 million needed?

WORKING CAPITAL MANAGEMENT

In Chapters 17, 18, and 19 we examined the principles of investment in the major types of current assets and the choice among the major sources of short-term financing. We will now look at issues in the overall management of current assets and current liabilities, which is called **working capital management**.[1] This chapter therefore serves as a summary of current asset management and financing, and it draws on Chapters 14 and 16 as well.

This chapter is divided into three sections. In the first section we discuss the concept of working capital. The second section contains the central concern of the chapter, the interrelationships between current assets and current liabilities and the choice between short-term and long-term financing. The last section covers the relationship between working capital and long-term investment decisions.

WORKING CAPITAL: DEFINITIONS

Working capital has traditionally meant current assets. The term originated in simpler times when the economy was based on agriculture. Fruit and vegetable processors, meat packers, and commodity dealers purchase agricultural products, process them, and sell them. Agricultural production is a seasonal business and normally the products are sold prior to the next season. Thus, at the beginning of the season these firms have very low levels of current assets. As crops are harvested, processed, and sold, current asset levels increase dramatically. The current assets of these firms are financed almost entirely with short-term sources. As inventory is sold, accounts receivable collected, and short-term debt repaid, both current asset and current liability levels are lowered until the bottom of the seasonal cycle is reached, typically in the late spring. This is "capital at work." The term "working capital" is sometimes used as a synonym for current assets, and the term "net working capital" is used to mean the quantity that results from subtracting the dollar value of current liabilities from the dollar value of current

---

[1] To understand this chapter, you should have studied Chapters 14 and 16 through 19.

assets. In this book "working capital" refers to current assets minus current liabilities (a synonym for net working capital), since this is standard in modern practice. Working capital management includes the management of all the types of current assets and short-term financing sources discussed in Chapters 17, 18, and 19. It also includes the decisions as to the appropriate amount of long-term financing used in financing the current assets of the enterprise.

Working capital represents the portion of current assets financed with long-term debt and equity. Any firm with a current ratio greater than 1.0 has positive working capital. For a given level of current liabilities, the greater the working capital of the firm, the larger is its current ratio. Long-term debt agreements often contain provisions requiring the firm to maintain a minimum level of working capital. Such provisions are intended to provide a degree of safety to the lender under the assumption that current assets are more likely to maintain reasonable liquidating value than other assets of the firm.

What determines the amount of working capital for a firm? Obviously, working capital is determined by the level of current assets and the level of current liabilities, since working capital is simply the difference between the two. But what considerations by management lead them to operate with a particular level of working capital?

First, we should note that the basic characteristics of the firm's operations have a great deal to do with the level and types of current assets and liabilities and, therefore, the level of working capital. Table 20-1 provides data on a variety of firms and industries. Note the wide variations among them. There are also significant differences among firms in a given line of business. For example, a typical small department store had working capital equal to 17 percent of sales in 1989. However, a fourth of the stores had working capital of less than 9 percent of sales and a fourth of the stores had working capital greater than 27 percent of sales.[2]

Second, the working capital management problems faced by financial managers differ by type of firm. For example, the management of working capital for a bowling alley is not only relatively simple, but is also not very important to the company's overall success. On the other hand, the working capital problems of Sears are both extremely complex and very important to the firm (see Table 20-1). Table 20-2 shows a general guide to the relative importance and complexity of the working capital management problems faced by financial managers of different types of firms rated on a scale of 0 (lowest) to 5 (highest). "Importance" is based primarily on the level of current assets relative to total assets. "Complexity" is based on the nature of the problems faced by the firms' managers. These ratings are based on domestic operations. International operations involve a significant increase in complexity.

---

[2] Robert Morris Associates 1989. Data on the distribution of working capital as a percentage of assets for different firms in the same industry were not available.

The interrelationships among the current assets and current liabilities greatly complicate working capital management. In Chapters 17, 18, and 19 we examined situations in which these interrelationships were either not present or were small enough to be safely ignored. However, for most lines of business, any decision that affects the firm's sales is likely to affect the levels of investment in cash, accounts receivable, and inventory. Changes in sales also are likely to affect purchases and, therefore, accounts payable. This is true regardless of the nature of the decisions being made—whether they involve credit or inventory policies, new production methods, marketing strategies, personnel policies,

TABLE 20-1
Working capital for firms and industries

	Working capital (% of assets)	Current assets (% of assets)	Current liabilities (% of assets)
ALCOA	13.8	26.6	12.8
Dow Chemical	11.4	36.6	25.1
H. J. Heinz	24.9	56.9	32.0
Sears (retail only)	50.1	82.5	32.4
Shell Oil	0.4	15.8	15.4
Union Pacific	0.8	16.5	15.7
Large manufacturers	8.2	32.6	24.4
Wholesalers	17.5	61.9	44.4
Retailers	21.3	49.9	28.6
Small companies (less than $100 million in assets)			
Boat builders	15.5	60.8	45.3
Chemical manufacturers	30.4	62.7	32.3
Computer manufacturers	32.0	70.9	38.9
Petroleum refiners	3.7	46.2	42.5
Chemical wholesalers	18.8	74.8	56.0
Electronics wholesalers	28.0	80.8	52.8
Boat dealers	20.5	80.6	60.1
Computer stores	14.9	72.9	58.0
Department stores	37.2	72.4	35.2
Vegetable farms	0.2	36.4	36.2
Air transportation	− 3.9	36.2	40.1
Bowling alleys	−13.2	13.6	26.8
Radio stations	3.3	28.7	25.4

Sources: Company annual reports, quarterly financial statistics, and Robert Morris Associates.

TABLE 20-2
Working capital management problems

Type of firm	Importance	Complexity
Small service firm—cash sales	0	0
Small service firm—credit sales	2	1
Small manufacturer	3	3
Small distribution firm—cash sales	4	2
Small distribution firm—credit sales	5	3
Large service firm—credit sales	2	2
Large manufacturer	3	5
Large distribution firm	5	5

or whatever. The basic rule is to choose the set of policies that has the highest net present value of cash flows. The difficulty is in translating this rule into practice—estimating the cash flows and determining the appropriate discount rate to apply to them. Also, in some situations it may be more convenient to use an internal rate of return or a net profit approach in the evaluation of policies.

Interrelationships among current assets and liabilities affect both investment and financing decisions. We show first how to evaluate current asset investments when they are present. The example we use also illustrates the complexity of the problems. Then we will discuss the factors affecting the choice of financing and the determination of the level of working capital.

*Current Asset
Investment: An
Example*

Suppose that Sam's Auto Parts, a local distributor of auto parts to service stations, is considering a $20,000 increase in inventory. This added investment is expected to increase sales by $1000 per week or $52,000 per year. Cost of goods sold and purchases will increase by $800 per week and the increase in sales will add $120 per week to cash operating expenses, which will be paid every 4 weeks. No bad debt losses are expected on the additional sales and no discounts are offered for early payment by customers. Sam's tax rate is 25 percent and taxes are paid quarterly. Sam expects that the increase in the level of operations will require additional minimum cash balances at the firm's bank of $200 beginning in week 1.

The following information describes Sam's operations:

Inventory order period	= 4 weeks
Period from receipt of goods to cash disbursement	= 2 weeks
Period from sales of goods to cash receipt	= 6 weeks

In week 0, Sam will receive the additional inventory. Sales are expected to increase in week 1 to the new level. Exhibit 20-1 shows the expected effect of the inventory decision on Sam's current assets and current liabilities at the end of each week through week 14 and for weeks 398 and 399. Week 398 is provided because this is the last week that Sam's cash position is expected to be negative. It is no worse than zero after week 398. The significance of this fact is discussed later.

There are several methods that can be used to evaluate the desirability of this decision. A simple procedure, which is often used in practice, is based on estimating the average additional investment in working capital that will result from a decision and comparing this investment with the additional annual cash flows that are expected. Either net present value, internal rate of return, or net profit may then be used as a criterion for evaluating the desirability of the decision. As we will see, this procedure provides an approximation to the actual expected net present value, internal rate of return, or net profit of the investment. It provides only an approximation because the timing and amount of cash flows are not precisely taken into account.

Applying this simplified procedure, the average additional investment in working capital is determined using data from Exhibit 20-1.

EXHIBIT 20-1
Impact of Sam's inventory decision on current assets and liabilities[a]

End of week	Available cash	Accounts receivable	Inventory	Accounts payable	Accrued expenses	Taxes payable
0	0	0	$20,000	$20,000	0	0
1	− $ 200	$1,000	19,200	20,000	$120	$ 20
2	− $20,200	$2,000	18,400	0	240	40
3	− 20,200	3,000	17,600	0	360	60
4	− 20,200	4,000	20,000	3,200	480	80
5	− 20,680	5,000	19,200	3,200	120	100
6	− 23,880	6,000	18,400	0	240	120
7	− 22,880	6,000	17,600	0	360	140
8	− 21,880	6,000	20,000	3,200	480	160
9	− 21,360	6,000	19,200	3,200	120	180
10	− 23,560	6,000	18,400	0	240	200
11	− 22,560	6,000	17,600	0	360	220
12	− 21,560	6,000	20,000	3,200	480	240
13	− 21,040	6,000	19,200	3,200	120	260
14	− 23,500	6,000	18,400	0	240	20
. . . .						
398	− 320	6,000	18,400	0	240	160
399	680	6,000	17,600	0	360	180

[a] Does not include the impact of any debt used to finance investment.

Average minimum cash balance	=	$ 200
+ Average accounts receivable	=	6,000
+ Average inventory	=	18,800
− Average accounts payable	=	1,600
− Average accrued expenses	=	300
− Average taxes payable	=	140
Average working capital investment	=	$22,960

Note that the averages are calculated to reflect normal operations (accounts receivable reach their normal value after week 5). In the calculation of average working capital investment, we subtract "spontaneous" current liabilities from current assets. These are the current liabilities that are generated as a normal part of the firm's operations and do not include discretionary short-term financing sources such as bank loans.

The expected annual cash flow from this investment is:

Annual cash revenues from sales	=	$52,000
− Annual cash cost of goods sold	=	41,600
− Annual cash operating expenses	=	6,240
− Annual taxes	=	1,040
Annual aftertax cash flow	=	$ 3,120

Treating this decision as a reversible investment (see the discussion at the beginning of Chapter 17), we calculate the internal rate of return to be 13.6 percent ($3120/$22,960). Suppose that the required rate of return (discount rate) for this investment is 11 percent per year. The investment looks like a good deal, since 13.6 percent is greater than 11 percent. Alternatively, for comparison with more accurate procedures, let's calculate the net present value assuming that the investment is perpetual. In this case, the NPV is:

$$NPV = \$3120(P/A, 11\%, \infty) - \$22,960$$
$$= \$3120/0.11 - \$22,960$$
$$= \$5404$$

Since the NPV is greater than zero, the investment is again found to be worthwhile.

A more accurate procedure is to calculate the net present value of the actual cash flows expected to result from this investment fully taking into account the timing of the cash flows. The relevant time period for these cash flows is a week, and a discount rate of 0.2 percent per week is equivalent to 11 percent per year.[3] Exhibit 20-2 shows the cash flows through week 14. After week 13, the cash flows repeat the same sequence for as long as the inventory decision is in effect. A diagram of these cash flows is shown in Figure 20-1.

---

[3] A discount rate of 0.2 percent per week is approximately equivalent to an effective rate of 11 percent per year with weekly compounding. $(1.11)^{1/52} - 1 = 0.00201$.

729

CHAPTER 20
Working capital
management

The NPV of the cash flows *at the beginning of week 1*, assuming that the cash flows are perpetual, is most easily calculated by calculating the present value of each stream of cash separately as follows (noting that discount rates of 0.8024 percent per four weeks and 2.63 percent per 13 weeks are equivalent to a discount rate of 0.2 percent per week):

EXHIBIT 20-2
Impact of Sam's inventory decision on cash flows

| Week | Receipts | Disbursements | | | Required increase in cash balances | Net cash flow | Cumulative net cash flow |
		Suppliers	Operating expenses	Taxes			
0	0	0	0	0		0	0
1	0	0	0	0	$200	−$ 200	−$ 200
2	0	$20,000	0	0		−$20,000	−$20,200
3	0	0	0	0		0	− 20,200
4	0	0	0	0		0	− 20,200
5	0	0	$480	0		− 480	− 20,680
6	0	$ 3,200	0	0		− 3,200	− 23,880
7	$1,000	0	0	0		1,000	− 22,880
8	$1,000	0	0	0		1,000	− 21,880
9	$1,000	0	$480	0		520	− 21,360
10	$1,000	$ 3,200	0	0		− 2,200	− 23,560
11	$1,000	0	0	0		1,000	− 22,560
12	$1,000	0	0	0		1,000	− 21,560
13	$1,000	0	$480	0		520	− 21,040
14	$1,000	$ 3,200	0	$260		− 2,460	− 23,500

FIGURE 20-1
Cash flows from Sam's inventory decision.

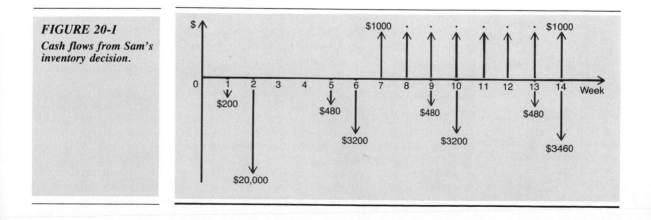

$$NPV = \$1000(P/F,\ 0.2\%,\ 5)(P/A,\ 0.2\%,\ \infty)$$
$$-\$20,000(P/F,\ 0.2\%,\ 1)$$
$$-\$3200(P/F,\ 0.2\%,\ 1)(P/A,\ 0.8024\%,\ \infty)$$
$$-\$480(P/A,\ 0.8024\%,\ \infty) - \$260(P/A,\ 2.63\%,\ \infty) - \$200$$
$$= \$1000(0.99)/0.002 - \$20,000(0.998)$$
$$-\$3200(0.998)/0.008024 - \$480/0.008024$$
$$-\$260/0.0263 - \$200$$
$$= \$495,000 - \$19,960 - \$398,006 - \$59,821$$
$$-\$9886 - \$200$$
$$= \$7127$$

We can compare the NPV of $7127, which is the most accurate estimate, with the NPV of $5404 calculated using the working capital investment approach. The error in the simpler procedure is 24 percent ($1723/$7127). In general the working capital investment method produces an underestimate of the actual expected NPV (or IRR or net profit) because it overstates the actual outlay involved and understates the benefits. The outlay is overstated because the outlays are assumed to occur at time 0, whereas they actually occur over several weeks or months.[4] The benefits are understated because they are assumed to begin in one year, whereas they actually begin much sooner. Therefore, the method is a conservative approach for evaluating these complex investment problems. Direct examination of the cash flows is not only more accurate but is also important for a different reason.

Examine the column labeled "Available Cash" in Exhibit 20-1. These figures are the same as those labeled "Cumulative Net Cash Flow" in Exhibit 20-2. The data in these two columns show the estimated impact on the firm's cash position from undertaking this investment. For example, the $-$23,880 for week 6 means that the sum of the incremental cash flows from weeks 0 through 6 resulting from the inventory increase equals $-$23,880. That is, the inventory increase of $20,000 results in an expected net cash outlay of $23,880 over the period from week 0 to week 6. The largest (negative) position is reached at the end of week 6, $-$23,880. Sam must be prepared to raise this much money to support the added inventory investment. The only way for Sam to obtain the amount and timing of this financing requirement is to forecast the actual cash flows. How long will the money be needed? The investment does not have a continuously positive cash position until week 399, almost eight years from the beginning. Therefore, despite the

---

[4] In addition, this simple method treats the additional accounts receivable as being a net cash outlay. As was discussed in Chapter 17, the cash investment in accounts receivable may be overstated if gross accounts receivable are used in the analysis. In this example, the cash outlay associated with accounts receivable is only the cost of the goods sold, $4800 (80 percent of $6000). Use of $4800 in place of the $6000 reduces working capital investment by $1200 and increases NPV to $6604. The resulting error decreases to 7.3 percent ($523/$7127). Use of cash investment adds complexity to the analysis and is still only an approximation. For an accurate evaluation, a forecast of cash flows is required.

profitability of this investment, it is expected to require financing for well over seven years or until it is reversed (reversal would produce a positive cash position). Unless conditions change, it will be profitable to continue the investment, and Sam must plan to provide financing for the investment for many years. Projections of the cash flows are essential in making the financing plans.

Working Capital and Financing Decisions

We have just seen that current asset expansion may be partially financed by current liabilities that arise as part of the firm's normal operations (accounts payable, accrued expenses, and so on). There are additional linkages between current assets and current liabilities that affect the level of working capital and that are important in deciding how to finance current assets.

We discussed the use of inventory and accounts receivable as collateral for loans in Chapter 19. Thus, for firms unable to obtain unsecured financing, the nature and quality of these current assets affect the availability and terms of short-term financing. We also noted in Chapter 19 that banks often require compensating balances as part of their loan terms. This means that the short-term financing decision influences the level of cash held.

How do financial managers deal with these interactions? Important tools are the pro forma financial statements presented in Chapter 16. Alternative financing policies are evaluated by forecasting their impact on the cash flows, balance sheets, and income statements of the firm. For example, decisions that require heavy use of short-term secured credit also require the availability of appropriate collateral. A projected balance sheet will show the levels of accounts receivable and inventory that might serve as collateral for loans. The level of working capital projected for the firm can also be checked against any requirements of long-term lenders. In making their decisions regarding the appropriate amount of short-term financing to support forecasted current asset investment, financial managers use the matching principle as an important guide.

The Matching Principle

The **matching principle**, one of the oldest principles in finance, can be stated as follows:

Finance short-term needs with short-term sources, and finance long-term needs with long-term sources.

The idea expressed in this principle is to "match" the maturity of the source of funds to the length of time the funds are needed.

The underlying logic is that, in the long run, the firm will be exposed to less risk and lower financing costs if the matching principle is followed. If the firm finances long-term needs with short-term borrowing, it will have to refinance (reborrow) its short-term debts as they become due, thereby exposing itself to added transaction costs (accounting and legal costs, fixed borrowing fees by lenders, etc.) and to the risk that new borrowing will be available only at higher interest rates with onerous terms. If the firm finances short-term needs with long-term sources, there will be times when there are excess funds that may have to be invested in low-yielding securities.

To see how the matching principle is applied, let's examine a graph of the total assets of the firm over time. For simplicity we will break the assets into only two types, current assets and fixed assets. Current assets include cash, marketable securities, accounts receivable, and inventory; fixed assets are long-term assets such as plant and equipment. In Figure 20-2 the fixed assets are shown increasing at a steady rate, as we are assuming a growing firm. Current assets are added to fixed assets to arrive at total assets. The matching principle states that the fixed assets of the firm should be financed with long-term sources (long-term debt plus equity), but what about current assets? Notice that in Figure 20-2 current assets have their ups and downs over time but they, too, are increasing on average. To see this more clearly, we can look at just the current assets over time in Figure 20-3. We have divided the current assets held by the firm into two types: temporary current assets and permanent current assets. Permanent current assets are the minimum investment in current assets that management has determined as being appropriate to support the current sales of the firm.

From Figure 20-3 the matching principle indicates that permanent current assets in addition to fixed assets should be financed with long-term sources. Only temporary current asset investment would be financed with short-term sources. The matching principle is not always followed by financial managers, in part because it does not consider the "permanent" short-term financing that arises from current liabilities. As the firm's sales grow over time, its current liabilities increase apart from

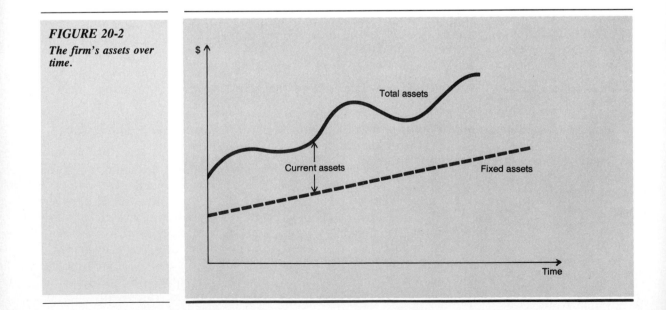

FIGURE 20-2
The firm's assets over time.

any explicit decisions made by financial management. Increases in sales result in increased employment and therefore higher average levels of wages and salaries payable. Increases in the volume of purchases lead to increased accounts payable even if all discounts are taken. Higher profits lead to higher taxes and therefore higher taxes payable. Thus a portion of increases in permanent current assets is financed by spontaneously generated increases in current liabilities. Only the increase in permanent working capital (permanent current assets minus permanent current liabilities) is to be financed by long-term sources under the matching principle. Furthermore, financial managers may be willing to trade off some risk in order to reduce financing costs. In order to understand this tradeoff between risk and financing cost we need to know about yield curves.

The Yield Curve

For most of the twentieth century interest rates on short-term debt securities have been less than interest rates on long-term debt securities. The typical situation is illustrated in Figure 20-4. A graph of interest rates on debt securities of a given type relative to the maturity of the debt is called a **yield curve**. At any point in time the financial manager of a firm can construct a yield curve showing the interest rate that the firm would have to pay on debt of a given maturity. In the typical case, the interest rate on short-term debt is less than the interest rate on long-term debt. However these relationships change over time. Often, short-term rates exceed long-term rates. For example, throughout 1981 the prime rate on bank loans was several percentage points higher than the interest rate on long-term Aaa bonds.

Yield curves can be developed for the securities of any borrower. The primary yield curve in the economy is the interest rate–maturity

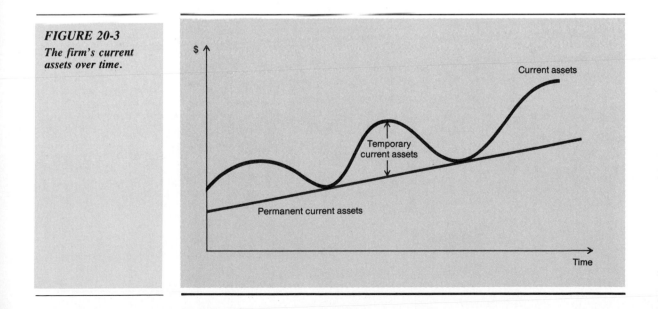

FIGURE 20-3
The firm's current assets over time.

relationship for United States government securities. The financial manager must understand the information provided by these relationships. The government securities yield curve is thought to be determined by three factors, as follows.[5]

1 The current level of short-term interest rates[6]
2 The expectations of investors and borrowers as to future interest rates
3 Premiums for risk of ownership of long-term securities (also called liquidity premiums)

When investors believe that interest rates will rise in the future, they will want to purchase short-term securities planning to reinvest at maturity at the higher rates. Thus the prices of short-term securities will rise, forcing down the interest rates on those securities. Simultaneously the prices of long-term securities will fall as investors sell them to buy short-term securities, and interest rates on long-term securities will rise. Conversely, when investors believe interest rates will fall, short-term interest rates will rise and long-term interest rates will fall as investors shift from short-term securities to long-term securities. The process stops when investors estimate that it is no longer profitable to make such shifts and the market comes into equilibrium. Thus, the yield curve reflects current expectations regarding future interest rates. However, expectations are not the only factor influencing yield curves. Even for securities issued by the United States government, investors must bear some risk

---

[5] A more comprehensive discussion of this topic is in Appendix 5A. We provide only the basic ideas here.

[6] See Chapter 2 for a discussion of the factors determining the current level of short-term interest rates.

FIGURE 20-4
A typical yield curve.

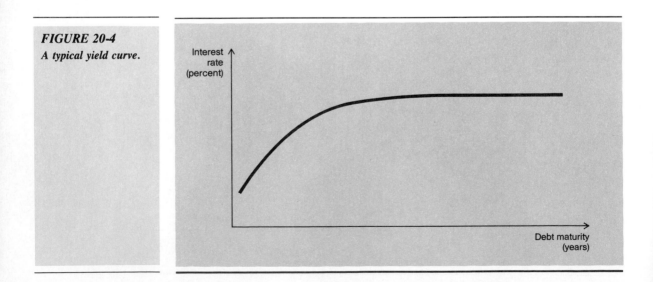

due to possible changes in interest rates. An increase in interest rates causes the prices of fixed income securities to fall. The longer the maturity of the security, the larger is the decline in price for a given change in interest rates. Thus long-term bonds are riskier than short-term bonds or bills. The result is that long-term bonds provide higher yields than short-term bonds to compensate investors for the additional risk.[7]

For business firms, long-term debt carries an additional premium because the interest and principal payments become less certain the further into the future they are; that is, there is more risk that the firm will default. Even AT&T bonds are risky in this sense. You may be fairly confident that AT&T will be able to pay its debts in 1995, but what about AT&T bonds maturing in 2010? Are you sure that satellite technology or some other factors will not put AT&T in a difficult financial position then? If you are not sure about AT&T, how about Burlington Northern Railroad, or IBM? These firms appear very safe today, but who knows what problems they might have in the future. The result is that the long-term debt of a business carries a higher risk premium than its short-term debt because of the difficulty in predicting long-run future outcomes.

The existence of risk premiums on long-term debt presents a dilemma to the financial manager. Financing exclusively through short-term debt has a lower expected interest cost to the firm, but it also is riskier. When the firm finances through twenty-year bonds, management knows the interest and principal payments that must be paid over the next twenty years if the firm is to avoid bankruptcy. If one-year notes are used, they must be repaid when due. If new securities must be issued to repay the one-year notes, the interest payments required after the first year are uncertain. Future interest payments will depend on the general level of interest rates at the time of the refinancing and the risk of the business at that time. Exclusive use of short-term debt would probably result in negative working capital for most firms and lenders often do not like to see current ratios of less than 1.0 for the firms to which they are providing credit. Moreover, use of short-term debt to finance permanent current assets and fixed assets means that the firm must continually refinance the debt as it comes due. Poor operating results in any year can make this difficult and expensive.

The pressure on financial managers remains. Should they strive for lower expected costs of financing by heavy use of short-term debt or should they reduce risk by following the matching principle? There is no clear-cut answer.

[7] Actually, the reason for higher interest rates on long-term debt instruments (positively sloped yield curve) is more complicated than described here. The shape of the yield curve depends on expected inflation, the preferred holding periods of investors, and the supply of debt instruments. However, since the yield curve for United States government securities is ordinarily positively sloped, it is likely that investors feel that the risk of long-term securities is greater than that of short-term securities, that is, the "risk premium" is larger the greater the term to maturity.

Liquidity for a firm is best defined as the ability to raise cash when needed. Assets are liquid if they can be rapidly converted into cash. Money market securities are an excellent source of asset liquidity. Potential liabilities (unused available credit) also provide liquidity. For example, if a firm has a line of credit of $200,000 and is currently borrowing only $50,000, it has $150,000 of liquidity from this borrowing source. Note that for assets, the larger is the amount held by the firm, the greater the firm's liquidity. Similarly, for potential liabilities the larger are the firm's potential liabilities, the greater its liquidity. Thus, a firm with a credit line of $200,000 that is borrowing only $50,000 has more liquidity than another firm with the same credit line but borrowing the full $200,000. To the extent that the firm has large investments in assets that are readily convertible into cash and has a large potential for increased borrowing, it is liquid.

There are two aspects to liquidity—planned liquidity and protective liquidity. Planned liquidity involves nothing more than the planning we stressed in Chapter 16. The financial manager must forecast cash needs and plan how those needs are to be met—through reductions in assets (usually marketable securities) increases in liabilities (drawing down established lines of credit), or the issuance of stock. Protective liquidity is the ability to meet unexpected cash demands. Unexpected cash demands are net cash outflows greater than those originally forecast. Unexpected cash demands can arise for many reasons. In some cases cash is needed to undertake unexpected investment opportunities. The inability to raise sufficient cash to undertake these investments results in foregone profits. In other cases cash is needed because of unexpected outflows—for example, a recall of defective products or a sudden increase in the prices of purchased goods. Cash may be needed because cash inflows are less than anticipated—for example, a strike that stops production, a slowdown in collections due to recession in the economy, a breakdown in a critical manufacturing step that cannot be fixed quickly, or a technological breakthrough that causes prices to drop dramatically.

Given the general uncertainty regarding cash flows, conservative financial managers maintain substantial liquidity. These managers make sure that they have committed credit lines well above the amount they expect to need. If the firm uses commercial paper, backup lines with banks will be maintained. They will keep marketable securities as a precautionary investment.

The net result of the financing and investment considerations discussed above is a tradeoff between risk and return in the working capital decision. Aggressive financial managers may be willing to operate with low levels of working capital. They will make heavy use of short-term debt and keep marketable securities to a minimum. They would expect to achieve maximum returns by this policy but they do subject the firm to greater risk. Conservative financial managers choose to operate with high levels of working capital. They avoid short-term debt except for temporary financing and maintain relatively large investments in liquid marketable securities. They opt for safety at a cost of foregone returns.

In all cases, the appropriate level of working capital is greatly influenced by the inherent characteristics of the business. For example, policies that would be considered reasonably safe and conservative for an electric utility (such as having zero working capital) would be considered highly risky for firms in most other industries. Therefore, in evaluating alternative policies, the financial manager should take into account the particular operating characteristics of the business. A helpful guide is to compare the firm's working capital position with those of other firms in the same industry, using procedures such as those discussed in Chapter 14. It is also essential to take into account the special features of the firm, since all companies in a given industry are not exactly alike.

WORKING CAPITAL AND BUSINESS EXPANSION

From our analysis of cash, accounts receivable, and inventory, we know that the amount of investment in current assets is closely related to the firm's sales volume. We also know that increased sales and inventory require higher purchases of raw materials or goods for resale and thus lead to increases in accounts payable. Further, we observed that part of the firm's other short-term liabilities depends on the general level of firm activity, wages payable, for example. This means that a firm planning investments in plant and equipment in order to expand output and sales must also plan for an increase in current asset investment. This increase in current assets, however, will be financed at least in part by "natural" costless increases in current liabilities.[8] But as long as some of the increased current assets are financed from sources other than current liabilities (that is, from cash flow from operations or from new stock or long-term debt), the result will be an increase in working capital investment by the firm. This additional investment must be considered in the analysis of the desirability of expansion. As we discussed earlier, there are two ways to incorporate the working capital changes into the analysis —as working capital investment or by direct forecasts of cash flows.

As an example of the working capital investment approach, consider a firm planning to invest $1 million in a plant to manufacture snowshoes. The expected annual sales from the facility are $1.8 million with anticipated aftertax cash flows of $200,000 per year. Assuming these cash flows will continue in perpetuity, the rate of return on the plant investment might be thought to be 20 percent ($200,000/$1,000,000). But wait. The financial manager must estimate the additional investment in raw materials, work-in-process, and finished goods inventory. Total additional inventory investment might be 20 percent of annual sales, or

---

[8] Here we would include only accounts payable that will be obtained when all discounts are taken. If discounts are foregone, trade credit is not costless and must be considered as part of the overall financing plan.

$360,000. If the firm purchases additional raw materials at a rate of $50,000 per month on terms of net 30, increased accounts payable will be (at no cost to the firm) $50,000. If the snowshoes will be sold on terms of net 60, accounts receivable will average two months' sales or 2 × ($1.8 million/12) = $300,000. The cash investment in these accounts is $200,000 (the cost of producing the goods sold to create the accounts receivable). The firm will probably also need additional cash balances to support the production and collection activity, say, 1 percent of annual sales, or $18,000. Additional current liabilities excluding any discretionary short-term financing might be 2 percent of annual sales, or $36,000. A summary of the additional working capital required is shown below.

Cash balance needed	$ 18,000
Cash investment in accounts receivable	300,000
Inventory investment	360,000
Total investment in current assets	$678,000
Less: Accounts payable	50,000
Other current liabilities	36,000
Required investment in working capital	$592,000

This additional investment in working capital must be included as part of the total investment. Thus total investment in the project will be $1 million in plant plus $592,000 in working capital for a total of $1,592,000. The actual rate of return on this project is therefore only 12.6 percent ($200,000/$1,592,000). Clearly, the financial manager would be making a big mistake to ignore working capital in evaluating the desirability of expansion.

However, we have seen that this approach to dealing with working capital changes provides only an approximation to the results of direct forecasting of cash flows and does not provide good estimates for determining the actual cash required to finance the project. It is best used in preliminary capital budgeting. Projects that are very good, very bad, or somewhere in between can be readily identified using the working capital investment approach. In final planning for a project, the cash flows are needed.

A more fundamental problem is the determination of what changes in working capital or cash flows will occur as a result of undertaking the project. How is the manager to determine the amount of working capital needed? In theory, each asset and liability must be analyzed in detail according to the principles of Chapters 17, 18, and 19. However, this is usually too time-consuming for the degree of accuracy possible, given the normal uncertainties inherent in any major expansion. Instead, the manager will use approximations based on the forecasting techniques of Chapter 16.

In addition to including working capital investment as part of initial investment, any anticipated changes in the level of investment over the life of the project must be included. Additions to working capital due to forecasting increases in sales volume reduce net cash flow in the period when the increase occurs. Reductions in working capital increase net cash flow. At the end of the investment period, working capital due to the project will fall to zero. The reduction in working capital investment is part of the salvage value of the total project (is a cash inflow).

SUMMARY

Working capital management is the management of current assets and current liabilities of the firm, which must be considered as a total package because of the many links between current assets and current liabilities. Working capital equals current assets minus current liabilities. Working capital is therefore the portion of the firm's current assets that is financed with long-term debt, preferred stock, and equity.

The matching principle states that short-term needs for money should be financed with short-term financing sources and that long-term needs for money should be financed with long-term sources. If the matching principle is followed, temporary investments in current assets should be financed with current liabilities such as trade credit, commercial paper, and short-term bank loans.

The relationship between interest rates and maturities of debt securities at a point in time is called a yield curve. The yield curve is determined by current short-term interest rates, by expectations of investors and borrowers as to future interest rates, and by the risk premiums required by investors. From the perspective of investors, the greater is the maturity of the debt, the more risky it is to own. However, from the perspective of the financial manager of a business firm, financing with short-term debt is more risky than financing with long-term debt.

Liquidity for a firm is the capability to raise cash quickly when it is needed. Assets provide liquidity if they can be rapidly converted into cash. The ability to borrow cash also provides liquidity. The financial manager should plan to provide liquidity for anticipated future cash needs. In addition, it is desirable for the firm to have liquidity available for unexpected cash needs.

Working capital requirements are an important part of capital budgeting decisions and should be included in the evaluation of each project.

QUESTIONS

1 Some data for two companies are shown below. Which one do you think has the more liquidity? Why?

Working capital	Company A	Company B
Current assets	$2,000	$2,200
Working capital	$1,500	$ 800
Total assets	$5,000	$5,000

2 The two partners of Kale and Collard Enterprises recently had the following argument:

    Kale: "At the end of this year we expect our growth in sales to require an increase in current assets of $400,000. In view of this need I suggest we seek long-term financing."

    Collard: "On the contrary, the $400,000 increase is due entirely to increased accounts receivable and inventory, for which $60,000 will be needed only for a few months. We should finance this $400,000 in additional current assets with a current liability such as a short-term bank loan."

Can you help Kale and Collard?

3 Indicate for the following situations whether you would expect the working capital of the firm in each case to increase, to decrease, or to remain at current levels. Explain why.

    a An electronics manufacturer has just completed new facilities that are expected to enable the firm to increase sales by 30 percent.

    b A clothing manufacturer discovers that a large part of the firm's inventory is unsalable and is therefore worthless.

    c A pencil manufacturer receives a large special order for an odd-sized pencil not normally produced.

    d The financial manager of a large corporation has received a staff study that indicates the corporation's liquidity is much too low because of increased uncertainty in the future cash flows and profits of the firm.

4 What is the matching principle?

5 Which one of the following three cases best describes a firm that is applying the matching principle? What financing policies do the other two firms appear to be using?

    a Firm *A* maintains a low current ratio compared to other firms in its industry although its proportion of debt to total assets equals the industry average. Sales for the firm have increased each year for the past four years at a stable rate.

    b Firm *B* has substantial credit lines available at commercial banks and is a frequent issuer of commercial paper; however, it often has no outstanding bank loans or commercial paper. The sales of this firm are somewhat seasonal and sales increased at annual rates varying between 4 percent and 20 percent over the past five years.

    c Firm *C* is a highly seasonal industry and its sales growth has been irregular. It often has substantial holdings of marketable securities in contrast to other firms in the industry and its working capital as a percentage of total assets is well above the industry average.

6 As financial manager of the Curve Company you have observed that for the past twelve months interest rates on long-term debt securities of Curve have averaged two percentage points higher

than the rates on short-term debt. In recent weeks interest rates in the economy have risen. The differential between long-term and short-term interest rates for Curve has decreased to one percentage point. What do you think is happening?

7 What are the two general sources of liquidity for a firm?

8 How does planned liquidity differ from protective liquidity?

9 Since liquidity is desirable, why don't all firms have lots of liquidity?

10 Bismark Shipyards is planning a new shipyard. Will the amount of working capital investment that must be considered in the decision depend on whether the new yard is a replacement for an existing facility or is in addition to existing facilities? Why or why not?

PROJECT

Plot the current yield curve for United States government securities and the yield on these securities one year ago. Try to explain why they appear as they do and what has changed from last year to the present. (A source for yields on United States government securities is *The Wall Street Journal*.) In your analysis do not include yields on any bonds that have coupon rates of $4\frac{1}{4}$ percent or less as yields on these securities are strongly influenced by special tax considerations. (They may be redeemed at par in settlement of estate taxes.)

*DEMONSTRATION
PROBLEMS*

DP1 Flake Enterprises is expecting sales next year to be $4.4 million, up $400,000 from last year. Inventory is expected to increase from $800,000 to $880,000 in order to support the higher level of sales. Purchases of goods average 60 percent of sales, and Flake pays its suppliers within 20 days, on average, taking all discounts available. How much of the $80,000 increase in inventory investment will be financed by spontaneous trade credit?

SOLUTION TO DP1:

Increase in inventory investment = $80,000
Purchases = 60% of annual sales
Increase in purchases = 60% of $400,000 increase in sales
$$= \$240,000 \text{ per year}$$
$$= \$240,000/360 \text{ days}$$
$$= \$666.67 \text{ per day}$$
Accounts payable = 20 days purchases
Increase in accounts payable = 20 days × $622 purchases per day
$$= \$13,333$$

Therefore, of the $80,000 increase in inventory, $13,333 will be financed by spontaneous trade credit.

DP2 As an assistant to the financial manager of Warble Birdseed Company, you have been provided with a forecast of Warble's cash flows. All cash inflows and outflows have been forecast except for any new financing, changes in short-term debt, and changes in securities investment. Payments to suppliers have been forecast assuming that all cash discounts available have been taken. Warble currently has $0.5 million invested in marketable securities. The cash flow forecast for the next six quarters is shown below. (Dollar figures are in millions.)

Quarter	1	2	3	4	5	6
Cash flow	$(3.0)	$(1.0)	$(2.0)	$3.0	$(1.5)	$1.5
Cumulative cash flow	$(3.0)	$(4.0)	$(6.0)	$(3.0)	$(4.5)	$(3.0)

a Based on the figures shown, how much "permanent" financing appears to be needed by Warble?

b What is the maximum amount of "temporary" financing and when is it forecast to be needed?

c Given the financing options shown below, which ones are consistent with the matching principle?

(1) Issue $5.5 million in long-term debt.

(2) Issue $2.5 million in long-term debt and issue 90-day commercial paper as needed.

(3) Issue $2.5 million in long-term debt and obtain a $3.0 million credit line.

(4) Issue commercial paper as needed.

SOLUTION TO DP2:

a Adjust the cumulative cash flows for the $0.5 million in securities which would be available to finance part of the initial cash outflow. The $2.5 million is the minimum cumulative cash outflow occurring in quarters 1 and 4. The answer is $2.5 million in permanent financing.

b Given the answer from *a*, the maximum temporary financing needed is in quarter 3 and amounts to $3.0 million.

c Options 2 and 3 are consistent with the matching principle since there will not be any excess cash (investment in securities) and short-term borrowing can be repaid within a year. Option 1 results in excess cash during quarters 1, 4, and 6. Option 4 wold require the firm to issue commercial paper continuously over the six quarters.

PROBLEMS

1 Determine the working capital for a company with the following balance sheet.

Assets		Liabilities and net worth	
Cash	$ 500	Notes payable	$ 3,000
Accounts receivable	8,500	Accounts Payable	2,500
Inventory	6,500	Long-term debt	6,000
Equipment	9,500	Net worth	13,500
Total	$25,000	Total	$25,000

2 The Ibex Company maintains inventory levels equal to 20 percent of its annual sales revenues. Total purchases of goods for inventory average 36 percent of annual sales. Sales for next year are expected to be $400,000 higher than last year. Ibex purchases goods on terms of net 30. If Ibex maintains its current policies, what will be the increase in inventory investment because of the increase in sales and how much of that increase will be financed by spontaneous trade credit?

3 As financial manager for Trident Electronics, you have completed the two-year cash flow forecast shown below. All cash inflows and outflows have been forecast, given the minimum cash balance of the firm, except that any new financing required and temporary investments in securities are not included in the cash inflows and outflows. Cash discounts are assumed to be taken when available. (Dollar figures are in millions.)

Quarter	1	2	3	4	5	6	7	8
Cash inflow (outflow)	$2.2	$(6.5)	$(4.0)	$1.3	$4.0	$(2.0)	$2.0	$(0.5)
Cumulative inflow (outflow)	$2.2	$(4.3)	$(8.3)	$(7.0)	$(3.0)	$(5.0)	$(3.0)	$(3.5)

a How much "permanent" financing appears to be needed by this firm?

b Given your answer from a, what is the maximum "temporary" financing required and when does it occur?

4 As Trident Electronics' financial manager (problem 3), you must develop a financial plan for the firm.

a Evaluate the following alternative financing proposals submitted by your staff. Which ones are consistent with the matching principle? Might any fail to meet the financing needs of the firm? Are any particularly unsuited for the firm in other ways?

(1) Obtain a line of credit for $3.0 million and issue $5.5 million of long-term debt in quarter 2.

(2) Plan to issue ninety-day commercial paper as needed.

(3) Obtain a two-year revolving credit agreement with a limit of $8.5 million.

(4) Obtain a line of credit for $5.5 million and issue $3.0 million in long-term debt in quarter 2.

(5) Issue $3.0 million of common stock in quarter 2 and use
trade credit as needed.

(6) Plan to finance with ninety-day bank loans as needed.

b Examine the implications of financing alternatives 1, 4, and 6,
assuming the following:

(1) Interest rate on long-term debt will be 15 percent.

(2) Interest rate on line of credit will be 14 percent.

(3) Interest rate on temporary investments will be 12 percent.
You should determine the actual loans and investments that
will be outstanding in each quarter and the total cost of the
three financing plans over the two-year period, treating the interest received on securities as an offset to interest expense on
debt. Rank the three alternatives with respect to interest cost
and with respect to financing risks. What do you observe?

5 Estimate the liquidity readily available for the following companies:

a Firm *A* has $40,000 in U.S. Treasury bills and bank credit
lines of $200,000. The firm has no bank loans currently out-
standing.

b Firm *B* has no marketable securities and a bank credit line of
$400,000. The firm is currently borrowing $150,000 from its
bank.

6 Fitite Corporation is planning to build a new textile mill in Flor-
ida.The mill is expected to provide additional sales as follows:

First year	Second year	Third year and on
$2.0 million	$2.5 million	$3.0 million per year

That is, the mill is not expected to be producing at its maximum
capacity of $3.0 million per year until the third year after opening.

The financial manager of Fitite estimates that, for every dollar
of sales, $0.25 must be invested in current assets. If all discounts
are taken and all bills are paid on time, accounts payable average
$0.04 per dollar of sales for products similar to those being pro-
duced in the new mill. Other current liabilities, such as wages
payable, typically average $0.05 per dollar of sales. Estimate the
working capital investment required for the new mill. How do
these requirements affect the cash flows associated with the project?

7 The financial manager of Western Distributors is considering a
proposal to expand into the Dallas, Texas, area. The proposal is
to lease warehouse space and invest in sufficient inventory to support expected sales of $260,000 per year. If the venture proves
successful, additional expansion (perhaps with purchased facilities) will be considered. The lease is for ten years, but may be
cancelled at the end of the first year. For the present, the major

issues are the prospective profitability of the proposal and its financing requirements.

Cost of goods sold (purchases) averages 75 percent of sales. Operating expenses, which include lease payments, are expected to be $52,000 per year. Western pays taxes quarterly at a marginal tax rate of 40 percent per year.

The initial inventory investment will be $45,000 and will be received in week "zero." After the initial order, purchases will be made every two weeks to replace goods sold. Western normally pays its suppliers one week after receipt of goods. This payment period is sufficient to qualify Western for all purchase discounts (which are reflected in the cost of goods sold and inventory figures given above). The first restocking order will be received in week 2, with payment in week 3.

The weekly cash payroll for the warehouse (included in operating expenses) is expected to be $700 and the remaining operating expenses result in cash payments of $1200 every four weeks starting in week 5. Cash payments for taxes will occur in the week that they are due, in weeks 13, 26, and so on. Taxes are based on sales less cost of goods sold and accrued operating expenses for the quarter. At the projected level of operations, Western will need $4000 in additional cash balances in a Dallas bank beginning in week 1.

Western offers its customers payment terms that result in cash collections four weeks on average after sales of goods. For purposes of this analysis, the financial manager wishes to assume that all customers pay four weeks after sale.

a What is the expected annual cash flow at a sales level of $260,000 per year?

b Assuming that sales are $5000 per week beginning in week 1 and that operating expenses also begin in week 1, forecast the weekly levels of current assets and liabilities associated with the proposal for the first 15 weeks of operations (weeks zero to 14). What is the expected average level of working capital investment under normal operations?

c What is the expected rate of return on working capital investment assuming that it is reversible? If the required rate of return (discount rate) for investments of this type is 11 percent, should the proposal be accepted?

d Calculate the net present value of the annual cash flow using a discount rate of 11 percent and assuming that it is perpetual. Should the proposal be accepted?

8 Using the information in problem 7, forecast the weekly cash flows from the Dallas proposal for weeks zero through 13. What is the maximum amount of financing that will be needed and when does it occur?

9 Using the results from problem 8, calculate the net present value of the proposal as of week 1 assuming that it is continued forever

at the same level of operation. Use a discount rate of 0.2 percent per week. (See Appendix 20A for interest rate factors). Is the proposal acceptable?

10 (THIS PROBLEM REQUIRES THE USE OF A COMPUTER).

The financial manager of Western Distributors (problem 7) is concerned that sales will not reach a rate of $260,000 per year ($5000 per week) immediately after operations begin. In addition, the marketing manager for Western has proposed to spend $24,000 ($2000 per week in tax-deductible cash expenses) in initial promotional activities. Using the information in problem 7, set up a spreadsheet that will provide weekly cash flows for the first 14 weeks for different sales levels in each week and different initial marketing budgets (assume the budgeted amount will be spent over the first 12 weeks in equal weekly amounts). Include a calculation of the net present value of these cash flows in the spreadsheet (this is one way to measure the initial investment in the project). The discount rate is 0.2 percent per week. What are the NPVs and the maximum amounts of financing needed for the first 14 weeks of the Dallas project under the following conditions:

a Sales start at $5000 per week and continue at this rate. The promotional budget is zero. *Note*: This is the solution to problem *8*.

b Sales start at $5000 per week and continue at this rate. The promotional budget is $24,000.

c Sales start at $1000 per week and increase by $500 per week until they reach $5000 per week. The promotional budget is $24,000.

11 (THIS PROBLEM REQUIRES THE USE OF A COMPUTER AND STUDY OF APPENDIX 17B. It is an extension of problem *10* and includes the solution to that problem.)

The financial manager of Western Distributors (problem *10*) is concerned about the profitability of the Dallas project with the added initial promotional expense of $24,000 and the possibility of lower initial sales. Since this is a pilot project for future expansion in the Dallas market, it is not necessary for the project to actually be desirable by itself. However, some measure of its desirability is needed before a decision can be made. Since the lease may be cancelled after one year, a one-year evaluation period seems appropriate. As assistant to the financial manager, undertake the following tasks:

a Develop a worksheet that provides weekly cash flows for weeks 1 through 56. Assume that the warehouse lease will not be continued and that all inventory will be sold by the end of week 52. Purchases will be ended prior to then so as to produce zero ending inventory given the rate of sales. Operating expenses will cease in week 52. Accounts receivable will continue to be collected after week 52 with no added expenses, although the bank account will be maintained until all accounts are collected.

b   Calculate the net present values and internal rates of return for the three sales and promotion assumptions in problem *10* (*a, b,* and *c*).

c   Evaluate the results in the context of the total situation faced by Western Distributors.

12   The Save-More Company operates a chain of drugstores in California. The firm's financial manager, C. K. Wu, is investigating the impact of establishing a new credit policy for the firm. For many years Save-More extended credit only to a select number of customers who were known personally by the managers of Save-More's stores. In an effort to increase sales and to compete more effectively, management changed its policy two years ago to one of extending thirty days of credit to anyone who asked for it. This policy proved successful in increasing sales but also caused a tremendous increase in accounts receivable and bad debt losses. C. K. thought that, by being somewhat more selective in extending credit and by adding an interest charge to accounts more than thirty days overdue, most of the benefits of the wide-open policy might be retained while reducing costs. The following estimates were requested by C. K. from the marketing staff and are based on an analysis of customer accounts (dollar figures are in thousands and are annual averages):

	Credit policy		
	Restrictive	Selective	Wide open
Sales revenues	$40,000	$50,000	$55,000
Other income[a]	0	200	0
Cost of goods sold	24,000	30,000	33,000
Operating expenses	10,000	12,000	13,000
Bad debt losses	0	200	500
Required cash balances	500	600	600
Accounts receivable	1,000	6,000	8,000
Inventory	6,000	7,000	7,500
Accounts payable	2,000	2,200	2,300
Accrued expenses	1,000	1,200	1,300
Taxes payable	300	400	450

[a] Interest charges under selective credit policy.

Save-More's tax rate is 40 percent. C. K. estimates that the appropriate discount rate for the restrictive policy is 10 percent per year. However, due to the greater risks associated with the selective and the wide-open policies, higher discount rates should be used. Discount rates of 11 percent for the selective policy and 12 percent for the wide-open policy are believed to be appropriate. Estimate the net present value of each policy assuming that they are continued in perpetuity. Use a "working capital investment" approach.

SELECTED INTEREST FACTORS
FOR WEEKLY ANALYSIS

Week	0.15 percent		0.2 percent		0.25 percent	
	P/F	P/A	P/F	P/A	P/F	P/A
1	0.9985	0.9985	0.9980	0.9980	0.9975	0.9975
2	0.9970	1.9955	0.9960	1.9940	0.9950	1.9925
3	0.9955	2.9910	0.9940	2.9880	0.9925	2.9851
4	0.9940	3.9850	0.9920	3.9801	0.9901	3.9751
5	0.9925	4.9776	0.9901	4.9701	0.9876	4.9627
6	0.9910	5.9686	0.9881	5.9582	0.9851	5.9478
7	0.9896	6.9582	0.9861	6.9443	0.9827	6.9305
8	0.9881	7.9463	0.9841	7.9285	0.9802	7.9107
9	0.9866	8.9329	0.9822	8.9107	0.9778	8.8885
10	0.9851	9.9180	0.9802	9.8909	0.9753	9.8639
11	0.9836	10.9016	0.9783	10.8691	0.9729	10.8368
12	0.9822	11.8838	0.9763	11.8454	0.9705	11.8073
13	0.9807	12.8645	0.9744	12.8198	0.9681	12.7753
14	0.9792	13.8438	0.9724	13.7922	0.9656	13.7410
15	0.9778	14.8215	0.9705	14.7627	0.9632	14.7042
16	0.9763	15.7978	0.9685	15.7312	0.9608	15.6650
26	0.9618	25.4808	0.9494	25.3109	0.9371	25.1426
27	0.9603	26.4411	0.9475	26.2584	0.9348	26.0774
28	0.9589	27.4000	0.9456	27.2040	0.9325	27.0099
39	0.9432	37.8536	0.9250	37.4818	0.9072	37.1149
40	0.9418	38.7954	0.9232	38.4049	0.9050	38.0199
41	0.9404	39.7358	0.9213	39.3263	0.9027	38.9226
52	0.9250	49.9877	0.9013	49.3405	0.8782	48.7048
53	0.9236	50.9113	0.8995	50.2401	0.8760	49.5809
54	0.9222	51.8336	0.8977	51.1378	0.8739	50.4548
55	0.9209	52.7544	0.8959	52.0337	0.8717	51.3264
56	0.9195	53.6739	0.8941	52.9279	0.8695	52.1959
57	0.9181	54.5920	0.8924	53.8202	0.8673	53.0633
58	0.9167	55.5088	0.8906	54.7108	0.8652	53.9285
59	0.9154	56.4241	0.8888	55.5996	0.8630	54.7915
60	0.9140	57.3381	0.8870	56.4866	0.8609	55.6524

PART FIVE

SPECIAL TOPICS

Part 5 discusses several issues relating to many—but not all—business firms. Chapter 21 describes various forms of leasing arrangements, indicates why leasing may have advantages over purchasing, and explains how the financial manager decides whether to lease or purchase a particular asset. Chapter 22 discusses the use of convertibles and warrants as a financing method. Chapter 23 covers mergers and acquisitions—when they are justified and how management should analyze a potential merger in determining its advisability.

CHAPTER TWENTY-ONE

LEASING

Virtually any asset that can be purchased can also be leased. A **lease** is a contract between the owner of an asset, called the **lessor**, and another party, called the **lessee**, who makes periodic payments to the owner for the *right* to use the asset. From the introduction of leasing by Phoenician shipowners 3000 years ago until the mid-1960s, only a few types of assets could be leased and the volume of lease transactions was not very large compared with the volume of purchases. However, in recent years the volume of leasing and the range of assets available for lease has grown dramatically. In addition to the well-established leasing operations in computers, office equipment, transportation equipment (railroad cars, autos, aircraft, ships), and machinery, leasing arrangements now extend to such areas as shipping containers, nuclear fuel cores, medical equipment, and pollution control devices. Approximately one-fifth of all new equipment in the United States is leased. A striking example of the importance of leasing is Anaconda Aluminum's $138,000,000 reduction mill near Sebree, Kentucky, which is entirely leased. That single plant represents approximately 3 percent of the entire United States aluminum production capacity. Even the United States Navy began leasing ships in 1971 when Congress failed to appropriate funds for the purchase of needed fuel tankers. Leasing, indeed, has come of age.

WHO PROVIDES LEASES?

As we noted, at least two parties are involved in a lease—the lessor (owner) and the lessee (user). In a **leveraged lease**, there is also a lender (for example, an insurance company), from whom the lessor borrows the funds to purchase the assets. Sometimes, a **lease packager** or an investment bank will arrange the lease agreement for a fee without participating directly as a lessor, lessee, or lender. In terms of dollar volume, the most important lessors of equipment are the manufacturers themselves; they represent roughly half the equipment leasing done in the United States. Banks account for approximately one-third of the equipment leasing, with most of the rest done by independent leasing companies.

TYPES OF LEASES

Operating Lease

An **operating lease** is a short-term lease (lease term is only a small fraction of the useful life of the asset). A long-term lease which allows the lessee (and sometimes the lessor) to cancel the lease at any time is also referred to as an operating lease. The lessor may provide services under the lease agreement such as maintenance, insurance, and the payment of property taxes. Vehicles, computers, copiers, amusement equipment, display fixtures, and furniture are among the assets commonly acquired on an operating lease basis. The term "operating lease" also refers to a lease which is not classified under accounting rules as a capital lease (see the discussion later in this chapter on accounting for leases).

Financial Lease

A **financial lease** (or **finance lease**) involves an intermediate or long-term commitment by the lessor and lessee. If the asset is equipment, the lease duration will generally equal at least half of the expected useful life of the assets. Maintenance or other services are not generally provided by the lessor under a financial lease although this is subject to negotiation.

Assets often covered by financial leases include real estate, office equipment, medical equipment, railroad cars, airplanes, and construction equipment. If the asset is real estate, the lessor may be an individual or a business firm, frequently an insurance company. An equipment lessor is commonly a manufacturer, a finance or leasing company, or a commercial bank. A common procedure for leasing equipment is for the lessee to determine the equipment it wants to lease and to settle on a purchase price with the manufacturer. The firm then finds a leasing company or bank, which will purchase the asset and lease it to the firm for a rental which provides an adequate return on the lessor's investment.

A financial lease will often provide a means for the lessee to continue possession of the property after the expiration of the initial lease. This may be allowed for under a renewal option that permits the lessee to obtain a new lease at a specified rental after the initial lease expires. The lease may also contain a purchase option that gives the lessee the right to buy the asset for a particular price at the lease's expiration.

The lease payment is a fixed obligation of the lessee and, as with debt interest, failure to make the rental payment can result in insolvency and bankruptcy court action. Although the lessor's claim against the lessee in the event of bankruptcy is usually somewhat less stringent than that of most creditors, it does provide for repossession of the leased asset and at least partial payment to the lessor of lease rentals applicable to the remaining term of the lease. Perhaps more relevant is that, for the going concern, leases involve a fixed charge like debt payments, and therefore fluctuations in firm income are absorbed by the lessee. In other words, a financial lease, like debt, involves the benefits and dangers of leverage.

Sale and Leaseback

A firm may sell an asset it already owns to another party and then lease it back from the buyer. In this way the firm can obtain cash (proceeds from the sale) and still have use of the asset. This arrangement is called a **sale**

and leaseback. Financial leases (rather than operating leases) are virtually always used in sale and leasebacks. The lease will ordinarily provide for an option either to renew the lease or to purchase the asset at the end of the lease term.

As with an ordinary financial lease, the buyer and lessor under a sale and leaseback agreement will frequently be an insurance company if the asset is real estate, or a leasing firm, finance company, or commercial bank if the asset is equipment. The lease provisions are the same as those described for financial leases in general.

Full-Service Lease

Under a full-service lease the lessor maintains and insures the assets and pays property taxes on the asset. This is similar to a **maintenance lease**, which obligates the lessor to provide maintenance services. A full-service lease is the opposite of a **net lease**, under which the rent payment is "net," i.e., the lessee pays maintenance costs, insurance, and property taxes.

Leveraged Lease

A **leveraged lease**, *or* **third-party lease**, involves a third party—a lender—in addition to the lessor and lessee. The lessor borrows part of the asset's purchase price from the lender, and the lease rentals are used to service the loan, any excess going to the lessor. Both the depreciation (for tax purposes) and the investment tax credit on the asset are allocated to the lessor. The loan is on a nonrecourse basis, i.e., the lender has a claim against the asset and the lease rentals if there is default on the loan but the lender may not demand additional payments from the lessor. Therefore, even in the unlikely event that the asset becomes worthless and the lessee becomes bankrupt, the most that the lessor could lose would be the down payment that it made in purchasing the asset. Of course, the loan will carry an interest rate which adequately compensates the lender for the risks involved.

Large lease transactions (e.g., the lease of a plane or ship) may involve the creation of a **trust** that acquires the asset to be leased. The trust obtains the funds to purchase the asset by selling an equity (ownership) interest in the trust to the lessor and selling **mortgage bonds** to other investors. These bonds are usually guaranteed by the lessee (that is, the lessee pays them off if the trust defaults on the bonds).[1] The periodic lease payments go to the trust, which uses them to pay off the bonds. Whatever is left over after making the bond payments is income to the ownership (lessor) interest in the trust.[2] This arrangement allows the lessor company to borrow some of the funds through the trust (by

---

[1] This means that if the trust defaults on the bonds, the bondholders can take possession of the trust's assets (including the leased assets); and if the assets are not worth enough to repay what is owed on the bonds, the lessee must pay what is still owed. The lessor is not liable for the bonds.

[2] Income from the trust is allocated to the lessor in computing corporate income taxes. The taxable trust income (or loss) is the rental payments less interest deduction on the mortgage bonds less depreciation on the asset.

issuing the mortgage bonds) to cover the asset's cost, while at the same time limiting the lessor's liability on the bonds (since the lessee guarantees the bonds).

Table 21-1 summarizes the characteristics of the major types of leases.

DEFINING A LEASE FOR TAX AND ACCOUNTING PURPOSES

True Leases and the IRS

With a **true lease** the lessor retains the tax benefits of ownership and the lessee deducts the lease rentals for tax purposes. The lessor claims the depreciation and owns the leased equipment at the end of the lease. Even if two parties regard an agreement as a lease, the agreement is a true lease (that is, a lease for tax purposes) only if it conforms to certain guidelines set forth in the law. If the agreement does not conform to the guidelines, the transaction will be treated for tax purposes as a *sale* of the asset to the user; this is so regardless of the intent or desires of the "lessor" and "lessee."

Three major guidelines appear in the tax law for determining whether an arrangement between a user and provider of an asset is a lease. The first and oldest guideline is Revenue Ruling 55-540, which essentially states that a transaction is a lease only if the lease rental payments do not effectively provide the "lessee" with an ownership interest in the asset.[3]

In 1975, the Internal Revenue Service issued Revenue Procedure 75-21, which covers leveraged leases and, in practice, also covers direct leases; this guideline expanded upon Revenue Ruling 55-540. Revenue Procedure 75-21 stipulates that for a transaction to be deemed a lease for tax purposes: [4]

---

[3] Evidence that ownership is being acquired would be, for example, if the lease rental were far above fair rental value or if the lessee had the option to purchase the asset for a price which is materially less than fair market value at the time the purchase option could be exercised.

[4] Only the major provisions of Revenue Procedure 75-21 are stated below.

TABLE 21-1
Types of leases

Type of lease	Parties involved	Duration	Does lessor maintain asset?
Operating lease	Lessor and lessee	Short-term	Often yes
Financial lease	Lessor and lessee	Long-term	Generally no
Sale and leaseback	Lessor (buyer) and lessee (seller)	Long-term	Generally no
Full-service	Lessor and lessee	Generally short-term	Yes
Leveraged lease	Lessor, lender, and lessee	Long-term	Generally no

1   The lessor must maintain at least a 20 percent "at risk" investment in the asset throughout the lease term.[5]

2   The residual value of the asset must equal 20 percent of the original cost of the asset without taking into account general inflation or deflation (i.e., netting out any value changes due to inflation or deflation); and the remaining useful life of the asset at the end of the lease term must be the larger of one year or 20 percent of the original estimated useful life of the asset.

3   The lessee may not have the right to buy the asset from the lessor for a price less than fair market value, and the lessor may not have the right to require any party (including the lessee) to buy the asset.

4   The lessee may not finance the asset's cost (e.g., by lending money to the lessor) and may not guarantee any indebtedness incurred by the lessor in connection with the asset.

5   The lessor must show that it expects to profit from the transaction apart from the tax benefits provided by the asset under the lease arrangement.

The major thrust of the above criteria is that the lessor must retain some of the nontax benefits of owning the asset (e.g., a material salvage value) and must assume some of the risks and responsibilities of ownership (e.g., of obtaining financing).[6]

The Economic Recovery Tax Act of 1981 (ERTA) temporarily changed the rules of the leasing game (the law was later changed again) for *corporate* lessors; the lease guidelines under ERTA have generally been referred to as the "safe-harbor" leasing provisions.[7] Under ERTA, a corporate lessor and a lessee could elect to treat a transaction as a lease for tax purposes as long as the lessor maintained at least a 10 percent " at risk" investment in the leased asset throughout the lease term and the lease had a duration satisfying a certain specified constraint.[8] ERTA made it much easier to deem a transaction a true lease since it imposed

---

[5] **At risk investment** is the sum of cash invested in the asset by the lessor plus any recourse debt incurred by the lessor in acquiring the asset. With **recourse debt** the creditor may legally demand payment of the debt, as well as take claim to the asset, if the lessor defaults on the debt. With **nonrecourse debt**, the loan is at most collateralized by the asset and the creditor may not turn to the borrower for payment if the borrower defaults on the loan. The 20 percent investment in the asset is computed by dividing the cash investment plus recourse debt by the depreciated tax basis of the asset; the depreciated tax basis of the asset at any point in time equals the original cost of the asset minus accumulated depreciation for tax purposes.

[6] If a lease arrangement does not meet the five criteria, the IRS or the courts may still allow the arrangement to be treated as a lease for tax purposes. The likelihood of treatment as a lease is greater the more closely the lease satisfies the five criteria.

[7] ERTA specified that, to be eligible for safe-harbor treatment, the lessor must be a corporation (or a group of corporations); the lessee need not be a corporation.

[8] A failure to elect to have the lease fall under the safe-harbor provisions would mean that the old law (in effect, Revenue Ruling 55-540 and Revenue Procedure 75-21) would apply to the lease.

no constraints on the financing of the asset (except for the 10 percent at risk lessor investment), on the level of the lease rentals, on the existence of a bargain purchase option (e.g., an option allowing the lessee to buy the asset for $1 at the end of the lease term would be acceptable), or on the profitability of the asset for the lessor. Companies with tax losses (who therefore could not take the investment tax credit or depreciation deductions) could easily arrange leases with profitable companies which could use the tax shelters to reduce their corporate income taxes. Under such leases the tax benefits enjoyed by the lessor would in part be passed on to the lessee in the form of low lease rentals.

After passage of ERTA, many firms chose to lease rather than to own operating assets. For example, in 1981 Ford sold to IBM $1 billion of machinery, equipment, and tooling (representing almost all of Ford's 1981 domestic capital spending). Ford had purchased the assets in 1981 but, because of its continuing losses, would not have been able to benefit from investment tax credits or depreciation. By selling the assets to IBM and then leasing them back, Ford ended up ahead by well over $100 million in cash. IBM received large tax savings by using the investment tax credits and depreciation to reduce its tax bill.

In the years after 1981, Congress changed the tax law several times. Safe-harbor leasing was completely phased out. The Tax Reform Act of 1986 made two changes of major importance to leasing. The first was the elimination of the investment tax credit (ITC). Under the prior law, many companies that could not use the ITC (because they paid very little or nothing in taxes) leased from firms that could take the ITC. The tax savings of the lessor due to the lessor's taking the ITC could be passed on to the lessee through lower lease rentals. The elimination of the ITC removed this incentive to lease. But offsetting this was a new incentive to leasing created by the corporate alternative minimum tax (AMT), which was introduced by the 1986 Tax Reform Act (see Chapter 3 on the AMT). An asset user paying the AMT may benefit by leasing from a lessor who is not subject to the AMT (which would be the case if the lessor uses very few tax shelters relative to its income). The reason is that a company that can avoid the AMT gains more from depreciation deductions than does a company that pays the AMT. Therefore, an asset user subject to the AMT can lease from a lessor that is unaffected by the AMT, and the depreciation benefits gained by the lessor can be passed on to the user in low lease rentals. This tax advantage has been a major spur to leasing by such firms as United Technologies Corporation, Goodyear Tire & Rubber Company, CSX Corporation, and Exxon Corporation.

Accounting for Leases

The Financial Accounting Standards Board (an arm of the American Institute of Certified Public Accountants) requires, under FASB Statement 13, that leases be classified *by the lessee* as either capital leases or operating leases. A **capital lease** transfers most or all of the benefits and risks of ownership to the lessee. If a lease is not a capital lease, it is an operating lease.[9] If one or more of the following conditions are met, the lease is deemed a capital lease by the lessee:[10]

1 The lease transfers ownership of the asset to the lessee at the end of the lease term.

2 The lease provides for a bargain purchase option.

3 The lease term equals or exceeds 75 percent of the asset's useful life.

4 At the beginning of the lease term, the present value of the lease payments equals or exceeds 90 percent of the current fair market value of the asset.[11]

If the lease is a capital lease, the balance sheet of the lessee shows the present value of the lease rental payments as an asset ("leased property under capital leases") and as a liability ("capital lease obligations"). This is illustrated in Exhibit 21-1.

[9] For excellent reviews of the FASB's Statement 13 (Statement of Financial Accounting Standards No. 13: Accounting for Leases) see J. J. Kalata, D. G. Campbell, and I. K. Shumaker, "Lease Finance Reporting," *Financial Executive* (March 1977), pp. 34–40; L. Schachner, "The New Accounting for Leases," *Financial Executive* (February 1978), pp. 40–47; J. R. Deming, "An Analysis of FASB No. 13," *Financial Executive* (March 1978), pp. 46–51.

[10] For a *lessor*, a lease is a capital lease if it meets one or more of the four conditions stated in the text below *and* if there is reasonable certainty concerning both the receipt of the lease rentals and the magnitude of the costs to be incurred by the lessor in connection with the lease. It is possible that a lease be categorized as a capital lease by the lessee but, because of uncertainties concerning rentals or lessor costs, be classified as an operating lease by the lessor.

[11] The interest rate used to compute the present value of the lease rentals is the lessee's incremental borrowing rate; however, if the lessee knows the lessor's implicit internal rate of return on the lease transaction, the lower of that rate and the lessee's marginal borrowing rate is used.

EXHIBIT 21-1
Balance sheet of a firm with capital lease obligations

Assets:	
Current assets	$1,000,000
Property and equipment	6,000,000
Leased property under capital leases	2,000,000
Liabilities and shareholders' equity:	
Current liabilities	$3,000,000
Long-term debt	1,000,000
Capital lease obligations	2,000,000
Shareholders' equity	3,000,000

International leasing involves a lessor in one country and a lessee in another. Both parties are commonly subsidiaries of the same MNC, and the lessor is often a wholly owned international leasing company, which leases to the other members of the multinational group. The most common rationale for international leasing is tax savings because of differences in tax laws in the lessor and lessee countries. A company in a low tax rate nation may find it profitable to lease from a subsidiary in a high tax rate country, which can better use the tax advantages of ownership. Many MNCs have been able to arrange *double-dip* leases between affiliates in two countries. In this arrangement, the lessor in one country defines the transaction so that it is treated as a purchase for tax purposes, and both parties enjoy the depreciation tax benefits of ownership. Taking advantage of such international tax loopholes requires a manager who has a good deal of expertise in international tax law and accounting regulations.

An additional reason for international leasing is to protect the assets of an MNC subsidiary in a politically unstable country. The foreign government will, perhaps, be more reluctant to expropriate the subsidiary's assets if they are considered the legal property of a firm outside the country. In addition, international leasing can be a way to circumvent exchange controls. Countries that block earnings repatriation (in the form of dividend or interest payments) may still allow the parent corporation to receive lease payments.

Back in Chapter 8, it was explained that the net benefit to the firm from purchasing an asset is its net present value. The asset should be purchased only if the net present value is positive. Leasing is an alternative way to obtain use of an asset. To determine whether leasing or buying an asset is better, the net present value of the asset's cash flows to the lessee under the lease must be compared with the net present value of the asset if purchased. The option (lease or purchase) with the greater net present value is superior and the asset is acquired if, and only if, that superior option has a zero or positive net present value (a zero net present value means that the superior option earns just the minimum acceptable rate of return). The analysis proceeds in the following steps:[12]

1 Compute the net present value of the asset's cash flows if the asset is purchased [signified NPV(purchase)]; this step is *identical to* that

---

[12] The lease or buy analysis presented here in the text assumes that firm debt and leasing are independent and is based on an equivalent method described in L. D. Schall, "The Lease or Buy and Asset Acquisition Decisions," *Journal of Finance* (September 1974). If debt and leasing are interdependent, Eq. (21-3) must have an additional term, $\tau \Delta R$; ΔR is the change in firm interest expense due to a change in firm debt resulting from leasing (on this see Schall, ibid., footnote 10). For a detailed analysis of the debt-leasing interdependency using a model consistent with the one presented here, see S. C. Myers, D. A. Dill, and A. J. Bautista, "Valuation of Financial Lease Contracts," *Journal of Finance* (June 1976). For a discussion of other leasing issues see M. H. Miller and C. W. Upton, "Leasing, Buying, and the Cost of Capital Services," *Journal of Finance* (June 1976); W. G. Lewellen, M. S. Long, and J. J. McConnell, "Asset Leasing in Competitive Capital Markets," *Journal of Finance* (June 1976).

described in Chapters 8, 9, and 10 (since these chapters were concerned with the evaluation of an asset purchase).

2 Compute the net present value of the cash flows generated for the firm by the asset if it is leased [signified NPV(lease)].

3 Compare NPV(purchase) with NPV(lease). The option—purchase or lease—with the higher NPV is superior, and the other option should be rejected. The superior option should be adopted if, and only if, its NPV is zero or positive.

The remainder of this section explains how the above analysis is performed. Before illustrating the approach, though, we should explain why it is generally *not* correct to use NPV(purchase) to accept or reject projects and *then* to do the lease versus purchase analysis of the accepted projects. Such a method would mean that any asset with a negative NPV(purchase) would be rejected and would not be considered further. Thus, it is possible that an asset have a negative NPV(purchase) but a positive NPV(lease), in which case rejecting the asset because NPV(purchase) is negative would mean passing up a good opportunity (the opportunity to lease the asset). For example, if a machine has an NPV(purchase) of −$500, under this method we would drop the machine from further consideration. But, if NPV(lease) = $800 for the machine, by rejecting the machine we would be losing the $800 present value obtainable with a lease. The approach recommended here prevents this type of mistake. Admittedly, there are cases in which it is clear (even without any formal present value analysis) that an asset should be acquired and that the only decision is whether to lease the asset or purchase it. In this case, we could either use the method recommended in this chapter or we could simply compute the net advantage to leasing the asset, and then lease it only if the net advantage is positive; the net advantage to leasing approach is described in Appendix 21B.

We should also point out that the method illustrated below assumes that leasing the asset does not affect the firm's borrowing against other assets; Appendix 21A discusses the complications which arise in the analyses when leasing does affect the level of firm debt.

With purchase of the asset, the firm assumes all the risks and benefits of ownership, including risks associated with the sale value (salvage value) of the asset when the firm no longer needs it. The company pays all the costs of maintaining the asset, e.g., upkeep expenses and property taxes. If the firm borrows to finance the asset, it pays interest and principal on that debt. All maintenance expenses, debt interest, and depreciation on the asset are tax deductible. On the other hand, with a lease the firm receives the benefits from using the asset but has no claim on its salvage value (which is reserved for the asset's owner). The lessee must make lease payments and may also be required to cover some or all of the maintenance expenses on the asset. Lease payments and lessee expenses associated with the asset are tax deductible for the lessee. The lessee cannot deduct depreciation on the asset, since this is a tax deduction for the lessor (owner).

The cash flow from purchasing the asset is computed in the manner described in Chapter 8. This cash flow in year t, CF(purchase)$_t$, equals

$$\left\{ \begin{array}{c} \text{Cash flow in year } t \\ \text{with purchase of asset} \end{array} \right\} = \text{CF(purchase)}_t$$

$$= \text{revenues}_t - \text{expenses}_t$$
$$- \text{capital expenditures}_t - \text{taxes}_t$$

$$= \text{revenues}_t - \text{expenses}_t$$
$$- \text{capital expenditures}_t$$
$$- \tau \, (\text{revenues}_t$$
$$- \text{expenses}_t - \text{depreciation}_t) \qquad (21\text{-}1)$$

where τ is the corporate tax rate. Equation (21-1) is identical to Eq. (8-1). "Capital expenditures" in Eq. (21-1) represents any additional capital outlays during the life of the asset (e.g., a new roof or lighting fixtures if the purchased asset were a manufacturing plant). If the asset is sold (e.g., near the end of its useful life), there is a cash inflow equal to the net aftertax proceeds from selling the asset, and this is reflected in Eq. (21-1) as a negative capital expenditure (i.e., as a positive cash flow). The example in Exhibit 21-2 illustrates how salvage value is treated. As explained in Chapter 8, in Eq. (21-1) interest on debt is not included in expenses. CF(purchase)$_t$ is discounted using the firm's cost of capital if the purchased asset is financed in the same way (same proportions of debt and equity financing) and is of the same risk as the company's other assets. The discount rate will differ from that used on the firm's other assets if the asset's financing or risk differs from that of the firm's other assets. The method for determining the discount rate in this latter case is described in Chapter 10. The analysis of an asset purchase is identical to that described in Chapters 8, 9, and 10. Once we have estimated the discount rate, k, we compute the net present value with purchase, which equals

$$\text{NPV(purchase)} = \frac{\text{CF(purchase)}_1}{1 + k} + \frac{\text{CF(purchase)}_2}{(1 + k)^2}$$
$$+ \cdots + \frac{\text{CF(purchase)}_n}{(1 + k)^n} - I \qquad (21\text{-}2)$$

CF(purchase)$_n$ includes the net aftertax salvage value of the asset assuming it is sold in year n. I is the initial cost of the asset.

With leasing, the cash flow in year t from the asset, CF(lease)$_t$, equals

$$\left\{ \begin{array}{c} \text{Cash flow in year } t \\ \text{with leasing of} \\ \text{the asset} \end{array} \right\} = \text{CF(lease)}_t$$

$$= \text{revenues}_t - \text{expenses}_t - \text{lease rental}_t$$
$$- \text{taxes}_t$$

$$= \text{revenues}_t - \text{expenses}_t - \text{lease rental}_t$$
$$- \tau(\text{revenues}_t - \text{expenses}_t - \text{lease rental}_t)$$
$$\qquad (21\text{-}3)$$

The expression in parentheses is the taxable income from the asset if it is leased. All of CF(lease)$_t$ goes to the company's stockholders [since there is no debt used to finance the asset and CF(lease)$_t$ is net of the lease rental payments]. The appropriate discount rate for CF(lease)$_t$ is a rate that reflects the riskiness of CF(lease)$_t$. This lease cash flow is likely to be riskier than CF(purchase)$_t$ since CF(purchase)$_t$ is the *total* aftertax stream to equity *and* to any debt used to purchase the asset, whereas CF(lease)$_t$ is the net cash flow over and above the amount payable to the lessor; that is, CF(lease)$_t$ is an equity cash flow after meeting the fixed charge in the form of the lease payment. The rate k_L for discounting CF(lease)$_t$ will therefore normally exceed the rate k in Eq. (21-1) for discounting the less risky CF(purchase)$_t$.[13] The important point here is that *the discount rate used to discount any cash flow is the rate that is appropriate given the risk of that cash flow; therefore, if CF(purchase)$_t$ is less risky than CF(lease)$_t$, k in Eq. (21-2) will be less than k_L in Eq. (21-4).* (The reader may find it helpful to review the discussion of risk-adjusted discount rates in Chapter 10.) The net present value of the lease cash flow equals

$$NPV(\text{lease}) = \frac{CF(\text{lease})_1}{1 + k_L} + \frac{CF(\text{lease})_2}{(1 + k_L)^2} + \cdots + \frac{CF(\text{lease})_n}{(1 + k_L)^n} \qquad (21\text{-}4)$$

Leasing is superior if NPV(lease) exceeds NPV(purchase), and purchase is superior if NPV(purchase) exceeds NPV(lease). The superior choice, lease or purchase, is accepted only if its NPV is zero or positive. For example, if NPV(lease) = $2000 and NPV(purchase) = $1000, lease is superior since NPV(lease) exceeds NPV(purchase); and the asset should be leased since NPV(lease) is positive. However, if NPV(lease) = −$1000 and NPV(purchase) = −$1500, lease is superior to purchase (it's less bad), but leasing is rejected along with purchase

---

[13] To clarify the point that the discount rate used to discount CF(purchase) in Eq. (21-1) is likely to be less than the discount rate applicable to CF(lease) in (21-3), notice that (21-1) is *not* net of payments to creditors (interest and principal) who may provide part of the funds to finance the firm's acquisition of assets. CF(purchase) is funds flow from the asset that goes to *both* shareholders and creditors and is therefore discounted using a rate (cost of capital) that is a *weighted average* of the firm's equity discount rate (signified k_s) and the firm's debt rate (signified k_B). For example, assume an asset with a CF(purchase) of $100 per year, where $60 per year is to go to shareholders and $40 per year is to go to bondholders, and let k_s = 12 percent and k_B = 9 percent. The rate k_s to discount the $60 equity cash flow (signified CF$_e$) would be 12 percent, the rate k_B to discount the $40 debt cash flow would be 9 percent, and the rate to discount the total $100 flow (signified k) would be between 9 percent and 12 percent, say, 10 percent (k = 10 percent). Observe that CF$_e$ = CF(purchase) − debt payments = $100 − $40 = $60. The equity rate k_s is greater than the weighted average k because equity flow CF$_e$ is riskier, due to financial leverage (see Chaps. 12 and 15), than total cash flow CF(purchase). Notice now that CF(lease) in Eq. (21-3) is net of the firm's lease payments. Deducting the lease payments is similar to deducting debt payments from CF(purchase) to compute CF$_e$. CF(lease) is like CF$_e$ in that both are riskier than the total cash flow from the asset before deduction of the fixed charges (debt or lease). It follows that CF(lease) of (21-3) is likely to be riskier than CF(purchase) of (21-1).

since NPV(lease) is negative. In this situation, acquiring the asset by lease or by purchase is unprofitable.

A numerical illustration will help to clarify the approach outlined above. Assume that the firm can purchase, for $3000, an asset with a useful life (to the firm) of five years. It is expected that the asset will be sold after five years for $200 (net of any taxes on the sale) and depreciation for tax purposes is to be on a straight-line basis, that is, $600 per year for five years ($3000/5 years). (Recall from Chapters 3 and 8 that, in computing depreciation for tax purposes, salvage value is assumed to be zero.) Purchase of the asset will increase the firm's expected revenues by $2400 per year and will raise its expected operating expenses (not including depreciation or debt interest) by $1000 per year. The corporate income tax rate is 50 percent. Assume that the discount rate for the asset is 10 percent. As shown in Exhibit 21-2, NPV(purchase) = $914.

The firm can also lease the asset for a yearly rental of $700. With the lease, the increase in expected revenues from using the asset is $2400 (as with purchase) and the increase in the firm's expected nondepreciation expenses is $900 (this differs from the $1000 increase in expenses with purchase since it is assumed that $100 of the asset's maintenance expenses will be covered by the lessor). The discount rate to be used in discounting the expected net cash flow from leasing the asset is 15 percent. This rate exceeds the 10 percent discount rate with purchase because we are assuming that the lease cash flow [Eq. (21-3)] is riskier than the purchase cash flow [Eq. (21-1)] (see footnote 14 and the associ-

---

EXHIBIT 21-2
Computation of the net present value of purchasing the asset

Year (1)	Revenues (2)	Nondepreciation expenses other than debt payments (3)	Depreciation (4)	Taxes {0.50[(2) − (3) − (4)]} (5)	Aftertax salvage value (6)	Net cash flow [(2) − (3) − (5) + (6)] (7)	10% present value factor (8)	Present value of net cash flow[a] [(7) × (8)] (9)
1	$2,400	$1,000	$600	$400		$1,000	0.9091	$ 909
2	2,400	1,000	600	400		1,000	0.8264	826
3	2,400	1,000	600	400		1,000	0.7513	751
4	2,400	1,000	600	400		1,000	0.6830	683
5	2,400	1,000	600	400	$200	1,200	0.6209	745
								$3,914

NPV(purchase) = present value of future cash flows − cost of asset
= $3,914 − $3,000 = $914

[a] Figures are rounded.

ated text discussion). Exhibit 21-3 shows the lease computations. Since NPV(lease) = $1341, and, as shown in Exhibit 21-2, NPV(purchase) = $914, the asset should be leased.

CONSIDERATIONS IN THE LEASING DECISION

The decision to lease or not to lease is often based in practice on certain commonly held notions about leasing. Below we examine these notions.

Availability of Cash

It is sometimes argued that leasing imposes less of a current cash drain on the firm than purchase, thus freeing capital for other purposes. This argument is correct in the unusual situation in which the firm can lease the asset but cannot borrow to buy the asset (and cannot buy the asset on an installment payment basis, which is in effect a borrowing arrangement). If the firm can purchase the asset using borrowed funds, the immediate cash outlay may be no greater than with leasing. Lease arrangements often require deposits or advance rental payments when the lease is set up, and these immediate cash payments may equal or exceed any equity investment (down payment) required in purchasing the asset.

Effect on the Firm's Borrowing Capacity

Lenders (as well as shareholders) pay serious attention to the company's ability to service its debt. Too much debt restricts the firm's capacity to borrow further. What of leasing? Is leasing a method of obtaining assets on credit without the penalty of a reduced capacity to incur additional debt? Clearly, a lease imposes a fixed charge on the firm and poses a

---

EXHIBIT 21-3
Computation of the net present value of leasing the asset

Year (1)	Revenues (2)	Nondepreciation expenses other than lease and debt payments (3)	Lease rental (4)	Taxes {0.50[(2) − (3) − (4)]} (5)	Net cash flow [(2) − (3) − (4) − (5)] (6)	15% present value factor (7)	Present value of net cash flow[a] [(6) × (7)] (8)
1	$2,400	$900	$700	$400	$400	0.8696	$ 348
2	2,400	900	700	400	400	0.7561	302
3	2,400	900	700	400	400	0.6575	263
4	2,400	900	700	400	400	0.5718	229
5	2,400	900	700	400	400	0.4972	199
							$1,341

NPV(lease) = present value of net cash flows with leasing = $1,341

[a] Figures are rounded.

similar threat to the firm's solvency as does debt (leaseholders can demand payment just as creditors can).[14] At issue here is whether lenders view the lease in this way or merely ignore outstanding leases in computing fixed charges of the firm. Until recently, leases often were not properly acknowledged by creditors. Therefore, the firm's ability to incur added debt was greater if the firm leased assets rather than purchased them with borrowed funds. Now, however, leases are usually recognized as fixed obligations similar to debt. This change in attitude is in part due to pressure from the Securities and Exchange Commission and The American Institute of Certified Public Accountants for improved financial disclosure by firms. As described earlier in the section on Accounting for Leases, financial statements now disclose major assets held under a lease and disclose the associated rental payment obligation. Because leases as well as debt are now taken into account by lenders, leasing and borrowing have similar effects on the firm's borrowing ability.

Convenience

Leasing is a very convenient way to obtain the services of an asset for a short period of time. Except for tax considerations, leasing is economically equivalent to buying an asset from a dealer and, at the time of purchase, negotiating an agreement to sell the asset back to the dealer for a predetermined price. Leasing has emerged in part to meet the needs of those who want short-term use with no uncertainty about cost (e.g., no uncertainty about what can be obtained for the asset when it is no longer needed). Furthermore, for those with a very short-term need for an asset, leasing is especially practical because it involves fewer legal costs and lower taxes than purchase and resale; purchase and resale would require two transfers of title and perhaps state sales taxes on each transfer.

Avoidance of Restrictions on the Firm

Lenders frequently impose restrictions on the firm with the idea of improving the firm's capacity to pay off the loan. Examples are limits on dividends, subordination clauses, and restrictions on new investment or sales of firm property. Lease agreements may also include such con-

---

[14] Leases and debt do differ in certain important respects. First, a lessor may obtain the asset being financed at the end of the lease term, whereas a creditor does not receive a physical asset. Second, creditors have a stronger claim than do lessors against a firm in the event that the borrower (lessee) firm suffers financial distress. Although both the lessor and a secured lender have a claim against the asset if payments are not properly made, there may be an amount due in excess of the value of the asset. The creditor can sue for that deficiency whereas a lessor is limited to one year's lease payment from a bankrupt firm and to three years' lease payments from a firm under reorganization. Third, a borrowing firm can always dispose of an asset and pay off the debt when it chooses but, if it leases the asset, it cannot necessarily terminate possession of a leased asset unless there is a lease cancellation option or the right to sublease the asset. That is, a lessee may be locked into an asset, whereas this can be avoided if the asset is owned. Fourth, constraints on the firm are more likely to be imposed by creditors than by lessors (for example, that the firm maintain a particular level of working capital, of net worth, etc.).

straints, but they are less frequent and are often less restrictive. However, in contrast with debt, a lease may involve constraints on the use of the leased property, for example, how many hours per week a machine may be used. These restrictions are meant to protect the asset (since it is still owned by the lessor) rather than to enhance the lessee's rental-paying ability.

Avoiding the restrictions of a debt arrangement by leasing instead is not costless. The debt restrictions protect the lender and reduce the lender's risk, thereby reducing the interest the lender demands on the debt. If a lessor does not require similar restrictions, the risk for the lessor will be greater than for a lender and, to compensate for this, the lease rentals will provide a higher rate of return to the lessor than to a lender. The benefit to the lessee firm of no restrictions on its operations is reflected in higher lease payments. Whether the lack of restriction is worth the added cost will depend on the situation.

Shifting of Risk of Obsolescence

Is leasing a way for an asset user to escape the risk that the asset will become obsolete and worthless? The answer is yes, but normally at a cost. Even with a financial lease, the lease term can be sufficiently short (e.g., 50 percent of the asset's expected economic life) that the lessee can avoid holding an obsolete asset. Alternatively, the lease may be long-term but have a cancellation clause (which allows the lessee to cancel the contract during its term). Therefore, the risk of obsolescence can be shifted to the lessor. But, here again the rental price on the asset will mirror the costs borne by the lessor. To be willing to assume the obsolescence risk, the lessor will require a higher rental than if such risk were assumed by the lessee. In effect then, the lessee ends up paying for the obsolescence risk.[15] But what if the lessor is better able than the user (lessee) to find a use for a somewhat outdated asset? This might occur because of the lessor's superior access to many potential users of the asset. Under these conditions, the cost of obsolescence may be less under leasing than under purchase by the user. This advantage will be at least partially passed on to the lessee (in the form of lower lease payments) as lessors compete for customers in a competitive market. In this case, the asset user (lessee) may gain by leasing rather than buying the asset since the impact of obsolescence is lower with lease than with purchase.[16]

---

[15] Even if the lessee pays the lessor for assuming the obsolescence risk, there may be an advantage for the lessee in this arrangement in that the lease rental payments are predictable (since they are specified in the lease contract), whereas the future impact of obsolescence on the value of the asset is uncertain. Therefore, the lessee is in a more predictable position by leasing rather than by buying. But, again, it should be emphasized that the lessee pays a higher rental to the lessor for having the latter assume the less predictable position. Whether the asset user is willing to pay the extra amount to a lessor in order to shift the uncertainty to the lessor (rather than for the user to buy the asset) will depend upon the particular circumstances.

[16] If there are dealers who buy and sell used assets and who, like lessors, have good access to potential asset users, leasing may offer no advantage relative to purchase and eventual resale to a used-asset dealer.

The owner of the asset receives salvage value (residual value); but the higher the expected salvage value, the lower the lease rentals need be in order that the lessor earn a satisfactory return on its investment. The anticipated salvage value is therefore reflected in the lease payments required on an asset, and there is no implied gain to a firm from owning relative to leasing. Indeed, if the lessor firm is especially capable of finding productive economic employment of the asset after it is used by the lessee, the salvage value may be greater for a lessor than for a user-lessee. This advantage would make leasing more economical than purchase by the user firm.[17] On the other hand, if the user anticipates that the asset will have a higher future value than others (lessors) expect—as might occur, for example, if the asset were real estate—then the firm might wish to purchase. This is a gamble on the part of the firm's management that its expectations are more likely to be fulfilled than those of the lessor.

An example that illustrates, in the extreme, how important residual value can be in some cases involves Gulf Oil's lease of a property in West Texas. In 1925, Gulf negotiated a fifty-year lease of the Waddell Ranch oil properties owned by wildcatter W. H. McFadden. Because oil output during the fifty-year lease was unexpectedly restricted by the Texas Railway Commission (which sets oil extraction rates in Texas), much of the oil remained in the ground when the lease expired in 1975. Gulf Oil foresaw this during the late 1960s and sued to have the lease extended. The Texas Supreme Court ruled against Gulf, declaring that the lease specified fifty years and the unexpected intervention of the Texas Railway Commission did not alter that fact. The stock of Southland Realty Company, the owner of Waddell Ranch, rose sharply after the court decision.

The firm can depreciate the asset for tax purposes if it purchases the asset but not if it leases the asset. However, since a *lessor* gets depreciation deductions and *will in a competitive market pass at least some of the tax benefits on to the lessee in the form of lower rental charges*, we cannot assume that depreciation encourages purchase rather than lease of the asset by the user.

In short, tax factors encourage that choice between leasing and purchase which minimizes the total taxes associated with the asset's use and ownership (ownership by the user with purchase or by the lessor with lease). Whether lease or purchase is preferred on the basis of tax considerations depends on such factors as the lessor's and lessee's tax brackets, the method of depreciating the asset (straight-line or accelerated), and the degree to which the asset is debt financed by its owner (the user under purchase or the lessor under a lease). These factors vary from case to case and the impact of taxes will therefore depend on the particular situation.

---

[17] See Footnote 16.

SUMMARY

Under a lease, the user of an asset (the lessee) pays the owner (the lessor) a rental per period for the usage right. An operating lease is a short-term lease whereas a financial lease covers a major portion of the asset's useful life. A sale and leaseback contract provides for the sale of the asset by the user, who then leases it back from the purchaser. A full-service lease requires that the lessor provide services to the lessee, including maintenance of the asset, payment of property taxes and insurance, etc. A leveraged lease (or third-party lease) involves not simply the lessor and lessee but also a lender who ordinarily provides a major portion of the asset's purchase price. The loan is on a nonrecourse basis, i.e., the lender has a claim to the asset and to the rental payments due under the lease but may not turn to the lessor for any amounts owed on the loan.

The tax law specifies requirements which must be met in order that a transaction be treated as a lease for tax purposes. Financial statements prepared in accordance with the guidelines set by the Financial Accounting Standards Board must disclose major leases. If the lease is a capital lease under these guidelines, the lessee lists, on its balance sheet, the present value of the future lease rentals as an asset and as an obligation (much like debt).

The purchase and lease alternatives for acquiring an asset can be evaluated by comparing their cash flows. The alternative with the higher net present value of cash flows is preferred and is adopted if its net present value is positive or zero.

A firm may prefer to lease rather than purchase because a lease imposes less of an immediate cash drain on the firm; but this is only true if the firm cannot borrow to buy the asset. Lease obligations are generally viewed by creditors as a form of debt, and they will reduce the firm's ability to borrow in the same way that borrowing to purchase an asset will. Leasing is an especially convenient and economical way to obtain the short-term use of an asset since it involves fewer legal costs, and sometimes lower total sales taxes, than a purchase. Leasing is a way to avoid the restrictions imposed by lenders and is a way to shift the risks of obsolescence; but the lease rental will reflect the risks borne by the lessor. The presence of a high salvage value on an asset does not imply that purchase is better than lease since the lease rental will take into account the salvage value the lessor will realize on the asset. Tax considerations may favor lease or purchase by the asset user, depending on the particular circumstances.

QUESTIONS

1 Describe the major difference between an operating lease and a financial lease.
2 What is a leveraged lease?
3 How is the discount rate used to evaluate a lease determined? Is the discount rate for evaluating the purchase of an asset the same as that used for evaluating the lease? Explain fully.
4 "The neat part about leasing is that there is less cash drain on a company than if it buys the asset outright." Evaluate this statement.

5   What rationale, if any, can be given for listing the leased assets and the present value of lease payments on the balance sheet?

6   Restrictive provisions are more often found in debt contracts than in lease contracts. Furthermore, the return required by lessors is usually greater than that required by creditors. Reconcile these facts.

7   How does a lease affect the cost of asset obsolescence to the asset user?

8   "The trouble with leasing from the lessee's standpoint is that the lessor, not the lessee, gets the advantage of taking depreciation for tax purposes." Evaluate this statement.

9   How do the expectations of the lessee and the lessor concerning an asset's salvage value affect the attitudes of each with regard to what is an acceptable lease rental?

10 Describe in words the proper way to evaluate a lease.

PROJECTS

1   Select a major asset used by one or more firms in your area and find out how you would negotiate the lease and the purchase of the asset.

2   Select several assets that can both be purchased and leased. For each asset, obtain data on the purchase price and the lease rental charged for the asset (assume some lease duration), and obtain an estimate of the likely salvage value of the asset at the end of the lease term you assume. Find out how the asset is depreciated under current tax law. Compute the aftertax rate of return earned by the lessor on the asset. Assume that the lessor is in the 34 percent tax bracket, and assume that the lessor pays the purchase price you determined for the asset.

DEMONSTRATION PROBLEMS

DP1 Rocket Technologies is evaluating the purchase or lease of new equipment. The estimated increase in annual revenues is $200,000, and the estimated increase in operating expenses is $90,000, regardless of whether the asset is purchased outright or leased from the manufacturer. The equipment costs $300,000 to purchase and has an estimated life of eight years, at the end of which time it can be sold for an aftertax salvage value of $20,000. If the asset is leased, the annual payments come to $50,000, payable at the end of each year for eight years. The company plans to depreciate its new equipment on a straight-line basis over five years (assume zero salvage value for tax depreciation computations). The proper discount rate with which to evaluate the leased equipment is 20 percent; for the purchased equipment, it is 18 percent. The firm's tax rate is 40 percent. What should Rocket Technologies do—purchase, lease, or not acquire the equipment? Show all calculations.

SOLUTION TO DP1:

Net Present Value of Purchase

$$\text{Depreciation expense} = \frac{\$300,000}{5 \text{ years}} = \$60,000$$

	Years 1–5	Years 6–8
Revenues	$200,000	$200,000
Operating expense	−90,000	−90,000
Prctax cash flow	$110,000	$110,000
Depreciation	−60,000	0
Taxable income	$ 50,000	$110,000
Tax at 40%	$ 20,000	$ 44,000

Net cash flow (years 1–5) = $110,000 − $20,000 = $90,000
Net cash flow (years 6–8) = $110,000 − $44,000 = $66,000
(excluding salvage value)

Salvage value (year 8) = $20,000
Net cash flow (year 8) = $20,000 + $66,000 = $86,000

NPV (purchase) = −$300,000 + $90,000(*P/A*, 18%, 5)
  + $66,000(*P/A*, 18%, 2)(*P/F*, 18%, 5)
  + $86,000(*P/F*, 18%, 8)
  = −$300,000 + $90,000(3.1272)
  + $66,000(1.5656)(.4371)
  + $86,000(.2660)
  = $49,489

Net Present Value of Lease

Revenues	$200,000
Operating expense	−90,000
Lease rental	−50,000
Pretax cash flow	$ 60,000
Taxable income	$ 60,000
Tax at 40%	$ 24,000
	$ 36,000

Net cash flow (year 1–8) = $60,000 − $24,000 = $36,000

NPV (lease) = $36,000(*P/A*, 20%, 8)
  = $36,000(3.8372)
  = $138,139

Conclusion   Since NPV(lease) exceeds NPV(purchase), and
since NPV(lease) is positive, the asset should be leased.

DP2   At the recent board of directors meeting of Crown Corporation, one of the directors argued that the company would be better off if it leased assets rather than bought them with borrowed money. He commented, "After all, you won't have a balance sheet showing debt on it. And that's good, 'cause we can borrow later on if we want to." Another director pointed out that lease payments are viewed as the equivalent to fixed charges on debt and that no one would be fooled by the lease versus debt issue. A third director thought the company would have to capitalize the leases in order to depict the true nature of the balance sheet.

If the firm has $80 million in assets before acquiring new assets, show what the balance sheet would look like if the assets were purchased with borrowed funds, and if the assets were leased (show the balance sheet both with and without balance sheet disclosure of the lease). The cost of the assets if purchased is $20 million. The present value of the lease rentals on the assets is also $20 million. The company currently has a book debt-equity ratio of 1:3.

SOLUTION TO DP2:

	Case A [Balance sheet with no disclosure of added $20 mil. in assets acquired by lease (same as balance sheet before assets are acquired)]	Case B (Balance sheet when using debt to purchase $20 mil. in assets)	Case C (Balance sheet with disclosure of added $20 mil. in assets acquired by lease)
Assets	$80	$100	$80
Assets under lease	0	0	20
Liabilities Bonds	20	40	20
Discounted lease payments	0	0	20
Owners' equity	60	60	60
Debt-equity ratio[a]	1:3	2:3	2:3

[a]Debt includes lease obligation under case C.

The capitalized value of the lease payments is treated as a form of debt. Cases B and C, then, are comparable in the information they provide. Case A understates the fixed obligations of the firm by concealing the lease obligation.

1   Lexington Products is in the process of evaluating the purchase or lease of new equipment. The estimated increase in annual revenues is $100,000, and the estimated increase in operating expense is $50,000, regardless of whether the asset is purchased outright or leased from the manufacturer. The equipment costs $195,000 to purchase and has an estimated life of twenty years, at the end of which time it can be sold for $5000. If the asset is leased, the annual payments come to $30,000, payable at the end of each year. The company plans to depreciate its new equipment on a straight-line basis with a salvage value of $5000. The financial manager has decided that the proper rate with which to evaluate the leased equipment is 20 percent; for the purchased equipment, it is 18 percent. The firm's tax rate is 40 percent. What should the company do: purchase or lease? Show all calculations.

2   As the financial manager of Glass Jewelry Stores, you must determine whether to lease new display cases or to buy them. The new cases will replace existing old-fashioned ones that, although usable, are not very attractive and have no significant market value. The new cases will raise before-tax net cash flow by $8000 per year before deducting an additional $200 per year upkeep expense on the new cases and before deducting any lease payments if the new cases are leased. If you buy the new cases, you must make a cash outlay of $30,000. The display cases are estimated to last fifteen years, at the end of which time you think you can sell them for $5000. However, the manufacturer will lease the same display cases for a period of fifteen years at the yearly rental rate of $4500 a year for the first nine years and $3500 a year thereafter. The lease payments are due at the end of each year. You estimate the new cases will require an additional $100 a year for maintenance and upkeep (above the upkeep costs of the existing old-fashioned cases) if you decide to lease rather than buy them. Your firm depreciates all such assets on a straight-line basis and is in the 40 percent tax bracket. The old cases are no longer being depreciated for tax purposes, and the new cases would be depreciated over fifteen years to a salvage value of $5000. You estimate that the purchase and lease cash flows have the same risk, both requiring a 15 percent discount rate. What should you do? Show all calculations.

3   You just sold your business and are considering a number of proposals on how you should invest your cash. Knox Corporation, a major builder in your city, has offered to construct and lease out an office building which Knox wants to sell you for $2,000,000. If you buy the property, you will receive a rental of $200,000 per year for the first five years, and $300,000 per year for the following thirteen years. You expect to sell the property at the end of the eighteen-year period for an aftertax price of $1.5 million. You will depreciate the building over eighteen years on a

straight-line basis; the building has a depreciable basis of $1,800,000 and depreciation will be $100,000 per year. Knox will manage and maintain the building, but you will pay the local property taxes (which are tax deductible for federal income tax purposes) of $30,000 per year. Your tax rate is 40 percent. You want at least a 15 percent aftertax return on your investments. Should you buy the building from Knox? Assume that you will pay cash for the property.

4 At the recent board of directors meeting of Durham Corporation, one of the directors argued that the company would be better off if it leased assets rather than bought them with borrowed money. He commented, "After all, you won't have a balance sheet showing debt on it. And that's good, 'cause we can borrow later on if we want to." Another director pointed out that lease payments are viewed as the equivalent to fixed charges on debt and that no one would be fooled by the lease versus debt issue. A third director thought the company would have to capitalize the leases in order to depict the true nature of the balance sheet.

If the firm has $20 million in assets before acquiring new assets, show what the balance sheet would look like under each of the proposed systems if the firm were to lease the assets or buy them with borrowed money. The cost of the assets to be acquired is $3 million. The firm can borrow the money to finance them at the market rate of 8 percent a year for twenty years. The annual lease payments, if the assets are leased, will be $160,000 for the twenty-year period. The company currently has a book debt-equity ratio of 3:7.

5 Vanguard Warehouses, Inc., can either purchase or lease a sophisticated security system for its warehouses. The system will increase annual revenues by $90,000 by attracting additional customers because of the increased safety at the warehouses and will *reduce* annual operating expenses by $60,000 by eliminating the need for around-the-clock guards (the annual savings are $62,000 with lease because maintenance of the system is provided by the lessor). The added revenues and cost savings occur over a ten-year period, at times 1, 2, . . . , 10. At the end of the ten years (at time 10) the system will be replaced. Vanguard's tax rate is 40 percent. The following table shows the data associated with purchase and lease. Using the information in the table, determine whether Vanguard should purchase the security system, lease it, or not acquire it at all.

Purchase	
Purchase price	$500,000
Life of system	10 years
Expected aftertax salvage value of system (at time 10)	$20,000
Added annual firm revenues from using the system	$90,000
Added annual firm expenses from using the system	($60,000)
Annual depreciation (using straight line)	$50,000
Discount rate on aftertax cash flow	15%

Lease	
Lease rental (payable at the beginning of the year, i.e., now, at time 1, at time 2, . . . , at time 9)	$125,000
Length of lease	10 years
Added annual firm revenues from using the system	$90,000
Added annual firm expenses from using the system (not including lease rental)	($62,000)
Discount rate on aftertax cash flow	18%

6 Gomez Office Equipment, Inc. (GOE), sells office equipment through a chain of retail outlets. GOE owns most of the outlets and leases the others. One of GOE's stores is in a shopping center that it completely owns. GOE has been offered $5 million for the center by Newport Development Corporation. This offer is at least as good as any GOE could get for the property. GOE management has decided that it will either sell the shopping center to Newport now or it will keep the center for five years and then sell it. GOE's tax basis in the property is $400,000; i.e., a sale for $5 million will produce a taxable capital gain of $4,600,000 ($5 million sales price *minus* the $400,000 tax basis). If GOE sells the center in five years, its tax basis will be zero (the taxable gain therefore being the price received for the property). GOE forecasts the cash flows shown below from the shopping center over the next five years:

Annual rental revenue	$800,000
Annual nondepreciation expenses other than debt payments	$150,000
Annual depreciation	
Years 1 and 2	$200,000
Years 3, 4, and 5	0

The nondepreciation expenses are for property taxes, insurance, maintenance, and so forth. The figures shown above are for the entire shopping center, including the part occupied by GOE (the rental revenue for the space occupied by GOE is zero).

Based on a detailed analysis performed by a major commercial real estate firm, GOE expects to be able to sell the shopping center in five years for $6.5 million.

If GOE sells the shopping center to Newport Development, it will lease back, for five years, the space its store currently occupies in the center. The lease rental will be $36,000 per year plus 3 percent of GOE's gross receipts from its store. Gross receipts are expected to be $250,000 in the first year and to grow at 4 percent per year over the next five years. Rentals are payable annually at the end of each year. All property taxes, insurance, and maintenance costs associated with the center will be paid by Newport Development.

Should GOE sell the shopping center to Newport Development now or keep the center and sell it in five years? In your analysis, use a 15 percent discount rate to compute all present values. Let GOE have a 30 percent tax rate on all income, including any capital gain from selling the property.

[*Note*: Problem *7* requires knowledge of Appendix 21A, and problem *8* requires a knowledge of Appendix 21B (Appendix 21A provides helpful background).]

7 Hardy Manufacturing is expanding its facilities. On March 1, 1991, Hardy will either purchase or lease equipment which it plans to use for four years and then replace with new equipment (whether or not it purchases or leases currently). Hardy's tax rate is 40 percent.

With *purchase* of the equipment: (a) the purchase price of the equipment is $4 million; (b) the equipment has an expected March 1, 1995, aftertax (i.e., net of taxes on any gain or loss from disposal of the asset) salvage value of $1 million; (c) the equipment will be depreciated at a rate of $800,000 per year; (d) the equipment will increase Hardy's annual revenues by $3 million and increase annual nondepreciation operating costs by $2 million; and (e) the discount rate for computing NPV(purchase) is 12 percent.

With *lease* of the equipment: (a) the annual lease rental is $950,000, with each rental payable at the end of each lease year (on March 1, 1992, March 1, 1993, March 1, 1994, and March 1, 1995); (b) the discount rate for discounting the net cash flow from leasing the asset (like col. 8 of Exhibit 21-8) is 13 percent; (c) the equipment will increase annual operating revenues by $3 million (same as with purchase) and increase annual nondepreciation operating costs by $1.9 million (the lessor will annually pay $100,000 of the costs associated with the equipment); and (d) Hardy will reduce its debt by $2 million, which we assume would have been payable at 11 percent per annum in annual installments as shown in the following table.

Payment date (1)	Principal (2)	Interest (3)	Total [(2) + (3)] (4)
March 1, 1992	$424,653	$220,000	$644,653
March 1, 1993	471,365	173,288	644,653
March 1, 1994	523,215	121,438	644,653
March 1, 1995	580,767	63,884	644,651[a]

[a] The annual payments are not exactly equal because of rounding off cents.

a Determine whether Hardy Manufacturing should purchase or lease the equipment. You may round all figures to the nearest thousand dollars.

b Assume all the information as stated in the problem above except that the lease payments are due at the *beginning* of each year (on March 1, 1991, March 1, 1992, March 1, 1993, and March 1, 1994). Determine whether Hardy Manufacturing should purchase or lease the equipment. You may round all figures to the nearest thousand dollars.

8 Anvil Steak Houses, Inc., is a chain of restaurants in the Southwest. In line with its policy of periodic refurbishing, it will replace the furniture in twenty of its restaurants on June 30, 1991. The remaining decision is whether to lease or to purchase the furniture. Anvil's tax rate is 40 percent.

With *purchase* of the furniture: (a) the purchase price is $900,000; (b) the furniture will be used for five years and then sold for an expected aftertax salvage value of $80,000; (c) the furniture will be depreciated over five years at the rate of $180,000 per year; and (d) the firm will increase its current debt to finance the purchase by $200,000, repayable in five equal annual installments at a 13 percent annual interest rate (the first payment on June 30, 1992, and the last payment on June 30, 1996). The amortization schedule on the $200,000 debt is shown below:

Payment date (1)	Principal (2)	Interest (3)	Total [(2) + (3)] (4)
June 30, 1992	$30,863	$26,000	$56,863
June 30, 1993	34,875	21,988	56,863
June 30, 1994	39,409	17,454	56,863
June 30, 1995	44,532	12,331	56,863
June 30, 1996	50,321	6,542	56,863

With *lease* of the furniture: (a) the annual lease rental will be $225,000 payable on June 30, 1992, June 30, 1993, June 30, 1994, June 30, 1995, and June 30, 1996; (b) $10,000 per year in property taxes on the furniture will be paid by the lessor (this tax is paid by Anvil if it purchases the furniture); and (c) Anvil will reduce its other debt by $600,000, which we assume would have been payable at 13 percent per annum in equal annual installments as shown in the table below:

Payment date (1)	Principal (2)	Interest (3)	Total [(2) + (3)] (4)
June 30, 1992	$ 92,589	$78,000	$170,589
June 30, 1993	104,625	65,964	170,589
June 30, 1994	118,227	52,362	170,589
June 30, 1995	133,596	36,993	170,589
June 30, 1996	150,963	19,626	170,589

Assume that the discount rate applicable to the additional firm cash flow with lease (relative to purchase) is 14 percent per year. What is the net advantage to leasing (NAL), and should Anvil lease or purchase the furniture?

The ▪ symbol indicates that all or a significant part of the problem can be solved using the *Computer Models* software that accompanies this text.

LEASE OR PURCHASE ANALYSIS WHEN LEASING AND FIRM DEBT ARE INTERDEPENDENT

DEBT AND LEASE INTER-DEPENDENCE

We pointed out in the text that Eq. (21-3) assumes that leasing an asset does not affect the firm's borrowing against other assets. This assumption is a simplification since borrowing and leasing both represent fixed obligations which must be periodically serviced by the firm, and the firm may wish to limit the *total* amount of such obligations (assuming any given set of productive assets being used by the firm). Leasing an asset might therefore motivate the firm to have a debt level which is lower than it would have if the asset were purchased. To illustrate how the lease or purchase problem is solved if debt and leasing are interdependent, assume that, with purchase, the following data apply to the asset:

Firm tax rate (τ) = 50 percent
Purchase price of asset = $2000
Useful life of asset = five years
Expected year 5 salvage value of asset = $100
Additional annual firm revenues from the asset = $1500
Additional annual firm nondepreciation operating expenses due to
  the asset = $750
Annual depreciation (for tax purposes) on the asset = $400

Assume that the $2000 asset purchase price would be financed 50 percent with debt and 50 percent with equity, i.e., $1000 from each financing source. The firm's balance sheet without the asset and with the asset assuming purchase is shown below.

A.

Firm balance sheet without the new asset		
Assets	$10,000	Debt	$5,000
		Equity	$5,000

B.

Firm balance sheet with purchase of the new asset			
Assets	$12,000	Debt	$6,000
		Equity	$6,000

The asset can be leased for a rental of $550 per year. Assume that the firm has a target of financing assets 50 percent with equity and 50 percent with *debt and/or lease obligations*. The firm's balance sheet with the lease of the new asset is shown below.

C.

Firm balance sheet with lease of the new asset			
Assets	$12,000	Debt	$4,000
		Lease obligation (present value of lease payments	$2,000
		Equity	$6,000

The $12,000 in balance sheet C assets includes the $2000 asset acquired under the lease. Notice that because of leasing the asset the firm has reduced its debt from $5000 in balance sheet A to $4000 in balance sheet C. The purpose of this $1000 debt reduction is to make the firm's debt *plus* lease obligations equal the $6000 of debt which would exist with purchase of the asset (see balance sheet B).

What is the cash flow impact of reducing firm debt by $1000 because the asset is leased? First, there is an immediate cash outlay of $1000 to retire the debt.[18] Second, there is a cash saving in future periods since interest and principal on the $1000 debt need no longer be paid. Third, there is a tax effect since the firm's tax deductible debt interest is lower than before. Assume that the retired debt of $1000 would have been amortized over a five-year period and carried an interest rate of 9 percent per annum. The amortization payments on the debt are shown in Exhibit 21-4. Given the above information, let's now examine how we could make the lease or purchase decision.

---

[18] The amount needed to retire the $1000 debt could actually be more or less than the $1000. For example, a 10 percent bond might be issued for $1000 and be callable at $1050; if interest rates fell to, say, 8 percent after the bond was issued, the bond would have a current market price greater than $1000; in this case to retire the bond the firm would either have to buy the bond in the market or call it for $1050 (either way it would cost more than $1000 to retire the bond). On the other hand if interest rates rise after the bond's issuance, say, to 12 percent, the bond could be purchased in the market for less than $1000 and retired.

To decide whether to purchase the asset, lease it, or not acquire it at all, we apply the following three steps: [19]

1 Compute the net present value of the asset's cash flows if the asset is purchased [signified NPV(purchase)]; this step is the same as step *1* on page 760.

2 Compute the net present value of the cash flow generated by the asset if the asset is leased [signified NPV(lease)]; this step is similar to step *2* on page 761 except that we will now take into account firm debt changes which result from leasing the asset.

3 Compare NPV(purchase) with NPV(lease). The option—purchase or lease—with a higher NPV is superior, and the other option should be rejected. The superior option should be adopted if and only if its NPV is zero or positive. This step is identical to step *3* on page 761.

Step *1* is shown in Exhibit 21-5. Under step *2* we have to take into account the change in the firm's debt from $5000 (balance sheet A) to $4000 (balance sheet C) which results from leasing the asset. As noted earlier, to retire the $1000, 9 percent debt a $1000 current payment to the creditor is necessary if the asset is leased. But, by repaying the debt, interest and principal payments are reduced by the amounts shown in Exhibit 21-4. Instead of CF(lease), of Eq. (21-3) on page 762, we have the following equation for years 1 through 5:

---

[19] Like other methods presently available in the literature, the lease versus purchase methods described in the text and in Appendixes 21A and 21B ignore personal tax effects, financial distress cost effects, and certain other costs of debt and leasing (e.g., the costs associated with monitoring agreements between the firm and its creditors or lessors). The methods presented here provide useful approximations in most practical situations.

EXHIBIT 21-4
Amortization schedule of $1000 debt retired with lease

Year (1)	Principal payment (2)	Interest payment (3)	Total payment (2) + (3) (4)
1	$167	$90	$257
2	182	75	257
3	198	59	257
4	216	41	257
5	237	21	258[a]

[a] To amortize the debt with *equal* installments would require $257.10 per year.

$$CF(lease)_t = revenues_t - expenses_t - lease\ rental_t$$
$$+ principal\ and\ interest\ saved_t - \tau(revenues_t$$
$$- expenses_t - lease\ rental_t + interest\ saved_t) \quad (21\text{-}4a)$$

$$= Eq.\ (21\text{-}3) + principal\ saved_t$$
$$+ (1 - \tau)\ (interest\ saved_t) \quad (21\text{-}4b)$$

The computations are shown in Exhibit 21-6. We are assuming that the lessor pays $100 of the asset's annual maintenance expense and therefore with lease the nondepreciation expenses other than lease and debt payments (col. 3 of Exhibit 21-6) are $650 per year, $100 less than the $750 nondepreciation expenses with purchase (col. 3 of Exhibit 21-5). NPV(lease) is $291, which is more than NPV(purchase) of $242; the present value of future aftertax cash flows is $49 greater with lease. Therefore, lease is preferred. The 14 percent discount rate in Exhibit 21-6 for discounting the net cash flow from leasing the asset is that rate which reflects the risk of the cash flow being discounted. The cash flow being discounted is like that of Eq. (21-3) *plus* a debt stream of principal and aftertax interest [see Eq. (21-4b) above]; since it is a mixture of the risky stream of Eq. (21-3) and a lower risk debt stream, it has a lower risk than the CF(lease)_t of Eq. (21-3).

EXHIBIT 21-5
Computation of the net present value of purchasing the asset

Year (1)	Revenues (2)	Nondepreciation expenses other than debt payments (3)	Depreciation (4)	Taxes {0.50[(2) − (3) − (4)]} (5)	Aftertax salvage value (6)	Net cash flow [(2) − (3) − (5) + (6)] (7)	10% present value factor (8)	Present value of net cash flow[a] [(7) × (8)] (9)
1	$1,500	$750	$400	$175		$575	0.9091	$ 523
2	1,500	750	400	175		575	0.8264	475
3	1,500	750	400	175		575	0.7513	432
4	1,500	750	400	175		575	0.6830	393
5	1,500	750	400	175	$100	675	0.6209	419
								$2,242

NPV(purchase) = present value of future cash flows − cost of asset + investment tax credit
= $2,242 − $2,000 = $242

[a] Figures are rounded.

EXHIBIT 21-6
Computation of the net present value of leasing the asset

Year (1)	Revenues (2)	Nondepre- ciation expenses other than lease and debt payments (3)	Lease rental (4)	Decrease in debt principal payments (5)	Decrease in debt interest payments (6)	Taxes[a] {0.50[(2) − (3) − (4) + (6)]} (7)	Net cash flow [(2) − (3) − (4) + (5) + (6) − (7)] (8)	14% present value factor (9)	Present value of net cash flow[a] [(8) × (9)] (10)
1	$1,500	$650	$550	$167	$90	$195	$362	0.8772	$ 318
2	1,500	650	550	182	75	188	369	0.7695	284
3	1,500	650	550	198	59	180	377	0.6750	254
4	1,500	650	550	216	41	171	386	0.5921	229
5	1,500	650	550	237	21	161	397	0.5194	206
									$1,291

NPV(lease) = present value of cash flows with leasing − current amount needed to retire $1000 debt
= $1,291 − $1,000 = $291

[a] Figures are rounded.

NET ADVANTAGE TO LEASING

It was explained in the text that, in general, it is not correct to decide whether or not to accept an investment using capital budgeting procedures and then, if the investment is acceptable, decide whether to lease the asset or to purchase it. The problem with this method is that the asset may have a negative NPV(purchase) and therefore be rejected even though its NPV with lease [NPV(lease)] is positive. That is, we would have rejected the profitable opportunity to lease the asset. In some situations, however, it is obvious (without any formal present value analysis) that a particular asset is so profitable that it should be acquired. In this case a shortcut approach to the lease or buy analysis is possible: We can simply compute the new present value of the difference between the cash flows with lease and the cash flows with purchase. The present value of the cash flow differences is the **net advantage to leasing**, or NAL. If NAL > 0, leasing is better; if NAL < 0, purchase is better; and, if NAL = 0, purchase and lease are equally desirable.

To illustrate the NAL method, we will use the example of Appendix 21A. The reader may find it helpful to review Appendix 21A. As before we will assume the following with purchase of the asset:

Firm tax rate (τ) = 50 percent
Purchase cost of asset = $2000
Useful life of asset = five years
Expected year 5 salvage value of asset = $100
Additional annual firm revenues from the asset = $1500
Additional annual firm nondepreciation operating expenses due to the asset = $750
Annual depreciation for tax purposes on the asset = $400
Increase in firm debt due to purchase of the asset = $1000

Exhibit 21-7 indicates the increase in firm debt payments resulting from the added $1000 of firm debt if the asset is purchased, where we are assuming an interest rate of 9 percent on marginal firm borrowing.

The asset can also be leased for $550 per year, in which case the data in Exhibit 21-6 apply (see page 783). With lease, the firm will *reduce* its debt by $1000 and firm debt payments will *fall* by the amounts shown in

Exhibit 21-4 (see page 781). We are assuming for simplicity that the firm's marginal borrowing rate is 9 percent and therefore Exhibits 21-4 and 21-7 are the same; they both show debt payments associated with a $1000 debt repayable at 9 percent interest over a five-year period.

The firm will have $2000 more debt with purchase than with lease, but with lease the firm will have a $2000 lease obligation (see balance sheets A, B, and C on pages 779 to 780). The added debt payments on the $2000 debt equal the sum of the amounts in Exhibits 21-4 and 21-6; Exhibit 21-8 shows the added debt payments on the $2000 of debt. Column 5 of Exhibit 21-8 indicates the corporate tax savings due to the payment of debt interest. Each dollar of interest paid reduces corporate taxes by $1 times the corporate tax rate (here assumed to be 50 percent).

EXHIBIT 21-7
Payments on additional $1000 with purchase of the asset

Year (1)	Principal payment (2)	Interest payment (3)	Total payment [(2) + (3)] (4)
1	$167	$90	$257
2	182	75	257
3	198	59	257
4	216	41	257
5	237	21	258[a]

[a] To amortize the debt with *equal* installments would require $257.10 per year.

EXHIBIT 21-8
Payments on added $2000 debt with asset purchase

Year (1)	Principal payment (2)	Interest payment (3)	Total payment [(2) + (3)] (4)	Firm tax savings due to interest tax deductibility [tax rate × (3)] (5)
1	$334	$180	$514	$90
2	364	150	514	75
3	396	118	514	59
4	432	82	514	41
5	474	42	516[a]	21

[a] To amortize the debt with *equal* installments would require $514.20 per year.

To compute the net advantage to leasing (NAL), we must look at the difference in firm cash flows with leasing and with purchase. If the asset is leased, there is no cash outlay at time 0 (when the asset is acquired); however, if the asset is purchased, there is a net current outlay of $2000, the purchase price of the asset. Therefore, the time 0 benefit from leasing the asset equals

Time 0 advantage of leasing = $2000

The *future* cash flow differences between leasing and purchase for years 1 through 5 can be determined by comparing Exhibits 21-5 and 21-6 (pages 782 and 783). Exhibit 21-9 shows the differences between the aftertax cash flows with lease and purchase. Column 7 is the difference between the firm's cash flow with lease and with purchase; since the figures are all negative, firm cash flow is smaller with lease than with purchase in years 1 through 5. The $2000 time 0 benefit with lease therefore requires a future sacrifice in years 1 through 5. To compute the NAL, we first determine the present value of col. 7 (which equals −$1951); the −$1951 means that the present value of the *future* firm aftertax cash flows with leasing is $1951 *less* than the present value of the *future* aftertax cash flows with purchase. We therefore deduct the $1951 from the $2000 to compute the NAL, implying an NAL of $49. Leasing is therefore superior to purchase since it produces a present value of aftertax cash flows which is $49 greater than with purchase. This is the same as the result arrived at in Appendix 21A.

How did we arrive at the 9.02 percent discount rate in col. 8 of Exhibit 21-9 which we used to compute the present value? The 9.02 percent rate is that rate which is appropriate given the risk of the cash flow in col. 7. This discount rate must produce the same $49 advantage with lease as was calculated in Appendix 21A since the Appendix 21A approach and the NAL approach must be consistent with one another. An alternative approach for computing the present value of the cash flows in Exhibit 21-9 is to discount each of cols. 2, 3, 4, 5, and 6 separately, using the rate appropriate to the risk of the cash flow being discounted. If the discount rates selected are correct, the NAL must equal the $49 implied by Exhibits 21-5 and 21-6 computations (assuming, of course, that the discount rates used in Exhibits 21-5 and 21-6 are correct). In practice, selecting the proper discount rate for computing a present value is very difficult and usually a good ballpark estimate is the best that can be hoped for.

EXHIBIT 21-9
Computation of the net advantage to leasing

Year (1)	Added aftertax operating expenses with purchase[a] (2)	Depreciation tax savings with purchase[b] (3)	Aftertax salvage value (4)	Aftertax lease rental[c] (5)	Interest tax savings with purchase[d] (6)	Added cash flow with lease [(2) − (3) − (4) − (5) − (6)] (7)	9.02% present value factor (8)	Present value [(7) × (8)] (9)
1	$50	$200		$275	$90	$(515)	0.9173	$ (472)
2	50	200		275	75	(500)	0.8414	(421)
3	50	200		275	59	(484)	0.7718	(374)
4	50	200		275	41	(466)	0.7079	(330)
5	50	200	$100	275	21	(546)	0.6493	(354)
								$(1,951)

Net advantage to leasing = $2000 − $1951 > 0; therefore, lease is preferable to purchase.

a Equal to (1 − tax rate) × (col. 3 of Exhibit 21-6 *minus* col. 3 of Exhibit 21-5).
b Equal to (tax rate) × (col. 4 of Exhibit 21-2).
c Equal to (1 − tax rate) × (col. 4 of Exhibit 21-6).
d Equal to col. 5 of Exhibit 21-8.

CHAPTER TWENTY-TWO

CONVERTIBLES AND WARRANTS

The securities used most often by corporations to raise long-term capital are common stock, bonds, and preferred stock. Convertibles and warrants are alternatives to these three basic securities. Convertibles and warrants have the special feature that either can be converted at the will of the owner into the issuing company's common stock. In this chapter we describe these securities and explain why they appeal to investors and to companies seeking capital.

CONVERTIBLES

Convertible bonds and preferred stock can be converted at the discretion of the security's owner into the common stock of the issuing firm. The owner may convert at any time or choose never to convert. The investor's decision regarding conversion is discussed below.

Conversion Price and Conversion Ratio

The **conversion price** is the dollars of par value of the convertible security paid per share of common stock acquired through conversion.[1] For example, if the conversion price of the stock is $50, a $1000 (par value) bond can be converted into twenty shares of common stock. That is,

$$\text{Conversion price} = \frac{\text{par value of convertible security}}{\text{number of common shares received}} \quad (22\text{-}1)$$

$$= \frac{\$1000}{20} = \$50$$

Similarly, if a share of convertible preferred with a par value of $100 is convertible into two shares of common stock, the conversion price is $50.

The **conversion ratio** is the number of common shares received for converting the convertible security. In the examples above, the conversion ratio is 20 for the convertible bond and 2 for the convertible preferred.

The convertible security agreement may contain a provision for a varying conversion price over time; for example, a bond may be convert-

---

[1] See Chapter 11 on par value.

ible into 10 shares of common stock from 1991 to 1993, into $9\frac{1}{2}$ shares of common stock from 1994 to 1996, and so on. Less frequently, the conversion option completely expires after a number of years.

The conversion ratio is adjusted if stock dividends or a stock split is declared. The adjustment ensures that holders of the convertible security will maintain their proportional shares of the firm's common stock. For example, a 10 percent stock dividend would result in a 10 percent increase in the conversion ratio.

Valuation of a Convertible

Investment Value of the Convertible Security   The **investment value** (pure security value) of a convertible security is the value that the security would have if it were not convertible but had all its other features. Investment value equals the present value of the interest plus maturity value of a convertible bond, or the present value of the dividend payments anticipated on a convertible preferred. For example, the investment value of a $1000 par 5 percent convertible bond with twenty years to maturity is the present value of the interest payments of $50 per year, plus the present value of the $1000 maturity value received twenty years hence. Applying the bond valuation procedure of Chapter 5, if the market interest rate on bonds of comparable risk but lacking the conversion option is 7 percent, the investment value of the bond is

$$\text{Investment value} = \frac{\$50}{1 + 0.07} + \frac{\$50}{(1 + 0.07)^2}$$

$$+ \cdots + \frac{\$50}{(1 + 0.07)^{20}} + \frac{\$1000}{(1 + 0.07)^{20}}$$

$$= \$50(P/A, 7\%, 20) + \$1000(P/F, 7\%, 20)$$

$$= \$50(10.594) + \$1000(0.2584) = \$788 \qquad (22\text{-}2)$$

A convertible security's market value will generally exceed its investment value. Why is this so? Because the investor not only receives the coupon (interest) payments and the maturity payment (or, with preferred stock, the preferred dividend payments) but also has the *additional advantage* of being able to convert the security into common stock at his or her option. The market value of a convertible equals its investment value plus the value of the option to convert.

Conversion Value of the Convertible Security   The **conversion value** of a security is the market value of the stock into which it is convertible. For example, assume that a $1000 bond is convertible into twenty shares of common stock with a market value of $46 per share. The conversion value of the bond is $920 (20 × $46). That is,

Conversion value = (number of shares of common stock received upon conversion) × (market price per share of common stock)

= (conversion ratio) × (market price per share of common stock)   (22-3)

If the market price of the common stock is high, conversion value can exceed investment value. Conversion value is shown in Figure 22-1; it rises as the market price of the common stock rises. Notice that conversion value can also be less than investment value, if the price of the common stock is low. Recall that our 5 percent bond has an investment value of $788, which in no way depends on the price of the common stock. But conversion value does depend on the market price of the common. If that market price were $30 per share, the conversion value would be $600 (20 shares × $30 per share), which is less than the investment value of $788. If the price per common share were $50, the conversion value of the convertible bond would be $1000, greater than investment value. Thus, conversion value can be above or below investment value depending upon whether the price of the common stock is high or low.

Market Value (Market Price) of the Convertible Security We have decided that the market value of the convertible security cannot be less than its investment value because the convertible security's market value equals the investment value of the bond or preferred stock plus the value of the right to convert. It is also true that market value can never be less than conversion value—this is so since the security is always worth at least as much as the common stock into which it can be converted. For example, if we know that we can convert a bond into $920 worth of stock ($920

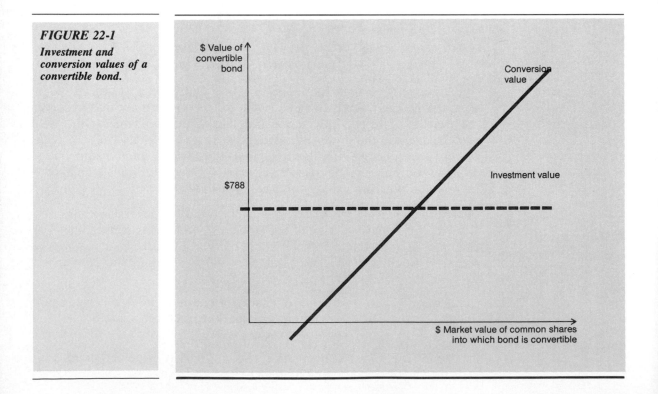

FIGURE 22-1

Investment and conversion values of a convertible bond.

conversion value), then we know that the convertible bond must be worth at least $920. Therefore, *market value is never less than investment value and never less than conversion value.*

The market value of the convertible security may exceed the investment and conversion values. Since the security also offers the option to convert, a premium above investment value may be paid for the convertible. The market value may also exceed the conversion value, since a convertible security not only offers the stock if one wishes to convert *but also has the investment value floor that common stock does not have.*

To illustrate, assume that the convertible bond in the above example has an investment value of $788 and is convertible into twenty shares of common stock with a market price of $60 per share; the conversion value of the bond is $1200, the market value of the twenty shares of common stock. But which is better, owning the convertible bond or owning the twenty shares of common stock? Clearly, the bond. The bond can always be converted into the twenty shares of common stock, so it must be worth at least as much as the twenty shares of common stock. The bond also has a "floor value," as explained above, equal to its investment value; no such floor exists for the twenty shares of common stock. Thus, if the common stock were to fall to $30 per share, the twenty shares of common stock would be worth $600. However, the convertible bond's value would not fall to $600; it would fall no further than the investment value floor of $788.[2] This added advantage of the convertible security gives it a value above the twenty shares of stock into which it can be converted (its conversion value). Of course, if the prices of the common stock and the convertible become extremely high, the investment value may become almost irrelevant and the value of the convertible security may approach its conversion value. For example, if the price of the common stock were $100 per share, conversion value of the convertible bond would be $2000 (20 shares × $100 per share). If it is extremely unlikely that the common stock will fall significantly, the floor provided by the investment value does not provide much of an advantage, and the convertible bond's market value will approximate its conversion value.

In summary, the market value of a convertible security will never be less than, and will generally exceed, both its investment value and its conversion value. See Figure 22-2. The **conversion premium** is the

---

[2] For the investment value to remain at $788, the market interest rate in Eq. (22-2) must be 7 percent. If the general level of interest rates rises and the stock's price falls, e.g., if the interest rate in Eq. (22-2) rises to 8 percent, the investment value would become $50($P/A$, 8%, 20) + $1000($P/F$, 8%, 20) = $705, which still exceeds the $600 value of the shares; the convertible bond would therefore have a market price of at least $705. If the interest rate on the bond were 10 percent in Eq. (22-2), then the investment value would be $50($P/A$, 10%, 20) + $1000($P/F$, 10%, 20) = $574; in this case, the convertible bond would be worth at least $600, since the bond's value must be no less than its investment value ($574) or the value of the stock into which it can be converted ($600).

amount by which the market value of the convertible exceeds the higher of its investment and conversion values (shaded area in Figure 22-2).

Dilution Effects of Conversion

Conversion generally lowers the earnings per share on the common stock. Let's see why. Assume that the firm has $10 million of twenty-year, 6 percent convertible bonds outstanding (not yet converted), which are convertible into common stock at a conversion price of $50 (therefore convertible into 200,000 shares of common). The firm also has 1 million shares of common stock outstanding before conversion. From Exhibit 22-1, which summarizes the position of the firm before and after conversion, we see that the earnings per share on the common stock drop from $3.30 to $3 due to conversion.[3] To see how this same concept works for convertible preferred stock, see problems *3* and *5*.

---

[3] It is possible that conversion will lead to a rise in earnings per share. This will occur if earnings per share before conversion are less than added aftertax earnings from eliminating the fixed charges, i.e., interest or preferred dividends on the convertible security divided by the number of new shares due to conversion. For example, assume that in Exhibit 22-1 the firm's convertible bonds were convertible into 50,000 shares of common stock instead of into 200,000 shares. After conversion there are 1,050,000 shares of common stock with earnings of $3.43 per share, which exceeds the preconversion earnings per share of $3.30. This occurred since earnings before conversion of $3 were less than added earnings from eliminating the interest on the convertibles divided by the number of new shares ($300,000/50,000 shares) = $6.

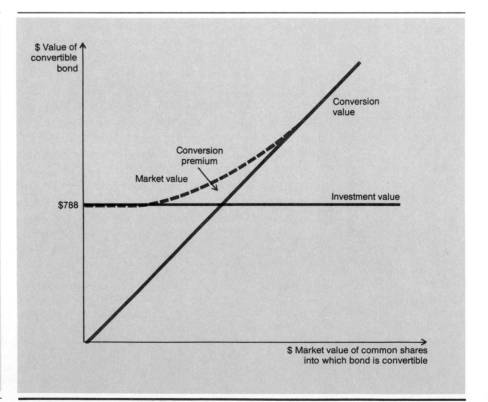

FIGURE 22-2
Value of a convertible bond. The market value of the convertible bond is never less than the investment value or conversion value. The market value of the convertible approaches conversion value if the common stock has a very high market value. The shaded area is the conversion premium, which is the excess of the convertible's market value over the higher of investment value and conversion value.

EXHIBIT 22-1
Effect of conversion on earnings per share

	Before conversion	After conversion
Earnings before interest and taxes	$7,200,000	$7,200,000
Bond interest	600,000	0
Earnings before taxes...................	$6,600,000	$7,200,000
Taxes (at 50%)........................	3,300,000	3,600,000
Earnings after taxes	$3,300,000	$3,600,000
No. of shares of common stock...........	1 million	1.2 million
Earnings per share	$3.30	$3.00

Appraisal of
Convertible
Securities

Many investors find convertible securities attractive because they provide a relatively safe investment income (and therefore an investment value floor) with the possibility of a large gain if the common stock appreciates significantly. However, the investor pays for the conversion right since the yield on a convertible security is less than that on a comparable security without the conversion privilege. For example, a twenty-year, $1000 nonconvertible bond of the firm with a coupon rate of 8 percent ($80 per year in interest payments) might sell at its face value of $1000, whereas a convertible bond with a coupon rate of only 6 percent ($60 per year in interest payments) might also sell at its face value of $1000. The nonconvertible bond yields 8 percent and the convertible bond yields 6 percent. The difference in yield is due to the conversion feature of the 6 percent bond. That is, investors are willing to accept the lower yield on the convertible bond because of the convertibility privilege.

It should be pointed out that convertible bonds often have a lower-priority position (subordinated position) than some or all of the issuing company's other debt obligations. The investor will want to take this factor into account.

The firm's decision to sell a convertible security must be based, like all financing decisions, on the firm's particular situation and on security market conditions. There is no reason to suppose that convertibles are, on the average, superior to other financing vehicles. It may appear that there is an advantage to the firm because convertible bonds or preferred stock can be sold at a yield less than that required if the securities were nonconvertible. However, whether such an advantage exists depends on the future trend in the company's common stock price. If the firm's stock does not appreciate much in value, then the common stockholders are better off since conversion will never occur. But if the firm prospers and the value of its stock rises, conversion will occur and the convertible security holders will effectively have bought the company's common stock at a bargain price. In this case, the firm's common shareholders are worse off than they would have been if the firm had initially issued nonconvertible securities. Therefore, the company's decision to issue convertibles essentially involves a gamble on the future course of the firm's stock.

Benefits may be provided by convertibles if the firm wishes to increase its debt (or preferred stock) outstanding in the short-run, but to replace the debt later with common stock financing. If the firm were to issue nonconvertible bonds now and stock later to pay off those bonds, it would incur flotation costs twice—now, and later when the stock is sold. With convertibles it could issue convertible debt now, which would be converted into common stock at the later date, with flotation costs incurred only in the current period. If a rise in the firm's common stock in a later period is anticipated, so that conversion can be expected to occur, this approach will avoid the refunding costs associated with replacing the nonconvertible debt with common stock.

Generally, convertible issues have a call provision that provides the firm with a means of compelling convertible security holders to convert to common stock if the stock price rises sufficiently. If the conversion value of the convertible security rises above the call price, the firm can merely call the securities and conversion will be forced. For example, assume a $1000 convertible bond convertible into twenty shares of City Corporation common stock. Let the call provision allow the firm to call the convertible for $1100. Assume that the price per share of City common stock is $65. The conversion value of the bond is $1300 (20 shares × $65 per share). City Corporation can call the bond, and security holders have the choice of converting or surrendering their bonds for the call price. An investor who does not convert receives the call price of $1100; an investor who does convert receives twenty shares of common stock with a total value of $1300. Obviously, investors will convert.

WARRANTS

A warrant is an option to buy a specified number of the firm's common stock at a stated price per share. Recall that a convertible security required surrender of the security in exchange for the common stock. A warrant requires a surrender of the warrant, *plus* the payment of additional cash—called the **exercise price**—in order to obtain the common stock. Warrants are issued by corporations for cash to investors who may exercise them (i.e., buy the stock) or may resell them to other investors. A warrant is like a stock right except that rights are issued free to existing stockholders who may sell them or exercise them by buying new shares. Warrants do not have to be exercised when they are bought but generally expire at a given date, although some are perpetual. Alleghany Corporation, Atlas Corporation, and Tri-Continental Corporation are among the few firms that have issued perpetual warrants.

In some cases, the exercise price of the common stock varies—generally moving upward—over time. For example, Indian Head warrants that expired in 1990 allowed the owner to purchase one share of common stock at $25 per share until May 15, 1975, at $30 per share until

May 15, 1980, at $35 per share until May 15, 1985, and $40 per share until
May 15, 1990.

Warrants are often issued with other securities (usually bonds or
preferred stock) in a unit or package. The warrants in this case may be
"detached" and sold separately by the investor.

Valuation of a Warrant

Theoretical Value of a Warrant The **theoretical value** of a warrant equals
the market value of the common stock purchased with the warrant minus
the total exercise price paid for the shares. This is analogous to the
conversion value of a convertible security. The theoretical value equals

Theoretical value of a warrant
$$= \text{(market price of common stock } - \text{ exercise price)}$$
$$\times \text{ (number of shares purchased with one warrant)} \quad (22\text{-}4)$$

For example, assume that Makitbig Company has warrants outstanding, each of which entitles the holder to purchase two shares of Makitbig
Company stock for $40 per share. These warrants expire one year from
now. If Makitbig common stock were selling for $45 per share, using
Eq. (22-4) the theoretical value of the warrant would be

Theoretical value of Makitbig warrant $= (\$45 - \$40) \times 2 = \$10$

By owning a warrant we can buy two shares of stock from the company
for $10 less than buying the shares on the open market. The theoretical
value can therefore be defined as the discount on the company's common stock that is allowed the warrantholder. If investors buy warrants
for their theoretical value and exercise them, they end up paying the
same price for the company's common stock as they would if they were
to buy the common stock directly in the market.

What if the market price of the common stock were equal to or below
the exercise price? Then the theoretical value of the warrant would be
zero (a warrant will never have a negative value).

Market Value of a Warrant An investor willing to purchase the common
stock at its market price would willingly pay the theoretical value for a
warrant, since it can be immediately exercised and the common stock
obtained. The theoretical value represents the minimum market value of
the warrant. Warrants, however, also offer investors the added option of
holding the warrant instead of purchasing shares.

Since warrants do not provide their owners any dividends or interest
payments, they do not have any investment value comparable to that for
a convertible security. The market value of a warrant is due entirely to
its potential conversion into common stock. However, the market price
of a warrant is generally greater than its theoretical value. The difference
between the market price of a warrant and its theoretical value is called
the **premium** on the warrant. Let's see why premiums arise and how they
depend on the price of the stock.

Suppose the price of Makitbig stock in the example above is $40. The
$40 exercise price of the Makitbig warrants is therefore equal to the
stock price and the theoretical value of the warrants is $0. Will the mar-

ket price and premium for the warrants be $0? Of course not. The owner of a Makitbig warrant will be able to realize a positive dollar return from owning the warrant if the stock price rises above $40 (the exercise price of the warrant) at any time prior to the expiration date of the warrant. The warrant will sell at a positive price (and premium) so long as there is a chance that the price of Makitbig common will exceed $40 prior to expiration of the warrant. Since the stock price is currently at $40, the chances are very good that the stock will rise in price (unless the warrant will expire momentarily) and therefore the premium will be relatively large. However, suppose that the stock price is $30, well below the exercise price. The theoretical value of the warrant is $0 in this case, just as before. But now, in order for the warrant to provide a positive dollar return from exercising it, the stock price must rise significantly above its current level. Therefore, the price (and premium) of the warrant will be much lower if Makitbig stock is selling for $30 than it would be if Makitbig stock were selling for $40. We can conclude that the further below the exercise price ($40) is the current price of the stock, the lower will be the warrant's premium and market price (market price = premium since the market price is less than the exercise price of $40).

What happens to the market price and the premium on the warrant if Makitbig's stock price goes over $40? The warrant's market price will rise reflecting the higher theoretical value of the warrant, but the premium will decrease. Therefore, at stock prices well above the exercise price, the market price of the warrant becomes approximately equal to its theoretical value; that is, the premium vanishes. This decline in the premium is due to the reduced advantage of owning the warrant relative to exercising it. To see why this is so, let's assume for a moment that the premium is a constant $5 regardless of Makitbig's stock price. As we will see, this assumption of a constant premium is not reasonable. Furthermore, for illustrative purposes, suppose that investors expect that Makitbig stock will provide the same probability distribution of annual rates of return at any given price for the stock. The assumed distribution is

Probability:	0.5	0.5
Rate of return:	−20%	40%

The expected rate of return on the stock is therefore 10 percent [$0.5 \times (-20\%) + 0.5 \times (40\%)$].

Exhibit 22-2 shows the rates of return expected on Makitbig warrants assuming that they will expire in one year and hence will be exercised within one year if it is profitable to do so. Observe that the expected rate of return declines as the stock price rises due to the increased theoretical value of the warrant plus our assumed constant premium of $5. Thus, for example, if $5 is a reasonable premium from the perspective of investors when the stock price is $40, the $5 premium is too high when the stock price is $45. The actual premium will decrease as the stock price increases. Therefore, in Exhibit 22-2, the premium will be less at a stock price of $45 than at a stock price of $40, and the premium will be less at a stock price of $50 than at a stock price of $45. As the stock price becomes very high, the premium almost completely disappears and the market price of the warrant will approximate its theoretical value.[4]

The general behavior of the price of Makitbig's warrants is illustrated in Figure 22-3. The market price of the warrant equals the premium for stock prices below the exercise price of $40. For stock prices below $40, changes in the market price of the warrant are the result of a changing premium. The market price of the warrant increases for stock prices above $40 due to the increased theoretical value; however, the premium declines as the stock price increases due to the reduced advantage of holding the warrant relative to exercising it.

Appraisal and Use of Warrants

Warrants have value beyond their theoretical value because they provide the opportunity of owning the common stock if the warrants are immediately exercised and the alternative of holding the unexercised warrant. As explained in the previous section, one may wish to hold the unexer-

[4] As the stock price goes up, both the expected rate of return on the warrant for any given fixed premium and the risk decline. Therefore, the net impact is difficult to analyze, but under reasonable assumptions it is possible to show that the premium should decline as the stock price rises (this is what we observe in practice). On this, see Paul A. Samuelson, "Rational Theory of Warrant Pricing," *Industrial Management Review* (Spring 1965).

EXHIBIT 22-2
Returns from Makitbig warrants

	Current stock price					
	$40		**$45**		**$50**	
Current market price of warrant[a]	$ 5		$15		$25	
Future stock price[b]	$32	$56	$36	$63	$40	$70
Dollar return from warrant[c]	$ 0	$32	$ 0	$46	$ 0	$60
Rate of return on warrant[d]	−100%	540%	−100%	207%	−100%	140%
Expected dollar return[e]	$16		$23		$30	
Expected rate of return on warrant[f]	220%		53.3%		20%	

[a] Theoretical value plus $5 premium.
[b] Based on constant probability distribution of rate of return applied to given stock price.
Probability: 0.5   0.5
Rate of return: −20%   40%

For example, if the current stock price is $40, the future stock price will be either [$40 − .20($40)] = $32 or [$40 + .40($40)] = $56.
[c] Assumes warrant for two shares of stock is exercised if stock price exceeds exercise price of $40. Thus, for example, if the current stock price is $40 and the future stock price is $56, the dollar return from the warrant = 2 × ($56 − $40) = $32.
[d] Equals [(Dollar return from warrant/current market price of warrant) − 1] × 100%.
[e] Based on equal probabilities of occurrence of 0.5. For example, $16 = .5($0) + .5($32).
[f] Based on equal probabilities of occurrence of 0.5. For example, 220% = .5(−100%) + .5(540%) = 220%.

cised warrant rather than the common stock since it offers the potential for a very high rate of return. Of course, there is also a high risk of loss. Also, until the warrants are exercised, the warrantholder receives no voting privileges or dividends.

The attraction of warrants for investors has led to their frequent use, especially by small dynamic firms as part of units of bonds, preferred stock, or common stock. A unit might be composed of a bond plus a warrant or of several shares of common stock plus a warrant. Various such combinations have appeared. Although warrants have characteristically been the tool of the smaller firm, in April 1970 AT&T, in a monumental offering, obtained $1.57 billion on an issue of bonds and warrants. This was the first time in over fifty years that the New York Stock Exchange accepted warrants for listing. As it turned out, the price of AT&T stock declined and the warrants become practically valueless, with few of them being exercised. Since 1970, other large firms have issued warrants, many of which are also listed on the New York Stock Exchange.

SUMMARY

A convertible bond or preferred stock can be transformed into the common stock of the corporation at the option of the holder. The value of a convertible as an income-producing security—providing bond interest or

FIGURE 22-3
Value of Makitbig warrants.

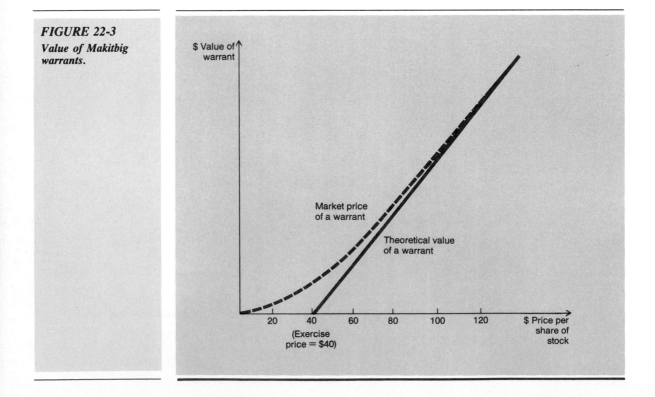

*preferred dividends—is referred to as its investment value. The market
value of the common stock into which the security can be converted is its
conversion value. The convertible's market value is the price it sells for in
the market, and this value will generally exceed both investment value and
conversion value. Conversion increases the number of common shares
outstanding and usually decreases earnings per share. A convertible
provides the investor with a relatively safe return in the form of interest or
preferred dividends and, in addition, the potential opportunity to participate
in the firm's growth and stock price increase. However, because of the
conversion advantage to the investor, the firm can pay a lower interest rate
or lower preferred dividend rate than would be the case if the conversion
option were not included. Whether a convertible is attractive to a given
investor will depend upon the investor's risk-return preferences and
expectations regarding the future price of the company's common stock.
Similarly, the firm's decision to issue a convertible security will depend
upon management's expectations regarding the company's stock price. An
advantage of convertible securities is that they allow the firm, in effect, to
issue debt in the short run and stock in the long run (when the convertible
is converted into common stock) without incurring flotation costs on two
separate issues.*

*The purchase of a warrant entitles the holder to purchase the
company's common stock at a specified price on any date preceding the
warrant's expiration. A warrant has a theoretical value equal to the market
value of the stock obtained with the warrant less the price paid for the
stock upon exercise. The theoretical value is the discount provided the
warrantholder on the price of the common stock. The market value of the
warrant will at least equal, and will generally exceed, its theoretical value.
Although historically the device of small firms, warrants have recently
enjoyed increased popularity as a financing method of larger companies.*

QUESTIONS

1 What is the investment value of a convertible security? Explain.
2 Explain what is likely to happen to the investment value of a convertible if the general level of interest rates rises.
3 Why is it that a convertible security's market price will generally
exceed its investment value?
4 "Convertible securities can be sold with a lower coupon rate than
nonconvertible securities. This means that their cost to the firm is
less than that of nonconvertible securities." Comment on this
statement.
5 What should the holder of a convertible bond do if the bonds are
called for redemption and the bond is selling:
   a at call price
   b below call price
   c above call price
6 Will dilution in earnings per share of common caused by conversion of convertible securities cause a decline in the value of the
shares?

7 What are the major differences between a warrant and a convertible security?

8 In terms of their earning dilution effects, compare the conversion of a convertible bond into the company's common stock with the exercise of a warrant to acquire the firm's stock.

9 "If the theoretical value of a warrant is equal to the market price of that warrant, an investor should be indifferent between the purchase of the warrant *and exercising it* and the purchase of the stock." Evaluate this statement, assuming there are no trading costs to consider.

10 Why might it be advantageous to hold a company's warrants rather than its common shares?

PROJECT

Select a convertible bond and obtain quarterly price data for a two-year period (for data, see, for example, *The Wall Street Journal*). For each quarter determine the convertible's investment value, conversion value, market value, and conversion premium. Satisfy yourself that the ideas presented in this chapter are valid for the convertible you selected.

Also obtain two years of quarterly price data for a warrant. Identify the warrant's market price and theoretical value for each quarter. Consider the market price and theoretical value behavior in light of the chapter material.

DEMONSTRATION PROBLEMS

DP1 A $100 par value preferred stock is convertible into common stock at a conversion price of $25, and the preferred stock is selling in the market at $228 per share. The preferred's investment value is $120. What is the approximate market price of the common stock? Show any calculations you make.

SOLUTION TO DP1:

$$\text{Conversion ratio} = \frac{\text{par value}}{\text{conversion price}}$$

$$= \frac{\$100}{\$25}$$

$$= 4$$

The market price of the preferred stock ($228) is far above its investment value ($120). Therefore, its conversion value apparently is determining its market value. Furthermore, since the market price of the preferred is so high, the conversion premium is likely to be nearly zero and the preferred's value is approximately equal to its conversion value. Therefore,

$$\frac{\text{Approximate price per}}{\text{share of common stock}} = \frac{\text{conversion value of preferred}}{\text{conversion ratio}}$$

$$= \frac{\$228}{4}$$

$$= \$57$$

DP2 Consider a $1000, 9 percent convertible, twenty-year bond maturing fifteen years from now. The bond is convertible into common stock at a conversion price of $100. The bond is also callable at $1140. Currently this bond is trading at $1120, and the common stock of the same firm sells at $105 a share. Straight bonds of this quality and maturity are currently traded on the market to yield 10 percent.

    a What is the conversion premium paid on the convertible bond?

    b At what common stock price would the holders of the convertible bond be indifferent to a choice of surrendering the bond if called or converting? (Ignore personal taxes in your computation.)

    c Suppose that the price per share for the common stock remains at $105 but the going rate of interest falls to 8 percent. What is the minimum possible market value of the bond?

SOLUTION TO DP2:

    a Investment value $= P = \$90(P/A, 10\%, 15)$
$$+ \$1000(P/F, 10\%, 15)$$

$$= \$90(7.6061) + \$1000(.2394)$$

$$= \$923.95$$

If the conversion price is $100, the bond is convertible into $1000/$100 = 10 shares.

Conversion value $= 10 \times \$105 = \$1050$

Conversion premium $=$ market value $-$ max(investment value, conversion value)

$$= \$1120 - \text{max}(\$923.95, \$1050)$$

$$= \$1120 - \$1050 = \$70$$

    b If the bond is surrendered, the bondholder gets $1040 (call price). If the bond is converted into stock selling for $P per share, the bondholder gets stock worth $10P$ (the conversion ratio is 10). Thus, for indifference between surrender and conversion:

$$10P = \$1140$$

$$P = \frac{\$1140}{10} = \$114$$

c Investment value becomes:

$$P = \$90(P/A, 8\%, 15) + \$1000(P/F, 8\%, 15)$$

$$= \$90(8.5595) + \$1000(.3152)$$

$$= \$1085.56$$

Since the investment value of $1085.56 is higher than the conversion value of $1050, the bond's market value floor is $1085.56.

DP3 A warrant sells for $25 and entitles the owner to purchase three shares of stock at an exercise price of $15 per share. The common stock sells for $22 per share.
a What is the theoretical value of the warrant?
b What is the premium at which the warrant is selling?

SOLUTION TO DP3:
a Theoretical value = (market price of common stock
− exercise price)
× (number of shares purchased with one warrant)

$$= (\$22 - \$15) \times 3 = \$21$$

b Premium = warrant market price
− theoretical value of warrant

$$= \$25 - \$21$$

$$= \$4$$

PROBLEMS

1 If the market price of a common share is $115, and you hold a warrant entitling you to purchase six shares at a price of $66 per share, what is the theoretical value of the warrant? [Ans.: Theoretical value = $490]

2 Hadrian, Inc., has outstanding an issue of $1000, 12 percent subordinated convertible debentures that are callable, will mature in fifteen years, and are convertible into common stock at a conversion price of $40. The market price of the common stock is $65. What is the conversion value of the convertible bonds? [Ans.: Conversion value = $1625]

3 A $150 par value preferred stock is convertible into common stock at a conversion price of $60, and the preferred stock is selling in the market at $230 per share. The preferred's investment value is $110. What is the approximate market price of the common stock? Show any calculations you make.

4 Assume that you own a $1000 convertible bond of the Barber Company maturing in six years. These bonds have a 13 percent coupon rate. The bonds are convertible into twenty shares of common stock. In addition, the bonds are callable at a call price of $1150. The Barber Company straight bonds (i.e., nonconvertible, noncallable) currently sell to yield 15 percent, and Barber's stock is selling at $55 a share. The straight bonds have the same risk as the convertibles would have if they didn't have the conversion feature.

a What is the conversion ratio for the convertible bond?

b What are the conversion price, the conversion value, and the investment value?

c What is the bond's current market value floor?

d What is the minimum price of the common stock at which shareholders will convert if the convertible bonds are called? (Ignore personal taxes in your computation.)

e Suppose the stock's price falls to $45 a share. In this case, what would be the bond's market value floor?

5 Lionel Pidgeon Industries has a $120 million, ten-year, 13 percent convertible bond issue outstanding. The company also has 120,000 shares of $11\frac{1}{2}$ percent, $500 par convertible preferred stock outstanding. Both the bonds and the preferred stock are callable. The bond's conversion price is $30 and the preferred conversion ratio is 20. The company is now in a position to call either or both issues. The current year's earnings before interest and taxes are expected to be $95 million. The firm currently has 1.5 million shares of common stock outstanding. Its tax rate is 50 percent. Show the effect on earnings per share of

a Conversion of the bonds only

b Conversion of the preferred stock only

c Conversion of both bonds and preferred stock

d Assume that the bonds' conversion price is $50 (instead of $30). Show what happens to EPS upon conversion of the bonds only and comment on the result.

6 Consider a $1000, 12 percent convertible, twenty-year bond maturing ten years from now. The bond is convertible into common stock at a conversion price of $50. The bond is also callable at $1120. Currently this bond is trading at $1100, and the common stock of the same firm sells at $42 a share. Straight bonds of this quality and maturity are currently traded on the market to yield 11 percent.

a What is the conversion premium paid on the convertible bond?

b At what common stock price would the holders of the convertible bond be indifferent between surrendering the bond if called or converting? (Ignore personal taxes in your computation.)

c Suppose that the price per share for the common stock remains at $42, but the going rate of interest falls to 9 percent. What is the minimum possible market value of the bond?

7 A share of Upsilon Corporation's common stock sells for $45. One warrant will purchase three shares of the common stock at an exercise price per share of $16. What is the theoretical value of the warrant? [Ans.: Theoretical value = $58]

8 A warrant sells for $450 and entitles the owner to purchase twenty shares of stock at an exercise price of $10 per share. The common stock sells for $25 per share.

a What is the theoretical value of the warrant?

b What is the premium at which the warrant is selling?

9 Fruhan, Inc., needs $5 million to introduce a new engine oil additive. The company would like to sell common stock, but the market is somewhat depressed and management believes that the current $25 a share for its stock does not reflect its true value. Two alternatives are being considered: (a) sell 5000 12 percent convertible bonds (each with a par value of $1000) with a conversion ratio of 20 or (b) sell 5000 12 percent bonds, each with a par value of $1000 and each with twenty warrants attached, with each warrant good to buy one share of common stock at $32. With a or b, Fruhan will receive $5 million in cash (the bonds are sold at par with zero underwriting costs). Before adopting a or b, the firm has the following liabilities and equity position:

Short-term loans....................................	$ 500,000
Common stock, $10 par.............................	2,000,000
Retained earnings...................................	500,000
Total claims.....................................	$3,000,000

The firm's rate of return on assets before interest and taxes is 30 percent; its tax rate is 50 percent. Thus the EBIT before a or b is adopted is $900,000 (30% × $3,000,000). The rate of return (in terms of EBIT) on investment of any new capital raised under a or b will also be 30 percent.

a Show the liabilities and equity position of the firm for both alternatives a and b after conversion.

b Assuming that the firm invests all its available funds, compute the earnings per share (EPS) for alternatives a and b. Explain the differences, if any.

c What considerations other than EPS could be important in reaching a decision as to which alternative to use?

In the spring of 1973, two events occurred in Chicago that sparked minor revolutions in the theory and practice of finance, created excitement among investors, caused concern in the chambers of the United States Congress, and generated long hours for the staff at the Securities and Exchange Commission. In April the Chicago Board of Trade launched a new venture, the Chicago Board Options Exchange (CBOE), an organized exchange for the trading of options in common stocks. A few weeks later the May–June issue of the *Journal of Political Economy* (published by the University of Chicago) was mailed out to subscribers. In the *Journal* was an article by two academicians, Fischer Black and Myron Scholes, entitled "The Pricing of Options and Corporate Liabilities." The "Option Pricing Model" developed by Black and Scholes has since taken a position in financial theory second only to the "Capital Asset Pricing Model" of Chapter 6.

Since 1973 the trading volume in options has exploded. For popular companies such as IBM and Kodak, more shares are now involved in options trading than in the stock themselves. In the academic literature there has been a parallel increase in journal articles analyzing options and other financial contracts using the perspective of option pricing theory. What are these options that people are so excited about and what new insights has the analysis of options provided? The answers to these questions are the topic of this essay.

THE OPTIONS MARKETS

Have you ever received a rain check when you tried to purchase an item on sale at a store but found the item was out of stock? If the store gives you a slip of paper saying that you can buy the item at the sale price when the item comes in, the store has given you a **call option** on the item. A call option in common stock is the right to purchase the stock at a fixed price ("exercise price" or "striking price") during a set period of time. A typical call contract provides the purchaser with the right to buy 100 shares of a particular stock at any time up to and including the expiration date of the call, which may be thirty days to one year from the time the call was first written. Note that the holder of a call does not have to buy the stock (or the item at the store); the call provides the option of buying or not buying at the holder's discretion. Warrants (discussed in Chapter 22) are a special type of call option issued by a company on the company's stock. A **put option** is the right to sell a given number of shares of a particular stock at a specified exercise price during a set period of time. The holder of a put has the option of selling or not selling the stock.

Options have been used in real estate transactions for many years. Land developers often purchase options on individual parcels of land in the process of attempting to put together a large enough area to make a development project economically feasible. Stockbrokers and dealers have traditionally bought and sold options for their customers. The opening of the CBOE meant that an organized market existed for purchase and sale of options on common stock. In particular, a good secondary market for options now exists. Thus, for example, the investor in a call option that will expire in six months has the choice of:

1 Selling the option to another investor at any time in the next six months

2 Exercising the option (buying the underlying stock for the price fixed in the contract) at any time in the next six months

3 Holding the option until it expires

Similarly, the holder of a put option can sell it to someone else, exercise it, or simply hold it until expiration. With an organized exchange it is now easy for the investor to find out what the current value of the option is, and the investor knows that it will be easy to sell the option at any time. These are the same sorts of advantages that exist for investors in stock listed on the stock exchanges as compared with those that trade "over-the-counter."

For whatever reasons, individuals and financial institutions have flocked to the options market. In 1973, 1.1 million option contracts traded on the CBOE; in 1974 volume went to 5.6 million. At this point other exchanges began options trading. The Amex, Philadelphia, Pacific, and Midwest stock exchanges began listing options. By 1980, the annual total volume of stock underlying the options traded exceeded the volume of actual shares traded on the New York Stock Exchange. The growth of the options market has dramatically exceeded expectations.

BUYING AND SELLING OPTIONS

An individual may write or buy a call option and may write or buy a put option. As explained above, the *buyer* of an option is entitled to purchase the underlying stock (a call option) or to sell the underlying stock (a put option) at the exercise price if the option is exercised within the specified time period. The *writer* of an option assumes the other side of the transaction. The writer of a call option is obligated, under the option agreement, to sell the underlying stock at the exercise price if the option is exercised before the option expires. The writer of a put option is obligated to buy the underlying stock at the exercise price if the option is exercised before the expiration date. For every call option and every put option there is a writer and a buyer; the individual investor may assume either of these roles.

To buy or write an option, an individual need only contact a securities broker. The broker will conduct the transaction, in return for which a commission is charged. A commission is charged both when an option is purchased or written and when it is exercised (it is generally the case that a commission is paid when a security—e.g., a share of stock—is purchased and again when it is sold).

Only the shares of certain companies have been approved for options trading on the exchanges. For the shares to be approved, there must be at least a certain number outstanding, the per share price must exceed a specified minimum, and the trading volume in the shares must exceed a certain level.

In addition to the strategy of buying or writing a put or call option, an investor can also engage in a **spread** or a **straddle** transaction. A spread position involves writing and buying calls (or writing and buying puts) on the same underlying stock, but the options have a difference in maturity date, striking price, or both. An example of a spread would be holding a call option to buy 100 shares of Ideal Corporation common stock at $50 per share and also writing a call option for 100 shares of Ideal stock with an exercise price of $55 per share. A straddle involves writing and buying an equal number of puts (or calls) for the same underlying stock, where the puts (or calls) bought and written have the same exercise price and the same expiration date. Writing a put and buying a put covering 100 shares of Ideal stock, both with an exercise price of $50 and both expiring on the same date, would be a straddle. An investor in a straddle generally anticipates wide price fluctuations in the underlying stock but is unsure as to whether the movement will be up or down.

APPLICATIONS OF
OPTIONS ANALYSIS

The discussion of warrant valuation in Chapter 22 applies equally well to other forms of call options. Moreover, the concept of an option has far broader applications than simply to real estate deals and to options on common stock. Common stock itself can be viewed as an option on the company. For example, suppose a firm has only one type of liability against it, a bank loan that must be paid in full in sixty days. The stockholders of the firm have an option on the firm. The exercise price of their option is the payment due on the

debt. If the stockholders believe the firm is worth more than the amount due on the debt, they can pay the bank and own the firm's assets. Otherwise they can let their option expire and the bank will own the firm.

Consider a much different application, a fixed-rate long-term loan with prepayment possible (that is, the borrower is permitted, if he or she chooses, to pay off the loan before maturity). The borrower in this case has been provided with an option to prepay the loan. If interest rates go up, the borrower need only make the required payments. If interest rates decline, the borrower can get a new loan at the lower rate and pay off the old loan. This option is valuable to the borrower; however, it is obtained at the expense of the lender. The lender has an incentive not to give something for nothing; therefore the lender may charge a somewhat higher interest rate on such loans (that is, a higher interest rate than if prepayment were forbidden), or more commonly, include penalties for early repayment.

CHAPTER TWENTY-THREE

HOLDING COMPANIES, MERGERS, AND CONSOLIDATIONS

This chapter discusses how and why two or more separate companies combine into one company. The common term for this combination process is "merger." The sections that follow describe the various kinds of business combinations, how firms arrange a merger, why they merge, and how a company decides whether or not a merger is a good idea. The Merger Game, which follows this chapter, examines the strategies companies use in taking over other companies and defending themselves against takeovers, and discusses the use of investment bankers who help companies in formulating and carrying out those strategies.

HOLDING COMPANIES, MERGERS, CONSOLIDATIONS, AND DIVESTITURES

A **holding company** is a corporation that has working control of one or more other corporations, called **subsidiaries**, through ownership of the subsidiaries' common stock. The sole purpose of the holding company is to own shares in other corporations. The holding company may achieve sufficient influence for control with as little as 20 percent, or an even smaller fraction, of a subsidiary's stock.

Holding companies are subject to an added tax on profit. Twenty percent of dividends received by the holding company from the domestic (United States) corporations in which it has an investment are taxed as corporate income.[1] If the holding company and the corporations it controls were merged into a single firm, this added tax could be avoided.[2]

A **merger** or **consolidation** is the unification of previously separate companies into a single corporation. Technically, a merger occurs if one of the two or more combining firms survives (e.g., if firm A and firm B merge and the new firm is called firm A). A consolidation is the union of

---

[1] For example, if corporation J pays holding company H $100 in dividends, $20 of these dividends would be taxable at the corporate tax rate. If the corporate tax rate were 40 percent, then company H would pay $8 in taxes on the dividends (0.40 × $20).

[2] Actually, the tax on 20 percent of dividends can be avoided if the holding company and its subsidiary form all or part of a consolidated group of corporate entities and file a consolidated federal income tax return. One of the requirements for a consolidated group is that the holding company own at least 80 percent of the subsidiary's stock.

firms into a new firm (e.g., firm *A* and firm *B* combined to form firm *C*). The merger or consolidation of firms that are in similar lines of business, e.g., two food wholesalers or two appliance manufacturers, is referred to as a **horizontal combination**. A **vertical combination** joins firms that are engaged in different stages of production of the same type of product, e.g., an oil producer and a refiner. A **conglomerate** is any group of firms in different lines of business that are controlled by a single corporation. The controlled firms in a conglomerate may be separate corporate entities (subsidiaries) or unincorporated divisions of the parent.

Since mergers, consolidations, and other business combinations involve essentially the same financial issues, we will use the term "merger" to refer to either a merger or a consolidation. Also, since one of the firms in a merger survives, the surviving firm can be viewed as acquiring the other (nonsurviving) firm; if firm *A* survives and firm *B* does not, we will often refer to the merger as the acquisition of firm *B* by firm *A*.

A **divestiture** (often referred to as a **spinoff**) is the sale of a division or subsidiary; it is the opposite of a merger. The failure to realize any benefits from a merger acquisition often motivates companies to divest themselves of previously acquired firms. Such giants as RCA, American Can, Kraft, and ITT have recently engaged in massive sell-offs of unwanted subsidiaries.

A **leveraged buyout** is a transaction in which a company, or a subsidiary or a division of a company, is bought by private investors who borrow to finance the purchase. Typically, the assets of the purchased company are used to collateralize the borrowing of the purchaser, and the acquired business is a publicly traded firm (or subsidiary or division of a publicly traded firm) which is taken private (not publicly traded) after the buyout. Very frequently, the private investors purchasing the company are existing managers of the business. For example, in 1984 Dupont sold, for $500 million, the commodity chemical operations it got in its 1981 purchase of Conoco. The buyers were Conoco managers, and their financing was from a group of bankers and insurers lead by Manufacturers Hanover Trust and Prudential Insurance.

The largest leveraged buyout in history (and the biggest takeover in history) was the 1988 $25.1 billion purchase of RJR Nabisco by an investment group led by Kohlberg Kravis Roberts & Company (KKR). The takeover resulted in RJR Nabisco "going private" and followed a fierce contest for control between KKR and another group comprised of RJR Nabisco CEO R. Ross Johnson and his financial backer, Shearson Lehman Hutton.

Leveraged buyouts have become very controversial in recent years, perhaps because of the high proportion of debt typically used in the takeovers. Ratios of debt to equity of 10 are common, and ratios of 25 or more have occurred. Studies indicate that, on average, company profitability increases after an LBO, and post-LBO employment is not significantly affected. One explanation for the improved performance is better incentives for management, who generally have a larger stake in the company after the leveraged buyout than before. Michael Jensen of

Harvard University argues that the large indebtedness after the LBO means greater vigilance on the part of management, who must run extra hard to ensure that the firm has sufficient cash flow to service the company's debt. On the negative side, the increase in shareholder wealth is in many cases partially offset by losses for investors who held the company's bonds before the LBO and who see a fall in the value of those bonds as they become riskier due to increased company debt. Economists are divided on the dangers posed by the increased debt loads produced by LBOs. To date, the record of LBOs seems to argue that they are good for the economy. But, if the economy were to enter a severe recession—or worse—it is likely that the leverage would become a social as well as corporate liability because of the resulting bankruptcies.

MERGER PROCEDURE

Negotiating the Merger

A merger is usually arranged through negotiations between the managements of the firms concerned. The negotiations are ordinarily initiated by the acquiring firm, which offers cash or securities to the other firm's stockholders. After a merger agreement has been worked out by the firms' managements, the agreement must then be approved by the companies' boards of directors. For the combination to proceed, approval must be secured from the stockholders of both firms; a majority—and frequently two-thirds—of the outstanding shares of each firm must be voted in favor of the merger. Following this and the filing of any papers with the state governments in which the corporations are domiciled, the exchange of assets for securities is made and the merger is consummated.

Mergers are not always friendly matches. Frequently, when firm *A* indicates an interest in purchasing firm *B*, the latter company's management spurns the advance. Firm *A* may attempt to circumvent the firm *B* management. One approach is to obtain the proxies (voting power) of the firm *B* shareholders and undertake a proxy fight. If firm *A* wins the proxy fight (that is, gets more proxies than firm *B* management does), it can vote to oust the firm *B* management and then proceed to promote the merger. Proxy fights are expensive and usually unsuccessful for the outsiders. An alternative strategy for circumventing the firm *B* management is for firm *A* to buy the firm *B* shares. This may begin with firm *A*'s purchasing some of the shares in the open market and then announcing that it will purchase some or all of the remaining firm *B* shares directly from the firm *B* shareholders. The offer announcement is called a **tender offer**. Tender offers sometimes succeed and sometimes don't, but they are more often successful than proxy fights. In response to the tender offer, the hostile firm *B* management may use various legal and financial tactics to fend off firm *A* (for details, see ''The Merger Game,'' which follows this chapter). Sometimes there are competing tender offers, with several companies offering to buy the shares of a particular ''target'' (the term for a company which another company wants to buy).

The Federal Trade Commission and the Justice Department both have the power to prevent a merger if it will, or potentially will, reduce competition. This power results primarily from three statutes: the Sherman Act of 1890, the Federal Trade Commission Act of 1914, and the Clayton Act of 1914 (as amended by the Celler-Kefauver Act of 1950). In special cases, a merger can also be disallowed by other government agencies such as the Department of Transportation or the Federal Communications Commission. For example, Civil Aeronautics Board approval is necessary for one airline to take over another airline.

A merger may be blocked if it substantially lessens or tends to lessen competition in a line of business. The courts have wide discretion in defining the relevant product line and geographic area of competition. For example, in its decision that Du Pont's control over the cellophane market did not constitute a monopoly, the courts defined the relevant market to include all types of wrapping (of which cellophane represents only a small fraction) rather than cellophane alone (over which Du Pont had a monopoly). In contrast, Reynolds Metals was forced to divest itself of Arrow Brands because of the combined firm's share of the sales of aluminum foil to florists alone. The absence of clear guidelines on what will and what will not be acceptable to government antitrust officials or the courts injects an added element of uncertainty to merger activities.

Companies may not be allowed to merge even if the threat to competition is only potential. Procter & Gamble, which had entered the bleach market in a big way by purchasing giant Clorox, was forced to divest itself of Clorox because the courts felt that the merger removed Procter & Gamble as a potential competitor of Clorox. The rationale for ordering the divestiture was that keeping P & G "on the fringes" of the market as a watchful potential entrant into the market would prevent Clorox from abusing its strong market position.

January 1982 saw two dramatic events in United States antitrust history—a settlement between the U.S. Justice Deparment and American Telephone and Telegraph Company, which resulted in AT&T's breakup; and the end of the government's thirteen-year antitrust suit against IBM, with the U.S. Justice Department simply dropping the case. Under the AT&T settlement, AT&T divested itself of its local telephone operating companies (by distributing stock in the companies to AT&T stockholders); the total physical assets of those companies is roughly $80 billion. In return, AT&T was allowed to retain its three remaining major components: its Western Electric manufacturing subsidiary, its Bell Laboratories research arm, and its long-distance operations—a combined entity with approximately $40 billion in physical assets. Additionally, AT&T was freed of restrictions from entering new markets, including cable television, newspapers, telecommunications, and computers.

The IBM victory reflected in large part changing market conditions. During the thirteen-year battle between IBM and the U.S. Justice Department, IBM's dominance in the computer field deteriorated as new technologies developed and as domestic and foreign competitors entered the market. This relative decline of IBM was in some measure due to the antitrust suit itself. To avoid strengthening the government's case in the suit, IBM was reluctant in the early and mid-1970s to use its full muscle in competing with other companies. It was only in the late 1970s that IBM again fought aggressively for market share. But, by that time, the industry had changed and many new and vigorous competitors had emerged. In 1982, IBM's competitive environment became still more ominous as another giant, AT&T, was unleashed from government constraints.

The Form of Property Exchanged

One firm's acquisition of another firm may involve a merger, the purchase of a controlling interest in the other firm (that is, a purchase of a majority of its stock), or the purchase of the other firm's assets. In each case, the buying company can pay cash, its securities (the buyer's common stock, preferred stock, bonds, etc.), or some combination of the two.

With a merger, acquiring firm A obtains all the assets and liabilities of selling firm B and the two companies are consolidated under single control. The shareholders of both firms must vote in favor of the merger. Usually at least two-thirds approval of the shareholders of each company is required. If, instead, A buys the stock of B but no formal merger occurs, approval by neither firm's shareholders is required. A problem does arise, though, in that complete consolidation of the two firms may be blocked by a recalcitrant shareholder of B; of course, if firm A owns a sufficient fraction of firm B's stock, it can deal with this situation by voting the shares of B in favor of a merger and then merging the two companies. The third option—the purchase of B's assets—does not require the approval of firm A's shareholders and requires the approval of the seller B's shareholders only if a major portion of B's assets are sold. Furthermore, A can pick and choose the assets it prefers and does not assume B's liabilities (some of which may be hidden). Firm B can either retain the proceeds from the asset sale or distribute them to shareholders.

Should firm A pay cash or securities in the acquisition? Firm A may prefer to pay cash if it has excess cash available; if not, it will have to issue debt or equity securities to make the purchase. Expectations concerning the price of A's stock are also relevant. For example, even if A has excess cash available, if its management feels that the firm's stock price is unreasonably inflated, management may prefer to use stock rather than cash (or stock rather than debt securities) in the purchase. Since what is paid in the acquisition is a matter of negotiation between A and B, the desires of the shareholders of firm B also affect the form of payment. The firm B shareholders will more likely prefer cash to firm A stock the better are the alternative investment opportunities available to the firm B shareholders and the less optimistic are the firm B shareholders about the future trend in the price of firm *A* stock. Taxes also affect the choice of form of payment in an acquisition. This is discussed next.

Tax Considerations

The taxes of the buyer and the seller in an acquisition depend on whether the acquisition is taxable or tax-free. Although the tax laws are quite complex, the primary condition that must be met for an acquisition to be tax-free is that a major part (how much depends on whether stock or assets are acquired and on other details) of the payment by buyer *A* to seller *B* be in the form of voting stock (common or preferred) of firm *A*. This is so whether the acquisition is an asset purchase, a purchase of stock, or a formal merger. If the acquisition is not tax-free, it is taxable.

Under a taxable exchange, the shareholders of selling firm *B* pay capital gains taxes (or take capital losses) on the sale just as though they had sold their shares in the stock market. Company *B* also pays corporate taxes on the difference between what is paid for the company's assets and their tax basis. Under a tax-free exchange, the firm *B* shareholders pay no taxes currently but may owe taxes in later years, and firm *B* pays very limited taxes on the exchange. The acquiring firm's taxes are also affected in that, with a taxable exchange, the tax basis (depreciated value for tax purposes) of the acquired firm's assets reflects the purchase price paid in the acquisition; with a tax-free exchange, the acquired assets have the same tax basis as before the merger.

To illustrate a taxable and a tax-free exchange assume that Bear Transportation Industries buys Honey Bus Company, Inc. Honey's physical assets are buses which were purchased by the firm in 1988 for $50 million; the buses are being depreciated on a straight-line basis over five years ($10 million per year in depreciation) and, in 1991, have a depreciated book value of $20 million. Assume that, because of inflation and good maintenance, the buses' 1991 fair market value is $40 million. In 1991 Bear buys Honey for $60 million. Assume that Honey's shareholders paid $50 million for their shares in 1987. Suppose that Honey's tax rate is 30 percent. Exhibit 23-1 shows the tax consequences of the acquisition. It is clear that, from a personal tax standpoint, there is an advantage to a tax-free exchange because the Honey shareholders can postpone the taxes on their capital gain. At the corporate tax level, there are offsetting factors, but in most cases a tax-free exchange also produces lower corporate taxes. The taxable exchange allows Bear to increase the depreciable tax basis of Honey's buses from the old basis of $20 million to the fair market value of $40 million. This means bigger depreciation deductions for Bear than under a tax-free exchange (under which the buses' depreciable basis would remain at $20 million). In most situations, however, this depreciation advantage is more than offset by the tax the acquired company must pay on the gain from the acquisition (Honey's corporate tax on the $40 million difference between the $60 million purchase price and the $20 million tax basis of Honey's assets).

The Tax Reform Act of 1986 made several significant changes in the tax law as it affects merger and acquisition activity. The most important was the repeal of the General Utilities doctrine. The General Utilities doctrine sharply limited the gain a corporation would recognize (for tax purposes) on the sale or distribution of appreciated property to its shareholders if the company were completely liquidated. A taxable exchange is deemed a complete liquidation for this purpose. Under the *new* law, in the Honey-Bear example, the $40 million difference between the purchase price and asset book value is taxable to the seller corporation, Honey. Therefore, with Honey's corporate tax rate of 30 percent, Honey must pay a corporate tax of $12 million (0.30 × $40 million) because of the taxable acquisition of Honey by Bear. In addition, the shareholders of Honey must pay a personal income tax on their gain from the transaction. So, if the Honey shareholders had paid $50 million for their shares in 1987, they have a $10 million gain ($60 million sale price less $50 million original cost) on which they must pay taxes. Under the *old* law (i.e., under the General Utilities doctrine), an acquired firm, such as Honey, would pay only limited taxes on the transaction (the tax would relate to previous depreciation taken by the acquired company and to the valuation of the acquired company's inventory), although the acquired company's shareholders would still have to pay the personal tax on their

---

EXHIBIT 23-1

Tax consequences of taxable and nontaxable acquisition

	Taxable acquisition	**Nontaxable acquisition**
1. Tax consequences for Honey shareholders	A long-term capital gain of $10 million is recognized in 1991 by Honey's shareholders.	No capital gain is recognized in 1991; the capital gain is deferred until the Honey shareholders sell their Bear stock.[a]
2. Tax consequences for Honey	Corporate tax of $12 million owed on $40 million gain	No tax owed
3. Tax consequences for Bear	The tax basis of the buses for computing Bear's depreciation is the buses' actual $40 million value; depreciation over the remaining 2-year life of the buses will be $20 million per year ($40 million/2 years).	The tax basis of the buses for computing Bear's depreciation is the buses' old basis of $20 million; depreciation over the remaining 2-year life of the buses will be $10 million per year ($20 million/2 years).

[a] If the Honey shareholders were to sell the Bear stock in 1994 for, say, $90 million, they would have a long-term capital gain of $40 million (= $90 million sales price *minus* $50 million original cost of the Honey shares).

gain ($10 million in Honey's case). The repeal of the General Utilities doctrine significantly affects the economics of mergers and makes tax-free acquisitions relatively more attractive than before.

The 1986 Tax Reform Act made two other important changes that affect acquisitions. The new law significantly limits the tax loss carryforwards of an acquired corporation (see Chapter 3 on loss carryforwards) which can be used by the acquiring firm. So, if A buys B in 1991 and B has losses from years before 1991 which it is carrying forward to 1991 and later years (to use to reduce taxes in those later years), A is more restricted under the new tax law in its ability to use these loss carryforwards against A's profits for years 1991 and thereafter. Second, under the new law a corporation cannot deduct for tax purposes any part of payments made to buy back shares from stockholders ("stock redemptions") or any of the expenses associated with that buy-back (e.g., costs associated with legal, accounting, appraisal, or investment banking services). Under the old law, the firm could deduct, in computing its corporate taxable income, both premiums paid above fair market value for stock and associated buy-back expenses. For example, if Mr. X purchased one million corporation A shares and threatened to buy up the remaining shares, A's management might buy back X's shares at a $10 per share premium (total premium = $10 million = 1 million shares × $10 per share). In return X would agree to stay away for some specified time period. Payments for stock in such situations are commonly referred to as "greenmail." Under the old tax law, the $10 million premium and other expenses could be deducted by corporation A in computing its taxable income. Theses items are no longer tax deductible.

Another relevant tax factor is the taxability of dividends received by one corporation from another corporation in which it owns stock. If firm A were to buy less than 80 percent of firm B's stock, 20 percent of any dividends paid by firm B to firm A would be included in firm A's taxable corporate income. This dividend tax at the corporate level is avoided if firm A owns 80 percent or more of firm B. This tax consideration might influence firm A in its choice between purchasing stock in firm B, purchasing firm B's assets, or effecting a formal merger with firm B.

MERGER TRENDS

During the 1960s mergers and acquisitions in this country reached an historic peak, exceeding the previous high achieved during the boom of the late 1920s. As indicated in Figure 23-1, the uptrend in business combinations from the early 1930s to the end of the 1960s (1968 was the peak year) was followed by a sharp decline and, in recent years, a recovery. The post-1968 decline resulted in large part from more vigorous antitrust law enforcement, more stringent tax laws, and poor performance by many conglomerates that had grown through merger. In addition, during the 1960s, the availability of desirable acquisition candidates declined (and their prices rose) as many of these companies were purchased. By the mid-1970s, a cautious realism emerged out of the hyperemotional enthusiasm of the 1960s and the negativity of the early

1970s. In the 1960s, firms often made acquisitions without carefully considering the ultimate consequences. The result, in many cases, was severe disappointment for the acquiring company. The largely intuitive and hasty approach is now shunned, and acquisition decisions usually follow exhaustive study. Outside experts (particularly commerical and investment banks, CPA firms, and merger specialists) are often used in the merger process. Merger evaluation and analysis will be the subject of much of this chapter.

REASONS FOR MERGER

Our analysis of investment opportunities in Chapters 8, 9, and 10 focused on investments in new assets which involved the *internal* expansion of the firm. Mergers involve the acquisition of other business entities and are referred to as *external* expansion. The primary benefits of mergers are the resulting synergies and tax savings.

Operating Advantages and Synergies

Mutual benefits produced by the merger are called **synergies**. Examples are lower costs of production, management, financing, research, and marketing. The most common economies are reductions of duplicate fixed costs of production and management, since fewer plants and smaller total managerial staff may be needed as a result of the merger. Even if the merged firms produce different products, it is often possible to reduce accounting and personnel departments and top-level managerial staffs simply by eliminating duplication and inefficiencies. Research

FIGURE 23-1

Historical trends in mergers and acquisitions by manufacturing and mining concerns. (Source: Mergers Status Review.)

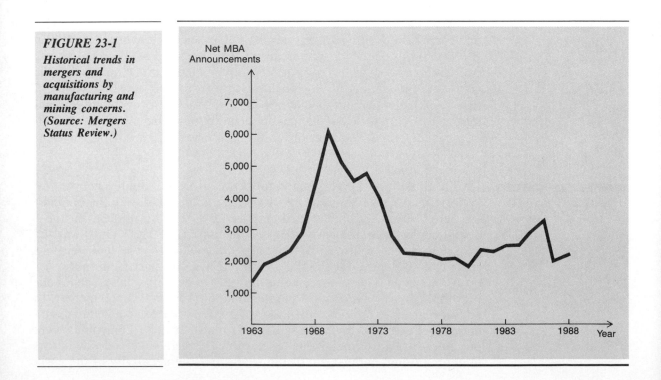

economies may also be achieved by eliminating similar research efforts and the repetition of mistakes already made by the other firm's researchers. Marketing economies may be produced through savings in advertising (by reducing the need to attract each other's customers), and also from the advantages of offering a more complete product line since a wider product line may provide larger sales per unit of sales effort and per sales person. A saving often arises from consolidating departments involved with financial activities, e.g., accounting, credit, billing, and purchasing. And, there may be significant economies of scale in acquiring capital through public offerings. Flotation costs per dollar of capital raised drop rapidly as issue amounts increase up to $10 million (see Chapter 11, Table 11-5).

Strategic pricing advantages may also accrue through the acquisition of monopolistic power or something approaching it. However, this advantage involves serious legal risks and may be short-lived because of enforcement of antitrust regulations.

The concept of synergy was the rationale used by many conglomeratiers during the 1960s to justify their ambitious expansion into many unrelated industries. The idea was that by placing many companies under a single management, a cross-fertilization of ideas and managerial expertise would result. In some cases it worked, or at least the conglomerates in question were successful. Notable examples are Textron, ITT, and MCA. But there are also casualties, including such former high fliers as Ling-Temco-Vought, Whittaker Corporation, and Memorex Corporation, all of which expanded into various unrelated fields and suffered large losses. Even Litton Industries, once the archetype of the successful conglomerate, experienced severely deflated earnings and financial difficulties in the early 1970s that necessitated a major overhaul of operations. By the 1980s, Litton had reorganized and returned to profitability. However, the days of glory were long past.

The mixed results of acquisition are also reflected in the experience of otherwise successful corporate giants that strayed into unfamiliar areas. Boise Cascade's failure in mobile home and engineering ventures, RCA's enormous losses in computers, Union Carbide's unprofitable diversification into petroleum, pharmaceuticals, and semiconductors, and Amcord's unsuccessful diversification into non-cement-related areas are prominent examples. Of course, there are also examples of unsuccessful mergers of companies within the same industry. The important point here is that in most cases the likelihood of achieving synergistic benefits from merger is enhanced if the acquiring company expands into fields with which it is familiar. Although this would appear to be good common sense, it is a principle that has often been ignored.

Tax Benefits

There are two major tax considerations favoring merger. First, the tax treatment of liquidations of stock to raise money to pay estate taxes is very generous. As a result, the heirs of a company's deceased owner often find it advantageous to sell their inherited stock in the company to another firm. The second tax consideration relates to the offsetting of profits and losses for tax purposes. With merger, the losses (or tax credits) of one company can be used to offset the profits of the other. The result is that lower total taxes are paid by the combined company. For example, if firm *A* were earning $3 million per year and firm *B* were losing $1 million per year, a merged company composed of firm *A* and firm *B* would have a net income of $2 million per year (assuming no synergies or diseconomies from the merger). Without merger, firm *A* would pay taxes on $3 million of income and firm *B* would pay no taxes; whereas with merger taxes would have to be paid only on income of $2 million.[3]

Internal versus External Growth

Instead of acquiring another company, a firm could, of course, attempt to build the operation from scratch through internal investment.[4] But, sometimes external expansion (merger) has special advantages. Expansion is more rapid if an existing firm is purchased. In some cases, it may be impossible to duplicate an operation, particularly if a patent or mineral right is monopolized by that company or if the product manufactured has a commanding position in its market. Even if duplication is possible, an attempt to create a similar business operation internally is usually more risky than acquiring a going concern. A newly created operation may not be able to match an existing company's performance record, or acquire similar product markets and staff. This risk element is magnified if the industry of the acquired company already has adequate capacity. Increasing that capacity through internal investment would therefore be profitable only if an existing producer were displaced, whereas a business combination would merely involve consolidating existing capacity. The latter would probably be the less risky alternative.

Keep in mind that, although acquiring an existing firm can have the advantages over internal investment noted above, the stockholders of the takeover candidate will ordinarily demand a price for their stock that reflects the company's value. For the would-be purchaser, this price

---

[3] If the firm incurring the loss can carry back its losses against past profits and thereby receive a rebate of past taxes, no gain from merging with a profitable company would accrue. Losses can also be carried forward, so that in future profitable years previous losses can be deducted from the profits, thus reducing taxable income by that earlier loss. However, the firm must wait for this carryforward benefit until it makes a profit. Furthermore, losses can be carried back only three years and forward fifteen years, implying that continuous losses over many years (e.g., due to large research outlays) may never be canceled against profits. In this case of extended losses, a merger with a currently profitable firm would be advantageous. On loss carrybacks and carryforwards, see Chapter 3.

[4] Internal investment should be contrasted with internal financing of investment, where the latter refers to the use of retained earnings (earnings not paid out as dividends) rather than externally raised funds (through the sale of new stock or through borrowing) to finance investment. On internal and external financing, see Chaps. 11 and 13.

may be high enough to negate the advantages of merger over internally generated expansion.

Portfolio Diversification: A Poor Rationale for Mergers

You remember from Chapter 6 that portfolio diversification is a way for an *investor* to reduce risk. Does it follow that a *firm* should diversify (e.g., by buying other companies) in order to provide its shareholders with less risky returns (that is, with returns from a diversified portfolio of corporate assets)? Is firm diversification *for diversification's sake alone* a good rationale for corporate merger? In general, the answer is no. The reason is that investors can do their own diversifying and there is no advantage to shareholders from companies doing their diversifying for them. An investor could buy 1 percent of firm *A*'s shares and 1 percent of firm *B*'s shares, and this would be just as good as buying 1 percent of a merged company made up of firms *A* and *B*. Merger will produce no benefits for shareholders simply as a result of firm diversification. For merger to produce benefits, there must be greater total cash flows from the merged firms, for example, as a result of operating synergies or tax savings.[5]

Two usually minor exceptions to the rule that firm diversification does not pay should be mentioned. First, a firm may be able to reduce the possibility of financial distress (that is, of not having sufficient cash to service debt) or even bankruptcy by merging with a company which has cash flows which follow a different pattern.[6] A second exception applies to stockholders who have most of their wealth invested in a single stock. For example, assume that Curly Mills has most of his savings tied up in the stock of Mills Mills Incorporated (MM Inc.). Also assume that Curly paid $2 per share for the stock and the stock is now selling for $10 per share. If Curly wants to diversify, he will have to sell his MM Inc. stock and pay capital gains taxes. However, if MM Inc. diversifies, Curley can achieve diversification without selling his stock and can thereby avoid the capital gains taxes. This kind of situation is particularly relevant to closely held family corporations.

DO MERGERS PRODUCE GAINS?

Do mergers produce gains for investors? The evidence is that the selling firm's shareholders enjoy significant gains from a merger but that the buying firm's shareholders experience no significant gains or losses

---

[5] The reader should review the Chap. 10 discussion of Company Diversification and Project Analysis on pages 437–439; the same underlying principle applies to firm asset diversification whether it is accomplished through ordinary capital investments or through merger acquisitions.

[6] For example, if High Corporation's cash flow tends to be high during booms and low during recessions and Low Corporation's cash flow tends to be low during booms and high during recessions, merging High and Low will result in a merged company with a cash flow which is more insulated from the business cycle than the cash flow of either High or Low alone.

(some studies show small average gains or losses for buyers).[7] Using different data samples, the average percentage premium above pre-merger share price paid by the buyer for the seller's stock was found by Shad to be 20 percent, by Mandelker to be 14 percent, and by Bradley and Korn to be 53 percent.[8] Premiums vary enormously and are sometimes more than 100 percent. For example, in 1981 Standard Oil Company of Ohio paid a 130 percent premium for Kennecott Corporation. Amax, Inc., *rejected* a bid from Standard Oil Company of California which involved a premium of over 100 percent, presumably because it was too low. The premium paid by Du Pont for Conoco was a "mere" 80 percent.

The moral we can draw from the above evidence is clear: it pays to be bought. This fact has not been overlooked by the investment community. The investor newsletters of the large brokerage firms regularly list companies which are potential "targets" (companies targeted for acquisition by other companies). Merger "arbitragers" speculate in stocks of firms which are likely merger candidates. And investment bankers and law firms provide advice—often on a continuing basis—to company managements who are worried that another firm might come along and offer a large premium to the company's shareholders and effect a take-over (on this, see "The Merger Game" following this chapter).

We should be careful in interpreting the finding that buyers on average neither gain nor lose significantly from a merger. First, since buyers are normally much larger than sellers, it may be that the changes in the buyer's stock price from the merger is simply not ordinarily large enough to be picked up by empirical tests. A company with shares worth $1 billion might buy another firm for $100 million and gain, or lose, $20 million as a result; but a gain or loss of $20 million is only 2 percent of the buyer's equity value, simply a small blip that is not easy to detect from available data (especially since many other factors affect the company's share price). Second, none of the merger studies takes into account the costs incurred by the acquiring company in pursuing a long-term merger program (these costs may have been incurred over many years). It might be that, if the costs were netted out, we would find that acquiring firms actually end up with net losses from their merger activities.

---

[7] See, for example, S. R. Shad, "The Financial Realities of Mergers," *Harvard Business Review* (November–December 1969) pp. 133–146; G. Mandelker, "Risk and Return: The Case of Merging Firms," *Journal of Financial Economics* (December 1974), pp. 303–335; T. C. Langetieg, "An Application of a Three-Factor Performance Index to Measure Stockholder Gains from Merger," *Journal of Financial Economics* (December 1978), pp. 365–383; P. Dodd and R. Ruback, "Tender Offers and Stockholder Returns: An Empirical Analysis," *Journal of Financial Economics* (December 1977), pp. 351–373. For an excellent collection of papers on the consequences of corporate mergers, see *Journal of Financial Economics* (April 1983).

[8] See Shad, op. cit. and Mandelker, op. cit.; and see J. W. Bradley and D. M. Korn, "Bargains in Valuation Disparities: Corporate Acquiror versus Passive Investor" *Sloan Management Review* (Winter 1979), pp. 51–64.

Given that shareholders of acquired companies on average benefit from takeovers, it is of some interest whether measures taken by a corporation to prevent a takeover hurt shareholders. Such measures are virtually always instituted at the behest of management (see the essay ''The Merger Game'' after this chapter for details on antitakeover tactics). There is some evidence that takeover defenses decrease shareholder wealth, but only if they are not ratified by shareholder vote. For example, antitakeover corporate charter amendments submitted to stockholder vote seem to reduce the price of the company's stock only insignificantly. Other maneuvers taken at the initiative of management without shareholder ratification do appear to significantly reduce share value.[9]

ANALYZING AN ACQUISITION

The shareholders of both the acquiring and the acquired firms want the merger to improve their wealth positions. Only if the long-run returns per share of common stock of the acquiring firm are improved is the merger acceptable to the buyer. Similarly, the seller is better off only if the cash or securities received in the merger are worth more than the securities surrendered. We will now examine how the price paid for an acquired firm is determined. For clarity, purchase with cash and purchase with securities will be examined separately.

Purchase with Cash

If the payment for the selling company is in cash, then the decision from the standpoint of the buyer can be handled in the same way as any new investment using the capital budgeting methods described in Chapters 8, 9, and 10. Only if the net present value of the aftertax net cash flow from the new assets is positive is the acquisition a good investment. The simplest case is that in which only the assets and not the liabilities of the selling firm are obtained. In this case, the investment in the assets [I of Eq. (8-2) of Chapter 8] for computing the acquisition's net present value is simply the cash price paid for the assets.

If the acquisition for cash also involves the assumption of the selling firm's liabilities, the present value of the seller's debt that is assumed must be added to the cost of the assets (cash paid to the seller's stockholders) to determine the initial outlay in computing NPV. The acquisition then would be acceptable to the buyer only if the present value of the future aftertax flow from the acquired firm exceeds the cash paid to the seller's stockholders plus the present value of the seller's debts that are assumed. For example, if firm A merges with firm B by paying firm B's stockholders $1 million in cash and also assumes firm B's liabilities of $500,000, the computation of the net present value of the acquisition is as

[9] See H. DeAngelo and E. Rice, ''Antitakeover Charter Amendments and Stockholder Wealth,'' *Journal of Financial Economics* (April 1983), pp. 329–360; and P. Malatesta and Ralph A. Walking, ''Poison Pill Securities: Stockholder Wealth, Profitability and Ownership Structure,'' working paper (September 1986), pp. 1–40.

shown in Exhibit 23-2. It is assumed in the example that the assets of firm *B* will generate an aftertax cash flow of $180,000 per year for twenty-five years and that the discount rate on the new investment is 10 percent.[10] Notice that the situation here is therefore identical to a capital budgeting decision in which firm *A* buys $1.5 million in assets and finances the acquisition with $500,000 of debt and $1 million in retained earnings (the firm's cash). In both cases, firm *A* ends up with firm *B*'s assets and an added debt of $500,000. The Exhibit 23-2 computation produces an NPV of $133,860, implying that the merger is profitable to firm *A*.

In determining their willingness to sell their shares for $1 million, firm *B*'s stockholders will have analyzed the anticipated future performance of firm *B* without the merger, tax effects, and other considerations discussed earlier. Only those shareholders who want the funds to spend on current consumption, or to reinvest in what they view as better opportunities than firm *B*, will be satisfied with the merger agreement. To assure that the selling firm's stockholders will approve the acquisition, the price per share offered by the acquiring firm for the selling

---

[10] This discount rate will depend upon the risk of the investment. It is assumed here for simplicity that the firm's debt-equity ratio will not be significantly changed as a consequence of the merger. On these points, see Chaps. 7 and 12.

EXHIBIT 23-2
Evaluating the purchase for cash of company B by company A

Pretax cash flow from new assets		$ 260,000
Less taxes:		
Pretax cash flow	$260,000	
Depreciation	60,000	
Taxable income................................	$200,000	
Tax (0.40 × taxable income)[a]		80,000
Aftertax cash flow		$ 180,000
Initial outlay:		
Payment to *B*'s (seller's) stockholders		$1,000,000
Assumption of *B*'s debt		500,000
Total initial outlay		$1,500,000

Applicable cost of capital adjusted for risk of the investment = 10%
NPV = $180,000 (*P/A*, 10%, 25) − initial outlay
    = (9.0770 × $180,000) − $1,500,000
    = $133,860

Conclusion: Merger is profitable since NPV = $133,860.

[a] A corporate tax rate of 40 percent is assumed.

firm's stock is often significantly above the stock's premerger market price.

In a merger in which stock is issued in payment to the selling firm's stockholders, stockholders will find the merger desirable only if the value of their shares is higher with the merger than without the merger. The number of shares that the buying firm (*A*) will issue in acquiring the selling firm (*B*) is determined as follows:

1 The acquiring firm will compare the value per share of firm *A* with and without the merger.
2 The selling firm will compare the value of firm *B* with the value of the shares that they would receive from firm *A* under the merger.
3 The managements of firms *A* and *B* will negotiate the final terms of the merger in light of *1* and *2*; the ultimate terms of the merger will reflect the relative bargaining positions of the two firms.

The fewer of *A*'s shares that *A* must pay *B*, the better off are the stockholders of *A* and the worse off are the stockholders of *B*. However, for the merger to be effected, the shareholders of both the buying firm and the selling firm will have to anticipate some benefit from the merger.

To illustrate points 1, 2, and 3 for a simple case (Exhibit 23-3), we will assume that the value of a share can be computed by applying an appropriate price-earnings ratio to its current earnings.[11] Assume that the expected annual earnings of firms *A* and *B* without merger are $200,000 and $100,000, respectively, a total of $300,000 per year. Earnings are expected to remain level in the future. With merger, the expected total annual earnings are $350,000, an increase of $50,000 per year due to the economies generated by the merger. The information missing from Exhibit 23-3 cannot be supplied until the number of firm *A*'s shares to be issued in purchasing firm *B* is determined. In Exhibit 23-4 the effects of issuing 20,000, 30,000, and 37,500 new shares of firm *A* in purchasing firm *B* are shown. With 20,000 new shares there are 70,000 postmerger firm *A* shares and *B*'s stockholders obtain two-sevenths (20,000/70,000) of the merged firm, that is, obtain shares worth $1 million ($\frac{2}{7}$ × $3.5 million postmerger firm value). The merger has no effect on firm *B*'s shareholder wealth, since the value of the firm *B* stock surren-

---

[11] The analysis applies regardless of how investors value shares. For example, if the value of a share is equal to the present value of expected future dividends (see Chapter 5), then in Exhibit 23-3 substitute "Dividends per share" for "Earnings per share" in row 3, and substitute "Price-dividend ratio" for "Price-earnings ratio" in row 5; the price-dividend ratio for the perpetuity case considered here is simply $(1/k)$, where k is the discount rate for computing the present value of the dividends and $(1/k)$ is the perpetuity factor $(P/A, k, \infty)$. Rather than expected future dividends, one could also discount expected future equity cash flow (firm cash flow minus payments to creditors) to value the firm's shares. Until recently, earnings analysis was a more popular method than discounted cash flow (or discounted dividends) for evaluating merger prospects. By the mid-1980s, however, large companies had come to rely as heavily on the discounted cash flow approach as on earnings analysis in assessing merger candidates.

EXHIBIT 23-3
Premerger and postmerger financial data

	Premerger firm A	Premerger firm B	Postmerger firm A
1. Current earnings per year	$200,000	$100,000	$350,000
2. Shares outstanding	50,000	10,000	?
3. Earnings per share [(1)/(2)]	$4	$10	?
4. Price per share	$40	$100	?
5. Price-earnings ratio [(4)/(3)]^a	10X	10X	10X
6. Value of firm [(2) × (4)]	$2,000,000	$1,000,000	$3,500,000
7. Expected annual growth rate in earnings in foreseeable future	0	0	0

^{a} The price-earnings ratio equals either [(4)/(3)] or [(6)/(1)].

dered is also $1 million. The exchange ratio in col. b is the number of new firm A shares issued (20,000) per firm B share obtained (10,000), which equals 2. Firm A's stockholders have shares worth $2.5 million after the merger and are therefore $500,000 better off as a consequence of the acquisition.[12]

If 37,500 new firm A shares were issued, firm B's shareholders would own a fraction ($\frac{375}{875}$) of the postmerger firm with a total share value of $1,500,000. Firm A's stockholders would own a fraction ($\frac{500}{875}$) of the merged company's shares and have shares worth $2 million. In this case, firm B's stockholders gain and firm A's stockholders neither gain nor lose from the combination. For any number of shares issued between 20,000 and 37,500 (e.g., 30,000), both firm A's stockholders and firm B's stockholders benefit from the merger. If less than 20,000 shares were offered to B, B's stockholders would lose in the exchange, and exactly 20,000 shares would leave B's stockholder with no gain or loss. Similarly, an offer of more than 37,500 shares of firm A's stock for firm B would result in a reduction in the wealth of firm A's stockholders, and

[12] We can compute the number of shares which makes the shareholders of A no better and no worse off (signify this number as n_A^*, where $n_A^* = 37,500$ in the example), and the number of shares which makes the shareholders of B no better and no worse off (signified n_B^*, where $n_B^* = 20,000$ in the example). Let n_A' be the number of firm A shares before the merger ($n_A' = 50,000$ in the example). n_A^* and n_B^* satisfy the following equations:

$$\begin{array}{ll} \text{Value of firm } A \\ \text{shares without merger} \end{array} = \left[\frac{n_A'}{n_A' + n_A^*} \right] \times \left[\begin{array}{l} \text{value of firm } A \\ \text{shares after the merger} \end{array} \right] \qquad \text{(a)}$$

$$\begin{array}{ll} \text{Value of firm } B \\ \text{shares without merger} \end{array} = \left[\frac{n_B^*}{n_A' + n_B^*} \right] \times \left[\begin{array}{l} \text{value of firm } A \\ \text{shares after the merger} \end{array} \right] \qquad \text{(b)}$$

where $[n_A'/(n_A' + n_A^*)]$ in (a) is the fraction of postmerger firm A owned by the A shareholders after the merger if n_A^* shares are paid; and $[n_B^*/(n_A' + n_B^*)]$ in (b) is the fraction of postmerger firm A owned by the B shareholders after the merger if n_B^* shares are paid.

exactly 37,500 shares would leave A's stockholders no better and no worse off. Since A's and B's shareholders want a gain from the merger, the final bargain must be between 20,000 and 37,500 of firm A's shares paid for firm B.

What will the ultimate bargain produce? That depends on the relative bargaining positions of firm A and firm B. If firm A has many other merger candidates of equal desirability to firm B, little more than 20,000 shares might be necessary to induce firm B to negotiate. If firms similar to B are rare and B's owners are aware of that fact, and if, in addition, many other merger-hungry firms such as A are seeking merger partners, close to 37,500 shares might be required to buy firm B. This is largely what has happened in recent years. Successful small companies are actively sought by larger firms for marriage, the result being high prices for the small companies.

The above example simplifies the problem in several respects. First, as noted earlier, the stockholders of the two firms may have differing expectations regarding the futures of the firms if left unmerged and if merged. Furthermore, earnings may be growing and not level, as in the above illustration. Thus, for example, firm A might be growing rapidly, firm B growing slowly, and the new merged firm might have an expected growth rate close to that of firm A. In this case, firm B's shareholders would be trading shares with a claim to low growth earnings for shares with rapidly increasing earnings. The greater the growth potential of the new shares of the merged company relative to the old firm B's shares, the fewer the new shares firm A needs to issue to acquire firm B. Indeed, firm B's stockholders might be willing to trade in their shares for new shares with lower *current* earnings because of the greater growth rate in earnings per share. For example, if current earnings of firm B were $100,000 and growing at 2 percent per year, the owners of firm B might be willing to trade these shares for firm A's shares providing current

---

EXHIBIT 23-4

Impact of alternative numbers of firm A's shares issued to buy firm B on the total value of shares owned by stockholders of firms A and B

Number of firm A's shares issued to firm B stockholders (a)	Exchange ratio [(a)/10,000 firm B's shares] (b)	Number of firm A's shares outstanding after merger [50,000 + (a)] (c)	Postmerger fraction of firm owned by firm B shareholders [(a)/(c)] (d)	Value of shares owned by firm B shareholders [(d) × $3.5 million] (e)	Postmerger fraction of firm owned by original firm A shareholders [50,000/(c)] (f)	Value of shares owned by firm A shareholders [(f) × $3.5 million] (g)
20,000	2	70,000	$\frac{2}{7}$	$1,000,000	$\frac{5}{7}$	$2,500,000
30,000	3	80,000	$\frac{3}{8}$	1,312,500	$\frac{5}{8}$	2,187,500
37,500	3.75	87,500	$\frac{375}{875}$	1,500,000	$\frac{500}{875}$	2,000,000

earnings of only $80,000 but a growth rate of, say, 10 percent per year. In short, future earnings are as important (usually more important) than current earnings in determining the desirability of the merger to the parties concerned.

Are the book values and liquidation values of firm B's assets, and the quantity of firm B's liquid assets, relevant in appraising firm B as an acquisition possibility? None of these factors was mentioned above. We can begin by dismissing book values entirely since they are based on historical costs and generally do not reflect real economic worth.

To obtain cash (for example, for exploiting investment opportunities), firm A can issue its own securities (debt or equity) or sell some of its assets; it can also buy a company that has excess liquid assets (that are readily converted to cash), or buy an illiquid company and either sell some of its fixed assets or issue securities against those assets. That is, there are many ways to obtain liquidity and they should be compared on the basis of overall cost and benefit. It is true that purchasing a company with surplus liquidity is a convenient way to obtain cash, but it is clearly not the only way or necessarily the cheapest way.

ACCOUNTING TREATMENT OF MERGERS

In accounting practice, a merger is recorded as a purchase or as a pooling of interests. The primary differences between the two methods are in the value placed on the assets of the purchased firm for representation on the combined entity's balance sheet and for computing depreciation for the combined firm and in the representation of the combined firms income after merger. Note that the treatment of a merger for tax purposes (taxable or nontaxable) is an issue that is separate from whether a merger is a pooling or a purchase; it is the latter topic that we discuss in this section.

Under the purchase method, the acquired assets are carried on the books at the price paid (in cash or stock) for the selling company's stock plus any liabilities of the selling company assumed by the acquiring firm. To illustrate, assume that firm A purchases firm B by paying firm B's shareholders in firm A stock worth $1,500,000 (fair market value of the stock) and assume that the purchase method of accounting is used. From the premerger balance sheet in Exhibit 23-5 note that the firm B's owners' equity is only $800,000 and therefore the acquisition involves a $700,000 premium over book value paid to firm B's owners ($1,500,000 in firm A's stock for $800,000 of equity interest). This means that firm B's assets are being valued at $700,000 more than they appear on firm B's books, that is, are valued at $1,700,000. The acquired assets are valued on the postmerger books at $1,700,000; total assets are therefore $4,700,000 for the combined company ($3 million of firm A's assets + $1,700,000). The depreciation deduction (for accounting purposes) for the merged company in forthcoming years will be computed using the $4,700,000 as the depreciation base.

Under the pooling of interests approach, the assets are valued just as they were on the acquired firm's books. The depreciation base for the combined company will consequently be $4 million. Thus, if a merger involves payment for a firm's shares in excess of their book value, a pooling of interest involves lower asset values and lower depreciation charges in future periods (and therefore higher accounting income) than does a merger accounted for as a purchase.

The second difference between purchase and pooling is that with purchase the income on the financial statements of the acquiring firm includes the income of the acquired firm only from the date of the merger, whereas with pooling the income of the acquiring firm is restated retroactively to include the income of the acquired firm in all previous periods. For example, assume that firm A buys firm B on July 1, 1992, and that A has earned $3 million per year since its beginning in 1970. B has earned $1 million per year since its beginning in 1970. With purchase, A's financial statements after the merger will show 1992 earnings of $3,500,000 ($3 million of A's earnings plus the earnings of B after the July 1, 1992 merger) and will show pre-1992 earnings of $3 million (that is, will not include any of B's earnings in the premerger years). In contrast, with pooling, the earnings of A will be stated as $4 million for all years from 1980 (when B was started) to 1992, that is, the earnings of the two firms are simply combined for all time periods. Thus, when the historical earnings of firm A are presented in firm A's financial statements after the merger, those historical earnings will appear to be larger if the merger of A and B was a pooling of interests than if the merger was a purchase.

We have assumed thus far that the price paid for the acquired firm does not include a premium above the fair market value of the acquired firm's assets if those assets were sold individually. Such a premium is commonly referred to as goodwill and arises if the acquired firm has added value from such things as a strong market position, unusually talented personnel, and so forth. Goodwill is amortized in the financial statements and therefore deducted in computing the earnings reported to

---

EXHIBIT 23-5
Premerger and postmerger balance sheets of firms A *and* B *under the purchase method and the pooling of interests method of accounting for the merger*

	Premerger balance sheets		Postmerger balance sheet of merged firm	
	Firm A	Firm B	Purchase method	Pooling of interests method
Assets (net of depreciation)	$3,000,000	$1,000,000	$4,700,000	$4,000,000
Liabilities	1,000,000	200,000	1,200,000	1,200,000
Owners' equity	2,000,000	800,000	3,500,000	2,800,000

stockholders; however, the amortized goodwill is not deductible for tax purposes. Accounting earnings will be negatively affected by the amortized goodwill with purchase accounting but not with pooling of interests accounting, since the latter records assets at book values rather than at the purchase price.

Opinion 16 of the Accounting Principles Board of the American Institute of Certified Public Accountants specifies the conditions under which a pooling of interests accounting for a merger may be used. If these conditions are not met, the merger is to be treated as a purchase. One condition that must be satisfied for the pooling of interests method to be applicable is that the owners of the acquired firm must maintain their proportionate ownership claim (with voting rights) in the surviving firm. This would occur if they received voting common stock in payment for their stock in the acquired firm, whereas it would not occur if preferred stock, bonds, or cash were exchanged for the selling firm's shares. Use of the pooling of interests approach also requires that the combined entity intends to retain most or all of the purchased assets for at least two years after the merger and that the purchase be effected in a single transaction (no payments contingent upon the firm's future performance).

SUMMARY

A holding company is a firm that controls one or more other companies (called subsidiaries) through ownership of the subsidiary firms' common stock. In this chapter we use the term "merger" to signify the combination of two or more firms into one. Mergers take many forms, including horizontal, vertical, and conglomerate combinations. A merger may result from a friendly agreement between the managements of the combining companies (with the approval of the shareholders of both companies) or may involve the unfriendly takeover of one company by another. An unfriendly takeover ordinarily entails the buyer's purchase of the seller's shares by means of a tender offer. The Federal Trade Commission, the U.S. Justice Department, and certain other government agencies can block a merger if it will reduce competition.

A company can purchase a controlling interest in another company, can buy the other company's assets, or can combine with the other company through merger. A purchase can involve payment in the form of cash or of the securities of the purchasing company. A purchase is taxable to the selling firm (or its stockholders) if payment is in cash or bonds, whereas the taxes are postponed (a nontaxable exchange) if the voting stock of the purchasing firm is used in payment. From a tax standpoint, the sellers will usually prefer a nontaxable exchange whereas the acquiring firm will usually prefer that it be taxable. The buying company prefers a taxable purchase because this generally implies a higher depreciation base (higher depreciation deductions for tax purposes) in future years. The choice between payment in voting stock or in cash or nonvoting securities may also depend upon nontax considerations, such as the availability of excess cash in the buying company's coffers, the desire for cash by the selling firm's stockholders, and the expectations regarding the future performance of the acquiring firm's stock that would be used as payment in the purchase. A merger can produce benefits in the form of production economies, tax reductions, and reduction of risk through diversification. External growth through merger can provide certain advantages over internal expansion, including greater speed, lower risk, and the ability to purchase assets only obtainable by buying another firm. Merging simply to produce a better portfolio of assets for shareholders is generally a poor policy since shareholders can do their own diversifying.

In a purchase for cash, the decision to sell will be based upon a comparison by the sellers of the cash offered for their firm with the value of the firm being sold. The purchasing firm can treat the purchase as a capital budgeting problem, purchasing the new company only if the net cash flow from the acquired enterprise has a present value exceeding the purchase price. If payment is in the form of stock of the purchasing company, although a capital budgeting approach is still valid, an easier approach is to examine earnings per share with and without the merger. For both parties to agree to the merger, the shareholders of both firms must perceive an increase in their wealth positions. Particularly if there are real benefits from the merger (for example, production economies or tax benefits), both parties can gain—that is, both can end up with stock worth more than the value without the merger.

From an accounting standpoint, a merger is treated as a purchase or as a pooling of interests. The primary differences between the two methods are in recording the value of the acquired firm's assets on the acquiring firm's balance sheet and in the representation of the combined firm's historical earnings.

QUESTIONS

1　Contrast a holding company, a merger, and a consolidation.
2　Differentiate between horizontal and vertical combinations.
3　State the steps involved in a tender offer.
4　Certain production economies can result from mergers. What are some of these economies?
5　How can a reduction in the variability (uncertainty) of firm income occur through merger?
6　Explain when one can regard a reduction in the income uncertainty or variability resulting from a merger as a good thing, that is, as a benefit of the merger. When is it not a benefit?
7　What advantages are there to external growth through merger? Disadvantages?
8　What advantages does the straight purchase of assets have over a merger?
9　From a taxation point of view the form of payment for acquired firms can be important. Explain why. If only tax conditions were important, what form of payment would the seller and the buyer prefer?
10　It has been argued that a prosperous firm can acquire firms with operating losses and thereby incur a tax savings. Explain how this can come about.

PROJECT

Find an example of a tender offer being advertised in *The Wall Street Journal*. If you owned 100 shares of stock of the firm for which the tender offer is being made, would you be willing to tender your shares? You should analyze the offer carefully before making your decision (see Appendix 5A on sources of information about the firm involved).

DEMONSTRATION PROBLEMS

DP1 Melody Dance Studios is contemplating the acquisition of Grange Theaters. Melody can acquire Grange Theaters for $7 million but must pay off Grange's $4 million in liabilities. The pretax cash flow from Grange Theaters is estimated at $2 million a year for twenty years. The $7 million in Grange Theaters' assets are to be depreciated over twenty years on a straight-line basis (with no salvage value). At the end of the 20 years Melody expects to sell Grange Theaters for an aftertax price of $10 million. Melody is in a 40 percent tax bracket, and Grange Theaters will be operated with no debt. Investments with risk comparable to that of Grange Theaters should yield 20 percent after taxes. Determine whether the acquisition is advisable for Melody.

SOLUTION TO DP1:

Pretax cash flow		$ 2,000,000
Less taxes:		
Pretax cash flow	$2,000,000	
Depreciation	350,000	
Taxable income	1,650,000	
Taxes (.4 × taxable income)	660,000	660,000
Aftertax cash flow		$ 1,340,000
Initial cash outlay:		
Payment to Grange's stockholders		$ 7,000,000
Assumption of Grange's liabilities		$ 4,000,000
Initial outlay		$11,000,000

Applicable cost of capital adjusted for risk of the investment is 20%.

$$\text{NPV} = \$1,340,000(P/A, 20\%, 20) + \$10,000,000(P/F, 20\%, 20)$$
$$- \$11,000,000$$
$$= \$1,340,000(4.8696) + \$10,000,000(.0261) - \$11,000,000$$
$$= \$6,525,264 + \$261,000 - \$11,000,000$$
$$= -\$4,213,736$$

The merger is unprofitable.

DP2 Swindler Corporation and Solop Incorporated have decided to merge if satisfactory terms can be worked out. Swindler will issue new shares which it will pay to the Solop shareholders in exchange for their Solop shares. The boards of the two companies have decided that the number of Swindler shares to be issued shall be in the range of 100,000 to 200,000. Construct a table showing the consequences for the Solop and Swindler shareholders if 100,000, 150,000, and 200,000 shares are issued in the acquisition. Use the data below in developing your solution.

| | Without merger | | With merger |
	Swindler	Solop	
Earnings per year	$3,000,000	$1,000,000	$4,500,000
Shares outstanding	500,000	50,000	?
Earnings per share	$6	$20	?
Price per share	$60	$200	?
Price-earnings ratio	10X	10X	10X
Value of shares	$30,000,000	$10,000,000	$45,000,000

SOLUTION TO DP2:

Number of Swindler shares issued to Solop stockholders (a)	Exchange ratio [(a)/50,000 Solop shares] (b)	Number of Swindler shares outstanding after merger [500,000 + (a)] (c)	Postmerger fraction of firm owned by Solop shareholders [(a)/(c)] (d)	Value of shares owned by Solop shareholders [(d) × $45,000,000] (e)	Postmerger fraction of firm owned by original Swindler shareholders [500,000/(c)] (f)	Value of shares owned by Swindler shareholders [(f) × $22,050,000] (g)
100,000	2	600,000	1/6	$ 7,500,000	5/6	37,500,000
150,000	3	650,000	15/65	10,384,615	50/65	34,615,385
200,000	4	700,000	2/7	12,857,143	5/7	32,142,857

Earnings per share under each of the terms specified will be $7.50, $6.92, and $6.43. The price per share under each of the terms will be $75, $69.23, and $64.28. If 100,000 Swindler shares are issued, Swindler shareholders gain and Solop shareholders lose from the merger. If 150,000 or 200,000 Swindler shares are issued, both the Swindler and Solop shareholders gain from the merger.

1 What are the tax advantages of merging Camper Farms and Sandman Sleepwear, where Camper has an annual taxable income of $8 million and Sandman has an annual loss of $5 million? Assume that Camper has a 40 percent tax rate and that Sandman pays no taxes.

2 Sport Ties, Inc., is contemplating the acquisition of The National Shoe Company. Sport Ties can acquire National Shoe for $4.5 million but must pay off National Shoe's $2.6 million in liabilities. The pretax cash flow from National Shoe is estimated at $1.1 million a year for twenty years. The $4.5 million in National Shoe assets are to be depreciated over twenty years on a straight-line basis (with no salvage value). Sport Ties is in a 50 percent tax bracket, and National Shoe will be operated with no debt. Investments with risk comparable to that of National Shoe should yield 18 percent after taxes. Determine whether the acquisition is advisable for Sport Ties.

3 Gargantua Clothing is considering the acquisition of Little Annie Dress Company. Gargantua will pay $1.5 million to buy Little Annie's assets; Gargantua will assume Little Annie's liabilities of $280,000. The pretax cash flow of Little Annie is estimated at $800,000 a year for thirty-five years. The $1.5 million in assets are to be depreciated on a straight-line basis (with no salvage value). Little Annie is to be operated with no debt. Gargantua is in a 50 percent tax bracket. It estimates that investment at this level of risk should yield 16 percent. You are asked to determine whether the merger should be made. How would you do this? Show all calculations.

4 Type-It, Inc, is considering a merger with Write-It, Inc. The data below are in the hands of both boards of directors. The merger is expected to generate significant production economies and increased earnings. The issue at hand is how many Type-It shares Write-it should get. Both boards are focusing their attention on earnings per share, for this potentially affects the value of the shares to be received and given. Both boards have agreed that the number of shares to be considered should be 200,000, 400,000 and 600,000. Construct a table demonstrating the potential impact of each scheme on each set of shareholders.

	Without merger		With merger
	Type-It	**Write-It**	
Earnings per year	$5,000,000	$1,500,000	$7,350,000
Shares outstanding	300,000	100,000	?
Earnings per share	$16.67	$15	?
Price per share	$50	$45	?
Price-earnings ratio	3X	3X	3X
Value of firm	$15,000,000	$4,500,000	$22,050,000

5 Scratch Fur is considering a merger with Trap, Inc. The data below are in the hands of both boards of directors. The issue at hand is how many shares of Scratch should be exchanged for Trap. Both boards are considering three possibilities: 20,000, 25,000, and 30,000 shares. Construct a table demonstrating the potential impact of each scheme on each set of shareholders.

	Scratch	Trap	Combined
Current earnings per year	$150,000	$90,000	$312,500
Shares outstanding	60,000	$200,000	?
Earnings per share	$2.50	$.45	?
Price per share	$20	$3.60	?
Price-earnings ratio	8X	8X	8X
Value of firm	$1,200,000	$720,000	$2,500,000

6 Firm *A* acquires firm *B* for $60 million in stock and the assumption of $50 million in liabilities. The acquired assets have a book value of $80 million. The premerger balance sheet of the two firms are set forth below. Demonstrate how the balance sheet of the combined firm will look under both the purchase method and the pooling of interests method of accounting.

	Firm *A*	Firm *B*
Assets	$150,000,000	$80,000,000
Liabilities	$95,000,000	$50,000,000
Owners' equity	$55,000,000	$30,000,000

The ▪ symbol indicates that all or a significant part of the problem can be solved using the *Computer Models* software package that accompanies this text.

It's a rare week that the financial press does not report the details of at least one corporate courtship turned sour, with one company desperately fleeing the unwanted attentions of the other. This essay describes some of the tactics, and some of the tacticians, involved in this popular drama. We begin by describing three especially interesting business takeovers: the RJR Nabisco takeover, the Du Pont takeover of Conoco, and Texaco's purchase of Penzoil.

THE RJR NABISCO TAKEOVER

On October 20, 1988, F. Ross Johnson, CEO of RJR Nabisco, and his financial backer, Shearson Lehman Hutton, presented their offer to purchase all RJR stock for $17.3 billion, a $75 per share bid that was roughly 45 percent above the price at which RJR stock was trading at the time. Within four days, on October 24, Kohlberg Kravis Roberts & Company (KKR) entered the contest with a bid of $20.7 billion. Efforts by Johnson and KKR to develop a joint proposal failed, and others entered the bidding, topped by an offer from First Boston worth $27.1 billion. On November 20, the RJR board announced a new deadline for final offers. In the end, on November 30, KKR won the auction when the RJR board accepted its $25.1 billion offer over another with roughly the same value made by Johnson. KKR successfully defended its position as the leader in the LBO game by negotiating the largest business takeover in history.

The RJR leveraged buyout drew comments of various sorts from skeptical observers. Some were very critical of F. Ross Johnson for initially offering what turned out to be much less than the company's equity value. If Johnson was the company's CEO and presumably representing shareholders, why did he try to buy them out at a bargain price? In his own defense, Johnson argues that the price he offered was well above the stock's market price at the time. Critics also question the heavy borrowing by KKR in its purchase of RJR Nabisco. After the LBO, RJR Nabisco had roughly $23 billion of debt and, according to Henry Kravis (one of the principal partners of KKR), about $7 billion in equity value. Kravis asserts that this debt to equity ratio of 3 to 1 is actually quite low for a leveraged buyout. (It is true that LBOs typically involve debt-equity ratios of 10 or 12 to 1.) Soon after the LBO was completed it appeared that the takeover was successful and that the new RJR Nabisco—now a private company—would be able to service its debt. However, the track record was still very short and was established during a period of general expansion of the U.S. economy. Time will tell whether KKR's victory in the bidding for RJR Nabisco was actually a success for KKR or good fortune for F. Ross Johnson.

THE DU PONT-CONOCO MERGER

It didn't appear at the time to be an especially noteworthy occasion. Dome Petroleum's chairman, John Gallagher and its president, William Richards, had come to see Conoco's chairman, Ralph E. Bailey, to discuss the possible acquisition by Dome of certain Conoco properties in Canada. Dome's proposal was for it to purchase 20 percent of Conoco's stock in a public tender offer and then surrender the stock to Conoco in exchange for the Canadian properties. Bailey listened but was noncommittal. Somehow, Gallagher misunderstood and thought that he had the go-ahead. About a week after the meeting, on May 5, 1981, Dome made its tender offer for 20 percent of the Conoco shares at $65 per share, about $15 more than the price Conoco shares had been trading at in recent weeks. The response of the stockholders was more than Dome had anticipated. Banks, pension funds, and other institutions held a majority of Conoco stock and were eager to sell not just 20 percent, but 51 percent—control of Conoco—to Dome at the $65 tender price. Although Conoco had huge oil, gas, and coal holdings, estimated by some to be worth $160 per share, Conoco had been having trouble with the United Mine Workers and had worrisome exposure because it held large reserves in Libya. Nevertheless, $65 per share was a bargain price for a controlling interest in Conoco. At least that was the view of Edgar Bronfman, Chairman of Seagram, which had recently been outbid by Fluor Corporation in an attempt to buy St. Joe Minerals. On May 31, Bronfman met with the Conoco board and proposed that Seagram buy for cash, at $70 to $75 per share, 35 percent of Conoco. Bronfman even agreed to a "standstill agreement" under which Seagram would vote with management for the next fifteen years. But the Conoco board was not satisfied with this proposal, since after the fifteen-year pact expired Seagram could effectively control the company. The discussions reached an impasse and Bronfman left. Meanwhile, on another floor at Conoco headquarters, Dome was negotiating with Conoco an exchange of $245 million in cash plus the 2 million shares of Conoco it had bought through its tender offer in return for

Conoco's Canadian oil and gas properties.

At this point, Conoco was not sure what Seagram would do next. As a precaution Conoco asked investment bank Morgan Stanley to prepare a list of potential "white knights" which might be interested in merging with Conoco should Seagram decide to attempt a takeover. Over the coming weeks, Du Pont's chairman, Edward Jefferson, heard about the goings-on at Conoco and on June 24 called Bailey to inquire about the matter. The next day, on June 25, Seagram made a tender offer for 41 percent of Conoco's stock at $73 per share. Shearson Loeb Rhoades and Lazard Frères were now serving as Seagram's investment bankers. After the Seagram tender offer, Mobil and Texaco called Bailey. Bailey spurned the Mobil advances. The Conoco board also decided against the Texaco offer of $85 per share in cash because of potential antitrust problems. Bailey then called Du Pont's Jefferson to propose a merger. Du Pont accepted, but only on the condition that it could buy 16 million shares from Conoco's treasury for $87.50 a share before making a public tender offer. On July 6, Du Pont made its offer for all of Conoco's outstanding shares: $87.50 for the first 40 percent of the stock and 1.6 Du Pont shares per Conoco share for the remaining Conoco shares.

On July 12, Seagram counterattacked by raising its bid to $85 per share for 51 percent of Conoco's stock. Du Pont responded by increasing its offer to $95 per share for the first 40 percent of the stock and 1.7 shares of Du Pont shares per share of Conoco for the rest of the stock. On July 16 a new player entered the game: Mobil announced it would pay $90 a share for the first 50 percent of Conoco and Mobil securities worth $90 per share for the remainder.

Over the next three weeks, Du

Pont, Seagram, and Mobil increased their offers in a bidding war which ended on August 5 with Du Pont's victory. In the end, Seagram acquired 28 million Conoco shares which it exchanged for 47.5 million new Du Pont shares. Seagram thus became the largest single Du Pont stockholder, with 20.1 percent of the stock (the Du Pont family and trusts own approximately 19.8 percent).

After the merger, the total market value of Du Pont stock was about $11 billion. The merger had created a new energy-chemical giant. Du Pont now had a guaranteed source of petroleum and ownership of the nation's largest single coal reserve; in 1981 Conoco's proven United States reserves were 403 million barrels of oil, 2.7 trillion cubic feet of natural gas, and 14 billion tons of coal. In exchange for Conoco, the Conoco shareholders (including Seagram) received cash and Du Pont stock worth nearly $7.5 billion.

THE TEXACO-PENZOIL CASE

Mergers can be full of surprises, as Texaco found out after acquiring Getty Oil for $10.1 billion. In January 1984, officials of Penzoil and Getty Oil verbally agreed in principle that Penzoil would acquire Getty for $112.50 per share. Shortly thereafter Texaco offered Getty $128 a share. Getty promptly jilted Penzoil and agreed to the match with Texaco. Penzoil responded with a lawsuit against Texaco for $7.53 billion in damages, arguing that it would have to spend at least that much to replace the oil and gas reserves it hoped to acquire with Getty. A sympathetic jury decided that Penzoil and Getty had a binding contract and awarded Penzoil the $7.53 billion plus an additional $3 billion in punitive damages—the largest legal judgement in U.S. history. The $10.53 billion award exceeded the entire market value of Texaco's stock. After attempts by Penzoil and Texaco to arrange an out-of-court settlement failed, in April 1987 Texaco filed for bankruptcy under Chapter 11 of the Federal Bankruptcy Code. In December, 1987, after the shuttle diplomacy of financier and Texaco stockholder Carl Icahn, Texaco agreed to pay Penzoil $3 billion to settle the suit. The agreement allowed Texaco to emerge from bankruptcy and begin its recovery.

KNOWING HOW TO SAY NO IMPOLITELY

If an acquiror has sufficient resources and determination, it can at some price induce the shareholders of a target firm to sell out. But without the cooperation of the target firm's management—cooperation that is often absent—the target may carry too high a price tag to be acceptable to the potential acquiror. The acquiror has several methods for attempting to purchase another company: peaceful negotiation with the other company's management, a proxy fight, or a purchase of the target firm's shares (in the open market or through a tender offer). If the peaceful approach doesn't work, the most common takeover tactic is to simply sidestep the target's management and try to buy its shares.

The target's management may resist a merger because it feels the offer is inadequate, that the combination does not make good business sense, that the target's management will be replaced if the takeover succeeds, or for some other reason. In these situations, the acquisition attempt is regarded as hostile—the result often being a furious attempt by the target's management to protect its "sleeping beauty" from the grasp of the attacking "black knight." Many companies keep "black books" listing defense tactics known in the trade as "shark repellent." In addition to simply appealing to the company's shareholders not to sell their shares to the shark, there are numerous defensive weapons available to the target's management.

One technique to repel an attacker is to find a "white knight," another merger partner that will pay a higher price, provide a better operating fit, or offer a more attractive future to management than is expected if the black knight succeeds. Du Pont was a white knight for Conoco, which was battling it out against black knights Seagram and Mobil. A variation of the white knight stratagem is the "lockup." The lockup involves the target's selling stock or a part of the company to a friendly buyer, thereby making a takeover either less attractive or more difficult. For example, Pullman, Inc. granted options to Wheelabrator-Frye Inc., to purchase parts of Pullman's operations. This reinforced Pullman in its attempts to ward off McDermott, Inc. A special breed of lockup was attempted by Continental Airlines when, to thwart a hostile takeover attempt by Texas International Airlines, it proposed to give its employees a 51 percent ownership of Continental by issuing new shares and in effect selling the shares to its employees under an employee stock ownership plan (ESOP). Although the plan never materialized, it was interesting testimony to the ingenuity of human beings under siege.

Still another tactic was used by St. Joe Minerals Corporation to block a $45 per share bid by Seagram. St. Joe's management threatened to liquidate the company (sell off its assets and distribute the proceeds to its shareholders). The issue was ultimately resolved when Fluor Corporation bought St. Joe for $60 per share, more than Seagram was willing to pay.

Legal ploys are common defenses. The target firm can take the attacker to court so as either to delay or block the merger, an approach used, for example, by Conoco against Seagram, McGraw-Hill against American Express, and Continental Airlines against Texas International Airlines. A farsighted management may adopt another tack: to change the rules of the game by encouraging shareholders to amend the corporate charter so that a very large majority of shares (e.g., 80 percent) is needed to approve a merger.

Another legal stratagem is the "poison pill," a deterrent to potential acquirors which becomes effective if a takeover is attempted or succeeds. For example, the corporate charter might be amended to include a provision that the company buy back (redeem) at a high specified price the shares of the minority shareholders who do not sell their shares to an acquiring firm. The idea here is that paying off the minority shareholders could wipe out a major portion of the company's assets, making it an unattractive acquisition. Another poison pill would involve according to the company's shareholders the right to buy shares in an acquiring company at a significant discount from market price, if a hostile takeover were to succeed.

One way to avoid being acquired is to beome an acquiror. There are several variants of this approach. One is to simply buy other firms, financing the purchases with new stock. Expanding the size of the company and the number of shares makes it more costly and more difficult for another firm to obtain control. An extra edge is gained if, in purchasing other companies, the target makes an acquisition that might result in antitrust action if the hostile acquiror were to succeed in effecting the merger. The target company can also buy back its own shares from the firm attempting the takeover. The payment for the stock (often referred to as "greenmail") virtually always produces a large profit for the firm selling back the target's shares. Under the buy-back agreement, the aggressor agrees to cease from any further takeover attempts for some period (say 10 years). The largest "greenmail" payment to date was the 1984 repurchase by Texaco of 9.9% of its stock from the Bass Brothers (Texas Oil folks) for $1.28 billion. Other major buy-backs were Walt Disney's 1984 purchase of 11.1% of its stock from Saul Steinberg for $325.5 million, Gulf and Western's 1983 acquisition of 9.4% of its stock from Carl Lindner for $210.1 million, and Warner Communications 1984 buy-back of 8.6% of its stock from Rupert Murdoch for $181.6 million. Many critics have argued, with good justification, that "greenmail" is the target management's way to prevent a takeover that may jeopardize the management's jobs. The target's shareholders, of course, foot the bill.

The heated struggle between Curtiss-Wright, the aerospace conglomerate, and Kennecott Corporation, the nation's largest copper company, illustrates two other aggressive defense tactics: the target making a target out of the aggressor, and the countertender offer for one's own shares. A couple of years after losing a 1978 proxy fight to take over Kennecott, Curtiss-Wright announced that it was going to increase its stock holdings in Kennecott from 14.3 percent to 25 percent. Kennecott management began to fear a takeover attempt by Curtiss-Wright. They decided on a preemptive strike: a Kennecott takeover of Curtiss-Wright. The copper company offered $40 per share for Curtiss-Wright, nearly twice the then going price. In response, Curtiss-Wright made a $44 (and then a $46) counteroffer for its

own stock, thereby blocking Kennecott. Kennecott then started buying Curtiss-Wright stock in the open market and eventually accumulated 32 percent of the company's shares. In the end, in early 1981, Kennecott and Curtiss-Wright negotiated a truce which included Kennecott's exchanging the Curtiss-Wright shares it held for the Kennecott shares held by Curtiss-Wright. Shortly thereafter, in 1981, Standard Oil of Ohio bought Kennecott for $2 billion.

Many managements have arrived at the same conclusion: If you can't save the ship, at least save the captain. This idea has spawned a rash of bailout agreements between companies and their managements to protect top officers from the unpleasantness of a takeover by another company. For example, Conoco chairman Ralph Bailey was guaranteed his salary through April 1, 1989—a perc worth $3.5 million. Wetterau Inc., a St. Louis food company, agreed to grant huge cash payments to sixteen executives—including $1.25 million to its chairman—if the company were unwillingly acquired. Needless to say, this type of "golden parachute" arrangement has become highly controversial. Indeed, under a new tax provision enacted in 1984, if the parachute payment is more than three times the executive's annual compensation during his or her last five years of employment, a large tax penalty is imposed on the executive receiving the payment and on the company making the payment. In spite of this, not only has the number of golden parachutes grown since the enactment of the tax penalty, but their size and scope have increased. For example, the 1986 merger of General Electric and RCA will result in "golden pond" payments of $33.3 million to 62 of RCA's top executives.

THE MERGER BROKERS

Companies looking for a merger partner or trying to defend themselves against hostile takeovers often turn to specialists—investment bankers, lawyers, accountants, proxy solicitors, and public relations firms. Expert advice does not come cheap. Four months of legal and strategic battling was involved in the successful 1980 effort by Pullman Inc. to fight off McDermott Inc., and instead be acquired by Wheelabrator-Frye Inc., for $646 million. The total fees to investment bankers, lawyers, accountants, and others paid by the three companies was $17 million. First Boston alone collected $6 million. The $13.4 billion purchase of Gulf by Socal produced $63 million in fees to investment bankers ($46.5 million to Salomon Brothers and Merrill Lynch for advising Gulf Oil, and $16.5 million to Morgan Stanley for helping Socal). In the $7.5 billion Du Pont-Conoco merger, First Boston (which advised Du Pont) and Morgan Stanley (which advised Conoco) each received approximately $15 million.

Failure to consummate the transaction does not derail the gravy train. Forest products company Mead Corporation successfully fought a nine-month battle to prevent its takeover by Occidental Petroleum. The fight cost the two firms $15 million.

Ordinarily the investment bankers' fee is the largest professional expense in a major takeover. In a transaction involving several hundred million dollars, investment bankers advising the buyer will customarily receive $1.5 million to $3 million. Sometimes the fee is tied to the success of the offer. When Phillip Morris paid $515.5 million for 7-Up ($47 per share), Lehman Bros. received $1.9 million in fees instead of the $3,150,000 that it would have received if the purchase had been at the earlier tender offer price of $41 per share.

The seller's investment banker usually earns a percentage of the purchase price, roughly in the neighborhood of one-half percent, although this can vary from 0.1 percent for billion-dollar deals to well over 1 percent for transactions under $100 million. The fee is likely to be higher for hostile takeovers than for peaceful ones. First Boston's $6 million fee in the Pullman-Wheelabrator merger was about 1 percent of the purchase price. A common guideline on small deals is the 5–4–3–2–1 formula, under which the merger specialist gets a 5 percent commission on the first $1 million of the merger's cost, 4 percent on the second million, and so on.

Are the professionals who provide the advice and counsel worth the cost? Although in some cases companies have partially supplanted the services of investment bankers with those of the somewhat less expensive financial consulting firms, it is almost certain that as long as there are mergers—especially of the hostile variety—the services of bankers and lawyers will be in demand.

SUGGESTED READINGS

CHAPTER 1

Anthony, Robert N., "The Trouble with Profit Maximization," *Harvard Business Review,* 38 (November–December 1960), pp. 126–134.
Donaldson, Gordon, "Financial Goals: Management vs. Stockholders," *Harvard Business Review,* 41 (May–June 1963), pp. 116–129.
Geneen, Harold S., "Why Directors Can't Protect the Shareholders," *Fortune,* 110 (September 17, 1984), pp. 28–32.
Gitman, Lawrence, and Charles E. Maxwell, "Financial Activities of Major U.S. Firms," *Financial Management,* 14 (Winter 1985), pp. 57–65.
Jensen, M. C., and W. H. Meckling, "Can the Corporation Survive?" *Financial Analysts Journal* (January–February 1978), pp. 31–37.
Sherman, Stratford P., "Pushing Corporate Boards to Be Better," *Fortune* (July 18, 1988), pp. 58–67.

CHAPTER 2

Friedman, Milton, "Factors Affecting the Level of Interest Rates," *Proceedings of the Conference on Savings and Residential Financing* (U.S. Savings and Loan League, 1968), pp. 11–27.
Instruments of the Money Market, 5th ed., Federal Reserve Bank of Richmond, 1981.
Seligman, Daniel, "Why Americans Don't Save Enough," *Fortune,* 109 (April 2, 1984), pp. 26–36.
"Signals from the Future: The Emerging Financial Services Industry," *Economic Review,* Federal Reserve Bank of Atlanta, 68 (September 1983), pp. 20–32.
Sivesind, Charles M., "Mortgage-Backed Securities: The Revolution in Real Estate Finance," *Quarterly Review,* Federal Reserve Bank of New York, 4 (Autumn 1979), pp. 1–10.
Van Horne, James C., *Financial Market Rates and Flows,* 2d ed. (Englewood Cliffs, NJ: Prentice-Hall, 1984), pp. 79–102.

CHAPTER 3

Aharony, Joseph, Charles P. Jones, and Itzhak Swary, "An Analysis of Risk and Return Characteristics of Corporate Bankruptcy Using Market Data," *Journal of Finance,* 35 (September 1980), pp. 1001–1016.
Altman, Edward I., "Corporate Bankruptcy Potential, Stockholder Returns, and Share Valuation," *Journal of Finance,* 24 (December 1969), pp. 887–900.
Farrell, Kevin, "The Small Pay More," *Venture* (August 1984), pp. 58–62.
Gehan, Raymond F., "How the Accelerated Cost Recovery System Affects Property," *Financial Executive,* 50 (March 1982), pp. 12–15.

842

SUGGESTED READINGS

Gordon, Myron, ''Toward a Theory of Financial Distress,'' *Journal of Finance,* 26 (May 1971), pp. 347–356.
Hoeber, Ralph C., et al., *Contemporary Business Law,* 2d ed. (New York: McGraw-Hill, 1982), chaps. 39–42.

CHAPTER 4

Grant, Eugene L., et al., *Principles of Engineering Economy,* 8th ed. (New York: John Wiley & Sons, 1990).

CHAPTER 5

Bauman, W. Scott, ''Investment Returns and Present Values,'' *Financial Management,* 27 (September–October 1971), pp. 107–118.
Fisher, Thomas R., and William E. Fruhan, ''Is Your Stock Worth Its Price?'' *Harvard Business Review,* 59 (May–June 1981), pp. 124–132.
Van Horne, James C., *Financial Market Rates and Flows,* 2d ed. (Englewood Cliffs, NJ: Prentice-Hall), pp. 103-133.

CHAPTER 6

Malkiel, Burton G., *A Random Walk Down Wall Street,* 4th ed. (New York: W. W. Norton, 1985).
Modigliani, Franco, and Gerald A. Pogue, ''An Introduction to Risk and Return: Concepts and Evidence, Part I,'' *Financial Analysts Journal,* 30 (March–April 1974), pp. 68–80.
Mullins, David W., Jr., ''Does the Capital Asset Pricing Model Work?'' *Harvard Business Review,* 60 (January–February 1982), pp. 105–114.

CHAPTER 7

Brennan, Michael J., ''A New Look at the Weighted Average Cost of Capital,'' *Journal of Business Finance,* 5 (Spring 1973), pp. 24–30.
Gitman, Lawrence J., and Vincent A. Mercurio, ''Cost of Capital Techniques Used by Major U.S. Firms: Survey and Analysis of Fortune's 1000,'' *Financial Management,* 11 (Winter 1982), pp. 21–29.
Solomon, Ezra, ''Measuring a Company's Cost of Capital,'' *Journal of Business,* 28 (October 1955), pp. 240–252.

CHAPTER 8

Corr, Arthur V., ''Capital Investment Planning,'' *Financial Executive,* 50 (April 1982), pp. 12–15.
Lewellen, Wilbur G., H. P. Lanser, and J. J. McConnell, ''Payback Substitutes for Discounted Cash Flow,'' *Financial Management,* 2 (Summer 1973), pp. 17–25.
Ross, Marc, ''Capital Budgeting Practices of Twelve Large Manufacturers,'' *Financial Management,* 15 (Winter 1986), pp. 15–22.
Woods, John C., and Maury R. Randall, ''The Net Present Value of Future Investment Opportunities: Its Impact on Shareholder Wealth and Implications for Capital Budgeting Theory,'' *Financial Management,* 18 (Summer 1989), pp. 85–92.

CHAPTER 9

Anderson, Gerald L., ''International Project Financing,'' *Financial Executive,* 45 (May 1977), pp. 40–45.
Fogler, H. Russell, ''Ranking Technique and Capital Rationing,'' *Accounting Review,* 47 (January 1972), pp. 134–143.
Hendricks, James A., ''Capital Budgeting Practices Including Inflation Adjustments: A Survey,'' *Managerial Planning* (January–February 1983), pp. 22–28.
Oblak, David J., and Roy J. Helm, Jr., ''Survey and Analysis of Capital Budgeting Methods Used by Multinationals,'' *Financial Management,* 9 (Winter 1980) pp. 37–41.

Rappaport, Alfred, and Robert A. Taggart, Jr., "Evaluation of Capital Expenditure Proposals under Inflation," *Financial Management,* 11 (Spring 1982), pp. 5–13.

Rummel, R. J., and David A. Heenan, "How Multinationals Analyze Political Risk," *Harvard Business Review,* 56 (January–February 1978), pp. 67–76.

Shapiro, Alan C., "Capital Budgeting for the Multinational Corporation," *Financial Management,* 7 (Spring 1978), pp. 7–16.

CHAPTER 10

Harris, Robert S., Thomas J. O'Brien, and Doug Wakeman, "Divisional Cost-of-Capital Estimation for Multi-Industry Firms," *Financial Management,* 18 (Summer 1989), pp. 74–84.

Hertz, David B., "Risk Analysis in Capital Investment," *Harvard Business Review,* 42 (January–February 1964), pp. 95–106.

———, "Investment Policies That Pay Off," *Harvard Business Review,* 46 (January–February 1968), pp. 96–108.

Lewellen, Wilbur G., and Michael S. Long, "Simulation versus Single-Value Estimates in Capital Expenditure Analysis," *Decision Sciences,* 3 (1972).

Magee, John F., "How to Use Decision Trees in Capital Investment," *Harvard Business Review,* 42 (September–October 1964), pp. 79–96.

Van Horne, James C., "An Application of the Capital Asset Pricing Model to Divisional Required Returns," *Financial Management,* 9 (Spring 1980), pp. 14–19.

Weston, J. Fred, "Investment Decisions Using the Capital Asset Pricing Model," *Financial Management,* 2 (Spring 1973), pp. 25–33.

CHAPTER 11

Arnold, Jasper H., III, "How to Negotiate a Term Loan," *Harvard Business Review,* 60 (March–April 1982), pp. 131–138.

Clemente, Holly A., "Innovative Financing," *Financial Executive,* 50 (April 1982), pp. 14-19.

Donaldson, Gordon, "In Defense of Preferred Stock," *Harvard Business Review,* 40 (July–August 1962), pp. 123–136.

Finnerty, John D., "Financial Engineering in Corporate Finance: An Overview," *Financial Management,* 17 (Winter 1988), pp. 14–33.

Furst, Richard W., "Does Listing Increase the Market Price of Common Stocks?" *Journal of Business,* 43 (April 1970), pp. 174–180.

Marks, Kenneth R., and Warren A. Law, "Hedging Against Inflation with Floating-Rate Notes," *Harvard Business Review,* 58 (March–April 1980), pp. 106–112.

Militello, Frederick C., Jr., "Swap Financing," *Financial Executive* (October 1984), pp. 34–39.

Rosenberg, M., and A. Young, "Firm Repurchasing Stock: Financial, Security Market, and Operating Characteristics," *University of Michigan Business Review* (May 1978), pp. 17–22.

Smith, Clifford W., Jr., "Raising Capital: Theory and Evidence," *Midland Corporate Finance Journal,* 4 (Spring 1986), pp. 6–22.

Winger, Bernard J., C. R. Chen, J. D. Martin, J. W. Petty, and S. L. Hayden, "Adjustable Rate Preferred Stock," *Financial Management,* 15 (Spring 1986), pp. 48–57.

CHAPTER 12

Marsh, Paul, "The Choice Between Equity and Debt: An Empirical Study," *Journal of Finance,* 37 (March 1982), pp. 121–144.

Myers, Stewart C., "The Capital Structure Puzzle," *Journal of Finance,* 39 (July 1984), pp. 575–592.

Scott, David F., Jr., and D. J. Johnson, "Financing Policies and Practices in Large Corporations," *Financial Management* (Summer 1982), pp. 51–59.

Scott, David F., Jr., and John D. Martin, "Industry Influence on Financial Structure," *Financial Management,* 4 (Spring 1975), pp. 67–73.

Sihler, William W., "Framework for Financial Decisions," *Harvard Business Review,* 49 (March–April 1971), pp. 123–125.

Weston, J. Fred, "What MM Have Wrought," *Financial Management,* 18 (Summer 1989), pp. 29–38.

CHAPTER 13

Asquith, Paul, and David W. Mullins, Jr., "Signalling with Dividends, Stock Repurchases, and Equity Issues," *Financial Management,* 15 (Autumn 1986), pp. 27–44.

Baker, H. Kent, G. E. Farrelly, and R. B. Edelman, "A Survey of Management Views on Dividend Policy," *Financial Management,* 14 (Autumn 1985), pp. 78–84.

Black, Fisher, "The Dividend Puzzle," *Journal of Portfolio Management,* 2 (Winter 1976).

Eiseman, Peter C., and Edward A. Moses, "Stock Dividends: Management's View," *Financial Analysts Journal,* 34 (July–August 1978), pp. 77–80.

Haugen, Robert A., and Lemma W. Senbet, "Corporate Finance and Taxes: A Review," *Financial Management,* 15 (Autumn 1986), pp. 5–21.

Higgins, Robert C., "The Corporate Dividend-Savings Decision," *Journal of Financial and Quantitative Analysis,* 7 (March 1972), pp. 1527–1541.

Soter, Dennis S., "The Dividend Controversy—What It Means for Corporate Policy," *Financial Executive,* 47 (May 1979), pp. 38–43.

Wansley, James W., William R. Lane, and Salil Sarkar, "Managements' View on Share Repurchase and Tender Offer Premiums," *Financial Management,* 18 (Autumn 1989), pp. 97–110.

West, Richard R., and Alan B. Brouilette, "Reverse Stock Splits," *Financial Executive,* 38 (January 1970), pp. 12–17.

CHAPTER 14

Altman, Edward I., "Financial Ratios, Discriminant Analysis, and the Prediction of Corporate Bankruptcy," *Journal of Finance,* 23 (September 1968), pp. 589–609.

Beaver, William, "Financial Ratios as Predictors of Failure," *Empirical Research in Accounting: Selected Studies, 1966* (Institute of Professional Accounting, January 1967), pp. 71–111.

Dambolena, Ismael G., and Sarkis J. Khoury, "Ratio Stability and Corporate Failure," *Journal of Finance,* 35 (September 1980), pp. 1017–1026.

Helfert, Erich A., *Techniques of Financial Analysis,* 5th ed. (Homewood, IL: R. D. Irwin, 1982), chaps. 1–2.

Largay, James A., III, and Clyde P. Stickney, "Cash Flows, Ratio Analysis, and the W. T. Grant Company Bankruptcy," *Financial Analysts Journal,* 36 (July–August 1980), pp. 51–54.

CHAPTER 15

Heath, Loyd C., "Let's Scrap the Funds Statement," *The Journal of Accountancy* (October 1978), pp. 94–103.

Kelvie, William E., and John M. Sinclair, "New Techniques for Break-Even Charts," *Financial Executive,* 36 (June 1968), pp. 31–43.

Packer, Stephen B., "Flow of Funds Analysis—Its Uses and Limitations," *Financial Analysts Journal,* 20 (July–August 1964), pp. 117–123.

Raun, D. L., "The Limitations of Profit Graphs, Break-Even Analysis, and Budgets," *Accounting Review,* 39 (October 1964), pp. 927–945.

CHAPTER 16

Chambers, John C., et al., "How to Choose the Right Forecasting Technique," *Harvard Business Review,* 49 (July–August 1971), pp. 45–74.

Georgoff, David M., and Robert G. Murdick, "Manager's Guide to Forecasting," *Harvard Business Review,* 86 (January–February 1986), pp. 110–120.

Parker, George C., and Edilberto L. Segura, "How to Get a Better Forecast," *Harvard Business Review,* 49 (March–April 1971), pp. 99–109.

Preston, Gerald R., "Considerations in Long-Range Planning," *Financial Executive,* 36 (May 1968), pp. 44–49.

Wheelwright, Steven C., and Daniel G. Clarke, "Corporate Forecasting: Promise and Reality," *Harvard Business Review,* 54 (November–December 1976), pp. 40–68.

CHAPTER 17

Carpenter, Michael D., and Jack E. Miller, "A Reliable Framework for Monitoring Accounts Receivable," *Financial Management,* 8 (Winter 1979), pp. 37–41.

Schiff, Michael, "Credit and Inventory Management—Separate or Together," *Financial Executive,* 40 (November 1972), pp. 28–33.

Snyder, Arthur, "Principles of Inventory Management," *Financial Executive,* 32 (April 1964), pp. 13–21.

CHAPTER 18

Cohen, Allen M., "Treasury Terminal Systems and Cash Management Information Support," *Journal of Cash Management,* 3 (August–September 1983), pp. 9–18.

Gitman, Lawrence J., Edward A. Moses, and I. Thomas White, "An Assessment of Corporate Cash Management Practices," *Financial Management,* 8 (Spring 1979), pp. 32–41.

Kamath, Rawindra, S. Khaksari, H. H. Meier, and J. Winklepeck, "Management of Excess Cash: Practices and Developments," *Financial Management,* 14 (Autumn 1985), pp. 70–77.

Reed, Ward L., Jr., "Profits from Better Cash Management," *Financial Executive,* 40 (May 1972), pp. 40–56.

CHAPTER 19

Conover, C. Todd, "The Case of the Costly Credit Agreement," *Financial Executive,* 39 (September 1971), pp. 40–48.

Diener, Royce, "Analyzing the Financing Potential of a Small Business," in I. Pfeffer (ed.), *The Financing of Small Business* (New York: Macmillan, 1967), pp. 211–228.

CHAPTER 20

Donaldson, Gordon, "Strategy for Financial Emergencies," *Harvard Business Review,* 47 (November–December 1969), pp. 67–79.

Johnson, James M., David R. Campbell, and James L. Wittenbach, "Problems in Corporate Liquidity," *Financial Executive,* 48 (March 1980), pp. 44–53.

Osteryoung, Jerome S., Gordon S. Roberts, and Daniel E. McCarty, "Ride the Yield Curve When Investing Idle Funds in Treasury Bills?" *Financial Executive,* 47 (April 1979), pp. 10–15.

Van Horne, James C., "A Risk-Return Analysis of a Firm's Working Capital Position," *Engineering Economist,* 14 (Winter 1969), pp. 71–88.

CHAPTER 21

Anderson, Paul F., and John D. Martin, "Lease vs. Purchase Decisions: A Survey of Current Practice," *Financial Management,* 6 (Spring 1977), pp. 41–47.

Bierman, Harold, Jr., "Buy Versus Lease with an Alternative Minimum Tax," *Financial Management,* 17 (Winter 1988), pp. 87–91.

Bower, R. S., "Issues in Lease Financing," *Financial Management,* 2 (Winter 1973), pp. 25–33.

Ingberman, Monroe, Joshua Ronen, and George H. Sorter, "How Lease Capitalization Under FASB Statement No. 13 Will Affect Financial Ratios," *Financial Analysts Journal,* 35 (January–February 1979), pp. 28–31.

Schall, Lawrence D., "The Evaluation of Lease Financing Opportunities," *Midland Corporate Finance Journal,* 3 (Spring 1985), pp. 48–65.

Schall, Lawrence D., "Analytic Issues in Lease vs. Purchase Decisions," *Financial Management,* 16 (Summer 1987), pp. 17–20.

Smith, Pierce R., "A Straightforward Approach to Leveraged Leasing," *The Journal of Commercial Bank Lending* (July 1973), pp. 19–39.

Sorensen, Ivar W., and Ramon E. Johnson, "Equipment Financial Leasing Practices and Costs: An Empirical Study," *Financial Management,* 6 (Spring 1977), pp. 33–40.

Sorensen, Ivar W., and Ramon E. Johnson, "Equipment Financial Leasing Practices and Costs: An Empirical Study," *Financial Management,* 6 (Spring 1977), pp. 33–40.

CHAPTER 22

Brennan, Michael J., and Eduardo S. Schwartz, "The Case for Convertibles," *Journal of Applied Corporate Finance,* 1 (Summer 1988), pp. 55–64.

Hayes, Samuel L., III, and Henry B. Reiling, "Sophisticated Financing Tool: The Warrant," *Harvard Business Review,* 47 (January–February 1969), pp. 137–150.

Melicher, Ronald W., and J. Ronald Hoffmeister, "Issuing Convertible Bonds," *Financial Executive,* 48 (June 1980), pp. 20–23.

Rush, David, and Ronald Melicher, "An Empirical Examination of Factors Which Influence Warrant Prices," *Journal of Finance,* 29 (December 1974), pp. 1449–1466.

Soldofsky, Robert M., "Yield-Rate Performance of Convertible Securities," *Financial Analysts Journal,* 27 (March–April 1971), pp. 61–65.

CHAPTER 23

Biggadike, Ralph, "The Risky Business of Diversification," *Harvard Business Review,* 57 (May–June 1979), pp. 103–111.

Bradley, Michael, "Interfirm Tender Offers and the Market for Corporate Control," *Journal of Business,* 53 (October 1980), pp. 345–376.

Emmett, Robert, "How to Value a Potential Acquisition," *Financial Executive,* 50 (February 1982), pp. 16–19.

Hector, Gary, "Is Any Company Safe from Takeover?" *Fortune* (April 2, 1984), pp. 18–20.

Hogarty, Thomas F., "The Profitability of Corporate Mergers," *Journal of Business,* 44 (July 1970), pp. 317–327.

Jarrell, Gregg A., and Annette B. Poulsen, "The Returns to Acquiring Firms in Tender Offers: Evidence from Three Decades," *Financial Management,* 18 (Autumn 1989), pp. 12–19.

Jensen, Michael C., "The Takeover Controversy: Analysis and Evidence," *Midland Corporate Finance Journal,* 4 (Summer 1986), pp. 6–32.

Interest rate of ⅓ percent

N	Compound amount — Future value of a present amount F/P	Present value — Present value of a future amount P/F	Annuity compound amount — Future value of an annuity F/A	Sinking fund — Annuity providing a future amount A/F	Annuity present value — Present value of an annuity P/A	Capital recovery — Annuity repaying a present amount A/P	N
1	1.0033	.9967	1.0000	1.0000	.9967	1.0033	1
2	1.0067	.9934	2.0033	.4992	1.9900	.5025	2
3	1.0100	.9901	3.0100	.3322	2.9801	.3356	3
4	1.0134	.9868	4.0200	.2488	3.9669	.2521	4
5	1.0168	.9835	5.0334	.1987	4.9504	.2020	5
6	1.0202	.9802	6.0502	.1653	5.9306	.1686	6
7	1.0236	.9770	7.0704	.1414	6.9076	.1448	7
8	1.0270	.9737	8.0940	.1235	7.8813	.1269	8
9	1.0304	.9705	9.1209	.1096	8.8518	.1130	9
10	1.0338	.9673	10.1513	.0985	9.8191	.1018	10
11	1.0373	.9641	11.1852	.0894	10.7831	.0927	11
12	1.0407	.9609	12.2225	.0818	11.7440	.0851	12
13	1.0442	.9577	13.2632	.0754	12.7017	.0787	13
14	1.0477	.9545	14.3074	.0659	13.6561	.0732	14
15	1.0512	.9513	15.3551	.0651	14.6074	.0685	15
16	1.0547	.9481	16.4063	.0610	15.5556	.0643	16
17	1.0582	.9450	17.4610	.0573	16.5006	.0606	17
18	1.0617	.9419	18.5192	.0540	17.4424	.0573	18
19	1.0653	.9387	19.5809	.0511	18.3812	.0544	19
20	1.0688	.9356	20.6462	.0484	19.3168	.0518	20
21	1.0724	.9325	21.7150	.0461	20.2493	.0494	21
22	1.0760	.9294	22.7874	.0439	21.1787	.0472	22
23	1.0795	.9263	23.8633	.0419	22.1050	.0452	23
24	1.0831	.9232	24.9429	.0401	23.0283	.0434	24
25	1.0868	.9202	26.0260	.0384	23.9484	.0418	25
26	1.0904	.9171	27.1128	.0369	24.8655	.0402	26
27	1.0940	.9141	28.2032	.0355	25.7796	.0388	27
28	1.0977	.9110	29.2972	.0341	26.6906	.0375	28
29	1.1013	.9080	30.3948	.0329	27.5986	.0362	29
30	1.1050	.9050	31.4961	.0317	28.5036	.0351	30
31	1.1087	.9020	32.6011	.0307	29.4056	.0340	31
32	1.1124	.8990	33.7098	.0297	30.3046	.0330	32
33	1.1161	.8960	34.8222	.0287	31.2006	.0321	33
34	1.1198	.8930	35.9382	.0278	32.0936	.0312	34
35	1.1235	.8901	37.0580	.0270	32.9837	.0303	35
36	1.1273	.8871	38.1816	.0262	33.8708	.0295	36

N	Compound amount — Future value of a present amount F/P	Present value — Present value of a future amount P/F	Annuity compound amount — Future value of an annuity F/A	Sinking fund — Annuity providing a future amount A/F	Annuity present value — Present value of an annuity P/A	Capital recovery — Annuity repaying a present amount A/P	N
48	1.1732	.8524	51.9596	.0192	44.2888	.0226	48
60	1.2210	.8190	66.2990	.0151	54.2991	.0184	60
72	1.2707	.7869	81.2226	.0123	63.9174	.0156	72
84	1.3225	.7561	96.7541	.0103	73.1593	.0137	84
96	1.3764	.7265	112.9185	.0089	82.0393	.0122	96
108	1.4325	.6981	129.7414	.0077	90.5718	.0110	108
120	1.4908	.6708	147.2498	.0068	98.7702	.0101	120
132	1.5516	.6445	165.4714	.0060	106.6477	.0094	132
144	1.6148	.6193	184.4354	.0054	114.2168	.0088	144
156	1.6806	.5950	204.1721	.0049	121.4896	.0082	156
168	1.7490	.5717	224.7128	.0045	128.4777	.0078	168
180	1.8203	.5494	246.0904	.0041	135.1922	.0074	180
192	1.8945	.5279	268.3390	.0037	141.6439	.0071	192
204	1.9716	.5072	291.4940	.0034	147.8430	.0068	204
216	2.0520	.4873	315.5923	.0032	153.7994	.0065	216
228	2.1356	.4683	340.6725	.0029	159.5227	.0063	228
240	2.2226	.4499	366.7745	.0027	165.0219	.0061	240
252	2.3131	.4323	393.9399	.0025	170.3059	.0059	252
264	2.4074	.4154	422.2120	.0024	175.3830	.0057	264
276	2.5055	.3991	451.6360	.0022	180.2613	.0055	276
288	2.6075	.3835	482.2588	.0021	184.9487	.0054	288
300	2.7138	.3685	514.1293	.0019	189.4526	.0053	300
312	2.8243	.3541	547.2981	.0018	193.7801	.0052	312
324	2.9394	.3402	581.8183	.0017	197.9383	.0051	324
336	3.0591	.3269	617.7449	.0016	201.9337	.0050	336
348	3.1838	.3141	655.1353	.0015	205.7726	.0049	348
360	3.3135	.3018	694.0489	.0014	209.4613	.0048	360
∞					300.0000	.0033	∞

Interest rate of ½ percent

N	Compound amount — Future value of a present amount (F/P)	Present value — Present value of a future amount (P/F)	Annuity compound amount — Future value of an annuity (F/A)	Sinking fund — Annuity providing a future amount (A/F)	Annuity present value — Present value of an annuity (P/A)	Capital recovery — Annuity repaying a present amount (A/P)	N
1	1.0050	.9950	1.0000	1.0000	.9950	1.0050	1
2	1.0100	.9901	2.0050	.4988	1.9851	.5038	2
3	1.0151	.9851	3.0150	.3317	2.9702	.3367	3
4	1.0202	.9802	4.0301	.2481	3.9505	.2531	4
5	1.0253	.9754	5.0503	.1980	4.9259	.2030	5
6	1.0304	.9705	6.0755	.1646	5.8964	.1696	6
7	1.0355	.9657	7.1059	.1407	6.8621	.1457	7
8	1.0407	.9609	8.1414	.1228	7.8230	.1278	8
9	1.0459	.9561	9.1821	.1089	8.7791	.1139	9
10	1.0511	.9513	10.2280	.0978	9.7304	.1028	10
11	1.0564	.9466	11.2792	.0887	10.6770	.0937	11
12	1.0617	.9419	12.3356	.0811	11.6189	.0861	12
13	1.0670	.9372	13.3972	.0746	12.5562	.0796	13
14	1.0723	.9326	14.4642	.0691	13.4887	.0741	14
15	1.0777	.9279	15.5365	.0644	14.4166	.0694	15
16	1.0831	.9233	16.6142	.0602	15.3399	.0652	16
17	1.0885	.9187	17.6973	.0565	16.2586	.0615	17
18	1.0939	.9141	18.7858	.0532	17.1728	.0582	18
19	1.0994	.9096	19.8797	.0503	18.0824	.0553	19
20	1.1049	.9051	20.9791	.0477	18.9874	.0527	20
21	1.1104	.9006	22.0840	.0453	19.8880	.0503	21
22	1.1160	.8961	23.1944	.0431	20.7841	.0481	22
23	1.1216	.8916	24.3104	.0411	21.6757	.0461	23
24	1.1272	.8872	25.4320	.0393	22.5629	.0443	24
25	1.1328	.8828	26.5591	.0377	23.4456	.0427	25
26	1.1385	.8784	27.6919	.0361	24.3240	.0411	26
27	1.1442	.8740	28.8304	.0347	25.1980	.0397	27
28	1.1499	.8697	29.9745	.0334	26.0677	.0384	28
29	1.1556	.8653	31.1244	.0321	26.9330	.0371	29
30	1.1614	.8610	32.2800	.0310	27.7941	.0360	30
31	1.1672	.8567	33.4414	.0299	28.6508	.0349	31
32	1.1730	.8525	34.6086	.0289	29.5033	.0339	32
33	1.1789	.8482	35.7817	.0279	30.3515	.0329	33
34	1.1848	.8440	36.9606	.0271	31.1955	.0321	34
35	1.1907	.8398	38.1454	.0262	32.0354	.0312	35
36	1.1967	.8356	39.3361	.0254	32.8710	.0304	36
48	1.2705	.7871	54.0978	.0185	42.5803	.0235	48
60	1.3489	.7414	69.7700	.0143	51.7256	.0193	60
72	1.4320	.6983	86.4089	.0116	60.3395	.0166	72
84	1.5204	.6577	104.0739	.0096	68.4530	.0146	84
96	1.6141	.6195	122.8285	.0081	76.0952	.0131	96
108	1.7137	.5835	142.7399	.0070	83.2934	.0120	108
120	1.8194	.5496	163.8793	.0061	90.0735	.0111	120
132	1.9316	.5177	186.3226	.0054	96.4596	.0104	132
144	2.0508	.4876	210.1502	.0048	102.4747	.0098	144
156	2.1772	.4593	235.4473	.0042	108.1404	.0092	156
168	2.3115	.4326	262.3048	.0038	113.4770	.0088	168
180	2.4541	.4075	290.8187	.0034	118.5035	.0084	180
192	2.6055	.3838	321.0913	.0031	123.2380	.0081	192
204	2.7662	.3615	353.2311	.0028	127.6975	.0078	204
216	2.9368	.3405	387.3532	.0026	131.8979	.0076	216
228	3.1179	.3207	423.5799	.0024	135.8542	.0074	228
240	3.3102	.3021	462.0409	.0022	139.5808	.0072	240
252	3.5144	.2845	502.8741	.0020	143.0908	.0070	252
264	3.7311	.2680	546.2259	.0018	146.3969	.0068	264
276	3.9613	.2524	592.2514	.0017	149.5110	.0067	276
288	4.2056	.2378	641.1158	.0016	152.4441	.0066	288
300	4.4650	.2240	692.9940	.0014	155.2069	.0064	300
312	4.7404	.2110	748.0719	.0013	157.8091	.0063	312
324	5.0327	.1987	806.5469	.0012	160.2602	.0062	324
336	5.3431	.1872	868.6285	.0012	162.5688	.0062	336
348	5.6727	.1763	934.5392	.0011	164.7434	.0061	348
360	6.0226	.1660	1004.5150	.0010	166.7916	.0060	360
∞					200.0000	.0050	∞

Interest rate of ⅔ percent

N	Compound amount — Future value of a present amount (F/P)	Present value — Present value of a future amount (P/F)	Annuity compound amount — Future value of an annuity (F/A)	Sinking fund — Annuity providing a future amount (A/F)	Annuity present value — Present value of an annuity (P/A)	Capital recovery — Annuity repaying a present amount (A/P)	N
48	1.3757	.7269	56.3499	.0177	40.9619	.0244	48
60	1.4898	.6712	73.4769	.0136	49.3184	.0203	60
72	1.6135	.6198	92.0253	.0109	57.0345	.0175	72
84	1.7474	.5723	112.1133	.0089	64.1593	.0156	84
96	1.8925	.5284	133.8686	.0075	70.7380	.0141	96
108	2.0495	.4879	157.4295	.0064	76.8125	.0130	108
120	2.2196	.4505	182.9460	.0055	82.4215	.0121	120
132	2.4039	.4160	210.5804	.0047	87.6006	.0114	132
144	2.6034	.3841	240.5084	.0042	92.3828	.0108	144
156	2.8195	.3547	272.9204	.0037	96.7985	.0103	156
168	3.0535	.3275	308.0226	.0032	100.8758	.0099	168
180	3.3069	.3024	346.0382	.0029	104.6406	.0096	180
192	3.5814	.2792	387.2092	.0026	108.1169	.0092	192
204	3.8786	.2578	431.7973	.0023	111.3267	.0090	204
216	4.2006	.2381	480.0861	.0021	114.2906	.0087	216
228	4.5492	.2198	532.3830	.0019	117.0273	.0085	228
240	4.9268	.2030	589.0204	.0017	119.5543	.0084	240
252	5.3357	.1874	650.3588	.0015	121.8876	.0082	252
264	5.7786	.1731	716.7882	.0014	124.0421	.0081	264
276	6.2582	.1598	788.7312	.0013	126.0315	.0079	276
288	6.7776	.1475	866.6454	.0012	127.8684	.0078	288
300	7.3402	.1362	951.0265	.0011	129.5645	.0077	300
312	7.9494	.1258	1042.4111	.0010	131.1307	.0076	312
324	8.6092	.1162	1141.3907	.0009	132.5768	.0075	324
336	9.3238	.1073	1248.5646	.0008	133.9121	.0075	336
348	10.0976	.0990	1364.6448	.0007	135.1450	.0074	348
360	10.5357	.0914	1490.3596	.0007	136.2835	.0073	360
∞					150.0000	.0067	∞

N	Compound amount — Future value of a present amount (F/P)	Present value — Present value of a future amount (P/F)	Annuity compound amount — Future value of an annuity (F/A)	Sinking fund — Annuity providing a future amount (A/F)	Annuity present value — Present value of an annuity (P/A)	Capital recovery — Annuity repaying a present amount (A/P)	N
1	1.0067	.9934	1.0000	1.0000	.9934	1.0067	1
2	1.0134	.9868	2.0067	.4983	1.9802	.5050	2
3	1.0201	.9803	3.0200	.3311	2.9604	.3378	3
4	1.0269	.9738	4.0402	.2475	3.9342	.2542	4
5	1.0338	.9673	5.0671	.1974	4.9015	.2040	5
6	1.0407	.9609	6.1009	.1639	5.8625	.1706	6
7	1.0476	.9546	7.1416	.1400	6.8170	.1467	7
8	1.0546	.9482	8.1892	.1221	7.7652	.1288	8
9	1.0616	.9420	9.2438	.1082	8.7072	.1148	9
10	1.0687	.9357	10.3054	.0970	9.6429	.1037	10
11	1.0758	.9295	11.3741	.0879	10.5724	.0946	11
12	1.0830	.9234	12.4499	.0803	11.4958	.0870	12
13	1.0902	.9172	13.5329	.0739	12.4130	.0806	13
14	1.0975	.9112	14.6231	.0684	13.3242	.0751	14
15	1.1048	.9051	15.7206	.0636	14.2293	.0703	15
16	1.1122	.8991	16.8254	.0594	15.1285	.0661	16
17	1.1196	.8932	17.9376	.0557	16.0217	.0624	17
18	1.1270	.8873	19.0572	.0525	16.9089	.0591	18
19	1.1346	.8814	20.1842	.0495	17.7903	.0562	19
20	1.1421	.8756	21.3188	.0469	18.6659	.0536	20
21	1.1497	.8698	22.4609	.0445	19.5357	.0512	21
22	1.1574	.8640	23.6107	.0424	20.3997	.0490	22
23	1.1651	.8583	24.7681	.0404	21.2579	.0470	23
24	1.1729	.8526	25.9332	.0386	22.1105	.0452	24
25	1.1807	.8470	27.1061	.0369	22.9575	.0436	25
26	1.1886	.8413	28.2868	.0354	23.7988	.0420	26
27	1.1965	.8358	29.4754	.0339	24.6346	.0406	27
28	1.2045	.8302	30.6719	.0326	25.4648	.0393	28
29	1.2125	.8247	31.8763	.0314	26.2896	.0380	29
30	1.2206	.8193	33.0889	.0302	27.1088	.0369	30
31	1.2287	.8138	34.3094	.0291	27.9227	.0358	31
32	1.2369	.8085	35.5382	.0281	28.7312	.0348	32
33	1.2452	.8031	36.7751	.0272	29.5343	.0339	33
34	1.2535	.7978	38.0203	.0263	30.3320	.0330	34
35	1.2618	.7925	39.2737	.0255	31.1246	.0321	35
36	1.2702	.7873	40.5356	.0247	31.9118	.0313	36

Interest rate of ¾ percent

N	Compound amount — Future value of a present amount — F/P	Present value — Present value of a future amount — P/F	Annuity compound amount — Future value of an annuity — F/A	Sinking fund — Annuity providing a future amount — A/F	Annuity present value — Present value of an annuity — P/A	Capital recovery — Annuity repaying a present amount — A/P	N
1	1.0075	.9926	1.0000	1.0000	.9926	1.0075	1
2	1.0151	.9852	2.0075	.4981	1.9777	.5056	2
3	1.0227	.9778	3.0226	.3308	2.9556	.3383	3
4	1.0303	.9706	4.0452	.2472	3.9261	.2547	4
5	1.0381	.9633	5.0756	.1970	4.8894	.2045	5
6	1.0459	.9562	6.1136	.1636	5.8456	.1711	6
7	1.0537	.9490	7.1595	.1397	6.7946	.1472	7
8	1.0616	.9420	8.2132	.1218	7.7366	.1293	8
9	1.0696	.9350	9.2748	.1078	8.6716	.1153	9
10	1.0776	.9280	10.3443	.0967	9.5996	.1042	10
11	1.0857	.9211	11.4219	.0876	10.5207	.0951	11
12	1.0938	.9142	12.5076	.0800	11.4349	.0875	12
13	1.1020	.9074	13.6014	.0735	12.3423	.0810	13
14	1.1103	.9007	14.7034	.0680	13.2430	.0755	14
15	1.1186	.8940	15.8137	.0632	14.1370	.0707	15
16	1.1270	.8873	16.9323	.0591	15.0243	.0666	16
17	1.1354	.8807	18.0593	.0554	15.9050	.0629	17
18	1.1440	.8742	19.1947	.0521	16.7792	.0596	18
19	1.1525	.8676	20.3387	.0492	17.6468	.0567	19
20	1.1612	.8612	21.4912	.0465	18.5080	.0540	20
21	1.1699	.8548	22.6524	.0441	19.3628	.0516	21
22	1.1787	.8484	23.8223	.0420	20.2112	.0495	22
23	1.1875	.8421	25.0010	.0400	21.0533	.0475	23
24	1.1964	.8358	26.1885	.0382	21.8891	.0457	24
25	1.2054	.8296	27.3849	.0365	22.7188	.0440	25
26	1.2144	.8234	28.5903	.0350	23.5422	.0425	26
27	1.2235	.8173	29.8047	.0336	24.3595	.0411	27
28	1.2327	.8112	31.0282	.0322	25.1707	.0397	28
29	1.2420	.8052	32.2609	.0310	25.9759	.0385	29
30	1.2513	.7992	33.5029	.0298	26.7751	.0373	30
31	1.2607	.7932	34.7542	.0288	27.5683	.0363	31
32	1.2701	.7873	36.0148	.0278	28.3557	.0353	32
33	1.2796	.7815	37.2849	.0268	29.1371	.0343	33
34	1.2892	.7757	38.5646	.0259	29.9128	.0334	34
35	1.2989	.7699	39.8538	.0251	30.6827	.0326	35
36	1.3086	.7641	41.1527	.0243	31.4468	.0318	36

N	Compound amount — Future value of a present amount — F/P	Present value — Present value of a future amount — P/F	Annuity compound amount — Future value of an annuity — F/A	Sinking fund — Annuity providing a future amount — A/F	Annuity present value — Present value of an annuity — P/A	Capital recovery — Annuity repaying a present amount — A/P	N
48	1.4314	.6986	57.5207	.0174	40.1848	.0249	48
60	1.5657	.6387	75.4241	.0133	48.1734	.0208	60
72	1.7126	.5839	95.0070	.0105	55.4768	.0180	72
84	1.8732	.5338	116.4269	.0086	62.1540	.0161	84
96	2.0489	.4881	139.8562	.0072	68.2584	.0147	96
108	2.2411	.4462	165.4832	.0060	73.8394	.0135	108
120	2.4514	.4079	193.5143	.0052	78.9417	.0127	120
132	2.6813	.3730	225.1748	.0045	83.6064	.0120	132
144	2.9328	.3410	257.7116	.0039	87.8711	.0114	144
156	3.2080	.3117	294.3943	.0034	91.7700	.0109	156
168	3.5089	.2850	334.5181	.0030	95.3346	.0105	168
180	3.8380	.2605	378.4058	.0026	98.5934	.0101	180
192	4.1981	.2382	426.4104	.0023	101.5728	.0098	192
204	4.5919	.2178	478.9183	.0021	104.2966	.0096	204
216	5.0226	.1991	536.3517	.0019	106.7869	.0094	216
228	5.4938	.1820	599.1727	.0017	109.0635	.0092	228
240	6.0092	.1664	667.8869	.0015	111.1450	.0090	240
252	6.5729	.1521	743.0469	.0013	113.0479	.0088	252
264	7.1894	.1391	825.2574	.0012	114.7876	.0087	264
276	7.8638	.1272	915.1798	.0011	116.3781	.0086	276
288	8.6015	.1163	1013.5375	.0010	117.8322	.0085	288
300	9.4084	.1063	1121.1219	.0009	119.1616	.0084	300
312	10.2910	.0972	1238.7985	.0008	120.3770	.0083	312
324	11.2564	.0888	1367.5139	.0007	121.4882	.0082	324
336	12.3123	.0812	1508.3037	.0007	122.5040	.0082	336
348	13.4673	.0743	1662.3006	.0006	123.4328	.0081	348
360	14.7306	.0679	1830.7435	.0005	124.2819	.0080	360
∞					133.3333	.0075	∞

Interest rate of 1.00 percent

N	Compound amount — Future value of a present amount — F/P	Present value — Present value of a future amount — P/F	Annuity compound amount — Future value of an annuity — F/A	Sinking fund — Annuity providing a future amount — A/F	Annuity present value — Present value of an annuity — P/A	Capital recovery — Annuity repaying a present amount — A/P	N
1	1.0100	.9901	1.0000	1.0000	.9901	1.0100	1
2	1.0201	.9803	2.0100	.4975	1.9704	.5075	2
3	1.0303	.9706	3.0301	.3300	2.9410	.3400	3
4	1.0406	.9610	4.0604	.2463	3.9020	.2563	4
5	1.0510	.9515	5.1010	.1960	4.8534	.2060	5
6	1.0615	.9420	6.1520	.1625	5.7955	.1725	6
7	1.0721	.9327	7.2135	.1386	6.7282	.1486	7
8	1.0829	.9235	8.2857	.1207	7.6517	.1307	8
9	1.0937	.9143	9.3685	.1067	8.5660	.1167	9
10	1.1046	.9053	10.4622	.0956	9.4713	.1056	10
11	1.1157	.8963	11.5668	.0865	10.3676	.0965	11
12	1.1268	.8874	12.6825	.0788	11.2551	.0888	12
13	1.1381	.8787	13.8093	.0724	12.1337	.0824	13
14	1.1495	.8700	14.9474	.0669	13.0037	.0769	14
15	1.1610	.8613	16.0969	.0621	13.8651	.0721	15
16	1.1726	.8528	17.2579	.0579	14.7179	.0679	16
17	1.1843	.8444	18.4304	.0543	15.5623	.0643	17
18	1.1961	.8360	19.6147	.0510	16.3983	.0610	18
19	1.2081	.8277	20.8109	.0481	17.2260	.0581	19
20	1.2202	.8195	22.0190	.0454	18.0456	.0554	20
21	1.2324	.8114	23.2392	.0430	18.8570	.0530	21
22	1.2447	.8034	24.4716	.0409	19.6604	.0509	22
23	1.2572	.7954	25.7163	.0389	20.4558	.0489	23
24	1.2697	.7876	26.9735	.0371	21.2434	.0471	24
25	1.2824	.7798	28.2432	.0354	22.0232	.0454	25
26	1.2953	.7720	29.5256	.0339	22.7952	.0439	26
27	1.3082	.7644	30.8209	.0324	23.5596	.0424	27
28	1.3213	.7568	32.1291	.0311	24.3164	.0411	28
29	1.3345	.7493	33.4504	.0299	25.0658	.0399	29
30	1.3478	.7419	34.7849	.0287	25.8077	.0387	30
31	1.3613	.7346	36.1327	.0277	26.5423	.0377	31
32	1.3749	.7273	37.4941	.0267	27.2696	.0367	32
33	1.3887	.7201	38.8690	.0257	27.9897	.0357	33
34	1.4026	.7130	40.2577	.0248	28.7027	.0348	34
35	1.4166	.7059	41.6603	.0240	29.4086	.0340	35
36	1.4308	.6989	43.0769	.0232	30.1075	.0332	36

N	Compound amount — Future value of a present amount — F/P	Present value — Present value of a future amount — P/F	Annuity compound amount — Future value of an annuity — F/A	Sinking fund — Annuity providing a future amount — A/F	Annuity present value — Present value of an annuity — P/A	Capital recovery — Annuity repaying a present amount — A/P	N
48	1.6122	.6203	61.2226	.0163	37.9740	.0263	48
60	1.8167	.5504	81.6697	.0122	44.9550	.0222	60
72	2.0471	.4885	104.7099	.0096	51.1504	.0196	72
84	2.3067	.4335	130.6723	.0077	56.6485	.0177	84
96	2.5993	.3847	159.9273	.0063	61.5277	.0163	96
108	2.9289	.3414	192.8926	.0052	65.8578	.0152	108
120	3.3004	.3030	230.0387	.0043	69.7005	.0143	120
132	3.7190	.2689	271.8959	.0037	73.1108	.0137	132
144	4.1906	.2386	319.0616	.0031	76.1372	.0131	144
156	4.7221	.2118	372.2091	.0027	78.8229	.0127	156
168	5.3210	.1879	432.0970	.0023	81.2064	.0123	168
180	5.9958	.1668	493.5802	.0020	83.3217	.0120	180
192	6.7562	.1480	575.6220	.0017	85.1988	.0117	192
204	7.6131	.1314	661.3078	.0015	86.8647	.0115	204
216	8.5786	.1166	757.8606	.0013	88.3431	.0113	216
228	9.6666	.1034	866.6588	.0012	89.6551	.0112	228
240	10.8926	.0918	989.2554	.0010	90.8194	.0110	240
252	12.2740	.0815	1127.4002	.0009	91.8527	.0109	252
264	13.8307	.0723	1285.0653	.0008	92.7697	.0108	264
276	15.5347	.0642	1458.4726	.0007	93.5835	.0107	276
288	17.5613	.0569	1656.1259	.0006	94.3056	.0106	288
300	19.7885	.0505	1876.8466	.0005	94.9466	.0105	300
312	22.2981	.0448	2129.8139	.0005	95.5153	.0105	312
324	25.1261	.0398	2412.6101	.0004	96.0201	.0104	324
336	28.3127	.0353	2731.2720	.0004	96.4680	.0104	336
348	31.9035	.0313	3090.3481	.0003	96.8655	.0103	348
360	35.9496	.0278	3494.9641	.0003	97.2183	.0103	360
∞					100.0000	.0100	∞

APPENDIX A Interest rate of 1.25 percent

Interest rate of 1.25 percent

N	Compound amount — Future value of a present amount — F/P	Present value — Present value of a future amount — P/F	Annuity compound amount — Future value of an annuity — F/A	Sinking fund — Annuity providing a future amount — A/F	Annuity present value — Present value of an annuity — P/A	Capital recovery — Annuity repaying a present amount — A/P	N
1	1.0125	.9877	1.0000	1.0000	.9877	1.0125	1
2	1.0252	.9755	2.0125	.4969	1.9631	.5094	2
3	1.0380	.9634	3.0377	.3292	2.9265	.3417	3
4	1.0509	.9515	4.0756	.2454	3.8781	.2579	4
5	1.0641	.9398	5.1266	.1951	4.8178	.2076	5
6	1.0774	.9282	6.1907	.1615	5.7460	.1740	6
7	1.0909	.9167	7.2680	.1376	6.6627	.1501	7
8	1.1045	.9054	8.3589	.1196	7.5681	.1321	8
9	1.1183	.8942	9.4634	.1057	8.4623	.1182	9
10	1.1323	.8832	10.5817	.0945	9.3455	.1070	10
11	1.1464	.8723	11.7139	.0854	10.2178	.0979	11
12	1.1608	.8615	12.8604	.0778	11.0793	.0903	12
13	1.1753	.8509	14.0211	.0713	11.9302	.0838	13
14	1.1900	.8404	15.1964	.0658	12.7706	.0783	14
15	1.2048	.8300	16.3863	.0610	13.6005	.0735	15
16	1.2199	.8197	17.5912	.0568	14.4203	.0693	16
17	1.2351	.8096	18.8111	.0532	15.2299	.0657	17
18	1.2506	.7996	20.0462	.0499	16.0295	.0624	18
19	1.2662	.7898	21.2968	.0470	16.8193	.0595	19
20	1.2820	.7800	22.5630	.0443	17.5993	.0568	20
21	1.2981	.7704	23.8450	.0419	18.3697	.0544	21
22	1.3143	.7609	25.1431	.0398	19.1306	.0523	22
23	1.3307	.7515	26.4574	.0378	19.8820	.0503	23
24	1.3474	.7422	27.7881	.0360	20.6242	.0485	24
25	1.3642	.7330	29.1354	.0343	21.3573	.0468	25
26	1.3812	.7240	30.4996	.0328	22.0813	.0453	26
27	1.3985	.7150	31.8809	.0314	22.7963	.0439	27
28	1.4160	.7062	33.2794	.0300	23.5025	.0425	28
29	1.4337	.6975	34.6954	.0288	24.2000	.0413	29
30	1.4516	.6889	36.1291	.0277	24.8889	.0402	30
31	1.4698	.6804	37.5807	.0266	25.5693	.0391	31
32	1.4881	.6720	39.0504	.0256	26.2413	.0381	32
33	1.5067	.6637	40.5386	.0247	26.9050	.0372	33
34	1.5256	.6555	42.0453	.0238	27.5605	.0363	34
35	1.5446	.6474	43.5709	.0230	28.2079	.0355	35
36	1.5639	.6394	45.1155	.0222	28.8473	.0347	36
48	1.8154	.5509	65.2284	.0153	35.9315	.0278	48
60	2.1072	.4746	88.5745	.0113	42.0346	.0238	60
72	2.4459	.4088	115.6736	.0086	47.2925	.0211	72
84	2.8391	.3522	147.1290	.0068	51.8222	.0193	84
96	3.2955	.3034	183.6411	.0054	55.7246	.0179	96
108	3.8253	.2614	226.0226	.0044	59.0865	.0169	108
120	4.4402	.2252	275.2171	.0036	61.9828	.0161	120
132	5.1540	.1940	332.3198	.0030	64.4781	.0155	132
144	5.9825	.1672	398.6021	.0025	66.6277	.0150	144
156	6.9442	.1440	475.5395	.0021	68.4797	.0146	156
168	8.0606	.1241	564.8450	.0018	70.0751	.0143	168
180	9.3563	.1069	668.5068	.0015	71.4496	.0140	180
192	10.8604	.0921	788.8326	.0013	72.6338	.0138	192
204	12.6063	.0793	928.5014	.0011	73.6540	.0136	204
216	14.6328	.0683	1090.6225	.0009	74.5328	.0134	216
228	16.9851	.0589	1278.8054	.0008	75.2900	.0133	228
240	19.7155	.0507	1497.2395	.0007	75.9423	.0132	240
252	22.8848	.0437	1750.7879	.0006	76.5042	.0131	252
264	26.5637	.0376	2045.0953	.0005	76.9984	.0130	264
276	30.8339	.0324	2386.7139	.0004	77.4055	.0129	276
288	35.7906	.0279	2783.2493	.0004	77.7648	.0129	288
300	41.5441	.0241	3243.5296	.0003	78.0743	.0128	300
312	48.2225	.0207	3777.8020	.0003	78.3410	.0128	312
324	55.9745	.0179	4397.9611	.0002	78.5708	.0127	324
336	64.9727	.0154	5117.8136	.0002	78.7687	.0127	336
348	75.4173	.0133	5953.3856	.0002	78.9392	.0127	348
360	87.5410	.0114	6923.2796	.0001	79.0861	.0126	360
∞					80.0000	.0125	∞

Interest rate of 1.50 percent

N	Compound amount — Future value of a present amount — F/P	Present value — Present value of a future amount — P/F	Annuity compound amount — Future value of an annuity — F/A	Sinking fund — Annuity providing a future amount — A/F	Annuity present value — Present value of an annuity — P/A	Capital recovery — Annuity repaying a present amount — A/P	N
1	1.0150	.9852	1.0000	1.0000	.9852	1.0150	1
2	1.0302	.9707	2.0150	.4963	1.9559	.5113	2
3	1.0457	.9563	3.0452	.3284	2.9122	.3434	3
4	1.0614	.9422	4.0909	.2444	3.8544	.2594	4
5	1.0773	.9283	5.1523	.1941	4.7826	.2091	5
6	1.0934	.9145	6.2296	.1605	5.6972	.1755	6
7	1.1098	.9010	7.3230	.1366	6.5982	.1516	7
8	1.1265	.8877	8.4328	.1186	7.4859	.1336	8
9	1.1434	.8746	9.5593	.1046	8.3605	.1196	9
10	1.1605	.8617	10.7027	.0934	9.2222	.1084	10
11	1.1779	.8489	11.8633	.0843	10.0711	.0993	11
12	1.1956	.8364	13.0412	.0767	10.9075	.0917	12
13	1.2136	.8240	14.2368	.0702	11.7315	.0852	13
14	1.2318	.8118	15.4504	.0647	12.5434	.0797	14
15	1.2502	.7999	16.6821	.0599	13.3432	.0749	15
16	1.2690	.7880	17.9324	.0558	14.1313	.0708	16
17	1.2880	.7764	19.2014	.0521	14.9076	.0671	17
18	1.3073	.7649	20.4894	.0488	15.5726	.0638	18
19	1.3270	.7536	21.7967	.0459	16.4262	.0609	19
20	1.3469	.7425	23.1237	.0432	17.1686	.0582	20
21	1.3671	.7315	24.4705	.0409	17.9001	.0559	21
22	1.3876	.7207	25.8376	.0387	18.6208	.0537	22
23	1.4084	.7100	27.2251	.0367	19.3309	.0517	23
24	1.4295	.6995	28.6335	.0349	20.0304	.0499	24
25	1.4509	.6892	30.0630	.0333	20.7195	.0483	25
26	1.4727	.6790	31.5140	.0317	21.3986	.0467	26
27	1.4948	.6690	32.9867	.0303	22.0676	.0453	27
28	1.5172	.6591	34.4815	.0290	22.7267	.0440	28
29	1.5400	.6494	35.9987	.0278	23.3761	.0428	29
30	1.5631	.6398	37.5387	.0266	24.0158	.0416	30
31	1.5865	.6303	39.1018	.0256	24.6461	.0406	31
32	1.6103	.6210	40.6883	.0246	25.2671	.0396	32
33	1.6345	.6118	42.2986	.0236	25.8790	.0386	33
34	1.6590	.6028	43.9331	.0228	26.4817	.0378	34
35	1.6839	.5939	45.5921	.0219	27.0756	.0369	35
36	1.7091	.5851	47.2760	.0212	27.6607	.0362	36
40	1.8140	.5513	54.2679	.0184	29.9158	.0334	40
44	1.9253	.5194	61.6889	.0162	32.0406	.0312	44
48	2.0435	.4894	69.5652	.0144	34.0426	.0294	48
52	2.1689	.4611	77.9249	.0128	35.9287	.0278	52
56	2.3020	.4344	86.7975	.0115	37.7059	.0265	56
60	2.4432	.4039	96.2147	.0104	39.3803	.0254	60
64	2.5631	.3856	106.2096	.0094	40.9579	.0244	64
68	2.7523	.3633	116.8179	.0086	42.4442	.0236	68
72	2.9212	.3423	128.0772	.0078	43.8447	.0228	72
76	3.1004	.3225	140.0274	.0071	45.1641	.0221	76
80	3.2907	.3039	152.7109	.0065	46.4073	.0215	80
84	3.4926	.2863	166.1726	.0060	47.5786	.0210	84
88	3.7069	.2698	180.4605	.0055	48.6822	.0205	88
92	3.9344	.2542	195.6251	.0051	49.7220	.0201	92
96	4.1758	.2395	211.7202	.0047	50.7017	.0197	96
100	4.4320	.2256	228.8030	.0044	51.6247	.0194	100
104	4.7040	.2126	246.9341	.0040	52.4944	.0190	104
108	4.9927	.2003	266.1778	.0038	53.3137	.0188	108
112	5.2990	.1887	286.6023	.0035	54.0858	.0185	112
116	5.6242	.1778	308.2801	.0032	54.8131	.0182	116
120	5.9693	.1675	331.2882	.0030	55.4985	.0180	120
∞					66.6667	.0150	∞

Interest rate of 2.00 percent

N	Compound amount — Future value of a present amount — F/P	Present value — Present value of a future amount — P/F	Annuity compound amount — Future value of an annuity — F/A	Sinking fund — Annuity providing a future amount — A/F	Annuity present value — Present value of an annuity — P/A	Capital recovery — Annuity repaying a present amount — A/P	N
1	1.0200	.9804	1.0000	1.0000	.9804	1.0200	1
2	1.0404	.9612	2.0200	.4950	1.9416	.5150	2
3	1.0612	.9423	3.0604	.3268	2.8839	.3468	3
4	1.0824	.9238	4.1216	.2426	3.8077	.2626	4
5	1.1041	.9057	5.2040	.1922	4.7135	.2122	5
6	1.1262	.8880	6.3081	.1585	5.6014	.1785	6
7	1.1487	.8706	7.4343	.1345	6.4720	.1545	7
8	1.1717	.8535	8.5830	.1165	7.3255	.1365	8
9	1.1951	.8368	9.7546	.1025	8.1622	.1225	9
10	1.2190	.8203	10.9497	.0913	8.9826	.1113	10
11	1.2434	.8043	12.1687	.0822	9.7868	.1022	11
12	1.2682	.7885	13.4121	.0746	10.5753	.0946	12
13	1.2936	.7730	14.6803	.0681	11.3484	.0881	13
14	1.3195	.7579	15.9739	.0626	12.1062	.0826	14
15	1.3459	.7430	17.2934	.0578	12.8493	.0778	15
16	1.3728	.7284	18.6393	.0537	13.5777	.0737	16
17	1.4002	.7142	20.0121	.0500	14.2919	.0700	17
18	1.4282	.7002	21.4123	.0467	14.9920	.0667	18
19	1.4568	.6864	22.8406	.0438	15.6785	.0638	19
20	1.4859	.6730	24.2974	.0412	16.3514	.0612	20
21	1.5157	.6598	25.7833	.0388	17.0112	.0588	21
22	1.5460	.6468	27.2990	.0366	17.6580	.0566	22
23	1.5769	.6342	28.8450	.0347	18.2922	.0547	23
24	1.6084	.6217	30.4219	.0329	18.9139	.0529	24
25	1.6406	.6095	32.0303	.0312	19.5235	.0512	25
26	1.6734	.5976	33.6709	.0297	20.1210	.0497	26
27	1.7069	.5859	35.3443	.0283	20.7069	.0483	27
28	1.7410	.5744	37.0512	.0270	21.2813	.0470	28
29	1.7758	.5631	38.7922	.0258	21.8444	.0458	29
30	1.8114	.5521	40.5681	.0246	22.3965	.0446	30
31	1.8476	.5412	42.3794	.0236	22.9377	.0436	31
32	1.8845	.5306	44.2270	.0226	23.4683	.0426	32
33	1.9222	.5202	46.1116	.0217	23.9886	.0417	33
34	1.9607	.5100	48.0338	.0208	24.4986	.0408	34
35	1.9999	.5000	49.9945	.0200	24.9986	.0400	35
36	2.0399	.4902	51.9944	.0192	25.4888	.0392	36
40	2.2080	.4529	60.4020	.0166	27.3555	.0366	40
44	2.3901	.4184	69.5027	.0144	29.0800	.0344	44
48	2.5871	.3865	79.3535	.0126	30.6731	.0326	48
52	2.8003	.3571	90.0164	.0111	32.1449	.0311	52
56	3.0312	.3299	101.1583	.0098	33.5047	.0298	56
60	3.2810	.3048	114.0515	.0088	34.7609	.0288	60
64	3.5515	.2816	127.5747	.0078	35.9214	.0278	64
68	3.8443	.2601	142.2125	.0070	36.9936	.0270	68
72	4.1611	.2403	158.0570	.0063	37.9841	.0263	72
76	4.5042	.2220	175.2076	.0057	38.8991	.0257	76
80	4.8754	.2051	193.7720	.0052	39.7445	.0252	80
84	5.2773	.1895	213.8666	.0047	40.5255	.0247	84
88	5.7124	.1751	235.6177	.0042	41.2470	.0242	88
92	6.1832	.1617	259.1618	.0039	41.9136	.0239	92
96	6.6929	.1494	284.6467	.0035	42.5294	.0235	96
100	7.2446	.1380	312.2323	.0032	43.0984	.0232	100
104	7.8418	.1275	342.0919	.0029	43.6239	.0229	104
108	8.4883	.1178	374.4129	.0027	44.1095	.0227	108
112	9.1880	.1088	409.3981	.0024	44.5581	.0224	112
116	9.9453	.1005	447.2673	.0022	44.9725	.0222	116
120	10.7652	.0929	488.2582	.0020	45.3554	.0220	120
∞					50.0000	.0200	∞

APPENDIX A Interest rate of 3.00 percent

Interest rate of 3.00 percent

N	Compound amount — Future value of a present amount F/P	Present value — Present value of a future amount P/F	Annuity compound amount — Future value of an annuity F/A	Sinking fund — Annuity providing a future amount A/F	Annuity present value — Present value of an annuity P/A	Capital recovery — Annuity repaying a present amount A/P	N
1	1.0300	.9709	1.0000	1.0000	.9709	1.0300	1
2	1.0609	.9426	2.0300	.4926	1.9135	.5226	2
3	1.0927	.9151	3.0909	.3235	2.8286	.3535	3
4	1.1255	.8885	4.1836	.2390	3.7171	.2690	4
5	1.1593	.8626	5.3091	.1884	4.5797	.2184	5
6	1.1941	.8375	6.4684	.1546	5.4172	.1846	6
7	1.2299	.8131	7.6625	.1305	6.2303	.1605	7
8	1.2668	.7894	8.8923	.1125	7.0197	.1425	8
9	1.3048	.7664	10.1591	.0984	7.7861	.1284	9
10	1.3439	.7441	11.4639	.0872	8.5302	.1172	10
11	1.3842	.7224	12.8078	.0781	9.2526	.1081	11
12	1.4258	.7014	14.1920	.0705	9.9540	.1005	12
13	1.4685	.6810	15.6178	.0640	10.6350	.0940	13
14	1.5126	.6611	17.0863	.0585	11.2961	.0885	14
15	1.5580	.6419	18.5989	.0538	11.9379	.0838	15
16	1.6047	.6232	20.1569	.0496	12.5611	.0796	16
17	1.6528	.6050	21.7616	.0460	13.1651	.0760	17
18	1.7024	.5874	23.4144	.0427	13.7535	.0727	18
19	1.7535	.5703	25.1169	.0398	14.3238	.0698	19
20	1.8061	.5537	26.8704	.0372	14.8775	.0672	20
21	1.8603	.5375	28.6765	.0349	15.4150	.0649	21
22	1.9161	.5219	30.5368	.0327	15.9369	.0627	22
23	1.9736	.5067	32.4529	.0308	16.4436	.0608	23
24	2.0328	.4919	34.4265	.0290	16.9355	.0590	24
25	2.0938	.4776	36.4593	.0274	17.4131	.0574	25
26	2.1566	.4637	38.5530	.0259	17.8768	.0559	26
27	2.2213	.4502	40.7096	.0246	18.3270	.0546	27
28	2.2879	.4371	42.9309	.0233	18.7641	.0533	28
29	2.3566	.4243	45.2189	.0221	19.1885	.0521	29
30	2.4273	.4120	47.5754	.0210	19.6004	.0510	30
31	2.5001	.4000	50.0027	.0200	20.0004	.0500	31
32	2.5751	.3883	52.5028	.0190	20.3888	.0490	32
33	2.6523	.3770	55.0778	.0182	20.7658	.0482	33
34	2.7319	.3660	57.7302	.0173	21.1318	.0473	34
35	2.8139	.3554	60.4621	.0165	21.4372	.0465	35
36	2.8983	.3450	63.2759	.0158	21.8323	.0458	36
40	3.2620	.3066	75.4013	.0133	23.1148	.0433	40
44	3.6715	.2724	89.0484	.0112	24.2543	.0412	44
48	4.1323	.2420	104.4084	.0096	25.2667	.0396	48
52	4.6509	.2150	121.6962	.0082	26.1662	.0382	52
56	5.2346	.1910	141.1538	.0071	26.9655	.0371	56
60	5.8916	.1697	163.0534	.0061	27.6756	.0361	60
64	6.6311	.1508	187.7017	.0053	28.3065	.0353	64
68	7.4633	.1340	215.4436	.0046	28.8670	.0346	68
72	8.4000	.1190	246.6672	.0041	29.3651	.0341	72
76	9.4543	.1058	281.8098	.0035	29.8076	.0335	76
80	10.6409	.0940	321.3630	.0031	30.2008	.0331	80
84	11.9754	.0835	365.3805	.0027	30.5501	.0327	84
88	13.4796	.0742	415.9854	.0024	30.8605	.0324	88
92	15.1714	.0659	472.3789	.0021	31.1362	.0321	92
96	17.0755	.0586	535.8502	.0019	31.3812	.0319	96
100	19.2186	.0520	607.2877	.0016	31.5989	.0316	100
104	21.6307	.0462	687.6913	.0015	31.7923	.0315	104
108	24.3456	.0411	778.1863	.0013	31.9642	.0313	108
112	27.4012	.0365	880.0391	.0011	32.1168	.0311	112
116	30.8403	.0324	994.6754	.0010	32.2525	.0310	116
120	34.7110	.0288	1123.6396	.0009	32.3730	.0309	120
∞					33.3333	.0300	∞

Interest rate of 4.00 percent

N	Compound amount — Future value of a present amount — F/P	Present value — Present value of a future amount — P/F	Annuity compound amount — Future value of an annuity — F/A	Sinking fund — Annuity providing a future amount — A/F	Annuity present value — Present value of an annuity — P/A	Capital recovery — Annuity repaying a present amount — A/P	N
40	4.8010	.2083	95.0255	.0105	19.7928	.0505	40
44	5.6165	.1780	115.4129	.0087	20.5488	.0487	44
48	6.5705	.1522	139.2632	.0072	21.1951	.0472	48
52	7.6866	.1301	167.1647	.0060	21.7476	.0460	52
56	8.9922	.1112	199.8055	.0050	22.2198	.0450	56
60	10.5196	.0951	237.9907	.0042	22.6235	.0442	60
64	12.3065	.0813	282.6619	.0035	22.9685	.0435	64
68	14.3968	.0695	334.9209	.0030	23.2635	.0430	68
72	16.8423	.0594	396.0566	.0025	23.5156	.0425	72
76	19.7031	.0508	467.5766	.0021	23.7312	.0421	76
80	23.0498	.0434	551.2450	.0018	23.9154	.0418	80
84	26.9650	.0371	649.1251	.0015	24.0729	.0415	84
88	31.5452	.0317	763.6310	.0013	24.2075	.0413	88
92	36.9035	.0271	897.5868	.0011	24.3226	.0411	92
96	43.1718	.0232	1054.2960	.0009	24.4209	.0409	96
100	50.5049	.0198	1237.6237	.0008	24.5050	.0408	100
104	59.0836	.0169	1452.0911	.0007	24.5769	.0407	104
108	69.1195	.0145	1702.9877	.0006	24.6383	.0406	108
112	80.8600	.0124	1996.5012	.0005	24.6908	.0405	112
116	94.5948	.0106	2339.8705	.0004	24.7357	.0404	116
120	110.6626	.0090	2741.5640	.0004	24.7741	.0404	120
8					25.0000	.0400	8

N	Compound amount — Future value of a present amount — F/P	Present value — Present value of a future amount — P/F	Annuity compound amount — Future value of an annuity — F/A	Sinking fund — Annuity providing a future amount — A/F	Annuity present value — Present value of an annuity — P/A	Capital recovery — Annuity repaying a present amount — A/P	N
1	1.0400	.9615	1.0000	1.0000	.9615	1.0400	1
2	1.0816	.9246	2.0400	.4902	1.8861	.5302	2
3	1.1249	.8890	3.1216	.3203	2.7751	.3603	3
4	1.1699	.8548	4.2465	.2355	3.6299	.2755	4
5	1.2167	.8219	5.4163	.1846	4.4518	.2246	5
6	1.2653	.7903	6.6330	.1508	5.2421	.1908	6
7	1.3159	.7599	7.8983	.1266	6.0021	.1666	7
8	1.3686	.7307	9.2142	.1085	6.7327	.1485	8
9	1.4233	.7026	10.5828	.0945	7.4353	.1345	9
10	1.4802	.6756	12.0061	.0833	8.1109	.1233	10
11	1.5395	.6496	13.4864	.0741	8.7605	.1141	11
12	1.6010	.6246	15.0258	.0666	9.3851	.1066	12
13	1.6651	.6006	16.6268	.0601	9.9856	.1001	13
14	1.7317	.5775	18.2919	.0547	10.5631	.0947	14
15	1.8009	.5553	20.0236	.0499	11.1184	.0899	15
16	1.8730	.5339	21.8245	.0458	11.6523	.0858	16
17	1.9479	.5134	23.6975	.0422	12.1657	.0822	17
18	2.0258	.4936	25.6454	.0390	12.6593	.0790	18
19	2.1068	.4746	27.6712	.0361	13.1339	.0761	19
20	2.1911	.4564	29.7781	.0336	13.5903	.0736	20
21	2.2788	.4388	31.9692	.0313	14.0292	.0713	21
22	2.3699	.4220	34.2480	.0292	14.4511	.0692	22
23	2.4647	.4057	36.6179	.0273	14.8568	.0673	23
24	2.5633	.3901	39.0826	.0256	15.2470	.0656	24
25	2.6658	.3751	41.6459	.0240	15.6221	.0640	25
26	2.7725	.3607	44.3117	.0226	15.9828	.0626	26
27	2.8834	.3468	47.0842	.0212	16.3296	.0612	27
28	2.9987	.3335	49.9676	.0200	16.6631	.0600	28
29	3.1187	.3207	52.9663	.0189	16.9837	.0589	29
30	3.2434	.3083	56.0849	.0178	17.2920	.0578	30
31	3.3731	.2965	59.3283	.0169	17.5885	.0569	31
32	3.5081	.2851	62.7015	.0159	17.8736	.0559	32
33	3.6484	.2741	66.2095	.0151	18.1476	.0551	33
34	3.7943	.2636	69.8579	.0143	18.4112	.0543	34
35	3.9461	.2534	73.6522	.0136	18.6646	.0536	35
36	4.1039	.2437	77.5983	.0129	18.9083	.0529	36

APPENDIX A — Interest rate of 5.00 percent

Interest rate of 5.00 percent

N	Compound amount — Future value of a present amount F/P	Present value — Present value of a future amount P/F	Annuity compound amount — Future value of an annuity F/A	Sinking fund — Annuity providing a future amount A/F	Annuity present value — Present value of an annuity P/A	Capital recovery — Annuity repaying a present amount A/P	N
1	1.0500	.9524	1.0000	1.0000	.9524	1.0500	1
2	1.1025	.9070	2.0500	.4878	1.8594	.5378	2
3	1.1576	.8638	3.1525	.3172	2.7232	.3672	3
4	1.2155	.8227	4.3101	.2320	3.5460	.2820	4
5	1.2763	.7835	5.5256	.1810	4.3295	.2310	5
6	1.3401	.7462	6.8019	.1470	5.0757	.1970	6
7	1.4071	.7107	8.1420	.1228	5.7864	.1728	7
8	1.4775	.6768	9.5491	.1047	6.4632	.1547	8
9	1.5513	.6446	11.0266	.0907	7.1078	.1407	9
10	1.6289	.6139	12.5779	.0795	7.7217	.1295	10
11	1.7103	.5847	14.2068	.0704	8.3064	.1204	11
12	1.7959	.5568	15.9171	.0628	8.8533	.1128	12
13	1.8856	.5303	17.7130	.0565	9.3936	.1065	13
14	1.9799	.5051	19.5986	.0510	9.8986	.1010	14
15	2.0789	.4810	21.5786	.0463	10.3797	.0963	15
16	2.1829	.4581	23.6575	.0423	10.8378	.0923	16
17	2.2920	.4363	25.8404	.0387	11.2741	.0887	17
18	2.4066	.4155	28.1324	.0355	11.6896	.0855	18
19	2.5270	.3957	30.5390	.0327	12.0853	.0827	19
20	2.6533	.3769	33.0660	.0302	12.4622	.0802	20
21	2.7860	.3589	35.7193	.0280	12.8212	.0780	21
22	2.9253	.3418	38.5052	.0260	13.1630	.0760	22
23	3.0715	.3256	41.4305	.0241	13.4886	.0741	23
24	3.2251	.3101	44.5020	.0225	13.7986	.0725	24
25	3.3864	.2953	47.7271	.0210	14.0939	.0710	25
26	3.5557	.2812	51.1135	.0196	14.3752	.0696	26
27	3.7335	.2678	54.6691	.0183	14.6430	.0683	27
28	3.9201	.2551	58.4026	.0171	14.8981	.0671	28
29	4.1161	.2429	62.3227	.0160	15.1411	.0660	29
30	4.3219	.2314	66.4388	.0151	15.3725	.0651	30
31	4.5380	.2204	70.7608	.0141	15.5928	.0641	31
32	4.7649	.2099	75.2988	.0133	15.8027	.0633	32
33	5.0032	.1999	80.0638	.0125	16.0025	.0625	33
34	5.2533	.1904	85.0670	.0118	16.1929	.0618	34
35	5.5160	.1813	90.3203	.0111	16.3742	.0611	35
36	5.7918	.1727	95.8363	.0104	16.5469	.0604	36

N	Compound amount — Future value of a present amount F/P	Present value — Present value of a future amount P/F	Annuity compound amount — Future value of an annuity F/A	Sinking fund — Annuity providing a future amount A/F	Annuity present value — Present value of an annuity P/A	Capital recovery — Annuity repaying a present amount A/P	N
40	7.0400	.1420	120.7996	.0083	17.1591	.0583	40
44	8.5572	.1169	151.1430	.0066	17.6628	.0566	44
48	10.4013	.0961	188.0254	.0053	18.0772	.0553	48
52	12.5428	.0791	232.8562	.0043	18.4181	.0543	52
56	15.3674	.0651	287.3482	.0035	18.6985	.0535	56
60	18.6792	.0535	353.5837	.0028	18.9293	.0528	60
64	22.7047	.0440	434.0933	.0023	19.1191	.0523	64
68	27.5977	.0352	531.9533	.0019	19.2753	.0519	68
72	33.5451	.0298	650.9027	.0015	19.4038	.0515	72
76	40.7743	.0245	795.4864	.0013	19.5095	.0513	76
80	49.5614	.0202	971.2288	.0010	19.5965	.0510	80
84	60.2422	.0166	1184.8448	.0008	19.6680	.0508	84
88	73.2248	.0137	1444.4964	.0007	19.7269	.0507	88
92	89.0052	.0112	1760.1045	.0006	19.7753	.0506	92
96	108.1864	.0092	2143.7282	.0005	19.8151	.0505	96
100	131.5013	.0076	2610.0252	.0004	19.8479	.0504	100
104	159.8406	.0063	3176.8120	.0003	19.8749	.0503	104
108	194.2372	.0051	3865.7450	.0003	19.8971	.0503	108
112	236.1574	.0042	4703.1473	.0002	19.9153	.0502	112
116	287.0508	.0035	5721.0151	.0002	19.9303	.0502	116
120	348.9120	.0029	6958.2397	.0001	19.9427	.0501	120
∞					20.0000	.0500	∞

Interest rate of 6.00 percent

N	Compound amount — Future value of a present amount — F/P	Present value — Present value of a future amount — P/F	Annuity compound amount — Future value of an annuity — F/A	Sinking fund — Annuity providing a future amount — A/F	Annuity present value — Present value of an annuity — P/A	Capital recovery — Annuity repaying a present amount — A/P	N
1	1.0600	.9434	1.0000	1.0000	.9434	1.0600	1
2	1.1236	.8900	2.0600	.4854	1.8334	.5454	2
3	1.1910	.8396	3.1836	.3141	2.6730	.3741	3
4	1.2625	.7921	4.3746	.2286	3.4651	.2886	4
5	1.3382	.7473	5.6371	.1774	4.2124	.2374	5
6	1.4185	.7050	6.9753	.1434	4.9173	.2034	6
7	1.5036	.6651	8.3938	.1191	5.5824	.1791	7
8	1.5938	.6274	9.8975	.1010	6.2098	.1610	8
9	1.6895	.5919	11.4913	.0870	6.8017	.1470	9
10	1.7908	.5584	13.1808	.0759	7.3601	.1359	10
11	1.8983	.5268	14.9716	.0668	7.8869	.1268	11
12	2.0122	.4970	16.8699	.0593	8.3838	.1193	12
13	2.1329	.4688	18.8821	.0530	8.8527	.1130	13
14	2.2609	.4423	21.0151	.0476	9.2950	.1076	14
15	2.3966	.4173	23.2760	.0430	9.7122	.1030	15
16	2.5404	.3936	25.6725	.0390	10.1059	.0990	16
17	2.6928	.3714	28.2129	.0354	10.4773	.0954	17
18	2.8543	.3503	30.9057	.0324	10.8276	.0924	18
19	3.0256	.3305	33.7600	.0296	11.1581	.0896	19
20	3.2071	.3118	36.7856	.0272	11.4699	.0872	20
21	3.3996	.2942	39.9927	.0250	11.7641	.0850	21
22	3.6035	.2775	43.3923	.0230	12.0416	.0830	22
23	3.8197	.2618	46.9958	.0213	12.3034	.0813	23
24	4.0489	.2470	50.8156	.0197	12.5504	.0797	24
25	4.2919	.2330	54.8645	.0182	12.7834	.0782	25
26	4.5494	.2198	59.1564	.0169	13.0032	.0769	26
27	4.8223	.2074	63.7058	.0157	13.2105	.0757	27
28	5.1117	.1956	68.5281	.0146	13.4062	.0746	28
29	5.4184	.1846	73.6398	.0136	13.5907	.0736	29
30	5.7435	.1741	79.0582	.0126	13.7648	.0726	30
31	6.0881	.1643	84.8017	.0118	13.9291	.0718	31
32	6.4534	.1550	90.8898	.0110	14.0840	.0710	32
33	6.8406	.1462	97.3432	.0103	14.2302	.0703	33
34	7.2510	.1379	104.1838	.0096	14.3681	.0696	34
35	7.6861	.1301	111.4348	.0090	14.4982	.0690	35
36	8.1473	.1227	119.1209	.0084	14.6210	.0684	36

N	Compound amount — Future value of a present amount — F/P	Present value — Present value of a future amount — P/F	Annuity compound amount — Future value of an annuity — F/A	Sinking fund — Annuity providing a future amount — A/F	Annuity present value — Present value of an annuity — P/A	Capital recovery — Annuity repaying a present amount — A/P	N
40	10.2857	.0972	154.7620	.0065	15.0463	.0665	40
44	12.9855	.0770	199.7580	.0050	15.3832	.0650	44
48	16.3939	.0610	256.5645	.0039	15.6500	.0639	48
52	20.6969	.0483	328.2814	.0030	15.8614	.0630	52
56	26.1293	.0383	418.8223	.0024	16.0288	.0624	56
60	32.9877	.0303	533.1282	.0019	16.1614	.0619	60
64	41.6462	.0240	677.4367	.0015	16.2665	.0615	64
68	52.5774	.0190	859.6228	.0012	16.3497	.0612	68
72	66.3777	.0151	1089.6286	.0009	16.4156	.0609	72
76	83.8003	.0119	1380.0056	.0007	16.4678	.0607	76
80	105.7960	.0095	1746.5999	.0006	16.5091	.0606	80
84	133.5650	.0075	2209.4167	.0005	16.5419	.0605	84
88	168.6227	.0059	2793.7123	.0004	16.5678	.0604	88
92	212.8823	.0047	3531.3721	.0003	16.5884	.0603	92
96	268.7590	.0037	4462.6505	.0002	16.6047	.0602	96
100	339.3021	.0029	5638.3681	.0002	16.6175	.0602	100
104	428.3611	.0023	7122.6844	.0001	16.6278	.0601	104
108	540.7960	.0018	8996.5995	.0001	16.6358	.0601	108
112	682.7425	.0015	11362.3743	.0001	16.6423	.0601	112
116	861.9466	.0012	14349.1103	.0001	16.6473	.0601	116
120	1088.1877	.0009	18119.7958	.0001	16.6514	.0601	120
∞					16.6667	.0600	∞

APPENDIX A Interest rates of 7.00 and 8.00 percent

Interest rate of 8.00 percent

N	Capital recovery — Annuity repaying a present amount (A/P)	Annuity present value — Present value of an annuity (P/A)	Sinking fund — Annuity providing a future amount (A/F)	Annuity compound amount — Future value of an annuity (F/A)	Present value — Present value of a future amount (P/F)	Compound amount — Future value of a present amount (F/P)	N
1	1.0800	.9259	1.0000	1.0000	.9259	1.0800	1
2	.5608	1.7833	.4808	2.0800	.8573	1.1664	2
3	.3880	2.5771	.3080	3.2464	.7938	1.2597	3
4	.3019	3.3121	.2219	4.5061	.7350	1.3605	4
5	.2505	3.9927	.1705	5.8666	.6806	1.4693	5
6	.2163	4.6229	.1363	7.3359	.6302	1.5869	6
7	.1921	5.2064	.1121	8.9228	.5835	1.7138	7
8	.1740	5.7466	.0940	10.6366	.5403	1.8509	8
9	.1601	6.2469	.0801	12.4876	.5002	1.9990	9
10	.1490	6.7101	.0690	14.4866	.4632	2.1589	10
11	.1401	7.1390	.0601	16.6455	.4289	2.3316	11
12	.1327	7.5361	.0527	18.9771	.3971	2.5182	12
13	.1265	7.9038	.0465	21.4953	.3677	2.7196	13
14	.1213	8.2442	.0413	24.2149	.3405	2.9372	14
15	.1168	8.5595	.0368	27.1521	.3152	3.1722	15
16	.1130	8.8514	.0330	30.3243	.2919	3.4259	16
17	.1096	9.1216	.0296	33.7502	.2703	3.7000	17
18	.1067	9.3719	.0267	37.4502	.2502	3.9960	18
19	.1041	9.6036	.0241	41.4463	.2317	4.3157	19
20	.1019	9.8181	.0219	45.7620	.2145	4.6610	20
21	.0998	10.0168	.0198	50.4229	.1987	5.0338	21
22	.0980	10.2007	.0180	55.4568	.1839	5.4365	22
23	.0964	10.3711	.0164	60.8933	.1703	5.8715	23
24	.0950	10.5288	.0150	66.7648	.1577	6.3412	24
25	.0937	10.6748	.0137	73.1059	.1460	6.8485	25
26	.0925	10.8100	.0125	79.9544	.1352	7.3964	26
27	.0914	10.9352	.0114	87.3508	.1252	7.9881	27
28	.0905	11.0511	.0105	95.3388	.1159	8.6271	28
29	.0896	11.1584	.0096	103.9659	.1073	9.3173	29
30	.0888	11.2578	.0088	113.2832	.0994	10.0627	30
35	.0858	11.6546	.0058	172.3168	.0676	14.7853	35
40	.0839	11.9246	.0039	259.0565	.0450	21.7245	40
45	.0826	12.1084	.0026	386.5056	.0313	31.9204	45
50	.0817	12.2335	.0017	573.7702	.0213	46.9016	50
55	.0812	12.3186	.0012	848.9232	.0145	68.9139	55
60	.0808	12.3766	.0008	1253.2133	.0099	101.2571	60
∞	.0800	12.5000					∞

Interest rate of 7.00 percent

N	Compound amount — Future value of a present amount (F/P)	Present value — Present value of a future amount (P/F)	Annuity compound amount — Future value of an annuity (F/A)	Sinking fund — Annuity providing a future amount (A/F)	Annuity present value — Present value of an annuity (P/A)	Capital recovery — Annuity repaying a present amount (A/P)	N
1	1.0700	.9346	1.0000	1.0000	.9346	1.0700	1
2	1.1449	.8734	2.0700	.4831	1.8080	.5531	2
3	1.2250	.8163	3.2149	.3111	2.6243	.3811	3
4	1.3108	.7629	4.4399	.2252	3.3872	.2952	4
5	1.4026	.7130	5.7507	.1739	4.1002	.2439	5
6	1.5007	.6663	7.1533	.1398	4.7665	.2098	6
7	1.6058	.6227	8.6540	.1156	5.3893	.1856	7
8	1.7182	.5820	10.2598	.0975	5.9713	.1675	8
9	1.8385	.5439	11.9780	.0835	6.5152	.1535	9
10	1.9672	.5083	13.8164	.0724	7.0236	.1424	10
11	2.1049	.4751	15.7836	.0634	7.4987	.1334	11
12	2.2522	.4440	17.8885	.0559	7.9427	.1259	12
13	2.4098	.4150	20.1406	.0497	8.3577	.1197	13
14	2.5785	.3878	22.5505	.0443	8.7455	.1143	14
15	2.7590	.3624	25.1290	.0398	9.1079	.1098	15
16	2.9522	.3387	27.8881	.0359	9.4466	.1059	16
17	3.1588	.3166	30.8402	.0324	9.7632	.1024	17
18	3.3799	.2959	33.9990	.0294	10.0591	.0994	18
19	3.6165	.2765	37.3790	.0268	10.3356	.0968	19
20	3.8697	.2584	40.9955	.0244	10.5940	.0944	20
21	4.1406	.2415	44.8652	.0223	10.8355	.0923	21
22	4.4304	.2257	49.0057	.0204	11.0612	.0904	22
23	4.7405	.2109	53.4361	.0187	11.2722	.0887	23
24	5.0724	.1971	58.1767	.0172	11.4693	.0872	24
25	5.4274	.1842	63.2490	.0158	11.6536	.0858	25
26	5.8074	.1722	68.6765	.0146	11.8258	.0846	26
27	6.2139	.1609	74.4838	.0134	11.9867	.0834	27
28	6.6488	.1504	80.6977	.0124	12.1371	.0824	28
29	7.1143	.1406	87.3465	.0114	12.2777	.0814	29
30	7.6123	.1314	94.4608	.0106	12.4090	.0806	30
35	10.6766	.0937	138.2369	.0072	12.9477	.0772	35
40	14.9745	.0668	199.6351	.0050	13.3317	.0750	40
45	21.0025	.0476	285.7493	.0035	13.6055	.0735	45
50	29.4570	.0339	406.5289	.0025	13.8007	.0725	50
55	41.3150	.0242	575.9286	.0017	13.9399	.0717	55
60	57.9464	.0173	813.5204	.0012	14.0392	.0712	60
∞					14.2857	.0700	∞

Interest rate of 10.00 percent

N	Compound amount — Future value of a present amount F/P	Present value — Present value of a future amount P/F	Annuity compound amount — Future value of an annuity F/A	Sinking fund — Annuity providing a future amount A/F	Annuity present value — Present value of an annuity P/A	Capital recovery — Annuity repaying a present amount A/P	N
1	1.1000	.9091	1.0000	1.0000	.9091	1.1000	1
2	1.2100	.8264	2.1000	.4762	1.7355	.5762	2
3	1.3310	.7513	3.3100	.3021	2.4869	.4021	3
4	1.4641	.6830	4.6410	.2155	3.1699	.3155	4
5	1.6105	.6209	6.1051	.1638	3.7908	.2638	5
6	1.7716	.5645	7.7156	.1296	4.3553	.2296	6
7	1.9487	.5132	9.4872	.1054	4.8684	.2054	7
8	2.1436	.4665	11.4359	.0874	5.3349	.1874	8
9	2.3579	.4241	13.5795	.0736	5.7590	.1736	9
10	2.5937	.3855	15.9374	.0627	6.1446	.1627	10
11	2.8531	.3505	18.5312	.0540	6.4951	.1540	11
12	3.1384	.3186	21.3843	.0468	6.8137	.1468	12
13	3.4523	.2897	24.5227	.0408	7.1034	.1408	13
14	3.7975	.2633	27.9750	.0357	7.3667	.1357	14
15	4.1772	.2394	31.7725	.0315	7.6061	.1315	15
16	4.5950	.2176	35.9497	.0278	7.8237	.1278	16
17	5.0545	.1978	40.5447	.0247	8.0216	.1247	17
18	5.5599	.1799	45.5992	.0219	8.2014	.1219	18
19	6.1159	.1635	51.1591	.0195	8.3649	.1195	19
20	6.7275	.1486	57.2750	.0175	8.5136	.1175	20
21	7.4002	.1351	64.0025	.0156	8.6487	.1156	21
22	8.1403	.1228	71.4027	.0140	8.7715	.1140	22
23	8.9543	.1117	79.5430	.0126	8.8832	.1126	23
24	9.8497	.1015	88.4973	.0113	8.9847	.1113	24
25	10.8347	.0923	98.3471	.0102	9.0770	.1102	25
26	11.9182	.0839	109.1818	.0092	9.1609	.1092	26
27	13.1100	.0763	121.0999	.0083	9.2372	.1083	27
28	14.4210	.0693	134.2099	.0075	9.3066	.1075	28
29	15.8631	.0630	148.6309	.0067	9.3696	.1067	29
30	17.4494	.0573	164.4940	.0061	9.4269	.1061	30
35	28.1024	.0356	271.0244	.0037	9.6442	.1037	35
40	45.2593	.0221	442.5926	.0023	9.7791	.1023	40
45	72.8905	.0137	718.9048	.0014	9.8628	.1014	45
50	117.3909	.0085	1163.9085	.0009	9.9148	.1009	50
55	189.0591	.0053	1880.5914	.0005	9.9471	.1005	55
60	304.4816	.0033	3034.8164	.0003	9.9672	.1003	60
∞					10.0000	.1000	∞

Interest rate of 9.00 percent

N	Compound amount — Future value of a present amount F/P	Present value — Present value of a future amount P/F	Annuity compound amount — Future value of an annuity F/A	Sinking fund — Annuity providing a future amount A/F	Annuity present value — Present value of an annuity P/A	Capital recovery — Annuity repaying a present amount A/P	N
1	1.0900	.9174	1.0000	1.0000	.9174	1.0900	1
2	1.1881	.8417	2.0900	.4785	1.7591	.5685	2
3	1.2950	.7722	3.2781	.3051	2.5313	.3951	3
4	1.4116	.7084	4.5731	.2187	3.2397	.3087	4
5	1.5386	.6499	5.9847	.1671	3.8897	.2571	5
6	1.6771	.5963	7.5233	.1329	4.4859	.2229	6
7	1.8280	.5470	9.2004	.1087	5.0330	.1987	7
8	1.9926	.5019	11.0285	.0907	5.5348	.1807	8
9	2.1719	.4604	13.0210	.0768	5.9952	.1668	9
10	2.3674	.4224	15.1929	.0658	6.4177	.1558	10
11	2.5804	.3875	17.5603	.0569	6.8052	.1469	11
12	2.8127	.3555	20.1407	.0497	7.1607	.1397	12
13	3.0658	.3262	22.9534	.0436	7.4869	.1336	13
14	3.3417	.2992	26.0192	.0384	7.7862	.1284	14
15	3.6425	.2745	29.3609	.0341	8.0607	.1241	15
16	3.9703	.2519	33.0034	.0303	8.3126	.1203	16
17	4.3276	.2311	36.9737	.0270	8.5436	.1170	17
18	4.7171	.2120	41.3013	.0242	8.7556	.1142	18
19	5.1417	.1945	46.0185	.0217	8.9501	.1117	19
20	5.6044	.1784	51.1601	.0195	9.1285	.1095	20
21	6.1088	.1637	56.7645	.0176	9.2922	.1076	21
22	6.6586	.1502	62.8733	.0159	9.4424	.1059	22
23	7.2579	.1378	69.5319	.0144	9.5802	.1044	23
24	7.9111	.1264	76.7898	.0130	9.7066	.1030	24
25	8.6231	.1160	84.7009	.0118	9.8226	.1018	25
26	9.3992	.1064	93.3240	.0107	9.9290	.1007	26
27	10.2451	.0976	102.7231	.0097	10.0266	.0997	27
28	11.1671	.0895	112.9682	.0089	10.1161	.0989	28
29	12.1722	.0822	124.1354	.0081	10.1983	.0981	29
30	13.2677	.0754	136.3075	.0073	10.2737	.0973	30
35	20.4140	.0490	215.7108	.0046	10.5668	.0946	35
40	31.4094	.0318	337.8824	.0030	10.7574	.0930	40
45	48.3273	.0207	525.8587	.0019	10.8812	.0919	45
50	74.3575	.0134	815.0836	.0012	10.9617	.0912	50
55	114.4083	.0087	1260.0918	.0008	11.0140	.0908	55
60	176.0313	.0057	1944.7921	.0005	11.0480	.0905	60
∞					11.1111	.0900	∞

APPENDIX A   Interest rates of 11.00 and 12.00 percent

Interest rate of 12.00 percent

N	Compound amount — Future value of a present amount — F/P	Present value — Present value of a future amount — P/F	Annuity compound amount — Future value of an annuity — F/A	Sinking fund — Annuity providing a future amount — A/F	Annuity present value — Present value of an annuity — P/A	Capital recovery — Annuity repaying a present amount — A/P	N
1	1.1200	.8929	1.0000	1.0000	.8929	1.1200	1
2	1.2544	.7972	2.1200	.4717	1.6901	.5917	2
3	1.4049	.7118	3.3744	.2963	2.4018	.4163	3
4	1.5735	.6355	4.7793	.2092	3.0373	.3292	4
5	1.7623	.5674	6.3528	.1574	3.6048	.2774	5
6	1.9738	.5066	8.1152	.1232	4.1114	.2432	6
7	2.2107	.4523	10.0890	.0991	4.5638	.2191	7
8	2.4760	.4039	12.2997	.0813	4.9676	.2013	8
9	2.7731	.3606	14.7757	.0677	5.3282	.1877	9
10	3.1058	.3220	17.5487	.0570	5.6502	.1770	10
11	3.4785	.2875	20.6546	.0484	5.9377	.1684	11
12	3.8960	.2567	24.1331	.0414	6.1944	.1614	12
13	4.3635	.2292	28.0291	.0357	6.4235	.1557	13
14	4.8871	.2046	32.3926	.0309	6.6282	.1509	14
15	5.4736	.1827	37.2797	.0268	6.8109	.1468	15
16	6.1304	.1631	42.7533	.0234	6.9740	.1434	16
17	6.8660	.1456	48.8837	.0205	7.1196	.1405	17
18	7.6900	.1300	55.7497	.0179	7.2497	.1379	18
19	8.6128	.1161	63.4397	.0158	7.3658	.1358	19
20	9.6463	.1037	72.0524	.0139	7.4694	.1339	20
21	10.8038	.0926	81.6987	.0122	7.5620	.1322	21
22	12.1003	.0826	92.5026	.0108	7.6446	.1308	22
23	13.5523	.0738	104.6029	.0096	7.7184	.1296	23
24	15.1786	.0659	113.1552	.0085	7.7843	.1285	24
25	17.0001	.0588	133.3339	.0075	7.8431	.1275	25
26	19.0401	.0525	150.3339	.0067	7.8957	.1267	26
27	21.3249	.0469	169.3740	.0059	7.9426	.1259	27
28	23.8839	.0419	190.6989	.0052	7.9844	.1252	28
29	26.7499	.0374	214.5828	.0047	8.0218	.1247	29
30	29.9599	.0334	241.3327	.0041	8.0552	.1241	30
35	52.7996	.0189	431.6635	.0023	8.1755	.1223	35
40	93.0510	.0107	767.0914	.0013	8.2438	.1213	40
45	163.9876	.0061	1358.2300	.0007	8.2825	.1207	45
50	289.0022	.0035	2400.0132	.0004	8.3045	.1204	50
55	509.3206	.0020	4236.0050	.0002	8.3170	.1202	55
60	897.5969	.0011	7471.6411	.0001	8.3240	.1201	60
8					8.3333	.1200	8

Interest rate of 11.00 percent

N	Compound amount — Future value of a present amount — F/P	Present value — Present value of a future amount — P/F	Annuity compound amount — Future value of an annuity — F/A	Sinking fund — Annuity providing a future amount — A/F	Annuity present value — Present value of an annuity — P/A	Capital recovery — Annuity repaying a present amount — A/P	N
1	1.1100	.9009	1.0000	1.0000	.9009	1.1100	1
2	1.2321	.8116	2.1100	.4739	1.7125	.5839	2
3	1.3676	.7312	3.3421	.2992	2.4437	.4092	3
4	1.5181	.6587	4.7097	.2123	3.1024	.3223	4
5	1.6851	.5935	6.2278	.1606	3.6959	.2706	5
6	1.8704	.5346	7.9129	.1264	4.2305	.2364	6
7	2.0762	.4817	9.7833	.1022	4.7122	.2122	7
8	2.3045	.4339	11.8594	.0843	5.1461	.1943	8
9	2.5580	.3909	14.1640	.0706	5.5370	.1806	9
10	2.8394	.3522	16.7220	.0598	5.8892	.1698	10
11	3.1518	.3173	19.5614	.0511	6.2065	.1611	11
12	3.4985	.2858	22.7132	.0440	6.4924	.1540	12
13	3.8833	.2575	26.2116	.0382	6.7499	.1482	13
14	4.3104	.2320	30.0949	.0332	6.9819	.1432	14
15	4.7846	.2090	34.4054	.0291	7.1909	.1391	15
16	5.3109	.1883	39.1899	.0255	7.3792	.1355	16
17	5.8951	.1696	44.5008	.0225	7.5488	.1325	17
18	6.5436	.1528	50.3959	.0198	7.7016	.1298	18
19	7.2633	.1377	56.9395	.0176	7.8393	.1276	19
20	8.0623	.1240	64.2028	.0156	7.9633	.1256	20
21	8.9492	.1117	72.2651	.0138	8.0751	.1238	21
22	9.9336	.1007	81.2143	.0123	8.1757	.1223	22
23	11.0263	.0907	91.1479	.0110	8.2664	.1210	23
24	12.2392	.0817	102.1742	.0098	8.3481	.1198	24
25	13.5855	.0736	114.4133	.0087	8.4217	.1187	25
26	15.0799	.0663	127.9988	.0078	8.4881	.1178	26
27	16.7386	.0597	143.0786	.0070	8.5478	.1170	27
28	18.5799	.0538	159.8173	.0063	8.6016	.1163	28
29	20.6237	.0485	178.3972	.0056	8.6501	.1156	29
30	22.8923	.0437	199.0209	.0050	8.6938	.1150	30
35	38.5749	.0259	341.5896	.0029	8.8552	.1129	35
40	65.0009	.0154	581.8261	.0017	8.9511	.1117	40
45	109.5302	.0091	986.6386	.0010	9.0079	.1110	45
50	184.5648	.0054	1668.7712	.0006	9.0417	.1106	50
55	311.0025	.0032	2818.2042	.0004	9.0617	.1104	55
60	524.0572	.0019	4755.0658	.0002	9.0736	.1102	60
8					9.0909	.1100	8

Interest rate of 13.00 percent

N	Compound amount — Future value of a present amount F/P	Present value — Present value of a future amount P/F	Annuity compound amount — Future value of an annuity F/A	Sinking fund — Annuity providing a future amount A/F	Annuity present value — Present value of an annuity P/A	Capital recovery — Annuity repaying a present amount A/P	N
1	1.1300	.8850	1.0000	1.0000	.8850	1.1300	1
2	1.2769	.7831	2.1300	.4695	1.6681	.5995	2
3	1.4429	.6931	3.4069	.2935	2.3612	.4235	3
4	1.6305	.6133	4.8498	.2062	2.9745	.3362	4
5	1.8424	.5428	6.4803	.1543	3.5172	.2843	5
6	2.0820	.4803	8.3227	.1202	3.9975	.2502	6
7	2.3526	.4251	10.4047	.0961	4.4226	.2261	7
8	2.6584	.3762	12.7573	.0784	4.7988	.2084	8
9	3.0040	.3329	15.4157	.0649	5.1317	.1949	9
10	3.3946	.2946	18.4197	.0543	5.4262	.1843	10
11	3.8359	.2607	21.8143	.0458	5.6869	.1758	11
12	4.3345	.2307	25.6502	.0390	5.9176	.1690	12
13	4.8980	.2042	29.9847	.0334	6.1218	.1634	13
14	5.5348	.1807	34.8827	.0287	6.3025	.1587	14
15	6.2543	.1599	40.4175	.0247	6.4624	.1547	15
16	7.0673	.1415	46.6717	.0214	6.6039	.1514	16
17	7.9861	.1252	53.7391	.0186	6.7291	.1486	17
18	9.0243	.1108	61.7251	.0162	6.8399	.1462	18
19	10.1974	.0981	70.7494	.0141	6.9380	.1441	19
20	11.5231	.0868	80.9468	.0124	7.0248	.1424	20
21	13.0211	.0768	92.4699	.0108	7.1016	.1408	21
22	14.7138	.0680	105.4910	.0095	7.1695	.1395	22
23	16.6266	.0601	120.2048	.0083	7.2297	.1383	23
24	18.7881	.0532	136.8315	.0073	7.2829	.1373	24
25	21.2305	.0471	155.6196	.0064	7.3300	.1364	25
26	23.9905	.0417	176.8501	.0057	7.3717	.1357	26
27	27.1093	.0369	200.8406	.0050	7.4086	.1350	27
28	30.6335	.0326	227.9499	.0044	7.4412	.1344	28
29	34.6158	.0289	258.5834	.0039	7.4701	.1339	29
30	39.1159	.0256	293.1992	.0034	7.4957	.1334	30
35	72.0685	.0139	546.6808	.0018	7.5856	.1318	35
40	132.7816	.0075	1013.7042	.0010	7.6344	.1310	40
45	244.6414	.0041	1874.1646	.0005	7.6609	.1305	45
50	450.7359	.0022	3459.5071	.0003	7.6752	.1303	50
55	830.4517	.0012	6380.3979	.0002	7.6830	.1302	55
60	1530.0535	.0007	11761.9498	.0001	7.6873	.1301	60
∞					7.6923	.1300	∞

Interest rate of 14.00 percent

N	Compound amount — Future value of a present amount F/P	Present value — Present value of a future amount P/F	Annuity compound amount — Future value of an annuity F/A	Sinking fund — Annuity providing a future amount A/F	Annuity present value — Present value of an annuity P/A	Capital recovery — Annuity repaying a present amount A/P	N
1	1.1400	.8772	1.0000	1.0000	.8772	1.1400	1
2	1.2996	.7695	2.1400	.4673	1.6467	.6073	2
3	1.4815	.6750	3.4396	.2907	2.3216	.4307	3
4	1.6890	.5921	4.9211	.2032	2.9137	.3432	4
5	1.9254	.5194	6.6101	.1513	3.4331	.2913	5
6	2.1950	.4556	8.5355	.1172	3.8887	.2572	6
7	2.5023	.3996	10.7305	.0932	4.2883	.2332	7
8	2.8526	.3506	13.2328	.0756	4.6389	.2156	8
9	3.2519	.3075	16.0853	.0622	4.9464	.2022	9
10	3.7072	.2697	19.3373	.0517	5.2161	.1917	10
11	4.2262	.2366	23.0445	.0434	5.4527	.1834	11
12	4.8179	.2076	27.2707	.0367	5.6603	.1767	12
13	5.4924	.1821	32.0887	.0312	5.8424	.1712	13
14	6.2613	.1597	37.5811	.0266	6.0021	.1666	14
15	7.1379	.1401	43.8424	.0228	6.1422	.1628	15
16	8.1372	.1229	50.9804	.0196	6.2651	.1596	16
17	9.2765	.1078	59.1176	.0169	6.3729	.1569	17
18	10.5752	.0946	68.3941	.0146	6.4674	.1546	18
19	12.0557	.0829	78.9692	.0127	6.5504	.1527	19
20	13.7435	.0728	91.0249	.0110	6.6231	.1510	20
21	15.6676	.0638	104.7684	.0095	6.6870	.1495	21
22	17.8610	.0560	120.4360	.0083	6.7429	.1483	22
23	20.3616	.0491	138.2970	.0072	6.7921	.1472	23
24	23.2122	.0431	158.6586	.0063	6.8351	.1463	24
25	26.4619	.0378	181.8708	.0055	6.8729	.1455	25
26	30.1666	.0331	208.3327	.0048	6.9061	.1448	26
27	34.3899	.0291	238.4993	.0042	6.9352	.1442	27
28	39.2045	.0255	272.8892	.0037	6.9607	.1437	28
29	44.6931	.0224	312.0937	.0032	6.9830	.1432	29
30	50.9502	.0196	356.7868	.0028	7.0027	.1428	30
35	98.1002	.0102	693.5727	.0014	7.0700	.1414	35
40	188.8835	.0053	1342.0251	.0007	7.1050	.1407	40
45	363.6791	.0027	2590.5648	.0004	7.1232	.1404	45
50	700.2330	.0014	4994.5213	.0002	7.1327	.1402	50
55	1348.2388	.0007	9623.1343	.0001	7.1376	.1401	55
60	2595.9187	.0004	18535.1333	.0001	7.1401	.1401	60
∞					7.1429	.1400	∞

APPENDIX A Interest rates of 15.00 and 16.00 percent

Interest rate of 15.00 percent

N	Compound amount — Future value of a present amount — F/P	Present value — Present value of a future amount — P/F	Annuity compound amount — Future value of an annuity — F/A	Sinking fund — Annuity providing a future amount — A/F	Annuity present value — Present value of an annuity — P/A	Capital recovery — Annuity repaying a present amount — A/P	N
1	1.1500	.8696	1.0000	1.0000	.8696	1.1500	1
2	1.3225	.7561	2.1500	.4651	1.6257	.6151	2
3	1.5209	.6575	3.4725	.2880	2.2832	.4380	3
4	1.7490	.5718	4.9934	.2003	2.8550	.3503	4
5	2.0114	.4972	6.7424	.1483	3.3522	.2983	5
6	2.3131	.4323	8.7537	.1142	3.7845	.2642	6
7	2.6600	.3759	11.0668	.0904	4.1604	.2404	7
8	3.0590	.3269	13.7268	.0729	4.4873	.2229	8
9	3.5179	.2843	16.7858	.0596	4.7716	.2096	9
10	4.0456	.2472	20.3037	.0493	5.0188	.1993	10
11	4.6524	.2149	24.3493	.0411	5.2337	.1911	11
12	5.3503	.1869	29.0017	.0345	5.4206	.1845	12
13	6.1528	.1625	34.3519	.0291	5.5831	.1791	13
14	7.0757	.1413	40.5047	.0247	5.7245	.1747	14
15	8.1371	.1229	47.5804	.0210	5.8474	.1710	15
16	9.3576	.1069	55.7175	.0179	5.9542	.1679	16
17	10.7613	.0929	65.0751	.0154	6.0472	.1654	17
18	12.3755	.0808	75.8364	.0132	6.1280	.1632	18
19	14.2318	.0703	88.2118	.0113	6.1982	.1613	19
20	16.3665	.0611	102.4436	.0098	6.2593	.1598	20
21	18.8215	.0531	118.8101	.0084	6.3125	.1584	21
22	21.6447	.0462	137.6316	.0073	6.3587	.1573	22
23	24.8915	.0402	159.2764	.0063	6.3988	.1563	23
24	28.6252	.0349	184.1678	.0054	6.4338	.1554	24
25	32.9190	.0304	212.7930	.0047	6.4641	.1547	25
26	37.8568	.0264	245.7120	.0041	6.4906	.1541	26
27	43.5353	.0230	283.5688	.0035	6.5135	.1535	27
28	50.0656	.0200	327.1041	.0031	6.5335	.1531	28
29	57.5755	.0174	377.1697	.0027	6.5509	.1527	29
30	66.2118	.0151	434.7451	.0023	6.5660	.1523	30
35	133.1755	.0075	881.1702	.0011	6.6166	.1511	35
40	267.8635	.0037	1779.0903	.0006	6.6418	.1506	40
45	538.7693	.0019	3585.1285	.0003	6.6543	.1503	45
50	1083.6574	.0009	7217.7163	.0001	6.6605	.1501	50
55	2179.6222	.0005	14524.1479	.0001	6.6636	.1501	55
60	4383.9987	.0002	29219.9916	.0000	6.6651	.1500	60
∞					6.6667	.1500	∞

Interest rate of 16.00 percent

N	Compound amount — Future value of a present amount — F/P	Present value — Present value of a future amount — P/F	Annuity compound amount — Future value of an annuity — F/A	Sinking fund — Annuity providing a future amount — A/F	Annuity present value — Present value of an annuity — P/A	Capital recovery — Annuity repaying a present amount — A/P	N
1	1.1600	.8621	1.0000	1.0000	.8621	1.1600	1
2	1.3456	.7432	2.1600	.4630	1.6052	.6230	2
3	1.5609	.6407	3.5056	.2853	2.2459	.4453	3
4	1.8106	.5523	5.0665	.1974	2.7982	.3574	4
5	2.1003	.4761	6.8771	.1454	3.2743	.3054	5
6	2.4364	.4104	8.9775	.1114	3.6847	.2714	6
7	2.8262	.3538	11.4139	.0876	4.0386	.2476	7
8	3.2784	.3050	14.2401	.0702	4.3436	.2302	8
9	3.8030	.2630	17.5185	.0571	4.6065	.2171	9
10	4.4114	.2267	21.3215	.0469	4.8332	.2069	10
11	5.1173	.1954	25.7329	.0389	5.0286	.1989	11
12	5.9360	.1685	30.8502	.0324	5.1971	.1924	12
13	6.8858	.1452	36.7862	.0272	5.3423	.1872	13
14	7.9875	.1252	43.6720	.0229	5.4675	.1829	14
15	9.2655	.1079	51.6595	.0194	5.5755	.1794	15
16	10.7480	.0930	60.9250	.0164	5.6685	.1764	16
17	12.4677	.0802	71.6730	.0140	5.7487	.1740	17
18	14.4625	.0691	84.1407	.0119	5.8178	.1719	18
19	16.7765	.0596	98.6032	.0101	5.8775	.1701	19
20	19.4608	.0514	115.3797	.0087	5.9288	.1687	20
21	22.5745	.0443	134.8405	.0074	5.9731	.1674	21
22	26.1864	.0382	157.4150	.0064	6.0113	.1664	22
23	30.3762	.0329	183.6014	.0054	6.0442	.1654	23
24	35.2364	.0284	213.9776	.0047	6.0726	.1647	24
25	40.8742	.0245	249.2140	.0040	6.0971	.1640	25
26	47.4141	.0211	290.0883	.0034	6.1182	.1634	26
27	55.0004	.0182	337.5024	.0030	6.1364	.1630	27
28	63.8004	.0157	392.5028	.0025	6.1520	.1625	28
29	74.0085	.0135	456.3032	.0022	6.1656	.1622	29
30	85.8499	.0116	530.3117	.0019	6.1772	.1619	30
35	180.3141	.0055	1120.7130	.0009	6.2153	.1609	35
40	378.7212	.0026	2360.7572	.0004	6.2335	.1604	40
45	795.4438	.0013	4965.2739	.0002	6.2421	.1602	45
50	1670.7038	.0006	10435.6488	.0001	6.2463	.1601	50
55	3509.0488	.0003	21925.3050	.0000	6.2482	.1600	55
60	7370.2014	.0001	46057.5085	.0000	6.2492	.1600	60
∞					6.2500	.1600	∞

APPENDIX A Interest rates of 18.00 and 20.00 percent

Interest rate of 20.00 percent

N	Compound amount / Future value of a present amount / F/P	Present value / Present value of a future amount / P/F	Annuity compound amount / Future value of an annuity / F/A	Sinking fund / Annuity providing a future amount / A/F	Annuity present value / Present value of an annuity / P/A	Capital recovery / Annuity repaying a present amount / A/P	N
1	1.2000	.8333	1.0000	1.0000	.8333	1.2000	1
2	1.4400	.6944	2.2000	.4545	1.5278	.6545	2
3	1.7280	.5787	3.6400	.2747	2.1065	.4747	3
4	2.0736	.4823	5.3680	.1863	2.5887	.3863	4
5	2.4883	.4019	7.4416	.1344	2.9906	.3344	5
6	2.9860	.3349	9.9299	.1007	3.3255	.3007	6
7	3.5832	.2791	12.9159	.0774	3.6046	.2774	7
8	4.2998	.2326	16.4991	.0606	3.8372	.2606	8
9	5.1598	.1938	20.7989	.0481	4.0310	.2481	9
10	6.1917	.1615	25.9587	.0385	4.1925	.2385	10
11	7.4301	.1346	32.1504	.0311	4.3271	.2311	11
12	8.9161	.1122	39.5805	.0253	4.4392	.2253	12
13	10.6993	.0935	48.4966	.0206	4.5327	.2206	13
14	12.8392	.0779	59.1959	.0169	4.6106	.2169	14
15	15.4070	.0649	72.0351	.0139	4.6755	.2139	15
16	18.4884	.0541	87.4421	.0114	4.7296	.2114	16
17	22.1861	.0451	105.9306	.0094	4.7746	.2094	17
18	26.6233	.0376	128.1167	.0078	4.8122	.2078	18
19	31.9480	.0313	154.7400	.0065	4.8435	.2065	19
20	38.3376	.0261	186.6880	.0054	4.8696	.2054	20
21	46.0051	.0217	225.0256	.0044	4.8913	.2044	21
22	55.2061	.0181	271.0307	.0037	4.9094	.2037	22
23	66.2474	.0151	326.2369	.0031	4.9245	.2031	23
24	79.4968	.0126	392.4842	.0025	4.9371	.2025	24
25	95.3962	.0105	471.9811	.0021	4.9476	.2021	25
26	114.4755	.0087	567.3773	.0018	4.9563	.2018	26
27	137.3706	.0073	681.8528	.0015	4.9636	.2015	27
28	164.8447	.0061	819.2233	.0012	4.9697	.2012	28
29	197.8136	.0051	984.0680	.0010	4.9747	.2010	29
30	237.3763	.0042	1181.8816	.0008	4.9789	.2008	30
∞					5.0000	.2000	∞

Interest rate of 18.00 percent

N	Compound amount / Future value of a present amount / F/P	Present value / Present value of a future amount / P/F	Annuity compound amount / Future value of an annuity / F/A	Sinking fund / Annuity providing a future amount / A/F	Annuity present value / Present value of an annuity / P/A	Capital recovery / Annuity repaying a present amount / A/P	N
1	1.1800	.8475	1.0000	1.0000	.8475	1.1800	1
2	1.3924	.7182	2.1800	.4587	1.5656	.6387	2
3	1.6430	.6086	3.5724	.2799	2.1743	.4599	3
4	1.9388	.5158	5.2154	.1917	2.6901	.3717	4
5	2.2878	.4371	7.1542	.1398	3.1272	.3198	5
6	2.6996	.3704	9.4420	.1059	3.4976	.2859	6
7	3.1855	.3139	12.1415	.0824	3.8115	.2624	7
8	3.7589	.2660	15.3270	.0652	4.0776	.2452	8
9	4.4355	.2255	19.0859	.0524	4.3030	.2324	9
10	5.2338	.1911	23.5213	.0425	4.4941	.2225	10
11	6.1759	.1619	28.7551	.0348	4.6560	.2148	11
12	7.2876	.1372	34.9311	.0286	4.7932	.2086	12
13	8.5994	.1163	42.2187	.0237	4.9095	.2037	13
14	10.1472	.0985	50.8180	.0197	5.0081	.1997	14
15	11.9737	.0835	60.9653	.0164	5.0916	.1964	15
16	14.1290	.0708	72.9390	.0137	5.1624	.1937	16
17	16.6722	.0600	87.0680	.0115	5.2223	.1915	17
18	19.6733	.0508	103.7403	.0096	5.2732	.1896	18
19	23.2144	.0431	123.4135	.0081	5.3162	.1881	19
20	27.3930	.0365	146.6280	.0068	5.3527	.1868	20
21	32.3238	.0309	174.0210	.0057	5.3837	.1857	21
22	38.1421	.0262	206.3448	.0048	5.4099	.1848	22
23	45.0076	.0222	244.4868	.0041	5.4321	.1841	23
24	53.1090	.0188	289.4945	.0035	5.4509	.1835	24
25	62.6686	.0160	342.6035	.0029	5.4669	.1829	25
26	73.9490	.0135	405.2721	.0025	5.4804	.1825	26
27	87.2598	.0115	479.2211	.0021	5.4919	.1821	27
28	102.9666	.0097	566.4809	.0018	5.5016	.1818	28
29	121.5005	.0082	669.4475	.0015	5.5098	.1815	29
30	143.3706	.0070	790.9480	.0013	5.5168	.1813	30
∞					5.5556	.1800	∞

Interest rate of 30.00 percent

N	Compound amount — Future value of a present amount (F/P)	Present value — Present value of a future amount (P/F)	Annuity compound amount — Future value of an annuity (F/A)	Sinking fund — Annuity providing a future amount (A/F)	Annuity present value — Present value of an annuity (P/A)	Capital recovery — Annuity repaying a present amount (A/P)	N
1	1.3000	.7692	1.0000	1.0000	.7692	1.3000	1
2	1.6900	.5917	2.3000	.4348	1.3609	.7348	2
3	2.1970	.4552	3.9900	.2506	1.8161	.5506	3
4	2.8561	.3501	6.1870	.1616	2.1662	.4616	4
5	3.7129	.2693	9.0431	.1106	2.4356	.4106	5
6	4.8268	.2072	12.7560	.0784	2.6427	.3784	6
7	6.2749	.1594	17.5828	.0569	2.8021	.3569	7
8	8.1573	.1226	23.8577	.0419	2.9247	.3419	8
9	10.6045	.0943	32.0150	.0312	3.0190	.3312	9
10	13.7858	.0725	42.6195	.0235	3.0915	.3235	10
11	17.9216	.0558	56.4053	.0177	3.1473	.3177	11
12	23.2981	.0429	74.3270	.0135	3.1903	.3135	12
13	30.2875	.0330	97.6250	.0102	3.2233	.3102	13
14	39.3738	.0254	127.9125	.0073	3.2487	.3078	14
15	51.1859	.0195	167.2863	.0060	3.2682	.3060	15
16	66.5417	.0150	213.4722	.0046	3.2832	.3046	16
17	86.5042	.0116	285.0139	.0035	3.2948	.3035	17
18	112.4554	.0089	371.5180	.0027	3.3037	.3027	18
19	146.1920	.0068	483.9734	.0021	3.3105	.3021	19
20	190.0496	.0053	630.1655	.0016	3.3158	.3016	20
21	247.0645	.0040	820.2151	.0012	3.3198	.3012	21
22	321.1839	.0031	1067.2796	.0009	3.3230	.3009	22
23	417.5391	.0024	1388.4635	.0007	3.3254	.3007	23
24	542.8008	.0018	1806.0026	.0006	3.3272	.3006	24
25	705.6410	.0014	2348.8033	.0004	3.3286	.3004	25
26	917.3333	.0011	3054.4443	.0003	3.3297	.3003	26
27	1192.5333	.0008	3971.7776	.0003	3.3305	.3003	27
28	1550.2933	.0006	5164.3109	.0002	3.3312	.3002	28
29	2015.3813	.0005	6714.6042	.0001	3.3317	.3001	29
30	2619.9956	.0004	8725.9855	.0001	3.3321	.3001	30
8					3.3333	.3000	8

Interest rate of 25.00 percent

N	Compound amount — Future value of a present amount (F/P)	Present value — Present value of a future amount (P/F)	Annuity compound amount — Future value of an annuity (F/A)	Sinking fund — Annuity providing a future amount (A/F)	Annuity present value — Present value of an annuity (P/A)	Capital recovery — Annuity repaying a present amount (A/P)	N
1	1.2500	.8000	1.0000	1.0000	.8000	1.2500	1
2	1.5625	.6400	2.2500	.4444	1.4400	.6944	2
3	1.9531	.5120	3.8125	.2623	1.9520	.5123	3
4	2.4414	.4096	5.7656	.1734	2.3616	.4234	4
5	3.0518	.3277	8.2070	.1218	2.6893	.3718	5
6	3.8147	.2621	11.2588	.0888	2.9514	.3388	6
7	4.7684	.2097	15.0735	.0663	3.1611	.3163	7
8	5.9605	.1678	19.8419	.0504	3.3289	.3004	8
9	7.4506	.1342	25.8023	.0388	3.4631	.2888	9
10	9.3132	.1074	33.2529	.0301	3.5705	.2801	10
11	11.6415	.0859	42.5661	.0235	3.6564	.2735	11
12	14.5519	.0687	54.2077	.0184	3.7251	.2684	12
13	18.1899	.0550	68.7596	.0145	3.7801	.2645	13
14	22.7374	.0440	86.9495	.0115	3.8241	.2615	14
15	28.4217	.0352	109.6868	.0091	3.8593	.2591	15
16	35.5271	.0281	138.1085	.0072	3.8874	.2572	16
17	44.4089	.0225	173.6357	.0058	3.9099	.2558	17
18	55.5112	.0180	218.0446	.0046	3.9279	.2546	18
19	69.3889	.0144	273.5558	.0037	3.9424	.2537	19
20	86.7362	.0115	342.9447	.0029	3.9539	.2529	20
21	108.4202	.0092	429.6809	.0023	3.9631	.2523	21
22	135.5253	.0074	538.1011	.0019	3.9705	.2519	22
23	169.4066	.0059	673.6264	.0015	3.9764	.2515	23
24	211.7582	.0047	843.0329	.0012	3.9811	.2512	24
25	264.6978	.0038	1054.7912	.0009	3.9849	.2509	25
26	330.8722	.0030	1319.4890	.0008	3.9879	.2508	26
27	413.5903	.0024	1650.3612	.0006	3.9903	.2506	27
28	516.9879	.0019	2063.9515	.0005	3.9923	.2505	28
29	646.2349	.0015	2580.9394	.0004	3.9938	.2504	29
30	807.7936	.0012	3227.1743	.0003	3.9950	.2503	30
8			4.0000			.2500	8

Interest rate of 50.00 percent

N	Compound amount — Future value of a present amount — F/P	Present value — Present value of a future amount — P/F	Annuity compound amount — Future value of an annuity — F/A	Sinking fund — Annuity providing a future amount — A/F	Annuity present value — Present value of an annuity — P/A	Capital recovery — Annuity repaying a present amount — A/P	N
1	1.5000	.6667	1.0000	1.0000	.6667	1.5000	1
2	2.2500	.4444	2.5000	.4000	1.1111	.9000	2
3	3.3750	.2963	4.7500	.2105	1.4074	.7105	3
4	5.0625	.1975	8.1250	.1231	1.6049	.6231	4
5	7.5938	.1317	13.1875	.0758	1.7366	.5758	5
6	11.3906	.0878	20.7813	.0481	1.8244	.5481	6
7	17.0859	.0585	32.1719	.0311	1.8829	.5311	7
8	25.6289	.0390	49.2578	.0203	1.9220	.5203	8
9	38.4434	.0260	74.8867	.0134	1.9480	.5134	9
10	57.6650	.0173	113.3301	.0088	1.9653	.5088	10
11	86.4976	.0116	170.9951	.0058	1.9769	.5058	11
12	129.7463	.0077	257.4927	.0039	1.9846	.5039	12
13	194.6195	.0051	387.2390	.0026	1.9897	.5026	13
14	291.9293	.0034	581.8585	.0017	1.9931	.5017	14
15	437.8939	.0023	873.7878	.0011	1.9954	.5011	15
16	656.8408	.0015	1311.6817	.0008	1.9970	.5008	16
17	985.2613	.0010	1968.5225	.0005	1.9980	.5005	17
18	1477.8919	.0007	2953.7838	.0003	1.9986	.5003	18
19	2216.8378	.0005	4431.6756	.0002	1.9991	.5002	19
20	3325.2567	.0003	6648.5135	.0002	1.9994	.5002	20
21	4987.8851	.0002	9973.7702	.0001	1.9996	.5001	21
22	7481.8276	.0001	14961.6553	.0001	1.9997	.5001	22
23	11222.7415	.0001	22443.4829	.0000	1.9998	.5000	23
24	16834.1122	.0001	33666.2244	.0000	1.9999	.5000	24
25	25251.1683	.0000	50500.3366	.0000	1.9999	.5000	25
∞					2.0000	.5000	∞

Interest rate of 40.00 percent

N	Compound amount — Future value of a present amount — F/P	Present value — Present value of a future amount — P/F	Annuity compound amount — Future value of an annuity — F/A	Sinking fund — Annuity providing a future amount — A/F	Annuity present value — Present value of an annuity — P/A	Capital recovery — Annuity repaying a present amount — A/P	N
1	1.4000	.7143	1.0000	1.0000	.7143	1.4000	1
2	1.9600	.5102	2.4000	.4167	1.2245	.8167	2
3	2.7440	.3644	4.3600	.2294	1.5889	.6294	3
4	3.8416	.2603	7.1040	.1408	1.8492	.5408	4
5	5.3782	.1859	10.9456	.0914	2.0352	.4914	5
6	7.5295	.1328	16.3238	.0613	2.1680	.4613	6
7	10.5414	.0949	23.8534	.0419	2.2628	.4419	7
8	14.7579	.0678	34.3947	.0291	2.3306	.4291	8
9	20.6610	.0484	49.1526	.0203	2.3790	.4203	9
10	28.9255	.0346	69.8137	.0143	2.4136	.4143	10
11	40.4957	.0247	98.7391	.0101	2.4383	.4101	11
12	56.6939	.0176	139.2348	.0072	2.4559	.4072	12
13	79.3715	.0126	195.9287	.0051	2.4685	.4051	13
14	111.1201	.0090	275.3002	.0036	2.4775	.4036	14
15	155.5681	.0064	386.4202	.0026	2.4839	.4026	15
16	217.7953	.0046	541.9883	.0018	2.4885	.4018	16
17	304.9135	.0033	759.7837	.0013	2.4918	.4013	17
18	426.8789	.0023	1064.6971	.0009	2.4941	.4009	18
19	597.6304	.0017	1491.5760	.0007	2.4958	.4007	19
20	836.6826	.0012	2089.2064	.0005	2.4970	.4005	20
21	1171.3556	.0009	2925.8889	.0003	2.4979	.4003	21
22	1639.8978	.0006	4097.2445	.0002	2.4985	.4002	22
23	2295.8569	.0004	5737.1423	.0002	2.4989	.4002	23
24	3214.1997	.0003	8032.9993	.0001	2.4992	.4001	24
25	4499.8796	.0002	11247.1990	.0001	2.4994	.4001	25
∞					2.5000	.4000	∞

GLOSSARY

accelerated depreciation Any method of depreciating an asset that produces higher depreciation in earlier years than in later years.

accounting rate of return The rate of return on an investment computed as accounting profit divided by some measure of investment; e.g., average profit per year divided by initial investment.

acid test ratio See **quick ratio**.

activity ratio A financial ratio that indicates how efficiently a firm uses its assets; inventory turnover, average collection period, fixed-asset turnover, and total-asset turnover are activity ratios.

adjustable rate preferred stock Preferred stock with a dividend that varies with some stipulated market interest rate (e.g., the U.S. Treasury bill rate).

after-acquired property A provision in a bond indenture that provides that all property acquired by the firm in the future will also serve as collateral for the bonds.

agency issue See **best efforts issue**.

annuity A series of equal periodic payments or receipts.

arrangement An adjustment between a debtor and a creditor for the settlement of the debtor's obligations; usually covers small- and medium-sized debtor firms.

authorized shares Shares authorized under the company's charter for issuance. For example, a firm with 1 million authorized shares may issue up to but no more than 1 million shares unless the corporate charter is amended to increase this number.

availability time (float) Time period between the date of deposit of a check in the bank and the date of availability of the deposited cash for use by the depositor. Availability float is the amount of the deposit multiplied by the availability time.

balance sheet method Forecasts of future financing requirements and available cash based only on forecast income statements and balance sheets.

bankruptcy The condition in which a firm (or individual) is unable to pay its debts, and its assets are consequently surrendered to a court for administration.

bearer security Security for which ownership is primarily evidenced by possession of the certificate (compare with **registered securities**).

benefit-cost ratio For an investment, the ratio of the present value of its future cash flows to its initial cost. The benefit-cost ratio method uses the ratio to evaluate investment opportunities.

best efforts issue Issuing securities without underwriting. Securities are sold on a commission basis by the investment bankers with no guarantee of the total amount that will be sold.

beta A measure of the response of the rate of return on an asset or a portfolio of assets to changes in the rate of return of the entire capital market, and a measure of the risk of an asset or portfolio in the Capital Asset Pricing Model.

blanket mortgage A mortgage that covers many assets; e.g., a blanket mortgage covering several buildings in a real estate complex.

blocked funds Funds that cannot be converted into another currency due to exchange controls.

bond A long-term promise to pay a specified dollar amount; a long-term debt security.

book value The original cost of an asset minus total depreciation deductions made to date; this is the value indicated by the firm's financial statements.

break-even point The level of output at which the firm is just breaking even, i.e., earning a zero profit.

broker One who arranges the purchase and sale of assets; e.g., a securities (stock) broker, a mortgage broker, and a real estate broker. A broker does not buy or sell the asset but simply brings buyers and sellers together (contrast with **dealer**).

business risk Risk arising from the uncertainty of the future revenues and expenses (not including debt interest) of a firm (i.e., riskiness of the firm's EBIT).

call option See **option**.

call premium The difference between the call price and the face value of a bond.

call price The price that the firm must pay per bond to bondholders if the bonds are called (repurchased by the firm directly from bondholders).

call provision A stipulation in a bond or preferred stock agreement that the firm has the right to repurchase (call) the outstanding bonds or preferred stock at a given price from the securityholder.

capital asset A physical asset (plant and equipment) used by a firm in producing goods or services.

Capital Asset Pricing Model (CAPM) A model of equilibrium rates of return (prices) in the financial markets. The CAPM provides an explicit equation for the expected rate of return on an asset and for the equilibrium value of an asset.

capital budget A statement of the firm's planned investments, generally based upon estimates of future sales, costs, production needs, and availability of capital.

capital gains (losses) The difference between the original cost of an asset and its selling price. Capital gains (losses) are *realized* when the asset is sold.

capital income Income produced from investing money, such as dividends and interest. See also **earned income**.

capital market line A line showing the relationship between the expected rate of return and the risk borne by investors in the capital markets.

capital rationing The use of funds by the firm in a situation in which the funds are limited, i.e., no additional capital can be obtained regardless of the profitability of the investment opportunity.

capital structure The composition of a firm's financing; often refers to the proportions of long-term debt, preferred stock, and common equity on the firm's balance sheet.

cash budget Planned cash receipts and payments for one or more future periods.

cash flow from an investment The dollars coming to the firm (**cash inflow**) or paid out by the firm (**cash outflow**) as a result of adopting the investment.

cash flow forecasts Forecasts of cash receipts and payments for one or more periods.

CBOE Chicago Board Options Exchange.

certainty equivalent An amount, to be received for certain at a particular point in time, which is equal in desirability to a risky cash flow occurring at the same point in time.

chattel mortgage A pledge of personal property as collateral on a debt.

clientele effect The attraction of investors who purchase the company's stock because they prefer the company's policies, such as the company's long-run dividend policy.

closed-end mortgage A mortgage that forbids the borrower from using the security (collateral) provided by the mortgage to cover any additional debt unless the additional debt is of lower priority than the existing debt backed by the mortgage.

coefficient of variation The standard deviation of a variable divided by the variable's expected level, for example, standard deviation of cash flow divided by the expected cash flow.

collateral Property pleged by a borrower as security on a loan.

collateral trust bonds Bonds that are secured by marketable securities, inventories, or intangible assets (e.g., patents).

collection period The time period from the date of sale of the firm's product to the date of receipt of cash (currency or check) from the customer.

combined leverage The combination of operating and financial leverage.

commercial paper Short-term debt issued by corporations to the public.

common stock A document that represents the ownership of a corporation.

compensating balance Money that must be on deposit at a bank to compensate the bank for services; may be a requirement of a loan.

competitive bid A bid for securities that are ultimately sold to the investment banker that bids the highest price for the issue.

composition An agreement between the firm and its creditors under which creditors receive less than the amount due to them in satisfaction of the debt (e.g., $0.50 on the dollar).

compound interest Interest that is paid or received on interest accumulated from prior periods.

concentration bank A bank used to concentrate deposits.

conglomerate A group of firms in different lines of business that are controlled by a single corporation.

consolidation The combination of two or more firms into a completely new firm (e.g., firm *A* consolidating with firm *B* to form firm *C*).

contractual (financial) Inability to fulfill debt commitments.

conversion premium The difference between a convertible's market value and the higher of its investment and conversion values.

conversion price The price, in terms of dollars of par of the convertible security, paid per share of common stock acquired through conversion.

conversion ratio The number of common shares received for converting a convertible security.

conversion value The market value of the common stock into which the convertible security can be converted.

convertible bond A bond that can be converted at the option of the owner into common stock of the corporation.

convertible security A security (usually a bond or preferred stock) that can be converted at the option of the holder into some other type of security (usually common stock) issued by the same corporation.

corporation A business that has been chartered by a state and whose owners are not personally responsible for the business's debts.

correlation coefficient A measure of how closely the two variables move together; this covariation is also indicated by the **covariance** of the two variables.

cost of capital The minimum acceptable rate of return on an investment undertaken by a company; often measured as an average of the rates on the individual securities issued by the company.

cost recovery The term used for depreciation for tax purposes under the Economic Recovery Tax Act of 1981.

coupon The interest payment to the bondholder made periodically (usually semiannually).

coupon rate The percentage of a bond's par value that is paid each year as interest to the bondholder (a $1000 face value bond with a 6 percent coupon rate pays $60 per year in interest).

covariance A measure of the statistical relationship between two variables.

covenant A promise by the firm, included in the debt contract, to perform a certain act (e.g., to pay interest on the debt); a **restrictive covenant** is one that imposes constraints upon the firm in order to protect the debtholders' interests (e.g., a restriction on dividends or a requirement that the firm maintain a particular current ratio).

cover To eliminate risk of a position by taking an offsetting position. For example, to buy or sell a futures contract in the forward exchange market to protect against a loss that may occur as a result of exchange rate changes.

cum dividend With the dividend (compare with **ex-dividend**).

cum rights With rights; shares which entitle the owner to rights to buy shares of the company's stock are cum rights (compare with **ex-rights** and also see **rights**).

cumulative dividends Unpaid preferred dividends from prior years that must be paid before any dividends are paid to common stockholders.

cumulative preferred stock Preferred stock for which any past unpaid preferred dividends must be paid in full before any dividends are issued on the firm's common stock.

cumulative voting A system of electing directors under which a significant minority of the shares is ensured of being able to elect at least one director.

currency exchange rate The rate at which one nation's monetary unit can be exchanged for another nation's monetary unit.

current ratio Current assets divided by current liabilities; a measure of a firm's liquidity.

current yield (on a bond) The annual interest paid on a bond divided by the current price of the bond.

dealer One who is in the occupation of buying or selling some type of asset; e.g., a securities dealer (contrast with **broker**).

debenture A long-term debt instrument issued by a corporation that is not secured by specific property but instead by the general credit of the corporation.

debt capacity The maximum amount of debt that can feasibly be outstanding for a firm at a given point in time.

debt ratio Total firm debt divided by total assets; a measure of a firm's debt burden.

decision tree analysis A way of formulating a problem—often represented by a figure that looks like a tree—which involves choosing a best alternative or strategy. Dynamic programming is a solution technique for efficiently solving such a problem.

degree of combined leverage (DCL) The percentage change in aftertax earnings per share from a 1 percent change in sales.

degree of financial leverage (DFL) The percentage change in aftertax earnings per share from a 1 percent change in EBIT.

degree of operating leverage (DOL) The percentage change in earnings before interest and taxes (EBIT) from a 1 percent change in sales.

depletion A tax deduction reflecting the using up of a natural resource.

depository bank A bank used for deposit of receipts from customers.

depreciation A deduction of part of the cost of an asset from income in each year of the asset's life. **Economic depreciation** is the decline in the value of an asset over time.

dilution A reduction in earnings per share due to an increase in the number of shares outstanding.

direct issue Securities sold directly to investors by the issuing firm.

disbursement bank A bank in which a firm maintains deposit accounts for disbursement purposes, i.e., to make payments by check to suppliers of goods and services.

disbursement time (float) The time period between the date payment (a check) is mailed (or given) to a supplier of goods or services to the firm and the date the firm loses use of the money (check is presented to the firm's bank). Disbursement float is the amount of the payment multiplied by the disbursement time.

discount (bond) The difference between the face value and market value of a bond if the face value is greater; e.g., the discount is $100 on a $1000 (face value) bond selling in the market for $900.

disintermediation The withdrawal of money from financial intermediaries in order to reinvest it in the securities issued by business firms and governmental units.

diversification Investing in more than one risky asset at a time.

divestiture The sale of a division or subsidiary of a company.

dividend payout ratio The proportion of earnings paid out in dividends.

earned income Income produced by an individual's personal services. See also **capital income**.

EBIT Earnings before debt interest and income taxes are deducted.

economic failure The inability of the firm to earn an adequate return on investment regardless of the company's financial structure.

economic order quantity The amount of purchased goods per order that minimizes the cost of inventory.

efficient frontier A curve that indicates the expected returns and standard deviations of all efficient portfolios.

efficient market A market in which asset prices reflect available information instantaneously.

efficient portfolio A portfolio which provides the lowest risk (standard deviation) for its expected return and the highest expected return for its level of risk.

EPS Earnings per share.

equipment trust certificate Bonds that are secured by equipment.

equity investment That portion of firm investment financed from retained earnings or from the sale of equity securities such as common stock or warrants.

Eurobond A bond denominated in a currency that is foreign to the country in which the bond is sold. For example, a dollar denominated bond sold in France.

Eurocurrency Bank deposits in a currency that is foreign to the country in which the bank is located. For example, German marks deposited in a British bank.

Eurodollars United States dollar deposits in foreign banks. The Eurodollar is one type of Eurocurrency.

exchange rate The ratio of the value of one currency relative to another; the rate at which one currency may be exchanged for another.

ex-dividend Without the dividend; the term describes a purchase of shares under which the purchaser is not entitled to the latest dividend (compare with **cum dividend**).

exercise price The dollar amount that must be paid for a share of common stock when it is bought by exercising a warrant or a call option. The exercise price is sometimes referred to as the **option price.**

expected cash flow An average of the possible cash flows in a period; this average equals the sum of all possible cash flows each multiplied by its probability of occurrence.

ex-rights Without rights; shares which do not entitle the owner (buyer) to rights to buy shares of the company's stock are ex-rights (compare with **cum rights** and also see **rights**).

extension An agreement between the firm and its creditors to postpone payments on the firm's debt.

external financing Raising money by issuing new securities or by borrowing.

external investment Expansion by acquiring another firm (contrast with **internal investment**).

extra dividend A dividend payment, in addition to the firm's regular dividend, which is paid only if the firm has been particularly profitable during the period.

face value See **maturity value.**

factoring Selling accounts receivable. The purchasing firm is called a **factor.**

field warehouse An area set aside on a borrower's premises in which goods used as collateral are placed.

financial asset A claim to a present or future payment of dollars; e.g., a corporate bond that is a claim to future interest and principal payments by a corporation.

financial failure See **contractual failure.**

financial intermediaries Financial institutions that borrow money from some people in order to lend it to others.

financial lease A lease that is noncancellable (except by mutual consent of both lessor and lessee) and that generally has a duration equal to most of the economic life of the asset.

financial leverage The effect of debt financing on stockholder income. Often also used to refer to the use of debt financing by a firm. May also include the impact of preferred stock financing on stockholder income.

financial ratio A ratio of dollar magnitudes obtained from a firm's financial statements that reflects some aspect of the firm's performance.

financial risk The uncertainty as to the future returns to a firm's owners resulting from the use of debt or preferred stock.

fixed charge A payment by the firm required under a contractual agreement; e.g., interest on debt, sinking fund contributions, and lease payments.

fixed cost A cost that does not change as output changes.

floating rate bond Bond with an interest rate which varies with short-term interest rates.

floor plan Loan agreement used to finance "large-ticket" items such as automobiles and appliances. Each item is separately identified as being collateral for the loan.

flotation costs The accounting, legal, underwriting, and other costs of issuing securities (new stock, bonds, etc.).

forward contract A futures contract in a currency.

forward rate The rate of exchange as set currently for a transaction to occur at a specified future time.

FRICTO An acronym for flexibility, risk, income, control, timing, and other considerations in the evaluation of alternative financing methods.

full service lease Lease under which the lessor (owner) maintains and insures the asset and pays property taxes on the asset.

fundamental analysis The analysis of a company's stock based upon the company's business performance and financial position (contrast with **technical analysis**).

fundamentalist Someone who believes that analysis of information about a company can be helpful in determining whether the securities of the company would be a good investment.

funded debt A term used to refer to any long-term debt of the firm; sometimes used to refer to any debt for which there is a written agreement covering the indebtedness.

funding See **refunding**.

funds A term that normally refers either to cash or to working capital (current assets minus current liabilities).

funds flow The flow of funds through the firm; this flow is described by a sources and uses statement.

future value The value at a future date of money that has been paid or received in prior periods.

futures contract A contract for future delivery of a specified amount of an asset (commodity, currency, or security) at a fixed price on a particular date in the future.

general lien Claim against all assets of a given type; used to secure a loan.

general partnerships A business in which each partner is personally responsible for any debts of the business.

going public The selling of stock by the issuing corporation to the general public for the first time.

holding company A firm that owns a controlling interest in one or more other firms (which are referred to as subsidiaries).

horizontal combination The union of firms which are in similar lines of business, e.g., two electronics manufacturers.

illiquidity The condition in which a firm (or individual) has inadequate cash to meet its obligations.

income bond A bond that pays interest only to the extent that the firm issuing the bond has earnings (EBIT) to cover the interest.

incremental internal rate of return method A method for comparing two or more mutually exclusive investments using the IRR approach. This method examines the IRR on the additional (or "incremental") cash flow produced by one investment relative to any mutually exclusive alternative in order to determine which is more profitable.

indenture The contract between the corporation and the bondholders specifying the provisions of the debt agreement.

initial public offering The first offering of stock to the general public, at which time the stock is registered with the Securities and Exchange Commission.

insolvency The condition in which a firm (or individual's) liabilities exceed its assets.

interim financing Short-term loans to be repaid from long-term debt or other financing in the future.

internal financing Financing with money both earned and retained in the business.

internal investment A firm's investment that involves the direct acquisition of productive assets rather than the acquisition of another firm or the productive assets of another firm (**external investment**).

internal rate of return The discount rate that discounts an investment's expected net cash flows to a net present value of zero.

interrelated investment opportunities Investments that affect each other's cash flows.

investment banker Financial institution specializing in underwriting and selling new securities issues.

investment company A company whose primary business is the purchase and ownership of government securities and the stocks and bonds of other firms. Mutual funds, closed-end investment companies, and venture capital firms are investment companies.

investment tax credit An income tax credit that is given to firms for investing in plant and equipment.

investment value The value that a convertible security would have if it were not convertible but had all its other features.

IPO See **initial public offering.**

legal list A list of securities that fiduciary institutions (e.g., insurance companies and banks) may, under various state laws, acquire as investments.

lessee The user of a leased asset who pays the lessor for the usage right.

lessor The owner of a leased asset.

letter of credit A written statement by a bank that money will be paid provided conditions specified in the letter are met.

letter stock Privately placed common stock for which, under SEC regulation, the purchaser is required to provide a letter indicating that the stock is not intended for resale.

leverage The degree of firm borrowing.

leverage ratio A financial ratio that measures a firm's debt burden; the debt, times interest earned, and fixed-charges coverage ratios are leverage ratios.

leveraged buyout The sale of a subsidiary or division of a company to parties (often the purchased company's management) who borrow to make the purchase.

leveraged lease (or "third-party lease") An arrangement under which the lessor borrows funds to cover part or all of the purchase price of the asset.

limited liability A legal term that means that the owner of a business is not personally responsible for its debts; only the owner's investment in the business is available to its creditors.

limited partnerships A business in which some partners (the general partners) are personally responsible for any debts, but the other partners (the limited partners) are not.

line of credit An agreement by a bank to loan money to a customer as needed up to a stated maximum amount.

liquidation The sale of a firm's assets when the company is dissolved.

liquidity premium The additional return earned on securities of greater term to maturity.

liquidity ratio A financial ratio that measures a firm's ability to fulfill short-run financial commitments; the current and quick ratios are liquidity ratios.

listed stock Stock that is traded on an organized securities exchange.

lock box A post office box to which local payments to a company will be sent. A local bank will collect the payments and deposit them in the company's account.

loss carryback (-forward) Using a business loss in the current year as a deduction from taxable income in prior years (carryback) or future years (carryforward).

mail time (float) The time period between the date a customer mails payment (currency or check) to a company and the date the company receives the payment. Mail float is the amount of the payment multiplied by the mail time.

maintenance lease A lease under which the lessor pays for all maintenance and upkeep of the asset.

majority rule voting A system of electing directors under which a majority of the shares has the power to elect the entire board of directors.

margin The amount paid by an investor in acquiring a security, usually expressed as a percentage of the security's purchase price. The Federal Reserve sets minimum margin requirements for securities traded on the organized securities exchanges.

market rate of discount The rate of discount used by investors to discount returns of a particular level of risk.

market value (or market price) The value that an asset (e.g., a security such as a share of stock or a physical asset such as a machine) is bought and sold for in the market.

matching principle A principle that holds that the firm should finance short-term needs with short-term sources and long-term needs with long-term sources.

maturity date The date on which the firm is to retire a bond by repaying the principal (maturity value); that is, when the bond matures.

maturity value The amount the firm promises to pay the bondholder, in addition to interest, when the bond matures. The maturity value is also referred to as the bond's **par value, face value,** or **principal value.**

merger The combination of two or more firms with one of them surviving (e.g., firm *A* merging with firm *B* with firm *A* surviving).

minimum acceptable rate of return The lowest rate of return that an investment can be expected to earn and still be acceptable; same as the investment's **cost of capital.**

mortgage A pledge of specific property given by a borrower as security on a loan.

mortgage bond A bond secured by a mortgage.

multinational company A company that has direct investments in more than one country.

mutual fund A company that invests in securities using money raised from selling shares to individual investors at their net asset value (market value of assets divided by number of shares). Shares will be redeemed by the fund at their net asset value at the request of the investor. Also called "open-end investment companies."

mutually exclusive alternatives Alternatives or options of which only one can be adopted (adopting one eliminates the chance of adopting any of the others).

negative pledge clause A provision in a bond agreement that the firm will issue no new debt which will take priority over the bonds covered by the agreement.

negotiated underwriting A process of issuing securities whereby a firm selects an investment banker and negotiates the terms of the issue.

net lease A lease under which the lessee pays all maintenance and upkeep of the asset.

net present value The present value of the future cash flows of an investment less the investment's current cost.

net profit Aftertax net income to stockholders; sometimes also used to refer to the annual annuity that is equivalent to a given net present value.

net working capital See **working capital**.

note (loan) Written and signed evidence of a debt.

note (United States) A type of United States government security with an original maturity of one to ten years. Similar to a bond but with a shorter maturity.

open account A credit arrangement under which sales are made to the buyer without a formal debt agreement (such as a note).

open-end mortgage A mortgage that allows the security (collateral) provided by the mortgage to be used as collateral on additional debt. A **limited open-end mortgage** allows the issuance of further debt up to some specified limit.

operating lease A lease that is cancellable by the lessee at any time upon due notice to the lessor. Also refers to a short-term lease that is cancellable by the lessor or lessee upon due notice to the other party.

operating leverage The existence of fixed operating costs in the firm's cost structure.

operating margin Operating income divided by sales; a measure of a firm's profitability.

option A right to buy (call) or sell (put) a specified amount of a particular asset (e.g., Ford common stock) at a given price within a specified period of time.

over-the-counter market A market for securities made up of securities dealers who may or may not be members of an organized exchange.

owner of record The individual recorded on the corporation's books as the owner of the company's outstanding securities.

par value The stated value of a security. The par value of a bond is its maturity value, the amount paid per bond at maturity. The par value of a share of preferred stock is the amount on which preferred dividends are based (a $100 par value 6 percent preferred stock pays $6 annually in dividends). The preferred's par value is also the amount owed to the preferred shareholder upon liquidation or bankruptcy of the corporation. The par value of common stock is the value of a share of stock set by the board of directors and is generally less than market value; the primary significance of this value is that, in most states, the firm may not pay dividends if such dividends reduce common shareholders' equity in the firm below the total par on all common stock outstanding.

participating preferred stock Preferred stock with a provision for increased dividends if the firm's earnings exceed some minimum amount.

partnership A business owned by two or more people who agree on how the profits will be divided and who are personally liable for firm debts. See also **limited partnerships.**

payback period The amount of time required for an asset to generate enough cash flow to just cover the initial outlay for that asset.

payback period method A capital budgeting technique that specifies that an investment is acceptable only if it has a payback period less than or equal to some specified time period, e.g., three years.

personal property All property other than **real property.**

pooling of interests A method of accounting for a business combination under which the assets of the acquired firm are subsequently carried on the merged firm's books at the same value that they were carried by the selling firm.

portfolio A combination of assets owned for investment.

preemptive right The stockholder's right to purchase additional stock of the company before it is offered for sale to outsiders.

preferred stock Stock that has a claim against income and assets before common stock but after debt.

premium (bond) The difference between the market value and the face value of a bond if the market value is greater; e.g., the premium is $200 on a $1000 (face value) bond selling in the market for $1200.

premium (warrant) The difference between the market value and the theoretical value of the warrant.

present value The value of money at a given date that will be paid or received in future periods.

price-earnings ratio The price per share of stock divided by the annual earnings per share.

primary markets The market in which financial assets are originally issued.

prime rate Interest rate charged by banks on short-term loans to large, low-risk businesses.

principal The amount on which interest is paid by a borrower or the amount on which interest is received by a lender.

principal value The **maturity value** of a bond.

private issue Security issue sold to only a few investors that need not be registered with the Securities and Exchange Commission. Also called **private placement.**

processing time (float) The time period between the date a company receives payment from a customer and the date the payment is deposited in the company's bank. Processing float is the amount of the payment multiplied by the processing time.

profitability index A measure of the profitability of an investment computed by dividing the net present value (or simply present value of future cash flows) by the initial cost of the investment.

profitability ratio A financial ratio that indicates the net returns on sales or assets; net operating margin, profit margin on sales, return on total assets, and return on net worth are profitability ratios.

proprietorship A business owned by an individual who is personally responsible for all its debts.

prospectus Information supplied to potential investors in a new securities issue that describes the current condition and history of the firm.

protective covenant See **covenant.**

proxy The authorization given by a shareholder to another party to exercise the shareholder's voting rights at a stockholders' meeting.

public issue Security issue sold to many investors. Large issues of most types of securities must be registered with the Securities and Exchange Commission.

public warehouse A place where goods belonging to other people are stored; sometimes used to maintain control over collateral.

purchase method A method of accounting for a business combination in which the assets of the acquired firm are carried on the merged firm's books at the price paid for them in the merger acquisition.

pure residual dividend policy See **residual dividend policy**.

put option See **option**.

quick ratio (or acid test ratio) A measure of the firm's liquidity equal to [(current assets − inventory) ÷ current liabilities].

rate of return The interest rate earned on an investment; may be the actual rate or an expected rate.

real property Land and buildings.

realized capital gain See **capital gains**.

red herring Preliminary prospectus in a securities offering.

refunding The issuance of new securities to pay off outstanding old debt; **funding,** on the other hand, specifically refers to issuing long-term debt to pay off short-term debt.

registered security Security whose ownership is recorded by the issuing company's registrar (compare with **bearer security**).

reorganization An adjustment under Chapter 11 of the Bankruptcy Reform Act for settlement of the firm's debts; covers most public corporations except railroads.

residual dividend policy A policy under which all equity investment is financed first with retained earnings and then, if such earnings are inadequate, by selling additional equity securities such as common stock and warrants. Earnings that are left over after equity investment is made are paid out as a dividend. A **pure residual dividend policy** requires that the above residual policy be followed every year; a **smoothed residual dividend policy** requires following a residual policy over the long run with dividends kept stable from year to year.

restrictive provisions Restrictions on various activities of a borrower included as part of a loan agreement to protect the lender. See **covenant**.

retained earnings The earnings in a given period that have been retained by the firm rather than paid out as dividends; also refers to the balance sheet account that is the sum of all earnings retained to date.

reverse split The reduction in the number of the firm's shares produced by exchanging all outstanding shares for a smaller number of new shares; each shareholder's percentage ownership of the firm is unaffected.

revolving credit Legal commitment by a bank to loan money to a customer as needed up to a stated maximum amount. The time period covered by the agreement may extend for several years.

rights A privilege offered to stockholders of buying a specified number of additional shares of the company's stock before the stock is offered to outsiders for sale. A stockholder is issued one right per share of stock already owned.

rights-off See **ex-rights**.

rights-on See **cum rights**.

sale and leaseback An arrangement under which the user of the asset sells the asset and then leases it back from the purchaser.

salvage value (residual value) The money that the firm can receive for an asset after it has held it for a period of time.

secondary market The market in which previously issued financial assets are traded.

security market line A line indicating the relationship between the risks and expected rates of return of available assets (securities) in the market.

semistrong-form efficient market A market in which asset prices instantaneously reflect all publicly available information.

sensitivity analysis Analysis of the effect on a project's cash flows or profitability of possible changes in factors which affect the project (sales, various costs, etc.).

serial bonds Bonds issued at the same time but which mature at different times in the future. For example, a $50 million serial bond issue may provide for $5 million of bonds maturing in five years, another $5 million of bonds maturing in six years, etc., until all bonds have matured in fourteen years.

simulation The use of a set of mathematical relationships to duplicate the operations of a system (e.g., a firm), in order to analyze the system. Simulation could be used to analyze the effect of a new project on firm profits.

sinking fund contribution A periodic payment made by the firm into a fund ("sinking fund") that will be paid to bondholders in retiring the bonds.

sinking fund provision A stipulation in the bond agreement (indenture) that the firm establish a sinking fund. The fund is used to retire part or all of the bonds by buying them on the open market, calling them, or retiring them at maturity.

skewness A measure of the nonsymmetry of a probability distribution.

Small Business Administration (SBA) A federal agency established to aid small businesses.

Small Business Investment Company (SBIC) A financial institution established under certain federal laws to provide financing to small businesses.

smoothed residual dividend policy See **residual dividend policy.**

spinoff The sale of a division or subsidiary of a company.

spot rate The current rate of exchange between two currencies; the rate of exchange at which currencies are presently being traded.

standard deviation A measure of the degree of dispersion of a probability distribution; a higher standard deviation of a cash flow implies a greater uncertainty regarding its level. Standard deviation is the square root of the **variance.** To adjust for scale in making risk comparisons between projects, a useful parameter is the project cash flow's **coefficient of variation,** which equals the cash flow's standard deviation divided by the expected cash flow.

stated value A value set by the board of directors for no-par stock. Stated value has essentially the same meaning as **par value,** in that dividends may not be paid which reduce shareholders' equity below the stated value of all the outstanding shares.

stock dividend New shares distributed to existing shareholders as a dividend.

stock exchange A financial institution that provides a central location for the purchase and sale of stocks.

stock split An increase in the number of firm shares effected by giving stockholders additional shares in proportion to the number of shares already owned.

strong-form efficient market A market in which asset prices instantaneously reflect all available information (compare with **weak-form efficient market** and **semistrong-form efficient market**).

subordination Relegation to a lower-priority position in receiving interest and principal; if an issue of debentures is subordinated to other debt, the latter debt is paid the amount due before the **subordinated debentures** receive anything.

syndicate A group of investment bankers formed to handle a large security issue, or a group of lenders formed to handle a large loan.

synergy Benefits from joining two or more economic units; e.g., the benefits from merging two firms if the merger lowers the cost per unit of output.

taxable income The income of an individual or business on which income taxes are levied as defined by the tax laws. Various deductions are made from total income to arrive at taxable income.

technical analysis The analysis of a firm's stock based on historical trends in the stock's market price (contrast with **fundamental analysis**).

technician Someone who believes that analysis of the history of past prices of an asset can be useful in forecasting the future price of the asset.

term to maturity The amount of time until a debt instrument matures; a twenty-year bond that was issued five years ago has a term to maturity of fifteen years.

term structure (of interest rates) The relationship between the market interest rate and the term to maturity of fixed-income securities that differ only in their term to maturity.

theoretical value For a warrant, the market price minus the option price of the common stock acquired with the warrant multiplied by the number of shares purchased per warrant; this is equal to the value of the common stock acquired with the warrant less the exercise price paid for that stock.

third-party lease See **leveraged lease**.

trade credit Credit on goods purchased by a company from its supplier on open account.

transfer price The price charged by one part of a company or group of companies for goods or services provided to another part of the same company or group of companies, e.g., the price charged one subsidiary by another subsidiary.

Treasury bill A security issued at a discount by the United States government with a maturity of one year or less, paying its face value at maturity with no interest payments.

Treasury stock Shares repurchased from a stockholder by the issuing company.

trustee In bankruptcy, a court-appointed official who draws up a reorganization plan and supervises the firm's assets until the plan goes into effect. In a public bond issue, an individual or firm who represents the bondholders in dealing with the issuing company.

underwriting The purchase of securities from the issuing company by an investment banker for resale to the public.

variable cost A cost that changes as output changes.

variable rate loan A loan with an interest rate that varies according to the general level of interest rates. The interest rate is not fixed over the period of the loan.

variance See **standard deviation**.

venture capital Money invested in a small or new business as an investment by persons not directly managing the business.

vertical combination The union of firms engaged in different stages of production for the same type of product; e.g., a food retailer and food wholesaler.

warrant An option to buy a security (e.g., a share of stock) issued by the firm that issued the warrant.

weak-form efficient market Market in which asset prices instantaneously reflect information contained in the past history of asset prices (compare with **semistrong-form efficient market** and **strong-form efficient market**).

with dividend See cum dividend.

with rights See cum rights.

working capital Current assets *minus* current liabilities (sometimes referred to as **net working capital**).

yield to maturity The rate of return earned on a bond if it is purchased at a given price and held to maturity.

yield curve A plot of **yield to maturity** and **term to maturity** for fixed income securities that differ only in their term to maturity. Often used as a synonym for the **term structure of interest rates.**

INDEX

DATE DUE

MAR 2 '97			
APR 20 '98			
MAY 1 8 '98			

FUTURE VALUE OF $1 IN N PERIODS (F/P, i, N)

N	0.33%	0.50%	0.67%	0.75%	0.83%	1%	2%	3%	4%	5%	6%	7%
1	1.0033	1.0050	1.0067	1.0075	1.0083	1.0100	1.0200	1.0300	1.0400	1.0500	1.0600	1.0700
2	1.0067	1.0100	1.0134	1.0151	1.0167	1.0201	1.0404	1.0609	1.0816	1.1025	1.1236	1.1449
3	1.0100	1.0151	1.0201	1.0227	1.0252	1.0303	1.0612	1.0927	1.1249	1.1576	1.1910	1.2250
4	1.0134	1.0202	1.0269	1.0303	1.0338	1.0406	1.0824	1.1255	1.1699	1.2155	1.2625	1.3108
5	1.0168	1.0253	1.0338	1.0381	1.0424	1.0510	1.1041	1.1593	1.2167	1.2763	1.3382	1.4026
6	1.0202	1.0304	1.0407	1.0459	1.0511	1.0615	1.1262	1.1941	1.2653	1.3401	1.4185	1.5007
7	1.0236	1.0355	1.0476	1.0537	1.0598	1.0721	1.1487	1.2299	1.3159	1.4071	1.5036	1.6058
8	1.0270	1.0407	1.0546	1.0616	1.0686	1.0829	1.1717	1.2668	1.3686	1.4775	1.5938	1.7182
9	1.0304	1.0459	1.0616	1.0696	1.0775	1.0937	1.1951	1.3048	1.4233	1.5513	1.6895	1.8385
10	1.0338	1.0511	1.0687	1.0776	1.0865	1.1046	1.2190	1.3439	1.4802	1.6289	1.7908	1.9672
11	1.0373	1.0564	1.0758	1.0857	1.0956	1.1157	1.2434	1.3842	1.5395	1.7103	1.8983	2.1049
12	1.0407	1.0617	1.0830	1.0938	1.1047	1.1268	1.2682	1.4258	1.6010	1.7959	2.0122	2.2522
13	1.0442	1.0670	1.0902	1.1020	1.1139	1.1381	1.2936	1.4685	1.6651	1.8856	2.1329	2.4098
14	1.0477	1.0723	1.0975	1.1103	1.1232	1.1495	1.3195	1.5126	1.7317	1.9799	2.2609	2.5785
15	1.0512	1.0777	1.1048	1.1186	1.1326	1.1610	1.3459	1.5580	1.8009	2.0789	2.3966	2.7590
16	1.0547	1.0831	1.1122	1.1270	1.1420	1.1726	1.3728	1.6047	1.8730	2.1829	2.5404	2.9522
17	1.0582	1.0885	1.1196	1.1354	1.1515	1.1843	1.4002	1.6528	1.9479	2.2920	2.6928	3.1588
18	1.0617	1.0939	1.1270	1.1440	1.1611	1.1961	1.4282	1.7024	2.0258	2.4066	2.8543	3.3799
19	1.0653	1.0994	1.1346	1.1525	1.1708	1.2081	1.4568	1.7535	2.1068	2.5270	3.0256	3.6165
20	1.0688	1.1049	1.1421	1.1612	1.1805	1.2202	1.4859	1.8061	2.1911	2.6533	3.2071	3.8697
21	1.0724	1.1104	1.1497	1.1699	1.1904	1.2324	1.5157	1.8603	2.2788	2.7860	3.3996	4.1406
22	1.0760	1.1160	1.1574	1.1787	1.2003	1.2447	1.5460	1.9161	2.3699	2.9253	3.6035	4.4304
23	1.0795	1.1216	1.1651	1.1875	1.2103	1.2572	1.5769	1.9736	2.4647	3.0715	3.8197	4.7405
24	1.0831	1.1272	1.1729	1.1964	1.2204	1.2697	1.6084	2.0328	2.5633	3.2251	4.0489	5.0724
25	1.0867	1.1328	1.1807	1.2054	1.2306	1.2824	1.6406	2.0938	2.6658	3.3864	4.2919	5.4274
30	1.1050	1.1614	1.2206	1.2513	1.2827	1.3478	1.8114	2.4273	3.2434	4.3219	5.7435	7.6123
40	1.1424	1.2208	1.3045	1.3483	1.3937	1.4889	2.2080	3.2620	4.8010	7.0400	10.2857	14.9745
50	1.1810	1.2832	1.3941	1.4530	1.5143	1.6446	2.6916	4.3839	7.1067	11.4674	18.4202	29.4570
60	1.2210	1.3489	1.4898	1.5657	1.6453	1.8167	3.2810	5.8916	10.5196	18.6792	32.9877	57.9464
80	1.3050	1.4903	1.7016	1.8180	1.9424	2.2167	4.8754	10.6409	23.0498	49.5614	105.79	224.23
120	1.4908	1.8194	2.2196	2.4514	2.6963	3.3004	10.7652	34.7110	110.66	348.91	1,088	3,358

N	8%	9%	10%	11%	12%	13%	14%	15%	16%	18%	20%	25%
1	1.0800	1.0900	1.1000	1.1100	1.1200	1.1300	1.1400	1.1500	1.1600	1.1800	1.2000	1.2500
2	1.1664	1.1881	1.2100	1.2321	1.2544	1.2769	1.2996	1.3225	1.3456	1.3924	1.4400	1.5625
3	1.2597	1.2950	1.3310	1.3676	1.4049	1.4429	1.4815	1.5209	1.5609	1.6430	1.7280	1.9531
4	1.3605	1.4116	1.4641	1.5181	1.5735	1.6305	1.6890	1.7490	1.8106	1.9388	2.0736	2.4414
5	1.4693	1.5386	1.6105	1.6851	1.7623	1.8424	1.9254	2.0114	2.1003	2.2878	2.4883	3.0518
6	1.5869	1.6771	1.7716	1.8704	1.9738	2.0820	2.1950	2.3131	2.4364	2.6996	2.9860	3.8147
7	1.7138	1.8280	1.9487	2.0762	2.2107	2.3526	2.5023	2.6600	2.8262	3.1855	3.5832	4.7684
8	1.8509	1.9926	2.1436	2.3045	2.4760	2.6584	2.8526	3.0590	3.2784	3.7589	4.2998	5.9605
9	1.9990	2.1719	2.3579	2.5580	2.7731	3.0040	3.2519	3.5179	3.8030	4.4355	5.1598	7.4506
10	2.1589	2.3674	2.5937	2.8394	3.1058	3.3946	3.7072	4.0456	4.4114	5.2338	6.1917	9.3132
11	2.3316	2.5804	2.8531	3.1518	3.4785	3.8359	4.2262	4.6524	5.1173	6.1759	7.4301	11.6415
12	2.5182	2.8127	3.1384	3.4985	3.8960	4.3345	4.8179	5.3503	5.9360	7.2876	8.9161	14.5519
13	2.7196	3.0658	3.4523	3.8833	4.3635	4.8980	5.4924	6.1528	6.8858	8.5994	10.6993	18.1899
14	2.9372	3.3417	3.7975	4.3104	4.8871	5.5348	6.2613	7.0757	7.9875	10.1472	12.8392	22.7374
15	3.1722	3.6425	4.1772	4.7846	5.4736	6.2543	7.1379	8.1371	9.2655	11.9737	15.4070	28.4217
16	3.4259	3.9703	4.5950	5.3109	6.1304	7.0673	8.1372	9.3576	10.7480	14.1290	18.4884	35.5271
17	3.7000	4.3276	5.0545	5.8951	6.8660	7.9861	9.2765	10.7613	12.4677	16.6722	22.1861	44.4089
18	3.9960	4.7171	5.5599	6.5436	7.6900	9.0243	10.5752	12.3755	14.4625	19.6733	26.6233	55.5112
19	4.3157	5.1417	6.1159	7.2633	8.6128	10.1974	12.0557	14.2318	16.7765	23.2144	31.9480	69.3889
20	4.6610	5.6044	6.7275	8.0623	9.6463	11.5231	13.7435	16.3665	19.4608	27.3930	38.3376	86.7362
25	6.8485	8.6231	10.8347	13.5855	17.0001	21.2305	26.4619	32.9190	40.8742	62.6686	95.3962	264.6978
30	10.06	13.27	17.45	22.89	29.96	39.12	50.95	66.21	85.85	143.37	237.38	807.79
40	21.72	31.41	45.26	65.00	93.05	132.78	188.88	267.86	378.72	750.38	1,470	7,523
50	46.90	74.36	117.39	184.56	289.00	450.74	700.23	1,084	1,671	3,927	9,100	70,065